COMPLAINT AND REFORM
IN ENGLAND

Complaint and Reform in England
1436-1714

FIFTY WRITINGS OF THE TIME ON POLITICS,
RELIGION, SOCIETY, ECONOMICS,
ARCHITECTURE, SCIENCE, AND EDUCATION

Arranged with Introductions by

WILLIAM HUSE DUNHAM, JR.

and

STANLEY PARGELLIS

1968
OCTAGON BOOKS, INC.
New York

Reprinted 1968
by special arrangement with Oxford University Press, New York, Inc.

OCTAGON BOOKS, INC.
175 FIFTH AVENUE
NEW YORK, N. Y. 10010

LIBRARY OF CONGRESS CATALOG CARD NUMBER: 68-16771

Printed in U.S.A. by
NOBLE OFFSET PRINTERS, INC.
NEW YORK 3, N. Y.

TO

WALLACE NOTESTEIN

ACKNOWLEDGEMENT

THE members of the Reference and Cataloguing Departments and the Rare Book Room of the Yale University Library have, with inexhaustible patience, given the editors much bibliographical aid. For many ideas, constructive suggestions, and friendly encouragement we are indebted to Franklin Le V.Baumer, John M.Berdan, Lewis P.Curtis, Ralph H.Gabriel, John A.Gee, Wallace Notestein, Ashley W.Oughterson, and Hartley Simpson. The clerical work, no small factor in this book, was faithfully and efficiently performed by A.M.Lee, A.R.McWilliams,Jr., M.Virshup, and B.Williams.

The heads of the following organizations have kindly granted the necessary permission to reprint from the scholarly editions published under their auspices:

The Early English Text Society, Fish, *A Supplication for the Beggars*; *The Decay of England*.

The Maine Historical Society, Hakluyt, *Western Discoveries*.

The Oxford University Press, Fortescue, *The Governance of England*; Beale, *A Treatise of the Office of a Councillor*.

H.M. Public Record Office, The Manuscripts, *An Argument for the Independence of the Spirituality; Articles for Priests Unlearned*.

The Society for Promoting Christian Knowledge, *An Admonition to the Parliament*.

The University Press, Cambridge, Smith, *De Republica Anglorum*.

The Yale University Press, Lupset, *An Exhortation to Young Men*.

The illustrations are from originals in the Bodleian Library, the British Museum, and the Yale University Library who have granted permission to reproduce them.

W.H.D., JR.
S.P.

CONTENTS

LIST OF ILLUSTRATIONS

INTRODUCTION

It is man's beliefs that truly constitute his state.

JOSÉ ORTEGA Y GASSET

POLITICAL theories, aesthetic principles, religious beliefs, economic and educational programs, scientific opinions, and concepts of social organization which were current in England between 1436 and 1714 constitute the variety of matter contained in this book. They have been taken from fly-sheets, pamphlets, tracts, and larger works which circulated among Renaissance Englishmen. In a few cases where an extensive circulation may be doubted, the piece was chosen for one of two reasons. Either it presents briefly and succinctly conventional points of view, as the two manuscript papers on the church in the 1530's, or else it is known to have influenced persons of power. Hakluyt's essay on overseas expeditions, unpublished until 1877, was seen in manuscript by Elizabeth and Walsingham. In so far as possible, writings that could be printed *in toto* have been chosen, but sometimes a specific belief is more clearly stated in part of a larger work. In such cases sizable portions have been extracted, and wherever abridgement has been necessary, it is always indicated. The spelling, punctuation, and capitalization have been modernized which has, in a few instances, disclosed a literary merit hitherto lost amidst the awkward orthography of our ancestors.

The book has been designed to show the beliefs and ideas which shaped the civilization of England during two crucial centuries of her history. Behind the movements, forces, and currents of thought which are said to make history, there were actual human beings with profound convictions. These men gave reality to historical abstractions. To know the life of the past, the lively men who made it must be sought. The men themselves are gone, but the words through which they conveyed their beliefs remain. Their prejudices and complaints, their vindications of the *status quo*, their will to set things right, their modes of thought, their manner of argument, their emotional reactions to national events, and the habits, customs, and material trappings of English life, all these appear in their writings and enliven the history of past conflicts, victories, and defeats.

What some men wrote, others read. But all that was written during two hundred years cannot be reviewed, and to ascertain what was commonly believed in the past a repertory of ideas must be devised. The works of the great thinkers have already been reprinted. But another approach to the common thought of England is through the vulgar writings of pamphleteers, popularizers, and propagandists who prepared common beliefs for dissemination among the rank and file of literate Englishmen. Their publications contain the opinions held by large groups of people, or by very aggressive minorities, which often determined the day by day course of England's history. The selections which follow were chosen as representative statements of major beliefs and convictions which drove on the men who pushed English civilization to and fro as modernism came on and medievalism wore away.

The thought of the great thinkers of the time is not really neglected. Their names may not appear, but their ideas repeatedly occur. Biographically, Calvin, Locke, and Bacon are omitted: intellectually, they are present in numerous guises familiar to their less sophisticated contemporaries. The first puritan manifesto of 1572, *An Admonition to the Parliament*, presents the version of Calvinism which more directly affected the lives of Englishmen than did Calvin's own *Institutes*. The Royal Society described by Sprat was a realization of Bacon's idea for an academy of wisdom, ' Solomon's House.' The long forgotten Anthony Ascham quoted from Hobbes as well as from Aristotle; and it was Luther's God whom Lady Jane Grey worshipped. Though the thought of the master was often no longer pure and undefiled, it was made carnate by men and women who believed in it, fought, and sometimes died for it.

Many of these vital beliefs had a currency in the eighteenth and nineteenth centuries, and some are operative today. The convictions that England should ' keep the narrow seas ' by navalism and that she should gain prosperity by protective tariffs, prevalent in 1436, still have adherents. In 1584 Richard Hakluyt devised the principal arguments for imperialism used ever since. Sir William Smith expounded the Tory mind of any age. The ways to get on in the world—Beale's advice to prospective statesmen, Powell's formulae for social advancement, Audley's tags for material success—suggest a certain changelessness in a changing world. Man's conflict with nature prompted not only Hakluyt's *Western Discoveries*, but Lowe's book on surgery and medicine, and Sprat's justification of experimental knowledge. From the classical world, that reservoir of ideas which have refurbished western culture since the fifteenth century, Englishmen drew much. Classical ideas are scattered through many of these writings; they are concentrated in those on architecture and education. And a few ideas which were given a scant hearing in their day survived, or were revived, to colour later English civilization. Only recently the notions of the Levellers were cited by a mediator of American labour disputes. Beliefs are hard to kill, they often enjoy resurrection, and fundamental ones seldom change in essence.

However, some beliefs which once affected the lives of many men now seem outmoded and discarded. Witchcraft and bleeding, along with losing causes—the divinity of kings and the exclusive verity of medieval catholicism—must be included in even a rough pattern of English thought during the Tudor and Stuart periods. That these beliefs were real and vital factors in determining the outcome of historical conflicts becomes clear when reading parliamentary speeches like those of Queen Elizabeth, Wentworth, and Roe.

The authors of these writings did not live or write in tightly sealed compartments. Their ideas, like their lives, frequently flowed from one category into another, and often a single writing covers several main divisions of human thought. An arrangement according to modern classifications—politics, economics, science, or aesthetics—would have been misleading. A self-conscious specialization generally did not exist. A chronological arrangement is used as it preserves the sequence in which the writings appeared. They have been incorporated into the *Chronology of English History*, which follows this introduction, to show their relationship to one another and to the events in England's history. This outline indicates the circumstances which brought each writing into being or were affected by it. The pages opposite the *Chronology* contain the terms of life of the authors, when known, so that the historical events to which they were exposed may be ascertained. These happenings often determined the character of the author and sometimes explain why he wrote. Likewise, the biographical sketches of the authors are inserted to suggest the personality behind each selection. In the case of the anonymous tracts and the statutes concerning witchcraft, apparel, and poor relief, the notes explain their inclusion and relate them to the general history of England. A brief note on the preceding page is inserted before each illustration to give bibliographical data and to suggest the points in the intellectual and cultural history of England thereby demonstrated.

Yale University.   W.H.D., Jr.
    21 *July* 1937.   S.P.

A CHRONOLOGY OF ENGLISH HISTORY

John Fortescue
1390–1400 ?

1400

1410

1420

1430

1440

1450

1460

A CHRONOLOGY OF ENGLISH HISTORY

	1399	The deposition of Richard II.
	1399–1413	*The Reign of Henry IV.*
1400		Glendower's rising. The death of Chaucer.
	1401	The statute *De haeretico comburendo.*
	1403	The rebellion of the Percies of Northumberland.
	1408	The defeat and death of the earl of Northumberland.
1410		The parliamentary petition to disendow the church.
	1413–1422	*The Reign of Henry V.*
	1415	War against France and the battle of Agincourt.
	1417	Henry V's second expedition into France.
1420		The Treaty of Troyes. Henry V's marriage to Catherine of France.
	1421	The birth of Henry VI. Henry V's third expedition into France.
	1422–1461	*The Reign of Henry VI.*
	1422–1435	The regency in France of John, duke of Bedford.
	1429–1431	The campaigns of Dunois and Joan of Arc.
1430		The forty shilling freehold franchise act.
	1435	The unsuccessful peace conference at Arras.
	1435–1438	The donation of books for a library at Oxford by Humphrey, duke of Gloucester.
	1436	The loss of Paris to the French.
		The Libel of English Policy.
1440		Henry VI founded Eton.
	1441	Henry VI founded King's College, Cambridge.
	1445	The marriage of Henry VI and Margaret of Anjou.
	1447	The death of Humphrey, duke of Gloucester. The death of Cardinal Beaufort.
1450		Jack Cade's rebellion in Kent. The loss of Normandy.
	1453	The loss of Aquitaine and the end of the Hundred Years War. The birth of Prince Edward of Lancaster.
	1454	Henry VI's illness, the protectorate of the duke of York.
	1455	The battle of St. Alban's. The beginning of the Wars of the Roses.
		The second protectorate of the duke of York.
	1457	The trial and imprisonment of Reginald Pecock, bishop of Chichester.
1460		The duke of York claimed the crown.

John Fortescue   1460

                                                        1470

Died 1476

                                                        1480

                                                        1490

Thomas Lupset
    1495

            Simon Fish   1500
              1500 ?

                                                        1510

1460

1461	The battle of Towton.
1461–1483	*The Reign of Edward IV.*
1463	**The act in restraint of excessive array.**
1464	The marriage of Edward IV and Elizabeth Woodville.
1465	The capture of Henry VI.
1468–1470	Fortescue's *De Laudibus Legum Angliae.*
1469–1470	Malory's *Morte d'Arthur.*

1470
      The restoration of Henry VI by Richard, earl of Warwick.

1471	The battle of Tewkesbury and the restoration of Edward IV. The deaths of Henry VI, Prince Edward of Lancaster, the earl of Warwick.
1471–1476	**Sir John Fortescue, The Governance of England.**
1475	Edward IV's invasion of France and the agreement of Pecquiny.
1476	The first English printing press of William Caxton at Westminster.

1480

1483	**The act in restraint of excessive apparel.**
1483	*The Reign of Edward V, 9 April to 25 June.*
1483–1485	*The Reign of Richard III.*
1485	The Battle of Bosworth Field.
1485–1509	*The Reign of Henry VII.*
1486	The marriage of Henry VII and Elizabeth of York.
1487	The Yorkist pretender, Lambert Simnel.

1490

1492	The Treaty of Étaples.
1492–1499	Perkin Warbeck's risings.
1494	Poynings' act.
1496	The *Magnus Intercursus.*
1497	The Cabots' voyage to Newfoundland and Nova Scotia. John Colet's lectures on St. Paul's Epistles at Oxford.
1499	Erasmus' first visit to England at Oxford.

1500

1501	The marriage of Prince Arthur to Catherine of Aragon.
1502	The marriage of Princess Margaret to James IV of Scotland. The death of Prince Arthur.
1503	Prince Henry's betrothal to Catherine of Aragon.
1509–1547	*The Reign of Henry VIII.*
1509	Dean Colet's foundation of St. Paul's School. The marriage of Henry VIII and Catherine of Aragon. The execution of Empson and Dudley.

1510

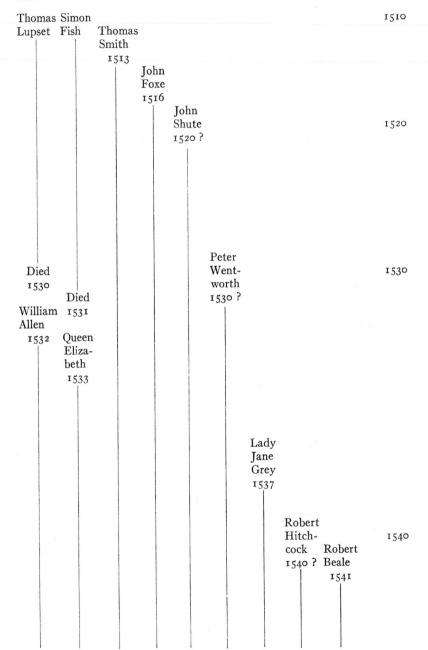

Thomas Simon   1510
Lupset Fish   Thomas
             Smith
             1513
                   John
                   Foxe
                   1516
                         John
                         Shute   1520
                         1520 ?

                                        Peter
Died   Went-   1530
1530   worth
         Died   1530 ?
William   1531
Allen
1532   Queen
         Eliza-
         beth
         1533

                                           Lady
                                         Jane
                                         Grey
                                         1537

                                                 Robert
                                                 Hitch-   1540
                                                 cock   Robert
                                                 1540 ?   Beale
                                                         1541

1510

1512–1513	Henry VIII's first war against France.
1515	The parliamentary attack on benefit of clergy, mortuary fees, and papal decrees.
1516	Sir Thomas More's *Utopia*.
1517	Martin Luther's attack on indulgences at Wittenburg.
1519	Charles V elected Holy Roman Emperor.

1520

1521	Henry VIII's *Assertio septem sacramentorum*. Henry VIII *Fidei Defensor*.
1525	Tyndale's English *Bible*.
1527	The sack of Rome and the imprisonment of Pope Clement VII. The divorcing of Catherine of Aragon considered.
1528	**Simon Fish, The Supplication for the Beggars; Thomas Lupset, An Exhortation to Young Men.**
1529	The fall of Wolsey. The opening of the Reformation Parliament.

1530

1531	Henry VIII Supreme Head of the Church of England by convocation.
1532	**An Argument for the Independence of the Spirituality.** The requirement of royal consent for church laws.
1533	The marriage of Henry VIII and Anne Boleyn. Thomas Cranmer archbishop of Canterbury. The decree of Henry VIII's divorce from Catherine of Aragon.
1534	The abolition of papal authority in England by acts of parliament.
1535	**Articles for Priests Unlearned.** The execution of More and Fisher.
1536	The dissolution of the smaller monasteries. The ' Ten Articles.' The Pilgrimage of Grace. The execution of Anne Boleyn. The marriage of Henry VIII and Jane Seymour. Henry VIII endowed Trinity College, Cambridge.
1539	The *Great Bible* in English. The ' Six Articles.' The final dissolution of the monasteries.

1540

	The execution of Thomas Cromwell.
1541	Henry VIII king of Ireland.
1542	War against Scotland. The birth of Mary Stuart.
1543–1546	War against France. The sale of monastic lands and debasement of the currency.
1547–1553	*The Reign of Edward VI.*
1547	Edward Seymour, duke of Somerset, governor and protector of the realm.

Allen Eliza- Smith Foxe Shute Went- Grey Hitchcock   Beale
    beth   worth

floret   1550
                                            Nicholas
                                            Breton 1551
                                              Richard
                                              Hakluyt
                                              1552 ?
                        Died
                        1554

                                                          1560

                        Henry
                        Wotton
            Died   1568
            1570 ?   1570
                                  floret
            Thomas
            Powell
            1572 ?   William
                                    Laud
Died   1573
1577

Ephraim   1580
Pagitt
1577 ?   David
            Thom-   Jen-
            as Roe   kins
            1581 ?   1582

1549   The first act of Uniformity and the first *Book of Common Prayer*.
          Kett's rebellion in East Anglia. The failure of the ' commonwealth party.'
1550   The earl of Warwick (duke of Northumberland 1551) in power.

1550–1553 **The Decay of England.**
1552   The second act of Uniformity and the second *Book of Common Prayer*.
1553   The ' Forty-two Articles.' Lady Jane Grey queen for nine days.
1553–1558 *The Reign of Mary.*
1554   The marriage of Mary and Philip II. **The execution of Lady Jane Grey.**
          The restoration of papal authority in England.
1555   Latimer and Ridley burned at Oxford. The Muscovy Company.
1557   War against France.
1558–1603 *The Reign of Elizabeth.*
1558–1560 Anthony Jenkinson's travels through Russia.
1559   The acts of Supremacy and Uniformity. John Knox in Scotland.
1560   The restoration of the currency. The Treaty of Edinburgh.

1561   Mary Stuart's return from France to Scotland.
1563   The ' Thirty-nine Articles.' The Apprentice act.
          The act against conjurations, enchantments, and witchcrafts.
          John Foxe, The Acts and Monuments.
          John Shute, The First and Chief Grounds of Architecture.
1565   **Sir Thomas Smith, De Republica Anglorum.**
1568   Mary Stuart's flight to England.
1569   The plot of Norfolk and the northern earls.
1570   Pope Pius V's excommunication of Elizabeth.

1571   The Ridolfi plot.
1572   **An Admonition to the Parliament.**
1576   **Peter Wentworth's Speech in the house of commons.**
1576–1578 Frobisher's three voyages seeking the northwest passage.
1578–1580 Drake's voyage around the world.
1579   Spanish-papal rebellion in Ireland. The Eastland Company.
          The Chelmsford Witchcraft Pamphlet.
1580   **Robert Hitchcock, A Politic Plat.**

1581   The Jesuit mission under Campion and Parsons. The Levant Company.
1584   **Richard Hakluyt, Western Discoveries.**
1585   **Elizabeth's Speech to parliament. The Middlesex Witchcraft Pamphlet.**

Al- Eliza- Pa- Foxe Pow- Roe Went- Wot- Jen- Hitch- Laud Beale Bre- Hak-
len beth gitt | ell worth ton kins cock ton luyt

Died
1587

1590

Died
1591 ?

Died
1594

Died
1596

1600

Died
1601

Died
1603

Gerrard
Winstanley
1609

1610

Died
1616
Anthony William
Ascham Smith
1618 1616 ?
1620

Marcha-
mont
Nedham
1620

Died
1626

1585–1587 Davis's voyages to Baffin's Bay. Leicester's expedition in the Netherlands.

1586 The Babington plot.

1587 The execution of Mary Stuart. Raleigh's unsuccessful colonization of Virginia.

1588 **Cardinal Allen, An Admonition to the Nobility. Elizabeth's Speech at Tilbury.**
The defeat of the Spanish Armada. The Martin Marprelate Tracts.

1590 The first three books of Spenser's *Faerie Queene.*

1591 The return of Ralph Fitch from Persia and India.
Shakespeare's *Love's Labour's Lost* (?).

1592 **Robert Beale, A Treatise of the Office of a Councillor.**

1593 **Elizabeth's Speech to Parliament.**
The hanging of the Puritans—Penry, Barrow, and Greenwood.

1594 The first four books of Richard Hooker, *The Laws of Ecclesiastical Polity.*

1597 **Peter Lowe, The Whole Art of Chirurgery.**

1598 **Act for the Relief of the Poor and Impotent.**

1599 Essex in Ireland.

1600 The East India Company.

1601 The abolition of monopolies.
Elizabeth's Golden Speech to parliament.
The rebellion and execution of Essex.

1603–1625 *The Reign of James I.*

1604 Peace with Spain. The Hampton Court Conference.

1605 The Gunpowder Plot.

1607 The successful settlement of Virginia.

1608 The settlement of the plantation of Ulster.

1610

1611 The authorized, King James, version of the *Bible.*

1614 The East India Company's ships victorious over the Portuguese off Surat.

1615 Sir Thomas Roe's embassy to the Great Mogul of India.

1616 The dismissal of Sir Edward Coke as chief-justice of the king's bench.

1618 **Nicholas Breton, The Court and Country.**

1620 The settlement of the Pilgrims at Plymouth, Massachusetts.

1621 The impeachment of Francis Bacon.
Parliamentary opposition to James I's foreign policy.

1622 **Tom Tell-Troath.**

1623 The visit of Charles and Buckingham to Madrid.

1624 **Sir Henry Wotton, The Elements of Architecture.** War with Spain.

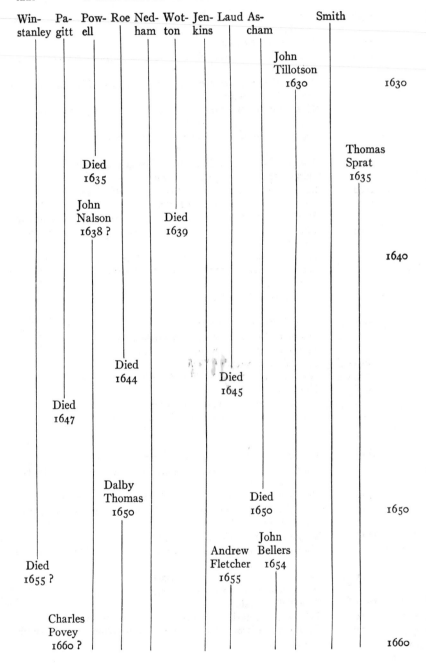

Win- Pa- Pow- Roe Ned- Wot- Jen- Laud As-   Smith
stanley gitt ell   ham ton kins   cham

John
Tillotson
1630   1630

Died   Thomas
1635   Sprat
                                 1635

John
Nalson   Died
1638 ?   1639

                                   1640

Died
1644   Died
                 1645
Died
1647

Dalby
Thomas   Died
1650   1650   1650

                         John
              Andrew Bellers
Died   Fletcher 1654
1655 ?   1655

Charles
Povey
1660 ?   1660

1625–1649 *The Reign of Charles I.*
1625   The marriage of Charles I and Henrietta Maria of France.
1627–1629 War with France.
1628   The Petition of Right. The assassination of Buckingham.
1629–1640 Charles I's rule without parliament.
1630

1631   **Thomas Powell, Tom of all Trades.**
1632–1639 Thomas Wentworth lord-deputy of Ireland.
1633   William Laud archbishop of Canterbury.
1634   The levying of ship-money. The settlement of Maryland.
1637   Hampden's case. The rejection of Laud's Litany in Scotland.
            The imprisonment of Prynne and Lilburne by the court of star
            chamber.
            William Laud, A Speech delivered in Star Chamber.
1639   The first Bishops' War. Wentworth made chief minister.
1640   The Short Parliament. The second Bishops' War.
            The Description of a Puritan.
1640   The Long Parliament.

1641   The Catholic rising in Ireland. The execution of Wentworth.
            Sir Thomas Roe, His Speech in Parliament.
1642–1646 The first Civil War.
1643   The Westminster Assembly of Divines. The Solemn League
            and Covenant.
            Touching the Fundamental Laws.
1644   **Ephraim Pagitt, Heresiography.**
1645   The organization of the New Model.
1646   The surrender of Oxford and the end of the first Civil War.
1647   The first 'Agreement of the People.'
1648   The second Civil War. Pride's Purge and the Rump parliament.
1649   The execution of Charles I and the establishment of the
            Commonwealth.
            **David Jenkins, God and the King. Anthony Ascham, The
            Original and End of Civil Power. Gerrard Winstanley, A
            Letter to Lord Fairfax.**
            Cromwell's conquest of Ireland.
1650   Cromwell's defeat of the Scots.

1651   The Navigation Act. Hobbes's *Leviathan.*
1652–1654 The first Dutch War.
1653   The Instrument of Government and the establishment of the
            Protectorate.
1655   The rule of the major-generals.
1655–1659 War with Spain.
1658   The death of Cromwell. Richard Cromwell Lord Protector.
1659   The abolition of the Protectorate. **The Leveller.**
1660   The restoration of Charles II. **A New Litany for these Times.**

Povey Nal- Thomas Ned- Jen- Fletcher Bellers Tillot- Smith Sprat   1660
    son   ham kins   son

Died
1663

William
Cowper
1664

John
Toland
1670

1670

Died
1678

1680

Died
1686

1690

1660

1660–1685 *The Reign of Charles II.*
1661–1679 The Cavalier parliament.
1661   The Savoy Conference.
1661–1665 The Clarendon Code.
1662   The Royal Society. **The Way to be Rich.**
1663   The plantation of the Carolinas. Milton's *Paradise Lost.*
           Marchamont Nedham, A Discourse concerning Schools.
1665–1667 The second Dutch War.
1665   The Great Plague.
1666   The Fire of London.
1667   The impeachment and exile of Clarendon. The Cabal.
           **Omnia Comesta a Belo. Thomas Sprat, The History of the
           Royal Society.**

1670   The Treaty, and Secret Treaty, of Dover.

1672   Charles II's Declaration of Indulgence. The Stop of the
           Exchequer.
1672–1674 The third Dutch War.
1673   The Test Act. The fall of the Cabal.
1674   **Verbum Sapienti.**
1674–1678 Danby's ministry.
1677   The marriage of Mary, daughter of James II, to William of
           Orange.
1678   Titus Oates's Popish Plot. The impeachment of Danby.
           Bunyan's *Pilgrim's Progress.*
1679   The Exclusion Bill. Dissolution of the Cavalier Parliament.
           John Nalson, A Letter from a Jesuit at Paris.
           John Tillotson, Of the Trial of the Spirits.

1680

1681   The Oxford Parliament. Dryden's *Absalom and Achitophel.*
1682   The settlement of Pennsylvania and Delaware.
           **Sir William Smith, Charge at the Quarter Sessions for
           Middlesex.**
1685–1689 *The Reign of James II.*
1685   Monmouth's rebellion.
1686   The revival of the court of high commission. Hales's case.
1687   James II's Declaration of Indulgence. Newton's *Principia.*
1688   James II's second Declaration of Indulgence. The seven
           bishops' case.
           The birth of James, the Old Pretender.
           The landing of William of Orange and the flight of James II.
1689–1694 *The Reign of William and Mary.*
1689   The Toleration act, the Mutiny act, and the Bill of Rights.
           Locke's *Essay on Government.* War of the League of Augsburg.

1690   **Dalby Thomas, Historical Account of the West Indies.**

Toland Povey Thomas Cowper Fletcher Bellers Tillotson Smith Sprat   1690

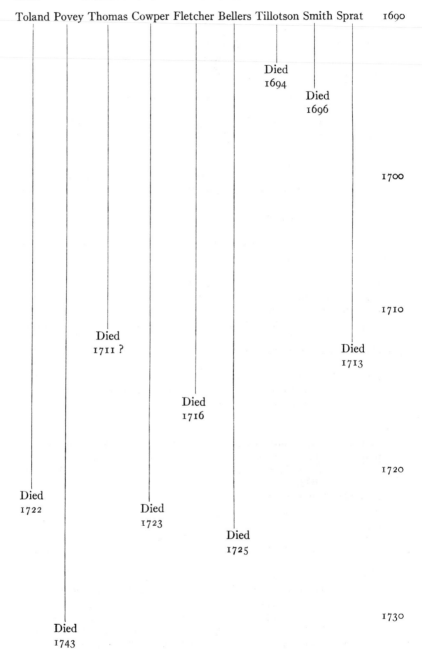

Died
1694

Died
1696

1700

1710

Died
1711 ?

Died
1713

Died
1716

1720

Died
1722

Died
1723

Died
1725

1730

Died
1743

1690

1692	The defeat of the French fleet off La Hogue.
1693	The beginning of the National Debt.
1694	The founding of the Bank of England.
1694–1702	*The Reign of William III.*
1695	The expiration of the licensing of the press act.
1696	**John Bellers, Supplement to the Proposal for a College of Industry.**
1698	The New East India Company. The first Partition Treaty. **John Toland, The Danger of Mercenary Parliaments.**
1698–1700	The Darien Company.

1700   The second Partition Treaty.

1701	**Charles Povey, The Unhappiness of England.** The act of Settlement.
1701–1713	The War of the Spanish Succession.
1702–1714	*The Reign of Anne.*
1704	**Andrew Fletcher, Proposals for the Reformation of Schools.** The capture of Gibraltar. The battle of Blenheim.
1707	The union of England and Scotland.
1708	The union of the two East India Companies.

1710   The trial of Dr. Sacheverell.

1711	**Representation of the Present State of Religion.** The South Sea Company. The Occasional Conformity Act. Property qualifications for members of parliament. The dismissal of Marlborough.
1712	The creation of twelve Tory peers.
1713	The Treaty of Utrecht and the Asiento Treaty.
1714	The Schism Act. **William Cowper, An Impartial History of Parties.**
1714–1727	*The Reign of George I of the House of Hanover.*

1720

1730

COMPLAINT AND REFORM
IN ENGLAND

THE LIBEL OF ENGLISH POLICY
1436

'A manual of statesmanship in rude verse,' the *Libel* was probably written in 1436. Although its author is unknown, it may have been prepared by Adam Moleyns, or Molyneux, then clerk of the king's council, afterwards bishop of Chichester. He was associated with the peace-party throughout his public career.

The poem contains views on England's foreign trade, international relations, and the importance of sea-power. It advocates a protective policy in the regulation of trade for the promotion of English interests, and, as a forecast of the economic and political policies of the next two centuries, the *Libel* brings into focus the nationalistic forces germinating in the early fifteenth century.

The present version is considerably abridged and edited, although the main arguments have been retained. In some instances where the versification has demanded the retention of the original word, a modern equivalent is given in brackets. To attain clarity the most reasonable reading has been chosen from the texts printed by Thomas Wright (*Political Poems and Songs*, Vol.II, 1861), Wilhelm Hertzberg (*The Libell of Englishe Policye*, Leipzig, 1878), and Sir George Warner, Oxford, 1926.

Here begins the prologue of the process of the Libel of English Policy, exhorting all England to keep the sea environ, and namely the narrow sea, showing what profit comes thereof, and also what worship and salvation to England and to all Englishmen.

The true process of English policy,
Of outerwards to keep this realm in rest
Of our England, that no man may deny,
Nor say of sooth but one of the best
Is this, that who says south, north, east, and west,
Cherish merchandise, keep the admiralty,
That we be masters of the narrow sea.

For Sigismond the great emperor,
Which yet reigns, when he was in this land
With King Henry the fifth, prince of honour,
Here much glory, as he thought, he found;
A mighty land, which had taken on hand
To war in France and make mortality
And ever well kept round about the sea.

And to the king thus he said, ' My brother,'
   When he perceived two towns Calais and Dover,
' Of all your towns to choose of one and other,
   ' To keep the sea and soon to come over
   ' To war outwards and your realm to recover,
' Keep these two towns sure to your majesty,
' As your two eyes to keep the narrow sea.'

For if this sea be kept in time of war
   Who can here pass without danger and woe?
Who may escape, who may mischief defer?
   What merchandise may forby be agoo [gone]?
   For needs he must take truce every foe
Flanders, and Spain, and others, trust to me,
Or else hindered all for this narrow sea.

Therefore I cast me by a little writing
   To show at eye this conclusion,
For conscience and for mine acquitting
   Against God and against abusion [abuse],
   And cowardice and to our enemy's confusion;
For four things our noble [a coin] shows to me,
King, ship, and sword, and power of the sea.

Where been our ships? where been our swords become?
   Our enemies bid for the ship set a shape.
Alas! our rule halts, it is benumb;
   Who dare well say that lordship should take keep?
   I will essay, though mine heart begin to weep,
To do this work, if we would ever the [thrive],
For very shame, to keep about the sea.

Shall any prince, what so be his name,
   Which has nobles much like ours,
Be lord of sea, and Flemings to our blame
   Stop us, take us, and so make fade the flowers
   Of English state, and disdain our honours?

For cowardice, alas! it should so be;
Therefore I begin to write now of the sea.

Of the commodities of Spain and of Flanders. The first chapter.

Know well all men that profit in certain
Commodities called, coming out of Spain,
And merchandise, who so well know what that is,
Been figs, raisins, wine bastard, and dates;
And licorice, Seville oil, and grain,
White Castile soap, and wax, is not in vain;
Iron, wool, wadmole,[1] goatfell, kidfell also,
For point-makers [2] full needful be the two;
Saffron, quicksilver, which are Spain's merchandy,
Is into Flanders shipped full craftily,
Unto Bruges, as to her staple fair,
The haven of Sluys they have for her repair,
Which is called the Swyn, their ships guiding,
Where many vessel and fair are abiding.
But these merchants, with their ships great,
And such chaffer as they buy and get
By the ways, must need take on hand
By the coasts to pass of our England,
Betwixt Dover and Calais, this is no doubt,
Who can well else such matter bring about.
     And when these said merchants discharged be
Of merchandise in Flanders near the sea,
Then they be charged again with merchandy
That to Flanders longeth full richly;
Fine cloth of Ypres, that named is better than ours,
Cloth of Curtrike, fine cloth of all colours,
Much fustian and also linen cloth.
But you Flemings, if you be not wroth,
The great substance of your cloth, at the full,
You know you make it of our English wool.

1. A coarse woollen cloth.
2. Makers of the points, or laces, with which the hose were fastened.

Then may it not sink in man's brain,
But that it must, this merchandise of Spain,
Both out and in by our coasts pass;
He that said nay, in wit was like an ass.
Thus if this sea were kept, I dare well say,
We should have peace with the grounds twain.
For Spain and Flanders is as each other's brother,
And neither may well live without other.
They may not live to maintain their degrees,
Without our English commodities,
Wool and tin; for the wool of England
Sustains the Flemish commons, I understand.
Then if England would this wool restrain
From Flanders, this follows in certain,
Flanders of need must with us have peace,
Or else she is destroyed, without lees [truly].
Also if Flanders thus destroyed be,
Some merchandy of Spain will never ithe [thrive];
For destroyed it is, and, as in chief,
The wool of Spain it comes not to proof,
But if it be toseed ³ and mixed well
Amongst English wool the greater deal.
For Spanish wool in Flanders draped is [made into cloth],
And ever has been, that men have mind of this;
And yet wool is one of the chief merchandy
That belongs to Spain, who so will espy;
It is of little value, trust unto me,
With English wool but if it mixed be.
Thus if the sea be kept, then hearken hither,
If these two lands come not together,
So that the fleet of Flanders pass nought
That in the narrow sea it be not brought
Into La Rochelle, to seek the fumose [smoky] wine,
Nor into Britain's bay for salt so fine,
What is then Spain? what is Flanders also?
As who said, nought, the thrift is ago [gone].

3. Picked, pulled, as wool, etc. A term used among clothiers.

For the little land of Flanders is
But a staple to other lands, I wis,
And all that grows in Flanders, grain and seed,
May not a month find him meat and bread.
What has then Flanders, be Flemings lief or loath,
But a little mader and Flemish cloth?
By draping of our wool in substance
Live her commons, this is her governance;
Without which they may not live at ease,
Thus must they starve, or with us must have peace.

Of the commodities of Portugal. The second chapter.

The merchandise also of Portugal
To divers lands come into sale.
Portuguese with us have truth in hand,
Whose merchandise comes much into England.
They been our friends with their commodities,
And we English pass into their countries.
Her land has oil, wine, osey [a wine], wax, and grain;
Figs, raisins, honey, and cordweine; [4]
Dates and salt, hides, and such merchandy.

. . . .

The commodities of Petty Brittany, with her rovers on the sea. The third chapter.

Furthermore to write I am fain,
Somewhat speaking of the Little Britain;
Commodities thereof there is and was,
Salt and wines, creste cloth [a linen], and canvas;
And the land of Flanders surely
Is the staple of their merchandy;
Which merchandise may not pass away,
But by the coast of England, this is no nay.
And of this Britain, who so truth believes,

4. Spanish leather, brought from Cordova.

Are the greatest rovers and the greatest thieves
That have been in the sea many one year,
That our merchants have bought full dear.
For they have taken notable goods of ours
On this said sea, these false coloured pelours [thieves],
Called of Saint Malo, and elsewhere,
Which to their duke none obeisance will bear.
With such colours we have been hindered sore,
And feigned peace is called no war herefore.
Thus they have been in divers coasts many
Of our England, more than rehearse can I;
In Norfolk coasts, and other places about,
And robbed and burnt and slain by many a route,
And they have also ransomed town by town,
That into the realms of the best have run their son[s];
Which have been ruth unto this realm and shame;
They that the sea should keep are much to blame.
For Britain is of easy reputation,
And Saint Malo turns him to reprobation.

A story of King Edward III his ordinance for Britain.

Here bring I in a story to me lent,
That a good squire, in time of parliament,
Took unto me well written in a scrowe [scroll],
That I have command both with high and low,
Of which all men accorden into one,
That it was done not many years agone,
But when noble King Edward the third
Reigned in grace, right thus it betide.
For he had a manner jealousy
To his merchants, and loved them heartily.
He felt the ways to rule well the sea,
Whereby merchants might have prosperity,
That from Harfleur and Houndfleur did he make,
And great wars that time were undertake
Betwixt the king and the duke of Britain;

At last to fall to peace both were they fain.
Upon the which, made by convention,
Our merchants made them ready bound
Toward Britain to load their merchandy,
Winning them friends, and went forth boldly.
But soon anon our merchants were itake,
And we sped never the better for truth's sake.
They lost their goods, their money, and spending;
But their complaint come unto the king.
Then wax he wroth, and to the duke he sent
And complained that such harm was hent
By convention, and peace made so refused.
Which duke sent again, and him excused,
Rehearsing that the mount of Saint Michael
And Saint Malo would never a dele [part]
Be subject unto his governance,
Nor be under his obeisance;
And so they did without him that deed.
But when the king anon had taken heed,
He in his heart set a judgment,
Without calling of any parliament,
Or great tarry to take long advice,
To fortify anon he did devise
Of English towns three, that is to say
Dartmouth, Plymouth, the third it is Fowey,
And gave them help and notable puissance,
With insistence set them in governance
Upon Petty Britain for to war.
That good seamen would no more defer,
But beat them home, and made they might not route,
Took prisoners, and learned them for to loot.
And again the duke an example wise
Wrote to the king, as he first did devise,
Him excusing; but our meny [people] wode [furious]
With great power passed over the flood,
And warred forth into the duke's land,
And had nigh destroyed free and bond.

But when the duke knew that the towns three
Should have lost all his natal country,
He undertook by surety true, not false,
For Mount Saint Michael and Saint Malo als[o],
And other parts of the Little Britain,
Which to obey, as said was, were not fain,
The duke himself for all did undertake,
With all his heart a full peace did he make.
So that in all the lifetime of the king
Merchants had peace without warring.

He make a statute for Lombards in this land,
That they should in no wise take on hand
Here to inhabit, here to charge and to discharge,
But forty days, no more time had they large.
This good king, by wit of such appreffe [contrivance],
Kept his merchants and the sea from mischief.

*Of the commodities of Scotland, and draping of her wool in Flanders. The
fourth chapter.*

Moreover, of Scotland the commodities
Are fells, hides, and of wool the fleece.
And all these must pass by us away
Into Flanders by England, sooth to say.
And all her wool was draped for to sell
In the towns of Poperinghe and of Bell,
Which my lord of Gloucester with ire
For her falsehood set upon a fire.
And yet they of Bell and Poperinghe
Could never drape their wool for anything,
But if they had English wool withal.
Our goodly wool that is so general
Needful to them in Spain and Scotland als[o],
And other coasts; this sentence is not false.
You worthy merchants, I do it upon you,
I have this learned, you know well where and how;

You know the staple of that merchandy
Of this Scotland is Flanders sikerly [surely].
And the Scots been charged, known at the eye,
Out of Flanders with little mercery,
And great plenty of haberdasher's ware,
And half their ships with cartwheels bare,
And with barrows, are laden as in substance.
Thus most rude ware be in their chevesaunce [bargain];
So they may not forbear this Flemish land.
Therefore if we would manly take on hand
To keep this sea from Flanders and from Spain,
And from Scotland, like as from Petty Britain,
We should right soon have peace for all their boasts;
For they must need pass by our English coasts.

*Of the commodities of Prussia, and High Dutch men, and Easterlings. The
fifth chapter.*

Now go we forth to the commodities
That come from Prussia in two manner degrees;
For two manner people have such use,
This is to say, High Dutch men of Pruse
And Easterlings, which might not be forborne
Out of Flanders, but it were verily forlorne.
For they bring in the substance of the beer
That they drink full too good cheap, not dear.
You have heard that two Flemings together
Will undertake, or they go any whither,
Or they rise once, to drink a barrel full
Of good beer; so sore they haul and pull,
Under the board they pissen as they sit;
This comes of covenant of a worthy wit.
Without Calais, in their breech they cakked [went to stool],
When they fled home, and when they leisure lacked
To hold their siege, they went like as a doe;
Well was that Fleming that might trusse [pack off] and go.
For fear they turned back, and hied fast;

My lord of Gloucester made them so aghast
With his coming, and sought them in their land,
And burnt and slew as he had taken on hand;
So that our enemies durst not bide nor stir,
They fled to mewe [5], they durst no more appear.

. . . .

Now beer and bacon been from Prussia brought
Into Flanders, as loved and far-sought;
Osmonde [iron], copper, bow-staves, steel, and wax,
Pelter-ware gray [hides], and pitch, tar, board, and flax,
And Cologne thread, fustian, and canvas,
Card, buckram, of old time thus it was.
But the Flemings among these things dear
In common love best bacon and beer.
Thus are they hogs, and drunken well ataunt [so much],
Farewell Fleming, hay, haro, hay, avaunt.
Also Prussia men make here adventure
Of plate of silver, of wedges good and sure
In great plenty, which they bring and buy
Out of lands of Bealme [Bohemia] and Hungary;
Which is increase full great unto this land.
And they been laden, I understand,
With woollen cloth all manner of colours,
By dyers crafts full diverse that been ours.
And they adventure full greatly into the Bay
For salt, that is needful without nay.
Thus if they would not our friends be,
We might lightly stop them in the sea;
They should not pass our streams without leave,
It would not be, but if we should them grieve.

*Of the commodities of the Genoese, and their great carracks. The sixth
chapter.*

The Genoese come in sundry wises
Into this land, with divers merchandises,

5. *Mewe:* A close place; strictly speaking, the place where falcons were put to moult.

In great carracks arrayed without lack,
With cloths of gold, silk, and pepper black
They bring with them, and of woad great plenty,
Wool, oil, wood ashes, by vessels in the sea,
Cotton, rock-alum, and good gold of Gene [Genoa].
And they be charged with wool again, I ween,
And woollen cloth of ours of colours all.
And they adventure, as oft it does befall,
Into Flanders with such things as they buy,
That is their chief staple sekerly;
And if they would be our full enemies,
They should not pass our streams with merchandise.

*The commodities and niceties of Venetians and Florentines, with their
galleys. The seventh chapter.*

The great galleys of Venice and Florence
Be well laden with things of complacence,
All spicery and of grocer's ware,
With sweet wines, all manner of chaffer,
Apes, and japes, and marmosettes tailed,
Nifles, trifles, that little have availed,
And things with which they cleverly blear our eye,
With things not enduring that we buy;
For much of this chaffer that is wastable
Might be forborne for dear and deceivable.
And that I ween, as for infirmities,
In our England is such commodities,
Without help of any other land,
Which by wit and practice be they found,
That all ill humours might be voided sure;
Which that we gather with our English cure,
That we should have no need to scammony [plant used in medicine],
Turbit, euforbe [a plant], correct diagredie,
Rhubarb, senna, and yet they been too needful;
But I know things also speedful,
That grow there, as these things said;

Let of this matter no man be dismayed,
But that a man may void infirmity
Without drugs fetched from beyond the sea.
And yet there should except be one thing,
It were but sugar, trust to my saying.
He that trusts not to my saying and sentence,
Let him better search experience.

. . . .

Another example of deceit.

Now listen well how they made us a baleys [rod]
When they borrowed at the town of Calais,
As they were wont, their wool that was them lent,
For year and year they should make payment,
And some time also two year and two year;
This was fair loan, but yet will you hear
How they to Bruges would their wools carry,
And for them take payment without tarry,
And sell it fast for ready money in hand?
For fifty pounds of money of loss they would not wonde [stop]
In a thousand pounds, and live thereby,
Till the day of payment easily,
Some gain again in exchange making,
Full like usury, as men make undertaking.
Then when this payment of a thousand pound[s]
Was well content, they should have chaffer sound,
If they would from the staple full
Receive again three thousand pounds in wool.
And thus they would, if we will believe,
Wipe our nose with our own sleeve;
Though this proverb be homely and undue,
Yet by likeliness it is for sooth full true.
In Cotswold also they ride about,
And all England, and buy without doubt,
What them list, with freedom and franchise,
More than we English may get in any wise.

But would God that, without longer delays,
These galleys were unfreighted in forty days,
And in those forty days charged again;
And that they might be put to certain
To go to host, as we there with them do.
It were expedient that they did right so
As we do there; if the king would it,
Ah! what worship would fall to English wit!
What profit also to our merchandy,
Which would of need be cherished heartily!
For I would know why now our navy fails,
When many a foe us at our door assails,
Now in these days, that, if there come a need,
What navy should we have it is to dread.
In Denmark were full noble conquerors
In time passed, full worthy warriors,
Which when they had their merchandise destroyed,
To poverty they fell, thus were they annoyed;
And so they stand at mischief at this day;
This learned I late, well written, this no nay.
Therefore beware, I can no better will,
If grace it will of other men's peril;
For if merchants were cherished to their speed,
We were not likely to fail in one need.
If they be rich, then in prosperity
Shall be our land, lords, and commonalty.
And in worship now think I on the son
Of merchandy, Richard of Whittington,
That lode-star and chief chosen flower,
What has by him our England of honour?
And what profit has been of his riches?
And yet lasts daily in worthiness,
That pen and paper may not me suffice
Him to describe, so high he was of price;
Above merchants to set him one of the best,
I can no more, but God have him in rest.

. . . .

Conclusion of this depending of keeping of the sea.

Then I conclude, if never so much by land
Were by carts brought unto their hand,
If well the sea were kept in governance,
They should by sea have no deliverance,
We should them stop, and we should them destroy,
As prisoners we should them bring to noy [injury];
And so we should of our cruel enemies
Make our friends for fear of merchandise,
If they were not suffered for to pass
Into Flanders; but we be frail as glass,
And also brittle, not tough, never abiding,
But when grace shines soon are we sliding.
We will it not receive in any wise;
That make lust, envy, and covetise.
Expound me this, and you shall sooth it find.
Bear it away, and keep it in your mind.

Then should worship unto our noble be,
In feet and form to lord and majesty;
Like as the seal the greatest of this land
On the one side has, as I understand,
A prince riding with his sword drawn,
In the other side sitting, sooth it is in saw,
Betokening good rule and punishing
In very deed of England by the king.
And it is so, God blessed might he be;
So one likewise I would were on the sea.
By the noble that sword should have power,
And the ships on the sea about us here.
What needs a garland, which is made of ivy,
Show a tavern wineless, also thrive I;
If men were wise, the Frenchman and Fleming
Should bear no state in sea by warring.

Of Hankin Lyons.

> Then Hankin Lyons [a pirate] should not be so bold
> To stop us, and our ships for to hold,
> Unto our shame; he had be beaten thence.
> Alas! Alas! why did we this offence,
> Fully to shed the old English fames,
> And the profits of England, and their names?
> Why is this power called of covetise
> With false colours cast before our eyes?
> That if good men called warriors
> Would take the sea for the common succours,
> And purge the sea unto our great avail,
> And win them good, and have up the sail,
> And on our enemies their lives to jeopard,
> So that they might their prizes well depart,
> As reason would, justice, and equity,
> To make this land have lordship of the sea.

. . . .

*Of the commodities of Ireland, and policy and keeping thereof, and con-
quering of wild Irish, with an incident of Wales. The ninth chapter.*

> I cast to speak of Ireland but a little,
> Commodities of it I will entitle,
> Hides, and fish, salmon, hake, herring,
> Irish woollen, linen cloth, falding [rough cloth],
> And martens good, been their merchandise,
> Hart's hides, and other of venery,
> Skins of otter, squirrel, and Irish hare,
> Of sheep, lamb, and fox, is their chaffer,
> Fells of kid and conies great plenty.
> So that if Ireland help us to keep the sea,
> Because the king called is *rex Angliae*,
> And is *dominus* also *Hiberniae*,
> Of old possessed by progenitors,
> The Irishmen have cause like to ours

Our land and theirs together defend,
That no enemy should hurt nor offend
Ireland nor us, but as one commonalty
Should help to keep well about the sea.
For they have havens great and goodly bays,
Sure, wide, and deep, of good assays,
At Waterford and coasts many one,
And, as men see, in England be there none
Better havens for ships in to ride,
No more sure for enemies to abide.
Why speak I thus so much of Ireland?
For also much as I can understand
It is fertile for things that there do grow
And multiply, look who so lust to know;
So large, so good, and so commodious,
That to declare is strange and marvellous.
For of silver and gold there is the ore
Among the wild Irish, though they be poor;
For they are rude, and know thereon no skill;
So that if we had there peace and good will,
To mine and refine, and metal for to pure,
In wild Irish might we find the cure.
As in London says a jeweller,
Which brought from thence gold ore to us here,
Whereof was refined metal good and clean,
As the touch, no better could be seen.
Now here beware and heartily take intent,
As you will answer at the last judgment,
That for sloth and for racheshede [carelessness]
You remember, with all your might take heed
To keep Ireland, that it be not lost;
For it is a buttress and a post
Under England, and Wales another.
God forbid but each were other's brother,
Of one allegiance due unto the king.
But I have pity, in good faith, of this thing,
That I shall say, with advisement,

I am afeared that Ireland will be shent,
It must away, it will be lost from us,
But if thou help, thou Jesus gracious,
And give us grace all sloth to leave beside.
For much thing in my heart is hide,
Which in another treatise I cast to write,
Made all only for that soil and site
Of fertile Ireland, which might not be forborne,
But if England were nigh as good as gone.
God forbid that a wild Irish wirling
Should be chosen for to be their king,
After their conquest of our last puissance,
And hinder us by other lands alliance.
Wise men say, which fools not, nor doubt,
That wild Irish so much of ground have got
There upon us, as likeliness may be,
Like as England to shires two or three
Of this our land is made comparable,
So wild Irish have won unto us unable
It to defend, and of no power
That our ground there is a little corner,
To all Ireland in true comparison.
It needs no more this matter to expose,
Which if it be lost, as Christ Jesus forbid,
Farewell Wales, then England comes to dread
For alliance of Scotland and of Spain,
And other more, as the Petty Britain,
And so have enemies environ round about.
I beseech God that some prayers devout
Might let the said appearance probable
Thus disposed without feigned fable;
But all only for peril that I see
Thus imminent as likely for to be.

And well I wot that from hence to Rome,
And, as men say, in all Christendom,
Is no ground nor land to Ireland like,

So large, so good, so plenteous, so rich,
That to this word *dominus* doth belong.
Then me seems that right were, and not wrong,
To get that land, and it were piteous
To us to lose this high name *dominus*.
And all this word *dominus* of name
Should have the ground obedient, wild and tame.
That name and people together might accord,
And all the ground be subject to the lord;
And that it is possible to be subject
Unto the king, well shall it be detect
In the little book that I of spake;
I trow reason all this will undertake.
And I know well with Ireland how it stand;
Alas! fortune begins so to scant,
Or else grace, that dead is governance.
For so diminishes parts of our puissance
In that land, that we lose every year
More ground and more, as well as you may hear.
I heard a man speak to me full late,
Which was a lord of full great estate,
That expenses of one year done in France
Werred [expended] on men well willed of puissance,
This said ground of Ireland to conquer,
And yet because England might not forbear
These said expenses gathered in one year,
But in three years or four gathered up here,
Might win Ireland to a final conquest
In one sole year, to set us all in rest.
And how soon would this be paid again,
What were it worth yearly, if we not feign,
I will declare, who so lust to look,
I trow full plainly in my little book.
But covetise and singularity
Of one profit, envy, cruelty,
Have done us harm, and do us every day,
And musters made that shame it is to say,

Our money spent all to little avail;
And our enemies so greatly do prevail,
That what harm may fall and overthwart,
I may hardly write more for sore of heart.

. . . .

Of the commodious stockfish of Iceland, and keeping of the sea, namely the
narrow sea, with an incident of the keeping of Calais. The tenth chapter.

Of Iceland to write is little need,
Save of stockfish; yet for sooth indeed
Out of Bristol, and coasts many one,
Men have practised by needle and by stone
Thither-wards within a little while
Within twelve years, and without peril
Gone and come, as men were wont of old
Of Scarborough unto the coasts cold;
And now so many ships this year there were,
That much loss for unfreight they bore;
Iceland might not make them to be fraught
Unto the havens thus much harm they caught.
Then here I end of the commodities
For which need is well to keep the seas;
East and west, south and north they be;
And chiefly keep sharply the narrow sea,
Between Dover and Calais, and as thus
That foes pass not without good will of us,
And they abide our danger in the length,
What for our coasts and Calais in our strength.

. . . .

After the chapters of commodities of divers lands, shows the conclusion of
keeping of the sea environ by a story of King Edgar, and two incidents
of King Edward the third and King Henry the fifth. The eleventh chapter.

Now see we well then that this round sea
To our noble be pariformity [similitude],

Within the ship is showed there the sail
And our king of royal apparel,
With sword drawn, bright and extent,
For to chastise enemies violent,
So should he be lord of the sea about,
To keep enemies from within and without,
To behold through Christianity
Master and lord environ of the sea,
All living men such a prince to dread
Of such a reign to be afeared indeed.
Thus prove I well that it was thus of old,
Which by a chronicle anon shall be told,
Right curious, but I will interpret
It into English, as I did it get.
Of King Edgar, one most marvellous
Prince living, witty, and chivalrous,
So good that none of his predecessors
Was to him like in prudence and honours.
He was fortunate, and more gracious
Than others before, and more glorious.
He was beneath no man in holiness,
He passed all in virtuous sweetness.
Of English kings was none so commendable
To English men, nor less memorable
Than Cyrus was to Persia by puissance;
And as great Charles was to them of France,
And as to the Romans was great Romulus,
So was to England this worthy Edgarus.
I may not write more of his worthiness,
For lack of time, nor of his holiness;
But to my matter I him exemplify,
Of conditions twain and of his policy.
Within his land was one, this is no doubt,
And another in the sea without.
That in time of winter and of werre [war],
When boisterous winds put seamen into ferre [fear],
Within his land about by all provinces

He passed through, perceiving his princes,
Lords, and others of the commonalty,
Who was oppressor, and who to poverty
Was drawn and brought, and who was clean in life,
And who was fallen by mischief and by strife
With overloading and extortion;
And good and bad of each condition
He espied: and his ministers als[o],
Who did truth, and which of them was false;
How the right and laws of his land
Were execute[d], and who durst take on hand
To disobey his statutes and decrees,
If they were well kept in all countries.
Of these he made subtle investigation
By his own espy and other men's relation.
Among other was his great business
Well to be ware that great men of riches
And men of might in city nor in town,
Should to the poor do no oppression.
Thus was he wont, as in this winter tide,
In such enserchise [inquiry] busily to abide;
This was his labour for the public thing,
Thus was he occupied, a passing holy king.

Now to the purpose; in the summer fair,
Of lusty season, when cleared was the air,
He had ready ships made before,
Great and huge, not few but many a score,
Full three thousand and six hundred also,
Stately enough on any sea to go.
The chronicles say these ships were full boisterous;
Such things belong to kings victorious.
In summer time would he have in wone [custom],
And in custom, to be full ready soon,
With multitude of men of good array,
And instruments of war of best assay;
Who could them well in any wise describe,

It were not light for any man alive.
Thus he and his would enter ships great,
Habiliments having and the fleet
Of sea-wars, that joyful was to see
Such a navy, and lord of majesty
There present in person them among,
To sail and row environ all along,
So regally about the English isle,
To all strangers terror and peril;
Whose sons went out in all the world about,
Unto great fear of all that be without,
And exercise to knights and his meyné [household]
To him belonging of his native country.
For courage must of need have exercise,
Thus occupied for eschewing of vice.
This knew the king, that policy espied,
Winter and summer he was thus occupied.
Thus conclude I by authority
Of chronicle, that environ the sea
Should been ours subject unto the king,
And he be lord thereof for any thing,
For great worship, and for profit also,
To defend his land from every foe.
That worthy king I leave, Edgar by name,
And all the chronicle of his worthy fame;
Save only this I may not pass away,
A word of mighty strength till that I say,
That granted him God such worship here,
For his merits, he was without peer,
That sometime at his great festivity
Kings and earls of many a country,
And provinces many, were there present,
And many lords come thither by assent
To his worship; but in a certain day
He bade ships be ready of array
For to visit Saint John's Church he list,
Rowing unto the good holy Baptist.

He assigned to earls, lords, knights,
Many ships right goodly to sights;
And for himself and eight kings mo[re]
Subject to him, he made keep one of tho[se],
A good ship, and entered into it,
With eight kings, and down did they sit,
And each of them an oar took in hand,
At oar-holes eight, as I understand;
And he himself at the ship behind
As steersman, it him became of kind.
Such another rowing, I dare well say,
Was not seen of princes many a day.
Lo, then, how he on waters had the price,
In land, in sea, that I may not suffice
To tell aright the magnanimity
That King Edgar had upon the sea.

An incident of the lord of the sea, King Edward the third.

Of King Edward I pass, and his prowess
On land, on sea, you know his worthiness.
The siege of Calais, you know well all the matter,
Round about by land and by the water,
How it lasted, not years many ago,
After the battle of Crécy was idoo [done];
How it was closed environ about,
Old men saw it which live, this is no doubt.
Old knights say that the duke of Burgoyne,
Late rebuked for all his golden coin,
Of ship and sea made no besieging there,
For want of ships that durst not come for fear.
It was no thing besieged by the sea,
Thus call they it no siege for honesty.
Guns assailed, but assault was there none,
No siege, but flight, well was he that might gone.
This manner carping have knights far in age,
Expert of old this manner language.

But King Edward made a siege royal,
And won the town, and in especial
The sea was kept, and thereof he was lord,
Thus made he nobles coined of record.
In whose time was no navy in the sea
That might withstand the power of his majesty.
Battle of Sluys you may read every day,
How it was done, I leave and go my way;
It was so late done that you it know,
In comparison within a little throw.
For which to God give we honour and glory,
For lord of sea the king was with victory.

*Another incident of keeping of the sea, in the time of the marvellous warrior
and victorious prince, King Henry the fifth, and of his great ships.*

And if I should conclude all by the king,
Henry the fifth, what was his purposing,
When at Hampton he made the great dromons [ships of war],
Which passed other great ships of all the commons,
The Trinity, the Grace-Dieu, the Holy-Ghost,
And other more which as now be lost,
What hope you was the king's great intent
Of those ships, and what in mind he meant?
It was not else but that he cast to be
Lord round about environ of the sea.
And when Harfleur had his siege about,
There came carracks horrible, great, and stout,
In the narrow sea willing to abide
To stop us there with multitude of pride.
My lord of Bedford came on and had the cure;
Destroyed they were by that discomfiture.
This was after the king Harfleur had won,
When our enemies to besiege had begun,
That all was slain or taken by true relation,
To his worship and his English nation.
There was present the king's chamberlain

At both battles, who knows this in certain;
He can it tell otherwise than I;
Ask him, and wit; I pass forth hastily.
What had this king of high magnificence,
Of great courage, of wisdom, and prudence,
Provision, foresight, audacity,
Of fortitude, justice, ability,
Discretion, subtle avisiveness [good counsel],
Temperance, nobleness, and worthiness,
Science, prowess, devotion, equity,
Of most estate his magnanimity,
Like to Edgar and the said Edward,
A branch of both, like them as in regard.
Where was in life a man more victorious,
And in so short time prince so marvellous?
By land and sea so well he him acquit,
To speak of him I stony [am confounded] in my wit.
Thus here I leave the king with his nobleness,
Henry the fifth, with whom all my process
Of this true book of pure policy,
Of sea keeping, intending victory,
I leave endly, for about in the sea
No better was prince of strenuity.
And if he had to this time lived here,
He had been prince named without peer.
His great ships should have been put in preffe [proof],
Unto the end that he meant of in cheffe [chief].
For doubt it not, but that he would have be
Lord and master about the round sea,
And kept it sure, to stop our enemies hence,
And won us good, and wisely brought it thence,
That no passage should be without danger
And his licence on sea to move and stir.

Of unity, showing of our keeping of the sea, with one final process of peace
by authority. The twelfth chapter.

Now then for love of Christ and of his joy,
Bring it England out of trouble and noye,
Take heart and wit, and set a governance,
Set many wits without variance
To one accord and unanimity,
Put to good will for to keep the sea.
First for worship and profit also,
And to rebuke of each evil willed foe;
Thus shall riches and worship to us belong;
Then to the noble shall we do no wrong,
To bear that coin in figure and in deed,
To our courage and our enemies to dread.
For which they must dress them to peace in haste,
Or else their thrift to standen and to waste,
As this process hath proved by and by,
All by reason and expert policy,
And by stories which proved well this part;
And else I will my life put in jeopart,
But many lands would seek here peace for need,
The sea well kept, it must be do for dread.
Thus must Flanders for need have unity
And peace with us, it will none other be,
Within short while, and ambassadors
Would been here soon to treat for their succours.
This unity is to God pleasaunce
And peace after the wars variance;
The end of battle is peace sikerly,
And power causes peace finally.
Keep then the sea about in special,
Which of England is the round wall;
As though England were likened to a city,
And the wall environ were the sea.
Keep then the sea, that is the wall of England,
And then is England kept by God's hand;

That is, for any thing that is without,
England were at ease without doubt.
And thus should every land one with another
Entrecomen [intercommunicate] as brother with his brother,
And live together warless in unity,
Without rancour, in very charity,
In rest and peace, to Christ's great pleasance,
Without strife, debate, and variance.
Which peace men should ensearch with business,
And knit it sadly holding in holiness.
The apostle says, if you list to see,
' Be ye busy for to keep unity
' Of the spirit in the bond of peace,'
Which is needful to all, without lese.
The prophet bids us peace for to inquire,
To pursue it, this is holy desire.
Our Lord Jesus says, ' Blessed might they be
' That make peace, that is tranquility.'
' For peace makers,' as Matthew writes aright,
' Shall be called the sons of God almight.'
God give us grace the ways for to keep
Of his precepts, and sluggishly not to sleep
In shame of sin, that our very foe
May be to us converse and turned to.
For in Proverbs a text is to purpose,
Plain enough, without any gloss,
' When men's ways please unto our Lord,
' It shall convert and bring to accord
' Man's enemies unto peace very,
' In unity, to live to God's pay.'
Which unity, peace, rest, and charity,
He that was here clad in humanity,
That came from heaven, and mounted up with our nature,
Ere he ascended, he gave to us cure,
And left with us peace against strife and debate,
Might give us peace so well iradicate [rooted]
Here in this world, that after all this feste

We may have peace in the land of behest [promise],
Jerusalem, which of peace is the sight,
With his brightness of eternal light.
There glorified in rest with his tuition
The deity to see with full fruition,
He second person in divineness,
Who us assume, and bring us to the bliss. Amen.

Here ends the true process of the Libel of English Policy, exhorting all England to keep the sea environ, and namely the narrow sea; showing what worship, profit, and salvation comes thereof to the realm of England.

Go forth, libel, and meekly show thy face,
    Appearing ever with humble countenance;
And pray my lords thee to take in grace
    In opposaile [inquiry], and cherishing thee advance
To hardiness, if that not variance
    Thou hast from truth by full experience,
Authors and reasons: if ought fail in substance,
    Remit to them that gave thee this science.
That since it is sooth, in very faith,
    That the wise lord baron of Hungerford
Hath thee overseen, and verily he says
    That thou art true, and thus he doth record,
Next the gospel; God wot, it was his word,
    When he thee read all over in a night.
    Go forth, true book, and Christ defend the right.

Explicit libellus de policia conservativa maris.

ACTS FOR THE REFORMATION OF EXCESSIVE ARRAY

1363–1533

THE base of these selections is the act for the reformation of excessive array prepared in 1461 but not enacted until 1463. The elaborate scheduling of the apparel suitable to various degrees of social status demonstrates three points: first, the character of the various 'estates and degrees' in English society and the close connection between wealth and status; then the economic protection afforded by this act to native craftsmen; and finally, the keen desire of the new Yorkist government to establish social order— 'peace, unity, and concord.'

The principles involved in this act were not new but medieval. Its prototype is the act of 1363 which has been included to show the evolution of social categories during the century before 1463. A similar act of 1533 attests a further elaboration of social degree and describes a more sophisticated society embellished with titles of honour, prizes, and badges for successful attainment. The increase in wealth since 1463 is obvious from the sumptuousness of the apparel mentioned.

The original economic motive—the protection of domestic industry—still persisted in 1533. The moral aspirations of the governors of English society appear in the preambles of the three acts, and the role of local government in the enforcement of national legislation is clearly apparent. However, the distinction between enactment and enforcement must be remembered, and the success of these acts in regulating conduct, save perhaps in excluding foreign goods, may be doubted. They may better be considered to reflect the social ideals than the actual state of society.

The following version has been taken from the *Statutes of the Realm* and has been modified for the sake of clarity.

STATUTES OF THE REALM

37 Edward III, cc.8–15, 1363

[Original in French]

THE DIET AND APPAREL OF SERVANTS.

VIII. ITEM, For the outrageous and excessive apparel of divers people, against their estate and degree, to the great destruction and impoverishment of all the land; it is ordained, that grooms, as well servants of lords, as they of mysteries and artificers, shall be served to eat and drink once a day of flesh or of fish, and the remnant of other victuals, as of milk, butter, and cheese, and other such victuals, according to their estate: and that they have cloths for their vesture, or hosing, whereof the whole cloth shall not exceed 2 marks, and that they wear no cloth of higher price, of their buying, nor nothing of gold nor of silver embroidered, enamelled, nor of silk, nor nothing pertaining to the said things; and their wives, daughters, and children of the same condition in their clothing and apparel, and they shall wear no veils passing 12 pence a veil.

THE APPAREL OF HANDICRAFTSMEN AND YEOMEN.

IX. ITEM, That people of handicraft and yeomen shall not take nor wear cloth of a higher price for their vesture or hosing than within 40 shillings the whole cloth; nor stone, nor cloth of silk nor of silver, nor girdle, knife, button, ring, garter, nor brooch, ribbon, chains, nor any such other things of gold or of silver, nor any manner of apparel embroidered, enamelled, nor of silk; and that their wives, daughters, and children be of the same condition in their vesture and apparel; and that they wear no veil of silk, but only of yarn made within the realm, nor no manner of fur, nor of budge [lamb's skin], but only lamb, cony, cat, and fox.

APPAREL OF ESQUIRES AND GENTLEMEN.

X. ITEM, That esquires and all manner of gentlemen, under the estate of a knight, which have no land nor rent to the value of £100 a year, shall not take nor wear cloth for their clothing or hosing of a higher price, than within the price of 4 marks and a half the whole cloth, by way of buying nor otherwise; and that they wear no cloth of gold, nor silk, nor silver, nor any manner of clothing embroidered, ring, buttons, nor brooch of gold, ribbon, girdle, nor any other apparel, nor harness, of gold nor of silver, nor anything of stone, nor any manner of fur; and that their wives, daughters, and children be of the same condition, as to their vesture and apparel, without any turning up or purfle [decorated border]; and that they wear no manner of apparel of gold or silver, or of stone. But that esquires, which have land or rent to the value of £200 a year and above, may take and wear cloths of the price of 5 marks the whole cloth, and cloth of silk and of silver, ribbon, girdle, and other apparel reasonably garnished of silver; and that their wives, daughters, and children may wear fur turned up of miniver [white squirrel], without ermines or lettice [skunk?] or any manner of stone, but for their heads.

APPAREL OF MERCHANTS, CITIZENS, AND HANDICRAFTSMEN.

XI. ITEM, That merchants, citizens and burgesses, artificers, people of handicraft, as well within the City of London, as elsewhere, which have clearly goods and chattels to the value of £500, and their wives and children may take and wear in the manner as the esquires and gentlemen which have land to rent to the value of £100 a year; and that the same merchants, citizens, and burgesses, which have clearly goods and chattels to the value of £1000, and their wives and children may take and wear in the manner as esquires and gentlemen, which have land and rent to the value of £200 a year: and no groom, yeoman, or servant of merchant, artificer or people of handicraft shall wear otherwise in apparel than is above ordained of yeomen of lords.

APPAREL OF KNIGHTS.

XII. ITEM, That knights, which have land or rent within the value of £200 shall take and wear cloth of 6 marks the whole cloth for their vesture and of none higher price: and that they wear not cloth of gold, nor clothes, mantle, nor gown furred with miniver nor of ermines, nor any apparel embroidered with stones, nor otherwise; and that their wives, daughters, and children be of the same condition; and that they wear no turning up of ermines, nor of lettices, nor any manner of apparel of stone, but only for their heads. But that all knights and ladies, which have land or rent over the value of 400 marks a year, to the sum of £1000 shall wear at their pleasure, except ermines and lettices and apparel of pearls and stone, but only for their heads.

APPAREL OF THE CLERGY.

XIII. ITEM, That clerks, which have degree in any church, cathedral, college, or schools, or clerk of the king that hath such estate that requires fur, shall do and use according to the constitution of the same; and all other clerks, which have 200 marks of land a year, shall wear and do as knights of the same rent; and other clerks within the same rent shall wear as the esquires of £100 of rent: and that all those, as well knights as clerks, which by this ordinance may wear fur in winter, in the same manner shall wear lawn [fine linen] in the summer.

APPAREL OF PLOUGHMEN.

XIV. ITEM, That carters, ploughmen, drivers of the plough, oxherds, cowherds, shepherds, deyars [swineherds], and all other keepers of beasts, threshers of corn, and all manner of people of the estate of a groom, attending to husbandry, and all other people, that have not forty shillings of goods, nor of chattels, shall not take nor wear any manner of cloth, but blanket and russet wool of twelve-pence; and shall wear the girdles of linen according to their estate; and that they come to eat and drink in the manner as pertains to them, and not excessively. And it is ordained, that if any wear or do contrary to any of the points aforesaid, that he shall forfeit to the king all the apparel that he has so worn against the form of this ordinance.

CLOTHIERS SHALL MAKE CLOTHS ACCORDINGLY.

XV. ITEM, To the intent that this ordinance, for the taking and wearing of cloths, be maintained and kept in all points without blemish; it is ordained, that all the makers of cloths within the realm as well men as women, shall conform in making their cloths according to the price limited by this ordinance; and that all the drapers shall buy and purvey their sorts according to the same price; so that so great a plenty of such cloths be made and set to sale in every city, borough, and merchant town, and elsewhere within the realm, that for default of such cloths the said ordinance be in no point broken; and the said clothmakers and drapers shall be constrained in any way that shall seem best to the king and his council. And this ordinance of new apparel shall begin at Candlemas [2 February] next coming.

STATUTES OF THE REALM

38 Edward III, c.2, 1364

[Original in French]

THE STATUTE 37 EDW.III, C.5, REPEALED.

II. ITEM, As to that which was ordained at the last parliament of living and of apparel, and that no English merchant should use but one merchandise: it is ordained that all people shall be as free as they were at all times before the said ordinance, and namely as they were in the time of the king's grandfather, and his other good progenitors.

ALL BUYING AND SELLING DECLARED FREE.

And that all merchants, as well aliens as denizens, may sell and buy all manner of merchandise, and freely carry them out of the realm, paying the customs and subsidies thereof due.

EXCEPT AS TO EXPORT OF WOOLS AND OF GOLD AND SILVER.

Except that the English merchants shall not pass out of the realm with wools or woolfells; and that none carry out of the realm gold nor silver, in plate nor in money, saving the victuallers of fish that fish for herring and other fish, and they that bring fish within the realm in small vessels, which meddle not with other merchandise; and that according to the arbitrament of the chancellor.

STATUTES OF THE REALM
3 Edward IV, c.5, 1463
[Original in French]

APPAREL OF PERSONS ACCORDING TO THEIR SEVERAL RANKS.

ITEM, Pray the commons in the said parliament assembled, to our said sovereign lord the king, to call to his gracious remembrance that in the times of his noble progenitors divers ordinances and statutes were made in this realm of England for the apparel and array of the commons of the same realm, as well of men as of women, so that none of them ought to use nor wear any inordinate and excessive apparel, but only according to their degrees; which statutes and ordinances notwithstanding, for default of punishment and putting them in due execution, the commons of the said realm, as well men as women, have worn and daily do wear excessive and inordinate array and apparel to the great displeasure of God and impoverishing of this realm of England and to the enriching of strange realms and countries, to the final destruction of the husbandry of this said realm:

KNIGHTS UNDER THE ESTATE OF A LORD AND THEIR WIVES.

Our said sovereign lord the king, by the advice and assent of the said lords spiritual and temporal, and at the special request of the said commons assembled in the said parliament, and by authority of the same, hath ordained and established that no knight under the estate of a lord, other than lords' children, nor no wife of such knight, from the Feast of the Purification of Our Lady, [2 February], which shall be in the year of our Lord God 1465, shall wear any manner cloth of gold, or any corsets wrought with gold, or any fur of sables; and if any such knight do the contrary, or suffer his wife or child, the same child being under his rule or governance, to do the contrary, that then he shall forfeit for every such default £20 to the king.

KNIGHTS BACHELORS AND THEIR WIVES.

And also that no bachelor knight, nor his wife, from the said feast, shall wear any cloth of velvet upon velvet, but such knights which be of the Order of the Garter, and their wives, upon pain to forfeit to the king's use for every such default 20 marks. And also that no person under the estate of a lord, from the said feast, wear any manner of cloth of silk, being of the colour of purple; upon pain to forfeit to the king for every default £10. And also that no esquire nor gentleman, nor none other under the degree of a knight, nor none of their wives, except the sons of lords and their wives, and the daughters of lords, esquires for the king's body, and their wives, shall wear from the said feast any velvet, satin branched, nor any counterfeit cloth of silk resembling the same, or any corsets wrought like to velvet or to satin branched, or any fur of ermine; upon pain to forfeit for every default 10 marks to the king's use. And also that no esquire nor gentleman, nor none other under the degrees above rehearsed, shall wear, from the said feast, any damask or satin, except the menial esquires, sergeants, officers of the king's household, yeomen of the crown, yeomen of the king's chamber, and esquires and gentlemen having possessions to the yearly value of £40 and their wives and widows having like possessions, and the daughters unmarried of persons having possessions to the value of £100 by the year; upon pain to forfeit to the king for every default 100 shillings.

THE STEWARD, TREASURER, ETC., OF THE KING'S HOUSEHOLD.

Provided always, that the steward, chamberlain, treasurer, and comptroller of the king's household, and knights for his body and their wives may wear furs of sables and ermines.

THE MAYORS OF LONDON.

And that the mayors of the City of London, which be or have been

or hereafter for the time shall be, and their wives, may wear such array
as before is limited to bachelor knights and to their wives.

ALDERMEN AND RECORDERS OF LONDON.

And that such which be or have been or for the time shall be aldermen or recorders of the same city, and all mayors and sheriffs of cities,
towns, and boroughs of this realm of England, such as be counties
corporate, and all mayors and bailiffs of all other cities, and of every
of the Cinque Ports, and the barons of the same ports, such as have
been chosen and assigned, or hereafter shall be chosen and assigned
to do their service at the coronation of the king our sovereign
lord, or of my lady the queen, and mayors and bailiffs of boroughs
corporate, being shire towns, and the mayors and bailiffs of Colchester and Lynn, and the recorders of the said cities, boroughs,
and towns, being counties corporate, and of all other cities, now being
recorders, or which have been or in time to come shall be, and the aldermen of the same, and their wives in like manner, may use and wear
such array as before is limited to esquires and gentlemen before specified,
having possessions to the yearly value of £40.

PERSONS NOT HAVING POSSESSIONS OF THE YEARLY VALUE OF £40.

And also our said sovereign lord the king hath ordained and established in this present parliament that no man but such as have possessions to the yearly value of £40 or above, shall wear, from the said feast,
any fur of martens, lettice [skunk?], pure gray, or pure miniver [white
squirrel]; nor no wife, son, daughter, nor servant of any man, the same
son and daughter being in his rule and governance, nor no widow but
such as hath possessions of the said yearly value of £40, shall use nor
wear any of the said furs, or any girdle garnished with gold or silver, in
any part of the same gilt, or any corset of silk made out of this realm of
England, or any coverchiefs, whereof the price of a plight [a recognized
length] shall exceed the sum of 3 shillings 4 pence; upon pain to forfeit
to the king for every default thereof 5 marks.

PROVISO FOR THE OFFICERS OF THE KING'S HOUSEHOLD, AND OTHERS.

Provided always, that the said menial esquires, sergeants, officers of
the king's household, yeomen of the crown, yeomen of the king's chamber, and esquires and gentlemen having possessions of the said yearly
value of £40, and the aforesaid mayors, recorders, aldermen, sheriffs and
bailiffs of every of the said cities, towns, and boroughs, and the said

barons of the Cinque Ports and their wives, may wear the said furs of martens, foins [beech-martens], lettice, pure gray, or pure miniver, and also that their said wives may use and wear gilt girdles, and coverchiefs of the price of 5 shillings the plight.

PERSONS NOT HAVING 40S. PER ANNUM.

And moreover, he hath ordained and established, that no man but such as hath possessions of the yearly value of 40 shillings shall wear in array for his body, from the said feast, any fustian, bustian, nor fustian of Naples, scarlet cloth in grain, nor any fur but black or white lamb; all mayors, aldermen, sheriffs, barons of the Cinque Ports, bailiffs of cities and boroughs, and others before provided, and their wives, and the menial servants of yeomen's degree, of lords, knights, esquires, and other gentlemen having possessions of the said yearly value of £40 excepted; upon pain of 40 shillings to be forfeit to the king for every such default.

APPAREL OF YEOMEN.

And also, he hath ordained and established that no yeoman, nor none other person under the same degree, from the said Feast of St. Peter called Ad Vincula [1 August], which shall be in the year of our Lord 1465, shall use nor wear in array for his body any bolsters nor stuffing of wool, cotton, nor caddis [padding], nor any stuffing in his doublet, but only lining according to the same; upon pain to forfeit to the king's use for every such default 6 shillings and 8 pence. Also our said sovereign lord the king, by the advice and assent aforesaid, has ordained and established, that no knight under the estate of a lord, esquire, gentleman, nor none other person, shall use or wear from the Feast of All Saints [1 November], which shall be in the year of our Lord 1465, any gown, jacket, or coat, unless it be of such length that the same, he being upright, may cover his privy members and buttocks; upon pain to forfeit to the king for every default 20 shillings.

PENALTY ON TAILORS.

Also by the assent aforesaid, it is ordained, that no tailor after the said feast, shall make to any person any gown, jacket, or coat, of less length, or doublet stuffed, contrary to the premises, upon the same pain for every default.

LENGTH OF PIKES TO SHOES AND BOOTS.

And also hath ordained and established in the said present parliament that no knight under the estate of a lord, esquire, gentleman, nor other person shall use nor wear, after the said Feast of St. Peter [1 August], any shoes or boots having pikes passing the length of two inches; upon pain to forfeit to the king for every default 3 shillings and 4 pence.

PENALTY ON SHOEMAKERS.

And if any shoemaker make any pikes of shoes or boots after the said Feast of St. Peter to any of the said persons, contrary to this ordinance, he shall likewise forfeit to the king for every default 3 shillings 4 pence.

APPAREL OF SERVANTS IN HUSBANDRY, LABOURERS, ETC.

Also he has ordained and established, by the advice and assent aforesaid, that no servant of husbandry, nor no common labourer nor servant nor any artificer dwelling out of a city or borough, after the said Feast of All-Saints [1 November], shall use nor wear in their clothing any cloth, whereof the broad yard shall pass the price of 2 shillings; nor that any of the said labourers nor servants suffer any of their wives to wear after the same feast any clothing of higher price than before is limited to their husbands; nor that they suffer any of their said wives, after the same feast, to wear any coverchiefs, whereof the price of the plight shall pass 12 pence; nor that none of the same servants nor labourers, after the same feast, shall wear any close hose, whereof the pair shall pass in price 14 pence; nor that the same servants nor labourers, nor none of their wives, from the said feast, shall wear any girdle garnished with silver; upon pain to forfeit for every default to the king 3 shillings 4 pence. And because that coverchiefs daily brought into this realm do induce great charge and cost in the same, and in effect in waste, our said sovereign lord the king, by the authority aforesaid, has ordained and established that no person, after the Feast of St. Michael the Archangel [29 September] which shall be in the year of our Lord 1465, shall sell in any part within this realm, any lawn [fine linen], nifles [light or flimsy cloth], umple [kind of linen], or any other manner of coverchiefs, whereof the plight shall exceed 10 shillings, upon pain to forfeit to the king for every plight sold at a higher price 13 shillings 4 pence.

JUSTICES OF THE PEACE AND MAYORS MAY HEAR AND DETERMINE OFFENCES.

And also he has ordained and established that the justices of the peace of every county, mayors of cities and boroughs within this realm shall have authority and power to inquire, hear, and determine all and every of the said defaults and forfeitures, as well by inquiry as by due examination of every of the said offenders contrary to this ordinance; and the matters and causes, concerning the said offences and forfeitures, to determine by like process and in like manner and form before attainder in this behalf, as is commonly used by them of trespass done with force and arms against the king's peace; and after the attainder like execution.

REMOVAL OF SUCH PROCEEDING INTO THE KING'S BENCH.

And if any matter touching any of the said offences be removed from any of the said justices of peace or mayors before the king, that then the justices assigned for pleas before the king to be holden shall have power to award such process and execution in this behalf, as before is limited.

APPLICATION OF FORFEITURES.

Also he has ordained and established that all the said forfeitures and every of them shall be levied, applied, and employed to the use and expenses of the king's household.

PROVISO FOR PERSONS OFFICIATING AT DIVINE SERVICE.

Provided always that this statute of array be in no wise prejudicial or hurtful to any person using or wearing any ornament, vesture, or apparel in doing of divine service. Nor that this ordinance extend to the justices of any bench of our sovereign lord the king, master or warden of the rolls, master of the king's chancery, barons of the king's exchequer, nor chancellor of the same, which now be or hereafter shall be.

FOR SCHOLARS OF THE UNIVERSITIES.

Provided also that the scholars of the universities of this realm, and scholars of any university out of this realm, may wear such array as they may wear by the rule of the said universities, notwithstanding this ordinance. Provided also that henchmen, heralds, pursuivants, sword-bearers to mayors, messengers, and minstrels, nor none of them, nor players in their interludes shall not be comprised within this statute; nor any persons wearing any purses, brooches, or crowns for caps of children, shall be comprised within the same. Provided also that this ordinance do in no wise extend to any manner of array necessary to be worn in war or in the feats of the same.

STATUTES OF THE REALM
22 Edward IV, c.1, 1483
[Original in French]

Here Begin the Statutes Made at Westminster in the Twenty-Second Year.

OUR lord the king, Edward the Fourth, at his parliament held at Westminster the twentieth day of January, in the two-and-twentieth year of his reign, to the honour of God, and for the weal of his people of this his realm, by the advice and assent of the lords spiritual and temporal, and at the request of his commons, in the said parliament assembled, and by the authority of the same parliament, has ordained and established certain statutes and ordinances in the manner and form following:

I. FORMER STATUTES RESPECTING APPAREL.

FIRST, Because that our sovereign lord the king has conceived by a petition made to him by his commons that divers statutes and ordinances touching the restraint of the excessive apparel of the people of his said realm were made and ordained, and that for the non-due execution of the same statutes his said realm was fallen into great misery and poverty, and like to fall into greater unless a better remedy be provided. Whereupon our said sovereign lord the king, by the advice, assent, and authority aforesaid, has ordained and established that no manner of person of what estate, degree, or condition that he be, shall wear any cloth of gold, or silk of purple colour, but only the king, the queen, the king's mother, the king's children, his brother and sisters, upon pain of forfeiture for every default £20. And that none under the estate of a duke shall wear any cloth of gold of tissue, upon pain of forfeiture for every default 20 marks. And that no man under the estate of a lord shall wear plain cloth of gold, upon pain to forfeit for every default 10 marks; and that no man under the degree of a knight shall wear any velvet in his doublets nor gowns; and that no man under the same degree wear any damask or satin in his gowns, but only esquires for the king's body, upon pain to forfeit for every default 10 shillings, and that no yeomen of the crown, nor other men under the degree of an esquire or gentleman, shall wear in their doublets damask or satin, nor gowns of camlet, upon pain to forfeit for every default 40 shillings. And that no man under the estate of a lord wear any manner of woollen cloth made out of this realm of England, Ireland, Wales, and Calais, nor wear any furs of sables, upon pain to forfeit for every default £10. And also it is ordained and established by the said authority that no servant of husbandry nor common labourer, nor servant to any artificer out of city or borough, shall wear in their clothing any cloth, whereof the broad yard shall pass the price of 2 shillings; nor that any of the said servants or labourers shall suffer their wives to wear any clothing of higher price than is before limited to their husbands; nor they shall not suffer their wives to wear any reile [neckerchief] called a kerchief, whose price exceeds 20 pence, nor none of the said servants or labourers shall wear any hose, whereof the pair shall pass 18 pence, upon pain to forfeit for every default 3 shillings 4 pence. Moreover, it is ordained that the justices of peace in every county, mayors, sheriffs, bailiffs, masters and other chief officers of cities, boroughs, towns of the Cinque Ports and other corporate towns within this realm, shall have power and authority to inquire, hear, and determine all the said defaults and forfeitures, and every of them, to be made or had within their several jurisdictions, as well by inquiry as by due examination, and the matters and causes concerning the said offences and forfeitures to determine by like process and judgment, and in like manner and form before attainder in this behalf, as is before the justices of peace commonly used of trespass done with force and arms against the king's peace, and after attainder like execution.

. . . .

FORMER ACTS REPEALED.

Also it is ordained by the authority aforesaid that all other ordinances and statutes before this time made of array or apparel shall be by the authority of this present parliament void and of no force nor effect; and that this act begin and take effect after the Feast of Epiphany next coming [6 January 1484], and not before. And it is ordained and enacted by the authority aforesaid that no manner person under the estate of a lord shall wear from the said feast any gown or mantle unless it be of such length, that, he being upright, it shall cover his privy members and buttocks; upon pain to forfeit to our sovereign lord the king at every default, 20 shillings; and like examination, process, and judgment shall be therein had as in the premises is ordained. Provided always that this present act for apparel shall not be prejudicial to the liberty in wearing of cloth and fur, purple and cloth of gold only excepted, of Sir Thomas Montgomery, Sir Thomas Burgh, Sir Thomas Vaughan, Sir John Don, Sir William Parr, Sir Thomas St. Leger, Sir Thomas Bourchier, Sir Thomas Grey, nor of Master Oliver, the king's secretary, nor any of them. And provided also that the same act be not prejudicial to Master John Gunthorp, dean of the king's chapel; nor to Sir John Elrington, treasurer of the king's house nor to any of them as above.

STATUTES OF THE REALM

24 Henry VIII, c.xiii, 1533

An Act for Reformation of Excess in Apparel

[Original in English]

[Abridged]

INEFFICIENCY OF FORMER LAWS AGAINST EXCESS IN APPAREL.

WHERE before this time divers laws, ordinances, and statutes have been with great deliberation and advice provided, established, and devised for the necessary repressing, avoiding, and expelling of the inordinate excess daily more and more used in the sumptuous and costly array and apparel customably worn in this realm, whereof hath ensued and daily do chance such sundry high and notable inconveniences as be to the great, manifest, and notorious detriment of the common weal, the subversion of good and politic order in knowledge and distinction of people according to their estates, pre-eminences, dignities, and degrees, and to the utter impoverishment and undoing of many inexpert and light persons inclined to pride, mother of all vices; which good laws notwithstanding, the outrageous excess therein is rather from time to time increased than diminished, either by the occasion of the perverse and forward manners and usage of people, or for that errors and abuses once rooted and taken into long custom be not facilely and at once without some moderation for a time relinquished and reformed: In consideration whereof and for a reasonable order and remedy like to be observed, performed, and continually kept, it is by the king's highness, the lords spiritual and temporal, and the commons in this present parliament assembled and by authority of the same enacted, established, and ordained in the manner and form following:

NONE BUT THE KING AND ROYAL FAMILY SHALL WEAR PURPLE SILK, OR CLOTH OF GOLD TISSUE.

FIRST, that no person or persons of what estate, dignity, degree, or condition soever they be, from the feast of the Purification of Our Lady [2 February] which shall be in the year of our Lord 1533, use or wear in any manner of their apparel or upon their horse, mule, or any other beast any silk of the colour of purple, nor any cloth of gold tissue, but only the king, the queen, the king's mother, the king's children, the king's brethren and sisters, and the king's uncles and aunts; except that it shall be lawful to all dukes and marquises to wear and use in their doublets and sleeveless coats, cloth of gold tissue and in no other of their garments, so that the same to be worn by such dukes and marquises shall not exceed the price of £5 a yard.

KNIGHTS OF THE GARTER.

Provided that this word, purple, extend not to any mantle of the Order of the Garter.

CLOTH OF GOLD, SILVER, OR TINSELLED SATIN ON CLOTH OR SILK EMBROIDERED WITH GOLD OR SILVER.

And that no man under the estate of an earl from the said feast use or wear in his apparel of his body or upon his horse, mule, or other beast, or harness of the same beast, any cloth of gold or of silver or tinselled satin, or any other silk or cloth mixed or embroidered with gold or silver, nor also any furs of sables; except that it shall be lawful for viscounts, the Prior of Saint John's Jerusalem within this realm, and barons to wear in their doublets or sleeveless coats, cloth of gold, silver, or tinsel.

FOREIGN WOOLLEN CLOTH.

Also it is enacted that no man under the estate of a duke, marquis, earl, and their children, or under the degree of a baron, unless he be a knight that is Companion of the Garter, from the said feast, wear in any part of his apparel any woollen cloth made out of this realm of England, Ireland, Wales, Calais, Berwick, or the Marches of the same, except in bonnets. Nor also wear in any manner of apparel of his body or on his horse, mule, or other beast, or harness of the same beast, any velvet of the colours of crimson, scarlet, or blue, nor any furs of black genets [civet-cat] or lucerns [lynx], nor any manner of embroidery: And that no man unless he be a knight, after the said feast wear any collar of gold named a Collar of S. And that no man under the degree of a baron's son or of a knight, except he may spend yearly in lands or tenements, rents, fees, or annuities to his own use for the term of his life or for the term of another man's life or in the right of his wife £200 over all charges, shall after the said feast, use or wear any chain or gold bracelet, brooch, or other ornament of gold on any part of his or their apparel or the apparel of his or their horse, mule, or other beast, except every such chain, jewel, brooch, or ornament be in weight one ounce of fine gold or above, and except rings of gold to be worn on their fingers with stones or without; nor also shall wear any manner of velvet in their gowns, coats with sleeves or other outermost garments, nor any furs of leopards, nor also shall wear any manner of embroidery, pricking, or printing with gold, silver, or silk in any part of their apparel or on their horses, mules, or other beasts. And that no man under the said estates and degrees other than such as may spend in lands, or tenements, rents, fees, or annuities as is aforesaid £100 a year above all charges, shall after the said feast wear any satin, damask, silk, camlet [wool and silk], or taffeta in his gown, coat with sleeves, or other outermost apparel or garment, nor any manner of velvet otherwise than in sleeveless jackets, doublets, coifs [close-fitting caps], partlets [neckerchiefs], or purses, nor also shall he wear any fur whereof the like kind grows not within this realm of England, Ireland, Wales, Calais, Berwick, or the Marches of the same, except foins [beech martens], genets, called gray genets, and budge [lamb's skin]. And that no man under the said degrees, (other than the son and heir apparent of a knight, or the son and heir apparent of a man of 300 marks a year over all charges, and such other men as may spend in lands and tenements, rents, fees, annuities, or other yearly profits as is aforesaid £40 a year over all charges), from the said feast may wear in their gowns or any of their outermost apparel any camlet, or silk, nor may he wear in any other part of his apparel any silk other than satin, damask, taffeta, or sarcenet [soft silk] in his doublets, and sarcenet, camlet, or taffeta in the lining of his gowns, and the same or velvet in their sleeveless coats, jackets, jerkins, coifs, caps, purses, or partlets, the colours of scarlet, crimson, and blue always excepted; nor shall he wear any fur of foins or genets called gray genets, nor any other furs whereof the like kind is not grown within this realm . . . nor shall he wear any manner of anklets, buttons, or brooches of gold, silver gilt, or counterfeit gilt, nor shall he wear any chain of gold of less weight and value than ten ounces of Troy weight of fine gold.

PERSONS HAVING £20 A YEAR.

And that no man under the said degrees other than such gentlemen that may spend in lands or tenements, rents, fees, or annuities as is aforesaid £20 a year over all charges from and after the said feast wear any manner of silk in any apparel of his body or of his horse, mule, or other beast, except it be satin, taffeta, sarcenet, or damask in his doublet or coif, and camlet in his sleeveless jackets, and a lace of silk for his bonnet or points [kerchiefs], laces, girdles, or garters made or wrought in England or Wales; nor shall he wear any furs of black cony [rabbit] or budge. And that no man under the said degrees other than such as may spend in lands and tenements, rents, fees, or annuities, £5 a year over all charges, from and after the said feast wear any manner of cloth of the colours of scarlet, crimson, or violet ingrained, nor any silk in their doublets or jackets, nor any other cloth in any garment above the price of 6s.8d. the broad yard, nor any other thing made out of this realm except camlet in their doublets and jackets.

SERVANTS AND YEOMEN, AND PERSONS HAVING LESS THAN 40S. A YEAR.

And that no serving-man nor other yeoman taking wages or such other as he may not spend in freehold 40s. a year, shall wear any cloth in his hose above the price of 2s. the yard; and that none of their hose be garded [trimmed] or mixed with any other thing that may be seen on or through the outer part of their hose but with the selfsame cloth only, nor in his gown, coat, jacket, or other garment any cloth above the price of 3s.4d. the broad yard, except it be his master's livery, nor any manner of fur except cony called gray cony, black lamb or white lamb of English, Welsh, or Irish growing. Nor shall he wear any shirt,

shirt band, under or upper cap, coif, bonnet, or hat garnished, mixed, made, or wrought with silk, gold, or silver; nor shall he wear any bonnet or shirt band made or wrought out of this realm of England or Wales.

SILK RIBBONS IN BONNETS, BADGES OF THEIR LORDS, PRIZES WON AT
WRESTLINGS, ETC., SILVER WHISTLES, ETC.

Nevertheless, it shall be lawful for him to wear a silk ribbon for his bonnet, and also the cognizance or badge of his lord or master, and a horn tipped with silver gilt or ungilt; and also they and all other persons to wear on their bonnets all such prizes of silver, gilt, or ungilt as they may win by wrestling, shooting, running, leaping, or casting of the bar; and also masters of the ships or other vessels and mariners to wear whistles of silver, with the chain of silver to hang the same upon; any former clause in this act heretofore mentioned to the contrary notwithstanding.

HUSBANDMEN.

And that no husbandman from the said feast wear in his hose any cloth above the price of two shillings the yard, or any cloth in his gown above the price of four shillings the broad yard, or in his coat or jacket above the price of 2s.8d. the broad yard; nor in his doublet any other thing than is wrought within this realm, fustian and canvas only excepted, nor any manner of fur in any his apparel. And that no servingman in husbandry or journeyman in handicrafts taking wages, after and from the feast aforesaid wear in his hose any cloth above the price of 16d. the yard, nor shall wear any cloth in his gown, jacket, or coat above the price of 2s.8d. the broad yard, nor in his doublet any other thing than fustian, canvas or leather, or woollen cloth nor any manner of fur in any of his apparel.

PROVISO FOR SERVANTS OF THE ROYAL FAMILY, ETC.

PROVIDED always that all such officers and servants waiting or attending upon the king, the queen, the prince or princess daily, yearly, or quarterly in their households or being in their exchequer roll, as shall be licensed by his grace to use any manner of apparel on their bodies, horses, mules, or other beasts otherwise than is before expressed, shall be able to lawfully do the same according to the licence which shall be given unto them in that behalf: the same licence to be declared in writing by the king's highness, or the lord steward of his most honourable household, or the lord chamberlain knowing the king's most gracious pleasure in the same.

Provided also that the vice chamberlain, steward, treasurer, and comp-

troller of the French queen's honourable household, after and from the
said feast may wear in their gowns, coats, jackets, doublets, and other
apparel velvet, satin, and damask being of the colours of black, tawny,
or russet, and also chains and brooches of gold of such value as they will
at their liberty, this present act or anything therein mentioned to the
contrary notwithstanding.

LORD CHANCELLOR AND OTHER OFFICERS OF STATE.

Provided also that the lord chancellor and the lord treasurer of England,
the president of the king's council and the lord privy seal, of what estate
or degree so ever they be besides those offices, may wear in their apparel
velvet, satin, and other silks of any colours, except purple, and any
manner of furs, except black genets, anything in this act mentioned, to
the contrary notwithstanding.

APPAREL OF THE CLERGY.

II. Be it further enacted, that after the said feast, none of the clergy,
under the dignity of a bishop, abbot, or prior being a lord of the parliament, wear in any part of his or their apparel of their bodies or on their
horses, any manner of stuff made out of this realm of England, Ireland,
Wales, Calais, Berwick, or the Marches of the same; except that it
shall be lawful to all archdeacons, deans, provosts, masters and wardens
of cathedral and collegiate churches, prebendaries, doctors, or bachelors
in divinity, doctors of the one law or the other, and also doctors of other
sciences, which have taken that degree or be admitted in any university
to wear sarcenet in the lining of their gowns, black satin or black camlet
in their doublets, and sleeveless coats, and black velvet or black sarcenet
or black satin in their tippets [scarf], and riding hoods or girdles, and
also cloth of the colours of scarlet nurrey [purple-red] or violet and furs
called gray black budge, foins, shanks [from legs of sheep], or miniver
[white squirrel] in their gowns and sleeveless coats, anything before mentioned to the contrary notwithstanding. And that none of the clergy,
under the degrees aforesaid, wear any manner of furs other than black
cony, budge, gray cony, shanks, calaber [foreign squirrel], gray fitch
[skunk], fox, lamb, otter, and beaver. And that none of the clergy under
the degrees aforesaid, other than masters of art and bachelors of the one
law or the other admitted in any university or such other of the said
clergy as may spend yearly £20 over all charges, shall wear in their tippets
any manner of sarcenet or other silk.

[*Note*:   The following proviso is inserted at the bottom of the original
act, with reference to be inserted after the clause now numbered as II.
of this act.]

VII.   PROVISO FOR ORNAMENTS FOR DIVINE SERVICE.

[PROVIDED always that this act nor anything therein contained be
hurtful or prejudicial to any spiritual or temporal person in and for the
wearing any ornaments of the church used for executing divine service,
or for wearing their amices [religious cap], mantles, habits, or garments
of religion which they be used or bound unto by their offices; nor also
to any graduates, beadles, or ministers to the graduates in universities
and schools, for wearing of their habits or hoods with furs, linings, or
otherwise after such form as heretofore they have been accustomed to do.]

PROVISO FOR JUDGES, SERGEANTS, MAYORS, RECORDERS, SHERIFFS, AND OTHER PUBLIC OFFICERS.

III. PROVIDED also that this act or anything therein contained
shall not extend nor be hurtful or prejudicial to any of the king's most
honourable council, nor to justices of the one bench or the other, the
barons of the king's exchequer, the master of the rolls, sergeants-at-law,
the masters of the chancery, nor to any of the council of the queen,
prince, or princesses, apprentices of the law, the royal physicians, mayors,
recorders, aldermen, sheriffs, bailiffs elect, and all other head officers of
cities, towns, and boroughs corporate, wardens of occupations, the
barons of the Cinque Ports, that is to say, to all the said officers and
persons that now be or heretofore have been in like place, office, or
authority, or hereafter for the time shall be, as well during the time
after they have been in any such place, office, or authority; but that they
shall at all times be able to wear, after the said feast, all such apparel in
and upon their bodies, horses, mules, and other beasts, and also citizens
and burgesses shall be able to wear such hoods of cloth and of such colours
as they have heretofore used to wear, anything in this act mentioned to
the contrary notwithstanding . . . Nor shall this act or anything therein
mentioned extend to ambassadors or other personages sent from outward princes, or to noblemen or others coming into the king's realm
to visit, see, or salute his grace, or to see the country, and not minded
to make long or continual sojourn in the same; nor to any hench-

man, herald, or pursuivant-at-arms, minstrels, player in interludes, sights, revels, jousts, tournaments, barriers, solemn watches, or other martial feats or disguisings, or to men of war, being in the king's wages of war, nor to any man for wearing of any apparel given unto him by the king's highness, the queen, the French queen, the prince or princess, nor to any swordbearer of the City of London, or of any city, borough, or town incorporate.

Nor also shall extend to any outer barrister of any of the Inns of Court for wearing in any of his apparel such silk and fur as is before limited for men that may spend in lands, tenements, rents, fees, or annuities for term of life £20 over all charges; nor to any other student of the Inns of Court or Chancery . . .

PENALTY UPON OFFENDERS: THE APPAREL UNDULY WORN AND 3s.4d. PER DAY.

IV. It is also further enacted that if any man use or wear at any time after the said feast any apparel or other the premises contrary to the tenure and form aforesaid, then he so offending shall forfeit the same apparel so by him used or worn upon his person, horse, mule, or other beast, or the value thereof and also 3s.4d. in the name of a fine for every day that he shall so wear the same contrary to the tenure and purport of this act; and that every man that will, may lawfully sue for the same by action of detinue to be commenced within 15 days next after the beginning of the term next ensuing after any such time and cause of forfeiture so given, in which action the defendant shall not be allowed to wage his law; nor shall any essoin or protection be allowed him in that behalf; the one-half of the which forfeiture and fine shall be to the king's highness and the other half to him or them that will sue for the same in form and within the time before limited.

JUSTICES OF THE PEACE MAY PUNISH OFFENDERS.

V. And it is further enacted by the authority aforesaid that it shall be lawful to the justices of peace in their sessions, the sheriff in his turn, the steward in any leet or lawday, the aldermen in their wards, and to all other persons having authority to inquire of bloodshed and frays, to inquire of every of the said offences and forfeitures and the parties offending against this statute and so presented shall make fine in manner and form and after the rate aforesaid.

THE GOVERNANCE OF ENGLAND
by Sir John Fortescue
1471–1476

Sir John Fortescue (1390?–1476?), having attended Exeter College, Oxford, and Lincoln's Inn, of which he was governor in 1425, became a sergeant-at-law in 1429–30. Ten years later he acted as a judge of assize on the Norfolk circuit, was made a king's sergeant and, in 1442, chief justice of the king's bench. He was an active member of Henry VI's 'court' party, and political circumstances involved Fortescue in politics to a degree unusual for one pursuing a judicial career. He adhered to the Lancastrians during the Wars of the Roses, going into exile with them after the battle of Towton, 1461. Two years later he went with Queen Margaret and Prince Edward to the continent and then in 1464 to Paris.

Between 1468 and 1470 Fortescue wrote, for the edification of Prince Edward, his more famous book, *De Laudibus Legum Angliae*, wherein he praises the merits of the English law, the law courts, and the jury system; describes the Inns of Court and compares English justice and government to that of France. Already he had written 1461–63, *De Natura Legis Naturae* and tracts against the Yorkist claim to the English throne. Fortescue's pro-Yorkist attitude in the *Governance of England* resulted from the course of political events during 1471.

Henry VI had been restored to the English throne in October 1470 through the collaboration of Richard, earl of Warwick, and Louis XI with whom Fortescue had negotiated in behalf of Queen Margaret. The former chief justice had drawn up a program of government for the Lancastrians and had advocated a reorganization of the council in a plan similar to that described in the *Governance*. But the Lancastrian government fell before the counter-attack of Edward IV; Henry VI and Prince Edward were both killed, and Fortescue considered the Lancastrian cause obsolete. He made his peace with Edward IV by retracting his previous arguments against the House of York and was pardoned in October 1471. Later he was admitted to the king's council, and sometime between 1471 and 1476 he wrote the *Governance of England*, incorporating therein his old plan for conciliar reform and adding thereto eulogistic thanks to God for having 'sent King Edward IV to reign upon us.'

His otherwise analytical essay on practical government is prefaced with a summary of the distinction, more fully developed in the *De Laudibus Legum Angliae*, between *ius regale* and *ius politicum et regale*. Fortescue's aversion to the absolute rule of a prince explains the later popularity of the *De Laudibus* which was published six times before 1600, four times in the next century, and three in the eighteenth. His thesis, over-emphasized, misinterpreted, and trumpeted by parliamentary propagandists since the seventeenth century, has obscured the fact that Fortescue stood for a strong executive under a centralized system of government such as the Tudor monarchs devised. The law, not parliament, Fortescue contended, should limit royal absolutism. His proposal that the council should prepare legislation for parliament [*Governance,* c.15] shows how far he was from entertaining any notion of parliamentary sovereignty in the modern sense.

Most of the basic principles of Fortescue's political philosophy may be found in the *Governance of England* which was printed in 1714 and 1719. It was properly edited in 1885 by Charles Plummer whose text is here reprinted unabridged.

Chapter I

The difference between *Dominium Regale* and *Dominium Politicum et Regale*

THERE be two kinds of kingdoms, of the which that one is a lordship called in Latin *dominium regale*, and that other is called *dominium politicum et regale*. And they differ in that the first king may rule his people by such laws as he makes himself. And therefore he may set upon them taxes and other impositions, such as he will himself, without their assent. The second king may not rule his people by other laws than such as they assent unto. And therefore he may set upon them no impositions without their own assent. This diversity is well taught by Saint Thomas, in his book which he wrote *Ad Regem Cipri de Regimine Principum*. But yet it is more openly treated in a book called *Compendium Moralis Philosophie*, and somewhat by Giles in his book *De Regimine Principum*. The children of Israel, as says Saint Thomas, after that God had chosen them *in populum peculiarem et regnum sacerdotale*, were ruled by him under judges *regaliter et politice* into the time that they desired to have a king, as then had all the gentiles, which we call pagans that had no king but a man that reigned upon them *regaliter tantum*. With which desire God was greatly offended, as well for their folly, as for their unkindness; that since they had a king, which was God, that reigned upon them politically and royally, and yet would change him for a king, a very man, that would reign upon them only royally. And therefore God menacing them made them to be terrified by thunder and other frightful things from heaven. And when they would not thereby leave their foolish desire, he charged the prophet Samuel to declare unto them the law of such a king as they asked; which among other things said that he would take from them their land and give it to his servants, and set their children in his carts, and do to them such other many harmful things, as in the eighth chapter of the first Book of Kings it may appear. Whereas before that time, while they were ruled by God royally and politically under judges, it was not lawful to any man for to take from them any of their goods, or to grieve their children that had not offended. Whereby it may appear that in those days *regimen politicum et regale* was distinguished *a regimine tantum regale*; and that it was better to the people to be ruled politically and royally, than to be ruled only royally. Saint Thomas also in his said book praises *dominium politicum et regale* because the prince that reigns by such lordship may not freely fall into tyranny, as may the prince that reigns *regaliter tantum*. And yet they both be equal in estate and in power, as it may lightly be showed and proved by infallible reason.

Chapter II

Why one king reigns *Regaliter*, and another *Politice et Regaliter*

IT may peradventure be marvelled by some men why one realm is a lordship only royal and the prince thereof rules it by his law called *Jus regale*; and another kingdom is a lordship royal and politic, and the prince thereof rules it by a law called *Jus politicum et regale*; since these two princes be of equal estate. To this doubt it may be answered in this manner. The first institution of these two realms upon the incorporation of them is cause of this diversity. When Nimrod by might for his own glory made and incorporated the first realm and subdued it to himself by tyranny, he would not have it governed by any other rule or law, but by his own will; by which and for the accomplishment thereof he made it. And therefore though he had thus made him a realm, Holy Scripture disdained to call him a king, *quia rex dicitur a regendo*; which thing he did not, but oppressed the people by might, and therefore he was a tyrant and called *primus tirrannorum*. But holy writ calls him *robustus venator coram Domino*. For as the hunter takes the wild beast for to slay and eat him, so Nimrod subdued to himself the people with might to have their service and their goods, using upon them the lordship that is called *dominium regale tantum*. After him Belus that was first called a king, after him his son Ninus, and after him other pagans, that by example of Nimrod made themselves realms, would not have them ruled by other laws than by their own wills. Which laws be right good under good princes, and their kingdoms be then most resembled to the kingdom of God which reigns upon man ruling him by his own will. Wherefore many Christian princes use the same law; and therefore it is that the laws say, *quod principi placuit, legis habet vigorem.* And thus I suppose first began in realms *dominium tantum regale.* But afterward, when mankind was more civilized and better disposed to virtue, great communities, as was the fellowship that came into this land with Brutus, willing to be united and made a body politic called a realm, having a head to govern it; as after the saying of the philosopher, every community united of many parts must needs have a head;—then they chose the same Brutus to be their head and king. And they and he upon this incorporation, institution, and uniting of themselves into a realm, ordained the same realm to be ruled and governed by such laws as they all would assent unto; which law therefore is called *politicum,* and because it is administered by a king, it is called *regale. Policia dicitur a poles, quod est plures, et ycos, scientia; quo regimen politicum dicitur regimen plurium scientia sive consilio ministratum.* The king of Scots reigns upon his people by this law, *videlicet, regimine politico et regali.* And as Diodorus Siculus says in his book *De Priscis Historiis,* the realm of Egypt is ruled by the same law, and therefore the king thereof changes not his laws without the assent of his people. And in like form as he says is ruled the kingdom of Saba in *Felici Arabia,* and the land of Libya; and also the more part of all the realms of Africa. Which manner, rule, and lordship the said Diodorus in that book praises greatly; for it is not only good for the prince, that may thereby the more surely do justice than by his own arbitrament; but it is also good for his people that receive thereby such justice as they desire themself. Now as meseems it is shown openly enough, why one king reigns upon his people *dominio tantum regali,* and that other reigns *dominio politico et regali;* for that one kingdom began of and by the might of the prince, and that other began by the desire and institution of the people of the same prince.

Chapter III

Here be shown the fruits of *Jus Regale* and the fruits of *Jus Politicum et Regale*

AND how so be it that the French king reigns upon his people *dominio regali*, yet Saint Louis sometime king there, nor any of his progenitors set never taxes or other imposition upon the people of that land without the assent of the three estates, which when they be assembled be like to the court of the parliament in England. And this order kept many of his successors into late days, that Englishmen made such war in France, that the three estates durst not come together. And then for that cause and for great necessity which the French king had of good for the defence of that land, he took upon him to set taxes and other impositions upon the commons without the assent of the three estates; but yet he would not set any such charges, nor has set, upon the nobles for fear of rebellion. And because the commons there, though they have grudged, have not rebelled or been hardy to rebel, the French kings have yearly since set such charges upon them and so augmented the same charges as the same commons be so impoverished and destroyed, that they are scarcely able to live. They drink water, they eat apples, with bread right brown made of rye; they eat no flesh but if it be right seldom a little lard, or of the entrails and hides of beasts slain for the nobles and merchants of the land. They wear no woollens, but if it be a poor coat under their outermost garment, made of great canvas, and called a frock. Their hose be of like canvas, and pass not their knee, wherefore they be gartered and their thighs bare. Their wives and children go barefoot; they are able in no other wise to live. For some of them that were wont to pay to his lord for his tenement, which he hires by the year, a crown, pays now to the king over that crown five crowns. Upon which they be compelled by necessity so to watch, labour, and grub in the ground for their sustenance, that their nature is wasted, and the kind of them brought to nought. They go crooked and be feeble, not able to fight nor to defend the realm; nor have they weapons, nor money to buy them weapons withal. But verily they live in the most extreme poverty and misery, and yet dwell they in one of the most fertile realms of the world. For this cause the French king has not men of his own realm able to defend it, except his nobles, which bear not such impositions, and therefore they be right strong of their bodies; by which cause the said king is compelled to make his armies and retinues for the defence of his land of strangers, as Scots, Spaniards, Aragonese, Germans, and of other nations, or else all his enemies might overrun him; for he has no defence of his own except his castles and fortresses. Lo, this is the fruit of his *Jus regale*. If the realm of England, which is an isle and therefore may not lightly get succour of other lands were ruled under such a law and under such a prince, it would be then a prey to all other nations that would conquer, rob, or devour it; which was well proved in the time of the Britons, when the Scots and the Picts so beat and oppressed this land that the people thereof sought help of the Romans to whom they had been tributary. And when they could not be defended by them, they sought help of the duke of Britain then called Little Britain, and granted therefore to make his brother Constantine their king. And so he was made king here, and reigned many years, and his children after him, of which great Arthur was one of their issue. But blessed be God, this land is ruled under a better law; and therefore the people thereof be not in such penury, nor thereby hurt in their persons, but they be wealthy, and have all things necessary to the sustenance of nature. Wherefore they be mighty and able to resist the adversaries of this realm and to beat other realms that do or would do them wrong. Lo, this is the fruit of *Jus politicum et regale*, under which we live. Somewhat now I have shown the fruits of both laws, *ut ex fructibus eorum cognoscetis eos*.

Chapter IV

Here is shown how the revenues of France be made great

SINCE our king reigns upon us by laws more favourable and good to us than be the laws by which the French king rules his people, it is reasonable that we be to him more good and more profitable than be the subjects of the French king unto him; which it would seem that we be not, considering that his subjects yield to him more in a year, than we do to our sovereign lord in two years, howsobeit that they do so against their wills. Nevertheless when it is considered how a king's office stands in two things, one to defend his realm against their enemies without by the sword; another that he defend his people against wrongdoers within by justice, as it appears by the said first Book of Kings; which the French king does not, though he keep justice between subject and subject, since he oppresses them more himself than would have done all the wrongdoers of the realm, though they had no king. And since it is a sin to give no meat, drink, clothing, or other alms to them that have need, as shall be declared in the day of doom, how much a greater sin is it to take from the poor man his meat, his drink, his clothing, and all that he has need of. Which verily does the French king to many a thousand of his subjects, as it is before openly declared. Which thing though it be now coloured *per jus regale*, yet it is tryanny. For, as Saint Thomas says, when a king rules his realm only to his own profit and not to the good of his subjects, he is a tryrant. King Herod reigned upon the Jews *dominio regali*; yet when he slew the children of Israel, he was in that a tyrant, though the laws say, *quod principi placuit, legis habet vigorem*. Wherefore Ahab, which reigned upon the children of Israel by like law, and desired to have had Naboth his subject's vine-yard, would not by that law take it from him, but preferred him the value thereof. For these words said the prophet, *predic eis jus regis*, be not else to say but *predic eis potestatem regis*. Wherefore as oft as such a king does any thing against the law of God, or against the law of nature, he does wrong, notwithstanding the said law declared by the prophet. And it is so, that the law of nature wills in this case that the king should do to his subjects as he would be done to himself if he were a subject; which may not be that he would be almost destroyed as be the commons of France. Wherefore, albeit that the French king's revenues be by such means much greater than be the revenues which the king our sovereign lord has of us, yet they be not well taken, and the might of his realm is almost destroyed thereby. By which consideration I would not that the king's revenues of this realm were made great by any such means. And yet of necessity they must be greater than they be at this day. And truly it is very necessary that they be always great; and that the king have abundantly wherewith his estate may be honourably kept for right many causes, of which some shall now be remembered.

Chapter V

The harm that comes of a king's poverty

FIRST, if a king be poor, he shall by necessity make his expenses, and by all that is necessary to his estate, by credit and borrowing; whereby his creditors will win from him the fourth or the fifth penny of all that he dispenses. And so he shall lose when he pays, the fourth or the fifth penny of his revenues, and thus be thereby always poorer and poorer, as usury and loans increase the poverty of him that borrows. His creditors shall always grudge for lack of their payment and defame his highness of misgovernance and default of keeping of days; which if he keep, he must borrow also much at the days, as he did first; for he shall be then poorer than he was by the value of the fourth or fifth part of his first expenses, and so be always poorer and poorer, unto the time he be the poorest lord of his land. For such manner of borrowing makes the great lords to be poorer than their tenants. What dishonour is this and abating of the glory of a king. But yet it is most to his insecurity. For his subjects will rather go with a lord that is rich and may pay their wages and expenses, than with their king that has nought in his purse, but they must serve him, if they will do so, at their own expense. *Item*, if the king be poor, he shall of necessity make his gifts and rewards by assignments, for which he shall have but little thanks. For the poorer man had liefer an hundred marks in hand, than an hundred pound by assignment, which peradventure shall cost him right much ere he can get his payment, and peradventure be never paid thereof. And often times for lack of money the king shall be fain to give away his land to such as would have been fainer of a hundred pounds in hand, than of forty pounds worth land yearly, to the great abating of his revenues and depopulation of his realm. But the greatest harm that comes of a king's poverty is that he shall by necessity be compelled to find extraordinary means of getting of goods; as to accuse some of his subjects that be innocent, and upon the rich men more than the poor because that they may better pay; and to show rigour there as favour ought to be shown, and favour there as rigour should be shown, to perversion of justice and perturbation of the peace and quiet of the realm. For, as the philosopher says in his *Ethics, Impossibile est indigentem operari bona.* It needs not now to specify more of the harms which come to a realm by the poverty of their king, howbeit they be many more than we have shown yet; for every wise man may see them openly enough. But we must hold it for undoubted that there may no realm prosper or be worshipful under a poor king.

Chapter VI

Ordinance for the king's ordinary charges

AND since it is necessary that the king be always rich, which may not be unless he have revenues sufficient for the yearly maintenance of his estate; it is behooveful that we first estimate, what his yearly charges and expenses be likely to draw unto. For after that need his revenues to be proportioned; but yet they need to be greater than will be the charges, for doubt of sudden cases which may fall to him and to his realm. For Saint Bernard says that if a man's expenses be equal to his livelihood, a sudden chance may destroy his estate. The king's yearly expenses stand in charges ordinary and in charges extraordinary. His charges ordinary may not be eschewed, and therefore it needs that there be livelihood assigned for the payment thereof; which livelihood be in no wise put to no other use. And if it happen that any patent be made of any part thereof to other use, that then that patent be void and of no effect. Which thing if it be firmly established, the king's ordinary charges may always be paid in hand, and the provision for them may always be made in season; which shall be worth to the king the fourth or the fifth part of the quantity of his expenses for ordinary charges. This may in nothing restrain the king's power. For it is no power to be able to alienate and put away; but it is power to be able to have and keep to himself. As it is no power to be able to sin and to do ill, or to be able to be sick, wax old, or that a man may hurt himself. For all these powers come of impotency. And therefore they may properly be called non-powers. Wherefore the holy spirits and angels that may not sin, wax old, be sick, or hurt themselves have more power than we, that may harm ourselves with all these defaults. So is the king's power more, in that he may not put from him possessions necessary for his own sustenance, than if he might put them from him and alienate the same to his own hurt and harm. Nor is this against the king's prerogative, by which he is exalted above his subjects; but rather this is to him a prerogative. For no man save he may have again the land that he has once alienated. This livelihood assigned for the ordinary charges shall afterwards be never asked of the king, nor his highness shall think for that that he has the more livelihood to be given away; but by reason hereof he will the more restrain his gifts of other of his livelihood, considering that then it will not be great, and therefore he shall have more need of it than they that will ask it. The ordinary charges, which the writer hereof can now remember, be these: the king's household, his wardrobe. And how so be it that the king list now, or will hereafter, make his household less than it was wont to be; yet his highness shall then have therefore about his person, for his honour and surety, lords, knights, and squires, and others, in also great number, or greater than his household was wont to be, to his charges peradventure also greatly, as his household well ruled was wont to stand him in. Wherefore herein it needs not to consider or to purvey, but only for the king's house, which he may resume or change into his new manner or other form at his pleasure, and as it shall be thought after the seasons most expedient. The expenses of which household may soon be estimated by those who of old time have been officers therein, and by the clerks of the exchequer. The second ordinary charge is the payment of the wages and fees of the king's great officers, his courts, and his council. Which charge will always be great, and these men need to be always readily paid. For indigence in them is not only unworshipful, but it may do the most harm that may fall of any need in any estate of the land, after the king's most great estate. The third charge ordinary is the payment of the keeping of the marches, wherein we bear much greater charges yearly than do the Scots, which oftentimes is for the favour that we do to the persons that keep them, which favour the Scots do not. The fourth charge is the keeping of Calais, which charge is well enough known. The fifth charge is for the king's works, of which the yearly expenses may not be estimated, but yet the accounts of the clerks of the works will show the likelihood thereof, while the king makes no new works. The keeping of the sea I reckon not among the ordinary charges, howbeit the charge thereof is yearly born, because it is not estimable, and the king has therefore the subsidy of poundage and tonnage. Nor the less be that a reason why poundage and tonnage may not be reckoned as parcel of the revenues which the king has for the maintenance of his estate, because it ought to be applied only to the keeping of the sea. And though we have not always war upon the sea, yet it shall be necessary that the king have always some fleet upon the sea for the repressing of rovers, saving of our merchants, our fishers, and the dwellers upon our coasts; and that the king keep always some great and mighty vessels for the breaking of an army when any shall be made against him upon the sea. For then it shall be too late to make such vessels. And yet without them all the king's navy shall not suffice to board with carracks and other great vessels, nor yet to be able to break a mighty fleet gathered of purpose. Now, as I suppose, we have reckoned the greatest part of the king's ordinary charges. Wherefore we will consider next his extraordinary charges, as far as may be possible to us.

Chapter VII

The king's extraordinary charges

THE king's extraordinary charges be so casual that no man may know them in certain. But yet he may estimate what sum they be not like to exceed, but if there fall a case over much exorbitant; and then it shall be reason, and also necessary, that all the realm bear for that case a singular charge. Such of the said extraordinary charges as the writer hereof can now remember be these. First the king shall oftentimes send out of this land his ambassadors, as well to the pope, as to divers kings, princes, and nations; and otherwhiles he shall send his procurators and messengers to the general councils. Which ambassadors, procurators, and messengers shall need to be honourably accompanied and well be seen, as well for the worship of the realm as for the advancing of the matters for which they shall be sent, to the king's right great charge, which shall be more or less after their long or short stay in their voyage. *Item,* the king shall bear yearly charges unknown in receiving of legates and messengers sent from the pope, and of ambassadors sent from kings and other princes, and also from great communities beyond the sea, which will put the king to great expenses while they be here, and at their departing they must needs have great gifts and rewards; for that befits the king's magnificence and liberality, also it is necessary for the worship of his realm. *Item*, since it is not good that he reward such as do and shall do to him service or other manner of pleasures with the possessions and revenues of his crown, nor with other possessions of his inheritance—for they be much more necessary for the sustenance of his great estate—it shall therefore be necessary, that the king make such rewards with money out of his coffers, and that some of them have so largely thereof as they may buy themselves land withal, if they will. For by this means the king's estate shall always be kept unblemished. And of some man his highness shall have more thanks for money than for land; and also money is the most convenient reward to him that has not long served. This charge will always be great, and so inestimably great that in some years a great lord's livelihood shall not suffice to bear it, though he would sell great part thereof. And truly, when the king rewards his servants in this manner, he shows great favour to all his realm. *Item*, it shall need that the king have such treasure as he may make new buildings when he will for his pleasure and magnificence; and as he may buy him rich clothes, rich furs, other than be wont to fall under the yearly charges of his wardrobe, rich stones, fine linen, belts, and other jewels and ornaments convenient to his estate royal. And oftentimes he will buy rich hangings and other apparel for his houses; vessels, vestments, and other ornaments for his chapel; buy also horses of great price, trappings, and do other such noble and great costs, as befits his royal majesty, of which it is not now possible to the writer hereof to remember the especialities. For if a king did not so, nor might do, he lived then not like his estate, but rather in misery and in more subjection than does a private person. *Item*, the king shall oftentimes send his commissioners in great might, and also his judges, to repress and punish rioters and risers; for which cause he shall other-whiles ride in his own person mightily accompanied. Which thing will not be done without great costs; for no man is bound to serve him in such cases at his own expense. *Item*, if there come a sudden army upon this land by sea or by land, the king must encounter them with a like army, or a greater; for the expenses whereof he shall not so suddenly have any aid of his people. Wherefore he must then do the expenses with money out of his coffers, or put all his land in jeopardy. Lo, now we have remembered great part of the king's extraordinary charges; and before we have showed great part of his ordinary charges. Wherefore now it is time that it be showed how the king may have revenues and livelihood sufficient to bear these two charges.

Chapter *VIII*

If the king's livelihood suffice not, his subjects ought to make it sufficient

IT is shown before how necessary it is that livelihood sufficient be assigned for the king's ordinary charges, and that the same livelihood be only applied thereto and not aliened in time coming. For that assignment may in no wise hurt the king, considering that if any part of the revenues thereof remain over the payment of the same ordinary charges, that so remaining is the king's own money, which he may then employ to other use at his own pleasure. And it is undoubted that the king has livelihood sufficient which may be so assigned for his ordinary charges. Wherefore we have now nothing else to be searched but what livelihood the king has for the payment of his charges extraordinary, over so much livelihood as shall be assigned for his charges ordinary; and if he have not livelihood sufficient thereto, how then his livelihood may be made sufficient. For his realm is bound by right to sustain him in everything necessary to his estate. For, as Saint Thomas says, *Rex datur propter regnum, et non regnum propter regem.* Wherefore all that he does ought to be referred to his kingdom. For though his estate be the highest estate temporal in the earth, yet it is an office, in which he administers to his realm defence and justice. And therefore he may say of himself and of his realm, as the pope says of himself and of the church, in that he writes, *servus servorum Dei.* By which reason, right as every servant ought to have his sustenance of him that he serves, so ought the pope to be sustained by the church, and the king by his realm. For *nemo debet propriis expensis militare.* And our lord says, *dignus est operarius cibo suo.* Wherefor the apostle says, *communicet is qui catezizatur verbo, ei qui se catezizat, in omnibus bonis.* Wherefore since every realm is bound to sustain its king, yet much more be we bound thereto upon whom our king reigns by so favourable laws as is before declared.

Chapter IX

Here he shows the perils that may come to the king by
over-mighty subjects

BUT since the said extraordinary charges be so uncertain that they be
not estimable, it is not possible to put in certain, what livelihood will
yearly suffice to bear them. Wherefore we need in this case to use conjecture and imagination, as to think that there is no lord's livelihood in
England sufficient to bear the king's extraordinary charges. Then needs
it that the king's livelihood, above such revenues as shall be assigned
for his ordinary charges, be greater than the livelihood of the greatest
lord in England. And peradventure, when livelihood sufficient for the
king's ordinary charges is fixed and assigned thereto, it shall appear that
divers lords of England have also much livelihood of their own, as then
shall remain in the king's hands for his extraordinary charges; which
were inconvenient and would be to the king right dreadful. For then
such a lord may spend more than the king, considering that he is charged
with no such charges extraordinary or ordinary as is the king, except an
household, which is but little in comparison of the king's house. Wherefore if it be thus, it shall be necessary that there be purveyed for the
king much greater livelihood than he has yet. For man's courage is so
noble, that naturally he aspires to high things, and to be exalted, and
therefore enforces himself to be always greater and greater. For which
the philosopher says, *omnia amamus sed principari maius.* Whereof it
has come that oftentimes when a subject has had also great livelihood
as his prince, he has anon aspired to the estate of his prince, which by
such a man may soon be got. For the remnant of the subjects of such a
prince, seeing that if so mighty a subject might obtain the estate of their
prince, they should then be under a prince double so mighty as was their
old prince—which increase any subject desires, for his own discharge
of that he bears to the sustenance of his prince—and therefore will be
right glad to help such a subject in his rebellion. And also such an enterprise is the more feasible, when such a rebel has more riches than his
sovereign lord. For the people will go with him that best may sustain
and reward them. This manner of doing has been so often practised
almost in every realm that their chronicles be full of it. In the realm of

France was never change of their king, since it was first inhabited by Frenchmen, but by the rebellion of such mighty subjects; as Childeric king of France, descended of Clovis, which was first Christian king of France, was put down by Pepin son to Charles Martel, which was the most mighty subject that unto that time was ever seen in the realm of France. And afterwards Charles, descended of Charlemagne, son to the said Pepin by nine or by ten generations, was put from the kingdom of France by Hugh Capet, son to Hugh Magnus, earl of Paris, which then was the mightiest subject of France, and therefore created and called *Dux Franciae*. And in our days we have seen a subject of the French king's in such might, that he has given battle to the same king and put him to flight, and afterwards besieged him being in Paris his greatest city, and so kept there, unto the time his said king had made such end with him, his adherents, and followers as he desired. We have also seen late in our realm some of the king's subjects give him battle, by occasion that their livelihood and offices were the greatest of the land, and else they would not have done so.

The earls of Leicester and Gloucester, which were the greatest lords of England, rose against their king Henry the third, and took him and his son prisoners in the field. Which manner of behaviour the king of Scots that last died dreading to be practised in his land, put out of the same land the Earl Douglas whose livelihood and might was nearly equivalent to his own, moved thereto by no other cause, save only dread of his rebellion. The chronicles of every realm, and in especial of Spain and Denmark, be full of such examples; and so be also the Book of Kings in Holy Scripture; wherefore it needs not to write more herein. And also it may not be eschewed, but that the great lords of the land by reason of new descents falling unto them, by reason also of marriages, purchases, and other titles, shall oftentimes grow to be greater than they be now, and peradventure some of them to be of livelihood and power like a king; which shall be right good for the land while they aspire to none higher estate. For such was the duke of Lancaster, that warred the king of Spain, one of the mightiest kings of Christendom, in his own realm. But this is written only to the intent that it be well understood how necessary it is that the king have great possessions and peculiar livelihood for his own surety; namely, when any of his lords shall happen to be so excessively great as there might thereby grow peril to his estate.

For certainly there may no greater peril grow to a prince than to have a subject equally powerful to himself.

Chapter X

How that the crown is best to be endowed

Now that the likeness of the king's charges ordinary and extraordinary be showed, and over that how necessary it is that he have great livelihood above the same charges, in which it needs that he exceed greatly every man of the land, which livelihood undoubtedly he has not at this day; it is therefore behooveful that we now search how the king may have such livelihood; but first, of what commodities it may best be taken. The king of France might not at one time spend of his domains, as in lordships, and other patrimony peculiar, as much as might then the king of England; which may well appear by that the queen of France has but five thousand marks yearly to her dower, whereas the queen of England has ten thousand marks. For in those days there was but little more of the realm of France in the king's hands, than that part which is called the Isle of France. For all the remnant of the realm as Burgundy, Normandy, Guienne, Champagne, Langue d'oc, and Flanders, with many other such great lordships, were then in the hands of the dussepers [twelve peers], and of other princes and great lords. For which cause the gabelle of the salt, and the fourth of the wines were granted to the king by the three estates of France, which was no little subsidy. For there is no man in France that may eat salt but if he buy it of the king; and that is now set to so great price that the bushel, which the king buys for three pence or four pence, is sold to his people for two shillings and a penny, and otherwhiles more. And the fourth pipe of the wines that be made in France may be no little thing, since the tilling of the vine is the greatest commodity of the realm; but that commodity we have not in this land. Wherefore there is no part of those manners of subsidy that might be good for our sovereign lord, but if it were that he might sell to his subjects the salt that comes hither. In which thing he shall have more grudging of the people than profit. For in France the people salt but little meat, except their bacon, for they would buy little salt; but yet they be compelled to buy more salt than they would. For the king's officers bring to their houses every year as much salt as by their conjecture is reasonable to the number of the men, women, and children that dwell therein, for which they shall pay though they will not have so much. This rule would be sore abhorred in England, as well by the merchants that be wont to have their freedom in buying and selling of salt, as by the people that use much to salt their meats more than do the Frenchmen; by occasion whereof they will then at every meal grumble against the king that treats them more rigorously than his progenitors have done. And so his highness shall have thereof, but as had the man that sheared his hog, much cry and little wool. In Flanders, and in other lordships of the dukes of Burgundy downward, he takes certain impositions made by himself upon every ox, every sheep, and upon other things sold; and also upon every vessel of wine, every barrel of beer, and other victuals sold in his lordships, which is no little revenue to him; but yet he does it in spite of the people, which God defend that the king our sovereign lord should do upon his people, without their grants of assent. Nevertheless with their assent such manner of subsidy, if there could not be found a better means of increasing of the king's revenues, were not unreasonable. For therein and in the gabelle of the salt, every man shall bear the charge thereof equally. But yet I would not that such a new charge were put upon the people in our sovereign lord's days, with which his progenitors charged them never, if a better remedy could be found. King Solomon charged his people with greater impositions than they were wont to bear before his days. And because his son King Roboam would not ease them thereof, the ten parts of the people divided in twelve parts, departed from him, and chose them a new king, and came never after that time under his subjection. Of which departing God said himself afterwards, *a me factum est istud*. Which is an example that it is not good a king to oversore charge his people. Wherefore, me thinks that if the king might have his livelihood for the sustenance of his estate in great lordships, manors, fee-farms, and such other domains, his people not charged, he should keep to him wholly their hearts, exceed in lordships all the lords of his realm, and there should none of them grow to be like unto him, which thing is most to be feared of all the world. For then within few years there should not remain lordships in his realm, by which they might grow so great. Nor they might grow such by marriages, but if the king willed it. For to him fall all the great marriages of his land, which he may dispose as he lists. And by descent there is not like to fall greater heritage to any man than to the king. For to him be cousins the most and greatest lords of the realm. And by escheats there may not so much land fall to any man as to the king, because that no man has so many tenants as he; and also no man may have the escheats of treason but himself. And by purchases, if this be done, there shall no man so well increase his livelihood as the king. For there shall none of his tenants alienate livelihood without his licence, wherein he may best prefer himself. Nor there shall no livelihood be kept so whole as the king's, considering that he may not honestly sell his land, as other men may do; and also his selling would be the hurt of all his realm. Such was the selling of Chirke and Chirkelands, whereof never man see a precedent, and God defend that any man see more such hereafter. For selling of a king's livelihood is properly called dilapidation of his crown, and therefore is of great infamy. Now we have found, undoubtedly, what manner revenues is best for the endowment of the crown. But since it is said before that the king has not at this day sufficient thereto, it is most convenient that we now search how his highness may have sufficient of such revenues, which we found now best therefore.

Chapter XI

Here is shown what of the king's livelihood given away may best be taken again

THE holy patriarch Joseph, while he, under Pharaoh king, governed the land of Egypt, ruled and so treated the people thereof that they granted to pay, and paid to the same king, the fifth part of their grains and of all other things that grew to them yearly of the earth; which charge they bear yet, and ever shall bear. Wherefore their prince, which now is the sultan of Babylon, is one of the mightiest princes of the world; and that notwithstanding the same Egyptians be the most rich commons that live under any prince. Whereby we learn that it shall not only be good to our prince, but also to us ourselves, that he be well endowed; for else the patriarch would not have made such a treaty. The French king in one thing, that is to say in wine, takes more of his people than does the sultan, for he takes the fourth penny thereof. But yet he takes nothing of their grains, wools, or of any other goods that grows to them of their land. The king our sovereign lord had betimes, since he reigned upon us, livelihood in lordships, lands, tenements, and rents, nearly to the value of the fifth part of his realm, above the possessions of the church. Of which livelihood, if it had been kept still in his hands, he had been more mighty in good revenues than any of the said two kings, or any king that now reigns upon Christian men. But this was not possible to have been done. For to some part thereof the heirs of them that some-time owned it be restored; some by reason of entails, some by reason of other titles, which the king has considered and thought them good and reasonable. And some of the said livelihood his good grace has given to such as have served him so notably, that as their renown will be eternal, so it befitted the king's magnificence to make their rewards everlasting in their heirs, to their perpetual memory and honour. And also the king has given part of this livelihood to his most worshipful brothers, which not only have served him in the manner aforesaid, but be also so nigh in blood to his highness that it befitted not his magnificence to have done in otherwise. Nevertheless, some men have done him service for which it was reasonable that his grace had rewarded them; and for lack of money, the king then rewarded them with land. And to some men he has done in likewise above their merits through importunity of their suits. And it is supposed that some of them have gotten a hundred pounds worth land, that would have held themselves content with two hundred pounds in money, if they might have had it in hand. Wherefore it is thought that if such gifts, and namely those which have been made inconsiderately or above the merits of them that have them, were re-formed; and they rewarded with money, or offices, and some with liveli-hood term of life, which after their deaths would then return to the crown, the king should have such livelihood as we now seek for, suffi-cient for the maintenance of his estate. And if it would not then be so great, I hold it for undoubted that the people of his land will be well willing to grant him a subsidy upon such commodities of his realm as be before specified, as shall accomplish that which shall be lacking to him of such livelihood; so that his highness will establish the same livelihood then remaining to abide perpetually to his crown without translating thereof to any other use. For else when that shall happen hereafter to be given away, it shall need that his commons be charged with a new subsidy, and thus be kept always in poverty.

Chapter XII

Here is shown what harm would come to England if the commons thereof were poor

SOME men have said that it were good for the king that the commons of England were made poor, as be the commons of France. For then they would not rebel as now they do oftentimes; which the commons of France do not, nor may do, for they have no weapons, nor armour, nor goods to buy it withal. To these manner of men may be said with the philosopher, *ad pauca respicientes de facili enunciant*. This is to say, they that see but few things will soon say their advices. Forsooth these folk consider little the good of the realm of England, whereof the might stands most upon archers, which be no rich men. And if they were made more poor than they be, they should not have wherewith to buy them bows, arrows, jackets, or any other armour of defence, whereby they might be able to resist our enemies when they list to come upon us; which they may do in every side, considering that we be an island; and, as it is said before, we may not soon have succour of any other realm. Wherefore we shall be a prey to all our enemies, but if we be mighty of ourselves, which might stands most upon our poor archers; and therefore they need not only have such habiliments as now is spoken of, but also they need to be much exercised in shooting, which may not be done without right great expenses, as every man expert therein knows right well. Wherefore the making poor of the commons, which is the making poor of our archers, shall be the destruction of the greatest might of our realm. *Item*, if poor men may not lightly rise, as is the opinion of these men, which for that cause would have the commons poor, how then, if a mighty man made a rising should he be repressed, when all the commons be so poor that after such opinion they may not fight, and by that reason not help the king with fighting? And why makes the king the commons every year to be mustered, since it were good they had no arms nor were able to fight? O, how unwise is the opinion of these men; for it may not be maintained by any reason! *Item*, when any rising has been made in this land before these days by commons, the poorest men thereof have been the greatest causers and doers therein. And thrifty men have been loath thereto, for dread of losing of their goods. But yet oftentimes they have gone with them through menacing that else the same poor men would have taken their goods, wherein it seems that poverty has been the whole cause of all such risings. The poor man has been stirred thereto by occasion of his poverty for to get goods and the rich men have gone with them because they would not be poor by losing of their goods. What then would fall, if all the commons were poor? Truly it is like that this land then should be like unto the realm of Bohemia, where the commons for poverty rose upon the nobles and made all their goods to be common. *Item*, it is the king's honour, and also his office, to make his realm rich; and it is dishonour when he has but a poor realm, of which men will say that he reigns but upon beggars. Yet it were much greater dishonour, if he found his realm rich and then made it poor. And it were also greatly against his conscience, that ought to defend them and their goods, if he took from them their goods without lawful cause; from the infamy whereof God defend our king and give him grace to augment his realm in riches, wealth, and prosperity, to his perpetual laud and worship. *Item*, the realm of France gives never freely of their own goodwill any subsidy to their prince, because the commons thereof be so poor as they may not give anything of their own goods. And the king there asks never subsidy of his nobles, for dread that if he charged them so, they would conspire with the commons and peradventure put him down. But our commons be rich, and therefore they give to their king, at sometimes a fifteenth and a tenth, and oftentimes other great subsidies, as he has need for the good and defence of his realm. How great a subsidy was it, when the realm gave to their king a fifteenth and a tenth for five years, and the ninth fleece of their wools, and also the ninth sheaf of their grains, for the term of five years. This might they not have done if they had been impoverished by their king, as be the commons of France; nor such a grant has been made by any realm of Christendom, of which any chronicle makes mention; nor none other may or has cause to do so. For they have not so much freedom in their own goods, nor be treated by so favourable laws as we be, except a few regions before specified. *Item*, we see daily how men that have lost their goods and be fallen into poverty become anon robbers and thieves; which would not have been such if poverty had not brought them thereto. How many a thief then were like to be in this land if all the commons were poor. The greatest surety, truly, and also the most honour that may come to the king is that his realm be rich in every estate. For nothing may make his people to arise but lack of goods or lack of justice. But yet certainly when they lack goods they will arise, saying that they lack justice. Nevertheless if they be not poor, they will never arise but if their prince so leave justice that he give himself all to tyranny.

Chapter XIII

Only lack of heart and cowardice keep the Frenchmen from rising

POVERTY is not the cause why the commons of France rise not against their sovereign lord. For there were never people in that land more poor than were in other time the commons of the country of Caux, which was then almost deserted for lack of tillers, as it now well appears by the new husbandry that is done there, namely in grubbing and stocking of trees, bushes, and groves, grown while we were their lords of the country. And yet the said commons of Caux made a marvellous great rising and took our towns, castles, and fortresses, and slew our captains and soldiers, at such a time as we had but few men of war lying in that country. Which proves that it is not poverty that keeps Frenchmen from rising, but it is cowardice and lack of heart and courage, which no Frenchman has like unto an Englishman. It has been oftentimes seen in England that three or four thieves for poverty have set upon six or seven true men and robbed them all. But it has not been seen in France that six or seven thieves have been hardy to rob three or four true men. Wherefore, it is right seldom that Frenchmen be hanged for robbery, for they have no hearts to do so terrible an act. There be therefore more men hanged in England in a year for robbery and manslaughter than there be hanged in France for such manner of crime in seven years. There is no man hanged in Scotland in seven years together for robbery. And yet they have oftentimes hanged for larceny and stealing of goods in the absence of the owner thereof. But their hearts serve them not to take a man's goods, while he is present and will defend it; which manner of taking is called robbery. But the Englishman is of another courage. For if he be poor and see another man having riches, which may be taken from him by might, he will not spare to do so, but if that poor man be right true. Wherefore it is not poverty, but it is lack of heart and cowardice that keeps the Frenchmen from rising.

Chapter XIV

Here it is shown why it needs that there be a resumption and a grant of goods made to the king

THIS search which we now have made, for to understand how harmful it would be to the king and to his realm if his commons were poor, has been a digression from the matter in which we labour; that is to say, for to understand how the king may best have sufficient and lasting livelihood for the sustenance of his estate. Wherefore, it behooves that we now resort to the point in which we left, which, as I remember, was this. We found by great causes that it was needful that all such gifts as have been made of the king's livelihood inconsiderately, as not deserved, or above the merits of him that have gotten them, were reformed; so as they which have done any service be not unrewarded. Which thing, as methinks, may not perfectly be done without a general resumption made by authority of parliament; and that there be given to the king by the same authority a great subsidy, with which his highness, by the advice of his council, may reward those that have deserved rewards, and ought not therefore to have part of his revenues, by which his estate must needs be maintained; or ought not have so much of the revenues as they have now, or not so great estate in the same. Considering that all such giving away of the king's livelihood is harmful to all his liegemen, which shall thereby, as is before shown, be compelled to a new charge for the sustenance of his estate. But yet, ere any such resumption be made, it shall be good that a worshipful and a notable council be established, by the advice of which all new gifts and rewards may be moderated and made, as if no such gifts or rewards had been made before this time. Provided always that no man be harmed, by reason of such resumption, in the arrears of such livelihood as he shall then have, which shall run after that resumption and before the said new gifts and rewards. And when such a council is fully created and established, it shall be good that all supplications which shall be made to the king for any gift or reward be sent to the same council and there debated and deliberated; first whether the suppliant has deserved such reward as he asks; and if he has deserved it, yet it needs that it be deliberated whether the king may give such reward as he asks of his revenues, saving to himself sufficient for the sustenance of his estate. For else such giving were no virtue, but a spice of prodigality, and as for so much it were dilapidation of his crown. Wherefore, no private person will, by reason of liberality or of reward, so abate his own livelihood as he may not keep such estate as he did before. And truly it were better that a private person lacked his reward which he has well deserved, than that by his reward the good public and all the land were hurt. Wherefore to eschew these two harms, it may then be advised by the council how such a person may be rewarded with office, money, marriage, franchises, privileges, or such other things, of which the crown has great riches. And verily if this order be kept, the king shall not be grieved by importunity of suitors, nor they shall by importunity or influence obtain any unreasonable desires. O what quiet shall grow to the king by this order; and in what rest shall then his people live, having no colour of grudging with such as shall be about his person, as they were wont to have for the giving away of his land, and also for the miscounselling of him in many other cases; nor of murmur against the king's person, for the misgovernance of his realm! For in this council may be determined every case of difficulty, ere the king do anything therein. And the wise man says, *ubi multa consilia, ibi salus.* And truly such a continual council may well be called, *multa consilia,* for it is often, and every day counsels.

Chapter XV

How the king's council may be chosen and established

THE king's council was wont to be chosen of great princes and of the greatest lords of the land, both spiritual and temporal, and also of other men that were in great authority and offices. Which lords and officers had nearly as many matters of their own to be treated in the council as had the king. Wherefore, when they came together, they were so occupied with their own matters and with the matters of their kin, servants, and tenants, that they tended but little, and otherwhiles nothing, to the king's matters. And also there were but few matters of the king's, unless the same matters touched also the said councillors, their cousins, their servants, tenants, or such other as they owed favour unto. And what lower man was there sitting in that council that durst say against the opinion of any of the great lords? And why might not then men make by means of corruption some of the servants and counsellors of some of the lords to move the lords to partiality, and to make them also favourable and partial as were the same servants, or the parties that so moved them? Then could no matter treated in the council be kept private. For the lords oftentimes told their own counsellors and servants, that had sued to them for those matters, how they had sped in them and who was against them. How may the king be counselled to restrain giving away of his land, of giving of offices, corodies, or pensions of abbeys, by such great lords to other men's servants, since they most desire such gifts for themselves, and their servants? Which things considered, and also many other which shall be shown hereafter, it is thought good that the king had a council chosen and established in the form that follows, or in some other form like thereto. First, that there were chosen twelve spiritual men and twelve temporal men of the wisest and best disposed men that can be found in all the parts of this land; and that they be sworn to counsel the king after a form to be devised for their oath. And, in especial, that they shall take no fee, nor clothing, nor no rewards of any man, except only of the king; like as the justices of the king's bench and of the common pleas be sworn, when they take their offices. And that these twenty-four be always councillors, but if there be any fault found in them, or that it list the king, by the advice of the more part of them, change any of them. And that every year be chosen by the king four lords spiritual and four lords temporal to be for that year of the same council, in like form as the said twenty-four shall be. And that they all have a head or a chief to rule the council, one of the said twenty-four, and chosen by the king, having his office at the king's pleasure; which may then be called, *capitalis consiliarius*. It shall not be necessary that the twelve spiritual men of this council have so great wages as the twelve temporal men; because they shall not need to keep a household in their country, while they be absent, as the temporal men must needs do for their wives and children. By which consideration the spiritual judges in the court of parliament of Paris take but two hundred francs by the year, whereas the temporal judges thereof take by the year three hundred francs. The said eight lords also, which by reason of their baronies and estates be to the king *consiliari nati,* and therefore ought to counsel him at all times when he will, need not to have great wages for their attendance to his council, which shall last but for a year. For temporal men, which by reason of their inheritance and livelihood be made sheriffs for a year, take of the king little and almost nothing for their service of that year. And though that wages of the said twenty-four councillors seems a new and a great charge to the king, yet when it is considered how great wages the great lords and other men, which were of the king's council in times past, took for their attendance thereto, which manner of council was nothing so behooveful to the king and to his realm as this will be, which wages shall thenceforward cease; the wages of the twenty-four councillors shall appear no great charge to the king. And I can suppose that some king before this time has given to some one man that has served him as much livelihood yearly as the said wages will come to. And if the same wages be thought too great charge unto the king, the aforesaid councillors may be in less number, as to be sixteen councillors of private persons, with two lords spiritual and two lords temporal; so as then they be in all but twenty persons. These councillors are able to continually, at such hours as shall be assigned to them, commune and deliberate upon the matters of difficulty that fall to the king; and then upon the matters of the policy of the realm; as how the going out of money may be restrained, how bullion may be brought into the land, how also plate, jewels, and money late borne out may be gotten again; of which right wise men may soon find the means. And also how the prices of merchandise grown in this land may be held up and increased, and the prices of merchandise brought into this land abated. How our navy may be maintained and augmented, and upon such other points of policy, to the greatest profit and increase that ever came to this land. How also the laws may be amended in such things as they need reformation in; whereby the parliaments shall be able to do more good in a month to the mending of the law than they shall be able to do in a year, if the amending thereof be not debated and by such council ripened to their hands. There may be of this council, when they list come thereto, or that they be desired by the said councillors, the great officers of the land, as chancellor, treasurer, and privy seal; of which the chancellor, when he is present, may be president and have the supreme rule of all the council. Also the judges, the barons of the exchequer, the clerk of the rolls, and such lords as the aforesaid councillors will desire to be with them for matters of great difficulty, may be of this council when they be so desired, and else not. All other matters which shall concern this council, as when a councillor dies, how a new councillor shall be chosen, how many hours of the day this council shall sit, when they shall have any vacation, how long any of them may be absent, and how he shall have his leave, with all other articles necessary for the behaviour and rule of this council, may be conceived at leisure and put in a book, and that book kept in this council as a register or an ordinary, how they shall do in everything.

Chapter XVI

How the Romans prospered while they had a great council

THE Romans, while their council called the senate was great, got, through the wisdom of that council, the lordship of great part of the world. And afterwards Julius, their first emperor, counselled by the same senate, got the monarchy nearly of all the world. Upon which Octavian, their second emperor, commanded all the world to be described as subject unto him. But after this, when ill disposed emperors, as Nero, Domitian, and others had slain a great part of the senators and despised the counsel of the senate, the estate of the Romans and of their emperors began to fall down, and has fallen always since, into such decay that now the lordships of the emperor be not so great as be the lordships of some king which, while the senate was whole, was subject to the emperor. By which example it is thought, that if the king have such a council as is before specified, his land shall not only be rich and wealthy, as were the Romans, but also his highness shall be mighty and of power to subdue his enemies and all other that he shall list to reign upon. Of such examples many of the books of chronicles be full; and in especial the chronicles of the Lacidemonians and of the Athenians, which, while they prospered, were best counselled and most did after counsel of any people of the world, except the Romans. But when they left such counsel, they fell into non-power and poverty; as of the city of Athens it may well appear, by that it is now but a poor village and sometime was the most worshipful city of Greece.

Chapter XVII

Here follows advertisements for the giving of the king's offices

IF it will like the king to give no office into the time that his intent therein be communed with his council and their opinion by his highness understood in the same, he shall be able to so reward his servants with offices as there shall be little need to give them much of his livelihood, and his offices shall then be given to such as shall only serve himself. Whereby he shall have then a greater might and a guard of his officers, when he list to call them, than he has now of his other paid men under the estate of lords. For the might of the land, after the might of the great lords thereof, stands most in the king's officers. For they are able best to rule the countries where their offices be, which is in every part of the land. A poor bailiff may do more in his bailiwick than any man of his degree dwelling within his office. Some forester of the king's, that has no other livelihood, may bring more men to the field well arrayed, and namely for shooting, than may some knight or squire of right great livelihood, dwelling by him and having no office. What then may greater officers do, stewards of great lordships, receivers, constables of castles, master foresters, and such other officers; besides the higher officers, as justices of foresters, justices and chamberlains of countries, the warden of the ports, and such other? Forsooth, it is not lightly estimable what might the king may have of his officers, if every of them had but one office and served no other man but the king. Nor is it easy to be estimated how many men may be rewarded with offices, and how greatly, if they be discreetly given. The king gives more than a thousand offices, besides those that my lord the prince gives, of which I reckon the officers as the king's officers. Of these officers some may spend by the year, by reason of his office, two hundred pounds, some a hundred pounds, some a hundred marks, some forty pounds, some fifty marks, and so downward. So as the least of them, though he be but a parker, taking but two pence on a day, yet he has by the year three pounds ten pence, besides his dwelling in the lodge, his cow for his milk, and such other things going about him, and the fees of his office, so as that office is to him as profitable as would be a hundred shillings of fee or rent, which is a fair living for a yeoman. How many men then of every estate and of every degree, and how greatly, may the king reward with offices without giving away of his livelihood. For sooth, the greatest lord's livelihood in England may not suffice to reward so many men, though he would divide it every part amongst his servants; nor two of the greatest lords of England may make so great a might as the king may have only of his officers, if they were wholly and only his servants and every of them had but one office. To this say such lords and other men, such as ask of the king offices for their servants, that they and all their servants shall always serve the king, and his officers shall do him the better service, by reason they be in their service; for they will help him to do so and suffer not in their company but such as will do so. Whereto may be said, that it is true they shall do the king service while they be in their company; but so should they have done, though the king had never made them his officers. Wherefore the king shall not be the better served, that he has given his offices to their servants, but rather worse. For our lord said, *Nemo potest duobus dominis servire*. And so the king shall lose the offices, as for any singular service he shall have for them, or that the same officers should think themselves beholden unto the king for their offices which his highness has given them at the contemplation of their masters and for no reward of any service that they have done or shall do unto himself. By consideration whereof their old masters shall be better served by them than they were before; and so be more mighty in their countries to do what they will; and the king in less might and have the fewer officers to repress them when they do amiss. And this has caused many men to be such brokers and suitors to the king, for to have his offices in their countries to themselves and to their men, that almost no man in some country durst take an office of the king but he first had the good will of the said brokers and engrossers of offices. For if he did not so, he should not after that time have peace in his country; whereof have come and grown many great troubles and debates in divers countries of England. Which matters thoroughly considered, it seems very good that no man have any office of the king's gift but he be first sworn that he is servant to no other man, or will serve any other man, or take his clothing or fee while he serves the king. And that no man have more offices than one, except that the king's brothers may have two offices; and such men as serve the king about his person, or in his council, may have in their counties a parkership for their disport when they come home, or such an other office, as they may well keep by their deputies.

Chapter XVIII

Advertisement how corodies and pensions may best be given

AND if it will like the king to give no corody nor pension, which he has by right of his crown, of every abbey, priory, and other houses founded upon hospitality by any of his progenitors, into the time that his intent therein be communicated and deliberated with his aforesaid council, and that his highness have understood their opinion in the same; then shall men of his household be rewarded with corodies and have honest sustenance in their old days when they may no longer serve; and the clerks of his chapel that have wives, or be not advanced, be rewarded with pensions without great abating of the king's revenues for their rewards or sustenance. For such corodies and pensions were first given to the king for the same intent. But now of late time, other men than the king's servants have asked them, and by importunate suit have gotten great parts of them to the king's great harm and hurt of his said servants; which by the cause thereof live in the greater penury, and in no surety of their sustenance in time coming when they shall not be able to do the king service.

Chapter XIX

How great good will grow of the firm endowing of the crown

AND when the king, by the means aforesaid or otherwise, has gotten again his livelihood, if then it would like his most noble grace to establish and, as who says, amortise the same livelihood to his crown so as it may never be alienated therefrom without the assent of his parliament, which then would be as a new foundation of his crown, he shall be thereby the greatest founder of the world. For whereas other kings have founded bishoprics, abbeys, and other houses of religion, the king shall then have founded a whole realm and endowed it with greater possessions and better than ever was any realm in Christendom. This manner of foundation may not be against the king's prerogative or his liberty, no more than is the foundation of an abbey, from which he may take no part of the possessions which he has once given them without the assent of their convent. But this manner of endowment of his crown shall be to the king a greater prerogative, in that he has then enriched his crown with such riches and possessions as never king shall be able to take from it without the assent of his whole realm. Nor this may be to the hurt of the prerogative or power of his successors; for, as it is shown before, it is no prerogative or power to be able to lose any good, or to be able to waste, or put it away. For all such things come of impotency, as does power to be sick or wax old. And truly, if the king do thus, he shall do thereby daily more alms than shall be done by all the foundations that ever were made in England. For every man of the land shall by this foundation every day be the merrier, the surer, fare the better in his body and all his goods, as every wise man may well conceive. The foundation of abbeys, of hospitals, and such other houses, is nothing in comparison hereof. For this shall be a college in which shall sing and pray for evermore all the men of England spiritual and temporal. And their song shall be such among other anthems: Blessed be our Lord God, for that he has sent King Edward the fourth to reign upon us. He has done more for us than ever did king of England or might have done before him. The arms that have fallen in getting of his realm be now by him turned into the good and profit of us all. We shall now be able to enjoy our own goods, and live under justice, which we have not done of long-time, God knows. Wherefore of his alms it is that we have all that is in our home.

Chapter XX

Advertisement for making of patents of gifts

It is not meant by the premises but that the king without the assent of his parliament shall give to such as do him singular service land for term of their lives. For thereby his crown may not be disinherited; for that land will soon come again. But then it were good that the same land be no more given; for else importunate suitors will gape upon such reversions and oftentimes ask them ere they befall. And when they have fallen, the king shall have no rest with such suitors unto the time his highness have given again all such land as he has once given. By continuance thereof that land shall not serve him but for gifts, as do offices, corodies, and pensions. And truly it were good that of all the king's gifts his patents made mention that they were passed, *de auisamento consilii sui*; and namely for a year or two. For if such an order be kept, men will not be so hasty to ask rewards, unless they be of right good merits; and many men will then be of better governance, for the king's council should deem them worthy to be rewarded. And they that obtain not that they desire shall have then little colour of grudge, considering that they lack it by the discretion of the king's council. And the king shall have hereby great rest and be well defended against such importunate suitors. And yet he may leave this order when that him list.

Explicit

A SUPPLICATION FOR THE BEGGARS

by Simon Fish

1528–1529

and

THE STORY OF SIMON FISH

as told by JOHN FOXE in his

Acts and Monuments 1563

JOHN FOXE (1516–1587), the martyrologist, was a student of Brasenose College and Fellow of Magdalen College, Oxford, 1539–1545. When tutor to the children of Henry Howard, earl of Surrey, from 1548 to 1553, he published tracts advocating advanced views in religion. Queen Mary released from prison the catholic duke of Norfolk, the grandfather of Foxe's pupils, who promptly dismissed the tutor. In 1554 Foxe went to Strasburg where he published a small volume on the lives of Huss and Wycliffe. At the end of the year he joined the English *emigrés* at Frankfort and entered into controversy with Knox and Cox over the use of Edward VI's second Book of Common Prayer. Next he proceeded to Basle where he published reports of the protestant persecutions in England. In September 1559 he published in Latin a book of 732 pages on the saints and martyrs, which was translated into English and elaborated into the first (1563) edition of the famous *Acts and Monuments*.

Foxe, once more in London, resided at the new duke of Norfolk's house in Aldgate, received a small pension from him which was inadequate to relieve his chronic poverty, and proceeded to labour on more elaborate editions of his book. In 1570 he preached a powerful sermon against the bull excommunicating Elizabeth for which he was rewarded with a prebend in Salisbury. That year he issued another edition, dedicated to Queen Elizabeth, of the *Acts and Monuments* in two volumes of 934 pages and 1378 pages each. Five editions in all appeared in the sixteenth century and four more during the seventeenth. Convocation ordered copies to be placed in the cathedral churches, and many parsons saw to it that copies were chained to the eagle brass in their parish churches. In this way, and through abridgements and epitomes, *Foxe's Book of Martyrs* came to be the great source book for protestant history among the laity, and its effect in shaping Anglican religious thought and history is beyond estimate.

The text of Fish's *Supplication* is taken from that edited by F.J.Furnivall, *The Early English Text Society*, Extra Series, No.xiii (1871), while that of Foxe's commentary on Fish is from the 1570 edition of the *Acts and Monuments*.

SIMON FISH (died 1531) was a graduate of Oxford and a resident at Gray's Inn about 1525. He belonged to a circle of young men hostile to Wolsey and the wealth of the church. He acted a role in an interlude ridiculing Wolsey after which, fearful of the cardinal's wrath, he fled to the Netherlands. Here he joined Tyndale, soon to return to London as an agent distributing Tyndale's *New Testament*. In 1527 he was back in

83

the Netherlands where he wrote the *Supplication for the Beggars*, probably in 1528 since London is said to have been ' flooded with copies of it ' before the opening of the 1529 reformation parliament. It provoked an answer, the *Supplication of Souls* (1529?), from Sir Thomas More, then lord chancellor. Fish's tract was printed again in 1546 and in Foxe's *Acts and Monuments*, but at the outset it began a vogue for many pamphlets similar in form and spirit. At the end of 1529 Fish seems to have returned to London. He was suspected of heresy, and his tract was condemned by Archbishop Warham. Later More contended that Fish saw the error of his ways, repented, foreswore his heresies and returned to the church. In any event his career was stopped by the plague in 1531. Most of the information about him is derived from this account by Foxe.

THE STORY OF MASTER SIMON FISH

BEFORE the time of Master Bilney and the fall of the cardinal, I should have placed the story of Simon Fish, with the book called *The Supplication of Beggars*; declaring how, and by what means, it came to the king's hand, and what effect thereof followed after, in the reformation of many things; especially of the clergy. But the missing of a few years in this matter breaketh no great square in our story, though it be now entered here, [under the year 1531] which should have come in six years before. The manner and circumstance of the matter is this:

After that the light of the gospel, working mightily in Germany, began to spread his beams here also in England, great stir and alteration followed in the hearts of many; so that coloured hypocrisy and false doctrine and painted holiness began to be espied more and more by the reading of God's word. The authority of the bishop of Rome, and the glory of his cardinals, was not so high, but such as had fresh wits, sparkled with God's grace, began to espy Christ from Antichrist; that is, true sincerity from counterfeit religion; in the number of whom was the said Master Simon Fish, a gentleman of Gray's Inn. It happened the first year that this gentleman came to London to dwell, which was about A.D. 1525, that there was a certain play or interlude made by one Master Roo, of the same inn, gentleman, in which play partly was matter against the Cardinal Wolsey; and when none durst take upon them to play that part which touched the said cardinal, this aforesaid Master Fish took upon him to do it. Whereupon great displeasure ensued against him upon the cardinal's part, insomuch as he, being pursued by the said cardinal the same night that this tragedy was played, was compelled of force to void his own house, and so fled over the sea unto Tyndale: upon occasion whereof, the next year following, this book was made (being about the year 1527); and so, not long after, in the year (as I suppose) 1528, was sent over to the Lady Ann Bulleyne, who then lay at a place not far from the court. Which book her brother seeing in her hand, took it and read it, and gave it her again, willing her earnestly to give it to the king, which thing she so did. This was (as I gather) about A.D. 1528.

The king, after he had received the book, demanded of her who made it: whereunto she answered and said, a certain subject of his, one Fish, who was fled out of the realm for fear of the cardinal. After the king had kept the book in his bosom three or four days as is credibly reported, such knowledge was given by the king's servants to the wife of the said Simon Fish, that she might boldly send for her husband without all peril or danger: whereupon she, thereby being encouraged, came first and made suit to the king for the safe return of her husband; who, understanding whose wife she was, showed a marvellous gentle and cheerful countenance towards her, asking where her husband was. She answered, ' If it like your grace, not far off.' ' Then,' saith he, ' fetch him, and he shall come and go safe without peril, and no man shall do him harm ': saying moreover, that he had much wrong that he was from her so long; who had been absent now the space of two years and a half. In the which meantime the cardinal was deposed, as is afore showed, and Master More set in his place of the chancellorship.

Thus Fish's wife, being emboldened by the king's words, went immediately to her husband, being lately come over, and lying privily within a mile of the court, and brought him to the king; which appeareth to be about A.D. 1530. When the king saw him and understood he was the author of the book, he came and embraced him with loving countenance. Who after long talk for the space of three or four hours, as they were riding together on hunting, the king at length dimitted him, and bade him take home his wife, for she had taken great pains for him; who answered the king again, and said, he durst not so do, for fear of Sir Thomas More, then chancellor, and Stokesley, then bishop of London. This seemeth to be about A.D. 1530.

The king, taking his signet off his finger, willed him to have him recommended to the lord chancellor, charging him not to be so hardy to work him any harm. Master Fish, receiving the king's signet, went and declared his message to the lord chancellor, who took it as sufficient for his own discharge, but he asked him, if he had anything for the discharge of his wife? For she, a little before, had by chance displeased the friars, for not suffering them to say their gospels in Latin in her house, as they did in others, unless they would say it in English. Whereupon the lord chancellor, though he had discharged the man, yet leaving not his grudge towards the wife, the next morning sent his man for her to appear before him; who, had it not been for her young daughter, which then lay sick of the plague, had been like to come to much trouble. Of the which plague, her husband, the said Master Fish, deceasing within half a year, she afterwards married to one Master James Bainham, Sir Alexander Bainham's son, a worshipful knight of Gloucestershire; the which aforesaid Master James Bainham not long after was burned, as incontinently after, in the process of this story, shall appear.

And thus much concerning Simon Fish, the author of the *Book of Beggars*, who also translated a book called *The Sum of the Scripture*, out of the Dutch.

Now cometh another note of one Edmund Moddis the king's footman, touching the same matter.

This Master Moddis, being with the king in talk of religion and of the new books that were come from beyond the seas, said, if it might please his grace to pardon him, and such as he would bring to his grace, he should see such a book as it was a marvel to hear of. The king demanded what they were. He said, ' Two of your merchants, George Elyot and George Robinson.' The king appointed a time to speak with them. When they came afore his presence in a privy closet, he demanded what they had to say or to show him. One of them said, that there was a book come to their hands, which they had there to show his grace. When he saw it, he demanded if any of them could read it. ' Yea,' said George Elyot, ' if it please your grace to hear it.' ' I thought so,' said the king, ' for if need were, thou canst say it without book.'

The whole book being read out, the king made a long pause, and then said, ' If a man should pull down an old stone wall, and begin at the lower part, the upper part thereof might chance to fall upon his head.' And then he took the book, and put it into his desk, and commanded them, upon their allegiance, that they should not tell to any man that he had seen the book, &c. The copy of the foresaid book, entitled *Of the Beggars*, here ensueth.

A SUPPLICATION FOR THE BEGGARS

To the king our sovereign lord

MOST lamentably complain their woeful misery unto your highness, your poor daily beadsmen, the wretched hideous monsters (on whom scarcely for horror any eye dare look), the foul, unhappy sort of lepers, and other sore people, needy, impotent, blind, lame, and sick, that live only by alms, how that their number is daily so sore increased that all the alms of all the well-disposed people of this your realm is not half enough for to sustain them, but that for very constraint they die for hunger. And this most pestilent mischief is come upon your said poor beadsmen by the reason [that] there is in the times of your noble predecessors passed craftily crept into this your realm an other sort (not of impotent but) of strong puissant and counterfeit holy, and idle beggars and vagabonds which since the time of their first entry by all the craft and wiliness of Satan are now increased under your sight not only into a great number, but also into a kingdom. These are (not the herds, but the ravenous wolves going in herds' clothing devouring the flock) the bishops, abbots, priors, deacons, archdeacons, suffragans, priests, monks, canons, friars, pardoners, and summoners. And who is able to number this idle ravenous sort which (setting all labour aside) have begged so importunately that they have gotten into their hands more than the third part of all your realm. The goodliest lordships, manors, lands, and territories are theirs. Besides this they have the tenth part of all the corn, meadow, pasture, grass, wool, colts, calves, lambs, pigs, geese, and chickens. Over and besides the tenth part of every servant's wages the tenth part of the wool, milk, honey, wax, cheese, and butter. Yea, and they look so narrowly upon their profits that the poor wives must be accountable to them of every tenth egg or else she gets not her rites at Easter, shall be taken as an heretic; hereto have they their four offering days; what money pull they in by probates of testaments, privy tithes, and by men's offerings to their pilgrimages, and at their first masses?

Every man and child that is buried must pay somewhat for masses and dirges to be sung for him or else they will accuse the dead's friends and executors of heresy; what money get they by mortuaries, by hearing of confessions (and yet they will keep thereof no counsel) by hallowing of churches, altars, super-altars, chapels, and bells, by cursing of men and absolving them again for money? What a multitude of money gather the pardoners in a year? How much money get the summoners by extortion in a year, by citing the people to the commissary's court and afterward releasing their appearance for money? Finally, the infinite number of begging friars, what get they in a year? Here if it please your grace to mark you shall see a thing far out of joint. There are within your realm of England 52,000 parish churches. And this standing, that there be but ten households in every parish, yet are there five hundred thousand and twenty thousand households. And of every of these households has every of the five orders of friars a penny a quarter for every order, that is for all the five orders five pence a quarter for every house. That is for all the five orders twenty pence a year of every house. *Summa*: five hundred thousand and twenty thousand quarters of angels. That is 260 thousand half-angels. *Summa*: 130 thousand angels. *Summa totalis* 43 thousand pounds and £333,6s.,8d., sterling; whereof not four hundred years past they had not one penny. Oh grievous and painful exactions thus yearly to be paid, from the which the people of your noble predecessors the kings of the ancient Britons ever stood free. And this will they have or else they will procure him that will not give it them to be taken as an heretic; what tyrant ever oppressed the people like this cruel and vengeable generation? What subjects shall be able to help their prince that be after this fashion yearly polled? What good Christian people can be able to succour us poor lepers, blind, sore, and lame, that be thus yearly oppressed? Is it any marvel that your people so complain of poverty? Is it any marvel that the taxes, fifteenths, and subsidies that your grace most tenderly of great compassion has taken among your people to defend them from the threatened ruin of their commonwealth have been so slothfully, yea painfully, levied? Seeing that almost the utmost penny that might have been levied has been gathered before yearly by this ravenous, cruel, and insatiable generation. The Danes, neither the Saxons, in the time of the ancient Britons should never have been able to have brought their armies from so far hither unto your land

to have conquered it if they had had at that time such a sort of idle glut-
tons to find at home. The noble King Arthur had never been able to
have carried his army to the foot of the mountains to resist the coming
down of Lucius the emperor if such yearly exactions had been taken of
his people. The Greeks had never been able to have so long continued
at the siege of Troy if they had had at home such an idle sort of cormorants to find. The ancient Romans had never been able to have put
all the whole world under their obeisance if their people had been thus
yearly oppressed. The Turk now in your time should never be able to
get so much ground of Christendom if he had in his empire such a sort
of locusts to devour his substance. Lay then these sums to the aforesaid
third part of the possessions of the realm that you may see whether it
draw nigh unto the half of the whole substance of the realm or not, so
shall you find that it draws far above. Now let us then compare the number of this unkind idle sort unto the number of the lay people, and we
shall see whether it be indifferently shifted or not that they should have
half. Compare them to the number of men, so are they not the hundredth
person. Compare them to men, women, and children, then are they not
the four-hundredth person in number. One part therefore in four-
hundredth parts divided were too much for them except they did labour;
what an unequal burden is it that they have half with the multitude and
are not the four-hundredth person of their number? What tongue is
able to tell that ever there was any commonwealth so sore oppressed
since the world first began?

And what do all these greedy sort of sturdy, idle, holy thieves with
these yearly exactions that they take of the people? Truly nothing but
exempt themselves from the obedience of your grace. Nothing but translate all rule, power, lordship, authority, obedience, and dignity from your
grace unto them. Nothing but that all your subjects should fall into disobedience and rebellion against your grace and be under them. As they
did unto your noble predecessor King John: which for because that he
would have punished certain traitors that had conspired with the French
king to have deposed him from his crown and dignity (among the which
a clerk called Stephen whom afterward against the king's will the pope
made bishop of Canterbury was one) interdicted his land. For the which
matter your most noble realm wrongfully (alas for shame) has stood tributary (not unto any kind, temporal prince, but unto a cruel, devilish

bloodsupper drunken in the blood of the saints and martyrs of Christ)
ever since. Here were an holy sort of prelates that thus cruelly could
punish such a righteous king, all his realm and succession, for doing
right!

Here were a charitable sort of holy men that could thus interdict a
whole realm, and pluck away the obedience of the people from their
natural liege lord and king, for none other cause but for his righteousness.
Here were a blessed sort, not of meek herds but of bloodsuppers that
could set the French king upon such a righteous prince to cause him to
lose his crown and dignity to make effusion of the blood of his people,
unless this good and blessed king of great compassion, more fearing and
lamenting the shedding of the blood of his people than the loss of his
crown and dignity against all right and conscience, had submitted himself unto them. O case most horrible that ever so noble a king, realm,
and succession should thus be made to stoop to such a sort of bloodsuppers; where was his sword, power, crown, and dignity become whereby
he might have done justice in this manner? Where was their obedience
become that should have been subject under his high power in this
matter? Yea, where was the obedience of all his subjects become that
for maintenance of the commonwealth should have helped him manfully
to have resisted these bloodsuppers to the shedding of their blood? Was
not all together by their policy translated from this good king unto them?
Yea, and what do they more? Truly nothing but apply themselves by all
the sleights they may to have to do with every man's wife, every man's
daughter, and every man's maid, that cuckoldry and bawdry should
reign over all among your subjects, that no man should know his own
child, that their bastards might inherit the possessions of every man to
put the right begotten children clear beside their inheritance in subversion of all estates and godly order. These be they that by their ab-
staining from marriage do let the generation of the people whereby all
the realm at length if it should be continued shall be made desert and
unhabitable.

These be they that have made an hundred thousand idle whores in
your realm which would have gotten their living honestly, in the sweat
of their faces, had not their superfluous riches elected them to unclean
lust and idleness. These be they that corrupt the whole generation of
mankind in your realm, that catch the pox of one woman and bear them

to another, that be burnt with one woman, and bear it to another, that
catch the leprosy of one woman, and bear it to another, yea some one
of them shall boast among his fellows that he has meddled with an hundred women. These be they that when they have once drawn men's
wives to such incontinency spend away their husband's goods, make the
women to run away from their husbands, yea, run away themselves both
with wife and goods, bring both man, wife, and children to idleness,
theft, and beggary. Yea, who is able to number the great and broad,
bottomless ocean sea full of evils that this mischievous and sinful generation may lawfully bring upon us unpunished; where is your sword,
power, crown, and dignity become that should punish (by punishment
of death even as other men are punished) the felonies, rapes, murders,
and treasons committed by this sinful generation? Where is their obedience become that should be under your high power in this matter? Is
not all together translated and exempt from your grace unto them? Yes,
truly. What an infinite number of people might have been increased to
have peopled the realm if these sort of folk had been married like other
men. What breech of matrimony is there brought in by them? Such
truly as was never since the world began among the whole multitude of
the heathen.

Who is she that will set her hands to work to get three pence a day
and may have at least twenty pence a day to sleep an hour with a friar,
a monk, or a priest? What is he that would labour for a groat a day and
may have at least twelve pence a day to be bawd to a priest, a monk, or a
friar? What a sort are there of them that marry priests' sovereign ladies
but to cloak the priest's incontinency and that they may have a living of
the priest themselves for their labour? How many thousands do such
lubricity bring to beggary, theft, and idleness which should have kept
their good name and have set themselves to work had not been this
excess treasure of the spirituality? What honest man dare take any man
or woman in his service that has been at such a school with a spiritual
man? Oh the grievous shipwreck of the commonwealth, which in
ancient time before the coming in of these ravenous wolves was so prosperous: that then there were but few thieves: yea, theft was at that time
so rare that Caesar was not compelled to make penalty of death upon
felony as your grace may well perceive in his institutes. There was
also at that time but few poor people and yet they did not beg but there

was given them enough unasked, for there was at that time none of these ravenous wolves to ask it from them as it appears in the acts of the apostles. Is it any marvel though there be now so many beggars, thieves, and idle people? Nay, truly.

What remedy: make laws against them. I am in doubt whether you are able: are they not stronger in your own parliament house than yourself? What a number of bishops, abbots, and priors are lords of your parliament? Are not all the learned men in your realm in fee with them to speak in your parliament house for them against your crown, dignity, and commonwealth of your realm, a few of your own learned council only excepted? What law can be made against them that may be available? Who is he, (though he be grieved never so sore) for the murder of his ancestor, ravishment of his wife, of his daughter, robbery, trespass, mayhem, debt, or any other offence, dare lay it to their charge by any way of action, and if he do then is he, by and by, by their wiliness accused of heresy; yea, they will so handle him e'er he pass that except he will bear a faggot for their pleasure he shall be excommunicate, and then be all his actions dashed. So captive are your laws unto them that no man that they list to excommunicate may be admitted to sue any action in any of your courts. If any man in your sessions dare be so hardy to indict a priest of any such crime he has e'er the year go out such a yoke of heresy laid in his neck that it makes him wish that he had not done it. Your grace may see what a work there is in London, how the bishop rages for indicting of certain curates of extortion and incontinency the last year in the warmoll [wardmote] quest. Had not Richard Hunne commenced action of *praemunire* against a priest he had been yet alive and not heretic at all but an honest man.

Did not divers of your noble progenitors—seeing their crown and dignity run into ruin and to be thus craftily translated into the hands of this mischievous generation—make divers statutes for the reformation thereof, among which the statute of mortmain was one? To the intent that after that time they should have no more given unto them. But what availed it? Have they not gotten into their hands more lands since than any duke in England has, the statute notwithstanding? Yea, have they not for all that translated into their hands from your grace half your kingdom thoroughly? The whole name as reason is for the anciety of your kingdom which was before theirs and out of the which theirs is grown only abiding with your grace? And of one kingdom made twain: the spiritual kingdom, (as they call it) for they will be named first, and your temporal kingdom. And which of these two kingdoms suppose you is like to overgrow the other; yea, to put the other clear out of memory? Truly the kingdom of the bloodsuppers, for to them is given daily out of your kingdom. And that that is once given them comes never from them again. Such laws have they that none of them may neither give nor sell nothing; what law can be made so strong against them that they either with money or else with other policy will not break and set at naught? What kingdom can endure that ever giveth thus from him and receives nothing again? O how all the substance of your realm forthwith your sword, power, crown, dignity, and obedience of your people runs head-long into the insatiable whirlpool of these greedy goulafres [whirlpools] to be swallowed and devoured.

Neither have they any other colour to gather these yearly exactions into their hands but that they say they pray for us to God to deliver our souls out of the pains of purgatory without whose prayer they say, or at least without the pope's pardon, we could never be delivered thence, which if it be true then is it good reason that we give them all these things all were it a hundred times as much; but there be many men of great literature and judgment that for the love they have unto the truth and unto the commonwealth have not feared to put themselves into the greatest infamy that may be, in abjection of all the world, yea, in peril of death to declare their opinion in this matter which is that there is no purgatory, but that it is a thing invented by the covetousness of the spirituality only to translate all kingdoms from other princes unto them, and that there is not one word spoken of it in all Holy Scripture. They say also that if there were a purgatory, and also if that the pope with his pardons for money may deliver one soul thence, he may deliver him as well without money; if he may deliver one, he may deliver a thousand: if he may deliver a thousand he may deliver them all, and so destroy purgatory. And then is he a cruel tyrant without all charity if he keep them there in prison and in pain till men will give him money.

Likewise say they of all the whole sort of the spirituality that if they will not pray for no man but for them that give them money, they are tyrants and lack charity, and suffer those souls to be punished and pained uncharitably for lack of their prayers. These sort of folks they call heretics, these they burn, these they rage against, put to open shame and make them bear faggots. But whether they be heretics or no, well I wot that this purgatory and the pope's pardons is all the cause of translation of your kingdom so fast into their hands wherefore it is manifest it cannot be of Christ, for he gave more to the temporal kingdom, he himself paid tribute to Caesar; he took nothing from him but taught that the high powers should be always obeyed; yea, he himself (although he were most free lord of all and innocent) was obedient unto the high powers unto death. This is the great scab why they will not let the New Testament go abroad in your mother tongue lest men should espy that they by their cloaked hypocrisy do translate thus fast your kingdom into their hands, that they are not obedient unto your high power that they are cruel, unclean, unmerciful, and hypocrites, that they seek not the honour of Christ but their own, that remission of sins are not given by the pope's pardon, but by Christ, for the sure faith and trust that we have in him. Here may your grace well perceive that except you suffer their hypocrisy to be disclosed all is like to run into their hands and as long as it is covered so long shall it seem to every man to be a great impiety not to give them. For this I am sure, your grace thinks (as the truth is) I am as good a man as my father, why may I not as well give them as much as my father did. And of this mind I am sure are all the lords, knights, squires, gentlemen, and yeomen in England; yea, and until it be disclosed all your people will think that your statute of mortmain was never made with no good conscience seeing that it takes away the liberty of your people in that they may not as lawfully buy their souls out of purgatory by giving to the spirituality as their predecessors did in times past.

Wherefore if you will eschew the ruin of your crown and dignity let their hypocrisy be uttered, and that shall be more speedful in this matter than all the laws that may be made, be they never so strong. For to make a law for to punish any offender except it were more for to give other men an example to beware to commit such like offence, what should it avail. Did not Doctor Allen most presumptuously now in your time against all his allegiance, all that ever he could to pull from you the knowledge of such pleas as belong unto your high courts unto another court in derogation of your crown and dignity? Did not also Doctor Horsey and his accomplices most heinously, as all the world knows, murder in prison

that honest merchant Richard Hunne? For that he sued your writ of
praemunire against a priest that wrongfully held him in plea in a spiritual
court for a matter whereof the knowledge belonged unto your high
courts. And what punishment was there done that any man may take
example of to beware of like offence? Truly none but that the one paid
five hundred pounds (as it is said to the building of your star chamber)
and when that payment was once past the captains of his kingdom (because he fought so manfully against your crown and dignity) have heaped
to him benefice upon benefice so that he is rewarded ten times as much.
The other (as it is said) paid six hundred pounds for him and his accomplices which for because that he had likewise fought so manfully against
your crown and dignity was immediately (as he had obtained your most
gracious pardon) promoted by the captains of his kingdom with benefice
upon benefice to the value of four times as much; who can take example
of this punishment to beware of such like offence? Who is he of their
kingdom that will not rather take courage to commit like offence seeing
the promotions that fell to these men for their so offending? So weak
and blunt is your sword to strike at one of the offenders of this crooked
and perverse generation.

And this is by the reason that the chief instrument of your law, yea,
the chief of your council, and he which has your sword in his hand to
whom also all the other instruments are obedient, is always a spiritual
man which has ever such an inordinate love unto his own kingdom that
he will maintain that, though all the temporal kingdoms and commonwealths of the world should therefore utterly be undone; here leave we
out the greatest matter of all lest that we, declaring such an horrible
carrion of evil against the ministers of iniquity, should seem to declare
the one only fault or rather the ignorance of our best beloved minister
of righteousness, which is to be hid till he may be learned by these small
enormities that we have spoken of to know it plainly himself. But what
remedy to relieve us, your poor, sick, lame, and sore beadsmen? To
make many hospitals for the relief of the poor people? Nay truly. The
more the worse, for ever the fat of the whole foundation hangs on the
priest's beards. Divers of your noble predecessors, kings of this realm,
have given lands to monasteries to give a certain sum of money yearly
to the poor people whereof for the ancient of the time they give never
one penny; they have likewise given to them to have a certain mass said

daily for them whereof they say never one. If the abbot of Westminster should sing every day as many masses for his founders as he is bound to do by his foundation, one thousand monks were too few; wherefore if your grace will build a sure hospital that never shall fail to relieve us all your poor beadsmen, so take from them all these things. Set these sturdy lobies [louts] abroad in the world to get them wives of their own, to get their living with their labour in the sweat of their faces according to the commandment of God: Genesis iii, to give other idle people by their example occasion to go to labour. Tie these holy idle thieves to the carts to be whipped naked about every market town till they will fall to labour that they by their importunate begging take not away the alms that the good Christian people would give unto us sore impotent miserable people your beadsmen. Then shall as well the number of our aforesaid monstrous sort as of the bawds, whores, thieves, and idle people decrease. Then shall these great yearly exactions cease. Then shall not your sword, power, crown, dignity, and obedience of your people be translated from you. Then shall you have full obedience of your people. Then shall the idle people be set to work. Then shall matrimony be much better kept. Then shall the generation of your people be increased; then shall your commons increase in riches. Then shall the gospel be preached. Then shall none beg our alms from us. Then shall we have enough and more than shall suffice us, which shall be the best hospital that ever was founded for us; then shall we daily pray to God for your most noble estate long to endure.

Domine salvum fac regem.

Against this *Book of the Beggars*, above prefixed, being written in the time of the cardinal, another contrary book or supplication was devised and written shortly upon the same, by one Sir Thomas More, knight, chancellor of the duchy of Lancaster, under the name and title of *The Poor Silly Souls Puling out of Purgatory*. In the which book, after that the said Master More, writer thereof, hath first divided the whole world into four parts, that is, into heaven, hell, middle earth, and purgatory; then he maketh the dead men's souls, by a rhetorical ' prosopopoea,' to speak out of purgatory pin-fold, sometimes lamentably complaining, sometimes pleasantly dallying and scoffing, at the author of the *Beggars*'

Book; sometimes scolding and railing at him, calling him fool, witless, frantic, an ass, a goose, a mad dog, a heretic, and all that naught is. And no marvel, if these silly souls of purgatory seem so fumish and testy; for heat (you know) is testy, and soon inflameth choler. But yet those purgatory souls must take good heed how they call a man fool and heretic so often; for if the sentence of the gospel doth pronounce them guilty of hell-fire, which say, ' Fatue,' ' Fool,' it may be doubted lest those poor, silly, melancholy souls of purgatory, calling this man fool so oft as they have done, do bring themselves thereby out of purgatory-fire to the fire of hell, by the just sentence of the gospel; so that neither the five wounds of St. Francis, nor all the merits of St. Dominic, nor yet of all the friars, can release them, poor wretches! But yet, forsomuch as I do not, nor cannot think, that those departed souls either would so far overshoot themselves, if they were in purgatory, or else that there is any such fourth place of purgatory at all (unless it be in Master More's *Utopia*), as Master More's poetical vein doth imagine, I cease therefore to burden the souls departed, and lay all the wit in Master More, the author and contriver of this poetical book, for not keeping *decorum personae*, as a perfect poet should have done. They that give precepts of art, do note this in all poetical fictions, as a special observation, to foresee and express what is convenient for every person, according to his degree and condition, to speak and utter. Wherefore if it be true that Master More saith, in the sequel of his book, that grace and charity increaseth in them that lie in the pains of purgatory, then is it not agreeable that such souls, lying so long in purgatory, should so soon forget their charity, and fall arailing in their supplication so fumishly, both against this man, with such opprobrious and unfitting terms, and also against John Badby, Richard Hawdon, John Gose, Lord Cobham, and other martyrs of the Lord, burned for his word; also against Luther, William Tyndale, Richard Hunne, and other more, falsely belying the doctrine by them taught and defended; which is not like that such charitable souls of purgatory would ever do, neither were it convenient for them in that case; which indeed, though their doctrine were false, should redound to the more increase of their pain. Again, where the bishop of Rochester defineth the angels to be ministers to purgatory-souls, some will think, peradventure, Master More to have missed some part of his *decorum*, in making the evil spirit of the author and the devil to be messenger between middle-earth and purgatory, in bringing tidings to the prisoned souls both of the book and of the name of the maker.

Now, as touching the manner how this devil came into purgatory, laughing, grinning, and gnashing his teeth, in sooth it maketh me to laugh, to see the merry antics of Master More. Belike then this was some merry devil, or else had eaten with his teeth some nasturtium before; which, coming into purgatory to show the name of this man, could not tell his tale without laughing. ' But this was,' saith he, ' an enmious and an envious laughing, joined with grinning and gnashing of teeth.' And immediately upon the same, was contrived this scoffing and railing supplication of the puling souls of purgatory, as he himself doth term them. So then, here was enmying, envying, laughing, grinning, gnashing of teeth, puling, scoffing, railing, and begging; and all together to make a very black *sanctus* in purgatory. Indeed we read in Scripture, that there shall be weeping and gnashing of teeth in hell, where the souls and bodies of men shall be tormented. But who would ever have thought before, that the evil angel of this man that made the *Book of Beggars*, being a spiritual and no corporal substance, had teeth to gnash, and a mouth to grin? But where then stood Master More, I marvel, all this mean while, to see the devil laugh with his mouth so wide that the souls of purgatory might see all his teeth? Belike, this was in Utopia, where Master More's purgatory is founded; but because Master More is hence departed, I leave him with his merry antics. And as touching his book of purgatory, which he hath left behind, because John Frith hath learnedly and effectuously overthrown the same, I will therefore refer the reader to him, while I repair again (the Lord willing) to the history.

After that the clergy of England, and especially the cardinal, understood these books of *The Beggars' Supplication* aforesaid, to be strewed abroad in the streets of London, and also before the king, the said cardinal caused not only his servants diligently to attend to gather them up, that they should not come into the king's hands, but also, when he understood that the king had received one or two of them, he came unto the king's majesty, saying, ' If it shall please your grace, here are divers seditious persons which have scattered abroad books containing manifest errors and heresies;' desiring his grace to beware of them. Whereupon the king, putting his hand in his bosom, took out one of the books, and delivered it unto the cardinal. Then the cardinal, together with the bishops, consulted how they might provide a speedy remedy for this mischief, and thereupon determined to give out a commission to forbid the reading of all English books, and namely, this *Book of the Beggars*, and the New Testament of Tyndale's translation, which was done out of hand by Cuthbert Tunstal, bishop of London, who sent out his prohibition unto his archdeacons with all speed, for the forbidding of that book and divers other more; the tenor of which prohibition here followeth.

A prohibition sent out by Cuthbert Tunstal, bishop of London, to the archdeacons of his diocese, for the calling in of the New Testaments translated into English, with divers other books; the catalogue whereof hereafter ensueth.

Cuthbert, by the permission of God, bishop of London, unto our well-beloved in Christ, the archdeacon of London, or to his official, health, grace, and benediction. By the duty of our pastoral office, we are bound diligently, with all our power, to foresee, provide for, root out, and put away, all those things, which seem to tend to the peril and danger of our subjects, and especially the destruction of their souls. Wherefore we, having understanding, by the report of divers credible persons, and also by the evident appearance of the matter, that many children of iniquity, maintainers of Luther's sect, blinded through extreme wickedness, wandering from the way of truth and the catholic faith, craftily have translated the New Testament into our English tongue, intermeddling therewith many heretical articles, and erroneous opinions, pernicious and offensive, seducing the simple people; attempting, by their wicked and perverse interpretations, to profanate the majesty of the Scripture, which hitherto hath remained undefiled, and craftily to abuse the most holy word of God, and the true sense of the same, of the which translation there are many books imprinted, some with glosses, and some without, containing in the English tongue that pestiferous and most pernicious poison dispersed throughout all our diocese of London in great number; which truly, without it be speedily foreseen, without doubt will contaminate and infect the flock committed unto us, with most deadly poison and heresy; to the grievous peril and danger of the souls committed to our charge, and the offence of God's divine majesty. Wherefore, we, Cuthbert, the bishop aforesaid, grievously sorrowing for the premises, willing to withstand the craft and subtlety of the ancient enemy and his ministers, which seek the destruction of my flock, and with a diligent care to take heed unto the flock committed to my charge, desiring to provide speedy remedies for the premises, do charge you jointly and severally, and by virtue of your obedience straightly enjoin and command you that by our authority you warn, or cause to be warned, all and singular, as well exempt as not exempt, dwelling within your archdeaconries, that within thirty days' space, whereof ten days shall be for the first, ten for the second, and ten for the third and peremptory term, under pain of excommunication and incurring the suspicion of heresy, they do bring in, and really deliver unto our vicar-general, all and singular such books as contain the translation of the New Testament in the English tongue; and that you do certify us, or our said commissary, within two months after the day of the date of these presents, duly, personally, or by your letters, together with these presents, under your seals, what you have done in the premises, under pain of contempt.

Given under our seal, the xxiii of October, in the v year of our consecration, *anno* 1526.

The like commission, in like manner and form, was sent to the three other archdeacons of Middlesex, Essex, and Colchester, for the execution of the same matter, under the bishop's seal.

The names of the books that were forbidden at this time, together with the New Testament:

The *Supplication of Beggars*; the *Revelation of Antichrist*, of Luther; the New Testament of Tyndale; the *Wicked Mammon*; the *Obedience of a Christian Man*; an *Introduction to Paul's Epistle to the Romans*; a *Dialogue betwixt the Father and the Son*; *Oeconomicae Christianae*; *Unio dissidentium*; *Piae Precationes*; *Captivitas Babylonica*; *Johannes Hus in Oseam*; *Zwinglius in Catabaptistas*; *De pueris instituendis*; *Brentius de administranda Republica*; Luther *ad Galatas*; *De libertate Christiana*; Luther's exposition upon the *Pater Noster*.

AN EXHORTATION TO YOUNG MEN

Persuading them to walk in the pathway that leadeth to honesty and goodness: written to a friend of his by Thomas Lupset, Londoner, 1529.

THOMAS LUPSET (1495–1530) was born in London near St. Paul's cathedral, and by
1508 he had become a member of Dean Colet's household. He received a liberal education at the dean's grammar school of St. Paul's. He went on to Pembroke Hall, Cambridge, where he at once revolted against the traditional scholasticism. Save for the
lectures by Erasmus, Lupset found little to his liking at the university and by 1516
had returned to London. After a year he became a student at Paris where he supervised the printing of two of Linacre's translations of Galen into Latin and the second
edition of More's *Utopia*. By 1519 he was in residence at Corpus Christi College, Oxford,
recently founded by Bishop Fox to promote the new learning, serving as university
lecturer on Greek and Latin literature and enjoying ' a very high reputation.'

In 1523 Lupset went to Padua as a member of Reginald Pole's household. During
this sojourn he visited both Venice and Paris and returned to England in 1527. He was
then engaged as tutor for Wolsey's illegitimate son, Thomas Winter. Sometime between his arrival in England and his departure for Paris in 1528 with Winter, he conducted a class for two pupils, Christopher Smith and Edmond Withypoll, both Londoners. For Withypoll, the son of a prosperous member of the Company of Merchant
Taylors, Lupset wrote *An Exhortation to Young Men*. The youth was to become a
successful merchant, a great landed proprietor, and an acquaintance of Gabriel Harvey,
the friend of Edmund Spenser. The expectancy that Withypoll would become engrossed in trade led Lupset to emphasize the danger of neglecting both physical and
spiritual health in the pursuit of wealth. The suggestion that Edmond order his life
according to the relative importance of the soul—derived from Plato—and the advice
on which books to read illustrate the rapid development of humanism in England
between 1510 and 1530.

An Exhortation to Young Men was printed in 1535, 1538, and 1544. The text has not
been abridged and is taken from J.A.Gee, *The Life and Works of Thomas Lupset*,
1928.

TO MY WITHYPOLL

IT happeneth at this time (my heartily beloved Edmond) that I am in
such place, where I have no manner of books with me to pass the time
after my manner and custom. And though I had here with me plenty of
books, yet the place suffereth me not to spend in them any study. For
you shall understand that I lie waiting on my lord cardinal, whose hours
I must observe, to be always at hand, lest I be called when I am not by:

101

the which should be straight taken for a fault of great negligence. Wherefore, now that I am well satiated with the beholding of these gay hangings that garnish here every wall, I will turn me and talk with you. For you must know that my mind hath long coveted to show what affection I bear toward you: the which hitherto peradventure I never uttered unto you so plainly that you might take thereof any perfect knowledge. And that I so did keep in such outward tokens, whereof when you were with me you should have perceived my love: the cause was none other but that indeed I loved you. For long I have been taught that the master never hurteth his scholar more than when he uttereth and showeth by cherishing and cockering the love that he beareth to his scholars. I think you lacked with me no cherishing, but of cockering you had very little, because I was loath to hurt you: the which loathness came, I say, of that I loved you. But now inasmuch you be of age and also by the common board of houseling admitted into the number of men, to be no more in the company of children, and specially for as much as my rule over you is ceased, I will not defer any longer the expressing of mine heart that no less loveth and favoureth you than if nature had made you either my son or my brother. For this always is my mind: if I have a friend in whom I find such faith and honesty that I inwardly joy in heart with him, I reckon straight that all his be mine without any exception: so that in very deed I take to my care, as mine own, all things that be in my friend's care. This mind had I to my friend Andrew Smith, whose son Christopher, your fellow, I ever took for my son, and now I think plainly that he is so in very deed. This strength hath true love in friendship, the which hath likewise joined your father in such manner to my heart that me think you should be no more his son than you be mine. And though I can suffer your father to take the rule of you more than I do, yet I cannot suffer that he should care more for your profit than I do. For as I desire and wish that you never have need of me, so surely if you ever should have, it should well then appear that as nature hath given you one father, so your father's friendship hath provided for you another father. Wherefore good Edmond reckon no less affection in me to do you good than is in your own father, whose only study and care is to see you grow and prosper toward the state of an honest man: and I to further you to the same, am as desirous as he is, and as much as I can, I will help you both with my counsel and power such as I have.

If you will call to your mind all the frays that have been between you and me, or between me and Smith, you shall find the causes ever depended of a care I had for your and his manners when I saw certain phantasies in you or him that jarred from true opinions, the which true opinions, above all learning, I would have masters ever teach their scholars. But now that you be of better ability to take counsel, I will begin to show you my mind, in staying you for the whole course of your life, that you may in time learn what is to be done to be a good and an honest man. You be yet in the first entry of your life, and now is the time to have a guide that may faithfully conduct you in the right way. For there be so many paths, and for the most part all bypaths be more worn with the steps of your foregoers than is the very true path of living, that if you go alone, you may peradventure long wander out of the straight way. Wherefore as near as I can, I will in few words appoint unto you certain marks upon the which if you diligently look, you cannot err nor fail of the way that leadeth to the reward of an honest good man, whose virtue savoureth pleasantly to heaven, pleaseth the world, and nourisheth himself with an incomparable delight and gladness, that continually reigneth in his clean and pure conscience. With these marks and tokens, the which I would you looked still upon, I will assign you certain authors, in whose works I would you should bestow your leisure, when you may have time to read that by them you may at the full be instructed in all things appertaining to virtue: and in all your life I would you meddled not greatly with any other books, than with these that I shall name unto you. It is not the reading of many books that getteth increase of knowledge and judgment: for the most part of them that readeth all indifferently confound their wits and memory without any notable fruit of their reading. It must be a diligent reader that shall take the profit of his labour and diligence. No man (specially of them that have other occupations) can use reading but in very few works, the which I would should be picked out of the best sort, that the fruit of the reader's diligence may be the greater. I see many lose their time when they think to bestow their time best, because they lack judgment or knowledge to pick out the books, the which be worthy to be studied. And in everything an order well observed bringeth more profit than any labour or pain beside. Wherefore, my good Withypoll, take heed to my lesson. I am in doubt whether you have any other lover that can and will show you a like tale: but well I am assured that you have none that can thus teach you with a better will, to have you take profit by him, than I do: and of me how long you shall have this use, it is in God's will to determine. As much as lieth in me, I will now procure and provide that these letters shall keep to your use the sum of my counsel, by the which if you order your will, I put no doubt but first the grace of God shall be rooted in you, and next you shall live with a merry heart, and finally never to lack the commodities requisite for the short time in this world, in the which case you shall obtain the worship and dignity of a good and an honest man, whose conditions I had rather see you have with poverty than in great abundance to be a man of small honesty. You may be good, honest, and rich: and so study to be, or else think never of riches: for otherwise you shall deceive yourself and do contrary to that way that as well worldly wisdom as the truth of our faith showeth you. But now hear what I say.

First and last (mine own good Withypoll) remember earnestly to have in your mind three certain things, the which be of such value that he that forgetteth either their dignity and nature, or else the degrees and order of them, he cannot please neither God, nor himself, nor the world. I say, in all the course of your life there be three things to be looked so upon, that the first of them must be first of you regarded, the second next after, and the third in his place after the two. Beware, as of deadly poison, that you ruffle not them without care, one before the other, as to take the third in the place of the first, or the second after the third, or both the second and the third before the first. In this conclusion you shall (as I have said) both offend God and displease yourself, and also nothing content the world. Like as the most part of men nowadays trespass all for the reachfulness and negligence in not keeping these three things under the dignity and degree according as they ought to be observed and kept. And what be we (my good Edmond) if we be out of God's favour? Odious to ourself, and despiteful to men. Therefore again I exhort you to the intent you may eschew this abominable condition and grow to be admitted in the blessed number of them that rest in the grace of God, in the cleanness of their conscience, and in the favour of the world, to be judged a good, a wise, and an honest man. For this final end mine exhortation is now that you in all your acts in the whole course of your life remember these three things that I will re-hearse unto you. But I say to you that you must not only remember these three things, but also specially have in mind the degrees of them, so that ever the first of them be chiefly in your thought above all other; and then in his place put the second, and let not the third be regarded but as his place requireth, that is, when you have done with the first, and also with the second. There lieth more weight and value upon the knowing and keeping of this tale, that I shall tell you, than if I could show you the way within few months to be a man of great power, both in exceeding abundance of riches and also in passing authority of rule. Therefore as well for the fruit that followeth, if you do after mine ex-hortation, as for the infinite hurts that you cannot escape if you should forget that I say: I warn and warn you again, hear this lesson with a glad ear and print the same in your mind to execute with lively diligence the effect of this counsel, wherein is contained your life and death, your joy and sorrow, as well in this world as in that shall be hereafter. These three things be the soul, the body, and the substance of this world. The first place hath by good reason the soul, seeing it is a thing immortal that is created and made after the figure and shape of almighty God. The next and second room hath the body, as the case and sepulchre of the soul and nearest servant to the secrets of the spirit. The third room occupieth the riches and goods of this world as the necessary instruments or tools for the body, the which cannot want nor lack such things. Let then the eye of your inward mind first and chiefly ever behold the first thing in you, that is your soul. Next thereto have a respect to your body. And thirdly consider the world. Care for your soul as for your chief jewel and only treasure. Care for your body for the soul's sake. Care for the world for the body's sake. Beware above all things that you go not backward, as he doth that careth first to be a rich man, next to be an healthy man, and thirdly to be a good man: where he should do clean contrary, first to study for goodness, next for health, and then for wealth. You see so great blindness among men that some folk so careth for riches that very little they look for the health of the body and nothing at all they mind the state of the soul. I say to you, some folks do thus: I would to God I might not truly report that for the most part all men in manner nowadays do nor other wise. Look upon either the spiritual sort or the temporal, and much ado you shall have, in the great swarming multitude of this blind sort, to find out them that first above all things care for their soul, next for their body, and thirdly for goods of this world. You shall see merchants spare no travail nor jeopardy of the body to get these goods. They be (to say the truth) so occupied in the study of this third thing, that scant they have time to care for the second: and as for the first, they pass nothing thereupon, it seemeth a thing least in their thought, where of conveniency the same care, study, and thought that they give to the obtaining of these worldly goods, they should spend it all in the maintenance of the first thing, that is the soul: and the small little regard that they take for the first should be bestowed for the third: and more than they do, they should cherish the second. The same confusion is with us scholars: for our first study is to get promotion, to get these goods, to live wealthily. In this care we busily be occupied continually. Somewhat more we cherish our bodies than doth the merchant: but our cherishing is for the longer use of these goods, not, as it should be, for the soul's sake. And as for the soul, we have as little regard as other men have, although we speak thereof more than peradventure other men do.

This overthwart confusion of these three things marreth all. And plainly I may say, that all mischief cometh only of this misorder, that we put the chief care of our study to the third thing and not to the first, as of duty we ought to do the contrary. If my purpose were to show you what other men do and not rather what I would have you do, I would farther proceed to express unto you how far out of square our life is nowadays, and how blessed a life we should have in this transitory world, if the care of our soul were first and chiefly in men's minds like as the care of the worldly substance occupieth our hearts above all other things. If it were as it ought to be, that in our phantasy reigned the study for the soul, then should be here that celestial kingdom, the which Christ teacheth us to pray for in our paternoster where we crave of God that his rule and reign may come among us. But as I despair that commonly this study and care cannot be changed from these worldly riches to the soul, so I am full of good hope that you will take heed to your life, to order therein your desires in this due manner, more regarding what should be done than what is done. When you see and know the right path, I trust you will not walk in the crooked highway. The truth shall more draw you to love and to follow virtue than the common example shall entice you to follow vice, the which no man can love, not the sinner himself.

But now mine own good Edmond, here of these three things somewhat more you must print in your mind with a perfect persuasion that your soul is the chief treasure that you have: whereupon your continual thought and care must be to keep it, to defend it, to nourish it, to comfort it by all ways and means possible for you. In this study you must spend all your wits: night and day you must think on this thing: what so ever you do, you must direct your act to this thing. If you be occupied in the state of your body, either to drive away sickness or to sustain health, let it be for the service your body oweth to the soul. If you travail for goods of this world, to get your own living, or to help your friend, or else to provide for your children, when God shall send you them, let your travail be for the necessities of the body, and so finally for the soul. Consider what the goods of the world be, how they be but instruments for the body. Use then the world in his kind. Look again upon your body, how it is preciouser than the goods: use him then in his worthiness and hurt not your body for a thing of less value. And as you have nothing, neither your body nor your goods, to be compared with the dignity of your soul, so, my sweet Withypoll, let nothing be in your reputation above this chief and principal jewel, the which must only for himself be cared for, and all other things in this life must be cherished for it. I stick much with you in repeating one thing, but marvel not though I so do. For I see us all in this world so blinded, partly by a use and custom from the cradle, in the magnificence of these goods, partly by the example of them with whom we be daily conversant, that scant after long crying, it can now be heard, that the soul must be chiefly cared for. And except grace work with you, that you yourself will consent to the truth, it is not possible to persuade you that the very true way of living is this, to care chiefly for the soul and to care for all other things only for the soul's sake. This saying, though it be true, yet I say, it cannot be heard: inasmuch the lives of all them, with whom you shall be continually conversant, shall cry out clean contrary against my saying. For on all sides you shall see men sweating in a continual work, both of body and of mind, to get these worldly goods without any mention made of the soul's state: the which the very friars care little for, as it openly appeareth. But ever I say to you, look what Christian men should do, and if you see men so do, be glad of that sight and follow the same: if you see the contrary, flee from the example and cleave ever fastly to the truth with a sorrowful heart for the loss of other men that so blindly rush forth in the train of a vicious living, where the soul is so little cared for.

That this first thing may be the better in your study, I will briefly touch somewhat of those things that appertain hereto: to have you know what nourisheth and comforteth the soul, and what hurteth and annoyeth the same. The soul cannot but ever live, it hath no end of living: yet we may say, that the soul liveth and dieth: it liveth in the grace of God and dieth in the malice of the devil. The soul's life is the light of virtue: his death is the darkness of sin. You have a free will given you, whereby you may either quicken or slay at your own pleasure your soul in the bright paradise of life, and you may set your soul in the black dungeon of death. Let therefore this will of yours ever study to procure for the soul's life, the which is your own life: and in the same study you shall deliver the soul from his death, the which is the perpetual pain ordained for sin, that separateth the image of God from his patron. I say sin pluckleth your soul from God, whose image your soul should bear. Therefore in all your acts so do that you willingly displease not God: who cannot be pleased but with a pure and clean conscience, pure and clean if you suffer no sin to remain so long in your desire and mind that it cankereth the thought. Your thought is cankered with the long residence of sin, when either you be weak in the study of virtue, or else make very little of a fault, or defend your vice, or nuzzle yourself in a custom of an inordinate desire. The frailness of our flesh is so great that it can not be but that sin shall come to our desire: but it is our blame if sin tarry and abide within us. God hath given us a mighty power over ourself: we may when we will correct our desires and drive out all sin. If you know not what is sin, nor what is virtue, by the fear and love of God, you shall know both. The fear of God will teach you to flee sin and follow virtue. The love of God will teach you to follow virtue and flee sin: whereby your privy and secret conscience shall better and more clearly perceive what is to be done, and what is not, than any definition or description can appoint out to you. Therefore, my dear Withypoll, enwrap yourself fast and sure in the fear and love of God: from your first rising to your rest draw forth the day in all your business as this loving fear and fearful love shall secretly admonish and warn you: and die rather than you would pursue any lust against your knowledge of God's pleasure.

What merchandise so ever you occupy, remember, it is the business of the third care, for the which you may not leave any point of this first care, that belongeth to the soul. Likewise if you be occupied about the body, remember, it is the work of the second care, the which also must be ordered under the first, the which first must always stick in your mind, stirred up and led in all desires and appetites by the said fear and love of God. Do never that thing wherein you fear God's displeasure.

More particularly in writings you shall learn this lesson, if you would sometime take in your hands the New Testament and read it with a due reverence. For I would not have you in that book forget with whom you talk. It is God that there speaketh, it is you a poor creature of God that readeth. Consider the match and meek down your wits. Presume not in no case to think that there you understand ought: leave devising thereupon: submit yourself to the expositions of holy doctors: and ever conform your consent to agree with Christ's church. This is the surest way that you can take, both before God and man. Your obedience to the universal faith shall excuse you before God, although it might be in a false belief: and the same obedience shall also keep you out of trouble in this world, where you see how foolish meddlers be daily sore punished, both to their own undoing and also to the great sorrow and lamenting of their lovers and friends. Surely the truth is as I have said, that it is your part to obey and to follow the church: so that both for your soul's sake, and for your bodily quietness, with the comfort of your friends, I exhort you to meddle in no point of your faith otherwise than the church shall instruct and teach you. In the which obedience read for your increase in virtue the story of our master Christ, that lively expresseth the whole course of a virtuous life. And there you shall hear the Holy Ghost command you to seek first afore all things the kingdom of heaven, and then (saith the spirit of God) all other things appertaining to the body and world shall by themselves follow without your care.

In reading the gospels I would you had at hand Chrysostom and Jerome, by whom you might surely be brought to a perfect understanding of the text. And hereafter at leisure, I would you read the *Ethics* of Aristotle; either under some expert philosopher or else with comment of Futtiratius. And let Plato be familiar with you, specially in the books that he writeth *De re publica*. Also you shall find much for your knowledge in the moral philosophy of Cicero as in his books *De officiis, de senectute, de fato, de finibus, de academicis, questio. Thusc.* Specially read with diligence the works of Seneca of whom you shall learn as much of virtue as man's wit can teach you. These works I think sufficient to show you what is virtue and what is vice: and by reading of these you shall grow into a high courage to rise in a judgment above the common sort to esteem this world according to his worthiness, that is far under the dignity of the virtues, the which the mind. of man conceiveth and rejoiceth in. These books shall lift you up from the clay of this earth and set you in a hill of high contemplation, from whence you shall look down and despise the vanity that foolish men take in the deceitful pomp of this short and wretched life. More books I will not advise you, for your soul's study, to read than these: except it be *Enchiridion*, that Erasmus writeth, a work doubtless, that in few leaves containeth an infinite knowledge of goodness. Think not, my good Edmond, that I overcharge you. For I know what pleasure you have in reading: and in better books you cannot bestow your pleasure than in these, the which be in number but few, and yet they shall do you more good than the reading here and there of many other. I would to Jesus I had in your age followed like counsel in reading only these works, the which now at last by a great loss of time in reading of other I have chosen out for my purpose to refresh with them the rest of my life. And I counsel you now to begin to do the same when time and convenient leisure shall be given you to read any book.

The second care is for the body, the which you must cherish as much as may stand with the service of your former thought and study for your chief treasure. Have a respect to keep your body in good health, the which resteth in the air and in your diet. Abide not where corruption or infection is: eat not nor drink not out of time or measure: nor yet of such meats and drinks as be more delicate and pleasant than wholesome. Know the measure of your stomach before you overload your belly. Choke not your appetite, but feed your hunger. Drown not your lust, but quench your thirst, and ever for your soul's sake keep you from gluttony. Fast sometime, both for devotion and also for your health. Sleep rather too little than too much: as much as you take from sleep, so much you add to your life. For sleep is death for the time. Exercise you continually: for in labour your body shall find strength: and lustiness is gotten by the use of your limbs. Let never the sun rise before you: you shall have to all your affairs the longer day: and ever for your soul's sake flee from idleness, the which is not only in him that doth nothing, but also in him that doth not well: and idle you be, when you be not well occupied. Be temperate in your lusts touching the bodily pleasure: the time shall not be long till your friends by God's grace will provide you of an honest mate. In the mean season let the fear and love of God keep you in chastity, the which appertaineth to your chief care: for needs you must so do, seeing that otherwise lechery shall sore defile your soul, the which you must regard before the body's appetite. For this part I would you read, as your leisure shall be, a little work of Galen *De bona valetudine tuenda.* And in the works aforenamed, you shall find many things that shall instruct you well for this part also, and likewise for the third, the which third ever hath occupied men's stomachs more than either the first or the second. Wherefore as well in Holy Scripture, as in the other philosophers, and especially in Seneca, you shall find many lessons that appertain to the third care. This third care is for the goods in this world. In this part I can give you small advice of myself, because I have had but small experience herein: yet ever I see that you may not in the study of getting these goods leave or slake the chief care, for the first thing, nor yet the secondary care, for the body. Labour you must for your living in a due order, as in the third degree of your things. If matins, mass, or a sermon be to be heard, set your merchandise apart for the season and prefer the matins of your soul that looketh to have such ghostly food. If the time require to have you take a meal, either a dinner or a supper for your refection, let not your merchandise defer the going thereto in a due time. For remember that business is one degree above your merchandise. If you espy a poor man to be in need of your help, haste to help him before any care of making a bargain, for that work of mercy pertaineth to your chief jewel: and therefore your soul shall grow in the grace of God. Break not much, to the hurt of your health, the convenient time of going to bed for any occupations or reckonings in your study for these goods. For remember that rest and sleep pertain to the second thing, where your counting book belong to the third. In making your bargain, keep faith and promise: deceive no man with any guile or false colour. For let it be ever in your phantasy how the gains that you should get with such untrue dealing be contained under your third, that is to say, under your least care, where the breaking of faith and promise, with false deceit and untrue dealing, sore hurteth your soul, in whom resteth your chief thought. And by falsehood, you could not get so much of riches as by the same you should lose of honesty and goodness. Wherefore travail ever as the degrees of these three things shall require. If an infinite heap of worldly goods might be got with a small hurt and damage of the soul, forsake rather that great heap than you would suffer this small hurt. There can be no comparison between the soul's health and the riches: the least drop that can be of your soul's part, must ponder and weigh more in your thought than all this world beside can do.

Let not any similitude deceive your judgment. As if, perchance, a man would reason that the goods of the soul be all gold, the goods of the world be all lead: although that gold is ever better than lead, yet there may be a great quantity of lead that shall be valued above the small portion of gold. So in your phantasy a great gain and lucre of the worldly goods may seem better than a small point of our soul's substance. Wherefore, he will conclude that with a little loss of honesty or goodness we may venture to get a great advantage in this world: and some little small portion we may borrow of our soul to win by that means a great sum of riches. Beware, good Withypoll, of such reasoning, and to the death, to gain all the whole royalty of this whole world, never trespass against your soul in the smallest jot that can be imagined. As if you might be made a lord of great might and power with abundance of possessions and goods, only for the speaking in witness of one word against the truth, with grudge of your conscience: forsake you all that offer, rather than you would feel the privy bite of your offence. For if you look well, you shall see that there is a greater value of gains in the smallest jot of virtue than is in the most power of riches: and that the loss of the smallest mote pertaining to your soul's state is more hurt and damage than the refusing or foregoing of all that is under heaven. So that I say it is not like between the soul's goods and the goods of this world as it is between gold and lead valued above a pennyweight of gold: where there is no title so small of virtue that is not to be valued without comparison above the whole power of the earth and seas throughout Asia, Africa, and Europe. The proof of my saying dependeth hereupon that every jot, every tittle, every mote of virtue, wherein is contained the soul's wealthy state, hath appointed his proper state and place in the heaven and kingdom of God: and all the spiritual goods, both small and great, be under God, of whom virtue receiveth her reward: of the which reward he that loseth any manner portion, loseth more than the loss of the whole dominion and rule of this world, whose prince is the devil, that reigneth over all them as over his bond servants, the which can find in their hearts to forsake virtue to win these false and vain goods that stand to us in no earthly stead but for the short time of a few years in this life, where the possessions of virtue be everlasting. Thus I show you, good Edmond, that your care to get these worldly goods must be subdued under due order as in this third place. But what be these goods, and what way you may lawfully get them, I doubt not but your father will in time convenient show you. He is of that sort of men the which hath by long approved honesty purchased him a good name and is thereby beloved and regarded of good men: whose steps if you follow, you shall by God's grace come to like worship, and be of like or more ability to leave to your children sufficient to pass this life with. Here remember, the more your father loveth you, the less is your third care: and the less that your third care is, the more leisure you have to think upon your chief jewel, the which God hath given you to be ordered after your will, in the which jewel you shall after this life well passed have the fruition of God's presence, wherein resteth the joy ineffable of the blessed lambs. The goats, that is to say the greedy souls of this third care, the which never mindeth or very little and weakly mindeth the first care, shall remain for ever more in the painful darkness, where is nothing but crying out and lamenting, with fretting stomachs and snaring of teeth, as the gospel shall teach you. In the which book of God you shall hear what an hard thing it is for a rich man to enter into heaven: because that most commonly rich men spend all their care and thought out of order, only for this world, and seldom or never they think of their soul: and when they think thereof, they so think that they put that care far under the care of these worldly businesses, doing clean contrary to this order, the which God would have us to keep. The which order though you shall see very little regarded of all sorts of men, yet good Edmond regard you it, and have pity of them that regard it not. It is the Son of God, the which saith, Many be called to heaven, but few be chosen. Enforce yourself to be among the few, and forsake the multitude. Be not drawn to an evil opinion, neither with the example of popes, cardinals, and priests, nor with the example of princes, lords, knights, gentlemen, and merchants, nor yet with the example of monks and friars. You may by yourself know what is the right path: follow you courageously the same and forsake the common highway of sinners.

Yet before I leave this third care, I will show you my mind, what is chiefly in this part to be cared for as the best portion of worldly riches. Surely I reckon no possession of lands, nor yet no substance of merchandise, nor yet no abundance of money, to be comparable to a good friend. Therefore above all things in this world, procure to have plenty of friends and make of them your count, as of your best and most precious goods. Always your friend shall be more profitable to you than any treasure or power beside can be. How you shall know them that be worthy to be your friends, and by what means, and what way friends be both gotten and also kept, you shall best learn in Cicero's little book *De amicitia*. I cannot say in this thing any point that is left of him, wherefore I remit you to that work. Another point touching this care of worldly goods is to use accordingly your wife, when the time shall come that you shall have one. For to obtain substance of goods, it lieth as much in the wife to keep that you bring home, as in your travail to bring home. And surely unless she be the keeper and sparer, the husband shall little go forward in his labour of getting. And the very truth is that there is no evil housewife but for her faults the good man is to be blamed. For I am utterly of this opinion, that the man may make, shape, and form the woman as he will. I would go farther with you in this thing and show somewhat of the way to order your household, if I saw not this matter so largely treated of divers philosophers, of whom you shall hear as much as may be said in this thing. Specially I would you read with most diligence the proper book that Xenophon writeth hereof: it is called *Oeconomia*, that is to say, the craft to order and keep an house, where this author giveth such counsel, for all the course of an honest man's life in this world to grow in riches, under the means of discretion and wisdom, that no man in my mind can say more therein or better: the

which judgment of mine I doubt not but you will approve, when you
have read the said work: it is translated out of Greek into Latin by one
Raphael, but in his translation the work loseth a great part of the grace
that it hath in the Greek tongue, and also his translation in many places
is false: and it plainly appeareth that Raphael understood not well what
Xenophon wrote in Greek. I have therefore, for divers of my friends'
sake, translated the same work out of Greek tongue into English, and
you shall have the same with my goodwill when your pleasure is to
read it.

I would also for some part of this third care have you read the seventh
and eighth books of Aristotle's *Politics*, for to hear his counsel concerning
the bringing up of children and the use of other certain things.

This is the effect and sum, mine own good Edmond, of my counsel,
touching the three said things: in the which I reckon to rest the whole
course of your life: and if you observe and keep them in their degrees
and order accordingly, you shall surely content God, next please yourself, and thirdly satisfy the world. On the contrary part, misorder these
cares and you shall run into the vengeance of God, into the hate of yourself, and into the indignation of all men. Behold I pray you these hungry
and greedy wretches that make of the third thing their first thought and
care: what life lead they in the slander of all their acquaintance? What
death have they in sight of their privy conscience when they remember
their false swearings, their deceitful bargains, their plain robberies, their
pollings, their cruel exactions, their oppressings of the poor men? What
hope have they of God's favour when they remember all their care and
thought hath been for the wealth of this world? The which when they
leave and forsake, they despair of all other wealthiness: inasmuch their
minds never earnestly cared for that wealth the which ever endureth.

This remembrance of their misorder is an heavy burden to their
conscience. It cannot be otherwise. Consider now again how clear and
light his mind is that in all his life hath ever chiefly studied for the soul's
wealth, that remembreth ever how his care hath been for the reward of
virtue. Of this man how well doth every man speak? What joy and
comfort embraceth the conscience of this man when the hand of God
calleth him from his short life to that perpetual life, for the which he
hath so much laboured? The other, be he never so rich, is called a false
fellow, a wretched knave. This man, be he never so poor, is called an

honest person, a good man, for whom the heaven gates standeth open, whilst the other falleth to endless torments. This is the end of misorder, and this is the end of good order, in breaking and keeping the degrees of the forsaid three things. Wherefore I cannot warn you too often to take heed of this counsel: and you cannot too often hear the same. The jeopardy is not small if you should forget this tale: it is no less peril than utter shame in this world, with death everlasting. Wheresoever is slander, there is shame: greater slander there can be none than followeth on all sides the unjust rich man. And he ever, where some ever he be, gathereth unjustly riches that careth chiefly for these worldly promotions: the which man hath (I say) both in his life extreme shame and also after this life extreme punishment. You be not forbidden to get riches, but the inordinate desire of getting riches is abominable both in the sight of God and man: your desire is inordinate, if it be not ordered under the degree of your chief care, as now often enough hath been repeated. I would now leave you and make an end of these three cares and studies appertaining to your soul, body, and goods: saving that because I somewhat know your disposition, I will particularly touch one thing or two that you must most earnestly beware of: because you be much naturally inclined otherwise to fall into certain points that sore disquieteth the mind, hurteth the body, and hindereth the profits of this life: so that friendly I will admonish you of one or two things that pertain to all your three charges.

Take heed, my good Withypoll, of your passion toward wrath, ire, and anger: resist as much as you can the provocation of your stomach to this vehement pang. Be not light erred in hearing a word of displeasure. Consider the kind of life that you take: you must be conversant with many and divers merchants, among whom every one thinketh himself both lord and master. In such company chanceth to be often disdainful looks, proud countenances, scorns, mocks, scoffs, comparisons, biting taunts, odious checks, spiteful reproaches, with fretting envy, and with many other corrupt affections, whereby riseth much debate, and sometimes there followeth plain fury, that maketh men more like wild beasts, for the time of their madness, than to reasonable creatures. It is a great grace in him that feeleth his heart aggrieved, and yet showeth not outwardly his grief. This prudent dissimulation more avengeth his quarrel than any rendering of words could do. For it is a deadly stroke that the patient man giveth in this soft and mild suffering the rages of an angry fool. Look well upon them both: he that suffereth and saith naught is like a man, the railer or taunter is like a beast or a fool. The sufferer always both in his time of suffering and also afterward, when all fumes be ceased, hath a great praise of all that beholdeth him, and ever he hath cause of rejoicing and gladness: where the other fretteth with himself, and scant the next day after he can show his face: behind whose back his company reporteth the folly of his hastiness, and sore they blame him for his uncomely behaviour. Let the quarrel be what you lust, ever by your patience and sufferance you shall have advantage of him that provoketh you, and finally, for your often forebearing, a name of soberness, wisdom, and discretion: whereof shall follow great credence and a love of all honest persons toward you: where he that will suffer naught, but will ease his stomach in giving mock for mock, check for check, shall be taken for a wrangler, a brawler: and few or none honest men will gladly meddle with him.

To rule this passion of ire you shall be much more stronger than mine exhortation can make you, if you will (as I have counselled you before) have Plato your familiar. And Seneca shall be a meet physician for to help your mind against these grievous pangs. The best is not to be angry, the next is not to show in words or countenance your anger: but remember, if it chance that you be angered, and that you have in showing your anger moved and stirred some other to be displeased, beware that you nourish not this grief, spit out of your stomach all peevishness, and seek atonement as soon as it can be possible. If the party speak not to you, speak you to him: it is no shame to be agreed, it is a foul shame to continue in anger: and in the mean season your prayer to God is void, for out of charity, and out of favour and grace of God. It is the ground and only stay of our religion to love together like brothers all under one Father that looketh over us in heaven, for whose sake, see that you never sleep with grudge against any person: in so doing you shall finally obtain that no man will bear you grudge, and for your love you shall have love plentifully of God and of the world: Begin, mine own good Withypoll, to overthrow this beastly passion of wrath before your age make your stomach stubborn. Overcome now in time sullenness before men have regard of your displeasure: accustom yourself with mildness, softness, patience, sufferance, and especially with gentleness, that cannot abide an heart mindful of any grief. To your inferior be pitiful, buxom, and ready in offering yourself, both to take and keep friendship. With your fellow and companion strive not, compare not: but always study to increase familiarity by loving manners and easily forget injuries. Let no displeasure be taken of you, how many some ever displeasures be given you. To your better and superior if you obey and give place, it shall be reputed to your commendation and praise. There is no man so vile but his love may stand in stead to you, and of the poorest man's hatred you may have some time hurt.

Thus I say both for the worldly wisdom and also for the bonds of your faith, you must take heed to this warning: and the more you be inclined not only to be quickly angry, but also to nourish long your anger, the more diligence you must betimes take to correct and amend your nature, remembering always your chief care, that pertaineth to the first thing, the which is with nothing more hurted and hindered in his way to grace ward than with breaking of love and charity. And as often as you be angry, so often pluck you your soul from the presence of God. By the same passion also you disquiet your body, and oftentimes follow diseases by the fierce pursuing of a grief, and sometime by rages chanceth plain battle, and thereof your body standeth ever in jeopardy. Also nothing more hindereth the gains of your third care than doth unpatient chiding with others. For it causeth many to forbear company: and by that ever followeth loss of occupying. And sometime a good word behind your back may advantage you more than a long sailing into Spain, and an evil word likewise may do you more hurt than a loss of a ship. Let no man have cause to be angry with you, and ever you be sure to be well reported by.

One other thing or two I would warn you of, with as many words as I have done of the said passion, if I thought not that by the reading of the said works you shall much better than I can show you not only flee from all misbehaviours and corrupt uses of ill fantasies, but also follow the clean picked virtues, and by your own study grow to be a perfect man in the favour of God and all others. No man shall counsel you better than you shall do your own self, if in reading you will examine secretly your conscience, whether such properties be in you as you read or no. If they be in you and be dispraised, determine with yourself to amend them: if they be not in you and be good, determine with yourself to get them. As in reading you shall hear above all other faults dispraised an untrue tongue, which bringeth a man out of credence, a thing very hurtful for merchants, whose craft you be like to exercise: and beside, it sore offendeth the ears of God to hear his best beloved creature make that noise against his knowledge and privy conscience: where nothing garnisheth man's voice better than truth of his tale. This thing chiefly apperteineth to the care of the soul, that is your first charge. It maketh also for the second and for the third care. For surely when the mind is disquieted with the remembrance of the offence in lying, the body hath his part of ill rest: And by the same untrue speaking, much hurt and damage ensueth against your credence, a thing I say most necessary to be kept and maintained of all them that seek by merchandise any lucre or gains. Therefore let your mind, my good Withypoll, never delight to utter any lie. Either speak not, or speak truly. What fault soever you may do, let it not be defended with a false tale: for that were to flee out of the smoke into the fire, as to do a worse fault in choking an ill, and in the mean season your soul suffereth a sore stroke. Thus ever as you read of this matter, have mind of yourself to take fruit of your reading.

In consideration also of all three parts, that is to say, both for the defence of your soul's state, and for the wealth of your body, and also for the worldly good's sake, use in all your acts a certain commendable wisdom, never to be none of these busy meddlers: leave other men's faults, leave correcting that you have no power in, leave teaching of that you know not. Let the gospel be ordered by them that be admitted for doctor's thereof. Let the priests be blamed of them that have the rule of the order. Let common ceremonies and all old customs alone. Put ever your trust in the power and will of God, and obey to the consent of the church without quarrelling or resisting. Go you forth your way after the meek steps of a true Christian man. Let the world bluster and blow as it will, be you none of the blowers. Scourge who will, be you none of the scourgers. For believe me, sooner shall the rod than the child that is beaten be cast into the fire. In eschewing all meddling, you shall save your goods, you shall keep your body from travail, and by the same means you shall best provide a sure buckler for your soul. For under the cloak of obedience, chance what chance shall, your soul is ever sure for taking any hurt: the justice of God will keep you harmless, howso-

ever the tempest of enormities overfloweth this world. If you should be
malapert and presume to be a doer: report me to you, what may in this
world happen to your undoing both in goods and body: and by the same
trouble you shall be cast from the succour of God, who abideth not any
presumption. You fall into presumption, when you grudge against your
rulers, though they be worthy of all dispraises. You presume, when you
meddle with them that be not under you. You presume, when you take
in hand to amend this or that where your part is not to speak. And especially you be presumptuous, when you dare craik that you know God's
will. Leave therefore, my good Edmond, all manner of meddling and
pray to God to accept your obedience. Pray also bitterly that his will
may be fulfilled in this world among us, as the angels fulfil it in heaven.
Thus pray, and meddle no farther. For I assure you, it is so to be done.

Many more things might be said for these three cares, but to you I
reckon it enough this much that I have here touched. Yet one word or
two more shall not be superfluous. For I would not have you deceived
by any word that I have here used. As peradventure you might be, if I
should thus leave you. Seeing that I have bid you first to care for your
soul, next to care for your body, and thirdly to care for the goods of this
world. Moreover I said, there be goods of the soul, goods of the body,
goods of this life. But let these words be to you as not spoken in their
exact and proper signification. For to speak truly, there is no care but
one, nor there be no goods but of one. We must have a certain slight
regard to our body, and a slighter regard to the world: but care we may
not for neither of these two. You know that to care were to take an
inward weighty thought: the which must not be taken but for a thing
of great worthiness, and also of more surety than is either our body or
the world. Only our soul is the thing to be cared for: and these small
commodities, with certain pretty pleasures of the body and of the world,
cannot truly be named goods: for in very deed they be not good. For this
word good includeth a dignity in him that savoureth of God and heaven:
so that those things be only worthy to be called goods, the which have a
perpetuity and steadfastness of godly substance. Other things variable,
changeable, flittering, such as may be taken from us maugre our heed,
be not worthy of this high name. Neither the body nor yet fortune hath
any goods: our spirit and mind only hath things that truly be called goods,
the which be so constantly and surely ours that ever they remain with

us in spite of all chances and all our adversaries. Mercy, pity, devotion, meekness, soberness, patience, faithfulness, charity, and such other virtues be the very true goods, the which we may justly reckon ours, and for them we should continually labour. For these be the substance that our soul must have, to be with them richly decked and garnished that we may have our holy day array and our nuptial vesture according, to come to the great feast that Christ saith we shall once be called to. All these false goods of the body's lustings, beauty, fairness, strength, health: and also these trifling goods of fortune, royal houses, large heritance, great rents, implements, costly apparel, gold, silver, honour, power, friendship, nobility, and what you will else in this world: all these vain things, both of body and fortune, can make but a ragged garment for our soul, the which shall be with extreme shame drawn from the said feast if it come in God's presence with these beggarly rags. This saying, good Withypoll, I speak to ease and comfort your mind: for by this tale that is true, you now learn that although before I said you should have three cares in this life, yet indeed you have but one care, the which is to care for the true goods that be to be purchased for the soul's wealthy state. Wherefore of your three cares, strike off two, if you will speak of earnest care. Yet I will stick a little more with you in this point: for fain I would you should see a true mark, whereby you may govern and rule all your phantasies and opinions. If your phantasy be well directed to the true mark, you cannot miss of the right path to virtue, the which bringeth man thither where he shall receive the inestimable reward for his travail. I say your soul only must be cared for: and this only care must be to get and keep the true goods that be only the goods of the mind. Other goods be not called properly goods. You see how these pretty commodities of the body, and also these small gifts of fortune, maugre our heed, be taken from us, as I cannot escape always sickness, I cannot escape misfortunes: I cannot flee from the cruel hands of tyrants, I may be cast into tortures, I may rot in fetters, I may lose all my substance, by water, by fire, by thieves, or by other violent robbery. Against these chances no man can resist, no care nor thought prevaileth to assure us, either of our bodies, or of such goods. Wherefore learn you that I say, before God we have no goods, but only the goods of the spirit and mind, the which goods (as I have said) be so sure ours, that they cannot be taken from us but with our own will consenting to the loss of them. In this spiritual possession every man is an invincible emperor. We may despise all violence of princes, all worldly chances touching the keeping of virtue, maugre the whole power of the devil and all his retinue. Hereof learn and mark, mine Edmond, wherein you may be hurted, that your care may the better be bestowed. For to care, where you have no hurt, it is needless: or not to care, where you be hurt, is a blind ignorance.

We be hurt when we lose any part of God's favour: we lose God's favour, when we lose any goods of the mind: we lose the goods of the mind, when we either rejoice of the having bodily and worldly goods, or make sorrow of the lacking the same. We be not hurted when God continueth his favour, when we decay not in the strength of mind: we decay not in the strength of mind when we be not overcome, neither with the gladness of the body's and world's prosperity, nor with bewailing of their adversity. Thus you see, neither in the goods of the body, nor in the goods of the world, you can either take or escape hurt: it is only the virtue of your mind, wherein you must search whether you be safe or hurt.

Now when you know the place of your hurt, know also what may do you hurt, that you may be more chary of your hurter. You see once the place wherein you may be hurted is your secret mind, a very sure place. For it is not fire, nor water, nor thief, that can come there: it is no prince's sword that can pierce into this place, it is no misluck of fortune that can light upon your spirit: finally there is no devil of hell that can fasten a stroke upon you to do you in this place any hurt. This should be a greater gladness unto you, to consider in how strong a tower you be from all hurt: but see then again, who it is that may hurt you. For surely you cannot be hurted but of one, in whom is power to do hurt: this is your own free will. This will of yours, and nothing else, hath power to hurt you. See shortly in example, how your lands be taken from you, you be spoiled of your goods, fire burneth up your house, you be haled to prison, you be beaten, you be torn with whips, you be drawn upon the racks, you lie in chains, you come forth to open shame, you suffer cold, you be gnawed with hunger and thirst, finally you be put to death. What of all this? Yet I cannot say that you be hurted: I see that with all this the favour and grace of good may continue with you as it did with the holy martyrs. And also before Christ's passion holy Job suffered all this and was not hurted. This is a great comfort for you to see that nothing can hurt you but only your own self. This is the high grace of God, that so hath made man to be over all a mighty conqueror, that can take no hurt but of himself. Wherefore I trust you will live ever safe and sound. For I will not think that ever you will be so mad as to hurt yourself. Then, for these trifles of the body and world, take no care: it is neither the second thing nor the third thing that can be so unto you that in either of them you can be hurted. Marry take heed, lest by the displeasures done in the second and in the third, you of madness take occasion to be hurted, and willingly hurt yourself in the first thing, the which only is the place where you may be hurted. And none beside your own will hath power to hurt you there: as if in the time of the loss of worldly goods, you will fret in anger, you will despise God, you will curse and ban, you will enforce to be avenged, you cry out in fury and madness: now take you thought and care, for surely you be hurted, and your chief jewel hath a great loss. For God withdraweth from your soul a great part of his grace: so that this hurt you do to your own self by this forwardness. Likewise whilst your body is tormented, either with sickness or otherwise: if you therefore forsake patience and swell in wrath, you be then hurt indeed, but of none other person beside yourself only. Thus you may take from the second and the third, in the which two you cannot be hurted, an occasion to hurt yourself and to have thereof a great cause of a sore and an earnest care for the peril that your soul thereby falleth in.

To confirm you the faster in these right opinions, I would you read the little book of Epictetus, entitled his *Enchiridion*, well translated into Latin by Angelus Politian. But to say the truth the work is so briefly and darkly written that without a comment or a good master you shall not perceive the fruit of the text. I am in mind, if I may have thereto leisure, to translate the comment of Simplicius upon the said work, and then shall you find such sweetness in that book, that I believe it will ravish you into an higher contemplation than a great sort of our religious men come to. And one thing believe me, my good Withypoll, that in reading of these old substantial works, the which I have named unto you, shall beside the perfection of knowledge, engender a certain judgment in you, that you shall never take delight nor pleasure in the trifles and vain inventions that men nowadays write to the inquieting of all good order: by reason that the most part of men that read these new flittering works, lack perfect judgment to descrive a weighty sentence from a light clause, the which judgment cannot be gotten but by a long exercising of our wits with the best sort of writers. And to me it is a pitiful thing to behold the foolish dreams of these young clerks in men's hands: and to see these noble old works of the holy fathers and philosophers lie untouched. Where if these new writers speak any thing well, it is picked out of these ancient books. But whatsoever these petty clerks pick out nowadays, for the most part it is defaced and brought out of good fashion with their evil handling.

I will now make an end: it is sufficient to a willing mind, such as I trust is in you, to have with a friend's finger the way appointed where you must walk if you will proceed in virtue: the which is only the thing that maketh a man both happy in this world and also blessed in the world to come. Believe you my counsel, and use the same, or else hereafter you will peradventure bewail your negligence.

Fare ye well.

At More, a place of my lord cardinal's, in the feast of Saint Bartholomew, 1529.

AN ARGUMENT FOR THE INDEPENDENCE
OF THE SPIRITUALITY
1532

An Argument for the Independence of the Spirituality, 1532, and *Articles for Priests Unlearned*, 1535, present concisely the arguments on each side in the conflict between Henry VIII and the church of Rome. The crux of the issue concerned sovereignty and jurisdiction: whether the clergy should remain independent from, or should submit to royal authority.

The 1532 paper is taken from a manuscript in the Public Record Office, London, (*State Papers* 6, vol.1/8) and has, presumably, never been printed. However, it may have circulated in manuscript copies as did so many pamphlets during the early sixteenth century. In any event it contains the conventional arguments then commonly put forward in defence of the clergy, and it may be considered typical of this kind of controversial writing. Another paper written by Cardinal Fisher, bishop of Rochester, contains similar arguments, but, unhappily, it is badly mutilated and incomplete.

The orthodox point of view of the defenders of the clergy in the 1530's is countered in the *Articles for Priests Unlearned* (*State Papers* 6, vol.5/5). This paper, also anonymous, presents the arguments favouring Henry VIII's supremacy over the English clergy. Its opening suggests that it may have been composed at official instigation as a part of Henry's far-reaching propaganda campaign. Its incompleteness leads one to doubt whether it was actually circulated, although it may be an early draft of a tract that was. While the objectives of these two papers are diametrically opposed, the same fundamentally medieval method of argument has been employed in each. The processes of thinking and the authorities cited are the same. The few lines written at the end to instruct ' priests which be learned ' supposes that the author was planning to use the same tactics that he directed towards the ignorant to convince the intelligent of the rightness of Henry's supreme headship. The use of similar arguments and similar authorities in each tract to support opposite contentions shows that the medieval-mindedness of the proponents of the break from Rome was as great as that of its opponents.

That the bishops have immediate authority of Christ to make such laws as they shall think expedient for the weal of men's souls.

IN every commonwealth that had any pretence of godly frame or godly order, there was amongst them a convenient portion of men deputed, *ad cultum dei*, that is to say to the service of God, and to be his ministers and to offer up to him sacrifices for the weal of other and to be a mean to pacify the wrath and the indignation of God against sin, and to purchase his gracious favour and liberal bounteousness in all things necessary to the life of man. For albeit so that many nations and countries did honour many false gods, yet was there impressed in all their hearts on [one?] general consent that he or they whom they reputed as god or gods was to be honoured and worshipped of all men, and that for his honour duly and seriously to be kept, certain ministers, which should principally intend that same, ought to be thus deputed and assigned. Wherefore, as the most famous histories do write and testify, there was in every nation such ministers appointed to do and keep certain ceremonies pertaining to the special honour of such as they reputed to be the god or gods of that nation. For indeed the devil and his angels had seduced the hearts of many people from the worshipping of him that is the only true god and made them to give honour unto many false gods.

Yet, nevertheless, all nations, were they never so much pagans and heathen, they verily thought that those that were the ministers of their gods should be had for the dignity of that office in much reputation and reverence before all other for the which also they provided for them sufficient possessions to live upon; they endowed them with great liberties and were conformable unto their counsels and ordinance which thing the Holy Scripture besides the other gentile histories doth testify. For Moses, in the Book of Genesis c. 47, doth write that in the great famine which endured in Egypt by the space of seven years, all the people for want of corn and victual was compelled to sell their lands unto the king save only the priests which were deputed unto the service of their gods. Those priests were not compelled to sell their lands and possessions which before that time was given unto them by kings and princes of that country, but they were allowed also for to have out of the king's provision their sustenance and sufficient living all that time that the hunger so endured.

In the region of Ethiopia likewise the chief honour and reverence was given unto the priests and ministers of their gods: for they of this country divided amongst them four degrees of men to whom honour should be done. One was of the judges of men's lives and they were in the lowest degree of honour. And other above them was of the nobles. The third was of the most singular wise and politic men which had with their wisdom adjoined virtue and innocency. The fourth and the highest was of priests of the which number they did choose them a king of these priests. St. Austin in a sermon maketh mention that he went thither to see them and giveth them a wonderful praise.

In the region of India also much honour, singular authority, great possessions, many liberties was given to the priests as Diodorus and other writers of stories maketh mention, and as Strabo writeth they were called Brahmans, men of high learning and of singular virtue.

In France also before that it was Christianized there were such priests which the gentile stories doth testify were called druids, and they were had in great reverence and highly privileged as many great stories doth remember.

Amongst the Romans likewise the Roman writers do witness of great honour, great possessions, great liberties that were given unto priests whom they called *flamines* and by them there were ordered and instructed in all things appertaining unto the religion of their gods, as in seeking the favour of them and in avoiding their displeasure and indignation.

And according to the manner of the Romans the people here within this realm of England before it was converted unto the faith of Christ called their priests also *flamines*, as our own stories do make mention, and was ordered and advised by them in all things belonging to their gods concerning the weal and comfort which as they supposed was derived from their gods unto the whole country by the mediation and sacrifice of the ministers that were mediators as they thought between their gods and the people.

Not only these nations that we have rehearsed thus did, but that people which were peculiarly chosen of almighty God, I mean the Hebrews. Amongst them by the ordinance of God was deputed like priests and mediators between God and the people and had in great honour and reverence and had their possessions assigned and appointed for them with many great liberties and privileges, albeit the office of the priesthood was not ordained nor intended of God that it should always continue but cease and have an end after the coming of our Saviour Christ. Yet, nevertheless, during the time of Moses' law their authority was such that the people was bounden to obey them in all things concerning the weal of their souls. And not only that people, but kings and pagans of other nations also did the same as it appeareth in the first and second book of Esdras, the king of the Persians did trust thereby to win the favour of God to themselves, their realms, and their children.

Forasmuch, then, as in every commonwealth the people had certain persons deputed for the ceremonies of worshipping of or them whom they reputed to be their god or gods, much rather in the commonweal of Christendom such ought to be deputed and assigned for the ceremonies of worshipping him which is the only true god. It is therefore most convenient for them to have between them and God such priests and ministers that might of [sic] offer prayer and other sacrifices unto him for the weal of all the people and to appease his wrath and indignation against their sin. And also to minister unto the people the spiritual treasure of his manifold graces.

Of these ministers and priests the prophet Isaiah spake many days before the coming of our Saviour Christ and prophesied saying, *Sacerdotes dei vocabimini ministri dei nostri dicetur vobis.* That is to say it shall be said unto you that you be the ministers of our Lord God. And to this same purpose Saint Paul saith of himself and of all such ministers, *Sic nos existimet homo sicut ministros Christi et dispensatores misteriorum dei.* Let men so think of us that we be the ministers of Christ and the dispensers of his high mysteries.

When the gentiles and all the heathen nations with their kings and princes thus favourably entreated their priests which were but ministers unto the idols and false gods and had them in this reverence and gaveth so great possessions and privileged them with such liberties and were obedient unto them as concerning the order of their lives, how much rather shall now the Christian kings and princes and the true Christian people that were so dearly redeemed by that most precious blood of Christ Jesus and have received so many wonderful benefits and so excellent sacraments. Whereof he hath ordained the priests of the new law ministers and dispensers, how much, I say, ought they now to have in honour and reverence these very priests and ministers of Christ's church, consecrated unto the service of almighty God. How favourable should they entreat them in all things. How glad to defend their rights, privileges, and liberties, how ready to obey their wholesome counsels and ordinances which they devise and ordain for the weal of their souls. And that thus it ought to be in very deed we shall prove by 12 manner of ways.

1. The first by the testimonies of Holy Scripture.
2. The second by the example of the apostles that made such laws.
3. The third by the examples of such punishments as they took upon the offenders.
4. The fourth by the customable usage of general councils.

5. The fifth by the testimonies of ancient doctors.

6. The sixth by the example of holy saints' acts and deeds.

7. The seventh by the names that they be called by in the Scripture of God.

8. The eighth by the punishment of the gentiles for misentreating the priests of their idols.

9. The ninth by the punishment of the gentiles for misentreating the priests of the Jews.

10. The tenth by the punishment of the Jews for condemning of their own priests.

11. The eleventh by the punishment of emperors and kings for condemning of the priests of Christ.

12. The twelfth by the great prosperity that was given to such Christian princes for the obeying unto such priests.

By Scriptures first this shall appear for Saint Paul saith, *Qui bene presunt presbiteri duplici honore digni habeantur.* That is . . . (Here the author breaks off leaving the treatise unfinished.)

The beginning for priests which be unlearned, concerning the king's title of supreme head of the church of England.

You shall understand that I am commanded by mine ordinary to declare unto you at this time and at certain other times to me appointed, specially two things, one concerning the king's grace's title of supreme head of the church of England in earth immediately under Christ, and the other concerning the abolishing of that jurisdiction which the bishops of Rome have heretofore exercised and usurped within his realm. As concerning the first, that is the king's said title of supreme head, I think it is not unknown unto you and, if it be, I now declare unto you how that as well by the authority of the king's high court of parliament as also by the authority and consent of all the clergy of this his realm assembled in both the convocations of the primates of Canterbury and York, it is and hath been concluded and determined as a most certain truth and verity founded as well in Holy Scripture as also upon other most evident grounds, considerations, causes, and authorities confirmed by the testimonies of the most ancient interpreters of Scripture, that the king's highness is and of right hath been and ought to be reputed and taken the only chief and supreme head of the church of England immediately under Christ in earth—and to have the highest and most supreme jurisdiction, power, and governance over the same. And for proof and confirmation thereof, I allege unto you first the authority of Saint Paul in the thirteenth chapter to the Romans where he chargeth all men excepting no degree or sort of men to obey the high *potestates*, that is to say their kings and princes, and Saint Paul there avoweth and proveth that forasmuch as all power of princes proceedeth of God, all sorts of men be bounden necessarily to obey and be subject unto them not only for fear but also for conscience and duty, for the same is the ordinance of God. And whosoever resisteth their power resisteth the ordinance of God and cometh thereby into everlasting damnation and that Saint Paul in this place by these words power or *potestate* meaneth prince, it is evident for two causes: one because he speaketh of a sword of punishment which

2—The illustration opposite is the title page of the Great Bible of April 1539. The border is a wood-cut, attributed to Holbein, whose patron, Henry VIII, ' is made the prominent person in the design.' The Supreme Head of the Church of England vies with the Bible ' as the great object of the whole' engraving. The Word of God Henry hands to Cromwell and Cranmer, who, in turn, give it to the laity and the clergy. Below, the people cheer, with ' Vivats' and ' God save the king,' the king whose program for saving God for England included the translation of the Bible into English.

Above the king is God, from whom flow two apt biblical quotations: ' I have found a man after mine own heart, which shall fulfil all my will' (Acts xiii,22) and ' the word also that cometh out of my mouth shall not turn again void unto me, but shall accomplish my will' (Isaiah lv,11). From Henry VIII come three more biblical quotations which read in the Great Bible: ' Such things command and teach' (I Timothy iv,11); ' judge righteously between every man and his brother, and the stranger that is with him. See that ye know no faces in judgment, but hear the small as well as the great, and be afraid of no man, for the judgment is God's' (Deuteronomy i,16–17, quoted in full); and finally from Daniel (vi,26) Henry proclaims, ' My commandment is, in all my dominion and kingdom, that men fear and stand in awe of [Daniel's God. For he is] the living God, which abideth ever.'

These quotations which appear in Latin on the title page were taken from the Vulgate, for the numeration of the two Psalms is that of the Vulgate and not that of the 1539 version. That in the upper right-hand corner is the 105th verse of Psalm cxix: ' Thy word is a lantern unto my feet, and a light unto my paths.' At the left, Cranmer quotes from I Peter v,1–2: ' Feed you Christ's flock,' while on the right Cromwell repeats the 14th verse of Psalm xxxiv: ' Eschew evil and do good: seek peace and ensue it.' And the preacher in the pulpit below recites from I Timothy ii,1–2: ' I exhort therefore, that above all things, prayers, supplications, intercessions, and giving of thanks be had for all men: for kings, and for all that are in authority, that we may live a quiet and peaceable life, with all Godliness and honesty.' Each of these quotations from the Great Bible varies somewhat from the reading in the King James' version of 1611. In that year the Great Bible ' assumed the form ever since known as the Authorized Version,' but even today the Psalter in the Book of Common Prayer ' still follows, with slight variations, the Great Bible.'

This was the first translation to be issued through public authority. In 1530 a commission to inquire into the expediency and necessity of an English translation had reported adversely. But in 1534 the convocation of Canterbury petitioned the king for just such a Bible, and finally in 1538 Cromwell sponsored Miles Coverdale's work in revising Matthew's Bible of 1537 for this purpose. He used, for this revision, Sebastian Münster's Latin translation of the Hebrew Old Testament, and the Vulgate and the Erasmian Greek texts of the New, along with the Complutensian Polyglot of 1520.

Matthew's Bible was a compilation made from Tyndale's New Testaments, the first of which reached England in 1526, and Coverdale's Bible of 1535, the first complete English translation. Thomas Matthew was probably an alias for John Rogers, a fellow worker with Tyndale, so it was Rogers, Tyndale, and Coverdale who were really responsible for the English Bibles of Henry VIII's reign. The Great Bible was printed by Grafton and Whitchurch in London, but it was begun at Paris by Francis Regnault. On 17 December 1538 the French inquisitor-general interdicted the printing, but Coverdale and Grafton, who were there, saved some of the sheets which they transported with presses, type, and workmen to London. Six editions, known as Cranmer's version, followed before the end of 1541, making an estimated total of 21,000 copies. In September 1538 Cromwell had enjoined the clergy to have this Bible set up in some convenient place in each parish church where the parishioners might read it.

¶ The Byble in
Englyshe, that is to saye the content of all the holy scrypture, bothe
of ý olde and newe testament, truly
translated after the veryte of the
Hebrue and Greke textes, by ý dy-
lygent studye of dyuerse excellent
learned men, expert in the forsayde
tonges.

¶ Prynted by Rychard Grafton &
Edward Whitchurch.

Cum priuilegio ad imprimen-
dum solum.

1539

they bear, the other because he speaketh of tribute to be given to them which two things pertain only to kings and princes and other *potestates*. And to this sentence of Saint Paul agreeth Saint Peter in the second chapter of his first epistle, which biddeth us all to be subject to kings as to them which excel and pass all other and not only to them but also to such as they send to govern under them.

Further you shall understand that this truth and sentence concerning king's powers was not begun by the commandment of Saint Paul and Saint Peter in the New Testament, but it was one open verity and clear case afore in the Old Testament, as it appeareth plainly in the twelfth chapter of the Sapience where it is written: Hear you kings which have multitudes of people under you, for the power over them is given to you of God. And this power is given to kings not only over the laymen but also over all sorts of men as is aforesaid, wherefore good King Jehoshaphat did exercise this power indifferently over all when he appointed to the priests what they should do in ministration of justice, and to his nobles what they should do in the ministration of the same appointing to either of them their limits and bounds, as it is written in the nineteenth chapter of the second book of the Paralipomenon which the said good king would not have been [done?] if the governance, ruling, and ordering of all his people, as well priests as other, had not appertained to him. Like power used that good King Josiah, when he commanded the highest priest Hilkiah to see the temple, which was then ruinous, repaired as it is when in the twenty-second chapter of the second Book of Kings. Likewise the good King Hezekiah calling the priests and Levites his sons commanded them to go into the temple and to purify the house of God and after commanded the priests descended from Aaron to make sacrifice upon the altar of our Lord as it is when in the twenty-ninth chapter of the Paralipomenon. And the said king did not only command the priests and Levites as his subjects, but also did constitute and ordain the companies of priests and Levites as they were divided and ordered every man in his proper office both priests and Levites as it is written in the thirtieth chapter of the Paralipomenon.

Further kings had not only power to command priests to such things as they thought convenient and meet to be done, but they had also power and authority to remove and punish the highest priest for his offences by the power of death. As King Solomon removed the great bishop

Abiathar from his room and office, because he had ministered Adonijah to be king and said further to him, that he was worthy to die, but he would not kill him then because he bore the Ark of our Lord before David his father, but he constituted Zadok in his place to be highest priest. Saul, king of Israel, had no such reverence to the highest priest Ahimelech whom he judged to have committed treason against him, and therefore gave sentence of death against him saying *Morte moriere*, that is to say, thou shall die, and caused the said Ahimelech and four score and five other priests of his house and family to be put to death in one day for the said offence, as it is written in the first Book of Kings, the twenty-second chapter. Also Alexander, the son of Antiochus, being the king of Crete in the hundredth and threescoreth year of the reign of Greeks, put down Alcimus [?] which was chief bishop or priest of Israel and constituted Jonathan the brother of Judas Maccabeus to be the great priest or bishop over the Jews—and the same Jonathan being a nobleman and full of zeal of the laws of God and of his country took the said office at the said King Alexander's hand as you shall find in the first book of the Maccabees the tenth chapter. And for this rule and power that kings have to punish every man which doth amiss and to promote and defend such as be good, Saint Paul and Saint Peter call princes the ministers of God. Wherefore Saint Augustine in the fifth epistle entreating the word of the prophet David spoken to princes which are these: See that you serve our Lord and fear him.

In the twenty-ninth chapter of Exodus it is written that Moses himself being the supreme head, duke, or prince of the children of Israel, made Aaron the great bishop and his children priests, and he himself certain sacrifices at their consecration. He also washed them and clothed them with meet, devised clothes according to their office, and entered or initiated the hands of Aaron and his children to do sacrifice causing them to lay their hands upon the head of the calf which stood before the tabernacle of testimony ready to be sacrificed, which Moses himself sacrificed and took of the blood thereof and imbued therewith both the ends of the altar with his finger and poured out the rest of the blood at the foot of the altar; here you may note that Moses, being a temporal prince and chief head and captain of the children of Israel, not only made priests but also the highest bishop. And not only did sacrifice to God at the time of their consecration, but also applied their hands to the thing ready to be sacrificed as giving them authority to do sacrifice to good, not much unlike the manner which bishops now use in making of priest when they put into their hands a chalice in token that they give them authority to sing mass, and of this place it evidently appeareth that a good temporal prince offered sacrifice to God and consecrated the chief bishop and his priest under him, which be two excellent powers given by God to Moses being the ruler and prince of the children of Israel.

And as touching the power and authority to preach and teach the word of God that office was as highly committed to him by the Father and the Holy Trinity in his time as that office was committed to the apostles in their time and executed as diligently for . . .

[Here the text breaks off and the page is left unfinished. On the back of the page are four Latin quotations from the Old Testament. The next page is blank, but the back contains the following:]

And this is spoken indifferently of all kings, as well of Jews and pagans as Christian, for when the emperors of Rome were pagans it was laid to Christian men's charge: that they neither loved, favoured, nor obeyed the emperor, whereunto answereth Tertullian in a certain book of his written to one Scapula, the president or ruler of Carthage, in this manner: a Christian man knowing the emperor to be ordained and constituted of God must needs love him, reverence and honour him, and desire of God his wealth and health. And a little after in the said book he writeth this: we Christian men worship the emperor as a man next to God and inferior to God alone. And the said Tertullian hath like . . . in a book of his called the defence of Christian men against gentiles, writing this: numbering God first, the emperors or kings be second, and after God they be first of all. You may perceive by this saying of Tertullian (which lived within one-hundred and twenty-eight years after Christ and his apostles) that it is no new invention that kings be the supreme head next God of all such as be their subjects. And that Christ's kings be the supreme heads of the church of Christ being under their rule and dominion.

[At the bottom of the same page the author has apparently started a new treatise, for in the margin he has written: ' The beginning for priests which be learned.']

Where Saint Paul in the third chapter to Titus commandeth him and by him all other which ought to show the will of God to the people to admonish them to be subject to princes and *potestates*, and to be obedient to their commandments, therefore I following the said commandment of Saint Paul require you to be subject and obedient to the commandments of our most noble prince and his laws and most specially concerning two things. One . . .

[Here the author breaks off, and this is the end of the manuscript.]

CERTAIN CAUSES GATHERED TOGETHER
WHEREIN IS SHOWED THE DECAY OF ENGLAND

Only by the great multitude of sheep, to the utter decay of household keeping, maintenance of men, dearth of corn, and other notable discommodities approved by six old proverbs.

PROVERBS 20—*A King that sitteth in judgment, and looketh well about him, driveth away all evil.*

[1550–1553]

This anonymous sheep-tract is one of several supplications and petitions written about 1550 to procure relief for small men from rural distress. The mid-century 'dearth in time of plenty,' fully described by John Hales in *The Common Weal of this Realm of England*, 1549, resulted from economic and financial maladjustments. Henry VIII's last war against France had impoverished the government, led to debasement of the currency, and accelerated the rise in prices already begun by the gold from the new world. Foreign trade was out of balance; wages, with their maximum set by statute, lagged behind prices; and new processes of manufacture and new agricultural arrangements threw men out of work. In the rural south of England the new agriculture often meant the enclosure of small farms or common land either for sheep pasture or for more efficiently farmed arable.

The public mind of rural England held these enclosures to be the grievance on which to blame these misfortunes. Popular agitation through risings and writings caught the sympathy of the ' Commonwealth's Party ' in parliament. Latimer lent powerful invective, Cranmer sympathy, and Protector Somerset good intentions in support ' of poor men's causes.' In the house of commons, John Hales led the attack being made on enclosures through bills introduced between 1547 and 1549. He served on the commission appointed by Somerset in 1548 to survey the extent of the enclosing that had taken place, but juries packed and intimidated by the magnates reduced the results of this philanthropic gesture to negligible proportions.

The text of *The Decay of England* is that edited by J.M.Cowper in *Four Supplications*, Early English Text Society, extra series, vol.xiii (1871) p.93.

TO THE KING'S MOST HONOURABLE COUNCIL, AND THE LORDS OF THE PARLIAMENT HOUSE

THE first article and point, as we do think, it is great pity (so the will of God it were) that there is not corn enough within this realm of England, at all times necessary to certify and suffice the king's subjects for the space of one year, two, or three, if there were no corn sown in this realm by the said space.

We do say that the king's majesty, mercifully hearing the petition of these his grace's poor subjects, may at all times remedy it, when it shall please his majesty, being for a commonwealth for his grace's subjects, and to the great increase of this noble realm of England.

We say, as reason doth lead us, that sheep and sheepmasters doth cause scantity of corn, which we do think it may be well approved by reason of six proverbs; for and if all our livings and all our commodities were divided in parts, by reason of the same six proverbs, we that be the king's majesty's poor subjects do lose six of our commodities, then have we three losses which make nine; by reason of the same three losses, we, the king's majesty's subjects, do lose the third part of our living, then have we the tenth part, which we call a remedy, beseeching your noble grace to remedy when your majesty shall please.

As touching the first proverb of the six, we do think

> The more sheep, the dearer is the wool.
> The more sheep, the dearer is the mutton.
> The more sheep, the dearer is the beef.
> The more sheep, the dearer is the corn.
> The more sheep, the scantier is the white meat.
> The more sheep, the fewer eggs for a penny.

In the first proverb, the more sheep, the dearer is the wool, our complaint is for Oxfordshire, Buckinghamshire, and Northamptonshire; and as for all other shires, we refer it to the plaintiffs.

We shall desire you, and all other that read and see the true intents and meanings of this our doings, to pardon our ignorance; yet notwithstanding, we desire you somewhat to attender the premises, seeing it is done and put forth for the commodity of the king's majesty's realm and for the wealth of his grace's poor subjects.

In the said Oxfordshire, Buckinghamshire, and Northamptonshire, there be many men of worship dwelling within the said three shires and have great lands to live upon, the which we pray to God to give them joy of and well to occupy it. Many of these worshipful men set no store nor price upon the maintenance of tillage of their lands as before time have been used, neither breeding nor feeding of cattle, but many of them doth keep the most substance of their lands in their own hands. And where tillage was wont to be, now is it stored with great number of sheep: and they that have great number of sheep must needs have great store of wool, and we cannot think who should make the price of wool but those that have great plenty of sheep. And we do partly know that there be some dwelling within these three shires, rather than they will sell their wool at a low price, they will keep it a year or twain, and all to make it dear and to keep it a dear price. And by this means the first proverb to be true: The more sheep, the dearer is the wool.

In the second proverb, as we do think: The more sheep, the dearer is the mutton.

As by reason, the most substance of our feeding was wont to be on beef, and now it is on mutton. And so many mouths goeth to mutton, which causeth mutton to be dear.

In the third proverb, as we do think: The more sheep, the dearer is the beef.

As by reason that breeding and feeding, is not set by as it hath been in times past; and whereas sheep are kept upon the pasture grounds where breeding and feeding of beefs were wont to be kept, and now there is nothing kept there but mutton.

The fourth proverb: The more sheep, the dearer is the corn.

By reason tillage is not used, occupied, and maintained as it hath been before time, but sheep kept upon the ground where tillage was wont to be kept and maintained.

The fifth proverb: The more sheep, the scanter is the white meat.

By reason tillage is not used, occupied, and maintained, nor maintenance of houses and hospitality, whereas cattle was wont to be fed and bred; by reason of keeping of cattle, should increase white meat; and now there is nothing kept there but only sheep.

The sixth proverb: The more sheep, the fewer eggs for a penny.

By reason cottages go down in the country, whereas poultry was wont to be bred and fed, now there is nothing kept there but sheep, which cause the eggs to be sold for four a penny.

Thus be the six proverbs true, as we do think, desiring you to give hearing unto them, and that it may be well amended for the commonwealth of the king's poor subjects.

Then have we three losses, that maketh nine.

The first loss, as we do think, there is not so many ploughs used, occupied, and maintained within Oxfordshire as was in King Henry the seventh's time, and since his first coming there lacketh forty ploughs; every plough was able to keep six persons, down lying and uprising in his house, the which draweth to twelve score persons in Oxfordshire.

And where that the said twelve score persons were wont to have meat, drink, raiment, and wages, paying scot and lot to God and to our king, now there is nothing kept there but only sheep. Now these twelve score persons had need to have living:—whither shall they go? into Northamptonshire? and there is also the living of twelve score persons lost: whither shall then they go? forth from shire to shire and to be scattered thus abroad within the king's majesty's realm, where it shall please almighty God; and for lack of masters, by compulsion driven, some of them to beg and some to steal.

The second loss, as we do think: that there is never a plough of the forth ploughs, but he is able to till and plough to certify six persons, and every plough to sell thirty quarters of grain by the year; or else he can full ill pay six, seven, eight pounds by the year. Forty ploughs, thirty quarters every plough, draweth to two hundred quarters in Buckinghamshire, two hundred quarters in Oxfordshire, and two hundred quarters in Northamptonshire, and so forth from shire to shire in certain shires within the king's majesty's realm of England. What shall the twelve two hundred quarters of corn do in Oxfordshire? We do think it will maintain the king's markets and sustain the king's subjects; and likewise in Buckinghamshire, and also in Northamptonshire and so from shire to shire in certain shires within the king's majesty's realm. Furthermore it is to be considered what this twelve hundred quarters of corn is able to do within Oxfordshire; it is able to certify and suffice fifteen score people by the year bread and drink and allow to every person two quarters of wheat and two quarters of malt by the year; whereas in the first the whole living of twelve score persons, meat, and drink, and raiment, uprising and down lying, paying scot and lot to our God and to our king. And the second loss, bread and drink for fifteen score persons by the year, which the whole number draweth to five hundred and forty persons in Oxfordshire; and so in Buckinghamshire, and so likewise in Northamptonshire, and so forth from shire to shire within the king's majesty's realm.

And if it be as we do think that there be four score ploughs in every one of these shires less than there was, then is there the living lost of a thousand and four score persons in every one of these foresaid shires. This is the second loss, as we do think, and call for remedy for it.

The third loss, as we do think: We do lose in the said three shires keeping of household and hospitality and maintaining of tillage and household keeping; we do lack corn and also lose our cattle; for where any household is kept, there is kept kine and calves; and of our kine there cometh milk, butter, and cheese; and all this doth sustain the king's majesty's subjects; and for this we have nothing but sheep.

And furthermore, where households be kept, there is hogs, pigs, and bacon, capons, hens, ducks, eggs, fruit, and many other commodities that are necessary and needful to be had for the maintenance and living of the king's majesty's poor subjects to live by; and for that we have nothing but sheep. This is the third loss.

The tenth is, which we do call for remedy, and we desire of God and the king's majesty if it shall please his highness to be so good and gracious unto his poor subjects, that there might be in every shire and hundred as many ploughs used, occupied, and maintained, as many households kept, as was by King Henry the seventh's time, first coming. And then unfeigned, as we do think, we should have corn enough, cattle enough, and sheep enough; then will sheep and wool be in more men's hands; we shall have also white meat enough and all things necessary. And thus Jesus preserve our dread sovereign lord and king!

As we do think, we have two losses more that we have not spoken: the first loss is for lack of household keeping and maintenance of tillage. It is great decay to artillery: for that do we reckon that shepherds be but ill archers. And as we do further think, it loseth the king's majesty in provision for his noble households, that is to say in wheat, malt, beans, muttons, veals, hay and oats, and poultry, and all manner such provisions that belongeth to his majesty's household, as we do think, five thousand marks by the year with the left. In a trial as we do think, if it should please the king's majesty's officers to call in his grace's purveyors and examine them where they have had within their time for his grace's provisions of his wars and for his majesty's household, whereas there is now nothing to be gotten: for they that keep the said lands hath put the foresaid lands to pastures, themselves buyeth all manner of grain and corn to keep their household withal.

Furthermore, if it shall please the king's highness and his noble council for to have a further trial of this matter and to assure it to be true, take all craftsmen dwelling in cities and towns, day labourers that laboureth by water or by land, cottagers and other householders, refusing none, but only them that hath all this abundance, that is to say, sheep or woolmasters and enclosers, the lamentations of the king's majesty's subjects will make any true hearted body to seek and call for remedy, which we beseech the Lord to amend. Amen.

Furthermore, as we do think, this realm doth decay by this means: it is to understand and know that there are in England towns and villages to the number of fifty thousand and upward, and for every town and village, take them one with another throughout all, there is one plough decayed since the first year of the reign of King Henry the seventh. And in some towns and villages all the whole town decayed since that time; and if there be for every town and village one plough decayed, since the first year of the reign of King Henry the seventh, then is there decayed fifty thousand ploughs and upward.

The which fifty thousand ploughs, every plough were able to maintain six persons: that is to say, the man, the wife, and four other in his house, less and more. Fifty thousand ploughs, six persons to every plough, draweth to the number of three hundred thousand persons were wont to have meat, drink, and raiment, uprising and down lying, paying scot and lot to God and to the king. And now they have nothing but goeth about in England from door to door and ask their alms for God's sake. And because they will not beg, some of them doth steal, and then they be hanged, and thus the realm doth decay, and by none other ways else, as we do think. Beseeching your highness (of your most noble grace) and honourable lordships, the premises tenderly considered before you in examination upon the premises, that we may have a remedy in this behalf. And we shall daily pray for the conservation of your highness, and for your full noble lordships.

Finis.

Imprinted at London
*in Paul's church-yard at
the sign of Saint Austin*
by Hugh Singleton.

THE EXAMINATION AND EXECUTION OF
LADY JANE GREY
1554

as told by John Foxe in his
Acts and Monuments
1563

For the biographical sketch of John Foxe,
see above, p.83.

THE 12th day of February was beheaded the Lady Jane, to whom was sent Master Fecknam, alias Howman, from the queen, two days before her death, to commune with her and to reduce her from the doctrine of Christ to Queen Mary's religion: the effect of which communication here follows:

The communication had between the Lady Jane and Fecknam.

FECKNAM: 'Madam, I lament your heavy case; and yet I doubt not but that you bear out this sorrow of yours with a constant and patient mind.'

JANE: 'You are welcome unto me, sir, if your coming be to give Christian exhortation. And as for my heavy case, I thank God, I do so little lament it, that rather I account the same for a more manifest declaration of God's favour toward me than ever he showed me any time before. And therefore there is no cause why either you, or others which bear me goodwill, should lament or be grieved with this my case, being a thing so profitable for my soul's health.'

FECKNAM: 'I am here come to you at this present, sent from the queen and her council, to instruct you in the true doctrine of the right faith: although I have so great confidence in you, that I shall have, I trust, little need to travail with you much therein.'

JANE: 'Forsooth, I heartily thank the queen's highness, which is not unmindful of her humble subject: and I hope, likewise, that you no less will do your duty therein both truly and faithfully, according to that you were sent for.'

FECKNAM: 'What is then required of a Christian?'

JANE: 'That he should believe in God the Father, the Son, and the Holy Ghost, three persons and one God.'

FECKNAM: 'What? is there nothing else to be required or looked for in a Christian, but to believe in God?'

JANE: 'Yes, we must believe in him, we must love him with all our heart, with all our soul, and with all our mind, and our neighbour as ourself.'

FECKNAM: 'Why? then faith justifies not, nor saves not.'

JANE: 'Yes verily, faith, as St. Paul says, only justifies.'

FECKNAM: 'Why? St. Paul says, " If I have all faith without love, it is nothing." '

JANE: 'True it is; for how can I love him whom I trust not, or how can I trust him whom I love not? Faith and love go both together, and yet love is comprehended in faith.'

FECKNAM: 'How shall we love our neighbour?'

JANE: 'To love our neighbour is to feed the hungry, to clothe the naked, and give drink to the thirsty, and to do to him as we would do to ourselves.'

FECKNAM: 'Why? then it is necessary unto salvation to do good works also, and it is not sufficient only to believe.'

JANE: 'I deny that, and I affirm that faith only saves: but it is meet for a Christian, in token that he doth follow his master Christ, to do good works; yet may we not say that they profit to salvation. For when we have done all, yet we be unprofitable servants, and faith only in Christ's blood saves.'

FECKNAM: 'How many sacraments are there?'

JANE: 'Two: the one the sacrament of baptism, and the other the sacrament of the Lord's Supper.'

FECKNAM: 'No, there are seven.'

JANE: 'By what scripture find you that?'

FECKNAM: 'Well, we will talk of that hereafter. But what is signified by your two sacraments.?'

JANE: 'By the sacrament of baptism I am washed with water and re-generated by the Spirit, and that washing is a token to me that I am the child of God. The sacrament of the Lord's Supper, offered unto me, is a sure seal and testimony that I am, by the blood of Christ, which he shed for me on the cross, made partaker of the everlasting kingdom.'

FECKNAM: 'Why? what do you receive in that sacrament? Do you not receive the very body and blood of Christ?'

JANE: 'No surely, I do not so believe. I think that at the supper I neither receive flesh nor blood, but only bread and wine: which bread when it is broken, and the wine when it is drunk, put me in remembrance how that for my sins the body of Christ was broken, and his blood shed on the cross; and with that bread and wine I receive the benefits that come by the breaking of his body and shedding of his blood, for our sins on the cross.'

FECKNAM: 'Why, does not Christ speak these words, "Take, eat, this is my body?" Require we any plainer words? Does he not say, it is his body?'

JANE: 'I grant, he says so; and so he says, "I am the vine, I am the door"; but he is never the more for that the door nor the vine. Does not St. Paul say that he calls things that are not, as though they were? God forbid that I should say that I eat the very natural body and blood of Christ: for then either I should pluck away my redemption, either else there were two bodies, or two Christs, or else twelve bodies. One body was tormented on the cross, and then if they did eat another body, then either he had two bodies, either else if his body were eaten, then it was not broken upon the cross; or else if it were broken upon the cross, it was not eaten of his disciples.'

FECKNAM: 'Why, is it not as possible that Christ, by his power, could make his body both to be eaten and broken, as to be born of a woman without seed of man, and as to walk upon the sea, having a body, and other such like miracles as he wrought by his power only?'

JANE: 'Yes verily, if God would have done at his supper any miracle, he might have done so: but I say, that then he minded no work nor miracle, but only to break his body and shed his blood on the cross for our sins. But I pray you answer me to this one question: Where was Christ when he said, "Take, eat, this is my body"? Was he not at the table, when he said so? He was at that time alive, and suffered not till the next day. Well, what took he, but bread? what broke he, but bread? and what gave he, but bread? Look, what he took, he broke: and look, what he broke, he gave: and look, what he gave, they did eat: and yet all this while he himself was alive, and at supper before his disciples, or else they were deceived.'

FECKNAM: ' You ground your faith upon such authors as say and un-
say both with a breath; and not upon the church, to whom you ought
to give credit.'

JANE: ' No, I ground my faith on God's word, and not upon the
church. For if the church be a good church, the faith of the church
must be tried by God's word; and not God's word by the church,
neither yet my faith. Shall I believe the church because of antiquity,
or shall I give credit to the church that takes away from me the half
part of the Lord's Supper, and will not let any lay man receive it in
both kinds but themselves? Which thing, if they deny to us, then deny
they to us part of our salvation. And I say, that it is an evil church,
and not the spouse of Christ, but the spouse of the devil, that alters
the Lord's Supper, and both takes from it and adds to it. To that
church, say I, God will add plagues; and from that church will he
take their part out of the book of life. Do they learn that of St. Paul,
when he ministered to the Corinthians in both kinds? Shall I believe
this church? God forbid!'

FECKNAM: ' That was done for a good intent of the church, to avoid
a heresy that sprang on it.'

JANE: ' Why, shall the church alter God's will and ordinance for a
good intent? How did King Saul? God the Lord defend!'

With these and such like persuasions he would have had her leaned
to the church, but it would not be. There were many more things whereof
they reasoned, but these were the chiefest. These words following were
spoken openly.

After this, Fecknam took his leave, saying that he was sorry for her:
' For I am sure,' quoth he, ' that we two shall never meet.'

JANE: ' True it is,' said she, ' that we shall never meet, except God
turn your heart; for I am assured, unless you repent and turn to God,
you are in an evil case. And I pray God, in the bowels of his mercy,
to send you his Holy Spirit; for he has given you his great gift of utterance, if it pleased him to open the eyes of your heart.'

A Letter written by the Lady Jane in the end of the New Testament in
Greek, the which she sent unto her sister Lady Katherine, immediately
before she suffered.

I have here sent you, good sister Katherine, a book, which, although it be not outwardly trimmed with gold, yet inwardly it is more worth than precious stones. It is the book, dear sister, of the law of the Lord. It is his testament and last will, which he bequeathed unto us wretches; which shall lead you to the path of eternal joy: and, if you with a good mind read it, and with an earnest mind do follow it, it shall bring you to an immortal and everlasting life. It will teach you to live, and learn you to die. It shall win you more than you should have gained by the possession of your woeful father's lands. For as, if God had prospered him, you should have inherited his lands; so, if you apply diligently this book, seeking to direct your life after it, you shall be an inheritor of such riches, as neither the covetous shall withdraw from you, neither thief shall steal, neither yet the moths corrupt. Desire with David, good sister, understand the law of the Lord your God. Live still to die, that you by death may purchase eternal life. And trust not that the tenderness of your age shall lengthen your life; for as soon (if God call) goeth the young as the old: and labour always to learn to die. Defy the world, deny the devil, and despise the flesh, and delight yourself only in the Lord. Be penitent for your sins, and yet despair not: be strong in faith, and yet presume not; and desire, with St. Paul, to be dissolved and to be with Christ, with whom even in death there is life. Be like the good servant, and even at midnight be waking, lest, when death cometh and stealeth upon you like a thief in the night, you be, with the evil servant, found sleeping; and lest, for lack of oil, you be found like the five foolish women; and like him that had not on the wedding garment, and then you be cast out from the marriage. Rejoice in Christ, as I trust I do. Follow the steps of your Master Christ, and take up your cross: lay your sins on his back, and always embrace him. And as touching my death, rejoice as I do, good sister, that I shall be delivered of this corruption and put on incorruption. For I am assured, that I shall, for losing of a mortal life, win an immortal life, the which I pray God grant you, send you of his grace to live in his fear, and to die in the true Christian faith, from the which (in God's name), I exhort you that you never swerve, neither for hope of life, nor for fear of death. For if you will deny his truth to lengthen your life, God will deny you, and yet shorten your days. And if you will cleave unto him, he will prolong your days, to your comfort and his glory: to the which glory God bring me now, and you hereafter, when it pleaseth him to call you. Fare you well, good sister, and put your only trust in God, who only must help you.

These are the words that the Lady Jane spake upon the scaffold, at the hour of her death. First, when she mounted upon the scaffold, she said to the people standing thereabout, ' Good people, I am come hither to die, and by a law I am condemned to the same. The fact against the queen's highness was unlawful, and the consenting thereunto by me: but, touching the procurement and desire thereof by me, or on my behalf, I do wash my hands thereof in innocency before God, and the face of you, good Christian people, this day ': and therewith she wrung her hands, wherein she had her book. Then said she, ' I pray you all, good Christian people, to bear me witness that I die a true Christian woman, and that I do look to be saved by no other mean but only by the mercy of God, in the blood of his only Son Jesus Christ: and I confess that when I did know the word of God, I neglected the same, loved myself and the world; and therefore this plague and punishment is happily and worthily happened unto me for my sins; and yet I thank God of his goodness that he hath thus given me a time and respite to repent. And now, good people, while I am alive, I pray you assist me with your prayers.' And then, kneeling down, she turned her to Fecknam, saying: ' Shall I say this psalm? ' And he said, ' Yea.' Then said she the psalm of *Miserere mei Deus* in English, in most devout manner, throughout to the end; and then she stood up, and gave her maiden, mistress Ellen, her gloves and handkerchief, and her book to master Bruges, wherewith she untied her gown, and the hangman pressed upon her to help her off with it; but she, desiring him to let her alone, turned towards her two gentlewomen, who helped her off therewith, and also with her frowes, paste, and neckerchief, giving to her a fair handkerchief to knit about her her eyes.

Then the hangman kneeled down and asked her forgiveness, whom she forgave most willingly. Then he willed her to stand upon the straw; which doing, she saw the block. Then she said, ' I pray you dispatch me quickly.' Then she kneeled down, saying, ' Will you take it off, before I lay me down? ' And the hangman said, ' No, madam.' Then tied she the kerchief about her eyes, and feeling for the block, she said, ' What shall I do? Where is it? Where is it? ' One of the standers-by guiding her thereunto, she laid her head down upon the block, and then stretched

3—The illustration opposite is the woodcut title-page of the 1570 edition of John Foxe, *Acts and Monuments*. The cut was also used in the 1583 edition but without the descriptive type at the bottom. The pictorial narratives of ' the persecuted church ' and ' the persecuting church ' are typical of the propaganda used during the sixteenth century to bolster the cause of the reformed religion and to discredit popery. The episodes depicted from the religious life of each faith show the main points of difference between the old and new religions. The protestants are enjoying sermons, bible reading, prayer, and the Light of personal inspiration. Their course leads to martyrdom by fire and a glorious salvation in heaven. The features of catholicism especially obnoxious to the reformers—beads, processions, candles, monks, and relics; the idolatrous mass with the doctrine of transubstantiation designated by the elevation of the host—are shown as leading to eternal damnation amidst the devils of hell.

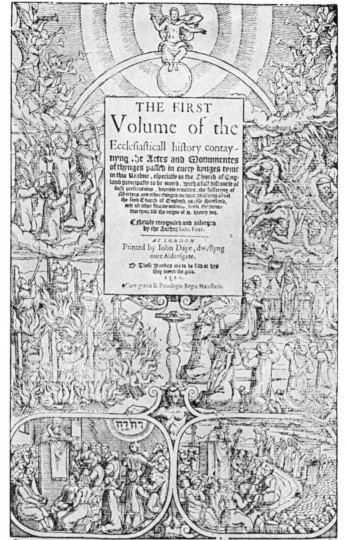

THE FIRST
Volume of the
Ecclesiasticall history contay-
nyng the Actes and Monumentes
of thynges passed in every kynges tyme
in this Realme, especially in the Church of England principally to be noted, with a full discourse of
such persecutions, horrible troubles, the sufferyng of
Martyrs, and other thynges incident, touching aswel
the sayd Church of England, as also Scotland,
and all other forreine nations, from the primitive tyme, till the reigne of K. Henry viij.

Newly recognised and inlarged
by the Author Iohn Foxe.

AT LONDON
Printed by Iohn Daye, dwellyng
over Aldersgate.

These Bookes are to be sold at hys
shop vnder the gate.
1570.

Cum gratia & Priuilegio Regiæ Maiestatis.

{ The Image of the persecuted Church. }   { The Image of the persecutyng Church. }

forth her body, and said, ' Lord, into thy hands I commend my spirit'; and so finished her life, in the year of our Lord God 1553[1554], the 12th day of February.

The Lady Jane to a learned man of late fallen from the truth of God's most holy word for fear of the world. [Master Harding, late Chaplain to the Duke of Suffolk, her father.]

So oft as I call to mind the dreadful and fearful sayings of God, that he which lays hold upon the plough and looks back again is not meet for the kingdom of heaven; and, on the other side, to remember the comfortable words of our Saviour Christ to all those that, forsaking themselves, do follow him: I cannot but marvel at thee, and lament thy case, that thou which sometime was the lively member of Christ, but now the deformed imp of the devil; sometime the beautiful temple of God, but now the stinking and filthy kennel of Satan; sometime the unspotted spouse of Christ, but now the unshamefaced paramour of Antichrist; sometime my faithful brother, but now a stranger and apostate; yea, sometime a stout Christian soldier, but now a cowardly runaway. So oft, I say, as I consider the threatenings and promise of God to all those that faithfully love him, I cannot but speak to thee, yea rather cry out upon thee, thou seed of Satan, and not of Judah, whom the devil has deceived, the world has beguiled, and the desire of life subverted, and made thee of a Christian an infidel. Wherefore hast thou taken upon thee the testament of the Lord in thy mouth? Wherefore hast thou preached the law and the will of God to others? Wherefore hast thou hitherto yielded thy body to the fire and to the bloody hands of cruel tyrants? Wherefore hast thou instructed others to be strong in Christ, when thou thyself do now so shamefully shrink, when thou thyself do now so horribly abuse the testament and law of the Lord? When thou thyself preachest not to steal, yet most abominably stealest, not from men, but from God, and as most heinous sacrilege, robbest Christ thy Lord of his right members, thy body and thy soul; when thou thyself dost rather choose to live miserably with shame to the world, than to die, and gloriously with honour to reign with Christ, in whom even in death is life? And when I say thou thyself art most weak, then thou ought to show thyself most strong. For the strength of a fort is not known before the assault, but thou yieldest thy hold before any battery made. O wretched and unhappy man, what art thou, but dust and ashes? And wilt thou resist thy Maker that fashioned thee and framed thee? Wilt thou now forsake him that called thee from the custom gathering among the Romish Antichristians, to be an ambassador and messenger of his eternal words? He that first framed thee, and since thy first creation and birth preserved thee, nourished and kept thee, yea, and inspired thee with the spirit of knowledge (I cannot say of grace), shall he not now possess thee? Darest thou deliver up thyself to another, being not thine own but his? How canst thou, having knowledge, or how darest thou neglect the law of the Lord, and follow the vain traditions of men; and whereas thou hast been a public professor of his name, become now a defacer of his glory? Yea, wilt thou refuse the true God, and worship the invention of man, the golden calf, the whore of Babylon, the Romish religion, the abominable idol, the most wicked mass? Wilt thou torment again, rend and tear the most precious body of our Saviour Christ, with thy bodily and fleshly teeth? Without the breaking whereof upon the cross, our sinful sins could else no ways be redeemed? Wilt thou take upon thee to offer up any sacrifice unto God for our sins, considering that Christ offered up himself, as Paul says, upon the cross, a lively sacrifice once for all? Can neither the punishment of the Israelites (which, for their idolatry, so oft they received) move thee, neither the terrible threatenings of the ancient prophets stir thee, nor the curses of God's own mouth, fear thee to honour any other God than him? Wilt thou so regard him, that spared not his dear and only Son for thee, so diminishing, yea, utterly extinguishing his glory, that thou wilt attribute the praise and honour to idols, which have mouths and speak not, eyes and see not, ears and yet hear not; which shall perish with them that made them?

What says the prophet Baruch, where he recited the epistle of Jeremiah, written to the captive Jews? Did he not forewarn them that in Babylon they should see gods of gold, silver, wood, and stone borne upon men's shoulders, to cast a fear before the heathen? But be not you afraid of them, says Jeremiah, nor do as other do. But when you see others worship them, say you in your hearts, It is thou, O Lord, that ought only to be worshipped; for, as for the timber of those gods, the carpenter framed them and polished them: yea, gilded be they, and laid over with silver and vain things, and cannot speak. He shows, moreover, the abuse of their deckings, how the priests took off their ornaments, and apparelled their women withal: how one holds a sceptre, another a sword in his hand, and yet can they judge in no matter, nor defend themselves, much less any other, from either battle, or murder, nor yet from gnawing of worms, nor any other evil thing. These, and such like words, speaketh Jeremiah unto them, whereby he proves them but vain things and no gods. And at last he concludes thus: Confounded be they that worship them. They were warned by Jeremiah, and thou as Jeremiah hast warned others, and art warned thyself by many scriptures in many places. God says he is a jealous God, which will have all honour, glory, and worship given to him only. And Christ says, in the fourth of Luke, to Satan which tempted him, even to the same Satan, the same Beelzebub, the same devil, which hath prevailed against thee: It is written, saith he, thou shalt honour the Lord thy God, and him only shalt thou serve.

These, and such like, do prohibit thee and all Christians to worship any other god than which was before all worlds, and laid the foundations both of heaven and earth. And wilt thou honour a detestable idol, invented by Romish popes, and the abominable college of crafty cardinals? Christ offered himself up once for all, and wilt thou offer him up again daily at thy pleasure? But thou wilt say, thou dost it for a good intent. O sink of sin! O child of perdition! Dost thou dream therein a good intent, where thy conscience bears thee witness of the promise of God's wrath toward? How did Saul? Who for that he disobeyed the word of the Lord for a good intent, was thrown from his worldly and temporal kingdom. Shalt thou, then, that dost deface God's honour and rob him of his right, inherit the eternal and heavenly kingdom? Wilt thou, for a good intent, dishonour God, offend thy brother, and endanger thy soul, wherefore Christ hath shed his most precious blood? Wilt thou, for a good intent, pluck Christ out of heaven, and make his death void, and deface the triumph of his cross by offering him up daily? Wilt thou, either for fear of death, or hope of life, deny and refuse thy God, who enriched thy poverty, healed thy infirmity, and yielded to thee his victory, if thou couldst have kept it? Dost thou not consider that the thread of thy life hangeth upon him that made thee, who can (as his will is) either twine it harder to last the longer, or untwine it again to break it the sooner? Dost thou not then remember the saying of David, a notable king, to teach thee, a miserable wretch, in his hundred and fourth psalm, where he says thus: When thou takest away thy spirit, O Lord, from men, they die and are turned again to their dust; but when thou lettest thy breath go forth, they shall be made, and thou shalt renew the face of the earth. Remember the saying of Christ in his gospel: Whosoever seeketh to save his life, shall lose it: but whosoever will lose his life for my sake, shall find it. And in another place, Whosoever loveth father or mother above me, is not meet for me. For he that will be my disciple must forsake father and mother and himself and take up his cross, and follow me. What cross? The cross of infamy and shame, of misery and poverty, of affliction and persecution, for his name's sake. Let the oft falling of those heavenly showers pierce thy stony heart. Let the two-edged sword of God's holy word shear asunder the sewed-together sinews of worldly respects, even to the very marrow of thy carnal heart, that thou mayest once again forsake thyself and embrace Christ. And, like as good subjects will not refuse to hazard all in the defence of their earthly and temporal governor, so fly not like a white-livered milksop from the standing wherein thy chief captain Christ hath set thee in array of this life. *Viriliter age, confortetur cor tuum, sustine Dominum.* Fight manfully, come life, come death: the quarrel is God's, and undoubtedly the victory is ours.

But thou wilt say, I will not break unity. What? Not the unity of Satan and his members? Not the unity of darkness, the agreement of Antichrist and his adherents? Nay, thou deceivest thyself with fond imaginations of such a unity as is among the enemies of Christ. Were not the false prophets in a unity? Were not Joseph's brethren and Jacob's sons in a unity? Were not the heathen, as the Amalekites, the Perizzites and Jebusites, in a unity? I keep no order but rather look to my matter. Were not the Scribes and Pharisees in a unity? Doth not King David testify, *Convenerunt in unum adversus Dominum?* Yea, thieves, murderers, conspirators, have their unity. But what unity? Even Tully says of amity: *Amicitia*, says he, *non est, nisi inter bonos.* But mark, my friend (yea, friend, if thou art not God's enemy); there is no unity but where Christ knitteth the knot among such as be his. Yea, be well assured, that where his truth is resident, there it is verified that he himself says: *Non veni mittere pacem in terram, sed gladium*, etc., to set one against another, the son against the father, and the daughter against the mother-in-law. Deceive not thyself, therefore, with the glittering and glorious name of unity; for Antichrist hath his unity, not yet in deed, but in name. The agreements of ill men is not a unity but a conspiracy.

Thou hast heard some threatenings, some curses, and some admonitions, out of the Scripture, to those that love themselves above Christ. Thou hast heard, also the sharp and biting words to those that deny him for love of life. Saith he not that he that denieth me before men, I will deny him before my Father in heaven? And to the same effect writeth Paul, Hebrews vi: It is impossible, saith he, that they which be once lightened, and have tasted of the heavenly gift, and be partakers of the Holy Ghost, and have tasted of the good word of God, if they fall and slide away, it is impossible that they should be renewed again by repentance, crucifying again to themselves the Son of God, and making him a mocking-stock. And again saith he, If we shall willingly sin, after we have received the knowledge of his truth, there is no oblation left for sin, but the terrible expectation of judgment and fire which shall devour the adversaries. Thus St. Paul writes, and this thou readest; and dost thou not quake and tremble?

Well, if these terrible and thundering threatenings cannot stir thee to cleave unto Christ and forsake the world, yet let the sweet consolations and promises of the Scriptures, let the example of Christ and his apostles, holy martyrs, and confessors encourage thee to take faster hold by Christ. Hearken what he saith: Blessed are you when men revile you and persecute you for my sake: rejoice and be glad, for great is your reward in heaven; for so persecuted they the prophets that were before you. Hear what Isaiah the prophet saith: Fear not the curse of men; be not afraid of their blasphemies and revilings; for worms and moths shall eat them up like cloth and wool: but my righteousness shall endure for ever, and my saving health from generation to generation. What art thou then, saith he, that fearest a mortal man, the child of a man, which fadeth away like the flower and forgettest the Lord that made thee, that spread out the heavens, and laid the foundation of the earth? I am thy Lord thy God, that maketh the sea to rage, and to be still, who is the Lord of Hosts: I shall put my word in thy mouth and defend thee with the turning of a hand. And our Saviour Christ saith to his disciples, They shall accuse you and bring you before princes and rulers, for my name's sake; and some of you they shall persecute and kill: but fear you not, saith he, nor care you not what you shall say: for it is my Spirit that speaketh within you. The hand of the highest shall defend you, as hairs of your head are numbered, and none of them shall perish. I have laid up treasure for you, saith he, where no thieves can steal, nor moth corrupt. And happy are you, if you abide to the end; fear not them, saith Christ, that hath power only of the body, but fear him that hath power both over the body and soul. The world loveth her own, and if ye were of the world, the world would love you, but you are mine. Therefore the world doth hate you.

Let these and suchlike consolations, cut out of the Scriptures, strengthen you to Godward: let not the examples of holy men and women go out of your mind, as Daniel and the rest of the prophets; of the three children of Eleazar, that constant father; of the seven of the Maccabees' children; of Peter, Paul, Stephen, and other apostles and holy martyrs in the beginning of the church, as of good Simeon, archbishop of Seloma, and Zetrophone, with infinite others under Sapor, the king of the Persians and Indians, who condemned all torments devised by the tyrants, for their Saviour's sake. Return, return again into Christ's war, and, as becometh a faithful warrior, put on that armour that St. Paul teacheth to be most necessary for a Christian man. And, above all things, take to you the shield of faith and be you provoked by Christ's own example to withstand the devil, to forsake the world, and to become a true and faithful member of his mystical body, who spared not his own body for our sins.

Throw down thyself with the fear of his threatened vengeance, for this so great and heinous an offence of apostasy: and comfort thyself, on the other part, with the mercy, blood, and promise of him that is ready to turn unto you, whensoever you turn unto him. Disdain not to come again with the lost son, seeing you have so wandered with him. Be not ashamed to turn again with him from the swill of strangers to the delicates of your most benign and loving Father, acknowledging that you have sinned against heaven and earth: against heaven, by staining his glorious name and causing his most sincere and pure word to be evil spoken of through you: against earth, by offending your so many weak brethren, to whom you have been a stumbling-block through your sudden sliding. Be not abashed to come home again with Mary, and weep bitterly with Peter, not only with shedding the tears of your bodily eyes, but also pouring out the streams of your heart—to wash away, out of the sight of God, the filth and mire of your offensive fall. Be not abashed to say with the publican, Lord be merciful unto me a sinner. Remember the horrible history of Julian of old, and the lamentable case of Spira of late, whose case, methinks should be yet so green in your remembrance, that, being a thing of our time, you should fear the like inconvenience, seeing you are fallen into the like offence.

Last of all, let the lively remembrance of the last day be always before your eyes, remembering the terror that such shall be in at that time, with the runagates and fugitives from Christ, which, setting more by the world than by heaven, more by their life than by him that gave them their life, did shrink, yea did clean fall away, from him that never forsook them: and, contrariwise, the inestimable joys prepared for them, that feared no peril, nor dreading death, have manfully fought and victoriously triumphed over all power of darkness, over hell, death, and damnation, through their most redoubted captain, Christ, who now stretcheth out his arms to receive you, ready to fall upon your neck and kiss you, and, last of all, to feast you with the dainties and delicates of his own precious blood: which undoubtedly, if it might stand with his determinate purpose, he would not let to shed again, rather than you should be lost. To whom with the Father, and the Holy Ghost, be honour, praise, and glory everlastingly. Amen.

> Be constant, be constant; fear not for pain:
> Christ hath redeemed thee, and heaven is thy gain.

THE FIRST AND
CHIEF GROUNDS OF ARCHITECTURE

Used in all the ancient and famous monuments with a farther and more ample discourse upon the same than hitherto hath been set out by any other. Published by John Shute, Painter and Architect. Imprinted at London in Fleet Street near to Saint Dunstan's Church by Thomas Marshe, 1563.

JOHN SHUTE (fl. 1550–1570) was an architect, limner, and miniature painter of contemporary distinction, but no work by him has been authenticated. The little known of him has been derived from the tract here printed which is the principal Elizabethan treatise upon architecture. Most of its contents are derived from Vitruvius' *Ten Books of Architecture*. Vitruvius, a superintendent of *ballistæ* under the Roman Emperor Augustus, had enjoyed 'no great reputation as an architect,' but his book was to become the manual for the architects of the sixteenth century. Palladio in Italy developed his rules and principles for building from Vitruvius and incorporated them into his *Four Books of Architecture*, 1570; Guillaume Philander dedicated his *Annotations on Vitruvius*, 1546, to the French king, Francis I; and Philibert de l'Orme formulated his architectural style, which was dominant in sixteenth-century France, from the same source. Vitruvius' book had been recovered in the fifteenth century with the finding of a manuscript copy at the monastery of St. Gall, and from this event the classical influence upon European architecture may be dated. Shute's knowledge came, then, from Vitruvius, from the buildings he saw in Italy, and from his practical experience as a builder in England.

The original edition of 1563 contains some mathematical tables on measurements and four illustrations of classical columns, one of which is here reproduced. A second edition was published in 1584. This text is taken from the 1563 edition and has been considerably abridged as indicated.

THE CONTENTS OF THIS BOOK

Briefly collected and set out for the help of the reader.

The discourse from time to time how this science of architecture hath increased.

What the office and duty is, of him that will be a perfect architect, or master of buildings.

The first pillar that was found out by the Ionians, upon the symmetry of a strong man, being six times the length of his foot in height, was renewed again by the Tuscans, and of them taketh his name to be called Tuscana.

The second pillar called Dorica builded to his perfection in Greece, by Dorus, and of him taketh his name whose height is seven times his thickness which thickness is called the diameter.   Folio vii.

The third pillar called the Ionica was set in the temple of Apollo and Diana, finished and builded by the Ionians, whose height is eight times his thickness.   Folio ix.

The fourth pillar called Corinthia, found in the city of Corinth by Calimachus the excellent architect, whose height is nine diameters.   Folio xi.

The fifth pillar named Composita or Italica made to his perfection in the time of Vespasian by the ancient Romans, whose height is 10 diameters.   Folio xiv.

Of another ancient pillar, necessary to the before named pillars found out to his perfection by the Athenians called Atticurga or Attica.   Folio xvi.

The placing of the five orders, namely, AREOSTYLOS, DIASTYLOS, EUS–TYLOS, SYSTYLOS, and PICNOSTYLOS.   Folio xvii.

A rule of Vitruvius given for these three pillars, Dorica, Ionica, Corinthia, for the placing or displacing of them one above another.   Folio xviii.

A rule for the diminishing of the pillar under the capital.   eodem.

An example to be observed for the increase of the height of Epistilium.   eodem.

To The Most High and Excellent,
Princess Elizabeth, by the Grace of God
Queen of England, France, and Ireland,
Defender of the Faith, etc.

It is both rightly and excellently affirmed of Marcus Tullius Cicero, in his first book *De officiis* (right excellent princess and my most gracious sovereign lady) that no man is born into this world for his private and singular weal because our country chiefly, partly our parents, and partly our kinsfolk, do require as it were a duty of us, and recompense for that the which we have received, and like as the members of man's body be divers in number and have according to their diversity divers and peculiar properties, so is it in a good and well settled commonweal: in which there is no office so base, or handy work so simple which is not necessary and profitable for the same. And as the members of the body doing without impediments their natural duties, the whole body is in an healthful harmony and able to perform all that belongeth to the same. So is it in a public weal when all men in their calling, do labour not only for their own gain, but also for the profit and commodity of their country, which things when I according to my small capacity did weigh with myself, I was as it were stirred forward to do my duty unto this my country wherein I live and am a member.

And so much the rather, for that being servant unto the right honourable duke of Northumberland [in] 1550, it pleased his grace for my further knowledge to maintain me in Italy there to confer with the doings of the skilful masters of architecture, and also to view such ancient monuments hereof as are yet extant. Whereupon at my return, presenting his grace with the fruits of my travails, it pleased the same to show them unto that noble King Edward VI, your majesty's most dear brother of famous memory, whose delectation and pleasure was to see it, and such like. And having the said tricks and devices as well of sculpture and painting, as also of architecture, yet in my keeping, I thought it good at this time to set forth some part of the same for the profit of others, especially touching architecture: wherein I do follow not only the writings of learned men, but also do ground myself on my own experience and practice, gathered by the sight of the monuments in Italy.

And because all the members of the body have chiefly and principally a duty to the head, as governor of the whole, and without which all the other cannot live, so my duty enforceth me most sovereign lady (the perfect and natural head next unto God of this our commonweal) to show a token of the same unto your highness, in presenting these my poor and simple labours whereunto I am rather boldened considering your highness' delight in all kind of good learning and perfect skill in the tongues and sciences. Most humble beseeching your royal majesty to vouchsafe to let this my small travail and work pass under your noble protection and defence: and I according to my bond and duty shall pray to God for your long life and prosperous reign, with peace and tranquility to his honour and glory. Amen.

Your majesty's most humble
and obedient subject.

JOHN SHUTE.

John Shute painter and architect:
unto the loving and friendly readers.

AMONGST all other things (gentle and loving reader) wherewith the divine providence of almighty God hath most liberally and plentifully endowed mankind, there is nothing either for the dignity and worthiness of the thing itself, or for the wonderful estimation and price which in all times it hath been in, more excellent, precious, and commendable than learning knowledge and science, the which alone causeth mortal men to be most like immortal gods: and as it taketh out of their minds that rude and uncomely admiration wherewith through ignorance the simple in most name trifles are wonderfully occupied. So to the wise be monuments and works skilfully practised and carefully left both commendable and marvellous: yea and such, as neither the injuries of any storms and tempest can clean waste and consume, no nor (as it seemeth) the envy of man or the spoil of enemies deface and overthrow, neither that which is greatest of all, time itself can deface or cast out of mind. And among all other studies there is none in my simple judgment of this sort that deserveth greater praise, than that which is of the Greeks named Architectonica, and of the Latins Architectura (I think not altogether unfit nor unaptly by me termed in English, the art and trade to raise up and make excellent edifices and buildings) the which like as in all other ages hath been in marvellous account and estimation, as full well appeareth by divers learned philosophers and famous princes that embraced the same, as Plato, Aristotle, Pliny, who were excellent therein as their works will witness. Alexander Magnus, Julius Caesar, Vespasian, Adrian, with many other ancient Greeks and Romans which laboured to advance their name thereby who left many arguments of their virtue, high intents, and doings by the same with many other famous, of which Pliny maketh mention. Vitruvius and Frontyne, of later days men praiseworthy, very studious and painful therein, so in us seemeth it not only to crave the wonted commendation, but also to be most necessary and profitable as well by the condition of the time as necessity of the thing itself.

And surely such is the amplitude and largeness (I may well say perfection) of this faculty, that without some acquaintance with many other arts ye shall not enter into the deep secrets: for it hath a natural society and as it were by a certain kindred and affinity is knit unto all the mathematicals which sciences and knowledges are friends and a maintainer of divers rational arts: so that without a mean acquaintance or understanding in them neither painters, masons, goldsmiths, embroiderers, carvers, joiners, glaziers, gravers in all manner of metals, and divers others more can obtain any worthy praise at all. Now all these, being branches of that foresaid foundation stock or science, shall bring forth the fruits of it to their great profits, and commodity of the realm, which continuing and thoroughly practised in the same by time shall increase riches, worship, and fame. Considering with myself the manifold commodities and profits that should redound to a great many lovers of the same, and contrariwise what a loss and hindrance it hath been to them that lack the languages and learning who of necessity hath remained in ignorance to their great loss and discommodity of the realm. Notwithstanding, I know well there hath been a multitude and at this time be very many learned men who hath (through travail received) the full perfection of the prudent lady Scientia, of whom so deeply learned I crave pardon for my rude rashness that I having but tasted a certain sweetness of her excellence and liberality, wherefore natural love hath drawn me to advance her reputation and honour, according to my poor ability and good will, the thing nothing garnished as it ought to be, but most briefly and plainly with such demonstrations that it might edify them which of a long time have desired and reached at it to attain.

Also for the encouraging of those which earnestly studied and favoured it, I thought it therefore good to set out and commit to writing in our native language part of those things which (both by great labour and travail, at the first for my private commodity I searched out and for my own pleasure out of divers as well Latin and Italian, as French and Dutch writers) I have diligently gathered. As also passed many countries and regions to see, both in Rome amongst the antiquities and in the most notable places of Italy, where are most excellent buildings, and intending to write of architecture or buildings, I thought it best neither with the lightest or least profitable part thereof to begin, nor altogether after the most slender sort to handle that which I purposed to entreat upon.

I have therefore taken my first entrance into the writing of this art, at the five antique pillars or columns, commonly named of the places and persons partly where and of whom they were invented, and partly of their virtues and properties of those that they were likened unto, which pillars' names are these as followeth: Tuscana, Dorica, Ionica, Corinthia, and Composita. The treatise of these pillars, as it hath in it most delectation and pleasure in the beauty and comeliness of the workmanship appertaining unto them, so though at the beginning it be mingled with a little asperity and as it were bitterness (for the difficulty and hardness wherewith as both principals and also other things of any excellency at the first are customed to be, it is somewhat cumbrous) yet it is both so necessary and profitable, that neither without it any man may attain to any estimable part of the rest of this science, and with it as by a clue of thread or plain pathway a man may most easily pierce and lightly pass over the most dark and unknown corners of the whole process thereof.

But to speak of the worthiness of this part of architecture: it seemeth almost altogether superfluous, wherefore taking these to suffice in the part to be said, I will now show what trade and order I do follow in the declaration of the measures, proportions, and garnishments of these before-mentioned pillars. For so much therefore as in teaching of all arts three things are chiefly to be considered, that is to say, diligence in giving the precepts, aptness in choosing plain and evident examples, and last of all practice and experience of the teacher. I have for the first part taken for my author chiefly to be followed the noble and excellent writer Vitruvius, one of the most perfectest of all the antiques, and for that neither any one man, in what art soever it be, is absolute, and that other singular men of the antiques and he in many points do disagree and differ, which Sebastianus Serlius, a marvellous cunning artificer in our time in many places of his works learnedly doth declare. I have added unto him upon whatsoever in anything seemed needful the opinion and meaning of the said expert writer Sebastianus, here and there also, where I thought meet, I have joined the mind and judgment of one Gulielmus Philander, a notable man which about the year of our Lord 1546 wrote unto the French king *Annotations upon Vitruvius*, concerning this matter or such like. Now for examples which are necessarily required to the opening of such dark matters, I have everywhere through the whole process of this present treatise after the precepts to the lightening of them set both demonstration and figure, and as for practice and experience of these things which I teach, I assure thee, most gentle reader and all other that shall be readers, so this my little work that I have put no tittle in any part thereof concerning the proportion and symmetry, to use the accustomed term of the art of the forenamed columns, which I have not as well seen and measured in Italy, from whence they came first unto us amongst the antique works, that I might with so much more perfection write of them as both the reading of the thing and seeing it in deed is more than only bare reading of it.

This small and simple treatise of mine I cannot tell whitherwith, like felicity brought to his perfection as with no small labour and study for this time ended, I thought meet as the first fruits of my poor attempt and endeavours to leave as a duty and debt of me to be paid, and that well received of all men, I shall think myself most happy, and if not of all persons, yet at the leastwise of such as be honest esteemers and accepters of other men's diligence and studies. The which if it come to pass, both I shall be glad of my labours in these things bestowed and for the love of my natural countryman be furthermore encouraged hereafter to attempt greater things. Thus almighty God preserve the ungodly exercises to his pleasure for ever. Amen.

The discourse from time to time
how this science of architecture increased.

IN the beginning of the world, nature by necessity did first invent strange manner of covertures or houses for the people to inhabit in, but of all such order and form of buildings as were before Noah's flood, it shall not need to make rehearsal. But after the flood of Noah, the people again, when they were increased and multiplied, did daily more and more seek for their commodity to be defended from the heat of the sun and coldness of the air: some succoured themselves under the shadow of trees, and other, taking occasion thereby, devised to set up forked stakes, with the forks upwards, and thereupon laid boughs. Afterwards they still devised and daily did practise more and more in that kind. And in time, they, perceiving the use of cutting with iron, did set upright trees as they had before, with their stakes being done with their hands, and because they should not cleave with the heaviness of their burdens above at the top, they compassed them about with rings of iron, and called them pillars or columns. The form and shape of which pillars they did imitate, fashioning them of stone.

And then they, calling to their remembrance the flood of Noah, which had drowned all the world, devised to build the tower of Babylon. So they added instead of the ring above at the top of their pillars, these which our author Vitruvius calleth Astragali and Apophigis. So in process of time, divers witty men ever adding some thing thereto, at the last it came to some perfection. Then did they begin to devise and practise after divers fashions, and builded a great part of the tower. In which building came the division of tongues or languages, whereby these builders were parted and scattered abroad upon the face of the earth, and inhabited many strange countries, and began to build in Egypt, and after that in many other places, as seemeth by the works, which Belus, Ninus, and Semiramis builded, which were spread so far, as some men do suppose that Trier in low Dutchland should have been builded of the brother of Ninus, as ye may perceive by Berosus, Herodotus, and many other that are writers and witnesses of the same.

Yea, shortly after was made Memphis, the which now is named Alkayre, the which was builded by a king of Egypt, having in compass round about, one hundred and fifty stades, or as some interpret it, so many furlongs, and in like manner the ancient city of Thebes in Greece, besides many other cities which were made before and after. In the which it is to be supposed, that there were sumptuous temples and palaces. So that they were expert and began in that science to come to more perfection.

And immediately after a witty man named Dorus (the son of Helemer and Optix the Nymph) invented and made the first pillar drawn to perfection, and called it Dorica, after his own name. Shortly after him, there was Ion, son of Xuthus, that was made governor of a part of Caria, which he had won, he in that country builded these cities following, Priam, Samum, Teorem, Colophonem, Nachium, Erithren, Phoceam, Clazomenas, Lebedum Melyten, of the which the citizens afterward drove out of the country the Carians, and called it Ionia, after their king's name, and then they made their churches and temples of their gods, and first began with Apollo his temple, as they had seen it in Greece before. And they not knowing any measure of pillars considered how to make a just symmetry, that it might be comely and also strong, took their measure by the foot of a strong-fashioned man, finding him to be in height six times the length of his foot, and so by that measure finished all the parts of the pillar, and called it Dorica, because they had seen it in the works of Dorus, and so therewith finished the temple of Apollo; after that they devised to make a temple to the goddess Diana, wherein they did devise another symmetry for that temple as they had done for the temple of Apollo, and fashioned it after the just measure of a woman, to the end and purpose it should be more beautiful and slender, making it eight diameters in height, and called it Ionica, after their country, adding thereunto in the stead of her show, that which Vitruvius nameth Spira, and in the capital, was set Voluta, in the stead of her hair, which trussed up with a lace, on either side of her head, for an ornature and garnishment of the capital, they also fashioned the body of the pillar, and filled it with Canalicoli and Striges, as though it were the pleats of her garments. Then they being more delighted with the beautifulness of the height thereof added also another diameter, unto the foresaid Dorica, and made it seven diameters in height.

After that in the city of Corinth was buried a certain maiden, after whose burial her nurse (who lamented much her death), knowing her delights to have been in pretty cups and such like conceit in her lifetime, with many other proper things appertaining only to the pleasure of the eye, took them and brake them, and put them into a little pretty basket, and did set the basket on her grave, and covered the basket with a square paving stone. That done, with weeping tears she said, Let pleasure go with pleasure, and so the nurse departed. It chanced that the basket was set upon a certain root of an herb called Acanthus, in French Branckursine, or bearfoot with us, now in the springtime of the year, when every root spreadeth forth his leaves, in the increasing they did run up by the sides of the basket, until they could rise no higher for the stone that covered the basket, which being square and casting his four corners over the sides of the round basket, constrained the branches of the herb to draw downwards again with a certain compass, and so grew to the fashion that Vitruvius calleth Voluta. So is there also other smaller that come out of the cauls and stalks and are named in Greek Helices, and the basket being hidden underneath with a multitude of leaves. In this city one Calimachus, an excellent architect, passing or going thereby, regarding the beautiful work of nature, afterwards using then the measures of the foresaid pillars, making the pillar Ionic, upon the which pillar or scapus thereof, he set the capital, the which he had seen upon the tomb of the maiden, the which garnished beautifully the whole pillar, which capital, was in height the thickness of the pillar, and named it Corinthia, because it was made in the city of Corinth, by the hands of Calimachus, who for the excellence of that art was named Catatechnos,

4—The illustration opposite is a drawing entitled 'Ionica' from John Shute, *The First and Chief Grounds of Architecture*. It depicts the Ionic style for column and pediment, and the book contains several similar ones of the other classic orders. This, with illustrations 5 and 9, is to demonstrate the introduction of classic principles into architecture and the evolution from the Gothic to the Anglo-classic style. Shute's drawings are tangible evidence of the new mathematical approach to building and of the importation of Italo-classic forms into England. They do much to compensate for the technical aridity of his treatise and probably had as much effect in popularizing the classic tradition in architecture as had his learned disquisition. Shute's meticulousness for mathematical proportions, rules, and principles in building show an interest in classicism deeper than surface ornamentation and provide a definite point of departure for a study of the classic influence in English artistic enterprise. The drawings were done, presumably, by the author himself, very likely during his sojourn in Italy.

CYMATIVM
CYMOTIV. G

REGVLA
SIMA   L
CORONA K
DENTICVLI
ZOPHORVS
CYMATIVM B
FASCIA 3 E
FASCIA 2 D
FASCIA I C
ABACVS   V
FRONS
Y ECHINVS
ASTRAGALVS

VOLVTA

CAPVS

S

TORVS O
ASTRAGALLO
PLINTHVS N
CYMA H
TIVM H
SIMA   R

M P SCOTIA SVPE
RIOR.

SECTION
L ASTRAGALVS

ICHNOGRAPHIA

I   O   N   I   C   A

ASTRAGALVS D
TORVS F
CIPLINTHVS

E SIMA EVER
SA.

and after that this work growing more and more to perfection came to the Romans, and so throughout all Italy, and many other places, yea, and was thoroughly practised by them.

Then the Tuscans, beginning to build, having knowledge of the pillar, which was first invented by the Ionians, upon the symmetry of a strong man, invented to build strongly after the manner aforesaid, yea, and to garnish also their cities and towns beautifully with a pillar of their own device which yet at this present time remaineth whole in the city of Florence and in the countries thereabout they formed and fashioned that pillar, which to this day is named after the said country Tuscana. The Romans, then well practised in their measures of all the rest of their columns, and also desirous to increase so noble an art by some noble accession, beholding and regarding the beautifulness of these foresaid pillars, that is to say, Tuscana, Dorica, Ionica, Corinthia, gathered out of each of the same pillars that which they thought most fair, and made a pillar of pleasure or triumph, after the most excellent manner that ever was before. This pillar was first builded to his perfection in the time of Titus, Vespasianus, who set it at his triumph in the highest place of his arch triumphal, and called it Composita, or as some do name it here Italica. These pillars, partly for their beauty and comeliness, partly for their fortitude and strength, the writers of them have resembled and likened to certain feigned gods and goddesses. As namely Tuscana is applied unto Atlas, the king of Mauritania: Dorica, unto Hercules and the god Mars: Ionica, to Diana, or Apollo: Corinthia unto Vesta or somelike virgin, and Composita, unto Pandora of Hesiodus, the which he feigneth to have been endued with divers of those graces and cunning, wherewith the before-named gods and goddesses were endued, so that it seemeth by the ancient writers and authors, which have made rehearsal of these things, that they have been had in great estimation and price, as ye may well perceive by Isis, which builded a temple in Egypt for her father Jupiter, because her husband Osiris and she were in great estimation, and also, for their beautiful inventions and wisdom, were honoured as gods.

This may well be gathered by their pillars and ornaments that belong thereunto, the which were noted and marked with Hebrew letters, and also by the sepulchres of Amasis, which was made more than 1500 years before the birth of Christ, in the which one of the pyramids was 360,000 men's work, the space of twenty years, the which remaineth in Egypt to be seen at this present day, and many other beautiful buildings of that nation. Read, Diado, *Sic.* li.1, 2. Also it seemeth by many other writers, that after Babel decayed, incontinently the Hebrews most triumphantly flourished in this point. Thus we may perceive that the Hebrews received their knowledge of the Babylonians, and the Greeks received it of the Hebrews, in like case the Latins and the Italians received theirs from the Greeks, the which our author Vitruvius doth not deny, in making demonstrations to a Latin work with Greek letters as upon the invention of the Greeks, which concerning his science in Architectura, in the which thing Vitruvius seemeth much to be commended as one that did not disdain to acknowledge the authors and writers out of whom he received his knowledge. In so much as in his seventh book of Architecture, he affirmeth (by naming the notablest of them) that they which have left these things in writing are to be commended, whose names also I thought not altogether the meetest to be omitted, and therefore do rehearse these. Theodorus, which wrote of the Dorica, Etesiphon and Metageves, who wrote of the Ionica which was set in the temple of Diana at Ephesus. Then Hermogenes hath written of Diana in Magnesia, after Argelius, which made the rehearsal of the Corinths. Fifthly Sathirus and Pitheus, who did speak of Mansolea in Halicarnasus, last both Cares, Briaxes, Scopas, Praxiteles, and many other, as Nexaria, Theosides, Philemon, Demophilos, Pollis, Leonides, Silamon, Melanpus, Sarnacus, Euphranor, all the which verily are to be thanked and commended thoroughly. For by them we know and perceive (as though we saw in a looking-glass) the things, that have been seen, done, and made long before.

Nevertheless, it hath been withdrawn and hidden (as almost all other knowledges, for a long season hath been) through ignorance, for so it came to pass by the injury of time, that all sciences and learning have been kept secret and not spoken of, in so much that at this day there are many which name this order of building to be of the new fashion. But it cannot be new that hath so many ancient authors and masters thereof, whom namely the noble writer or author Pliny hath in so great estimation, that for their sake he blameth all them greatly that have written and wrought anything and have not named the authors and masters, of whom they take their invention especially of such great and unspeakable work, of which the honour and fame hath been as much unto the maker thereof as it was unto them that caused those things to be made. But now of thy things we have spoken enough, let us therefore speak somewhat of the worthiness of this science, and of the office of an architect.

What the office and duty is of him that will be
a perfect architect or master of buildings.

ARCHITECTURE (by the common consent of many notable men) as Cesarius saith, is of all arts the most noble and excellent, containing in it sundry sciences and knowledges wherewith it is furnished and adorned, as full well Vitruvius doth affirm and declare by his writing. For, saith he, an architect must be sharp of understanding and both quick and apt to conceive the true instructions and meanings of them that have written thereof: and must also be a perfect distributor of the great mysteries that he hath perceived and experimented, that plainly and briefly he may discuss and open demonstrations of that which shall be done or meet to those persons that shall be the founders of any noble works; wherefore he ought first to be a very good grammarian, then to have expert knowledge in drawing and protracting the thing, which he hath conceived. Next he must have a good sight in geometry, consequently in optic, and in such like sciences he must have good perseverance. Likewise in arithmetic he must be very perfect, and in histories singularly well seen. He must also have a good sight in music, and some knowledge in physic, not altogether ignorant in astronomy, he must also besides all this be in philosophy very expert.

The causes why all these sciences before named ought to be in him that is a perfect architect and master of building be of Vitruvius in this sort rehearsed. If he have (saith he) learning he shall strengthen his memory with all written books, and through drawing utter his fantasy and show the trick or fashion of the thing that he goeth about to make. And geometry teacheth us the order of rules, compasses, squares, quadrants, and just water-levels with many other knowledges that proceedeth thereof, as Euclid and other authors and also Sebastian Serlius, in his first chapter, rehearseth optic, showeth us how and by what means the lights should be set into the house, and how they should be brought from place to place, as to serve the whole house, and every place therein, which optica, is properly called perspective, and is of a further speculation, than therein can or needeth to be expressed: which of Sebastian Serlius, in his second book, first, second, and third chapters, is partly declared arithmetic, teacheth us innumerable points most necessarily required to the perfect knowledge of this art, for without it, we can neither know or yet discuss the measures and hard sentences or questions of symmetry, neither how to account the cost and charges of our labours.

An architect also must have a knowledge in histories; there be moreover multitude of causes in buildings, and very many ornatures and garnishings of which he must needs give answer, from whence they come, and for what purpose they are made; as for an example, if a master workman should make images, figured like women, clothed and garnished after a beautiful sort, which are named Cariatides, and set them in his work for pillars and make over their head Mutilos and Coronas, if it were demanded of him to what purpose those images were made, then he should answer that Caria, a town in Peloponnesus, traitorously conspired with the Persians against the Greeks. But the Greeks getting the victory over their enemies, agreed with one accord and besieged Caria, and won the city, killed the men and took the women, carrying them as bond women not suffering them to put off their rich ornaments and jewels, to the intent that the show of their triumph might be thereby the more glorious. So they subdued, were brought into bondage. For this cause and other such like, the chief masters of architecture made in their common places and palaces such women to bear up the burden of their buildings, the which was a remembrance and a memorial of their punishments for their malice against the Greeks, sustained by the Cariatides, that is to say, by the women of Caria: in like case did the Lacedemonians, when they with so little a power overcame such a great host of the Persians and slew them. After which conquest in their triumph, they builded a gallery which should remain unto them for a perpetual and everlasting token of victory and did set therein the figures and counterfeits of the Persians, which before were their prisoners, in their strange apparel, standing in their palaces, supporting their galleries, wherefore they were feared of their enemies thereby, and also yet encouraged the hearts of the citizens against their other enemies and back friends. Upon this example Pausanias did afterward make the counterfeits of the same Persians, and upon their heads he laid Epistilia and Coronas, setting betwixt them Zophorus, the which was garnished and figured with the jewels that they had taken from them, being their enemies, as cups, goblets, chains, girdles, and such like other jewels, which were plentiful among the Persians, and under their feet were set Stylobata, wherein were written their titles. Many such histories an architect ought of necessity to know.

Next unto this doth follow music, which also is very necessary for an architect, for these causes must he have, as it were, a foresight in it, that thereby the principal chambers of the house should with such order be made that the voice or noise of musical instruments should have their perfect echo, resounding pleasantly to the ears of those that shall be hearers thereof, as also the Romans used in all their palaces and for many other necessities thereunto belonging, of the which Vitruvius maketh further demonstration, as the refreshing of the melancholic minds, which are always travailing for further knowledge.

But now consequently followeth the cause why he should have sight in physic, which through the knowledge of astronomy perfectly doth declare the movings of the heavens, and whereunto by their natural inclinations they be disposed, as also the understanding of the plagues or coasts of the world, which the Greeks call climata, to the intent that he may show what ground plots stand in the most wholesome air to build upon. And which also be the sweet and wholesome waters; the most fertile and fruitful places, as namely for those plots that stand contrary to this order are not meet or necessary to build upon. This wholesome ground so found whereon ye shall build, ye must first have knowledge how to cast your ground plot, wherein you must divide all your several places of offices appertaining to the furniture of your house, your principal chambers of rest and libraries, and such other like must receive their lights from the east, for that the sun by natural heat at his rising draweth to him all corrupt humours and evil vapours of the earth and quickeneth the spirits of man and beast, and if ye will cast therein bains or hothouses, with winter chambers and parlours they shall receive light from the west. For that side is defended from the south winds which are grievous and contagious and also great wasters of all kinds of buildings, as may well be perceived by old edifices. Your study places, where you would write, draw, or devise, or the places where your cellars should be cast, ought to receive their light from the north, by cause in that part are the lights, which are steadfast. As for lights other ways appointed, I refer to the builders of those works. But Vitruvius maketh no further mention thereof.

Now also it belongeth to an architect to have the knowledge of astronomy, whereby he should directly know the four principal places, which are east, west, north, and south with that, which they call Equinoctium, and Solsticium, and the movings of the stars, for without this knowledge none can attain unto the making of horologes, quadrants, clocks, dials, in the sun, necessary to be set in goodly edifices.

It belongeth also to an architect to have sight of philosophy, which teaching to be of a noble courage as Vitruvius saith, and also gentle, courteous, faithful, and modest, not given to avarice and filthy lucre, as not to be troubled or corrupted with rewards or gifts, but with gravity and sageness to conceive all honour and dignity in all things concerning his good name and estimation. Let him also take a charge of works in hand, being desired and not desirous of works. He, which would be an expert architect, ought to have all these sciences and knowledges. To him that hath any science or knowledge and judgment therewith conceived, it is most evident and plain.

Nevertheless it will sound strangely to some that a man should learn so many sciences for the attaining of one, and keep all them in memory for the practice of the same; yet it is necessary and also meet that although he be not perfect in them or every of them, yet he should have some knowledge in them and so it behooveth, neither it is requisite that he should be so perfect a grammarian as was Aristarchus, and yet not altogether without it. Nor in music like unto Aristoxenis, neither in painting like Appelles nor Plastes, or statuary like unto Miron or Policrates, neither in physic like unto Hippocrates, but yet in this and other not altogether ignorant. But if a man might be perfect in all the sciences as were Aristarchus, Samrius, Plulolaus, Architas, Tarentinus, Apollonius, Pergeus, Eratosthenes, Sireneus, Archimedes, Scopinas (for all these were strongly weaponed with all these sciences before rehearsed), he should be able to answer to all questions thereto appertaining.

But I may pray as Vitruvius doth, saying, I pray, O Caesar, and all other that read this my writings, if there be anything disagreeing to any of these sciences, bear with me for I confess myself (saith he) not to be perfect in any of the other sciences. But he nameth himself to be an architect, wherein he thinketh himself perfect. But I, the setter forth of this treatise in English, acknowledge myself not to be a perfect architect (as he saith) nor yet grammarian, and though I have put myself in press, it is not through the deep knowledge above rehearsed, but I do it for to put in use an entrance or beginning to them which be therein ignorant and desire further knowledge in these things, as hereafter appeareth by the declaration hereof.

Tuscana

The manner and form of the five principal pillars, and their proper names with all their compounds thereto belonging, and their setting in their just places by the order and rule of Symmetria, and marked with the letters *A.B.C.* whereunto is made this pillar Tuscana, as it is figured, invented, and made by the Ionians, upon the symmetry of a strong man. Renewed and found again by the Tuscans and of them taketh his name.

Tuscana

This pillar is the strongest and most able to bear the greatest of burden of all the others. And that same his strength cometh by his shortness, therefore he is likened unto Atlas, king of Mauretania, and the pillar is named Tuscana, whose height must be with the basis and capital 6 times his thickness in height. But if you will set stylobata, or pedestate, under the pillar, then shall ye begin from the ground upward, even after this sort. Ye shall make a four square stone, like unto a die. The quantity of the square as great as ye will, according to your purpose. Or ye may draw a ground plot on a table, in that square ye shall make a round compass, so great as it may be within that square, and then within that compass make another square, and then within that square, make ye another compass, the which compass shall be the just thickness of your pillar. The which Vitruvius calleth the diameter, and then shall your uttermost compass be for the projecture, or sailing out or hanging over of the foot of the pillar which projecture the Greeks do name or call it Ecphoron. Now the foot of the pillar, which is named basis, or base, which base, stretcheth out to the uttermost compass, and the square without that compass is the just breadth of the pedestal, which is marked with *A.* That breadth or height of that square divide you into four parts. Give tenia under marked with *B.* so much as one of these parts, for his just height also. Tenia, above marked with *C.* as much to his height: this done, the pedestal, is 6 such parts in his whole height, like unto the pillar, which is 6 diameters in height as is before mentioned, the which measures be plainly showed in the middle pillar, which is your ground plot, wherein is found the height, breadth, and thickness and also the projectures of the whole work. Thus I conclude an end of the pedestal, with his measures.

Basis or Spira

Now upon the pedestal which is marked with an *A*. you shall let your base, or foot of the pillar, being in height half the thickness of the pillar, and that height ye shall divide into 2 parts. Give one part unto Plinthus which ought to be round, and is marked with this letter *D*. The second part give unto the height of Torus, marked with *E*. with apophigis, which Vitruvius calleth libmus. This projecture of this base shall stand out on either side of the pillar so much as the one compass is greater than the other, as is before rehearsed in making of the ground plot in the pedestal.

Scapus or Columna

Upon the foot of the pillar, directly and upright set scapus, whose mark is *F*., the which scapus is the body of the pillar and is 5 diameters in height, that is to say 5 times his thickness in height. The which thickness under at the lowest part of scapus you shall divide into 4 parts, whereof at the head of the scapus shall be 3. So shall the pillar under the capital be diminished the fourth part: whereas all the other pillars are diminished the sixth part. For the which pillar I have found or invented another way in the diminishing of it than is declared for the diminishing of other pillars, the which hereafter followeth. Divide the height of scapus into 3 parts. Upon the lower part standing on the base, make half a compass, as great as you may, being within the thickness of the pillar. Then draw down right the thickness of the pillar under the capital downwards upon the third part of the height of scapus, whereupon was made the half-compass, then shall those 2 lines make 2 crosses upon each side of the half-compass, one cross. Then measure from the cross downward even by the side of the half-compass, unto the strike under the half-compass, and divide it into six lines overthwart the half-compass and mark them also with 1,2,3,4,5,6 as you may plainly see in your ground plot. That done, take a pair of compasses and set the one foot of the compass in the middle of the pillar, under the capital, and the other point of the compass ye shall bring downward until ye come to the prick, where the half-compass was made with, let that point of the compass under the capital stand, and with the other point of the compass draw upward, compassing from the third part of the pillar unto the height of the pillar, that the one part of the compass be just as high as the other. Then have ye made the round side of your quadrant: the which line so drawn shall be divided into 6 parts: which parts ye shall draw overthwart the pillar, and mark them also from the capital downward with 1,2,3,4,5,6. Then shall ye begin after this manner and draw from the end of the strike within the half-compass, the which is marked with 2 upward unto the strike above marked 2, to the line above drawn overthwart the pillar, and also from the strike 3 drawn upward unto the strike above marked with 3, and so from 4 to 4 and from 5 to 5 and also from 6 to 6. The which lines lead downward perpendicularly. Then shall ye close up the side of the pillar, as I have closed the one side, and left the other open that you may see it and understand it the better. Then take a rule and draw from the smallest of the pillar, under the capital, drawing downward to the line 2, the which is drawn overthwart the pillar, and so draw from 2 downward unto 3 and also from 3 to 4, from 4 to 5, from 5 to 6. So have you diminished just the 2 third parts of the height of scapus. I say not that you should use justly no more but these 6 lines unto the diminishing of this pillar and these other pillars following, I do but show you by this briefness, the plain and true way: by the which way notwithstanding ye may occupy so many lines as shall be needful. The more in number, the perfecter shall the diminishing be. Now at the top of scapus, you shall make astragalus, and apophigis, marked with G. and shall be high the sixth part of the modulus, that is the twelfth part of the diameter. That part you shall divide into 3 parts, whereof give the two highest parts to astragalus, and the third unto his apophigis, also beneath at the food of scapus there is a square edge or apophigis inferior being in height so much as the height of astragalus, that standeth at the top of scapus, their projecture be like unto their heights.

Capital or Capituli

Upon the body or top of the pillar, the head or capituli shall be set, being in height one modulus, that is to say half a diameter, that height you shall divide into 3 parts, give the one part to hypotrachelium, marked with *H.* The second part ye shall divide into 4 parts. Three of them ye shall give to echinus, marked with *I.*, the fourth part give to annulus, also that part which remaineth give to plinthus which is the highest part whose mark is *K.*, the projecture or hanging over shall be so much as the pillar is diminished on each side, the which is correspondent to the thickness of scapus beneath. Thus writeth Sebastian Serlius, of the projecture of this capital. Nevertheless I have seen in some places in Italy that the projecture have been like to their height because the pillar is so much diminished, it should be therefore the more comely to have the greater projecture, and yet shall those two ways not differ much one from the other. But yet of these two ways let us take the most fair. I have also seen this pillar so placed that it hath been 7 diameters in height, whereas he supported no other pillars but his own trabiacions. So endeth the form and measures of the capitulum.

Epistilium

Upon the capital shall be laid or set epistilium, named also trabes called in our English tongue the architrave, the which is marked with *L.* and is a modulus in height. The which height ye shall divide into 6 parts whereof tenia, to be the sixth part, and the other 5 parts is for trabs. So done: upon the epistilium you shall set zophorus being also a modulus in height and is marked with *M.*, upon zophorus shall be set coronix being in height also a modulus, and that height you shall divide into 4 parts, give one part unto cimatium under corona marked with *N.*, but the other side of it is called tenia, and give likewise 2 parts unto corona marked with *O.*, and the fourth part which remaineth give unto cimatium over corona which is marked with *P.* In corona ye shall make denticulos, the which are made like teeth and their projectures shall be like unto their heights, saving only corona which hangeth his height and half his height over. And thus endeth the measures of the pillar called Tuscana. Now ye shall understand that the pillar which standeth in the middle is your ground plot, but the other which standeth by him is made upon the selfsame measure but that it is otherwise garnished, which garnishments bring other measures for them. And as touching this pillar, I shall begin from the lowest part of the pedestal being tenia inferior, dividing his height into 8 parts. Give 3 parts unto plinthus and 4 parts give also to sima reversa, and the eighth part remaineth for the small edge upon sima, upon the which is set the body of the pedestal; also the upper tenia, ye shall divide his height into 5 parts, give 2 parts unto hypotrachelium, and also 2 parts unto cimatium, and the fifth part give unto his edge at the top of the pedestal, now basis or base belonging to the said pillar is the height of a modulus, or half the thickness of the pillar whose height ye shall divide into 2 parts. Give plinthus one part and the second part divide you into 3 parts. Give 2 parts unto torus, and the third part divide also into 3 parts. Give 2 parts to sima and the third part ye shall give the edge under sima. So endeth the measures of the basis or base, upon the which base shall be set scapus, or the body of the pillar, made after the manner and order as before is mentioned upon the which shall be set the capital; the one capital is like to the other saving that it hath upon echinus a little edge which setteth forth plinthus with a more beautiful projecture. As concerning the architrave or epistilium, that is as before rehearsed a modulus in height, which height ye shall divide into 6 parts. Tenia occupieth the sixth part, the other 5 parts ye shall divide into 2 parts. Give one part unto the half of trochilus, the other part is left for the flat square that resteth upon the capital and so endeth the epistilium. Now as touching the frieze or zophorus, being also a modulus in height, as is before rehearsed of the other, is like unto it but that this swelleth outward the fourth part of a round compass, that is drawn above a square being the height and breadth of a modulus wherewith endeth zophorus, upon the which shall be set coronix, the one side is like unto the other in the measures, but that in this side cymatium is set under corona, and upon the other side tenia is set under corona, being of one height. This done and finished according to this rule, so endeth the measures and garnishment of the first pillar called Tuscana.

Now for as much as that you have understanding how all the parts of this pillar, and the rest of the pillars that shall be, hath their measures, ornatures, and names, finished out of ichnographia or ground plot upwards to the very top of the same work, wherefore I thought it good for the more perfection and exercises of the gentle reader to make a rehearsal of all the parts and parcels downward again ending in ichnographia where I began first. These be the names Trabeationis, Cymatium mar. P., Corona mar. O., Tenia mar. N., Zophorus mar. M., Tenia in epistilium mar. L., Capituli. Plinthus mar. K., Echinus et Annullus mar. I.,

Hypotrachelium mar. H., Columna mar. F., Astragalus mar. G., Apophiges superior and inferior Spira five Basis. Torus mar. E., Plinthus mar. D., Stylobatae. Tenia pro Coronice mar. C., Tenia pro Basis mar B., Ichnographia mar. A. being the perfect square or ground plot the beginning and foundation of this work.

Of another authentic pillar and a necessary companion to the before-named pillars made by the Athenians to his perfection named Atticurga.

Of this pillar Plinius maketh rehearsal and as he saith is a corner pillar, being four square, whose diameter marked with *A.* (saith he) is like unto the round pillars, which he standeth by, but in the diagonal line marked *B.* he is thicker than the round pillars. It is that pillar which Vitruvius nameth Atticurga or Attica, made by the Athenians, the which nation used also the measures of Corinthia in their pillars. So that the capital of this foresaid pillar is much like to the capital of Corinthia. The spira, or base of the said Attica, wherewith also they used to garnish Corinthia, Vitruvius also witnesseth of such a pillar, declaring and saith that spira Attica should be like unto spira or base Ionica. Thus have you all the manner and measures of pillars that any notable masters of architecture or authors thereof have written. As in order do follow. Tuscana containeth in height 6 diameters, Dorica 7 diameters in height, Ionica 8 diameters in height, Corinthia 9 diameters in height, and Composita containeth 10 diameters in height. Now of this foresaid pillar Atticurga, I find no mention made of his height. But of the multitude of his canaliculi, which be 7 on either side of the pillar. And as touching his height, whereof no mention is made, it is to be thought that he must bear such height as the rest of the pillars, for Vitruvius saith that the highest pillar passeth not 10 diameters in height so that his height may be agreeable to the height of those round pillars that are joined with him, whether they be Composita or Corinthia, which I myself have seen in Rome in the arch triumphant of Severus, being joined with Composita, also in Pantheon where his three sides plainly are seen, the fourth standing in the wall, the capital and base is like to the round pillars wherewith he standeth, being Corinthia. The projecture of his base was like unto spira Attica, the which is half a modulus on either side of the base, the which Vitruvius more plainly at large declareth.

The change of the five pillars orderly to be used each of them in his
kind which order of buildings be named of Vitruvius as followeth
Picnostylos, Sistylos, Diastylos, Ariostylos, Eustylos, whose
pictures ensueth demonstrated in order.

Now forsomuch as I have rehearsed the beginning and the institution
of this art of architecture, naming the writers and authors of the said
science, and declared the measures geometrical thereto belonging in
their symmetries, with all their garnishments: it is therefore also requisite
to rehearse and to let you understand by what means the order of the
before-named pillars shall be altered in their standing, adding, or abating
to and fro, every of them accordingly as they shall be placed, by which
knowledge or like knowledges many may come to the right perfection;
upon which occasion it shall be declared what mention Vitruvius doth
make in the third book and second chapter and also the opinion of Sebastianus Serlius and others upon the same, how far and how near the pillars
shall be set asunder: saying that this order of picnostylos ought thus to
be made, that which is the space between the 2 pillars shall be a diameter
and a half the pillar being in height 10 diameters. Sistylos is that which
hath 2 diameters betwixt the 2 pillars, whose height shall be 9 diameters
and a half. Diastylos shall thus be made, the pillars shall stand 3 diameters
one from another, whose height shall be 8 diameters and a half. Ariostylos
is that which hath the space or breadth between the pillars 4, 5, or 6
diameters, and at the furthest 7 diameters, the which pillars commonly
are 8 diameters in height: but in the eustylos the authors differ. The one
saith that his measure is like diastyli, and the other saith that it ought
to be like sistyli, and so because diastyli is 8 diameters and a half and
sistyli 9 and a half, therefore our author hath made between them both
an uniformity and causeth eustylos to be 9 diameters in height. This
done, areostyli is 8 diameters in height, diastyli 8 diameters and a half,
eustylos 9 diameters, sistyli 9 and a half, and picnostyli 10 diameters.
Now like as Tuscana, Dorica, Ionica, Corinthia, and Composita increase their heights by diameters, so do these 5 here before rehearsed
increase their heights by modulus or half-diameters, and you shall also
garnish and fashion them according to their lengths, as I have by their
length showed before their similitude and strength, which you shall see
and perceive more plainly in the demonstrations following.

Areostylos

Beginning with this first being areostylos, as Cesarianus saith, ought to be in height 8 diameters, and the distance between the 2 pillars to be 4, 5, or 6 diameters as is before rehearsed, which pillar for his strength is likened or to be sembled unto Tuscana necessary for all foundations and fortifications both to withstand great force, and support weighty burdens, as the master builder can use him, which is to be seen in divers places in Italy, calling it rustic or rough-hewed stone, and in other places to be otherwise garnished.

Diastylos

The second order as I have placed it, is that which Vitruvius calleth diastylos, whose height (saith he) is: 8 diameters and a half, and the distance between the 2 pillars ought to be 3 diameters or 4 at the furthest, which pillar is likened unto Dorica made to his perfection in the temple of Mars which also is a pillar to garnish cities and gates, somewhat pleasant and strong as is to be seen in divers places as also gates of palaces with the outer galleries.

Eustylos

The third order is that which Vitruvius calleth eustylos, the which our author hath brought to a uniformity, saying the pillar to be in height 9 diameters, and the distance between the 2 pillars to be 2 diameters and a quarter, as Gulielme Philander affirmeth, but at the furthest 2 diameters and a half or 3, which pillar is likened unto Ionica builded to his perfection in the temple of Diana and Apollo and to be used in many mean edifices to be garnished accordingly.

Sistylos

The fourth order is that which Vitruvius calleth sistylos, whose height (saith he) is 9 diameters and a half, whose pillars standeth distant one from the other 2 diameters, or 2 and a half at the furthest, and after this manner it was made in the temple of Fortune, which pillar is likened unto Corinthia, whose measures are slender and serveth to garnish princes' palaces and for divers other things necessary which multitude needeth not to be rehearsed, but as time shall serve they may be practised and brought in use to divers uses most necessary.

Picnostylos

The first and last order is that which Vitruvius calleth picnostylos whose height (saith he) is 10 diameters, whose pillars standeth distant from each other a diameter and a half or 2 at the furthest, and thus was it made in the temple of Venus which pillar is sembled or to be compared unto Composita, having in it the full beauty of all the foresaid measures and garnishments, for all excellent artificers beautifully to set forth whether it be in gold or silver or other rich stone or fine woods, in marketry or embossing or carving as shall be thought pleasant and necessary for noble and mighty princes or for divers other estates, lovers of excellency or cunning.

Another rule given by Vitruvius for these three orders
of pillars Dorica, Ionica, Corinthia, to be
used as followeth.

Now if you will begin with the order of Dorica, you shall divide his height with the base and capital into 15 parts, one of those parts shall be the height of the base and as much unto the height of the capital, which shall be the modulus of the work. If it shall be the order of Ionica, you shall divide the height of scapus, with the base and capital into 8 parts and a half, and one of those parts shall be the diameter of the whole work, whose base shall be a modulus in height, his capital shall be as before is rehearsed in Ionica. Also if you will make an order of Corinthia, ye shall make it as I have now rehearsed of this last pillar, saving only that in the stead of the capital of Ionica ye shall set the capital of Corinthia, which is a diameter in height. Now ye shall understand that Vitruvius doth not will Dorica, Ionica, and Corinthia to stand one upon another, but he willeth the edifice to be all of Dorica, or else all of Ionica, or all of Corinthia, and they to stand one upon another, always diminishing, so that the higher they stand, the lesser or slenderer they must be, for, as he saith, a tree is nowhere so great, as at the ground, and so groweth smaller and smaller upward unto the top. Likewise he willeth the lowest pillar to be strongest made upon the measure, as before is said, and the second pillar that standeth over him both in height and breadth shall diminish his fourth part. And his architrave, frieze, or cornice shall be in height the fifth part of the height of that pillar, and so setting the one upon the other, diminishing after this said order. Some of the antiques aforesaid have observed these orders and measures, as Sebastianus doth witness in his third book and fourth chapter that there are many edifices of the antiques wherein all the orders of these pillars have been set one upon another: garnishing them accordingly as it is yet to be seen in the Amphitiatrum named Colliseum in Rome whose excellent and praiseworthy doing shall be more plainly set forth hereafter.

Here is another necessary rule appointed of Vitruvius
for the diminishing of scapus, under the capital
by the increasing of his height.

Vitruvius, in his third book and third chapter, saith thus: if scapus amount in height from 15 foot unto 20, the diameter is to be divided into 6 parts and a half, and the thickness of the pillar under the capital shall be 5 and a half. And if scapus amount from 20 unto 30 foot, then shall the diameter be divided into 7 parts, whereof 6 parts shall be the thickness of the pillar under the capital, and so augmenting and diminishing after this order until scapus, if it were possible, should amount to the number of 110 foot which is the end of this table that standeth here beside wherein ye may perceive in every 10 foot increasing in height doth show the thickness of scapus under the capital, so that the 110 foot in height of scapus, the diameter to be divided into 11 parts, then shall be the thickness of scapus, under the capital 10 of those 11 parts, and so forth if need shall require.

Another example to be observed very necessary for the
master builder or architect that is for the enlarg-
ing of the epistilium, when the pillar amounteth
to certain heights.

Vitruvius in the latter end of his third book declaring when the pillar, that is to say base, scapus, and capital, amounteth from 15 foot to 20 foot in height, then shall the height of the whole pillar be divided into 13 parts, on such a part shall be the height of the epistilium, also if the pillar do increase from 20 to 25 foot then shall the pillar be divided into 12 parts and a half whereof the height of the epistilium shall occupy one such part, also if the pillar surmount from 25 to 30 foot the height of the pillar must be divided into 12 parts, whereof the height of the epistilium shall occupy one such part, and so forth as the column increaseth in height so increaseth the height of epistilium, as in this table is evidently discussed the increasing from 15 to 60 foot increased by 5 at once, the which pillar of 60 foot in height shall be divided into 9 parts whereof the epistilium occupieth for his height one such part, and so passing forward as necessity shall require in order as before mentioned.

There be also divers other orders of measures and example that the antiques always used in their times, which should be too tedious for the hearer, and too long for the reader, having no figures out of the which springeth both desire and also encouragement to the same. Thus ending this treatise of the introduction and measures of these foresaid pillars, which are the original first grounds and entering into this noble science of architecture, practised and allowed by right mighty and worthy potentates, and emperors for perpetual memory of their victorious and triumphant feats, the elegance thereof, of all antiquity hath been and yet presently is as a perfect example and a mirror to behold, learn and take true measures, as well to all such as delight in durable edifices and buildings, as also to all noble personages and architectures, which do or shall take pleasure to erect and build the like to any beauty and perfection according to the device and minds of the foresaid authors, Vitruvius, and Sebastianus Serlius, to whom, undoubtedly, the praise and commendation is chiefly to be attributed and given. I submit my travail unto all other that in any part be or shall be of more perfect and deeper learning, knowledge, and experience, and of like well willing affection, wherewith I do offer this my poor attempts and final travails.

CONJURATIONS, ENCHANTMENTS, AND WITCHCRAFTS.

1563—1579—1585

THE history of witchcraft as a secular crime may be begun with the act of 1563 against conjurations, enchantments, and witchcrafts. This statute was introduced in the 1559 parliament, where it reached the engrossing stage, but was not enacted until the next parliament. A similar act had been passed in 1542, but it had been repealed under Edward VI, and the Elizabethan agitation against indulgers in the occult seems to have sprung up afresh.

On the continent at this time the mania of witch-persecution was rife. From the Rhineland and Switzerland came back to England many Marian exiles who had been exposed to the propaganda of the protestant reformers against witches. Specifically, John Jewel, Elizabeth's new bishop of Salisbury, who had visited Frankfort, Strasburg, and Zurich, preached a sermon denouncing witches before the queen in 1559–60. His formal cry of alarm against the cult declared:

> This kind of people (I mean witches and sorcerers) within these few last years are marvellously increased within this your grace's realm. These eyes have seen most evident and manifest marks of their wickedness. Your grace's subjects pine away even unto death, their colour fadeth, their flesh rotteth, their speech is benumbed, their senses are bereft. Wherefore your poor subjects' most humble petition unto your highness is that the laws touching such malefactors may be put in due execution.

This sermon, the church-historian Strype alleged, brought about the law enacted in 1563 to suppress this social and spiritual danger.

But the government had yet another reason to check the superstition. In 1561 it was found, in disclosing a conspiracy to proclaim Mary Stuart queen of England, that two conjurers had prophesied Elizabeth's death. The numerous real and imagined plots against Elizabeth made her councillors peculiarly sensitive to even the most fantastic rumours. To assure royal security the state stepped in to stop superstitious activities tending towards social disturbances.

However, after the death of Mary Stuart, a decline in persecution set in. Two-thirds of the executions took place early in Elizabeth's reign. The leniency of the courts after 1587 suggests the political motive for persecution to have been genuine. The publication of chap-books, following a notorious or sensational trial for witchcraft, fostered the mania for persecution. These pamphlets were brought out like modern newspaper extras ' to catch the public before the sensation had lost its flavour,' and they were generally of a partisan character defending the judge rendering the decision. In them may be found details ' that give many glimpses into the everyday life of the lower classes in town and country.' [1]

The first pamphlet here printed describes the case of Elizabeth Francis in 1579. The

1. Wallace Notestein, *A History of Witchcraft in England, 1558–1718.*

woman had been accused, along with others, in 1566 but had escaped conviction. Her second trial proves a continuity of the witchcraft movement at Chelmsford, and the same Essex village suffered a third alarm in 1589 when three more executions took place. The proximity of Chelmsford to London, the centre of the belief in witchcraft, may account for the consistency of the public mania. The later trials are marked by an elaboration of judicial procedure and an increase in the variety of the testimony produced. The trials described in these two chap-books show that the charges of witchcraft were brought against members of the lower social orders—persons on poor relief, whores, and the mothers of bastards. The personal insignificance, and perhaps social obnoxiousness, of many of the victims suggests a rationalization of social sins into the occult by the respectable citizenry. The commonplace character of the charges themselves is paralleled by the similar charges brought against witches in Germany at this time as described in the Fugger News Letters.

The Act of 1563 is taken from the *Statutes of the Realm* and has not been abridged. The two chap-books are from the private collection of Mr. Wallace Notestein, and that of 1585 he believes to be a unique copy. Both have been transcribed *in toto* and no alteration save in spelling and punctuation has been made.

STATUTES OF THE REALM
5 Elizabeth, A.D. 1563

Chapter XVI
An Act Against Conjurations, Enchantments, and Witchcrafts

WHERE at this present, there is no ordinary nor condign punishment provided against the practisers of the wicked offences of conjurations and invocations of evil spirits, and of sorceries, enchantments, charms, and witchcrafts, the which offences by force of a statute made in the 33 year of the reign of the late King Henry the eighth were made to be felony, and so continued until the said statute was repealed by the act and statute of repeal made in the first year of the reign of the late King Edward the sixth; since the repeal whereof many fantastical and devilish persons have devised and practised invocations and conjurations of evil and wicked spirits, and have used and practised witchcrafts, enchantments, charms, and sorceries, to the destruction of the persons and goods of their neighbours and other subjects of this realm, and for other lewd intents and purposes contrary to the laws of almighty God, to the peril of their own souls, and to the great infamy and disquietness of this realm: for reformation whereof be it enacted by the queen's majesty with the assent of the lords spiritual and temporal and the commons in this present parliament assembled, and by the authority of the same, that if any person or persons after the first day of June next coming, use, practise, or exercise any invocations or conjurations of evil and wicked spirits, to or for any intent or purpose; or else if any person or persons after the said first day of June shall use, practise, or exercise any witchcraft, enchantment, charm, or sorcery, whereby any person shall happen to be killed or destroyed, that then as well every such offender or offenders in invocations or conjurations as is aforesaid, their counsellors and aiders, as also every such offender or offenders in witchcraft, enchantment, charm, or sorcery whereby the death of any person doth ensue, their aiders and counsellors, being of either of the said offences lawfully convicted and attainted, shall suffer pains of death as a felon or felons, and shall lose the privilege and benefit of sanctuary and clergy: saving to the wife of such person her title of dower, and also to the heir and successor of such person his or their titles of inheritance, succession, and other rights, as though no such attainder of the ancestor or predecessor had been had or made.

PENALTY ON PRACTISING WITCHCRAFT, ETC., TO THE BODILY HARM OF ANY ONE; FIRST OFFENCE, ONE YEAR'S IMPRISONMENT AND PILLORY; SECOND OFFENCE, FELONY WITHOUT CLERGY.

And further be it enacted by the authority aforesaid, that if any person or persons, after the said first day of June next coming, shall use, practise, or exercise any witchcraft, enchantment, charm, or sorcery, whereby any person shall happen to be wasted, consumed, or lamed in his or her body or member, or whereby any goods or cattles of any person shall be destroyed, wasted, or impaired, then every such offender or offenders their counsellors and aiders, being thereof lawfully convicted, shall for his or their first offence or offences, suffer imprisonment by the space of one whole year, without bail or mainprise, and once in every quarter of the said year, shall in some market town, upon the market day or at such time as any fair shall be kept there, stand openly upon the pillory by the space of six hours, and there shall openly confess his or her error and offence; and for the second offence, being as is aforesaid lawfully convicted or attainted, shall suffer death as a felon, and shall lose the privilege of clergy and sanctuary: saving to the wife of such person her title of dower, and also to the heir and successor of such person, his or their titles of inheritance, succession, and other rights, as though no such attainder of the ancestor or predecessor had been had or made.

PEERS SHALL BE TRIED BY PEERS.

Provided always, that if the offender, in any of the cases aforesaid for which the pains of death shall ensue, shall happen to be a peer of this realm, then his trial therein to be had by his peers, as it is used in cases of felony or treason and not otherwise.

PENALTY ON PRACTISING WITCHCRAFT, ETC., TO DISCOVER TREASURE, OR TO PROVOKE UNLAWFUL LOVE, ETC., FIRST OFFENCE, ONE YEAR'S IMPRISONMENT AND PILLORY; SECOND OFFENCE, FORFEITURE OF GOODS AND IMPRISONMENT FOR LIFE.

And further to the intent that all manner of practise, use, or exercise of witchcraft, enchantment, charm, or sorcery should be from henceforth utterly avoided, abolished, and taken away; be it enacted by the authority of this present parliament, that if any person or persons shall from and after the said first day of June next coming, take upon him or them, by witchcraft, enchantment, charm, or sorcery, to tell or declare in what place any treasure of gold or silver should or might be found or had in the earth or other secret places, or where goods or things lost or stolen should be found or become, or shall use or practise any sorcery, enchantment, charm, or witchcraft, to the intent to provoke any person to unlawful love, or to hurt or destroy any person in his or her body, member, or goods; that then every such person or persons so offending, and being thereof lawfully convicted, shall for the said offence suffer imprisonment by the space of one whole year without bail or mainprise, and once in every quarter of the said year shall in some market town, upon the market day or at such time as any fair shall be kept there, stand openly upon the pillory by the space of six hours, and there shall openly confess his or her error and offence; and if any person or persons, being once convicted of the same offences as is aforesaid, do eftsoons perpetrate and commit the like offence, that then every such offender being thereof the second time convicted as is aforesaid, shall forfeit unto the queen's majesty her heirs and successors, all his goods and chattels and suffer imprisonment during life.

A DETECTION OF DAMNABLE DRIFTS

Practised by three witches arraigned at Chelmsford in Essex, at the last assises there holden, which were executed in April 1579.

To the reader.

Accept this pamphlet (Christian reader) view, and peruse it with discretion, and heedfulness. No trifles are therein contained worthy to be contained, nor pernicious fantasies deserving to be condemned. But contrariwise in this pretty plot may wholesome herbs of admonitions for the unwary, and careless, and sweet flowers to recreate the wearied senses, be gathered. For on the one side the clear sight may espy the ambushments which Satan, the secret workmaster of wicked drifts, hath placed in most parts of this realm, either by crafty conveyances to creep into the conceits of the simple, or by apparent treachery to undermine and spoil the states of such as God permitteth him to have power over. And on the other side the eye that is wimpled may hereby be advertised of the darkness wherewith his understanding is overcast, and putting off the veil of vanity, may reclaim his concept, and esteem of the impiety of the offenders and villainy of their acts, according to the word of God, and weightiness of the case. And if in time past he hath escaped their sorceries, let him not the less fear the harms that may hereafter ensue. For the Devil by the sufferance of almighty God is as well able to plague the person that most presumeth of safety, as any have been who in this treatise are mentioned. Some with much ado can be awaked out of their drowsy dreams, though they be told that their neighbour's house is on fire. But when their own walls are invaded with like flames, they shall find that it had been better to have come an hour too soon, to quench those foreign fires, than to have risen one minute too late to extinguish the same creeping into their own chambers. If therefore thou be assured that thy neighbour, either in body, family, or goods, is impaired by damnable witchcraft, or perceivest by information or otherwise aught of such devices intended to be practised, or likely presumption of such devilish deeds contrived, for charity to thy Christian brother, and tender regard of thine own state, prevent or stop the mischief by all possible means. And for thine own part with prayer, and assured faith in the merits of Christ Jesus shield thyself, so shall neither the Devil nor his angels have power, over thee or thine.

Farewell.

The Confession of Elizabeth Frances, late of Hatfield in Essex.

Imprimis, the said Elizabeth Frances confessed that about Lent last (as she now remembereth) she came to one Poole's wife, her neighbour, and required some old yeast of her, but being denied the same, she departed towards one goodwife Osborne's house, a neighbour dwelling thereby, of whom she had yeast, and in her way going towards the said goodwife Osborne's house, she cursed Poole's wife and bade a mischief to light upon her, for that she would give her no yeast; whereupon suddenly in the way she heard a great noise, and presently there appeared unto her a spirit of a white colour in seeming like to a little rugged dog, standing near her upon the ground, who asked her whither she went? She answered for such things as she wanted, and she told him therewith that she could get no yeast of Poole's wife and therefore willed the same spirit to go to her and plague her, which the spirit promised to do, but first he had her give him somewhat, then she having in her hand a crust of white bread, did bite a piece thereof and threw it upon the ground, which she thinketh he took up and so went his way, but before he departed from her she willed him to plague Poole's wife in the head, and since then she never saw him, but she hath heard by her neighbours that the same Poole's wife was grievously pained in her head not long after, and remaineth very sore pained still, for on Saturday last past this examinate talked with her.

2. Item, this Elizabeth Frances saith further, that she knoweth one Elizabeth Lord, a widow, dwelling in the same parish of Hatfield and so hath done of long time, of whom she heard, that about seven or eight years past she brought drink in a cruse, and gave it to one John Frances, servant to goodman Some of the same parish, shortly after the taking of which drink he sickened and died.

3. Item, she further confesseth that she likewise knoweth that the same Widow Lord, was said to have bewitched one Joan Roberts, servant to old Higham, in a piece of an apple-cake which she gave her, upon the eating whereof she presently sickened and not long after died.

4. Item, she also confesseth that she knows one Mother Osborne, a widow in the same town, to be a witch, and that she hath a mark in the end of one of her fingers like a pit, and another mark upon the outside of her right leg, which she thinketh to be pluckt out by her spirit: and that one Mother Waterhouse, her own sister (long since executed for witchcraft), had the selfsame marks, which she termeth (nips) and she saith that this Mother Osborne lying lame and complaining of her sore leg, she, the said Elizabeth Frances, came unto her and required to see her leg, which being showed unto her, she, the said Elizabeth, had to put it into the bed again, saying: that she herself knew that the same came by want of well serving of God. And thus much for Elizabeth Frances.

The Evidence given against Ellen Smith of Maldon.

There was one John Chaundeler dwelling in Maldon, whose wife, named Alice Chaundeler, was mother unto this Ellen Smith, and for witchcraft was executed long before, after whose execution he went unto his daughter-in-law Ellen Smith, and demanded certain money of her, which she had received of her mother his wife, by means of which money they fell out, and in falling out the said Ellen in great rage said unto him, that it had been better for him he had never fallen out with her, and so it came to pass; for the same John Chaundeler confessed before his death, that after the same hour that she had said so unto him, he never ate any meat that digested in him, but ever it came up again as soon as it was down, by which means he consumed, and wasted away to his death.

2. The son of the foresaid Ellen Smith, of the age of thirteen years, or thereabouts, came to the house of one John Eastwood of Maldon, for to beg an alms, who chid the boy away from his door, whereupon he went home and told his mother, and within a while after the said Eastwood was taken with very great pain in his body, and the same night following, as he sat by the fire with one of his neighbours, to their think-

ing they did see a rat run up the chimney, and presently it did fall down again in the likeness of a toad, and taking it up with the tongs, they thrust it into the fire, and so held it in forcibly; it made the fire burn as blue as azure, and the fire was almost out, and at the burning thereof the said Ellen Smith was in great pain and out of quiet, whereupon dissemblingly she came to the house of the foresaid John Eastwood, and asked how all that were there did, and he said well I thank God, and she said I thought you had not been well, and therefore I came to see how you did, and so went her way.

3. Also it was avouched, and by this prisoner confessed, that whereas her daughter, and the daughter of one Widow Webb of Maldon aforesaid, did fall out and fight, the same Ellen Smith offended thereat, meeting goodwife Webb's daughter the next day, gave her a blow on the face, whereupon so soon as the child came home she sickened, and languishing two days, cried continually, ' away with the witch, away with the witch,' and so died. And in the morning immediately after the death of the same child, the said goodwife Webb espied (as she thought) a thing like to a black dog go out at her door, and presently at the sight thereof she fell distraught of her wits.

4. Besides, the son of this Mother Smith confessed that his mother did keep three spirits, whereof the one called by her Great Dick was enclosed in a wicker bottle: the second named Little Dick was put into a leather bottle: and the third termed Willet she kept in a wool-pack. And thereupon the house was commanded to be searched. The bottles and pack were found, but the spirits were vanished away.

The effect of the evidence against Mother Staunton, late of Wimbish in Essex, who was arraigned, but not executed, for that no manslaughter or murder was objected against her.

Imprimis, this Mother Staunton, late of the parish of Wimbish in Essex, came to the house of one Thomas Pratt of Brokewalden, John Farrour of Liblebury being present, and one Thomas Swallow, and the said Mother Staunton, being demanded by one of them how she did, she answered, that a knave had beaten her, saying she was a witch; then said he again, in good faith Mother Staunton, I think you be no witch; no master, quoth she, I am none indeed, although I can tell what belongeth to that practise; of which words, the goodman of the house took witness of the aforenamed parties, and delivered a bill, subscribed with their hands thereof, to Master George Nichols.

2. Item, the said Mother Staunton came to his house another time, and after certain words of anger between him and her, he rased her face with a needle; what, quoth she, have you a flea there? And the next night after, the said Pratt was so grievously taken with torment of his limbs, that he never thought to have lived one hour longer, which also was subscribed and sent.

3. Item, she came the third time by his door with grains, and he demanding a few of her, she asked what he would do with them, I will give them, said he, to my chickens, and snatching a handful from her, did so. But after they had tasted of them, three or four dozen of them died, and only one chicken escaped of them all.

4. Item, she came on a time to the house of one Richard Saunder of Brokewalden, and being denied yeast, which she required of his wife, she went her way murmuring, as offended with her answer, and after her departure, her young child in the cradle was taken vehemently sick, in a marvellous strange manner, whereupon the mother of the child took it up in her arms to comfort it, which being done, the cradle rocked of itself, six or seven times, in presence of one of the earl of Surrey's gentlemen, who seeing it stabbed his dagger three or four times into the cradle ere it stayed: merrily jesting and saying, that he would kill the Devil, if he would be rocked there.

5. Item, the said Mother Staunton came on a time to the house of one Robert Petty of Brokewalden, and being denied by his wife divers things, which she demanded at once, and also charged with the stealing of a knife from thence, she went her way in great anger, and presently after her departure, the little child of the said Petty fell so strangely sick as for the space of a week, as nobody thought it would live.

6. Item, the said Staunton's wife came also to one William Torner's house of Brokewalden upon a Friday, as she had done often in times past, and being denied of certain things which she craved, as a piece of leather etc., she asked the goodwife how many children she had, who answered one, which child being then in perfect health, was presently taken with such a sweat and coldness of body, and fell into such shrieking

and staring, wringing and writhing of the body to and fro, that all that saw it, were doubtful of the life of it.

7. Item, she came on a time to the house of Robert Cornell of Suersem, and craved a bottle of milk of his wife, but being denied it, she departed for a little while, leaving her own bottle behind her, and took another with her that belonged to the aforesaid Cornell; after three days she came again, and requested her own bottle, and restored the other, craving milk as before; the wife of the house always suspecting her to be a witch denied her request, and barred the doors against her, whereupon she sat down upon her heels before the door, and made a circle upon the ground with a knife. After that she digged it full of holes within the compass, in the sight of the said wife, her man, and her maid, who demanding why she did so: she made answer, that she made a shiting house for herself after that sort, and so departed. The next day the wife coming out at the same door, was taken sick, and began to swell from time to time, as if she had been with child, by which swelling she came so great in body as she feared she should burst: and to this day is not restored to health.

Item, she came often to the house of one John Hopwood of Walden, and had continually her requests, at the last being denied of a leathern thong, she went her way offended and the same night his gelding in the stable, being the day before in very good case, died suddenly, and afterward being burdened with all, she never denied it.

Item, she coming to the house of John Cornell the younger of Wimbish, and being denied her demand, she took offence, and immediately after his cattle instead of sweet milk, yielded gore stinking blood, and one of his kine fell into such miserable plight that for a certain space he could by no means recover her.

Item, she came on a time to the vicar's house at Wimbish, and being denied her errand by his wife (he being as then from home) his little son in the nurse's lap was taken with such vehement sickness, that the beholders supposed no less, but it would straight have died, the said Mother Staunton sitting by, and having touched the child before it grew sick: but within one hour after the vicar came home the child recovered perfectly, and played as before.

Item, also she came on a time to the house of one Robert Lathbury, of the same town, who disliking her dealing, sent her home empty, but presently after her departure, his hogs fell sick and died, to the number of twenty, and in the end he burned one, whereby as he thinketh, he saved the rest: he also had a cow strangely cast into a narrow gripe, and being holpen out in the presence of Master Henry Mordaunt, notwithstanding the diligent care that was taken of her, she was in few days three times like to be lost in the mire. And thus much for Mother Staunton.

The effect of the evidence given in against Mother Nokes late of Lamberd parish in Essex.

A certain servant to Thomas Spicer of Lamberd End in Essex yeoman, sporting, and passing away the time in play with a great number of youth, chanced to snatch a pair of gloves out of the pocket of this Mother Nokes' daughter, being a young woman of the age of twenty-eight years, which he protesteth to have done in jest. Her mother perceiving it demanded the gloves of him, but he giving no great ear to her words departed towards the fields to fetch home certain cattle. Immediately upon his departure quoth the same Mother Nokes to her daughter, let him alone, I will bounce him well enough, at what time he being suddenly taken, and reft of his limbs fell down. There was a boy then in his company by whom he sent the gloves to Mother Nokes. Notwithstanding his master was fain to cause him to be set home in a wheelbarrow, and to be laid into a bed, where with his legs across he lay bedrid eight days, and as yet hath not attained to the right use of his limbs.

Further it was avouched that Mother Nokes had said that her husband lay with one tailor's wife of Lamberd End, and with reproachful words reviled her, saying at last; thou hast a nurse child but thou shalt not keep it long, and presently thereupon the child died.

Another affirmed that when he had reproved the said tailor's wife and Mother Nokes as they were at church, and willed them to agree better, the same Mother Nokes in a fume answereth that she cared for none of them all, as long as Tom held on her side, meaning her fiend.

The same man having a servant of his at plough, this Mother Nokes going by asked the fellow a question but getting no answer of him she went her way. Forthwith one of his horses fell down. At his coming home to dinner, he told his master how the same horse was swollen about the head. His master at first supposing that it came by a stripe, was greatly offended at the ploughman, but afterwards understanding of Mother Nokes going by, and the circumstance before mentioned, went to the said Mother Nokes and chid and threatened to have her to her answer. Howbeit the horse died.

Finis.

THE SEVERAL FACTS OF WITCHCRAFT

Approved and laid to the charge of Margaret Harkett, of the town of Stanmore, in the county of Middlesex, for the which she was arraigned and condemned at the session's house, before her majesty's justices the 17 of February, and executed for the same at Tyburn this 19 of February 1585.

On Wednesday being the seventh day of February last past Anno 1585, Margaret Harkett of the Town of Stanmore, in the County of Middlesex widow about threescore years of age, was arraigned, examined, found guilty and condemned at the Sessions of Gaol Delivery, for the City of London and Middlesex: at the Sessions house in the Old Bailey, where by the several oaths of sundry honest persons, these matters were proved, *videlicet*. That she came to a close in the same town of Stanmore, belonging to one Joan Frynde, whose pease being ripe and ready to gather, she (without the consent of the said Joan Frynde or any other household) did gather a basket full, and filled her apron also with the said pease, and when she was ready to depart, this Joan Frynde who owned the close came, and demanded why she did gather those pease without leave, wherefore she willed her to deliver her the pease that were in her basket, and those that were in her lap she would give her.

But this ungodly woman did fling the pease down on the ground, saying, if you make so much ado for a few pease, take them all, the next year I will have enough of my own, and you shall have few enough. So she cursed the same ground and stamped on it and went her ways, and never since that time that the woman could have any pease grow in her ground or any other corn would grow in the same place.

William Frynde's wife, of the said Town of Stanmore, brought home a child to nurse from Westminster where the parents dwelt: who brought

the child and showed it to her husband, but he said unless he knew the
parents of the child, he would not suffer her to keep it: this witch being
at her house the same time, owing her a grudge, said, what will you do
with a nurse child, you will but starve it, sure I will warrant you the
child shall not prosper: and the child shortly after did fall sick, and consumed to the death in most strange manner, so that in three weeks following the child died, and was consumed and parched like a green leaf that
had been hanged to dry in a chimney.

She came to the house of one William Goodwin of the same town
for the yeast, the servants denied that there was any in the house: notwithstanding, the stand was new filled, and the servants were loath to
take of the yeast. Whereat this witch said you shall have less, and so
went her ways, and the next day following, though none of the house
did draw out any drink out of the same stand, yet was it found dry without drink or yeast, except a few hard dried dregs.

She came thither also another time for oat-meal, and they would
give her none: and forthwith a lamb (which was kept in the same
house), being in the room where the witch was, fell down and died
presently.

She came into a gentleman's ground called Master Mashe of Stanmore,
where she was stealing of wood, and the bailie taking her with the manour,
made her to leave it behind her: and gave her two or three small blows
over the back not hurting her: whereat she said he should repent it, and so
she went her ways. Shortly after this bailie fell into a frenziness, so that
he became stark mad, being bound and chained in his bed: could get no
remedy, until it pleased God that this witch came home to his house,
and at his bedside she kneeled down and asked him forgiveness: whereat
he cried, away with the witch, break her neck downstairs, for she hath
bewitched me, and God be thanked was afterward restored to his health
and wits, and is now very well.

She came to one of her neighbours to borrow a horse, knowing him to
have four very good indifferent geldings, the worst worth four marks:
and he denied her thereof, but she said she would be even with him, and
shortly after all his four geldings were dead, and died suddenly one after
another.

She came to one John Frynde, of the age of twenty years, the son of
Thomas Frynde being of the same town, and offered him a pair of shoes

to sell, her price was ten pence, and he offered her six pence and would give her no more. Whereat she was sore vexed, because at that time she had need of money: this was in the latter end of summer, so the fellow thinking nothing, went to gathering of pears from off the tree, and upon a sudden fell down to the ground, and did hurt his cods with the said fall, so that he was constrained to keep in the house. But this witch did openly make report in the town, that he was burned with a whore, and that he came to her and desired to have his pleasure of her: which speeches came to the fellow's ear, who a quarter of a year after he was recovered did meet this witch in the town: where he asked why she gave out such lewd speeches of him, being most unjust, demanding of her, if ever he spake to her in any such sort, but she answered that he knew best: then he charged her that he thought his harm came by her means, I, said she, I have not done with thee yet: so he went about his business and being come home, he complained of his back and his belly, saying assuredly that he thought she had bewitched him: so his pain increased more and more, and he began to grow into a consumption, and wasted away like as the child before mentioned, like a parched or withered leaf, hanged up in the smoke of a chimney, and died three months after, and before he died his side did burst, and his guts and backbone was rotted in sunder, so that his guts and bowels being rotten did issue forth of his belly: and died hereof in most pitiful and grievous manner, the said party taking it upon his death, that her witchcraft and sorcery was the cause of his death.

After whose death the townsmen made complaint of her dealing to the justice, who commanded one Master Norwood, a gentleman in the town, to go search her house: this gentleman went thither and did search her house, yet desired the justice not to apprehend her, until there were some further trial made of her. But she promised for their searching, she would requite them shortly: and forthwith, the next morning one of the gentleman's best milch kine, which was worth four mark, being well over night, was found dead. The gentleman fearing some greater injury by her, did then command his servants that they should give her nothing if she came thither to crave anything, so within two days after she came for buttermilk, but they denied her thereof: and after that they could never make cheese or butter since.

Then was she apprehended and brought before the justice, by whom she was examined, and by him committed to the gaol of Newgate, where she remained until the sessions, held for gaol delivery of London and Middlesex: And then by twelve honest substantial men for the causes aforesaid, was found guilty and worthy of death: where she had judgment and was executed accordingly.

Finis.

DE REPUBLICA ANGLORUM.

The manner of government or policy of the realm of England, compiled by the honourable Sir Thomas Smith, knight, doctor of both the laws, and one of the principal secretaries unto the two most worthy princes, King Edward the sixth, and Queen Elizabeth. *Seen and allowed.* At London, printed by Henrie Midleton for Gregorie Seton, anno domini, 1583.

SIR THOMAS SMITH (1513–1577), physician, mathematician, astronomer, architect, historian, orator, councillor, member of parliament, ambassador, and gardener was a veritable Renaissance *uomo universale*. He studied law at Paris, Orleans, and Padua after attending the Saffron Walden grammar school and Queen's College, Cambridge, where he was a fellow in 1530 and became a master of arts in 1533. In 1544 he was appointed regius professor of civil law and vice-chancellor of the university. Two years later he was ordained a priest and in 1548 was made dean of Carlisle and provost of Eton. He also served as one of the two principal secretaries of state for Protector Somerset, but on the fall of Somerset's party he lost his office and was sent to the Tower.

There he aided Stephen Gardiner, bishop of Winchester, who was able to repay Smith for his political assistance during Mary's reign. Smith was a member of Mary's first parliament, but then retired to his studies and his architecture until returned again to parliament in 1559 when he served on the commission to revise the Prayer Book. From 1562 to 1566 he was English ambassador at Paris, and it was while in France that he wrote the *De Republica Anglorum*. In a letter from Bordeaux, dated 6 April 1565, to his friend Haddon, he wrote of the book:

> And because in my absence I feel a yearning for our commonwealth, I have put together three books here at Toulouse describing it, taking as the title *De Republica Anglorum*; and in these I have set forth almost the whole of its form, especially those points in which it differs from the others. But it differs in almost all; with the consequence that the work has grown larger than I expected. I have written it moreover in the language of our own country, in a style midway between the historical and the philosophical, giving it the shape in which I imagined that Aristotle wrote of the many Greek commonwealths books which are no longer extant. I have furnished fruitful argument for those who would debate after the fashion of philosophers on single topics and raise nice points as to justice and injustice, and whether what is held yonder in England as law be the better, or what is held here and in those regions which are administered in accordance with the Roman Law. For all things, almost, are different, and I have set them forth on both sides in rough general outline. 'Why not send the books to me?' (you say). 'I desire eagerly to see what you have done.' They still lie among the rough scrawls of my note-books; when they have been fully written out and given to the world in book-form, I shall send them to you. For you were accustomed to think (as the well-known writer puts it) that our trifles had some value. You will certainly say, if I mistake not, when you read them through, that I am not ill-versed in our country's institutions. But it needs

must be that in this brief essay there should be gaps, and a few points not filled in, because I brought with me not a single book and had no man of law to consult. Accordingly I have written only as much as was supplied by my memory, for the time being, of matters I had seen or read. Those parts that are imperfect I shall be able to complete at my leisure when I have returned home.[1]

Back in England in 1566, Smith promoted a colony at Ards, County Down, Ireland, over which he placed his illegitimate son, Thomas. With Cecil and Leicester, he formed the ' Society of the New Art '—the art of turning iron into copper. In 1571 he was made a privy councillor and the next year was sent to France to discuss Alençon's marriage to Elizabeth. On his return he was made a principal secretary of state and succeeded Cecil as chancellor of the Order of the Garter.

Although the *De Republica Anglorum* was not printed until 1583, eleven editions had been issued by 1690, and it was done into Dutch in 1673 and into German in 1688. The book is recommended by Beale in his treatise on the office of principal secretary (below p.382) and enjoyed considerable contemporary popularity. The chapters here printed are grouped together to describe crown and parliament and the structure of English society. They are taken from L.Alston's scholarly edition, the University Press, Cambridge, 1906. No abridgements within the chapters have been made save that indicated in c.8 of Book III, but in a few instances the variant readings supplied by the editor have been substituted for greater intelligibility.

BOOK I.

The first source or beginning of an house or family called οἰκονομία.

Chapter 11

THEN if this be a society, and consisteth only of freemen, the least part thereof must be of two. The naturalest and first conjunction of two toward the making of a further society of continuance is of the husband and of the wife after a diverse sort each having care of the family: the man to get, to travail abroad, to defend: the wife, to save that which is gotten, to tarry at home to distribute that which cometh of the husband's labour for the nurtriture of the children and family of them both, and to keep all at home neat and clean. So nature hath forged each part to his office, the man stern, strong, bold, adventurous, negligent of his beauty, and spending. The woman weak, fearful, fair, curious of her beauty, and saving. Either of them excelling other in wit and wisdom to conduct those things which appertain to their office, and therefore where their

1. L.Alston, Thomas Smith, *De Republica Anglorum,* pp.xiii–xiv.

wisdom doth excel, therein it is reason that each should govern. And without this society of man and woman, the kind of man could not long endure. And to this society men are so naturally born that the prince of all philosophers in consideration of natures was not afraid to say that a man by nature is rather desirous to fellow himself to another and so to live in couple, than to adherd himself with many. Although of all things or living creatures a man doth show himself most politic, yet can he not well live without the society and fellowship civil. He that can live alone, saith Aristotle, is either a wild beast in a man's likeness, or else a god rather than a man. So in the house and family is the first and most natural (but private) appearance of one of the best kinds of a commonwealth, that is called the Aristocracy where a few and the best do govern, and where not one always: but sometime and in some thing, one, and some-time and in some thing another doth bear the rule. Which to maintain for his part God hath given to the man great wit, bigger strength, and more courage to compel the woman to obey by reason or force, and to the woman beauty, fair countenance, and sweet words to make the man to obey her again for love. Thus each obeyeth and commandeth other, and they two together rule the house. The house I call here the man, the woman, their children, their servants bond and free, their cattle, their household stuff, and all other things which are reckoned in their possession, so long as all these remain together in one, yet this cannot be called Aristocracy, but metaphorical, for it is but an house, and a little spark resembling, as it were, that government.

The first and natural beginning of a kingdom, in Greek Βασιλεία.

Chapter 12

But for so much as it is the nature of all things to increase or decrease, this house thus increasing and multiplying by generation, so that it can-not well be comprehended in one habitation, and the children waxing bigger, stronger, wiser, and thereupon naturally desirous to rule, the father and mother sendeth them out in couples as it were by provining or propagation. And the child by marriage beginneth as it were to root towards the making of a new stock, and thereupon another house or family. So by this propagation or provining first of one, and then another, and so from one to another in space of time, of many houses was made a street or village, of many streets and villages joined together a city or borough. And when many cities, boroughs, and villages were by common and mutual consent for their conservation ruled by that one and first father of them all, it was called a nation or kingdom. And this seemeth the first and most natural beginning and source of cities, towns, nations, kingdoms, and of all civil societies. For so long as the great grandfather was alive and able to rule, it was unnatural for any of his sons or offspring to strive with him for the superiority, or to go about to govern or anywise to dishonour him from whom he had received life and being. And therefore such a one doth bear the first and natural example of an absolute and perfect king. For he loved them as his own children and nephews, cared for them as members of his own body, provided for them as one having by long time more experience than any one or all of them. They again honoured him as their father of whose body they came, obeyed him for his great wisdom and forecast, went to him in doubtful cases as to an oracle of God, feared his curse and malediction as proceeding from God's own mouth. He again used no rigour: for each pain put upon them, he esteemed as laid upon himself.

The first and natural beginning of the rule of a few of the best men called in Greek Ἀριστοκρατεία.

Chapter 13

But when that great grandfather was dead, the sons of him and brethren among themselves not having that reverence to any, nor confidence of wisdom in any one of them, nor that trust the one to the other, between whom (as many times it fareth with brethren) some strifes and brawlings had before arisen: to defend themselves yet from them which were walsh and strangers, necessarily agreed among themselves to consult in common, and to bear rule for a time in order, now one, now another: so that no one might bear always the rule, nor any one be neglected. And by this means if any one failed during his year or time by ignorance, the next (being either wiser of himself, or else by his brother's error and fault) amended it. And in the meanwhile, at divers and most times when urgent necessity did occur, they consulted all those heads of families together within themselves, how to demean and order their matters, best for the conservation of themselves, and each of their families, generally and particularly. Thus a few being heads and the chief of their families, equal in birth and nobility, and not much different in riches, governed their own houses and the descendants of them particularly, and consulted in common upon public causes, agreeing also upon certain laws and orders to be kept amongst them. So the best, chiefest, and sagest did rule, and the other part had no cause to strive with them, nor had no cause nor appearance to compare with any of them, neither for age nor discretion, nor for riches or nobility. The rulers sought each to keep and maintain their posterity, as their sons and nephews, and such as should succeed them and carry their names when they were dead, and so render them being mortal by nature immortal by their fame and succession of posterity: having most earnest care to maintain still this their cosinage and common family as well against foreign and barbarous nations, which were not of their progeny, tongue, or religion, as against wild and savage beasts. This seemeth the natural source and beginning or image of that rule of the fewer number, which is called of the Greeks Ἀριστοκρατεία and of the Latins *optimatum respublica*.

The first original or beginning of the rule of the multitude, called πολιτεία or Δημοκρατία.

Chapter 14

Now as time bringeth an end of all things, these brethren being all dead, and their offspring increasing daily to a great multitude, and the reverence due the old fathers in such and so great number of equals failing by the reason of the death or doting of the elders: each owing their merits of education apart to their fathers and grandfathers, and so many arising and such equality among them, it was not possible that they should be content to be governed by a few. For two things being such as for the which men in society and league do most strive, that is honour and profit, no man of free courage can be contented to be neglected therein, so that they were fain of necessity to come to that, that the more part should bear the price away in election of magistrates and rulers. So that either by course or by lot each man in turn might be received to bear rule and have his part of the honour, and (if any were) of the profit, which came by administration of the commonwealth. For whosoever came of that old great grandfather's race, he acounted himself as good of birth as any other. For service to the commonwealth all or such a number had done it, as they could not be accounted few. And if a few would take upon them to usurp over the rest, the rest conspiring together would soon be master over them, and ruinate them wholly. Whereupon necessarily it came to pass that the commonwealth must turn and alter as before from one to a few, so now from a few to many and the most part, each of these yet willing to save the politic body, to conserve the authority of their nation, to defend themselves against all other, their strife being only for empire and rule, and who should do best for the commonwealth, whereof they would have experience made by bearing office and being magistrates. This I take for the first and natural beginning of the rule of the multitude which the Greeks called Δημοκρατία: the Latins some *Respublica* by the general name, some *populi potestas*, some *census potestas*, I cannot tell how latinly.

That the common wealth or policy must be according to the nature of the people.

Chapter 15

By this process and discourse it doth appear that the mutations and changes of fashions of government in commonwealths be natural and do not always come of ambition or malice: and that according to the nature of the people, so the commonwealth is to it fit and proper. And as all these three kinds of commonwealths are natural, so when to each party or espece and kind of the people that is applied which best agreeth like a garment to the body or shoe to the foot, then the body politic is in quiet, and findeth ease, pleasure, and profit. But if a contrary form be given to a contrary manner of people, as when the shoe is too little or too great for the foot, it doth hurt and encumber the convenient use thereof, so the free people of nature tyrannized or ruled by one against their wills, were he never so good, either fail of courage and wax servile, or never rest until they either destroy their king and them that would subdue them, or be destroyed themselves. And again another sort there is which without being ruled by one prince but set at liberty cannot tell what they should do, but either through insolency, pride, and idleness will fall to robbery and all mischief, and to scatter and dissolve themselves, or with foolish ambition and private strife consume one another and bring themselves to nothing. Of both these two we have histories enough to bear witness, as the Greeks, Romans, Samnites, Danes, Vandals, and others. Yet must you not think that all commonwealths, administrations, and rulings began on this sort, by provining or propagation, as is before written, but many times after a great battle and long war the captain who led a multitude of people, gathered peradventure of divers nations and languages, liking the place which he hath by force conquered, tarrieth there and beginneth a commonwealth after this manner, and for the most part a kingdom. As the Goths and Lombards in Italy, the Frenchmen in Gaul, the Saracens in Spain and part of France, the Saxons in Great Britain, which is now called England: of which when that one and chief prince is dead, the nobler sort consult among themselves, and either choose another head and king, or divide it into more heads and rulers; so did the Lombards in Italy, and the Saxons in England; or take at the first a common rule and popular estate, as the Swiss did in their cantons and do yet at this day; or else admit the rule of a certain few, excluding the multitude and communalty, as the Paduans, Veronese, and Venetians have accustomed.

The division of the parts and persons of the commonwealth.

Chapter 16

To make all things yet clear before, as we shall go, there ariseth another division of the parts of the commonwealth. For it is not enough to say that it consisteth of a multitude of houses and families which make streets and villages, and the multitude of the streets and villages make towns, and the multitude of towns the realm, and that freemen be considered only in this behalf, as subjects and citizens of the commonwealth, and not bondmen who can bear no rule nor jurisdiction over freemen, as they who be taken but as instruments and the goods and possessions of others. In which consideration also we do reject women, as those whom nature hath made to keep home and to nourish their family and children, and not to meddle with matters abroad, nor to bear office in a city or commonwealth no more than children and infants: except it be in such cases as the authority is annexed to the blood and progeny, as the crown, a duchy, or an earldom for there the blood is respected, not the age nor the sex. Whereby an absolute queen, an absolute duchess or countess, those I call absolute which have the name, not by being married to a king, duke, or earl, but by being the true, right, and next successors in the dignity, and upon whom by right of the blood that title is descended: these I say have the same authority although they be women or children in that kingdom, duchy, or earldom, as they should have had if they had been men of full age. For the right and honour of the blood, and the quietness and surety of the realm, is more to be considered than either the tender age as yet impotent to rule, or the sex not accustomed (otherwise) to intermeddle with public affairs, being by common intendment understood, that such personages never do lack the counsel of such grave and discreet men as be able to supply all other defects. This (as I said) is not enough. But the division of these which be participant of the commonwealth is one way of them that bear office, the other of them that bear none: the first are called magistrates, the second private men. Another the like was among the Romans of *patricii* and *plebei*, the one striving with the other a long time, the *patricii* many years excluding the *plebei* from bearing rule, until at last all magistrates were made common between them: yet was there another division of the Romans into *senatores*, *equites*, and *plebs*: the Greeks had also εὐγενεῖς καὶ Δημαγτιχαις. The French have also at this day *les nobles* and *la populare*, or *gentils hommes* and *villaines*. We in England divide our men commonly into four sorts, gentlemen, citizens, yeoman artificers, and labourers. Of gentlemen the first and chief are the king, the prince, dukes, marquises, earls, viscounts, barons, and these are called κατ 'ἐξοχὴν the nobility, and all these are called lords and noblemen: next to these be knights, esquires, and simple gentlemen.

Of the first part of gentlemen of England called *nobilitas maior*.

Chapter 17

Dukes, marquises, earls, viscounts, and barons either be created by the prince or come to that honour by being the eldest sons, as highest and next in succession to their parents. For the eldest of duke's sons during his father's life is called an earl, an earl's son is called by the name of a viscount, a viscount's son a baron, or else according as the creation is. The creation I call the first donation and condition of the honour (given by the prince, for good service done by him and advancement that the prince will bestow upon him) which with the title of that honour is commonly (but not always) given to him and to his heirs, males only: the rest of the sons of the nobility by the rigour of the law be but esquires, yet in common speech, all dukes and marquises' sons, and the eldest son of an earl be called lords. The which name commonly doth agree to none of lower degree than barons, excepting such only as be thereunto by some special office called. The barony or degree of lords doth answer to the dignity of the senators of Rome, and the title of our nobility to their *patricii*; when *patricii* did betoken *senatores aut senatorum filios*. *Census senatorius* was in Rome at divers times divers, and in England no man is created baron, except he may dispend of yearly revenue one thousand pounds or one thousand marks at the least. Viscounts, earls, marquises, and dukes more according to the proportion of the degree and honour, but though by chance he or his son have less, he keepeth his degree: but if the decay be excessive, and they be not able to maintain the honour (as *senatores Romani* were *amoti senatu*) so sometimes they are not admitted to the upper house in the parliament, although they keep the name of lord still.

Of the second sort of gentlemen which may be called *nobilitas minor*, and first of knights.

Chapter 18

No man is a knight by succession, not the king or prince. And the name of prince in England κατ ᾽ἐξοχὴν betokeneth the king's eldest son or prince of Wales: although the king himself, his eldest son, and all dukes be called by general name princes. But as in France the king's eldest son hath the title of the dauphin, and he or the next heir apparent to the crown is monsire, so in England the king's eldest son is called κατ ᾽ἐξοχὴν the prince. Knights therefore be not born but made, either before the battle to encourage them the more to adventure their lives, or after the conflict, as advancement for their hardiness and manhood already showed: or out of the war for some great service done, or some good hope through the virtues which do appear in them. And they are made either by the king himself, or by his commission and royal authority given for the same purpose, or by his lieutenant in the wars, who hath his royal and absolute power committed to him for that time. And that order seemeth to answer in part to that which the Romans called *equites Romanos*, differing in some points, and agreeing in other, as their commonwealth and ours do differ and agree: for never in all points one commonwealth doth agree with another, no nor long time any one commonwealth with itself. For all changeth continually to more or less, and still to divers and diverse orders, as the diversity of times do present occasion, and the mutability of men's wits doth invent and essay new ways to reform and amend that wherein they do find fault. *Equites Romani* were chosen *ex censu*, that is, according to their substance and riches. So be knights in England most commonly, according to the yearly revenue of their lands being able to maintain that estate: yet all they that had *equestrem censum*, *non legebantur equites*. No more are all made knights in England that may spend a knight's land or fee, but they only whom the king will so honour. The number of *equites* was uncertain, and so it is of knights at the pleasure of the prince. *Equites Romani* had *equum publicum*. The knights of England have not so, but find their own horse themselves in peace time, and most usually in wars.

Census equester was among the Romans at divers times of diverse value: but in England whosoever may dispend of his free lands £40 sterling of yearly revenue by an old law of England either at the coronation of the king, or marriage of his daughter, or at the dubbing of the prince, knight, or some such great occasion, may be by the king compelled to take that order and honour or to pay a fine, which many not desirous of honour as of riches, had rather disburse. Some who for causes are not thought worthy of that honour and yet have ability, neither be made knights though they would, and yet pay the fine. £40 sterling at that time when this order began maketh now £120 of current money of England: as I have more at large declared in my book of the diversity of standards or the valour of moneys.

When the Romans did write *senatus populusque Romanus*, they seemed to make but two orders, that is of the senate and of the people of Rome, and so in the name of people they contained *equites* and *plebem*: so when we in England do say the lords and the commons, the knights, esquires, and other gentlemen, with citizens, burgesses, and yeomen be accounted to make the commons. In ordaining of laws the senate of lords of England is one house, where the archbishops and bishops also be, and the king or queen for the time being as chief: the knights and all the rest of the gentlemen, citizens, and burgesses which be admitted to consult upon the greatest affairs of the realm be in another house by themselves, and that is called the house of the commons, as we shall more clearly describe when we speak of the parliament. Whereupon this word knight is derived, and whether it do betoken no more but that which *miles* doth in Latin, which is a soldier, might be moved as a question. The word soldier now seemeth rather to come of sold and payment, and more to betoken a waged or hired man to fight than otherwise, yet Caesar in his *Commentaries* called *soldures* in the tongue *gallois* men who devoted and swore themselves in a certain band or oath, one to another and to the captain, which order if the Almains did follow, it may be that they who were not hired but being of the nation, upon their own charges and for their advancement, and by such common oath or band that did follow the wars, were (possibly) κατ'ἐξοχὴν called knights or *milites*, and now among the Almains some are called lanceknights as soldiers of their band not hired, although at this day they be for the most part hirelings. Or peradventure it may be that they which were next about the prince as his guard or servants, picked or chosen men out of the rest being called in the Almain language *knighten* which is as much to say as servants: these men being found of good service, the word afterward was taken for an honour, and for him who maketh profession of arms. Our language is so changed that I dare make no judgment thereof. Now we call him knight in English that the French calleth *chevalier*, and the Latin *equitem* or *equestris ordinis*.

And when any man is made a knight, he kneeling down is stroken of the prince, with his sword naked upon the back or shoulder, the prince saying: *sus* or *sois chevalier au nom de Dieu* and (in times past) they added *St. George*, and at his rising the prince saith, *avauncer*. This is the manner of dubbing of knights at this present. And that term dubbing was the old term in this point, and not creation. At the coronation of a king or queen, there be Knights of the Bath made with long and more curious ceremonies. But howsoever one be dubbed or made a knight, his wife is by and by called a lady as well as a baron's wife: he himself is not called lord, but hath to his name in common appellation added this syllable, sir, as if he were before named Thomas, William, John, or Richard, afterward he is always called Sir Thomas, Sir William, Sir John, Sir Richard, and that is the title which men give to knights in England. This may suffice at this time to declare the order of knight-hood, yet there is another order of knights in England which be called the Knights of the Garter. King Edward the third, after he had obtained many notable victories, King John of France, King James of Scotland, being both prisoners in the Tower of London at one time, and King Henry of Castile the bastard, expulsed out of his realm, and Don Petro restored unto it by the prince of Wales and duke of Aquitaine called the Black Prince, invented a society of honour, and made a choice out of his own realm and dominions, and all Christendom: and the best and most excellent, renowned persons in virtues and honour, he did adorn with that title to be knights of his order, gave them a garter decked with gold, pearl, and precious stones, with the buckle of gold, to wear daily on the left leg only, a kirtle, gown, cloak, chaperon, collar, and other august and magnifical apparel both of stuff and fashion exquisite and heroical, to wear at high feasts, as to so high and princely an order was meet: of which order he and his successors kings and queens of England to be the sovereign, and the rest by certain statutes and laws among themselves, be taken as brethren and fellows in that order, to the number of xxvi. But because this is rather an ornament of the realm than any policy or government thereof, I leave to speak any further of it.

Of Esquires.

Chapter 19

Escuier or esquier (which we call commonly squire) is a French word, and betokeneth *scutigerum* or *armigerum*, and be all those which bear arms (as we call them) or *armories* (as they term them in French) which to bear is a testimony of the nobility or race from whence they do come. These be taken for no distinct order of the commonwealth, but do go with the residue of the gentlemen: save that (as I take it) they be those who bear arms, testimonies (as I have said) of their race, and therefore have neither creation nor dubbing: or else they were at the first costerels or the bearers of the arms of lords or knights, and by that being taught in arms had that name for a dignity and honour given to distinguish them from a common soldier called in Latin *gregarius miles*.

Of Gentlemen.

Chapter 20

Gentlemen be those whom their blood and race doth make noble and known, Εὐγενεῖς in Greek, the Latins call them all *nobiles*, as the French *nobles*. Εὐγενεῖα or *nobilitas* in Latin is defined, honour or title given, for that the ancestor hath been notable in riches or virtues, or (in fewer words) old riches or prowess remaining in one stock. Which if the successors do keep and follow, they be *vere nobiles* and Εὐγενεῖς: if they do not, yet the fame and wealth of their ancestors serve to cover them so long as it can, as a thing once gilted though it be copper within, till the gilt be worn away. This hath his reason, for the etymology of the name serveth the efficacy of the word. *Gens* in Latin betokeneth the race and surname, so the Romans had *Cornelios, Sergios, Appios, Fabios, Aemilios, Pisones, Julios, Brutos, Valerios*, of which who were *Agnati*, and therefore kept the name, were also *gentiles*: and remaining the memory of the glory of their progenitors' fame, were gentlemen of that or that race. This matter made a great strife among the Romans, when those which were *novi homines* were more allowed, for their virtues new and newly shown, than the old stock of ancient race newly defaced by the cowardice and evil life of their nephews and descendants could make the other to be. Thus the *Cicerones, Catones*, and *Marii* had much ado with those ancients, and therefore said *Juvenalis*:

> *Malo pater tibi sit Tersites, dummodo tu sis*
> *Æacidi similis vulcaniaque arma capessas,*
> *Quam te Thersiti similem producat Achilles.*

But as other commonwealths were fain to do, so must all princes necessarily follow, that is, where virtue is to honour it: and although virtue of ancient race be easier to be obtained, as well by the example of the progenitors, which encourageth, as also through ability of education and bringing up, which enableth, and the lastly enraced love of tenants and neighbours to such noblemen and gentlemen, of whom they hold and by whom they do dwell, which pricketh forward to ensue in their fathers' steps. So if all this do fail (as it were great pity it should) yet such is the nature of all human things, and so the world is subject to mutability, that it doth many times fail: but when it doth, the prince and commonwealth have the same power that their predecessors had, and as the husbandman hath to plant a new tree where the old faileth, so hath the prince to honour virtue where he doth find it, to make gentlemen, esquires, knights, barons, earls, marquises, and dukes, where he seeth virtue able to bear that honour or merit, to deserve it, and so it hath always been used among us. But ordinarily the king doth only make knights and create barons or higher degrees: for as for gentlemen, they be made good cheap in England. For whosoever studieth the laws of the realm, who studieth in the universities, who professeth liberal sciences, and to be short, who can live idly and without manual labour, and will bear the port, charge, and countenance of a gentleman, he shall be called master, for that is the title which men give to esquires and other gentlemen, and shall be taken for a gentleman: for true it is with us as is said, *Tanti eris aliis quanti tibi fueris*: (and if need be) a king of heralds shall also give him, for money, arms newly made and invented, the title whereof shall pretend to have been found by the said herald in perusing and viewing of old registers, where his ancestors in times past had been recorded to bear the same: or if he will do it more truly and of better faith, he will write that for the merits of that man, and certain qualities which he doth see in him, and for sundry noble acts which he hath performed, he by the authority which he hath as king of heralds and arms giveth to him and his heirs these and these arms, which being done I think he may be called esquire, for he beareth ever after those arms. Such men are called sometime in scorn gentlemen of the first head.

Whether the manner of England in making gentlemen so easily is to be allowed.

Chapter 21

A man may make doubt and question whether this manner of making gentlemen is to be allowed or no, and for my part I am of that opinion that it is not amiss. For first the prince loseth nothing by it, as he should do if it were as in France: for the yeomen or husbandmen is no more subject to tail or tax in England than the gentleman: no, in every payment to the king the gentleman is more charged, which he beareth the gladlier and dareth not gainsay for to save and keep his honour and reputation. In any show or muster or other particular charge of the town where he is, he must open his purse wider and augment his portion above others, or else he doth diminish his reputation. As for their outward show, a gentleman (if he will be so accounted) must go like a gentleman, a yeoman like a yeoman, and a rascal like a rascal: and if he be called to the wars he must and will (whatsoever it cost him) array himself and arm him according to the vocation which he pretendeth: he must show also a more manly courage and tokens of better education, higher stomach, and bountifuller liberality than others, and keep about him idle servants, who shall do nothing but wait on him. So that no man hath hurt by it but he himself, who hereby perchance will bear a bigger sail than he is able to maintain. For as touching the policy and government of the commonwealth, it is not those that have to do with it, which will magnify themselves, and go in higher buskins than their estate will bear: but they which are to be appointed are persons tried and well known, as shall be declared hereafter.

Of Citizens and Burgesses.

Chapter 22

Next to gentlemen be appointed citizens and burgesses, such as not only be free and received as officers within the cities, but also be of some substance to bear the charges. But these citizens and burgesses be to serve the commonwealth in their cities and boroughs or in corporate towns where they dwell. Generally, in the shires they be of none account, save only in the common assembly of the realm to make laws, which is called the parliament. The ancient cities appoint four and each borough two to have voices in it, and to give their consent or dissent in the name of the city or borough for which they be appointed.

Of Yeomen.

Chapter 23

Those whom we call yeoman, next unto the nobility, knights, and squires, have the greatest charge and doings in the commonwealth, or rather are more travailed to serve in it than all the rest: as shall appear hereafter. I call him a yeoman whom our laws do call *legalem hominem*, a word familiar in writs and inquests, which is a freeman born English, and may dispend of his own free land in yearly revenue to the sum of 40s. sterling: this maketh (if the just value were taken now to the proportion of moneys) £6 of our current money at this present. This sort of people confess themselves to be no gentlemen, but give the honour to all which be or take upon themselves to be gentlemen, and yet they have a certain pre-eminence and more estimation than labourers and artificers, and commonly live wealthily, keep good houses, and do their business, and travail to acquire riches: these be (for the most part) farmers unto gentlemen, which with grazing, frequenting of markets, and keeping servants not idle as the gentleman doth, but such as get both their own living and part of their master's: by these means do come to such wealth, that they are able and daily do buy the lands of unthrifty gentlemen, and after setting their sons to the schools at the universities, to the laws of the realm, or otherwise leaving them sufficient lands whereon they may live without labour, do make their said sons by those means gentlemen. These be not called masters, for that (as I said) pertaineth to gentlemen only: but to their surnames men add goodman: as if the surname be *Luter*, *Finch*, *White*, *Brown*, they are called goodman *Luter*, goodman *White*, goodman *Finch*, goodman *Brown*, amongst their neighbours, I mean not in matters of importance or in law. But in matters of law and for distinction, if one were a knight they would write him (for example sake) Sir *John Finch* knight, so if he be an esquire, *John Finch* esquire, if he be not esquire, *John Finch* gentleman, if he be no gentleman, *John Finch* yeoman. For amongst the gentlemen they which claim no higher degree, and yet to be exempted out of the number of the lowest sort thereof, be written esquires. So amongst the husbandmen, labourers, lowest and rascal sort of the people such as be exempted out of the number of the rascability of the popular sort be called and written yeomen, as in the degree next unto gentlemen. These are they which old Cato calleth *aratores* and *optimos cives in republica*: and such as of whom the writers of commonwealths praise to have many in it. Aristoteles namely reciteth Πόμα μεσήτια ἄριστα: these tend their own business, come not to meddle in public matters and judgments but when they are called, and glad when they are delivered thereof, are obedient to the gentlemen and rulers, and in war can abide travail and labour as men used to it, yet wishing it soon at an end that they might come home and live of their own. When they are forth they fight for their lords of whom they hold their lands, for their wives and children, for their country and nation, for praise and honour against they come home, and to have the love of their lord and his children to be continued towards them and their children, which have adventured their lives to and with him and his. These are they which in the old world gat that honour to England, not that either for wit, conduction, or for power they are or were ever to be compared to the gentlemen, but because they be so many in number, so obedient at the lord's call, so strong of body, so hard to endure pain, so courageous to adventure with their lord or captain going with, or before them, for else they be not hasty nor never were, as making no profession of knowledge of war. These were the good archers in times past, and the stable troop of footmen that affaide all France, that would rather die all than once abandon the knight or gentleman their captain, who at those days commonly was their lord, and whose tenants they were, ready (besides perpetual shame) to be in danger of undoing of themselves and all theirs if they should show any sign of cowardice or abandon the lord, knight, or gentleman of whom they held their living. And this they have amongst them from their forefathers told one to another. The gentlemen of France and the yeomen of England are renowned, because in battle of horsemen France was many times too good for us, as we again alway for them on foot. And gentlemen, for the most part, be men at arms and horsemen, and yeomen commonly on foot: howsoever it was, yet the gentlemen had always the conduction of the yeomen, and as their captains were either afoot or upon a little nag with them, and the kings of England in foughten battles remaining always among the footmen, as the French kings amongst their horsemen. Each prince thereby, as a man may guess, did show where he thought his strength did consist. What a yeoman is I have declared, but from whence the word is derived it is hard to say: it cannot be thought that yeoman should be said as young men, for commonly we do not call any a yeoman till he be married and have children, and as it were have some authority among his neighbours. Yonker in low Dutch betokeneth a mean gentleman or gay fellow. Possibly our yeomen, not being so bold as to name themselves gentlemen when they came home, were content when they had heard by frequentation with low Dutchmen of some small gentleman (but yet that would be counted so) to be called amongst them yonker man, and the calling so in wars by mockage or in sport the one another when they came home yonker man, so yeoman: which word now signifieth among us a man well at ease and having honestly to live, and yet not a gentleman: whatsoever that word yonker man, yonke man, or yeoman doth more or less signify to the Dutch men.

Of the fourth sort of men which do not rule.

Chapter 24

The fourth sort or class amongst us is of those which the old Romans called *capite censii proletarii* or *operae*, day-labourers, poor husbandmen, yea merchants or retailers which have no free land, copyholders, and all artificers, as tailors, shoemakers, carpenters, brickmakers, bricklayers, masons, etc. These have no voice nor authority in our commonwealth, and no account is made of them but only to be ruled, not to rule other, and yet they be not altogether neglected. For in cities and corporate towns for default of yeomen, inquests and juries are impanelled of such manner of people. And in villages they be commonly made churchwardens, aleconners, and many times constables, which office toucheth more the commonwealth, and at the first was not employed upon such low and base persons. Wherefore, generally to speak of the commonwealth, or policy of England, it is governed, administered, and manured by three sorts of persons, the prince, monarch and head governor, which is called the king, or if the crown fall to a woman, the queen absolute, as I have heretofore said: in whose name and by whose authority all things are administered. The gentlemen, which be divided into two parts, the barony or estate of lords containing barons and all that be above the degree of a baron (as I have declared before): and those which be no lords, as knights, esquires, and simply gentlemen. The third and last sort of persons is named the yeomanry. Each of these hath his part and administrations, in judgments, corrections of defaults, in election of offices, in appointing and collection of tributes and subsidies, or in making laws, as shall appear hereafter.

BOOK III

Of wives and marriages.

Chapter 6

The wives in England be as I said *in potestate maritorum*, not that the husband hath *vitae ac necis potestatem*, as the Romans had in the old time of their children, for that is only in the power of the prince, and his laws, as I have said before, but that whatsoever they have before marriage, as soon as marriage is solemnized, is their husband's, I mean of money, plate, jewels, chattels, and generally all movables. For as for land and heritage followeth the succession and is ordered by the law as I shall say hereafter: and whatsoever they get after marriage, they get to their husbands. They neither can give nor sell any thing either of their husband's or their own. Theirs no movable thing is by the law of England *constanti matrimonio*, but as *peculium servi aut filii familias*: and yet in movables at the death of her husband she can claim nothing, but according as he shall will by his testament, no more than his son can: all the rest is in the disposition of the executors if he die testate. Yet in London and other great cities they have that law and custom, that when a man dieth his goods be divided into three parts. One third is employed upon the burial and the bequests which the testator maketh in his testament. Another third part the wife hath as her right, and the third third part is the due and right of his children equally to be divided among them. So that a man there can make testament but of one third of his goods: if he die intestate, the funerals deducted, the goods be equally divided between the wife and the children.

By the common law of England if a man die intestate, the ordinary (which is the bishop by common intendment) sometime the archdeacon, dean, or prebendary by privilege and prescription, doth commit the administration of the goods to the widow or the child, or next kinsman of the dead, appointing out portions to such as naturally it belongeth unto, and the ordinary by common understanding hath such gravity and discretion as shall be meet for so absolute an authority, for the most part following such division as is used in London, either by thirds or halves. Our forefathers newly converted to the Christian faith had such confidence in their pastors and instructors and took them to be men of such conscience that they committed that matter to their discretion, and belike at the first they were such as would seek no private profit to themselves thereby, that being once so ordained hath still so continued. The abuse which hath followed was in part redressed by certain acts of parliament made in the time of King Henry VIII, touching the probate of testaments, committing of administration and mortuaries. But to turn to the matter which we now have in hand, the wife is so much in the power of her husband, that not only her goods by marriage are straight made her husband's, and she loseth all her administration which she had of them: but also where all English men have name and surname, as the Romans had, *Marcus Tullius, Caius Pompeius, Caius Iulius*, whereof the name is given to us at the font, the surname is the name of the gentility and stock which the son doth take of the father always, as the old Romans did, our daughters so soon as they be married lose the surname of their father, and of the family and stock whereof they do come, and take the surname of their husbands, as transplanted from their family into another. So that if my wife was called before *Philippe Wilford* by her own name and her father's surname, so soon as she is married to me she is no more called *Philippe Wilford*, but *Philippe Smith*, and so must she write and sign: and as she changeth husbands, so she changeth surnames, called always by the surname of her last husband. Yet if a woman once marry a lord or a knight, by which she is called my lady with the surname of her husband, if he die and she take a husband of a meaner estate, by whom she shall not be called lady, (such is the honour we do give to women) she shall still be called lady with the surname of her first husband and not of the second.

I think among the old Romans those marriages which were made *per coemptionem in manum,* and *per aes* and *libram* made the wife *in manu et potestate viri,* whereof also we had in our old law and ceremonies of marriage a certain memory as a view and *vestigium.* For the woman at the church door was given of the father or some other man next of her kin into the hands of the husband, and he laid down gold and silver for her upon the book, as though he did buy her, the priest belike was in stead of *Lipripeus:* our marriages be esteemed perfect by the law of England, when they be solemnized in the church or chapel, in the presence of the priest and other witnesses. And this only maketh both the husband and the wife capable of all the benefits which our law doth give unto them and their lawful children. Insomuch that if I marry the widow of one lately dead, which at the time of her husband's death was with child, if the child be born after marriage solemnized with me, this child shall be my heir, and is accounted my lawful son, not his whose child it is in deed, so precisely we do take the letter where it is said, *pater est quem nuptiae demonstrant.* Those ways and means which Justinian doth declare to make bastards to be lawful children, *muliers* or rather *melieurs* (for such a term our law useth for them which be lawful children) be of no effect in England; neither the pope nor emperor, nor the prince himself never could legitimate a bastard to enjoy any benefit of our law, the parliament hath only that power.

Although the wife be (as I have written before) *in manu et potestate mariti,* by our law yet they be not kept so strait as in mew and with a guard as they be in Italy and Spain, but have almost as much liberty as in France, and they have for the most part all the charge of the house and household (as it may appear by Aristotle and Plato the wives of the Greeks had in their time), which is indeed the natural occupation, exercise, office, and part of a wife. The husband to meddle with the defence either by law or force, and with all foreign matters which is the natural part and office of the man, as I have written before. And although our law may seem somewhat rigorous toward the wives, yet for the most part they can handle their husbands so well and so dulcely, and specially when their husbands be sick: that where the law giveth them nothing, their husbands at their death of their good will give them all. And few there be that be not made at the death of their husbands either sole or chief executrices of his last will and testament, and have for the most part the government of the children and their portions: except it be in London, where a peculiar order is taken by the city much after the fashion of the civil law.

All this while I have spoken only of movable goods: if the wife be an inheretrix and bring land with her to the marriage, that land descendeth to her eldest son, or is divided among her daughters. Also the manner is that the land which the wife bringeth to the marriage or purchaseth afterwards, the husband cannot sell nor alienate the same, no not with her consent, nor she herself during the marriage, except that she be sole examined by a judge at the common law: and if he have no child by her and she die, the land goeth to her next heirs at the common law: but if in the marriage he have a child by her, which is heard once to cry, whether the child live or die, the husband shall have the usufruct of her lands (that is the profit of them during his life), and that is called the courtesy of England.

Likewise if the husband have any land either by inheritance descended or purchased and bought with his money, if he die before the wife, she shall have the usufruct of one third part of his lands. That is, she shall hold the one-third part of his lands during her life as her dowry, whether he hath child by her or no. If he hath any children, the rest descendeth straight to the eldest: if he hath none, to the next heir at the common law: and if she mislike the division, she shall ask to be endowed of the fairest of his lands to the third part.

This which I have written touching marriage and the right in movables and unmovables which cometh thereby, is to be understood by the common law when no private contract is more particularly made. If there be any private pacts, covenants, and contracts made before the marriage betwixt the husband and the wife, by themselves, by their parents, or their friends, those have force and be kept according to the firmity and strength in which they are made, and this is enough of wives and marriage.

Of Children.

Chapter 7

Our children be not *in potestate parentum*, as the children of the Romans were: but as soon as they be *puberes*, which we call the age of discretion (before that time nature doth tell they be but as it were *partes parentum*), that which is theirs they may give or sell, and purchase to themselves either lands and other movables, the father having nothing to do therewith. And therefore *emancipatio* is clean superfluous, we know not what it is. Likewise *sui haeredes*, complaints *de inofficioso testamento* or *praeteritorum liberorum non emancipatorum* have no effect nor use in our law, nor we have no manner to make lawful children but by marriage, and therefore we know not what is *adoptio* nor *arrogatio*. The testator disposeth in his last will his movable goods freely as he thinketh meet and convenient without controlment of wife or children. And our testaments for goods movable be not subject to the ceremonies of the civil law but made with all liberty and freedom and *iure militari*. Of lands as you have understood before, there is difference: for when the owner dieth, his land descendeth only to his eldest son, all the rest, both sons and daughters, have nothing by the common law, but must serve their eldest brother if they will, or make what other shift they can to live: except that the father in lifetime do make some conveyance and estates of part of his land to their use, or else by devise, which word amongst our lawyers doth betoken a testament written, sealed, and delivered in the lifetime of the testator before witness: for without those ceremonies a bequest of lands is not available. But by the common law if he that dieth hath no sons but daughters, the land is equally divided among them, which portion is made by agreement or by lot. Although as I have said ordinarily and by the common law, the eldest son inheriteth all the lands, yet in some countries all the sons have equal portion, and that is called gavelkind and is in many places in Kent. In some places the youngest is sole heir, and in some places after another fashion. But these being but particular customs of certain places and out of the rule of the common law, do little appertain to the disputation of the policy of the whole realm and may be infinite. The commonwealth is judged by that which is most ordinarily and commonly done through the whole realm.

Of Bondage and Bondmen.

Chapter 8

After that we have spoken of all the sorts of free men according to the diversity of their estates and persons, it resteth to say somewhat of bondmen which were called *servi*, which kind of people and the disposition of them and about them doth occupy the most part of Justinian's Digests and Code. The Romans had two kinds of bondmen, the one which were called *servi*, and they were either which were bought for money, taken in war, left by succession, or purchased by other kind and lawful acquisition, or else borne of their bond women and called *vernae*: all those kind of bondmen be called in our law villains in gross, as you would say immediately bond to the person and his heirs. Another they had as appeareth in Justinian's time, which they called *adscripticii glebae* or *agri censiti*. These were not bond to the person, but to the manor or place, and did not follow him who had the manors, and in our law are called villains regardants, for because they be as members, or belonging to the manor or place. Neither of the one sort nor of the other have we any number in England. And of the first I never knew any in the realm in my time: of the second so few there be, that it is not almost worth the speaking. But our law doth acknowledge them in both those sorts. Manumission of all kinds of villains or bondmen in England is used and done after divers sorts, and by other and more light and easy means than is prescribed in the civil law, and being once manumitted, he is not *libertus manumittentis*, but simply *liber*: howbeit sith our realm hath received the Christian religion which maketh us all in Christ brethren, and in respect of God and Christ *conservos*, men began to have conscience to hold in captivity and such extreme bondage him whom they must acknowledge to be his brother, and as we use to term him Christian, that is who looketh in Christ and by Christ to have equal portion with them in the Gospel and salvation. Upon this scruple, in continuance of time and by long succession, the holy fathers, monks, and friars in their confession, and specially in their extreme and deadly sicknesses, burdened the consciences of them whom they had under their hands: so that temporal men by little and little, by reason of that terror in their conscience, were glad to manumit all their villains: but the said holy fathers, with the abbots and priors, did not in like sort by theirs, for they had also conscience to impoverish and despoil the churches so much as to manumit such as were bond to their churches, or to the manors which the church had gotten, and so kept theirs still. The same did the bishops also, till at the last and now of late some bishops to make a piece of money manumitted theirs partly for argent, partly for slanders, that they seemed more cruel than the temporalty: after the monasteries coming into temporal men's hands have been occasion that now they be almost all manumitted. The most part of bondmen when they were there, yet were not used with us so cruelly nor in that sort as the bondmen at the Roman civil law, as appeareth by their comedies, nor as in Greece as appeareth by theirs: but they were suffered to enjoy copyhold land to gain and get as other serfs that now and then their lords might fleece them and take a piece of money of them, as in France the lords do tail them whom they call their subjects at their pleasure, and cause them to pay such sums of money as they list to put upon them. I think both in France and England the change of religion to a more gentle, humane and more equal sort (as the Christian religion is in respects of the Gentiles) caused this old kind of servile servitude and slavery to be brought into that moderation, for necessity first to villains regardants, and after to servitude of lands and tenures, and by little and little finding out more civil and gentle means and more equal to have that done which in time of heathenness servitude or bondage did, they almost extinguished the whole. For although all persons Christians be brethren by baptism in Jesu Christ, and therefore may appear equally free: yet some were and still might be christened being bond and serf, and whom as the baptism did find so it did leave them, for it changeth not civil laws nor compacts amongst men which be not contrary to God's laws, but rather maintaineth them by obedience. Which seeing men of good conscience, having that scruple whereof I wrote before, have by little and little found means to have and obtain the profit of servitude and bondage which gentility did use and is used to this day amongst Christians on the one part, and Turks and Gentiles on the other part, when war is betwixt them upon those whom they take in battle. Turks and Gentiles I call them, which using not our law the one believeth in one God, the other in many gods, of whom they make images. For the law of Jews is well enough known, and at this day so far as I can learn amongst all people Jews be held as it were in a common servitude, and have no rule or dominion as their own prophecies do tell that they should not have, after that Christ was promised to them, was of them refused for when they would not acknowledge him, obstinately forsaking their health in soul for the life to come and honour in this world for the time present, not taking the good tidings, news, and evangel brought to them for their disobedience by the great grace of God, and by the promise of the prophets fructified in us which be Gentiles and brought forth this humanity, gentleness, honour, and godly knowledge which is seen at this present. But to return to the purpose.

This persuasion, I say, of Christians not to make nor keep his brother in Christ, servile, bond, and underling for ever unto him, as a beast rather than as a man, and the humanity which the Christian religion doth teach, hath engendered through realms not near to Turks and barbarians, a doubt, a conscience, and scruple to have servants and bondmen: yet necessity on both sides of the one to have help, on the other to have service, hath kept a figure or fashion thereof. So that some would not have bondmen, but *adscripticii glebae*, and villains regardant to the ground, to the intent their service might be furnished and that the country being evil, unwholesome, and otherwise barren should not be desolate. Others afterwards found out the ways and means, that not the men but the land should be bound and bring with it such bondage and service to him that occupieth it, as to carry the lord's dung unto the fields, to plough his ground at certain days, sow, reap, come to his court, swear faith unto him, and in the end to hold the land but by copy of the lord's court roll, and at the will of the lord. This tenure is called also in our law, villain, bond, or servile tenure: . . .

Another kind of servitude or bondage is used in England for the necessity thereof, which is called apprenticehood. But this is only by covenant, and for a time, and during the time it is *vera servitus*. For whatsoever the apprentice getteth of his own labour, or of his master's occupation or stock, he getteth to him whose apprentice he is; he must not lie forth of his master's doors, he must not occupy any stock of his own, nor marry without his master's licence, and he must do all servile offices about the house, and be obedient to all his master's commandments, and shall suffer such correction as his master shall think meet, and is at his master's clothing and nourishing, his master being bound only to this which I have said, and to teach him his occupation, and for that he serveth some for seven or eight years, some nine or ten years, as the master and the friends of the young man shall think meet or can agree: altogether (as Polidore hath noted) *quasi pro emptitio servo*: nevertheless that neither was the cause of the name apprentice, neither yet doth the word betoken, that which Polydore supposeth, but it is a French word, and betokeneth a learner or a scholar. *Apprendre* in French is to learn, and *apprentise* is as much to say in French (of which tongue we borrowed this word and many more other) as *discipulus* in Latin: likewise he to whom he is bound is not called his lord but his master, as you would say his teacher. And the pactions agreed upon be put in writing, signed and sealed by the parties, and registered for more assurance: without being such an apprentice in London and serving out such a servitude in the same city for the number of years agreed upon, by order of the city amongst them, no man being never so much born in London, and of parents Londoners, is admitted to be a citizen or free man of London: the like is used in other great cities of England. Besides apprentices, others be hired for wages, and be called servants or serving men and women throughout the whole realm, which be not in such bondage as apprentices but serve for the time for daily ministry, as *servi* and *ancillae* did in the time of gentility and be for other matters in liberty as full free men and women.

But all servants, labourers, and others not married must serve by the year: and if he be in covenant, he may not depart out of his service without his master's licence, and he must give his master warning that he will depart one quarter of a year before the term of the year expireth, or else he shall be compelled to serve out another year. And if any young man unmarried be without service, he shall be compelled to get him a master whom he must serve for that year, or else he shall be punished with stocks and whipping as an idle vagabond. And if any man married or unmarried, not having rent or living sufficient to maintain himself, do live so idly, he is inquired of and sometime sent to the jail, sometime otherwise punished as a sturdy vagabond: so much our policy doth abhor idleness. This is one of the chief charges of the justices of peace in every shire. It is taken for ungentleness and dishonour and a show of enmity, if any gentleman do take another gentleman's servant (although his master hath put him away) without some certificate from his master, either by word or writing, that he hath discharged him of his service. That which is spoken of men-servants, the same is also spoken of women-servants. So that all youth that hath not sufficient revenues to maintain itself, must needs with us serve, and that after an order as I have written. Thus necessity and want of bondmen hath made men to use free men as bondmen to all servile services: but yet more liberally and freely, and with a more equality and moderation than in time of gentility slaves and bondmen were wont to be used, as I have said before. The first and latter fashion of temporal servitude and upon paction is used in such countries as have left off the old accustomed manner of servants, slaves, bondmen and bondwomen, which was in use before they had received the Christian faith. Some after one sort, and some either more or less rigorously according as the nature of the people is inclined or hath devised amongst themselves for the necessity of service.

BOOK II

Of the parliament and the authority thereof.

Chapter I

The most high and absolute power of the realm of England consisteth in the parliament. For as in war where the king himself in person, the nobility, the rest of the gentility, and the yeomanry are, is the force and power of England: so in peace and consultation where the prince is to give life, and the last and highest commandment, the barony for the nobility and higher, the knights, esquires, gentlemen, and commons for the lower part of the commonwealth, the bishops for the clergy be present to advertise, consult, and show what is good and necessary for the commonwealth, and to consult together, and upon mature deliberation every bill or law being thrice read and disputed upon in either house, the other two parts first each apart, and after the prince himself in presence of both the parties doth consent unto and alloweth—that is the prince's and the whole realm's deed: whereupon justly no man can complain, but must accommodate himself to find it good and obey it.

That which is done by this consent is called firm, stable, and *sanctum*, and is taken for law. The parliament abrogateth old laws, maketh new, giveth orders for things past, and for things hereafter to be followed, changeth rights and possessions of private men, legitimateth bastards, establisheth forms of religion, altereth weights and measures, giveth forms of succession to the crown, defineth of doubtful rights whereof is no law already made, appointeth subsidies, tails, taxes, and impositions, giveth most free pardons and absolutions, restoreth in blood and name as the highest court, condemneth or absolveth them whom the prince will put to that trial: and to be short, all that ever the people of Rome might do either in *centuriatis comitiis* or *tributis*, the same may be done by the parliament of England, which representeth and hath the power of the whole realm both the head and the body. For every Englishman is intended to be there present, either in person or by procuration and attorneys, of what pre-eminence state, dignity, or quality soever he be, from the prince (be he king or queen) to the lowest person of England. And the consent of the parliament is taken to be every man's consent.

The form of holding the parliament.

Chapter 2

The prince sendeth forth his rescripts or writs to every duke, marquis, baron, and every other lord temporal or spiritual who hath voice in the parliament, to be at his great council of parliament such a day (the space from the date of such a writ is commonly at the least forty days): he sendeth also writs to the sheriffs of every shire to admonish the whole shire to choose two knights of the parliament in the name of the shire, to hear and reason, and to give their advice and consent in the name of the shire, and to be present at that day: likewise to every city and town which of anciety hath been wont to find burgesses of the parliament, so to make election that they might be present there at the first day of the parliament. The knights of the shire be chosen by all the gentlemen and yeomen of the shire, present at the day assigned for the election: the voice of any absent can be counted for none. Yeomen I call here (as before) that may dispend at the least 40s. of yearly rent of free land of his own. These meeting at one day, the two who have the more of their voices be chosen knights of the shire for that parliament: likewise by the plurality of the voices of the citizens and burgesses be the burgesses elected. The first day of the parliament the prince and all the lords in their robes of parliament do meet in the higher house, where, after prayers made, they that be present are written, and they that be absent upon sickness or some other reasonable cause (which the prince will allow) do constitute under their hand and seal some one of those who be present as their procurer or attorney to give voice for them, so that by presence or attorney and proxy they be all there, all the princes and barons and all archbishops and bishops, and (when abbots were) so many abbots as had voice in parliament. The place where the assembly is, is richly tapised and hanged, a princely and royal throne as appertaineth to a king, set in the midst of the higher place whereof. Next under the prince sitteth the chancellor, who is the voice and orator of the prince. On the one side of that house or chamber sitteth the archbishops and bishops, each in his rank, on the other side the dukes and barons. In the midst thereof upon woolsacks sitteth the judges of the realm, the master of the rolls, and the secretaries of state. But these that sit on the woolsacks have no voice in the house, but only sit there to answer their knowledge in the law, when they be asked if any doubt arise among the lords: the secretaries to answer of such letters or things passed in council whereof they have the custody and knowledge: and this is called the upper house, whose consent and dissent is given by each man severally and by himself, first for himself, and then severally for so many as he hath letters and proxies, when it cometh to the question, saying only content or not content, without further reasoning or replying. In this meantime the knights of the shires and burgesses of the parliament (for so they are called that have voice in parliament and are chosen as I have said before, to the number betwixt 300 and 400) are called by such as it pleaseth the prince to appoint, into another great house or chamber by name, to which they answer and declaring for what shire or town they answer: then they are willed to choose an able and discreet man to be as it were the mouth of them all and to speak for and in the name of them and to present him so chosen by them to the prince: which done they coming all with him to a bar, which is at the nether end of the upper house, there he first praiseth the prince, then maketh his excuse of unability, and prayeth the prince that he would command the commons to choose another. The chancellor in the prince's name doth so much declare him able, as he did declare himself unable, and thanketh the commons for choosing so wise, discreet, and eloquent a man, and willeth them to go and consult of laws for the commonwealth. Then the speaker

5—The illustration opposite shows Queen Elizabeth at the opening of parliament in the parliament chamber at Westminster Palace. It is taken from an engraving, attributed to Renold Elstrack (1570–c.1625), in Thomas Milles, *Nobilitas Politica vel Civilis*, 1608. Milles compiled his book from manuscripts left by his uncle, Robert Glover (died 1588) who probably wrote the chapter for which this illustration was made. This chapter describes the pomp and ceremony at the opening of parliament 22 November 1584, but the book was not published until 1608, and there is reason to suppose that the engraving was made nearer 1608 than 1584. If the attribution to Elstrack is correct, the drawing was probably made after 1598 when his earliest dated work appeared. Then, too, the throne on the queen's left, labelled ' *P. Walliae*,' (prince of Wales) seems very inappropriate for a parliament of Elizabeth who was always so sensitive about the question of her successor. But it might be included in a view of her parliament chamber which was made and published during the reign of James I. A picture of parliament in 1523, when there was no prince of Wales, omits this throne and also the one on the queen's right labelled *R. Scotiae*. The safest conclusion is that the view was engraved during James I's reign, before 1608, and that the two minor thrones were Jacobean, rather than Elizabethan, garnishings.

The manner of sitting in parliament as shown in this picture may be worked out from Milles' (Glover's) verbal description of the 1584 parliament and from the view of parliament in D'Ewes' *Journal* (1680) said to be derived from the 1608 engraving. The lord chancellor and lord high treasurer stand behind the queen as labelled, the former's woolsack remaining empty before the throne. Of the ' great sacks of red cloth filled with wool,' the two at the sides of the table are occupied by ' the master of the rolls, the queen's secretary, the judges, the barons of the exchequer, and certain lawyers, as well civilians as common lawyers.' On the sack at the foot of the table sits ' the clerk of the parliament, with the clerk of the crown, behind whom the other clerks write, resting upon their knees.' On the sack below this one sit the barons. The sacks (or benches) at the left are occupied by the lords spiritual, those on the right by the other lords temporal. The lords on the queen's right bear the cap of maintenance and the earl marshal's baton; of the men on her left, one carries the sword, and the other two may be the lord steward and the garter king-of-arms. In the foreground, behind the bar, stands the speaker of the house of commons flanked by the gentleman usher of the black rod on his right, and possibly the serjeant-at-arms of the house of commons at his left. (Cf. A.F.Pollard, *The Evolution of Parliament*, 1926, pp.383–385.)

SVMMI ET SVPREMI SENACVLI PARLAMENTARIS IN ANGLIA TYPVS.

Milites Prouocarion & Burgenses (quas vocant) utrinq. qui Cameram Parlamenti inferiorem constituunt, Prolocutorem conducentes.

maketh certain requests to the prince in the name of the commons, first, that his majesty would be content that they may use and enjoy all their liberties and privileges that the common house was wont to enjoy. Secondly, that they might frankly and freely say their minds in disputing of such matters as may come in question and that without offence to his majesty. Thirdly, that if any should chance of that lower house to offend or not to do or say as should become him, or if any should offend any of them being called to that his highness' court, that they themselves might (according to the ancient custom) have the punishment of them. And fourthly, that if there came any doubt, whereupon they shall desire to have the advice or conference with his majesty or with any of the lords, that they might do it. All which he promiseth in the commons' names that they shall not abuse but have such regard as most faithful, true, and loving subjects ought to have to their prince.

The chancellor answereth in the prince's name, as appertaineth. And this is all that is done for one day, and sometime two. Besides the chancellor, there is one in the upper house who is called clerk of the parliament who readeth the bills. For all that cometh in consultation either in the upper house or in the nether house is put in writing first in paper, which being once read, he that will riseth up and speaketh with it or against it: and so one after another so long as they shall think good. That done they go to another, and so another bill. After it hath been once or twice read and doth appear that it is somewhat liked as reasonable, with such amendment in words and peradventure some sentences as by disputation seemeth to be amended: in the upper house the Chancellor asketh if they will have it engrossed, that is to say, put into parchment: which done, and read the third time, and that eftsoons if any be disposed to object disputed again among them, the chancellor asketh if they will go to the question; and if they agree to go to the question, then he saith, Here is such a law or act concerning such a matter, which hath been thrice read here in this house, are you content that it be enacted or no? If the not contents be more, then the bill is dashed, that is to say the law is annihilated and goeth no further. If the contents be the more, then the clerk writeth underneath: *Soit baille aux commons.* And so when they see time they send such bills as they have approved by two or three of those which do sit on the woolsacks to the commons: who asking licence, and coming into the house with due reverence, saith to the speaker: Master speaker, my lords of the upper house have passed among them and think good that there should be enacted by parliament such an act, and such an act, and so readeth the titles of that act or acts. They pray you to consider of them and show them your advice, which done they go their way. They being gone and the door again shut the speaker rehearseth to the house what they said. And if they be not busy disputing at that time in another bill, he asketh them straightway if they will have that bill or (if there be more) one of them.

In like manner in the lower house the speaker, sitting in a seat or chair for that purpose somewhat higher that he may see and be seen of them all, hath before him in a lower seat his clerk, who readeth such bills as be first propounded in the lower house, or be sent down from the lords. For in that point each house hath equal authority to propound what they think meet, either for the abrogating of some law made before or for making of a new. All bills be thrice in three diverse days read and disputed upon, before they come to the question. In the disputing is a marvellous good order used in the lower house. He that standeth up bareheaded is understanded that he will speak to the bill. If more stand up, who that first is judged to rise is first heard, though the one do praise the law, the other dissuade it, yet there is no altercation. For every man speaketh as to the speaker, not as to one another, for that is against the order of the house. It is also taken against the order to name him whom you do confute, but by circumlocution, as he that speaketh with the bill, or he that spake against the bill, and gave this and this reason. And so with perpetual oration not with altercation, he goeth through till he do make an end. He that once hath spoken in a bill though he be confuted straight, that day may not reply, no though he would change his opinion. So that to one bill in one day one may not in that house speak twice, for else one or two with altercation would spend all the time. The next day he may, but then also but once.

No reviling or nipping words must be used. For then all the house will cry, it is against the order: and if any speak unreverently or seditiously against the prince or the privy council, I have seen them not only interrupted, but it hath been moved after to the house, and they have sent them to the Tower. So that in such a multitude and in such diversity of minds and opinions there is the greatest modesty and temperance of speech that can be used. Nevertheless with much dulce and gentle terms, they make their reasons as violent and as vehement the one against the other as they may ordinarily, except it be for urgent causes and hasting of time. At the afternoon they keep no parliament. The speaker hath no voice in the house, nor they will not suffer him to speak in any bill to move or dissuade it. But when any bill is read, the speaker's office is as briefly and as plainly as he may to declare the effect thereof to the house. If the commons do assent to such bills as be sent to them first agreed upon from the lords thus subscribed, *Les commons ont assentus*, so if the lords do agree to such bills as be first agreed upon by the commons, they send them down to the speaker thus subscribed, *Les seigneurs ont assentus*. If they cannot agree, the two houses (for every bill from whence soever it doth come is thrice read in each of the houses) if it be understood that there is any sticking, sometimes the lords to the commons, sometimes the commons to the lords do require that a certain of each house may meet together, and so each part to be informed of other's meaning, and this is always granted. After which meeting for the most part not always either part agrees to other's bills. In the upper house they give their assent and dissent each man severally and by himself first for himself and then for so many as he hath proxy. When the chancellor hath demanded of them whether they will go to the question after the bill hath been thrice read, they saying only content or not content, without further reasoning or replying: and as the more number doth agree, so it is agreed on or dashed.

In the nether house none of them that is elected either knight or burgess can give his voice to another nor his consent nor dissent by proxy. The more part of them that be present only maketh the consent or dissent. After the bill hath been twice read, and then engrossed and eftsoons read and disputed on enough as is thought, the speaker asketh if they will go to question. And if they agree he holdeth the bill up in his hand and saith, As many as will have this bill go forward, which is concerning such a matter, say yea. Then they which allow the bill cry yea, and as many as will not, say no: as the cry of yea or no is bigger, so the bill is allowed or dashed. If it be a doubt which cry is the bigger, they divide the house, the speaker saying, as many as do allow the bill go down with the bill, and as many as do not sit still. So they divide themselves, and being so divided they are numbered who make the more part, and so the bill doth speed. It chanceth sometime that some part of the bill is allowed, some other part hath much contrariety and doubt made of it: and it is thought if it were amended it would go forward. Then they choose certain committees of them who have spoken with the bill and against it to amend it, and bring it in again so amended, as they amongst them shall think meet: and this is before it is engrossed, yea and some time after. But the agreement of these committees is no prejudice to the house. For at the last question they will either accept it or dash it as shall seem good, notwithstanding that whatsoever the committees have done.

Thus no bill is an act of parliament, ordinance, or edict of law, until both the houses severally have agreed unto it, after the order aforesaid, no nor then neither. But the last day of that parliament or session the prince cometh in person in his parliament robes and sitteth in his state: all the upper house sitteth about the prince in their states and order in their robes. The speaker with all the common house cometh to the bar, and there after thanks given first in the lords' name by the chancellor, etc. and in the commons' name by the speaker to the prince, for that he hath so great care of the good government of his people, and for calling them together to advise of such things as should be for the reformation, establishing, and ornament of the commonwealth: the chancellor in the prince's name giveth thanks to the lords and commons for their pains and travails taken, which he saith the prince will remember and recompense when time and occasion shall serve, and that he for his part is ready to declare his pleasure concerning their proceedings, whereby the same may have perfect life and accomplishment by his princely authority, and so have the whole consent of the realm. Then one reads the title of every act which hath passed at that session, but only in this fashion: An act concerning such a thing, etc. It is marked there what the prince doth allow, and to such he saith: *Le roy* or *la royne le veult*. And those be taken now as perfect laws and ordinances of the realm of England, and none other, and as shortly as may be put in print, except it be some private cause or law made for the benefit or prejudice of some private man, which the Romans were wont to call *privilegia*. These be only exemplified under the seal of the parliament, and for the most part not printed. To those which the prince liketh not, he answereth, *Le roy* or *la royne s'advisera*, and those be accounted utterly dashed and of no effect.

This is the order and form of the highest and most authentical court of England, by virtue whereof all those things be established whereof I spake before, and no other means accounted available to make any new forfeiture of life, member, or lands of any English man, where there was no law ordained for it before. Now let us speak of the said parts when they be several.

Of the monarch, king or queen of England.

Chapter 3

The prince whom I now call (as I have often before) the monarch of England, king or queen, hath absolutely in his power the authority of war and peace, to defy what prince it shall please him, and to bid him war, and again to reconcile himself and enter into league or truce with him at his pleasure or the advice only of his privy council. His privy council be chosen also at the prince's pleasure out of the nobility or barony, and of the knights and esquires, such and so many as he shall think good, who doth consult daily, or when need is of the weighty matters of the realm, to give therein to their prince the best advice they can. The prince doth participate to them all, or so many of them as he shall think good, such legations and messages as come from foreign princes, such letters or occurrences as be sent to himself or to his secretaries, and keepeth so many embassades and letters sent unto him secret as he will, although these have a particular oath of a councillor touching faith and secrets administered unto them when they be first admitted into that company. So that herein the kingdom of England is far more absolute than either the dukedom of Venice is, or the kingdom of the Lacedemonians was. In war time, and in the field the prince hath also absolute power so that his word is a law, he may put to death or to other bodily punishment whom he shall think so to deserve without process of law or form of judgment. This hath been sometime used within the realm before any open war in sudden insurrections and rebellions, but that not allowed of wise and grave men, who in that their judgment had consideration of the consequence and example, as much as of the present necessity, especially, when by any means the punishment might have been done by order of law. This absolute power is called martial law, and ever was and necessarily must be used in all camps and hosts of men, where the time nor place do suffer the tarriance of pleading and process, be it never so short, and the important necessity requireth speedy execution, that with more awe the soldier might be kept in more straight obedience without which never captain can do anything available in the wars.

The prince useth also absolute power in crying and decreeing the money of the realm by his proclamation only. The money is always stamped with the prince's image and title. The form, fashion, manner, weight, fineness, and baseness thereof is at the discretion of the prince. For whom should the people trust more in that matter than their prince, seeing the coin is only to certify the goodness of the metal and the weight, which is affirmed by the prince's image and mark? But if the prince will deceive them and give them copper for silver or gold, or enhance his coin more than it is worth, he is deceived himself, as well as he doth go about to deceive his subjects. For in the same sort they pay the prince his rents and customs. And in time they will make him pay ratably or more for meat, drink, and victuals for him and his, and for their labour: which experience doth teach us now in our days to be done in all regions. For there ever hath been, and ever will be, a certain proportion between the scarcity and plenty of other things, with gold and silver, as I have declared more at large in my book of money. For all other measures and weights, as well of dry things as of wet, they have accustomed to be established or altered by the parliament and not by the prince's proclamation only.

The prince useth also to dispense with laws made, whereas equity requireth a moderation to be had, and with pains for transgression of laws, where the pain of the law is applied only to the prince. But where the forfeit (as in popular actions it chanceth many times) is part to the prince, the other part to the declarator, detector, or informer, there the prince doth dispense for his own part only. Where the criminal action is intended by inquisition (that manner is called with us at the prince's suit) the prince giveth absolution or pardon: yet with a clause, *modo stet rectus in curia*, that is to say, that no man object against the offender. Whereby notwithstanding that he hath the prince's pardon if the person offended will take upon him the accusation (which in our language is called the appeal) in cases where it lieth, the prince's pardon doth not serve the offender.

The prince giveth all the chief and highest offices or magistracies of the realm, be it of judgment or dignity, temporal or spiritual, and hath the tenths and first fruits of all ecclesiastical promotions, except in the universities and certain colleges which be exempt.

All writs, executions, and commandments be done in the prince's name. We do say in England the life and member of the king's subjects are the king's only, that is to say no man hath high nor mesne justice but the king nor can hold plea thereof. And therefore all those pleas which touch the life or the mutilation of man, be called pleas of the crown, nor can be done in the name of any inferior person than he or she that holdeth the crown of England. And likewise no man can give pardon thereof but the prince only: although in times past there were certain county palatines, as Chester, Durham, Ely, which were high justices, and writs went in their name, and also some lord marchers of Wales, which claimed like privilege. All these are now worn away. The supreme justice is done in the king's name, and by his authority only.

The prince hath the wardship and first marriage of all those that hold lands of him in chief. And also the government of all fools natural, or such as be made by adventure of sickness, and so continue, if they be landed. This being once granted by act of parliament (although some inconvenience hath been thought to grow thereof, and sith that time it hath been thought very unreasonable) yet once annexed to the crown who ought to go about to take the club out of Hercules' hand. And being governed justly and rightly I see not so much inconvenience in it, as some men would make of it: divers other rights and pre-eminences the prince hath which he called prerogatives royal, or the prerogative of the king which be declared particularly in the books of the common laws of England.

To be short the prince is the life, the head, and the authority of all things that be done in the realm of England. And to no prince is done more honour and reverence than to the king and queen of England, no man speaketh to the prince nor serveth at the table but in adoration and kneeling, all persons of the realm be bareheaded before him: insomuch that in the chamber of presence where the cloth of estate is set, no man dare walk, yea though the prince be not there, no man dare tarry there but bareheaded. This is understood of the subjects of the realm: for all strangers be suffered there and in all places to use the manner of their country, such is the civility of our nation.

AN ADMONITION TO THE PARLIAMENT
1572

' THE *Admonition to the Parliament* of 1572 was the first open manifesto of the puritan party; and it marks the point at which puritanism began to be a hostile force, determined to do away with the existing system of polity and worship in the English Church.' [1] The authorship of the tract has never been definitely established although two contemporary clergymen, John Field and Thomas Wilcox, claimed the honour and suffered a year's imprisonment in Newgate for the same. However, the pamphlet is generally recognized as of prime importance in the growth of Elizabethan puritanism. Its purpose was to coalesce into a unified movement the sporadic efforts to purify the Church of England after 1558.

The puritan attack on the Prayer Book at the 1563 convocation had failed, the vestiarian controversy of 1566 lacked cohesion and clouded the essential issues by quarrelling over minutiae, and so the more far-sighted puritans were coming to adopt a program opposing not only the externals of worship, but the order of service and the government of the church. With this shift in the objectives of their attack, there came also a shift in the puritans' methods. Their activity was carried from the councils of the church into the political arena of the nation. By 1571 their forces were becoming organized; Cartwright was gaining the leadership and was directing the attack. In the parliament of that year a series of ecclesiastical bills was introduced, only to be quashed by the queen who asserted her royal supremacy in matters ecclesiastical. The attack was resumed in the next parliament of 1572. A bill ' to legalize the puritan disorders in worship ' reached the engrossing stage, but its potential force was destroyed by the substitution of a compromise measure. Even this alternative was doomed, for the queen forbade parliamentary consideration of any religious bills not previously approved by the clergy.

However, before this parliament ended 30 June 1572, the *Admonition* addressed to it was out. It probably resulted from a private meeting of puritans in London and was produced by secret presses. In reality an appeal to the country at large, it aroused public opinion and rapidly gained notoriety. On 27 June the bishop of Lincoln preached against it at Paul's Cross. The first edition was exhausted, despite the efforts at censorship, and a revised edition went into two printings. Attacks on the manifesto, counter-attacks, and rejoinders followed, and a *Second Admonition to the Parliament*, attributed rather doubtfully to Cartwright, came out in February 1573. The popularity of the first *Admonition* is further attested by the efforts of the clergy to check its circulation, and the despair they felt appears in the correspondence of Archbishop Parker and the bishops of Peterborough and London. The secret presses had put forth so many offensive tracts by June 1573 that the issue was fairly joined when the queen's proclamation condemned the rites, ceremonies, and devices of the puritans and the ' books under the title of *An Admonition to the Parliament*.' At the end of the year the arrest of Cartwright

1. W.H.Frere and C.E.Douglas, *Puritan Manifestoes.*

was ordered, but he was already in exile. The *Admonition* had ' done its work ' in rallying the militant forces of puritanism and in providing a clear exposition of the principles on which the puritans might base their political action.

The text is taken from W.H.Frere and C.E.Douglas, *Puritan Manifestoes*, The
Church Historical Society, London, 1907. It has not been abridged save for the omission
of a note on *errata* as indicated by asterisks. The supplementary essay entitled, *A View
of Popish Abuses*, is included, but *To the Christian Reader* and *The Letters* of Rudolph
Gualter and Theodore Beza are omitted.

TO THE GODLY READERS, GRACE AND PEACE FROM GOD, Etc.

Two treatises you have here ensuing (beloved in Christ) which you
must read without partiality or blind affection. For otherwise you shall
neither see their meaning, nor refrain yourselves from rashly condemning
of them without just cause. For certain men there are of great countenance, which will not lightly like of them, because they principally concern their persons and unjust dealings: whose credit is great, and whose
friends are many, we mean the lordly lords, archbishops, bishops, suffragans, deans, doctors, archdeacons, chancellors, and the rest of that
proud generation, whose kingdom must down, hold they never so hard:
because their tyrannous lordship can not stand with Christ's kingdom.
And it is the special mischief of our English church, and the chief cause
of backwardness and of all breach and dissension. For they whose authority is forbidden by Christ will have their stroke without their fellow servants, yea, though ungraciously, cruelly, and popelike they take upon
them to beat them, and that for their own childish articles, being for the
most part against the manifest truth of God: first, by experience their
rigour hath too plainly appeared ever since their wicked reign, and especially for the space of these five or six years last past together. Of the
enormities, which with such rigour they maintain, these treatises do in
part make mention, justly craving redress thereof. But the matters do
require a larger discourse. Only the authors of these thought it their parts
to admonish you at this time of those inconveniences which men seem
not to think upon, and which without reformation can not but increase
further dissension: the one part being proud, pontifical and tyrannous:
and the word of God for the other part express and manifest, as if it

pleased the state to examine the matters, it would be evident. And would to God that free conference in these matters might be had. For howsoever learned and many they seem to be, they should and may in this realm find enough to match them and shame them too, if they hold on as they have begun. And out of this realm they have all the best reformed churches throughout Christendom against them. But in a few words to say what we mean. Either must we have right ministry to God and a right government of his church, according to the scriptures set up (both which we lack) or else there can be no right religion, nor yet for contempt thereof can God's plagues be from us any while deferred. And therefore though they link in together, and slanderously charge poor men (whom they have made poor) with grievous faults, calling them puritans, worse than the Donatists, exasperating and setting on, such as be in authority against them: having hitherto miserably handled them, with revilings, deprivations, imprisonments, banishments, and such like extremities, yet is these poor men's cause never the worse: nor these challengers the better: nor God his hand the further off, to link in with his against them: nor you (Christian brethren) must never the rather without examination condemn them. But thankfully take this taste which God by these treatises offereth you, and weigh them by the word of God, and do your endeavour every one in his calling to promote his cause. And let us all, with more earnest prayer than we are wont, earnestly commend it to God his blessing, and namely, that it will please him by his spirit, to lighten the heart of our most gracious sovereign, and the rest in authority, to the benefit of his small flock and the overthrow of their proud enemies, that Godliness may by them proceed in peace and God his glory through Jesus Christ be thoroughly advanced. Which we call God to witness, is our only labour and suit. And so presently we leave you: heartily beseeching God to grant it. Amen.

AN ADMONITION TO THE PARLIAMENT.

Seeing that nothing in this mortal life is more diligently to be sought for and carefully to be looked unto than the restitution of true religion and reformation of God's church: it shall be your parts (dearly beloved) in this present parliament assembled, as much as in you lieth to promote the same and to employ your whole labour and study; not only in aban-

doning all popish remnants both in ceremonies and regiment, but also
in bringing in and placing in God's church those things only which the
Lord himself in his word commandeth. Because it is not enough to take
pains in taking away evil, but also to be occupied in placing good in the
stead thereof. Now because many men see not all things, and the world
in this respect is marvellously blinded, it hath been thought good to
proffer to your godly considerations a true platform of a church reformed,
to the end that it being laid before your eyes, to behold the great unlike-
ness betwixt it and this our English church: you may learn either with
perfect hatred to detest the one, and with singular love to embrace, and
careful endeavour to plant the other: or else to be without excuse before
the majesty of our God, who (for the discharge of our conscience, and
manifestation of his truth) hath by us revealed unto you at this present,
the sincerity and simplicity of his Gospel. Not that you should either
wilfully withstand, or ungraciously tread the same under your feet, for
God doth not disclose his will to any such end, but that you should yet
now at the length with all your main and might, endeavour that Christ
(whose easy yoke and light burden we have of long time cast off from us)
might rule and reign in his church by the sceptre of his word only.

May it therefore please your wisdoms to understand, we in England
are so far off from having a church rightly reformed, according to the
prescript of God's word, that as yet we are not come to the outward face
of the same. For to speak of that wherein all consent, and whereupon
all writers accord. The outward marks whereby a true Christian church
is known are preaching of the word purely, ministering of the sacraments
sincerely, and ecclesiastical discipline which consisteth in admonition
and correction of faults severely. Touching the first, namely the ministry
of the word, although it must be confessed that the substance of doctrine
by many delivered is sound and good, yet herein it faileth, that neither
the ministers thereof are according to God's word proved, elected, called,
or ordained: nor the function in such sort so narrowly looked unto, as
of right it ought, and is of necessity required. For whereas in the old
church a trial was had both of their ability to instruct, and of their Godly
conversation also: now, by the letters commendatory of some one man,
noble or other, tag and rag, learned and unlearned, of the basest sort of
the people (to the slander of the Gospel in the mouths of the adversaries)
are freely received. In those days no idolatrous sacrificers or heathenish

priests were appointed to be preachers of the Gospel: but we allow, and like well of popish mass-mongers, men for all seasons, King Henry's priests, King Edward's priests, Queen Mary's priests, who of a truth (if God's word were precisely followed) should from the same be utterly removed. Then they taught others, now they must be instructed themselves, and therefore like young children they must learn catechisms. Then election was made by the common consent of the whole church: now every one picketh out for himself some notable good benefice, he obtaineth the next advowson, by money or by favour, and so thinketh himself to be sufficiently chosen. Then the congregation had authority to call ministers: instead thereof now, they run, they ride, and by unlawful suit and buying prevent other suitors also. Then no minister placed in any congregation, but by the consent of the people, now, that authority is given into the hands of the bishop alone, who by his sole authority thrusteth upon them such as they many times as well for unhonest life, as also for lack of learning, may, and do justly dislike. Then, none admitted to the ministry, but a place was void beforehand, to which he should be called: but now, bishops (to whom the right of ordering ministers doth at no hand appertain) do make 60, 80, or a 100 at a clap, and send them abroad into the country like masterless men. Then, after just trial and vocation they were admitted to their function by laying on of the hands of the company of the eldership only: now there is (neither of these being looked unto) required an alb, a surplice, a vestment, a pastoral staff, beside that ridiculous, and (as they use it to their new creatures) blasphemous saying, Receive the Holy Ghost. Then every pastor had his flock, and every flock his shepherd, or else shepherds: now they do not only run frisking from place to place (a miserable disorder in God's church) but covetously join living to living, making shipwreck of their own consciences, and being but one shepherd (nay, would to God they were shepherds and not wolves) have many flocks. Then the ministers were preachers: now bare readers. And if any be so well disposed to preach in their own charges, they may not without my lord's licence. In those days known by voice, learning, and doctrine: now they must be discerned from other by popish and antichristian apparel, as cap, gown, tippet, etc. Then, as God gave utterance they preached the word only: now they read homilies, articles, injunctions, etc. Then it was painful: now gainful. Then poor and ignominious: now rich and glorious. And therefore titles, livings, and offices by antichrist devised are given to them, as metropolitan, archbishop, lord's grace, lord bishop, suffragan, dean, archdeacon, prelate of the garter, earl, county palatine, honour, high commissioners, justices of peace and quorum, etc. All which, together with their offices, as they are strange and unheard of in Christ's church, nay plainly in God's word forbidden: so are .they utterly with speed out of the same to be removed. Then ministers were not tied to any form of prayers invented by man, but as the spirit moved them, so they poured forth hearty supplications to the Lord. Now they are bound of necessity to a prescript order of service and book of common prayer in which a great number of things contrary to God's word are contained, as baptism by women, private communions, Jewish purifyings, observing of holidays, etc., patched (if not all together, yet the greatest piece) out of the pope's *portuis*. Then feeding the flock diligently: now teaching quarterly. Then preaching in season and out of season: now once in a month is thought sufficient, if twice, it is judged a work of supererogation. Then nothing taught but God's word, now prince's pleasures, men's devices, popish ceremonies, and antichristian rites in public pulpits defended. Then they sought them: now they seek theirs.

These and a great many other abuses are in the ministry remaining, which unless they be removed and the truth brought in, not only God's justice shall be poured forth, but also God's church in this realm shall never be built. For if they which seem to be workmen are no workmen in deed but in name, or else work not so diligently and in such order as the workmaster commandeth, it is not only unlikely that the building shall go forward, but altogether impossible that ever it shall be perfected. The way therefore to avoid these inconveniences and to reform these deformities is this: your wisdoms have to remove advowsons, patronages, impropriations, and bishop's authority, claiming to themselves thereby right to ordain ministers, and to bring in that old and true election which was accustomed to be made by the congregation. You must displace those ignorant and unable ministers already placed and in their rooms appoint such as both can and will by God's assistance feed the flock. You must pluck down and utterly overthrow without hope of restitution, the court of faculties, from whence not only licences to enjoy many benefices are obtained, as pluralities, trialities, totquots, etc., but all things for the most part, as in the court of Rome are set on sale, licences to marry, to eat flesh in times prohibited, to lie from benefices and charges, and a great number beside of such like abominations. Appoint to every congregation a learned and diligent preacher. Remove homilies, articles, injunctions, a prescript order of service made out of the mass book. Take away the lordship, the loitering, the pomp, the idleness, and livings of bishops, but yet employ them to such ends as they were in the old church appointed for. Let a lawful and a Godly seignory look that they preach, not quarterly or monthly, but continually: not for filthy lucre sake, but of a ready mind. So God shall be glorified, your consciences discharged, and the flock of Christ (purchased with his own blood) edified.

Now to the second point, which concerneth ministration of sacraments. In the old time the word was preached before they were ministered: now it is supposed to be sufficient if it be read. Then, they were ministered in public assemblies, now in private houses. Then by ministers only, now by midwives and deacons equally. But because in treating of both the sacraments together we should deal confusedly, we will therefore speak of them severally. And first for the Lord's Supper, or Holy Communion.

They had no introit, for Celestinus a pope brought it in about the year 430. But we have borrowed a piece of one out of the mass book. They read no fragments of the Epistle and Gospel: we use both. The Nicene creed was not read in their communion: we have it in ours. There was then accustomed to be an examination of the communicants which now is neglected. Then they ministered the sacrament with common and usual bread: now with wafer cakes, brought in by Pope Alexander, being in form, fashion, and substance like their God of the altar. They received it sitting: we kneeling, according to Honorius' decree. Then it was delivered generally, and indefinitely, *Take ye and eat ye*: we particularly, and singularly, *Take thou, and eat thou*. They used no other words but such as Christ left: we borrow from papists, *The body of our Lord Jesus Christ which was given for thee, etc.* They had no *Gloria in excelsis* in the ministry of the sacrament then, for it was put to afterward: we have now. They took it with conscience: we with custom. They shut men by reason of their sins from the Lord's Supper: we thrust them in their sin to the Lord's Supper. They ministered the sacrament plainly: we pompously, with singing, piping, surplice and cope wearing. They simply as they received it from the Lord: we, sinfully, mixed with man's inventions and devices. And as for baptism, it was enough with them if they had water, and the party to be baptized faith, and the minister to preach the word and minister the sacraments.

Now, we must have surplices devised by Pope Adrian, interrogatories ministered to the infant, godfathers, and godmothers, brought in by Heginus, holy fonts invented by Pope Pius, crossing and such like pieces of popery, which the church of God in the apostle's times never knew (and therefore not to be used), nay (which we are sure of) were and are man's devices brought in long after the purity of the primitive church. To redress these your wisdoms have to remove (as before) ignorant ministers, to take away private communions and baptisms, to enjoin deacons and midwives not to meddle in minister's matters, if they do to see them sharply punished. To join assistance of elders and other officers, that seeing men will not examine themselves, they may be examined and brought to render a reason of their hope. That the statute against wafer cakes may more prevail than an injunction. That people be appointed to receive the sacrament, rather sitting, for avoiding of superstition, than kneeling, having in it the outward show of evil from which we must abstain. That excommunication be restored to his old former force. That papists nor other, neither constrainedly nor customably, communicate in the mysteries of salvation. That both the sacrament of the Lord's Supper and baptism also, may be ministered according to the ancient purity and simplicity. That the parties to be baptized, if they be of the years of discretion, by themselves and in their own persons, or if they be infants, by their parents (in whose room if upon necessary occasions and businesses they be absent, some of the congregation knowing the good behaviour and sound faith of the parents) may both make rehearsal of their faith, and also if their faith be sound and agreeable to Holy Scriptures desire to be in the same baptized. And finally, that nothing be done in this or any other thing but that which you have the express warrant of God's word for.

Let us come now to the third part which concerneth ecclesiastical discipline. The officers that have to deal in this charge are chiefly three: ministers, preachers, or pastors of whom before, seniors or elders, and deacons. Concerning seniors, not only their office but their name also is out of this English church utterly removed. Their office was to govern the church with the rest of the ministers, to consult, to admonish, to correct, and to order all things appertaining to the state of the congregation. Instead of these seniors in every church, the pope hath brought in and we yet maintain, the lordship of one man over many churches, yea over sundry shires. These seniors then, because their charge was not overmuch, did execute their offices in their own persons without substitutes. Our lords bishops have their under officers, as suffragans, chancellors, archdeacons, officials, commissaries, and such like. Touching deacons, though their names be remaining, yet is the office foully perverted and turned upside down, for their duty in the primitive church was to gather the alms diligently and to distribute it faithfully, also for the sick and impotent persons to provide painfully, having ever a diligent care that the charity of Godly men were not wasted upon loiterers and idle vagabonds. Now it is the first step to the ministry, nay, rather a mere order of priesthood. For they may baptize in the presence of a bishop or priest, or in their absence (if necessity so require) minister the other sacrament, likewise read the Holy Scriptures and homilies in the congregation, instruct the youth in the catechism, and also preach, if he be commanded by the bishop. Again, in the old church every congregation had their deacons. Now they are tied to cathedral churches only, and what do they there? Gather the alms and distribute to the poor? Nay, that is the least piece or rather no part of their function. What then? To sing a gospel when the bishop ministereth the communion. If this be not a perverting of this office and charge, let everyone judge. And yet lest the reformers of our time should seem utterly to take out of God's church this necessary function, they appoint somewhat to it concerning the poor, and that is, to search for the sick, needy, and impotent people of the parish and to intimate their estates, names, and places where they dwell to the curate that by his exhortation they may be relieved by the parish or other convenient alms. And this as you see is the nighest part of his office, and yet you must understand it to be in such places where there is a curate and a deacon: every parish cannot be at that cost to have both, nay, no parish so far as can be gathered at this present hath. Now then, if you will restore the church to his ancient officers, this you must do. Instead of an archbishop or lord bishop, you must make equality of ministers. Instead of chancellors, archdeacons, officials, commissaries, proctors, doctors, summoners, churchwardens, and such like: you have to plant in every congregation a lawful and Godly seignory. The deaconship must not be confounded with the ministry, nor the collectors for the poor may not usurp the deacon's office: but he that hath an office must look to his office, and every man must keep himself within the bounds and limits of his own vocation. And to these three jointly, that is, the ministers, seniors, and deacons, is the whole regiment of the church to be committed. This regiment consisteth especially in ecclesiastical discipline, which is an order left by God unto his church, whereby men learn to frame their wills and doings according to the law of God, by instructing and admonishing one another, yea and by correcting and punishing all wilful persons, and condemners of the same. Of this discipline there is two kinds, one private, wherewith we will not deal because it is impertinent to our purpose, another public, which, although it hath been long banished, yet if it might now at the length be restored, would be very necessary and profitable for the building up of God's house. The final end of this discipline is the reforming of the disordered and to bring them to repentance and to bridle such as would offend. The chiefest part and last punishment of this discipline is excommunication by the consent of the church determined, if the offender be obstinate, which how miserably it hath been by the pope's proctors and is by our new canonists abused, who seeth not? In the primitive church it was in many men's hands: now one alone excommunicateth. In those days it was the last censure of the church and never went forth but for notorious crimes: now it is pronounced for every light trifle. Then excommunication was greatly regarded and feared: now because it is a money matter, no whit at all esteemed. Then for great sins, severe punishment, and for small offences, little censures: now great sins either not at all punished, as blasphemy, usury, etc., or else slightly passed over with pricking in a blanket, or pinning in a sheet, as adultery, whoredom, drunkenness, etc. Again, such as are no sins (as if a man conform not himself to popish orders and ceremonies, if he come not at the whistle of him who hath by God's word no authority to call, we mean chancellors, officials, doctors, and all that rabble) are grievously punished, not only by excommunication, suspension, deprivation, and other (as they term it) spiritual coercion, but also by banishing, imprisoning, reviling, taunting, and what not? Then the sentence was tempered according to the notoriousness of the fact. Now on the one side either hatred against some persons carryeth men headlong into rash and cruel judgment: or else favour, affection, or money, mitigateth the rigour of the same, and all this cometh to pass because the regiment left of Christ to his church is committed into one man's hands, whom alone it shall be more easy for the wicked by bribing to pervert than to overthrow the faith and piety of a zealous and Godly company, for such manner of men indeed should the seigniors be. Then it was said, Tell the church: now it is spoken, Complain to my lord's grace, primate and metropolitan of all England, or to his inferior, my lord bishop of the diocese, if not to him, show the chancellor or official, or commissary or doctor. Again, whereas the excommunicate were never received till they had publicly confessed their offence, now for paying the fees of the court, they shall by master official, or chancellor, easily be absolved in some private place. Then the congregation, by the wickedness of the offender grieved, was by his public penance satisfied. Now absolution shall be pronounced, though that be not accomplished. Then the party offending should in his own person hear the sentence of absolution pronounced. Now bishops, archdeacons, chancellors, officials, commissaries, and such like, absolve one man for another. And this is that order of ecclesiastical discipline which all Godly wish to be restored, to the end that every one by the same may be kept within the limits of his vocation and a great number be brought to live in Godly conversation. Not that we mean to take away the authority of the civil magistrate and chief governor, to whom we wish all blessedness and for the increase of whose Godliness we daily pray: but that Christ being restored into his kingdom to rule in the same by the sceptre of his word and severe discipline, the prince may be better obeyed, the realm more flourish in Godliness, and the Lord himself more sincerely and purely according to his revealed will served than heretofore he hath been, or yet at this present is. Amend therefore these horrible abuses, and reform God's church, and the Lord is on your right hand, you shall not be removed for ever. For he will deliver and defend you from all your enemies, either at home or abroad, as he did faithful Jacob and good Jehoshaphat. Let these things alone, and God is a righteous judge, he will one day call you to your reckoning. Is a reformation good for France? And can it be evil for England? Is discipline meet for Scotland? And is it unprofitable for this realm? Surely, God hath set these examples before your eyes to encourage you to go forward to a thorough and a speedy reformation. You may not do as heretofore you have done, patch and piece, nay rather go backward, and never labour or contend to perfection. But altogether remove whole Antichrist, both head, body, and branch, and perfectly plant that purity of the word, that simplicity of the sacraments, and severity of discipline, which Christ hath commanded and commended to his church. And here to end, we desire all to suppose that we have not attempted this enterprise for vainglory, gain preferment, or any other worldly respect: neither yet judging ourselves so exactly to have set out the state of a church reformed, as that nothing more could be added, or a more perfect form and order drawn: for that were great presumption to arrogate so much unto ourselves, seeing that as we are but weak and simple souls, so God hath raised up men of profound judgment and notable learning. But thereby to declare our good wills toward the setting forth of God's glory and the building up of his church, accounting this, as it were, but an entrance into further matter, hoping that our God, who hath in us begun this good work, will not only in time hereafter make us strong and able to go forward therein: but also move other, upon whom he hath bestowed greater measure of his gifts and graces, to labour more thoroughly and fully in the same.

The God of all glory so open your eyes to see his truth that you may not only be inflamed with a love thereof, but with a continual care seek to promote, plant, and place the same amongst us, that we the English people, and our posterity, enjoying the sincerity of God's gospel for ever, may say always: The Lord be praised. To whom with Christ Jesus his son our only saviour, and the Holy Ghost our alone comforter, be honour, praise, and glory, for ever and ever. Amen.

Finis.

A VIEW OF POPISH ABUSES YET REMAINING IN THE ENGLISH CHURCH, FOR THE WHICH GODLY MINISTERS HAVE REFUSED TO SUBSCRIBE.

Abide patiently the Lord's leisure. Cast thy care upon the Lord, and he will bring it to pass, he will do it.

The jeopardous time is at hand, that the wrath of God shall be declared from heaven upon all ungodliness of those seducers that withhold the truth in unrighteousness and set his commandments at naught for their own traditions.

WHEREAS immediately after the last parliament, held at Westminster, begun in anno 1570 and ended in anno 1571, the ministers of God's holy word and sacraments were called before her majesty's high commissioners and enforced to subscribe unto the articles if they would keep their places and livings, and some for refusing to subscribe were unbrotherly and uncharitably entreated and from their offices and places removed: may it please therefore this honourable and high court of parliament, in consideration of the premises, to take a view of such causes as then did withhold and now doth the foresaid ministers from subscribing and consenting unto those foresaid articles by way of purgation to discharge themselves of all disobedience towards the church of God and their sovereign, and by way of most humble entreaty, for the removing away and utter abolishing of all such corruptions and abuses as withheld them, through which this long time brethren have been at unnatural war and strife among themselves to the hinderance of the gospel, to the joy of the wicked, and to the grief and dismay of all those that profess Christ's religion and labour to attain Christian reformation.

The First Article.

First, that the book commonly called the book of common prayers for the church of England, authorized by parliament, and all and every the contents therein be such as are not repugnant to the word of God.

Albeit, right honourable and dearly beloved, we have at all times born with that which we could not amend in this book and have used the same in our ministry so far forth as we might: reverencing those times and those persons in which and by whom it was first authorized, being studious of peace and of the building up of Christ's church, yet now being compelled by subscription to allow the same and to confess it not to be against the word of God in any point but tolerable: we must needs say as followeth that this book is an unperfect book, culled and picked out of that popish dunghill, the mass book full of all abominations. For some and many of the contents therein be such as are against the word of God, as by his grace shall be proved unto you. And by the way, we cannot but much marvel at the crafty wiliness of those men whose parts it had been first to have proved each and every content therein to be agreeable to the word of God, seeing that they enforce men by subscription to consent unto it or else send them packing from their callings.

1. They should first prove that a reading service by the word of God going before and with the administration of the sacraments is according to the word of God; that private communion, private baptism, baptism ministered by women, holidays ascribed to saints, prescript services for them, kneeling at communion, wafer cakes for their bread when they minister it, surplice and cope to do it in, churching of women, coming in veils, abusing the psalm to her, *I have lifted up mine eyes unto the hills*, *etc.*, and such other foolish things, are agreeable to the written word of the Almighty. But their craft is plain. Wherein they deceive themselves, standing so much upon this word repugnant, as though nothing were repugnant or against the word of God but that which is expressly forbidden by plain commandment, they know well enough and would confess, if either they were not blinded or else their hearts hardened, that in the circumstances each content wherewith we justly find fault, and they too contentiously for the love of their livings maintain, smelling of their old popish priesthood, is against the word of God. For besides that this prescript form of service as they call it is full of corruptions, it maintained an unlawful ministry unable to execute that office.

By the word of God, it is an office of preaching, they make it an office of reading: Christ said, Go preach, they in mockery give them the Bible and authority to preach, and yet suffer them not except that they have new licences. So that they make the chiefest part preaching but an accessory, that is as a thing without which their office may and doth consist. In the scriptures there is attributed unto the ministers of God the knowledge of the heavenly mysteries, and therefore as the greatest token of their love, they are enjoined to feed God's lambs, and yet with these such are admitted and accepted as only are bare readers that are able to say service and minister a sacrament. And that this is not the feeding that Christ spake of, the scriptures are plain. Reading is not feeding, but it is as evil as playing upon a stage and worse too. For players yet learn their parts without book, and these, a many of them can scarcely read within book. These are empty feeders, dark eyes, ill workmen to hasten in the Lord's harvest, messengers that cannot call, prophets that cannot declare the will of the Lord, unsavoury salt, blind guides, sleepy watchmen, untrusty dispensers of God's secrets, evil dividers of the world, weak to withstand the adversary, not able to confute, and to conclude, so far from making the man of God perfect to all good works, that rather the quite contrary may be confirmed.

By this book bare reading is good tilling, and single service saying is excellent building, and he is shepherd good enough that can as popish priests could out of their *portuis* say fairly their divine service. Nay, some in the fullness of their blasphemy have said that much preaching bringeth the word of God into contempt, and that four preachers were enough for all London, so far are they from thinking it necessary and seeking that every congregation should have a faithful pastor. Paul was not so wise as these politic men when he said, We cannot believe except we hear, and we cannot hear without a preacher, etc., seeing we may hear by reading and so believe without a preacher. Foolishly he spake, when he said he must be apt to teach, since every man of the basest sort of the people is admitted to this function of such as Jeroboam did sometimes make his priests. We will say no more in this matter, but desire you to consider with us what small profit and edification this silly reading hath brought to us these thirteen years past (except perhaps by some Circumcellion or new apostle we have had now and then a fleeing sermon) surely our sins are grown ripe, our ignorance is equal with the ignorance of our leaders, we are lost, they cannot find us, we are sick, they cannot heal us, we are hungry, they cannot find us, except they lead us by other men's lights and heal us by saying a prescript form of service, or else feed us with homilies that are too homely to be set in the place of God's scriptures. But drunken they are and show their own shame, that strive so eagerly to defend their doings that they will only not acknowledge their imperfections, but will enforce other men to allow them.

2. In this book also, it is appointed that after the creed, if there be no sermon, an homily must follow either already set out, or hereafter to be set out. This is scarce plain dealing, that they would have us consent unto that which we never saw, and which is to be set out hereafter, we having had such cause already to distrust them, by that which is already

set out, being corrupt and strange, to maintain an unlearned and reading ministry: and since it is plain that men's works ought to be kept in, and nothing else but the voice of God and Holy Scriptures, in which only are contained all fullness and sufficiency to decide controversies, must sound in his church, for the very name Apocrypha testifieth that they ought rather to be kept close than to be uttered.

3. In this book days are ascribed unto saints and kept holy with fasts on their evens and prescript service appointed for them, which beside that they are of many superstitiously kept and observed, are also contrary to the commandment of God. Six days shalt thou labour, and therefore we for the superstition that is put in them dare not subscribe to allow them.

4. In this book we are enjoined to receive the communion kneeling, which beside that it hath in it a show of papistry doth not so well express the mystery of this Holy Supper. For as in the Old Testament eating the Paschal lamb standing signified a readiness to pass, even so in receiving it now sitting according to the example of Christ, we signify rest, that is, a full finishing through Christ of all the ceremonial law and a perfect work of redemption wrought that giveth rest for ever. And so we avoid also the danger of idolatry, which was in times past too common, and yet is in the hearts of many who have not yet forgotten their breaden God, so slenderly have they been instructed. Against which we may set the commandment: Thou shalt not bow down to it, nor worship it.

5. As for the half communion, which is yet appointed like to the commemoration of the mass, we say little of it, saving that we may note how near the translator bound himself to the mass book that would not omit it. We speak not of the name of priest wherewith he defaceth the minister of Christ (because the priest that translated it would perhaps fain have the ministers of Christ to be joined with him) seeing the office of priesthood is ended, Christ being the last priest that ever was. To call us therefore priests as touching our office is either to call back again the old priesthood of the law, which is to deny Christ to be come or else to keep a memory of the popish priesthood of abomination still amongst us. As for the first, it is by Christ abolished, and for the second it is of Antichrist and therefore we have nothing to do with it. Such ought to have no place in our church, neither are they ministers of Christ sent

to preach his gospel, but priests of the pope to sacrifice for the quick and the dead, that is to tread under their feet the blood of Christ. Such ought not to have place amongst us as the scriptures manifestly teach. Besides that we never read in the New Testament that this word priest as touching office is used in the good part.

6. Sixthly, in this book three or four are allowed for a fit number to receive the communion, and the priest alone together with one more, or with the sick man alone, may in time of necessity, that is, when there is any common plague, or in time of other visitation, minister it to the sick man, and if he require it, it may not be denied. This is not I am sure like in effect to a private mass: that scripture, Drink ye all of this, maketh not against this, and private communion is not against the scriptures.

7. And as for private baptism that will abide the touchstone. Go ye, saith Christ and teach, baptizing them, etc. Now teaching is divorced from communions and sacraments. They may go alone without doctrine. Women that may not speak in a congregation may yet in time of necessity minister the sacrament of baptism, and that in a private house. And yet this is not to tie necessity of salvation to the sacraments, nor to nuzzle men up in that opinion. This is agreeable with the scriptures, and therefore when they bring the baptized child, they are received with this special commendation: I certify you that you have done well, and according unto due order, etc. But now we speak in good earnest, when they answer this: let them tell us, how this gear agreeth with the scriptures and whether it be not repugnant or against the word of God.

8. The public baptism, that also is full of childish and superstitious toys. First in their prayer they say that God by the baptism of his son Jesus Christ did sanctify the flood Jordan and all other waters, to the mystical washing away of sin, attributing that to the sign which is proper to the work of God in the blood of Christ, as though virtue were in water to wash away sins. Secondly, they require a promise of the godfathers and godmothers (as they term them) which is not in their powers to perform. Thirdly, they profane holy baptism, in toying foolishly, for that they ask questions of an infant, which cannot answer, and speak unto them as was wont to be spoken unto men and unto such as being converted answered for themselves and were baptized. Which is but a mockery of God, and therefore against the Holy Scriptures. Fourthly,

they do superstitiously and wickedly institute a new sacrament, which is proper to Christ only, marking the child in the forehead with a cross, in token that hereafter he shall not be ashamed to confess the faith of Christ. We have made mention before of that wicked divorce of the word and sacraments. We say nothing of those that are admitted to be witnesses, what ill choice there is made of them, how convenient it were seeing the children of the faithful only are to be baptized, that the father should and might, if conveniently, offer and present his child to be baptized, making an open confession of that faith wherein he would have his child baptized and how this is used in well ordered churches.

9. As for matrimony that also hath corruptions too many. It was wont to be counted a sacrament, and therefore they use yet a sacramental sign, to which they attribute the virtue of wedlock. I mean the wedding ring, which they foully abuse and dally withal in taking it up and laying it down. In putting it on they abuse the name of the Trinity, they make the new married man according to the popish form to make an idol of his wife, saying: With this ring I thee wed, with my body I thee worship, etc. And because in popery no holy action might be done without a mass, they enjoin the married persons to receive the communion (as they do their bishops and priests when they are made, etc.) other petty things out of the book, we speak not of, as that women contrary to the rule of the apostle come and are suffered to come bare-headed with bagpipes and fiddlers before them to disturb the congregation, and that they must come in at the great door of the church or else all is marred.

10. As for confirmation which was in times past apostolical and so called of the ancient fathers, yet as they use it by the bishop alone to them that lack both discretion and faith, it is superstitious and not agreeable to the word of God, but popish and peevish; we speak not of other toys used in it; and how far it differeth, and is degenerated from the first institution, they themselves that are learned can witness.

11. They appoint a prescript kind of service to bury the dead: and that which is the duty of every Christian, they tie alone to the minister, whereby prayer for the dead is maintained and partly gathered out of some of the prayers, where they pray that we with this our brother and all other departed in the true faith of thy holy name may have our perfect consummation and bliss both in body and soul. We say nothing of the threefold peal because that is rather licensed by injunction than com-

manded in their book; nor of their strange mourning by changing their garments, which if it be not hypocritical, yet it is superstitious and heathenish, because it is used only of custom; nor of burial sermons, which are put in place of trentales, whereout spring many abuses, and therefore in the best reformed churches are removed; as for the superstitions used both in country and city for the place of burial, which way they must lie, how they must be fetched to church, the minister meeting them at church stile with surplice with a company of greedy clerks, that a cross white or black must be set upon the dead corpse, that bread must be given to the poor, and offerings in burial time used, and cakes sent abroad to friends, because these are rather used of custom and superstition than by the authority of the book. Small commandment will serve for the accomplishing of such things. But great charge will hardly bring the least good thing to pass, and therefore all is let alone, and the people as blind and as ignorant as ever they were. God be merciful unto us.

12. Churching of women after childbirth smelleth of Jewish purification: their other rites and customs in their lying in and coming to church is foolish and superstitious as it is used. She must lie in with a white sheet upon her bed and come covered with a veil, as ashamed of some folly. She must offer, but these are matters of custom, and not in the book. But this Psalm (as is noted before) is childishly abused, I have lift up mine eyes unto the hills, from whence cometh my help. The sun shall not burn thee by day, nor the moon by night. They pray that all men may be saved and that they may be delivered from thundering and tempest, when no danger is nigh. That they sing *Benedictus, Nuncdimittis* and *Magnificat*, we know not to what purpose, except some of them were ready to die, or except they would celebrate the memory of the Virgin, and John Baptist, etc. Thus they profane the Holy Scriptures.

13. In all their order of service there is no edification according to the rule of the apostle, but confusion, they toss the Psalms in most places like tennis balls. The people some standing, some walking, some talking, some reading, some praying by themselves, attend not to the minister. He again posteth it over, as fast as he can gallop. For either he hath two places to serve, or else there are some games to be played in the afternoon, as lying for the whetstone, heathenish dancing for the ring, a

bear or a bull to be baited, or else Jack-an-apes to ride on horseback, or an interlude to be played, and if no place else can be gotten, it must be done in the church, etc. Now the people sit and now they stand up. When the Old Testament is read or the lessons, they make no reverence, but when the gospel cometh, then they all stand up. For why, they think that to be of greatest authority and are ignorant that the scriptures came from one spirit. When Jesus is named, then off goeth the cap and down goeth the knees with such a scraping on the ground that they cannot hear a good while after, so that the word is hindered, but when any other names of God are mentioned, they make no curtsy at all as though the names of God were not equal or as though all reverence ought to be given to the syllables. We speak not of ringing when matins is done and other abuses incident. Because we shall be answered that by the book they are not maintained, only we desire to have a book to reform it. As for organs and curious singing, though they be proper to popish dens, I mean to cathedral churches, yet some others also must have them. The queen's chapel and these churches must be patterns and precedents to the people of all superstitions.

14. Their pontifical (which is annexed to the book of common prayer and whereunto subscribing to the articles, we must subscribe also) whereby they consecrate bishops, make ministers and deacons, is nothing else but a thing word for word drawn out of the pope's pontifical wherein he showeth himself to be antichrist most lively. And as the names of archbishops, archdeacons, lord bishops, chancellors, etc., are drawn out of the pope's shop together with their offices, so the government which they use by the life of the pope which is the canon law is antichristian and devilish and contrary to the scriptures. And as safely may we by the warrant of God's word subscribe to allow the dominion of the pope universally to reign over the church of God as of an archbishop over an whole province or a lord bishop over a diocese, which containeth many shires and parishes. For the dominion that they exercise, the archbishop above them and they above the rest of their brethren, is unlawful and expressly forbidden by the word of God.

15. Again in that they are honoured with the titles of kings and great rulers, as lord, lord's grace, metropolitan, primate of all England, honour, etc., it is against the word of God.

Moreover, in that they have civil offices, joined to the ecclesiastical, it is against the word of God. As for an archbishop to be a lord president, a lord bishop, to be a county palatine, a prelate of the garter, who hath much to do at St. George's feast when the Bible is carried before the procession in the cross's place, a justice of peace, or justice of quorum, an high commissioner, etc., and therefore they have their prisons, as clinks, gatehouses, colehouses, towers, and castles, which is also against the scriptures. This is not to have keys but swords, and plain tokens they are that they exercise that which they would so fain seem to want, I mean dominion over their brethren.

16. In that the lord bishops, their suffragans, archdeacons, chancellors, officials, proctors, doctors, summoners, and such ravening rabblers take upon them, which is most horrible, the rule of God's church, spoiling the pastor of his lawful jurisdiction over his own flock given by the word, thrusting away most sacrilegiously that order which Christ hath left to his church, and which the primitive church hath used, they show they hold the doctrine with us, but in unrighteousness, with an outward show of Godliness, but having denied the power thereof, entering not in by Christ but by a popish and unlawful vocation. We speak not how they make ministers by themselves alone, and of their sole authority, and that in secret places, of their election and probation, that it is of him to whom by no right it belongeth. And that when they have made them, either they may tarry in their college and lead the lives of loitering losels, as long as they live, or else gad abroad with the bishop's bulls like to Circumcellions, to preach in other men's charges where they list or else get benefices by friendship, or money, or flattery where they can catch them, or to conclude: If all these fail, that they may go up and down like beggars and fall to many follies: or else as many have done set up bills at Paul's, or at the Royal Exchange and in such public places to see if they can hear of some good masters to entertain them into service. Surely, by the canon law, by which the bishops reign and rule, they ought to keep those ministers which they make as long as they have no livings and places. We know three or four bishops in this realm would have kept such houses as never none did in this land, if this rule had been observed. They clapt them out so fast by hundreds, and they make them pay well for their orders, and surely to speak the truth they were worthy, for the bishops (what odds so ever there were of their gifts) yet in their letters gave them all a like commendation. They put on their surplices

or else subscribed like honest men. Fie upon these stinking abominations.

17. We should be too long to tell your honours of cathedral churches,
the dens aforesaid of all loitering lubbers, where master dean, master
vicedean, master canons or prebendaries the greater, master petty canons,
or canons the lesser, master chancellor of the church, master treasurer,
otherwise called Judas the pursebearer, the chief chanter, singing men,
special favourers of religion, squeaking choristers, organ players, gospellers, epistelers, pentioners, readers, vergers, etc., live in great idleness and
have their abiding. If you would know whence all these came, we can
easily answer you that they came from the pope as out of the Trojan
horse's belly, to the destruction of God's kingdom. The church of God
never knew them, neither doth any reformed church in the world know
them.

18. And birds of the same feather are covetous patrons of benefices,
parsons, vicars, readers, parish priests, stipendiaries, and riding chaplains,
that under the authority of their masters spoil their flocks of the food of
their souls. Such seek not the Lord Jesus but their own bellies, clouds
they are without rain, trees without fruit, painted sepulchres full of dead
bones, fatted in all abundance of iniquity, and lean locusts in all feeling,
knowledge, and sincerity.

TO PROVE THAT THE REGIMENT OF THE CHURCH SHOULD BE SPIRITUAL,
READ EPHE.XI.23. I THES.V.I3. I TIM.V.2. HEB.X.30.

19. What should we speak of the archbishop's court, since all men
know it, and your wisdoms cannot but see what it is. As all other courts
are subject to this by the pope's prerogative, yea, and by statute of this
realm yet unrepealed, so is it the filthy quagmire and poisoned plash of
all the abominations that do infect the whole realm. We speak not of
licences granted out of this court to marry in forbidden times, as in lent,
in advent, in the gang week, when banners and bells with the priest in
his surplice singing gospels and making crosses rangeth about in many
places, upon the ember days, and to forbidden persons, and in exempt
places. We make no mention of licences to eat white meat and flesh in
lent, and that with a safe conscience, for rich men that can buy them
with money, nor we say nothing how dearly men pay for them. As for
dispensations with beneficed boys, tolerations for non-residents, bulls
to have two benefices, to have three, to have more, and as many as they

list or can get, these are so common, that all Godly and good men are compelled with grief of heart to cry out upon such abominations. We omit excommunication for money, absolution for the same, and that by absolving one man for another, which how contrary it is to the scriptures the complaints of many learned men by propositions in open schools proposed, by writings in printed books set out, and by preaching in open pulpits have been sufficiently witnessed. To conclude, this filthy court hath full power together with the authority of this petty pope, metropolitan and primate of all England, to dispense in all causes wherein the pope was wont to dispense, under which are contained more cases and causes than we are able to reckon. As for my lord's grace of York, we deal not with him. We refer him to that learned epistle, which Beza wrote unto him about these matters.

20. And as for the commissaries court, that is but a petty little stinking ditch that floweth out of that former great puddle robbing Christ's church of lawful pastors, of watchful seniors and elders, and careful deacons. In this court as in the other, one alone doth excommunicate, one alone sitteth in judgment, and when he will, can draw back the judgment which he hath pronounced, having called upon the name of God, and that for money which is called the changing of penance. In this court, for non-payment of two pence, a man shall be excommunicated if he appear not when he is sent for, if he do not as his ordinary would, from whom he had his popish induction and institution and to whom he hath sworn, *canonicam obedientiam*, canonical obedience, if he learn not his catechism like a good boy without book, when it were more meet he should be able to teach others. To conclude: if he be not obedient to all these lord bishops' officers, by and by he must be cut off by excommunication. And as it is lightly granted and given forth, so if the money be paid and the court discharged, it is as quickly called in again. This court pulleth parishes, scourgeth the poor hedge priests, ladeth churchwardens with manifest perjuries, punisheth whoredoms and adulteries with toyish censures, remitteth without satisfying the congregation, and that in secret places, giveth out dispensations for unlawful marriages, and committeth a thousand such like abominations. God deliver all Christians out of this antichristian tyranny where the judges, advocates, and proctors for the most part are papists, and as for the scribes and notaries as greedy as cormorants, and if they all should perhaps see this

writing, they would be as angry as wasps and sting like hornets. Three of them would be enough to sting a man to death for why they are high commissioners.

All this we say springeth out of this pontifical which we must allow by subscription, setting down our hands, that it is not repugnant or against the word of God, we mean this antichristian hierarchy and popish ordering of ministers, strange from the word of God and the use of all well reformed churches in the world.

21. We have almost let pass one thing worthy the remembrance, which is that they take upon them blasphemously, having neither promise nor commandment to say to their new creatures, Receive the Holy Ghost. As though the Holy Ghost were in their power to give without warrant at their own pleasure.

And thus much be spoken as touching this book, against which to stand is a wonder to two sorts of men, the one ignorant, the other obstinate. The Lord give those that be his understanding in all things that they may have judgment: as for the other whom the God of this world hath blinded, lest they should see and confess the truth and so be saved, and that do in the full growth of wickedness maliciously resist the truth, God confound them, that peace may be upon Israel and his saving health upon this nation. Amen.

The Second Article.

That the manner and order appointed by public authority about the administration of the sacraments and common prayers, and that the apparel by sufficient authority appointed for the ministers within the church of England be not wicked nor against the word of God, but tolerable, and being commanded for order and obedience sake, are to be used.

For the order of administration of sacraments and common prayer, enough is said before, all the service and administration is tied to a surplice, in cathedral churches they must have a cope, they receive the communion kneeling, they use not for the most part common bread according to the word of God and the statute, but starch bread according to the injunction. They commonly minister the sacraments without preaching the word.

And as for the apparel, though we have been long born in hand and yet are that it is for order and decency commanded, yet we know and have proved that there is neither order, nor comeliness, nor obedience in using it. There is no order in it, but confusion: no comeliness, but deformity: no obedience, but disobedience, both against God and the prince. We marvel that they could espy in their last synod, that a gray amice, which is but a garment of dignity, should be a garment (as they say) defiled with superstition, and yet that copes, caps, surplices, tippets, and such like baggage, the preaching signs of popish priesthood, the pope's creatures, kept in the same form to this end, to bring dignity and reverence to the ministers and sacraments, should be retained still and not abolished. But they are as the garments of the idol, to which we should say, avaunt and get thee hence. They are as the garments of Balamites, of popish priests, enemies to God and all Christians. They serve not to edification, they have the show of evil (seeing the popish priesthood is evil), they work discord, they hinder the preaching of the Gospel, they keep the memory of Egypt still amongst us and put us in mind of that abomination whereunto they in times past have served, they bring the ministry into contempt, they offend the weak, they encourage the obstinate. Therefore can no authority by the word of God with any pretence of order and obedience command them, nor make them in any wise tolerable, but by circumstances they are wicked and against the word of God.

If this be not plain enough by that which is already set forth, we mind by God's grace to make it plainer and should do it better, if it were as lawful for us (as for our adversaries) to publish our minds in print. Then should appear what slender stuff they bring that are so impudent by open writing to defend it. And if it might please her majesty, by the advice of you right honourable in this high court of parliament to hear us, by writing or otherwise to defend ourselves, then (such is the equity of our cause) that we would trust to find favour in her majesty's sight. Then those patched pamphlets made by sudden upstarts and new converts should appear in their colours, and truth have the victory and God the glory. If this cannot be obtained, we will by God's grace address ourselves to defend his truth by suffering, and willingly lay our heads to the block, and this shall be our peace, to have quiet consciences with our God, whom we will abide for, with all patience, until he work our full deliverance.

The Third Article.

That the articles of religion which only concern the true Christian faith and the doctrine of the sacraments comprised in a book imprinted: Articles whereupon it was agreed by both archbishops, etc., and every of them contain true and godly Christian doctrine.

For the articles concerning that substance of doctrine using a godly interpretation in a point or two, which are either too sparely or else too darkly set down, we were and are ready according to duty to subscribe unto them. We would to God that as they hold the substance together with us, and we with them: so they would not deny the effect and virtue thereof. Then should not our words and works be divorced, but Christ should be suffered to reign, a true ministry according to the word instituted, discipline exercised, sacraments purely and sincerely ministered. This is that we strive for and about which we have suffered not as evil-doers, but for resisting popery and refusing to be strong with the tail of antichristian infection, ready to render a reason of our faith, to be stopping of all our enemies' mouths. We therefore for the church of God's sake, which ought to be most dear unto you, beseech you for our sovereign's sake, upon whom we pray that all God's blessings may be poured abundantly. We pray you to consider of these abuses to reform God's church according to your duties and callings, that as with one mouth we confess one Christ, so with one consent this reign of antichrist may be turned out headlong from amongst us, and Christ our Lord may reign by his word over us. So your seats shall be established and settled in great assurance, you shall not need to fear your enemies: for God will turn away his threatened plagues from us. Which he in mercy do, for his Christ's sake.

Amen.

Finis.

A SPEECH IN THE HOUSE OF COMMONS

By Peter Wentworth

8 February 1576

Peter Wentworth (1530?–1596) was a member of six parliaments. During his first in 1571, he noted Sir Humphrey Gilbert's 'disposition to flatter and fawn upon the prince,' and he spoke 'for the maintenance of free speech, to preserve the liberties of the house, and to reprove liars.' He served on a committee which rejected several of the Thirty-nine Articles and was conspicuous for his aggressive puritanism. Contemporaries considered him 'a man of hot temper and impatient for the new discipline.' On the opening day of parliament, 1576, he made the memorable speech here printed. He himself said it had been written two or three years previously; he was not permitted to conclude it, was examined before a committee sitting in the star chamber, and was sent to the Tower. In spite of his connections through his second wife, Elizabeth, sister of Sir Francis Walsingham and aunt by marriage of Sir Philip Sidney and Robert Devereux, earl of Essex, he was returned to the Tower of London in 1587, 1593, and died there in 1596. While living in the Tower he wrote a reply to Dolman [Parsons] concerning the succession to the throne, which was printed in 1598 and entitled, *A Pithie Exhortation to Her Majesty for establishing her successor to the Crowne.*

The speech is taken from Sir Simon D'Ewes, *Journal,* 1693 Edition, pp.236–244.

This present journal of the house of commons containeth in it not only many good passages touching the ordinary usages and privileges of the house, but is plentifully stored also with divers extraordinary and rare occurrences touching the maintenance of the liberties of the house, not only from the indignity of private persons, but also against the pressures of the lords of the upper house; in which also there wanted not the zealous endeavour of the house for reformation of divers ecclesiastical matters, and the remarkable imprisonment of a member of the same by themselves: in which I have supplied many passages and speeches which were wanting in the original journal book itself, in the due places, out of several copies of them I had by me. Yet to avoid confusion, whatsoever is transcribed out of the said copies is distinguished by some annotation or animadversion, both before and after it. And lastly it may here fitly be observed, that this being but the second session of the fourth parliament of her majesty's reign, the house of commons, as did also the lords of the upper house, fell to their ordinary business upon their first meeting in manner and form following, viz.

On Wednesday the eighth day of February, the bill that upon actions upon the case brought for slanderous words or writings, the country may be traversed, was read the first time.

Peter Wentworth, Esquire, one of the burgesses for the borough of Tregony in the county of Cornwall, was for unreverent and undutiful words uttered by him in his house of our sovereign lady the queen's majesty sequestered, that the house might proceed to conference and consideration of his said speech. Which speech I have transcribed out of a copy I had by me, and added it to this journal: viz.

Mr. Speaker, I find written in a little volume these words in effect: Sweet is the name of liberty, but the thing itself a value beyond all inestimable treasure. So much the more it behooveth us to take care lest we, contenting ourselves with the sweetness of the name, lose and forego the thing, being of the greatest value that can come unto this noble realm. The inestimable treasure is the use of it in this house. And therefore I do think it needful to put you in remembrance that this honourable assembly are assembled and come together here in this place for three special causes of most weighty and great importance.

The first and principal is to make and abrogate such laws as may be most for the preservation of our noble sovereign.

The second . . .

The third is to make or abrogate such laws as may be to the chiefest surety, safe-keeping, and enrichment of this noble realm of England. So that I do think that the part of a faithful-hearted subject is to do his endeavour to remove all stumbling-blocks out of the way that may impair or any manner of way hinder these good and Godly causes of this our coming together. I was never of parliament but the last and the last session, at both which times I saw the liberty of free speech, the which is the only salve to heal all the sores of this commonwealth, so much and so many ways infringed, and so many abuses offered to this honourable council, as hath much grieved me even of very conscience and love to my prince and state. Wherefore to avoid the like I do think it expedient to open the commodities that grow to the prince and whole state by free speech used in this place, at the least so much as my simple wit can gather of it, the which is very little in respect of that that wise heads can say therein, and so it is of the more force.

First, all matters that concern God's honour through free speech shall be propagated here and set forward, and all things that do hinder it removed, repulsed, and taken away.

Next, there is nothing commodious, profitable, or any way beneficial for the prince or state, but faithful and loving subjects will offer it in this place.

Thirdly, all things discommodious, perilous or hurtful to the prince or state shall be prevented, even so much as seemeth good to our merciful God to put into our minds, the which no doubt shall be sufficient, if we do earnestly call upon him and fear him, for Solomon saith, ' The fear of God is the beginning of wisdom, wisdom,' saith he, ' breatheth life into her children, receiveth them that seek her, and will go beside them in the way of righteousness ': so that our minds shall be directed to all good, needful, and necessary things, if we call upon God with faithful hearts.

Fourthly, if the envious do offer any thing hurtful or perilous to the prince or state in this place, what incommodity doth grow thereby? Verily I think none, nay will you have me to say my simple opinion therein, much good cometh thereof; how forsooth, for by the darkness of the night the brightness of the sun showeth more excellent and clear, and how can truth appear and conquer until falsehood and all subtleties that should shadow and darken it be found out? For it is offered in this place a piece of fine needle-work unto them that are most skilful therein, for there cannot be a false stitch (God aiding us) but will be found out.

Fifthly, this good cometh thereof, a wicked purpose may the easier be prevented when it is known.

Sixthly, an evil man can do the less harm when it is known.

Seventhly, sometime it happeneth that a good man will in this place (for argument sake) prefer an evil cause, both for that he would have a doubtful truth to be opened and manifested, and also the evil prevented; so that to this point I conclude, that in this house which is termed a place of free speech, there is nothing so necessary for the preservation of the prince and state as free speech, and without it is a scorn and mockery to call it a parliament house, for in truth it is none, but a very school of flattery and dissimilation, and so a fit place to serve the Devil and his angels in, and not to glorify God and benefit the commonwealth.

Now to the impediments thereof which by God's grace and my little experience I will utter plainly and faithfully, I will use the words of Elcha, ' Behold, I am as the new wine which hath no vent and bursteth the new vessels in sunder, therefore I will speak that I may have a vent, I will open my lips and make answer, I will regard no manner of person, no man will I spare, for if I should go about to please men, I know not how soon my Maker will take me away.' My text is vehement the which by God's sufferance I mean to observe, hoping therewith to offend none; for that of very justice none ought to be offended for seeking to do good and saying of the truth.

Amongst other, Mr. Speaker, two things do great hurt in this place, of the which I do mean to speak: the one is a rumour which runneth about the house and this it is, take heed what you do, the queen's majesty liketh not such a matter, whosoever prefereth it, she will be offended with him; or the contrary, her majesty liketh of such a matter, whoso-ever speaketh against it she will be much offended with him.

The other: sometimes a message is brought into the house either of commanding or inhibiting, very injurious to the freedom of speech and consultation, I would to God, Mr. Speaker, that these two were buried in Hell, I mean rumours and messages; for wicked undoubtedly they are, the reason is, the Devil was the first author of them, from whom pro-ceedeth nothing but wickedness: now I will set down reasons to prove them wicked.

First, if we be in hand with anything for the advancement of God's glory, were it not wicked to say the queen liketh not of it, or commanded that we shall not deal in it? Greatly were these speeches to her majesty's dishonour, and an hard opinion were it, Mr. Speaker, that these things should enter into her majesty's thought; much more wicked and un-natural were it that her majesty should like or command anything against God, or hurtful to herself and the state. The Lord grant this thing may be far from her majesty's heart. Here this may be objected, that if the queen's majesty should have intelligence of anything perilous or beneficial to her majesty's person or the state, would you not have her majesty give knowledge thereof in this house, whereby her peril may be pre-vented, and her benefit provided for? God forbid, then were her majesty in worse case than any of her subjects. And in the beginning of our speech I showed it to be a special cause of our assembly, but my intent is, that nothing should be done to God's dishonour, to her majesty's peril, or the peril of the state. And therefore I will show the inconven-iences that grow of these two.

First, if we follow not the prince's mind, Solomon saith, the king's displeasure is a messenger of death: this is a terrible thing to weak nature, for who is able to abide the fierce countenance of his prince, but if we will discharge our consciences, and be true to God, and prince and state, we must have due consideration of the place and the occasion of our coming together, and especially have regard unto the matter wherein we both shall serve God, and our prince and state faithfully, and not dissembling as eye pleasers, and so justly avoid all displeasures both to God and our prince: for Solomon saith, In the way of the righteous there is life, as for any other way it is the path to death. So that to avoid everlasting death and condemnation with the high and mighty God, we ought to proceed in every cause according to the matter, and not according to the prince's mind; and now I will show you a reason to prove it perilous always to follow the prince's mind. Many times it falleth out, that a prince may favour a cause perilous to himself and the whole state; what are we then if we follow the prince's mind, are we not unfaithful unto God, our prince and state? Yes truly, we are chosen of the whole realm, of a special trust and confidence by them reposed in us, to foresee all such inconveniences. Then I will set down my opinion herein, that is, he that dissembleth to her majesty's peril, is to be counted as an hateful enemy; for that he giveth unto her majesty a detestable Judas his kiss; and he that contrarieth her mind to her preservation, yea though her majesty would be much offended with him, is to be adjudged an approved lover, for faithful are the wounds of a lover, saith Solomon, but the kisses of an enemy are deceitful: And it is better, said Antisthenes, to fall amongst ravens than amongst flatterers, for ravens do but devour the dead corpse, but flatterers the living. And it is both traitorous and hellish through flattery to seek to devour our natural prince, and that do flatterers; therefore let them leave it with shame enough.

Now to another great matter that riseth of this grievous rumour, what is it forsooth? whatsoever thou art that pronouncest it, thou dost pronounce thy own discredit; why so? for that thou dost what lieth in thee to pronounce the prince to be perjured, the which we neither may nor will believe, for we ought not without too manifest proof to credit any dishonour to our anointed, no we ought not without it to think any evil of her majesty, but rather to hold him a liar what credit soever he be of; for the queen's majesty is the head of the law, and must of necessity maintain the law, for by the law her majesty is made justly our queen, and by it she is most chiefly maintained: hereunto agreeth the most excellent words of Bracton, who saith, The king hath no peer nor equal in his kingdom; he hath no equal, for otherwise he might lose his authority of commanding, sithence that an equal hath no rule of commandment over his equal. The king ought not to be under man, but under God and under the law, because the law maketh him a king: let the king therefore attribute that to the law, which the law attributeth unto him, that is, dominion and power; for he is not a king in whom will and not the law doth rule, and therefore he ought to be under the law. I pray you mark the reason why my authority saith, the king ought to be under the law, for saith he, He is God's vicegerent here upon earth, that is, his lieutenant to execute and do his will, the which is law or justice, and thereunto was her majesty sworn at her coronation, as I have heard learned men in this place sundry times affirm; unto the which I doubt not but her majesty will for her honour and conscience sake have special regard; for free speech and conscience in this place are granted by a special law, as that without the which the prince and state cannot be preserved or maintained: so that I would wish every man that feareth God, regardeth the prince's honour, or esteemeth his own credit, to fear at all times hereafter to pronounce any such horrible speeches, so much to the prince's dishonour; for in so doing he showeth himself an open enemy to her majesty, and so worthy to be condemned of all faithful hearts. Yet there is another inconvenience that riseth of this wicked rumour, the utterers thereof seem to put into our heads, that the queen's majesty hath conceived an evil opinion, diffidence, and mistrust in us her faithful and loving subjects; for if she had not, her majesty would then wish that all the things dangerous to herself should be laid open before us, assuring herself that loving subjects, as we are, would without schooling and direction, with careful minds to our powers, prevent and withstand all perils that might happen unto her majesty; and this opinion I doubt not but her majesty hath conceived of us, for undoubtedly there was never prince that had faithfuller hearts than her majesty hath here; and surely there were never subjects had more cause heartily to love their prince for her quiet government than we have. So that he that raiseth this rumour, still increaseth but discredit in seeking to sow sedition as much as lieth in him, between our merciful queen and us her most loving and faithful subjects, the which by God's grace shall never lie in his power, let him spit out all his venom and therewithal show out his malicious heart; yet I have collected sundry reasons to prove this a hateful and a detestable rumour, and the utterer thereof to be a very Judas to our noble queen, therefore let any hereafter take heed how he publish it, for as a very Judas unto her majesty and enemy to the whole state, we ought to accept him.

Now the other was a message, Mr. Speaker, brought the last sessions into the house, that we should not deal in any matters of religion, but first to receive from the bishops: surely this was a doleful message, for it was as much as to say, Sirs, you shall not deal in God's causes, no, you shall in no wise seek to advance his glory; and in recompense of your unkindness, God in his wrath will look upon your doings, that the chief cause that you were called together for, the which is the preservation of their prince, shall have no good success. If some one of this house had presently made this interpretation of this said message, had he not seemed to have the spirit of prophecy? Yet truly I assure you Mr. Speaker, there were divers of this house that said with grievous hearts, immediately upon the message, that God of his justice could not prosper the session; and let it be holden for a principle, Mr. Speaker, that counsel that cometh not together in God's name cannot prosper: for God saith, Where two or three are gathered together in his name there am I in the midst among them. Well, God, even the great and mighty God, whose name is the Lord of Hosts, great in council, and infinite in thought, and who is the only good director of all hearts, was the last session shut out of doors; but what fell out of it forsooth? His great indignation was therefore poured upon this house, for he did put into the queen's majesty's heart to refuse good and wholesome laws for her own preservation, the which caused many faithful hearts for grief to burst out with sorrowful tears and moved all papists traitors to God and her majesty, who envy good Christian government, in their sleeves to laugh all the whole parliament house to scorn; and shall I pass over this weighty matter so slightly? Nay, I will discharge my conscience and duties to God, my prince and country. So certain it is, Mr. Speaker, that none is without fault, no not our noble queen, sith then her majesty hath committed great fault, yea, dangerous faults to herself.

Love, even perfect love void of dissimulation, will not suffer me to hide them, to her majesty's peril, but to utter them to her majesty's safety: and these they are, it is a dangerous thing in a prince unkindly to abuse his or her nobility and people, and it is a dangerous thing in a prince to oppose or bend herself against her nobility and people, yea, against most loving and faithful nobility and people. And how could any prince more unkindly intreat, abuse, oppose herself against her nobility and people, than her majesty did the last parliament? Did she not call it of purpose to prevent traitorous perils to her person, and for no other cause? Did not her majesty send unto us two bills, willing us to make choice of that we liked best for her safety, and thereof to make a law, promising her majesty's royal consent thereunto? And did we not first choose the one, and her majesty refused it, yielding no reason, nay yielding great reasons why she ought to have yielded to it? Yet did we nevertheless receive the other, and agreeing to make a law thereof, did not her majesty in the end refuse all our travails? And did not we, her majesty's faithful nobility and subjects, plainly and openly decipher ourselves unto her majesty and our hateful enemies; and hath not her majesty left us all to the open revenge? Is this a just recompense in our Christian queen for our faithful dealings? The heathen do requite good for good, then how much more is it to be expected in a Christian prince? And will not this her majesty's handling, think you, Mr. Speaker, make cold dealing in any of her majesty's subjects toward her again? I fear it will. And hath it not caused many already, think you, Mr. Speaker, to seek a salve for the head that they have broken? I fear it hath, and many more will do the like if it be not prevented in time. And hath it not marvellously rejoiced and encouraged the hollow hearts of her majesty's hateful enemies and traitorous subjects? No doubt but it hath: and I beseech God that her majesty may do all things that may grieve the hearts of her enemies, and may joy the hearts that unfeignedly love her majesty. And I beseech the same God to endue her majesty with his wisdom, whereby she may discern faithful advice from traitorous sugared speeches, and to send her majesty a melting, yielding heart unto sound counsel, that will may not stand for a reason: and then her majesty will stand when her enemies are fallen, for no estate can stand where the prince will not be governed by advice. And I doubt not but that some of her majesty's council have dealt plainly and faithfully with her majesty herein; if any have, let it be a sure token to her majesty to know them for approved subjects; and whatsoever they be that did persuade her majesty so unkindly to intreat, abuse, and to oppose herself against her nobility and people, or commend her majesty for so doing, let it be a sure token to her majesty to know them for sure traitors and underminers of her majesty's life and remove them out of her majesty's presence and favour: for the more cunning they are, the more dangerous are they unto her majesty. But was this all? No, for God would not vouchsafe that his Holy Spirit should all that session descend upon our bishops; so that that session nothing was done to the advancement of his glory. I have heard of old parliament men that the banishment of the pope and popery and the restoring of true religion had their beginning from this house, and not from the bishops; and I have heard that few laws for religion had their foundation from them; and I do surely think, before God I speak it, that the bishops were the cause of that doleful message, and I will show you what moveth me so to think: I was amongst others the last parliament sent unto the bishop of Canterbury for the articles of religion that then passed this house. He asked us why we did put out of the book the articles for the homilies, consecrating of bishops, and such like? Surely, Sir, said I, because we were so occupied in other matters, that we had no time to examine them how they agreed with the word of God: What, said he, surely you mistook the matter, you will refer yourselves wholly to us therein? No, by the faith I bear to God, said I, we will pass nothing before we understand what it is; for that were but to make you popes; make you popes who list, said I, for we will make you none. And sure, Mr. Speaker, the speech seemed to me to be a pope-like speech, and I fear lest our bishops do attribute this of the pope's canons unto themselves, *Papa non potest errare*; for surely if they did not, they would reform things amiss, and not to spurn against God's people for writing therein as they do; but I can tell them news, they do but kick against the prick, for undoubtedly they both have and do err, and God will reveal his truth, maugre the hearts of them and all his enemies, for great is the truth and it will prevail: and to say the truth, it is an error to think that God's spirit is tied only to them; for the heavenly spirit saith, First seek the Kingdom of God and the righteousness thereof, and all these things (meaning temporal) shall be given you; these words were not spoken to the bishops only, but to all; and the writ, Mr. Speaker, that we are called up by, is chiefly to deal in God's cause: so that our commission both from God and our prince is to deal in God's causes: therefore the accepting of such messages, and taking them in good part do highly offend God, and is the acceptation of the breach of the liberties of this honourable council; for is it not all one thing to say, Sirs, you shall deal in such matters only, as to say, you shall not deal in such matters? And so as good to have fools and flatterers in the house, as men of wisdom, grave judgment, faithful hearts, and sincere consciences, for they being taught what they shall do can give their consents as well as the others. Well, he that hath an office, saith St. Paul, let him wait on his office, or give diligent attendance upon his office. It is a great and special part of our duty and office, Mr. Speaker, to maintain the freedom of consultation and speech, for by this, good laws that do set forth God's glory and for the preservation of the prince and state are made. St. Paul in the same place saith, Hate that which is evil, cleave unto that which is good: then with St. Paul, I do advise you all here present, yea and heartily and earnestly desire you from the bottom of your hearts to hate all messengers, tale-carriers, or any other thing whatsoever it be that any manner of way infringes the liberties of this honourable council; yea, hate it or them as venomous and poison unto our commonwealth, for they are venomous beasts that do use it; therefore I say again and again, hate that which is evil and cleave unto that which is good; and this being loved and faithful hearted, I do wish to be conceived in fear of God, and of love to our prince and state. For we are incorporated into this place to serve God and all England, and not to be time-servers, as humour-feeders, as cancers that would pierce the bone, or as flatterers that would fain beguile all the world, and so worthy to be condemned both of God and man; but let us show ourselves a people endued with faith, I mean with a lively faith, that bringeth forth good works, and not as dead. And these good works I wish to break forth in this sort, not only in hating the enemies before-spoken against, but also in open reproving them as enemies to God, our prince and state that do use them, for they are so. Therefore I would have none spared or forborn that shall from henceforth offend herein, of what calling soever he be, for the higher place he hath the more harm he may do; therefore if he will not eschew offences, the higher I wish him hanged. I speak this in charity, Mr. Speaker, for it is better that one should be hanged than that this noble state should be subverted. Well I pray God with all my heart to turn the hearts of all the enemies of our prince and state, and to forgive them that wherein they have offended, yea and to give them grace to offend therein no more; even so I do heartily beseech God to forgive us for holding our peaces when we have heard any injury offered to this honourable council; for surely it is no small offence, Mr. Speaker, for we offend therein against God, our prince and state, and abuse the confidence by them reposed in us. Wherefore God, for his great mercy's sake, grant that we may from henceforth show ourselves neither bastards nor dastards therein, but that as rightly begotten children, we may sharply and boldly reprove God's enemies, our prince's and state; and so shall every one of us discharge our duties in this our high office, wherein he hath placed us, and show ourselves haters of evil, and cleavers to that that is good, to the setting forth of God's glory and honour, and to the preservation of our noble queen and commonwealth: for these are the marks that we ought only in this place to shoot at. I am thus earnest, I take God to witness, for conscience sake, love, love unto my prince and commonwealth, and for the advancement of justice; for justice, saith an ancient father, is the prince of all virtues, yea the safe and faithful guard of man's life, for by it empires, kingdoms, people, and cities be governed, the which if it be taken away, the society of man cannot long endure. And a king, saith Solomon, that sitteth in the throne of judgment and looketh well about him, chaseth away all evil; in the which state and throne God for his great mercy's sake grant that our noble queen may be heartily vigilant and watchful; for surely there was a great fault committed both in the last parliament; and since also that was as faithful hearts as any were unto the prince and state received most displeasure, the which is but an hard point in policy, to encourage the enemy, to discourage the faithful-hearted, who of fervent love cannot dissemble, but follow the rule of St. Paul, who saith, let love be without dissimulation.

Now to another great fault I found the last parliament committed by some of this house also, the which I would desire of them all might be left; I have seen right good men in other causes, although I did dislike them in that doing, sit in an evil matter against which they had most earnestly spoken; I mused at it, and asked what it meant, for I do think it a shameful thing to serve God, their prince or country, with the tongue only, and not with the heart and body. I was answered that it was a common policy in this house to mark the best sort of the same, and either to sit or arise with them; that same common policy I would gladly have banished this house, and have grafted in the stead thereof, either to rise or sit as the matter giveth cause: For the eyes of the Lord behold all the earth to strengthen all the hearts of them that are whole with him. These be God's own words, mark them well, I heartily beseech you all; for God will not receive half part, he will have the whole. And again, he misliketh those two-faced gentlemen, and here be many eyes that will to their great shame behold their double dealing that use it. Thus I have holden you long with my rude speech, the which since it tendeth wholly with pure conscience to seek the advancement of God's glory, our honourable sovereign's safety, and to the sure defence of this noble isle of England, and all by maintaining of the liberties of this honourable council, the fountain from whence all these do spring; my humble and hearty suit unto you all is to accept my good will, and that this that I have here spoken out of conscience and great zeal unto my prince and state may not be buried in the pit of oblivion, and so no good come thereof.

Upon this speech the house, out of a reverend regard of her majesty's honour, stopped his further proceeding before he had fully finished his speech. The message he meant and intended was that which was sent by her majesty to the house of commons in the said fourteenth year of her reign upon Wednesday the twenty-eighth day of May, by Sir Francis Knolles, knight, treasurer of her majesty's household, inhibiting them for a certain time to treat or deal in the matter touching the Scottish queen. Now follows the proceeding of the house upon this speech out of the original journal book itself.

Mr. Wentworth being sequestered the house as aforesaid for his said speech, it was agreed and ordered by the house upon the question (after sundry motions and disputations had therein) that he should be presently committed to the sergeants ward as prisoner, and so remaining should be examined upon his said speech for the extenuating of his fault therein, by all the privy council being of this house, the master of the requests, the captain of the guard, the treasurer of the chamber, the master of the jewel-house, the master of the wardrobe, the lieutenant of the Tower, Sir Thomas Scott, Sir Rowland Hayward, Mr. Attorney of the duchy, Mr. Henry Knolles the elder, Mr. Sampoole, Mr. Randall, Mr. Birched,

Mr. Marsh, who were appointed to meet this afternoon between two and three of the clock at the star-chamber and to make report at this house tomorrow next. And then the said Peter Wentworth was brought to the bar, and committed thereupon to the said sergeants ward according to the said order.

This afternoon-passages being thus transcribed for the most part out of the original journal book of the house of commons, now follows the examination of the said Mr. Wentworth before the committees before appointed, which is transcribed out of a memorial or copy thereof set down by the said Mr. Wentworth himself, being as followeth.

Post Meridiem

A true report of that which was laid to my charge in the star chamber by the committees of the parliament house (viz. the house of commons) that same afternoon (viz. Wednesday, February the eighth) after that I had delivered the speech in the house that forenoon, and my answer to the same.

COMMITTEES: First, where is your late speech you promised to deliver in writing?

WENTWORTH: Here it is, and I deliver it upon two conditions. The first is, that you shall peruse it all, and if you can find any want of good will to my prince and state in any part thereof, let me answer all as if I had uttered all. The second is, that you shall deliver it unto the queen's majesty; if her majesty or you of her privy council can find any want of love to her majesty of the state therein also, let me answer it.

C.: We will deal with no more than you uttered in the house.

W.: Your honours cannot refuse to deliver it to her majesty, for I do send it to her majesty as my heart and mind, knowing it will do her majesty good, it will hurt no man but myself.

C.: Seeing your desire is to have us deliver it to her majesty, we will deliver it.

W.: I humbly require your honours so to do.

C.: Then the speech being read, they said, here you have uttered certain rumours of the queen's majesty, where and of whom heard you them?

W.: If your honours ask me as councillors to her majesty, you shall pardon me; I will make you no answer: I will do no such injury to the place from whence I came; for I am now no private person, I am a public, and a counsellor to the whole state in that place where it is lawful for me to speak my mind freely, and not for you as councillors to call me to account for anything that I do speak in the house; and therefore if you ask me as councillors to her majesty, you shall pardon me, I will make no answer; but if you ask me as committees from the house, I will make you the best answer I can.

C.: We ask you as committees from the house.

W.: I will then answer you, and the willinger for that mine answer will be in some part so imperfect as of necessity it must be. Your question consisteth of these two points, where and of whom I heard these rumours? The place where I heard them was the parliament house; but of whom, I assure you I cannot tell.

C.: This is no answer to say you cannot tell of whom, neither will we take it for any.

W.: Truly your honours must needs take it for an answer, when I can make you no better.

C.: Belike you have heard some speeches in the town of her majesty's misliking of religion and succession; you are loath to utter of whom and did use speeches thereupon.

W.: I assure your honours I can show you that speech at my own house, written with my hand two or three years ago. So that you may thereby judge that I did not speak it of anything that I heard since I came to town.

C.: You have answered that, but where heard you it then?

W.: If your honours do think I speak for excuse's sake, let this satisfy you. I protest before the living God I cannot tell of whom I heard these rumours: yet I do verily think that I heard them of a hundred or two in the house.

C.: Then of so many you can name some.

W.: No surely, because it was so general a speech, I marked none; neither do men mark speakers commonly when they be general: and I assure you if I could tell, I would not. For I will never utter anything told me, to the hurt of any man, when I am not enforced thereunto, as in this case I may choose. Yet I would deal plainly with you, for I would tell your honours so, and if your honours do not credit me, I will voluntarily take an oath, if you offer me a Book, that I cannot tell of whom I heard those rumours. But if you offer me an oath of your authorities, I will refuse it, because I will do nothing to infringe the liberties of the house. But what need I to use these speeches? I will give you an instance whereupon I heard these rumours to your satisfying, even such a one as if you will speak the truth you shall confess that you heard the same as well as I.

C.: In so doing we will be satisfied, what is that?

W.: The last parliament (by which it may be conceived he meant and intended that parliament in *anno* 13 *Reginae Eliz.*) he that is now speaker (viz. Robert Bell, esquire, who was also speaker in the first session of this present parliament in *anno* 14 *Reginae eiusdem*) uttered a very good speech for the calling in of certain licences granted to four courtiers, to the utter undoing of six or eight thousand of the queen's majesty's subjects. This speech was so disliked of some of the council that he was sent for and so hardly dealt with that he came into the house with such an amazed countenance that it daunted all the house in such sort, that for ten, twelve, or sixteen days there was not one in the house that durst deal in any matter of importance. And in those simple matters that they dealt in, they spent more words and time in their preamble, requiring that they might not be mistaken, than they did in the matter they spake unto. This inconvenience grew unto the house by the councillors' hard handling of the said good member, whereupon this rumour grew in the house. Sirs, you may not speak against licences, the queen's majesty will be angry, the council will be too too angry, and this rumour I suppose there is not one of you here but heard it as well as I. I beseech your honours discharge your consciences herein as I do.

C.: We heard it we confess, and you have satisfied us in this; but how say you to the hard interpretation you made of the message that was sent into the house? (The words were recited.) I assure you I have never heard an harder interpretation of a message.

W.: I beseech your honours, first, was there not such a message sent unto the house?

C.: We grant that there was.

W.: Then I trust you will bear me record that I made it not; and I answer you that so hard a message could not have too hard an interpretation made by the wisest man in England. For can there by any possible means be sent a harder message to a council gathered together to serve God, than to say you shall not seek to advance the glory of God? I am of this opinion that there cannot be a more wicked message than it was.

C.: You may not speak against messages, for none sendeth them but the queen's majesty.

W.: If the message be against the glory of God, against the prince's safety, or against the liberty of this parliament house whereby the state is maintained, I neither may nor will hold my peace. I cannot in so doing discharge my conscience, whosoever doth send it. And I say, that I heartily repent me, for that I have hitherto held my peace in these causes, and I do promise you all (if God forsake me not) that I will never during life hold my tongue, if any message is sent wherein God is dishonoured, the prince perilled, or the liberties of the parliament impeached; and every one of you here present ought to repent you of these faults and to amend them.

C.: It is no new precedent to have the prince to send messages. (Then were two or three messages recited sent by two or three princes.)

W.: Sirs (said I), you do very evil to allege precedents in this order. You ought to allege good precedents to comfort and embolden men in good doing, and evil precedents to discourage and terrify men to do evil.

C.: But what meant you to make so hard interpretation of messages?

W.: Surely I marvel what you mean by asking this question. Have I not said, so hard a message could not have too hard an interpretation; and have I not set down the reason that moved me in my speech, that is to say, that for the receiving and accepting that message, God has poured so great indignation upon us that he put into the queen's majesty's heart to refuse good and wholesome laws for her own preservation; which caused many loving and faithful hearts for grief to burst out with sorrowful tears, and moved all papists, traitors to God, to her majesty, and to every good Christian government, in their sleeves to laugh the whole parliament house to scorn. Have I not thus said, and do not your honours think it did so?

C.: Yes truly. But how durst you say that the queen's majesty had unkindly abused herself against the nobility and people?

W.: I beseech your honours tell me how far you can stretch these words of her unkindly abusing and opposing herself against her majesty's nobility and people? Can you apply them any further than I have applied them, that is to say, in that her majesty called the parliament of purpose to prevent traitorous perils to her person, and for no other cause, and in that her majesty did send unto us two bills, willing us to take our choice of that we liked best for her majesty's safety and thereof to make a law promising her royal consent thereunto; and did we not first choose the one, and her majesty refused it? Yet did not we nevertheless receive the other? And agreeing to make a law thereof, did not her majesty in the end refuse all our travails? And did not the lord keeper in her majesty's presence in the beginning of the parliament show this to be the occasion that we were called together? And did not her majesty in the end of the parliament refuse all our travails, is not this known to all here present and to all the parliament house also? I beseech your honours discharge your consciences herein and utter your knowledge simply as I do, for in truth herein her majesty did abuse her nobility and subjects, and did oppose herself against them by the way of advice.

C.: Surely we cannot deny it, you say the truth.

W.: Then I beseech your honours show me if it were not a dangerous doing to her majesty in these two respects. First in weakening, wounding, and discouraging the hearts of her majesty's loving and faithful subjects, thereby to make them the less able or the more fearful and unwilling to serve her majesty. Another time, on the other side was it not a raising up and encouraging the hearts of her majesty's hateful enemies to adventure any desperate enterprise to her majesty's peril and danger?

C.: We cannot deny but that it was very dangerous to her majesty in those respects.

W.: And is it not a loving part of a subject to give her majesty warning to avoid danger?

C.: It is so.

W.: Then why do your honours ask how I dare tell a truth, to give the queen's majesty warning to avoid her danger?

I answer you thus, I do thank the lord my God, that I never found fear in myself to give the queen's majesty warning to avoid her danger, be you all afraid thereof if you will, for I praise God I am not, and I hope never to live to see that day, and yet I will assure your honours that twenty times and more, when I walked in my grounds revolving this speech to prepare against this day, my own fearful conceit did say unto me that this speech would carry me to the place whither I shall now go, and fear would have moved me to have put it out; then I weighed whether in good conscience, and the duty of a faithful subject, I might keep myself out of prison, and not to warn my prince from walking in a dangerous course; my conscience said unto me that I could not be a faithful subject if I did more respect to avoid my own danger than my prince's danger: herewith all I was made bold and went forward as your honours heard, yet when I uttered those words in the house, that there was none without fault, no not our noble queen; I paused and beheld all your countenances, and saw plainly that those words did amaze you all. Then I was afraid with you for company, and fear bade me to put out those words that followed, for your countenances did assure me that not one of you would stay me of my journey; yet the consideration of a good conscience and of a faithful subject did make me bold to utter it in such sort as your honours heard, with this heart and mind I spake it, and I praise God for it, and if it were to do again I would with the same mind speak it again.

C.: Yea but you might have uttered it in better terms, why did you not so?

W.: Would you have me to have done as you of her majesty's privy council do, to utter a weighty matter in such terms as she should not have understood, to have made a fault; then it would have done her majesty no good, and my intent was to do her good.

C.: You have answered us.

W.: Then I praise God for it. And as I made a courtesy, another spake these words.

C.: Mr. Wentworth will never acknowledge himself to make a fault, nor say that he is sorry for anything that he doth speak, you shall hear none of these things come out of his mouth.

W.: Mr. Seckford, I will never confess that to be a fault to love the queen's majesty whilst I live, neither will I be sorry for giving her majesty warning to avoid danger while the breath is in my body; if you do think it a fault to love her majesty, or to be sorry that her majesty should have warning to avoid her danger, say so, for I cannot; speak for yourself, Mr. Seckford.

A POLITIC PLAT

For the honour of the prince, the great profit of the public state, relief of the poor, preservation of the rich, reformation of rogues and idle persons, and the wealth of thousands that know not how to live. Written for a New Year's gift to England, and the inhabitants thereof, by Robert Hitchcock, late of Caversfield in the county of Buckingham, gentleman. Imprinted at London, by John Kingston. 1 January, 1580.

ROBERT HITCHCOCK (fl. 1570–1591), a gentleman from Buckinghamshire, is known almost solely from his writings which denote him a military man. In 1586 he was to raise 150 volunteers from his county for service in the Netherlands. From there he brought back and translated from the Italian *The Quintessence of Wit* by Francisco Sansovino. He dedicated a military tract to the earl of Essex in 1591, and among his unpublished papers is a proposal to the queen to station ships of war in the channel to annoy foreign enemies.

His *Politic Plat*, advocating the development of English fisheries, proposes a new solution to an old problem. Tudor governments had sought to encourage the fishing industry for commercial and naval purposes by decreeing Fish Wednesdays as well as Fish Fridays. Fish days had been legislated in 1549, 1559, and 1564. In 1585 Wednesday was dropped, but the policy of Fish days was to be revived again in the seventeenth century.

At the time Hitchcock's proposal was considered more than a crack-pot's dream, and Thomas Digges introduced the subject of the fishery plan into parliament. Unfortunately, an early prorogation stopped the progress of the plan and cut short any likelihood of its ultimate realization. However, Thomas Mun, a leading Jacobean economist, commended Hitchcock's scheme, and Tobias Gentleman and John Keymer wrote books developing the arguments presented in the *Politic Plat*.

The present edition has been abridged by about one-third and is taken from the original 1580 edition.

To the friendly reader.

FORASMUCH as the almighty God hath blessed and enriched this noble kingdom with the sweet dew of his heavenly goodness; and stored therein many hidden rich and pleasant treasures for our benefits, to reveal unto us when his good pleasure is: I think therefore, every man is rather born to profit his native soil and commonwealth in revealing

6—The illustration opposite is a view of the first Royal Exchange, the interior facing west, engraved by Wenceslaus Hollar in 1644. Sir Thomas Gresham, Elizabeth's brilliant financier, founded the Royal Exchange at his own expense. The building was designed by the Flemish Henri de Pas, after the Italianized Antwerp Exchange, and was erected between 1566 and 1570. Not only was the Exchange the material embodiment of the spirit of Gresham and the new men of commerce, but it was also a practical demonstration of the classic principles in architecture advocated by Shute three years before. It was one of the first buildings in England with more than a ' classic overlay on a Gothic framework,' and it admirably illustrates the transition occurring in English architecture. This building served the needs of finance and commerce until its destruction in the great fire of 1666 after which a truly Anglo-classic edifice replaced it.

Wenceslaus Hollar's drawings (illustrations 1,5,10,13) provide the most artistic information about London and its buildings between 1637 and 1677. Hollar, a Bohemian, was born in Prague in 1607. He was working in Germany in 1636 when the earl of Arundel, on an embassy to the Emperor Ferdinand, found him and attached him to his legation. The next year Hollar etched plates of the works of art in the earl's collections in England. About 1639 he was made drawing master to the royal princes. He remained in England until 1644 when, after fighting for the Royalists and being captured, he escaped to Antwerp. There he did 350 plates in six years, many of the English scenes being done from sketches he had previously made. He returned to England in 1652, and during the Restoration he received court employment and was appointed the king's 'scenographer, or designer of prospects.' However, his material fortune was never great, and he died in 1677 in financial distress though 'having led a painful and labourious life' during which he made over 2700 plates. Sir Seymour Haden, the famous etcher, appraised the quality of Hollar's work thus:

> 'If anyone want truth without pretension let him go to Hollar. If he want perfection of "biting" and the precise degree of gradation required, let him also go to Hollar. If he want to live in the time illustrated, let him again go to Hollar. People sometimes say to me, "What is it you see in Hollar?" and I always answer, "Not quite, but nearly everything."'

For Hollar's life and reproductions of his engravings, see A.M.Hind, *Wenceslaus Hollar*, London, 1922.

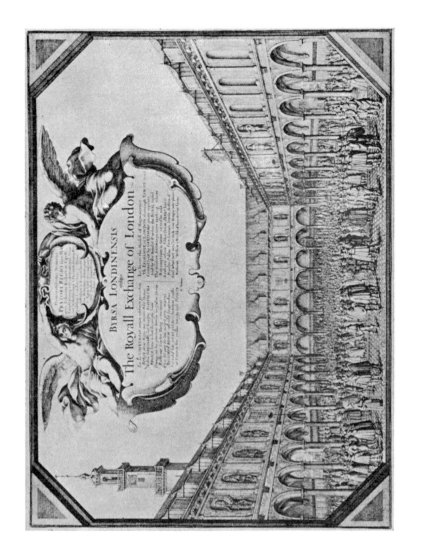

the same secrets and hidden treasure to his country, if they be showed to him; than to seek after his own private gain and glory thereby. So I have taken upon me, good gentle reader, to unfold some of the same hidden treasures to my country; which I suppose is manifested unto me. Albeit there be a great number that can more sweetly, and with pleasanter words and sugared style, than I, set out the matter to thee, if they knew it, in far better method and order; yet the zeal and duty I bear to my country, being partly fed with hope of thy good patience, gentle reader, and partly emboldened with the forewarning that Ecclesiastes c.ii. giveth, which is that no man shall be condemned before his tale be told, and inquisition thereof made: whereby righteous judgment may thereof follow lest he, as Solomon saith, procure to himself folly and shame, in giving sentence of a matter before he hear it.

These things, I say, have moved me to put forth my simple mind in writing to my country; and praying thee, of thy good courtesy, to peruse it, and to thoroughly weigh the depths thereof in the balance of thy grave judgment: and if thou find the pith and kernel of my labour fruitful to thee and thy country, as I doubt nothing thereof but thou shalt; then may it be, that it hath pleased God to pour out his knowledge as well upon a soldier as upon a great clerk, for now and then wisdom may be shrouded under an unclean cloak. And I doubt not also, but the same reasons and duty that bound me these many years to travail in this action, to my great cost and charge, to find out the way and perfection thereof, shall also bind thee and move thee effectually to favour it; to further it in the parliament house; and to defend my imperfection against a sort of Momus sect and Zoilus' band, that can rather find fault with the man than with the matter, be it never so well, or any way put to their helping hands to amend the same (if it be not orderly). My care hath been to please my country, and the honest and grave sort thereof; which if this my travail shall do and content, I have cause to thank almighty God for it, and think my time well spent.

For in this little book, gentle reader, thou shalt find (if the same be executed according to law) it importeth much matter, bringing great plenty and much wealth and benefit to all the inhabitants of this realm; it provideth for the poor in honest and decent manner, bringing them to a good and a godly vocation of life: with many other special benefits to this kingdom and commonwealth; which for tediousness' sake, lest I weary thee, I refer thee to the book itself, where thou mayest at large see them with the eye, judge them by thy good discretion, wisdom, and favour, and further them by thy good help and assistance at convenient time.

So fare thee heartily well,

ROBERT HITCHCOCK.

The Epistle to England.

For me, O noble and renowned England! to write to thee, that hath bred and brought forth so many famous, honourable, wise, and learned men; who be not only most expert in all politic government, but also most happily furnished each way with all manner of knowledge, cunning, and wisdom, thoroughly seen in all the noble sciences and arts liberal: both thou and they may think, and think truly, overmuch boldness and mere arrogancy in me, that neither am furnished of good letters, knowledge, histories, or other means to make a plausible way of that, or for that I wish should have good success at thy hands, or of good opinion at theirs. Much more I am afraid lest thou hold it outrage and presumption for me to dedicate unto thee, and trouble thee with the patronage and defence of this my device; a fruitless thing, as some may deem it, before it be thoroughly considered of them.

But since I am void of presumption, all manner of ways (God be my record), and am one of thine own brood, fostered up with the fat of thy loins; and take not upon me to discourse of vanities, but of the setting out of part of thy flowing goodness that hath so embalmed this thy region with secret riches: though a world of eyes be poring in my face, I trust in thy own cause and for thine own sake, and the goodness of the matter itself, and for such reasons and arguments as I have set down, to find a great number of willing hearts, and well disposed minds—that with open mouth will confess the invention sound and good; and the means to bringing it to pass, both easy and profitable—to further their native soil and the benefit thereof, with this my simple action I take in hand of displaying part of thy riches.

And, therefore, the grave and wise men of this land, of their good grace and favour, I trust undoubtedly will accept, and take in good part, this my good will and long travail, and shroud and defend me and my book, under the wings of their wisdom, as under a sure anchor-hold, against the rash opinions of those that rather wilfully than wisely will imagine no politic provision can come from the bulwark of a soldier that hath trailed the pike.

But as God raiseth instruments to set out his glory in divers ways, and by divers degrees; so let it not be grievous to thee, O England! nor to the better sort of men, that one of thine own, though not so finely as others, do set abroad part of thy riches, wealth, and glory to enrich thy own peculiar people withal; and hath opened the golden stream of thy secret storehouse to the inhabitants of the same. But likewise, open thou by thy divine providence the hearts of the wise, grave, and rich of this land that they will affect it, embrace it, put their helping hands to it, and willingly further it by all possible means they can, for the common profit of the inhabitants. Inasmuch as, by God's means, so great a benefit is offered with small care, little toil, and no cost to make all this land blessed, the people thereof happy, strong, and invincible.

If I should particularly discourse the several commodities that flow from it, in particularity, and the number of all sorts of people within this land that shall be maintained thereby, I should but weary you with a long tale and keep you from the matter I desire you should know.

Therefore commending the goodness thereof to your wisdom and myself to your favourable exposition, I end.

Yours humbly, in all that I may, at commandment
during life, for the honour of prince and country,
ROBERT HITCHCOCK.

· · · · · · · · ·

Hitchcock's New Year's Gift to England

The great care that the queen's majesty and her noble progenitors have taken to banish and root out of their dominions that loathsome monster idleness (the mother and breeder of vagabonds) is most apparent by their wholesome laws and provisions, made from time to time; beginning at the worthy reign of King Edward III, King Richard II, and so descending to her majesty's most prudent and virtuous government: wherein as well public provisions hath been to help the commonwealth, as some sharp and severe punishment provided, if common policy would not serve. Yet, nevertheless, all these laws, so circumspectly made, could not, nor cannot banish that pestilent canker out of this commonwealth by any degree; but that the same increaseth daily more and more: to the great hurt and impoverishing of this realm.

For remedy whereof, almighty God, by the most commodious situation of this island, and his blesssings, both of the land thereof and of the sea wherewith it is environed, hath provided a most convenient means; both for labour for the idle, and for food, benefit, and riches for the inhabitants. Whereby, the lusty vagabonds and idle persons (the roots, buds, and seeds of idleness) shall at all hands and in all places be set on work, and labour willingly, and thereby prove good subjects, and profitable members of this commonwealth. This realm and the inhabitants bordering as well upon the sea as upon the land throughout the same, in short time to be marvellously enriched. Nine thousand mariners more than now presently there is, to serve in her majesty's ships at all times if need be. The coins of gold and silver that issue plentifully out of this realm to stay and abide within this land: for restraint whereof both her highness and her noble progenitors have made divers laws and statutes, but yet never could do the same. A ready means to cause foreign wares to be brought hither. Her majesty's custom and subsidies greatly augmented. Her navigation greatly increased. The towns bordering on the sea coasts, now in ruins and void of English inhabitants, to be peopled and inhabited by her majesty's own peculiar subjects; to the great strength of this realm and terror of the enemy.

Besides the help that shall be ministered to two hundred and twenty-five decayed towns in England and Wales; with a stock of two hundred pounds to every decayed town to set the poor on work. And to eight principal port towns within this land, appointed for sundry causes appertaining to this Plat eight thousand pounds; which is to every principal port town one thousand pounds, to be a stock for ever. Besides four hundred fishing ships to continue for ever. And two good ships of war, furnished warlike, to defend the fishing ships. All which things, God willing, may be performed within three years, without cost or charge to any man, as by this Plat shall appear. And also an infinite number of people, as well rich and poor, set to work by divers means and degrees; which things will relieve many a poor man, and save many a tall fellow from the gallows.

For performance whereof. First, there must be made four hundred fishing ships, after the manner of Flemish busses, of the burden of three score and ten tons the ship, or more, but none under: which will cost two hundred pounds the ship, with the furniture, if it be ready furnished to the sea in all things necessary. Every ship requireth one skilful master to govern it, twelve mariners or fishermen, and twelve of the strong, lusty beggars or poor men taken up through this land.

Which in the whole amounteth to the number of ten thousand persons, at the first manning of the ships. So that with a little experience, this realm hath clearly increased nine thousand mariners more than were in this land before.

These ships so made, furnished, and manned must be appointed to such roads and haven towns as border upon the sea coasts compassing this realm round about; beginning at London, and so orderly proceeding, according to the table hereunto annexed. And being thus placed, having with them to the seas for their victuals, sufficient bread, beer, butter, and cheese; with barrels (empty), cask, and salt; with order also not to return until they be fully laden: shall go yearly a-fishing and kill herrings upon the coasts of England and Ireland, presently in all ways as they kill them, to gill them, salt, pickle, and barrel them, after the Flemish manner, with 'salt upon salt,' which is the best kind of salt. And shall fish for herrings yearly during the time of herring fishery, which is fourteen or fifteen weeks. In which time, by God's grace, every ship will kill, at the least, fifty last of the best sort of herrings; amounting in the whole to twenty thousand last. Every last, being sold but for £10, which is 16s.8d. the barrel, draweth to £200,000 yearly for the best herrings only. Perhaps they may laden their ships twice yearly with herrings; and then this sum is doubled in that time of herring fishing.

And to the end that the herrings shall be wholesome for the subject, stranger, or for whomsoever shall buy them, and that the good usage thereof may gain credit where they shall happen to be uttered, they shall account in making of their herrings upon the sea, so as sixteen barrels made there, make but twelve barrels at their home-coming to their several ports; when they shall be new sorted, severed, couched, and truly and justly packed by such honest and substantial men as shall be sworn and purposely chosen for that intent, and they to have two pence of every barrel, according to the statute for that purpose provided:

dividing the full herrings into two several sorts, marking the biggest and best herrings with this several mark B: the second, with the second mark M: also the shotten herrings [empty herrings that have cast their spawn] with this proper mark S. To the end no man may be abused. Every barrel containing two and thirty gallons, according to the statute made 22 Edward IV, c. 2, which twelve barrels make a last.

Out of which said number of 20,000 last of herrings, nine or ten thousand last will be a sufficient rate or portion to satisfy this whole realm. The residue, being 10,000 or 11,000 last, drawing to £100,000, being ordered as aforesaid, will be of as great estimation in France, as the Flemish herrings be: and will be sold and uttered in divers parts of that region; as in Normandy, in Nantes, in Bordeaux, and in Rochelle. And the further south that the countries do lie, the better utterance for fish. For these herrings, return will be made of all such necessaries as we want in this realm, viz., wine and woads (for which is always paid ready gold), salt, canvas, glass, dowlass, and divers other things. The custom also for the queen's majesty, being paid upon every last of that which shall be transported and sold beyond the sea, cometh to £5,000, after the rate of poundage, for this number of herrings only.

The other part of this great blessing of God may aptly be taken and applied, viz., these 400 busses or fishing ships, may take cod and ling and Newfoundland fish: the advantage and profit whereof, this realm and subjects, of late years, for the most part, have lost, and suffered strangers (the Flemings and other nations) to take. Who, seeing our careless dealing, have not only taken this beneficial fishing from us, but very warily doth sell the same commodity unto us; and thereby carrieth out of this land both gold and silver and a marvellous quantity of double double beer, and other things: satisfying us with these fishes, which through our own sloth, we lose; which being taken by ourselves, as a special blessing of God appointed unto us, and so sold to them and others, it must needs follow that we should save a great mass of gold within this land. And for that fish they now utter unto us, we should receive of them the commodities of the Low Countries, viz., Holland cloth, rape oil, hops, madder, all sorts of wire, and divers other merchandise; or else their ready gold and money, whereby this realm and subjects should be mightily enriched.

This great benefit is no less to be valued for the profit of this realm and subjects, than the benefit only of the herrings. For every ship, being but of the burden of 70 tons, if God bless it with safe return from New-foundland, will bring home to his port in August 20,000 of the best and middle sort of wet [fresh] fish (at the least) called blank fish, and 10,000 dry fish; which being sold on the ship's return, as it may be, at New-haven [Havre] in France but for forty shillings the hundred of wet fish (which is not four pence the fish), and twenty shillings the hundred of dry fish (which is not two pence the fish), amounteth to £500 at the least.

Likewise any other of the ships, but of the like burden, going a-fishing to the Ward House [near North Cape], to Iceland, to the North Seas of England and Scotland, or to Ireland, cometh home, at the same time, laden with 15,000 cod, and 10,000 ling: which being sold but for forty shillings the hundred, one with another, amounteth to £500.

And besides that, every ship will bring home to his port four or five ton of oil made of the fish livers, worth to be sold for £12 the ton.

The way how this Plat shall be brought to pass and performed, with-out cost or charges to any man, is by borrowing of £80,000 for three years; which forty men in a shire will and may easily accomplish, if every man lend but £50, upon good assurance, after the rate of ten pounds yearly upon every £100 lent: which sums shall be repaid again within three years, at two payments.

In what sort this money shall be levied is set down in the first table following.

The second table doth declare to whom, and to what principal port towns the money shall be delivered, how it shall be used, who shall give assurance for the same, and therewith provide the foresaid ships.

The third table doth show to what haven towns these fishing ships shall be placed; and how the money shall be levied to make payment of the money borrowed, and to answer all charges.

And in the fourth table is set down how many decayed towns, in every shire, shall have a continual stock of £200 apiece, to set the poor on work for ever. Also how every man shall be pleased and liberally con-sidered, that shall be appointed to the execution of this Plat. And how the payments of the money borrowed, with the interest money for the time of forbearance, shall be made and paid at two payments. . . .

Objections; and the answers of the author.

First, what moves you to think that there will be found forty men in every shire of England, that will lend £50 a man, for three years, in this covetous time, when every man is for himself?

THIS realm of England and Wales is very populous, and the most part be the poorer sort of people, who daily do harken when the world should amend with them. They are indifferent in what sort, so that their state were relieved; and so perhaps apt to assist rebellion, or to join with whomsoever dare invade this noble island, if any such attempt should be made. Then are they meet guides to bring the soldiers or men of war to the rich men's wealth. For they can point with their finger, ' There it is! ' ' Yonder it is! ' ' Here it is! ' ' And he hath it! ' and, ' She hath it that will do us much good! ' and so procure martyrdom with murder to many wealthy persons, for their wealth. Therefore the wise and wealthy men of this land had need, by great discretion, to devise some speedy help therein; that this poorer sort of people may be set to some good arts, science, occupations, crafts, and labours, by which means they might be able to relieve themselves of their great need and want. And being brought to such vocation of life, having some good trade to live upon, there is no doubt but that they will prove good and profitable subjects; and be careful to see this commonwealth flourish; and will spend their lives and blood to defend the same, and their little wealth, their liberties, their wives, and children. For having nothing, they are desperate; but having some little goods, they will die before they lose it. Wherefore if this matter be looked into with eyes of judgment, there is no doubt of borrowing the money upon the assurance and interest. For I do know in some shires four men that will gladly lend so much money as the whole shire is appointed to lend. In Holland and Zealand the rich men make so sure account of their fishing, that they appoint their children's portions to be increased by that use.

I pray you, show me by what occasion or means this huge number of beggars and vagabonds do breed here in England; and why you appoint twelve of them to every ship? I think they may carry the ship away and become pirates.

If you consider the poverty that is, and doth remain in the shire towns and market towns within this realm of England and Wales; which towns being inhabited with great store of poor householders, who by their poverty are driven to bring up their youth idly, and if they live until they come to man's estate, then are they past all remedy to be brought to work. Therefore at such time as their parents fail them, they begin to shift, and acquaint themselves with some one like brought up, that hath made his shift with dicing, cosening, picking or cutting of purses: or else, if he be of courage, plain robbing by the wayside, which they count an honest shift for the time, and so come they daily to the gallows.

Hereby grows the great and huge number of beggars and vagabonds which, by no reasonable means or laws, could yet be brought to work, being thus idly brought up. Which perilous state and imminent danger that they now stand in, I thought it good to avoid by placing twelve of these poor people into every fishing ship; according to this Plat.

Who when they shall find and perceive that their diet for all the whole year is provided, and that two voyages every year will yield to every man for his pains £20 clear, and for ever to continue; by which honest trade they shall be able to live in estimation amongst men; whereas before they were hated, whipped, almost starved, poor and naked, imprisoned, and in danger daily to be marked with a burning iron for a rogue and to be hanged for a vagabond. When they shall find these dangers to be avoided by their travail, and thereby an increase of wealth to ensue: they will be glad to continue this good and profitable vocation, and shun the other. Besides that it is well known that six mariners or seafaring men are able to rule and govern twelve land men that be not acquainted with the sea: and therefore it is to be doubted that this kind of people will prove pirates; they be so base-minded. For the heart, mind, and value of a man is such, and his spirit is so great, that he will travel all the kingdoms of princes to seek entertainment, rather than he will show his face to beg or crave relief of thousands of people that be unworthy to unbuckle his shoes: and in his great want, will take with force and courage from them that hath, to serve his necessity; thinking it more happy to die speedily than to live defamed and miserably. Of which sort of people, at the breaking up of wars, there are a great number of worthy and valiant soldiers, that have served in the wars with invincible minds: who, through want of living, either depart as aforesaid; or else, if they tarry in England, hanging is the end of the most part of them.

How may so many ships be provided, for want of timber, masts, cables, pitch, and iron? And where shall masters and mariners be had; with other needful things, as salt, nets, and cask?

To that, I must put you in mind of Holland, Zealand, and Friesland, that of late years, have flourished with ships, mariners, and fishermen; and thereby proved of marvellous wealth. No country more so. And all the timber they used for their ships came from the dominions of other princes. Their cables, masts, pitch, and tar came from the countries under the king of Denmark; the sails for their ships, the thread for their nets came from Normandy and Brittany; their salt came from France, Portugal, and Spain; and their iron came from the countries of other princes.

We need not doubt of these things. For there are ships presently to be bought (for the sums of money appointed for every ship) both here in this realm, and in Holland, France, and in other places. And if there were not, I could name the places in this realm where there is plenty of timber. If you do remember the great and wonderful woods of timber trees that are in Ireland, you will shake off that doubt. And for iron; that there is great plenty made within this land, I may call to witness the inhabitants of the Forest of Dean, the county of Sussex, with other places. And for all other needful things the havens, ports, and realm of England lieth nearer to those countries where plenty is than those of the Flemings do.

And for masters there are plenty of coast men, which will gladly serve that place, that be sufficient men. And for mariners there is great store of poor fishermen all along the coast of England and Wales, that will willingly serve in these fishing ships, and use the craft of fishing: their gain will be so great. And for salt there is great plenty made at the Witchs [Droitwich, Nantwich, Northwich] in Cheshire, and in divers other places; besides many salt houses standing upon the coast of England that make salt by seething of salt sea water. And besides there is the great store of salt that will be brought yearly into England by the merchants and others, to make 'salt upon salt.' Also for cask there is a great store of oak, ash, and beech growing in many places of England; so that there can be no want of cask if there be use to use it; nor yet of any other thing aforesaid, if good consideration be had.

This Plat, being put into execution, will breed such store of mariners that whensoever the noble navy of England shall be set to the seas for the safeguard of this land; there shall be no want of mariners to serve in the same: whereas now they be both scant and hard to be found. Look back into Holland, where practice is used; and see what store is there!

You appoint ten thousand last of herrings to be sold in France. How can that be, so long as the Flemings, the Frenchmen, and other nations do fish; who have already won the credit of their fish? They shall sell, when we cannot; then where shall the fish taken by us be uttered?

There is no doubt but there will be ten thousand last of herrings to spare, this realm being served, if these four hundred fishing ships with these fishermen be appointed to the seas: for they will take their place to fish within the queen's majesty's seas; and so shall serve both England and France plentifully, and also better cheap than the Flemings are able to do. And the herrings, cod, and Newland fish, being used in such sort as the Flemings do, will be of as great estimation as theirs be, and may yearly be sold and uttered in France; as at Dieppe that serves and victuals all Picardy; at Newhaven [Havre] that serves all base [lower] Normandy; and at the town of Rouen, that serves all the high countries of France; for thither cometh yearly three hundred lighters, called gabers, with wines, of ten or twelve hundred tons a gaber; and their best return is fish and salt. And for the other parts of France, as Rochelle and Bordeaux; also the merchants that travel into Spain, Portugal, Italy, Barbary, and Africa, carrying fish: the further south and south-west that the fish, well used, is carried, the dearer it is and greatly desired. Wherefore let all men fish that will, of what country soever, for there is fish in plenty in these northern seas for them all, if there were a thousand sail of fishing ships more than there is; and the English nation shall and may weary them out for their travail and labour; where they fish is not far; their ports, harbours, and roads be at hand; their ships cost the fishermen nothing. Therefore the Englishmen shall better be able to sell good cheap than any other nation; by means whereof they shall sell when others cannot. And so the Flemings, being put from uttering their herrings in France, shall be driven to leave their great ships; and to fish in smaller vessels near the shore to serve their own turns: as heretofore they have caused us to do for fear of them and every tempest; triumphing at our folly, for not taking this great benefit and blessing of God poured into our laps.

How do you know that nine or ten thousand last of herrings will serve all England? And when wars shall happen between England and France, where shall we sell the rest of our herrings and other fish; the Flemings being provided for by their own people?

By estimation, five thousand last of herrings do serve London; out of which portion, all the shires about London are served. And by the like estimation, five thousand last more will serve all England.

And if wars should happen between France and England, then the Italians, Spaniards, Flemings, and other nations do bring into England all sorts of French commodities, as wines, woad, lockromes [lockrams, a kind of linnen], and canvas of all sorts. These merchants will daily look for profit: and in time of wars nothing doth pass with less danger, sooner is vented and made ready money, than these herrings, cod, ling, and Newland fish. So there is no doubt of utterance for fish, either in wars or in peace.

Let experience of other countries serve for this wholly. And I think it good to let you understand how herrings were sold in France, *anno* 1577.

The best Flemish herrings were sold for £24 10s. the last. Yarmouth herrings (who, of late, do use and order their herring as the Flemings do) were sold for £20 12s. the last. Irish herrings, for £18 the last. Coast herrings and Scotch herrings, for £11 the last.

These differences be in herrings, which being used as is set down in this Plat, will be in all places (within a little time) equal in goodness with the Flemish herrings.

In what order do the Flemings, the Frenchmen, and others fish for herrings, cod, and Newland fish?

First behold this sea Plat or proportiture here set down showing how the same strangers do fish in their great ships upon the English coast: and how our English men, for fear of them and of every tempest, as aforesaid, do fish in small vessels near the shore.

The Flemings set out of Flanders, Holland, and Zealand yearly at Bartholomewtide [24 August] four or five hundred busses, to fish for herrings upon the east coast of England; where before they fish, they ask leave at Scarborough, as evermore they have done: with which honour (and no profit) this realm and subjects hath hitherto been vainly fed. And amongst them, this is the order. One man provides the ship, another the victuals and salt, the third the cask, the fourth the nets: and when the ships come home they divide the fish.

There goeth out of France commonly five hundred sail of ships yearly in March to Newfoundland, to fish for Newland fish, and come home again in August. Amongst many of them, this is the order. Ten or twelve mariners do confer with a money man, who furnisheth them with money to buy ships, victuals, salt, lines, and hooks, to be paid his money at the ship's return, either in fish or money, with £35 upon the £100 in money lent.

Likewise here in England, in the West Country, the like order is used. The fishermen confer with the money man, who furnisheth them with money to provide victuals, salt, and all other needful things; to be paid £25 at the ship's return, upon the £100 in money lent. And for some of the same money, men do borrow money upon £10 in the £100, and put it forth in this order to the fishermen. And for to be assured of the money ventured, they will have it assured [insured]; giving £6 for the assuring of every £100 to him that abides the venture of the ship's return: as thus. A ship of Exeter is gone to the Ward House, to fish for cod and ling. The venture of the ship, salt, and victuals is £300. For £18 all is assured. So that if the ship never return, yet the money man gaineth declaro [clear] £48 and his principal again.

So by these reasons there seemeth great good to be done by fishing when other men being at such charges do prove rich by using this trade. Shall not the English nation that thus shall fish (the greatest charges cut off) be more able to sell good cheap than any others may: and so weary them out, as aforesaid.

You say that much gold goeth forth of this land for wines and other French commodities: I pray you, to what value in the year doth the wines of France brought into England amount unto? And what several sorts of English wares be sold in France to buy the same?

I do esteem to come into England every year ten thousand tuns of Gascony and Rochelle wines, which at twenty crowns the tun, amounteth in English payment, to £60,000. The fleet that goeth from London to Bordeaux, carrieth commonly victuals, ballast, and some cloth. For the money is always made over by exchange out of London, out of Flanders, and out of Spain. And the ships that go from other places of this realm, as from Bristol, Wales, Westchester, Newcastle, Hull, and elsewhere to the vintage, carrieth (contrary to the law) leather, calves' skins, butter and tallow, with ready gold, as they may provide it all the whole year before.

At Rouen in France, which is the chiefest vent [mart], be sold our English wares, as Welsh and Manchester cottons, Northern kerseys, whites, lead, and tin: which money is commonly employed in Normandy and Brittany in all sorts of canvas with other small wares, and in lockromes, glass, and dowlass [coarse linen], pouldavis, olyraunce [?], and myndernex [?]; part for ready money, part for commodities. And woad is commonly ladened at Bordeaux and uttered there to our nation and others for money or cloth, or else not [sold at all.] These sorts of wares bought in France, besides the wine, amounts by estimation to six times as much as all the English wares that be sold for in France every year. And for a truth this trade of fishing is the best, and of lightest cost that can be found, to counteract the values of the French commodities. Experience doth show the same by the Flemings, who with their green [undried] fish, barrelled cod, and herrings, carry out of England for the same, yearly, both gold and silver and other commodities, and at the least ten thousand tuns of double double beer, and hath also all kinds of French commodities continually, both in time of wars and peace, by their trade only of fishing. Thus the great sums of gold that are carried yearly out of this land to the vintage, as appeareth by this Plat following, will stay: and wines, nevertheless, and other French wares of all sorts will be had and obtained for herrings and fish.

When you put your fishing Plat into the parliament house, what did you conceive by the speech of such burgesses as you conferred with of the same?

In the eighteenth year of the queen's majesty's reign, five or six days before the parliament house broke up [i.e., March 1576], I had the burgesses of almost all the stately port towns of England and Wales at dinner with me at Westminster: amongst whom the substance of my Plat was read, and of every man well liked; so that some were desirous to have a copy of the same, and said that ' they would, of their own cost and charges, set so many ships to the sea as was to their towns appointed, without the assistance of any other.' Of the like mind were the burgesses of Rye; and some said it were good to levy a subsidy of two shillings [in the pound] on land, and sixteen pence [in the pound on] goods, for the making of these fishing ships. Of which mind the Speaker, Master Bell, was; saying, ' A parliament hath been called for a less cause.' Other some said, ' It were good to give a subsidy for this purpose to ship these kind of people in this sort; for if they should never return, and so avoided [got rid of], the land were happy: for it is but the riddance of a number of idle and evil-disposed people.' But these men that so do think, will be of another mind within two years next after this Plat takes effect, as when they shall see, by this occasion only, such a number of carpenters and shipwrights set on work; such a number of coopers employed; such numbers of people making lines, ropes, and cables; dressers of hemp, spinners of thread, and makers of nets; so many salt houses set up to make salt, and ' salt upon salt.' And what a number of mariners are made of poor men; and what a number of poor men are set on work in those shires all along upon the sea coast in England and Wales in splitting of fish, washing of fish, packing of fish, salting of fish, carrying and recarrying of fish, and serving all the countries [counties] in England with fish. And to serve all those occupations aforesaid, there must depend an infinite number of servants, boys, and day-labourers, for the use of things needful. And withal to remember how that about England and Wales, there is established in four score haven towns, five fishing ships to every town to continue for ever, which will breed plenty of fish in every market; and that will make flesh [butcher's meat] good cheap. And that by the only help of God and these fishermen, there shall be established within England and Wales, to 225 decayed towns a stock of £200 to every decayed town, which shall continue for ever to set the poor people on work. And to conclude, I do carry that mind, that within few years there will be of these fishing towns of such wealth, that they will cast ditches about their towns, and wall the same defensively against the enemy to guard them and their wealth in more safety. What Englishman is he, think you! that will not rejoice to see these things come to pass. And, for my part, I perceive nothing but good success is likely to come of this Plat.

To further the same, I gave a copy hereof to my lord of Leicester six years past [1573], another copy to the queen's majesty four years past [1575]. Also to sundry of her majesty's privy council, certain copies. And in the end [March 1576] of the last parliament, holden in the said eighteenth year of her majesty's reign, I gave twelve copies to councillors of the law, and other men of great credit; hoping that God would stir up some good man to set out this work, which the author (being a soldier, trained up in the wars and not in the schools, with great charges and travail of mind, for his country's sake) hath devised and laid as a foundation for them that hath judgment to build upon.

Amongst whom, Master Leonard Digges, a proper gentleman and a wise, had one copy, who, being a burgess of the house, took occasion thereupon to desire licence to speak his mind concerning this Plat, saying that he spake for the commonwealth of all England and for no private cause. He (by report) did so worthily frame his speech for the common weal of his country that he hath gained thereby both fame and great good liking of all the hearers; and so concluded, desiring that this device might be read: which, for want of time, was deferred until their next assembly in parliament.

Finis.

A PARTICULAR DISCOURSE

Concerning the great necessity and manifold commodities that are like to grow to this realm of England by the western discoveries lately attempted, written in the year 1584, by Richard Hakluyt of Oxford, at the request and direction of the right worshipful Mr. Walter Raleigh, now knight, before the coming home of his two barks, and is divided into xxi chapters, the titles whereof follow in the next leaf.

RICHARD HAKLUYT (1552?–1616) began his interest in geography during his schooling at Westminster School and at Christ Church, Oxford, where he took his bachelor's degree in 1574 and his master's three years later. An avid reader of Greek, Latin, Italian, French, Spanish, Portuguese, and English, he wrote in 1582 *Divers Voyages touching the Discovery of America*. The following year his patron, Lord Howard of Effingham, procured for Hakluyt the chaplaincy to Sir Edward Stafford, Elizabeth's ambassador at Paris. While there he was urged by Secretary Walsingham to make ' diligent inquiry of such things as may yield any light unto our western discovery.' Besides reports to Walsingham, Hakluyt also forwarded to Walter Raleigh views on western voyages. Hakluyt's research in the writings of French and Spanish explorers was embodied in *A particular discourse concerning . . . western discoveries*. This essay, written in 1584 but never printed until 1877, was shown in manuscript to Queen Elizabeth, Walsingham, and possibly Sir Philip Sidney during 1584–1585 when Hakluyt was in England.

He returned to Paris, however, and stayed there until 1588 when he came to England to publish *The principal navigations, voyages, and discoveries of the English nation made by sea or over land*. The first edition (1589) of this work, dedicated to Walsingham, was the nucleus of the large three-volume collection published from 1598 to 1600. In 1606 Hakluyt joined the petitioners to King James I for a patent for the colonization of Virginia and became one of the chief adventurers in the London or South Virginia Company. But long before all this, he had ' trumpeted ' the cause of the expeditions to America promoted by Raleigh and Gilbert and gave generously his advice drawn from his vast fund of second-hand knowledge of the New World. His *Voyages* proved a reservoir of geographical knowledge for the seventeenth century colonizers and explorers, and Froude styled this work ' the prose epic of the modern English nation.'

The *Discourse concerning western discoveries* reflects the scholarly and antiquarian character of his larger work and also contains concrete arguments for new explorations and the advantages likely to accrue to England thereby. The list of equipment appended at the end shows a practical attitude towards the problem of colonization. The present selections are taken from the only printed edition in *The Collections of the Maine Historical Society, Second Series, Documentary History, vol. II*, edited by Charles Deane. Save for the deletion of long quotations in foreign languages, no abridgement has been made within a single chapter.

Cap. I.

That this Western discovery will be greatly for the enlargement of the
gospel of Christ, whereunto the princes of the reformed religion are
chiefly bound, amongst whom her majesty is principal.

SEEING that the people of that part of America from 30 degrees in Florida
northward unto 63 degrees (which is yet in no Christian prince's actual
possession) are idolaters; and that those which Stephen Gomez brought
from the coast of Norumbega in the year 1524 worshipped the sun, the
moon, and the stars, and used other idolatry, as it is recorded in the
history of Gonsaluo de Ouiedo, in Italian, fol.52 of the third volume
of Ramusius; and that those of Canada and Hochelaga in 48 and 50
degrees worship a spirit which they call Cudruaigny, as we read in the
tenth chapter of the second relation of Jacques Cartier, who saith:
This people believe not at all in God, but in one whom they call Cudruaigny; they say that often he speaketh with them, and telleth them
what weather shall follow, whether good or bad, etc., and yet notwithstanding they are very easy to be persuaded, and do all that they saw
the Christians do in their divine service, with like imitation and devotion,
and were very desirous to become Christians, and would fain have been
baptized, as Verarsanus witnesseth in the last words of his relation, and
Jacques Cartier in the tenth chapter before recited—it remaineth to be
thoroughly weighed and considered by what means and by whom this
most godly and Christian work may be performed of enlarging the
glorious gospel of Christ, and reducing of infinite multitudes of these
simple people that are in error into the right and perfect way of their
salvation. The blessed Apostle Paul, the converter of the Gentiles, Rom.:
10, writeth in this manner: Whosoever shall call on the name of the
Lord shall be saved. But how shall they call on him in whom they have
not believed? And how shall they believe in him of whom they have
not heard? And how shall they hear without a preacher? And how shall
they preach except they be sent? Then it is necessary for the salvation
of those poor people which have sat so long in darkness and in the shadow
of death, that preachers should be sent unto them. But by whom should
these preachers be sent? By them no doubt which have taken upon them
the protection and defence of the Christian faith. Now the kings and
queens of England have the name of Defenders of the Faith. By which

title I think they are not only charged to maintain and patronize the faith of Christ, but also to enlarge and advance the same. Neither ought this to be their last work, but rather the principal and chief of all others, according to the commandment of our Saviour, Christ, Matthew 6: First seek the kingdom of God and the righteousness thereof, and all other things shall be ministered unto you.

PLANTING FIRST NECESSARY.

Now the means to send such as shall labour effectually in this business is by planting one or two colonies of our nation upon that firm where they may remain in safety and first learn the language of the people near adjoining (the gift of tongues being now taken away), and by little and little acquaint themselves with their manner, and so with discretion and mildness distil into their purged minds the sweet and lively liquor of the gospel. Otherwise, for preachers to come unto them rashly without some such preparation for their safety, it were nothing else but to run to their apparent and certain destruction, as it happened unto those Spanish friars, that, before any planting, without strength and company, landed in Florida where they were miserably massacred by the savages. On the other side, by mean of planting first, the small nation of the Portuguese towards the south and east have planted the Christian faith according to their manner and have erected many bishoprics and colleges to train up the youth of the infidels in the same, of which act they more vaunt in all their histories and chronicles than of anything else that ever they achieved. And surely if they had planted the gospel of Christ purely, as they did not, they might justly have more rejoiced in that deed of theirs than in the conquest of the whole country or in any other thing whatsoever. The like may be said of the Spaniards, who (as it is in the preface of the last edition of Osorius, *De rebus gestis Emanuelis*) have established in the West Indies three archbishoprics, to wit, Mexico, Luna, and Onsco, and thirteen other bishoprics there named, and have built above 200 houses of religion in the space of fifty years or thereabouts. Now if they, in their superstition, by means of their planting in those parts, have done so great things in so short space, what may we hope for in our true and sincere religion, proposing unto ourselves in this action not filthy lucre nor vain ostentation, as they indeed did, but principally the gaining of the souls of millions of those wretched people, the reducing of them from darkness to light, from falsehood to truth, from dumb idols to the living God, from the deep pit of hell to the highest heavens. In the 16 of the Acts of the Apostles, when Paul sought to preach in Asia and to go into Bithinia, the Holy Ghost suffered him not. But at Troas a vision appeared unto him by night. There stood a man of Macedonia and prayed him, saying: Come into Macedonia and help us. And after he had seen the vision, immediately he prepared to go into Macedonia, being assured that the Lord had called him to preach the gospel unto them. Even so we, whiles we have sought to go into other countries (I would I might say to preach the gospel), God by the frustrating of our actions seemeth to forbid us to follow those courses, and the people of America cry out unto us, their next neighbours, to come and help them and bring unto them the glad tidings of the gospel. Unto the prince and people that shall be the occasion of this worthy work and shall open their coffers to the furtherance of this most godly enterprise, God shall open the bottomless treasures of his riches and fill them with abundance of his hidden blessings; as he did to the good Queen Isabella, which being in extreme necessity, laid her own jewels to gage for money to furnish out Columbus for the first discovery of the West Indies.

And this enterprise the princes of the religion (among whom her majesty is principal) ought the rather to take in hand, because the papists confirm themselves and draw others to their side, showing that they are the true Catholic church because they have been the only converters of many millions of infidels to Christianity. Yea, I myself have been demanded of them, how many infidels have been by us converted? Whereunto, albeit I alleged the example of the ministers which were sent from Geneva with Villegagnon into Brazil, and those that went with John Ribault into Florida, as also those of our nation that went with Frobisher, Sir Frances Drake, and Fenton; yet in very deed I was not able to name any one infidel by them converted. But God, quoth I, hath his time for all men, who calleth some at the ninth and some at the eleventh hour. And if it please him to move the heart of her majesty to put her helping hand to this godly action, she shall find as willing subjects of all sorts as any other prince in all Christendom. And as for the boasting of your conversion of such multitudes of infidels, it may justly be counted rather a perversion, seeing you have drawn them as it were out of Scylla into Charybdis, that is to say, from one error into another. Now therefore I trust the time is at hand when by her majesty's forwardness in this enterprise, not only this objection and such like shall be answered by our fruitful labour in God's harvest among the infidels, but also many inconveniences and strifes amongst ourselves at home in matters of ceremonies shall be ended. For those of the clergy, which by reason of idleness here at home, are now always coining of new opinions, having by this voyage to set themselves on work in reducing the savages to the chief principles of our faith, will become less contentious, and be contented with the truth in religion already established by authority. So they that shall bear the name of Christians shall show themselves worthy of their vocation, so shall the mouth of the adversary be stopped, so shall contention amongst brethren be avoided, so shall the gospel among infidels be published.

Cap. II.

That all other English trades are grown beggarly or dangerous, especially dangerous in all the king of Spain his dominions, where our men are driven to fling their Bibles and prayer books into the sea and to forswear and renounce their religion and conscience and consequently their obedience to her majesty.

WE are now to consider the quality and condition of all the trades which at this day are frequented by our nation. And first, to begin southward, and so come to the north; leaving Brazil and Guinea where we have little to do, let us first speak of our trade in Barbary. If any of our ships trading thither be driven upon the coast of Spain, and that proof may be made that we have been there, they make it a very sufficient cause of confiscation of ship and goods, and so they thrust our men into the inquisition, charging them that they bring armour, munition, and forbidden merchandise to strengthen the infidels against these parts of Christendom; which thing is committed to print and confessed by all our merchants trading thither. And though our men escape the Spaniards' tyranny, yet at the death of the prince in Barbary, all our men's goods there are subject to the spoil, the custom of the country permitting the people to rob and rifle until another king be chosen without making any kind of restitution. Besides that inconvenience, the traffic groweth daily to worse terms than heretofore. I omit to show here how divers have been undone by their servants which have become renegades, of whom by the custom of the country their masters can have no manner of recovery, neither call them into justice.

THE DOMINIONS OF THE KING OF SPAIN.

In all the king of Spain's dominions our men are either enforced with wounded consciences to play the dissembling hypocrites, or be drawn to mislike with the state of religion maintained at home, or cruelly made away in the inquisition. Moreover, he being our mortal enemy, and his empire of late being increased so mightily, and our necessity of oils and of colours for our clothing-trade being so great, he may arrest almost the one-half of our navy, our traffic and recourse being so great to his dominions.

THE TRADE OF TURKEY.

For the new trade in Turkey, besides the great expenses in maintaining a kind of ambassador at Constantinople, and in sending of presents to Selim the Grand Seignior, and to divers of his insatiable bassoes, our merchants are fain with large rewards to gratify the Knights of Malta, in whose danger their ships must often pass. Moreover that trade is so much to the detriment of the state of Venice, and all the other states of Italy, that they are daily occupied in seeking how they may overthrow the same. Neither is it the least incommodity that our ships are continually assaulted by the corsairs and pirates and galleys of Algiers, by which they had a rich ship, called the Mary Martin, sunk this year; and the last year another was taken at Tripoli in Barbary, and the master with another hanged, and the rest made slaves. Besides, the bark Reynolds was arrested at Malta, and at length with much ado delivered.

FRANCE.

To leave the Levant and to come to France, the traffic there of mine own knowledge is grown to such decay, partly by the impositions and taxes which are daily devised by the king, partly by their subtle sleights and devices to confiscate our clothes for insufficient workmanship, and partly by their own labour in making more and better cloth than heretofore they were accustomed, that our men for the most part are weary of the country, and some of them utterly undone by their subtle and unconscionable wrangling. As for all Flanders and the Low Countries, these eighteen years most cruel civil wars have so spoiled the traffic there that there is nothing but poverty and peril, and that which is worse, there is no hope of any speedy amendment.

ESTLAND.

To come to the Easterlings and the trades with the cities within the Sound of Denmark, they being deprived of the old privileges of the Steelyard here in London have not only offered our men at home many injuries in their cities, but seek all the means they can devise wholly to cut off all our occupying that way; and to the same purpose have lately clean debarred our men of their accustomed and ancient privileges in all their great towns. Also the exactions of the king of Denmark at our passage in and out by the sound to Lübeck, Danzig, Elbing, Riga, Reval, and the Narva, besides the power that he hath to arrest all our ships within the Sound at his pleasure, are two no small inconveniences and mischiefs.

RUSSIA.

Our trade into Muscovy is the last, which was so chargeable in the beginning, what with the cost of the discovery, what with presents to the emperor, together with the disorderly dealing of their factors, that it stood them in fourscore thousand pounds before they brought it to any good pass. And now after long hope of gain, the Hollanders, as also the men of Dieppe, are entered into their trade by the emperor's permission; yea, whereas at the first our men paid no custom, of late years, contrary to their first privilege, they have been urged to pay it. Also the charges of bringing the emperor's ambassador hither and maintaining him here, and the setting forth of her majesty's ambassador thither with presents to the emperor, lying all upon the poor merchants' necks, is no easy burden unto their shoulders. And to increase the same, the king of Denmark requireth a tribute of them, though they touch not upon any of his dominions. And now the emperor of Russia being late dead, it is greatly feared that the voyage will be utterly overthrown or else become not worth the continuance.

Thus having regard unto the premises, it behooveth us to seek some new and better trade, of less danger and more security, of less damage and of more advantage; the rather to avoid the wilful perjury of such of our English nation as trade to Spain and other of King Philip's dominions, where this oath following is usually ministered unto the master of our ships. First, he willeth the master to make a cross with his forefinger and his thumb, laying one over the other crosswise. This being done, he saith these words following: You shall swear to speak the truth of all things that shall be asked of you, and if you do not, that God demand it of you; and the English master must say, Amen. You shall swear by that cross that you bring no man in your ship but such as are good Christians, and do believe as our catholic church of Rome doth believe. Next, that you bring no manner of books but such as are allowed by our catholic church of Rome; and that you use no manner of prayers but such as are allowed by our church of Rome. What merchandise bring you; such and such. We will and command you and your company to come on land to mass every Sunday and holy day, upon pain of discommunication. Then they open their chests and look if the master and mariners bring any books with them in their chests. This done, the officers that come with the priests ask of the master and mariners cheese, butter, beef, bacon, and candles, as beggars, and they give it to them for fear they have of them, and so they go from the ships with their wallets full of victuals. The master doth pay four royals of plate for the bark that bringeth them aboard to visit them. Thus is wilful perjury permitted by the governors if they know it. Thus the covetous merchant wilfully sendeth headlong to hell from day to day the poor subjects of this realm. The merchant in England cometh here devoutly to the communion and sendeth his son into Spain to hear mass. These things are kept secret by the merchants, and such as depend upon the trade of merchandise are loath to utter the same.

Cap. III.

That this western voyage will yield unto us all the commodities of Europe, Africa and Asia, as far as we were wont to travel, and supply the wants of all our decayed trades.

IN THE FIRST VOLUME OF RAMUSIUS, FOL. 374, PAG. 2.

THE next thing is that now I declare unto you the commodities of this new western discovery, and what merchandise are there to be had, and from thence to be expected; wherein first you are to have regard unto the situation of the places which are left for us to be possessed. The countries, therefore, of America where-unto we have just title, as being first discovered by Sebastian Cabot, at the cost of that prudent prince King Henry the seventh, from Florida northward to 67 degrees (and not yet in any Christian prince's actual possession), being answerable in climate to Barbary, Egypt, Syria, Persia, Turkey, Greece, all the islands of the Levant sea, Italy, Spain, Portugal, France, Flanders, High Almayne, Denmark, Eastland, Poland, and Muscovy, may presently or within a short space afford unto us, for little or nothing, and with much more safety, either all or a great part of the commodities which the aforesaid countries do yield us at a very dear hand and with manifold dangers.

First, therefore, to begin at the south from 30 degrees, and to quote unto you the leaf and page of the printed voyages of those which personally have with diligence searched and viewed these countries. John Ribault writeth thus, in the first leaf of his discourse, extant in print both in French and English: We entered (saith he) and viewed the country which is the fairest, fruitfulest, and pleasantest of all the world, abounding in honey, wax, venison, wild fowl, forests, woods of all sorts, palm trees, cypresses, cedars, bays, the highest and greatest, with also the fairest vines in all the world, with grapes according, which naturally without art or man's help or trimming will grow to tops of oaks and other trees that be of wonderful greatness and height. And the sight of the fair meadows is a pleasure not able to be expressed with tongue, full of herons, curlews, bitterns, mallards, egrets, woodcocks, and all other kind of small birds, with harts, hinds, bucks, wild swine, and all other kind of wild beasts, as we perceived well both by their footing there, and also afterwards in other places by their cry and roaring in the night. Also there be conies and hares, silkworms in marvellous number, a great deal fairer and better than be our silkworms. Again, in the sixth leaf and second page; They showed unto us by signs that they had in the land gold and silver and copper, whereof we have brought some home. Also lead like unto ours, which we showed them. Also turquoises and great abundance of pearls, which as they declared unto us they took out of oysters, whereof there is taken ever along the river's side and amongst the reeds and in the marshes in so marvellous abundance as it is scant credible. And we have perceived that there be as many and as great pearls found there as in any country in the world. In the seventh leaf it followeth thus: The situation is under 30 degrees, a good climate, healthful, and of good temperature, marvellous pleasant, the people good and of a gentle and amiable nature, which willing will obey, yea, be contented to serve those that shall with gentleness and humanity go about to allure them, as it is necessary for those that be sent thither hereafter so to do. In the eighth leaf: It is a place wonderful fertile and of strong situation, the ground fat, so that it is like that it would bring forth wheat and all other corn twice a year. In the ninth leaf it followeth: We found there a great number of pepper trees, the pepper being yet green and not ready to be gathered. In the tenth leaf: There we saw the fairest and the greatest vines with grapes according, and young trees and small woods very well smelling, that ever were seen. Thus have you briefly the sum of the commodities which were found by John Ribault and his company on the coast of America from 30 to 34 degrees.

Moreover, Doctor Monardus, that excellent physician of Seville, writing of the trees of the West Indies in his book called *Joyful News out of the Newfound World*, maketh mention of a tree called sassafras, which the Frenchman found in Florida, fol.46 of his book, in manner following: From the Florida they bring a wood and root of a tree that groweth in those parts, of great virtues and excellencies, healing therewith grievous and variable diseases. It may be three years past that I had knowledge of this tree, and a Frenchman that had been in those parts showed me a piece of it and told me marvels of the virtues thereof, and how many and variable diseases were healed with the water which was made of it, and I judged that which now I do find to be true and have seen by experience. He told me that the Frenchmen which had been in the Florida at the time when they came into those parts had been sick the most of them of grievous and variable diseases and that the Indians did show them this tree and the manner how they should use it, etc.; so they did and were healed of many evils; which surely bringeth admiration that one only remedy should work so variable and marvellous effects. The name of this tree, as the Indians term it, is called pauame, and the Frenchmen call it sassafras. To be brief, the Doctor Monardus bestoweth eleven leaves in describing the sovereignties and excellent properties thereof.

The nature and commodities of the rest of the coast unto Cape Breton I will show unto you out of the printed testimonies of John Verarsanus and Stephen Gomez, both which in one year, 1524, discovered the said countries, and brought home of the people; Verarsanus into France, and Gomez into Spain.

Verasanus, falling in the latitude of 34 degrees, describeth the situation and commodities in this manner: Beyond this we saw the open country rising in height above the sandy shore, with many fair fields and plains full of mighty great woods, some very thick and some very thin, replenished with divers sorts of trees, and pleasant and delectable to behold as is possible to imagine. And your majesty may not think that these are like the woods of Hyrcania, or the wild deserts of Tartary, and the northern coasts, full of fruitless trees; but full of palm, date trees, bays, and high cypresses, and many other sorts of trees to us unknown in Europe, which yield most sweet savours far from the shore; neither do we think that they, partaking of the east world round about them, are altogether void of drugs and spicery and other riches of gold, seeing the colour of the land doth altogether argue it. And the land is full of many beasts, as red deer, fallow deer, and hares, and likewise of lakes and pools of fresh water, with great plenty of fowls convenient for all pleasant game. This land is in latitude of 34 degrees with good and wholesome air, temperate, between hot and cold; no vehement winds do blow in these regions, etc. Again, in the fourth leaf as it is in English, speaking of the next country, he saith: We saw in this country many vines growing naturally, which springing up took hold of the trees as they do in Lombardy, which, if by husbandmen they were dressed in good order, without all doubt they would yield excellent wines; for having oftentimes seen the fruit thereof dried, which was sweet and pleasant and not differing from ours, we think they do esteem of the same, because that in every place where they grow, they take away the under branches growing round about, that the fruit thereof may ripen the better. We found also roses, violets, lilies, and many sorts of herbs and sweet and odoriferous flowers. And after, in the sixth leaf, he saith: We were oftentimes within the land v. or vi. leagues, which we found as pleasant as is possible to declare, apt for any kind of husbandry of corn, wine, and oil. For therein there are plains 25 or 30 leagues broad, open and without any impediment of trees, of such fruitfulness that any seed being sown therein will bring forth most excellent fruit. We entered afterwards into the woods, which we found so great and thick that an army (were it never so great) might have hid itself therein, the trees whereof were oaks, cypresses, and other sorts unknown in Europe. We found pomi appii, plums, and nuts, and many other sorts of fruits to us unknown. There are beasts in great abundance, as red deer and fallow deer, leopards, and other kinds which they take with their bows and arrows which are their chiefest weapons. This land is situate in the parallel of Rome in 41 degrees and 2 terces. And towards the end he saith: We saw many of the people wear earrings of copper hanging at their ears. Thus far out of the relation of Verarsanus.

STEPHEN GOMEZ.

Now to come to Stephen Gomez, which by the commandment of the Emperor Charles the Fifth discovered the coast of Norumbega. These are the words of Gonsalvo de Oviedo in his summary of the West Indies, translated into Italian, concerning him, fol.52: . . . [Here follows an excerpt in Italian from Oviedo's *Summary of the West Indies*.]

A CAPTAIN OF DIEPPE.

Another French captain of Dieppe, which had been alongst this coast, giveth this testimony of the people and country from 46 to 47 degrees, as it is in the third volume of voyages gathered by Ramusius, fol.423, *pag. secunda*: . . . [A short passage in Italian from the work mentioned in the preceding line follows here.]

STEPHEN BELLINGER.

This coast, from Cape Breton 200 leagues to the southwest, was again discovered at the charges of the cardinal of Bourbon by my friend Stephen Bellinger of Rouen, the last year, 1583, who found a town of fourscore houses, covered with the barks of trees, upon a river's side, and about 100 leagues from the aforesaid Cape Breton. He reporteth that the country is of the temperature of the coast of Gascony and Guienne. He brought home a kind of mineral matter supposed to hold silver, whereof he gave me some; a kind of musk called castor; divers beasts' skins, as beavers, otters, martens, lucerns, seals, buffs, deer skins, all dressed and painted on the innerside with divers excellent colours, as red, tawny, yellow, and vermilion—all which things I saw; and divers other merchandise he hath which I saw not. But he told me that he had 440 crowns for that in Rouen, which, in trifles bestowed upon the savages, stood him not in forty crowns. And this year, 1584, the Marquis de la Roche went with three hundred men to inhabit in those parts, whose voyage was overthrown by occasion that his greatest ship of 300 tons was cast away over against Burwage, and so the enterprise for this year ceaseth.

JACQUES CARTIER.

The nature and quality of the other part of America from Cape Breton, being in 46 degrees unto the latitude of 52 for 300 leagues within the land even to Hochelaga, is notably described in the two voyages of Jacques Cartier. In the fifth chapter of his second relation thus he writeth: From the 19 till the 28 of September we sailed up the river, never losing one hour of time, all which space we saw as goodly a country as possibly could be wished for, full of all sorts of goodly trees, that is to say, oaks, elms, walnut-trees, cedars, furs, ashes, box, willows, and great store of vines, all as full of grapes as could be, that if any of our fellows went on shore, they came home laden with them. There are likewise many cranes, swans, geese, mallards, pheasants, partridges, thrushes, blackbirds, turtles, finches, red-breasts, nightingales, sparrows, with other sorts of birds even as in France, and great plenty and store. Again in the xi[th] chapter of the said relation there is mention of silver and gold to be upon a river that is three months' sailing, navigable southward from Hochelaga; and that red copper is in Saguenay. All that country is full of sundry sorts of wood and many vines. There is great store of stags, red deer, fallow deer, bears, and other such like sorts of beasts, as conies, hares, martens, foxes, otters, beavers, squirrels, badgers, and rats exceeding great, and divers other sorts of beasts for hunting. There are also many sorts of fowls, as cranes, swans, outards, wild geese, white and gray, ducks, thrushes, blackbirds, turtles, wild pigeons, linnets, finches, red-breasts, stares, nightingales, sparrows, and other birds even as in France. Also, as we have said before, the said river is the plentifulest of fish that ever hath been seen or heard of, because that from the head to the mouth of it you shall find all kind of fresh and salt water fish, according to their season. There are also many whales, porpoises, sea horses, and adhothuis, which is a kind of fish which we have never seen nor heard of before. And in the xii[th] chapter thus: We understood of Donaconna and others that . . . there are people clad with cloth as we are, very honest, and many inhabited towns, and that they had great store of gold and red copper; and that within the land beyond the said first river unto Hochelaga and Saguenay, is an island environed round about with that and other rivers, and that there is a sea of fresh water found, and, as they have heard say of those of Saguenay, there was never man heard of that found out the beginning and end thereof. Finally, in the postcript of the second relation, we read these words: They of Canada say, that it is a moon's sailing to go to a land where cinnamon and cloves are gathered.

VASQUES DE CORONADO.

And now, because hitherto I have spoken of the outward coast, I will also allege the commodities of the inland, in the latitude of 37 degrees, about the city of Cevola, using the very words of Vasques de Coronado, in the third chapter of his *Relation*, written to Don Antonio di Mendoza, Viceroy of Mexico, which sent him thither with many Spaniards and 400 horses and a thousand Indians to discover those countries. He, speaking there of the city of Cevola, proceedeth in this manner: . . . [There follow quotations in Spanish from Coronado's *Relation* and de Gomera's *General History of the Indies*.]

Touching Newfoundland, because no man hath better searched it out and all the commodities thereof than those that were there the last year, 1583, the space of eighteen days on land, with Sir Humphrey Gilbert, I will make rehearsal thereof, as I find it committed to print in a learned discourse, entitled *A True Report of the late Discoveries and Possession taken in the Right of the Crown of England, of the Newfound Lands, etc.* The words are these in the first leaf: Then Sir Humphrey went to view the country, being well accompanied with most of his captains and soldiers. They found the same very temperate, but somewhat warmer than England at that time of year, replenished with beasts and great store of fowl of divers kinds and fishes of sundry sorts, both in the salt water and in the fresh, in so great plenty as might suffice to victual an army, and they are very easily taken. And in the fifth chapter of the said discourse I read in this manner: But let us omit all presumptions, how vehement soever, and dwell upon the certainty of such commodities as were discovered and found by Sir Humphrey Gilbert and his assistants in Newfoundland in August last; for there may very easily be made pitch, tar, resin, soap ashes in great plenty, yea, as it is thought, enough to serve the whole realm of every of these kinds; and of train oil such quantity as if I should set down the value that they do esteem it at, which have been there, it would seem incredible.

STEPHANUS PARMENIUS, OF BUDA.

To this in effect agreeth what which one Stephanus Parmenius, a learned Hungarian, born in Buda, and lately my bedfellow in Oxford, wrote unto me out of Newfoundland, being of Sir Humphrey's company: . . . [Here follows a letter in Latin from Stephen Parmenius and a quotation from Ramusius' *Voyages*, in Italian.]

The rest of this coast from 60 to 63 is described by Frobisher, and in fresh memory, so that I shall not need to make repetition thereof.

Thus, having alleged many printed testimonies of these credible persons, which were personally between 30 and 63 degrees in America, as well on the coast as within the land, which affirmed unto the princes and kings which set them out, that they found there gold, silver, copper, lead, and pearls in abundance; precious stones, as turquoises and emeralds; spices and drugs, as pepper, cinnamon, cloves, rhubarb, musk called castor, turpentine; silkworms, fairer than ours of Europe; white and red cotton; infinite multitudes of all kind of beasts with their tallow and hides dressed and undressed; cochineal, found last year by the men of St. Jean-de-Luz, and many other kinds of colours for clothing; millions of all kinds of fowls for food and feathers; salt for fishing; excellent vines in many places for wines; the soil apt to bear olives for oil; all kinds of fruits, as oranges, almonds, filberts, figs, plums, mulberries, raspis, pomi appii, melons; all kind of odoriferous trees and date trees, cypresses, cedars, bays, sapines, honey and wax; and in Newfoundland abundance of pines and fir trees, ashes, and other like, to make masts and deal boards, pitch, tar, rosin; and hemp for cables and cordage; and up within the Grand Bay, exceeding quantity of all kind of precious furs (whereof I saw twenty thousand French crowns worth the last year brought to Paris to Valeron Perosse and Matthew Grainer, the king's skinners); also, such abundance of train oil to make soap, and of fish as a third part of Europe is furnished therewith,—I may well and truly conclude with reason and authority, that all the commodities of all our old decayed and dangerous trades in all Europe, Africa, and Asia haunted by us, may in short space for little or nothing, and many for the very workmanship, in a manner be had in that part of America which lieth between 30 and 60 degrees of northerly latitude, if by our slackness we suffer not the French or others to prevent us.

Cap. IV.

That this enterprise will be for the manifold employment of numbers
of idle men, and for breeding of many sufficient, and for utterance
of the great quantity of the commodities of our realm.

It is well worth the observation to see and consider what the like voyages
of discovery and planting in the East and West Indies hath wrought in
the kingdoms of Portugal and Spain; both which realms, being of themselves poor and barren and hardly able to sustain their inhabitants, by
their discoveries have found such occasion of employment that these
many years we have not heard scarcely of any pirate of those two nations;
whereas we and the French are most infamous for our outrageous, common, and daily piracies. Again, when heard we almost of one thief
amongst them? The reason is, that by these, their new discoveries, they
have so many honest ways to set them on work, as they rather want men
than means to employ them. But we, for all the statutes that hitherto
can be devised, and the sharp execution of the same in punishing idle
and lazy persons for want of sufficient occasion of honest employment,
cannot deliver our commonwealth from multitudes of loiterers and idle
vagabonds. Truth it is, that through our long peace and seldom sickness
(two singular blessings of Almighty God) we are grown more populous
than ever heretofore; so that now there are of every art and science so
many, that they can hardly live one by another, nay, rather they are
ready to eat up one another; yea, many thousands of idle persons are
within this realm, which, having no way to be set on work, be either
mutinous and seek alteration in the state, or at least very burdensome
to the commonwealth, and often fall to pilfering and thieving and other
lewdness, whereby all the prisons of the land are daily pestered and stuffed
full of them, where either they pitifully pine away, or else at length are
miserably hanged, even twenty at a clap out of some one jail. Whereas
if this voyage were put in execution, these petty thieves might be condemned for certain years in the western parts, especially in Newfoundland, in sawing and felling of timber for masts of ships and deal boards;
in burning of the firs and pine trees to make pitch, tar, rosin, and soap-
ashes; in beating and working of hemp for cordage; and, in the more
southern parts, in setting them to work in mines of gold, silver, copper,

lead, and iron; in dragging for pearls and coral; in planting of sugar cane, as the Portuguese have done in Madeira; in maintenance and increasing of silkworms for silk, and in dressing the same; in gathering of cotton whereof there is plenty; in tilling of the soil there for grain; in dressing of vines whereof there is great abundance for wine; olives, whereof the soil is capable, for oil; trees for oranges, lemons, almonds, figs, and other fruits, all which are found to grow there already; in sowing of woad and madder for dyers, as the Portuguese have done in the Azores; in dressing of raw hides of divers kinds of beasts; in making and gathering of salt, as in Rochelle and Bayonne, which may serve for the new land fishing; in killing the whale, seal, porpoise, and whirlpool for train oil; in fishing, salting, and drying of ling, cod, salmon, herring; in making and gathering of honey, wax, turpentine; in hewing and shaping of stone, as marble, jet, crystal, freestone, which will be good ballast for our ships homewards, and after serve for noble buildings; in making of cask, oars, and all other manner of staves; in building of forts, towns, churches; in powdering and barrelling of fish, fowls, and flesh, which will be notable provision for sea and land; in drying, sorting, and packing of feathers, whereof may be had there marvellous great quantity.

Besides this, such as by any kind of infirmity cannot pass the seas thither, and now are chargeable to the realm at home, by this voyage shall be made profitable members, by employing them in England in making a thousand trifling things, which will be very good merchandise for those countries where we shall have most ample vent thereof.

And seeing the savages of the Grand Bay, and all along the mighty river that runneth up to Canada and Hochelaga, are greatly delighted with any cap or garment made of coarse woollen cloth, their country being cold and sharp in the winter, it is manifest we shall find great utterance of our cloths, especially of our coarsest and basest northern doosens, and our Irish and Welsh friezes and rugs; whereby all occupations belonging to clothing and knitting shall be freshly set on work, as cappers, knitters, clothiers, woolmen, carders, spinners, weavers, fullers, shearmen, dyers, drapers, hatters, and such like, whereby many decayed towns may be repaired.

In sum, this enterprise will minister matter for all sorts and states of men to work upon; namely, all several kinds of artificers, husbandmen, seamen, merchants, soldiers, captains, physicians, lawyers, divines, cosmographers, hydrographers, astronomers, historiographers; yea, old folks, lame persons, women, and young children, by many means which hereby shall still be ministered unto them, shall be kept from idleness, and be made able by their own honest and easy labour to find themselves, without surcharging others. For proof of the last part of my allegation I will use but only this one example following.

In the year of our Lord 1564, at what time the Flemish nation were grown, as it were, to the fulness of their wealth and to the height of their pride, and not remembering what wonderful gain they had yearly by the wools, cloths, and commodities of England, began to condemn our nation and to reject our cloths and commodities, a subject of the then two earls of Emden, a man of great observation, wrote a notable discourse to the young earls, to take occasion of that present time by offer of large privileges in Emden to the Englishmen. In which discourse, the said subject, for the better inducement of the said two young earls, doth write of his own knowledge, as he in his discourse affirmeth, and as also by his report appeareth in the 22nd book of Sleydan's *Commentaries*, that, *anno* 1550, Charles the fifth, then emperor, would have had the Spanish inquisition brought into Antwerp and into the Netherlands; whereabout there was much ado, and that neither the suit of the town of Antwerp, nor the request of their friends, could persuade the emperor from it, till at the last they told him plainly, that if the inquisition came into Antwerp and the Netherlands, that the English merchants would depart out of the town and out of his countries; and upon declaration of this suggestion, search was made what profit there came and commodity grew by the haunt of the English merchants. Then was it found by search and inquiry, that within the town of Antwerp alone, there were fourteen thousand persons fed and maintained only by the working of English commodities, besides the gains that merchants and shippers with other in the said town did get, which was the greatest part of their living, which were thought to be in number half as many more; and in all other places of his Netherlands by the endraping of English wool into cloth, and by the working of other English commodities, there were thirty thousand persons more maintained and fed; which in all amounteth to the number of 51,000 persons. And this was the report that was given to this mighty emperor whereby the town of Antwerp and the Netherlands were saved from the inquisition. And in the end of the 45th article of the same discourse, also, he setteth down by particular account how the subjects of the same emperor in the Netherlands did gain yearly only by the wool and woollen cloth that came each year out of England, almost £600,000. I say almost six hundred thousand pounds sterling, besides the gains they had for sundry other things, that were of marvellous sums.

Now if her majesty take these western discoveries in hand, and plant there, it is like that in short time we shall vent as great a mass of cloth in those parts as ever we did in the Netherlands, and in time much more; which was the opinion of that excellent man, Mr. Robert Thorne, extant in print in the last leaf saving one of his discourse to Doctor Lea, ambassador for King Henry the eighth, in Spain, with Charles the emperor, whose words are these: And although (saith he) we went not into the said islands of spicery, for that they are the emperor's or king's of Portugal, we should by the way, and coming once to the line equinoctial find lands no less rich of gold and spicery as all other lands are under the said line equinoctial; and also should, if we may pass under the north, enjoy the navigation of all Tartary, which should be no less profitable to our commodities of cloth than those spiceries to the emperor and king of Portugal.

This being so, it cometh to pass that whatsoever cloth we shall vent on the tract of that firm, or in the islands of the same, or in other lands, islands, and territories beyond, be they within the circle arctic or without, all these cloths, I say, are to pass out of this realm full wrought by our natural subjects in all degrees of labour. And if it come about in time that we shall vent that mass there that we vented in the Base Countries, which is hoped by great reason, then shall all that cloth pass out of this realm in all degrees of labour full wrought by the poor natural subjects of this realm, like as the quantity of our cloth doth pass that goeth hence to Russia, Barbary, Turkey, Persia, etc. And then consequently it followeth that the like number of people allieged to the emperor shall be set on work in England of our poor subjects more than hath been; and so her majesty shall not be troubled with the pitiful outcries of cappers, knitters, spinners, etc.

And on the other side we are to note, that all the commodities we shall bring thence, we shall not bring them wrought, as we bring now the commodities of France and Flanders, etc., but shall receive them all substances unwrought, to the employment of a wonderful multitude of the poor subjects of this realm in return. And so to conclude, what in the number of things to go out wrought and to come in unwrought, there need not one poor creature to steal, to starve, or to beg as they do. OBJECTION.

And to answer objections: where fools for the swarming of beggars allege that the realm is too populous, Solomon saith, that the honour and strength of a prince consisteth in the multitude of the people. And if this come about, that work may be had for the multitude, where the realm hath now one thousand for the defence thereof, the same may have five thousand. For when people know how to live, and how to maintain and feed their wives and children, they will not abstain from marriage as now they do. And the soil thus abounding with corn, flesh, milk, butter, cheese, herbs, roots, and fruits, etc., and the seas that environ the same so infinitely abounding in fish, I dare truly affirm, that if the number in this realm were as great as all Spain and France have, the people being industrious, I say, there should be found victuals enough at the full in all bounty to suffice them all. And taking order to carry hence thither our cloths made in hose, coats, cloaks, hoods, etc., and to return thither hides of their own beasts, tanned and turned into shoes and boots, and other skins of goats, whereof they have store, into gloves, etc., no doubt but we shall set on work in this realm, besides sailors and such as shall be seated there in those western discovered countries, at the least 100,000 subjects, to the great abating of the good estate of subjects of foreign princes, enemies, or doubtful friends, and this *absque injuria*, as the lawyers say, albeit not *sine damno*. And having a vent of linen, as the Spaniards have in the rest of that firm, we may set our people in making the same, infinitely on work, and in many other things besides, which time will bring about, though now, for want of knowledge and full experience of this trade, we cannot enter into just account of all particulars.

Cap. V.

That this voyage will be a great bridle to the Indies of the king of Spain, and a mean that we may arrest at our pleasure for the space of ten weeks or three months every year one or two hundred sail of his subjects' ships at the fishing in Newfoundland.

THE cause why the king of Spain, these three or four years last past, was at such intolerable charges in furnishing out so many navies to win Tercera, and the other small islands of the Azores adjacent to the same, was the opportunity of the places in intercepting his West Indian fleet at their return homeward, as a matter that toucheth him indeed to the quick. But the planting of two or three strong forts upon some good havens (whereof there is great store) between Florida and Cape Breton would be a matter in short space of greater damage as well to his fleet as to his western Indies; for we should not only oftentimes endanger his fleet in the return thereof, but also in few years put him in hazard in losing some part of Nova Hispania.

Touching the fleet, no man (that knoweth the course thereof, coming out between Cuba and the Cape of Florida, along the gulf or strait of Bahama) can deny that it is carried by the current north and northeast towards the coast which we purpose, God willing, to inhabit; which happened to them not two years past, as Mr. Jennings and Mr. Smith, the master and master's mate of the ship called the *Toby*, belonging to Bristol, informed me, and many of the chiefest merchants of that city, whereof they had particular advertisement at Cadiz in Spain a little before by them that were in the same fleet the selfsame year, and were in person driven upon the same coast and saw the people, which they reported to be big men somewhat in making like the Hollanders, and lighted on a town upon a river's side, which they affirmed to be above a quarter of a mile in length. Besides the current, it is also a thing without controversy, that all southern and southeastern winds enforce the Spanish fleet returning home near or upon the aforesaid coast, and consequently will bring them into our danger, after we shall be there strongly settled and fortified.

We are moreover to understand that the savages of Florida are the Spaniard's mortal enemies and will be ready to join with us against them, as they joined with Captain Gourgues, a Gascon, who, being but a private man and going thither at his own charges, by their aid won and razed the three small forts which the Spaniards about twenty years ago had planted in Florida after their traitorous slaughter of John Ribault; which Gourgues slew and hanged up divers of them on the same trees whereon the year before they had hanged the French. Yea, one Holocotera, brother to one of the kings of the savages, leaping up on an high place with his own hands slew a Spanish cannonier as he was putting fire to a piece of ordnance; which story is at large in print set forth by Monsieur Poplynier in his book entitled *Trois Mondes*.

Also, within the land on the north side of Nova Hispania, there is a people called Chichimici, which are big and strong men and valiant archers, which have continual wars with the Spaniards and do greatly annoy them. The Spanish histories which I have read, and other late discourses, make great mention of them. Yea, Miles Philips, who was fourteen years in those parts and presented his whole travel in writing to her majesty, confesseth this to be most certain.

Now if we (being thereto provoked by Spanish injuries) would either join with these savages or send or give them armour, as the Spaniards arm our Irish rebels, we should trouble the king of Spain more in those parts than he hath or can trouble us in Ireland, and hold him at such a bay as he was never yet held at. For if (as the aforesaid Miles Philips writeth) it be true that one negro which fled from his cruel Spanish master is received and made captain of multitudes of the Chichimici, and daily doth grievously afflict them, and hath almost enforced them to leave and abandon their silver mines in those quarters, what damage might divers hundreds of Englishmen do them, being grown once into familiarity with that valiant nation.

And this is the greatest fear that the Spaniards have, to wit, our planting in those parts and joining with those savages, their neighbours, in Florida and on the north side of Nova Hispania. Which thing an English gentleman, Captain Muffet, who is now in France, told divers times this last winter in my hearing and others of credit, namely, that when he was in Spain, prisoner, not long since, he heard the treasurer of the West Indies say that there was no such way to hinder his master as to plant upon the coast near unto Florida, from whence by great rivers any man might easily pass far up into the land and join with his enemies,

whereof he stood in continual fear; and said, moreover, that that was
the occasion why such cruelty was used towards John Ribault and his
company upon his seeking to settle there.

THE BENEFIT OF PLANTING ABOUT CAPE BRETON OR NEWFOUNDLAND.

Finally, if we list not to come so near Florida, this is a matter of no
small moment, that if we fortify ourselves about Cape Breton, near
Newfoundland, partly by the strength of our fortification, and partly
by the aid of our navy of fishermen, which are already commanders of
others there, having our double forces thus joined together, we shall be
able upon every sudden to seize upon one or two hundred Spanish and
Portuguese ships, which for ten weeks or three months are there on fishing every year. This, I say, will be such a bridle to him and such an
advantage unto us, as we cannot possibly imagine a greater. And thus
the French served them in the time of Mounsieurs being in Flanders,
carrying away out of some harbours three or four Spanish and Portuguese
ships at once; and more they would have taken if our Englishmen, and,
namely, one of mine acquaintance of Ratcliff, had not defended them.
And hither of necessity they must yearly repair, being not able to make
their provision for land and sea of fish in any place else, except on the
coast of Ireland, and at Cape Blank in Africa, which two are nothing
worth in comparison of this third place.

So shall we be able to cry quittance with the king of Spain if he should
go about to make any general arrest of our navy, or rather terrify him
from any such enterprise, when he shall bethink himself that his navy in
Newfoundland is no less in our danger than ours is in his dominions
wheresoever.

Cap. VI.

That the mischief that the Indian treasure wrought in time of Charles
    the late emperor, father to the Spanish king, is to be had in considera-
    tion of the queen's most excellent majesty, lest the continual coming
    of the like treasure from thence to his son, work the unrecoverable
    annoy of this realm, whereof already we have had very dangerous
    experience.

IT is written in the thirtieth article of the discourse before specified,
dedicated to the two young earls of Emden, as followeth, verbatim:

With this great treasure did not the Emperor Charles get from the French king the kingdom of Naples, the dukedom of Milan, and all other his dominions in Italy, Lombardy, Piedmont, and Savoy? With this treasure did he not take the pope prisoner, and sack the see of Rome? With this treasure did he not take the French king prisoner and maintain all the great wars with France since the year of our Lord 1540 to the year of our Lord 1560 as is declared in the twelfth and thirteenth articles of his book? With this treasure hath he not maintained many cities in Italy, as well against the pope as against the French king, as Parma, Florence, and such other? With this treasure did he not overthrow the duke of Cleves, and take Gelderland, Groningenland, and other dominions from him, which ought to be a good warning to you all, as it shall be most plainly and truly declared hereafter! With this treasure did he not get into his hands the earldom of Lingen in Westphalia? With this treasure did he not cause the earl of Assen, your subject, to rebel against your grace's father and against you? The cause you know best. And what work this treasure made amongst the princes and towns in Germany, when the duke of Saxony and the landgrave von Hessen were taken, Sleydan, our own countryman, by his chronicle declareth at large. And did not this treasure, named the Burgundish ass, walk and run in all places to make both war and peace at pleasure? And took he nothing from the empire then? Yes, truly, too much, as you shall hear. When the Emperor Charles was first made emperor, what were the towns and countries in the Netherlands that justly or properly came to him by birth and inheritance? There was Brabant, Flanders, Zealand, Holland, Artois, and Hainault. And yet there is a great question concerning Holland, how the Emperor Charles and his progenitors came by it, and what homage and duty they ought to do for the same; because thereby the house of Burgundy hath the mouth of the river of Rhine at their commandment, which is to the great loss, damage, and danger of Germany, as hereafter shall be declared. Here be all the countries that belonged to the house of Burgundy when the Emperor Charles was made emperor. But how much hath been added to the Netherlands since by him, contrary to his oath made? That are these towns and countries, as it appeareth in Sleydan's *Chronicle*; viz., Luxembourg, Limburg, Gelderland, the earldom of Zutphen, the city and strait of Utrecht, with all the lands in Overijsel, West Friesland, the city of Groningen, and Groningenland.

And, as before it is said, he hath by policy gotten into his hands the earldom of Lingen, standing in Westphalia; and by the like policy, with
money, he is become the defender of the earldom of Assen, which is
parcel of your grace's country of East Friesland. All these countries
and towns, with the treasure of the Netherlands, hath he taken from the
Empire.

Thus far proceedeth this excellent man in describing how Charles
the emperor employed his treasure to the afflicting and oppressing of
most of the greatest estates of Christendom. The effect of these treasures
which he had out of the West Indies, Peter Martyr of Angleria, in the
epistle dedicatory of his decades to the said Emperor Charles, truly
prognosticated in the beginning, beforehand, where he writeth thus
unto him: Come therefore and embrace this new world and suffer us
no longer to consume in desire of your presence. From hence, from hence
(I say), most noble young prince, shall instruments be prepared for you
whereby all the world shall be under your obeisance.

And in very deed it is most apparent that riches are the fittest instruments of conquest, and that the emperor turned them to that use.

KING PHILIP'S INJURIES OFFERED BY HIS TREASURES.

To leave the father and to come to the son, hath not King Philip
employed his treasure as injuriously to all princes and potentates of Europe? Is it not he that with his Indian treasure corrupted the *Quinqueviri*
in Portugal, that in the interregnum were appointed overseers of the
commonwealth, and so hath joined that kingdom to his, with all the
islands, towns, and dominions belonging to that crown? Is it not he that
with his treasure hath gone about to hire some ungodly murderer to make
away with Don Antonio, one while by open proclamation, and another
while *sotto capo*, underhand? Is it not he that by his treasure hath hired
at sundry times the sons of Belial to bereave the Prince of Orange of his
life? And hath he not suborned by hope of reward other most ungodly
persons to lay violent hands upon other Christian princes? Hath not he
these many years given large pensions to numbers of English unnatural
rebels? Doth he not support the seminaries of Rome and Rheims to be
thorns in the sides of their own commonwealths? Hath not he divers
times sent foreign forces into Ireland, furnished with money, armour,
munition, and victuals? Hath not he sent round sums of money into
Scotland, both to the king and those that are about him, to alter the estate

there and to trouble ours? And is it not known that this Spanish ass roameth up and down laden through all France, and, when it could not enter into the papist's gates, it hath sought to enter into the courts of the princes of the religion, to renew the late intermitted civil wars? What it hath done and now doth in all the Empire and the Low Countries, and is like to work in other places unless speedy order be taken to hinder it, is described at large by Monsieur de Sainte-Aldegonde, a German gentleman, in a pithy and most earnest exhortation (extant in Latin, Italian, French, English, and Dutch) concerning the estate of Christendom, together with the means to defend and preserve the same, dedicated to all Christian kings, princes, and potentates.

Cap. VII.

What special means may bring King Philip from his high throne, and make him equal to the princes his neighbours; wherewithal is showed his weakness in the West Indies.

FIRST, it is to be considered that his dominions and territories out of Spain lie far distant from Spain, his chiefest force; and far distant one from another; and are kept by great tyranny; and *quos metuunt oderunt.* And the people kept in subjection desire nothing more than freedom. And like as a little passage given to water, it maketh his own way; so give but a small mean to such kept in tyranny, they will make their own way to liberty; which way may easily be made. And entering into the consideration of the way how this Philip may be abased, I mean first to begin with the West Indies, as there to lay a chief foundation for his overthrow. And like as the foundation of the strongest hold undermined and removed, the mightiest and strongest walls fall flat to the earth; so this prince, spoiled or intercepted for a while of his treasure, occasion by lack of the same is given that all his territories in Europe out of Spain slide from him, and the Moors enter into Spain itself, and the people revolt in every foreign territory of his and cut the throats of the proud, hateful Spaniards, their governors. For this Philip already owing many millions, and of late years impaired in credit, both by lack of ability of long time to pay the same, and by his shameful loss of his Spaniards and dishonours in the Low Countries, and by lack of the yearly renew of his revenue, he shall not be able to wage his several garrisons kept in his several frontiers, territories, and places, nor to corrupt in prince's courts, nor to do many feats. And this weighed, we are to know what Philip is in the West Indies; and that we be not abused with Spanish brags, and made to believe what he is not; and so, drawn into vain fear, suffer fondly and childishly our own utter spoil. And therefore we are to understand that Philip rather governeth in the West Indies by opinion, than by might; for the small manred of Spain, of itself being always at the best slenderly peopled, was never able to rule so many regions, or to keep in subjection such worlds of people as be there, were it not for the error of the Indian people that think he is that he is not and that do imagine that Philip hath a thousand Spaniards for every single natural subject that he hath there. And like as the Romans, allured hither into Britain, pierced the land and planted here and there in the mouths of rivers and upon straits and kept colonies, as at Westchester upon the river of Dee, at York upon the river of Ouse, and upon the rivers of Thames and Severn, and yet in truth never enjoyed more of the countries round about than the English, planted at Boulogne and Calais, did of the French soil adjoining, nor in effect had the British nation at commandment; even so hath the Spaniard pierced the Indies and planted here and there very thinly and slenderly, without having the Indian multitude in subjection, or in their towns and forts any number to hold any of them against the meanest force of a prince; so as in truth the Spaniard is very weak there. And it is known to Sir Francis Drake and to Mr. Hawkins and Miles Philips (which Miles lived 14 years in New Spain), and to divers others of her majesty's subjects besides that have been there, that the islands there abound with people and nations that reject the proud and bloody government of the Spaniard, and that do mortally hate the Spaniard. And they also know that the Moors, and such as the Spaniards have brought thither for the mines and for slavery, have fled from them into the islands, and of themselves maintain in many places frontier wars against the Spaniard, and many times so prevail, and especially of late, that the Spaniards have been enforced to send the Spanish merchants themselves into the wars, although it be against the special privileges granted by Charles, the late emperor, to the merchants, as may plainly appear by Spanish merchants' letters taken by Sir Francis Drake passing in the sea of Sur toward Panama, to be conveyed into Spain. And it is thought that Sir Francis Drake and some other English are of so great credit with the Cimarrons and with those that maintain those frontier wars, that he might, bringing thither a few captains and some of our meaner soldiers late trained in the Base Countries, with archers and light furniture, etc., bring to pass that, joining with those inland people, King Philip might either be deprived of his government there or at the least of the taking of his yearly benefit of the mines. Thus with small charge and few men, now and then renewing this matter by a few sails to be sent thither for the comfort of such as shall be there resident, and for the encouragement of the Cimmarons, greater effect may follow than by meeting with his golden fleet, or by taking of his treasures once or twice at the sea; for by this means, or by a platform well to be set down, England may enjoy the benefit of the Indian mines, or at the least keep Philip from possessing the same.

Hereunto if we add our purposed western discoveries, and there plant and people royally, and fortify strongly, and there build ships and maintain a navy in special port or ports, we may by the same either encounter the Indian fleet or be at hand as it were to yield fresh supply, courage, and comfort by men or munition to the Chichimici and the Cimarrons and such other as shall be incited to the spoil of the mines; which in time will, if it be not looked to, bring all princes to weak estate, that Philip, either for religion or other cause, doth hate; as the aforesaid Monsieur de Aldegond, in his pithy and most earnest exhortation to all Christian kings, princes, and potentates to beware of King Philip's ambitious growing, doth wisely and most providently forewarn.

To this may be added (the realm swarming with lusty youths that be turned to no profitable use), there may be sent bands of them into the Base Countries in more round numbers than are sent as yet. For if he presently prevail there, at our doors, farewell the traffic that else we may have there (whereof wise men can say much). And if he settle there, then let the realm say adieu to her quiet state and safety.

If these enter into the due consideration of wise men, and if platforms of these things be set down and executed duly and with speed and effect, no doubt but the Spanish empire falls to the ground, and the Spanish king shall be left bare as Æsop's proud crow; the peacock, the parrot, the pie, and the popinjay, and every other bird having taken home from him his gorgeous feathers, he will, in short space, become a laughing stock for all the world; with such a main to the pope and to that side, as never happened to the see of Rome by the practice of the late king of famous memory, her majesty's father, or by all the former practices of all the protestant princes of Germany, or by any other advice laid down by Monsieur de Aldegond, hereafter by them to be put in execution. If you touch him in the Indies, you touch the apple of his eye; for take away his treasure, which is *nervus belli*, and which he hath almost out of his West Indies, his old bands of soldiers will soon be dissolved, his purposes defeated, his power and strength diminished, his pride abated, and his tyranny utterly suppressed. . . .

Cap. XII.

That the passage in this voyage is easy and short, that it cutteth not near the trade of any other mighty princes, or near their countries, that it is to be performed at all times of the year and needeth but one kind of wind; that Ireland, being full of good havens on the south and west side, is the nearest part of Europe to it, which by this trade shall be in more security and the sooner drawn to more civility.

In this voyage we may see by the globe that we are not to pass the burnt zone, nor to pass through the frozen seas, but in a temperate climate unto a country much like to those parts of Gascony and Guienne, where heretofore our nation for a long time have inhabited. And it requireth not, as long voyages do, the taking in of fresh water by the way in divers places, by reason it may be sailed in five or six weeks. Whereby the merchant need not to expect two or three years for one return, as in the voyage of Sir Francis Drake, of Fenton and William Hawkins; but may receive two returns every year in the selfsame ships, I say, and well repose themselves at their arrivals; which thing I myself have seen and understood in France this present year done by the Frenchmen; who, setting forth in January, brought their bank fish which they took on the Bank, forty or three score leagues from Newfoundland, to Rouen in great quantity, by the end of May, and afterward returneth this year again to the fishing, and are looked for at home towards the fifth of

November. To the speedy performance of which voyage this is a special furtherance: that whereas most of our other voyages of like length require two or three sorts of winds at the least, one only wind sufficeth to make this; which was no doubt the cause of the quick return of my friend Stephen Bellinger of Rouen, who departed from Newhaven in January, was twelve months, arrived at Cape Breton in 20 days space, and from thence discovered very diligently 200 leagues towards Norumbega, and had traffic with the people in ten or twelve places; found a town containing fourscore houses, and returned home with a diligent description of the coast, in the space of four months, with many commodities of the country which he showed me.

Moreover this passage is neither by the Straits of Gibraltar, nor on the coasts of Spain, Portugal, France, nor Flanders, neither by the Sound of Denmark, nor Wardhouse in Norway; so as in taking our course on the high seas we shall not be in danger of the corsairs in the Levant, nor of the galleys of Barbary, nor of the Turk, nor of any state of Italy, neither of the Spaniard, the French, nor the Dane, nor of any other prince nor potentate within the Sound in the north or in the northeast parts of the world.

We may also travel thither and perform the same at all times of the year, with the like facility as our merchants of Bristol, Weymouth, and other parts of the West Countries travel for woad to the isles of St. Michael and Tercera (which are half the way thither) all the year long. For this coast is never subject to the ice which is never lightly seen to the south of Cape Race in Newfoundland.

Besides this, in our way as we pass to and fro, we shall have in tempests and other necessities the ports of Ireland to our aid, and no nearer coast of any enemy. Moreover by the ordinary intercourse we may annoy the enemies to Ireland and succour the queen's majesty's faithful subjects and draw the Irish by little and little to more civility; and in short time we may yield them from the coasts of America whatsoever commodities they now receive at the hands of the Spaniards. So the Spaniards shall want the ordinary victuals they receive every year from thence, whereby they cannot continue traffic nor fall so aptly to practise against our government there as heretofore by their trade thither they have done and do daily, to the great expenses of her majesty, and no small endangering and troubling of our state.

And to conclude: in trading to these countries we shall not need, for fear of the Spanish bloody inquisition, to throw our Bibles and prayer books overboard into the sea before our arrival at their ports, as these many years we have done and yet do, nor take such horrible oaths as are exacted of our men by the Spanish searchers, to such daily wilful and high offence of almighty God, as we are driven to continually in following our ordinary traffic into the king of Spain's dominions; whereof at large we have spoken before in the second chapter.

Cap. XIII.

That hereby the revenues and customs of her majesty, both outward and inward, shall mightily be enlarged by the toll, excises, and other duties which without oppression may be raised.

THE manifold testimonies, verbatim alleged by me in the third chapter, of John Ribault, John Verarsanus, Stephen Gomez, Vasques de Coronado, Jacques Cartier, Gasper Corterialis, and others, which all were the discoverers of the coast and inland of America between 30 and 63 degrees, prove infallibly unto us that gold, silver, copper, pearls, precious stones, and turquoises, and emeralds, and many other commodities, have been by them found in those regions. To which testimonies I should have added many more if I had not feared to be tedious. Now the fifth part of all these aforenamed commodities cannot choose but amount to a great matter, being yearly reserved unto her majesty, according to the tenor of the patent granted by King Henry the seventh in the eleventh year of his reign to John Cabot and his three sons, Lewis, Sebastian, and Sancius; the words whereof it should not be amiss here to set down, as they are printed in my book of voyages. These are the words . . . [Here follow in Latin the words of the patent.]

What gains this imposition may turn unto the crown of England in short time we may more than guess, having but an eye to the king of Spain's revenues, which he now hath out of all his dominions in all the West Indies.

The like in all respects may be said of the revenues of the crown of Portugal, which, being of itself one of the smallest and poorest kingdoms of all Christendom, became in short space so rich and honourable soon after their entering into their southeastern discoveries, traffics, and conquests, that, before the death of their late young King Sebastian, their ambassadors would strive and challenge for the chiefest place with the ambassadors of the greatest kings of Christendom; as I have heard it divers times spoken at Paris at my lord's table by men of great honour and experience, in which city most princes and states of Christendom have their ambassadors commonly resident.

To leave them and to come to our nation, I say that among other means to increase her majesty's customs this shall be one, especially that by planting and fortifying near Cape Breton, what by the strength of our ships being hard at hand, and bearing the sway already amongst all nations that fish at Newfoundland, and what by the forts that there may be erected and held by our people, we shall be able to enforce them, having no place else to repair unto so convenient, to pay us such a continual custom as shall please us to lay upon them; which imposition of two or three hundred ships laden yearly with sundry sorts of fish, train oil, and many kinds of furs and hides, cannot choose but amount to a great matter, being all to be levied upon strangers. And this not only we may exact of the Spaniards and Portuguese, but also of the Frenchmen, our old and ancient enemies. What should I speak of the customs of the great multitudes of coarse clothes, Welsh frieze, and Irish rugs, that may be uttered in the more northerly parts of the land among the eskimos of the Grand Bay, and among them of Canada, Saguenay, and Hochelaga, which are subject to sharp and nipping winters, albeit their summers be hotter much than ours. Again, the multitudes of small iron and copper works, wherewith they are exceedingly delighted, will not a little increase the customs, being transported out of the land. I omit the rehearsal of a thousand other trifling wares, which, besides they may set many women, children, and impotent persons on work in making of them, would also help to the increasing of the customs. Lastly, whatsoever kind of commodities should be brought from thence by her majesty's subjects into the realm, or be thither transported out of the realm, cannot choose but enlarge the revenues of the crown very mightily and enrich all sorts of subjects generally.

Cap. XIV.

That this action will be for the great increase, maintenance, and safety of our navy, and especially of great shipping, which is the strength of our realm, and for the supportation of all those occupations that depend upon the same.

In the statutes most providently ordained for increase and maintenance of our navigation in the reigns of King Richard the second, King Henry the seventh, King Henry the eighth, and her majesty that now is, though many and sundry rewards were proposed to encourage our people unto the sea, yet still I find complaints of decay of the navy, notwithstanding so many goodly privileges to maintain fishermen, the ordaining of Wednesday to be a new fish day for the better utterance of their fish that they should take at sea; yea, albeit there hath been granted a certain proportionable allowance out of the exchequer to such as would build any ships of burden to serve the prince in time of war, yet very little hath been done in that behalf. For, setting the city of London apart, go your way into the west part of England and Wales and search how many ships of 200 tons and upwards those parts can afford, and you shall find (God wotteth) no such number as at the first you did imagine. At this day I am assured there are scarce two of 200 tons belonging to the whole city of Bristol, and very few or none of the like burden along the channel of Severn from Gloucester to the Land's End on the one side and Milford Haven on the other. Now, to remedy this great and unknown want, no enterprise possibly can be devised more fit to increase our great shipping than this western fortifying and planting. For in this action we are not to cut over the narrow seas, in a day or a night, between Flanders, France, or Ireland, in small barks of 20 or 30 tons; but we are to pass over the breast of the main ocean and to lie at sea a month or six weeks together, whereby we shall be constrained of ourselves, without charging of the prince, to build great ships, as well to avoid the danger of tempest as also for the commodity of portage, whereunto the greater ships in long voyages are most convenient, which the Portuguese and Spaniards have found out by long experience, who for that cause build ships of 5, 6, 7, 8 hundred and a thousand tons, to send into their Eastern and Western Indies.

The like whereof we shall be the rather invited to do, since by this voyage we shall have many things for little or nothing that are necessary for the furniture of great shipping. For being possessed of Newfoundland, which the last year was seized upon in her majesty's name, we may have tar, rosin, masts, and cordage for the very workmanship of the same. All which commodities cannot choose but wonderfully invite our men to the building of great shipping, especially having store of the best shipwrights of the world, whereof some, for want of employment at home, have been driven to fly into foreign parts, as into Denmark. Moreover, in the judgment of those that are expert in sea causes, it will breed more skilful, cunning, and stout pilots and mariners then other belonging to this land. For it is the long voyages (so they be not too excessive long, nor through intemperate climates, as those of the Portuguese into their West Indies) that harden seamen and open unto them the secrets of navigation; the natures of the winds; the currents and setting of the sea; the ebbing and flowing of the main ocean; the influence of the sun, the moon, and of the rest of the celestial planets, and force which they have at sundry seasons upon that mighty body: which skill in sea causes the Emperor Charles the fifth, knowing how much it did import his state, to the intent it might better increase amongst the Spaniards, in great providence erected a lecture of the art of navigation in Seville, and ordained that no man should take charge to the West Indies that had not heard the reader of the same for a certain space, and, upon due examination, were allowed as sufficient by him, and others adjoined unto him as assistants to examine matters of experience; which order, if it had been established in England, such gross and insufficient fellows as he that cast away the *Admiral* of Sir Humphrey's company, with an hundred persons in her, to the west of Newfoundland, this time twelve months, had not been admitted to take so great a charge.

But to return to the increase and maintenance of our ships and shipmen; I say this is not as the voyage to Muscovy, which is open not past four months, but may be passed and repassed at our pleasure at all times of the year, and so our mariners may be set on work all the year long. Neither is the trade likely to prove so small as that of Muscovy, wherein not past ten ships at the most are employed once a year. For here there is a great hope, the country being as big as all Europe, and nothing in fruitfulness inferior to it, as I have proved before at large in the third chapter, that we shall have two fleets as big as those of the king of Spain to his West Indies, employed twice in the year at the least, especially after our fortifying in the country, the certain place of our factory being there established; whereby it must needs come to pass that our navy shall be mightily increased and maintained, which will not only be a chief strength and surety in time of wars, as well to offend as defend, but will also be the maintenance of many masters, mariners, and seamen, whereby they, their wives and children, shall have their livings, and many cities, towns, villages, havens, and creeks near adjoining unto the sea coast, and the queen's subjects, as brewers, butchers, smiths, ropers, shipwrights, tailors, shoemakers, and other victuallers and handicraftsmen, inhabiting and dwelling near thereabouts, shall also have by the same great part of their living. For proof hereof we need not to seek any further than unto our neighbours of Spain and Portugal; who, since the first discovery of their Indies, have not only mightily enlarged their dominions, marvellously enriched themselves and their subjects, but have also by just account trebled the number of their ships, masters, and mariners—a matter of no small moment and importance; insomuch that now, of late, King Philip hath made the Marquis de la Cruz, which last year won Tercera, grand admiral of the Ocean Sea, and Prince d'Oria of Genoa, admiral in the Levant. A taste of this increase we have had in our own selves, even by our trade of fishing in Newfoundland; which, as it is well known, hath been occasion, that in sundry places of this realm divers tall ships have been built and set forth even of late days; and more would be if, whereas now having but two months or ten weeks of fishing, by this new planting they might be drawn more south-westerly, where the special fishing places are, both for plenty and greatness of fish; and being out of danger and impediment of ice, they might fish there safely the greatest part of the year; and by their nearness unto our forts there, built about Cape Breton, they might yield succour unto them, and likewise by their neighbourhood be themselves in more security.

A MEAN TO AVOID THE SUDDEN ARRESTS OF OUR NAVY.

Finally, their ships, their goods, and their persons should not be subject to sudden arrests of strangers, as they are in all other trades of Christendom; but should enjoy as great freedom, liberty, and security as they usually do in their native country; the havens, towns, and villages in those parts being occupied and possessed by their fellow subjects; which freedom and liberty will greatly encourage them to continue constantly in this new traffic. . . .

Cap. XVII.

That by these colonies the northwest passage to Cathay and China may easily, quickly, and perfectly be searched out as well by river and overland as by sea; for proof whereof here are quoted and alleged divers rare testimonies out of the three volumes of voyages gathered by Ramusius and other grave authors.

In the third volume of *Navigations and Voyages*, gathered and translated into Italian by Mr. John Baptista Ramusius, fol.417, page 2, I read of John Verarsanus as followeth: This unhappy end had this valiant gentleman, who, if this misfortune had not happened unto him (with the singular knowledge that he had in sea matters and in the art of navigation, being also favoured with the great liberality of King Francis), would have discovered and opened unto the world that part also of land even to the pole. Neither would he have contented himself with the outside and sea coast only, but would have passed further up within the land so far as he could have gone. And many that have known him and talked with him have told me that he said he had in mind to persuade the French king to send out of France a good number of people to inhabit certain places of the said coast, which be of air temperate and of soil most fertile, with very fair rivers and havens able to receive any navy. The inhabitants of which places might be occasion to bring to pass many good effects; and, amongst other, to reduce those poor, rude, and ignorant people to the knowledge of God and true religion, and to show them the manner of husbandry for the ground, transporting of the beasts of Europe into those exceeding large and champion countries; and in time might discover the parts within land, and see if, amongst so many islands there be any passage to the South Sea, or whether the firm land of Florida continue still even to the pole.

Upon occasion of these last words I think it not amiss to allege those testimonies tending to the proof of this long desired northwest passage, which, with no small care these many years, I have observed in my readings and conferences concerning the same matter.

7—The illustration opposite is a map of the world inserted in the first, 1589, edition of Hakluyt's *Principal Navigations*. Concerning it, Hakluyt wrote at the end of his preface: ' I have contented myself with inserting into the work one of the best general maps of the world only, until the coming out of a very large and most exact terrestrial globe, collected and reformed according to the newest, secretest, and latest discoveries, both Spanish, Portugal, and English, composed by M. Emmerie Molineux of Lambeth, a rare gentleman in his profession, being therein for divers years, greatly supported by the purse and liberality of the worshipful merchant, M. William Sanderson.' The map, *Typus Orbis Terrarum*, first appeared in the *Theatrum Orbis Terrarum* of Abraham Ortelius, Antwerp, 1570. But Hakluyt's comment shows that he had a more complete knowledge of the world than this map depicts. The Molyneux globes, two feet and two inches in diameter and the largest made up to that time, were not published until 1592 despite Hakluyt's implication in 1589 that they were about to appear. However, the 1570 map gives, perhaps, a fairer indication of the extent of the geographer's knowledge in 1584 when he wrote the ' Western Discoveries.' It graphically shows the belief in the existence of both northwest and northeast passages to Cathay, and it contains much of the semi-mythical nomenclature to be found in the ' Western Discoveries.'

1. My first authority is in the second volume of Ramusius, in the discourse of the discovery of the islands Friesland, Iceland, Greenland, Drogeo, and Icaria, made in the north by Sir Nicholas Zeny, knight, and Mr. Anthony, his brother, in the year 1380. In which discourse, among many other things tending to the proof of this passage, I find this recorded: *Scoprirono una isola detta Estotilanda posta in ponente lontana da Frislanda piu di mille miglia*; whereof I gather, that whereas still he calleth Estotiland an island, and that it is distant westward from Friesland more than a thousand miles, that the sea is open above five hundred miles further than Frobisher and his company discovered. For he himself confesseth that he never sailed past five or six hundred miles to the west of Friesland; and here is mention made, that those fishermen that discovered the island of Estotiland found it to be more than a thousand miles to the west of the same.

2. The second testimony to prove this northwest passage is in the preface of the aforesaid Ramusius before his third volume, where he allegeth, in manner following, that which Sebastian Cabot wrote unto unto him concerning this matter: Many years past I was written unto by Sebastian Cabot, our countryman, a Venetian, and a man of great experience and very singular in the art of navigation and in the knowledge of cosmography, who sailed along and beyond Nova Francia, at the charges of King Henry the seventh, king of England; and he signified unto me, that having sailed a long time west and by north beyond those islands unto the latitude of 67 degrees and [an half] under the north pole, on the 11th day of June, and finding the sea open and without any manner of impediment, he thought verily that he might have passed by that way unto Cathay, which is in the east; and he would have done it, if the mutiny of the shipmaster and unruly mariners had not enforced him to return homewards from that place. But it seemeth (saith Ramusius) that God doth yet reserve to some great prince the discovery of this voyage to Cathay by this way, which, for the bringing of the spicery from India into Europe, would be the most easy and shortest of all others hitherto found out. And surely this enterprise would be the most glorious and of most importance of all other that any could imagine to make their name much more eternal and immortal among all ages to come than these so great tumults and troubles of wars, which are to be seen continually in Europe among the miserable and unhappy Christians.

3. Thirdly, the report which the people of Hochelaga made to Jacques Cartier, in the eighth chapter of his second relation, of the river three months navigable to the southward, doth not a little confirm the same.

4. Fourthly, the relation of the people of Canada in the twelfth chapter, following on this manner: Moreover they told us, and gave us to understand, that there are people clad with cloth as we are, and that there are many inhabited towns and good people, and that they have great store of gold and red copper, and that up into the land, beyond the river first above mentioned, even to Hochelaga and Saguenay, there is an isle environed about with that and other rivers, which beyond Saguenay entereth into two or three great lakes; also that there is found a sea of fresh water, the head and end whereof there was never man found that had thoroughly searched, as far as they have heard say of them of Saguenay, for they (as they signified unto us) had not been there themselves.

5. Fifthly, in the end of that second relation this postcript is added as a special point, to wit: That they of Canada say that it is the space of a moon (that is to say a month) to sail to a land where cinnamon and cloves are gathered; and in the French original which I saw in the king's library at Paris, in the abbey of St. Martin's, it is further put down, that Donnaconna, the king of Canada, in his bark had travelled to that country where cinnamon and cloves are had; yea, and the names whereby the savages call those two spices in their own language are there put down in writing.

6. Sixthly, this passage is likewise proved by the double report of Vasques de Coronado. For first, he being at Cibola [New Mexico], which standeth in 37 degrees and a half of northerly latitude within the land, he had this information of the people of the place . . . whereby I gather that some part of the northern sea is within eight days journey of Cibola. Again, when he was afterwards at the town of Quivira, which is situated by the seaside in the latitude of 40 degrees, he found there ships with mariners, which had the pictures of a bird, called *alcatrazzi*, in silver upon their bonnets and on the foreparts of their ships; which signified that they were thirty days sailing to that place; whence it is said that they must needs be of Cathay or China, seeing there is none but Spanish shipping upon all the coast of the backside of Nova Spania.

7. Seventhly, the people of Florida, at the river of May, in 30 degrees,

signified to John Ribault and his company, that they might sail in boats from thence through the country by river to Cibola in 20 days. These are the words, viz.: As we now demanded of them concerning the town of Cibola (whereof some have written that it is not far from thence, and is situated within the land, and towards the sea called *Mare del Sur*), they showed us by signs, which we understood well enough, that they might go thither with their boats, by rivers, in 20 days.

8. Eighthly, Don Antonio di Castillo, ambassador to her majesty from Henry the king of Portugal, told me here in London, the year before his departure, that one Anus Corterial, captain of the Isle of Tercera, in the year 1574, sent a ship to discover the northwest passage, which, arriving on the coast of America in 57 degrees of latitude, found a great entrance very deep and broad, without impediment of ice, into which they passed above twenty leagues, and found it always to tend towards the south. The land lay low and plain on either side. They would have gone further, but their victuals drawing short, and being but one ship, they returned back, with hope at another time to make a full search of the passage, whereof they saw not small likelihood.

9. Ninthly, Don Antonio, king of Portugal, showed me in Paris this present summer, a great old round card (out of which Postellus took the form of his map), that had the northwest strait plainly set down in the latitude of 57 degrees.

10. Tenthly, there is a mighty large old map in parchment, made, as it should seem, by Verarsanus, traced all along the coast from Florida to Cape Breton, with many Italian names, which layeth out the sea, making a little neck of land in 40 degrees of latitude, much like the straight neck or isthmus of Darien. This map is now in the custody of Mr. Michael Locke.

11. Eleventhly, there is an old excellent globe in the queen's privy gallery at Westminster, which also seemeth to be of Verarsanus' making, having the coast described in Italian, which layeth out the very selfsame straight neck of land in the latitude of 40 degrees, with the sea joining hard on both sides, as it doth on Panama and Nombre di Dios; which were a matter of singular importance, if it should be true, as it is not unlikely.

12. Twelfthly, the judgment of Gerardus Mercator, that excellent geographer, which his son, Rumold Mercator, showed me in a letter of

his and drew out for me in writing, of wise men is not lightly to be regarded. These were his words: . . . You write (saith he to his son)
great matters, though very briefly, of the new voyage, whereat I wonder
that it was not these many years heretofore attempted; for there is no
doubt but there is a straight and short way open into the west, even to
Cathay. Into which kingdom, if they govern their voyage well, they
shall gather the most noble merchandise of all the world, and shall make
the name of Christ to be known to many idolators and heathen people.

13. Hereunto agreeth the relation of Monsieur de Leau, an honest
gent of Morleux, in Brittany, which told me this spring, in the presence
of divers English men at Paris, that a man of St. Malo this last year discovered the sea on the back side of Hochelaga.

14. Moreover, the relation of David Ingram confirmeth the same;
for, as he avoucheth and hath put it down in writing, he travelled two
days in the sight of the North Sea.

15. Again, the prohibition which King Philip hath made, that none
of his pilots shall discover to the northwards of 45 degrees, may seem
chiefly to proceed of these two causes: the one, lest passing further to
the north, they might fall upon the open passage from *Mare del Sur*
into our Northern Sea; the other, because they have not people enough
to possess and keep the same, but rather in time should open a gap for
other nations to pass that way.

16. Lastly, I will end with the earnest petition and constant assertion
of Ramusius, in his first volume, fol.374, where, speaking of the several
ways by which the spicery, both of old and of late years, hath been brought
into Europe, he useth these speeches in the person of another: Why
do not the princes (saith he), which are to deal in these affairs, send forth
two or three colonies to inhabit the country and to reduce this savage
nation to more civility, considering what a battle and fruitful soil it is,
how replenished with all kind of grain, how it is stored with all kinds of
birds and beasts, with such fair and mighty rivers, that Captain Cartier
and his company in one of them sailed up an hundred and twenty four
leagues, finding the country peopled on both sides in great abundance;
and, moreover, to cause the governors of those colonies to send forth
men to discover the north lands about Terra de Labrador, and west northwest towards the seas, which are to sail to the country of Cathay, and
from thence to the islands of Molucca. These are enterprises to purchase

immortal praise, which the Lord Antony de Mendoza, viceroy of Mexico, willing to put in execution, sent forth his captains, both by sea and land, upon the northwest of Nova Spania, and discovered the kingdoms of the seven cities about Cibola; and Franciscus Vasques de Coronado passed from Mexico by land towards the northwest 2850 miles, in so much as he came to the sea which lieth between Cathay and America, where he met with the Cathayan ships; and, no doubt, if the Frenchmen, in this their *Nova Francia*, would have discovered up further into the land towards the west northwest parts, they should have found the sea and have sailed to Cathay.

Thus far Ramusius.

God, which doth all things in his due time, and hath in his hand the hearts of all princes, stir up the mind of her majesty at length to assist her most willing and forward subjects to the performance of this most godly and profitable action; which was begun at the charges of King Henry the seventh her grandfather, followed by King Henry the eighth, her father, and left, as it seemeth, to be accomplished by her (as the three years golden voyage to Ophir was by Solomon), to the making of her realm and subjects most happy and herself most famous to all posterity. Amen. . . .

Cap. XXI.

A note of some things to be prepared for the voyage, which is set down rather to draw the takers of the voyage in hand to the present consideration than for any other reason; for that divers things require preparation long before the voyage, without the which the voyage is maimed.

Dead Victual.

Hog's flesh, barrelled and salted, in great quantity.

Beef, barrelled, in less quantity.

Stockfish, meal in barrels.

Oatmeal, in barrels, near couched.

Rice, sallet oil, barrelled butter.

Cheese, honey in barrels.

Currants, raisins of the sun.

Dried prunes, olives in barrels.

Beans, dried on the kill.

Peas, dried likewise.

Canary wines, hollocke.

Sacks racked.

Vinegar, very strong.

Aqua vitae.

Ciders of France, Spain, and England.

Beer, brewed specially in special time.

Turnip seed.
Parsnip seed.
Radish.
Carrot.
Navews.
Garlic.
Onions.
Leeks.
Melons.
Pompions.
Cucumbers.
Cabbage Cole.
Parsley.
Lettuce.
Endive.
Alexander.
Orege.[orach]
Thyme.
Rosemary.
Mustard Seed.
Fennell.
Any seeds, new and fresh to be sown

Victual
By
Roots
And
Herbs

The Increase, Renewal, and the Continuance of Victual at the Planting Places, and Men and Things Incident and Tending to the Same:

Boars, sows.

Conies, buck and doe.

Doves, male and female.

Cocks, hens.

Ducks, male and female, for low soils.

Turkeys, male and female.

Wheat, Rye, Barley.
Big, or barley beer.
Oats, beans.
Peas, faches.[vetches?]
Three square grain.
} To sow to victual by bread and drink, etc.

Sugar cane planters with the plants.

Vine planters.

Olive planters.

Gardeners for herbs, roots, and for all earth fruits.

Grafters for fruit trees.

Hunters, skilful to kill wild beasts for victual.

Warreners to breed conies and to kill vermin.

Fowlers.

Sea fishers.

Fresh-water fishers.

Knitters of nets.

Butchers.

Salters and seasoners of victual.

Salt makers.

Cooks.

Bakers.

Brewers.

Greyhounds to kill deer, etc.

Mastiffs to kill heavy beasts of ravine and for night watches.

Bloodhounds to recover hurt deer.

Provisions Tending to Force:

Men expert in the art of fortification.

Platforms of many forms readied to carry with you by advice of the best.

Captains of long and of great experience.

Soldiers well trained in Flanders to join with the younger.

Harquebusers of skill.

Archers, strong bowmen.

Bowyers.

Fletchers.

Arrow-head makers.

Bow-stave preparers.

Glue makers.

Morrice-pike makers and of halbert staves.

Makers of spades and shovels for pioneers, trenchers, and fort-makers.

Makers of baskets to carry earth to forts and rampiers.

Pioneers and spademen for fortification.

Saltpeter makers.

Gunpowder makers.

Target makers of horns, defensive against savages.

Oilethole doublet makers, defensive, light and gentle to lie in.

Turners of targets of elm, and of other tough woods light.

Ships,
Pinnaces,
Barks,
Busses with flat bottoms, } furnished with expert seamen.

Swift boats and barges to pass by wind and oar, covered with quilted canvas of defence against shot from the shore, to pierce rivers for discovery, and to pass to and fro, offensive and defensive against savages, devised by Mr. Bodenham of Spain.

Shipwrights in some number to be employed on the timber.

Oar makers, and makers of cable and of cordage.

Provisions Incident to the First Traffic and Trade of Merchandise:

Grubbers and rooters up of cypress, cedars, and of all other fair trees, for to be employed in coffers, desks, etc., for traffic.

Mattocks, narrow and long, of iron, to that purpose.

Millwrights, to make mills for speedy and cheap sawing of timber and boards for trade, and first traffic of surety.

Millwrights, for corn mills.

Sawyers, for common use.

Carpenters, for buildings.

Joiners, to cut out the boards into chests to be embarked for England.

Blacksmiths, to many great and needful uses.

Pitch-makers.

Tar-makers.

Burners of ashes for the trade of soap ashes.

Coopers, for barrels to inclose those ashes.

Tallow chandlers, to prepare the tallow to be encasked for England.

Wax chandlers, to prepare wax in like sort.

Dyers, to seek in that firm that rich cochineal and other things for that trade.

Mineral men.

Artisans, Serving Our First Planters, not in Traffic but for Buildings:

Brick makers.

Tile makers.

Lime makers.

Bricklayers.

Tilers.

Thatchers with reed, rushes, broom, or straw.

Sinkers of walls and finders of springs.

Quarrellers to dig tile.

Rough masons.

Carpenters.

Lathmakers.

Artisans, Serving Our First Planters, and in Part Serving for Traffic:

Barbers.

Launders.

Tailors.

Butchers.

Pail makers.

Burcachiomakers.

Bottlemakers of London.

Shoemakers, cobblers.

Tanners, white tawers.

Buff skin dressers.

Chamois skin dressers.

A present provision for raising a notable trade for the time to come:

The knit woollen cap of Toledo in Spain, called *bonetto rugio collerado*, so infinitely sold to the Moors in Barbary and Africa, is to be prepared in London, Hereford, and Ross, and to be vented to the people, and may become a notable trade of gain to the merchant, and a great relief to our poor people, and a sale of our wool and of our labour; and being such a cap that every particular person will buy and may easily compass, the sale will be great in short time, especially if our people wear them at their first arrival there.

Things Forgotten May Here Be Noted as They Come to Mind, and after Be Placed with the Rest, And after That in All Be Reduced into the Best Order.

That there be appointed one or two preachers for the voyage that God may be honoured, the people instructed, mutinies the better avoided, and obedience the better used, that the voyage may have the better success.

That the voyage be furnished with Bibles and with books of service. That the books of the discoveries and conquests of the East Indies be carried with you.

That the books of the discoveries of the West Indies, and the conquests of the same, be also carried, to keep men occupied from worse cogitations, and to raise their minds to courage and high enterprises, and to make them less careless for the better shunning of common dangers in such cases arising. And because men are more apt to make themselves subject in obedience to prescribed laws set down and signed by a prince, than to the changeable will of any captain, be he never so wise or temperate, never so free from desire of revenge, it is wished that it were learned out what course both the Spaniards and Portuguese took, in their discoveries, for government, and that the same were delivered to learned men that had passed most of the laws of the empire and of other prince's laws, and that thereupon some special orders, fit for voyages and beginnings, might upon deliberation be set down and allowed by the queen's most excellent majesty and her wise council; and, fair engrossed, might in a table be set before the eyes of such as go in the voyage that no man punished or executed may justly complain of manifest and open wrong offered.

That some physician be provided to minister by counsel and by physic, to keep and preserve from sickness, or by skill to cure such as fall into disease and distemperature.

A surgeon to let blood, and for such as may chance, by wars or otherwise, to be hurt is more needful for the voyage.

An apothecary to serve the physician is requisite; and, the physician dying, he may chance (well chosen) to stand in stead of the one and the other, and to send into the realm, by seed and root, herbs and plants of rare excellency.

If such plenty of honey be in these regions as is said, it were to good purpose to carry in the voyage such of the servants of the Russia Company as have the skill to make the drink called meth, which they use in Russia and Poland, and nearer, as in North Wales, for their wine; and, if you cannot carry any such, to carry the order of the making of it in writing, that it may be made for a need.

And, before many things, this one thing is to be called, as it were, with speed to mind, that the prisons and corners of London are full of decayed merchants, overthrown by loss at sea, by usurers, suretyship, and by sundry other such means, and dare or cannot for their debts show their faces; and in truth many excellent gifts be in many of these men, and their good gifts are not employed to any manner of use, nor are not like of themselves to procure liberty to employ themselves, but are, without some special mean used to starve by want or to shorten their times by thought; and for that these men, schooled in the house of adversity, are drawn to a degree higher in excellency, and may be employed to great uses in this purposed voyage, it were to great purpose to use means by authority for such as maliciously, wrongfully, or for trifling causes are detained, and to take of them and of others that hide their heads, and to employ them; for so they may be relieved, and the enterprise furthered in many respects.

A MOST NEEDFUL NOTE.

And, in choice of all artisans for the voyage, this general rule were good to be observed, that no man be chosen that is known to be a papist, for the special inclination they have of favour to the king of Spain.

That also, of those artisans which are protestants, that where you may have change and choice, that such as be most strong and lusty men be chosen, and such as can best handle his bow or his harquebus; for the more good gifts that the goers in the voyage have, the more is the voyage benefited. And therefore (many going), if every man's gifts and good qualities be entered into a book before they be received, they may be employed upon any necessity in the voyage in this or in that, according as occasion of need shall require.

Finis.

FOUR SPEECHES BY QUEEN ELIZABETH

1585—1601

QUEEN ELIZABETH addressed three of these speeches to her parliaments, the fourth to her army. The parliamentary speeches have been accepted as at least fair reports of what the queen said, and recently the authenticity of her remarks at Tilbury has been urged by Professor Neal.[1]

The first speech, that of 1585, concerns the church and the religious situation resulting from the Jesuits' counter-attack against the queen and her religious settlement after 1580. Parliament legalized the national association for the protection of Elizabeth and provided a council of regency in event of her murder. But her speech was directed more against the inroads being made into the established religion by the puritans. Since the *Admonition* of 1572, more concerted action to liberalize the church and a more cohesive organization of puritans had brought the religious issues to the forefront of national affairs. In 1585 Elizabeth stood solidly behind the conservative and orthodox Whitgift, her new archbishop of Canterbury.

The speech at Tilbury in 1588 was intended to rally the spirits of the special army assembled there to withstand an advance of Parma's soldiers should they effect a landing. Dr. Sharp, then serving as chaplain, says that he re-delivered the queen's speech the next day to the troops. The assumption that Sharp must have had a draft of the original from which to do this is the ground for supposing that his version is ' a copy, at two or three removes, of a speech actually written by Elizabeth.'

Her address in 1593 was to thank parliament for the three subsidies that had been voted after no little haggling between the two houses. The commons had wished to grant only two subsidies, but the lords held out for three. The need for this money arose from the cost of continuing the war against Spain both in the Netherlands and in France where Elizabeth was supporting Henry IV's Huguenot cause while Philip II championed the Catholic League.

Elizabeth's golden speech to her last parliament followed the controversy over the abuse of monopolies. Parliament had met in no good humour, and one diarist noted that few members cried ' God bless your majesty ' after the formal opening. Even a demand for four subsidies, which were granted, had not riled the house of commons so much as had monopolies. The parliamentary attack was seconded by popular petitions to the queen and street cries of the Londoners. Robert Cecil's failure to control the house of commons, which had frankly got out of hand, led Elizabeth herself to intervene. Gracefully giving way to her subjects' wishes, she revoked every patent then in force and summoned the commons to appear before her at Whitehall to hear her declaration—the acme of Tudor kingcraft.

The speeches are printed in full from the sources indicated.

1. J.E.Neale, ' The Sayings of Queen Elizabeth,' *History*, vol.X (1926), 226–7.

QUEEN ELIZABETH'S SPEECH TO PARLIAMENT

29 March 1585

[Sir Simon D'Ewes, *Journal of the House of Lords*, 1693, pp.328–329]

To the further amplifying of which also, here doth now in the next place ensue a most pious and gracious speech of her majesty's, uttered by her upon the conclusion of this parliament, which being not found in the original journal-book of the upper house, is therefore supplied out of a copy thereof I had by me, written by John Stow the chronicler with his own hand, being verbatim as followeth.

My lords and ye of the lower house, my silence must not injure the owner so much as to suppose a substitute sufficient to render you the thanks that my heart yieldeth you, not so much for the safe keeping of my life, for which your care appears so manifest, as for the neglecting your private future peril, not regarding other way than my present state.

No prince herein, I confess, can be surer tied or faster bound than I am with the link of your good will, and can for that but yield a heart and a head to seek for ever all your best; yet one matter toucheth me so near, as I may not overskip, religion, the ground on which all other matters ought to take root, and being corrupted, may mar all the tree. And that there be some fault-finders with the order of the clergy, which so may make a slander to myself and the church, whose over-ruler God hath made me, whose negligence cannot be excused, if any schisms or errors heretical were suffered. Thus much I must say that some faults and negligences may grow and be, as in all other great charges it happeneth, and what vocation without? All which if you my lords of the clergy do not amend, I mean to depose you. Look ye therefore well to your charges. This may be amended without heedless or open exclamations. I am supposed to have many studies, but most philosophical. I must yield this to be true, that I suppose few (that be no professors) have read more. And I need not tell you that I am so simple, that I understand not, nor so forgetful, that I remember not; and yet amidst my many volumes I hope God's Book hath not been my seldomest lectures, in which we find that which by reason (for my part) we ought to believe; that seeing so great wickedness and griefs in the world in which we live, but as way-faring pilgrims, we must suppose that God would never have made us but for a better place, and of more comfort than we find here. I know no creature that breatheth, whose life standeth hourly in more peril for it than mine own, who entered not into my state without sight of manifold dangers of life and crown, as one that had the mightiest and greatest to wrestle with. Then it followeth that I regarded it so much, as I left my life behind my care; and so you see that you wrong me too much (if any such there be) as doubt my coldness in that behalf; for if I were not persuaded that mine were the true way of God's will, God forbid that I should live to prescribe it to you. Take you heed lest Ecclesiastes say not too true, they that fear the hoary frost, the snow shall fall upon them. I see many over-bold with God Almighty, making too many subtle scannings of his blessed will, as lawyers do with human testaments. The presumption is so great as I may not suffer it (yet mind I not hereby to animate Romanists, which what adversaries they be to mine estate is sufficiently known) nor tolerate new-fangledness. I mean to guide them both by God's holy true rule. In both parts be perils, and of the latter I must pronounce them dangerous to a kingly rule, to have every man according to his own censure to make a doom of the validity and privity of his prince's government with a common veil and cover of God's word, whose followers must not be judged but by private men's exposition. God defend you from such a ruler that so evil will guide you. Now I conclude that your love and care neither is nor shall be bestowed upon a careless prince, but such as but for your good will passeth as little for this world as who careth least, with thanks for your free subsidy, a manifest show of the abundance of your good wills, the which I assure you but to be employed to your weal, I could be better pleased to return than receive.

THE SPEECH OF QUEEN ELIZABETH TO HER ARMY

Encamped at Tilbury, 1588

[From a letter by Dr. Leonel Sharp to the duke of Buckingham after 1623, Cabala, 1691, pp.343–4.]

I REMEMBER in '88 waiting upon the earl of Leicester at Tilbury camp, and in '89, going into Portugal with my noble master, the earl of Essex, I learned somewhat fit to be imparted to your grace.

The queen lying in the camp one night, guarded with her army, the old treasurer, Burleigh, came thither and delivered to the earl the examination of Don Pedro, who was taken and brought in by Sir Francis Drake, which examination the earl of Leicester delivered unto me to publish to the army in my next sermon. The sum of it was this.

Don Pedro, being asked what was the intent of their coming, stoutly answered the lords: What, but to subdue your nation and root it out.

Good, said the lords, and what meant you then to do with the catholics? He answered, We meant to send them (good men) directly unto heaven, as all that are heretics to hell. Yea, but, said the lords, what meant you to do with your whips of cord and wire? (Whereof they had great store in their ships.) What? said he, we meant to whip you heretics to death that have assisted my master's rebels and done such dishonours to our catholic king and people. Yea, but what would you have done, said they, with their young children? They, said he, which were above seven years old should have gone the way their fathers went, the rest should have lived, branded in the forehead with the letter L for Lutheran, to perpetual bondage.

This, I take God to witness, I received of those great lords upon examination taken by the council, and by commandment delivered it to the army.

The queen the next morning rode through all the squadrons of her army, as armed Pallas, attended by noble footmen, Leicester, Essex, and Norris, then lord marshall, and divers other great lords. Where she made an excellent oration to her army, which the next day after her departure, I was commanded to re-deliver to all the army together, to keep a public fast.

Her words were these.

My loving people, we have been persuaded by some that are careful of our safety to take heed how we commit ourself to armed multitudes for fear of treachery; but I assure you, I do not desire to live to distrust my faithful and loving people. Let tyrants fear. I have always so behaved myself that, under God, I have placed my chiefest strength and safeguard in the loyal hearts and good will of my subjects, and therefore I am come amongst you, as you see, at this time, not for my recreation and disport, but being resolved, in the midst and heat of the battle, to live or die amongst you all, to lay down my life for my God and for my kingdom and for my people, my honour, and my blood, even in the dust. I know I have the body but of a weak and feeble woman, but I have the heart and stomach of a king, and a king of England too, and think foul scorn that Parma or Spain, or any prince of Europe should dare to invade the borders of my realm; the which, rather than any dishonour shall grow by me, I myself will take up arms, I myself will be your general, judge, and rewarder of every one of your virtues in the field. I know, already for your forwardness, you have deserved rewards and crowns; and we do assure you, in the word of a prince, they shall be duly paid you. In the meantime my lieutenant-general shall be in my stead, than whom never prince commanded a more noble or worthy subject, not doubting but by your obedience to my general, by your concord in the camp, and your valour in the field, we shall shortly have a famous victory over those enemies of my God, of my kingdom, and of my people.

A SPEECH MADE BY
QUEEN ELIZABETH IN PARLIAMENT

Concerning the Spanish Invasion, 1593
[H. Townshend, *Historical Collections*, 1680, pp.48–49.]

THIS kingdom hath had many wise, noble, and victorious princes. I will not compare with any of them in wisdom, fortitude, or any other virtues; but saving the duty of a child, that is not to compare with his father, in love, care, sincerity, and justice, I will compare with any prince that ever you had, or shall have.

It may be thought simplicity in me, that all this time of my reign I have not sought to advance my territories and enlarge my dominions; for opportunity hath served me to do it. I acknowledge my womanhood and weakness in that respect; but though it hath not been hard to obtain, yet I doubted how to keep the things so obtained: that hath only held me from such attempts. And I must say, my mind was never to invade my neighbours or to usurp over any; I am contented to reign over mine own and to rule as a just prince.

Yet the king of Spain doth challenge me to be the quarreller and the beginner of all these wars; in which he doth me the greatest wrong that can be, for my conscience doth not accuse my thoughts wherein I have done him the least injury; but I am persuaded in my conscience, if he knew what I know, he himself would be sorry for the wrong that he hath done me.

I fear not all his threatenings; his great preparations and mighty forces do not stir me; for though he come against me with a greater power than ever was his invincible navy, I doubt not (God assisting me, upon whom I always trust) but that I shall be able to defeat and overthrow him. I have great advantage against him, for my cause is just.

I heard him say, when he attempted his last invasion, some upon the seacoast forsook their towns and flew up higher into the country and left all naked exposed to his entrance. But I swear unto you by God, if I knew those persons, or any that should do so hereafter, I will make them know and feel what it is to be so fearful in so urgent a cause.

The subsidies you give me I accept thankfully, if you give me your good wills with them; but if the necessity of the time and your preservations did not require it, I would refuse them. But let me tell you that the sum is not so much, but that it is needful for a prince to have so much always lying in her coffers for your defence and not to be driven to get it when we should use it.

You that be lieutenants and gentlemen of command in your countries, I require you to take care that the people be well armed and in readiness upon all occasions. You that be judges and justices of the peace, I command and straightly charge you that you see the laws to be duly executed and that you make them living laws, when we have put life into them.

Thus with most gracious thanks to both houses, the princely speech ended.

THE GOLDEN SPEECH OF
QUEEN ELIZABETH TO HER LAST PARLIAMENT,

30 November 1601
[H. Townshend, *Historical Collections*, 1680, pp. 262–266]

In the afternoon, the commons attended the queen at Whitehall, about three of the clock, to the number of one hundred and forty.

At length the queen came into the council-chamber; where sitting under the cloth of state, at the upper end, the speaker, with all the commons came in: and after three low reverences made, he spake to this effect:

Most sacred, and more than most gracious sovereign,

We your faithful, loyal, and most obedient subjects and commons here present, vouchsafed of your special goodness (to our unspeakable comforts), access to your royal presence: do in all duty and humbleness come to present that which no words can express, our most humble and thankful acknowledgment of your most gracious message, and most bounden and humble thanks for your majesty's most abundant goodness, extended and performed to us.

We cannot say (most gracious sovereign); we have called and been heard; we have complained and have been helped; though in all duty and thankfulness we acknowledge your sacred ears are ever open and ever bowed down to hear us, and your blessed hands ever stretched out to relieve us.

We acknowledge (sacred sovereign) in all duty and thankfulness; we acknowledge, that before we call, your preventing grace and all-deserving goodness do watch over us for our good; more ready to give than we can desire, much less deserve.

The attribute which is most proper unto God, to perform all he promiseth (most gracious sovereign, queen of all truth, of all constancy, of all goodness, never wearied of doing good unto us, which the deeds themselves do speak), that we must render unto you most zealous, most careful to provide all good things for us, most gracious, most tender to remove all grievance from us, which all your princely actions have ever showed. And even now, your most gracious published proclamation, of your own only mere motion, and special grace, for the good of all your people, doth witness unto us.

We come not (sacred sovereign) one of ten, to render thanks, and the rest to go away unthankful: but all, of all, in all duty and thankfulness, do throw down ourselves at the feet of your majesty. Neither do we present our thanks in words, or any outward thing, which can be nothing, which can be no sufficient retribution for so great goodness.

But, in all duty and thankfulness, prostrate at your feet, we present our most loyal and thankful hearts; even the last drop of blood in our hearts, and the last spirit of breath in our nostrils, to be poured out, to be breathed up for your safety.

After three low reverences made, he with the rest kneeled down, and her majesty began thus to answer herself; viz.

Mr. Speaker,

We have heard your declaration, and perceive your care of our state, by falling into the consideration of a grateful acknowledgment of such benefits as you have received; and that your coming is to present thanks unto us, which I accept with no less joy than your loves can have desire to offer such a present.

I do assure you, there is no prince that loveth his subjects better, or whose love can countervail our love. There is no jewel, be it of never so rich a price, which I set before this jewel; I mean your love: for I do more esteem of it than of any treasure or riches; for that we know how to prize, but love and thanks I count unvaluable.

And, though God hath raised me high; yet this I count the glory of my crown, that I have reigned with your loves. This makes me that I do not so much rejoice that God hath made me to be a queen, as to be a queen over so thankful a people.

Therefore, I have cause to wish nothing more than to content the subjects; and that is a duty which I owe: neither do I desire to live longer days, than that I may see your prosperity; and that's my only desire.

And as I am that person, that still (yet under God) hath delivered you; so I trust (by the almighty power of God), that I still shall be his instrument to preserve you from envy, peril, dishonour, shame, tyranny, and oppression; partly by means of your intended helps, which we take very acceptably, because it manifests the largeness of your loves and loyalty to your sovereign.

Of myself I must say this, I was never any greedy scraping grasper, nor a straight, fast-holding prince, nor yet a waster. My heart was never set on worldly goods, but only for my subject's good. What you do bestow on me, I will not hoard it up, but receive it to bestow on you again: yea, my own proprieties I count yours, and to be expended for your good; and your eyes shall see the bestowing of all, for your good. Therefore, render unto them from me, I beseech you, Mr. Speaker, such thanks as you imagine my heart yieldeth but my tongue cannot express.

Nota, all this while we kneeled; whereupon her majesty said: ' Mr. Speaker, I would wish you and the rest to stand up; for I shall yet trouble you with longer speech.'
So we all stood up, and she went on with her speech, saying:

Mr. Speaker,

You give me thanks; but I doubt me, that I have more cause to thank you all, than you me. And I charge you, to thank them of the lower house from me: for had I not received a knowledge from you, I might have fallen into the lapse of an error, only for lack of true information.

Since I was queen, yet did I never put my pen unto any grant, but that, upon pretext and semblance made unto me, it was both good and beneficial to the subject in general; though a private profit to some of my ancient servants, who had deserved well at my hands. But the contrary being found by experience, I am exceedingly beholding to such subjects as would move the same at the first. And I am not so simple to suppose but that there are some of the lower house whom these grievances never touched. And for them I think they spake out of zeal for their countries and not out of spleen, or malevolent affection as being parties grieved. And I take it exceedingly gratefully from them; because it gives us to know that no respects or interests had moved them other than the minds they bear to suffer no diminution of our honour and our subjects' loves unto us. The zeal of which affection, tending to ease my people, and knit their hearts unto me, I embrace with a princely care; for (above all earthly treasure) I esteem my people's love, more than which I desire not to merit.

That my grants should be grievous to my people and oppressions privileged under colour of our patents, our kingly dignity shall not suffer it: yea, when I heard it, I could give no rest unto my thoughts until I had reformed it.

Shall they think to escape unpunished that have thus oppressed you, and have been respectless of their duty and regardless of our honour? No, Mr. Speaker, I assure you, were it not more for conscience-sake than for any glory or increase of love, that I desire these errors, troubles, vexations, and oppressions done by these varlets and lewd persons, not worthy the name of subjects, should not escape without condign punishment. But I perceive they dealt with me like physicians, who administering a drug make it more acceptable by giving it a good aromatical savour, or when they give pills, do gild them all over.

I have ever used to set the last judgment-day before my eyes, as so to rule as I shall be judged to answer before a higher judge, to whose judgment-seat I do appeal, that never thought was cherished in my heart that tended not to my people's good. And now, if my kingly bounty have been abused and my grants turned to the hurt of my people contrary to my will and meaning; or if any in authority under me have neglected or perverted what I committed to them; I hope God will not lay their culps and offences to my charge; who though there were danger in re-pealing our grants, yet what danger would I not rather incur for your good, than I would suffer them still to continue?

I know the title of a king is a glorious title. But assure yourself, that the shining glory of princely authority hath not so dazzled the eyes of our understanding, but that we well know and remember that we also are to yield an account of our actions before the Great Judge.

To be a king and wear a crown is a thing more glorious to them that see it than it is pleasing to them that bear it: for myself, I was never so much enticed with the glorious name of a king, or royal authority of a queen, as delighted that God had made me his instrument to maintain his truth and glory and to defend this kingdom (as I said) from peril, dishonour, tyranny, and oppression.

There will never queen sit in my seat with more zeal to my country, care for my subjects, and that sooner with willingness will venture her life for your good and safety, than myself. For it is not my desire to live nor reign longer than my life and reign shall be for your good. And though you have had, and may have many princes, more mighty and wise, sitting in this state; yet you never had, or shall have any that will be more careful and loving.

Shall I ascribe anything to myself, and my sexly weakness? I were not worthy to live then; and of all, most unworthy of the great mercies I have had from God, who hath ever yet given me a heart, which never yet feared foreign or home enemy. I speak it to give God the praise, as a testimony before you, and not to attribute anything to myself. For I, O Lord, what am I whom practices and perils past should not fear? Or, what can I do? [These words she spake with a great emphasis.] That I should speak for any glory, God forbid.

This, Mr. Speaker, I pray you to deliver to the house, to whom heartily commend me. And so, I commit you all to your best fortunes and further councils. And I pray you, Mr. Comptroller, Mr. Secretary, and you of my council, that before these gentlemen depart into their countries, you bring them all to kiss my hand.

AN ADMONITION TO THE NOBILITY

And people of England and Ireland concerning the present wars made for the execution of his holiness' sentence, by the high and mighty king catholic of Spain. By the cardinal of England. A.D. MDLXXXVIII.

WILLIAM ALLEN (1532–1594), while an undergraduate at Oriel College, Oxford, fell under the influence of his tutor, the Reverend Morgan Philipps, a truly zealous catholic. He was made a Fellow of Oriel in 1550, received an M.A. in 1554, and two years later was made Principal of St. Mary's Hall, Oxford. He held this office until he fled for Flanders in 1560 where he joined the English Roman catholic exiles at Louvain. In 1562 he sought to improve his health by a return to Lancashire where he was active in rallying Romanists until 1565 when he left England for ever.

At Mechlin, Allen was ordained priest after which he began a seminary at Douay in 1568 for English catholics. From this school sprung the English colleges at Rheims and Rome. The three institutions to educate Englishmen within the catholic faith owed their existence to Allen who gained for them financial support and, in 1575, papal endorsement. For their benefit Allen wrote tracts on catholic doctrine, on the English catholics, and on the colleges themselves.

During a visit to Rome in 1579–80, Allen urged the Jesuits to undertake the English mission of Campion and Parsons. Five years later he settled in Rome permanently, and at the request of Philip II of Spain he was in 1587 made cardinal of England. For several years he had been involved in the political intrigues of Parsons, Mary Stuart, the Guises, and Philip II against Elizabeth and her government. After Mary Stuart's execution in 1587, Allen was one of those who contended that Philip II had the better title to the English throne. In 1588 *An Admonition to the Nobility and People of England* was written, probably by the advice of Parsons, and Allen ' was induced to put his signature to this violent and offensive document, which was probably printed at Antwerp.'

After the failure of the 1588 Armada, catholics sought to destroy all the copies they could which explains the present rarity of the tract. The text below is taken from the 1842 reprint by Eupater (I.Mendham), London, and has been cut by about one-fourth as indicated.

Gulielmus miseratione Divina S.R.E. Tituli Sancti Martini in Montibus Cardinalis Presbyter de Anglia nuncupatus, Cunctis Regnorum Angliae & Hiberniae Proceribus populis & personis, omnibusque Christi fidelibus salutem in Domino sempiternam.

RIGHT honourable worshipful and most dearly beloved in our Lord, no man can be ignorant that either by report, reading, or remembrance

351

list look back not much further than fifty years past, that this great misery and mutation of state and religion in this our realm of England by which our church (alas) is already overthrown, our country in extreme terms of perishing, and ourselves with what so ever is dear unto us, in daily dread of destruction and damnation, proceeded not first of the subjects' disorder or disobedience to their kings (as else where heresy often doth) and as we see in many of the next nations unto us it presently happeneth, where no popular mutiny, against their magistrates, hath caused their like calamity: but begun first and wholly in effect by our king that then was, Henry the eighth, and afterwards till this day, hath been specially pursued by our prince's pretensed laws and usurped sovereignty over our souls, to the which our nobility, priests, and people, by force and fear, have rather been drawn than by lawful consent yielded thereunto.

And albeit wicked and hypocritical kings be suffered sometimes or sent from God, for the subjects' sins and for our offences, great no doubt and grievous in every estate (let none excuse themselves, let none accuse others); and that we hereby may worthily also be thought to have deserved both our prince's fall and our own punishment, according to God's most holy commination, that when his people should cease to serve him in truth, and commit wickedness, both they and their king should perish together: nevertheless, to see and know the place specially affected, and the next immediate surge of our sores, where we expect remedy and not ruin, is necessary for our recovery. Wherein, though the case have long seemed well near desperate, yet God himself not forgetful of his old mercies, beholding from heaven our not voluntary but coacted miseries, and our most holy and zealous father in Christ *Sixtus the fifth*, his highest minister, and our chiefest magistrate and master in earth, to whom our Saviour hath given apostolic power to take vengeance upon disobedience, moved by the sorrows and sighs of so many afflicted souls, and instant prayers of all Christian people that pity our enforced perishing in schism and heresy, doth give us at this time, both better means, more hope, and readier help, than we could ever possibly have either deserved or desired: yea they have (not the pope alone but God himself surely, and other the most zealous and mightiest princes in Christendom by his induction) taken the whole care of our case into their own hands, and that with such sincere intention (whereof myself can best bear witness and assure you my dear countrymen) and in such sweet, moderate, and merciful sort, that in the appliance of the prepared remedy, neither the corps of our commonwealth, need to feel or fear any distress, nor any part (other than the principal affected, and some such few as will not follow this offer of God's ordinance) be wrong or wrenched thereby. For albeit often else, in like case of revolt from God's church and our fathers' faith, not only the kings, but also their countries, after divers dreadful censures and sentences, have been by supreme authority of Christ's vicar, given up to invasion, wars, wastes, and final destruction, and we now might by way of rigour and extreme justice, be both charged and chastised far more deeply than the church of Theatira for tolerating the wicked Jezebel, not now as then calling herself a prophetess, but the very chief spiritual governess under God, to teach and deceive God's servants, and to force them to fornication, to eat bread of idolatry in schismatical service. And also for that, by error of conscience or want of courage, we have so long unnaturally subdued our souls to our bodies, hazarded our eternal salvation, to save our transitory substance, obeyed man more than God, preferred the temporal title, not only of lawful civil authority, but of manifold usurped tyranny, above the supreme bishop's spiritual sovereignty, by Christ's express word established on earth, yielding to the one most servilely as to our household and home God, and as to a very national idol, subjection both of body and soul, and thereby disobeying, disgracing, despising, and blaspheming the other, as a foreign power, or rather as a strange devil or antichrist (a thing punishable in the old law by death reputed in the new for express contempt of Christ's own person, revenged in Core and his confederates by fearful fire from heaven, by horrible gaping of the ground they stood upon, and by sudden sinking down to hell). Yet all this notwithstanding, the pope's holiness, who according to his apostolic benignity, wholly inclined to mercy, following God's rule and example rather of sparing the wicked for the good, than punishing the innocent for the evil, that the soul which sinneth only may perish, doth most mercifully forget and forgive all the premises, as well in the whole body of the commonwealth as in every particular person that is penitent and weary of these horrible disorders and treasons committed against God, the see apostolic, holy church, and our country (incorrigible persons, and principal procurers of these mischiefs only excepted) and only meaneth in Christ's word and power given unto him, and in zeal of God's house, to pursue the actual deprivation of Elizabeth the pretensed queen, eftsoons declared and judicially sentenced, by his holiness' predecessors, Pius quintus and Gregory XIII, for an heretic and usurper and the proper present cause of perdition of millions of souls at home, and the very bane of all Christian kingdoms and states near about her. That in this one woman's condign correction, God's mighty arm that deposeth the proud and powerable persons from their seats may be feared and glorified, and the horrible and wicked outrages of Henry the eighth, her supposed father's house and person, together with God's vengeance on the same, may in some measure of his justice be accomplished, and our whole people put in happy hope of salvation and full freedom of conscience again, that all the just of the earth may say, *Lo this is she that took not God for her strength, but trusted to her treasures and prevailed in her wickedness.* And that all the world, and namely our own nation and people, to whom the matter so nearly appertaineth, may thoroughly judge as well of this woman's and her parent's deserts, as of his holiness and his mighty and godly confederates most happy intention; and how justly and needfully for our only benefit and succour, they proceed at this present to her chastisement and deposition; it may please all my most dear countrymen, and especially our peers and nobility, on whom the ancient honour and liberty of our church and country chiefly dependeth, and by whose sword and knighthood (specially given to them and their noble progenitors for defence of the catholic religion), our country hath often been delivered from the tyranny and vexation of divers disordered insupportable kings and cruel usurpers. May it please them (I say) to consider but a little with me, the condition of the person pursued, and censured by God's church, together with the weight, quality, and number of her offences, and horrible crimes, which being open almost to all the world before, and now briefly recorded by this writing, no man (I trust) shall marvel why Christ's vicar here in earth, with other high ministers, of God's justice, would or could deprive this tyrant of her usurped state and dominion, when no commonwealth by law of nature neither would nor might justly suffer any such, to rule or reign over any human society, though neither Christ, pope, faith, nor religion were known.

THE CHIEF POINTS OF THIS ADMONITION.

To proceed therefore briefly and plainly we will set down what manner of woman she is against whom this holy enterprise is made; of whom and in what manner descended; how intruded into that dignity wherein she standeth; how she hath behaved herself both at home and abroad; by what laws of God and man her punishment is pursued; how just, honest, and necessary causes all true Englishmen have to embrace and set forward the same, seeing it proceedeth from so lawful authority, so just grounds, so holy intentions, and tendeth to so happy an end, and is to be executed by so sure and sweet means, and chosen persons, as now shall be declared.

And first of all it is notorious to the whole world, that Henry the supposed father to this pretensed queen, besides the infinite quantity and enormous quality of his most execrable wickedness, for the which by all law of religion, reason, and nature, he deserved oftentimes to be deprived, was in fine, for his horrible sacrileges, murdering of saints, and rebellion against God's church, lawfully excommunicated and deprived by Paulus tertius in the year 1535, and therewithal by name and in particular all the issue that should proceed of his incestuous copulation with Anne Boleyn, was most justly declared illegitimate and uncapable of succession to the crown of England: and that as well by the sentence of the said Paul, and of his predecessor Clement VII in the year of our Lord 1533 (both which stand in their full force still) as by sundry acts of parliament made by Henry himself and never repealed legitimating her sister and declaring her to be base, she must needs be adjudged by law and nature unable to inherit the crown.

Neither may she here allege, that by consent of the states and commonwealth she is lawfully possessed: for that by force she intruded, and constrained many men to give their consents, deposing unjustly the lords of the clergy without whom no lawful parliament can be holden in that realm, nor statute made which hath force to authorize prince or bind subjects. Over and besides that she never had consent nor any approbation of the see apostolic, without which, she nor any other can be lawful king or queen of England, by reason of the ancient accord, made between Alexander III the year 1171 and Henry II then king when he was absolved for the death of Saint Thomas of Canterbury, that no man might lawfully take that crown nor be accounted as king till he were confirmed by the sovereign pastor of our souls which for the time should be. This accord afterwards being renewed, about the year 1210 by King John, who confirmed the same by oath to Pandulphus, the pope his legate, at the special request and procurement of the lords and commons, as a thing most necessary for the preservation of the realm from unjust usurpation of tyrants, and avoiding other inconveniences which they had proved, and might easily fall again by the disorder of some wicked king.

But howsoever she be descended or possessed of the crown, her manifold wickedness hath been so heinous and intolerable that for the same she hath been in person justly deposed by the sentences of three sundry popes, whereunto if we add the two former censures condemning her incestuous nativity and generation, we shall find that she hath been condemned by five declaratory judicial sentences of God's church.

PERSONABLE CRIMES OF ELIZABETH, AND FIRST OF HERESY.

And to begin with the highest and most heinous crime of all against God and his church she is convicted of many damnable heresies, and open rebellion against God's church and see apostolic, for which she is so notoriously known, termed, and taken for an heretic as well at home as abroad, that she was glad to provide by a special act of parliament, that none should call her heretic, schismatic, tyrant, usurper, or infidel, under pain of high treason.

SHE ARROGATETH SPIRITUAL DIGNITY.

She usurpeth by Luciferian pride the title of supreme ecclesiastical government, a thing in a woman, in all men's memory unheard of, nor tolerable to the masters of her own sect, and to catholics in the world most ridiculous, absurd, monstrous, detestable, and a very fable to the posterity.

BASTARDY.

She unlawfully intruded herself, as before I have said, into possession of the crown of England and the annexed dominions, not by any descent of inheritance or other lawful title, but only by enforced unjust laws partly made by her supposed father being then an excommunicated person, and partly coacted by herself and her accomplices in the beginning of her pretended reign, being indeed taken and known for an incestuous bastard, begotten and born in sin, of an infamous courtesan Anne Boleyn, afterwards executed for adultery, treason, heresy, and incest, amongst others with her own natural brother, which Anne, her said supposed father kept by pretensed marriage, in the life of his lawful wife, the most renowned and blessed lady Queen Katherine, daughter of Castile and Aragon, as he did before unnaturally know and keep both the said Anne's mother and sister.

PERJURY AND IMPIETY.

She is guilty of perjury and high impiety for that she did break, violate, and deride, the solemn oath and promise made in her coronation, for defence of the ecclesiastical liberties and privileges granted by the ancient Christian kings of our realm, and for the contempt of the holy ceremony used in the anointing and investing of all faithful princes: wherein her wickedness was so notorious, that the principal prelate that then was in the realm, and to whom by ancient order (the cardinal of Canterbury then being dead) that function appertained, durst not for fear of God, and respect of his conscience, nor did not anoint her.

ABOLISHING CATHOLIC RELIGION.

She did immediately upon her said intrusion, violently against all law and order (the whole clergy, and many of the nobility and commons constantly reclaiming) to the perdition of infinite souls, abolish the whole catholic religion and faith, that all the former faithful kings of our country honourably lived and died in; repealing at the same time all the godly acts that Queen Mary, the only lawful daughter of King Henry the eighth, made for the reconcilement of the realm, to the unity of God's universal church again; and revived all the impious statutes, made by her foresaid supposed father and brother against God, the church, the see apostolic, and all innocency, by which she severed herself and subjects violently from the society of all catholic countries, and from the fellowship of all faithful princes and priests in the world.

PROFANING SACRAMENTS.

She did at the same time abolish or profane all the holy sacraments of Christ's church, and above other in particular, the very blessed and sovereign sacrifice of Christ's body and blood, erecting for the same, and in disgrace thereof, high idolatry and polluted bread of schism and abominable desolation.

FORBIDDING PREACHERS.

She did shut up both pulpits and churches from all catholic priests, preachers, and people, caused all God's public true ancient honour, service, and solemnity, throughout the whole realm of England (a most lamentable case) and not long after in Ireland, to cease upon one day, constraining by great penalties and extreme punishment many thousand poor Christian souls of every degree and sex, to forsake that faith and religion, in which they and all their forefathers were baptized and brought up, ever since the realm was first converted to Christ, to the great torment of their minds and consciences and shortening of their days.

PROFANING OF CHURCHES AND ALL HOLIES.

She impiously spoiled all sanctified places of their holy images, relics, memories, and monuments of Christ our Saviour, and of his blessed mother and saints, her own detestable cognizance and other profane portraitures and paintings exalted in their places: and therewith hath overthrown, destroyed, and robbed, all holy altars, chalices, vestments, church books, and sacred vessels, with whatsoever was consecrated to God's true worship, and the reverence of Christian religion, in the ancient apostolic ministry of the holy sacraments.

VIOLATING SACRED PERSONS.

She hath seized upon the sacred persons of God's anointed, even of very bishops that had charge of her own soul, called them to account for their preachings and doctrine, convented them before her profane counsellors and commissioners, deposed and imprisoned them with all others that were of learning and dignity among the clergy, till by the misery of their captivity they be in effect wholly worn and wasted away.

IMPIOUS SCORNFULNESS.

She hath caused the priests of God violently to be plucked from the altar in the midst of the sovereign action, and to be carried in scornful manner revested through the streets, and exposed to all the ungodly villainy, irrision, fury, and folly of the simple and barbarous people: a thing, certes, that above all other kinds of irreligiosity most deserveth and soonest procureth God's vengeance.

SUPPRESSION OF MONASTERIES.

She hath suppressed all the religious houses of both sexes, so many as were restored after her father's former horrible spoil, dispersed the professed of the same, and robbed them of all their lands and possessions.

OPPRESSION OF CATHOLIC GENTLEMEN, AND EXTORTION.

She hath by unjust tyrannical statutes injuriously invaded the lands and goods of catholic nobles and gentlemen, that for conscience's sake have passed the seas: and molested, disgraced, imprisoned, and spoiled, many at home of all degrees, because they would not give oath and agreement to her antichristian and unnatural proud challenge of supremacy, nor honour the idol of her profane communion board, whereby some provinces be in manner wholly bereaved of their just gentlemen in administration of the laws, and the people exceedingly annoyed by loss of so good lords, and so great housekeepers, for lack of whom the poor daily perish.

DESTRUCTION OF THE NOBILITY.

Besides all which sacrileges, abominations, and extortions against God, his church, and her own people, she passingly hath endangered the kingdom and country by this great alteration of religion, which thing is never without inevitable peril, or rather sure ruin of the commonwealth; as also she hath done by great contempt and abasing of the ancient nobility, repelling them from due government, offices, and places of honour, thrusting them to shameful and odious offices of inquisition upon catholic men, to the great vexation and terror of their own consciences, forcing them through fear and desire of her favour, and of her base leaders, to condemn that in others, which in their hearts and consciences themselves like of, and putting into their houses and chambers, traitors, spies, delators, and promoters, that take watch for her of all their ways, words, and writings; by which the principal be already ruined most lamentably, and the rest stand in continual thraldom, danger, and dishonour: so jealous be all tyrants and usurpers of their state, and so loath they are to be seconded by any other than of their own creation.

NEW NOBILITY.

She hath instead of the foresaid, and to their shame and despite, advanced base and unpure persons, inflamed with infinite avarice and ambition, men of great partiality, bribery, and iniquity, to the highest honours and most profitable offices of her court and country, repelling from all public action, charge, and authority, under colour of religion, the wisest, godliest, learnedest, and sincerest of all sorts of men, to the special annoyance and dishonour of the whole state.

NEW CLERGY.

She hath intruded the very refuse of the worst sort of mortal men, infamous amorous apostates and heretics, to all the spiritual dignities and preferments in the realm, who by their insatiable covetousness and concupiscence, have made lamentable havoc, waste, and destruction of the ancientest (well-near) and honourablest spiritual states in Christendom, herself not a little helping to the spoil of the same.

HARBOURING STRANGERS.

She hath laid the country wide open to be a place of refuge and sanctuary of all atheists, anabaptists, heretics, and rebellious of all nations, and replenished sundry the coast towns and others, with innumerable strangers of the worst sort of malefactors and sectaries, to the great impoverishing of the inhabitants, and no small peril of the whole realm: this being taken to be certain, that the number and quality of them is such, that when time may serve and favour them, they may give a sturdy battle to the inhabitants of the realm.

POLLING THE PEOPLE.

She hath not spared to oppress her subjects (never having just wars with any king or country in the world) with manifold exactions not only by ordinary means of more frequent and large subsidies (for which only end she hath had more parliaments and more often prorogations thereof than ever any lawful prince had in so many years) but also by sundry shameful guiles of lotteries, laws, decrees, and falls of money and such like deceits: and hath employed the riches of the realm to set up and sustain rebels and heretics against their natural princes, to the great dishonour of our nation, damage and danger as well of our merchants, as of all other travellers; a public piracy and robbery both by sea and land, therewith authorizing by her letters of marque, and otherwise permitting, divers wicked persons to spoil whom they list, without sparing, some piece of the gain returning to some of her own chief counsellors and officers.

SELLING OF LAWS.

She doth for money and bribes, to the enriching of herself and servants, by licences, dispensations, pardons, and permissions, abolish or frustrate many profitable laws: as she doth to the same end multiply sundry frivolous acts, with great forfeits to the transgressors, wittingly forbearing (as it may be thought) the execution of the same, that after oblivion of the observation thereof, her courtiers and other lost cousins and companions (whom her excessive avarice will not suffer to reward of her own) may make prey by promoting the poor people, and so live and feed

on the carcass of the commonwealth: yea, even suck out the very blood
of poor afflicted catholic men's consciences, who besides those sacrilegious mass mulcts, and the new made spoils and intolerable extortions,
for not coming to their damnable idolatry of the communion (which
for the love of God's law they often incur and sustain, to the utter
lamentable ruin of them and their posterity) be fain by great importable
gifts to procure at her officer's hands, some little ease and release of the
intolerable fears and miseries that they live in. By which wicked traffic
and other pitiful pillage of the people, some of her creatures are grown
so great and insolent, that all states and degrees within the realm stand
in awe and danger of them.

LEICESTER. THE EARL OF ESSEX.

In which sort, besides others whom we need not note, she hath exalted
one special extortioner, whom she took up first of a traitor and worse
than naught, only to serve her filthy lust, whereof to have the more
freedom and interest; he (as may be presumed, by her consent) caused
his own wife cruelly to be murdered, as afterwards for the accomplishment of his like brutish pleasures with another noble dame it is openly
known he made away her husband; who now of an amorous minion
advanced to high office, degree, and excessive wealth, is become her
chief leader in all her wicked and unwonted course of regiment, her instrument of the destruction of the nobility, by many indirect means,
and of the ruining, abasing, disgracing, disauthorizing divers ancient
houses, names, and persons of renown; besides innumerable of the communalty perished most pitifully in sundry provinces for the feeding of
his infinite avarice and other his unsatiable companions and retainers,
living only of bribery, spoil, and robbery: whereby, and through the
favour of the pretended he hath this many a year overruled the chamber,
court, council, parliament, ports, forts, seas, ships, borders, men, munition, and all the country; hath had still at commandment all officers,
justices, benches, bars, and sessions, hath had the sale and monopoly
of all laws, offices, licences, forfeits, bishoprics, benefices and colleges;
hath made such traffic, chopping, and changing with his mistress, about
the treasures, prerogatives, lands, and commodities of the crown, that so
and by divers unspeakable treacheries, he hath enabled and fortified himself far above the measure of any English subject, and hath been the
principal disturber and destroyer of the provinces round about us, to the

impoverishment of the people at home, and decay of all traffic abroad, with extreme peril of the land.

HER DISHONEST LIFE.

With the foresaid person and divers others she hath abused her body, against God's laws, to the disgrace of princely majesty and the whole nation's reproach, by unspeakable and incredible variety of lust, which modesty suffereth not to be remembered, neither were it to chaste ears to be uttered how shamefully she hath defiled and infamed her person and country, and made her court as a trap, by this damnable and detestable art, to entangle in sin and overthrow the younger sort of the nobility and gentlemen of the land, whereby she is become notorious to the world, and in other countries a common fable for this her turpitude, which in so high degree namely in a woman and a queen, deserveth not only deposition, but all vengeance both of God and man, and cannot be tolerated without the eternal infamy of our whole country, the whole world deriding our effeminate dastardy that have suffered such a creature almost thirty years together, to reign both over our bodies and souls, and to have the chief regiment of all our affairs as well spiritual as temporal, to the extinguishing not only of religion but all chaste living and honesty.

REFUSING TO MARRY. HER TREASON AGAINST QUEEN MARY.

She could never be restrained from this incontinence, though the principal peers of the realm and others of high authority as deputies from the whole parliament and estates, made humble suit and supplication to her, that for pity and compassion of their desolate case, and of the danger that the whole realm and specially the nobility should be in, if she deceased without lawful issue, in such a number of competitors of the crown, she would therefore marry and procure (if it were God's pleasure) lawful heirs of her body to inherit her dominions after her: to whom sometimes she merely and mockingly answered, that she would die a maid queen, but afterwards in contempt and rebuke of all the states of the realm, and to the condemnation of chaste and lawful marriage (whereunto as to a bridle of her licentiousness, she is enemy) she forced the very parliament itself to give consent and to provide by a pretended law, not tolerable (nor ever I trow heard of before in a Christian free people) that none should so much as be named for her successor during her life, saving the natural, that is to say bastard born child of her own body. A wonderful thraldom, a lamentable case, that this high court, of old so renowned for freedom and justice, should now be at the devotion of one woman so far, as to authorize both her shameful incontinency and pernicious obstinacy against the honour and good of the whole realm: having no cause in the world why the next lawful heir may not better bear the naming, than her unlawful long concealed or feigned issue, saving that it might be prejudicial to her private and present peace, which she ever preferreth before the public, as she presumeth upon the experience and late remembrance of her own wicked practises against her sovereign, when the time was, measuring all other by her own impatient ambition: but indeed it proceedeth specially, upon the recognising of her unrightful possession, usurpers always standing in more awe of the next heir and successor, than the lawful princes commonly do.

THE PRETENSE OF MARRIAGE. THE EARL OF ARUNDEL AND OTHERS. THE EARL OF ARRAN. THE KING OF SWEDEN. ARCHDUKE CHARLES. THE DUKE OF HOLST. HENRY NOW KING OF FRANCE. MONSIEUR ALENÇON.

She, all this notwithstanding, in the mean season, as often before and afterward, promised marriage to some of the nobility at home, making many of them in single life to the danger of their souls, and decay of their families, to attend her pleasure: and no less deeply dallied and abused by dissembling almost all the great personages of Europe, to whom as well by letters, as by solemn embassies, she proffered herself, to the mockery and final delusion of them all, to her own infamy, and the danger of her people, and specially of late years she hath most pitifully and devilishly abused the late noble brother of France, by manifold hope and promise of her marriage and crown, by which bait, and her deceitful suggestion, the poor young gentleman was driven into those dangerous actions and dishonourable affairs of heretics and rebels, to his great dishonour, and likely shortening of his days.

HER UNNATURAL AFFECTION TOWARDS THE COUNTRY.

By all which dishonourable and unworthy dealing, the whole world may see that in atheism and epicureanism, she would (if it were possible and might be suffered as she hath begun) turn the life and whole weal of our country once most flourishing, to the feeding of her own disordered delights, being loath no doubt that any thing should be left after her life, that her rage and riot had not overrun, or that her realm should be extant any longer than she might make pleasure of it; most glad (as may seem) that so flourishing and ancient a commonwealth which she hath in manner brought to destruction in her life, might be buried in her ignominious ashes when she is dead. Wherein her affection is so passing unnatural, that she hath been heard to wish, that the day after her death she might stand in some high place between heaven and earth, to behold the scrambling that she conceived would be for the crown; sporting herself in the conceit and forsight of our future miseries, by her only unhappiness procured: not unlike to Nero, who intending for his recreation to set Rome on fire, devised an eminent pillar whereon himself might stand to behold it, but so God may provide for her, and us, that she may see and feel some part of this pastime in her days, or rather she only and a few of her accomplices feel the pain, who alone or principally have deserved it, if we be so wise as to follow God's ordinances.

CONFEDERATION WITH REBELS.

Besides all these outrages in her person and regiment, and besides sundry wicked attempts, and treasons before she came to the crown, against her prince and country at home, she hath showed such faithless dealing towards all near neighbours most just mighty and catholic kings abroad, that it is almost incredible. Some she hath ignominiously spoiled of great treasures; one that fled to her for promised succour and safety, yea, even her that was our true lawful and worthy sovereign, she hath against all law of God, nature, and nations, after long imprisonment at length also murdered; of some she hath surprised towns and territories; with some she hath in great simulation of friendship, in effect broken most ancient leagues and amity; against them all, she hath not only notoriously confederated herself with their rebels, huguenots, geuses [sea-beggars], publicans, and malcontents, giving them great succour both of men, munition, and money, with much continual encouragement and counsel in all their wicked attempts: but was and yet is known to be the first and principal fountain of all these furious rebellions, in Scotland, France, and Flanders, to the fall almost of all their whole states, and the great calamity of the church of God, whereby it is evident to all the world that herself reigneth unlawfully as an usurper and rebel, who only standeth and holdeth herself up all this while by joining with traitors and rebels, and succouring them against their lawful princes and sovereigns.

HER LEAGUE WITH THE TURK.

In this kind she hath by the execrable practices of some of her chief ministers, as by their own hands, letters, and instructions, and by the parties' confessions it may be proved, sent abroad exceeding great numbers of intelligencers, spies, and practisers, into most princes' courts, cities, and commonwealths in Christendom, not only to take and give secret notice of prince's intentions, but to deal with the discontented of every state for the attempting of somewhat against their lords and superiors, namely against his holiness and the king of Spain his majesty, whose sacred persons they have sought many ways wickedly to destroy, as furthermore it is evident, how she hath by messengers and letters dealt with the cruel and dreadful tyrant and enemy of our faith the Great Turk himself (against whom our noble kings have in old time so valiantly fought, and vowed themselves to all perils and peregrinations), for the invasion of some parts of Christendom, and interception of some defensible ports and places of the same, as for the disturbance of Christianity and annoyance of the principal defenders of the catholic religion, she hath at this day a ledger [ambassador] in his court.

By which Machiavellian, godless, and conscienceless course, unjust usurped regiments be always conducted; advanced not by counsel or courage, but by plain trumpery, treason, and cozenage, working their own peace, wealth, and felicity, by their neighbours' wars, woe, and misery, which never endeth well, nor endureth long, nor is in fine unrevenged; though the present prosperity, upholden by others' calamity, hath averted the sense, the simple, and worldly, from the beholding of that extreme plague, which always both by God's justice, and man's revenge ensueth of the same.

HER EXTREME PRIDE.

Which long felicity, notwithstanding, hath so puffed up this usurper in presumption and pride of heart, that besides all other insolences and glorious vanities and vaunts in her words, crakes, countenances, and gestures, in all her life and behaviour (in which kind she exceedeth all creatures living), she hath caused the annual day of her coronation in all parts of the realm to be sacredly kept and solemnified, with ringing, singing, shows, and ceremonies, and far more vacation from all servile labours than any day either of our blessed Lord or Lady, and which is more abominable, having abolished the solemn feast of our blessed Lady's

nativity, she hath caused her own impure birthday to be solemnly celebrated, and put into the calendar the very eve of the said holy feast and
put out the name of another saint the 17 of November, to place the
memory of her coronation; God grant she may repent, lest instead of
her excessive praises that her favourers and flatterers now give unto her,
she hear yet in her own days, the saying of the prophet against the proud
prince Nebuchadnezzar: How didst thou fall, Lucifer, from heaven,
that wast so orient in the mooring? How wast thou brought down to the
ground that woundedst nations, that subvertedst kingdoms, and saidst
in thy heart, I will be like the highest? Or feel the plague of one of the
Herods that for too much delighting in the people's praises and acclama-
tions, and for not giving glory to God, was suddenly stricken by God's
angel, eaten of worms, and died.

OBSTINATE IN MALICE. HER EXCOMMUNICATION AND CONTEMPT THEREOF.

Now of all these heinous horrible facts, not credible almost to be
achieved by one woman, and her accomplices not so many, she hath in
fine showed herself incorrigible, and altogether impatient of admonition,
whereof she never had want, as well by the writings of sundry her learned
subjects, as sometimes by the imperial majesty, and other temporal
princes, and namely by divers holy popes, whose nuncios she would
never admit to tell her (as of duty they thought themselves bound) God's
threatenings for all her foresaid and many other intolerable disorders of
belief, life, and government. But to accomplish all other impiety, and
to show herself wholly sold to sin, she hath now eighteen years stood
stubbornly, contemptuously, and obdurately, as in the sight of God by
her own wilful separation through schism and heresy judged and condemned before, so now by name notoriously excommunicated and deposed in the word of Christ and omnipotent power of God by sentence
given against her by holy Pius the fifth the highest court of religion
under the heavens. The which state of excommunication (though presently of the faithless, where there is no sense of religion, it be not felt
nor feared) is most miserable, most horrible, and most near to damnation
of all things that may happen to a man in this life: far more grievous
(saith a certain glorious doctor) than to be hewn in pieces with a sword,
consumed by fire or devoured of wild beasts: and it is expressed in the
scriptures by the state of King Pharaoh his obduration and execation in
wilful wickedness.

SHE MURDERED THE EXECUTORS OF THE POPE'S SENTENCE.

And she hath not only continued in this damnable contempt of the holy church's censures so long as we have said, but also commanded and caused the publishers, defenders, approvers, and all others that attempted most honourably and godly the execution thereof as well of the nobility as the clergy and commons, some being apprehended at home, and others traitorously bought and sold abroad and sent home, and all in cruel manner murdered, yea, and for their parts very willingly martyred to their eternal estimation, rather than they would live, serve, or see any such heretic, atheist, and usurper, from whose pretensed kingly authority, they were in consideration of all these her heinous crimes, clearly by Christ's own vicar, and the warrant of all the faithful world (that never took itself bound to obey a condemned heretic or an apostate) before God and man discharged.

THE MURDER OF BISHOPS AND PRIESTS. THE ARCHBISHOP OF CASSELS, AND
   THE BISHOP OF MAYON. THE SLAUGHTER OF THE QUEEN OF SCOTLAND.

In which her obstinacy and satanical obduration daily increasing she hath these late years imbrued her hands and country with the sacred blood of a number of most innocent, learned, and famous religious men, yea and holy bishops also, as well in England as Ireland, caused them pitifully to be racked, rent, chained, famished, beaten, buffeted, derided, abused, and by false accusation of crimes never intended, under pretence of treason against her usurped state and person, to be finally with all cruelty executed to the regret and shame of our nation and wonder of all the world. And finally to accomplish the measure of her inhuman cruelty, she hath this last year barbarously, unnaturally against the law of nations by a stature of riot and conspiracy, murdered the Lady Mary of famous memory, queen of Scotland, dowager of France, God's anointed, her next kinswoman, and by law and right the true owner of the crown of England.

THE JUSTICE OF THE SENTENCE AGAINST ELIZABETH.

All which her open enormities, and other her secret wickedness hidden from us (which must needs be great, and not numerable, in a caliph so long under God's and holy church's curse, and given up into a reprobate sense and hardness of heart) may put all faithful and reasonable men out of doubt, of the justice of the apostolic sentence and censure against her: being well assured that if any case may fall, in which a prince may justly be forsaken or resisted by his subjects, or if any crime in the world either in life, regiment, or religion, can deserve deposition of a king, that here all causes together do concur in the person of the pretensed, in the highest degree; none ever not amongst the heathen, so unprofitable, so evil, so faithless, so pernicious, no realm ever so far fallen from religion, public honesty, order and sincerity, as ours hath done in her unhappy usurped government.

A NECESSARY CONSIDERATION.

And here we may behold, the pitiful race of an unbridled, powerable sinner (woe be to our offences that have deserved the experience of so lamentable a case) this unworthy woman's supposed father, first, as now herself afterward, by reason of their height of earthly power, free from civil chastisement, could not be content therewith till they had also discharged themselves of all remorse of conscience, of all awe of religion, of all spiritual discipline, and put themselves in full freedom from pope, prelate, prophet, priest, and ghostly father (an example for all commonwealths in the world to beware of by us, for ever) and therefore not only in their hearts said against God and his anointed, let us shake off their yoke and break their bonds asunder; but openly and boldly both said, and made themselves heads of the church and spirituality, as well now of the souls, as they were before of the bodies: that all life, faith, religion, church, counsel, conscience, scripture, sacrament, ceremony, and whatsoever was in heaven or earth, might wholly hang at their hands, lusts, and likings. At which licentious irreligiosity, and antichristian pride, though the highest in heaven do in the meantime laugh, and by long patience not only forbear the present revenge thereof, but also by secret judgment for the parties' increase of damnation, or expectation of their repentance, or the people's deservings, suffer it in them by continual prosperity and prevailing against the good, to be much confirmed and increased, yet these stubborn Nimrods, that aspire so far, and would overreach the highest, cannot, nor shall not escape God's ire and furious wrath, neither in this life nor in the next. Fear not my dear countrymen, fear not, one generation is not yet past since this wickedness began; trust now in God, and in this self generation it shall be revenged, and in the person of this the foresaid king's supposed daughter (in whose parents' concupiscence all this calamity was conceived) shall be both punished and ended.

PSAL. 36 & 72.

Have patience therefore a little, and marvel not to see the ungodly flourish and feed himself with the wealth of the world: nothing being a more sure sign of wrath to come, nor more unlucky to a mortal man specially to a prince, than to have prosperity and good luck in wickedness, and so to be beset wholly with flatterers that rock him asleep in the peace of sin, that he may neither hear his duty, nor bear check or chastisement for the same.

GOD'S PROVIDENCE TOWARDS PRINCES.

It was God's great providence (who by his prophet warned kings to take discipline, and to serve him in fear, lest in his ire he should suffer them to fall to unrighteousness) that ever lightly the princes of his people had some prophets or priests their overseers, that might from time to time admonish them of their offences and enormities, but especially of their falling from God, and to denounce God's threatenings, yea and execute his sentence upon them: whom all righteous and godly princes did fear, reverence, honour, and obey, even as God's angels appointed for their custody; as contrariwise such as were wicked tyrants not contented to be bridled by the Almighty, did seek cruelly their death and destruction, that their disorders might pass with all liberty and licentiousness, and without God's own controlment in his life.

Kings (I say) being not otherwise subject to superiors, and often impatient of admonition of their inferiors, may easily fall. Their fall must needs tend to the danger of whole countries. Therefore in respect of them namely, great power, courage, and freedom of speech were granted by God, as well ordinarily to priests, as extraordinarily to some prophets and religious persons in all ages, specially in the time of the New Testament, as shall farther be declared hereafter. Saul the first temporal king that the Jews (then God's peculiar people) had, though chosen and inspired by God, was led and directed by Samuel, so long as he was in order: but afterward for aspiring to spiritual function, and other disobedience, was by God's appointment and sentence pronounced against him, by the said Samuel deposed of his kingdom, and another named David anointed by him in the life of the said Saul: who now after his deprivation and as it were after his excommunication, was invaded by an ill spirit, that provoked him, to kill not only him that was now made the rightful owner of his crown (as Elizabeth hath by God's permission accomplished her like devilish desires against the Lady Mary, queen of Scotland) but also to seek for Samuel's death his spiritual governor, yea, and to command all the holy priests of Nob (finding none so wicked as to execute his will saving profane Doeg the Edomite) to be cruelly slain as traitors and favourers of David the competitor of his kingdom. And so he stood many years against God, and kept the kingdom by tyrannical force notwithstanding he was accursed and deprived, as the pretensed hath done. David nevertheless (in whom was the right of the crown) was lawfully up in arms with one of the principal priests that escaped the foresaid murder, though not of such power as the pretensed king was, till at length the usurper whom he might lawfully have killed but for reverence of his former holy unction would not, being slain in battle, he obtained his right, first of a part of his kingdom and afterwards of the whole, of which the said Saul's son Ishbosheth did for two years usurp a part by the pretended right of his father. By which example thou needest not now marvel that King Henry or his daughter should so long reign after their deprivation and excommunication, and be suffered to their own damnation, to execute cruelty upon the bishops and priests, yea, and to kill them as traitors, whom they honoured for virtue and learning before, even such persons as any just king or commonwealth, would have bought and ransomed from death, by the worth of half a kingdom; or to commit other outrages, seeing the spirit of Satan entering into such by their excommunication, inciteth them to all mischief, and especially to hate God's church and ministers, by whom Christ executeth his sentence against them.

JEROBOAM I REG.13 & 14.

So did Jeroboam seek to apprehend the prophet that threatened vengeance and destruction to him for his schism, and separation of his people from the old ancient true worship of God in Jerusalem, and for erecting of a new altar in Bethel (in which all schism and division from the apostolic see is prefigured) and creating of naught, out of Aaron's order, new, hungry, base, and unordered priests, the very pattern of all these contemptible ministers, put up out of the array, and lawful succession of apostolic priesthood: a crime so highly afterward both in himself and his stock revenged, that none of his house was left to piss against a wall.

. . . .

MATT.16.

Now is Christ's prerogative in most ample and exact terms communicated to the chief priest and pastor of our souls, in other manner of clause than our pretensed monstrous spiritual governess can show for herself; fie on that secular pride and wilful blind heresy that so repugneth to God's express ordinance, and yet is wickedly upholden of her flatterers, though reproved both at home and abroad by the most notorious heretics and sectmasters of all sorts. Now all Christ's sheep without exception, be they princes, be they poor men, if they be Christian men, are put to Peter's feeding and government: now the keys of heaven given to Christ's vicar, to let in, to lock out, to bind, to loose, to pardon, to punish.

. . . .

APOSTOLICAL POWER.

Such, lo, now is the apostolical force and power of Christ's priesthood in the New Testament, so far above the authority of earthly kings, as the sun is clearer than the moon, heaven above the earth, the soul of man better than his body, and the commonweal of the catholic church formed by Christ, more excellent than any secular society ordained by man.

. . . .

And when by process of time the church became more potent, and some princes were fallen to contempt of religion, as it lightly happeneth by heresy or apostasy; and that excommunication or other ordinary ecclesiastical discipline would not serve being only spiritual penalty, and now not having ordinarily annexed that corporeal vexation, executed by Satan upon excommunicate persons and therefore so much feared in the primitive church: then as well the bishops and godly persons their own subjects did crave aid and arms of other Christian princes against them, as also the most holy and ancient popes of Rome did with all godly zeal incite the catholic kings to the same; that those whom the spiritual rod could not fruitfully chastise, might by external force be driven down, or to repentance of their disorder. There is no war in the world so just or honourable, as that which is waged for religion, whether it be foreign or civil: nor crime in the world deserving more sharp and zealous pursuit of extreme revenge, than falling from the faith to strange religions, whether it be in the superior or subjects.

. . . .

Provided nevertheless, always in this case, that we follow not our deceitful wills, as our adversaries do, condemning for God's enemies such princes or persons as the holy church (who must be our judge and informer in all these things) pronounceth and holdeth to be most just, godly, and catholic kings: but then must we take them for heretics, when our lawful bishops and popes do so adjudge them to be, and so command us to take them, yea, and charge us to forsake them. Then be we sure in conscience, discharged of our oath and obedience, which be bands of such quality and nature, that they hold not, nor have force, against justice, and where the matter is unlawful. And we have just cause to arm ourselves for defence of God's honour and our innocence, and to seek for succour at popes' and princes' hands.

. . . .

For shameful injuries done to the holy church, and for persecution of bishops and religious, was John one of our kings of England with his whole country interdicted, and at length forced to yield his crown and dominions to the courtesy of the pope's legate, as before is mentioned. NUBRIG. LIB.2, C.25 AND 34.

For like causes, and namely for being accessary to the murder of the blessed bishop St. Thomas of Canterbury, was Henry II driven by Alexander III to order and penance. Henry VIII also, for more horrible waste and desolation of religion, wherein he far surmounted all his ancestors, and all others that ever we read of since the time of Julian the Apostate: for arrogating the title of supreme head of the church, and forcing all his people to swear to his folly, and that his concubine Anne Boleyn was their queen and his lawful wife: for most cruel slaughter of catholic bishops, priests, religious and laymen: for infringing and utterly abolishing against his own oath, all the privileges and liberties granted to the church of England by holy King Edward and other his forefathers: for destroying all holy houses of religion, and sacrilegiously invading all their goods and possessions: for marrying, remarrying, changing, divorcing, and killing of his wives, when, where, and whom he list: for these and such-like unspeakable outrages he was excommunicated by Paulus tertius as hath before been declared.

ELIZABETH EXCOMMUNICATED AND DEPRIVED ANNO 1570.

And now lastly, not only for unjust intrusion and usurpation, but also for the foresaid crimes, and following her said supposed father's ways (who was *radix peccati* of our days, and offended the more grievously, because he first compelled the people of God to schism and sin, as Jeroboam did the Israelites) this woman was by good Pius quintus excommunicated and deprived, and all other subjects discharged of oath and obedience towards her, with charge eftsoons to all the subjects of the realm of England, or other her dominions, that from thence forth under like pain of excommunication and God's and holy church's curse, they should not acknowledge her for their princess or superior, nor obey, defend, and maintain her, but according to every one's power and ability, to concur to her deposition and condign punishment.

EXECUTION OF THE SENTENCE DEFERRED.

Which sentence most holy, just, and dreadful, though hitherto it have not been openly pursued, partly by reason of the decease of Pius quintus, the publisher, which ensued not long after, and partly for that the usurper's forces, rage, and cruelty were so great, that they could hardly be resisted by the only inhabitants of the realm without evident danger and destruction of very many noble and godly persons, in which case the church's censure so far as they concern only temporal matters, by the meaning of him that gave the sentence, doth not bind; and lastly for that his holiness that now is (as his predecessors before him) having exceeding tender care not only of our souls but of our bodies and goods also, have hitherto tolerated in us, our enforced subjection and obedience to her in civil affairs, especially upon expectation, and hope, that she would after so long and fatherly sweet patience of the supreme pastors of our souls, at the request of so many princes Christian, at the pitiful suits, cries, clamours, and complaints of so many of her own people, for the blood of so many men meekly yielded, and the unconsolable complaints of so many afflicted consciences, either acknowledge her fault, incline to mercy towards the catholics, and seek (as her supposed father desired to do in the end of his life) to reconcile herself to the church, or to come to some good order at least with the see apostolic, and grant her catholic nobility and people, leave to serve God after their conscience, and manner of all their forefathers. Though (I say) for all these causes and other more, the former judicial sentence hath not been all this while executed, yet now our holy father Sixtus the fifth, seeing this usurper and excommunicate person to be nothing moved either with pity of the

people, or apostolic authority, but still obstinately and obdurately to persist, and proceed in all her former mischiefs and wickedness, could not
contain or forbear any longer, not only himself to employ against so
monstrous and pernicious an heretic, rebel, usurper, and firebrand of
all mischief, the treasures spiritual and temporal, that the omnipotent
God hath given him for maintenance of justice, innocency, and religion;
but also by the foresaid examples of his predecessors and other holy
bishops, and by a special canon of the great general Council of Lateran
touching the chastisement of princes that will not purge their dominions
of heresy and heretics, hath seriously dealt with the chief and greatest
princes of his Christian catholic communion, that they would give
succour to their afflicted brethren and confederates, and join together
with him their supreme pastor, for chastisement of that wicked woman,
the bane of Christendom and all their kingdoms, the scourge of God, and
rebuke of womankind; as in this case everyone would have been most
ready, had they not been forced at this time to employ all their forces
against the heretics and rebels of their own dominions, and therefore
hath specially entreated Philip the high and mighty king catholic of
Spain, that for the greatness of power given him by the Almighty, for his
singular love towards that nation whereof by marriage of holy Queen
Mary of blessed memory he once was king, for the old love and league
betwixt the said country and the house of Burgundy, for the infinite
injuries and dishonours done to his majesty and people by Elizabeth,
and to conclude for his special piety and zeal towards God's house and
the see apostolic, together with the consideration of the fresh, barbarous
murder of his cousin the queen of Scotland, by which the sacred honour
and name of kingly dignity is dishonoured, and all lawful princes highly
interested; that for these and many other causes, his majesty would take
upon him in the name of God almighty, this sacred and glorious enterprise. Who at length, as well by this his holiness' authority and exhortation, as by his own unspeakable zeal and piety, moved also not a little
by my humble and continual suit together with the afflicted and banished
catholics of our nation, of all and every degree, who have been by his
special compassion and regal munificence principally supported in this
their long exile, hath consented at last, and taken upon him this so holy
and glorious an act, to the only honour of God, the benefit of the Christian world, and your delivery (my good brethren) from the yoke of heresy

and thraldom of your enemies, and for restitution of those realms and the subjects of the same to their ancient liberty of laws and conscience. For which causes his majesty hath in the name of the lord God of Hosts commanded sufficient royal and main forces both by sea and land to be gathered, and to be conducted into our country (if need be, and if the pretensed and principal offender will not otherwise come to order) by the most godly and valorous general, and captains that be of his majesty's service in all Christendom.

Of whose proceeding in this action, and as well of his holiness as his majesty's intention and meaning therein, we are to advertise you all, by these presents, and to forwarn you against all false slanderous and seditious speeches of the enemies, and heretics, by which they have many years and in wonderful manner deluded some strangers, to their undoing, and the ruin of their countries: and so comfort you against all other popular fears of the simple sort: that neither the conquest of the land, dispossessing of the English, destruction of catholics, ruin of ancient houses, abolishing of our old laws, liberties, or customs, is purposed; nor any other annoyance or alteration in the world to be made, saving so much as the estates of the realm shall agree upon with his holiness, and majesty, for the restitution and preservation of the catholic religion, and necessary punishment of the pretended. Assuring you all (my most dear countrymen) by my honour, and in the word of a cardinal, that there shall be as great care had of every catholic and penitent person, as possibly can be; for that is the pope's and king's express will and pleasure.

Whereof you may all be the more secure, that his majesty hath appointed for the execution of this affair, so worthy, fortunate, and victorious a prince, no less renowned for his piety, mercy, and clemency (whereof you have seen these years, hard by you, so many examples) than for his valour and manifold victories, obtained against the church's and the king's rebels: as on the other side, for your like security, one of the worthiest peers of Spain, for valour, virtue, and sweetness of nature, and with him a great number of the flower of that nobility, who have no need of any thing of yours, are appointed for your succour, that if by your fault or mishap, the matter should come to a battle, they might after the victory, overrule and restrain the fury of the common soldiers, lest they should ruin and sack the whole country.

And for the same cause, his holiness hath also, not for my deserts, but of especial care and love of our nation preferred me, being of your flesh and blood, to this high function; intending to send me as his legate, with full commission and commandment to treat and deal from time to time, as well with the states of the realm, as with his holiness, and the king's majesty for the sweeter managing of this godly and great affair, and with them to deliberate of all the best means, how with the least damage of our country, nobility, and gentry, and best preservation of the whole people, this godly purpose of restoring the catholic religion, and putting the realm in order (as well for the title of the crown as other controversies that may fall, betwixt the church and the commonwealth, or any member thereof, for what matter soever, since the time that heresy, schism, and disorder began) may be achieved.

Therefore, having now through God's merciful goodness full and sufficient help for your happy reconcilement to Christ's church, and to deliver yourselves, your country, and posterity from that miserable servitude of body and soul which you have so long been in, for the more easy achieving of this godly designment, and for your better information: his holiness confirmeth, reneweth, and reviveth the sentence declaratory of Pius quintus of blessed memory, and the censures of all other his predecessors, and every branch, clause, and article of them, against the said Elizabeth, as well concerning her illegitimation, and usurpation, and inability to the crown of England, as for her excommunication and deposition in respect of her heresy, sacrilege, and abominable life. And dischargeth all men from all oath, obedience, loyalty, and fidelity towards her; requiring and desiring in the bowels of Christ, and commanding under pain of excommunication and other penalties of the law; and as they look for the favours and protection to them and theirs, afore promised, and will avoid the pope, king's, and other princes' high indignation, that no man of what degree or condition soever, obey, abet, aid, defend, or acknowledge her for their prince, or superior, but that all and every one, according to their quality, calling, and ability, immediately upon intelligence of his holiness' will, by these my letters, or otherwise, or at the arrival of his catholic majesty's forces, be ready, to join to the said army, with all the powers and aids they can make, of men, munition, and victuals, to help towards the restoring of the catholic faith, and actual deposing of the usurper, in such sort and place, as by the chief managers of this affair and the general of this holy war shall be appointed for the best advancement of the cause.

In which case, upon especial desire I have to preserve and continue all your noble names and families, being loath that for the offence of the present possessors the whole house should perish or any other suffer, but the offenders themselves: promise to make humble supplication in your behalf, that the honours and possessions of all such offenders, may descend to the next heirs of that name and blood, so that he or they can be proved to join with the catholic army, with all the forces and friends they can make, immediately upon knowledge had of this present, and means to accomplish their desire.

Now therefore, my lords and dear countrymen, if you list follow this God's ordinance, and happy provision that he hath of his great mercy, made for your honours, liberty, and salvation, if you without delay join yourselves, as God, conscience, and nature bindeth you; if you take part one with another in so godly and honourable a quarrel, you shall attain your purpose without all bloodshed: where otherwise if you should either sit still, or refuse to help or sever yourselves one from another, or any of you seek to uphold (which God forbid) the usurper or her accomplices, being thus cursed by the church, and forsaken of God and of all good men, you that so do shall first incur the angels' curse and malediction upon the inhabitants of the land of Meros, who sat still, and would not help God nor venture their lives in his quarrel; and secondly be as deeply excommunicated as she is, and so you shall be guilty of your own ruin, and the blood of the people, and yet shall not prevail.

You shall fight against God, and against his anointed, against your next lawful king, against truth, faith, religion, conscience, and your dear country: you shall bootless defend, yea to your own present destruction and eternal shame, a most unjust usurper, and open injurer of all nations; an infamous, deprived, accursed, excommunicate heretic; the very shame of her sex, and princely name; the chief spectacle of sin and abomination in this our age; and the only poison, calamity, and destruction of our noble church and country.

Fight not, for God's love, fight not, in that quarrel, in which if you die, you are sure to be damned: fight not against all your ancestors' souls and faith, not against the salvation of all your dearest, wives, children, and whatsoever you would well to, either now or in the time to come.

Match not yourselves against the highest: this is the day no doubt of her fall, this is the hour of God's wrath towards her and all her partakers. Forsake her therefore betimes, that you be not enwrapped in her sins, punishment, and damnation. Trust me, there was never any persecutor of the church, but in himself or his next seed, he came to shame and confusion. Remember the end of Antiochus, Jason, Jezebel, Julian, Valens, and of other the apostatous and heretical emperors, with such like usurpers and oppressors of God's church, how speedily they passed to eternal ignominy.

COMFORTS AND HELPS OF THE CATHOLIC PART.

On the other side, you most noble and valiant champions of God's church, the honour of English knighthood and the defenders of the glory and liberties thereof, you, and all the blessed people, to whom God hath given so happy a lot, zeal and courage to fight for your fathers' faith, for your country's liberty, for Christ, for religion, and for the dread sovereign sacraments of our salvation; the honourablest quarrel, the likeliest and most commendable cause, in the sight of the present world, and the posterity, that possibly can be. If you win, you save your whole realm from subversion, and innumerable souls, present and to come, from damnation; if you die, you be sure to be saved, the blessing of Christ and his church, the pardon of his holiness, given to all, in most ample sort, that either take arms, die, or any way duly endeavour in this quarrel. The prayers of all Christian people, which be publicly promulgated for your safety and good success: the blood of all the blessed bishops, religious, priests, and laymen, shed in that land, cry to God at this hour for your victory, and vengeance to your enemies their persecutors. All the saints in heaven, whose holy churches, bodies, and memories, your enemies have spoiled and profaned, make now instant suit for your happy success. All the virtuous priests of your country, who, by the long tyranny of this time, have suffered manifold miseries and martyrdoms, both at home and abroad, to save their own souls, and win their dearest countrymen to salvation, they also stretch forth their consecrated hands night and day for your victory, and be present divers of them to serve every man's spiritual necessity, by confession, counsel, and all consolation in Christ Jesus, giving you testimony by their readiness to live and die with you, how just the cause of this holy fight is, and how happy and glorious is the blood that shall be shed therein.

With these blessed patrons both in heaven and earth; with the guard of all God's holy angels; with our blessed Saviour himself in the sovereign sacrament, present among you to your protection, communicating comfort and courage; and with the daily most holy oblation of Christ's own dear body and blood, making more forcible intercession from the earth for you than the blood of Abel; with so many divine unspeakable helps, if you were never so few you could not lose: without these and against these holies, our enemies (be they never so fierce, never so proud, never so many, never so well appointed) they cannot prevail, fear you not, they cannot. Though never so great show be made, never so many raised against you, because most of them be catholics or notoriously injured by heretics, they be armed for us, they cannot strike, they will not fight against their own consciences, be bold of it, they will not. Many others of them be indifferent of neither or no religion; whose wit and wariness will be such in this extremity, and in so just a cause to desire a change, that where by overthrow of the heretics many shall be advanced and by their good success no man bettered in so great hazard of things, they will never adore the sun setting nor follow the declining fortune of so filthy, wicked, and illiberal a creature or her so base and dishonourable leaders: who also have been at deadly variance among themselves these many years, and some of them mortally hating their mistress will never omit this opportunity to be delivered of her and revenged one of another.

The rest of them that be pure zealous heretics, which be very few in comparison, and not very well contented neither with the former regiment, of all men in the world most effeminate, delicate, and least expert in the wars: the angel of God will persecute them, and they shall fly in fear and torment of their own wicked minds, though none pursue them.

You may all remember how the late great traitor, the duke of Northumberland, was in the height of his pride and power forsaken of all his men, and forced to yield to a poor desolate catholic lady. All the world knoweth how the like usurper Richard III, being most worthily in the very field and fight abandoned of the nobility and people, was made an example of God's ire towards all tyrants and usurpers.

But how so ever it fall out through the sins of the people at home, the catholic forces are strong enough, their provision sufficient, their appointment passing, more expert captains than the enemy hath good soldiers, all resolute to die, not available for any to fly away, all exceedingly encouraged by the equity of the cause, and wonderfully confirmed by God's mercies so oft in our days showed in all quarrels of the catholic religion.

These fifty years there was never catholic army which stood to it, but had the victory: by mistrusting God, by overmuch trusting man, by flying or avoiding the battle, by yielding or compounding, sundry great and godly attempts have been frustrated: but in manly and confident combating for God and the church, none at all.

Call to mind the miraculous victories of Charles V, subduing all the powerable Lutheran princes in Germany to his and the catholic church's obeisance with passing small forces and in a few years or rather months space, the enemies being almost innumerable. Remember the three famous battles that the catholic cantons and people of the Swiss, being in number, power, and provision much inferior to the other, obtained by God's special grace and justice of the cause against the Zwinglians their neighbours, in one of which Zwinglius himself was slain, and in every one a marvellous number of heretics, and of catholics so few, that in such inequality of human helps, God must needs be the extraordinary worker of the same.

Read the histories of France and see whether the catholics have not had in manner always miraculous victories against the Calvinists: among many, the fights at Dreux, at Jarnac, at Saint Denis, at Moncontour, and especially the merciful work of God this last year whereby we saw the huge forces, as well of Germans as Swiss, by God's mighty arm and very small aid of man wonderfully defeated.

Recount furthermore all the famous and fortunate encounters of a very few catholics against the heretics and rebels in Flanders: as at Groningen, at Mock [Knocke?], at Mons, at Antwerp, at Iemblous [Jemappes?], and many other conflicts, where without loss almost at all, many thousands of God's and the king's enemies have been cut in pieces, our Lord God no doubt combating with his people against his enemies, as he did against Sennacherib, Nicanor, and other mentioned in holy writ.

Which thing, most noble and valiant gentlemen of England, may give you courage and comfort from God himself, even the Lord God of Hosts, to adventure yourselves in a quarrel most honourable, in a cause that the divine majesty hath showed himself, not only in other ages but even in all our eyes and memories to have singular care of. In a case of the extremest necessity of our just defence and arms that ever any Christian people had or can have.

Thus much, my good lords and most dear friends, I have thought good to forwarn you of the whole cause of these present sacred wars, and of his holiness' and catholic majesty's sincere intention therein; and both their incomparable affections towards our nation, whereof I could give you far more comfortable intelligence if I were personally present with you, as I trust I shall be very shortly, for that is fully meant by our holy father and his majesty, and of me so much desired that every short day seemeth a long year till I enjoy you in our Lord, though in the mean time I stand here wholly for your service; wherein as I have spent these many years of my banishment, so would I now as God shall appoint and need require, bestow my blood and the remnant of my life among you in my dearest country for the better accomplishment of that which all true Christians and godly English hearts do desire.

Our Lord God bless and direct you all to follow that in this action, and in all your life that shall be most agreeable to his glory, our country's good, and your own honour and salvation.

From my lodging in the Palace of St. Peter
in Rome this 28 of April 1588.
THE CARDINAL.

A TREATISE OF THE OFFICE OF A COUNCILLOR

by Robert Beale

1592

ROBERT BEALE (1541–1601), who wrote legal, political, and historical works, was a diplomatist, member of parliament, and a member of the Elizabethan Society of Antiquaries. Concerning him and his tract on the principal secretary, Professor Conyers Read wrote:

'This treatise . . . is written in a clerkly hand of the late sixteenth or early seventeenth century. It was evidently composed in 1592 for the benefit of Sir Edward Wotton who expected at that time to be appointed principal secretary. As a matter of fact he was not appointed then, nor three years later when the matter was broached again. The author is indicated to have been R.B., without much doubt Robert Beale . . . Beale was Walsingham's brother-in-law and secretary as well as clerk of the privy council. He was employed on several diplomatic missions and more than once took Walsingham's place as principal secretary when he was away from England. Beale was, besides, a stout champion of the puritans and a distinguished civil lawyer. He was unusually well qualified to write of the office of principal secretary and his observations are particularly interesting in this connexion because his knowledge of the office was gained during Walsingham's incumbency and undoubtedly reflected the situation as it existed in his term of office.'

The version below is from C.Read, *Mr. Secretary Walsingham and the Policy of Queen Elizabeth*, vol.I,423. Oxford, Clarendon Press, 1925. The spelling has been modernized, but it has not been abridged.

A TREATISE OF THE OFFICE OF A COUNCILLOR
and Principal Secretary to Her Majesty
DIVIDED INTO THREE PARTS

WHEREOF the first treateth of the diversity of councils in England, their jurisdictions and authorities.

The second, of things fit to be provided by a secretary for his better service both for foreign and domestic affairs.

The third, of matters ordinarily falling into consultation, and of the manner of giving counsel and advice to a prince or in the assembly of councillors, and of the setting down of dispatches incident and appertaining to the office of a secretary.

ISAIAH:x:1

Woe unto them that decree wicked decrees and write grievous things.

INSTRUCTIONS FOR A PRINCIPAL SECRETARY

Observed by R.B. for Sir Edward Wotton: Anno Domini, 1592.

Imprimis, my meaning is not to speak anything of such qualities as are fit to be in one that should be a prince's secretary or councillor. That argument hath been handled by others, and whom her majesty shall call to that place my simple judgment must think sufficiently qualified. Wherefore, mine intention shall be only to note such things as belong unto the practice of the place of a secretary, which consisteth partly in dealing with her majesty and partly with the rest of her highness' most honourable privy council.

Touching matters to be handled before the council, to avoid the number and trouble of many unnecessary suits, it were convenient to have at the first entrance the order renewed and observed which hath been many times made by the lords of the council: for them to attend unto matters of state either at home or abroad; to refer private suits to the masters of the requests or other ordinary courts of justice. And for this purpose you shall do well to acquaint yourself with the jurisdictions of the particular courts of this realm, whereof Mr. Lambert and Mr. Crompton have of late made special treaties. And yet, where there is great cause, I would not have her majesty's council wholly abridged of that prerogative, for in times past they did deal in such causes, as appeareth by the first book or register of the court of requests and many other precedents of great moment.

Of such things as the secretary is to proffer to the council, let him first have in a several paper a memorial or docket of those which he mindeth to propound and have dispatched at every sitting. He is to proffer the public before the private, and discern of things which require speedy answer before such as may tarry longer leisure. Especially let not such messengers long stay which come either from beyond the seas or other parts and must have allowances for their journeys and attendances.

When the council meeteth, have a care that the time be not spent in matters of small moment, but to dispatch such things as shall be propounded unto them, for you shall find that they will not meet so often as you would desire, sometimes for sickness and sometimes for other employments.

Defer and prolong not suitors or any business you have in hand, for otherwise more will come upon you than you shall be able to dispatch, for as Seneca said of the affairs of princes,

> *Nunquam placidam sceptra quietem,*
> *Certumque sui tenuere diem;*
> *Alia ex aliis cura fatigat*
> *Vexatque animos nova tempestas*

and for this purpose you shall do well to have a memorial in writing of things to be done, lest your memory deceive you.

Favour not secret or cabinet councils which do but cause jealousy and envy. Some will protect them by the example of Henry the seventh, who was indeed a politic prince, but they do not well either conceive or report the matter, for, coming from a civil war, he was forced to have the noblemen reside in their countries to see good orders kept in the execution of justice; besides he was not destitute of a council of bishops and nobles who both attended him and made dispatches, as appears first by the first book of the court of requests; secondly, the disinheriting of his mother-in-law by a great council. It is true this hath been observed in other states upon extraordinary occasions, as during the controversies between the houses of France and Burgundy, so upon the voyage of Charles the eighth into Naples and the opposition of the house of Aragon, so that of Charles the fifth and Francis the first. Seeing now in our state there is no competition, as the cases differ, so the reasons vary.

When there shall be any unpleasant matter to be imparted to her majesty from the council or other matters to be done of great importance, let not the burden be laid on you alone but let the rest join with you. Excuse yourself by your years and for lack of experience; do not overthrow yourself for any of their pleasures or other respect as Mr. Davison did, for if anything be misliked, it will be said that it was the secretary's doing, that they signed for company, that the letter was brought to them, etc. And many times letters are gotten in chambers by councillor's clerks going from one to another which often are called in question, whereof no record is kept in the council book. And therefore it were good to renew the order kept in King Edward's time, the next day after their lords had signed the letters, to set their hands to the entries of the book.

It hath been the manner that the secretary should abbreviate on the backside of the letters, or otherwise in a by-paper, the substantial and most material points which are to be propounded and answered, lest the rest of the lords will not have them all read, or shall not have leisure, and let him in a by-paper make a note briefly of their resolutions to every point, commanding the clerks of the council to approach and give good ear for his better direction to frame their lordships' letter or answer.

Afterwards, upon sight of the letters sent and the notes thus taken of their lordships' resolution, the clerk of the council may draw a letter or minute (if it be a great cause), written with large lines, to be perused by the secretary and likewise communicated to the lord treasurer before it be preferred to the other lords to be signed.

The secretary must have a care that the clerks of the council keep a perfect book of the lords' sittings, of the place, day, and number, and likewise of their letters signed; and when every month is ended, let the clerk attending make up in order the bundle for the month and keep a special note in a paper book of every letter or other specialty in the said bundle in form of a calendar, so as by the said calendar he may know in what month and bundle to find that which shall be asked for, with a blank on the other side of the said book to note to whom any of the said letters may be delivered, if any send for them.

Let the clerks of the council likewise keep a special book of all the bonds taken by months and days in form of a calendar, leaving one side of the paper book blank to note by what order and what day the same bond was discharged.

Let also the said clerks, besides the great book, keep a little note of such as may be committed from the council, and if the secretary commit any of himself, let his man keep a note of them and will him to put him in remembrance of them, that they lie not too long to their utter undoing, and so many times the punishment hath been greater than the offence, besides many times the time is forgotten and passeth away which the law hath appointed for their indictments and trials, and so the offence is not punished as it should be; and sometimes her majesty is put to greater charges than needeth for finding of them in prison. It hath been heretofore an use that against great festival days and her majesty's remove in summer time from London, the keepers of the prisons should be commanded by the lords of the council to bring in a catalogue of their prisoners and by whom they were committed, to be considered of by the lords as they should see cause.

Take heed to whom you give any warrant for the apprehension of any man or searching of houses, they may abuse you and use it for other purposes, as was seen in the star chamber in the case of Dr. Gollock and his companions and, unless there be great cause or you be so specially commanded by her majesty, take heed of any letters that may stay or hinder their ordinary course of justice between party and party or be against the law and liberty of the land, whereto the prince is sworn; and it is the inheritance both of the prince and subject.

When any businesses cometh into the secretary's hands, he shall do well for the ease of himself to distribute the same and to use the help of such her majesty's servants as serve underneath him, as the clerks of the council, the clerks of the signet, the secretary of the Latin and of the French tongue, and of his own servants.

Albeit the secretaries of the Latin and French tongue can sufficiently discharge their duties, yet, for that the matters whereof they shall write any letters as also her majesty's meaning and humour shall be better known unto you than them, you shall do well to consider first of the minutes of the letters, that by no scholastical, ambiguous, or general phrase any advantage may be taken, as Duke Casimir did at his being here and hath besides often happened.

If there be any occasion of treaties, obligations, or contracts with foreign princes or estates in Latin, besides former precedents and your own learning, you shall do well to use the help of the doctors of the civil law and some discreet and well experimented notaries, which were more used in former times than of late years. Remember the saying of the Lord Hastings, lord chamberlain to King Edward fourth, in commons: that the Englishmen have been more overtaken by the French in their treaties than in their wars. And surely, in whomsoever the fault was, the last contract with the United Provinces was penned to the great disadvantage of her majesty and the fault could never since be amended.

Burden not yourself with too many clerks or servants as Sir Francis Walsingham did. Let your secret services be known to a few; the Lord Treasurer Burghley, being secretary, had not above two or three. Some you may train up for the first in writing out and compiling such books as are necessary for your service, whom upon preferment of your other servants, and after some time of proof, you may call nearer unto you as they shall deserve and you shall see cause.

You must have a care that they which be about you be no advertisers of any matters but where and when and to whom you shall appoint.

Be not too credulous lest you be deceived; hear all reports but trust not all; weigh them with time and deliberation and be not too liberal of trifles; observe them that deal on both hands lest you be deceived; follow the advice of the poet,

> *Qui cavet ne decipiatur vix cavet cum etiam cavet:*
> *Etiam cum cavisse ratus est, saepe is cautor captus est.*

Other matters wherewith a secretary is to deal in may be distinguished into public services, either appertaining to the realm or else with other foreign states.

Imprimis, let him keep a journal in form of a calendar by day, month, and year of the time of the receipts of his letters and likewise of his despatches by post or otherwise.

If any of the posts be slack or do not their duties with such diligence as they ought to do, which will appear by the endorsements of the packets, the secretary must see the fault forthwith redressed, lest afterwards, when perhaps the service shall require more speed, it be hindered by bearing with their negligence. And for the better direction of this service, a secretary is to have a special care to such orders as have been heretofore made about these causes and to see them executed with all severity.

The secretary shall do well to appoint the clerks of the council to keep particular books of the messages which they shall send away from the council and to sign no messenger's bill unless the party bring back a certificate from him to whom the letters were sent. And the secretary's clerk is to keep the like book for such messages as he shall dispatch of himself and have a care that he be not abused by counterfeiting of hands and the queen surcharged as heretofore she hath been.

A secretary must have a special cabinet, whereof he is himself to keep the key, for his signets, ciphers, and secret intelligences, distinguishing the boxes or tills rather by letters than by the names of the countries or places, keeping that only unto himself, for the names may inflame a desire to come by such things.

A secretary is to have every year from the clerk of the crown a copy of the books of the justices of peace, of all the commissions that shall be from time to time for restraint of grain and other services, of all judges and principal gentlemen able for service, either civil or martial.

I could wish that the secretary should make himself acquainted with some honest gentlemen in all the shires, cities, and principal towns and the affection of the gentry. But let him take heed that he be not too light of credit, lest they abuse him and serve their private turns.

It is convenient for a secretary to seek to understand the state of the whole realm, to have Sir Thomas Smith's book, although there be many defects, which by progress of time and experience he shall be able to spy and amend.

Then to have a book or notice of all the noblemen, their pedigrees, and alliances among themselves and with other gentlemen.

A secretary must likewise have the book of Ortelius's maps, a book of the maps of England, with a particular note of the divisions of the shires into hundreds, lathes, wapentakes, and what noblemen, gentlemen and others be residing in every one of them; what cities, boroughs, market-towns, villages; and also a good description of the realm of Ireland, a note of the noblemen and surnames English or Irish of their septs, enraghes, [sic] galloglasses, kerns and followers, and if any other plots or maps come to his hands, let them be kept safely.

It is requisite that a secretary should have digested into ten or twelve several books these matters following:

1. Imprimis, of matters concerning religion, of recusants in every shire, of their bonds, placings, children, etc.; of the examinations of priests and traitors, to confer them together, which cannot be when some parcels are in one man's hands and some in another; and surely it were not amiss that some discreet person were appointed for that purpose, things would be better remembered and sooner dispatched;

2. The commission and instructions for the principality and marches of Wales;

3. The commission and instructions of her majesty's council in the North, the commission of the lord lieutenant, the commissions of the

wardens over against Scotland, the establishment of Berwick, a role of the officers and bands, the laws of the marches;

4. A note of the forts along the sea coasts of this realm, who be their captains, how they be furnished, when, and how they be repaired, by notes out of the office of the ordinance, etc.;

5. A note of the office of the ordinance and armoury, powder, and munition within the realm and in what places;

6. A book of the names of her majesty's ships, of their reparation and furnitures and of the mariners and soldiers that are requisite;

7. A book of the rates of victuals to serve either by sea or land;

8. A collection of the late musters in every shire for some few years, what able men, what furniture and what kind of armour, what numbers have been of late years taken out of them for any service abroad, so as they be not overburdened;

9. A book of the privileges of Guernsey and Jersey, of the ancient customs of Normandy and of the said Isles, of the orders of the lords of the council upon their appeals, of the provisions and munition in the said Isles;

10. Of the affairs of the realm of Ireland and the ordinary commission and instructions of the lord deputies and presidents, the special letters to be kept that are sent thither.

A secretary should not be unacquainted with the estate of such English corporations and companies as trade into the parts of beyond the seas, as the Merchant Adventurers, the merchants trading the East Countries, those of Spain, Muscovy and such like.

Likewise he should not be unacquainted with the number of the strangers, denizens, and others, both in London and in other places of this realm. And surely, for want of consuls and governors to each nation as in times past, there is grown a great ignorance and confusion in the trade by one colouring another, plurality of trades and by other abuses, which are to be redressed even for her majesty's profit and the good estate and quietness of the realm.

A secretary should not be unacquainted with the matters of her majesty's mint, of the standard, alloys and remedies of her coin, and likewise of other coins abroad, and of matters of exchange;

Likewise with her majesty's revenues, lands, customs, profits by wards, and such like; with the expenses, fees, annuities, pensions, and other charges, both ordinary and extraordinary, that her highness is at.

I could also wish that the secretary provide for himself a good extract of the late books of the subsidies and of the loans or privy seals; a collection of the subsidies, benevolences, reliefs, and other contributions granted by the subjects since the conquest; likewise a copy of the books of the undersheriffs and coroners in every shire; by which means he shall know the names of the gentry as also of the wealthier sort of yeomen in the whole land.

Many times there will be consultation for household matters, wherefore it is fit that a secretary should have some knowledge of the orders of the king's household, of the rate of the provisions, of the late compositions with every shire, to the intent he may not be ignorant but able to say somewhat as a councillor ought to do.

Finally, it is very requisite that a secretary should be so sufficiently instructed in the points of Christian religion which the church of England professeth as to be able to maintain the same and answer all traitors and other adversaries that he shall have to deal with. I could also wish that he should not be ignorant of all other controversies about rites and ceremonies and what hath been done concerning them, that he may not be carried away with the partial reports of such as only seek the maintenance of themselves and care not what untrue reports they give out to incense her majesty against true and loyal subjects who are not heard as they are. And whereas the ecclesiastical courts do by law and custom hold pleas of very many things which do touch both the bodies and goods of the subjects, it is a strange thing that their judges only take the oath of supremacy and no oath to deal uprightly in justice and according to the laws of the land, as was used in the time of King Henry the eighth. And such an oath hath been always exacted and ought to be in places of judgment. But seeing the ecclesiastical law is not yet reformed as it ought to be according to sundry acts of parliament, they do what they list in admitting unlearned and unhonest ministers, in suppressing of good preachers, in tolerating, under colour of justice, pluralities and non-residencies, in simoniacal choppings and changings of livings and other enormities and abuses, as it is no wonder to see the apostasy of this realm to popery and atheism by their defaults, unless some speedy remedy be taken which, by former examples in the times of King Joas and Josias and the long experience of this time, cannot be hoped for that it will ever proceed from the clergy.

Albeit all these things cannot be had at once, by reason of late years that things have been made more private than were fit for her majesty's service and no means used of instruction and bringing up of others in knowledge to be able to serve her majesty, yet those remembrances may serve as notes and heads whereto a secretary may refer such things as he may get and be acquainted with in the time of his service. And although there be no present use, yet he shall do well to inquire and look after such things, to cause some of his clerks to write them out and, for avoiding of confusion, to digest them into such heads to serve his turn where there shall be need.

In the collection of things I would wish a distinction used between that which is public and that which is private,—that is, a separation between those things which are her majesty's records and appertains unto her and those which a secretary getteth by his private industry and charge. Heretofore there was a chamber in Westminster where such things, towards the latter end of King Henry the eighth, were kept and were not in the secretary's private custody; but since, that order hath been neglected and those things which were public have been culled out and gathered into private books, whereby no means are left to see what was done before or to give any light of service to young beginners, which is not well; and therefore I would wish a secretary kept such things apart in a chest or place and not to confound them with his own. And the want of so doing was the cause that upon the death of Mr. Secretary Walsingham all his papers and books both public and private were seized on and carried away, perhaps by those who would be loath to be used so themselves.

But to return to the practice of the office of a secretary; whensoever any privy seal shall pass for any of the above-named services, let especial note be kept thereof in a book under their several titles, that you may be able to give a true information of the same and require an account if there be cause. It may be that, many times before the privy seal and warrants be obtained, there shall be necessary use of the money for which your letter or bond may be directed. Beware how you take such a charge upon you and remember the warrant be gotten in due time. I have heard it credibly reported that the old treasurer, the marquis of Winchester, did so oftentimes direct his warrants to the tellers of the exchequer and afterwards did forget to solicit the warrants as he should have done, and so by age and for want of memory did forget their particular employments and was cast in arrearages unto the queen, and I know that Sir Francis Walsingham was overtaken in this sort. The Lord Treasurer Burghley is more circumspect, not to pay anything before the warrant doth come, and you shall do well to follow him in this point.

Touching foreign services, I would wish that you did, as soon as you can, inform yourself of such things as have passed between this realm and other states, at the least for the space of one year before, to the intent you may join your service with that which went before.

It is a secretary's duty beforehand to consider of the estate of the realm and all the rest of the princes' estates with whom there have been and are any doings, and what dangers may happen and how they may be remedied. Security hath been always the bane [bene?] of all kingdoms and estates; and it hath been in the end seen that, when councils are daily taken and varied according to the uncertainty of affairs, either at home or abroad, upon sudden events, the wisest men have been often overtaken and put to hard shifts and have not known what counsel to give or take. As Dion well noteth of Pompey, who was both wise and valiant, thought that with the trampling of his foot to have made all Italy tremble; whence Thucydides saith that *Timor memoriam excutit; propter repentina et long praeter opinionem accidentia capiuntur consilia plerumque nociva.*

Wherefore, if occasion serve, no opportunity is to be omitted to compound all discontents with neighbours abroad, so as the same may be with the honour of God and benefit of the realm, and to procure as much friendship as may be; lest, by suffering things to run on carelessly at random, our enemies prevent us of the means and they cannot be recovered when we would wish it. The sins of the people of this land are generally such and so little teaching and reformation of them, that if Job, being an upright man, fearing God, eschewing evil, did every day by prayer and sacrifice seek to make an atonement for the sins which his children might have committed and even then had no quietness or rest, but feared that which afterwards came upon him, surely we ought to be afraid that that come not upon us which our sins have most manifestly deserved, and seek to prepare ourselves for all events, that we be not dismayed at any thing that may happen.

For the knowledge of thing [*sic*] heretofore passed between this realm and other foreign estates, besides that understanding which he may obtain by diligent reading and observation of the histories of all countries, he is to provide for himself a book of such treaties as have, at the least for the space of one hundred years, been between this realm and other princes and states abroad.

As for the Low Countries, the treaties of the intercourse, the colloquy of Bruges, the contracts with the estates general and all such as do depend upon them. The treaties with Spain and Portugal are to be had and likewise a collection of the unkindnesses offered by the king and how his pretences both for the Low Countries and Indies may be answered, that when there shall be any treaty or other occasion, you be not to seek.

For France, let him gather all the treaties before the last king's death and likewise such things as have passed with the king that now is for assistances and loans of monies.

In Italy, since the suppression of the pope, there have been little dealings, notwithstanding the practices with the pope. Intelligences from these parts are not to be neglected. The great duke of Tuscany hath caused our nation to be well used at Ligorno and, albeit he be allied with the duke of Lorraine, yet he is esteemed to be no great friend to the greatness of the Spaniard, and if his friendship were entertained it would serve to good purpose, for he hath a great party in Rome amongst the cardinals. The signory of Venice hath, before the time of Queen Mary, had their ambassadors resident here; since, by reason of religion and for other causes, they have omitted the continuance thereof. They malign the English traffic within the straits and if occasion served would do anything with Spain to cut it off, fearing lest the English trade by Muscovy into Persia would abridge any part of their commodity, by their trading to Alexandria and Aleppo. They have dealt with the king of Poland to hinder our merchants from repairing thither. In such cases therefore, *cum Cretensibus Cretisandum est*, to get as much good as may be by them and from them without impiety and dishonesty.

In Germany, the secretary of the Latin tongue can I think inform you what letters have been sent to the emperor, the princes and estates of Germany. And forasmuch as the matters of the Hanse towns is one day likely to come in question, a secretary shall do well to inform himself beforehand of that which may be said on both sides.

Heretofore many treaties have been with Denmark and some dealing for the taking away of the new impositions upon the English subjects in the time of his war with Sweden, passing the sound, and likewise for the trade into Muscovy; of these a secretary ought not to be ignorant.

The like may be said of former dealings with the princes of Italy, with the kings of Poland, Sweden, the Muscovite, the Turk, the king of Barbary and all others with whom this state hath had any doings.

Our neighbours of Scotland are not to be forgotten: what treaties have passed heretofore between both the realms and for these latter years, what benefits her majesty hath bestowed upon the king since his cradle. And for the matters of the late Scottish queen which may perhaps be one day called in question a secretary for the honour of the queen and the realm is by all the means he can to inform himself of all her actions, concerning the murder of her husband, her flight into England and likewise her practices against her majesty, especially that with Babington, and the cause of her just and necessary execution, without which neither her majesty's person nor estate could be upholden and preserved. A secretary is also to understand the affections and partialities between the nobility of Scotland, to keep some intelligence with the ministers and, by showing some justice and favour to such merchants as may have complaints here, to procure that they may make good report of the friendship of England among the boroughs of that realm, which for the most part are well affected in matters of religion and the best part of the strength of that realm. As the keeping of him bare and the maintenance of a faction of his own subjects against him, behaving of himself well, is not to be liked, so it is not convenient to leave him alone to be practised by others. And therefore, according to the counsel given to King Henry the eighth for King James the fifth of Scotland, his grandfather, it were requisite to have continually with him some gentleman that might follow him in all his exercises and pastimes, that might do her majesty good service and hinder the designs of others.

In the setting down of the notes touching foreign estates, I have been more particular, for that I would wish you to follow another course with them than hath been of many years heretofore used. Some have despised it either of ignorance or for some other forward conceit. The government of children and civil dissensions abroad have served our turns better than perhaps they will do hereafter. I have not a little wondered to see so many great actions overpassed wherein her majesty was notably interested and yet had no person to deal for her; as when the last French king was chosen king of Poland. If his brother had remained in France, and he there from whence all the provisions of the navy comes, and both had joined against us, what should we have done. And yet to prevent it her highness had nobody for her, when all the petty princes in Italy and Germany had both then and afterwards. What prince is more interested in the affairs of the Low Countries than her majesty is, yet none was employed either in the meeting at Cologne or in the agreement with the malcontents. These things impair her majesty's credit, make her to be left to herself and cause that she is not duly informed how things pass, nor hath any of her subjects so acquainted with foreign affairs as is fit for her majesty's service. The inconvenience will more appear hereafter than it doth at this present.

But to return to my former purpose for the information of a secretary.

If, when you shall be secretary, you shall be put to answer any ambassador, sent before your coming to the place, see his former instructions and commission, that either he may not swerve from it or else to procure him some farther warrant by her highness' own letter if cause shall so require.

If you be to make any new instructions for ambassadors, consider of the former precedents and well weigh what her majesty's meaning is and what is the best way to attain thereunto, how the state whereto he is directed is divided or affected in war or otherwise. And herein perhaps your Italian *Relationi* may stand you in some stead for the knowledge of foreign estâtes.

If the charge of foreign espials and intelligences be committed unto you, I will show you my opinion. Mr. Secretary Walsingham, with her majesty's allowance and his own purse, entertained in above forty several places. In the time of the ambassages of Mr. la Mott and Mr. Mauvesier he had some of his secretaries that betrayed the secrets both of the French and Scottish dealings. In Scotland he was well beloved of many of the nobility, ministers, and others, whom he relieved when they were banished into England; with money he corrupted priests, Jesuits, and traitors to betray the practices against this realm. But, seeing how much his liberality was misliked, I do not think that you can follow the like example.

Out of Italy you may be advertised by such as commonly every week write the occurrences from Venice, and herein you may use the help of some Italian or merchant that tradeth into those parts. And if there be any English gentleman that travelleth into those parts, you may require him to advertise you of what he shall hear and he will take it as a great favour at your hands.

In Germany you shall do well to acquaint yourself with some discreet person of the company of the Merchant Adventurers and those which trade into those parts, to advertise you from time to time what they may understand at Stade or Elvinge and you may give them some convenient allowance to set others on work about those matters. You shall do well also to require the clerks or secretaries of the said companies and others, that if they shall by any letters or report of mariners or travellers understand anything, to inform you thereof as soon as they can. I think also that you may easily get acquaintance with some in Augusta and Frankfort and likewise in the courts of the emperor, the palsgrave, landsgrave, and other princes, that may from time to time inform you of such matters as they shall understand.

In France there is not that need as was heretofore, considering the good amity that is between her majesty and the French king. And yet for Brittany, the governors of Guernsey and Jersey may be admonished to procure intelligences of the enemies' doings and to advertise you thereof. In former times some correspondence hath been kept with the governor of Calais which may serve for good purpose, and it were convenient to have some advertise from thence, Dieppe and Rouen.

In the United Provinces the councillor for her majesty with the states may inform you both of their actions and of such other intelligences as they shall have out of other places, acquainting himself with that person to whom they shall commit that charge, which commonly is one of the council of estate.

To understand how things pass under the government of the king's side, you may use the help of some honest merchants, seeing the posts are suffered to come weekly from Antwerp. But this must you keep to yourself for fear of danger to the party and besides you must see what others will do for money.

In Spain I know not any other course that can be holden but by money. Scottishmen are suffered to trade thither and if any such assured person may be found they may be used. A Frenchman had great allowance to reside upon the borders, but I think deserved not his entertainment.

But take heed they deal not double with you and abuse you with toys and matters of their own invention. And for dealing with such as the laws of the realm esteemeth traitors, together with all others that shall deal with them, beware by the example of old Sir Thomas Wyatt in the time of King Henry the eighth and lately of Sir John Perrot, and see first you have a good warrant to deal in such causes as Montague and Chomley had, saving themselves by special pardons and by their advice overthrowing the whole nobility and council.

And forasmuch as you may be called in question for such privy seals as you may have received for such services without imprest or account, as happened after the death of Sir Francis Walsingham, you shall do well to keep unto yourself a special note what sums you have delivered out and how the same privy seals have been employed and may be answered and discharged if cause require.

Things to be done with her majesty.

Have in a little paper a note of such things as you are to propound to her majesty and divide it into the titles of public and private suits as the lord treasurer and Mr. Secretary were wont to do. Justinian said: *Omnium rerum habere memoriam divinitatis potiusquam humanitatis est.* And it may be otherwise that many times one matter will make you forget another if you have not such a remembrance.

Learn before your access her majesty's disposition by some in the privy chamber with whom you must keep credit, for that will stand you in much stead, and yet yield not too much to their importunity for suits, for so you may be blamed, nevertheless pleasure them when conveniently you may.

Show yourself willing to pleasure any of her majesty's kin, for although perhaps nothing be obtained, yet it will be well taken, as though you did it in respect they appertain unto her.

Do not burden yourself with many suits but refer them unto others of the chamber or household under whom they serve; so shall you content the parties, defer honour unto others who would be jealous of your sole credit, and keep yourself to do good to men of special honesty and desert.

When her highness is angry or not well-disposed, trouble her not with any matter which you desire to have done unless extreme necessity urge it.

When her highness signeth, it shall be good to entertain her with some relation or speech whereat she may take some pleasure.

To bills for lands and leases there must be first gotten the hands of the lord treasurer and chancellor of the exchequer and of her majesty's attorney and solicitor general.

To pardons, the hands of the justices of the assizes before whom the party hath been convicted. And if the pardon contains any restitution of lands or goods it is requisite that her majesty's learned council and the officers of the exchequer should be first acquainted therewith. And take heed lest in the draught of the pardon, under the colour to pardon one offence, you be not abused with a general clause of *Necnon omnes alias murdras* [*sic*] *et felonias,* reaching to things not spoken or thought of, as some have been heretofore.

In common things the hand of the clerks of the signet may suffice. For benefices the hand of some bishop must be gotten.

Let the clerks of the signet keep special notes in their books what bills be procured to be signed by yourself, what by the masters of the requests or any others, lest the same happen to be called in question. And likewise let them keep notes of such bills as pass by immediate warrant; the account will be the better kept of the fees appertaining to your office in the hanaper.

When any privy seal shall be directed to the secretary without imprest or account, for any reward to any other whose name her majesty would not have known, let him keep a special book to himself how and to whom the same was employed, lest there be an account afterwards demanded as was after the death of Mr. Secretary Walsingham.

If you be commanded to write any matter of importance, do what you can to procure that the same may be done by a special letter from her majesty herself, or if that may not be, set it down in writing. Make as though you doubted whether you had conceived her highness' mind or not and read it before her and alter it as she will have it. Keep that minute and a note of the day, lest afterwards you be charged with it, as was the case of Mr. Davison and Sir Edward Wotton in Scotland.

If it shall be needful to publish any proclamations, consider well of the matter and look unto former precedents, and therefore it shall be needful for you to have the book of proclamations printed in the time of King Edward the sixth and all the rest as many as you can get, dividing them according to their matters into several bundles, to avoid confusion and long search. If the matter be according to law then urge it, and for this purpose you shall do well to have always at hand the abridgements of Rastell and Pulton. If it be of any matter of law that is not contained in the said books, then let the draft be made by the queen's learned council and perused by the judges and so pass accordingly. As new evils require new remedies, so if no provision hath been heretofore made that may be enforced by law, then her majesty by her prerogative may take order in many things by proclamation. And herein it is good to see what hath been done in like cases in other countries. And to this purpose the books of the edicts and ordinances in France and of the pragmatics in Spain may stand you in some stead. But be circumspect in applying of those precedents to this estate to avoid an opinion of being newfangled and a bringer in of new customs. Show the necessity and cause and likewise the common benefit, that it may not be thought to tend to any private respects, and let the threatening of the penalties be such as may not seem strange or excessive, against the law and liberty of the land.

Be not dismayed with the controlments and amendments of such things which you shall have done, for you shall have to do with a princess of great wisdom, learning, and experience. It is reported of King Henry the eighth that when Sir William Peter, at the first time that he was secretary, seemed to be dismayed for that the king crossed and blotted out many things in a writing which he had made, the king willed him not to take it in evil part, for it is I, said he, that made both Cromwell, Wriothesly, and Paget good secretaries and so must I do to thee. The princes themselves know best their own meaning, and there must be time and experience to acquaint them with their humours before a man can do any acceptable service.

Use no peremptory contestations or replies, but deliver your opinion simply and the commodities and inconveniences that are like to ensue on both sides. Give no occasion that either her majesty or any other do think that you do it as though you esteemed your own wit better than theirs, but only of conscience and duty, so as if things fall out otherwise, her highness may see your single and upright dealing and that she may conceive that you are not carried, sometimes one way and sometimes another, to serve private turns, as perhaps she may be persuaded others have done.

It is written of Xerxes, when he called all his captains and officers, intending to make wars upon Greece, he used these speeches: *Ne viderer meo tantum consilio hoc aggressus convocavi vos, ceterum mementote mihi parendum magis, quam persuadendum est.* Princes find such flatterers and councillors as Cambises and Rehoboam did to follow their humours, yea many times will urge their councillors, as it is reported King Henry the eighth was wont to do to Sir Edward Montague, the chief justice and others. But consider you your duty and if you cannot do as much good as you would, yet decline *a malo.* Remember there is a higher Lord that will exact an account and is able to lay a more grievous punishment of soul and body than any prince can do.

If, not following your advice and counsel, things shall not fall out well as you advised, insult not, magnifying your own opinion and condemning hers, but with patience and meekness help to remedy that which may be amiss. Afterwards, when the like occasion may fall out, you may use it as a persuasion, but yet humbly and dutifully. Remember what Arrian saith in the life of Alexander: *Illud satis scio nullum unquam antiquorum regum in tantam post peccatum poenitentiam venisse ut illud vellet agnoscere. Plerique quamvis se deliquisse sciunt, id tamen tanquam iure factum existimantur,* etc., and therefore you must be contented and have patience.

So likewise towards your fellow councillors behave yourself as Maecenas counselled Augustus, *quorum consilium sequendum existimabis eos collauda et honora nam illorum inventis gratiam tibi paries: quorum vero reieceris nemquaquam eos aut ignominia afficies aut culpabis,* etc.

Be not therefore violent to have all faults reformed at once, for as an emperor said: *Multa simul Pluto corrigi non possunt.* And such was the answer that Antonius Pius the emperor made (as Capitolinus writeth) to his councillors that sollicited him to such a sudden and hasty reformation. According to the necessities of time, place, and persons seek to do good as much as you may, not exceeding the bounds of your calling and duty. In the time of King Edward the sixth it was an unseasonable advice given to the duke of Somerset to grant forth commissions for inclosures. His adversaries used this as an occasion both to raise popular insurrections and to overthrow his credit and authority.

Take heed you do not addict yourself to any faction that you may find among the councillors. You shall find they will only use you for their own turns and that done set little by you afterwards. Many times also men have been in danger without due desert and undone by suspicion of such men and matters. And the jealousy of princes is such that they cannot abide any councillor should depend on any other than themselves, neither is it convenient. Seek therefore by all the means you can to deserve well of them all and suffer yourself to be rather carried with the matter than with the man, as shall be most meetest for the service of God and her majesty.

If there arise any partialities and factions, do you endeavour rather to compound than to increase them or to have them continued to the hurt of the state, for by such means neither good came to any prince or sound advice in council given where they were maintained—so Proverbs: 26:2. Remember touching England the wise and politic discourse of Philip de Comines how Queen Margaret, wife to King Henry the sixth, by maintenance of such debate between the duke of Somerset and the earl of Warwick, overthrew her husband, her son, herself, and almost the whole realm. Although, God be thanked, there be no such strong parties now, yet considering our enemies, which attend any occasions, it is better they were suppressed than continued.

Bear reproofs, false reports, and such like crosses, if they be private and touch you not deeply, with silence or a modest answer. But if it be in company or touch your allegiance, honour, or honesty, mine advice is that you answer more roundly, lest your silence cause standers-by to think ill of you and to retain it in memory and thereupon to work your farther indignation and discredit. The not bearing of it may perhaps cause that the like injury shall not be offered unto you again, or at the least other men, who commonly take such words for truth, will suppose them rather to proceed of choler than any just cause; otherwise the old saying is true: *Veterem iniuriam tolerando, novam provocamus.* But, *ne quid nimis.*

Beware that before God and the whole world you can give a good account of your counsels and actions to be void of impiety, covetousness, envy, maliciousness, injustice and fraud. Remember the saying of Plato: ' Whilst a man's body is in good health, we like well of those that seek to satisfy our appetites and so indeed minister occasions of sickness. And when the sickness cometh, we attribute the whole cause, not to them who were in fault, but to the physician who doth not cure us as we would: ' *sic in republica, quando erumpit morbus presentes criminamus consultores atque iniuria afficimus; priores illos, qui causam morbi dederunt laudibus efferimus.* But Isocrates said: *Aequum non est ut calamitatum culpas in eos casus transferamus qui postremo acciderunt, sed delicti accusari debent, qui insecuti infortunii materiam dederunt*; nevertheless the world most commonly judgeth otherwise.

Wherefore you must be circumspect and pray to God, from whom every good gift proceedeth, to direct you by his Holy Spirit. Do nothing against his word, which ought to be your lantern, way, and direction. First, briefly examine all your counsels and actions according to the rule of the ten commandments, doing nothing that is prohibited in any of them, for (as the apostle saith), *non est faciendum malum ut eveniat bonum.* And the prophet crieth out, A woe them that take counsel without him and write grievous things, who shall not escape in the day of the visitation of the Lord.

Grieve not your own conscience and keep yourself as near as you may to the maintenance of the laws and liberties of the land. Decline from evil and do good. Beware of too much worldly policy and human wit. Be not self conceited and think not as they do of whom the poet speaketh: *Qui faciunt intelligendo et nihil intelligunt.* So shall the Lord prosper you against all such as either by open malice or secret practices shall seek your overthrow.

Be diligent: Remember the saying of Salust: *Non votis aut supplicationibus muliebribus auxilia divina parantur; vigilando, agendo, bene consulendo, etc., ubi enim secordiae et atque ignaviae tradideris, nequaquam Deum implores: iratus et infestus est.*

Be not one in speech and another in action, as Bion chargeth Seneca, *quod in plerisque contra facere visus esset, quam philosopharetur.*

Be clean handed, and although it were a hard matter to abridge one that shall occupy that place of all taking of that which will be offered, yet it is utterly to be avoided in matters which concern either the honour of God or justice. The Lord will bless you otherwise sufficiently and your enemies shall have less occasion to seek your discredit and overthrow, who most commonly, in the supplantation of men, look rather to some part of the spoil or prey than either to just matter or the service of God, prince, or country.

By the reading of histories you may observe the examples of times past, judging of their success. Agrippa, a great counsellor to Augustus the emperor, was by Dion accounted happy that he could so use his master's favour *ut neque ei unquam molestus esset, neque invidiae aliorum obnoxius: Augusto imperium stabilivit, et populum beneficiis ita devinixit ut omnium maxime popularis judicaretur.*

Thus have I passed over these things whereof I thought it necessary to inform you, being ready to pleasure you in what else I may.

A DISCOURSE OF
THE WHOLE ART OF CHIRURGERY

by Peter Lowe

1597

PETER LOWE (1550?–1612) was responsible for the real progress in medicine and surgery in Glasgow at the end of the sixteenth century. He had studied at Paris about 1565 and had become a Master of the Faculty of Surgery there. In the second edition of his *Chirurgery* he wrote of himself that ' he was Doctor in the Faculty of Chirurgery at Paris and ordinary surgeon to the French king and queen, that he had practised in France, Flanders, and elsewhere the space of 22 years, thereafter being Chirurgeon maior to the Spanish regiments at Paris 2 years, next following the French king, my master, in the wars 6 years, where I took commodity to practise all points and operations of chirurgery.' In 1596 he published at London *An Easie, Certaine, and Perfect Method to Cure and Prevent the Spanish Sickness*. The next year his great work, *The Whole Art of Chirurgery*, the first treatise in English on surgery, was printed in London.

In the spring of 1598 he was in Glasgow, and in March 1599 it was ' agreed of new and contracted betwixt the town and Doctor Lowe for 80 marks money by year ' that he should attend the poor of Glasgow. That year his cosmopolitanism brought him under the censure of the clerical inquisitors, and he twice stood ' at the pillar ' of the kirk. Lowe worked hard to eliminate the charlatans and empirics who practised in Glasgow, and he eventually succeeded in founding a college such as that he had known at Paris. On 29 November 1599 King James, by his charter, ' makes, constitutes, and ordains Master Peter Lowe, our chirurgeon and chief chirurgeon to our dearest son the prince, with the assistance of Mr. Robert Hamilton, professor of medicine, and their successors, indwellers of our City of Glasgow.' Lowe and Hamilton were empowered to examine and licence all persons professing surgery in Glasgow and Western Scotland, and this charter of foundation of the Faculty of Physicians and Surgeons is that under which the Faculty exercises its authority today. Although never president of the Faculty, Lowe was repeatedly one of the four quartermasters, and his memory has been venerated by that Faculty for three centuries.

The Whole Art of Chirurgery of over 450 pages discusses medicine as well as surgery. The first edition of 1597 was revised by Lowe in 1612 and reprinted in 1634 and 1654. The selections below are from the 1612 edition which contains numerous woodcut illustrations.

To my very worshipful, learned, and well experimented good friends, Gilbert Primrose, sergeant chirurgeon to the king's majesty; James Harvey, chief chirurgeon to the queen's majesty; those of the worshipful company

*of chirurgeons in London, and Edinburgh, and all such well experimented
men in this kingdom, who are licensed to profess the divine art of chirurgery: Peter Lowe wisheth all happiness of life.*

ALL men of virtue, and well affectioned to the commonwealth (worshipful brethren), ought without all dissimulation to endeavour themselves
by all means possible, to intrust such as err and do ignorantly in that
which is profitable to the commonwealth: as also to make such know
that which is hurtful and unprofitable, to the effect the simple or common sort may choose that which is commodious and profitable, and
reject that which is hurtful. For these, and divers other good considerations, ought all men (chiefly you who have authority, learning, and
knowledge in the art) to stop such as work unskilfully: as I doubt not,
to the grief of all honest men, this art is seen daily abused by a number
of ignorant, malicious people, who pass away (but trial, or punishment)
like as cozeners, quack-salvers, charlatans, witches, charmers, and divers
other sorts of abusers; whose names I will for the present omit, in hope
they will desist, their own consciences accusing them; but, alas, I doubt
not, but the most part of them lack both soul, conscience, and fear of
God, are of more unhappy life, ignorant, and void of all skill, giving
ever to the diseased *quid pro quo*, promising marvels and to cure all
things in short space: which I grant is a sure maxim, as I could give
over-many examples to the destruction of many, and grief of those to
whom they appertain. Of those abusers, there are eight or nine divers
sorts: for some run from one town to another promising to heal all
things by vomitaries, and laxates, chiefly with antimony, praecipitatum,
which is powder of quicksilver, laureola, hellebore, colocynth, aesula,
catapus, and divers other poisonable medicaments, full of venom uncor-
rected, without either weight or measure: those are the death of infinite
numbers, who for the most part end their days by cruel vomiting, insatiable going to the stool, with syncops and intolerable dolour of the
stomach and intestines; of those, some die the first or second day; the
most robust, the seventh or eighth day at the farthest. Another sort of
those deceivers allege to have their knowledge by reading some other
vulgar books, those fellows promise rare things and are garnished with
some words that are obscure and not common, nor well can be understood to themselves or by their auditor. But to make it the more plausible,

they ever thrust in those obscure words in any purpose, and to make the matter to have more faith, they interlace scripture, with sighs and sobs and divers other circumstances. The third takes upon him to heal all things by charms, and praying to saints of the like name that the sickness is of, alleging the diseases to be some saint's evil, as for example: such as become paralytic through a deflux of humours on the nerves, they term it to be a blast of evil wind, and by praying to St. Blaot, it shall heal: such as are hydropic, do pray to St. Hidrop: such as lose their sight, pray to St. Cleere: those who hear evil or hath disease in their ears, pray to St. Owen: such as hath the gut called chiragra, or any other disease in the hands, pray to St. Main, with divers other which were long to repeat. Those deceitful ignorant people consider not that all those diseases were long before any of those saints. The fourth sort allege to have the curation of all diseases from their parents, as heritage, and those be impudent deceivers. The fifth sort vaunts to be skilful in such like diseases, by experience upon themselves, alleging them to be most skilful in the cure of the French pox, because he was cured himself sundry times of the same disease. The sixth takes upon him to cure all things by poisonable vomitaries only, chiefly antimony, by the which those deceivers pervert all orders divine and human, in towns and nations, as ever hath been observed in physic, that hath many evils happening, expressly condemned by Hippocrates and divers other of the learned. The seventh sort of those ignorants, having some ulcers in their legs or arms a certain space, takes upon him to heal all sores, alleging by some revelation to have an unguent called *unguentum ad omnes plagas*: this fellow with the rest doth cure all their abuses and mischiefs with a truce or stone. The eighth sort who having almost drunk out one of his eyes and useth some few remedies for the same, professeth himself to be a fine eyenest. The ninth sort who hath been cut of the stone, or rupture, or seen beasts cut, takes upon him to be most excellent in the rupture, or stone. All those with divers others take on them to have done many cures, yet they forget the infinite murdered by them. Such mischiefs were never suffered among the infidels, much less should be amongst Christians, to the great dishonour of God and his laws. I read at Rome in the time of Cato, that ignorants were banished that commonwealth, the learned only and expert retained for the preservation of the public weal, with power to such, to punish all abusers who durst be so bold to transgress the commandments, constitutions, statutes, and ordinances divine and human. I might recite here many authorities both of the ancient and new writers, as well of ethnics as Christians, whereof sufficient witnesses remain of the great pains they have taken in keeping the canons of this art, and punishing of impostors, in such sort that they were esteemed as gods. Seeing those ethnics have been so curious in this matter, how justly may we that take the name of Christians be evil thought of for suffering of such abusers in our art: yet I hope all honest men, especially you, who are towards his majesty, will be earnest in purchasing of privileges and laws for restraining of all ignorant abusers in this kingdom, like as is granted to men of our art in other civil countries, to the great aid and comfort of all kings of those parts. It pleased his sacred majesty to hear my complaint about some fourteen years ago, upon certain abusers of our art, of divers sorts and ranks of people, whereof we have good store, and all things failing, unthrifts and idle people do commonly meddle themselves with our art, who ordinarily do pass without either trial or punishment. The matter being considered, and the abuse weighed by his majesty and honourable council, thought not to be tolerated, for the which I got a privilege under his highness' privy seal, to try and examine all men upon the art of surgery, to discharge and allow in the west parts of Scotland, who were worthy or unworthy to profess the same. The which I observed as I might, although there be men of greater authority and sufficiency to punish, and correct such, if they would. But such is the iniquity of time that abusers are commonly overseen by such as ought to punish them: in such sort that one blind guides another, and most commonly fall both into the ditch. In the mean time are permitted to use charms, lies, execrable oaths, mortiferous poison, fallacious and uncertain experiments, whereby they destroy both friend and foe, ever detracting the true professors of the art. Now worshipful brethren, in respect of those enormities with divers more, which were long to repeat, I doubt not but all you who are learned and true professors, having access and credit with his majesty, will seek and obtain such privileges and laws, as well to correct and punish abusers, as also to withstand the frivolous or fantastical opinions of such as use them, and neither for request nor lucre to admit any such ignorant abusers to profess our art, but say with the learned philosopher, Plato, Socrates, and the world are our friends, but the verity above all. Which verity maketh the flourishing of all commonwealths, arts, and sciences. The which if you endeavour yourself to prosecute, no doubt but that God of verity who doth recompense each one according to his merits, as also doth punish transgressors, shall reward you accordingly. The which God I beseech to bless and prosper each one of you in your calling, with good success in your cures, happy end in this world, and life eternal hereafter. From my house in Glasgow, the 20 day of December in the year of our Lord God, 1612.

Your loving friend,

PETER LOWE.

A DISCOURSE OF
THE WHOLE ART OF CHIRURGERY

By Peter Lowe, Scottishman

This discourse is divided into ten books; the first whereof containeth fourteen chapters, whose contents be these:

Chap. 1. Of the original, antiquity, and excellency of surgery.
2. Of surgery in general, the operations and instruments thereof.
3. Of natural things in general.
4. Of the elements and consideration thereof.
5. Of the temperaments and complexion of man's body.
6. Of the four humours, in particular and general.
7. Of members, and parts principal of the body.
8. Of virtues and faculties, and whereof they proceed.
9. Of actions, and operations of virtues.
10. Of spirits, and whereof they proceed.
11. Of age.
12. Of the entertainments of old age.
13. Of remedies to be used by aged people.
14. Of colour, figure, and kind.

Chapter I

Of the original, beginning, antiquity, and excellency of surgery

CONSIDERING with myself, that all men are naturally obliged to serve the commonwealth by some honest profession, and that no man is able to discharge that duty and benefit to his native country, except he learn in his tender age the science wherein the ornament thereof consisteth; after full deliberation I applied myself to the study of surgery, which is, by the consent of all learned men, not only a science very profitable and necessary to all sorts of people, but also most ancient and honourable, as manifestly testifieth all the antiquity: in reading whereof we find the invention of surgery ascribed (for the excellency thereof) to the gods themselves, to wit, to Aesculapius, son of Apollo, from the which Podalire and Machaon his sons learned the same and cured sundry and divers which were deadly hurt at the siege of Troy, as reported Homer the poet. Clemens Alexandrinus saith that the first operator was Mizram, son to Ham the nephew of Noah, and after him Apis and Orizis kings of Egypt. Cornelius Celsus saith that it was found and exercised long before any other sciences. But passing with silence Apollo, Aesculapius, Machaon, Podalire, and all that sort of gods, as also Hippocrates, Galen, Pythagoras, Empedocles, Parmenides, Pimander, Democritus, Chiron, Paeon, Heraclides, Diocles, Caristus, Herophilus, Erastratus, Sanctus Cosmus, and Damianus two worthy Arabs, Mesues, Avicenna, Averroes, Paulus, with infinite others Arabs, Hebrews, Greeks, and Latins, and all the ancient philosophers, together with Alexander the Great, Josina the ninth, king of Scotland, who lived before Christ 161 years, Marcus Antonius, and divers others emperors, kings and princes, which professed the same, as is evidently showed unto us by the Holy Scriptures and profane writers, like as by the writs of the learned, who professed the same, that the medicine surgeon with the medicaments was invented and approved by God himself, for in the 20th chapter of the second book of the Kings we read how Isaiah healed by God's commandment Ezechias by laying a fig on his bites and sores: as also in the 6th and 10th chapter of Tobias, how the angel commanded him to slay a fish called Cassidill, and to take the gall thereof to the web of the eyes. In the 12th and 13th of Leviticus God commanded the Israelites when they entered in Capernaum, that if there appeared any signs of leprosy, like as pustules of divers colours upon the skin, that such should be brought before Aaron, and rejected for lepers, by such signs as is set down in that chapter. But what, not only was it invented by the divine power, but in like manner expressly commanded in the 8th chapter of Ecclesiastes and divers other places, that the professors thereof should be honoured by all men, for God created him to the effect that he remain with thee to assure thee, and them which are with thee, and that thou defraud him not of his wages, for God created the medicines of the earth, and the wise will not disdain the same: for he gave this science to man, that he may be glorified in his marvellous works, for he is the curer of all things. Now seeing I have sufficiently both by the scripture and otherwise proved the excellency of surgery, it is not needful to compare the same with other arts and sciences, for if any art be praised because it was and is professed of noble men, you may clearly perceive that the gods, emperors, kings, and princes have practised the same. If we consider the sentence of the divine philosopher Plato, that things good are difficile, there is nothing harder than surgery, the which will occupy a man all his lifetime, to seek out the nature of things pertaining thereto. If things be praised for their strength and force, what thing is of more strength than to restore man to his health, which otherwise was altogether lost: some man may perchance object to me and allege that many professors of surgery, with their charms, herbs of poison, and false promises, destroy many people who would easily have recovered their health if they had given no credit to such dissemblers. I answer that such deceivers deserve and merit to be grievously punished and banished out of all countries, as I have said in my *Epistle to Chirurgeons.* I read for the restraining of such abusers that the wise jurisconsult Ulpian in the 50th and last book of the *Digests* expressly defended that any baillie, governor of province, or judge, should choose, constitute, or license any of our profession, but to leave that to the doctors and masters of each city, to choose the best experimented to the end the country and cities may be the more safely with their families and friends committed to their charge. Justinian *Libro de gestis* inhibits any to practise but such as are lawfully admitted by the masters of the art. The said Justinian likewise saith, that those of our profession were in such estimation that their wives and families were maintained in all liberty and exempted from all public charges, subsidies, tributes, imposts, watching, warding, riding in hosts, or inquests, and all other such common charges, which laws are all yet observed in France, Italy, and divers other civil parts. Would to God it were so in this isle, so God would be glorified, his highness' subjects well served, and honest men relieved of great burden; as no doubt the best disposed do think. And so I end this chapter of the antiquity and excellency of the divine art of surgery.

Chapter II

Of operations and instruments of surgery

INTERLOCUTORS: PETER LOWE, DOCTOR OF SURGERY,
AND JOHN LOWE, HIS SON

PE. You might have perceived by my former discourse touching the original of surgery and the excellency thereof, the great desire I have to profit you therein and to give good example to all those who would profess the same. In consideration whereof, I am determined to confer with you in that matter, seeing leisure doth permit me, as also because I am mindful to cause you to remain in Paris for your further instruction, and passing of the degrees there accustomed in the said art, for the which I will in these three books following, as also in every general chapter ensuing, set down so briefly as I can, the form and method that the doctors of surgery in Paris useth in their first examination tentative, where the provost of the said college and six other masters that he will choose, will examine you exactly upon the whole grounds of surgery, according to the which form I will begin and demand of you in few words the whole principal points of surgery: but according to Cicero, seeing all doctrine whatsoever which is grounded upon reason should begin at the definition, to the end we may the better understand that whereof we entreat, first then will I ask of you what is surgery?

JOHN. It is a science or art, that showeth the manner how to work on man's body, exercising all manual operations necessary to heal men, inasmuch as is possible by using of most expedient medicines. It is an old Greek word composed of the word *Cheir* which signifieth hand, and *Ergon* which signifieth operation. Yet no operation manual is comprehended under surgery, but such as is practised on the body of man for healing of diseases.

PE. Why say you art or science?

JOHN. Because it is divided into theory and practice as saith Hieronymus Mantuo.

PE. What is surgery theory?

JOHN. It is that part which teacheth us by rules only the demonstrations, which we may know without using any work of the hand, and therefore we call it science.

PE. What is practice?

JOHN. It is that part which consisteth in operation of the hand, according to the precepts in healing infirmities, as aposthumes against nature, biles, wounds, fractures, bones that be out of their natural place, with divers other operations belonging to the work of the hand, as you shall hear in the first book.

PE. Ere you go further, let us know what is the subject of this art.

JOHN. Man's body, which as Abdales the Saracen saith, the most divine and admirable thing in the world.

PE. Seeing the subject is so excellent, it is necessary that the surgeon be learned and wise, as well for the preservation of sickness as recovery of health.

JOHN. It should be so.

PE. How ought the surgeon to learn his art?

JOHN. Aristotle, the prince of philosophers, counselleth us to begin at general things, thereafter to proceed to things more particular, from easy and facile things, to obscure and difficile, as is observed in all other sciences.

PE. How many operations useth the surgeon most commonly?

JOHN. Five.

PE. Which be they?

JOHN. The first, is to take away that which is hurtful and superfluous, as to take away tumours against nature, lumps, cankers, warts, and such like; to draw the water out of the hydropics; to take away a sixth finger or toe; to drain forth a child being dead, out of the mother's womb; to cut a leg being gangrened or mortified, and such like. Secondly, to help and add to nature that which it wanteth, as to put an artificial ear, nose, or eye, a hand or leg, a platen in the roof of

8—The illustrations opposite are from the many woodcuts used to illustrate Peter Lowe, *The Whole Art of Chirurgery*, the second, 1612, edition. They are included to show the nature of the surgical instruments of the day, and they indicate the graphic means employed by Lowe in his effort to improve the quality of surgery. The book contains many similar drawings of surgical instruments, anatomy, methods of sewing up wounds, and artificial devices—legs, trusses, and the like. The chart of the veins to be opened for bleeding suggests the state of Lowe's knowledge of anatomy and the emphasis placed on that panacea which was customarily employed until the nineteenth century. The woodcuts show the practical character of the book and the influence of practice rather than theory upon the progress of surgery.

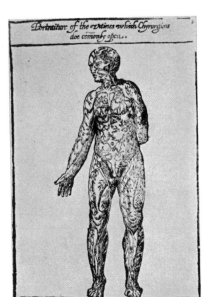

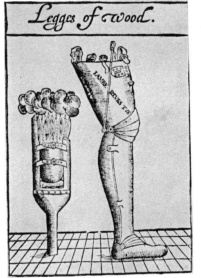

Legges of Wood.

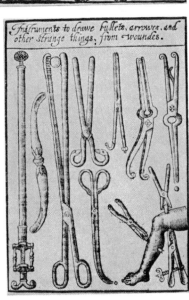

Instruments to drawe bullets, arrowes, and other strange things, from woundes.

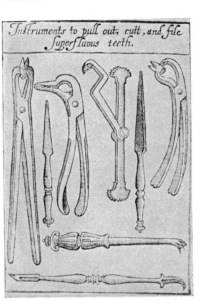

Instruments to pull out, cutt, and file superfluous teeth.

the mouth, which is needful to those who by the Spanish sickness or like disease, have the roof of the mouth falling, as is set down in my treatise of the Spanish sickness. The third is to put in the natural place, that which is out of his place, as to put in guts, the cawle, or net that covereth the guts, called the epiplon or omentum, after they be fallen in the scrotum, inguen, or umbilic; to put bones in their own place, being out of joint. The fourth, to separate that which is contained, as apposthumes, opening a vein, scarifying, applying of host-leeches, ventolies, by cutting the ligament under the tongue, cutting two fingers grown together, by cutting the prepuce of the yard, by cutting the natural conduit of women being closed naturally together, or else by accident, as oft chanceth after wounds, ulcers, and such like. The fifth, to join that which is separated, as in healing broken bones, bones that be out of their place, healing of wounds, ulcers, fistulas, and such like.

PE. What method is to be observed of the surgeon in working those operations?

JOHN. First, to know the disease; next, to do the operation as soon as may be, surely and without false promises or deceits to heal things that cannot be healed: for there are some, who being void of knowledge or skill, promise for lucre's sake, to heal infirmities, being ignorant both of the diseases and the remedies thereof. These faults be often committed of some, who usurping the name of surgeon, being unworthy thereof, have scarce the skill to cut a beard, which properly pertaineth to their trade.

PE. It seemeth by your words that there are some infirmities pertaining to our art which are incurable.

JOHN. There be divers, like as cancer occult, leprosy, elephantic particular: also when the diseased refuse the remedy proper for the cure thereof, as to cut a member being mortified, to make incision of the hydropic: and also when by the curing of the malady, there ensueth a greater disease, like as to stay altogether suddenly the hemorrhoids which have long run, or any other natural evacuation voluntary: (I saw in Paris a woman that had a flux of blood which flowed quarterly, sometime monthly, the which being stopped, she died immediately thereafter) to cut the varice in the leg, or elsewhere, because the humour taketh the course oftentimes to some principal part, which is cause of death, also in healing the biles which come in the legs or arms, called *malum mortuum*.

PE. What remedies then are most expedient to be used in those diseases?

JOHN. Remedies palliative and preservative to let the evil that it increase not, as we shall intreat of each of them in their several places.

PE. To do all those operations, what qualities are required of the surgeon?

JOHN. There are divers, and first of all as Celsus saith, that he be learned, chiefly in those things that appertain to his art, that he be of a reasonable age, and have a good hand, as perfect in the left as in the right, that he be ingenious, subtle, wise, and tremble not in doing his operations, that he have a good eye, and good experience in his art before he begin to practise the same, also that he have seen and observed of a long time of learned surgeons, that he be well mannered, affable, hardy in things certain, fearful in things doubtful and dangerous, discreet in judging of sickness, chaste, sober, pitiful, that he take his reward according to his cure and ability of the patient, not regarding avarice.

PE. What conditions ought the patient to have?

JOHN. Divers also, and first he must have a good opinion of the surgeon, that he have a good hope to be cured of him, to be obedient to his counsels, for that availeth much in healing of maladies, that he endure patiently that which is done for the recovery of his health.

PE. Which are the instruments that the surgeon ought to use in his operations?

JOHN. They are of two sorts, for some are common, others are proper; and the instruments and remedies common be also of two sorts, for some be medicinals, some be ferramentals.

PE. Why do you call them common?

JOHN. Because they serve indifferently to divers parts, and may be used in all parts of the body.

PE. Which are the medicinals?

JOHN. They consist in ordaining good regiment in things natural, unnatural, and against nature, in letting of blood, also in applying plasters, cataplasms, liniments, powders, unguents, and such like.

PE. Which be the instrumentals ferramentals?

JOHN. Some are to cut as razors, some to burn as cauters actuals, some to draw away, as tenals incisives, pincets, tirballs, some are to sound,

as to sound a wound, the stone in the bladder, and such like: some are
to sew wounds and knit veins and arteries, as needles.

PE. Which are the proper instruments?

JOHN. Those which serve to one part only, as in the head a trepan,
with sundry other capitals: in the eye an instrument called *speculum
oculi*, a needle proper to abate the cataract: in the ear a squirt for
deafness, or to draw forth anything inclosed in the ear: some in the
mouth as *speculum oris*, or *dilatorium* for convulsion: others are proper
for the pleurisy, others for the hydropsy: some to draw the stone,
which are made of divers fashions: some are proper for women, as
speculum matricis, sundry are proper for the birth, as you shall hear in
my treatise of the sickness of women: some are for the fundament, as
speculum ani: some for broken bones, and such as be out of their place,
as machines, laks, glossocomes, as is set down by Oribasius in his
book called *Antidotarium*.

PE. Which of those remedies are most necessary to be had always with
him?

JOHN. Arnoldus de Villa Nova counselleth always to have six to help
in necessity for things that are common: the first as astringent or
retentive, to stay a bleeding or fluxion that cometh in any part:
the second is basilicon, to make matter in a wound or an aposthume:
the third, some cleaning salve, as *apostulorum* or *diapeo*: the fourth,
is to fill up a wound or bile with flesh that is hollow, like as *unguentum
aureum*: the fifth, is *cerat galen*, or *rosat mesues*, proper to appease a
great dolour or heat which oft chanceth: the sixth, is called *desic-
cativum rubeum*, or such like, to dry and cicatrice the skin.

PE. How many kinds of ferraments ought the surgeon commonly to
carry with him?

JOHN. Divers, as a pair of shears, a razor, pincets, a lancet, a sound, a
tirball, a needle, and a cannon for needles.

PE. How many things are to be observed by the surgeon before he undertake any operation?

JOHN. According to Haly Abbas, there are five; the first, to know well
the temperament of the patient; the second, he must know the sickness and nature thereof: the third, whether it be curable or not: the
fourth, remedies proper and meet for the disease: the fifth, the right
way to apply such remedies as be needful: of all those he ought to

give good reasons and authority, of such famous men as have written of this science.

PE. In how many things consisteth chiefly the contemplation of surgery?

JOHN. In three things, according to Fuchius.

PE. Which are they?

JOHN. The first are those things that concur to the making and constitution of our body and therefore are called things natural. The second are those things which conserve the body from sickness and, being rightly used, nourish the same; our ancients call them things unnatural, because if they be immoderately and ill used, they be altogether contrary to our bodies. The third are those things indeed which are contrary to our bodies and therefore are called things contrary to nature, as Galen writeth.

PE. Tell me something more particularly of those contemplations of surgery.

JOHN. I am content, if your leisure permit.

PE. Then we will in the next chapter, proceed to natural things.

Chapter III

Of natural things in general

JOHN. May it please you to prosecute the discourse of natural things, seeing we have already entreated of surgery in general, of the operations and instruments surgicals.

PE. I like very well of this method, then tell me how many natural, things afe reckoned by the surgeon?

JOHN. Seven; the first is called elements. The second is temperament or complexion. The third, humours. The fourth, members. The fifth, virtues or faculties. The sixth, the works and effects of virtues. The seventh, spirits.

Chapter IV

Of elements

PE. Seeing, according to your former division of natural things, elements is the first, then tell me what is an element?

JOHN. It is the most simple part whereof any thing is made and in the destruction thereof is lastly resolved.

PE. How many elements are there?

JOHN. Two according to the contemplation of surgery, viz. simples or intelligibles, and composed or sensibles.

PE. Which are the intelligibles?

JOHN. Those which are known only by speculation and judgment, the which was first observed by Hippocrates.

PE. How many are they in number?

JOHN. They are four, according to Aristotle, to wit, the fire, the air, the water, and the earth, the which have divers qualities, hot, cold, moist, and dry.

PE. Are these four elements otherwise distinguished?

JOHN. They are distinguished also according to their lightness and heaviness.

PE. Which are the light?

JOHN. The fire and the air, and seeketh upward by reason of their lightness.

PE. What are the heavy?

JOHN. The water and the earth; for by reason of the heaviness they move downwards.

PE. Which are the sensible elements?

JOHN. They are similar or like parts of our body, as saith Galen.

PE. How many are they in number?

JOHN. Twelve, to wit, the bones, the cartilages, flesh, nerves, arteries, panicles, ligaments, tendons, membranes, the skin, the fat grease, the marrow: to the which similar parts, some add parts made of the superfluity of our body, as the hair and nails, which are also profitable.

. . . .

Chapter VI

Of humours

PE. Thou knowest that the most part of all sicknesses proceedeth and are entertained by some humour, and sometime by sundry humours together; therefore it is most necessary that the surgeon know per-

fectly the humours of our bodies, to the end he give the better order
for the curation of maladies: then tell me what is an humour?

JOHN. It is a thin substance into the which our nourishment first is
converted: or it is a natural juice wherewith the body is entertained,
nourished, or preserved.

PE. Whereof proceedeth the humours?

JOHN. Of the juice or chyle which is made in the stomach, of the aliment we are nourished with, changed by the natural heat of the
stomach and parts near thereto: thereafter brought by the veins
meseraikes to the liver, and maketh the four humours which differ in
nature and kind.

PE. How many humours are there?

JOHN. There are four, which represent the four elements, as well by
the substance as qualities, whereof every thing is made; Galen calleth
them the elements of the body.

PE. Which are the four humours?

JOHN. The blood, the phlegm, the choler, and melancholy.

PE. What is blood?

JOHN. It is an humour hot, aerious, of good consistence, red-coloured,
sweet-tasted, most necessary for nourishment of the parts of our body,
which are hot and humid, engendered in the liver, retained in the
veins, and is compared to the air, as saith Galen.

PE. What is phlegm?

JOHN. It is an humour cold and humid, thin in consistence, white-
coloured, when it is in the veins it nourisheth the parts cold and humid,
it lubrifieth the moving of the joints and is compared to water.

PE. What is choler?

JOHN. It is an humour hot and dry, of thin and subtle substance, black-
colored, bitter-tasted, proper to nourish the parts hot and dry, it is
compared to the fire.

PE. What is melancholy?

JOHN. It is humour cold and dry, thick in consistence, sour-tasted,
proper to nourish the parts that are cold and dry, and is compared to
the earth or winter.

PE. How many sorts of blood are there?

JOHN. Two, natural and unnatural.

PE. How many ways degenerateth the blood from the natural?

JOHN. Two ways; first by some alteration or transmutation of the substance, as when it becometh more gross and more subtle than it should be, or else by adustion, when the most subtle becometh in choler, and the most gross in melancholy.

Secondly, through unnatural proportion and evil mixture with the rest of the humours, and then it taketh divers names: as for example, if with the blood there be abundance of pituit, such is called phlegmatic, if the choler exceed the choleric, and so forth in the rest.

PE. How many sorts of phlegm are there?

JOHN. Two in like manner, natural and unnatural.

PE. How many kinds of pituit unnatural are there?

JOHN. According to Galen there are four sorts; the first called *vitrea*, because the humour is like unto melted glass, it is cold and proceedeth of gluttony and idleness, it provoketh to vomit, causeth great pain in the parts where it falleth, as on the teeth and intestines.

The second is called the sweet phlegm, because in spitting of it, it seemeth sweet, it provoketh the body to sleep.

The third is called bitter phlegm, because in spitting, it seemeth bitter, it is cold and maketh the body hungry.

The fourth is salt phlegm, it maketh the body dry and thirsty. There are some who make another kind called gypsy, because of the form and hardness it hath like lime called gypsum: it is often in the joints and is reckoned under *vitrea*.

PE. How many sorts of choler be there?

JOHN. Two in like manner, natural and unnatural.

PE. How many ways becometh the choler unnatural?

JOHN. Two ways; first, when it spilleth, rotteth, and is burnt, and then it is called choler adust by putrefaction. The other is made of the mixture of the other humours.

PE. Into how many kinds is it divided?

JOHN. In four, as saith Galen. The first, is called vitellin, because of the colour and thick substance: it is like the yolk of an egg, it is engendered in the liver and veins, when by the unnatural heat it both dissipate and consume.

The second is called verricuse, because this colour representeth a wart called *verruca*.

The third is called eruginus, because it is like the rust of brass or copper called *aerugo*.

The fourth is called the blue choler, because it is blue like azure. These three last humours, as saith Galen, are engendered in the stomach by vicious meats and evil juice, which cannot be digested and converted into good juice.

PE. How many sorts of melancholy are there?

JOHN. Two, natural and adust.

PE. How many kinds of unnatural or adust are there?

JOHN. Two, the first is that whereof cometh the humour melancholy, which is like the lee of blood when it is very hot and adust; or by some hot fever, that the blood doth putrify, as saith Avicen, and differeth from the natural melancholy as the dregs of wine burnt from the unburnt. Galen saith, that humour which is like the lees of wine, when it becometh more hot, it engendereth an humour against nature called *atra bilis*, of the which no beast can taste.

PE. Knowing these four humours and their generations, we must know in like manner, that in our bodies there is concoction, therefore tell me how many kinds of concoctions are there?

JOHN. There are three, as saith Johannes Bacchanellus. The first, is made in the stomach which converteth the meat we eat into the substance called chyle, in the which the four humours are not, but potentially. The second, is done in the liver, which maketh of the chyle the mass sanguinary, as saith Galen. The third, is made through all the body, of which are engendered the four humidities which the Arabians call humours nourishing, or elementaries, as saith Avicen. The first has no name and is thought to be the humour which droppeth from the mouth of the vein. The second is called ros, the which after it is drunken into the substance of the body, it maketh it humid, whereof it taketh the name. The third is called cambium. The fourth is called gluten and is the proper humidity of the similar parts.

PE. Have not these humours a certain time in the which they reign more than other in man's body?

JOHN. Yes indeed, for the blood reigneth in the morning from three hours until nine: in like manner in the springtime the choler from nine in the morning until three in the afternoon, as in summer: the phlegm from three in the afternoon until nine at night, as in autumn:

the melancholy, from nine at night until three in the morning, like as in winter, and this is the opinion of Hippocrates and Galen as touching humours. Such things being well understood, you may know what humour reigneth in the sick, and what time he shall be most grieved.

. . . .

The Ninth Book

Chapter I

Of bleeding and the things therein to be observed

Bleeding, which the Greeks call *Phlebotomia*, and the Latins *venaesectio*, is an incision of the vein artificially done, either to retain, divert, or evacuate blood and other humours contained within the body; for the which Avicen doth term it *universalem evacuationem*, and that for divers reasons; first, because it doth take away abundance of humours which often are contained in the veins above measure; next, it doth evacuate both good and evil humours, which are contained with the blood through the whole body above, and is a thing most necessary to be known by all chirurgeons, not only for the healing of maladies, but also for the conservation of our bodies from sickness, and sometime both for healing and preserving; for the which it is most necessary that the chirurgeon should know the number of the veins and their true situation, to the end he take not one for another: for sometimes the situation is variable, and in parts not accustomed, very difficile to be opened. The surgeon must also know the way to open them, with such things as should be observed before and after bleeding, with the effects following thereupon, which be divers, reckoned by the learned; of the which Saturn maketh some mention in these verses:

Exhilaret tristes, iratos placet, amantes,
Ne sint amantes. Phlebotomia facit.

which is to say, It maketh glad the pensive, and mitigates the wrathful, it impedeth lust, and such as are sick from being mad, especially by letting blood of the cephalic vein. There be divers particular commodities which do proceed of bleeding, saith Galen, and divers other learned writers:

first, it quickeneth the spirit and purgeth the brains, helpeth the memory and maketh the senses more subtle, clarifieth and sharpeneth the sight, voice, and wit, heateth the marrow, and wasteth such superfluous humours which make the marrow in the bones to be cold, it purifieth the whole senses, and removeth those fumes which ascend to the head and trouble the senses; it stayeth vomiting, and laxe, as saith Avicen, for it draweth the humour from the centre to the circumference; it profiteth much against immoderate waking, for it taketh away humours from the which divers sharp vapours ascend to the head and stayeth sleep: it removeth heaviness, dullness, and sluggishness of the body, helpeth difficulty of hearing, by taking away such humours as do provoke thick vapourous spirits, and send to the head and passages of the ears the same: it refresheth the pores and strength of the body, helpeth digestion, evacuateth chill blood, and is a natural evacuation of all the whole humours of our body, by the which infinite maladies are cured, those be the commodities for the most part which do ensue of bleeding and are set down by Saturn in these verses:

Lumina clarificat, sincerat Phlebotomia,
Mentes, et cerebrum, callidas facit esse medullas,
Viscera purgabit, stomachum, ventremque coercet,
Puros dat sensus, dat somnum, taedia tollit,
Auditus, vocem, vires, producit et auget.

Seeing the commodities of this remedy is so worthy and necessary for man's health, how justly may we blame those malicious ignorants that condemn the same, contrary to the opinion of the most learned and against all reason and experience; now it followeth to know the number of the veins which ordinarily are opened by the learned, for curing of maladies, which be 41 in number, viz. 17 in the head, 6 in the arms, which is three in each one, 6 in the hands, 4 in the fundament, which is two in each side; 8 in the legs, the which veins must be opened diversely, the great ones are opened long-ways, the little ones overthwart; that which is in the tip of the nose, is opened by pricking of it, not lifting the skin. As touching the particular opening of every vein, and the commodities following thereupon, you shall hear in the chapter following particularly.

. . . .

ACTS CONCERNING THE PUNISHMENT OF BEGGARS AND THE RELIEF OF THE POOR
1531—1598

The acts of 1598 to relieve poverty and to punish vagabonds codified and supplemented previous legislation on this subject. Extracts from earlier statutes have been included to demonstrate the evolution of England's national policy towards the problem of poverty. During the sixteenth century, voluntary charity and municipal relief proved inadequate to cope with the increasing economic distress. The Tudor solution, organized relief on a national basis supported by compulsory poor rates, was reached in the act of 1598. This statute, confirmed and slightly amended in 1601, was made permanent in 1640 and, with some modifications, governed the relief of the poor until 1834.

The primary principle, derived from an act of 1349, was the recognition of two types of poor. Distinction was made between the aged, impotent poor and the beggars and vagabonds. Of the latter those willing to work were to be given work, the unwilling were to be punished for their medieval sin of idleness. The problem confronting Tudor statesmen was to devise machinery for assisting those deserving aid or willing to work and for punishing the indolent. From 1531 to 1598 new principles and practices were added stage by stage.

The punishment of rogues was assigned to the justices of the peace in 1531, and a clear distinction between the deserving and undeserving was drawn. 'Out of this early recognition of a duty towards the impotent poor the whole system of poor relief was destined to grow.' Five years later, each parish was made legally responsible for the relief of its own poor, and a systematic collection of alms was prescribed. The voluntary giving of alms was put under moral compulsion in 1563, and a compulsory poor rate was assessed on all in 1572 when overseers of the poor were also added to the administration of relief. Means of providing work for the poor were developed further in 1576, and all these practices, and others, relating to vagabondage and poor relief, were incorporated in the act of 1598. The principle of a social obligation to the deserving poor had been consciously recognized in England before the death of Elizabeth.

STATUTES OF THE REALM
22 Henry VIII, A.D. 1531
Chapter XII

An Act Concerning Punishment of Beggars and Vagabonds.

I. INCREASE OF BEGGARS AND VAGABONDS, AND THE EVILS RESULTING THEREFROM;

WHERE in all places throughout this realm of England, vagabonds and beggars have of long time increased and daily do increase in great and excessive numbers by the occasion of idleness, mother and root of all vices, whereby hath insurged and sprung and daily insurgeth and springeth continual thefts, murders, and other heinous offences and great enormities to the high displeasure of God, the inquietation and damage of the king's people, and to the marvellous disturbance of the common weal of this realm. And whereas many and sundry good laws, straight statutes, and ordinances have been before this time devised and made as well by the king our sovereign lord as also by divers his most noble progenitors, kings of England, for the most necessary and due reformation of the premises, yet that notwithstanding the said numbers of vagabonds and beggars be not seen in any part to be diminished, but rather daily augmented and increased into great routs and companies as evidently and manifestly it doth and may appear. Be it therefore enacted by the king our sovereign lord and by the lords spiritual and temporal and the commons in this present parliament assembled and by authority of the same; that the justices of the peace of all and singular the shires of England within the limits of their commissions and all other justices of peace, mayors, sheriffs, bailiffs, and other officers of all and every city, borough, ridings, or franchises within the realm of England, within the limits of their authorities, shall from time to time as often as need shall require by their discretions divide themselves within the said shires, cities, boroughs, ridings, or franchises whereof they be justices of peace, mayors, sheriffs, bailiffs, or officers, and so being divided shall make diligent search and inquiry of all aged poor and impotent persons which live or of necessity be compelled to live by alms of the charity of the people that be or shall be hereafter abiding within every hundred, rape, wapentake, city, borough, parish, liberty, or franchises within the limits of their division, and after and upon such search made the said justices of peace, mayors, sheriffs, bailiffs, and other officers, that is to say, every of them within their limits of their authorities whereunto they be divided shall have power and authority by their discretions to enable to beg within such hundred, rape, wapentake, city, town, parish, or other limits as they shall appoint such of the said impotent persons which they shall find and think most convenient within the limits of their division to live of the charity and alms of the people, and to give in commandment to every such aged and impotent beggar (by them enabled) that none of them shall beg without the limits to them so apppointed, and shall also register and write the names of every such impotent beggar (by them appointed) in a bill or roll indented, the one part thereof to remain with themselves, and the other part by them to be certified before the justice of peace at the next sessions, after such search had, to be holden within the said shires, cities, towns, or franchises, there to remain under the keeping of the *custos rotulorum.* And that the said justices of peace, mayors, sheriffs, bailiffs, and other officers, that is to say, as they be divided, shall have power and authority to make such and so many seals to be engraved with the names of the hundreds, rapes, wapentakes, cities, boroughs, towns, or places within the which they shall appoint and limit every such impotent person to beg, and commit the said seals to the custody of such of them or to the custody of such others as they shall think convenient, and shall make and deliver to every such impotent person by them enabled to beg, a letter containing the name of such impotent person, and witnessing that he is authorized to beg and the limits within which he is appointed to beg, the same letter to be sealed with such of the said seals as shall be engraved with the name of the limit wherein such impotent person shall be appointed to beg in, and to be subscribed with the name of one of the said justices or officers abovesaid. And if any such impotent person so authorized to beg, do beg in any other place than within such limits that he shall be assigned unto, that then the justices of peace, mayors, sheriffs, bailiffs, constables, and all other the king's officers and ministers, shall by their discretions punish all such persons by imprisonment in the stocks by the space of two days and two nights, giving them but only bread and water, and after that, cause every such impotent person to be sworn to return again without delay to the hundred, rape, wapentake, city, borough, town, parish, or franchise where they be authorized to beg in.

II. BEGGARS WITHOUT LICENCES SHALL BE WHIPPED, OR SET IN THE
   STOCKS, ETC.

And it is enacted, that no such impotent person (as is above said) after the feast of the nativity of Saint John the Baptist next coming shall beg within any part of this realm, except he be authorized by writing under seal as is above said. And if any such impotent person after the said feast of Saint John be vagrant and go abegging having no such letter under seal as is above specified, that then the constables and all other inhabitants within such town or parish where such person shall beg shall cause every such beggar to be taken and brought to the next justice of peace or high constable of the hundred; and thereupon the said justice of peace or high constable shall command the said constables and other inhabitants of the town or parish which shall bring before him any such beggar, that they shall strip him naked from the middle upwards and cause him to be whipped within the town where he was taken or within some other town where the same justice or high constable shall appoint, if it shall seem to the discretion of the said justice of peace or high constable that it be convenient so to punish such beggar to him brought. And if not, then to command such beggar to be set in the stocks in the same town or parish where he was taken by the space of three days and three nights there to have only bread and water; and thereupon the said justice or high constable before whom such beggar shall be brought shall limit to him a place to beg in and give to him a letter under seal in form above remembered and swear him to depart and repair thither immediately after his punishment to him executed.

III. ALL PERSONS ABLE TO LABOUR WHO SHALL BEG, OR BE VAGRANTS, SHALL BE WHIPPED AND SENT TO THEIR PLACE OF BIRTH, ETC., THERE TO LABOUR, ETC.

And be it further enacted by the authority aforesaid that if any person or persons being whole and mighty in body and able to labour, at any time after the said feast of Saint John be taken in begging in any part of this realm, or if any man or woman being whole and mighty in body and able to labour having no landmaster nor using any lawful merchandise, craft, or mystery, whereby he might get his living after the same feast, be vagrant and can give none reckoning how he doth lawfully get his living, that then it shall be lawful to the constables and all other the king's officers, ministers, and subjects of every town, parish, and hamlet to arrest the said vagabonds and idle persons and them bring to any of the justices of peace of the same shire or liberty, or else to the high constable of the hundred, rape, or wapentake within which such persons shall be taken; and if he be taken within any city or town corporate, then to be brought before the mayor, sheriffs, or bailiffs of every such town corporate; and that every such justice of peace, high constable, mayors, sheriffs and bailiffs by their discretions shall cause every such idle person so to him brought to be had to the next market-town or other place, where the said justices of peace, high constable, mayors, bailiffs, or other officers shall think most convenient by his or their discretions, and there to be tied to the end of a cart naked and be beaten with whips throughout the same market-town or other place till his body be bloody by reason of such whipping; and after such punishment and whipping had, the person so punished by the discretion of the justice of peace, high constable, mayor, sheriffs, bailiffs, and other officers, before whom such person shall be brought, shall be enjoined upon his oath to return forthwith without delay in the next and straight way to the place where he was born, or where he last dwelled before the same punishment by the space of three years, and there put himself to labour, like as a true man ought to do; and after that done every such person so punished and ordered shall have a letter sealed with the seal of the hundred, rape, wapentake, city, borough, town, liberty, or franchise, wherein he shall be punished witnessing that he hath been punished according to this statute and containing the day and place of his punishment and the place whereunto he is limited to go and by what time he is limited to come thither, within which time he may lawfully beg by the way, showing the same letter, and otherwise not. And if he do not accomplish the order to him appointed by the said letter, then to be eftsoons taken and whipped and so as often as any default shall be found in him contrary to the order of this statute, in every place to be taken and whipped till he be repaired where he was born or where he last dwelled by the space of three years, and there put his body to labour for his living, or otherwise truly get his living without begging as long as he is able so to do; and if the person so whipped be an idle person and no common beggar, then after such whipping he shall be kept in the stocks till he hath found surety to go to service or else to labour after the discretion of the said justice of peace, mayors, sheriffs, bailiffs, high constables, or other such officers before whom any such idle person being no common beggar shall be brought, if by the discretion of the same justice of peace, mayor, sheriff, bailiff, high constable, or other such head officer, it be so thought convenient and that the party so punished be able to find surety or else to be ordered and sworn to repair to the place where he was born or where he last dwelled by the space of three years, and to have like letter and such further punishment if he eftsoons offend this statute as is above appointed to and for the common strong and able beggars, and so from time to time to be ordered and punished till he put his body to labour or otherwise get his living truly according to the law. And that the justices of the peace of every shire, riding, city, town and liberty shall have power and authority within the limits of their commissions to inquire of all mayors, bailiffs, constables, and other officers and persons that shall be negligent in executing of this act. And if the constables and inhabitants within any town or parish where any such impotent person or strong beggar doth happen to beg contrary to the form of this statute be negligent, and take not every such impotent and strong beggar that so shall beg against the form of this statute and order, and punish every such beggar as is above limited, that then the township or parish where such default shall be, shall lose and forfeit for every such impotent beggar that shall be suffered to beg within the said township or parish not being taken, ordered, and punished according to the form of this statute, 3s.4d., and for every strong beggar that shall happen to beg within any such township or parish not being taken and ordered as is above limited by this statute, 6s.8d., the one half of all which forfeitures to be to the king our sovereign lord and the other half to him that will sue for the same by any bill of information before the king's justices of his peace in their general sessions to be holden in the shire or within any liberty where such default shall happen. . .

IV. FOR PUNISHMENT OF SCHOLARS, SAILORS, FORTUNE-TELLERS, ETC., BEING BEGGARS OR VAGABONDS.

And be it enacted by the authority aforesaid that scholars of the universities of Oxford and Cambridge that go about begging, not being authorized under the seal of the said universities, by the commissary chancellor or vice-chancellor of the same; and all and singular shipmen pretending losses of their ships and goods of the sea going about the country begging without sufficient authority witnessing the same, shall be punished and ordered in manner and form as is above rehearsed of strong beggars; and that all proctors and pardoners going about in any country or countries without sufficient authority, and all other idle persons going about in any countries or abiding in any city, borough, or town, some of them using divers and subtle crafty and unlawful games and plays and some of them feigning themselves to have knowledge in physic, physiognomy, palmistry, or other crafty sciences whereby they bear the people in hand, that they can tell their destinies, deceases, and fortunes, and such other like fantastical imaginations to the great deceit of the king's subjects, shall upon examination had before two justices of peace whereof the one shall be of the quorum if he by provable witness be found guilty of any such deceits be punished by whipping at two days together after the manner before rehearsed. And if he eftsoons offend in the said offence or any like offence then to be scourged two days and the third day to be put upon the pillory from 9 of the clock till 11 before noon of the same day and to have one of his ears cut off; and if he offend the third time to have like punishment with whipping, standing on the pillory, and to have his other ear cut off, and that justices of peace have like authority in every liberty and franchise within their shires where they be justices of peace for the execution of this act in every part thereof, as they shall have without the liberty or franchise.

STATUTES OF THE REALM

27 Henry VIII, A.D. 1536.

Chapter XXV.

An Act for Punishment of Sturdy Vagabonds and Beggars.

RECITAL OF STATUTE 22 HEN. VIII. C. 12. ¶3. REQUIRING BEGGARS TO REPAIR TO THEIR TOWNS, ETC.

WHERE in an act made at Westminster in the 22nd year of the reign of our sovereign lord King Henry the eighth among other things it was ordained, established, and enacted, that every strong and valiant beggar and vagabond after he were whipped for his vagabondcy and idleness should depart from the place where he was whipped directly unto such town, hundred, and county where he was born, or where he had dwelled by the space of three years next before, there to continue and abide, and also that aged poor and impotent people should in likewise repair into every hundred within the said counties there to remain and continue according to the meaning and purport of the said act, upon pains limited in the same act more plainly appeareth. And forasmuch as it was not provided in the said act how and in what wise the said poor people and sturdy vagabonds should be ordered at their repair and at their coming into their countries, nor how the inhabitants of every hundred should be charged for the relief of the same poor people, nor yet for the setting and keeping in work and labour of the aforesaid valiant vagabonds at their said repair into every hundred of this realm, it is therefore now ordained and established and enacted by the king our sovereign lord, the lords spiritual and temporal and the commons in this present parliament assembled and by the authority of the same, that all and every the mayors, aldermen, sheriffs, bailiffs, constables, householders, and all other head officers and ministers of every city, shire, towns, and parishes of this realm, at the repair and coming thither of such poor creature or sturdy vagabond as is contained in the said act, shall most charitably receive the same and order the same in manner and form following, that is to say: that all the governors and ministers of every of the same cities, shires, towns, hundreds, wapentakes, lathes, rapes, ridings, tithings, hamlets, and parishes as well within liberties as without, shall not only succour, find, and keep all and every of the same poor people by way of voluntary and charitable alms, within every of the same cities, shires, towns, hundreds, wapentakes, lathes, rapes, tithings, hamlets, and parishes as well within liberties as without, to be succoured, relieved, and helped with such and convenient and necessary alms as shall be thought meet by their discretions, in such wise as none of them of very necessity shall be compelled to wander idly and go openly in begging to ask alms in any of the same cities, shires, towns, and parishes; but also to cause and to compel all and every the said sturdy vagabonds and valiant beggars to be set and kept to continual labour, in such wise as by their said labours they and every of them may get their own livings with the continual labour of their own hands; and every mayor, alderman, sheriff, bailiff, constable, and all other head officers and ministers of every county, city, town, and parish within this realm, or within any the king's dominions as well within liberties as without, and all other persons inhabitants within any of the same, shall endeavour themselves to order and direct the poor people, valiant beggars, and sturdy vagabonds in such wise as the effect of this present act shall be duly observed and put in due execution; upon pain that every parish shall lose and forfeit twenty shillings for every month in which it is omitted and undone; and that to be inquired of at every quarter sessions and to be duly presented and found by the verdict of 12 men.

. . . .

IV. OFFICERS AND CHURCHWARDENS SHALL GATHER ALMS FOR THE
MAINTENANCE OF IMPOTENT, AND EMPLOYMENT OF STURDY, BEGGARS.

ITEM, It is ordained and enacted by the authority aforesaid that all
and every the mayors, governors, and head officers of every city, borough,
and town corporate, and the churchwardens or two others of every
parish of this realm shall in good and charitable wise take such discreet
and convenient order, by gathering and procuring of such charitable and
voluntary alms of the good Christian people within the same with boxes
every Sunday, holy day, and other festival day, or otherwise among
themselves, in such good and discreet wise as the poor, impotent, lame,
feeble, sick, and diseased people, being not able to work, may be provided,
helped, and relieved, so that in no wise they nor none of them be suffered
to go openly in begging; and that such as be lusty or having their limbs
strong enough to labour may be daily kept in continual labour, whereby
every one of them may get their own substance and living with their
own hands; upon pain that all and every the mayors, governors, aldermen, head officers, and other the king's officers and ministers of every
of the said cities, boroughs, towns corporate, hundreds, parishes, and
hamlets shall lose and forfeit for every month that it is omitted and undone, the sum of twenty shillings.

. . . .

IX. THE CLERGY SHALL EXHORT PEOPLE TO ALMS FOR THE PURPOSES
OF THIS ACT.

ITEM, It is enacted by authority aforesaid that every preacher,
parson, vicar, curate of this realm, as well in all and every their sermons,
collations, biddings of the beads as in time of all confessions and at the
making of the wills or testaments of any persons at all times of the year,
shall exhort, move, stir, and provoke people to be liberal and bountifully
to extend their good and charitable alms and contributions from time to
time for and toward the comfort and relief of the said poor, impotent,
decrepit, indigent, and needy people, as for the setting and keeping to
continual work and labour of the foresaid rufflers, sturdy vagabonds, and
valiant beggars in every city, ward, town, hundred, and parish of this
realm as well within liberties as without.

. . . .

XV. THE PARSON SHALL KEEP YEARLY ACCOUNTS OF THE PRODUCE
AND APPLICATION OF ALMS, IN EVERY PARISH.

And it is ordered by the authority aforesaid that the parson, vicar, or parish priest or some other honest man of every parish of this realm, without taking or demanding anything for the same, shall keep a book of reckoning, and therein shall enter, write, and make mention from time to time in one place or part of the book as well of all and every such sums of money as shall be gathered by the charitable alms of the inhabitants of every of the same parishes, as to make mention in one other place of the same book how, upon whom, and in what wise any part of the same money shall be spent, and so from year to year from one year to another year he shall keep a new book, the book to be bought and paid for by the constable and churchwardens for the time being at the common collections, and always shall remain in the custody of two or three of them or of some other indifferent man by their consents and not with the parson, vicar, or parish priest.

STATUTES OF THE REALM

5 Elizabeth, A.D. 1563

Chapter III

An Act for the Relief of the Poor

. . . .

II. ON SUNDAY AFTER MIDSUMMER DAY YEARLY, THE HEAD OFFICERS OF
CITIES, ETC., AND THE PARSON AND CHURCHWARDENS OF PARISHES,
SHALL APPOINT COLLECTORS OF ALMS, TO GATHER AND DISTRIBUTE
THE SAME TO THE POOR, ETC.

AND further be it enacted by the authority aforesaid that yearly upon the Sunday next before the feast day of the nativity of St. John Baptist, commonly called Midsummer day, in every city, borough, and town corporate, the mayor, bailiffs, or other head officers for the time being, and in every other parish of the country the parson, vicar, or curate and churchwardens shall have written in a register or book to be provided by them as well the names of the inhabitants and householders within their city, borough, town corporate, or parish, as also the names of all such impotent, aged, and needy persons as be within their city, borough, town corporate, or parish which are not able to live of themselves nor with their own labor; and shall openly in the church and quietly after divine service call the said householders and inhabitants together, among whom the mayor or other head officers and two of the chief inhabitants in every such city, borough, and town corporate such as the mayor or other head officers shall think meet, and the parson, vicar, or curate and churchwardens in every other parish, shall elect, nominate, and appoint yearly two able persons or more, to be gatherers and collectors of the charitable alms of all the residue of the people inhabiting in the parish whereof they be chosen collectors for the relief of the poor. Which collectors, the Sunday next after their election, or the Sunday following if need require, when the people are at the church at divine service, shall gently ask and demand of every man and woman what they of their charity will be contented to give weekly towards the relief of the poor, and the same to be written in the said register or book. And the said gatherers, so being elected and chosen, shall justly gather and truly distribute the same charitable alms weekly by themselves or their assignees to the said poor and impotent persons of the said cities, boroughs, towns corporate, and parishes, without fraud or covin, favour or affection; and after such sort that the more impotent may have the more help, and such as can get part of their living to have the less, and by the discretion of the collectors to be put in such labour as they be fit and able to do, but none to go or sit openly a-begging, upon pain limited in the aforesaid statutes; and if the said mayors, bailiffs, head officers, parson, vicar, curate, and churchwarden, or any of them, fail in the doing and executing of the premises in form above declared, he or they so making default to forfeit for every such default forty shillings, to be employed to the use of the poor of that parish where he or they do inhabit, to be levied by the collectors of the same parish, by way of distress or otherwise as is appointed in this act for levying of like forfeitures.

. . . .

VII. PERSONS REFUSING TO CONTRIBUTE THEIR ALMS SHALL BE
   EXHORTED, AND IF THEY OBSTINATELY REFUSE SHALL BE BOUND BY
   THE BISHOP, ETC., TO APPEAR AT THE NEXT GENERAL SESSIONS OF
   JUSTICES, OR REFUSING TO BE SO BOUND, MAY BE IMPRISONED.

And be it further enacted by the authority aforesaid, that if any person
or persons being able to further this charitable work, do obstinately
and forwardly refuse reasonably to give towards the help and relief of
the poor, or do wilfully discourage others from so charitable a deed, the
parson, vicar, or curate and churchwardens of the parish wherein he
dwelleth shall then gently exhort him or them towards the relief of the
poor; and if he or they will not so be persuaded, then upon the certificate
of the parson, vicar, or curate of the parish to the bishop of the diocese
or ordinary of the place, chancellors or their commissaries or guardian
of the spiritualities, the same bishop, ordinary chancellors or commissaries, or guardian of the spiritualities shall send for him or them, to
induce or persuade him or them by charitable means and ways to extend
their charity to the poor, as in this act is well meant and intended; and
if the person or persons so sent for, of his or their forward or wilful mind
shall obstinately refuse to give weekly to the relief of the poor according
to his or their abilities, that then the bishop or ordinary of the diocese,
chancellors or their commissaries, shall have full power and authority
by virtue of this act, to bind the said obstinate and wilful persons so
refusing unto the queen by recognisance, in the sum of ten pounds, with
condition thereupon to be endorsed, that the said obstinate person so
refusing shall personally appear before the justices of peace of the county
where the same person shall then inhabit and dwell, if it be out of any
city, borough, or town corporate, and if it be within any city, borough,
or town corporate, then before the mayors, bailiffs, or other head officers
of every such city, borough, or town corporate, at the next general sessions to be holden before the said justices within the said county, or at
the next court to be holden before the said mayor, bailiffs, or other head
officers within every such city, borough, or town corporate, and that
the same obstinate person shall not from thence depart without licence,
of the said justices if he dwell out of any city, borough, or town corporate,
or of the said mayor, bailiffs, or other head officers if he dwell within
any such city, borough, or town corporate; and if any such obstinate
person shall refuse to be bound as is aforesaid, that then the said bishop,

ordinary, chancellor, or commissary, shall have authority by this act to commit the said obstinate person to prison, there to remain without bail or mainprise until the said obstinate person shall become bound as is aforesaid.

VIII. THE SESSIONS MAY ASSESS SUCH PERSONS TO RELIEF OF THE POOR;
     AND ON REFUSAL TO PAY THEY MAY BE IMPRISONED.

And further be it enacted by the authority aforesaid, that the said justices or such of them as shall be at the said sessions, or the mayor, bailiffs, or other head officers of every such city, borough, or town corporate, if the said obstinate persons do appear before them, shall charitably and gently persuade and move the said obstinate persons to extend his or their charity towards the relief of the poor of the parish where he or she inhabiteth and dwelleth; and if he or she shall obstinately and wilfully stand in the same, and will not be persuaded therein by the said justices, mayor, bailiffs, or other head officers, that then it shall and may be lawful to and for the said justices if it be out of any city, borough, or town corporate, and if it be within any city, borough, or town corporate, for the mayor, bailiffs, or other head officers of the same city, borough, or town corporate, with the churchwardens where the said obstinate person shall inhabit, or one of them, to assess, tax, and limit, upon every such obstinate person so refusing, according to their good discretions, what sum the said obstinate person shall pay weekly towards the relief of the poor within the said parish where he or she shall inhabit and dwell; and if the said person so assessed and taxed shall refuse to pay the sum that shall be so reasonably limited, taxed, and appointed, then the said justices of the peace or two of them whereof the one to be of the quorum, or the said mayor, bailiffs, or other head officers of every such city, borough, or town corporate, shall have full power and authority by virtue of this act, upon complaint and certificate to them by the collectors and churchwardens of the same parish where the said obstinate person shall dwell, to commit the said obstinate person and persons so refusing to pay to prison to the next gaol, there to remain without bail or mainprise till he or they have paid the said sum so appointed, taxed, and limited, together with the arrearages thereof, if any such shall fortune to be.

. . . .

XII. PARISHES IN CITIES SHALL CONTRIBUTE TO RELIEVE EACH OTHER.

And be it also enacted, that in all cities, boroughs, and towns corporate within which be divers parishes, the mayor and head officers of every the same cities, boroughs, and towns corporate, shall consider the state and ability of every such parish; and if the same mayor and officers shall understand by their discretion that the parishioners of any one of the said parishes is of such wealth and haviour, that they have no poverty amongst them, or be able sufficiently to relieve the poverty of the parish where they inhabit and dwell, and also to help and succour poverty elsewhere further, that then the said mayor and officers, with the assent of two of the most honest and substantial inhabitants of every such wealthy parish, shall consider the neediness of the inhabitants of the other parish or parishes within the same city or town corporate, and move, induce, and persuade the parishioners of the wealthier parish charitably to contribute somewhat according to their ability toward the weekly relief, succour, and consolation of the poor and needy within the other parish or parishes aforesaid where need is.

STATUTES OF THE REALM

14 Elizabeth, A.D. 1572

Chapter V

An Act for the Punishment of Vagabonds, and for Relief of the Poor and Impotent

WHERE all the parts of this realm of England and Wales be presently with rogues, vagabonds, and sturdy beggars exceedingly pestered, by means whereof daily happeneth in the same realm horrible murders, thefts, and other great outrages, to the high displeasure of almighty God, and to the great annoyance of the common weal; and for avoiding confusion by reason of numbers of laws concerning the premises standing in force together; be it enacted . . .

XXI. PERSONS REFUSING TO CONTRIBUTE, ETC., MAY BE COMMITTED BY TWO JUSTICES UNTIL COMPLIANCE.

And be it further enacted, that if any person or persons being able to further this charitable work will obstinately refuse to give towards the

help and relief of the said poor people, or do wilfully discourage others
from so charitable a deed, the said obstinate person or wilful discourager
shall presently be brought before two justices of the peace, whereof one
to be of the quorum, of the same county, to show the cause of his obstinate
refusal or wilful discouragement, and to abide such order therein as the
said justices shall appoint; if he refuse so to do, then to be committed to
the next gaol for the said shire, there to remain until he be contented
with their said order and do perform the same.

. . . .

XXV. PENALTIES APPLIED TO USE OF THE POOR.

Be it also enacted by the authority of this present parliament, that all
the forfeitures appointed or to grow by this statute (except the forfeitures
of justices of peace) shall wholly go and be employed to the use of the
poor aforesaid, and shall be levied by distress by the discretion of the
justices of the same county or two of them, or other head officers aforesaid: and that the justices of peace in all shires of England shall in their
quarter sessions next after Easter yearly examine the performance or
non-performance of this statute, according to the tenor thereof, as they
are bound to do the statute of labourers; and at their said sessions shall
yearly appoint new collectors and new overseers for the causes aforesaid,
and shall then also agree upon new views and searches of the said impotent people within every their limits for the year following, if need
shall be; and further at their said sessions shall take order by their good
discretions for all and every thing and things that may in any wise further
the intent of this act.

STATUTES OF THE REALM

18 Elizabeth, A.D. 1576

Chapter III

An Act for the Setting of the Poor on Work, and for the Avoiding of Idleness

. . . .

IV. FOR SETTING THE POOR, ETC., AT WORK, STORES OF WOOL, HEMP, FLAX, IRON, ETC., SHALL BE PROVIDED IN CITIES AND TOWNS, TO BE COMMITTED TO THE CARE OF PERSONS TO BE APPOINTED COLLECTORS AND GOVERNORS OF THE POOR, WHO SHALL EMPLOY THE POOR IN WORKING UP SUCH WOOL, ETC., AND PAY THEM FOR THE SAME; AND SHALL SELL THE WARES SO WROUGHT, TO KEEP UP THE STOCK OF MATERIALS.

ALSO to the intent youth may be accustomed and brought up in labour and work, and then not like to grow to be idle rogues, and to the intent also that such as be already grown up in idleness and so rogues at this present, may not have any just excuse in saying that they cannot get any service or work, and then without any favour or toleration worthy to be executed, and that other poor and needy persons being willing to work may be set on work: be it ordained and enacted by the authority aforesaid, that in every city and town corporate within this realm, a competent store and stock of wool, hemp, flax, iron, or other stuff by the appointment and order of the mayor, bailiffs, justices, or other head officers having rule in the said cities or towns corporate (of themselves and all others the inhabitants within their several authorities to be taxed, levied, and gathered) shall be provided. And that likewise in every other market town or other place within every county of this realm, where (to the justices of peace or greater part of them in their general sessions yearly next after Easter within every limit shall be thought most meet and convenient) a like competent store and stock of wool, hemp, flax, iron, or other stuff as the country is most meet for, by appointment and order of the said justices of peace or the greater part of them in their said general sessions (of all the inhabitants within their several authorities, to be taxed, levied, and gathered) shall be provided, the said stores and stocks in such cities and towns corporate, to be committed to the hands and

custody of such persons as shall by the mayor, bailiffs, justices, or other
head officers having authority in every such city or town corporate be
appointed, and in other towns and places to such persons as to the said
justices of peace or the greater part of them in their said general sessions
of the peace in their several counties shall be by them appointed; which
said persons so appointed as aforesaid, shall have power and authority
(by the advice of them who do appoint them) to dispose, order, and give
rules for the division and manner of working of the said stocks and stores,
who shall from henceforth be called the collectors and governors of the
poor, to the intent every such poor and needy person, old or young, able
to do any work, standing in necessity of relief, shall not for want of work
go abroad either begging or committing pilferings or other misdemeanour
living in idleness; which collectors and governors of the poor from time
to time (as cause requireth) shall and may of the same stock and store,
deliver to such poor and needy person a competent portion to be wrought
into yarn or other matter within such time and in such sort as in their
discretions shall be from time to time limited and prefixed, and the same
afterwards being wrought, to be from time to time delivered to the said
collectors and governors of the poor, for which they shall make payment
to them which work the same according to the desert of the work and
of new deliver more to be wrought; and so from time to time to deliver
stuff unwrought and receive the same again wrought as often as cause
shall require; which hemp, wool, flax, or other stuff wrought from time
to time shall be sold by the said collectors and governors of the poor
either at some market or other place, and at such time as they shall think
meet, and with the money coming of the sale to buy more stuff in such
wise as the stocks or store shall not be decayed in value; and if hereafter
any such person able to do any such work shall refuse to work or shall
go abroad begging or live idly, or taking such work, shall spoil or embezzle the same in such wise that after admonition given, the minister
and churchwardens of the parish and collectors and governors of the
poor, or the more part of them shall think the same person not meet
to have any more work delivered out of the same store and stock, that
then upon certificate thereof made under their hands and brought by
one of said collectors and governors of the poor to the hands of such
person or persons as shall in that county have the oversight and government of one of the houses of correction hereafter mentioned in this act,

in convenient apparel meet for such a body to wear, he, she, or they from such town, place, or parish shall be received into such house of correction, there to be straightly kept, as well in diet as in work, and also punished from time to time as to the said persons having the oversight and government of the said house of correction shall be appointed as hereafter in this act is declared; all which stocks and stores shall be provided and delivered to the hands of the said collectors and governors of the poor before the first day of November next coming and at all times hereafter as occasion shall serve; and that every person refusing to pay or not paying such sum of money towards the said stocks and stores, as upon them or any of them shall be by order aforesaid taxed, and at such time as by the same order shall be appointed, shall for every default forfeit double so much as he or they shall be so taxed unto.

V. HOUSES OF CORRECTION SHALL BE PROVIDED IN EACH COUNTY FOR
    PUNISHING AND EMPLOYING ROGUES AND UNSETTLED POOR, ETC.

And moreover be it ordained and enacted by the authority aforesaid, that within every county of this realm, one, two, or more abiding houses or places convenient in some market town or corporate town or other place or places, by purchase, lease, building, or otherwise by the appointment and order of the justices of peace or the more part of them in their said general sessions, (of the inhabitants within their several authorities to be taxed, levied, and gathered) shall be provided, and called the house or houses of correction, and also stock and store and the implements to be in like sort also provided for setting on work and punishing not only of those which by the collectors and governors of the poor for causes aforesaid to the said houses of correction shall be brought, but also of such as be or shall be inhabiting in no parish, or be or shall be taken as rogues, or once punished as rogues, and by reason of the uncertainty of their birth or of their dwelling by the space of three years, or for any other cause ought to be abiding and kept within the same country; which said house or houses of correction, with stocks, stores, and implements appointed for such houses of correction shall be provided in every county within one year next after this present session of parliament (if the same conveniently may be), and if in the said time the same cannot conveniently be, then within such time as to the justices of peace or the more part of them in their said general sessions of the peace in every county within their several jurisdictions shall be thought meet and convenient, so as it exceed not two years after taxation in such county, for that purpose made, or else the money levied to be repaid; and that every person refusing to pay or not paying such sum or money towards the making, obtaining, and furnishing of the said houses of correction, and buying of stocks and stores, and for the relief and sustentation of such persons as shall be appointed to the said houses of correction, upon them or any of them, shall be by order aforesaid taxed, and at such time as by the same order shall be appointed shall for every default forfeit double so much as he or they shall be so taxed unto.

VI. JUSTICES IN SESSION SHALL APPOINT OVERSEERS OF SUCH HOUSES OF CORRECTION, AND COLLECTORS OF RATES:

And be it also further enacted by the authority aforesaid, that the said justices of peace, or the more part of them, in their said general sessions in every county, shall and may appoint from time to time persons which shall be overseers of every such house of correction, which said persons shall be called the censors and wardens of the houses of correction, and shall have the rule, government, and order of such houses of correction, according to such orders as by the said justices of peace, or the more part of them, in their general sessions in every county shall be prescribed; and shall also by like authority appoint others for the gathering of such money as shall be taxed upon any person or persons within their several jurisdictions, towards the maintenance of the said houses of correction, which shall be called the collectors for the houses of correction; and if any person or persons refuse to be collector and governor of the poor or censor and warden or collector of or for any the houses of correction, that every person so refusing shall forfeit and lose the sum of five pounds.

STATUTES OF THE REALM

39 Elizabeth, A.D. 1598

Chapter III

An Act for the Relief of the Poor

CHURCHWARDENS AND FOUR OVERSEERS, TO BE APPOINTED BY JUSTICES OF PEACE YEARLY IN EASTER WEEK, SHALL EMPLOY CHILDREN AND PAUPERS, AND RAISE MONEY FOR STOCKS OF HEMP, ETC., AND FOR RELIEF OF IMPOTENT POOR, AND PUTTING CHILDREN APPRENTICE, ETC.

BE it enacted by the authority of this present parliament, that the church-wardens of every parish, and four substantial householders there being subsidy men, or for want of subsidy men four other substantial house-holders of the said parish, who shall be nominated yearly in Easter week, under the hand and seal of two or more justices of the peace in the same county, whereof one to be of the quorum, dwelling in or near the same parish, shall be called overseers of the poor of the same parish; and they or the greater part of them shall take order from time to time by and with the consent of two or more such justices of peace for setting to work of the children of all such whose parents shall not by the said persons be thought able to keep and maintain their children, and also all such persons married or unmarried as having no means to maintain them, use no ordinary and daily trade of life to get their living by; and also to raise weekly or otherwise (by taxation of every inhabitant and every occupier of lands in the said parish in such competent sum and sums of money as they shall think fit) a convenient stock of flax, hemp, wool, thread, iron, and other necessary ware and stuff to set the poor on work, and also com-petent sums of money for and towards the necessary relief of the lame, impotent, old, blind, and such other among them being poor and not able to work, and also for the putting out of such children to be appren-tices, to be gathered out of the same parish according to the ability of the said parish; and to do and execute all other things as well for the disposing of the said stock as otherwise concerning the premises, as to them shall seem convenient. Which said churchwardens and overseers so to be nominated, and such of them as shall not be let by sickness or other just excuse to be allowed by such two justices of peace or more, shall meet together at the least once every month in the church of the said parish, upon the Sunday in the afternoon after divine service, there to consider of some good course to be taken, and of some meet order to be set down in the premises; and shall within four days after the end of their year, and after other overseers nominated as aforesaid, make and yield up to such two justices of peace a true and perfect account of all sums of money by them received or rated and assessed and not received, and also of such stock as shall be in their hands or in the hands of any of the poor to work, and of all other things concerning their said office, and such sum or sums of money as shall be in their hands, shall pay and deliver over to the said churchwardens and overseers newly nominated and appointed as aforesaid: upon pain that every one of them absenting themselves without lawful cause as aforesaid from such monthly meeting for the purpose aforesaid, or being negligent in their office, or in the execution of the orders aforesaid, being made by and with the assent of the said justices of peace, to forfeit for every such default twenty shillings.

II. PARISHES MAY BE RATED IN AID OF OTHERS.

And be it also enacted, that if the said justices of peace do perceive that the inhabitants of any parish are not able to levy among themselves sufficient sums of money for the purposes aforesaid, that then the said justices shall and may tax, rate, and assess as aforesaid any other of other parishes, or out of any parish within the hundred where the said parish is, to pay such sum and sums of money to the churchwardens and overseers of the said poor parish for the said purposes, as the said justices shall think fit, according to the intent of this law; and if the said hundred shall not be thought to the said justices able and fit to relieve the said several parishes not able to provide for themselves as aforesaid, then the justices of peace at their general quarter sessions or the greater number of them, shall rate and assess as aforesaid, any other of other parishes, or out of any parish within the said county for the purposes aforesaid, as in their discretion shall seem fit.

III. RATES, ETC., MAY BE LEVIED BY DISTRESS.

And that it shall be lawful for the said churchwardens and overseers or any of them by warrant from any such two justices of peace to levy as well the said sums of money of every one that shall refuse to contribute according as they shall be assessed, by distress and sale of the offender's goods, as the sums of money or stock which shall be behind upon any account to be made as aforesaid, rendering to the party the overplus; and in defect of such distress, it shall be lawful for any such two justices of the peace to commit him to prison, there to remain without bail or mainprise till payment of the said sum or stock; and the said justices of peace or any one of them to send to the house of correction such as shall not employ themselves to work being appointed thereunto as aforesaid; and also any two such justices of peace to commit to prison every one of the said churchwardens and overseers which shall refuse to account, there to remain without bail or mainprise, till he have made a true account and satisfied and paid so much as upon the said account shall be remaining in his hands.

IV. CHURCHWARDENS, ETC., MAY BIND POOR CHILDREN APPRENTICE.

And be it further enacted, that it shall be lawful for the said churchwardens and overseers or the greater part of them, by the assent of any two justices of the peace, to bind any such children as aforesaid to be apprentices where they shall see convenient, till such man child shall come to the age of four-and-twenty years, and such woman child to the age of one-and-twenty years; the same to be as effectual to all purposes as if such child were of full age and by indenture of covenant bound him or herself.

V. HOUSES, ETC., MAY BE ERECTED ON WASTES FOR RESIDENCE OF POOR; OR COTTAGES APPROPRIATED TO INMATES.

And to the intent that necessary places of habitation may more conveniently be provided for such poor impotent people, be it enacted by the authority aforesaid, that it shall and may be lawful for the said churchwardens and overseers or the greater part of them, by the leave of the lord or lords of the manor whereof any waste or common within their parish is or shall be parcel, and upon agreement before with him or them made in writing under the hands and seals of the said lord or lords, or otherwise according to any order to be set down by the justices of peace of the said county at their general quarter sessions or the greater part of them, by like leave and agreement of the said lord or lords in writing under his or their hands and seals, to erect, build, and set up in fit and convenient places of habitation in such waste or common, at the general charges of the parish or otherwise of the hundred or county as aforesaid, to be taxed, rated, and gathered in manner before expressed, convenient houses of dwelling for the said impotent poor; and also to place inmates or more families than one in one cottage or house; one act made in the one-and-thirtieth year of her majesty's reign, entitled an act against the erecting and maintaining of cottages, or any thing therein contained to the contrary notwithstanding.

VI. APPEAL AGAINST RATES TO THE QUARTER SESSIONS.

Provided always, that if any person or persons shall find themselves grieved with any assessment or tax or other act done by the said church-wardens and other persons or by the said justices of peace, that then it shall be lawful for the justices of peace at their general quarter sessions or the greater number of them, to take such order therein as to them shall be thought convenient, and the same to conclude and bind all the said parties.

VII. PARENTS OR CHILDREN SHALL MAINTAIN THEIR RELATIONS;
    PENALTY, 20S. PER MONTH.

And be it further enacted, that the parents or children of every poor, old, blind, lame, and impotent person or other poor person not able to work, being of sufficient ability, shall at their own charges relieve and maintain every such poor person, in that manner and according to that rate, as by the justices of peace of that county where such sufficient persons dwell or the greater number of them at their general quarter sessions shall be assessed; upon pain that every one of them to forfeit 20s. for every month which they shall fail therein.

VIII. MAYORS, ETC., SHALL EXECUTE THIS ACT IN CORPORATIONS.

And be it further hereby enacted, that the mayors, bailiffs, or other head officers of every corporate town within this realm being justice or justices of peace, shall have the same authority by virtue of this act within the limits and precincts of their corporations, as well out of sessions as at their sessions, as is herein limited, prescribed, and appointed to any of the justices of peace in the county for all the uses and purposes in this act prescribed, and no other justice of peace to enter or meddle there.

IX. PARISHES IN TWO COUNTIES, ETC.

And be it also enacted, that if it shall happen any parish to extend itself into more counties than one, or part to lie within the liberties of any city or town corporate and part without, that then as well the justices of peace of every county, as also the head officers of such city or town corporate, shall deal and intermeddle only in so much of the said parish as lieth within their liberty and not any further.

X. ALL BEGGARS DECLARED ROGUES.

And be it further enacted by the authority aforesaid, that from the first day of November next ensuing the end of this session of parliament, no person or persons whatsoever, shall go wandering abroad and beg in any place whatsoever, by licence or without, upon pain to be esteemed, taken, and punished as a rogue: provided always, that this present act shall not extend to any poor people which shall ask relief of victuals only in the same parish where such poor people do dwell, so the same be in such time only and according to such order and direction as shall be made and appointed by the churchwardens and overseers of the poor of the same parish according to the true intent and meaning of this act.

XI. PENALTIES APPLIED TO USE OF THE POOR.

And further be it enacted by the authority aforesaid, that all penalties and forfeitures before mentioned in this act shall go and be employed to the use of the poor of the same parish, and towards a stock and habitation for them and other necessary uses and relief, as before in this act are mentioned and expressed, and shall be levied by the said churchwardens and overseers or one of them, by warrant from any two such justices of peace, by distress and sale as aforesaid; or in defect thereof, it shall be lawful for any two such justices of peace to commit the offender to prison, there to remain without bail or mainprise till the said forfeitures shall be satisfied and paid.

XII. RATES TO BE LEVIED IN EVERY PARISH.

And forasmuch as all begging is forbidden by this present act; be it further enacted by the authority aforesaid, that the justices of peace of every county or place corporate, or the more part of them in their general sessions to be holden next after the end of this session of parliament, or in default thereof at the quarter sessions to be holden about the feast of Easter next, shall rate every parish to such a weekly sum of money as they shall think convenient, so as no parish be rated above the sum of 6 pence nor under the sum of an halfpenny weekly to be paid, and so as the total sum of such taxation of the parishes in every county amount not above the rate of two pence for every parish in the said county; which sums so taxed shall be yearly assessed by the agreement of the parishoners within themselves, or, in default thereof, by the church-wardens and constables of the same parish or the more part of them, or in default of their agreement, by the order of such justice or justices of peace as shall dwell in the same parish, or (if none be there dwelling) in the parts next adjoining: and if any person shall refuse or neglect to pay any such portion of money so taxed, it shall be lawful for the said church-wardens and constables, or in their defaults for the justices of the peace, to levy the same by distress and sale of the goods of the party so refusing or neglecting, rendering to the party the overplus, and in default of such distress, it shall be lawful to any justice of that limit to commit such persons to prison, there to abide without bail or mainprise till he have paid the same.

XIII. SUCH RATES SHALL BE APPLIED TO PRISONERS IN THE KING'S BENCH AND MARSHALSEA, AND TO HOSPITALS, ALMS-HOUSES, ETC., TO BE COLLECTED BY CHURCHWARDENS, AND PAID TO HIGH CONSTABLE, AND BY HIM TO THE TREASURER OF THE JUSTICES, ETC.

And be it also enacted, that the said justices of the peace at their general quarter sessions to be held at the time of such taxation shall set down what competent sum of money shall be sent quarterly out of every county or place corporate for the relief of the poor prisoners of the king's bench and marshalsea, and also of such hospitals and alms-houses as shall be in the said county, and what sums of money shall be sent to every one of the said hospitals and alms-houses, so as there be sent out of every county yearly twenty shillings at the least to the prisoners of the king's bench and marshalsea; which sums ratably to be assessed upon every parish, the churchwardens of every parish shall truly collect and pay over to the high constable in whose division such parish shall be situate, from time to time quarterly, ten days before the end of every quarter; and every such constable at every such quarter sessions in such county, shall pay over the same to two such justices of the peace, or to one of them, as shall be by the more part of the justices of peace of the county elected to be treasurers of the said collection; which treasurers in every county so chosen shall continue but for the space of one whole year, and then give up their charge with a due account of their receipts and disbursements at their meeting in the quarter sessions to be holden after the feast of Easter in every year to such others as shall from year to year in form aforesaid successively be elected; which said treasurers or one of them shall pay over the same to the lord chief justice of England and knight marshal for the time being equally to be divided to the use aforesaid, taking their acquittance for the same, or in default of the said chief justice, to the next ancientest justice of the king's bench as aforesaid. And if any churchwarden or high constable or his executors or administrators shall fail to make payment in form above specified, then every churchwarden his executors or administrators so offending shall forfeit for every time the sum of ten shillings; and every high constable his executors or administrators shall forfeit for every time the sum of twenty shillings; the same forfeitures, together with the sums behind, to be levied by the said treasurer and treasurers by way of distress and sale of the goods as aforesaid in form aforesaid, and by them to be employed towards the charitable uses comprised in this act.

XIV. SURPLUS OF STOCK SHALL BE APPLIED TO HOSPITALS, ETC.

And be it further enacted, that all the surplusage of money which shall be remaining in the said stock of any county, shall by discretion of the more part of the justices of peace in their quarter sessions, be ordered distributed and bestowed for the relief of the poor hospitals of that county, and of those that shall sustain losses by fire, water, the sea, or other casualties, and to such other charitable purposes for the relief of the poor, as to the more part of the said justices of peace shall seem convenient.

XV. FINE ON TREASURER FOR NEGLECT, ETC.

And be it further enacted, that if any treasurer shall wilfully refuse to take upon him the said office of treasurership or refuse to distribute and give relief according to such form as shall be appointed by the more part of the said justices of peace, that then it shall be lawful for the justices of peace in their quarter sessions, or in their default for the justices of assize at the assizes to be held in the same county, to fine the same treasurer by their discretion; the same fine to be levied by sale of his goods, and to be persecuted by any two of the said justices of peace whom they shall authorize.

XVI. PROVISO FOR SOLDIERS AND MARINERS ASKING RELIEF.

Provided always nevertheless, that every soldier being discharged of his service, or otherwise lawfully licensed to pass into his country, and not having wherewith to relieve himself in his travel homewards, and every seafaring man landing from sea, not having wherewith to relieve himself in his travel homewards, having a testimonial under the hand of some one justice of peace of or near the place where he was landed or was discharged, setting down therein the place and time where and when he landed or was discharged, and the place of the party's dwelling place or birth unto which he is to pass, and a convenient time to be limited therein for his passage, shall and may, without incurring the danger or penalty of this act, in the usual ways directly to the place unto which he is directed to pass, and within the time in such his testimonial limited for his passage, ask and receive such relief as shall be necessary in and for his passage; this act or any thing therein contained to the contrary notwithstanding.

. . . .

XVIII. CONTINUANCE OF ACT.

Provided always, that his act shall endure no longer than to the end of the next session of parliament.

Chapter IV

An Act for Punishment of Rogues, Vagabonds, and Sturdy Beggars

FORMER ACTS AS TO VAGABONDS, ETC., REPEALED.

FOR the suppressing of rogues, vagabonds, and sturdy beggars, be it enacted by the authority of this present parliament, that from and after the feast of Easter next coming, all statutes heretofore made for the punishment of rogues, vagabonds, or sturdy beggars, or for the erection or maintenance of houses of correction, or touching the same, shall for so much as concerneth the same be utterly repealed: and that from and after the said feast of Easter, from time to time it shall and may be lawful to and for the justices of peace of any county or city in this realm or the dominions of Wales, assembled at any quarter sessions of the peace within the same county, city, borough, or town corporate, or the more part of them, to set down order, to erect and to cause to be erected one or more houses of correction within their several counties or cities; for the doing and performing whereof, and for the providing of stocks of money and all other things necessary for the same, and for raising and governing of the same, and for correction and punishment of offenders thither to be committed, such orders as the same justices or the more part of them shall from time to time take, reform, or set down in any their said quarter sessions in that behalf shall be of force and be duly performed and put in execution.

II. DEFINITION OF ROGUES, VAGABONDS, AND STURDY BEGGARS.

And be it also further enacted by the authority aforesaid, that all persons calling themselves scholars going about begging, all seafaring men pretending losses of their ships or goods on the sea going about the country begging, all idle persons going about in any country either begging or using any subtle craft or unlawful games and plays, or feigning themselves to have knowledge in physiognomy, palmistry, or other like crafty science, or pretending that they can tell destinies, fortunes, or such other like fantastical imaginations; all persons that be or utter themselves to be proctors, procurers, patent gatherers, or collectors for gaols, prisons, or hospitals; all fencers, bearwards, common players of interludes and minstrels wandering abroad (other than players of interludes belonging to any baron of this realm, or any other honourable personage of greater degree, to be authorized to play, under the hand and seal of arms of such baron or personage); all jugglers, tinkers, peddlars, and petty chapmen wandering abroad; all wandering persons and common labourers being persons able in body using loitering and refusing to work for such reasonable wages as is taxed or commonly given in such parts where such persons do or shall happen to dwell or abide, not having living otherwise to maintain themselves; all persons delivered out of gaols that beg for their fees, or otherwise do travel begging; all such persons as shall wander abroad begging, pretending losses by fire or otherwise; and all such persons not being felons wandering and pretending themselves to be Egyptians, or wandering in the habit, form, or attire of counterfeit Egyptians; shall be taken, adjudged, and deemed rogues, vagabonds, and sturdy beggars, and shall sustain such pain and punishment as by this act is in that behalf appointed.

III. ALL SUCH VAGABONDS, ETC., FOUND BEGGING, SHALL BE
WHIPPED AND PASSED TO THE PARISH OF THEIR BIRTH OR LAST
RESIDENCE, ETC., OR SENT TO THE HOUSE OF CORRECTION, ETC.

And be it enacted by the authority aforesaid, that every person which is by this present act declared to be a rogue, vagabond, or sturdy beggar, which shall be at any time after the said feast of Easter next coming taken begging, vagrant, wandering, or misordering themselves in any part of this realm or the dominion of Wales, shall upon their apprehension by the appointment of any justice of the peace, constable, headborough or tithingman of the same county, hundred, parish, or tithing where such

person shall be taken, the tithingman or headborough being assisted
therein with the advice of the minister and one other of that parish, be
stripped naked from the middle upwards and shall be openly whipped
until his or her body be bloody, and shall be forthwith sent from parish
to parish by the officers of every the same, the next straight way to the
parish where he was born, if the same may be known by the party's
confession or otherwise; and if the same be not known, then to the parish
where he or she last dwelt before the same punishment by the space of
one whole year, there to put him or herself to labour as a true subject
ought to do; or not being known where he or she was born or last dwelt,
then to the parish through which he or she last passed without punishment; after which whipping the same person shall have a testimonial
subscribed with the hand and sealed with the seal of the same justice of
the peace, constable, headborough, or tithingman and of the minister of
the same parish, or any two of them, testifying that the same person
hath been punished according to this act, and mentioning the day and
place of his or her punishment, and the place whereunto such person is
limited to go, and by what time the said person is limited to pass thither
at his peril. And if the said person through his or her default do not accomplish the order appointed by the said testimonial, then to be eftsoons
taken and whipped, and so as often as any default shall be found in him
or her contrary to the form of this statute, in every place to be whipped
till such person be repaired to the place limited; the substance of which
testimonial shall be registered by the minister of the parish in a book to
be provided for that purpose, upon pain to forfeit five shillings for every
default thereof. And the party so whipped and not known where he or
she was born or last dwelt by the space of a year, shall by the officers of
the said village where he or she so last past through without punishment,
be conveyed to the house of correction of the limit wherein the said
village standeth, or to the common gaol of that county or place, there to
remain and be employed in work until he or she shall be placed in some
service, and so to continue by the space of one whole year, or not being
able of body until he or she shall be placed, to remain in some alms-house
in the same county or place.

IV. DANGEROUS ROGUES MAY BE COMMITTED TO GAOL, AND
BANISHED OUT OF THE REALM, AND CONVEYED TO PLACES
ASSIGNED BY THE PRIVY COUNCIL; AND RETURNING SHALL BE FELONS
WITHOUT CLERGY.

Provided always and be it enacted, if any of the said rogues shall appear to be dangerous to the inferior sort of people where they shall be taken, or otherwise be such as will not be reformed of their roguish kind of life by the former provisions of this act, that in every such case it shall and may be lawful to the said justices of the limits where any such rogues shall be taken, or any two of them, whereof one to be of the quorum, to commit that rogue to the house of correction, or otherwise to the gaol of that county, there to remain until their next quarter sessions to be holden in that county, and then such of the same rogues so committed, as by the justices of the peace then and there present or the most part of them shall be thought fit not to be delivered, shall and may lawfully by the same justices or the most part of them be banished out of this realm and all other the dominions thereof, and at the charges of that country shall be conveyed unto such parts beyond the seas as shall be at any time hereafter for that purpose assigned by the privy council unto her majesty, her heirs or successors, or by any six or more of them, whereof the lord chancellor or lord keeper of the great seal, or the lord treasurer for the time being to be one, or otherwise be judged perpetually to the galleys of this realm, as by the same justices or the most part of them it shall be thought fit and expedient; and if any such rogue so banished as aforesaid shall return again into any part of this realm or dominion of Wales without lawful licence or warrant so to do, that in every such case such offence shall be felony, and the party offending therein suffer death as in case of felony; the said felony to be heard and determined in that county of this realm or Wales in which the offender shall be apprehended.

. . . .

VII. REGULATIONS FOR DISEASED POOR RESORTING TO BATH AND
BUXTON.

Be it further enacted by the authority aforesaid, that no diseased or impotent poor person shall at any time resort or repair from their dwelling places to the city of Bath or town of Buxton, or either of them, to the baths there for the ease of their griefs, unless such person do forbear to beg, and be licensed to pass thither by two justices of the peace of the county where such person doth or shall then dwell or remain, and provided for to travel with such relief for and towards his or her maintenance as shall be necessary for the same person for the times of such his or her travel and abode at the city of Bath and town of Buxton, or either of them, and return thence, and shall return home again, as shall be limited by the said licence; upon pain to be reputed, punished, and used as rogues, vagabonds, and sturdy beggars declared by this present act; and that the inhabitants of the same city of Bath and town of Buxton shall not in any wise be charged by this act with the finding or relieving of any such poor people.

. . . .

XIV. PROVISO FOR RELIEF OF SHIPWRECKED MARINERS.

Provided always nevertheless, that every seafaring man suffering shipwreck, not having wherewith to relieve himself in his travels homewards, but having a testimonial under the hand of some one justice of the peace of or near the place where he landed, setting down therein the place and time where and when he landed, and the place of the party's dwelling or birth unto which he is to pass, and a convenient time therein to be limited for his passage, shall and may without incurring the danger and penalty of this act, in the usual ways directly to the place unto which he is directed to pass, and within the time in such his testimonial limited for his passage, ask and receive such relief as shall be necessary in and for his passage.

. . . .

Chapter V

An Act for Erecting of Hospitals or Abiding and Working Houses for the Poor

35 ELIZ. C.7. ¶9, AS TO HOUSES OF CORRECTION, REQUIRED TO BE EXTENDED TO HOSPITALS;

WHEREAS at the last session of parliament provision was made, as well for maimed soldiers by collection in every parish, as for other poor, that it should be lawful for every person during twenty years next after the said parliament, by feoffment, will in writing, or other assurance, to give and bequeath in fee simple as well to the use of the poor as for the provision, sustentation, or maintenance of any house of correction or abiding houses, or of any stocks or stores, all or any part of his lands, tenements, or hereditaments; her most excellent majesty understanding and finding that the said good law hath not taken such effect as was intended, by reason that no person can erect or incorporate any hospital, houses of correction, or abiding places, but her majesty, or by her highness' special licence by letters patents under the great seal of England in that behalf to be obtained: her majesty, graciously affecting the good success of so good and charitable works, and that without often suit unto her majesty, and with as great ease and little charge as may be, is of her princely care and blessed disposition to and for the relief and comfort of maimed soldiers, mariners, and other poor and impotent people, pleased and contented that it be enacted by the authority of this present parliament, and be it enacted by the authority of this present parliament, that all and every person and persons seised of an estate in fee simple, their heirs, executors, or assigns at his or their wills and pleasures, shall have full power, strength, licence, and lawful authority, at any time during the space of twenty years next ensuing, by deed enrolled in the high court of chancery, to erect, found, and establish one or more hospitals, maisons de dieu, abiding places or houses of correction, at his or their will and pleasure, as well for the finding, sustentation, and relief of the maimed, poor, needy, or impotent people, as to set the poor to work, to have continuance for ever, and from time to time to place therein such head and members and such number of poor as to him his heirs and assigns shall seem convenient; and that the same hospitals or houses so founded, shall be incorporated and have perpetual successions for ever in fact, deed, and name, and of such head members and numbers of poor, needy, maimed, or impotent people as shall be appointed, assigned, limited, or named by the founder or founders, his or their heirs, executors, or assigns, by any such deed enrolled; and that such hospital, maison de dieu, abiding place or house of correction, and the persons therein placed, shall be incorporated, named, and called by such name as the said founder or founders, his heirs, executors, or assigns shall so limit, assign, and appoint; and the same hospital, maison de dieu, abiding place, or house of

correction so incorporated and named, shall be a body corporate and
politic, and shall by that name of incorporation have full power, authority,
and lawful capacity and ability to purchase, take, hold, receive, enjoy,
and have to them and to their successors for ever, as well goods and chattels
as manors, lands, tenements, and hereditaments being freehold of any person or persons whatsoever, so that the same exceed not the yearly value
of two hundred pounds above all charges and reprises to any one such
abiding house, hospital, maison de dieu, or house of correction; and so
as the same or any part thereof be not held of our sovereign lady the
queen, her heirs or successors, immediately in chief, or else of our said
sovereign lady the queen, or any other person by knight service, without
licence or writ of ad quod dampnum, or the statute of mortmain, or any
other statute or law to the contrary notwithstanding.

. . . .

THE COURT AND COUNTRY

Or a brief discourse dialogue-wise set down between a courtier and a country-man. Containing the manner and condition of their lives with many delectable and pithy sayings worthy observation. Also, necessary notes for a courtier. Written by N.B.Gent. Printed at London by G.Eld for John Wright, and are to be sold at his shop at the Sign of the Bible without Newgate, 1618.

NICHOLAS BRETON (1551–1626?), a professional writer in an age scornful of professionalism, was the son of a wealthy London citizen who died in 1559. His mother married about 1567 George Gascoigne, the poet and soldier, a courtier of expensive tastes who seems to have encouraged Breton to write. He was at Oxford for a time, though he took no degree, and later travelled on the continent. His literary career began in 1575 and lasted for fifty-one years. He wrote both verse and prose, and his prose output alone was as great as that of any Elizabethan. It shows considerable variety of form, but little innovation. Breton wrote devotional tracts, a favourite form of Elizabethan literature; a book of characters, following a fashion which was to be highly developed in the seventeenth century; a collection of familiar letters, *A Poste with a Packet of Mad Letters*, after a conventional organization; and dialogues such as the one printed here. He was deeply interested in religion, but in piety and the contemplation of God's mercy rather than controversy, and in country life. No flatterer, he dedicated his *Wonders worth the Hearing* in these words: ' Scholar I hold you none, but I know you understand English, and can conceive an honest meaning better than a brain full of more business.'

The text is taken from W.C.Hazlitt, *In-edited Tracts*, Roxburghe Library, 1868, and is not abridged.

To The Reader.

AMONG many passages that I have met with in the world it was my hap of late to light on a kind controversy between two kinsmen, a courtier and a countryman, who meeting together upon a time, fell to persuading one another from their courses of life; the courtier would fain have drawn the countryman to the court, and the countryman the courtier to the country. The reasons for their delights and love to their manner of lives I have set down as I found them; but whatsoever they alleged for their contentments, it seemed they were resolved upon their courses, for in the end they left where they begun every man to his own humour, and so brake off. Now what profit or pleasure may arise by the reading of them, I refer to their discretion that can best make use of them.

Matter of state is not here meddled with; scurrility here is none: no taxing of any person nor offence justly to any whosoever: but passages of
wit, without the malice of any evil mind. And in sum, matter of good
substance, and mirth enough to drive away a great deal of melancholy;
and so leaving it to your patience to read, and to your pleasure to esteem
of as you see cause: both to courtiers and countrymen that are kind and
honest men, I rest, to wish content in the course of a happy life, and
so remain

Your well wishing countryman,

N.B.

*To the Worshipful and Worthy Knight, the favourer of all good virtues and
studies, Sir Stephen Poll, of Blackmoor in Essex; and to his worthy Lady,
health, honour, and eternal happiness.*

Worthy Knight,

Being well acquainted with your true knowledge of the honour of the
court, and the pleasure of the country: your judicial observation in your
travels abroad, and your sweet retired life at home: finding my service
indebted to many of your undeserved bountiful favours, and willing, in
some fruits of my labour, to show the thankfulness of my love I have
adventured to present your patience with a short discourse, in the manner of a dialogue, between a courtier and a countryman, touching the
lives of either. What matter of worth is in it I will leave to your discretion
to consider of, with my bounden service to the honour of your command,
hoping that either here or in the country it will be a pretty passage of idle
time with some matter of mirth to remove melancholy. And so in prayer
for your health, and your good lady's, to whom, with yourself, dedicating
this short dialogue, I rest

Yours, humbly devoted to be commanded,

Nich. Breton.

The Courtier and the Country-man

COURTIER: Cousin, well met; I see you are still for the country, your
    habit, your countenance, your footing and your carriage do all plainly
    show you are no changeling, but every day alike, one, and the same.
COUNTRY-MAN: I am so indeed, and wish that you were so too: for
    then should you not be so great an eye-sore to your friends, nor such

an enemy to yourself: for, I fear the place you live in is more costly than profitable; where, for one that goes up the weather a number go down the wind, and perhaps the place not so truly full of delight as the passage through a meaner compass.

COURTIER: Oh cousin, you cannot but confess that blind men can judge no colours, and you that live plodding to purchase a pudding, cannot but distaste any meat that may compare with it, though in many degrees of goodness it exceed it: for, should I tell you truly what I know of it, you would soon alter your opinion to a point of better judgment. Oh, the gallant life of the court, where so many are the choices of contentment, as if on earth it were the paradise of the world: the majesty of the sovereign, the wisdom of the council, the honour of the lords, the beauty of the ladies, the care of the officers, the courtesy of the gentlemen, the divine service of the morning and evening, the witty, learned, noble, and pleasant discourses all day, the variety of wits, with the depth of judgments, the dainty fare, sweetly dressed and neatly served, the delicate wines and rare fruits, with excellent music and admirable voices, masks and plays, dancing and riding; diversity of games, delightful to the gamesters' purposes; and riddles, questions and answers; poems, histories, and strange inventions of wit, to startle the brain of a good understanding; rich apparel, precious jewels, fine proportions, and high spirits, princely coaches, stately horses, royal buildings, and rare architecture, sweet creatures and civil behaviour: and in the course of love such carriage of content as sets the spirit in the lap of pleasure, that if I should talk of the praise of it all day, I should be short of the worth of it at night.

COUNTRY.: And there withal you waked; or else you are like a musician that only plays upon one string: but, touch the bass, with the treble, the mean, with the counter tenor, and then see how the strings will agree together, and whether the voices do not rather fain than sing plain, for fear the ditty may disgrace the note, and so the music be not worth the hearing. But if all be as you say, yet take the evening with the morning, and all the week with the holiday, the sour with the sweet, and the cost with the pleasure, and tell me then if once in seven years, when your state is weakened and your land wasted, your woods untimbered, your pastures unstored, and your houses decayed: then tell me whether you find the proverb true, of the courtier young and old: though sometime a bell-wether may be fat, when many a better sheep cannot hit on so good a feeding. But since you speak so scornfully of the country life, if you were or could be so happy as to apprehend the true content in the course of it, you would shake the head and sigh from the heart to be so long from the knowledge of it, and never be at rest till you were gotten to it. Oh, the sweet of the country life, in which are so many and so true varieties of pleasures as keep the spirit ever waking, and the senses ever working for the full content of the whole creature, insomuch that if there may be a simile of heaven on earth, it is only in the precinct of the country passage, where both nature and reason behold and envy that satiety of pleasure that is not easily to be expressed. And to answer directly to some of your points of praise, let me tell you, though we see not our sovereign every day, yet we pray for him every hour; and holding ourselves unworthy of his presence, are glad when we may get a sight of his majesty.

Now, for councillors of state, we reverence their persons, and pray for their lives in their labours for our peace. And for your lords, we have landlords that agree best with our minds, whom using with due reverence, paying them their rent, and now and then for some small remembrances we can have friendly talk withal, and learn good lessons of them for many things to be looked into. And upon the bench at a quarter sessions, when they give a charge, hear them speak so wisely, that it would do one's heart good to hear them: and sometime in the holidays, when they keep good houses, make many a good meal's meat with them. And in the time of the year when the harvest is in, go a-hunting, and hawking, coursing and fishing with them: and sometime to continue good neighbourhood, meet and make matches for shooting and bowling with them, when we exercise the body in plain dealing, and not the brain in subtle device.

Now for your ladies, we have pretty wenches, that, though they be not proud, yet they think their penny good silver, and if they be fair it is natural, and having their mothers' wit they will do well enough for their fathers' understanding. And for your gentlemen, we have good yeomen that use more courtesy or at least kindness than curiosity, more friendship than compliments, and more truth than eloquence: and perhaps I may tell you, I think we have more ancient and true gentlemen that hold the plow in the field than you have in great places that wait with a trencher at a table; and I have heard my father say, that I believe to be true, that a true gentleman will be better known by his inside than his outside, for (as he said) a true gentleman will be like himself, sober, but not proud; liberal, and yet thrifty; wise, but not full of words; and better seen in the law, than be too busy with the laws; one that fears God; will be true to his king; and well knows how to live in the world, and whatsoever God sends, hath the grace to be content with it; loves his wife and his children, is careful for his family, is a friend to his neighbour, and no enemy to himself: and this (said my father) is indeed the true gentleman: and for his qualities, if he can speak well, and ride well, and shoot well, and bowl well, we desire no more of him. But for kissing of the hand, as if he were licking of his fingers, bending down the head, as if his neck were out of joint; or scratching by the foot, as if he were a corncutter; or leering aside, like a wench after her sweetheart; or winking with one eye, as though he were levying at a woodcock; and such apish tricks as came out of the land of Petito, where a monkey and a baboon make an urchin generation; and for telling of tales of the adventurous knight and the strange lady; and for writing in rhyme, or talking in prose, with more tongues than teeth in his head, and with that which he brought from beyond the seas, which he cannot be rid of at home, for swearing and braving, scoffing and stabbing, with such tricks of the devil's teaching, we allow none of that learning. Now, if you have any such where you live I know not; I hope with us there are none of them, but I am sure, if they come amongst us, we desire to be rid of them.

We have good husbands and honest widows; pure virgins and chaste bachelors; learned churchmen and civil townsmen; wholesome fare, full dishes, white bread, and hearty drink; clean platters and fair linen; good company, friendly talk, plain music, and a merry song: and so when God is praised and the people pleased, I think there is no course where a man may be better contented. Now, if it be true (but hope it is not) that I have heard, that in some such places as you live in, in the world, a great way hence beyond the sea, there be certain people that have brazen faces, serpents' tongues, and eagles' claws, that will intrude into companies, and persuade wickedness, and flatter follies; that catch hold of whatsoever they can light on for the service of lewdness, either money, lands, or leases, or apparel: and ever cramming, and yet ever craving. They are carriers of letters between lust and wantonness, tellers of old wives' tales, and singers of wenching ballads; swear and forswear, drink and gull, laugh and be fat, and for a little pleasure on earth go to the devil for ever. Now, these in the old time (but now-a-days I hope are out of use) were called parasites and panders, jesters or jugglers, much of the nature of gypsies, cunning as the devil to dive into a pocket, or to pick out the bottom of a purse; but I hope they are all dead, or at least you have few of them about you: if you have, I know not what use you can make of them, but I am sure we cannot away with them among us. I have heard, moreover, that you have among you certain eavesdroppers, that are tale carriers, that come among the roles of knaves. But for our houses in the country they are so far one from another, that if we catch any of them about us, we should carry him before the constable for a thief.

But now leaving to speak more of these things: for pleasures, believe it, we will put you down a world of steps; for, first of all we rise with the lark and go to bed with the lamb, so that we have the break of the day and the brightness of the sun to cheer our spirits in our going to our labours, which many of you bar yourselves of by making day of the night and night of the day, by sleeping after weariness upon the labour of wantonness, if not of wickedness, as they which work all day to bring the devil into hell at night, and labour all night for damnation in the morning: such I have heard of beyond sea, I pray God you have none about you: but for us in the country, I assure you we can abide no such doings. Now for the delight of our eyes, we have the May-painting of the earth, with divers flowers of dainty colours and delicate sweets: we have the berries, the cherries, the pease and the beans, the plums and the codlings, in the month of June: in July the pears and the apples, the wheat, the rye, the barley and the oats, the beauty of the wide fields, and the labours with delight and mirth, and merry cheer at the coming home of the harvest cart. We have, again, in our woods the birds singing: in the pastures the cow lowing, the ewe bleating, and the foal neighing, which with profit and pleasure makes us better music than an idle note and a worse ditty, though I highly do commend music, when it is in a right key. Again, we have young rabbits that in a sunny morning sit washing of their faces, while as I have heard beyond the seas there are certain old conies that in their beds sit painting of their faces: we have besides tumblers for our conies, and greyhounds for our courses, hounds for our chases, hawks of all kind for the field and the river and the wood: so that what can reason conceive that nature can desire but for the delight of both the country doth afford us?

Furthermore, at our meetings on the holidays between our lads and the wenches, such true mirth at honest meetings, such dancing on the green, in the market house, or about the may-pole, where the young folks smiling kiss at every turning, and the old folks checking with laughing at their children, when dancing for the garland, playing at stool-ball for a tansy and a banquet of curds and cream, with a cup of old nappy ale, matter of small charge, with a little reward of the piper, after casting of sheep's eyes, and faith and troth for a bargain, clapping of hands, are seals to the truth of hearts, when a pair of gloves and a handkerchief are as good as the best obligation, with a cap and a courtesy, hie ye home maids to milking, and so merrily goes the day away. Again we have hay in the barn, horses in the stable, oxen in the stall, sheep in the pen, hogs in the sty, corn in the garner, cheese in the loft, milk in the dairy, cream in the pot, butter in the dish, ale in the tub, and *aqua vitae* in the bottle, beef in the brine, brawn in the sauce, and bacon in the roof, herbs in the garden, and water at our doors, whole cloths to our backs, and some money in our coffers, and having all this, if we serve God withal, what in God's name can we desire to have more?

Now, for some of you, a man may take you many times in the nature of blind men, that you can scarcely see a penny in your purse, and your lands grown so light that you bear them all on your backs, and your houses so empty that in the cold of winter all the smoke goeth out at one chimney, when, if Brag were not a good dog, I know not how he would hold up his tail. Oh, the fine excuses of wit, or rather folly! Late business over night makes you keep your beds in the morning, when indeed it is for lack of meat to dinner, and perhaps no great banquet at supper, when a crust and an orange, a salad and a cup of sack makes a feast for a bravo: then after all, a stretch and a yawn, and a pipe of tobacco, wear boots for want of shoes, or else that the garters and the roses are at pawn. Now these are no courtiers, but hangers on upon those that sometimes in great places have an humour to fatten fleas.

Now for us in the country, we run no such courses but are content with that we have and keep somewhat for a rainy day: love neither to borrow nor lend but keep the stake still upright, spend as we may spare, and look to the main at the year's end: our meetings are for mirth and not mischief: and for quarrels we have none except the oil of the malt work up into the head and so distemper the brain that the tongue run out of order, when a fit of fisticuffs will soon make an end of all matters; so that we have pleasure with profit, mirth without madness, and love without dissembling, when the peace of conscience is an inward paradise. Now if you can show any better cards for the maintaining of your opinion, I pray you heartily let me hear it.

COURTIER: Oh, cousin, I am sorry to see your simplicity: what a deal of ado you have made about nothing! But I see the proverb holds true in you, he that lives always at home sees nothing but the same; and your education being but according to your disposition, somewhat of the meanest manner of good fashion, your wit rather being all in copy-hold than in *capite*, and your learning but to spell and put together, it were hard for you that never studied astronomy to speak of the nature of the stars; and therefore I can the better bear with your humour, because it is more natural than artificial, yet could I wish you would not so clownify your wit, as to bury your understanding all under a clod of earth. What! is man but as a beast, bred like a fore-horse, to go always right on and rather draw in a cart than trot in a better compass! Fie upon baseness, it is the badge of a beggar. No, let me tell you, if you were or could be acquainted with the life of a courtier, you would find such bewitching objects to the eyes and ravishing delights of the heart that you would hold the world as a wilderness to the palace of a prince and life but as a death that hath no taste of court comforts.

Oh, cousin, we have learning in such reverence, wisdom in such admiration, virtue in such honour, valour in such esteem, truth in such love, and love in so rare account, that there doth almost nothing pass in perfection that is not followed with great observation, where the favour of a prince makes a beggar a petty king, the countenance of a lord makes a clown a gentleman, and the look of a lady makes a groom a gay fellow. Oh, cousin, advancement and contentment are the fruits of court service, and the steps of hope to the state of honour: furthermore, for knowledge we have the due consideration of occurrence, the deciphering of characters, enditing of letters, hearing of orations, delivering of messages, congratulating of princes, and the form of ambassages, all which are such delights of the spirit as makes a shadow of that man that hath not a mind from the multitude to look into the nature of the spirit's honour.

Furthermore, we have in court officers of care, orders of discretion, eyes of brightness, ears of clearness, hearts of pureness, brains of wisdom, tongues of truth, minds of nobleness, and spirits of goodness, which though they be not in all, yet are they examples for all, and in the worthiest of all. Oh cousin, to hear a king or prince speak like a prophet, a queen like an angel, a councillor like an oracle, a lord like a councillor, a lady like a queen, a preacher like an apostle, and a courtier like a preacher: and then to note the majesty of the greatest, the reverence of the wisest, the honour of the worthiest, and the love of the best, to receive grace from the one, instruction from the other; favour from one, countenance from another; honour from one, and bounty from another: kindness from one, and comfort from another; where for the good [*sic*] all, love goeth through all, where exercises of wit are but trials of understanding, and the properties of speech are the proofs of judgment: where peace is the practice of power, justice the grace of wisdom, and mercy the glory of justice: where time is fitted to his use, and reason is the governor of nature, where privileges are protections for the unwilling offendant, and sanctuaries are the safety of the unhappily distressed: where the name of want hath no note, baseness no regard, wantonness no grace, nor wickedness entertainment, except the devil like an angel of light come unseen to the world: where the qualities of virtue are the grace of honour, and the breath of wisdom is the beauty of greatness: where art hath reward of labour, service the regard of duty, nature the effect of reason, and reason the respect of judgment: where idleness is hated, foolishness derided, wilfulness restrained, and wickedness banished: where wits refined, brains settled, bodies purged, and spirits purified

make a comfort of such creatures as come near unto heavenly
natures.

Believe me, cousin, there is no comparison between the court and
the country for the sweets of conceit in an understanding spirit which
can truly apprehend the true natures both of pleasures and profit.
Alas, let the cow low after her calf, and the ewe bleat after her lamb,
the ass bray, the owl sing, and the dog bark: what music is in this
medley? Let ignorance be an enemy to wit, and experience be the
mistress of fools, the stocks stand at the constable's door, and the gallows stand hard by the high way, what is all this to matter of worth?
To see lads lift up leaden heels, and wenches leer after their lubbers:
to see old folks play the fools to laugh at the birds of their own breed,
and the young colts whinny at their parting with their fillies, when
Madge must home to milking, and Simon must go serve the beasts:
What conceit is in all these courses but to trouble a good spirit with
spending time in idleness?

Oh, cousin, if thou wert once well entered into the life of a courtier,
thou wouldst never more be in love with the country, but use it as a
clean shirt, sometime for a refreshing, though it be far coarser for
wearing, and little cleaner than that which you put off. I could say
more that might easily persuade you to change your opinion and alter
your affection from the country to the court; but I hope this shall
suffice. If not, I pray you let me hear you speak to some purpose.

COUNTRY.: Say, quoth you! let me tell you, that all that you have said,
or I think you can say, doth, nor will work any more with my wit
to incline my humour to your will than a pill that lieth in the stomach
and more offends nature than purgeth humour: for, where there is
no corruption physic hath nothing to work upon, except by the
trouble of nature, to bring health into sickness. Do you think so
much of your strength as to remove a millstone with your little finger;
or are you so persuaded of your wit that with a word of your mouth
you can take away the strength of understanding? No such matter,
no haste but good: I pray you give me leave a little, and if I speak not
to your purpose, I will speak to mine own: and I will say as one Dante,
an Italian poet, once said in an obscure book of his, understand me
that can, I understand myself: and though my country book be written in a rough hand, yet I can read it and pick such matter out of it

as shall serve the turn for my instruction. What is here to do in persuading you know not what? To talk you care not how? Is this court eloquence? Is not the clownifying of wit the foolifying of understanding? Homespun cloth is not worth the wearing, water is a cold drink, and simpleness is but baseness, and a clown is but a rich beggar. Now truly, cousin, you are quite out: for, let me tell you that good words and good deeds are the best trials of good minds, and make the best passages among the best people: and so much for this matter.

Now to answer your proverbs, and as I can remember, most points of your discourses. First, let me tell you, that I hold it better to see something of mine own at home than travel so far that I see nothing of mine own abroad, for I have heard that rolling stones gather no moss. And for my education, if it hath been simple and my disposition not subtle, if I be not fashioned according to the world, I shall be the fitter for heaven: and for my wit, to deal truly with you, I had rather hold it in a copy of a good tenure than by the title of an idle brain to keep a fool's head in freehold. Now for my learning, I hold it better to spell and put together than to spoil and put asunder: but there are some that in their childhood are so long in their horn book, that do what they can, they will smell of the baby till they cannot see to read. Now we in the country begin and go forward with our reading in this manner, Christ's cross be my speed, and the Holy Ghost: for fear the devil should be in the letters of the alphabet, as he is too often when he teacheth odd fellows play tricks with their creditors, who instead of payments write IOU and so scoff many an honest man out of his goods.

And again, when he teacheth travellers that have taken a surfeit in the Low Countries to set down H and O to express the nature of their grief, and to jest out the time with B and R, or to bite men's good names with those letters to avoid actions of slander, and when they write you R, and they B, oh, fine knacks of more wit than honesty. But I hope there are none of these among you. But I have heard my father say that when he was young he saw many such in such places as you live in, but it was a great way hence beyond the salt water.

Now for astronomy, I think it be fallen from the height that it was in former time, for stars were wont to be in the heavens: now gallants hang them upon their heels, so bright in their spurs as if they were all young Phaethons that would ride Phœbus' horses, while the folly of pride should sit in the chair of ruin: but let them sit fast when they are up lest they break their necks in their falls.

Now for your nature and art, I think better of a natural art than an artificial nature. And for your fore-horse pace right on, I hope he is better than a resty jade that will not stir out of the stable or a kicking curtall that will set his rider beside the saddle; and better draw soundly in a cart than be lamed in a coach or be sick in a foot-cloth: and better a true trot than a fiddling amble. But let these humours pass.

Now for your bewitching objects, I doubt they will make abjects of subjects, and therefore I love no such devilish devices, when women's eyes will bewitch men's hearts and the breath of tongues will poison a man's wits. And for your ravishing delights it is a word that I well understand not, or at least, as I have heard, this ravishing is a word that signifieth robbing of wenches of the inner lining of their linen against their wills; and if it be so, it is a perilous delight that brings a man to the gallows, if not to the devil, for a little fit of pleasure: but if there be any better sense in it, I would be glad to understand it, though at this time I care not to be troubled with it.

Now for prince's palaces, they are too high buildings for our bricks; plain people are content with cottages and had rather pay tributes to their maintenance than have them too much in our view for blinding of our eyes with their golden brightness. Now for life and death, he that lives at quiet and will not be contented may change for the worse and repent it when he cannot help it. Oh cousin, I have heard my father say, that it is better to sit fast than to rise and fall, and a great wise man that knew the world to a hair would say that the mean was sure: better be in the middle room than either in the garret or the cellar: and another of an excellent world's wit that ran the ring with him in the walk of the world would say that honour was but ancient riches, and in high places, where frowns are deadly and favours are uncertain, there was more fear of the one than hope of the other: and a laborious week's wages well paid was better than a year's hope in paper: and therefore, he that would leave possessions for promises and assurances for hope were more full of wit than understanding and of conceit than judgment, for though there is no service to the

king, nor no fishing to the sea, yet there are so many suitors for rewards and so many beaters of the water that delays may be cold comforts of long hopes to the one, and the other angle all day and catch
a gudgeon at night: and therefore, though the world be like a well
with two buckets, that when one falleth, another riseth, yet the fall
is much swifter than the rising, and good reason, because the one goes
down empty and the other comes up laden. But to be plain, I have so
long been used to a quiet life that I would not leave it for a world.

Now for your notes of worth that you have set down in your court
commendations; I allow that all may be true, and they that thrive in
it may think well of it and hold it a kind of heaven upon earth: but
for myself, I remember certain notes that I read in a book of my
father's own writing that shall go with me to my grave; there were
not many but in my mind to good purpose: as first for greatness, my
mind to me a kingdom is: so that the quiet of the mind is a greater
matter than perhaps many great men possess. Then for wealth, godliness is great riches to him that is content with that he hath which
many great men sometime perhaps have less than meaner people.
Then for a good rule of life: fear God, and obey the king: which
perhaps some do not so well in the court as the country. Then for the
course of the law, love God above all and thy neighbour as thyself:
which if you do in the court as we do in the country, envy would
work no hatred, nor malice mischief: but love in all persons would
make a palace, a paradise, which in the best is more evident than in
the meanest apprehended: but God, whose love is the life of all, breed
such love in the lives of all that peace may ever live among all.

Now for learning, what your need is thereof I know not, but with
us, this is all we go to school for: to read common prayers at church
and set down common prices at markets; write a letter and make a
bond; set down the day of our births, our marriage day, and make
our wills when we are sick for the disposing of our goods when we
are dead: these are the chief matters that we meddle with, and we
find enough to trouble our heads withal; for if the fathers know their
own children, wives their own husbands from other men, maidens
keep their by-your-leaves from subtle bachelors; farmers know their
cattle by the heads, and shepherds know their sheep by the brand,
what more learning have we need of, but that experience will teach

us without book? We can learn to plough and harrow, sow and reap, plant and prune, thresh and fan, winnow and grind, brew and bake, and all without book; and these are our chief business in the country, except we be jurymen to hang a thief, or speak truth in a man's right, which conscience and experience will teach us with a little learning. Then what should we study for, except it were to talk with the man in the moon about the course of the stars? No, astronomy is too high a reach for our reason: we will rather sit under a shady tree in the sun to take the benefit of the cold air than lie and stare upon the stars to mark their walk in the heavens while we lose our wits in the clouds: and yet we reverence learning as well in the parson of our parish, as our schoolmaster, but chiefly, in our justices of peace, for under God and the king they bear great sway in the country. But for great learning, in great matters, and in great places, we leave it to great men. If we live within the compass of the law, serve God and obey our king, and as good subjects ought to do, in our duties and our prayers daily remember him, what need we more learning?

Now for wisdom, I heard our parson in our church read it in the holy book of God, that the wisdom of the world is but foolishness before God: and why then should a man seek to befool himself before God with more wit than is necessary for the knowledge of the world? The wise man must die as well as the fool, and when all are the sons of Adam we have a fair warning to be too busy with tasting of the tree of too much knowledge. I have read in the book of the best wisdom, that the fear of God is the beginning of wisdom, and surely, he that begins his lesson there may continue his learning the better and come to be a good scholar at last. Solomon, the wisest man that ever was, said that all was vanity and vexation of the spirit: and why then should a man vex his spirit with seeking to be as wise as a woodcock in beating his brains to get the possession of vanity? And yet I must confess, that lest vanity turn to villainy, it is good that the authority of wisdom have power to bridle the folly of self will. But for the great wisdom of councillors of state, judges of laws, governors of cities, generals of armies, or such great people in such great places, they go so far beyond our wits that we had rather be obedient to their wills than enter into the depth of their discretions and content ourselves with that wisdom which is most necessary for us, to love God above all and our neighbours as ourselves, to rise with the day rays, and go to bed without a candle, to eat when we are hungry, drink when we are thirsty, travel when we are lusty, and rest when we are weary: fear God, be true to the crown, keep the laws, pay scot and lot, breed no quarrels, do no wrongs, and labour all we may to have peace, both with God and man: speak truth and shame the devil: pitch and pay, say and hold, try and trust, believe no lies, tell no news: deceive not an enemy, nor abuse a friend, make much of a little and more as it may increase. These are the points of wisdom that we run the course of our card by.

Now for valour, it is seen best in the best quarrels, and Saint Paul said that he had fought the good fight to fight for the preservation of a state, the person of a king or prince, to keep my house from thieves, my children from dogs, and my family from famine, and my faith from fainting in the word of God, this hold we the good fight, and the true valour: not to stand upon puntos, not to endure a lie without death, challenge for a frown, and kill for a foul word, adventure all for nothing, or perhaps worse than nothing, lose lands, goods, life and soul and all in a murder or a bloody bargain, to please a punk, and to be counted a captain of the devil's army, or a gallant of the damned crew, except some few hours before his endwhile the worm of conscience bites him at the heart, a spark of grace enter into his soul, and make him at the gallows make a repentant rehearsal of a lewd life and leave a fair example at his death to all beholders, perhaps with these good words at his departing, all ye that here be, take example to be hanged by me.

Oh brave valour that makes many a sweeping eye, when my mother for my son and my sister for my brother, or my wife for my husband, or my father for my daughter, or mine uncle for mine aunt, sit and howl like dogs to see the works of the devil in the wicked of the world. Such kind of valour I have heard my father say that he hath marked in some places where he hath travelled, I know not where, a great way hence when he was young, where he found among a hellish company of accursed spirits, they were called valiant fellows, that durst say anything, do anything, or be anything, till they were worse than nothing: durst quarrel with any man, abuse any man, strike any man, kill any man, and care for no man, durst prate, lie, swear and forswear, scoff and swagger, drink and dice, drab and stab, durst be hanged and damned for a horrible fit of a frantic humour, and this was their valour. I pray God there be none such among you where you keep, I am sure there keep none such among us.

Now for truth, I hope there are more true hearts in the country than there are tongues in the city in many places, yea, and in greater places than I will speak of, but where they be, God bless them, and where they are not, God send them, and that is all that I say to them. But for ought I see there is so much falsehood in the world that I fear there is little truth on the earth: and in great places where protestations are without performances, and excuses are better than lies, lo here is either truth of love or love of truth? But a little, I think; I would there were more. But with us, truth is so beloved that a liar is held little better than a thief, and it is a lesson we learn our little children, speak truth, tell truth, take heed you lie not, the devil is the father of lies, and little better be his children; deal truly with all men, let your tongues and your hearts go together, Christ is truth, in his holy name be true, ever tell truth and shame the devil, be true to God in your belief and obedience to his word, be true to your king in the loyalty of your hearts, be true to your wives in the honesty of your bodies, and be true to your friends in performing your promises: this is the love we have to truth; if you have it so, it is a good blessing of God and makes a happy people.

And for love, if it be in the world, I think it is in the country, for where envy, pride, and malice, and jealousy make buzzes in men's brains, what love can be in their hearts, howsoever it slip from their tongues? No, no; our turtles ever fly together; our swans ever swim together, and our lovers live and die together. Now if such love be among you, it is worthy to be much made of; but if you like to-day and loath to-morrow, if you fawn to-day and frown to-morrow; if all your love be to laugh and lie down or to hope of gain or reward, that is none of our love. We love all goodness and only for goodness: first God, then ourselves, then our wives and children, then our family, and then our friends: and so hath love his course in our lives: and therefore if there be any observation in affection, I pray you let it be rather in the country than in any place where faith is not so fast but fancy can alter love upon a little humour of dislike.

Now for your favour, when one beggar grows rich by it, how many rich grow beggars through the hope of fortune: and therefore in my mind, better be lord over a little of a man's own than to follow a lord for the bare name of a gentleman, and better with a little to be counted a good man than with gaping after gudgeons to be thought I know not what. Truly, cousin, I think everything is best in his own nature: as one is bred, so let him be: for as a courtier cannot hold the plough but he will be soon seen to be no workman, so a country-man cannot court it, but he will show in somewhat from whence he comes.

And for a lady's look, I think we have wenches in the country that have as fair eyes as finer creatures, who when they list to look kindly will make many glad though few gay fellows. And for apparel, plain russet is our wearing, while pied coats among us we account players or fools, except they be better men than the best of our parish except our landlord.

Now for preferment and advancement, they be encouragements to some spirits that are born under the climbing climate, but for mine own part I love not to play the fly with a candle for fear of burning my wings, but will leave the ladder of honour to him that best knows how to climb and to sit fast when he is up. Now for your occurrences, what are they but news, sometimes true and sometimes false, which when they come to us they are commonly more costly than comfortable, and therefore we desire not to trouble ourselves? Now for deciphering of characters, I have heard my father say in the old time, that they were accounted little better than conjurations in which were written the names of devils that the college of hell used to conjure up in the world and belonged only to the study of sorcerers, witches, wizards, and such wicked wretches, as not caring for the plain word of God, go with scratches of the devil's claws into hell. But how true it is God knoweth: but that this is true, every man knoweth that it was a device of the devil at the first, to put into the head of a deceiving heart that having no true nor plain meaning in conscience, would write so, that no man should understand him but himself, or like himself, and only to hoodwink the world for looking into his wickedness. But what is the end of all wily beguiley? Seeking to deceive others, deceived himself most of all. Now letters of darkness devised by the devil for the followers of his designs in the courses of his deceit:

honest men in the country love to meddle with no such matters but so far as may be to God's glory and the good of a state, to find out the plots, and to prevent the mischief of a villainy, being done in God's holy name and by his grace. I hold it a fine quality to decipher a character, and lay open a knave. But for us in the country, we love no such brain-labours as may bring our wits into such a wood, that we know not how to get out of it. Now for enditing of letters: alas, what need we much ado about a little matter? If we can write, we commonly begin and end much after one manner: Trusting in God you are in good health, with all our friends: and so to the matter, either to borrow or to pay, or to know the price of your cattle, or for a merry meeting, or I thank you for my good cheer. And so with my hearty commendations, I commit you to God. From my house such a day. Your loving friend to his power. And then seal up the paper and write on the outside: To my loving cousin, neighbour, or friend, at his house in such a place, with speed, if the time require, and so no more ado. Except it be a love letter, and then a few idle words of,

Sweetheart, I commend me unto you, and have been as good as my promise, and have sent you a pair of gloves by Meg your brother's best beloved, and upon Friday (God willing) I will meet you at the market, and we will be merry and talk further of the matter, and if you be as I am, say and hold, I know my portion, and when yours is put to it we shall live the better. And so, keeping your handkerchief near my heart: till I see you, I rest

Yours during life in true love

W. T.

Now for your styles of honour and worship to this lord and that lady on the outside, and a deal of humility and ceremony on the inside, methinks it is a wearying of the mind before you come to the matter. And as I remember a great wise man that would dispatch many matters in little time, would thus ever read letters, in the beginning two words for the style, and other two at the end for the conclusion, so noting the treble above, and the bass beneath, he would soon in the midst find the substance of the music: and to tell truth, few words and plain and to the purpose, is better for our understanding than to go about with words to tell a long tale to little end.

Now if we cannot write, we have the clerk of the church, or the schoolmaster of the town to help us, who for our plain matters will serve our turns well enough, and therefore what need we trouble our heads with enditing of letters?

Now, for orations, they are fittest for scholars to allure an audience to attendance: but for us, we have more use of our hands to work for our livings than of our ears to hear the sound of a little breath. Yet I allow it among you in such places as you live in: but where truth is the best eloquence we make but two words to a bargain, and therefore for your long discourses we desire not to be wearied with them, but will leave them to you that have more use of them and have time to hearken to them.

Now for your messages, alas, cannot we give a cap and make a leg to our betters and deliver our minds in few words without we learn to look down as though we were seeking of a rabbit's nest, or that we had committed some such fault that we were ashamed to show our faces, or make a long congé as though we were making preparation to a galliard, when if a foot slip we may have a disgrace in the fall; and if a word be misplaced, it is half a marring to all the matter: and therefore for messages, our matters being not great, small instructions will serve our turns for the delivery of our minds.

Now for congratulating of princes, God bless them, they are too great men for us more than to pray for them; and their matters too high for our reason to reach after; it is enough for us to give a cake for a pudding, and a pint of wine for a pottle of beer: and when we kill hogs to send our children to our neighbours with these messages: My father and my mother have sent you a pudding and a chine, and desires you when you kill your hogs, you will send him as good again. Now for great folks, they have such great choice of presents, and of such great charge, and such great care in the delivery of them, that (Lord have mercy upon us) we in the country cannot tell what to say unto them, but, God bless them that have them and much good may they do them.

Now for ambassages and ambassadors, we know not what the word means and therefore little care to be troubled with the men; for when we hear of any man that comes from a strange country, we say, I pray God he comes for good, and then he is the better welcome.

Tush, talk to us of a basket or a basket-maker, and not of an ambassador nor ambassages; but make yourselves, that best know the meaning of them, the best use you can of them; for us, we care not to look after them, more than to pray for them, that as they do, or as they mean, so God bless them.

Now for your officers, their charge is so great that we desire not their places, for we hold a private quiet better than a public trouble: and a clean conscience worth a world of wealth. Now for your orders, perhaps your need of them is great where disorders may be grievous: for us in the country we have few, but in the churches for our seats, and at our meetings for our places, where, when master justice and the high constables are set, honest men like good fellows will sit together; except at a sessions or an assize we be called upon a jury, then as it pleaseth the clerk of the peace, set one afore another; and therefore for orders what need we trouble ourselves with other than we are used unto? I remember I have heard my father tell of a world of orders he had seen in divers places where he had travelled, where right good gentlemen, that had followed great lords and ladies had enough to do to study orders in their service: a trencher must not be laid nor a napkin folded out of order; a dish set down out of order, a capon carved, nor a rabbit unlaced out of order; a goose broken up, nor a pasty cut up out of order; a glass filled, nor a cup uncovered nor delivered out of order; you must not stand, speak, nor look out of order: which were such a business for us to go about that we should be all out of time ere we should get into any good order. But in that there is difference of places, and every one must have their due. It is meet for good manners to keep the rules of good orders. But how much more at rest are we in the country that are not troubled with these duties?

Now for your eyes of brightness, I fear you are not troubled with too many of them: late sitting up, long watching, and night business, as writings, readings, casting up of accounts, long watchings, and such like other business; besides gaming, playing at cards, tables and dice, or such sports as spend time, are all dangerous for weak sights and make a world of sore eyes. But as you said, some of the best sort are wiser in their actions and more temperate in their motions and therefore keep their sights in more perfection; which may be examples to others, if they have the grace to follow them. But for our eyes, if we do not hurt them with a strip of a twig in the wood, a fly in the air, or a mote in the sun, our eyes are as bright as crystal, so that we can see the least thing that may do us good; and if we can see the sun in the morning and the moon at night, see our cattle in our pastures, our sheep in the common, our corn in the fields, our houses in repair, and our money in our purses, our meat on our tables, and our wives with our children, and look up to heaven and give God thanks for all, we seek no better sight.

Now for the cleanness of your hands, I fear that now and then some of you have your hands so troubled with an itch that you must have them anointed with the oil of gold before you can fall to any good work: and some of you, that though your wits have good inventions, yet you cannot write without a golden pen, which indeed, best fits a fine hand. But for us in the country, when we have washed our hands, after no foul work nor handling any unwholesome thing, we need no little forks to make hay with our mouths to throw our meat into them.

Now for the pureness of your hearts; except kings, queens and princes, and such great persons, they make no comparison with country people, where yea and nay are our words of truth; faith and troth are our bonds of love, plain dealing, passages of honesty; and kind thanks continues good neighbourhood. A liar is hated, a scoffer scorned, a spendthrift derided, and a miser not beloved: a swaggerer imprisoned, a drunkard punished, and a juggler whipped, and a thief hanged, for our hearts will harbour no such guests. And for love, two eyes and one heart, two hands and one body, two lovers and one love ties a knot of such truth as nought but death can undo.

Now for brains of wisdom, I think he is wiser that keeps his own and spends no more than needs, than he that spends much in hope of a little and yet may hap lose that too at last. Now for tongues of truth, let me tell you, fair words make fools vain, and court holy-water will scarce wash a foul shirt clean, except it come from such a fountain as every man must not dip his finger in. But, cousin, when hearts and hands go together, words and deeds go together: these are the tongues that will not falter in their tales, but tell truth in the face of the wide world; and therefore excepting the best that may be examples to the rest, I think if truth be anywhere she is in the country.

Now for the nobleness of minds: it fitteth the persons in their places: but for us in the country, we had rather have old nobles in our purses, than a bare name of noble without nobles: the reason may be that we do not know the nature of nobleness so well as we do of nobles, and therefore we hear only so much of the cost of it, that we have no heart to look after it: but where it is truly we honour it, and say, God bless them that have it, and if they be worthy of it well may they keep it, and that is all I say to it.

Now to spirits of goodness, alas, there is not one in the world. Christ Jesus our Saviour said so, there is none good but God: and if there be any on the earth, I think a good belief and a good life doth best express the nature of it.

To conclude with virtue, in which you lay up all the treasures of life, I doubt not it is in the best, I would it were so in all with you, but be it where it pleaseth God to send it once, I verily believe it to be as truly in the country as in places of higher compass: and by your leave, let me tell you of a riddle of my father's own writing, touching that rare and precious jewel.

> There is a secret few do know,
> And doth in special places grow,
> A rich man's praise, a poor man's wealth,
> A weak man's strength, a sick man's health;
> A lady's beauty, a lord's bliss,
> A matchless jewel where it is:
> And makes where it is truly seen,
> A gracious king and glorious queen.

And this said he, is virtue, which though he understood in the court, yet he made use of it in the country. Now therefore good cousin, be content with your humour, and let me alone with mine; I think I have answered all your positions: and let me tell you, whatsoever you say, I verily believe that ere you die, I shall find you rather in the rule of peace in the country, than in the trial of patience in the court, except the heaven's highest grace, and under heaven our earth's highest honour, make you happier in their favours than the whole world else can make you. And now, what say you further unto me?

COURTIER: I say this to you, kind cousin, that your father's lessons have made you better learned than I looked for, but yet let me tell you, had you seen but one of our shows in our triumphs, heard one of our songs on our solemn days, and tasted one of our dishes in our solemn feasts, you would never look more on a May-game, listen more to a lousy ballad, nor ever be in love with beef and pudding.

COUNTRY.: Oh cousin, stay the bells, I think you are deceived, for it may be that at one of these shows, I might see the fruits of my labours and my poor neighbours flung away in gauds and feathers; and perhaps have a proud humour, wish to be as wise as they that were no wiser than they should be; and therefore I think, better tarry at home than travel abroad to no better purpose.

Now for songs, a plain ditty well expressed is better with us than a fine conceit, as feigned in the voice as the matter. Now for your dishes of meat, I will tell you, I heard my father once report it for a truth, that a great man who lived where you live sent him for a great dainty a porpoise pie or two cold: which taking very thankfully and causing the messenger to stay dinner with him, he cut one of them up and very nicely taking out a piece of it, gave it to my mother, which she no sooner had in her mouth, but it had like to have marred all with her stomach, but she quickly conveyed it all under board, which my father seeing, said, why, how now, wife? What? do you love no good meat? Yes (quoth she) but I pray you taste of it yourself: which he no sooner did, but he made as much haste out of his mouth with it as she did; then did the children likewise the same, and the servants being by, their master offered each one a piece of it, who no sooner tasted of it, but they did so spit and spatter as if they had been poisoned; then he gave a piece to his dog, which smelled to it and left it: by and by after came in a miller and his dog to whom my father in like manner offered a piece, but neither man nor dog would eat of it: whereupon my father heartily laughing, with thanks to his great lord for his kind token, sent one of them back again to him with this message, Commend me, I pray you, to my good lord, and tell him I heartily thank his honour, and tell him, if either myself or my wife or my children or my servants or my dog or the miller or his dog would have eaten of it, I would never have sent one bit back again to him of it: but it may be that it is more wholesome than toothsome, and he may make a better friend with it: so, paying the messenger for his pains, sent him away with his message, which was no sooner delivered, but his lord heartily laughed at it. This was one of your fine dishes. Another a great lady sent him, which was a little barrel of caviar which was no sooner opened and tasted but quickly made up again and was sent back with this message, Commend me to my good lady and thank her honour and tell her we have black soup enough already; but if it be any better thing, I beseech her ladyship to bestow it upon a better friend that can better tell how to use it. Now if such be your fine dishes, I pray you let me alone with my country fare. And now, what say you else unto me?

COURTIER: I say this, that nature is no botcher, and there is no washing of a black Moor, except it be from a little dirty sweat: the ox will wear no socks, howsoever his feet carry their favour: and Diogenes would be a dog, though Alexander would give him a kingdom: and therefore though you are my kinsman, I see it is more in name than in nature: thy breath smells all of garlic, and thy meat tastes all of mammaday pudding, which, breaking at both ends, the stuffing runs about the pot. And since I see thou art like a millstone that will not easily be stirred, I will leave thee to thy folly, till I find thee in a better humour, for I see the music of thy mind hangeth all upon the bass string. Farewell.

COUNTRY.: Nay, soft awhile, let me not be in your debt for an ill word or two: I see truth is no liar; all in the court are not courtiers, nor every man that hath wit is not truly wise; for then no man would spend breath to no purpose: an ox's foot may be sweeter than a cod's head, when socks may be but safeguards for bare toes in broken stockings: garlic hath been in more grace than tobacco, and is yet in the country with them that love meat better than smoke. Diogenes is dead, and Alexander is in his grave; and better be a mannish dog than a dogged man. And if your good will be to your good words, you are more like a stranger than a kinsman; and for my pudding, I believe it will prove better than a tobacco pipe. So, rather desirous to be a millstone, not to stir at every motion than a feather in a weathercock to turn with every gale of wind, I will pray for your better wit than you have shown in a self wild humour; and so. till I find you in more patience and less passion, I will leave you till we meet again, hoping that you will be as I am, and will be a friend to forget all ill humours and ready to requite all kindnesses.

COURTIER: So will I; and so, farewell.

Thus they parted for that time, but what fell out at their next meeting: as you like of this, you shall hear more hereafter.

Finis.

TOM TELL–TROATH
Or

A free discourse touching the manners of the time. Directed to his majesty by way of humble advertisement.

BOTH the author and the date of publication of the following tract, abridged from the version printed in the *Harleian Miscellany*, are unknown. Perhaps the original circulated in manuscript before it was printed. It seems to have been written about 1622, but the only reference to it in contemporary sources is in a letter of advice written by a privy councillor to Charles I, suggesting action against the 'seditious libelling of Tom Telltroath and other pamphleteers of that nature.' It may not have been printed, therefore, until 1626. The tract shows the vehemence of the anti-Spanish and anti-catholic feeling in England in 1621.

SINCE they that have the honour to appertain unto you have neither the courage nor the conscience to acquaint you with the fearful discontents of the time, but suffer you to lose the people's hearts so slightly as if they were not worth their keeping, I, a poor unknown subject, who never had the happiness to come near your majesty but in the throng, nor to take any other oath in your service but that of allegiance, have ventured upon so much forwardness at this time of need (when all places are indeed void which covetousness and huge ambition seem to fill) as to thrust myself into the best office about you—better than either president of the council or earl marshal of England, and far more discontinued— the noble office of telling truth: wherein, if boldness makes me forget my discretion, loyalty, I hope, will beg my pardon. And the rather because I persuade myself I am not altogether without warrant for what I do; for it was my duty not long since to take notice of two proclamations come out in your majesty's name against immoderate talkings, wherein it is your gracious pleasure to make all your loving subjects of what-soever condition instruments of state by giving them, not a bare voluntary power, but a subpœna charge and commission to inform against all those that shall at any time hereafter offend in that kind. Now your majesty shall know that I am one of the greatest company-keepers in this town and therefore cannot but be guilty of hearing many things that I am bound to reveal in obedience to the royal command, which is the duty I propose to myself. At this present time the misery is I know not where to begin, nor whom to accuse in particular of so general a crime.

For I vow to God and your majesty, I can come into no meetings, but I find the predominant humour to be talking of the wars of Christendom and honour of their country, and such like treasons; and would to God they would stop there and profane no more the things that are above them; but such is the rage and folly of their tongues, that they spare not your majesty's sacred person; yea, I horror, to descant upon the royal style is now their common pastime. That you are true and lawful king there is none so devilishly affected as to deny; but some there are that find such fault with your majesty's government as they wish Queen Elizabeth were alive again; who, they say, would never have suffered the enemies of her religion to have unbalanced Christendom as they have done within these few years.

They make a mock of your word ' Great Britain,' and offer to prove that it is a great deal less than ' Little England ' was wont to be: less in reputation, less in strength, less in riches, less in all manner of virtue and whatsoever else is required to make a state great and happy.

They wonder you will call yourself ' King of France ' and suffer your best subjects there to be ruined; for Ireland, they say, you content yourself with the name and let others receive the profit.

As for the glorious title ' Defender of the Faith ' (which was wont to be a point of controversy between us and Rome) they say flatly that your faithful subjects have more cause to question that than the papists.

For they were never better defended in their lives: witness the judges' privy instructions, the pursuivant's open prohibitions, and your Spanish ambassador's more than parliament protections.

Lastly, that you are ' Head of the Church ' they dare not doubt, but of what church they would gladly know; the ' triumphant,' they say, it cannot be, for there are too many corruptions and vexations in it.

And how far it is from the ' militant,' they call heaven and earth to witness. Therefore they conclude it must be either the church ' dormant ' or none: and to say the truth, sir, we are the securest sinners in the world.

These are the things that have most readily offered themselves to my remembrance, because they follow one another in a kind of order. But if I should report all the disorderly and extravagant speeches I have heard of this nature I must be fain to rack my memory, and, I fear, your majesty's patience; yet rather than leave the least shadow of suspicion upon my plain dealing by seeming to curtail in the performance of so necessary a duty, I will venture to add these few.

They that take the affairs of your children abroad most to heart, not being able to discern the compassion of your bowels but judging things by the exterior of your actions, will hardly be persuaded that you are their father; because they see the lamentable estate whereto you suffer things to run comes nearer to destruction than the nature of fatherly correction.

They are not ignorant that your majesty hath made as though you would do something for them, but they also know the course you have taken hath been more formal than effectual, more chargeable than honourable; and are of opinion that either your ambassadors have not negotiated as they ought or else have met with very ill masters of requests abroad, since they have not been able all this while to get their petition answered.

The very papists themselves, sir, repine at your error, and say that the prayers and monies that your majesty hath consumed of late in the unprofitable treaties might have been far better employed in redeeming your mother's soul out of purgatory; for, to get the enemy out of your children's country other ensigns might have been found a great deal more proper. In the meantime, they do not only bind but satisfy their pernicious hopes upon your majesty's patience. For, seeing how easily you tolerate all things abroad, they doubt not ere long but they shall also have toleration at home. Our godliest preachers do already pray against the evil day with so much earnestness as if that were at hand. And though there be orders given to preach nothing but ' court-divinity,' yet a man may easily perceive by the very choice of their texts and the very tears in their eyes that if they durst they would speak their consciences.

The perpetual walkers of Paul's do now despair to see their material church ever repaired, since the spiritual, and more worthy, is suffered to go to wrack. And some of them, not daring to meddle with affairs of state, because they are monied men, and yet not knowing how to hold their peace upon so sudden warning, think it their safest course to talk of nothing but ecclesiastical matters, wherein they all agree that your majesty hath pulled down the church more with your proceeding than you have raised it with your writings.

In your majesty's own taverns for one health that is begun to yourself there are ten drunk to the princes, your foreign children. And when the wine is in their heads, Lord have mercy on their tongues! Ever in the very gaming ordinaries, where men have scarce leisure to say grace, yet they take a time to censure your majesty's actions, and that in their old school terms. They say you have lost the fairest game at maw that ever king had, for want of making the best advantage of the five finger and playing the other helps in time. That your own card-holders play booty and give the sign out of your own hand. That he you played withall, hath ever been known for the greatest cheater in Christendom. In fine, there is no way to recover your losses and vindicate your honour, but with fighting with him that hath cozened you. At which honest, downright play you will be hard enough for him with all his tricks. I cannot forget how I have seen some, when they have lost all their money, fall a-cursing and swearing at the loss of Prague and the Palatinate, as though all the rancour of their hearts lay there. And, tell them of your majesty's proclamation, they answer in a chafe: ' You must give losers leave to speak.'

The merchants and tradesmen I, nor no man else, can accuse of being sensible of anything but what toucheth their own profit. All I find in them is they are extreme jealous the court will shortly put down their exchange, and apprehend, because one of their occupation is made treasurer, that therefore henceforward all things must be bought and sold there.

The lawyers seem not so much offended that your majesty hath removed the garland of their profession by putting the great seal into the hands of a churchman, as that you do not relieve your poor distressed children, according to the equity of their cause, who, they say, have been wrongfully outed; and that therefore you ought to grant them a writ of forcible re-entry, which (under correction) they conceive may be better executed by the general of an army than the sheriff of a county.

They that fly higher and fix their speculations upon the mysteries of the court do apparently perceive that the counsel of Gondomar hath taught some of your active ministers to juggle, only to make them passively capable of his own conjuring; and that, by the penetrating faculty of a yellow Indian demon, he hath at his command and is master of your cabinet without a key, and knows your secrets before the greatest part and most faithful of your council. And which is worse, they say your majesty knows it, and therefore suspect that yourself is bribed against yourself. Otherwise they think not the devil himself could so abuse the times we live in as to make things pass in that fashion as they do, contrary to all sense and conscience and reason of state.

Behold, sir, the second part of *vox populi*, by so much the more like itself than the first, by how much it comes short of it in wit and discretion; for, though the second cogitations are ever held the best, yet we see the common people for the most part, when they give themselves to talking, proceed from bad to worse and every time more foolishly than other. The reason is because they never think before they speak, but rashly vent whatsoever gets into their fancy, be it true, false, or probable, good, bad, or indifferent; nevertheless, by these overflowings of their mouths, your majesty may do well to guess at the abundance of their hearts. And my lords of your council may make use of their folly without disparaging of their own wisdom; which, if it be lawful for me to confess, the truth is the principal end I aim at; for it would never sink into my belief, that your majesty's meaning was to publish these kind of proclamations, to entrap your subjects and bring them to the block of punishment; but rather out of a politic design to sound their grief and make their complaints serve for so many directions to amendment. According to which persuasion, I have thought it sufficient to set down the bare discourses without troubling your majesty with the persons; for, if all that are infected with this ' king's-evil ' should be brought before you, I fear that both your majesty and your surgeon will want the virtue of curing all evils, which I wish you may do with as much ease as your own heart desires. And though, perhaps, I cannot end better than with saying *amen* to so good a prayer, yet now that I have begun to speak to the lord my king, let him not be offended with me, if I presume a little further, and offer at least a few of mine own conceptions by way of humble remonstrance; not that I can hope (however others have sped) to come from an informer to be a councillor, but, because I believe there are some things most worthy of your majesty's consideration that are fitter for an honest man to present than a great.

The great spectators of your majesty's wisdom (whose daily exercise is to multiply the object in the artificial glasses of fraud and flattery) are so distracted with the infinite faces of the counterfeits as they cannot discern the blemishes of the true. But we that know neither the use nor benefit of such court-perspectives and have no other way to understand your majesty than by your works, do to our great grief perceive a number of defects that cover the glory of your reign as in a cloud, and much allay the reverence due to the other excellencies of your person. For mine own part I cannot see them, and think it not enough to murmur as many do, but must show myself so affectionate to my prince and country as to advise your majesty of them; which I promise to do with as much humility as the matter will bear.

The general torrent and discontent that reigns with such a seditious noise over your whole kingdom; though (thanks be to God) it hath made no open breach upon your people's obedience, yet certainly hath very much weakened their affections, which hath ever been held dangerous and of so near neighbourhood as commonly there is no way to prevent the one without remedying the other.

The courses from whence that riseth are two:

I. Discord at home, and,
II. Dishonour abroad.

For the first, I must confess, I am not so well read in the new book of patents, as that I can make any long discourse upon that subject; and therefore to the lower house of parliament will leave it, which is the true crystal fountain that will not only present to your majesty's view, as in a mirror, all the foul spots of the common-weal, but serve you at the same time with waters, if you please, to wash them out. But for the other, which toucheth more to the quick all generous spirits and so excels in matter of complaint, as it receives redress, all other clamours ought to hold their peace; I dare pretend to know as much of it as another, and perhaps more than the share of a private gentleman. And, having been of late (by I know not what inclination of my genius) not only the chosen fruit of my outward observations, but the very nourishment of my sad and solitary thoughts, if then your majesty will give me leave to execute my melancholy office of telling truth and freely to advertise you what this grand grievance is that cries so loud for reparation in all voices, in all hearts, and it is a just resentment of the decay of our country's honour, a trade wherein we were wont to outbuy all our neighbours and make the great engrosser of your West Indies himself bankrupt. But, since your majesty came to be our sovereign, lest we should be too proud of so great an addition, it seems the hand of heaven hath thought fit to curb our felicity in this point, so that we have lived to see the brave stock of sovereign reputation, which our great queen, your predecessor, left us, quite banished and brought to nothing. And for acquiring of new, that is a thing so long since grown out of use as that may be very well reckoned amongst those other inventions we have lost through your injury of time.

The old compass of honour is quite forgot, and our pilots nowadays know no other route than that of their own fortunes, according to which they tack and untack all public affairs. No marvel then if we see your goodly vessels of this state misguided and shamefully exposed to all manner of danger: sometimes by being run aground upon your sands of shallow and uncertain policy; but most of all, by being kept at anchor, and full as it is of leaks and rotten ribs in the deep gulf of security: where that takes in more matter of ruin and corruption in six months than can be pumped out again in seven years. Nor can our statesmen excuse their negligence hereafter in saying the wind did not serve. For never did heavens blow more favourably to our advantage than that hath done of late, had we the grace but to have fitted our sails to the fairness of your occasion. But there hath been I know not what remora that hath hung a long time upon this unfortunate state, and still continues of that prodigious force as for ought I see (unless God of his mercy put his helping hand) it will rather sink us than suffer us to go forward in any course that tends to our prosperity.

In the meantime, our adverse parties have feardom enough and all is fish that comes to their nets, that it seems they have forbid us under pain of their high displeasure to deal any more in matters of worth; and reserving to themselves the rich prizes and triumphs of the time have thought that sufficient for us to shear our sheep and fetch home spices to make gingerbread. Not so much but the very pedlars whom we ourselves set up for our own use are now become our masters in the East Indies, and think themselves our fellows in any ground of Christendom.

These things are the more irksome unto us by reason we did least expect them at your majesty's hands. For who would have thought that we should have lost, but rather infinitely gained by changing the weaker sex for your more noble, to be our commander; and having withal to boot the only nation of the earth that could compare with us in valour to be our fellow-soldiers? But the event shows we are in nothing more miserable than in that we had so much reason to think ourselves happy; for now that we see how contrary to our hopes all things have succeeded and how vilely we have suffered our brave possibilities to pass away one after another, as in a dream our greatest comforts are changed into equal despair, and our most reputed blessings into most apparent curses.

Of all the benefits that descend from heaven to earth, there is none to be received with more praise and thankfulness than that of peace. But a man may have too much of his father's blessing; and I fear we have too much cause to complain of your majesty's unlimited peace, the excess whereof hath long since turned virtue into vice, and health into sickness. As long as other princes kept themselves within their bounds and followed your great example, it was a thing rather to be gloried in than any way reproached that your majesty was known throughout Christendom by the name of ' king of peace.' But now that both our sworn enemies and forsworn friends have taken up arms with one consent that defied your majesty's goodness by enterprising upon your nearest and dearest interest in all foreign parts; now that there is a question of God's glory as well as your own, and that the cause of both your children lies equally ableeding; now, I say, to continue the fault as still unmoved as if you were no king of this world, but stood already possessed of the kingdom of heaven by virtue of ' *beati pacifici*,' this certainly is such a strange piece of supererogation as will serve to astonish the present age and that to come but deserve well of neither. It will rather revoke in doubt your former merit and make us suspect that your peaceable disposition all this while hath not proceeded so much out of Christian piety and love of justice as out of mere impotency and desire of ease. Pardon me, O king, if I speak to you in a language you are not accustomed to hear.

It is a part of supremacy not to have your darling sin laid open, as my lords and bishops do very well observe; but it is now no time to balk and palliate that which all the world sees. For, though I fear it lies still in your bosom; yet the blazing star was not more spectable in our horizon nor gave people more occasion of talk. Heaven grant it may not be the cause of more mischief in Christendom than the other was a sign of. It is in your majesty's power to take away our fear and danger both at once if you will at length but know your own strength and take a resolution worthy of yourself.

There are two fair occasions that come, as it were, a-wooing to your majesty at this time, the least of which highly deserves the honour and good fortune of your maiden arms; so just, and so religious in all human and divine respects as I dare say that if the noble army of martyrs were sent down upon earth to make their fortunes anew they would choose no other quarrel to die in nor hope for a surer way to recover again the crown of glory.

The one is to re-establish your own children in Germany.

The other to preserve God's children in France.

Both of them so universally desired, and so conformable to Christian faith and good manners, that I doubt not but they have long since passed the press of conscience, though I know by what indirect means they are not suffered to come forth in public view. I shall not need to rip up these questions of state from the beginning and vex your majesty with proving particularly that which is best known to yourself; yet, because I see nothing done, I must needs say somewhat.

And first for the unfortunate princes your children. Though they may perhaps have committed a fault, which your majesty, in your singular wisdom, thought good to make them drink of (to purge them either of ill-counsel, or happily to quench in them betimes their dangerous thirst of ambition, which, not content with Rhine and Danuby, might afterwards attempt the ocean), yet to let them drink still, and so deep in the cup of afflictions as not to be able to stand upon their legs, but reel up and down without hope of recovery, is the scorn and opprobry of the nations of the earth.

Hac ratione potes justus fortasse videri:
At non crudelis non potes esse pater.

But some will say your majesty hath often advised them to return to themselves; and, which is more, that you sent one of late of purpose to lead them home. But, alas! in their case how vain is all comfort without hands! And how ill hath this, the promising endeavour sped: the guide you sent (as expert as he made himself in the enemy's ways) is come short of his undertaking, and, instead of giving end to the princes' misery, hath only lighted upon a handsome trick to cover his own shame. Had fortune so miraculously blessed his confidence as that he had performed this Hercules' labour without a lion's skin, he would have stained all wise men for ever, who, before he went, gave him for another last ambassador. It could never appear to them in the least form of likelihood; and having the credit due to gentlemen's complement that the Spanish council of war would be at the charge of getting a country by force of arms that they meant afterwards to restore at the kissing of a hand. They are known to be a people so circumspect and advised in all that they do as they never resolved upon the present without consulting the future, but make the reasons of both their equal warrant; and therefore, if they had made keeping of words in matters of this nature, they should questionless have judged it more convenient to have taken your majesty's for Bohemia, then have taken theirs for the Palatinate, which, before they would surrender, they were first obliged to conquer, and consequently to undertake a new warrant to no purpose. But, seeing they would not trust your majesty in so apparent a congruity, it is not to be wondered at that they have deceived you, but that they had the means to do so; for not only Ball, but every Balaam's ass, might easily foresee that your majesty's credulity was in the highway to perdition, and could not but bring you where the Spaniard would have you, who, how he useth all that are at his mercy, I am sorry to say your majesty is now to learn from so cursed a schoolmaster as himself, who will make no new scruple to whip you as your children with your own rods of iron, though he feignedly promised to use them only against the Turk; then it will be too late to wish you had believed Cassandra, the voice of your loving parliament, who, hearing of it, made a start out of their own business and could not be quiet till they had entreated your majesty to consider what a dangerous gift it was and how fit to be revoked. But your answer was that you had passed your royal word to the Spanish ambassador and could not break it; as if you were the only unfortunate prince in the world, that were tied to be faithful to your own prejudice. Had your minister in the court of Spain surreptitiously obtained a grant from that king of like importance, his catholic majesty would have been glad of so good an occasion to render it of no effect; and without standing on such gentle points of honour or framing to himself I know not what chimeras of jealousy between his own absolute power and his people's humble desire, would have been so far from expecting his parliament's opposition as he would rather have given them charge underhand to have made it, and by that means have recalled his benefit and preserved his thanks. But, if your majesty had made use of this expedient, there might perhaps some inconvenience ensued; for then, it is to be feared, the Spanish ambassador would have been discouraged from ever asking such unreasonable things again. Only the hope whereof makes him flatter the state and tell your majesty many a pleasant tale. We are not yet willing to be undeceived, for if we were, we should not stay till we saw the mountains that are promised us out of Spain vanish into smoke. The poor Palatinate shows us sufficiently what we are to look for from the Spaniard; who, if he were resolved to give us shortly so much of his own as is imagined, would never keep so grippingly from us that which is ours. But I cry the Spaniard's mercy; it is not he (good man) but the revengeful emperor that doth us this wrong; as if the emperor without him could wrong a mouse, or shows himself refractory to the least tittle of his known will. We may as well suppose the sea turbulent without wind, or the lower spheres to move without the *primum mobile*. I grant that we see the Spanish forces and the signs turn another way, but so as they involve, with a powerful and secret touch, the capture of the Palatinate and all the shires about it; without the which the emperor would be as quiet a lump of majesty as we could wish him, and his commissary, the duke of Bavaria, did nothing but what became him. It is the catholic usurper that sets them both a-work and plays least in sight himself. Between them they hold fast your children's patrimony, and play with your majesty as men do with little children at ' handy-dandy,—which hand will you have? ' when they are disposed to keep anything from them. Or as two that having joined together in a theft, he that took says, ' He has it not '; and he that hath it says, ' He took it not.' Which is a mockery more insufferable than the main injury and ought to pro- voke your majesty to the highest strain of indignation. For, if you persist in your obdurate patience and take still for payment all the artifices that their false dealing can coin, we shall be shrewdly tempted to believe for once what the author of all lies, to justify the king of Spain and the other princes of their religion, do constantly give out: that your majesty is sure of the Palatinate by treaty, and that you pretend the contrary to draw money from the parliament. Out of which opinion, if it be once suffered to take root, may grow a great deal of poison and fall upon your majesty as a just judgment of God; who, because you would wilfully trust your enemy to your hurt, may now see yourself so unhappy as not to be believed by your own subjects for your good. But, I hope, God, of his mercy, will avert so great a disaster, and give your majesty the grace to discover and destroy at the same instant this malicious invention; which may easily be done, if, without any more delay or reservations, you will now really and royally engage yourself in this righteous way. Nor let the scarcity of means and ways discourage you. For your majesty knows not what a secret treasure lies hid in your people's hearts, which (in so good an occasion as this) will be brought forth and laid at your feet in greater heaps than the world imagines. Your faithful parliament hath already made you a liberal offer of our lives and fortunes, and every good Englishman hath long since confirmed it in his particular devotion. It wholly depends upon your majesty's wisdom to make the right use of so great a gift; for therein consists all the danger, all the difficulty. The fundamental engines of war, as every man knows, are men and money; and, would to God your majesty's dominions were as well stored with the one as they are with the other; then should we not prostitute, as we do, to the great whore-master of Babylon, and for a few clods of earth give up the honour of our country and violate the love which we owe to religion. But his knowledge of our wants makes him presume on our easiness, and allure us to this base and impious adultery. Though, I verily believe, in this present occasion he and his bawds will be much deceived; for, if your majesty and your estates now assembled together, will tie the holy knot of union and make a firm covenant together, we shall not need to go so near hell for gold as Spanish mines; or, if we do, we will take a course to have it without being beholding to the devil: we shall be able to supply well enough for the business in hand out of that wherewith God Almighty hath blessed us. Only, I must advertise your majesty that we expect to see an army raised as well as subsidies. For, if we be at the charge of maintaining a war, it is reason we should partake of the honour and benefit of it; especially considering how hardly we can spare money and how easily men.

There are many thousands of your majesty's subjects, able and proper fellows, that lie languishing, ready to rebel for want of employment.

And, I hope none will deny but Englishmen can earn their wages at this work as well as any other nation. Sure I am that it is to be found in very good history that foreign princes have thought it none of their worst strategems to clothe a great part of their people in English cassocks to make themselves more terrible to the enemy. Count Mansfield is a gallant man and deserves not only to be well paid, but highly rewarded for the good service he hath done your majesty in that country. Had he not arrived there when he did, those few all worthy countrymen of ours that would not go away before they saw the last danger borne had been miserably sacrificed to the Spaniards' butchery,—which would have made a great many of us wear black in England for a while. But nothing would have lasted black so long as the story of it,—which, when posterity came to read, they would certainly have blurred that part of your majesty's reign with tears. But as he came thither by an accident, so (for ought I know) he may go away by another; and therefore it were fit to provide more certain soldiers for so certain a war. For (as my Lord Digby did very well show towards the end of his narration), Count Mansfield's army doth not consist of such as have their wives and children and friends dwelling in the Palatinate; but of such to whom all places are alike so they may set to work, and upon whom there can be no other tie than precise pay. How much better then were it for your majesty to satisfy the general desire and send over an army of good English; who, you may be sure, will neither change party nor spoil the country, but steadfastly adhere, as much out of affection as obligation, to the cause and persons of your children? Besides, if your majesty will take things aright, we do not contribute to this war so much to regain the Palatinate as to redeem the credit of our nation, which all the money in the kingdom is not able to do without action. There are, as I have heard, two reasons made to oppose this resolution; the one, the odds of the charge; the other, the difficulty of getting thither.

To the first, I answer briefly, that in matter of war, the best is ever cheapest, and the shortest, the best; I mean, not the shortest beginning, but the shortest ending. And, for the other, it is to be presumed that where your majesty shall make this war royal, by taking it upon yourself, you will not, for your own greatness' sake, be seen to send any forces but such as shall be able to make their way; if not, at least they may have their commission to take up lodgings by the way for those that shall come after, and so, though they come short of their journey's end, they may happily make an end of that they go for the sooner.

In plain terms, sir, the Palatinate is very ill-seated for us to war in; it being both remote from the sea and surrounded on all sides with our enemies, whom the pope hath tied together, like Samson's foxes' tails, to set these our parts of Christendom on fire; for which purpose they call themselves the catholic league, and have the catholic king for their head, who sticks close unto them in all adventures. Whereas your majesty, I know not for what crime, hath long since beheaded the poor protestant union, and left it as a body without a soul; yet it is not so dead and buried but that there is hope it will rise again at the first sound of your majesty's trumpets, and joyfully receive a second, and more durable, life, from your better resolutions,—of all the parts belonging to it the easiest to be resuscitated. And most useful for the present business are the united provinces of the Low Countries, as being the strongest and nearest to the head, during this time of dissolution.

They have been fain to do the office of a breast to give your children suck, but are indeed the arms; and would ere this, have carried them into their own country, had they not had their hands full of the common enemy at home. If then your majesty desires to remove the Spaniard's foot out of the Palatinate, the speediest course will be to give the Hollanders your helping hand in Flanders; or, if your strict alliance with Spain will not bear such an immediate act of hostility from yourself; you may, for love or money's sake, lend the prince, your son-in-law, an army to dispose of as he shall see cause; provided always that you council him underhand to his best advantage: so shall the Spaniard be paid in his own coin and our princes restored to their own possessions. Whereas, if you confine the action to the bare Palatinate, and content yourself with the dove's innocency, now that you see the enemy as wise as a thousand serpents, it will never have an end; but draw itself into such a continual circle of trouble as we may look to see a dozen years hence two such armies keeping one another at bay in the Palatinate, as do now in the Low Countries. I will not show so little respect to your majesty's judgment as to talk any longer in so clear a case, but will here conclude my reasons with my prayers, humbly beseeching your majesty to do yourself and Christendom right in this great affair. And let it be no longer heard that the Spaniard hath more wit than the English eye-sight; or the king of Spain's cousin-germains removed are nearer akin to him than your majesty's own children are to you.

It remains now that I speak a word or two in behalf of our brethren, God's children, in France, against the firebrands of hell, which have kindled a persecution without earthly matter, it being the heavenly cause of religion, and no other, for which they are made to suffer; wherein your majesty and state have as much interest as is possible for a man to have when his neighbour's house is on fire; indeed, so much as would ill become a private man to put you in mind of at any time but this, when, it seems, a dead sleep possesses all the land and we had rather perish than be disturbed.

The vigilant parliament hath lain *sentinel perdu* and discovered the enemy's approaches, but cannot be heard. The watched men of the balances that stand in the high places, though they cannot but see the danger, yet dare not give the alarm, for fear of disquieting your majesty. Lastly, and worst of all, the churchmen, who are the seers of Israel, and ought to descry from the holy place the troops of the Philistines and their plots, are they that do most of all connive at the stupidity of the time; all of them already, for excuse of their weakness, urge the strong opinions that they have of your majesty's ableness, for (say they) it is in vain either to advertise or advise your majesty of anything touching government, because, they are assured, you know as much of it as natural man can comprehend. And for mine own part, I think a great deal more; otherwise it could not be that your proceedings should so vary as they do from the whole current of human discretion.

I grant all wise princes have ever reserved to themselves certain cases of state, which the politicians call *arcana imperii*, and we should be too injurious to your majesty's wisdom and power, if we should grudge you the like privilege. But, alas, sir, we that have reasonable souls and cannot but use them in so important a matter, do find a great deal of difference between your majesty and other princes in this point. For, though they have locked up in the closet of their breasts their incommunicable purposes and so work upon divers occasions as that the effects have been seen to come abroad before the cause could be known, yet at last it comes to be evident that these their secret designs ever tended to the public good, and the instrumental means were only such heteroclites as did transcend, and not overthrow, common reason. Whereas your majesty's courses are not only inscrutable, but diametrically opposite to poor man's understanding: and so far from giving us any hope of good effects hereafter as they do already fulfil the utmost of our fears; insomuch that we have no way left to put ourselves out of astonishment and preserve your majesty's wisdom blameless, but by strainingly believing that, whereas all other princes have liberty to govern themselves according to the rules of worldly policy, your majesty's hands are tied from using such means and advantages by the corrective power of some secret revelation. And as David, who was ' a king after God's own heart,' might not for all that build God a temple because he had his hands in blood; so, happily, your majesty may not be suffered to do anything for the church of God because you have likewise your hands defiled with blood; for how can they be otherwise, being clast so straitly (as they are) with them that are red with the blood of the saints. One that knows the sweetness of your majesty's nature, and hath seen with what clemency and mercy you have swayed the sceptre, would think it little less blasphemy to accuse you of anything that is bloody. But God judges not like man. And who can hinder the Eternal from calling your majesty to account for all the ravage hath been done in his church of late, since you are his lieutenant of greatest trust, and have received of his heavenly grace both sufficient power and right to oppose such violent innovations? O, the good and divine providence of God that has given your majesty above all the princes of the earth such titles and royal attributes as do necessarily infer and transfer a right and protection upon these his poor, persecuted servants; for, whatsoever your majesty thinks of it, I do as verily believe as if there were a text for it in the Apocalypse, that the great God of the world in his omniscience and omnipotent prescience hath so disposed of states to the benefit of the church as to continue upon your majesty the title of France; to the end that little flock, which he hath thought good to plant there among so many wolves, might have by a just pretence ' the Defender of the Faith ' for theirs. If your majesty will not own this poor people, neither as you are the king of France nor ' Defender of the Faith,' yet ought you to preserve them for your England's sake; and do that for reasons of state which religion cannot obtain, for should the protestants of France be utterly extirpt and that puissant kingdom rendered as catholic as Spain, I hope our statesmen would not think England the same it was, nor your majesty behold your monarchy without griev-

9—The illustration opposite is a view of the house of commons in 1624. It is taken from British Museum MS. Harley, 159, a printed tract on the 1624 parliament. St. Stephen's Chapel, since 1548 the meeting place of the commons, was situated down towards the river from the north end of the White Hall in old Westminster Palace. It was a dingy, dungeon-like room and much too small, sixty by thirty-two feet, to accommodate the 480 or more members of the house. Here the house is shown in its most formal and magisterial capacity, sitting as a court to reprimand a delinquent kneeling at the bar. The sergeant-at-arms bears the mace, the symbol of the house's authority, the clerk of the house of commons with his assistant is at the table, and the speaker is voicing the house's displeasure. No significance was then attached to sitting on the right or left of the speaker, but members of the council were usually found 'about' or 'behind' the chair.

ing at so terrible an alteration. For mine own part, I should then begin to believe that the time were come Comines the Frenchman spoke of, who, being in discourse with an Englishman about the wars we had had so often and with so good success made in France, discreetly said, ' That God Almighty had brought the English into France to punish them for their sins; and when the sins of England should become greater than of France: he would likewise send the French thither to scourge them.' And how willingly that nation would embrace such an employment may be easily judged; whether we consider the old or the new cause of their hatred. The virtue of our ancestors sticks still in their stomachs, and the true profession of the Gospel enrages their consciences. They who believe they do God good service in cutting their own countrymen's and kinsmen's throats, because they are not papists, should doubtless think themselves damned if they should not do much more to strangers and their ancient enemies on the same occasion. Nor shall they want powerful incitements to so holy an enterprise. His holiness himself will be tempter, though (thanks be to God) he is nothing yet so cunning as the devil; for I know not by what pontifical fury he hath precipitated his instigations and suffered his malice to outrun the season. Would any (but Antichrist out of his wits) have so abused his most Christian child, the king of France, as to put him on the conquest of England before he was master of Rochelle? I must confess, when I first saw his apostolic letters, I had an opinion that some crafty huguenot had devised them to give your majesty a more sensible interest in their cause; but, having since been made certain they came from Rome, and that I find them inserted in a catholic writer, *avec privilege du roy*, I know not what to wonder at most, whether at them that say the pope can not err at all, or at him, that he should err so much.

. . . .

Behold the net St. Peter's successors hope to catch England with, wherein your majesty hath more to lose than any man I know. Be not therefore offended with your loving subjects if their hearts tremble, though not for fear, yet for grief, to see your majesty neglect both yourself and them in so pregnant and considerable an occasion. The pope needed not to have been so foolish as to advertise us; we should easily have been so wise of ourselves to understand how nearly the protestants of France concern England.

They are indeed so many hostages which God Almighty hath put into your majesty's hands to secure you and your majesty's dominions from all danger of that country, and to lose them were no other (in my opinion) than wilfully to tempt God to deliver us into the hands of our enemies. As long as God hath any children in France, we shall be sure to have brethren there. But, they once gone, your brother of France will quickly show whose child he is and how incompatible the obedience he owes him is with any goodwill he can bear your majesty. Since, then, the tie you have upon that prince's friendship is of so loose a knot, what can your majesty do better for yourself and yours than to keep his enmity still clogged by cherishing and maintaining so good a party in his country as those of the religion; who, you may be sure, will be so far at your devotion as to continue their public prayers for your prosperity.

Nor have the holy motions of God's spirit been altogether wanting to your majesty's heart in this point, at least, if we may believe what is unlawful to doubt—the protestation of your tongue. For it is most true that the first time the deputies of Rochelle presented themselves before your majesty, you received their lamentable remonstrances with all the shows of compassion, and sent them away astonished with your good words. Did you not then tell them that although your conscience would not suffer you to assist your own children in the war of Bohemia, because you were not well satisfied of the justice of their quarrel; yet for them, they might assure themselves, you would employ the utmost of your forces in their defence; that you had strictly examined all that had passed between their king and them and could not find wherein they had any way offended; that you were more engaged in their behalf than perhaps they know of. For when you renewed your alliance with this king after the death of his father, you caused an express article to be inserted, that those of the reformed religion, as long as they comported themselves as good subjects, should be maintained and enjoy the benefits of the edict in as ample manner, as they had done in his father's life-time; which being so rashly and wilfully infringed, you held yourself both in conscience and honour to take their cause in hand and see them righted, as you vowed to God you would? Considering this your resolution to the imprecations of so high a nature (although I doubt not but they proceeded of zeal); yet dare I not for the respect I owe unto your majesty but remember them in this place, and that nothing might be wanting to make innocency and religion credulous.

My lord of Buckingham himself fell upon his knees and besought your majesty to take them into your protection; insomuch that the poor men were almost ravished with joy at their good success and came away praising God for the favour they had found in your majesty's eyes. But, by the time they returned into their country (which was after some eight or nine months' soliciting), they hung down their heads and said they would as long as they lived call England the ' Land of Promise '; for, notwithstanding the great promises that your majesty made them, they met with no man but could tell them they would be deceived in their expectation; which they would not believe until they saw at last nothing done, because your majesty had told them (as became a great prince) that they were not a people with whom you had any reason to flatter or dissemble, for if you had not liked their cause you would have told them so at first. But, alas! what are they the better for your majesty's liking of their cause? That only shows the goodness of your own judgment, but doth no way lessen the bitterness of their calamity.

True it is, such was their humility and discretion, as they desired your majesty would first be pleased to try all peaceable means in their favour; not out of any hope they had that would produce any good effect, but because they knew it was a course most suitable to your majesty's inclination. Hereupon, your majesty thought good to send my lord of Doncaster into France to mediate their peace in the choice of whose person they held themselves as much gratified as in the embassage itself; for, though they were strangers and but newly arrived in the court, yet had they learned (as indeed who could not tell them) what a spotless and open-hearted affection that lord bare to the true service of God and his majesty. But in this employment his well wishes were his own, and his instructions your majesty's; and how far soever the one went before, he was now bound to follow the other. All he could do voluntarily was to use his best diligence in matter of time (as I assure myself he did) though it was his misfortune to meet with many heavy rubs. For, being arrived at the French king's camp, the cannon made such a noise at Montabaes as he could not of a long time be heard; and, when with much ado he had procured that favour, the answer he received was so unsavoury as both his business and himself fell sick upon it.

By occasion whereof, more time was spent in this one voyage than our ancestors were wont to employ in conquering half France; and, after all, he came home pitifully complaining of the ill-satisfaction he had received. Nevertheless, your majesty would not take his faithful account for final payment; but thought it worth the labour to send him once again, furnished (as the world conceived) with stranger charms than the first; but the effect showed all was one, for he found the young king as obstinate as ever in the pursuit of his arms and not to be persuaded to lay them down upon bare entreaties. And (to speak the truth) it was not to be expected at his hands. For he had no reason to increase the obligation his protestant subjects have to his majesty, by showing them any favour at your instance; since it is well known, a great part of the enmity he bears them proceeds merely out of a jealousy he hath that they have already too much dependence upon you. Had your majesty used your own persuasions for them, as Edward IV did to Louis XI, to make him let the duke of Brittany alone, I doubt not but his councils, as fierce a warrior as he is, would have advised him for the best; but this was a point of rhetoric beyond his lordship's commission; and all that was lawful for him to urge was easily avoided, either by flat refusal or by vain excusal. So, as he was forced the second time to return out of France without leaving behind him any sign that he had been there, that appeared here at home by my lord treasurer's accounts, there having been issued as much money out of the exchequer for the defraying this fruitless embassage as would have satisfied a great part of the church's necessities, as your majesty came after to consider, though too late, when you told the deputies you could have wished you had given them the money my lord of Doncaster had and would cost you in this treaty. And, without doubt, the one would have done them a great deal more good than the other. For they were so far from receiving any benefit by your majesty's intercession, as it did rather infinitely disadvantage them; it no ways slackened or appeased the fury of their prince, who continued his assaults upon them every day more cruelly than other.

And it was of that force with them, as not to aggravate matters and so render his majesty's pious endeavours more difficult, they imposed measure and modesty upon their arms; and in divers occasions, chose rather to suffer than employ the extremity of war in their defence. Besides, many of their party, seeing your majesty so far engaged in a treatise of peace, thought it no point of wisdom to declare themselves before they knew the issue of it, which could not but be a great weakness to them; so as the very prejudice they have received by your majesty's occasion (were there no other motive) obligeth you, in point of justice, to do something for them; and, in the name of God, what should hinder you, after so many vows and promises, from performing so easy and meritorious a work? Perhaps some false-hearted Achitophel hath buzzed into your apprehension that if you should relieve the protestants of France, the French king might likewise be drawn to assist the papists in England against your majesty; but (thanks be to God) we are not there yet.

For, though our papists have had more scope given them of late than all that love their country have wished; yet they are not grown to such a formidable light that this allusion should be thought of any consequence.

The protestants of France have laws made in their favour and towns given them for their security; but the papists of England can expect nothing from the laws of their country but penalty, nor challenge any other assurance than what proceeds from mere connivency. Besides, the tenets of the one are known to be so conformable to civil government as they are, and of right ought to be, permitted to assemble themselves both in provincial or national synods; whereas the other are justly denied this liberty because both their positions and dispositions are altogether repugnant to the peace and safety of the state. Well may they conspire in secret, two and two; but to rebel openly the constable will not suffer them; if they were in case to show themselves in right colours, we should quickly have news of their friends beyond the seas. There being a great prince in the world that openly professes the English catholics are as dear unto him as his own proper Castilians, it is not your majesty's example, but your wisdom, that must caution you from this danger. To hinder them from having any foreign assistance, there is no way but one—to keep them in such order as they may be incapable of it. The church of Rome, as it for the most part is grounded upon worldly policy, so it doth, above all excel in this—that it holds the parts firmly linked together and possesses, by I know not what fascination, with such a spirit of confederacy as they partake alike in both fortunes and passionably espouse one another's interests; whereas, if we pray once a week, more out of custom than any devotion, ' for the good estate of Christ's church,' we think we have performed the utmost of Christian duty. Hence it is that the catholic

COMPLAINT AND REFORM IN ENGLAND

cause makes such a noise in the world and carries all before it in these troublesome times; for amongst them it is not enough to profess religion without contributing to it; whereas we think God sufficiently honoured if we believe his truth; let him defend it as he will. Or, if at any time we be urged to fight for our religion, we use only the spiritual sword; whilst our adversaries they are victorious and confound more in a day with the one than St. Peter or St. Paul could ever convert with the other. The princes that have given their power to the beast send arms; and your majesty (that should fight the battles of the Lord), ambassadors. In a word, while your majesty amasseth yourself to convince an error or two of theirs, they find means to conquer a whole province of ours. Certainly these children of darkness are ' wiser in their generation than the children of light,' and shall rise up against us at the last day for bearing more affection to the Alcaron of Rome than we do to the gospel of Christ.

That I may yet give your majesty a more lovely touch of these things, let it be lawful for me to change the present state of religion throughout Christendom and see what will necessarily ensue. Suppose your majesty and the body of your estate were papists, and the recusants protestants. The French king and his major part of that kingdom, protestants, and the huguenots, papists; the king of Spain, the emperor, and all the tribe of Austria, of the confession of Augsburg; your children and other princes of Germany, their confederates, Roman catholics. Suppose, I say, the differences [were] in all parts the same, the sides only turned. Doth your majesty think you could have showed yourself deaf at such crying occasions, without seeing your whole kingdom in commotion? Or that they would have suffered you to take your pleasure a-hunting, whilst your children and brethren were made a prey to the common enemy?

No, assuredly; you would have found another manner of business of it; and seen yourself forced to prefer your safety before your ease; *Dieu et mon droit*, before *beati pacifici*; you should have seen the differences between a puritan parliament and a popish: and wondered at yourself for being so unequal as to fear the one and despise the other.

The pope's bulls and his fiercer beasts, the Jesuits, would have been continually upon your back and never left you neither safe nor quiet till they thrust you into action; and for one preacher of ours that chances to let a word fall from him to this purpose, you should have all theirs treat of nothing else. No prevention could have been used to make them either silent or sparing in a cause that so highly concerned their mother the church. What then,—shall the true religion, because it teacheth no doctrine but what agrees with the simplicity and pureness of the Gospel, be therefore neglected? God forbid. They that maintain the excommunication, deposition, and assassination of princes would desire no better ground than such an advantage for their opinion. And, if it could not but anger the very saints themselves to see their enemies triumph over them with such unlawful weapons, your majesty may say what you hear of puritans and, by the authority of your known disfavour, make that good word to be taken in an ill sense.

But, if my observation have not erred, in some parts of Christendom where I have lived, there is no religion like theirs, for a sovereign that desires to make himself absolute and dissolute. Insomuch that I wonder that such princes as profess religion only for policy's sake will suffer any other in their dominions. For let a protestant king (I mean one that rules over a people of that profession) be never so notoriously wicked in his person, nor so enormous in his government; let him stamp vice with his example and make it current by being his; let him remove the ancient boundwork of sovereignty and make every day new yokes and new scourges for his poor people; let him take rewards and punishments out of the hands of justice, and so distribute them without regard to right or wrong, as may make his followers doubt whether there be a heaven and hell,—which desperate point of unbelief is a great help and preparative to our preferment; in short, let him so excel in mischief, ruin, and oppression as Nero, compared with him, may be held a very father of the people; when he hath done all that can be imagined to procure hate and contempt, he shall not, for all that, have any occasion to fear, but may boldly go in and out to his sports without a public guard or a privy coat. And, though every day of his reign bring forth a new prodigy to grieve all that are honest and astonish all that are wise, yet shall he not need to take either the less drink when he goes to bed, or the more thought when he riseth. He may solace himself as securely in his bed-chamber as the grand signor in his seraglio; have lords spiritual for his mates, lords temporal for his eunuchs, and whom he will for his incubus. There may he kiss his minions without shame, and make his grooms his companions without danger; who, because they are acquainted with his secret sins, assume to themselves as much power and respect as catholic princes use

to give their confessors,—a pack of ravenous curs that know no difference between the commonwealth and one of their master's forests, but
think all other subjects beasts and only made for them to prey upon, that
lick their master's sores not whole, but smooth, and bark at every man
that dares be found circled with these sweet beagles. We may revel and
laugh, when all the kingdom mourns; and upon every foot of ground
his prerogative get, and cry with Tiberius, ' O people prepared for servitude! ' His poor protestant subjects will only think he is given them
of God for the punishment of their sins, and that he ought to be obeyed,
not because he is good, but because he is their king; not because he rules
according to justice and equity, but because his power is the ordinance of
God. Yea, the preachers of greatest note and credit will hold themselves
bound in duty to praise him against their consciences, and laying aside
divinity, make the pulpit a stage of flattery where you shall have them
endue him after a most poetical manner with more than all the virtues
and paint him so excellently good as would make all that hear them happy,
if they could believe the things of princes as well as those of God in spite
of their senses.

Nor do their fatherhoods this out of simplicity or ignorance (for they
are too well read in the black book of the court) but out of a politic and
officious purpose, to sweeten the people's minds and keep them from
rebelling.

These are the fruits and prosperities of the reformed religion, which,
teaching divine providence according to divine truth, ties the subject to
such wonderful patience and obedience as doth almost verify that bold
speech of Machiavelli, when he said, ' Christianity made men cowards.'
And if it be so advantageous to a bad prince, how much more to a good?
For though duties are and must be paid to both, yet is there a great deal
of difference in the manner and proportion; no more nor less than was
to be between the works of bare charity and mutual friendship: the one
receives the people's service and obedience as a mere alms, given for the
Lord's sake; the other as a free benevolence, wherein men extend themselves with the more alacrity, because they believe it is rather due to his
merit than to his power. The experience your majesty hath had in your
long and prosperous reign will better declare this truth than any discourse
of mine. I will therefore digress no farther in this point, but by way of
inference return to the mark I aim at which I doubt not but your maj-

esty's quick apprehension will sooner hit, than I can show; for can your
majesty but find it more than reasonable to favour or assist a religion
that you see deserves so well of princes and all human society? That
teacheth tumultuous hearts a harmony of heaven, and makes men obey
kings as the angels of God; that charitably beareth with bad, and abundantly requites the good: in short, a religion that hates the Jesuits with
a perfect hatred because they are our king's enemies. How ill-advised
then is that young prince that seeks with fire and sword to drive this
holy and only true opinion out of his kingdom? What can be pretended
by this his credulity, besides the pleasure of making martyrs? Would he
have all his subjects agree that it is lawful to kill kings, and none else to
write against consecrated knives? Would he have all his great ones to be
pensions of his ambitious neighbours, to wink at every public prejudice
that may serve to augment their state, and lessen his; and none left to
oppose the designs of his envious superiors in the Roman hierarchy, who
have a long while thought the crown of France too goodly a thing for
him or any Frenchman to possess? Conformable to which, there is a
famous work composed by a Spanish author, where, for the better managing of Christendom, his wisdom thinks it fit there should be two monarchies: a spiritual and a temporal; the pope to have the one, and his
majesty the other. But suppose little Louis the Just, by reason of his
strict alliance with Spain and his devout observance to Rome, may
promise himself more assurance of his life and empire than Henry the
Great, his more worthy father; nevertheless, if he were old enough to
be wise he would never teach his people so dangerous a lesson, once to
know their own strength; nor move them to take up arms in any occasion by compelling them to defend themselves in a just cause. How
fatal this indiscretion hath proceeded to as great princes as himself, both
ancient and modern examples do sufficiently instruct; but I cease to
wonder at him that hearkens to lying prophets and suffers himself to be
led away by the spirit of illusion. That which most disquiets my understanding is that your majesty should so much forget the part you have
in this good people, neuter betwixt his madness and their innocency. It
is nothing so grievous and scandalous in him to murder and scatter Christ's
flock, as it is in your majesty to look on, who is as well his deputy shepherd as his viceroy; indeed you are nothing, nor can be considered in any
capacity, function, or dignity, which doth not highly oblige you to take

the cause of these poor men to heart and employ your most potent means
for their preservation. Hitherto you have put God Almighty to do
miracles for them, who will not suffer them to perish, for his own
name's sake; but it is now expected, both of God and of man, that you
should put to the helping hand and command that reason with the sword
which you have so often in vain desired with your pen.

Your majesty shall no sooner exceed words and show yourself real in
this resolution, but the football will presently be on your side, and then
it will be your turn to receive ambassadors as fast as you have sent them
for the mediation of peace. That which is now held too much to grant,
your majesty may then think too little, and have more; for the profit
cannot but answer the honour; when you shall see it in your power to
sell the war to your subjects and the peace to your enemy at what rate
you please—a traffic far better becoming a great prince than that of
titles, offices, and such like petty commodities of court.

I would here make an end but that there is one motive more offers
itself to my conceit, which I think fit to prefer to your majesty's consideration. And that is this:

Your majesty hath ever expressed a desire, worthy yourself, to unite
the people as well as the countries of England and Scotland. And whosoever doth not contribute his best endeavours to so good a work is unworthy of either; only it is to be wished that your majesty would think
upon some better means than hitherto hath been used, such as may give
universal satisfaction, the true and most natural mother of union. It is
not to be done by choosing the minion alternatively out of each nation;
not by making Scotsmen lords of England, and Englishmen lords of
Scotland; nor yet by mixture of marriage, which, though it makes two
persons one, cannot make two people one; no, nor by the more subtle
way that is now practised, of making England as poor as Scotland.
These are too weak and counterfeit ingredients to compound a love-
potion for them that were wont to thirst after one another's blood; it
must be something of more virtue, that must charm the dissonant humours
of these two nations and make them forget whose fortune it was to be
envied, and whose to be contemned in times past; and, if anything on
earth do it, it will be their friendship at arms in some fortunate war,
where honour and danger may be equally divided, and no jealousy or
contention rise, but of well-doing; one victory obtained by the joint

valour of English and Scots will more indelibly christen your majesty's empire Great Britain, than any act of parliament or artifice of state.

If then your majesty will proceed in good earnest to the accomplishment of the fatherly desire, and relinquish the unwholesome and unnecessary policy of keeping the two nations in continual faction and counterpoise for the strengthening of your authority; what remains then but to bring forth your royal standard and make the conjunction of your arms the happy instrument of the people's union? They shall no sooner see the common ensign of honour, wherein they have both equal interest, but all other notes of diversity will be thought unworthy their remembrance; and then your enemy shall quickly find to his cost, that the two mighty and populous kingdoms of England and Scotland have but one head and one heart. Now, albeit your majesty have at this time as good choice of occasions as the world can afford, yet that of France seems most proper for this purpose. For, as that country was the cause of our ancient enmity, so would it be made to feel the first effects of our reconcilement, were it for nothing else but to cancel the strict alliance that was wont to be so suspected and prejudicial to England; had not the Scots of old been our back-friends and showed themselves in all occasions more affectionate to the French than us, your majesty might happily at this day have seen yourself king of France.

And yet, had we not preferred Scotland before France, your majesty had never come to be king of England; this will seem no riddle to them that are never so little acquainted with the history of those times: and, if England were able to make her party good both against Scotland and France, when their league offensive was at the strongest, what might not England and Scotland do now in France, where there is another manner of party than that of Burgundy to receive us? Surely, we might drive all the royalists into the sheepfold of Berris, and make another king of Burges. But I will not labour in vain to make your majesty's courage exceed your conscience: God Almighty, I know, hath filled your heart with dominion and so sealed it up from seditious thoughts, as that you esteem ' conquests no better than splendid robberies,' as you are pleased to express yourself in one of your late works of divinity: nor do I pretend to incite your majesty to anything but what may stand as well with your goodness as your greatness. Cursed be they that tell the king he may do all he can! For my part, I shall think myself blest of heaven if I may but obtain my humble desire, which goes no further than to what you ought; it is not spoil, nor the bellows of war, that I think worthy to move your majesty to forego the long contentment of peace. Nothing should make me so hardy for to wish it, were there any other hope but in your arms, to right the wronged world and acquit yourself of the duty to God and nature.

Behold (sir) as much as I am able to present; and perhaps more than I shall have thanks for; but that is the least part of my intention. The love to truth and your majesty's service deserve this and a great deal more of an honest man; and he that seeks reward of well-doing knows not the true value of a good conscience.

I shall be content to remain unknown, so as I make your majesty know what false and wicked men keep from you,—the misfortunes of government, and the just complaint of your subjects.

If I have offended your patience, your majesty may be pleased to consider how long yours hath offended all the world, and forgive me.

Let it not seem strange or evil in your majesty's eyes that I have used a few hearty words in a cause my soul loves above all that is mortal, and for the advancement whereof, I dare suffer as much as they deserve that dissuade you from it.

THE ELEMENTS OF ARCHITECTURE

Collected by Henry Wotton, Knight, from the best authors and examples. London, Printed by John Bill, MDCXXIV.

SIR HENRY WOTTON (1568–1639) was descended from a fifteenth century lord mayor of London and was the youngest son of a quiet and studious country gentleman of Bocton Hall, Kent. After Winchester and Oxford, where he knew John Donne, he spent five years in travel on the continent, living and learning Greek with the great French scholar Casaubon. He then entered the service of Essex, was employed on secret continental missions, and accompanied him on the Cadiz and Irish expeditions. After Essex's fall he left for Italy, to turn up at the court of James VI in Scotland masquerading as an Italian duke and representing the court of Tuscany. In 1604 James appointed him ambassador to Venice. On his trip south he wrote in a private album at Augsburg the famous definition which, when published, caused his temporary disgrace in 1612: *Legatus est vir bonus peregré missus ad mentiendum Reipublicae causa*—an ambassador is an honest man sent abroad to lie for the good of his country. A member of the 1613 parliament, he defended hereditary monarchy. He was ambassador to the Hague in 1614–1615; at Venice, 1616–1619; to Ferdinand II, 1620; and at Venice again, 1621–1623. The last fifteen years of his life he was Provost of Eton College, an appointment got through his friendship with Buckingham.

The tract printed here with abridgements was his first signed publication. It shows the ideals and standards of a travelled Englishman, of, indeed, an Italianate Englishman. All the architects Wotton praises, Palladio, Vignola, Ammanati, belong to the late Renaissance period. He described the essay as a hasty job: ' It was printed sheet by sheet, as fast as it was born, and it was born as soon as it was conceived; so as it must needs have the imperfections and deformities of an immature birth, besides the weakness of the parent.' His *Survey of Education* (1630) discussed what he called a kind of moral architecture, with emphasis upon the need of discovering the temperament and character of each child.

Wotton was a splendid type of cultured Elizabethan gentleman. The author of a few lyrics, the first to praise the young Milton extravagantly for his *Comus*, a collector of Italian pictures, famous as a wit, a fine letter-writer, pious, he was also a devoted friend of Izaak Walton, who wrote a life of him and quoted him in the *Compleat Angler* as one to whom fishing was ' rest to his mind, a cheerer of his spirits, a diversion of sadness, a calmer of unquiet thoughts, a moderator of passions, a procurer of contentedness.'

The Preface

I SHALL not need (like the most part of writers) celebrate the subject which I deliver. In that point I am at ease; for architecture can want no commendation, where there are noble men or noble minds; I will therefore spend this preface, rather about those from whom I have gathered my knowledge; for I am but a gatherer and disposer of other men's stuff at my best value.

Our principal master is Vitruvius, and so I shall often call him, who had this felicity that he wrote when the Roman empire was near the pitch; or, at least, when Augustus (who favoured his endeavours) had some meaning (if he were not mistaken) to bound the monarchy. This, I say, was his good hap; for in growing and enlarging times, arts are commonly drowned in action; but, on the other side, it was indeed an unhappiness to express himself so ill, especially writing (as he did) in a season of the ablest pens; and his obscurity had this strange fortune, that though he were best practised, and best followed by his own countrymen, yet, after the reviving and repolishing of good literature (which the combustions and tumults of the middle age had uncivilized) he was best, or, at least, first understood by strangers, for of the Italians that took him in hand, those that were grammarians seem to have wanted mathematical knowledge; and the mathematicians perhaps wanted grammar, till both were sufficiently conjoined in Leon Baptista Alberti the Florentine, whom I repute the first learned architect beyond the Alps: but he studied more indeed to make himself an author than to illustrate his master. Therefore, among his commentors, I must (for my private conceit) yield the chief praise unto the French, in Philander, and to the high Germans, in Gualterus Rivius, who, besides his notes, hath likewise published the most elaborate translation that, I think, is extant in any vulgar speech of the world, though not without bewailing, now and then, some defect of artificial terms in his own, as I must likewise, for if the Saxon (our mother tongue) did complain as justly (I doubt) in this point may the daughter: languages for the most part in terms of art and erudition, retaining their original poverty, and rather growing rich and abundant in complimental phrases and such froth. Touching divers modern men that have written out of mere practice, I shall give them their due upon occasion.

And now, after this short censure of others, I would fain satisfy an objection or two which seem to lie somewhat heavily upon myself. It will be said that I handle an art no way suitable either to my employments or to my fortune. And so I shall stand charged, both with intrusion, and with impertinency.

To the first I answer that though by the ever acknowledged goodness of my most dear and gracious sovereign, and by his long indulgent toleration of my defects, I have borne abroad some part of his civil service, yet when I came home and was again resolved into mine own simplicity, I found it fitter for my pen (at least in this first public adventure) to deal with these plain compilements and tractable materials than with the labyrinths and mysteries of courts and states; and less presumption for me, who have long contemplated a famous republic, to write now of architecture, than it was anciently for Hippodamus the Milesian, to write of republics who was himself but an architect.

To the second I must shrink up my shoulders, as I have learned abroad, and confess indeed that my fortune is very unable to exemplify and actuate my speculations in this art, which yet, in truth, made me the rather, even from my very disability, take encouragement to hope, that my present labour would find the more favour with others, since it was undertaken for no man's sake less than my own. And with that confidence I fell into these thoughts, of which there were two ways to be delivered, the one historical, by description of the principal works, performed already in good part, by Giorgio Vassari, in the lives of architects; the other logical, by casting the rules and cautions of this art into some comportable method, whereof I have made choice, not only as the shortest and most elemental, but indeed as the soundest; for, though in practical knowledges every complete example may bear the credit of a rule, yet, peradventure, rules should precede, that we may by them be made fit to judge of examples: Therefore, to the purpose, for I will preface no longer.

Of the Elements of Architecture. The First Part.

In architecture, as in all other operative arts, the end must direct the operation.

The end is to build well.

Well building hath three conditions: commodity, firmness, and delight. A common division among the deliverers of this art, though I know not how, somewhat misplaced by Vitruvius himself, *lib*.1, *cap*.3., whom I shall be willinger to follow as a master of proportion than of method. Now, for the attaining of these intentions, we may consider the whole subject under two general heads.

The seat and the work.

Therefore first, touching situation.

The precepts thereunto belonging do either concern the total posture (as I may term it) or the placing of the parts; whereof the first sort, howsoever usually set down by architects as a piece of their profession, yet are in truth borrowed from other learnings, there being between arts and sciences, as well as between men, a kind of good fellowship and communication of their principles.

For you shall find some of them to be merely physical, touching the quality and temper of the air, which being a perpetual ambient and ingredient, and the defects thereof incorrigible in single habitations (which I most intend), doth in those respects require the most exquisite caution, that it be not too gross, nor too penetrative; not subject to any foggy noisomeness, from fens, or marshes near adjoining; nor to mineral exhalations from the soil itself. Not undigested for want of sun, not unexercised for want of wind; which were to live (as it were) in a lake, or standing pool of air, as Alberti, the Florentine architect, doth ingeniously compare it.

Some do rather seem a little astrological, as when they warn us from places of malign influence, where earthquakes, contagions, prodigious births, or the like are frequent without any evident cause, whereof the consideration is peradventure not altogether vain. Some are plainly economical; as that the seat be well watered and well fuelled, that it be not of too steep and incommodious access to the trouble both of friends and family. That it lie not too far from some navigable river or arm of the sea for more ease of provision and such other domestic notes.

Some again may be said to be optical; such I mean as concern the properties of a well chosen prospect, which I will call the royalty of sight: for as there is a lordship (as it were) of the feet, wherein the master doth much joy when he walketh about the line of his own possessions; so there is a lordship likewise of the eye, which being a ranging and imperious, and (I might say) an usurping sense, can endure no narrow circumscription but must be fed both with extent and variety; yet, on the other side, I find vast and indefinite views which drown all apprehension of the uttermost objects condemned by good authors, as if thereby some part of the pleasure (whereof we speak) did perish. Lastly, I remember a private caution which I know not well how to sort, unless I should call it political. By no means to build too near a great neighbour; which were in truth to be as unfortunately seated on the earth as Mercury is in the heavens, for the most part, ever in combustion, or obscurity, under brighter beams than his own.

From these several knowledges, as I have said, and perhaps from some other, do architects derive their doctrine about election of seats, wherein I have not been so severe as a great scholar of our time, who precisely restraineth a perfect situation, at least for the main point of health, *ad locum contra quem sol radios suos fundit, cum sub ariete oritur*, that is, in a word, he would have the first salutation of the spring; but such notes as these, wheresoever we find them, in grave or slight authors, are to my conceit rather wishes than precepts, and in that quality I will pass them over. Yet I must withal say that in the seating of ourselves (which is a kind of marriage to a place) builders should be as circumspect as wooers; lest, when all is done, that doom befall us, which our master doth lay upon *Mitylene*, a town in truth (saith he) finely built, but foolishly planted. And so much touching that, which I termed the total posture.

The next in order is the placing of the parts; about which (to leave as little as I may in my present labour, unto fancy, which is wild and ir-regular) I will propound a rule of mine own collection, upon which I fell in this manner. I had noted, that all art was then in truest perfection, when it might be reduced to some natural principle; for what are the most judicious artisans but the mimics of nature? This led me to con-template the fabric of our own bodies, wherein the high Architect of the World had displayed such skill as did stupefy all human reason. There I found the heart as the fountain of life placed about the middle, for the more equal communication of the vital spirits. The eyes seated aloft, that they might describe the greater circle within their view. The arms projected on each side for ease of reaching. Briefly (not to lose ourselves in this sweet speculation) it plainly appeareth, as a maxim drawn from the divine light, that the place of every part is to be determined by the use.

So then, from natural structure, to proceed to artificial; and in the rudest things, to preserve some image of the excellentest. Let all the prin-cipal chambers of delight, all studies and libraries, be towards the east; for the morning is a friend to the muses. All offices that require heat, as kitchens, stillatories, stoves, rooms for baking, brewing, washing, or the like, would be meridional. All that need a cool and fresh temper, as cellars, pantries, butteries, granaries, to the north. To that same side likewise, all that are appointed for gentle motion, as galleries, especially in warm climes, or that otherwise require a steady and unvariable light, as Pinacothecia (saith Vitruvius) by which he intendeth (if I may guess at his Greek, as we must do often even at his Latin) certain repositories for works of rarity in picture or other arts, or by the Italians called *studioli*, which, at any other quarter where the course of the sun doth diversify the shadows, would lose much of their grace. And by this rule, having always regard to the use, any other part may be fitly accommodated.

I must here not omit to note that the ancient Grecians, and the Romans by their example, in their buildings abroad, where the seat was free, did almost religiously situate the front of their houses towards the south; perhaps that the master's eye, when he came home, might not be dazzled, or that, being illustrated by the sun, it might yield the more graceful aspect, or some such reason; but from this the modern Italians do vary; whereof I shall speak more in another place. Let thus much suffice at the present for the position of the several members, wherein must be 'had, as our author doth often insinuate, and especially *lib*.6, *cap*.10. a single regard to the nature of the region. Every nation being tied above all rules whatsoever to a discretion of providing against their own inconveniences; and therefore a good parlour in Egypt would perchance make a good cellar in England.

There now followeth the second branch of the general section touching the work.

In the work, I will first consider the principal parts, and afterwards the accessory or ornaments; and in the principal, first the preparation of the materials, and then the disposition which is the form.

Now, concerning the material part; although, surely, it cannot disgrace an architect which doth so well become a philosopher, to look into the properties of stone and wood; as that fir trees, cypresses, cedars, and such other aerial aspiring plants, being by a kind of natural rigour (which in a man I would call pride) inflexible downwards, are thereby fittest for posts or pillars, or such upright use; that, on the other side, oak, and the like true hearty timber, being strong in all positions, may be better trusted in cross and traverse work, for summers, or girding and binding beams, as they term them. And so likewise to observe of stone, that some are better within, and other to bear weather. Nay, to descend lower, even to examine sand and lime and clay (of all which things Vitruvius has discoursed, without any daintiness, and the most of new writers) I say, though the speculative part of such knowledge be liberal, yet, to redeem this profession, and my present pains from indignity, I must here remember that to choose and sort the materials for every part of the fabric is a duty more proper to a second superintendant over all the under artisans, called (as I take it) by our author, *officinator*, *lib*.6, *cap*.11. and in that place expressly distinguished from the architect, whose glory doth more consist in the designment and idea of the whole work, and his truest ambition should be to make the form, which is the nobler part (as it were) triumph over the matter; whereof I cannot but mention, by the way, a foreign pattern, namely the church of Santa Giustina in Padua: In truth, a sound piece of good art, where the materials being but ordinary stone, without any garnishment in sculpture, do yet ravish the beholder (and he knows not how) by a secret harmony in the proportions. And this indeed is that end, at which, in some degree, we would aim even in the privatest works: whereunto, though I make haste, yet let me first collect a few of the least trivial cautions belonging to the material provision.

Leon Batista Alberti is so curious as to wish all the timber cut out of the same forest and all the stone out of the same quarry.

Philibert de l'Orme, the French architect, goes yet somewhat further and would have the lime made of the very same stone which we intend to employ in the work; as belike imagining that they will sympathize and join the better, by a kind of original kindred; but such conceits as these seem somewhat too fine among this rubbage, though I do not produce them in sport. For surely the like agreements of nature may have oftentimes a discreet application to art. Always it must be confessed that to make lime without any great choice of refuse stuff, as we commonly do, is an English error of no small moment in our buildings. Whereas the Italians at this day, and much more the ancients, did burn their firmest stone, and even fragments of marble where it was copious, which in time became almost marble again, or at least of indissoluble durity, as appeareth in the standing theatres. I must not here omit, while I am speaking of this part, a certain form of brick described by Daniel Barbaro, patriarch of Aquilia, in the largest edition of his commentary upon

Vitruvius. The figure triangular, every side a foot long and some inch and a half thick, which he doth commend unto us for many good conditions; as that they are more commodious in the management, of less experience, of fairer show, adding much beauty and strength to the mural angles, where they fall gracefully into an indented work; so as I should wonder that we have not taken them into use, being propounded by a man of good authority in this knowledge; but that all nations do start at novelties and are indeed married to their own moulds. Into this place might aptly fall a doubt, which some have well moved, whether the ancient Italians did burn their brick or no; which a passage or two in Vitruvius hath left ambiguous. Surely, where the natural heat is strong enough to supply the artificial, it were but a curious folly to multiply both labour and expense; and it is besides very probable, that those materials, with a kindly and temperate heat, would prove fairer, smoother, and less distorted than with a violent; only they suffer two exceptions: first, that they are likely, by such a gentle drying, to be the more ponderous; an important circumstance to the main of the work in the compilement. The next is of no less moment: that they will want a certain sucking and soaking thirstiness, or a fiery appetite to drink in the lime, which must knit the fabric; but this question may be confined to the south where there is more sun and patience. I will therefore not hinder my course with this incident scruple, but close that part which I have now in hand about the materials with this principal caution; that sufficient stuff and money be ready before we begin; for when we build now a piece and then another by fits, the work dries and sinks unequally, whereby the walls grow full of chinks and crevices; wherefore such a pausing humour is well reproved by Palladio, *lib*.1. *cap*1. and by all other. And so having gleaned these few remembrances touching the preparation of the matter, I may now proceed to the disposition thereof, which must form the work. In the form, as I did in the seat, I will first consider the general figuration and then the several members.

Figures are either simple or mixed. The simple be either circular or angular, and of circular, either complete or deficient, as ovals, with which kinds I will be contented though the distribution might be more curious.

Now the exact circle is in truth a figure, which for our purpose hath many fit and eminent properties; as fitness for commodity and receit, being the most capable; fitness for strength and duration, being the most

10—The illustration on the opposite page is from an engraving of one of the many architectural drawings by Inigo Jones (1573–1652). It is plate 13, volume II, of William Kent, *The Designs of Inigo Jones*, London, 1770, and is there described as ' the principal plan with the elevation and section of a house, having an arcade to each front.' The rooms were to be eighteen feet high on the ground floor, fourteen feet high above, and the great room in the middle was to reach two stories with a gallery to the upper rooms as is apparent in the cross-section.

The drawing is to demonstrate Jones' role in blending the classic and native architectural traditions into the Anglo-classic style. Italo-classic forms had first appeared in arches, pilasters, and surface ornamentation in Henry VIII's reign, but the basic principles of classic architecture, advocated by Shute, led to the truly national English version achieved by Jones. He twice travelled in Italy, studied the writings of Vitruvius and wrote recipes into his copy of Palladio's treatise. But Jones' genius transcended imitation and created the style which culminated in the geometrical classicism of Christopher Wren. The classic values of symmetry, balance, unity, and simplicity are as apparent in this drawing as the geometrical forms, the mathematical precision, and the exterior decoration and ornamentation.

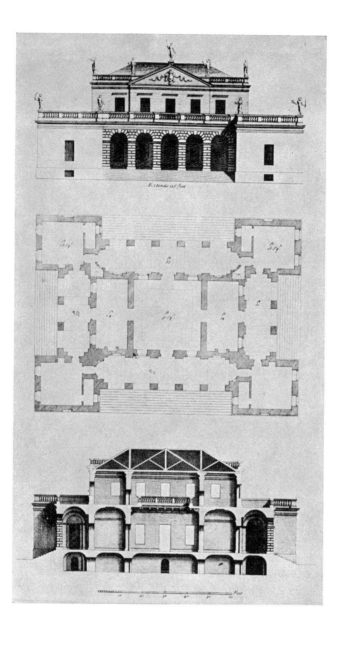

Extends 106 feet.

Feet

united in his parts; fitness for beauty and delight, as imitating the celestial orbs and the universal form. And it seems, besides, to have the approbation of nature, when she worketh by instinct, which is her secret school; for birds do build their nests spherically: but, notwithstanding these attributes, it is, in truth, a very unprofitable figure in private fabrics, as being of all other the most chargeable, and much room lost in the binding of the walls, when it comes to be divided: besides an ill distribution of light, except from the centre of the roof. So as anciently it was not usual, save in their temples and amphitheatres, which needed no compartitions. The ovals and other imperfect circular forms have the same exceptions, and less benefit of capacity: so as there remains to be considered in this general survey of figures, the angular and the mixed of both. Touching the angular, it may perchance sound somewhat strangely, but it is a true observation, that this art doth neither love many angles nor few; for, first, the triangle, which hath the fewest sides and corners, is of all other the most condemned, as being indeed both incapable and infirm (whereof the reason shall be afterwards rendered) and likewise unresolvable into any other regular form than itself in the inward partitions.

As for figures of five, six, seven, or more angles, they are surely fitter for military architecture, where the bulwarks may be laid out at the corners, and the sides serve for curtains, than for civil use; though I am not ignorant of that famous piece at Caprarola, belonging to the house of Farnese, cast by Baroccio into the form of a pentagon, with a circle inscribed, where the architect did ingeniously wrestle with divers inconveniences in disposing of the lights, and in saving the vacuities; but, as designs of such nature do more aim at rarity than commodity, so, for my part, I had rather admire them than recommend them.

These things considered, we are, both by the precepts and by the practice of the best builders, to resolve upon rectangular squares, as a mean between too few and too many angles; and through the equal inclination of the sides (which make the right angle) stronger than the rhomb or lozenge, or any other irregular square. But whether the exact quadrant or the long square be the better, I find not well determined, though, in mine own conceit, I must prefer the latter, provided that the length do not exceed the latitude above one-third part which would diminish the beauty of the aspect, as shall appear when I come to speak of symmetry and proportion.

Of mixed figures, partly circular, and partly angular, I shall need to say nothing; because, having handled the simple already, the mixed, according to their composition, do participate of the same respects. Only against these there is a proper objection, that they offend uniformity: whereof I am therefore opportunely induced to say somewhat, as far as shall concern the outward aspect, which is now in discourse.

In architecture there may seem to be two opposite affectations, uniformity and variety, which yet will very well suffer a good reconcilement, as we may see in the great pattern of nature, to which I must often resort: for surely there can be no structure more uniform than our bodies in the whole figuration; each side agreeing with the other, both in the number, in the quality, and in the measure of the parts. And yet some are round, as the arms, some flat, as the hands, some prominent, and some more retired. So as upon the matter we see that diversity doth not destroy uniformity, and that the limbs of a noble fabric may be correspondent enough, though they be various, provided always, that we do not run into certain extravagant inventions, whereof I shall speak more largely when I come to the parting and casting of the whole work. We ought likewise to avoid enormous heights of six or seven stories, as well as irregular forms; and the contrary fault, of low-distended fronts, is as unseemly: or again, when the face of the building is narrow and the flank deep: to all which extremes some particular nations or towns are subject, whose names may be civilly spared: and so much for the general figuration or aspect of the work.

Now concerning the parts in severalty. All the parts of every fabric may be comprised under five heads; which division I receive from Baptista Alberti, to do him right. And they be these,

The foundation,	The compartition,
The walls,	and
The appertitions, or overtures,	The cover.

About which I propose to gather the principal cautions; and as I pass along, I will touch also the natural reasons of art that my discourse may be the less mechanical.

First then, concerning the foundation which requireth the exactest care; for, if that happen to dance, it will mar all the mirth in the house: therefore, that we may found our habitation firmly, we must first examine the bed of earth (as I may term it) upon which we will build; and then the underfillings or substruction, as the ancients did call it: for the former, we have a general precept in Vitruvius, twice precisely repeated by him, as a point indeed of main consequence, first *lib.*1. *cap.*5. and again more fitly, *lib.*3. *cap.*3. in these words, as Philander doth well correct the vulgar copies: *Substructiones fundationes fodiantur* (saith he) *si queant inveniri ad solidum, et in solido.* By which words, I conceive him to commend unto us, not only a diligent, but even a jealous examination what the soil will bear; advising us not to rest upon any appearing solidity, unless the whole mould through which we cut has likewise been solid; but how deep we should go in this search, he hath nowhere to my remembrance determined, as, perhaps, depending more upon discretion than regularity, according to the weight of the work; yet Andrea Palladio hath fairly adventured to reduce it into rule: Allowing for that cavazione (as he calleth it) a sixth part of the height of the whole fabric, unless the cellars be under ground, in which case he would have us (as it should seem) to sound somewhat lower.

Some Italians do prescribe that, when they have chosen the floor or plot and laid out the limits of the work, we should first of all dig wells and cisterns and other under-conducts and conveyances, for the swillage of the house, whence may arise a double benefit, for both the nature of the mould or soil would thereby be safely searched; and moreover those open vents will serve to discharge such vapours, as, having otherwise no issue, might peradventure shake the building. This is enough for the natural grounding, which though it be not a part of the solid fabric, yet here was the fittest place to handle it.

There followeth the substruction, or ground work, of the whole edifice, which must sustain the walls; and this is a kind of artificial foundation as the other was natural. About which these are the chief remembrances. First, that the bottom be precisely level, where the Italians therefore commonly lay a platform of good board; then that the lowest ledge or row be merely of stone, and the broader the better, closely laid without mortar, which is a general caution for all parts in building that are contiguous to board or timber, because lime and wood are unsociable, and, if anywhere unfit confiners, then most especially in the foundation. Thirdly, that the breadth of the substruction be at least double of the insistent wall, and more or less, as the weight of the fabric shall require;

for, as I must again repeat, discretion may be freer than art. Lastly, I find in some a curious precept that the materials below be laid as they grew in the quarry, supposing them belike to have most strength in their natural and habitual posture; for, as Philip de l'Orme observeth, the breaking or yielding of a stone in this part, but the breadth of the back of a knife, will make a cleft of more than half a foot in the fabric aloft, so important are fundamental errors. Among which notes I have said nothing of pallification, or piling of the ground-plot, commanded by Vitruvius, when we build upon a moist or marshy soil, because that were an error of the first choice; and there all seats that must use such provision below (as Venice for an eminent example) would, perhaps, upon good enquiry, be found to have been at first chosen by the counsel of necessity.

Now the foundation being searched and the substruction laid, we must next speak of the walls.

Walls are either entire and continual or intermitted; and the intermissions be either pillars or pilasters; for here I had rather handle them, than as some others do, among ornaments.

The entire muring is by writers diversely distinguished; by some, according to the quality of the materials, as either stone or brick, etc., where, by the way, let me note, that to build walls and greater works of flint, whereof we want not example in our island, and particularly in the province of Kent, was (as I conceive) merely unknown to the ancients, who observing in that material a kind of metalic nature, or at least a fusibility, seem to have resolved it into nobler use; an art now utterly lost, or perchance kept up by a few chemics. Some again do not so much consider the quality as the position of the said materials: as when brick or squared stones are laid in their lengths with sides and heads together, or their points conjoined like a network (for so Vitruvius doth call it *reticulatum opus*) of familiar use (as it should seem) in his age, though afterwards grown out of request, even perhaps for that subtle speculation which he himself toucheth; because so laid, they are more apt, in swagging down, to pierce with their points than in the jacent posture, and so to crevice the wall; but to leave such cares to the meaner artificers, the more essential are these.

That the walls be most exactly perpendicular to the ground work; for the right angle (thereon depending) is the true cause of all stability, both in artificial and natural positions; a man likewise standing firmest when he stands uprightest. That the massiest and heaviest materials be the lowest, as fitter to bear than to be born. That the work as it riseth, diminish in thickness proportionally, for ease both of weight and of expense. That certain courses or ledges of more strength than the rest be interlaid like bones to sustain the fabric from total ruin if the under parts should decay. Lastly, that the angles be firmly bound, which are the nerves of the whole edifice, and therefore are commonly fortified by the Italians, even in their brick buildings, on each side of the corners with well squared stone yielding both strength and grace; and so much touching the entire or solid wall.

The intermissions (as hath been said) are either by pillars or pilasters.

Pillars, which we likewise call columns (for the word among artificers is almost naturalized), I could distinguish into simple and compound. But (to tread the beaten and plainest way) there are five orders of pillars, according to their dignity and perfection, thus marshalled:

The Tuscan,	The Corinthian,
The Doric,	and
The Ionic,	The Compound order;

or, as some call it, the Roman, others more generally, the Italian.

In which five orders, I will first consider their communities and then their proprieties.

Their communities (as far as I observe) are principally three. First, they are all round; for though some conceive, *coluna Atticurges*, mentioned by Vitruvius, *lib.*3. *cap.*3. to have been a squared pillar, yet we must pass it over as irregular, never received among these orders, no more than certain other licentious inventions, of wreathed, and vined, and figured columns, which our author himself condemneth, being in his whole book a professed enemy to fancies.

Secondly, they are all diminished, or contracted insensibly, more or less, according to the proportion of their heights, from one third part of the whole shaft upwards, which Philander doth prescribe by his own precise measuring of the ancient remainders, as the most graceful diminution; and here I must take leave to blame a practice grown (I know not how) in certain places too familiar, of making pillars swell in the middle, as if they were sick of some tympany, or dropsy, without any authentic pattern or rule, to my knowledge, and unseemly to the very judgment of sight. True it is, that in Vitruvius, *lib.*3. *cap.*2. we find these words, *De adjectione, quae adjicitur in mediis columnis, quae apud Grecos* ἔντασις *appellatur, in extremo libro erit formatio eius*; which passage seemeth to have given some countenance to this error; but of the promise there made, as of diverse other elsewhere, our master hath failed us, either by slip of memory or injury of time, and so we are left in the dark. Always sure I am, that, besides the authority of example which it wanteth, it is likewise contrary to the original and natural type in trees, which at first was imitated in pillars, as Vitruvius himself observeth, *lib.*5. *cap.*1. For whoever saw any cypress, or pine (which are there alleged) small below and above, and tumorous in the middle, unless it were some diseased plant, as nature (though otherwise the comeliest mistress) hath now and then her deformities and irregularities.

Thirdly, they have all their undersettings, or pedestals, in height a third part of the whole column, comprehending the base and the capital; and their upper adjuncts, as architrave, frieze, and cornice, a fourth part of the said pillar; which rule, of singular use and facility, I find settled by Jacobo Baroccio, and hold him a more credible author as a man that most intended this piece than any that vary from him in those dimensions.

These are their most considerable communities and agreements.

Their properties or distinctions will best appear by some reasonable description of them all, together with their architraves, friezes, and cornices, as they are usually handled.

. . . .

And so much touching the five orders of columns, which I will conclude with two or three not impertinent cautions:

First, that where more of these orders than one shall be set in several stories or contignations, there must be an exquisite care to place the columns precisely one over another, that so the solid may answer to the solid, and the vacuities to the vacuities, as well for beauty as strength of the fabric; and by this caution the consequence is plain that when we speak of intercolumniation or distance, which is due to each order, we mean in a Doric, Ionical, Corinthian porch, or cloister, or the like of one contignation, and not in storied buildings.

Secondly, let the columns above be a fourth part less than those below, saith Vitruvius, *lib.5. cap.1*. A strange precept, in my opinion, and so strange that peradventure it were more suitable, even to his own principles, to make them rather a fourth part greater; for *lib.3. cap.2.* where our master handleth the contractions of pillars, we have an optic rule that the higher they are, the less should be always their diminution aloft, because the eye itself doth naturally contract all objects more or less according to the distance; which consideration may, at first sight, seem to have been forgotten in the caution we have now given; but Vitruvius (the best interpreter of himself) hath in the same place of his fifth book, well acquitted his memory by these words: *Columnae superiores quarta parte minores, quam inferiores, sunt constituendae; propterea quod, operi ferendo quae sunt inferiora, firmiora esse debent*; preferring, like a wise mechanic, the natural reason, before the mathematical, and sensible conceits before abstracted. And yet *lib. 4. cap. 4.* he seemeth again to affect subtility, allowing pillars the more they are channelled, to be the more slender; because, while our eye (saith he) doth, as it were, distinctly measure the eminent and the hollowed parts, the total object appeareth the bigger, and so as much as those excavations do subtract is supplied by a fallacy of the sight; but here, methinks, our master should likewise have rather considered the natural inconvenience; for though pillars by channelling be seemingly engrossed to our sight, yet they are truly weakened in themselves; and therefore ought perchance in sound reason not to be more slender, but the more corpulent, unless appearances preponder truths, but *contra magistrum, non est disputandum*.

A third caution shall be that all the projected or jutting parts (as they are termed) be very moderate, especially the cornices of the lower orders; for whilst some think to give them a more beautiful and royal aspect, by their largeness, they sometimes hinder both the light within (whereof I shall speak more in due place) and likewise detract much from the view of the front without, as well appeareth in one of the principal fabrics at Venice, namely, the palace of the duke Grimani on the canal Grande, which, by this magnificent error, is somewhat disgraced. I need now say no more concerning columns and their adjuncts, about which architects make such a noise in their books, as if the very terms of architraves, and friezes, and cornices, and the like, were enough to graduate a master of this art; yet let me, before I pass to other matter, prevent a familiar objection; it will perchance be said that all this doctrine touching the five orders were fitter for the quarries of Asia, which yielded 127 columns of 60 foot high to the Ephesian temple, or for Numidia, where marbles abound, then for the spirits of England, who must be contented with more ignoble materials: to which I answer, that this need not discourage us: for I have often, at Venice, viewed with much pleasure, an *Atrium Graecium* (we may translate it an anti-porch, after the Greek manner) raised by Andrea Palladio, upon eight columns of the compounded order; the bases of stone without pedestals, the shafts or bodies of mere brick, three foot and a half thick in the diameter below, and consequently thirty-five feet high, as himself hath described them in his second book; than which mine eye hath never yet beheld any columns more stately of stone or marble; for the bricks having first been formed in a circular mould and then cut, before their burning, into four quarters or more, the sides afterwards join so closely and the points concentre so exactly that the pillars appear one entire piece; which short description I could not omit, that thereby may appear how in truth we want rather art than stuff to satisfy our greatest fancies.

After pillars the next in my distribution are pilasters, mentioned by Vitruvius, *lib*.5. *cap*.1. and scant anywhere else, under the name of parastates, as Philander conceiveth, which grammatical point (though perchance not very clear) I am contented to examine no farther. Always what we mean by the thing itself is plain enough in our own vulgar; touching which I will briefly collect the most considerable notes.

Pilasters must not be too tall and slender, lest they resemble pillars, nor too dwarfish and gross, lest they imitate the piles or piers of bridges: smoothness doth not so naturally become them as a rustic superficies, for they aim more at state and strength than elegancy. In private buildings they ought not to be narrower than one third, nor broader than two parts of the whole vacuity, between pilaster and pilaster; but to those that stand at the corners may be allowed a little more latitude by discretion for strength of the angles: in theatres and amphi-theatres, and such weighty works, Palladio observeth them to have been as broad as the half, and now and then as the whole vacuity. He noteth likewise (and others consent with him) that their true proportion should be an exact square; but, for lessening of expense and enlarging of room, they are commonly narrower in flank than in front: their principal grace doth consist in half or whole pillars applied unto them; in which case it is well noted by authors that the columns may be allowed somewhat above their ordinary length, because they lean unto so good supporters. And thus much shall suffice touching pilasters, which is a cheap, and a strong, and a noble kind of structure.

Now because they are oftener, both for beauty and majesty, found arched than otherwise, I am here orderly led to speak of arches, and, under the same head, of vaults; for an arch is nothing but a contracted vault, and a vault is but a dilated arch: therefore, to handle this piece both compendiously and fundamentally, I will resolve the whole business into a few theorems.

Theorem 1

All solid materials, free from impediment, do descend perpendicularly downwards, because ponerosity is a natural inclination to the centre of the world, and nature performeth her motions by the shortest lines.

Theorem 2

Bricks moulded in their ordinary rectangular form, if they shall be laid one by another in a level row, between any supporters sustaining the two ends, then all the pieces between will necessarily sink, even by their own natural gravity, and much more if they suffer any depression by other weight above them, because their sides being parallel, they have room to descend perpendicularly, without impeachment, according to the former theorem; therefore, to make them stand, we must either change their posture, or their figure, or both.

Theorem 3

If bricks moulded, or stones squared *cuneatim* (that is wedge-wise, broader above than below) shall be laid in a row level with their ends supported, as in the precedent theorem, pointing all to one centre, then none of the pieces between can sink till the supporters give way, because they want room in that figuration to descend perpendicularly. But this is yet a weak piece of structure, because the supporters are subject to much impulsion, especially if the line be long; for which reason this form is seldom used, but over windows or narrow doors. Therefore, to fortify the work as in this third theorem, we have supposed the figure of all the materials different from those in the second: so likewise we must now change the posture, as will appear in the theorem following.

Theorem 4

If the materials figured as before wedge-wise shall not be disposed levelly, but in form of some arch or portion of a circle, pointing all to the same centre: in this case, neither the pieces of the said arch can sink downwards, through want of room to descend perpendicularly: nor the supporters, or butments (as they are termed) of the said arch can suffer so much violence, as in the precedent flat posture for the roundness will always make the incumbent weight rather to rest upon the supporters than to shove them; whence may be drawn an evident corollary, that the safest of all arches is the semicircular, and of all vaults the hemisphere, though not absolutely exempted from some natural weakness, as Barnardino Baldi, abbot of Guastalla, in his commentary upon Aristotle's mechanics, doth very well prove; where, let me note by the way, that, when anything is mathematically demonstrated weak, it is much more mechanically weak: errors ever occurring more easily in the management of gross materials than lineal designs.

Theorem 5

As semicircular arches, or hemispherical vaults, being raised upon the total diameter, be of all other the roundest, and consequently the securest, by the precedent theorem; so those are the gracefullest, which, keeping precisely the same height, shall yet be distended one fourteenth part longer than the said entire diameter; which addition of distent will confer much to their beauty and detract but little from their strength.

This observation I find in Leon Batista Alberti; but the practice how to preserve the same height, and yet distend the arms or ends of the arch, is in Albert Dürer's geometry, who taught the Italians many an excellent line of great use in this art.

Upon these five theorems, all the skill of arching and vaulting is grounded: as for those arches, which our artisans call the third and fourth point, and the Tuscan writers *di terzo*, and *di quarto acuto*, because they always concur in an acute angle and do spring from division of the diameter into three, four, or more parts at pleasure; I say, such as these, both for the natural imbecility of the sharp angle itself, and likewise for their very uncomeliness, ought to be exiled from judicious eyes and left to their first inventors, the Goths or Lombards, amongst other relics of that barbarous age.

Thus, of my first partition of the parts of every fabric into five heads, having gone through the two former and been incidentally carried into this last doctrine touching arches and vaults, the next now in order are the apertion, under which term I do comprehend doors, windows, staircases, chimneys, or other conducts: in short, all inlets or outlets, to which belong two general cautions.

First, that they be as few in number and as moderate in dimension as may possibly consist with other due respects; for, in a word, all openings are weakenings.

Secondly, that they do not approach too near the angles of the walls; for it were indeed a most essential solecism to weaken that part which must strengthen all the rest: a precept well recorded, but ill practised by the Italians themselves, particularly at Venice, where I have observed diverse *pergoli*, or *meniana* (as Vitruvius seemeth to call them, which are certain ballified outstandings, to satisfy curiosity of sight) very dangerously set forth, upon the very point itself, of the mural angle.

Now, albeit, I make haste to the casting and comparting of the whole work (being indeed the very definitive sum of this art, to distribute usefully and gracefully a well chosen plot), yet I will first, under their several heads, collect briefly some of the choicest notes belonging to these particular overtures.

Of Doors and Windows

These inlets of men and of light I couple together, because I find their due dimensions brought under one rule, by Leon Alberti (a learned searcher) who, from the school of Pythagoras (where it was a fundamental maxim that the images of all things are latent in numbers) doth determine the comeliest proportion between breadths and heights; reducing symmetry to symphony, and the harmony of sound to a kind of harmony in sight, after this manner. The two principal consonances that most ravish the ear, are, by consent of all nature, the fifth and the octave; whereof the first riseth radically from the proportion, between two and three. The other from the double interval, between one and two, or between two and four, etc. Now, if we shall transport these proportions, from audible to visible objects, and apply them as they shall fall fittest (the nature of the place considered), namely, in some windows and doors, the symmetry of two to three in their breadth and length; in others the double, as aforesaid, there will indubitably result from either a graceful and harmonious contentment to the eye: which speculation, though it may appear unto vulgar artisans perhaps too subtle and too sublime, yet we must remember that Vitruvius himself doth determine many things in his profession by musical grounds, and much commendeth, in an architect, a philosophical spirit, that is, he would have him (as I conceive it) to be no superficial and floating artificer, but a diver into causes and into the mysteries of proportion. Of the ornaments belonging to both doors and windows, I shall speak in another place; but let me here add one observation, that our master (as appeareth by divers passages, and particularly *lib*.6. *cap*.9.) seems to have been an extreme lover of luminous rooms; and, indeed, I must confess that a frank light can misbecome by no edifice whatsoever, temples only excepted; which were anciently dark, as they are likewise at this day in some proportion. Devotion more requiring collected than diffused spirits. Yet, on the other side, we must take heed not to make a house (though but for civil use) all eyes like Argus; which in northern climes would be too cold, in southern, too hot; and therefore the matter indeed importeth more than a merry comparison. Besides, there is no part of structure either more expenseful than windows; or more ruinous; not only for that vulgar reason, as being exposed to all violence of weather, but because, consisting of so indifferent and unsociable pieces, as wood, iron, lead, and glass, and those small and weak, they are easily shaken; I must likewise remember one thing (though it be but a grammatical note) touching doors. Some were *fores* and some were *valvae*. Those (as the very word may seem to import) did open outwards, these inwards; and were commonly of two leaves or panes (as we call them) thereby requiring, indeed, a lesser circuit in their unfolding; and therefore much in use among the Italians at this day: but I must charge them with an imperfection, for though they let in as well as the former, yet they keep out worse.

Of Staircases

To make a complete staircase is a curious piece of architecture: the vulgar cautions are these:

That it have a very liberal light against all casualty of slips and falls.

That the space above the head be large and airy, which the Italians use to call *un belsfogolo*, as it were, good ventilation, because a man doth spend much breath in mounting.

That the half paces be well distributed, at competent distances, for reposing on the way.

That, to avoid encounters, and, besides, to gratify the beholder, the whole staircase have no niggard latitude, that is, for the principal ascent at least ten foot in royal buildings.

That the breadth of every single step or stair be never less than one foot, nor more than eighteen inches.

That they exceed by no means half a foot in their height or thickness; for our legs do labour more in elevation than in destination. These, I say, are familiar remembrances, to which let me add:

That the steps be laid where they join *con un tantino di scarpa*; we may translate it somewhat sloping, that so the foot may in a sort both ascend and descend together, which, though observed by few, is a secret and delicate description of the pains in mounting.

Lastly, to reduce this doctrine to some natural, or at least mathematical ground, our master (as we see *lib.9. cap.2.*) borroweth those proportions that make the sides of a rectangular triangle, which the ancient school did express in lowest terms by the numbers of 3, 4, and 5 that is, three for the perpendicular, from the stair-head to the ground; four for the ground-line itself; or recession from the wall, and five, for the whole inclination or slopeness in the ascent; which proportion, saith he, will make *Temperatas graduum librationes.* Hitherto of staircases which are direct: there are likewise spiral, or cockle stairs, either circular or oval, and sometimes running about a pillar, sometimes vacant, wherein Palladio (a man in this point of singular felicity) was wont to divide the diameter of the first sort into three parts, yielding one to the pillar and two to the steps; of the second into four, whereof he gave two to the stairs, and two to the vacuity, which had all their light from above, and this in exact ovals is a masterpiece.

Of Chimneys

In the present business, Italians, who make very frugal fires, are perchance not the best counsellors. Therefore from them we may better learn both how to raise fair mantles within the rooms, and how to disguise gracefully the shafts of chimneys abroad (as they use) in sundry forms (which I shall handle in the latter part of my labour) and the rest I will extract from Philip de l'Orme: in this part of his work more diligent than in any other, or, to do him right, than any man else.

First, he observeth very soberly, that who, in disposition of any building, will consider the nature of the region and the winds that ordinarily blow from this or that quarter, might so cast the rooms which shall most need fire, that he should little fear the incommodity of smoke, and therefore he thinks that inconvenience, for the most part, to proceed from some inconsiderate beginning. Or, if the error lay not in the disposition, but in the structure itself, then he makes a logical inquiry that either the wind is too much let in above at the mouth of the shaft, or the smoke stifled below; if none of these, then there is a repulsion of the fume by some higher hill or fabric that shall overtop the chimney and work the former effect; if likewise not this, then he concludes that the room which is infested must be necessarily both little and close, so as the smoke cannot issue by a natural principle, wanting a succession and supply of new air.

Now, in these cases, he suggesteth divers artificial remedies, of which I shall allow one a little description because it savoureth of philosophy, and was touched by Vitruvius himself, *lib.*1. *cap.*6. but by this man ingeniously applied to the present use. He will have us provide two hollow brass balls of reasonable capacity, with little holes open in both, for reception of water, when the air shall be first sucked out; one of these we must place with the hole upwards upon an iron wire that shall traverse the chimney a little above the mantle, at the ordinary height of the sharpest heat or flames, whereof the water within being rarified, and by rarifaction resolved into wind, will break out by the way, and so force up the smoke, which otherwise might linger in the tunnel by the way and oftentimes revert. With the other (said he) we may supply the place of the former when it is exhausted, or, for a need blow the fire in the meanwhile, which invention I have interposed for some little entertainment of the reader; I will conclude with a note from Palladio, who observeth that the ancients did warm their rooms with certain secret pipes that came through the walls, transporting heat (as I conceive it) to sundry parts of the house from one common furnace, I am ready to baptize them caliducts, as well as they are termed venti-ducts, and aquae-ducts that convey wind and water, which, whether it were a custom or delicacy, was surely, both for thrift and for use, far beyond the German stoves, and I shall prefer it likewise before our own fashion, if the very sight of a fire did not add to the room a kind of reputation, as old Homer doth teach us in a verse, sufficient to prove that himself was not blind as some would lay to his charge.

Touching conducts for the swillage and other necessities of the house (which how base soever in use, yet, for health of the inhabitants, are as considerable, and perhaps more than the rest), I find in our authors this counsel, that art should imitate nature in those ignoble conveyances and separate them from sight (where there wants a running water) into the most remote, and lowest, and thickest part of the foundation; with secret vents passing up through the walls like a tunnel to the wild air aloft, which all Italian artisans commend for the discharge of noisome vapours, though elsewhere to my knowledge little practised.

Thus, having considered the precedent appertions or overtures in severalty according to their particular requisites, I am now come to the casting or contexture of the whole work, comprehended under the term of compartition; into which (being the mainest piece) I cannot enter without a few general precautions, as I have done in other parts.

First, therefore, let no man that intendeth to build, settle his fancy upon a draft of the work in paper, how exactly soever measured, or neatly set off in perspective; and much less upon a bare plan thereof, as they call the *schiographia*, or ground lines, without a model or type of the whole structure, and of every parcel and partition in pasteboard or wood.

Next, that the said model be as plain as may be, without colours or other beautifying, lest the pleasure of the eye preoccupate the judgment, which advice omitted by the Italian architects, I find in Philip de l'Orme, and therefore (though France be not the theatre of best buildings) it did merit some mention of his name.

Lastly, the bigger that this type be, it is still the better, not that I will persuade a man to such an enormity as that model made by Antonio Labaco of Saint Peter's church in Rome, containing 22 foot in length, 16 in breadth, and 13 in height, and costing 4184 crowns; the price in truth of a reasonable chapel; yet in the fabric of some 40 or 50 thousand pounds charge, I wish 30 pounds at least laid out before hand in an exact model; for a little misery in the premises may easily breed some absurdity of greater charge in the conclusion.

Now, after these premonishments, I will come to the compartition itself, by which the authors of this art (as hath been touched before) do understand a graceful and useful distribution of the whole ground plot, both for rooms of office and of reception or entertainment, as far as the capacity thereof and the nature of the country will comport. Which circumstances in the present subject are all of main consideration and might yield more discourse than an elemental rhapsody will permit. Therefore (to anatomize briefly this definition) the gracefulness (whereof we speak) will consist in double analogy or correspondency. First, between the parts and the whole, whereby a great fabric should have great partitions, great lights, great entrances, great pillars or pilasters; in sum, all the members great. The next between the parts themselves, not only considering their lengths and breadths, as before, when we spake of doors and windows, but here likewise enters a third respect of height, a point (I must confess) hardly reducible to any general precept.

True it is that the ancients did determine the longitude of all rooms which were longer than broad by the double of their latitude (Vitruvius, *lib.*6 *cap.*5.) and the heighth by half of the breadth and length summed together. But when the room was precisely square, they made the height half as much more as the latitude; which dimensions the modern architects have taken leave to vary upon discretion, sometimes squaring the latitude, and then making the diagonal, or overthwart line, from angle to angle of the said square, the measure of the heighth sometimes more, but seldom lower than the full breadth itself; which boldness of quitting the old proportions some attribute first to Michael Angelo da Buonarroti, perchance upon the credit he had before gotten in two other arts.

The second point is usefulness, which will consist in a sufficient number of rooms of all sorts, and in their apt coherence without distraction, without confusion, so as the beholder may not only call it *una fabrica ben raccolta*, as Italians use to speak of well united works, but likewise that it may appear airy and spiritous, and fit for the welcome of cheerful guests, about which, the principal difficulty will be in contriving the lights and staircases, whereof I will touch a note or two: for the first I observe that the ancient architects were much at ease; for both the Greeks and the Romans (of whose private dwellings Vitruvius hath left us some description) had commonly two cloistered open courts, one serving for the women's side, and the other for the men, who, yet perchance, nowadays would take so much separation unkindly. Howsoever, by this means, the reception of light into the body of the building was very prompt, both from without and from within, which we must now supply either by some open form in the fabric or among graceful refuges by terracing any story which is in danger of darkness; or, lastly, by perpendicular lights from the roof, of all other the most natural, as shall be showed anon. For the second difficulty, which is casting of the staircases, that being in itself no hard point, but only as they are encumbrances of room for other use (which lights were not), I am therefore aptly moved here to speak of them. And first of offices.

I have marked a willingness in the Italian artisans to distribute the kitchen, pantry, bakehouse, washing rooms, and even the buttery, likewise under ground, next, above the foundation, and sometimes level with the plane or floor of the cellar, raising the first ascent into the house fifteen foot or more for that end, which, besides the benefit of removing such annoys out of sight, and the gaining of so much more room above, doth also, by elevation of the front, add majesty to the whole aspect: and with such a disposition of the principal staircase, which commonly doth deliver us into the plane of the second story, there may be wonders done with a little room, whereof I could allege brave examples abroad, and none more artificial and delicious than a house built by Daniele Barbaro, patriarch of Aquilia, before mentioned among the memorable commentors upon Vitruvius. But the definition (above determined) doth call us to some consideration of our own country, where, though all the other petty offices (before rehearsed) may well enough be so remote, yet, by the natural hospitality of England, the buttery must be more visible and we need, perchance, for our ranges a more spacious and luminous kitchen than the foresaid compartition will bear, with a more competent nearness likewise to the dining-room. Or else, besides other inconveniences, perhaps some of the dishes may straggle by the way: Here let me note a common defect that we have of a very useful room, called by the Italians *Il Tinello* and familiar, nay, almost essential in all their great families. It is a place properly appointed to conserve the meat that is taken from the table till the waiters eat, which, with us, by an old fashion, is more unseemly set by in the meanwhile.

Now, touching the distribution of lodging chambers: I must here take leave to reprove a fashion, which, I know not how, hath prevailed through Italy, though without ancient examples as far as I can perceive by Vitruvius. The thing I mean is that they so cast their partitions as, when all doors are open, a man may see through the whole house, which doth necessarily put an intolerable servitude upon all the chambers, save the inmost, where none can arrive but through the rest, or else the walls must be extreme thick for secret passages, and yet this also will not serve the turn without at least three doors to every room, a thing most unsufferable in cold and windy regions, and everywhere no small weakening to the whole work: therefore, with us that want no cooling, I cannot commend the direct opposition of such overtures, being indeed merely grounded upon the fond ambition of displaying to a stranger all our furniture at one sight, which, therefore is most maintained by them that mean to harbour but a few, whereby they make only advantage of the vanity, and seldom prove the inconvenience. There is likewise another defect (as absurdities are seldom solitary) which will necessarily follow upon such a servile disposing of inward chambers, that they must be forced to make as many common great rooms as there shall be several stories, which (besides that they are usually dark, a point hardly avoided, running as they do through the middle of the whole house) do likewise devour so much place, that thereby they want other galleries and rooms of retreat, which I have often considered among them (I must confess) with no small wonder; for I observe no nation in the world by nature more private and reserved than the Italian, and, on the other side, in no habitations less privacy, so as there is a kind of conflict between their dwelling and their being. It may here perchance be expected that I should at least describe (which others have done in drafts and designs) divers forms of plants and partitions and varieties of inventions; but speculative writers (as I am) are not bound to comprise all particular cases within the latitude of the subject which they handle; general lights and directions and pointings at some faults is sufficient. The rest must be committed to the sagacity of the architect, who will be often put to divers ingenious shifts when he is to wrestle with scarcity of ground. As sometimes to damn one room (though of special use) for the benefit and beauty of all the rest; another while, to make those fairest which are most in sight, and to leave the other (like a cunning painter) in shadow, *cum multis aliis*, which it were infinite to pursue. I will therefore close this part touching compartition as cheerfully as I can with a short description of a feasting or entertaining room after the Egyptian manner, who seem (at least till the time of Vitruvius) from the ancient Hebrews and Phoenicians (whence all knowledge did flow) to have retained, with other sciences in a high degree, also the principles and practice of that magnificent art. For, as far as I may conjecture by our master's text, *lib.*6. *cap.*5. (whereas in many other places he hath tortured his interpreters) there could no form for such a royal use be comparably imagined like that of the foresaid nation, which I shall venture to explain.

Let us conceive a floor or area of goodly length (for example, at least of 120 foot), with the breadth somewhat more than the half of the longitude, whereof the reason shall be afterwards rendered. About the two longest sides and head of the said room shall run an order of pillars, which Palladio doth suppose Corinthian (as I see by his design) supplying that point out of Greece, because we know no order proper to Egypt. The fourth side I will leave free for the entrance: on the foresaid pillars was laid an architrave, which Vitruvius mentioneth alone. Palladio adds thereunto (and with reason) both frieze and cornice, over which went up a continued wall, and therein half or three-quarter pillars, answering directly to the order below, but a fourth part less, and between these half columns above the whole room was windowed round about.

Now, from the lowest pillars there was laid over a contignation or floor, born upon the outward wall and the head of the columns with terrace and pavement, *sub dio* (saith our master) and so indeed he might safely determine the matter in Egypt, where they fear no clouds. Therefore, Palladio (who leaveth this terrace uncovered in the middle, and ballised about) did perchance construe him rightly, though therein discording from others; always we must understand a sufficient breadth of pavement, left between the open part and the windows, for some delight of spectators that might look down into the room; the latitude I have supposed, contrary to some former positions, a little more than half of the length, because the pillars standing at a competent distance from the outmost wall, will, by interception of the sight, somewhat in appearance diminish the breadth, in which cases (as I have touched once or twice before) discretion may be more licentious than art. This is the description of an Egyptian room for feasts and jollities. About the walls whereof we must imagine entire statues placed below and illuminated by the descending light from the terrace, as likewise from the windows between the half-pillars above, so as this room hath abundant and advantageous light, and, besides other garnishing, must needs receive much state by the very height of the roof, that lay over two orders of columns: and so, having run through the four parts of my first general division, namely, foundation, walls, appertitions, and compartition, the house may now have leave to put on his hat, having hitherto been uncovered itself, and consequently unfit to cover others; which point, though it be the last of this art in execution, yet it is always in intention the first, for who would build but for shelter? Therefore obtaining both the place and the dignity of a final cause, it hath been diligently handled by divers, but by none more learnedly than Bernardino Baldi, abbot of Gaustalla (before cited upon other occasion) who doth fundamentally and mathematically demonstrate the firmest knittings of the upper timbers which make the roof. But it hath been rather my scope in these elements to fetch the ground of all from nature herself, which indeed is the simplest mother of art. Therefore, I will now only deliver a few of the properest, and (as I may say) of the naturalest considerations that belong to this remaining piece.

There are two extremities to be avoided in the cover or roof; that it be not too heavy nor too light. The first will suffer a vulgar objection of pressing too much the under-work. The other containeth a more secret inconvenience; for the cover is not only a bare defence, but likewise a kind of band or ligature to the whole fabric, and therefore would require some reasonable weight. But of the two extremes, the house top-heavy is the worst. Next, there must be a care of equality, that the edifice be not pressed on the one side more than on the other; and here Palladio doth wish (like a cautelous artisan) that the inward walls might bear some good share in the burden and the outward be the less charged.

Thirdly, the Italians are very precise in giving the cover a graceful pendance or slopeness, dividing the whole breadth into nine parts, whereof two shall serve for the elevation of the highest top or ridge from the lowest; but in this point the quality of the region is considerable, for (as our Vitruvius insinuateth) those climes that fear the falling and lying of much snow ought to provide more inclining pentices; and comeliness must yield to necessity.

These are the usefullest cautions which I find in authors, touching the last head of our division, wherewith I will conclude the first part of my present travail. The second remaineth, concerning ornaments within or without the fabric, a piece not so dry as the mere contemplation of proportions. And therefore, I hope therein somewhat to refresh both the reader and myself.

Of the Elements of Architecture—The Second Part

Every man's proper mansion house and home, being the theatre of his hospitality, the seat of self-fruition, the comfortablest part of his own life, the noblest of his son's inheritance, a kind of private princedom, nay, to the possessors thereof, an epitome of the whole world, may well deserve by these attributes, according to the degree of the master, to be decently and delightfully adorned. For which end, there are two arts attending on architecture, like two of her principal gentlewomen to dress and trim their mistress, picture and sculpture, between whom, before I proceed any further, I will venture to determine an ancient quarrel about their precedency, with this distinction, that, in the garnishing of fabrics, sculpture, no doubt, must have the pre-eminence, as being indeed of nearer affinity to architecture itself, and, consequently, the more natural and more suitable ornament. But, on the other side (to consider these two arts as I shall do, philosophically and not mechanically) an excellent piece of painting is, in my judgment, the more admirable object, because it comes near an artificial miracle, to make divers distinct eminences appear upon a flat by force of shadows, and yet the shadows themselves not to appear; which I conceive to be the uttermost value and virtue of a painter, and to which very few have arrived in all ages.

In these two arts (as they are applicable to the subject which I handle) it shall be fit, first, to consider how to choose them, and next, how to dispose them. To guide us in the choice we have a rule somewhere (I well remember) in Pliny, and it is a pretty observation. That they do mutually help to censure one another. For picture is best when it standeth off, as if it were carved, and sculpture is best when it appeareth so tender as if it were painted; I mean, when there is such a seeming softness in the limbs as if not a chisel had hewed them out of stone or other material, but, a pencil had drawn and stroked them in oil, which the judicious poet took well to his fancy: *Excudunt alii spirantia mollius aera.*

But this generality is not sufficient to make a good chooser, without a more particular contraction of his judgment. Therefore, when a piece of art is set before us, let the first caution be, not to ask who made it, lest the fame of the author do captivate the fancy of the buyer: for, that excellent men do always excellently is a false conclusion, whereupon I observe among the Italian artisans three notable phrases, which well decipher the degrees of their works.

They will tell you that a thing was done *con diligenza*, *con studio*, and *con amore*; the first is but a bare and ordinary diligence, the second is a learned diligence, the third is much more, even a loving diligence; they mean not with love to the bespeaker of the work, but with a love and delight in the work itself, upon some special fancy to this or that story, and when all these concur (particularly the last) in an eminent author, then perchance *Titianus fecit*, or ὀφίδιας ἐποίει will serve the turn without farther inquisition; otherwise artisans have not only their growths and perfections, but likewise their veins and times.

The next caution must be (to proceed logically) that, in judging of the work itself, we be not distracted with too many things at once; therefore, first (to begin with picture) we are to observe whether it be well drawn or (as more elegant artisans term it) well designed; then whether it be well coloured, which be the two general heads; and each of them hath two principal requisites; for in well designing there must be truth and grace; in well colouring, force and affection; all other praises are but consequences of these.

Truth (as we metaphorically take it in this art) is a just and natural proportion in every part of the determined figure. Grace is a certain free disposition in the whole draft, answerable to that unaffected frankness of fashion in a living body, man or woman, which doth animate beauty where it is and supply it where it is not.

Force consisteth in the roundings and raisings of the work, according as the limbs do more or less require it; so as the beholder shall spy no sharpness in the bordering lines; as when tailors cut out a suit, which Italians do aptly term, according to that comparison, *contorni taglienti*; nor any flatness within the body of the figure, which how it is done, we must fetch from a higher discipline; for the optics teach us that a plane will appear prominent, and (as it were) embossed, if the parts farthest from the axle-tree, or middle beam of the eye, shall be the most shadowed. Because in all darkness there is a kind of deepness; but, as in the art of persuasion, one of the most fundamental precepts is the concealment of art; so here, likewise, the sight must be sweetly deceived by an insensible passage from brighter colours to dimmer, which Italian artisans call the middle tinctures; that is, not as the whites and yolks of eggs lie in the shell, with visible distinction, but as when they are beaten and blended in a dish; which is the nearest comparison that I can suddenly conceive.

Lastly, affection is the lively representation of any passion whatsoever, as if the figures stood not upon a cloth or board, but as if they were acting upon a stage; and here, I must remember, in truth, with much marvel, a note which I have received from excellent artisans, that, though gladness and grief be opposite in nature, yet they are such neighbours and confiners in art that the least touch of a pencil will translate a crying into a laughing face; which instance, besides divers other, doth often reduce unto my memoire that ingenious speculation of the Cardinal Cusanus, extant in his works, touching the coincidence of extremes. And thus much of the four requisites and perfections in picture.

In sculpture, likewise, the two first are absolutely necessary; the third, impertinent, for solid figures need no elevation by force of lights or shadows; therefore, in the room of this, we may put (as hath been before touched) a kind of tenderness, by the Italians termed *morbidezza*, wherein the chisel, I must confess, hath more glory than the pencil; that being so hard an instrument, and working upon so unpliant stuff, can yet leave strokes of so gentle appearance.

The fourth, which is the expression of affection (as far as it doth depend upon the activity and gesture of the figure) is as proper to the carver as to the painter; though colours, no doubt, have therein the greatest power; whereupon, perchance, did first grow with us the fashion of colouring even regal statues, which I must take leave to call an English barbarism.

Now in these four requisites, already rehearsed, it is strange to note that no artisan having ever been blamed for excess in any of the three last; only truth (which should seem the most innocent) hath suffered some objection, and all ages have yielded some one or two artificers so prodigiously exquisite that they have been reputed too natural in their drafts; which will well appear by a famous passage in Quintilian, touching the characters of the ancient artisans, falling now so aptly into my memory, that I must needs translate it, as in truth it may well deserve.

The place which I intend is extant in the last chapter save one of his whole work, beginning thus in Latin: *Primi, quorum quidem opera non vetustatis modo gratia visenda sunt clari pictores fuisse dicuntur, Polygnotus atque Aglaophon, etc. . . .*

This is that witty censure of the ancient artisans, which Quintilian hath left us, where the last character of Demetrius doth require a little philosophical examination: How an artificer, whose end is the imitation of nature, can be too natural? Which likewise, in our days, was either the fault, or (to speak more gently) the too much perfection of Albert Dürer, and perhaps also of Michael Angelo da Buonarroti, between whom I have heard noted, by an ingenious artisan, a pretty nice difference, that the German did too much express that which was, and the Italian that which should be, which severe observation of nature, by the one in her commonest, and by the other in her absolutest forms, must needs produce in both a kind of rigidity, and consequently more naturalness than gracefulness: this is the clearest reason why some exact symmetrists have been blamed for being too true, as near as I can deliver my conceit. And so much touching the choice of picture and sculpture: the next is the application of both to the beautifying of fabrics.

First, therefore, touching picture, there doth occur a very pertinent doubt, which hath been passed over too slightly, not only by some men, but by some nations; namely, whether this ornament can well become the outside of houses, wherein the Germans have so little scruple that their best towns are the most painted, as Augusta and Nuremberg. To determine this question in a word; it is true, that a story well set out with a good hand will everywhere take a judicious eye; but yet withal, it is as true, that various colours on the out-walls of buildings have always in them more delight than dignity. Therefore I would there admit no paintings but in black and white, nor even in that kind any figures (if the room be capable) under nine or ten foot high, which will require no ordinary artisan, because the faults are more visible than in small designs. In unfigured paintings, the noblest is the imitation of marbles and of architecture itself; as arches, friezes, columns, and the like.

Now, for the inside, here grows another doubt, whether *grotesca* (as the Italians) or antique work (as we call it) should be received, against the express authority of Vitruvius himself, *lib.7. cap.5.* where *pictura* (saith he) *fit eius, quod est, seu potest esse,* excluding by this severe definition all figures composed of different natures or sexes, as a Siren or Centaur, had been intolerable in his eye; but in this we must take leave to depart from our master; and the rather, because he spake out of his own profession; allowing painters (who have ever been as little limited as poets) a less scope in their imaginations, even than the gravest philosophers, who sometimes do serve themselves of instances that have no existence in nature; as we see in Plato's *Amphisboena*, and Aristotle's *Hirco-cervus*. And (to settle this point) what was indeed more common and familiar among the Romans themselves than the picture and statue of *Terminus*, even one of their deities? Which yet, if we well consider it, is but a piece of *grotesca*; I am, for these reasons, unwilling to impoverish that art, though I could wish such medley and motley designs confined only to the ornament of friezes and borders, their properest place. As for other storied works upon walls, I doubt our clime be too yielding and moist for such garnishment; therefore, leaving it to the dweller's discretion according to the quality of his seat, I will only add a caution or two about the disposing of pictures within.

First, that no room be furnished with too many, which in truth were a surfeit of ornament, unless they be galleries or some peculiar repository for rarities of art.

Next, that the best pieces be placed not where there is the least, but where there are the fewest lights; therefore, not only rooms windowed on both ends, which we call through-lighted, but with two or more windows on the same side, are enemies to this art; and sure it is, that no painting can be seen in full perfection, but (as all nature is illuminated) by a single light.

Thirdly, that in placing there be some care also taken how the painter did stand in the working, which an intelligent eye will easily discover, and that posture is the most natural; so as Italian pieces will appear best in a room where the windows are high; because they are commonly made to a descending light, which of all other doth set off men's faces in their truest spirit.

Lastly, that they be as properly bestowed for their quality as fitly for their grace; that is, cheerful paintings in feasting and banqueting rooms; graver stories in galleries, landscapes and boscage and such wild works in open terraces or in summer houses (as we call them) and the like.

And thus much of picture, which let me close with this note; that though my former discourse may serve perchance for some reasonable leading in the choice of such delights, yet let no man hope, by such a speculative erudition, to discern the masterly and mysterious touches of art, but an artisan himself; to whom, therefore, we must leave the prerogative to censure the manner and handling, as he himself must likewise leave some points, perchance of no less value to others; as, for example, whether the story be rightly represented, the figures in true action, the persons suited to their several qualities, the affections proper and strong, and such like observations.

Now for sculpture, I must likewise begin with a controversy as before (falling into this place) or let me rather call it a very mere fancy, strangely taken by Palladio, who, having noted in an old arch or two at Verona, some part of the materials already cut in fine forms, and some unpolished, doth conclude (according to his logic) upon this particular, that the ancients did leave the outward face of their marbles or freestone without any sculpture, till they were laid and cemented in the body of the building; for which likewise he findeth a reason (as many do now and then very wittily, even before the thing itself be true) that the materials being rough were more manageable in the mason's hand than if they had been smooth; and that so the sides might be laid together the more exactly; which conceit, once taken, he seems to have farther imprinted, by marking in certain storied sculptures of old time how precisely the parts and lines of the figures that pass from one stone to another do meet, which he thinks could hardly fall out so right (forgetting, while he speaks of ancient things, the ancient diligence) unless they had been cut after the joining of the materials; but all these inducements cannot countervail the sole inconvenience of shaking and disjointing the commissures with so many strokes of the chisel, besides an incommodious working on scaffolds; especially having no testimony to confirm it that I have yet seen among the records of art; nay, it is indeed rather true that they did square, and carve, and polish their stone and marble works, even in the very cave of the quarry, before it was hardened by open air; but (to leave disputation) I will set down a few positive notes for the placing of sculpture, because the choosing hath been handled before.

That, first of all, it be not too general and abundant, which would make a house look like a cabinet; and in this point moral philosophy, which tempereth fancies, is the superintendent of art.

That especially there be a due moderation of this ornament in the first approach; where our authors do more commend (I mean about the principal entrance) a Doric than a Corinthian garnishment; so as if the great door be arched with some brave head, cut in fine stone or marble for the key of the arch, and two incumbent figures gracefully leaning upon it towards one another, as if they meant to confer: I should think this a sufficient entertainment for the first reception of any judicious sight, which I could wish seconded with two great standing statues on each side of a paved way that shall lead up into the fabric, so as the beholder at the first entrance may pass his eye between them.

That the niches, if they contain figures of white stone or marble, be not coloured in their concavity too black; for though *contraria juxta se posita magis illucescunt* (by an old rule) yet it hath been subtly, and indeed truly, noted that our sight is not well contented with those sudden departments from one extreme to another; therefore let them have rather a duskish tincture than an absolute black.

That fine and delicate sculptures be helped with nearness, and gross with distance; which was well seen in the old controversy between Phidias and Alcamenes about the statue of Venus; wherein the first did show discretion and save labour, because the work was to be viewed at good height, which did drown the sweet and diligent strokes of his adversary: a famous emulation of two principal artisans celebrated even by the Greek poets.

That in the placing of standing figures aloft, we must set them in a posture somewhat bowing forward; because (saith our master *lib.3. cap.3.* out of a better art than his own) the visual beam of our eye, extended to the head of the said figures, being longer than to the foot, must necessarily make that part appear farther; so as to reduce it to an erect or upright position, there must be allowed a due advantage of stooping towards us; which Albert Dürer hath exactly taught in his forementioned geometry. Our Vitruvius calleth this affection in the eye a resupination of the figure: for which word (being in truth his own, for aught I know) we are almost as much beholding to him as for the observation itself. And let thus much summarily suffice touching the choice and use of these adorning arts. For to speak of garnishing the fabric with a row of erected statues about the cornice of every contignation or story, were discourse more proper for Athens or Rome, in the time of their true greatness, when (as Pliny recordeth of his own age) there were near as many carved images as living men; like a noble contention, even in point of fertility, between art and nature; which passage doth not only argue an infinite abundance, both of artisans and materials, but likewise of magnificent and majestical desires in every common person of those times, more or less, according to their fortunes. And true it is indeed that the marble monuments and memories of well deserving men, wherewith the very highways were strewed on each side, was not a bare and transitory entertainment of the eye, or only a gentle deception of time to the traveller; but had also a secret and strong influence, even into the advancement of the monarchy, by continual representation of virtuous examples; so as in that point art became a piece of state.

Now, as I have before subordinated picture and sculpture to architecture as their mistress, so there are certain inferior arts likewise subordinate to them: as, under picture, mosaic; under sculpture, plastic; which two I only nominate as the fittest to garnish fabrics.

Mosaic is a kind of painting in small pebbles, cockles, and shells of sundry colours; and of late days likewise with pieces of glass, figured at pleasure; an ornament, in truth, of much beauty and long life, but of most use in pavements and floorings.

Plastic is not only under sculpture, but indeed very sculpture itself; but with this difference, that the plasterer doth make his figures by addition, and the carver by subtraction, whereupon Michael Angelo was wont to say somewhat pleasantly that sculpture was nothing but a purgation of superfluities. For take away from a piece of wood or stone all that is superfluous, and the remainder is the intended figure. Of this plastic art, the chief use with us is the graceful fretting of roofs: but the Italians apply it to the mantling of chimneys with great figures; a cheap piece of magnificence, and as durable almost within doors as harder forms in the weather. And here, though it be a little excursion, I cannot pass unremembered again their manner of disguising the shafts of chimneys in various fashions, whereof the noblest is the pyramidal; being in truth a piece of polite and civil discretion to convert even the conduits of soot and smoke into ornaments; whereof I have hitherto spoken as far as may concern the body of the building.

Now there are ornaments also without, as gardens, fountains, groves, conservatories of rare beasts, birds, and fishes. Of which ignobler kind of creatures we ought not (saith our greatest master among the sons of nature) childishly to despise the contemplation; for in all things that are natural, there is ever something that is admirable. Of these external delights a word or two.

First, I must note a certain contrariety between building and gardening. For as fabrics should be regular, so gardens should be irregular, or at least cast into a very wild regularity. To exemplify my conceit: I have seen a garden (for the manner perchance incomparable) into which the first access was a high walk like a terrace, from whence might be taken a general view of the whole plot below; but rather in a delightful confusion, than with any plain distinction of the pieces. From this the beholder descending many steps was afterwards conveyed again, by several mountings and valings, to various entertainments of his scent and sight, which I shall not need to describe (for that were poetical); let me only note this, that every one of these diversities was as if he had been magically transported into a new garden.

But though other countries have more benefit of sun than we, and thereby more properly tied to contemplate this delight, yet have I seen in our own a delicate and diligent curiosity, surely without parallel among foreign nations: namely, in the garden of Sir Henry Fanshaw, at his seat in Ware Park where I well remember he did so precisely examine the tinctures and seasons of his flowers that, in their setting, the inwardest of those which were to come up at the same time should be always a little darker than the outmost and to serve them for a kind of gentle shadow, like a piece not of nature but of art, which mention (incident to this place) I have willingly made of his name for the dear friendship that was long between us; though I must confess, with much wrong to his other virtues, which deserve a more solid memorial than among these vacant observations. So much of gardens.

Fountains are figured, or only plain watered-works: of either of which, I will describe a matchless pattern.

The first, done by the famous hand of Michael Angelo da Buonarroti, in the figure of a sturdy woman, washing and winding of linen clothes; in which act she wrings out the water that made the fountain; which was a graceful and natural conceit in the artificer, implying this rule, that all designs of this kind should be proper.

The other doth merit some large expression; there went a long, straight, mossy walk of competent breadth, green and soft underfoot, listed on both sides with an aqueduct of white stone, breast-high, which had a hollow channel on the top, where ran a pretty trickling stream; on the edge whereof, were couched, very thick all along, certain small pipes of lead in little holes; so neatly that they could not be well perceived, till, by the turning of a cock, they did spout over changeably from side to side above man's height, in form of arches, without any intersection or meeting aloft, because the pipes were not exactly opposite; so as the beholder, beside that which was fluent in the aqueducts on both hands in his view, did walk as it were under a continual bower or hemisphere of water without any drop falling on him. An invention for refreshment surely far excelling all the Alexandrian delicacies and pneumatics of Hero.

Groves and artificial devices underground are of great expense and little dignity; which, for my part, I could wish converted here into those *cryptera*, whereof mention is made among the curious provisions of Tycho Brahe, the Danish Ptolemy, as I may well call him; which were deep concaves in gardens where the stars might be observed even at noon. For (by the way) to think that the brightness of the sun's body above doth drown our discerning of the lesser lights is a popular error; the sole impediment being that lustre, which by reflection doth spread about us from the face of the earth; so as the caves, before touched, may well conduce, not to a delicious, but to a learned pleasure.

In aviaries of wire to keep birds of all sorts, the Italians (though no wasteful nation) do, in some places, bestow vast expense; including great scope of ground, variety of bushes, trees of good height, running waters, and sometimes a stove annexed to contemper the air in winter. So as those chantresses, unless they be such as perhaps delight as much in their wing as in their voice, may live long, among so good provisions and room, before they know that they are prisoners, reducing often to my memory that conceit of the Roman stoic, who, in comparison of his own free contemplations, did think divers great and splendent fortunes of his time little more than commodious captivities.

Concerning ponds of pleasure near the habitation, I will refer myself to a grave author of our own (though more illustrious by his other work) namely *Sarisburiensis de Piscina*.

And here I will end the second part touching ornaments, both within and without the fabric.

Now as almost all those, which have delivered the elements of logic, do usually conclude with a chapter touching method, so I am here seized with a kind of critical spirit and desirous to shut up these building elements with some methodical direction how to censure fabrics already raised: for, indeed, without some way to contract our judgment, which, among so many particulars, would be lost by diffusion, I should think it almost harder to be a good censurer than a good architect; because the working part may be helped with deliberation, but the judging must flow from an extemporal habit. Therefore (not to leave this last piece without some light), I could wish him that cometh to examine any noble work, first of all to examine himself, whether perchance the sight of many brave things before (which remain like impressed forms) have not made him apt to think nothing good, but that which is the best; for this humour were too sour. Next, before he come to settle any imaginable opinion, let him by all means seek to inform himself precisely of the age of the work upon which he must pass his doom. And if he shall find the apparent decays to exceed the proportion of time, then let him conclude, without farther inquisition, as an absolute decree, that either the materials were too slight or the seat is nought. Now, after these premises, if the house be found to bear his years well (which is always a token of sound constitution), then let him suddenly run backwards (for the method of censuring is contrary to the method of composing) from the ornaments (which first allure the eye) to the more essential members, till at last he be able to form this conclusion, that the work is commodious, firm, and delightful; which (as I said in the beginning) are the three capital conditions required in good buildings, by all authors both ancient and modern. And this is, as I may term it, the most scientifical way of censuring. There are two other, which I must not forget. The first in Georgio Vassari, before his laborious work of the lives of architects, which is to pass a running examination over the whole edifice according to the properties of a well-shapen man. As whether the walls stand upright upon clean footing and foundation; whether the fabric be of a beautiful stature; whether for the breadth it appear well burnished; whether the principal entrance be on the middle line of the front or face, like our mouths; whether the windows, as our eyes, be set in equal number and distance on both sides; whether the offices, like the veins in our bodies, be usefully distributed and so forth. For this allegorical review may be driven as far as any wit will, that is at leisure.

The second way is in Vitruvius himself, *lib*.1. *cap*.2. where he summarily determineth six considerations, which accomplish this whole art.

Ordinatio.	*Symmetria.*
Dispositio.	*Decor,* and
Eurythmia.	*Distributio.*

Whereof (in my conceit) we may spare him the first two; for, as far as I can perceive, either by his interpreters or by his own text (which in that very place, where perchance he should be clearest, is of all other the cloudiest) he meaneth nothing by ordination but a well settling of the model or scale of the whole work. Nor by disposition, more than a neat and full expression of the first idea or designment thereof; which perchance do more than belong to the artificer than to the censurer. The other four are enough to condemn, or absolve, any fabric whatsoever. Whereof *eurythmia* is that agreeable harmony between breadth, length, and height of all the rooms of the fabric, which suddenly where it is taketh every beholder by the secret power of proportion: wherein let me only note this, that though the least error or offence that can be committed against sight is excess of height, yet that fault is nowhere of small importance, because it is the greatest offence against the purse.

Symmetria is the conveniency that runneth between the parts and the whole, whereof I have formerly spoken.

Decor is the keeping of a due respect between the inhabitant and the habitation. Whence Palladio did conclude that the principal entrance was never to be regulated by any certain dimensions, but by the dignity of the master; yet to exceed rather in the more than in the less is a mark of generosity and may always be excused with some noble emblem, or inscription, as that of the *Conte di Bevilacqua* over his large gate at Verona, where perchance had been committed a little disproportion.

Patet Janua: Cor magis.

And here likewise I must remember our ever memorable Sir Philip Sidney (whose wit was in truth the very rule of congruity), who well knowing that Basilius (as he had painted the state of his mind) did rather want some extraordinary forms to entertain his fancy than room for courtiers, was content to place him in a star-like lodge; which otherwise in severe judgment of art had been an incommodious figure.

Distributio is that useful casting of all rooms for office, entertainment, or pleasure, which I have handled before at more length than any other piece.

These are the four heads which every man should run over, before he pass any determinate censure upon the works that he shall view, wherewith I will close this last part touching ornaments. Against which (methinks) I hear an objection, even from some well-meaning man, that these delightful crafts may be divers ways ill applied in a land. I must confess, indeed, there may be a lascivious, and there may be likewise a superstitious use, both of picture and of sculpture: to which possibility of misapplication, not only these semi-liberal arts are subject, but even the highest perfections and endowments of nature. As beauty in a light woman, eloquence in a mutinous man, resolution in an assassinate, prudent observation of hours and humours in a corrupt courtier, sharpness of wit and argument in a seducing scholar, and the like. Nay, finally, let me ask, what art can be more pernicious than even religion itself, if itself be converted into an instrument of art: therefore, *ab abuti ad non uti, negatur consequentia.*

Thus having stitched in some sort together these animadversions touching architecture and the ornaments thereof, I now feel that contemplative spirits are as restless as active; for doubting with myself (as all weakness is jealous) that I may be thought to have spent my poor observation abroad about nothing but stone and timber and such rubbage, I am thereby led into an immodesty of proclaiming another work, which I have long devoted to the service of my country, namely, a philosophical survey of education, which is indeed a second building, or repairing of nature, and, as I may term it, a kind of moral architecture; whereof such notes as I have taken in my foreign transcursions or abode, I hope to utter without public offence, though still with the freedom of a plain Kentish man. In the meanwhile, I have let these other gleanings fly abroad, like the bird out of the ark, to discover what footing may be for that which shall follow.

Or the plain pathway to preferment. Being a discovery of a passage to promotion in all professions, trades, arts, and mysteries. Found out by an old traveller in the sea of experience, amongst the enchanted islands of ill fortune. Now published for common good. By Thomas Powell. *Summum hominis bonum bonus ex hac vita exitus.* London. Printed by B. Alsop and T. Fawcet, for Benjamin Fisher, and are to be sold at his shop at the sign of the Talbot in Aldersgate-street. 1631.

THOMAS POWELL (1572?–1635), 'the rollicking attorney and Welshman,' was a man of wide experience and well qualified to give cynical advice on the art of thriving. He was at Gray's Inn in 1593, published volumes of bad verse in 1598 and 1601, and wrote his first prose work in 1603, *A Welsh Bayte to spare Provender*, a justification of Elizabeth's treatment of papists and dissenters. In 1612—for the Thomas Powell who was a minor officeholder under James I was probably Powell the writer—he got a life grant of the keepership of the stables at Hampton Court; in 1613 he was appointed solicitor-general of the marches of Wales, a post he resigned in 1622; in 1620 he received as a life grant the office of keeping the ordnance in the Tower, not wholly a sinecure; and in 1622 he served as king's messenger, in attendance upon the privy council. His later prose works were of two sorts. He wrote serious and informative *vade mecums*: *Direction for Search of Records Remaining in the Chancerie, Tower, Exchequer* (1622); *The Attorney's Academy* (1623), a handbook to practise in courts of record; *The Attorney's Almanacke* (1627), a guide for removing cases from inferior to Westminster courts; and *The Repertorie of Records* (1631), an expansion of his earlier guide to the records. Sandwiched among such practical volumes were *The Mysterie of Lending and Borrowing, or The Tickling Torture* (1623), an amusing description of spongers and their victims; and *Tom of All Trades*, which can stand as the sincere if bitter account of a man grown wise in his world.

The text is taken from the publication of the New Shakespeare Society, 1876, edited by Frederick J.Furnivall.

TRINITY term was now ended; for by description of the time it could be no other parcel of the year. In that the scriveners at Temple-Bar had no employment but writing of blank bonds and texting of bills for letting of chambers in Chancery Lane. The vintners of Fleet Street discharged their journeymen; a general humility more than usual possessed the cookery of Ram Alley. The hostlers of Holborn had more than ordinary care to lay up their guests' boots, rather for fear of their slipping out of town than for any good observance towards them. And your country attorneys would no longer by any means endure the unwholesome air of an eightpenny ordinary. Every one that had wherewith to discharge his horse out of the stable strove who should first be gone. And amongst the rest myself made shift for so much money as wherewith to abate the fury of Mistress Overcount mine hostess, and so I departed likewise.

At the top of Highgate Hill I overtook a gentleman of Northamptonshire, riding homeward, whom I well knew; him I saluted cheerfully, and he received me lovingly. But in travelling together (me thought) he was not master of that mirthful disposition which he was wont to carry along with him to shorten the way betwixt his house and London. I gave him to understand how strange and notable this alteration appeared in him; and withal desired to know so much of the occasion thereof as might be impartable to a friend of so small growth. To which he answered thus: Sir, I come from London (it is true), from the term (it is certain true), from London and term. True and certain in nothing but expenses in all things; yet I would have you know that it is neither the thunderclap of dissolving an injunction, nor the doomsday of a decree, nor counsellor's fees, nor attorney's bills, in a language able to fright a man out of his wits can proscribe me my wonted mirth. It is something nearer and dearer (my dear friend) that robs me of that cheer which used to lift me up into the very sphere where Jove himself sits to bid all his guests welcome right heartily.

I remember me of children, six sons and three daughters, of whom I am the unhappy father. In that, besides the scars which my unthriftiness hath dinted upon their fortunes, the wounds of unequal times and a tempestuous age approaching are like to take away from them all hope of outliving the low water ebb of the evil day; all means of thriving by honest pains, study, or industry are bereft them. The common upon which industry should depasture is overlaid; numerousness spoils all, and poverty sells all at an under value.

In this case (sir) what can be advised? Whereunto I thus replied.

Sir, I have heedfully attended you in the delivery of your perplexed thoughts concerning the care which you have of your children, taking the true and even level of the declension of arts, the distent of trades and trading, the poverty of all professions, and the distemper, not of ours only, but of all Christian climates at this present, tending rather to a more contagion in the general air than a calmer temperament (for ought that yet appeareth): as for the storminess of the sea of state, foreign or domestic, let us leave the greater and lesser vessels that be exposed to it unto the proper pilots, masters, and mariners, who have the charge to attend the line or ply at the tackle; we are but poor passengers, and may assure ourselves to partake in their boon voyage, if they succeed well— as they may be certain to suffer in the same shipwreck with us, if we miscarry. I address me to give you the best advice I can, touching the preferment of every of your six sons and three daughters, in manner following.

It is true in most gentlemen, and very likely in you as in others living only upon the revenue of lands, that the height of their husbandry amounts to no more than to clear the last half-year's booking, and borrowing at the rent day that their credit may hold up and keep reputation till the next ensuing that again.

When you die, the eldest son claims the inheritance of what you leave, thanks God and nature for it, yourself least of all, and your fatherly providence never a whit.

If you take some course in your lifetime to make the rest of your children some small portions or estates out of the whole of your lands, it is ten to one but you destroy both him and them by that means.

For the heir, commonly striving to uphold the reputation of his ancestors, he abates nothing of his father's accustomed expenses towards the raising of those portions or estates so deducted. And they, on the other side, presume so much upon the hope thereof, that no profession will fit them. To be a minister (with them) is to be but a pedant; a lawyer, a mercenary fellow; a shopkeeper, a man most subject to the most wonderful crack, and a creature whose welfare depends much upon his wife's well-bearing and fair carriage. What is, then, to be done?

Surely it would be wished, seeing God and nature hath provided for the eldest, your younger sons, and your daughters especially, being worst able to shift, should be by you provided for in the first place, while your land is of virgin reputation, while it is chaste and undishonested by committing of single fornication with country creditors, that trade without sheets (that is) by pole-deed, only for saving of costs; or, at least, before it has defiled the bed of its reputation by prostituting to the adulterous embracings of a city scrivener. But especially, before it grow so impudent as to lie down in the market-place, and to suffer every petty clerk to bring its good name upon record and charge it that it was taken in the very fact between other men's sheets—as in this statute, or in that judgment: Take heed of that by any means. And be sure to match your eldest son when your credit is cried up to the highest, while your heir is yet in your power to dispose and will bend to your will, before his blood begin to feel the heat of any affections kindling about him, or before he can tell what difference is betwixt a black wrought waistcoat with a white apron, and a loose bodied gown without an apron. Put him off in his best clothes, (I mean) in the assurance of your lands; sell him at the highest rate. Then dichotomize the whole portion of his wife into several shares betwixt your other children. Not share and share alike, but to every each one, the more, according to their defects: let impotency, decrepitness, ill-favouredness, and incapacity rob the other of so much money as they have done them of comeliness, activity, beauty, and wit.

Put them not into any course of living according to any prescript order or method of your own election, but according to their inclination and addition, seeing that everyone, by instinct of nature, delighteth in that wherein he is like to be most excellent. And delight and pride in anything undertaken, make all obstacles in the way of attaining to perfection of no difficulty.

Now, in the next place, take heed that you put off those your sons whom you find fit and addicted to be bred in the ministry, or made up, to the law, or to be apprenticed, betimes, and before they take the taint of too much liberty at home.

And when they be put forth, call them not home speedily to revisit their father's house, no, not so much as hospitably by any means.

IN THE FIRST PLACE, TAKE YOUR DIRECTION FOR THE SCHOLAR

His education; his maintenance; his advancement.

For his education. The free-schools generally afford the best breeding in good letters.

So many of them also afford some reasonable means in aid of young scholars, for their diet, lodging, and teaching, given to them by the founders or benefactors of such schools.

Some of them be of the foundation of some kings and queens of this land; and they are commonly in the gift of the king, or his provost, or substitute in that behalf. Others be of the foundation of some bodies or societies incorporate; and they are commonly in the gift of such masters, wardens, presidents, and their senior fellows; such chief officers of any other title, or such master, wardens, and assistants, or such opposers, visitants, or committees of such bodies respectively as be appointed thereunto. Others be of the foundation of some private persons: and they are, for the most part, in the gift of the executor, heir, or feoffees of such donor, according to the purport of his will, or grant, or both.

Of every of which several kinds respectively are:

> Eton.
> Westminster.
> Winchester.
> The Merchant Taylors' School, London.
> The Skinners at Tunbridge.
> Sutton's Hospital.
> St. Bartholomew's.
> And very many other the like.

Briefly, few or no counties of this kingdom are unfurnished of such schools. And some have so many, that it is disputable whether the universities, with the Inns of Court and Chancery, have where to receive them or no.

Some of such free-schools, again, have scholarships appendant unto them, in the one of the universities, or both.

To which, upon election yearly, they are removable, as

> From Eton to King's College, Cambridge.
> From Westminster to Trinity College, Cambridge, or Christ Church, Oxon.
> From Winchester to New College, Oxon.
> From the Merchant Taylors' to St. John's, Oxon.
> And the like, from many the like.

Some other free-schools have pensions for preferment of their scholars, and for their maintenance in the university.

Some companies incorporate (especially of London, having no such pensions in certain) do usually out of the stock of their hall allow maintenance in this kind.

Besides that, there by many other private persons (upon my knowledge) who do voluntarily allow yearly exhibition of this nature.

Now if you would know how to find what is given to any such free-schools, and in whose disposing they now be,

Search

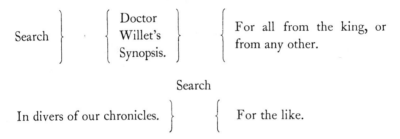

In the Tower of London, till the end of Richard the third.	For grants and for licence of mortmaine, *inde*.
And in the chapel of the Rolls, from thence till the present.	And for the like.
In the register of the prerogative court, for such things devised by will, by king, queen, or subject.	For such grants given by will.

And sometimes you shall find such things both in the Tower and the prerogative, and in the Rolls and prerogative respectively.

For the time since our reformed church of England began here,

| Search | Doctor Willet's Synopsis. | For all from the king, or from any other. |

Search

| In divers of our chronicles. | For the like. |

Next, add certain helps for discovery and attaining thereof.

First (if it may be) procure a sight of the ledger books, of such as in whom the disposition of such things resteth, which they keep for their own use.

Next, be acquainted with some of the disposers themselves.

Next, take the directions of the master or teacher of such free-schools.

Especially to be interested in the clerks or registers of such societies as have the disposing of any such things.

Also to use means by letters of persons powerful and useful to such disposers.

For (indeed) it is not the sound of a great man's name to a letter in these days, wherein they are grown so common and familiar to our societies (of London especially), can prevail so soon as the letter subscribed by the lord mayor, or other eminent officer of the city, to whose commandment they be immediately subjugate.

Lastly, if you use the means least seen, most used, and best allowed, together with these, for discovery and attaining of any such thing, it will not be beside the purpose, as I take it.

NOW SUPPOSE YOUR SON IS BROUGHT TO THE UNIVERSITY BY ELECTION OR AS PENSIONER.

The first thing you must take to your care is: in case he come not by election, but as a pensioner to live for the present upon your own charge, how to procure him a scholarship in the college where you bestow him.

Or in case he come elected into one, how to procure a farther addition of maintenance to him.

To bring him into a scholarship, place him with a senior fellow of the house (as tutor), though you allow to some junior fellow somewhat yearly for reading unto him.

This senior fellow, if the number of places void will bear it, may nominate your son for one in his own right; if it will not bear it, he may call to his aid some and so many suffrages of the rest, as, with the speaking merit of your son, may work your desire.

Then how to procure a pension for additament of means.

The chief skill is to find it out, being either in the gift of some body incorporate or of some private person, wherein the discovery is to be made (as aforesaid).

If you sue to a company consisting of many persons tradesmen, you must enquire who be the most potent patricians, and best reputed vestry wits amongst them, such as carry their gloves in their hands, not on their hands.

Amongst an assistance of many, only two or three strike the stroke, and hold the rest in a wonderful admiration of their extraordinary endowments. And how to speak sensibly to these two or three is no mystery; you know they are faithful fiduciaries in the election; and therefore, you must not presume to offer anything by any means. Only you may desire them to accept this poor piece of plate, with your name and arms upon it, and bind you unto their love, in keeping the memory of you hereafter. Do but try them in this kind, and attend the success. I tell you, this, with a buck at the renter warden's feast, may come somewhat near to the matter.

But for the pension to be obtained of a private person, the way is not the same. It proceedeth of the giver's mere charity, and must be taken by the hand of a desertful receiver. Though withal it may sometimes fall out, that merit is made by mediation, especially of some such reverend divine, as he doth most respect and frequent. For other, letters can little prevail with such persons.

The best note to discover a man inclinable to allow such a pension, is to examine how wealth and charity are equally and temporately mingled in him; and be sure, withal, that he be a man of some reasonable understanding in what he doth in this kind. For a fool's pension is like a new fashion, eagerly pursued at the beginning, but as scurvily left off in the proceeding.

Your next care is, in his due time to put on a fellowship, when he shall put off his scholarship, seeing the scholarship keeps him company no farther than to the degree of master of arts, and a quarter of a year after, in those colleges, where scholarships are longest lived, and in some not so long.

In some colleges the fellowship follows the scholarship of course; and as the one leaveth him, the other entertains him. But in the most it is not so, but comes by election. Which election passeth by the master and senior fellows, whereof every one doth name one, if the number to be elected will bear it; or if not, then they pass by most voices.

Where note, that the master hath a double voice, and in some places he hath the nomination of one, if there be two places void, yea, if there be but one at sometimes.

In colleges, the letters of great persons, especially of the lord's grace of Canterbury, and the university chancellor, have been of great prevailment; but it is not so now in these days.

There be beneficial gradations of preferment likewise, for fellows in their colleges; as lecturer, dean, bowser, vice-master, and master. But, for my part, I better like and commend those who, when they find themselves fit to put forth into the world, take the first preferment that is offered unto them, rather than such who live cloistered like votaries; who have sacraments to fill up their places, be it but to keep out others, such as use no exercise but wiping the dust off their books, and have an excellent activity in handling the fox-tail, such as hold no honour like to *supplicat reverentiis vestris*; and to be head bowser of the college, as good as to be chief butler of England.

These preferments of the college, all but that of the master, comes of course by order and antiquity. Therefore, no means but patient abiding needs for the acquiring of them in their due time.

I hasten to send your son out of the cloister of the commonwealth, and to show you how many ways of advancement are open unto him abroad, with the means to discover and attain.

AND FIRST FOR THE MINISTRY.

First, for his ease, let him look no farther than next to hand and enquire what benefices belong to their own college and are in the gift of their master and senior fellows (as most colleges have divers such); and amongst them, which are void at the present, or whose incumbent is not like to live long. And if he find out any such, then, if he know not, after so long continuance among them, to speak in his seniors' own dialect, let him never travel beyond Trumpington for me.

More indigitly, for attaining of such a benefice, let him enquire where the matins are read with spectacles, or where the good old man is lifted up into the pulpit, or the like, and make a way for succession accordingly.

Where note, that many times a fellow of the house may hold such a benefice together with his fellowship, or a pension, for increment of livelihood. And such ties as these are commonly the bond of matrimony, whereby they are so wedded to the college.

Next, he must climb up to the main top of speculation, and there look about him to discover what benefices are empty abroad, where the incumbent lives only upon the alms of *Confectio Alchermis*; or where one is ready to take his rise out of serge into satin, out of parsonage and a prebendary into a deanery and a donative, let him not be slow of footmanship in that case, by any means.

FOR BENEFICES ABROAD.

Benefices abroad are in the gift of

The king immediately,
Or the lord keeper for the king:
Some lord bishop:
Some dean and chapter:
Some body incorporate:
Some parish:
Some private patron.

You shall find in the Tower a collection of the patent rolls gathered of all presentations made by the king in those days to any church, prebendary, or chapel, in right of the crown, or otherways, from 1 of Edward the first, till the midst of Edward the third.

The king himself only and immediately presenteth in his own right to such benefices as belong to him, and are above twenty pounds value in the first fruits books.

For attaining of any which, I can advise you of no better course, than to learn the way to the back stairs.

The lord keeper presents for the king to all such benefices as belong to his majesty and are under twenty pounds value in the books.

Now to know which of these are full, and who are incumbents in any of these,

Search

The first fruits office.
The clerk, who hath the writing of the presentations.
The lord keeper's secretary being.

Where note, that the king hath used very seldom to grant any such living in reversion.

And the lord keeper now being, his care is so great in this, as in all cases of common good to provide for man's merit and cherish industry in the growing plants that no one can offer unto him a request of this kind without trespass to his good disposition.

In the next place, concerning benefices in the presentation of any of the lords bishops.

Note, that most bishoprics in England have presentation to divers benefices belonging to their sees.

For the number and present estate of these, search

    Their own ledgers.

    Their registers.

Inquire of

    Their auditors.

    Their stewards of their courts.

And sometimes you shall light upon some of their books of this kind in the hands of the heirs or executors of such as have born such offices under them.

He that is chaplain to such a lord bishop hath, for the most part, the best means, access, and opportunity, to attain to such a benefice.

The commendations of such a great personage, as to whom this patron oweth greatest respect, especially for his affairing in court, may do some good in the matter.

The like ways of discovery, and the like means of attaining any benefice in the presentation of any dean and chapter, are to be used with them respectively, as with the bishop's.

With every dean and chapter are likewise divers prebendaries to be obtained of their gift after the same manner and by the same means also.

The other bodies incorporate, besides those of colleges and deans and chapters, have many of them (especially of London and some subordinate societies thereof) right of the presentation to divers benefices.

Also some parishes, by prescription, do present to their own parochial benefices. And many patrons are content to present, according to the approbation of the parishioners, upon their hearing and allowing and due exclamation of the integrity of the life of such suitors, and no otherwise; divers governors, and gradations of the lands of divers hospitals, and *maisons de dieu*, have like right of presentation to benefices, as have other bodies incorporate. And the means of discovery and attaining are likewise the like.

In parishes and companies of tradesmen incorporate, some very few rule the roost.

Your alderman of the ward, his deputy, your common council-man, yea, sometime that petty epitomy of wardmote inquest, that little busy morsel of justice (the beadle of the ward), will make a strong party in the election, if he be put to it. The probatory sermon, that must be made upon such trial before such an auditory, would be according to the capacity in general, but more especially according to the humour and addiction of those whose wits the rest have in singular reverence, as Mr. Francis Fiat, a good understanding fishmonger (I assure you); you may give the style of right worshipful to them, though the best man of the company be but a wine cooper, and his judgment better in claret than in *contioclerum* a great deal.

If your son upon his trial can but fit their palates smoothly, which is hard to do, in regard that they are so hollow-mouthed, let him be sure, though he miss the benefice for want of preparation, yet ten to one but they will strain themselves to bring him in as a lecturer, which is a thing they reverence far beyond the parson of the parish by many degrees.

Lastly, for private patrons and the benefices in their gifts,

Search,

The bishop's register: for institution and presentation.
The archdeacon's register: for the induction.
The archbishop's register: if it be a peculiar.

It was my chance lately to see a book of all the benefices w thin the diocese of Canterbury, with the manner of their tithing in every each one respectively. In which I find that there are, or should be, with the register of every lord bishop, seven books kept for entry of the matters and business of their diocese, of which this of benefices is the chief.

The like I saw formerly of the diocese of St. David's, which confirms me in the institution and custom of keeping the said books also in other dioceses.

And seeing that several private patrons are of several dispositions; some more lucrative and covetous, others more charitable and religious; I can give you no other rule of attaining the benefice than this, viz.

That your son bring with him ability of learning, integrity of life, and conformity of behaviour, according to the order of the church established amongst us; and these shall make his way with the good and generous patron. But for the other patron, it makes no matter at all for learning, and a very little for manners, or whether he be a man conformable or no. Truly he is indifferent; for his part, very indifferent.

To such a patron your son must present himself thus (if he mean to be presented), according to present necessity: he must both speak and prove himself a man endowed with good gifts, for he shall have to deal with a patron of a quick capacity, more dexterous in apprehension than your son or you can be in delivery.

Be this patron what he will, your comfort is, the benefice must be filled, and that within a limited time; howsoever, it is dangerous to attend the ending of the day in this case (for seldom doth the clerks of the market get anything by their standing too long and above their accustomed hour).

Lapse by reason of simony and lapse for not presenting in due time both offer advancement to learning; but the first is as hard to discover as a witch, and the second as rare to find out as a faithful fiduciary or a fast friend.

The degrees of rising in the ministry are not easier known than practised by the industrious man.

Briefly, if all church livings in England were equally distributed, there is no one of the ministry, if he want not learning or good manners, needs want maintenance or good livelihood.

Here I could wish to God, that it might please the right reverend fathers of the church the lord bishops, that they would once in every of their times cause a true catalogue of all the benefices within their several dioceses, with the names of the patrons thereof, according to the last presentation, to be sent into the office of the first fruits, for the better information of all such as deserve and would gladly attain to some means of maintenance, which they may the better do by having recourse thither, there to take notice of all things of this nature. For I know that many sit down in their wants, having good means to many private patrons, only for lack of knowledge of the same.

Note that it is an usual thing in private patrons to grant reversion and advowson of such livings.

Myself intended heretofore to collect all such benefices, with their patrons, into a certain calendar, for such direction (as aforesaid), and made some passage into it. But the farther I went, the more impossible I found it. And I am now resolved, that without the bishop's assistance it cannot be done.

And so much for the Ministry.

THE LAWS PROMOTIONS FOLLOW.

BY CIVIL LAW AND COMMON LAW.

For breeding of your youth in the civil law, there are two colleges of especial note in our universities: the one is Trinity Hall in Cambridge; the other is New College in Oxford.

I remember me not of any free-school in England that have any place appendant in Trinity Hall in Cambridge. But in New College of Oxford, the free-school of Winchester hath claim both of scholarships and fellowships, the whole college consisting of none other, as I take it.

It is to be confessed, the charge of breeding a man to the civil law is more expensive, and the way more painful, and the books of greater number and price, than the common law requireth. But after the civil lawyer is once grown to maturity, his way of advancement is more beneficial, more certain, and more easy to attain, than is the common lawyer's; and all because their number is less, their learning more intricate. And they admit few or no solicitors to trample between them and the client. So that the fee comes to them immediately and with the more advantage.

The preferments at which they may arrive are these:
Chancellor to the bishop.
Archdeacon.
Commissary, where they have commissary official.
Judge and surrogate.
Advocate for the king.
Master of the chancery.
The king's proctor.
Advocate, and proctor at large.

In these courts, viz.
The high commission.
The delegates.
The prerogative.
The consistory.
The arches.
The bishop's courts.

The archdeacon's courts.

Chancellors, commissaries, and officials court.

The admiralty courts.

The court of the king's requests.

In times past the countenance of some bishop, especially of the lord archbishop, upon a civilian will much advance his practice as an advocate and give him promotion as a judge.

There are under the greater officers aforenamed divers other inferior officers, as

Register.

Actuary.

Examiner.

The number of the doctors (though I find them never to have been limited), yet it is certain that the time was within memory of man when the house of their commons did commonly give them all sufficient lodging and diet. And as for the number of proctors, they were of late times limited. How it is now, I know not.

FOR THE COMMON LAW.

For breeding of students at the common law, take directions for their method of study out of that tractate which Mr. Justice Dodridge did in his time pen for the purpose. Only (for my part) I do much commend the ancient custom of breeding of the younger students. First, in the Inns of Chancery; there to be the better prepared for the Inns of Court. And this must needs be the better way, seeing too much liberty at the first proves very fatal to many of the younger sort. I have observed and much commend also the breeding of some common lawyers in this kind, viz.

That when they have been admitted first into an Inn of the Chancery, they have been withal entered as clerks in the office of some prothonotary of the common pleas to add the skill of the practic to their speculation. And if a student be thus bred, by his foundation in the one and his experience in the other, he shall with more facility than others, who step into the Inn of Court at first, attain to an ability of practice.

Besides other ordinary requisite parts and arts in a common lawyer, skill in the records of all courts of record and in other antiquities of precedent, with some reading in the civil law, also will much enable him.

The common lawyer is to be bred only upon the purse. The charge most at the first. For after he hath spent some few years effectually, he may attain to the employment of some private friends, for advising with and instructing of greater counsel, whereby he shall add both to his means and knowledge.

It is true that I have known some attorneys and solicitors put on a counsellor's gown without treading the same usual path to the bar (as aforesaid). But indeed, I never look upon them but I think of the tailor, who in one of his customer's cast suits had thrust himself in amongst the nobility at a court mask, where, pulling out his handkerchief, he let fall his thimble and was so discovered and handled and dandled from hand to foot, till the guard delivered him at the great chamber door, and cried, ' farewell, good feeble! '

If the common lawyer be sufficiently able in his profession, he shall want no practice; if no practice, no profit.

The time was that the younger counsel had some such help, as to be a favourite, a kindred, to marry a niece, cousin, or a chamber-maid. But those days be past, and better supply their rooms.

As fellows of colleges in the universities get pensions or benefices to add to their livelihood, so barristers and counsellors of the Inns of Court advance their means by keeping of

> Courts of manors,
> Leets and barons,
> Swainmotes of forests,
> Stannaries,
> Cinque Ports, etc.

By places of

> Judges of inferior courts, as
> London, and other like corporations.
> The virge.
> The Tower of London.
> St. Katherine's, near the Tower.
> Borough of Southwark.
> The Clink.
> Wentworth, and like liberties.

By office of

Recorder of some corporate town.

Feodary of some counties.

The king's counsel in the marches of Wales, or at York, or judge
or counsel of some county palatine.

The greater places of preferment for common lawyers are the
judges at Westminster and elsewhere. The next are all the
several officers of the courts of Westminster, and elsewhere.

All which you shall find set forth briefly in Smith's *Commonwealth
of England* and part in mine own *Search of Records*. And all these together
afford sufficient maintenance for thousands of persons, who may be here
well provided for.

Here I should, and here I could, for better direction of younger
brothers, show what menial clerkships of large exhibition are under the
great officers of the land, the judges, the king's counsel, and other officers
which are not elsewhere published. And I know it would open a door
to many a proper man's preferment, especially under the lord keeper, as
secretaries for chancery business, and spiritual promotions, the commission of the peace, injunctions, the dockets. And other the like under the
lord treasurer, as secretaries for the business of the realm and the custom-
house; besides the inlets to so many preferments about the customs and
escheators; places under the lord treasurer, under the chancellor of the
exchequer, duchy and principality of Wales, and duchy of Cornwall,
as seal keeper, secretary, etc.

Under the master of the court of wards, as secretary; under the judges,
as marshal; clerk of the bails, etc.; under the barons of the exchequer, as
examiner; clerk of the bails, and other clerks.

Under the king's attorney general, as clerk of the patents, clerk
of the confessions and entries, clerk of the references, book bearer.
Under the solicitor general: clerk of the patents, book bearer. Besides many other clerks under the white staves of the court, and in
the counting house, and many several offices. All which, with hundreds more that I could name, with a plainer and more large deduction, were it not for fear that what I well intend for general good,
would be taken in offence for private prejudice. But for the clerkships

of the king's household, examine farther the Black Book of the Exchequer.

THE PHYSICIAN FOLLOWS.

And here I remember me of an old tale following, viz. At the beginning of the happy reign of our late good Queen Elizabeth, divers commissioners of great place, being authorized to enquire of, and to displace, all such of the clergy as would not conform to the reformed church, one amongst others was convented before them, who being asked whether he would subscribe or no, denied it, and so consequently was adjudged to lose his benefice and to be deprived his function; whereupon, in his impatience, he said,

' That if they (meaning the commissioners) held this course it would cost many a man's life.' For which the commissioners called him back again, and charged him that he had spoke treasonable and seditious words, tending to the raising of a rebellion or some tumult in the land; for which he should receive the reward of a traitor. And being asked whether he spake those words or no, he acknowledged it and took upon him the justification thereof; ' for,' said he, ' ye have taken from me my living and profession of the ministry; scholarship is all my portion, and I have no other means now left for my maintenance but to turn physician; and before I shall be absolute master of that mystery, (God he knows) how many men's lives it will cost. For few physicians use to try experiments upon their own bodies.'

With us, it is a profession can maintain but a few. And divers of those more indebted to opinion than learning, and (for the most part) better qualified in discoursing their travails than in discerning their patient's maladies. For it is grown to be a very housewives' trade, where fortune prevails more than skill. Their best benefactors: the Neapolitan, their grand seigneur; the sorpego, their gonfalonier; the sciatic, their great marshal, that calls the muster roll of them all together at every spring and fall—are all as familiar to her as the cuckoo at Cankwood in May; and the cure of them is the skill of every good old lady's cast gentlewoman; when she gives over painting, she falls to plastering, and shall have as good practice as the best of them for those kinds of diseases.

Marry, for women's griefs amongst physicians, the masculine is more worthy than the feminine.

Secrecy is the chief skill, and virility the best learning, that is required in a woman's physician. But I never read of many of those to be long lived, or honestly wived hitherto, in all my reading.

Hitherto I speak nothing in disrepute of the more reverend and learned sort of physicians, who are to be had in singular reverence and be useful to mankind next to the divine. Indeed, I rather pity them; and pitying, smile to see how prettily these young gamesters, male and female, lay about them and engross the greater part of patientry in all places wheresoever.

And here I may more fitly say (God knows) how many men's lives this abused opinion had of such gamesters costs; because they be not masters of that mystery and that science which requires the Greek tongue exactly, all the learning and skill of philosophy, history of all sorts (especially natural), knowledge of all vegetatives and minerals, and whatsoever dwells within the four elements; also skill in astronomy, astrology. And so much of the judicials upon all manner of calculations as may be well warranted; with much other kind of learning, art, and skill, whereof my young travailing physician and trading waiting woman never heard.

Their means of advancement are in these ways, viz.

To be physician of some college in one of the universities (as divers colleges have such places).

Physician to the king's or queen's person.

Physician to either of their households,

Or to some hospital (as most have such).

Or to some great persons who may prefer them hereafter, and be somewhat helpful in the meantime.

To a good old usurer, or one that hath got his great estate together unconscionably: for they fear nothing but death, and will buy life at any rate. There is no coward to an ill conscience.

It is not amiss to make way of acquaintance with gallants given to deep drinking and surfeiting; for they are patients at all times of the year.

Or a gentlewoman that would fain use the means to be pregnant.

Or your lascivious lady and your man in the periwig will help to furnish with a foot-cloth.

A citizen's wife of a weak stomach will supply the fringe to it.

And if all fail, and the bath will afford no room; let them find out some strange water, some unheard-of spring. It is an easy matter to discolour or alter the taste of it in some measure (it makes no matter how little). Report strange cures that it hath done. Beget a superstitious opinion in it, good fellowship shall uphold it, and the neighbouring towns shall all swear for it.

THE APPRENTICE FOLLOWS.

The first question is, to what trade you will put your son, and which is most worthy of choice. For the merchant, it requireth great stock, great experience in foreign estates, and great hazard and adventure at the best.

And this is not all: for it depends upon the peace of our state with foreign princes, especially those with whom we hold mutual traffic; or who lie in our way to intercept or impediment out trade abroad. Besides that, in time of war, they can hold no certainty of dealing, or supplying their factory in parts beyond the seas. Shipping is subject ever, at the let go, to be stayed, mariners to be pressed, and many other inconveniences attend them in such times; besides the burden of custom and imposition which all states impose more or less; so that unless we have peace with such neighbours, there is little hope in that profession in the ordinary and lawful way of trading.

Haply you will allege that some merchants thrive well enough when the wars most rage, and when the stream of state is most troubled. Some then hold it to be the best fishing; they that gain then (Sir), if they gain justifiably, gain not as merchants, but as men of war, which occupation a man may learn without serving seven years apprenticeship unto it.

And if they gain justifiably as merchants, it must be in some general stock of a society incorporated, who have purse to pass to and fro with sufficient power in the most dangerous times; and if such societies are tolerable at any time, it is at such times. How they be otherwise allowable, I leave to consideration.

For the shopkeeper, his welfare, for the most part, depends upon the prosperity of the merchant, for if the merchant sit still, the most of them may shut up their shop windows; little skill, art, or mystery, shall a man learn in shopkeeping. A man shall never in foreign parts, being put to his shifts out of his own meridian, live by the skill of weighing and measuring. The most use of advantage he can make of it is to benefit between the mart and the market, than which nothing is more uncertain, seeing there is no true judicial of the falling and rising of commodities, and the casualties that they are subject unto, (especially) in time of war.

Take this for a general rule, that those trades which ask most with an apprentice, are uncertainest of thriving, and require greatest stocks of setting up. Amongst trades, give me those that have in them some art, craft, or science, by which a man may live and be a welcome guest to all countries abroad, and have employment in the most stormy times at home, when merchants and shopkeepers are out of use (as)—

> An apothecary.
> A druggist.
> A surgeon.
> A lapidary.
> A jeweller.
> A printer.
> An engraver in stones and metal.
> One that hath skill in seasoning of shipwood.
> A carpenter of all sorts, especially of shipping.
> A smith of all sorts, especially of clocks, watches, guns, etc.
> A planter and gardener of all sorts.
> An engineer for making of patars, and the like engines of war; and hot presses for cloth, etc.; and engines to weigh any ship, or guns that are drowned, etc.; screws, etc.
> A maker of all sorts of instruments for navigation, compasses, globes, astrolabes.
> A drainer of grounds surmounded.
> A sail-maker, and
> A maker of cordage, tackle, etc.
> A limner.
> A clothier, a clothworker, and a dyer.
> A tailor, shoe-maker, glover, perfumer, and trimmer of gloves.
> An embroiderer.
> A feltmaker, a glazier, and one that can paint in glass.
> Briefly, any manufacture or trade, wherein is any science or craft.

Only those trades are of least use and benefit which are called house-wives trades (as brewer, baker, cook, and the like), because they be the skill of women as well as of men, and common to both.

I would have you know that the maker was before the retailer; and most shopkeepers are but of a sublimated trade, and retail but as attorneys to the maker. But if the maker (without dispute of freedom in any corporation) might set up shop and sell his commodity immediately, it would be a great deal better for the commonwealth than now it is.

Besides, it is no matter of difficulty, burden, or disgrace, for a shop-keeper, yea, a merchant, or a gentleman, to have the skill of some one of these manufactures, besides his revenue, or profession, to accompany him what fortune soever may carry him into countries unknown.

To my knowledge, a great earl lately of this land did think it no scorn to endeavour the attaining of the craft and trade of a farrier, wherein he grew excellent.

And when our acquaintance took first life with those of the Low Countries, upon a treaty wherein our ambassador strove to set forth the worthiness of our king and kingdom with the native commodities thereof, the Dutch (ignorantly conceiving that no man could attain to wealth without some good occupation or manufacture) asked him what handicraft our king was brought up unto, or what trade he had used to get so much wealth withal.

I admit the merchant royal that comes to his profession by travel and factory, full fraught, and free adventure, to be a profession worthy the seeking. But not the hedge-creeper that goes to seek custom from shop to shop with a creel under his arm, that leaps from his shop-board to the exchange, and after he is fame-fallen and credit-cracked in two or three other professions, shall wriggle into this and that when he comes upon the exchange, instead of enquiring after such a good ship, spends the whole hour in disputing, whether is the more profitable house-keeping, either with powder beef and brews, or with fresh beef and porridge; though (God wot) the black pot at home be guilty of neither: and so he departs when the bell rings and his guts rumble, both to one tune and the same purpose.

The merchant royal might grow prosperous were it not for such poor patching interloping lapwings, that have an adventure of two caldron of coals at Newcastle; as much oil in the Greenland fishing as will serve two cobblers for the whole year ensuing. And another at Rowsie, for as many fox-skins as will fur his Longlane gown, when he is called to the livery.

The shopkeeper is a cleanly trade, especially your linen-draper; which company hath the greatest commonalty and the largest privileges of all other, and yet they maintain nothing by charter, for (indeed) they have none.

But a manufacturer for my money, especially if he sell to the wearer immediately.

Now, for the better encouragement of men of trade, know that in most companies of tradesmen incorporate (especially in London), there is provision made by divers benefactors of their societies deceased for the enabling and setting up of young beginners, by stocks of money remaining in the hands of some few of the chief of their company (how faithfully disposed I leave to their own consideration), but surely the poorer sort complain much of the misemployment of it generally.

There is but one little crevice to peep in at their dealings, and that is between their master's conscience and the clerk's connivance, which is so narrow that you may sooner discern the South Pole through the main centre than discover their mystery.

Indeed, in times past, the clerkship of the company hath been bestowed upon some ancient decayed member of the company for his livelihood. But the attorney and scrivener and some petty clerks of the city, by the letters of, etc., pre-occupy those places.

And here I could wish, for righting of the dead, and relieving of the poorer members of such companies who are kept in ignorance, that some pains were taken in the prerogative office for the collating of all gifts of this nature to be published in print, that the meanest might thereby be able to call their grand masters to account if they abuse the trust in them reposited in this behalf. I acknowledge the youth of mine age to be determined, and (God knows) how poor a remain of life is left in my glass; yet if it may please those in whom the power resteth to give me leave to search (gratis) for all grants and gifts of pious use in all kinds whatsoever, I could willingly bestow that little of my lamp in collection of these things and publish them to posterity. Provided always that I and mine may have the privilege of imprinting the same for some fitting number of years to come.

THE NAVIGATOR.

Next to the man of trade, or rather equally with him, I must give the navigator his due, for that his profession is as full of science, as useful to the commonwealth, and as profitable to himself, as any trade whatsoever. If he attain the skill of knowing and handling the tackle, the certain art of his compass, the knowledge of languages, and dispositions of foreign nations where he travels and trades, he may rise from a squabbler to a master, from a master to be a general, honestly, and with good reputation, in a short time.

The navigator, his way of advancement and employment is by

The lords of his majesty's privy council,

The high admiral,

Commissioners for the king's navy,

Chief officers of the navies of societies incorporate,

Private merchants and the like, with the Trinity house.

But if he get to be an owner, he may trade as free as bird in air, as a man of war, or a man of trade and commerce. If he take heed that he intrench not upon the incorporated companies, especially the minotaur. He cannot do amiss (with God's assistance). He may live merrily and contentedly, be it but in trading as a mere carrier of home commodities imported from one port to another within the kingdom.

THE HUSBANDMAN.

The husbandman may likewise for the happy content of the life and the honest gain which it brings with it be worthy to invite a right good man's son to undergo the profession.

Your son whom you intend for a husbandman must be of a disposition part gentle and rustic, equally mixed together. For if the gentleman be predominant, his running nag will outrun the constable. His extraordinary strong beer will be too headstrong in office of churchwarden. And his well-mouthed dogs will make him out-mouth all the vestry. But if the clown be predominant, he will smell all brown bread and garlic. Besides, he must be of a hardier temper than the rest of his brethren, because the unhealthfullest corners of the kingdom are the most profitable for farmers. He must especially aim at a tenancy under the crown, or some bishop's see, dean and chapter, some college, some company, some hospital, or some other body incorporate. Wherein the auditor or receiver must be his best intelligencer and director. Young unthrifts acquaintance, when they first arrive at the age of one and twenty, and good old conscionable landlords that hold it a deadly sin to raise the rents of their grandfathers or hope to be delivered out of purgatory by their tenant's prayers, will do well.

> These professions before mentioned be (as it were) the orbs to receive all fixed stars, and such dispositions as may be put into any certain frame.
>
> But for a more libertine disposition, fit it with the profession of a courtier.
>
> For an overflowing and ranker disposition, make him a soldier.
>
> But, beyond this, he is a lost man, not worthy a father's remembrance or providence.

THE COURTIER'S WAYS OF ADVANCEMENT BE THESE:

By the general and most ancient rule of court, if you would have him to be preferred unto the king's service in the end, and in the meantime to have sufficient means of maintenance, place him with one of the white staves of the household.

By the more particular rule (if you can), put him unto the lord high steward his service (who, amongst the white staves), hath the chiefest hand in preferring to any office beneath stairs.

If the high steward be full, seek to the lord chamberlain, who hath the chief power to prefer to the places above stairs and to the wardrobe.

And, if there be no entrance there, then seek to the treasurer of the household, and next to the controller, the master of the household, the cofferer and the rest of the green cloth.

The master of the horse prefers to the avenary and other clerkship's offices and places about the stable.

The principal secretary hath heretofore had a great hand in preferring to the clerkships in the office of the signet, and the lord privy seal into the privy seal office.

The master of the great wardrobe into the clerkships and offices there; the master of the robes, the master of the jewel-house, the keeper of the privy purse, the master of the toils and tents, with some other the like, have whilom been the means of preferring divers their followers into the service of the king, in divers beneficial places and clerkships, in their several offices respectively.

The lord treasurer without the house prefers to his majesty's service, in most places in or about the custom-houses, in all the parts of England.

And, besides these, I find no means used of old for preferment into the king's service, for these kinds of places.

The yeomen of the guard were wont to come in for their personnage and activity by their captain's allowance.

And the bed-chamber men's servants ever were in way to be preferred for pages of the privy chamber, or grooms, or placed at the back stairs, not of right, but of custom.

For the clerks of the household, they were wont anciently to rise by certain degrees, according to the prescription of the Black Book; but how it is now, I know not.

For your better satisfaction of court offices, their order and fee, search the Black Book of the Exchequer and in the court; and for all offices whatsoever under the king throughout the whole kingdom, either in castle, park, chase, court, or house of the king's royalty or place soever, with the then fees of the same, I refer you to a book whereof many hundred copies are extant which was collected by the Lord Treasurer Burleigh and by him delivered to the late Queen Elizabeth of famous memory. And so much for the courtier.

THE SOLDIER FOLLOWS.

And the question is first,

Whether the better way of thriving is to be a sea-soldier or a land-soldier?

Questionless, the better way of thriving is to be a sea-soldier, in this kingdom of England, being an island, for that he is more useful to his country. More learning is required to be a sea-soldier than to be a land-soldier. A sea-soldier is certain of victuals and wages, where the land-soldier's pay will hardly find him sustenance. A sea-soldier may now and then chance to have a snap at a booty or a prize, which may in an instant make him a fortune for ever, where the land-soldier may in an age come to the ransacking of a poor fisher town at the most.

More valour is required in a sea-soldier than in a land-soldier; because the extremity of the place requires it. The sea captain is exposed to as much danger during the whole fight as the poorest man in the ship; where the land captain useth but to offer his men to the face of the enemy and then retreateth.

The way to rise to preferment at sea is by the admiral's countenance, and the vice-admiral's in the king's service, or in other service by the favour of great traded merchants and especially of your bodies incorporate and their chief officers: and more especially their president and treasurer for the time being.

His breeding is a matter of more moment than his age regardeth.

If he be true bred, he should be first made a perfect navigator, able to direct the steerage of their course, able to know the tackle, and appoint every sailor to his charge. He should know what number of sailors, what ordinance, and what munition, should be requisite for a ship of such a burden.

He should be a skilful cannoneer, and able to direct the gunner, to say what quantity of powder a piece of such bore and depth requireth, and of what weight the bullet should be where such a quantity of powder is used, whether the piece be sound or honeycombed. He should be able to know and direct what quantity of victual should be required for so many men for such a voyage and what quantity of powder and shot.

Also to oversee and direct the purser and steward in the expense of their victual without profuseness or too much parsimony.

Likewise skilful in all manner of fire-works and fitting engines for sea fight.

Briefly, he should be so complete, as that none should be able to teach him in his place, and he skilful to control every other in their places. He should be courteous and loving to his men; above all things, he should be zealous of the honour of God. See that the divine service be duly read on board evening and morning, and that swearing be severely punished. A sea captain is not a place for a young man to leap into instantly and immediately out of a ladies ushership, a great man's bedchamber, or a Littleton's discipleship.

It is not your feathered gallant of the court, nor your tavern roarer of the city, becomes this place, I assure you.

I find not any *Maison de dieu* for relieving of maimed mariners only, but that erected at Chatham by Sir John Hawkins, Knight, treasurer of the navy of the late Queen Elizabeth, wherein it was provided that there should be a deduction of sixpence by the month out of every man and boy their wages in every voyage towards the same, which I could wish were as well employed as collected.

THE LAND SOLDIER FOLLOWS.

If the land-soldier think to thrive and rise by degrees of service, from a common soldier to a captain, in this age, (alas) he is much deceived.

That custom is obsolete and grown out of use. Do what he can do in land service, he shall hardly rise by his single merit.

His happiness shall be but to fill his hungry belly and satiate himself upon a payday.

But if he be of kin, or a favourite to some great officer, he may carry the colours the first day, be a lieutenant the second, and a captain before he knows how many days go to the week in their regiment.

The land service where a man may learn most experience of war discipline is in the Low Countries by reason of the long exercise of wars and variety of stratagems there.

Beyond that, northward the service is both more unprofitable and more dangerous, and less experience is to be there learned.

The more your son turns his face to the south, the more profitable the land service is.

Lastly, if he have no friend or kindred to raise him in the land service, I assure you that there is no law against buying and selling of offices in the Low Countries, for aught that I have read; neither is it remarkable amongst them.

After the soldier returns home, it makes no matter what number of wounds he can reckon about him.

All the ways of relief for him that I can number are these:

A poor knight's place of Windsor; if the herald report him a gentleman, and the knights of the honourable Order of the Garter will accept him.

A brother of Sutton's Hospital; if the feoffees have not servants of their own to prefer before him.

A pensioner of the county; if the justices find him worthy, and that he was pressed forth of the same county.

Saint Thomas in Southwark, and St. Bartholomew's, Smithfield,
only till their wounds or diseases be cured and no longer; and
that if the masters of the said hospitals please to receive them.

For the Savoy, where soldiers had a foundation, I know none now.
And other houses appropriated for relief of soldiers, now in use, I
remember none.

For the chief are long since demolished, the Templars are gone, the
Knights of St. John of Jerusalem forgotten, that famous house upon
Lincoln Green is razed to the ground, and many the like, now better
known by the records than the remains of their ruins, with their revenue
are all diverted from the uses of their first foundation to private and
peculiar inheritances, which I pity more than the dissolution of all the
monasteries that ever were.

Here, you see, is preferment enough for your six sons, though you
bestow every one upon a several profession; only take this general rule
for all, viz.

To what course soever your sons shall betake them, be sure that they
all have grammar learning at the least, so shall they be able to receive
and retain the impression of any the said professions. And otherwise,
shall scarce possibly become masters in the same, or any one of them;
or if they do, it will be with more than ordinary pains and difficulty.

YOUR THREE DAUGHTER'S CHALLENGE THE NEXT PLACE.

For their portions I showed you before, how and when to raise them;
that is, by the marriage of your eldest son, or out of that part of your
personal estate which you may spare without prejudice of yourself.

FOR THEIR BREEDING.

I would have their breeding like to the Dutch woman's clothing,
tending to profit only and comeliness.

Though she never have a dancing school master, a French tutor, nor
a Scotch tailor to make her shoulders of the breadth of Bristol causeway,
it makes no matter, for working in curious Italian purls, or French
borders, it is not worth the while. Let them learn plain works of all

kind, so they take heed of too open seaming. Instead of song and music, let them learn cookery and laundry. And instead of reading Sir Philip Sydney's *Arcadia*, let them read the grounds of good housewifery. I like not a female poetess at any hand. Let greater personages glory their skill in music, the posture of their bodies, their knowledge in languages, the greatness and freedom of their spirits, and their arts in arraigning of men's affections at their flattering faces: this is not the way to breed a private gentleman's daughter.

If the mother of them be a good housewife, and religiously disposed, let her have the bringing up of one of them. Place the other two forth betimes, and before they can judge of a good manly leg.

The one in the house of some good merchant, or citizen of civil and religious government, the other in the house of some lawyer, some judge, or well reported justice or gentleman of the country, where the serving-man is not too predominant. In any of these she may learn what belongs to her improvement, for sempstry, for confectionary, and all requisites of housewifery. She shall be sure to be restrained of all rank company and unfitting liberty, which are the overthrow of too many of their sex.

There is a pretty way of breeding young maids in an exchange shop, or St. Martins Le Grand; but many of them get such a foolish crick with carrying the bandbox under their apron to gentlemen's chambers, that in the end it is hard to distinguish whether it be their belly or their bandbox makes such a goodly show.

And in a trade where a woman is sole chapman, she claims such a pre-eminence over her husband, that she will not be held to give him an account of her dealings, either in retail, or wholesale at any rate.

The merchant's factor and citizens' servant of the better sort cannot disparage your daughters with their society.

And the judges, lawyers, and justice's followers are not ordinary servingmen but men of good breed, and their education for the most part clerkly, whose service promiseth their farther and future advancement.

Your daughter at home will make a good wife for some good yeoman's eldest son, whose father will be glad to crown his sweating frugality with alliance to such a house of gentry.

The young man's fingers will itch to be handling of taffeta; and to be placed at the table and to be carved unto by Mistress Dorothy, it will make him and the good plain old Joan his mother to pass overall respect of portion or patrimony.

For your daughter at the merchant's, and her sister, if they can carry it wittily, the city affords them variety.

The young factor being fancy-caught in his days of innocency, and before he travel so far into experience as into foreign countries, may lay such a foundation of first love in her bosom as no alteration of climate can alter.

So likewise may Thomas the foreman of the shop, when beard comes to him as apprenticeship goes from him, be entangled and belimed with the like springs, for the better is as easily surprised as the worse.

Some of your clerkly men complain the moisture of their palms; others the sorpego in their wrists: both moving means.

With a little patience your daughter may light upon some counsellor-at-law, who may be willing to take the young wench, in hope of favour with the old judge. An attorney will be glad to give all his profits of a Michaelmas term, fees and all, but to woo her through a crevice. And the parson of the parish, being her ladies' chaplain, will forswear eating of tithe pig for a whole year, for such a parcel of glebe land at all times.

AND SO MUCH FOR YOUR SONS AND DAUGHTERS.

I now espy mine host of the Bull here in Saint Albans, standing at his door upon his left leg, like to the old drummer of parish-garden, ready to entertain us.

Therefore I will here conclude with that of the Poet,

> . . . *Navibus atque*
> *Quadragis petimus benevivere, quod petis hic est,*
> *Est Anglis, animus si te, non deficit equus.*

Finis.

A SPEECH DELIVERED IN THE STAR CHAMBER

On Wednesday, the XIVth of June, MDCXXXVII. At the censure of John Bastwick, Henry Burton, & William Prynne; concerning pretended innovations in the Church. By the most Reverend Father in God, William, L. Archbishop of Canterbury his Grace. London, Printed by Richard Badger. MDCXXXVII.

WILLIAM LAUD (1573–1645), bishop of London in 1628 and archbishop of Canterbury after 1633, shows in this speech both the ideals of dignity and beauty which he sought to attain in the church and his narrow impatience with diversity of religious opinion. William Prynne (1600–1669), however abusive and virulent his writing, was no man to dismiss as a mere libeller. An Oxford man, a lawyer, a theologian, an antiquarian, author during his life of some two hundred books and pamphlets, Prynne was a remarkably learned and cogent thinker even for that age. He began his polemics in 1627 with an attack on Arminianism, and for the rest of his life was continually in trouble with authority. Twice in 1630 he appeared before Star-chamber; for his *Histriomastix* (1632), a puritan diatribe against the stage, Laud determined to punish him. Its supposed vilification of the queen was construed as libel verging on treason, and Prynne was condemned to lose his ears on the pillory, to be disbarred, to be fined £5000, and to be imprisoned for life. His books were sold to pay his fine; but confinement in the Tower did not mean that he could not move about London nor write. His *News from Ipswich* (1636) was a scorching ten-page attack on prelates who suppressed Sunday lectures, prohibited sermons on fast days, and made changes in the collects. John Bastwick (1593–1654), a physician with whom Prynne collaborated, in his *Litany* (1636) accused bishops of encroaching on the prerogative. Henry Burton (1578–1648), a clergyman of Brownist leanings with whom Prynne had been associated in 1627, wrote in the same year his sermon *For God and the King*. The three were tried together. Their attempt to twist the case into an examination of the relations between church and king failed; the court intended to sentence them. Each was condemned to lose his ears on the pillory—Prynne in 1634 had saved the lower halves—to be fined, and to suffer perpetual imprisonment in remote places. In addition Prynne was branded S and L (seditious libeller) on either cheek. Laud's speech was delivered after sentence had been pronounced. Prynne spent three years in the Isle of Jersey and was released by the Long Parliament. He began at once to hound the man whose personal animosity he considered responsible for his tortures; his revenge came in 1644 when he appeared as public prosecutor in Laud's trial. Treason could not be proved, but an ordinance of attainder accomplished the same end.

. . . And I can say it clearly and truly, as in the presence of God, I have done nothing as a prelate, to the uttermost of what I am conscious, but with a single heart and with a sincere intention for the good government and honour of the church, and the maintenance of the orthodox truth and religion of Christ professed, established, and maintained in this church of England.

For my care of this church, the reducing of it into order, the upholding of the external worship of God in it, and the settling of it to the rules of its first reformation are the causes (and the sole causes, whatever are pretended) of all this malicious storm which hath lowered so black upon me and some of my brethren. And in the meantime, they which are the only or the chief innovators of the Christian world, having nothing to say, accuse us of innovation; they themselves and their complices in the meantime being the greatest innovators that the Christian world hath almost ever known. I deny not but others have spread more dangerous errors in the church of Christ; but no men, in any age of it, have been more guilty of innovation than they, while themselves cry out against it: *Quis tulerit Gracchos?*

And I said well, *Quis tulerit Gracchos?* For 'tis most apparent to any man that will not wink, that the intention of these men and their abettors was and is to raise a sedition, being as great incendiaries in the state (where they get power) as they have ever been in the church, Novatian himself hardly greater.

Our main crime is (would they all speak out, as some of them do) that we are bishops; were we not so, some of us might be as passable as other men.

And a great trouble 'tis to them, that we maintain that our calling of bishops is *jure divino*, by divine right. Of this I have said enough, and in this place, in Leighton's case, nor will I repeat. Only this I will say, and abide by it, that the calling of bishops is *jure divino*, by divine right, though not all adjuncts to their calling. And this I say in as direct opposition to the church of Rome as to the puritan humour.

And I say farther, that from the apostles' times, in all ages, in all places, the church of Christ was governed by bishops, and lay elders never heard of till Calvin's new-fangled device at Geneva.

Now this is made by these men as it were *contra regem*, against the king, in right or in power.

But that's a mere ignorant shift; for our being bishops *jure divino*, by divine right, takes nothing from the king's right or power over us. For though our office be from God and Christ immediately, yet may

11—The illustration opposite is Hollar's engraving of the trial of Archbishop Laud in 1644. It was used as the frontispiece to *A Breviate of the Life of William Laud*, written by William Prynne and published in London in 1644. The view shows the interior of the house of lords, with the famous Armada tapestries on the walls. The portrait of the debonair Prynne, looking unlike the avenging fury that he was, would seem to be authentic to judge from its similarity to the engraving of Prynne in *Canterburies Doome*, 1646. The lords refused to find Laud guilty of treason in this trial, and an ordinance of attainder (two years later) was necessary to send him to the block.

PROVERBS 11. 8:
The Righteous is delivered out of Trouble, and the wicked commeth in his stead.

A. The Arch-Bishop of *Canterbury*.
B. The Gentleman Vsher with his Black-Rod.
C. The Leiutenant of the Tower. D. The Bishops Councell.
E. The Clarke that reades the Evidence.
F. The Table where the Books and Papers given in evidence lay.
G. The Members of the House of Commons, and Mr. *Prynne* standing in the midst of them, H. Mr. *Henry Burton*.
I. I. I. The witnesses, Misttis *Bastwicke*. Mr. *Baker* the Messenger.
K. K. K. The People and Auditors, within and without the Barre.
L. L. The LORDS. M. M. The Judges, and Assistants.
N. The Speaker of the Lords House. T. The Hangings of 88. S. Mich. *Sparke*.

we not exercise that power, either of order or jurisdiction, but as God hath appointed us, that is, not in his majesty's or any Christian king's kingdoms, but by and under the power of the king given us so to do.

And were this a good argument against us as bishops, it must needs be good against priests and ministers too; for themselves grant that their calling is *jure divino*, by divine right, and yet I hope they will not say that to be priests and ministers is against the king or any his royal prerogatives.

Next, suppose our callings as bishops could not be made good *jure divino*, by divine right; yet *jure ecclesiastico*, by ecclesiastical right, it cannot be denied. And here in England the bishops are confirmed both in their power and means by act of parliament. So that here we stand in as good case as the present laws of the realm can make us. And so we must stand, till the laws shall be repealed by the same power that made them.

Now then, suppose we had no other string to hold by (I say suppose this, but I grant it not), yet no man can libel against our calling (as these men do) be it in pulpit, print, or otherwise, but he libels against the king and the state by whose laws we are established. Therefore all these libels, so far forth as they are against our calling, are against the king and the law, and can have no other purpose than to stir up sedition among the people.

If these men had any other intention, or if they had any Christian or charitable desire to reform anything amiss, why did they not modestly petition his majesty about it, that in his princely wisdom he might set all things right in a just and orderly manner? But this was neither their intention nor way. For one clamours out of his pulpit, and all of them from the press, and in a most virulent and unchristian manner set themselves to make a heat among the people, and so by mutiny to effect that which by law they cannot, and by most false and unjust calumnies to defame both our callings and persons. But for my part, as I pity their rage, so I heartily pray God to forgive their malice.

No nation hath ever appeared more jealous of religion than the people of England have ever been. And their zeal to God's glory hath been and at this day is a great honour to them. But this zeal of theirs hath not been at all times and in all places alike guided by knowledge. Now zeal, as it is of excellent use where it sees its way, so is it very dangerous company where it goes on in the dark. And these men, knowing the disposition of the people, have laboured nothing more than to misinform their knowledge and misguide their zeal, and so to fire that into a sedition, in hope that they whom they causelessly hate might miscarry in it.

For the main scope of these libels is to kindle a jealousy in men's minds that there are some great plots in hand, dangerous plots (so says Mr. Burton expressly) to change the orthodox religion established in England, and to bring in I know not what Romish superstition in the room of it. As if the external decent worship of God could not be upheld in this kingdom without bringing in of popery.

Now by this art of theirs give me leave to tell you that the king is most desperately abused and wounded in the minds of his people, and the prelates shamefully.

The king most desperately, for there is not a more cunning trickle in the world to withdraw the people's hearts from their sovereign than to persuade them that he is changing true religion, and about to bring in gross superstition upon them.

And the prelates shamefully, for they are charged to seduce and lay the plot, and be the instruments.

For his majesty first. This I know, and upon this occasion take it my duty to speak. There is no prince in Christendom more sincere in his religion, nor more constant to it, than the king. And he gave such a testimony of this at his being in Spain as I much doubt whether the best of that faction durst have done half so much as his majesty did in the face of that kingdom. And this you my lord the earl of Holland, and other persons of honour, were eye- and ear-witnesses of, having the happiness to attend him there. And at this day, as his majesty (by God's great blessing both on him and us) knows more, so is he more settled and more confirmed both in the truth of the religion here established and in resolution to maintain it.

And for the prelates. I assure myself they cannot be so base as to live prelates in the church of England, and labour to bring in the superstitions of the church of Rome upon themselves and it. And if any should be so foul, I do not only leave him to God's judgment, but (if these libellers or any other can discover that his base and irreligious falsehood) to shame also, and severe punishment from the state. And in any just way, no man's hand shall be more or sooner against him than mine shall be.

And for myself, to pass by all the scandalous reproaches which they have most injuriously cast upon me, I shall say this only.

First, I know of no plot nor purpose of altering the religion established.

Secondly, I have ever been far from attempting anything that may truly be said to tend that way in the least degree: and to these two I here offer my oath.

Thirdly, if the king had a mind to change religion (which I know he hath not, and God forbid he should ever have), he must seek for other instruments. For as basely as these men conceive of me, yet I thank God I know my duty well both to God and the king. And I know that all the duty I owe to the king is under God. And my great happiness it is (though not mine alone, but your lordship's and all his subjects with me) that we live under a gracious and a religious king that will ever give us leave to serve God first, and him next. But were the days otherwise, I thank Christ for it, I yet know not how to serve any man against the truth of God, and I hope I shall never learn it.

But to return to the business. What is their art to make the world believe a change of religion is endeavoured? What? Why, forsooth, they say there are great innovations brought in by the prelates, and such as tend to the advancing of popery.

Now that the vanity and falsehood of this may appear, I shall humbly desire your lordships to give me leave to recite briefly all the innovations charged upon us, be they of less or greater moment, and as briefly to answer them. And then you shall clearly see whether any cause hath been given of these unsavoury libels, and withall, whether there be any show of cause to fear a change of religion. And I will take these great pretended innovations in order, as I meet with them.

First, I begin with the *News from Ipswich*.

Where the first innovation is that the last year's fast was enjoined to be without sermons in London, the suburbs, and other infected places, contrary to the orders for other fasts in former times; whereas sermons are the only means to humble men, etc.

To this I say, first, that an after age may without offence learn to avoid any visible inconvenience observed in the former. And there was visible inconvenience observed in men's former flocking to sermons in infected places.

Secondly, this was no particular act of the prelates, but the business was debated at the council table, being a matter of state as well as of religion. And it was concluded for no sermons in those infected places upon this reason: that infected persons or families known in their own parishes might not take occasion upon those by-days to run to other churches, where they were not known, as many used to do to hear some humorous men preach. For on the Sundays when they better kept their own churches, the danger is not so great altogether.

Nor thirdly is that true, that sermons are the only means to humble men. For though the preaching of God's word, where it is performed according to his ordinance, be a great means of many good effects in the souls of men, yet no sermons are the only means to humble men. And some of their sermons are fitter a great deal for other operations: namely, to stir up sedition, as you may see by Mr. Burton's; for this his printed libel was a sermon first, and a libel too. And 'tis the best part of a fast to abstain from such sermons. . . .

3. The third innovation is that the prayer for seasonable weather was purged out of this last fast-book, which was (say they) one cause of shipwrecks and tempestuous weather.

To this I say, first, in the general: This fast-book, and all that have formerly been made, have been both made and published by the command of the king, in whose sole power it is to call a fast. And the archbishop and bishops to whom the ordering of the book is committed have power under the king to put in or leave out whatsoever they think fit for the present occasion, as their predecessors have ever done before them. Provided that nothing be in contrary to the doctrine or discipline of the church of England.

And this may serve in the general for all alterations in that or any other fast-book or books of devotion upon any particular occasions, which may and ought to vary with several times, and we may and do and will justify under his majesty's power all such alterations made therein.

Secondly, for the particular. When this last book was set out, the weather was very seasonable. And it is not the custom of the church, nor fit in itself, to pray for seasonable weather when we have it, but when we want it. When the former book was set out, the weather was extreme ill and the harvest in danger; now the harvest was in and the weather good.

Thirdly, 'tis most inconsequent to say that the leaving that prayer out of the book of devotions caused the shipwrecks and the tempests which followed. And as bold they are with God Almighty, in saying it was the cause. For sure I am God never told them that was the cause. And if God never revealed it, they cannot come to know it; yet had the bishops been prophets and foreseen these accidents, they would certainly have prayed against them.

Fourthly, had any minister found it necessary to use this prayer at any one time during the fast, he might with ease and without danger have supplied that want by using that prayer to the same purpose which is in the ordinary liturgy.

Fifthly, I humbly desire your lordships to weigh well the consequence of this great and dangerous innovation. The prayer for fair weather was left out of the book for the fast; therefore the prelates intend to bring in popery. And excellent consequence, were there any show of reason in it. . . .

5. The fifth innovation is that in the sixth order for the fast there is a passage left out concerning the abuse of fasting in relation to merit.

To this I answer that he to whom the ordering of that book to the press was committed did therefore leave it out; because in this age and kingdom there is little opinion of meriting by fasting.

Nay, on the contrary, the contempt and scorn of all fasting (save what humorous men call for of themselves) is so rank that it would grieve any Christian man to see the necessary orders of the church concerning fasting, both in Lent and at other set times, so vilified as they are.

6. The sixth innovation is that the Lady Elizabeth and her princely children are dashed (that's their phrase) out of the new collect, whereas they were in the collect of the former book.

For this first, the author of the *News* knows full well that they are left out of the collect in the latter editions of the common prayer-book, as well as in the book for the fast. And this was done according to the course of the church, which ordinarily names none in the prayer but the right line descending. Yet this was not done till the king himself commanded it, as I have to show under his majesty's hand.

Secondly, I beseech your lordships to consider what must be the consequence here. The queen of Bohemia and her children are left out of the collect, therefore the prelates intend to bring in popery; for that (you know) they say is the end of all these innovations. Now if this be the end and the consequence, truly the libellers have done very dutifully to the king, to poison his people with this conceit: that the Lady Elizabeth and her children would keep popery out of this kingdom, but the king and his children will not. And many as good offices as these have they done the king quite through these libels, and quite through his kingdoms. For my part, I honour the queen of Bohemia and her line as much as any man whatsoever, and shall be as ready to serve them, but I know not how to depart from my allegiance, as I doubt these men have done. . . .

8. The eighth innovation is that in the epistle the Sunday before Easter we have put out *In*, and made it *At the name of Jesus every knee shall bow*, which alteration, he saith, is directly against the act of parliament.

Here give me leave to tell you 'tis *At the name of Jesus* in the late learned translation made in King James his time. About which many learned men of best note in the kingdom were employed, besides some prelates.

But to this I answer: first, 'tis true the common prayer-book was confirmed by act of parliament, and so all things contained in it, at the passing of that act. But I hope if anything were false printed then, the parliament did not intend to pass those slips for current.

Secondly, I am not of opinion that if one word be put in for another, so they are both the same sense, that there is any great matter done against the act of parliament.

Thirdly, this can make no innovation. For *In the name* and *At the name of Jesus* can make no essential difference here. And Mr. Prynne (whose darling business it hath long been to cry down the honour due to the son of God at the mentioning of his saving name Jesus) knows the grammar well, *in a place* or *at a place*, etc.

Fourthly, if there were any error in the change of *In* into *At*, I do here solemnly protest to you I know not how it came. For authority from the prelates the printers had none, and such a word is easily changed in such a negligent press as we have in England. Or if any altered it purposely, for aught I know they did it to gratify the preciser sort. For therein they followed the Geneva translation and printed at Geneva, 1557, where the words are *At the name of Jesus*. And that is ninety-four years ago, and therefore no innovation made by us.

Fifthly, this I find in the queen's injunctions, without either word

In or *At.* ' Whensoever the name of Jesus shall be in any lesson, sermon, or otherwise pronounced in the church ('tis enjoined) that due reverence be made of all persons, young and old, with lowliness of curtsy and un-covering of the heads of the menkind, as thereunto doth necessarily belong, and heretofore hath been accustomed.' So here's necessity laid upon it, and custom for it, and both expressed by authority in the very beginning of the reformation, and is therefore no innovation now. . . .

11. The eleventh innovation is the reading of the second service at the communion table, or the altar.

To this first I can truly say that since my own memory this was in use in very many places, as being most proper (for those prayers are then read which both precede and follow the communion), and by little and little this ancient custom was altered, and in those places first where the emissaries of this faction came to preach. And now if any in authority offer to reduce it, this ancient course of the church is by-and-by called an innovation.

Secondly, with this the rubrics of the common prayer-book agree. For the first rubric after the communion tells us that upon holy-days, though there be no communion, yet all else that's appointed at the communion shall be read. Shall be read? That's true, but where? Why, the last rubric before the communion tells us that the priest, standing at the north side of the holy table, shall say the Lord's prayer with that which follows. So that not only the communion but the prayers which accompany the communion (which are commonly called the second service) are to be read at the communion table. Therefore if this be an innovation, 'tis made by the rubric, not by the prelates; and Master Burton's scoff that this second service must be served in for dainties savours too much of belly and profanation.

12. One thing sticks much in their stomachs, and they call it an innovation too. And that is bowing or doing reverence at our first coming into the church, or at our nearer approaches to the holy table, or the altar (call it whether you will). In which they will needs have it that we worship the holy table, or God knows what.

To this I answer, first, that God forbid we should worship anything but God himself.

Secondly, that if to worship God when we enter into his house or approach his altar, be an innovation, 'tis a very old one.

For Moses did reverence at the very door of the tabernacle (Num. 20). Hezekiah, and all that were present with him, when they had made an end of offering, bowed and worshipped (2 Chron.29). David calls the people to it with a *Venite*, O come let us worship and fall down, and kneel before the Lord our Maker (Psal.95). And in all these places (I pray mark it) 'tis bodily worship.

Nor can they say that this was Judaical worship, and now not to be imitated. For long before Judaism began, Bethel, the house of God, was a place of reverence (Gen.28). Therefore certainly of and to God. And after Judaical worship ended, *Venite, Adoremus*, as far upwards as there is any track of a liturgy, was the introitus of the priest, all the Latin church over.

And in the daily prayers of the church of England this was retained at the reformation, and that psalm in which is *Venite, Adoremus*, is commanded to begin the morning service every day. And for aught I know the priest may as well leave out the *Venite* as the *Adoremus*, the calling the people to their duty, as the duty itself when they are come.

Therefore even according to the service-book of the church of England the priest and the people both are called upon for external and bodily reverence and worship of God in his church. Therefore they which do it do not innovate. And yet the government is so moderate (God grant it be not too loose therewhile) that no man is constrained, no man questioned, only religiously called upon, *Venite, Adoremus*, Come let us worship.

For my own part I take myself bound to worship with body as well as in soul, whenever I come where God is worshipped. And were this kingdom such as would allow no holy table standing in its proper place (and such places some there are), yet I would worship God when I came into his house. And were the times such as should beat down churches, and all the curious carved work thereof, with axes and hammers, as in Psal.74 (and such times have been), yet would I worship in what place soever I came to pray, though there were not so much as a stone laid for Bethel. But this is the misery: 'tis superstition nowadays for any man to come with more reverence into a church than a tinker and his bitch come into an ale-house; the comparison is too homely, but my just indignation at the profaneness of the times makes me speak it.

And you my honourable lords of the garter, in your great solemnities, you do your reverence, and to almighty God, I doubt not, but yet it is *Versus Altare*, towards his altar, as the greatest place of God's residence upon earth. (I say the greatest, yea greater than the pulpit. For there 'tis *Hoc est corpus meum*, this is my body. But in the pulpit 'tis at most but *Hoc est verbum meum*, this is my word. And a greater reverence (no doubt) is due to the body than to the word of our Lord. And so in relation answerably to the throne where his body is usually present, than to the seat whence his word useth to be proclaimed. And God hold it there, at his word; for as too many men use the matter 'tis *Hoc est verbum diaboli*, this is the word of the devil, in too many places. Witness sedition and the like to it.) And this reverence ye do when ye enter the chapel, and when you approach nearer to offer. And this is no innovation, for you are bound to it by your order, and that's not new.

And idolatry it is not, to worship God towards his holy table. For if it had been idolatry, I presume Queen Elizabeth and King James would not have practised it, no not in those solemnities. And being not idolatry but true divine worship, you will I hope give a poor priest leave to worship God as yourselves do. For if it be God's worship, I ought to do it as well as you; and if it be idolatry, you ought not to do it more than I.

I say again, I hope a poor priest may worship God with as lowly reverence as you do, since you are bound by your order and by your oath, according to a constitution of Henry V (as appears), to give due honour and reverence *Domino Deo, et altarieius, in modum virorum ecclesiasticorum*: that is, to the Lord your God and to his altar (for there is a reverence due to that too, though such as comes far short of divine worship), and this in the manner as ecclesiastical persons both worship and do reverence.

The story which led in this decree is this: King Henry the fifth, that noble and victorious prince, returning gloriously out of France, sat at this solemnity, and finding the knights of the order scarce bow to God or but slightly, and then bow towards him and his seat, startled at it (being a prince then grown as religious as he was before victorious) and after asking the reason—for till then the knights of the order never bowed toward the king or his seat—the duke of Bedford answered, it was settled by a chapter act three years before. Hereupon that great king replied, No, I'll none of this, till you the knights do it *satis bene*, well enough, and with due performance to almighty God. And hereupon the forenamed act proceeded, that they should do this duty to almighty God, not slightly but *ad modum virorum ecclesiasticorum*, as low, as well, as decently as clergymen use to do it.

Now if you will turn this off, and say it was the superstition of that age so to do, Bishop Jewel will come in to help me there. For where Harding names divers ceremonies, and particularly bowing themselves and adoring at the sacrament—at the sacrament, I say, not adoring the sacrament; there Bishop Jewel (that learned, painful, and reverend prelate) approves all both the kneeling and the bowing and the standing up at the gospel (which as ancient as it is in the church, and a common custom, is yet fondly made another of their innovations); and further the bishop adds that they are all commendable gestures and tokens of devotion, so long as the people understand what they mean, and apply them unto God. Now with us the people did ever understand them fully and apply them to God, till these factious spirits and their like, to the great disservice of God and his church, went about to persuade them that they are superstitious if not idolatrous gestures; as they make everything else to be where God is not served slovenly. . . .

14. The fourteenth and the last innovation comes with a mighty charge, and 'tis taken out of an epistle to the temporal lords of his majesty's privy council. Of which epistle we got one sheet, and so (for aught I yet know) that impression staid. In that sheet is this charge. The words are:

'The prelates, to justify their proceedings, have forged a new article of religion, brought from Rome (which gives them full power to alter the doctrine and discipline of our church at a blow, as they interpret it), and have foisted it (*such is their language*) into the beginning of the twentieth article of our church. And this is in the last edition of the articles, anno 1628, in affront of his majesty's declaration before them, etc.'

The clause (which they say is forged by us) is this: the church (that is the bishops as they expound it) hath power to decree rites and ceremonies and authority in matters of faith (the word is *controversies* of faith, by their leave). This clause (say they) is a forgery fit to be examined and deeply censured in the star-chamber. For 'tis not to be found in the Latin or English articles of Edward VI or Queen Elizabeth, ratified by parliament.

And then in the margin thus: ' If to forge a will or writing be censurable in the star-chamber, which is but wrong to a private man, how much more the forgery of an article of religion, to wrong the whole church and overturn religion which concerns all our souls.'

This is a heavy charge, my lords. But I thank God the answer's easy.

And truly I grant that to forge an article of religion in whole or in part, and then to thrust it upon the church, is a most heinous crime far worse than the forging of a deed, and is certainly very deeply censurable in this court. And I would have humbly besought you that a deep censure might have been laid upon it, but that this sheet was found after, and so is not annexed to the information nor in judgment at this present before you.

But then, my lords, I must tell you I hope to make it as clear as the day that this forgery was not that this clause mentioned was added by the prelates to the article to gain power to the church, and so to serve our turns. But that that clause in the beginning of the article was by these men, or at least by some of their faction, razed out, and this to weaken the just power of the church to serve their turns.

They say (to justify their charge) that this clause is not to be found in the articles, English or Latin, or either Edward VI or Queen Elizabeth.

I answer: the articles of Edward VI and those made under Queen Elizabeth differ very much. And those of Edward VI are not now binding. So whether the clause be in or out of them, 'tis not much material.

But for the articles of the church of England, made in the queen's time and now in force, that this clause for the power of the church to decree ceremonies and to have authority in controversies of faith should not be found in English or Latin copies till the year 1628, that it was set forth with the king's declaration before it, is to me a miracle. But your lordships shall see the falsehood and boldness of these men.

What? Is this affirmative clause in no copy English or Latin till the year 1628? Why, my lords, I have a copy of the articles in English of the year 1612, and of the year 1605, and of the year 1593, and in Latin of the year 1563, which was one of the first printed copies if not the first of all. For the articles were agreed on but the nine and twentieth day of

January, anno 156$\frac{2}{3}$ $\begin{cases} \text{according to the English account.} \\ \text{according to the Julian account.} \end{cases}$

And in all these this affirmative clause for the church's power is in. And is not this strange boldness then to abuse the world, and falsely to say 'tis in no copy, when I myself out of my own store am able to show it to many, and so anciently?

But, my lords, I shall make it plainer yet. For 'tis not fit concerning an article of religion, and an article of such consequence for the order, truth, and peace of this church, you should rely upon my copies, be they never so many or never so ancient.

Therefore I sent to the public records in my office, and here under my officer's hand, who is a public notary, is returned me the twentieth article with this affirmative clause in it. And there is also the whole body of the articles to be seen.

By this your lordships see how free the prelates are from forging this part of the article. Now let these men quit themselves and their faction as they can, for their index expurgatorius and their foul rasure in leaving out this part of the article. For to leave out of an article is as great a crime as to put in; and a main rasure is as censurable in this court as a forgery.

Why, but then my lords, what is this mystery of iniquity?

Truly, I cannot certainly tell, but as far as I can, I'll tell you. The articles you see were fully and fairly agreed to and subscribed in the year 156⅔. But after this, in the year 1571, there were some that refused to subscribe, but why they did so is not recorded. Whether it were about this article or any other I know not. But in fact this is manifest, that in that year 1571 the articles were printed both in Latin and English, and this clause for the church left out of both. And certainly this could not be done but by the malicious cunning of that opposite faction. And though I shall spare dead men's names where I have not certainty, yet if you be pleased to look back and consider who they were that governed business in 1571, and rid the church almost at their pleasure, and how potent the ancestors these libellers began then to grow, you will think it no hard matter to have the articles printed, and this clause left out.

And yet 'tis plain that after the stir about subscription in the year 1571 the articles were settled and subscribed unto at last as in the year 1562, with this clause in them for the church. For looking farther into the records which are in mine own hands, I have found the book of 156⅔ subscribed by all the lower house of convocation in this very year of contradiction, 1571, Dr. John Elmar (who was after lord bishop of London) being there prolocutor, Alexander Nowell, dean of Saint Paul's, having been prolocutor in 156⅔, and yet living and subscribing in 1571. Therefore I do here openly in star-chamber charge upon that pure sect this foul corruption of falsifying the articles of the church of England; let them take it off as they can.

I have now done, and 'tis time I should, with the innovations charged upon the prelates and fit to be answered here.

Some few more there are, but they belong to matter of doctrine, which shall presently be answered, *justo volumine*, at large, to satisfy all wellminded people. But when Mr. Burton's book, which is the main one, is answered (I mean his book, not his railing), neither Prynne, nor Bastwick, nor any attendants upon Rabshakeh shall by me or my care be answered. If this court find not a way to stop these libellers' mouths and pens, for me they shall rail on till they be weary.

Yet one thing more I beseech you give me leave to add. 'Tis Master Burton's charge upon the prelates: that the censures formerly laid upon malefactors are now put upon God's ministers for their virtue and piety.

A heavy charge this too. But if he or any man else can show that any man hath been punished in the high commission, or elsewhere, by the prelates for virtue and piety, there is all the reason in the world we should be severely punished ourselves. But the truth is the virtue and piety for which these ministers are punished is for preaching schism and sedition, many of their sermons being as bad as their libels, as Burton's libel was one of his sermons first. But whether this stuff have any affinity with virtue and piety, I submit to any Christian reader.

And yet Mr. Burton is so confident of this innocency, even in this cause wherein he hath so foully carried himself, that he breaks forth into these words: ' I never so much as once dreamed that impiety and impudency itself in such a Christian state as this is, and under such a gracious prince, durst ever thus publicly have called me in question, and that upon the open stage, etc.'

You see the boldness of the man, and in as bad a cause as (I think) in this kind ever any man had.

I shall end all with a passage out of St. Cyprian, when he, then bishop of Carthage, was bitterly railed upon by a pack of schismatics. His answer was, and 'tis now mine: ' They have railed both bitterly and falsely upon me, and yet *non oportet me paria cum illis facere*, it becomes not me to answer them with the like, whether levities or revilings, but to speak and write that only which becomes *sacerdotem Dei*, a priest of God.'

Neither shall I in this give way (though I have been extremely vilified) to either grief or passion to speak, remembering that of the psalmist, Psalm 37, 'Fret not thyself, else shalt thou be moved to do evil.'

Neither yet by God's grace shall the reproaches of such men as these make me faint or start aside, either from the right way in matter of practice (they are St. Cyprian's words again) or *a certa regula*, from the certain rule of faith.

And since in former times some spared not to call the master of the house Beelzebub, how much more will they be bold with them of his household, as it is in St. Matthew, chapter 10. And so bold have these men been; but the next words of our Saviour are, Fear them not.

I humbly crave pardon of your lordships for this my necessary length, and give you all hearty thanks for your noble patience, and your just and honourable censure upon these men, and your unanimous dislike of them and defence of the church.

But because the business hath some reflections upon myself, I shall forbear to censure them, and leave them to God's mercy and the king's justice.

Finis.

THE DESCRIPTION OF A PURITAN,

From a dialogue wherein is plainly laid open the tyrannical dealing of lord bishops against God's children, with certain points of doctrine wherein they approve themselves according to Dr. Bridges his judgment to be truly the bishops of the devil. Published by the worthy gentleman Dr. Martin Marprelate. Reprinted in the time of parliament, anno dom. 1640.

THE following verses, which mark an early use of the heroic couplet for satirical purposes, were appended to a 1640 reprint of one of the last of the Martin-Marprelate tracts, originally printed about April 1589, probably by the Waldegrave press at La Rochelle. It was again reprinted in 1643, under the title, *The Character of a Puritan, and his Gallimaufrey of the Antichristian Clergie.* . .

HERE follows the description of a puritan, (as they are now termed) by profane papists and atheists, etc.

> Long hath it vext our learned age to scan,
>> who rightly might be termed a *puritan.*
> A puritan both layic and divine.
>> I will according to my skill define.
> A puritan, is he, that when he prays,
>> his rowling eyes up to the heavens doth raise.
> A puritan, is he, that cannot fare,
>> to deck his round head with a bonnet square.
> Whose Turkey robe, in his fair furred train
>> above his ankle, turneth up again:
> That at his belt a boss-clad Bible bears,
>> stampt with the true Geneva characters;
> Whose thin beat volume scorneth to admit,
>> the bastard monuments of humane writ.
> Whose hair, and ruffs, dare not his ears exceed:
>> that on high saints days wears his working weed.
> That crosses each doth hate, save on his pence,
>> and loathes the public rope of penitence.
> That in his censure each alike gainsays,
>> poets in pulpits, holy writ in plays.

Roods in the windows, and the marriage ring:
    the churching, veil, and midwives christening.
A puritan, is he, that listeth not to pray
    'gainst thunder, in the coldest winter day.
A puritan, is he, that quite denies
    the help of angels to a benefice.
That cannot brook a deputy, to serve
    and feed himself, but let his people starve.
That loves alike an organ in a choir,
    as th' elephant delights a swine to hear.
That never in his life did kneel before
    the gate of a cathedral chancel door.
A puritan, is he, that cannot dine,
    nor sup, without a double grace divine.
A puritan, is he, that through the year,
    two Lords-day sermons doth either preach or hear.
A puritan, is he, that will not lend,
    a gainful oath, to his distressed friend.
A puritan, is he, that for no meed
    will serve the time, and great men's humours feed.
That doth the self-accusing oath refuse:
    that hates the ale-house, and a stage, and stews.
A puritan, is he, whose austere life,
    will not admit a mistress and a wife.
That when his betters swear, doth bite the lip,
    nor will be drunken for good-fellowship.
That wisheth for the amendment of the best,
    blames the least ill, and doth the worst detest.
Reader, if such be termed a puritan,
    God make me wise, and thee an honest man.

SIR THOMAS ROE HIS SPEECH IN PARLIAMENT

Wherein he showeth the cause of the decay of coins and trade in this land, especially of merchant trade. And also propoundeth a way to the house, how they may be increased. London, printed for John Asten, 1641.

SIR THOMAS ROE (1581?–1644), was born at Low Leyton, Essex, grandson of a merchant tailor who became lord mayor of London. After an Oxford career, family wealth and connections got for him a post at Elizabeth's court, and in 1605 a knighthood from James I. In 1610 he sailed upon a voyage of exploration which took him three hundred miles up the Amazon, then unknown to Englishmen, and along the coast from the Amazon to the Oronoco. In 1614, at the request of the East India company, he went as ambassador to the Mogul emperor of Hindustan, where he concluded a commercial treaty giving the company factory concessions and laying foundations for future expansion. On the way home, in 1619, he settled disputes in Persia about the silk trade. A member of the 1621 parliament, he left in September as ambassador to the Ottoman Porte, where he obtained additional privileges for English merchants. During his eight-year absence he likewise mediated a peace treaty between Turkey and Poland, patched up an agreement with the Barbary pirates, and gained the support of the prince of Transylvania for Mansfeld's expedition. Arbitrator between Sweden and Poland in 1629, he brought about a six-years truce, and Gustavus Adolphus said that to Roe he owed the idea of carrying the war into Germany. He also arranged the claims of the city of Danzig, and on the way home concluded with Denmark a treaty long waiting settlement. From 1630 to 1636 he lived in retirement, on limited means; in 1638 as ambassador extraordinary to the congress of the Empire, France, and Sweden, he had some influence in restoring the palatinate. A privy councillor in 1640, he represented Oxford University in the Long Parliament.

The speech here printed was probably delivered, though not in finished form, sometime in November 1640, when the house was concerning itself with the state of trade. Roe's survey is applicable to the whole period since 1616. In December the house ordered fuller attendance at the grand committee of trade, so that subcommittees might be appointed; and ordered representatives of various merchant companies and groups to attend to give information. These were Roe's suggestions, and they represent the opinion of a shrewd, sagacious observer who had no contemporary equal in commercial affairs and who possessed the unwavering confidence of the house. Roe was a devout church-goer, an enthusiastic collector of Greek manuscripts, an explorer whose exploits are too little known, and the most outstanding English diplomat of the time.

IT is a general opinion that the trade of England was never greater, and it may be true that if it be so, yet it will not absolutely conclude that the kingdom doth increase in riches, for the trade may be very abundant,

599

and yet by consumption and importance of more than is expected, the stock may waste.

The balance would be a true solution of the question, if it could be rightly had: but by reason it must be made up by a medium of the books of rates it will be very uncertain.

Therefore we must seek another rule that is more sensible upon which we may all judge, and that may be by the plenty or scarcity of money; for it is a true rule, if money increase the kingdom doth gain by trade, if it be scarce it loseth.

Let us therefore consider, first whether our gold and silver be not decreased, and then by what means it is drained, and lastly, how it may be prevented and what remedies are appliable to effect it.

It is out of doubt our gold has gone to travel without licence that is visible beyond seas, and every receiver of sums of money must find it privately, and I fear the same of silver, for observing the species of late coining many half-crowns were stamped, which are no more to be seen, and by this measure I conclude the kingdom grows poor.

The causes of this decay of money may be many, it may be stolen out for profit, going much higher beyond seas, especially in France and Holland.

Much hath been drawn away by the stranger upon fears of our troubles, of which I have experience by exchanges, and exchanges are the great mystery, especially such as are used as a trade, and governed by bankers who make many returns in a year, and gain by every one more than the interest of a year, and the greatest danger to a state is when money is made merchandise, which should be but the measure thereof.

And here I will propose a problem, whether it were profitable to a kingdom or not, that the stranger for many years had a great stock here at interest, and still hath some, I confess it hath supplied the necessities of merchants, and helped to drive trade. But my *quaere* is this, suppose the first principal were truly brought in by the stranger, yet doubling every ten years, what becomes of the increase; have they not lived by our trade and the merchant adventurers, and soaked the kingdom of as many times principal as they have practised this usury many times ten years, and in the end drawn or carried all away; this is a point to a state very considerable.

Much coin hath been drawn away without doubt by the French, who have brought in wares of little bulk, perhaps without custom, but of dear price, and having turned it into gold have returned without investing any part thereof, and such petty merchants cannot be reached by the statute of employments.

Another cause of scarcity of coin may be the over-strict rule of the uncurrentness of any good coin, and that it must be sold here as bullion, in that case what stranger will bring in money; whereas if every good species current according to this alloy and weight in proportion to our coin, or rather a little higher, it will draw namely money by degrees into England, as lower grounds do water from higher, though they see not the channels: and we see France, Holland, and Germany admit all good coins, though foreign, for and above their intrinsic value.

But I will end this search by proposing some general remedies, for if I do now but make essays and give occasion to more subtle and particular disquisition,

1. To the first leak of stealing away coin, I would make it felony by an act: for if a man may justly suffer death for robbing of a private man, I see no injustice nor cruelty to inflict the same punishment upon him that robs a kingdom.

2. That the neighbour princes and states do cry up our money; and so entice it from us. This in my judgment ought to be provided for by our treaties, which was the old way, especially of commerce, by agreeing and publishing of placards according to a true par: for that prince that will make a treaty of commerce doth it for the use of the commodity, which certainly I would deny any prince that would not consent to keep moneys even by their true values, at least, that would set a higher price upon our money than the king hath done, and if our coin did either keep beyond the seas the English value, or were bullion and uncurrent, the stranger should have as little of our money as we have of theirs.

How to recover the stranger's money drawn away since our troubles is a hard endeavour and can no ways be brought to pass but by peace and trade, and the resolution of this will fall into the general remedy which I shall propose.

The peddling French trade must be met with by diligent search at the landing of these creamers, what they bring in, and by suffering none of them to pass any goods by private warrants: but that according as they shall be valued, they give bond to invest it in English commodity, natural, or naturalized, and that with surety. Nay, in this case not to allow them to exchange by bills; for it will not hurt the commonwealth if by any rigour they were beaten out of their private toyish traffic.

I shall not doubt to offend any but the mint, which may be recompensed to his majesty in his customs, if money be plentiful; for all goods will follow money. If I did propose the currentness of all goods and great species of foreign coins, for their true intrinsive value, according to the pay with ours, and if I say a little higher, according to our occasions, keeping our own coin pure and constant to be cried down as much under according to occasions, I think it will be a policy both reasonable and profitable, by experience tried in other states.

But leaving these empirical practices, I come now to the great and infallible rule and remedy, which is in plain English to settle and assure the ground of trade upon staple commodities, then like the Lady of Whitsuntide to her pipe-money, will dance after that; for as merchandise doth follow money, so doth money commodity.

I said at first it was a general opinion that trade never flourished more than now, and it may be so, but we must consider this be not accidental and changeable and depending more upon the iniquity or misery of the times than upon our own foundation and industry, and if that be so, then it is no sure ground for a state to rely upon; for if the causes change, the effects will follow.

Now it is true that our great trade depends upon the troubles of our neighbours, and we enjoy almost the trade of Christendom, but if a peace happen betwixt France, Spain, and the United Provinces, all these will share what we now possess alone, and therefore we must provide for that day, for nothing stands secure but upon his own foundation.

To make then our own trade secure, we must consider our own staple commodities, whereof wool is the chiefest, and seek the way to both, to keep up the price at home, and the estimation of all commodity made of that, and to be vented abroad.

Some other helps we have, as tin, lead, and such like, but I dare confidently affirm that nothing exported of our own growth hath balanced our riotous consumption at home, but those foreign commodities which I call naturalized, that is that surplus of our East India trade, which being brought home in greater quantity than are spent within the kingdom, are exported again and become in value and use as natural commodities, and therefore by the way, I hold it absolutely necessary to maintain that trade by a regulation with the Dutch, of which more reason shall be given, when that particular shall be taken into consideration.

We have yet another great help which is our own and wants only our industry to gather the harvest, which is our fishing and erecting of busses, both for the enriching of our kingdom and the breeding of mariners, and this by private industry (though to private loss) is beaten out ready, and shall be offered to the commonwealth if they please to accept of it. And to give you one only encouragement, I do avow that before the Dutch were lately interrupted by the Dunkirks, by their industry and our fish they made as great returns between Danzig and Naples as the value of all our cloth, which is one million yearly, and this in a due place I desire should have his due weight and consideration.

We have one help more if we knew how to use it, that is by the new drained lands in the fens, most fit for flax and hemp, to make all sorts of linen for the body, for the house and sails for ships. That is a Dutch and French trade, but in Holland one acre of ground is rented at three pounds, which if the Hollanders may have in the fens for 10 shillings or 12 shillings it will be easy to draw the manufacture into England, which will set infinite people awork, and we may be able to serve other nations with that which we buy dear from them. And then the state and kingdom will be happy and rich, when the king's customs shall depend upon commodities exported and those able to return all things which we want, and then our money must stay within our kingdom and all the trade return in money: to encourage you to this, I give you one example.

That if the several sorts of calicoes made of cotton wools in the Moguls and Dans dominions doth clothe from head to foot all Asia, a part of Europe, Egypt, much of Africa, and the eastern islands as far as Sumatra, which makes that prince without mines the richest prince in the world: and by his majesty's grace and privileges granted to the Dutch I am confident we may make and undersell in all linen cloth in all the nations in Europe.

But I have now wandered far from my theme, which was the decay of trade and of woollen commodity.

I must first therefore present to your consideration the causes thereof in my observations, whereof some are internal, and some external.

The internal have proceeded from her own false making, a stretchening, and such like practices, whereby indeed our cloth is discredited. I speak by experience from Danzig and Holland, northward to Constantinople, as I will instance in due time.

This false lucre of our own and the interruption in the dyeing and dressing projected and not overcome gave the first wound, though could it have been compassed, had doubled the value of our commodity.

This hath caused the Dutch, Silesians and Venetians to attempt the making of cloth, and now by experience (as I am informed) the half is not vented that was in the latter age.

Another internal cause hath risen from such impositions as hath made our cloth too dear abroad, and consequently taught others to provide for themselves.

Another internal cause hath sprung from pressaries upon tender consciences, that many of our clothiers and others have forsaken the kingdom and carried their arts with them, to the unexpressable detriment of the commonwealth.

The external causes have been the want of perfection and countenance to our merchants established abroad in factories by the state and by the treaties, whereby the capitulations have not been kept nor assured unto them, neither in Prussia, nor in the Sound, nor Hamburg, nor Holland, nor in the East: and this I dare say, that Laban never changed Jacob's wages so often as the Hollanders have forced our merchants to change their residences and the very course of this trade by laws and tricks for their own advantages, of which the merchant adventurers will more fully inform you.

Another external cause is [the] lamentable report [of] the increase of the pirates and the insecurity of the Mediterranean seas; whereby Bristol and the western ports that cannot have so great shipping as London are beaten out of trade and fishing, and if once those thieves shall find the way to Bank and Newfoundland they will undo the west parts of England.

I will trouble you with a consideration very considerable in our government, whether indeed London doth not monopolize all trade: in my opinion it is no good state of a body to have a fat head, thin guts, and lean members.

But to bring something before you of remedy, I say thus for my first ground, that if our cloth be not vented as in former years, let us embrace some other way to spend and vent our wools. Cloth is heavy and hot wearing and serves but one cold corner of the world: but if we embrace the new draperies and encourage the Walloons and others by privileges and naturalizations, we shall employ all the wool we have, set more people awork than by cloth, and a pound of wool in those stuffs true made will outsell two pounds in cloth, and thus we may supply France, Italy, Spain, Barbary, and some parts of Asia by such light and fine stuffs as will fit those warmer regions, and yet have sufficient for the cold climates to be spent and adventured in true made cloth, by the reputation both of our nation and commodity.

But in this course I must observe that these strangers so fit to be nourished, and being protestants, may have privileges to use their own rights in religion, so as they be not scandalous, as the Dutch and French had granted unto them by Queen Elizabeth. And certainly the settling of religion secure in England, the fear whereof made many weak minds to waver and abandon this country is and will be a great means to re-settle both the great and lesser manufacture of woollen commodities.

For the external causes we must fly to the sanctuary of his majesty's gracious goodness and protection, who I am confident, when the whole business shall be prepared for him, and that we have showed him our duty and love and settled his customs in such a bountiful way as he may reap his part of the fruit of trade, I am confident, I say, that he will vouchsafe you all favour fit to be conferred upon good subjects, and not only protect you abroad by his forces and authority, and by treaties with his neighbours, but by increasing the privileges of merchants at home, and confirming all their charters, the breach whereof hath been a great discouragement unto them, and without which duly observed they cannot regulate their trade.

There are some particulars in the Spanish trade perhaps worthy of animadversion, as underselling good commodity to make money or barter for tobacco, to the embasement of our own staple for smoke, which in a due place ought to be taken into regulation.

Another consideration for a ground of trade ought to be the nature of it, with whom, and for what we trade, and which trade is more principally to be nourished, which out of doubt are the northern trades, which are the root of all other, because the materials brought from those parts, as from Wx [Sweden], Muscovy, Norway, Prussia, and Livonia, are fundamental and of absolute necessity; for from these trades we get the materials of shipping, as pitch, tar, cordage, masts, and such like, which enable us to all the southern trades, of themselves of less use, being only wine, fruit, oranges, and curiosities for sauces, or effeminacy; but by these we sail to the East Indies, and may erect a company of the West Indies for the golden fleece which shall be prepared for you, whensoever you are ready for so great a consultation.

The right way to nourish these northern trades is by his majesty's favour to press the king of Denmark to justice, not to come as his intolerable taxes newly imposed upon trade in the passage of the Sound, in examples whereof the elector of Brandenburg joined with the king of Poland hath likewise more than trebled the ancient and capitulated duties, which if that they shall continue, I pronounce all the commerce of the Baltic sea so over-burdened that the Eastland company cannot subsist, nor without them and the Muscovy company the navigation, but that the materials for shipping will be doubled, which will eat out all trades. I have given you but essays, and struck little sparks of fire before you, my intention is but to provoke the wit and ability of others; I have drawn you a map wherein you cannot see things clearly and distinctly, only I introduce matter before you, and now I have done when I have showed you the way how to enlarge and bring every particular thing into debate.

To which end my motion and desire is this, that we may send to every several company of merchants trading in companies and under government and privileges, and to ask of them what is their grievances in their general trade (not to rake into private complaints), what is the causes of decay or abuses in their trades and of the want of money which is visible, and of the great losses both to the kingdom and to every particular by the late high exchanges, and to desire every one of these companies to set down their judgment in writing to the committee by a day appointed, and having from them all the general state of the complaints severally, we shall make some judgments of these relations one to another. This done, I desire to require all the same several companies upon their own papers to propose to us in writing the remedies appliable in their judgment, which materials having altogether and comparing one with another we shall discover that truth which we seek, that is whether trade and money decay or not, and how to remedy it.

But I have one request more, and so I will ease you of my loss of your time. That when from all these merchants we shall have before us so much matter and without such variety, and perhaps not without private and partial ends, that then you will give me leave to represent to you the names of some general and others disinterested and well-experienced in many particulars, who may assist our judgments in all the premises particularly in moneys and exchanges, and give us great light to prepare our result and resolution, to be by the whole house of commons represented to his majesty, and for expedition that a sub-committee may be named to direct this information from the merchants.

Finis.

TOUCHING THE FUNDAMENTAL LAWS

Or politic constitution of this kingdom, the king's negative voice, and the power of parliaments. To which is annexed, the privilege and power of the parliament touching the militia. London, printed for Thomas Underhill, and are to be sold at the sign of the Bible in Wood-street. MDCXLIII.

WHEN in its first year the Long Parliament attacked the king's assumption of sovereign power, it did so on the theory that he, his councillors and judges had breached the fundamental law of the land by which the liberties of the subject were protected. As to exactly the content of the fundamental law opinions varied, but not as to its existence. By that law the king's prerogative was held to be strictly defined, and any of his acts contrary to it were deemed not to be acts of the crown. The function of the courts was to interpret and declare decisions in accordance with it. Now parliament conceived of itself as the highest and supreme court. The statutes it passed were often rather declaratory of older law than enactments of new legislation. The judges in the ship-money case, for instance, were considered to have reversed a decision of the highest court as laid down in the Petition of Right. According to this theory the government of England was a limited monarchy, the king as supreme ruler bound nevertheless by the fundamental law which held even his prerogative and the liberties of Englishmen.

The step which parliament took in 1642, of immense significance for the future development of the English constitution, was to pass from this doctrine of the supremacy of the law to a doctrine of the sovereignty of parliament. The question of the control of the militia provided the occasion, and the assumption of the right to interpret the fundamental law provided the means. The Militia Ordinance of March rested upon the implication that in time of danger the fundamental law was the law of *salus populi*. As supreme judge of that law parliament was also judge of the necessity of evoking it.

There followed a pamphlet discussion as to the theoretical grounds for such assumption of sovereign power. This anonymous pamphlet, which appeared early in 1643, shows the extreme view which had been set forth in 1642 by Henry Parker (1602–1654) in *Observations upon some of his Majesties late Answers and Expresses.*

FUNDAMENTAL laws are not (or at least need not be) any written agreement like merestones between king and people, the king himself being a part (not party) in those laws, and the commonwealth not being like a corporation treated by charter, but treating itself. But the fundamental law or laws is a settling of the laws of nature and common equity (by common consent), in such a form of polity and government as that they may be administered amongst us with honour and safety. For the first of which therefore, we are governed by a king: and for the second, by a parliament, to oversee and take order that that honourable trust that is put into the hands of the king for the dignity of the kingdom be rightly executed, and not abused to the alteration of the politic constitution taken up and approved, or to the destruction of that for whose preservation it was ordered and intended. A principal part of which honour is that royal assent he is to give for the enacting of such good laws as the people shall choose, for they are first to consult their own safety and welfare, and then he who is to be intrusted with it is to give an honourable confirmation to it, and so to put an impress of safety and royal authority upon it.

Fundamental laws then are not things of capitulation between king and people, as if they were foreigners and strangers one to another (nor ought they or any other laws so to be, for then the king should govern for himself, not for his people). But they are things of constitution, treating such a relation, and giving such an existence and being by an eternal polity to king and subjects, as head and members; which constitution in the very being of it is a law held forth with more evidence, and written in the very heart of the republic far firmlier than can be by pen and paper, and in which sense we owe our allegiance to the king as head (not only by power, but influence) and so part of the constitution, not as a party capitulating for a prerogative against or contrary to it, which whosoever seeks to set up or side with do break their allegiance and rebel against the state, going about to deprive the king of his juridical and lawful authority conferred upon him by the constitution of this state, under the pretence of investing him with an illegal and unconstitutive power; whereupon may follow this grand inconvenience, the withdrawment of his peoples' allegiance, which, as a body connected with the head by the constitution of this kingdom, is owing to him; his person in relation to the body, as the enlivening and quickening head thereof, being sacred and taken notice of by the laws, in that capacity, and under that notion is made inviolate.

And if it be conceived that fundamental laws must needs be only extant in writing, this is the next way to bring all to confusion, for then by the same rule the king bids the parliament produce those laws that fundamentally give them their being, privileges, and power, (which by the way is not like the power of inferior courts that are springs of the parliament, dealing between party and party, but is answerable to their trust; this court being itself fundamental and paramount, comprehending law and equity, and being entrusted by the whole for the whole, is not therefore to be circumscribed by any other laws which have their being from it, not it from them, but only by that law which at first gave it its being, to wit, *salus populi*). By the same rule I say the parliament may also intreat the king to produce those laws that fundamentally give him his being, power, and honour. Both which must therefore be determined, but by laws, for they themselves are laws, yea the most supreme and fundamental law, giving law to laws themselves, but by the received constitution or polity, which they themselves are; and the end of their constitution is the law or rule of their power, to wit, an honourable and safe regiment of the commonwealth, which two whosoever goeth about to divide the one of them from the other, breaks the fundamental constitutive law or laws and polity of this kingdom, that ordinance of man which we are to submit unto; nor can or ought any statute or written law whatsoever, which is of later edition and inferior condition, being but an offspring of this root, be interpreted or brought in plea against this primary and radical constitution, without guilt of the highest treason and destructive enmity of the public weal and polity, because by the very constitution of this kingdom, all laws or interpretation of laws tending to confusion or dissolution, are *ipso facto* void. In this case we may allude and say that the covenant which was 400 years before the law, an after-act cannot disannull it.

OB[JECTION]. It may be objected, that this discourse seems to make our government to be founded in equity, not in law, upon that common rule of *salus populi*, which is alike common to all nations, as well as any: and so what difference?

ANS[WER]. The fundamental laws of England are nothing but the common laws of equity and nature reduced into a particular way of policy, which policy is the ground of our title to them and interest in them. For though it is true that nature hath invested all nations in an equal right to the laws of nature and equity by a common bounty, without respect of persons, yet the several models of external government and policy renders them more or less capable of this their common right: for though they have an equal right in nature to all the laws of nature and equity, yet having fundamentally subjected themselves by their politic constitutions unto a regal servitude, by barbarism or the like, they have thereby much disabled and divested themselves of that common benefit. But on the contrary, where the outward constitution or polity of a republic is purposely framed for the confirming and better conserving this common right of nature and equity (as in ours), there is not only a common right, but also a particular and lawful power joined with this right for its maintainance and supportation. For whereas other people are without all supreme power, either of making laws or raising monies, both these bodies of supremacy being in the arbitrary hands only of the sovereign magistrate amongst many nations, these with us are in the hands of the supreme government (not governor) or court of judicature, to wit the king and parliament; here the people (like freemen) give money to the king, he doth not take it; and offers laws to be enacted, doth not receive them so: now in such a constituted kingdom, where the very constitution itself is the fundamental law of its own preservation, as is this mixt regiment of ours, consisting of king and parliament as head and body, comprehending monarchy, aristocracy, and democracy; there the fundamental laws are like fundamental truths in these two properties: first, they are comprehended in a very little room, to wit, honour and safety; and secondly they have their influence into all other inferior laws which are to be subjected to them, and correspondent with them, as lawful children and natural branches.

OB. But in process of time there are many written laws which seem at least to contradict this fundamental constitution, and are not they binding notwithstanding it?

ANS. The constitution of this kingdom which gave it its being, and which is the radical and fundamental law thereof, ought therefor to command in chief, for that it never yields up its authority to those inferior laws which have their being from it, nor ought they which spring from it tend to the destruction of it, but on the contrary, it is to derive its radical virtue and influence into all succeeding laws, and they like branches are to make the root flourish, from whence they spring, with exhibiting the lively and fructifying virtue thereof, according to the nature and seasons of succeeding times; things incident in after-ages not being able to be foreseen, and particularly provided for at the beginning, saving in the fundamental law of *salus populi*, politicly established; nor can any laws growing out of that root bear any other fruit, than such as the nature thereof dictates; for, for a particular branch to ruin the whole foundation by a seeming sense contrary to it or differing from it, is very absurd; for then how can it be said, thou bearest not the root, but the root thee? Laws must always relish of and drink in the constitution or polity where they are made; and therefore with us, the laws wherein the king is nominated, and so seems to put an absolute authority into his hands, must never so be construed, for that were with a breath to blow down all the building at once: but the king is there comprehended and meant under a twofold notion; first, as trusted, being the head, with that power the law conferred upon him for a legal, and not an absolute purpose, tending to an honourable preservation, not an unnatural dissolution. Secondly, as meaning him juridically, not abstractly or personally, for so only the law takes notice of the king as a juridical person; for till the legislative power be absolutely in the king, so that laws come down from him to his people, and go not up from them to him, they must ever be so interpreted: for as they have a juridical being and beginning, to wit, in parliament, so must they have a suitable execution and administration, to wit, by the courts and legal ministers under the king's authority, which according to the constitution of this kingdom he can no more suspend for the good of his people than the courts can theirs; or if he do, to the public hazard, then have the courts this advantage, that for public preservation they may and must provide upon that principle, the king can do no wrong, neither in withholding justice, nor protection from his people. So that then *salus populi*, being so principally respected and provided for according to the nature of our constitution and polity, and so being *lex legum*, or the rule of all laws branching thence, then if any law do by variation of times, violence of tyranny, or misprision of interpreters, vary therefrom, it is a bastard and not a son, and is by the lawful parents either to be reduced or cast out, as gendering unto bondage and ruin of the inheritance by attempting to erect an absolute and arbitrary government. Nor can this equitable exposition of particular statutes taken from the scope of the politic constitution be denied without overthrow of just and legal monarchy (which ever tends to public good and preservation) and the setting up of an unjust and illegal tyranny, ruling, if not without law, yet by abused laws, turning them as conquered ordinance upon the people. The very scripture itself must borrow from its scope and principles for explanation of particular places, else it will be abused (as it is through that default) unto heresies. See we not how falsely Satan quoted true scripture to Christ when he tempted him, only by urging the letter without the equity, or true intention and meaning? We are to know and do things *verum verè, justum justè*, else we neither judge with righteous judgment, nor obey with just obedience.

OB. But is not the parliament guilty of exercising an arbitrary power, if their proceedings be not regulated by written laws, but by *salus populi*?

ANS. For the parliament to be bound up by written laws, is both destructive and absurd.

First, it is destructive, it being the fundamental court and law, or the very *salus populi* of England, and ordained, as to make laws, and see them executed, so to supply their deficiency according to the present exigency of things for public preservation by the prerogative of *salus populi* which is universally in them, and but particularly in particular laws and statutes, which cannot provide against all future exigents, which the law of parliament doth, and therefore are not they to be limits to this. And it would yet be further destructive, by cutting the parliament short of half its power at once, for it being a court both of law and equity (as appears by the power of making laws, which is nothing but equity reduced by common consent into polity) whenever it is circumscribed by written laws (which only is the property of inferior courts), it ceaseth to be supreme, and divests itself of that inherent and uncircumscribed power which *salus populi* comprehends.

Secondly, as it is destructive, so also it is absurd; for the legislative power which gives laws is not to receive laws, saving from the nature and end of its own constitution, which as they give it a being, so they endow it with laws of preservation both of itself and the whole, which it represents.

I would not herein be misunderstood, as if the parliament, when as it only doth the office of inferior courts, judging between party and party, were not limited by written laws: there I grant it is, because therein it only deals between *meum* and *tuum*, which particular written laws can and ought to determine: so that its superlative and uncircumscribed power I intend only as relating to the universe and the affairs thereof, wherein it is to walk by its fundamental principles, not by particular precepts or statutes, which are made by the parliament, between king and people, not between people and parliament: they are ordained to be rules of government to the king, agreeing with the liberty and property of the people, and rules of obedience to the people without detainment of their freedom by the exercise of an illegal, usurped, and unconsented power, whereunto kings (especially in hereditary monarchies) are very prone, which cannot be suspected by a parliament, which is representatively the public, intrusted for it, and which is like to partake and share with the public, being but so many private men put into authority *pro tempore*, by common consent, for common good.

Nor is the parliament hereby guilty of an arbitrary government, or is it destructive to the Petition of Right, when as in providing for public weal, it observes not the letter of the law; first, because as aforesaid, that law was not made between parliament and people, but by the people in parliament between the king and them, as appears by the whole tenor of it, both in the complaining and praying parts, which wholly relate to the king. Secondly, because of the common consent, that in the representative body (the parliament) is given thereunto, wherein England in her polity imitates nature in her instincts, who is wont to violate particular principles for public preservation, as when light things descend, and heavy ascend, to prevent a *vacuum*: and thirdly, because of the equitable power which is inherent in a parliament, and for public good is to be acted above and against any particular statute, or all of them: and fourthly, because the end of making that law, to wit, the public preservation, is fulfilled in the breaking of it, which is lawful in a parliament that is chosen by the whole for the whole, and are themselves also of the body, though not in a king, for therein the law saith, better a mischief than an inconvenience. But it may be objected, though it be not arbitrary for the parliament to go against written law, yet is it not so when they go against the king's consent, which the law, even the fundamental law, supposeth in parliamentary proceedings; this hath been answered, that the king is juridically and according to the intention of the law in his courts, so that what the parliament consults for the public good, that by oath, and the duty of his office, and nature of this polity he is to consent unto, and in case he do deny it, yet in the construction of the fundamental law and constitution of this kingdom, he is conceived to grant it, supposing the head not to be so unnatural to the body that hath chosen it for good and not for evil.

But it will be answered, where is the king's negative voice if the parliament may proceed without his consent? I answer: That there is no known nor written law that gives him any; and things of that nature are willingly believed till they be abused, or with too much violence claimed. That his majesty hath fundamentally a right of consent to the enacting of laws is true, which (as aforesaid) is part of that honourable trust constituted in him: and that this royal assent is an act of honour and not of absolute and negative power or prerogative, appears by these following reasons.

First, by his oath at the coronation mentioned in one of the parliament's declarations where he doth or should swear to confirm and grant all such good laws as his people *shall choose* to be observed, not *hath chosen*, for first, the word *concedis* in that oath were then unnecessary, the laws formerly enacted being already granted by foregoing kings, and so they need no more concession or confirmation, else we must run upon this shelf that all our laws die with the old king, and receive their being anew by the new king's consent. Secondly, hereby the first and second clause in that interrogatory, viz. *Concedis iustas leges et permittas protegendas*, are confounded and do but *idem repetere*; thirdly, *quas vulgus elegerit* implies only the act of the people in a disjunctive sense from the act or consent of the king, but laws already made have more than *quas vulgus elegerit*, they have also the royal consent too, so that that phase cannot mean them wherein the act or consent of the king is already involved.

Secondly, by the practice of requiring the royal assent even unto those very acts of subsidies which are granted to himself and for his own use, which it is supposed he will accept of, and yet *honoris gratia* is his royal assent craved and contributed thereunto.

Thirdly, by the king's not sitting in parliament to debate and consult laws, nor are they at all offered him by the parliament to consider of, but to consent to, which yet are transmitted from one house to another, as well to consult as consent to, showing thereby he hath no part in the consultory part of them (for that it belongs only to the people in parliament to discern and consult their own good), but he comes only at the time of enacting, bringing his royal authority with him, as it were to set the seal thereof to the indenture already prepared by the people, for the king is head of the parliament in regard of his authority, not in regard of his reason or judgment, as if it were to be opposed to the reason or judgment of both houses (which is the reason both of king and kingdom) and therefore do they as consult so also interpret laws without him, supposing him to be a person replenished with honour and royal authority not skilled in laws, nor to receive information either of law or council in parliamentary affairs from any, saving from that supreme court and highest council of the king and kingdom, which admits no counterpoise, being intrusted both as the wisest council and justest judicature.

Fourthly, either the chosen of the people in parliament is to be the ground and rule of the king's assent, or nothing but his pleasure; and so all bills, though never so necessary for public good and preservation, and after never so much pains and consultation of both houses, may be rejected, and so they made mere cyphers; and we brought to that pass, as either to have no laws, or such only as come immediately from the king (who oft is a man of pleasure, and little seen in public affairs, to be able to judge) and so the kingdom's great council must be subordinated either to his mere will, and then what difference between a free monarchy, and absolute, saving that the one rules without council, and the other against it, or at the best but to a cabinet council consisting commonly of men of private interests, but certainly of no public trust.

OB. But if the king must consent to such laws as the parliament shall choose *eo nomine*, they may then propound unreasonable things to him, as to consent to his own deposing, or to the lessening his own revenue, etc.

ANS. So that the issue is, whether it be fitter to trust the wisdom and integrity of our parliament, or the will and pleasure of the king in this case of so great and public concernment. In a word, the king being made the fountain of justice and protection to his people by the fundamental laws or constitution of this kingdom, he is therefore to give life to such acts and things as tend thereunto; which acts depend not upon his pleasure, but though they are to receive their greater vigour from him, yet are they not to be suspended at pleasure by him; for that which at first was intended by the kingdom for an honourable way of subsistence and administration must not be invested contrary to the nature of this polity (which is a free and mixt monarchy and not an absolute), to its destruction and confusion. So that in case the king in his person should decline his duty, the king in his courts are bound to perform it, where his authority properly resides; for if he refuse that honour which the republic by its fundamental constitution hath conferred upon him, and will not put forth the acts of it, for the end it was given him, viz. for the justice and safety of his people, this hinders not but that they who have as fundamentally reserved a power of being, well being in their own hands by the concurrence of parliamentary authority to the royal dignity, may thereby provide for their own subsistence, wherein is acted the king's juridical authority though his personal pleasure be withheld; for his legal and juridical power is included and supposed in the very being, and consequently in the acts of courts of justice, whose being he may as well suspend as their power of acting, for that without this is but a cypher; and therefore neither their being nor their acting so depend upon him, as not to be able to act and execute common justice and protection without him, in case he deny to act with them. And yet both so depend upon him, as that he is bound both in duty and honour, by the constitution of this polity to act in them and they from him, so that (according to that axiom in law) *the king can do no wrong*, because his juridical power and authority is always to control his personal miscarriages.

Se Defendendo.

God and nature hath ordained government for the preservation of the governed. This is a truth so undeniable as that none will gainsay it, saving in practice, which therefore being taken for granted, it must needs follow that to what end government was ordained, it must be maintained. For that it is not in the power of particular persons or communities of men to depart with self-preservation by any covenant whatsoever, nor ought it to be exacted by any superiors from their inferiors, either by oath or edict, because neither oaths nor statutes are obligatory further than they agree with the righteous laws of God and nature; further than so they ought neither to be made nor kept.

Let it be supposed then for argument sake, that the militia of the kingdom is in the power of the king, yet now as the case stands it is lawful for the parliament to reassume it, because though they passed it into his hands for the people's preservation, yet it was never intended that by it he might compass their destruction, contrary to the law of nature; whereby every man, yea everything is bound to preserve itself. And thus much in effect is confessed at unawares by the author of the *Reply to the Answer of the London Petition*: who affirmeth, saying, ' The king is invested with the sole power of training, arraying, and mustering,' and then gives the reason, ' because it is most consonant to reason as well as grounded on law, that he which is bound to protect, should be able to compass that end.' Which reason overthrows both his position and intention. 1. His position, for this is no reason why the sole power of the militia should be in the hands of the king; ' because he is bound to protect,' except he were bound solely to protect, that is, without the counsel and advice of parliament: but it hath been resolved that he is not sole judge of necessity, and therefore not sole protector against it, but together with his parliament, who consequently shares in the power of the militia. 2. It overthrows his intention, which is so to put the power of the militia into the hands of the king, as to enable him to do what he will with it, whenas yet he himself cannot but affirm, it is his to protect withall, so that when he ceaseth to use it to its end, it ceaseth to be in his power, or else let the man speak plain, and say, it is his to destroy as well as to protect.

OB. But the militia is passed to the king, absolutely without any condition of revocation expressed, or of limitation to circumscribe the use whereunto it ought to be employed.

1. ANS. Laws of God and nature neither are nor need to be expressed in contracts or edicts, for they are ever supposed to be supreme to human ordinances, and to challenge obedience in the first place, and other laws so far only as they are consonant to them, though these laws be further backed with oaths and protestations: as for instance, I give a man a sword, and swear I will never take it from him; yet if he actually assault me, or it manifestly appear he intends to cut my throat, or take my purse with it, I may lawfully possess myself of it again if opportunity serve. Because in such agreements betwixt man and man, the laws of nature neither are nor can be exempted, but are necessarily implied still to be of force, because no bonds can lawfully invalid them, and *id solum possumus quod jure possumus*. But it may be asked how it appears that the king intends to employ the militia to the destruction of his people. Why first because he hath refused to hearken to the wholesome counsel of his parliament, the representative body, and the highest court and counsel of the kingdom. 2. Because, *è contrario*, he hearkens to the counsels of notorious papists and malignants, men engaged against the public good and welfare of this kingdom, in a diametral opposition, so that if they perish it prospereth, and if it prosper they perish. 3. Because

he hath had a deep hand in contriving and plotting the ruin and extirpation of the parliament by secret and open violence, and in them of the
whole kingdom of whom they are the epitome, and as the king is the
head, so they are the heart. But further it may be replied, that the king
hath promised to maintain parliaments and govern by law. ANS. That
is so far as he knows his own heart, and as he can be master of himself. He sware the same at his coronation, and promised as much when
he granted the petition of right, but how they have been kept God
knows, and we are not ignorant. It may be his majesty may mean as
he speaks, but 1. Temptations may change his mind, as it hath done
too often, and as it did his that said to the prophet, is thy servant a dog
that he should do such things? and yet did them. The welfare of kingdoms is not to be founded upon bare spontaneous promises, but real
contracts. 2. He himself says he is not skilled in the laws, and we have
found it true, so that he must take information of them from some body;
from his parliament (that is his people that made them) he will not, and
are any fitter to be judges of the law than the highest court; if they may
be judges that are delinquents to the law, and malignants against it, and
have been grievous oppressors of the people, even against the known
laws (so much cried up) we are like to have just judges and righteous
lawyers.

2. ANS. If the militia be so absolutely the king's, as that all power
of defence and preservation of ourselves and our rights be taken from
us, to what purpose do we strive for liberty and property, and laws to
confirm them? These are but imaginary things, if they have no hedge
to fence them. If the militia be for the king, let us burn the statutes we
have already, and save a labour of making more. No man would think
it a good purchase to buy land, and when he hath paid his money, to
have it in the power of the seller to take it from him by his sword.

OB. It is true that kings are tied by oath and legal contracts to govern
by laws, and to maintain liberty and property to their people, which
puts them under an obligation of conscience to God, so that they are
responsible to him for the breach of fidelity and duty, but not to the
people who may mind them of their duty, but not compel them to it.

ANS. This objection hath two parts, first, that kings are only responsible to God. 2. That subjects must suffer wrong, but not by force
maintain their right. To the first I answer. That if kings be solely answer-

able to God, then contracts are in vain, for they shall answer for all their arbitrary and unjust tyranny over their people, though there were no contracts. That which makes us happier than other nations sure is not this, that the king for the breach of his duty hath more to answer at the day of judgment than other kings have; if that be all we have small cause to joy in our privileges, they are neither worth the blood that hath been shed for them, nor the money that hath been paid for them. Secondly, government must be considered under a twofold notion, divine and human. The genus which is government itself is divine, so that people are absolutely bound to have government, but not bound to have an absolute government; for the species or the *modus gubernandi* is human, and therefore the apostle says, ' Be subject to every ordinance of man,' that is, to every such kind of government as your lot falls to be under, by the constitution of the commonwealth you live in. Now government being thus of a mixt nature, the ordinance both of God and man, it is not only subject to God but also to men, to be regulated, amended, and maintained by the people: for as it is God's ordinance for their good, so doth he give them liberty too, provide it be not abused to their hurt; so that when God shall put an opportunity into their hands, they ought to improve it to the setting of government up right, or the keeping of it so from apparent violations. There was a time when both government and the manner of governing belonged to God, to wit, amongst the Israelites, for to that people he was both a God of morals and politics, and therefore he took it so ill for them to usurp upon his right, as to desire to change their government from judges to kings, but this was a peculiar right he assumed over that particular people only. To the second I answer thus. Every subject taken *divisim* and apart from the whole, is to suffer under abused authority, and to obey passively, rather than to break union or cause confusion; but no subject is bound to suffer by that which is not authority, as is the will of the magistrate. If a court of justice should unjustly condemn a man, he is patiently to undergo it, but if a judge or the king himself should violently set upon him to kill him, he may defend himself; for the ordinance of God and man both is affixed to the office, and not upon the person, to the authority and not unto the will, so that the person acting out of office and by his will may be resisted, though the ordinance may not. But the representative body of the commonwealth (which is all men *conjunctim*), they may not only oppose the person and his will, but even the office and authority itself when abused, and are bound to it both in conscience to God when he gives them opportunity, and in discharging of their trust to them that employed them. For first God calls to have the wicked removed from the throne, and whom doth he call upon to do it but upon the people (in case the king will not) or their trustees. For as he hath originally founded all authority in the people, so he expects a discharge of it from them for his glory, and the public weal, which are the ends of government, from which God and nature hath ordained it. Secondly, in discharge of their trust for the whole, for order sake, making them their representative actors, and putting that universal and popular authority that is in the body of the people, and which (for the public good and preservation) is above every man and all laws, into their hands, they may expect and challenge them by virtue of their stewardship to provide for their safety and well being against whomsoever shall oppose it, no one being above all; and therefore ought not that universal power, which by way of trust is conveyed over to the parliament, be betrayed into the hands of any by admitting or allowing any authority to be superior, by tolerating abuses and usurpations, as if they had not power to regulate them.

Finis.

HERESIOGRAPHY

Or a description of the heretics and sectaries sprang up in these latter times. Declaring, 1. Their original and first proceedings. 2. Their errors and blasphemies. 3. Their several sorts. 4. Their audacious boldness in these days. 5. The confutation of their errors. 6. How they have been punished and suppressed amongst us heretofore. The fourth edition, whereunto is added an alphabetical table. By Ephraim Pagitt. Mat.15: 17. Beware of false prophets, which come to you in sheep's clothing, but inwardly they are ravening wolves. London, Printed by W.W. for William Lee, and are to be sold at his shop in Fleet Street. 1647.

EPHRAIM PAGITT (1575?–1647) was the son of an Elizabethan divine who was deprived of his living for such puritan practices as refusing to make the sign of the cross in baptism, for not wearing a surplice, and for omitting parts of certain prayers. Ephraim was born in Northamptonshire, matriculated from Christ Church, Oxford, in 1593, and was appointed rector of a London church in 1601. A scholar and a great linguist, he published in 1635 his *Christianography*, a description of the various Christian churches in Europe, and in 1638 wrote a series of letters to the patriarchs of the Greek Orthodox church advertising and recommending his book. When the civil war broke out he retired to Deptford. A royalist by conviction, he nevertheless subscribed to the covenant, and in 1645 signed a petition to the parliament for the establishment of presbyterianism. It was for him a choice of evils; independency he abhorred and feared.

His *Heresiography* (1645), only the dedicatory epistles of which are here reproduced, is valuable chiefly by reason of its wide range. Every lapse from Calvinism Pagitt regarded with horror as a form of heresy. Anabaptists, Brownists, Independents, Familists, Adamites, Antinomians, Arminians, Socinians, Antitrinitarians, Millenarians, Hetheringtonians, Antisabbatarians, Traskites, Jesuits—he lumped them all under the same title. With that tremendous religious awakening which the civil war witnessed he had no sympathy. Its chief exponent in England had been John Everard, a Cambridge doctor of divinity who in the reign of James I had translated the works of such continental spiritual reformers as Hans Denck, Sebastian Franck, and Castellio. They had emphasized the gentleness of God, his kinship with man, the inward light in the soul. The Seeker movement in England, under which general term may be grouped together many different sects, was characterized by the same intensity of faith which marks every great religious revival, the certainty of conviction that God is knowable and attainable, and could become reality in every individual soul. ' This is He whom I have waited for and sought after from my childhood; this is He.' Such Christianity needed none of the symbols of the visible church.

12—The illustration opposite is the frontispiece to Pagitt's *Heresiography*, the fourth, 1647, edition. It is a sample of the typography and engraving used in the press campaigns during the Civil Wars. It shows a resort to visual appeal, as well as to argument, reason, and a vehement vocabulary, to discredit the multifarious religious sects that came in the wake of the English reformation. The six vignettes show the popular conceptions, or misconceptions, of the sectaries represented: the naked, baptizing Anabaptist; the paternalistic Familist; the wife-discarding Divorser; the worldly Jesuit; the Seeker on his quest for salvation; and the Antinomian relegating the moral law of the ten commandments to the background. These pictorial characterizations prove that the sectaries were considered human beings and not merely theological terms.

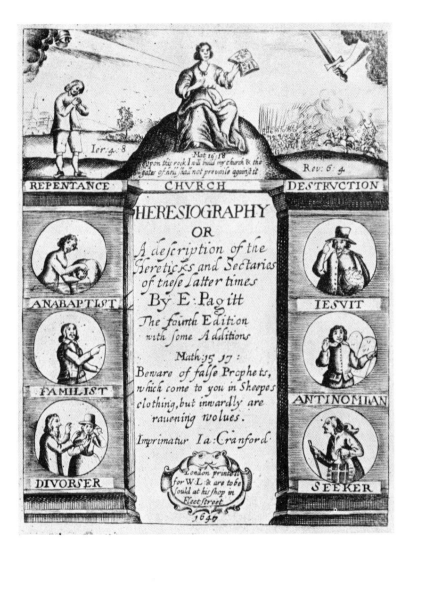

TO the right honourable Thomas Atkin, lord mayor of the city of London, and to the [aldermen] of the said city.

Right honourable and right worshipful, whereas I have lately published a Christianography, or a description of many great churches of Christians in the world: some of which are for extent larger than the church of Rome in Europe, for time more ancient, for succession as continual, for faith more sound: who believe with us the church of God to be catholic as it is in the Apostles' Creed, and not as it is set down in the new Trent Creed, confined to Rome, who renounce the pope's supremacy, some of them excommunicating him for a schismatic and heretic.

Who receive the Holy Communion in both kinds; they all drink of Christ's cup, and abhor the Romish decree made contrary to Christ's institution.

Who make no images to be worshipped.

Who do not acknowledge the figment of purgatory, nor use any prayers to be delivered from the feigned pains thereof.

Who have their prayers in their own tongue and mutter them not in Latin as the Romists do.

Who forbid not marriage (the prohibiting of which is called by St. Paul the doctrine of devils). Their priests may and do marry.

Who hold not popish transubstantiation.

Who prohibit not laymen the reading of the Holy Scriptures commanded by Christ himself.

Who do not join with Christ's intercession the suffrages of saints: nor with his justification the merit of works: nor with the satisfaction papal indulgences.

These points with some others which the ambition and avarice of the Romists hath lately hatched, they renounce with us.

This work I purposing to perfect and consummate to the glory of God, the great profit of the church, and establishing of men's consciences, they seeing the unity and agreement of the holy churches in the world with us; behold suddenly a numerous company of other heretics stole in upon us like the locusts, Rev.9.

As the unpure Familists, who blasphemously pretend to be godified like God, whereas indeed they are devilified like their father the devil.

The illuminated Anabaptists who blasphemously affirm the baptism of children to be the mark of the beast, and to come from Antichrist.

The Donatistical Brownists, who in times past hid themselves in holes, now lift up their heads and vent openly their errors, infecting our people.

The Antinomians, who teach, as I find, such a fair and easy way to heaven, viz. that a man need not be troubled by the law before faith, and that faith is not a going out of himself to take hold of Christ, but only a discerning that Christ is his, and that after this, such a man must see nothing in himself, have nothing, do nothing, need no sorrow nor repentance, nor be pressed to duties, need never pray unless moved by the spirit: if he fall into sin, never the more disliked of God, nor his condition the worse: and that he must abide in the height of comfort, though he fall into gross sin. The novelty of this doctrine takes so well, or rather ill, that multitudes of simple men and women dance after their pipes, they run after these men as if they were mad, crowding the churches, filling their doors and windows.

The Independents trouble also our poor church, who pretend that they have a perfect model of church government, which almighty God hath revealed to them, which many like better than the government of the reformed churches, being persuaded that in Independency they may have liberty to do what they list, having no government, hoping to be as free as their teachers, who will have none at all.

The Arminians also, an after-brood of the Pelagians, broach their erroneous opinions.

The Sabbatarians affirm the old Jewish Sabbath to be kept, and not the Lord's day.

The Antisabbatarians would have no particular Sabbath at all, but every day to be a Sabbath to a Christian man.

The Traskites, who would have us observe many Jewish ceremonies.

We have also Millenaries, who affirm that before the day of judgment Christ shall come down from heaven, and reign with the saints upon earth a thousand years, in which time they shall destroy all the wicked, binding their kings in chains, and nobles in links of iron.

We have Hetheringtonians, who hold a hodge-podge of many heresies, troubling our people's brains.

We have also Socinians, who teach that Christ died not to satisfy for our sins: and also his incarnation to be repugnant to reason, and not to be sufficiently proved by Scripture, with many other abominable errors.

We have Arians, who deny the deity of Christ.

We have an atheistical sect, who affirm that men's souls sleep with their bodies until the day of judgment.

We have atheists too many, as among others, one was committed by a justice of peace, who mocked and jeered at Christ's incarnation: his father was burned at Toulouse in France; he escaped unpunished among us: too many others we have.

They preach, print, and practise their heretical opinions openly: for books, *vide* the bloody tenet, witness a tractate of divorce, in which the bonds are let loose to inordinate lust: a pamphlet also in which the soul is laid asleep from the hour of death unto the hour of judgment, with many others.

Yea, since the suspension of our church government, everyone that listeth turneth preacher, as shoe-makers, cobblers, button-makers, hostlers, and such like, take upon them to expound the Holy Scriptures, intrude into our pulpits, and vent strange doctrine tending to faction, sedition, and blasphemy.

What mischief these sectaries have already done, we that have cure of souls in London find and see with great grief of heart: viz. our congregations forsaking their pastors; our people becoming of the tribe of Gad, running after seducers as if they were mad; infants not to be brought to the sacrament of baptism; men refusing to receive the Holy Communion, and the Lord's Prayer accounted abominable, etc. A volume will hardly contain the hurt that these sectaries have in a very short time done to this poor church; and doth not the commonwealth suffer with the church? Whence are all these distractions? Who are the incendiaries that have kindled and blown this fire among us, but these?

Considering with myself the former happiness of this kingdom, and the sudden change that is betide it, it being fallen from the height of prosperity to the lowest ebb of misery, and this not by the incursion of a foreign nation, but by its own children, who imbrue their hands in the blood one of another with no less inhumanity than the cannibals or men-eaters, without any reluctation at all; the son against the father, and the father against the son.

And moreover (which is worst of all) when I consider that some of our clergymen (who should like Moses stand in the gap to appease God's anger) do increase the same, not only by blowing the fire, but by their errors and schisms which they broach and foment among us; by which they do, as much as in them lieth, put men's souls in as great danger as their bodies.

And considering again how we are involved in a most cruel war without any hopes of peace, may not I cry out with the prophet, O that my head were full of water, and my eyes a fountain of tears, that I might weep for the slain of my people!

But all this being God's permitting, let us with patience possess our souls; let us trust in him, depend upon him, and in his good time he will deliver his church, and turn all to the best; and in the mean season every man do his best to quench this fire. For my own part these sad considerations made me leave my Christianography and write an Heresiography to describe the heretics and schismatics of this time, in which I set down their beginning among us; their heretical opinions and errors, confuting them; and also relate how other princes and commonwealths have suppressed them, and how severely some of them have been punished among us.

I know my reverend brethren have not been wanting to oppose these heretics in writing and preaching, in season and out of season, using all means to suppress these heresies, having to that end chosen special men to preach several lectures in several places: but without your help and the assistance of our religious patriots assembled in parliament, they do, and will increase upon us, do what we can.

This treatise I present to your lordship, and to this honourable senate. What can be more suitable or fitter for you, servants of the most high God, than that which tendeth to the glory of God, the edification of his church, and vindication of the truth against the illusion of sectaries and heretics?

What is more correspondent with the duty of Christian magistrates than to assist God's cause with your political authority? A question may be asked, whether it be lawful for magistrates to use the sword against the heretics? To this I answer; such whose heresies are blasphemous in doctrine, or dangerous to the state, deserve death: the reason is, because they corrupt the faith. If such as poison waters and fountains at which men and beasts drink deserve capital punishment, how much more they that as much as in them lieth go about to poison men's souls?

Yea, St. Augustine saith in his first tractate upon John; *Quantum in ipsis est, Christum in homine occidunt.*

The forenamed St. Augustine indeed wavered concerning this point for a time, as he confesseth in one of his epistles: but when he saw the city wherein he dwelt was reclaimed from Donatism by the magistrates' sword, he retracted his opinion.

And expecting the like success in this honourable city, I do implore your helps, and that for Jesus Christ's sake: and I pray you give me leave to put you in mind of the covenant we made in the presence of almighty God, the searcher of all hearts, with a true intent to perform the same, as we should answer at that great day when the secrets of all hearts should be disclosed, viz. that we should in like manner without respect of persons endeavour the extirpation of popery, prelacy, superstition, heresy, schism, profaneness, and whatsoever shall be found to be contrary to sound doctrine and the power of godliness, lest we partake in other men's sins, and thereby be in danger to receive of her plagues; and that the Lord may be one, and his name one in the three kingdoms. And this I beseech you in the name of God to take in hand, laying aside all human reasons.

Let not God's cause go to wrack, nor by worldly policies and human reasons be protracted or retarded.

The Turk will not suffer Mahomet to be blasphemed: as we are Christians let us stand for Christ.

How dangerous the fostering of heretics hath been, histories declare, viz. almighty God sent down fire from heaven and consumed Antioch, being a nursery of heretics. And also how the earth opened and swallowed Nicomedia, the meeting place of the blasphemous Arians: also in the commentaries of Sleiden, how the Anabaptists meeting first in conventicles, surprised Munster: and how hardly Amsterdam escaped them, Lambert Hortense writeth.

The plague is of all diseases most infectious: I have lived among you almost a jubilee, and seen your great care and provision to keep the city from infection, in the shutting up the sick, and in carrying them to your pest-houses, in setting warders to keep the whole from the sick, in making of fires, and perfuming the streets, in resorting to your churches, in pouring out your prayers to almighty God with fasting and alms to be propitious to you. The plague of heresy is greater, and you are now in more danger than when you buried five thousand a week: you have power to keep these heretics and sectaries from conventicles and shoaling together to infect one another. Fire is dangerous, many cities in Europe have been almost ruinated by it: I have seen your diligence and dexterity in quenching it in the beginning: your breaking open your pipes for water, making floods in your streets: your engines to cast the water upon the houses: your industry and pains is admirable.

Heresy is as dangerous as fire, use your best endeavours to quench it before it consumes us.

Thus not doubting, right honourable and right worshipful, of your best endeavours to suppress these heresies and sectaries by whom not only many poor souls were infected, but also the holy name of God is blasphemed; I cease, most humbly entreating almighty God to bless this city, and to give unto you the fruition of all temporal felicities in this life, and the never failing fulness of blessedness in the life to come.

To the Reader

Thou which hast a tender conscience, and desirest nothing so much as to know the right way to heaven, having many doubts which cause thee to leave thy own pastor, and run not only to other public congregations, but also to the private meetings of the Separatists and others for resolution.

For thy sake and safety I have published this treatise, in which thou mayest discern truth from error, having their errors set before thee, with the confutation of them out of the Holy Scripture.

Our Lord and Saviour in his holy sermon in the mount, telling his disciples of the narrow way that leadeth unto life, he especially forewarneth them of false prophets: Beware of false prophets which come to you in sheep's clothing, but inwardly they are ravening wolves. As if he should say, my dear disciples, you hearing of the way to heaven, will be inquiring after it, and especially of prophets; but let me forewarn you of false prophets, for instead of directing you, they will put you out of the way. False prophets will come, they are not sent: St. Paul asketh, how they can preach except they be sent? and this standeth with good reason: every true minister standeth in God's room, being the Lord's ambassador to deliver his will, who dare do this unsent? No man taketh his honour unto himself, but he that is called of God, saith my author to the Hebrews.

But whence come they now? from the schools of the prophets? no, many of them from the mechanic trades: as one from a stable, from currying his horses: another from his stall, from cobbling his shoes, and these sit down in Moses' chair to mend all, as ambassadors of Jesus Christ, as heralds of the most high God: these take upon them to reveal the secrets of almighty God to open and shut heaven, to save men's souls.

But to hear these fellows discourse of the holy Trinity, of God's eternal decree, and other deep points of divinity; you may hear the madmen in Bedlam prate as wisely as they: and are not their hearers that run after them as mad as they? Are they not bewitched, as St. Paul telleth the Galatians?

To you that are my disciples: daily experience showeth us whom the Anabaptists, Brownists, and other sectaries go about to seduce, viz. not drunkards, adulterers, swearers, and profane persons, whom the devil hath ensnared already, but such as are desirous of heaven. They lead captive (saith St. Paul) silly women who are always learning. They come unto you in sheep's clothing; that is, like zealous and holy Christians: for an example, the devil turned himself into an angel of light. Baal's priests used long prayers: the blasphemous Arians (as St. Basil writeth) were easily believed, because of their counterfeit holiness.

The Romish seducers pretend great sanctimony: the begging friars befooled the Christian world with their pretended holiness, with which they varnished their lewd lives. Generally they come to you with outward sanctimony, with a seeming contempt of the world; with long prayers, fasting, tears, alms-deeds, seeming-zeal, seeming-humility, seeming-harmlessness, etc.

They come to you in sheep's clothing, insinuating themselves into you, under colour of giving you good counsel: as the devil their chief, counselling our first parents to break God's commandment, promised to make them like God: and tempting Christ in the wilderness promised to give him all the kingdoms of the world, and the glory of them.

And that you may the better avoid their enchantments, I will show you the method they use in deceiving. As first, they endeavour to separate the sheep from their shepherds, bringing them into contempt with their people, affirming them to be unprofitable, unpowerful, taxing their conversations as profane, and doctrine as erroneous. Thus smiting your shepherds with their tongues, they draw you to their conventicles.

To palliate their errors, they pervert the Holy Scriptures, as that monster Arius pretended to have forty-two places of Scripture against the deity of Christ, and this he learned of his father the devil, who perverted part of the ninety-first Psalm to tempt our Lord to cast himself down from the pinnacle of the temple.

And for this cause these heretics are enemies to the ten commandments, being some of the law: to the Creed, being a brief of the Gospel, and to the Lord's Prayer, being a perfect form of prayer, containing all that can be asked, or prayed against, by which only a simple man may discern any heretic, contradicting any commandment of the Decalogue, article of the faith, and petition of the Lord's Prayer. And for this cause the church of Rome teacheth the laity them in Latin, and also they leave out part of the Decalogue in their catechisms: and for other heretics some do null the whole law, some the creed, and others the Lord's Prayer, affirming it to be abominable. Again, whatsoever outward show they make of holiness, they are indeed ravening wolves; therefore our Lord biddeth us beware of them. The word *beware* precedeth danger. As sheep are in danger among wolves, so are your souls in danger among false prophets.

The journey of the Israelites to the earthly Canaan was a type of our journey to the heavenly. And did not one false prophet Balaam do them more mischief in their journey than Og the king of Bashan, Sehon king of the Amorites, and all their enemies besides? yea, would the devil himself in his own likeness have been more noxious to the church of God than some heretics have been? As one heretic Arius, denying the deity of Christ, in a manner infected the whole world.

The like did one other heretic Eutiches, erring concerning his humanity, affirming the immensity of Christ's divine nature to have swallowed up his human. Now if Christ had not been man, how could he have died for us sinners? and if not God, how could he have wrought the salvation of mankind?

Alas, what danger are we in now, being environed with such a multitude of heretics? Our Lord telleth us again, by their fruits ye shall know them: they pretend that they are led by the spirit. The works of the spirit St. Paul setteth forth to be love, joy, peace, long-suffering, gentleness, goodness, faith, meekness, and temperance. If they were led by the Holy Spirit, these would be their characters. But St. Paul telleth us that in the latter days there shall come men, lovers of their own selves, boasters, proud, cursed speakers, disobedient to parents, unthankful, unholy. Mr. Calvin, that admirable man of God, whose name is yet terrible in the kingdom of popery, setteth down certain characters of these imposters, taken out of St. Augustine.

1. *Great boasters*, making ostentation of their own worth, like Simon Magus, who bewitched the people, saying that he himself was some great man: like the Gnostics, who had a high conceit of their own knowledge, as if they were the only knowing men of the whole world: their common talk is of their own worth and actions.

2. *Superbia tumidi*, blown up with pride, and among us many proud spirits having not those preferments which they thought themselves worthy of, have forsaken our church, and gone to Rome or Amsterdam.

3. *Calumnis insidiosi*, deceitful slanderers: and in this faculty of all other sects the Brownists excel: the Jesuits are not so bitter against our church as the Separatists, compare their writings. Michael the Archangel durst not give the devil such cursed speaking, nor rail upon him as they do upon us and God's church.

4. *Treacherously seditious*, not preaching peace, as Christ commanded his disciples to do, but division: yea, the Brownists arrogate to themselves the name of Separatists, which well they may, being separated from their mother church, from all the reformed churches, and maliciously divided amongst themselves.

5. Lest they should seem to be destitute of the light of truth, they arrogate to themselves the shadow of austerity and show of holiness.

6. Sacrilegious, what the appetite of all schismatics hath been in this way is notorious, caring not for the ruin of the whole church, upon condition that they might get somewhat. They have so taught, that some think there is no such sin as sacrilege at all.

Our Lord forewarning us of false prophets, and so lively describing them, and we having such characters and marks to know them: thou understanding the Decalogue, Creed, and Lord's Prayer, if thou be misled, thy sin will light upon thine own head. For is there any man so simple, but can tell when the doctrines they teach cross any of these?

And one thing more will aggravate your defection before almighty God, viz. your covenant and oath, wherewith you bound yourselves in the presence of God, to suppress all errors, heresies, and schism; God forbid but that you should keep your covenant which we ministered, and you received with great alacrity.

To draw to an end, Epiphanius writing of the heresies of his time, calleth his book Paenatium; that is, a medicinable box, containing saving medicaments against lying doctrine.

The end of my writing is not to hurt any man, but to give warning to well-minded souls, and especially to them that are entangled with errors, to pray to God to give them grace to see and renounce their errors, and to acknowledge the truth, that they may recover themselves out of the snare of the devil.

And if my pains shall do any good in the confirmation of any against seducers, in forewarning them to beware of private conventicles, and to keep them close to the public ministry of the word, and communion of saints in God's church, I shall think my labour well bestowed.

The God of peace grant that all they that confess his holy name, may agree in the truth of his holy word, and live in unity and godly love, Amen.

So prayeth thine in the Lord,

Old Ephraim Pagitt

GOD AND THE KING

Or the divine constitution of the supreme magistrate; especially in the kingdom of England: against all popular pretenders whomsoever. Published for the satisfaction of the weak: being a private discourse of a reverend judge, with some commanders of the army, for their satisfaction, by their desire. Dan. 2.37. *The God of heaven hath given thee a kingdom, and power.* Printed in the year, 1649.

DAVID JENKINS (1582–1663), 'the famous Welsh judge,' won that contemporary reputation during the civil wars by his testy and narrow obstinacy in maintaining the supremacy of the law against parliamentary declarations of sovereignty. Educated at Oxford, he read at Gray's Inn and was called to the bar in 1609. Though he did not wholly approve the domestic and ecclesiastical policies of Charles I, he became violent in his support of royal power. Having been appointed in 1643 judge of the south-western circuit in Wales, he went so far as to indict for high treason several parliamentarians in his district, and he bore arms himself, a man of sixty-two, 'his long rapier drawn, holding it on end.' In 1645 he was captured. Brought before the bar of the house of commons, he contemptuously and 'with much venom and spleen' denied its jurisdiction. Martyrdom indeed he sought; 'for a lawyer and a judge to die for obedience to the laws will be deemed by good men of this time a sweet smelling sacrifice.' He planned that at his execution, having previously strengthened his lungs with licorice and gingerbread, he should appear with Bracton's treatise hung on his left shoulder, the statutes-at-large on his right, and the Bible on a ribbon about his neck, and should read to the people that clear evidence which made the king supreme. The commons passed an ordinance for his attainder, but the lords, though twice reminded, never acted upon it. In 1649 the commons ordered him tried by the court in Wales, and in 1650, in retaliation for Ascham's murder in Madrid, by the High Court of Justice. But the old man never stood trial; moved from one place of confinement to another, he spent his time compiling reports of eight hundred leading cases in common law, and was released only at the Restoration.

The arguments in this pamphlet, written from Newgate prison, are those simple and logical ones he always advanced in oral and printed defence; 'heart of oak,' Anthony Wood called him, to whom the law of royal government was fundamental law.

To the reader.

In this argument the best and safest ground for the judgment and conscience is the word of God with the law of the land. And from both these the divine origin and supremacy of the king of England is declared and confirmed to thee.

633

As thou art English or Christian, thou canst not expect more than scripture and law for thy satisfaction.

And if thou acquiesce not in these, I shall not care to satisfy thee. And (for all thy professions of godliness and honesty) thou shalt be to me as a heathen and libertine.

Vale.

GOD'S DOMINION NATURAL AND UNIVERSAL.

God hath a natural dominion over and the universal government of the whole world, Zech.4:14; Psal.97:1; 99:1; 94:1:2;

THE SUPREME MAGISTRATE HATH HIS POWER FROM GOD. PSAL.95:3; I TIM.6:15.

The supreme magistrate (whosoever and wheresoever) hath his power by way of commission from God; I have said ye are gods, Psal.82:6; John 10:34. And they are called gods (saith M. Perkins) because they partake of his power in their authority, and of his glory in their majesty.

THE UTMOST OF THE MAGISTRATE'S POWER.

The utmost of the magistrate's power is the power of the sword, Rom.13:4, i.e., the power of life and death for the more effectual suppressing of vice and punishing and restraining of sin. And with this power is he armed by God, say the assembly of divines in their confession of faith, *Chap. of the Civil Magistrates.* Nor can the people confer this power on him, because

THE PEOPLE CANNOT CONFER THIS POWER.

1. As men they have not power over their own, much less over one another's lives, all and every of them being under the commandment *Non occides,* thou shalt not kill.

PSAL.94:1, 2.

2. As Christians they must not resist evil, Mat.5:39, nor revenge themselves, Rom.12:9. For it is written, vengeance is mine, I will repay, saith the Lord. And he maketh the magistrate his minister a revenger to execute wrath upon him that doth evil, Rom.13:4.

GOD CONSTITUTES THE SUPREME MAGISTRATE IN EVERY KINGDOM AND STATE.

And in this case the people can ordain outward forms only of offices and judicatories without divine authority or power. And so their seeming legal proceedings and executions of justice are indeed nothing else but real and revengeful murders. And as God conferreth the power, so doth he constitute the governor in every kingdom and state. He removeth kings and setteth up kings, Dan.2:21. He ruleth in the kingdom of men, and giveth it to whomsoever he will, Dan.4:17,32.

HOW HE MADE SAUL AND DAVID KINGS.

God gave order to Samuel to anoint first Saul, 1 Sam.9:15, then David king, 1 Sam.16:12. And afterwards he settled the kingdom in David's family, 2 Sam.7:11,12.

LUKE 12:11. 2 CHRON.9:8.

And God tells us by St. Paul that the higher power is his ordinance, Rom.13:1,2, and his minister, verse 4, ordained and constituted his lieutenant to rule and govern by him and for him.

HOW GOD MAKES KINGS AT THIS DAY.

And at this day he constituteth them in some places by the people's election, and with us by hereditary succession, Jam.1:1.

But howsoever constituted the supreme magistrate is God's ordinance, and he that resisteth him resisteth the ordinance of God, and they that resist shall receive to themselves damnation, Rom.13:2.

WHETHER THE KING BE THE SUPREME MAGISTRATE.

Now the great question and only doubt to be resolved is who with us is the supreme magistrate, whether the king or the lords and commons assembled in parliament.

ST. PAUL'S CHARACTER OF THE SUPREME MAGISTRATE APPLIED TO THE KING.

I answer and prove the king to be the supreme magistrate, that character which St. Paul gives of him, Rom.13.

The higher power to whom every soul is subject, verse 1.

And with us the king is that higher power, from whom all authority and jurisdiction is derived, 1 Edw.6,c.2.

And to whom every subject owes homage and faith of member, life, and earthly honour, 6 Edw.1. Com. on Littleton, 85.

The minister of God having the power of the sword for defence of the good and punishment of evil doers, verses 3,4.

And with us the king hath full power in all cases to do justice to all men, 24 Hen.8,c.12.

And the punishment of all offenders belongs to the king, Mary 1,c.1.

And all judges and ministers of justice have their power in this case by commission from him, 27 Hen.8,c.4.

Lastly, the sole power of pardoning treasons and felonies belongs to the king, ibid.

The person to whom tribute is due, and customs and fear and honour, verse 7, which is the king.

Wherefore we must needs be subject (to the king) not only for wrath but also for conscience sake, Rom. 13:5.

THE KING'S SUPREMACY ASSERTED BY THE LAWS OF THE LAND.

Secondly, the king's supremacy is asserted by the laws of the land and by several acts of parliament whereto the lords and commons themselves have assented.

BRACTON.

Bracton, a learned lawyer living in the time of Hen. 3, tells us every one is under the king, and he under none but God alone, Lib. 4, cap. 24, sect. 5.

The regality of the crown of England is immediately subject to God and to none other, 16 Rich. 2, c. 5.

24 HEN. 8, c. 12.

The realm of England is an empire and so hath been accepted in the world, governed by one supreme head and king, having the dignity and royal estate of the imperial crown of the same, unto whom a body politic compact of all sorts and degrees of people [has] been bounden and owing to bear next to God a natural and humble obedience.

25 HEN. 8, c. 21.

The commons acknowledge no superior to the king under God.

1 ELIZ. 1.

The oath of supremacy is framed declaring the king to be the one supreme governor in all causes and over all persons, &c.

And the said act is but a declaration of the ancient law, Cawdries Case, 5, part fol. 1.

And no person in any parliament hath a voice in the house of commons unless he take this oath, 5 Eliz. 1.

1 JAC. 1.

The lords and commons assembled in parliament tell us that in the high court of parliament all the body of the realm is either in person or by representation (upon their own free election), and they acknowledge King James to be their only rightful and lawful king, lord, and sovereign; and they submit themselves and their posterities to his majesty and his royal progeny and posterity for ever.

And in this present parliament in their addresses to the king do the lords and commons acknowledge him their gracious sovereign, and themselves his majesty's subjects.

Now the law makes not the servant greater than his master, nor the subject greater than the king; for that were to subvert order and measure.

Lastly, the king calls, adjourns, prorogues, and dissolves the two houses at pleasure; therefore he is superior to them.

Though at this time the exercise of that kingly power be suspended by the act of continuation, whereby nevertheless the two houses were enlarged in time only, not in power.

THE POWER OF THE LORDS AND COMMONS IN PARLIAMENT.

And whatsoever is pretended, the lords and commons assembled in parliament have in truth no more power than what the king's writ of summons gives them.

And the lords are summoned to consult and treat with the king upon matters of great concernment touching the king, the defence of the kingdom, and church of England. And the commons to do and consent to such things as shall be ordained by common counsel in parliament.

And this is all the power that the knights, citizens, and burgesses have from the places for which they serve.

THE KING THE REPRESENTATIVE OF GOD; THE PARLIAMENT OF THE PEOPLE.

The power of magistracy is not, cannot be, from the people, but from God; and so the king, the representative of God, must needs be superior to the parliament, the representative of the people.

THE ORDER IN GOVERNMENT.

Thus in the order of government God hath the first place throughout the world. And next under God is the supreme magistrate in all places of the world. And in England the king is the supreme governor, inferior to none but God alone, his minister to protect and punish; and under him the fountain of all authority, power, and justice in the kingdom, to whom every one owes homage, and the whole body of the realm a natural and humble obedience, as to their head, and faith and allegiance, as to their only rightful and lawful lord and sovereign.

HOW THE CROWN DESCENDS TO THE KING.

Now the means and manner whereby the king of England obtains the government thereof is set forth, 1 Jac.1., where the lords and commons assembled in parliament (being bounden thereunto both by the laws of God and man) do recognize and acknowledge that immediately upon the dissolution and decease of Elizabeth, late queen of England, the imperial crown of the realm of England and of all the kingdoms, dominions, and rights belonging to the same, did by inherent birthright and lawful and undoubted succession descend and come to his most excellent majesty, as being lineally, justly, and lawfully next and sole heir of the blood royal of this realm; and that by the goodness of God Almighty and lawful right of descent he was king of England, &c.

LIB.SECUND. HIST.MUND.

And so the saying of Sir Walter Raleigh is verified with us, kings are made by God and laws divine, and by human laws only declared to be kings. And thereupon he observes that David thought himself accountable only to God, to thee only have I sinned, Psal.51:4.

OBJECTION.

But parliaments have deposed kings and translated the crown from the heir of the blood royal to others.

SOLUTION.

The deposers were traitors by the resolution of all the judges of England, Coke, 2 part, Institutes: cap. of high treason.

And those that came to the crown by the title of the parliament were usurpers and kings only *de facto*, but not *de jure*.

Nor let us own the practices of exorbitant parliaments, but adhere to our legal oaths of supremacy and allegiance, wherein we have sworn to bear faith and true allegiance, as to the king's highness, so to his heirs and lawful successors, and him and them to defend to the utmost of our power against all conspiracies and attempts whatsoever which shall be made against his or their persons, their crown and dignity.

And whereas they (in former times) did set up kings and not by God, Hos.8:4.

SEE JUNIUS AND TREMELIUS UPON THE PLACES.

We have said we have no king, what shall a king do unto us? Hos.10:3.

Take all summed up in the confession of the church of Scotland concerning the civil magistrate.

THE CONFESSION OF THE CHURCH OF SCOTLAND.

We confess and acknowledge empires, kingdoms, dominions, and cities to be distincted and ordained by God; the powers and authorities in the same (be it of emperors in their empires; kings in their realms; dukes and princes in their dominions; and of other magistrates in their city) to be God's holy ordinance, ordained for the manifestation of his glory and for the singular profit and community of mankind, so that whosoever goeth about to take away or confound the whole state of civil policy, now long established, we affirm the same men not only to be enemies to mankind, but also wickedly to fight against God's expressed will.

Fear GOD: Honour the KING. 1 Pet.2:17.

Finis.

Γένεσις καὶ τέλος ἐξουσίας,

THE ORIGINAL & END OF CIVIL POWER

Or a discourse wherein is set forth and cleared what the people are; their natural bent to sociability and government; how they are the original and end of civil powers; where the supreme power doth properly reside; whether, when, and how the inferior magistrates and people may call to account, and punish the superior, and change the government, if they see it necessary. With some instances, where generals and commanders of armies have been assistant to the people to pull down wicked rulers, and set up new government and governors. By Eutactus Philodemius. London, printed 1649.

ANTHONY ASCHAM (1618–1650), born in Boston, Lincolnshire, was admitted to King's College, Cambridge, in 1634 as a scholar from Eton. He took his B.A. degree in 1638, his M.A. in 1642, and was a fellow of the college from 1637 to his death. He is said to have written the verses in *Pallas Armata: The Gentleman's Armorie; wherein the . . . use of the Rapier and of the Sword . . . is displayed* (1639). A parliamentarian, he was appointed tutor to the thirteen-year old James, duke of York, from the latter's capture at Oxford in 1646 to his arranged escape in 1648. That year Ascham printed *A Discourse: wherein is examined what is particularly lawfull during the confusions and revolutions of government,* a long pamphlet which was reprinted in 1649 with the title *Of the Confusions and Revolutions of Governments,* and again in 1689 as *A Seasonable discourse wherein is examined what is lawful during the confusions and revolutions of governments, especially in the case of a king deserting his kingdoms.* He was appointed agent of the Merchant Adventurers and of the republic at Hamburg in August 1649; and in January resident ambassador at Madrid. Milton as Latin secretary wrote the letters presenting him to the court of Spain. The day after he arrived (25 June 1650), he and his interpreter were murdered by English royalist officers, one of whom was a servant of Edward Hyde, later Lord Clarendon, who represented Charles II at Madrid. The murderers took sanctuary and were never formally tried by the Spanish government.

This pamphlet is the most elaborate of the efforts made to find a theoretical justification for the government of the Rump. Written two months after the king's execution, and a month after the arrest of the Leveller leaders, it was meant to answer both divine right and democratic arguments. Like Ireton, spokesman for the parliamentary leaders, Ascham slurred over that doctrine of fundamental law which parliament had advanced in 1640, which royalists used, and which was the core of Leveller thought.

To the Reader.

READER,

BEFORE I durst venture to publish these thoughts of mine, I have taken a little time to consult with myself, whether any man hath a supremacy,

640

viz., power of life and death over his own intellectual progeny; and I came to this result, that what was truly my own might be subject to the saddest of fates; and that my own will could justly design it to oblivion, vassallage or death. But if any thing herein were of God, I had no such power over it. I am no competent judge what is my own, and what is God's; and therefore, reader, if thou findest anything herein having on it the impress of truth, own it; thy good acceptance it may challenge. But if thou findest error in a borrowed varnish or enrobed in the garments of truth, which by endeavouring to personate truth would pass for current, let its nakedness be made manifest to the view of the world, and then let it serve thee for a foil to set forth truth the better by, and make it appear in its brighter lustre; and let me receive their better information, who would not be in love with anything that hath not its lineal descent and legitimation from truth. I have a belief, *That the people are the womb of all powers*; and that from thence all powers have received their warmth and lively vigour, and do continually receive their nutriment; the production and preservation of the civil powers (under God) are from the same root, the people; and as it is said in metaphysics, that those living creatures that receive their essence from the elements do thence receive their aliment; as the fruit hath not only its extraction but maturity from the tree, the tree hath its birth and life from the earth: so here, as the essence of civil forms of powers is from the people, so the preservation and support hereof is from them also. If that, and what I have here affirmed be truth, and yet notwithstanding it meet with thy cavils, know also it shall find champions, and will at length hold forth a serene countenance, unveiled from prejudices and the inglorious stains that may be cast upon it. Truth may be thrown down, but now not kept down. Read and try, and the gold that thou findest in the midst of my dross, make good use of; I have not studied to conform my self to the *placits* of men, but to the standard and rules of truth and righteousness, which will stand unshattered and unconquerable (though not unshaken) in the midst of a storm and tempestuous calumnies and obloquies of the whole world. If thou wilt not judge equally, judge as thou pleaseth of

Thy Well-wisher, but more
the Commonwealth's,

20 *April* 1649.

E. Philodemius

To the right honorable the parliament of England and Council of State.

Honourable Heroes

IF I have erred in this dedication, I must confess the error I have committed is willing and considerate. I did conceive it more safe and honourable to receive a wholesome check from so wise and noble personages, than to gain an aspect of favour, or be tickled with an ignorant applause from a lower patrociny. But if herein I have embased the current coin of truth and reason, by stamping my own image and inscription upon it, instead of that of God and nature, I must affirm that to be an unwilling and unconscious error, and I hope a gentle atonement and sacrifice may satisfy for it: I can have just recourse to that common plea that others have made before me, that my offence hath its rise from an error of love, not a love of error; and I hope (having not wilfully transgressed the marches and bounds of reason, and gone beyond the just and equal deportment of a Christian) there may be left unto me, the advantage of a possible and honest retreat into a better and sounder information, as to my sanctuary and safe reserve. The subject here treated of is sublime and generous, adequate to the most accomplish'd spirit, a spirit that can fix itself in an equidistant station between these two great and sharply controverted interest of populacy and magistracy, and yet get an exquisite knowledge of the just limits of their proper and distinct powers and rights. Heretofore the extreme on the magistrate's part was vigorously contested for and pursued, until at length it clashed with God's interest, and it proved like an earthern vessel dashed against an iron pot; and this age is witness with what a fatal blow God broke it into pieces: and now the other extreme is hotly contended for, by men as unacquainted with just and allowed policy, as they are with the disposition of them whom they speak for, as if the bulk of people in the moliminous confused body, were the supreme and sovereign power. The first extreme did presumptuously set God's seal of approbation to the unlimited vicious will of a degenerate magistrate; the last pulls down the great ordinance of magistracy under the unhallowed feet of an easily discontented vulgar; the Lord direct you, who have now the managery and government of the affairs of this poor tottered and divided state, to steer the right way to a harbour of rest; and make you wise to discern the disguised ends of these pretended popular champions, whose continual invectives against your late and present transactions of affairs bespeak them such opinionists of themselves, that they can better govern, than be willing to be governed; and hint unto us that the great design (by aspersing your proceedings, the reason or method whereof they do not comprehend or understand, and by elevating and crying up the power of the people above its due altitude) is your debasement; which (with their long sought for, and at last almost gained esteem among the credulous people) become steps of easier ascent into their wished seats of supremacy and domination. I have presumed too far in an epistle: I will trouble your patience no further, than to desire of him, who is only wise, and knoweth the councils, ways and aims of all men's hearts; Him, who is only powerful, weighing the mountains in balances, and holding the waters in the hollow of his hand, to be your mighty counsellor and preserver: So prayeth

Yours and Commonwealth's
Servant,

Grays-Inn this 20 of
April 1649.

E. PHILODEMIUS

The heads or principles treated upon in this discourse.

That the people (under God) are the efficient cause, and original of all just powers.

That the power or vigour which is in the people, whilest it remains there, untransferred into fewer hands, is (1) useless and unprofitable, (2) dangerous.

That Scripture not only commands, but even nature by its dictates prompts us to government, and inhibits anarchy.

That this or that form of government is not of divine unalterable institution, but originally an ordinance or creation of man.

That the end of government and of the species of it is the poeple's good and welfare, and the preservation of their rights.

That supreme power and authority, or royal majesty, doth regularly and formally reside in such person or persons as the people, by their consent or suffrage, set up to be magistrates and rulers over themselves, and no where else.

Some objections are answered and cleared.

Some men deviate from truth and reason by propounding to themselves vitiated principles to subserve their vile ends; and such men cannot choose but err, being willingly founded on a wrong bottom. Others there are who hold forth to themselves right principles, with which their squint-ends are so inconsistent that they draw out of such grounds and foundations false and wrested conclusions to suit with such ends; they direct their lives from the right centre to such part of the circumference that points at and best meets with their own profit, pleasure, honour, relations, self-interest and the like servile ends. The error of these last sort of men proceeds either from their slight consideration of the true nature and end of things, or from their willing inconsiderateness thereof. Should they therefore regularly proceed by a thorough digestion of things, and by an elaborate scanning and debate of them with themselves, they might easily become able to span and fathom reason in its fullest dimensions.

For as to find out maladies in their source and true nature is the first step to a real cure, by the application of fit and adequate remedies: so to know the original and true nature of things, is the basis and ground of all regular and unerring ratiocinations.

And if we fail in the right estate of things, our reasonings thereupon and thereabouts may and will be justly questionable as illegitimate, and so be stigmatized with the brand of an issue base-born and spurious, which otherwise it cannot be.

Therefore to avoid the error and brand before-mentioned, I shall endeavour to handle and treat of the heads and principles before set down, in the order and subordination they are put in, which I conceive to be most natural; and I shall begin with the first of them, and clear it to every unprejudiced judgment, to be a principle irrefragable and undeniable, the legitimate dictate of reason: reason itself being the apocalypse or revelation of nature, and having upon it the fair impress of nature's signet; nature also referring unto God, as its spring and author, and having in its face the pleasant lineaments of God's image, not rased out, though somewhat discharactered. The first principle as I shall speak of, is,

 1. The people (under God) are the original or efficient cause of all just powers.

God without doubt is the first cause, and original of government; and government in general hath on it the stamp of JUS DIVINUM. But God is not otherwise the original or spring of particular forms of government, than by a mere approbation or permission of those governors that are chosen and set up by means of the people's election. There is now no particular designation of this or that person to this or that kind of government by God immediately; or any divine institution of any particular civil form of government whatsoever. That place, Romans 13:1. ' Let every soul be subject to the higher powers, for there is no power but of God,' refers unto particular forms or species of government. The word ' power ' in the original (though in the abstract it signifies authority, right, dignity, prerogative, or liberty, and is so taken in many places of Scripture; yet here it is taken in the concrete, and) signifies magistrates, who are so of God, and not otherwise, than by permission or approbation as aforesaid: and it signifies in some places of Scripture *Jus et potestatem*, a lawful and rightful authority. And that which now makes an authority or power (I mean) any particular form or species of government lawful, besides the special approbation of God, is the peoples' free choice, for God hath so indulged man as neither to command or forbid this or that kind of government, but hath left all forms indifferent, and ordered it so, that the people's election, seconded with his approbation, should be the marks of its lawfulness, as shall be hereafter proved and made good.

Now having showed how God is the original of all just powers, I come to show you how the people are so. In the handling hereof, I shall first enquire, What is meant by people: secondly, by original: thirdly, by power: fourthly, by (just) power. The word ' all ' here (as I conceive) referring to particular forms and species of government, and so signifying as much as ' every ' and no more.

The word ' people ' will not need much explanation; yet it will be necessary that I give check to the common opinion what it signifies, it being taken for the vulgar and baser sort of men only: and therefore I shall first show what I conceive it to be: secondly, prove my opinion concerning it.

Now by people I mean every single or particular person within any nation or kingdom, high and low, noble and and ignoble, rich and poor, bond and free, without any limitation or restraint to any individual person whatsoever.

For proof hereof, Justinian in his institutes tells us the signification and extent of the word *populus*, a people, and how *plebs*, which signifies the vulgar sort of men, is distinguished from it; (saith he), The vulgar sort of men do differ, and are distinguished from the people, as the species differs from the genus; under the name people (which is a general word comprehending all degrees and sorts of men) are comprised not only the ordinary and inferior sort, but also the nobles, senators and great men; under the name *plebs*, or the vulgar, are now intended and understood (though some of the plebs in the Romans' time were of the posterity of those noblemen called *Curules magistratus*) the inferior and baser sort of men. And Minisinger the civilian, in his comment upon the aforementioned place of Justinian, saith, *In populo omnis pars civitatis, omnes ejus ordines continentur, plebs vero ea est, in qua gentes civium patriciae non insunt.* And Nicacius on the same place, *Populus nobilis, & ignobiles significat; plebs autem solum ignobiles.* So that is evident that the word ' people' includes and comprises under it the universal bulk or body of a nation, of a kingdom, or of the whole world, consisting of every individual person without any restriction to the greater, better, or more honourable sort of men on the one hand, or to the inferior plebeians or vulgar sort on the other hand.

What is meant by the peoples being the original of all just powers, is the second consideration. When they are said to be the original of all just powers, thereby is to be understood, their act of consent is the source and fountain from whence all forms of power and government flow.[1] They are the efficient and constituent cause of all forms of government. It is an old and true rule, *Omnis potestas fundata est in voluntate*, the people's will and common consent is the foundation of all just powers out of themselves. They are the *subjectum commune ditionis sive imperii*, the common subject of governments and empires. All sovereignties and royalties are virtually in the people, though it be formally in him or them whom the people set up over themselves. And that majesty or sovereignty that is united in one or more persons by the people's consent, is dispersedly in broken and scattered rays amongst the community or the universality of the people; and that vigour which every particular person hath in himself is naturally inherent in him, derived immediately to him from God, no creature on earth being the mediate instrument of it. And though the people by their consent do contract those scattered rays of power and concentre them into one or more persons, as best agrees with their own temper and constitutions of policy; yet they do not thereby pass away, or transfer to their rulers or magistrates their proper rights

1. Fortescue, *De Laudibus Legum Angliae*, pp.32,34.

and interests, but such an efficacy, vigour and virtue as to preserve their rights distinct, and to punish mutual intrenchments thereupon: without which they could not avoid precipitating themselves into popular ataxies and irregularities; which that place of Aristotle seems to hint at, viz., *Magistratus est custos & administrator communium honorum non propriorum*;[2] for which end each particular person hath a virtualness and potentiality (even in the freedom of nature) of communicating and deriving some oriency, life and lustre to that or those persons that by their consent have a designation to a government over them. . . .

Thirdly, by power is here understood this or that form of government, or distinct magistracy.

Fourthly, *just* power may be conceived to be this,[3] That this or that form of government (being originally from man) is not to be accounted just, i.e., the best and most excellent government, only because wise men say so, or because experience proves so, but (all forms thereof being indifferent in themselves, and neither commanded or prohibited by God, before the people's choice of such and such a form) because such a nation or people by a common consent set up such and such a government: for, saith Grotius,[3] in such a case (where forms are indifferent) *ex voluntate jus metiendum*, the justness (i.e.) the fitness and excellency of this or that government is to be measured and marked by the people's choice: for as there are many professions and callings in the world, and of those some professions are honourable, others base and of a low exteme; some callings profitable, others of little advantage; yet it is as just and lawful for a man to choose to himself (I speak only as to choice) the meanest, as well as the most honourable profession; and that calling which is of least profit, as well as that of greatest utility. It is just for him (I say) to make his free choice of this or that profession, this or that calling, which best pleases him and suits with his inclination or *placebo*, though the incommodity of his choice may be evidently prejudicial to him. And so we see that the original of all just powers is in the people; and that all particular forms of government arise from their voluntary submission, by which they set up over themselves with common consent one or more persons, for conservation of mutual rights, and avoidance of destructive mutual injuries; they are the fountain of all just powers and governments, which some wittily say is a wise conspiration of several different notes

2. *Politics*, V,C.1.   3. Grotius, *De jure belli et pacis*, lib.1, p.53.

into one sweet and harmonious tune of common interest. The second principle is,

> 2.   This power or vigour, whilst it remains in the bulk of the people, untransferred into fewer hands, is (1) useless and unprofitable to themselves, (2) dangerous.

This power and virtue, whilst it remains in the people themselves (as they are a community) is a *Potentia in Principiis*; the power they have, it is in its prémordials, it remains in a vast and thronged bulk of underived majesty; as the earth was, Gen.1.2. void and formless, or as the waters, v.9. of this chapter, which lay dispersed over the face of the earth, before God with his fiat did gather it together into one place. So whilst this power and rays of royalty lie uncontracted in the body of the people, and not contracted and united into one or few hands, it is first useless and unprofitable, and that (1) in respect of their temperamental inactivity and moliminousness of body, which doth so indispose them that they cannot draw forth into act, and exercise that virtual power they so have in themselves, for their own advantage and preservation: and (2) in respect of their distracted irregularity, they know not how to act and exercise it; their senses are their guides, which lead them into many tortuous meanders, and inextricable labyrinths, they know not how to gather up to themselves a just warning or foresight to prevent or avoid mischiefs. It is not the wisdom of some that leads them, but the will of most of the vulgar that hurries them; they have many eyes, yet they are so short-sighted that they rarely see, before they feel a disadvantage to themselves.

2.   The people's power and vigour, whilst it remains thus untransferred, is dangerous to themselves; they will soon range beyond the line and pale of private rights and proprieties, their appetites are their purveyors, and their wants are measured by their wills; they are like a strong and testy horse, but undisciplined, as unsensible of his own danger, as careless of him that rides him; confusion makes them desire order, and when they (we mean the most of them, who want discipline and government) have obtained their desired order, commonly they are so unfixed that they make a base retreat again into confusion; they love not war for its true end, nor peace for its rest and centre of repose, yet both for variety's sake. They (as one speaks of them) [4] assemble like bees at the

4. Peter Charon, *Treatise of Wisdom.*

sound of a bason, and dissolve again as a torrent violently breaks down its banks and mounds, they are constant in inconstancy. The same man saith of them thus, *Oderunt presentia, preterita celebrant, futura appetunt*; They hate things present, extol and admire things past, and greedily hunt after future things, or novelties. And now we come to the third head or principle (viz.)

3. That Scripture not only commands, but even nature by its dictates prompts us to government, and inhibits anarchy.

The people being a vast unwieldy body, uncemented by government, a besom unbound, or a rope of sand, easily and naturally become sensible of their inability and incapacity (as such a body) to govern themselves; and therefore to prevent those manifest inconveniences and precipices that they will inevitably fall into without an equal, orderly, and well-disposed government of the whole nature hath furnished every man with an innate principle of tendency to a sociableness: and Aristotle speaking of men's natural promptness to a sociableness, saith, *Non minimum appetunt convivere*,[5] the inward impulsive cause hereto (viz. to live together), is the law and instinct of nature; and the external moving cause of this *appetitus convivendi*, is commodiousness and conveniency of life (say most philosophers). It is an universal impress in nature that every man should desire to live together for the advantage afore-mentioned. And herein nature's dictates are most apparent and clear among the heathens and the most barbarous people in the world, who by their practice to live in companies and societies, to build houses, towns, and cities, and consequently to create kingdoms, show unto us the strong intensive bent that nature hath put upon all men towards a sociability; and this sociability doth as strongly and naturally incline men towards a government by rules and boundaries, for distinction and preservation of private rights, and by hedges and fences against all domestic and foreign wrongs; else society without government and laws would expose men to much damage, and that by every man's entrenching upon others' rights, and doing what he lists or seems good in his own eyes; therefore nature hath put upon man a tendency unto sociability, and so consequently unto government; that we may not advantage ourselves by others' wrongs, or others receive advantage by ours, are as well standing precepts of nature as rules in divinity.

5. *Politics*, III, C.4.

The famous and learned nobleman the Lord Verulam, in his treatise of the Advancement of Learning tells us that the force and efficacy of private right is this: That he that doth wrong, by the fact receives either profit or pleasure; by the example, incurs prejudice and peril; others are not partners with him in his profit or pleasure, but they take themselves interested in the example: and therefore they easily combine, and accord together to secure themselves by laws; lest injuries (*alternatim*) or by turns seize upon every particular.

So that as we see sociableness to have nature's stamp upon it, so we find government to bear the same impress and signature with that of sociableness; without society among people and tendency to cohabit and live together in companies, no government: without government, no laws, and without laws, no propriety and distinction, or severance of rights; and what then ensues, but miserable confusions and shoreless excesses by encroachments upon one another's native privileges and immunities; so that we may see clearly, that nature hath taught men to give up and concredit that power and vigour before mentioned, which they have in themselves, into such and such hands, for their own good, as shall be said hereafter.

That they have power of transferring the vigour of their right, strength, and interest into such and such hands is as clear as the sun in the firmament, the rule before mentioned doth evince, *Omnis potestas fundata est in voluntate,* all powers are founded upon the willing consent of the people, and here nature and reason hint to every common capacity, that they must necessarily fall into a vertiginous mace of errors and inextricable troubles and dangers, whilst that vigour they have in themselves remains useless and unactive as to their own good, and so easily conducive to their reciprocal disadvantage, which it must needs be, whilst it remains underived and uncontracted into one or few hands. The letters of the alphabet, when they are promiscuously thrown together in a heap, or scattered and dispersed asunder, are useless, and serve to no end, though they are the elements of all tongues and languages, and they will remain so until they be put together and set in that order as to make words and speech: so that vigour, virtue, and power which is in the people, though it be the element of all civil discipline and forms of government, yet whilst it is dispersed and confusedly lies in the bulk of the people, it remains useless and unprofitable, and doth not subserve its end; but when it is gathered together into one place, regulated and entrusted in the hands of one or more persons to be managed and acted by them, it is in its right place and serves its right end, as the alphabet disposed into words and speech.

Therefore (according to nature's instinct and the supreme *culpis* and ἀκμὴ of all politiques, *salus publica*) for the safety and benefit of the whole, and every individual (the general being but as it were a constellation of particulars) in their distinct nature, rights, and privileges, the people by a law of common consent (which is as was said before the foundation of all just powers, and which Grotius also affirms, saying, *Omne dominium voluntas humana introduxit*) do contract the aforesaid virtue and power into such and such hands for their own common advantage.

And when they who were before (as sand without lime) have thus dislodged out of themselves their power and vigour, and seated the same in one or more persons, and commissiorated them to give and manage laws, and make marches and boundaries to preserve their rights distinct, and to form rules and hedges to restrain and keep out mutual wrongs and injuries, which are the aims and ends at which all laws, decrees, and sanctions should level and be directed, then public laws made and actuated by such and such entrusted rulers and magistrates, become the guardians and protectors of private right, and that not only of the persons trusting, but also of the trusteds, who are as well the law's subservients, as to the punishments of it for doing evil, and to the encouragements of it for doing good as the persons trusting are; and such magistrates and governors (whom the people's power hath so dignified and enabled) become thereby dispensers and ministrants of such laws and sanctions, by making them to speak and sever men's rights, and to promulgate and apply the punishments and penalties of wrongful encroachments upon every man's propriety and interest, which laws and decrees are and would be otherwise dead and speechless, till so animated and inspirited in their execution by such and such designed and impowered rulers or magistrates. The fourth head is,

4. That this or that form of government is not of divine unalterable institution, but originally an ordinance or creation of man.

Though scripture and nature (whose commands, dictates, and avisos are ever infallible, being the very oracles of truth and reason) do teach all men docility and pliableness to society and cohabitation or living together (without which there is no living or being) and society inclines them to government (without which there is no well being) yet this or that special form of government or empire in its original can plead for itself no divine institution, or anything from natural instinct for its buttress or support, all forms of government whatsoever being in their origination and immediate root the ordinance and creation of man, and no way from God, but mediately and by permission or by approbation (as was said before) God permitting or putting his seal of establishment to it, when the people have chosen it: and when the choice of the people and the approbation or permission of God are united and concentred in one or more delegated or designed persons to be magistrates over them, then are they supreme, as in the forementioned place v.14. and then is such person or persons power sovereign, as shall be said hereafter. And if any one form of government were of divine institution, or from nature, then that particular form, and that only, should be the single, universal, and unalterable government throughout all empires, kingdoms, and dominions whatsoever in the whole world.

For instance sake, we may suppose that if that form of government styled monarchy could have called and pleaded Scripture and right nature (which in themselves are both unchangeable and ever the same) for its patronesses and preservers from so low a debasement (as some worthless men conceive it to be) as necessarily to have the consent of the populacy for its foundation and basis (which certain it hath and can have no other of right) then should it not have been so pinioned and close girt within the confines and circuit of a few kingdoms and territories, but must have swollen into a bulk of that bigness and dimension, as to be first an universal government and a body having in it all power entire and concentred, and like the refulgent sphere of the sun, dispersing the influence of its mandates and the streaming rays of its glory over the whole world: and secondly it must have been of that unalterableness and lasting permanency as that no transient fates of kingdoms might alter it, no such worm as other forms of government might gnaw the root of such a gourd and make it wither and perish; and thirdly it must have been the single empress of the world, the royal and magnetic lady, that should have inclined and drawn all the nations, empires, and kingdoms in the world to be enamoured with it, to pay unto it tributes of duty, and to offer to it presents of affection, to veil unto it, and court it.

But whose understanding is so bewitched or benighted as not to see the contrary?

It is obvious to every man, that hath not been born and bred up in a bottle, and never looked into the world but through a hole, that no one special form of government is divine or natural in its rise or root, for we find in scripture history several forms of government (viz.) by patriarchs, generals or commanders in chief, judges, high-priests, and kings: and in human stories, we read of government by popes, absolute and conditionate monarchs, of aristocracies and democracies; of governments by dukes, senators, consuls, dictators, and many more. All which several forms of governments should, yea could not have been, if any one of them ought to have been the single universal and unalterable government, and so have challenged and derived its legitimacy from divine institution, or from natural instinct. And now we are come to the fifth head or principle,

5. That the end of government and the species of it is the people's good and welfare and preserving of their rights.

As the people themselves are the original and efficient cause and their common consent the foundation of all just powers, so they and their peace and welfare are the final and only ends of it, besides God's glory, which is the ultimate end of all things. That power which they transfer (as before mentioned) out of themselves is merely fiduciary, and not inconditionate. It is deposited into such and such hands as the people's conservatories, and the conditionate ends of transferring such a majesty and dignity out of themselves unto those they make magistrates over them, is always either expressed or necessarily intended to be their own weal. The power of the whole people is committed or entrusted to one or a few, that the wisdom and faithfulness, care and activity of that one or those few, may redound and be employed to the benefit and preservation of the whole body. And whilst rulers and magistrates make this their joint end with the peoples, and draw all their lines to this centre, they may without hazard to their diadems or precipitating themselves into dangers, walk securely upon the highest stories of government and empire; but if they propound to themselves cross interfering ends to that of the people's good, and are not willing with Christ to lay down even their lives for their sheep or people; but rather study by gradual assents and insensible advances to build up a tyrannical fabric of government and measure the same by the vicious rules of their own wills, being puffed up with a foolish conceit of their own puissance and grandeur: they may for a while bid themselves go on and prosper, and say to themselves that they shall see no sorrow, yet they shall find at last their buildings to totter, and their strength to become impuissant, and the event and end of such unjust designs to prove tragical to themselves, and sceptres.

It cannot rationally be imagined that any nation or people whatsoever have, do, or indeed can intentionally give away that vigour they have in themselves to their kings and magistrates for their own hurt and destruction. The laws of God and nature never gave the people such commission to give it, or to their magistrates to receive and act it so inconditionately; and if the people by their suffrages should actually and expressly pass over such a power to their trustees so as to redound to their own ruin, it must needs be void *ipso facto*, because that would be out of the compass and circuits of the paramount laws of reason and their own safety, which are the elements of all good laws, out of which they are derived, and unto which they are designed, as to their end. It is irrational to think that any man or men can give to another that which they have not in themselves, for a power to ruin themselves they never had; and it is unnatural that any people should set up over themselves any one person or collectaneous body of men to be lords proprietaries of their rights and interests, and to hold an imperial and prerogative scourge over their backs, and keep them in a remediless condition, by labouring to work them to an embased flexibility to his or their wills, and so to emasculate their spirits, so as ever to prevent their free uttering of their just aggrievances; how contrary to nature as well as to the truth of God it is to deprive another man of his lawful right is easily demonstrable. Cicero tells us, that *Alteri datrahere, sui commodi causa, est contra naturam, quia si id fiat, societas hominum et communitas, evertetur necesse est* [6] (i.e.) to take away from another for thy own advantage sake is against nature, because thereby the societies of men and communities would be utterly and necessarily destroyed and overthrown. And Justinian in his *Reg. Juris* saith: that *Jure naturæ æquum est neminem cum alterius detrimento & injuriâ fieri locupletiorem* (i.e.) by the law of nature it is just and equal that no man do enrich himself to the detriment or wrong of another, we may not use our own industry to promote our own profit

6. *De officiis.*

and advantage, where another's right may be intrenched upon or prejudiced. And Grotius speaking of this injurious encroachment upon mutual rights, saith it is *furtum naturale jure prohibitum* (i.e.) a theft prohibited by nature. . . .

6. That supreme power and authority or royal majesty doth regularly and formally reside in such person or persons, as the people, by their consent and suffrage, set up to be magistrates and rulers over them, and no where else.

As it was said before, that the people were the *primum & commune subjectum potestatis & imperii*; the first and common subject of royal power, where it is virtually resiant, and from whence it hath its native and right origination, man being as Aristotle saith, *Animal politicum*; and having a natural appetite and strong bent upon him to be social and to live together in company with others; so now we conceive that *proprium & formale subjectum ditionis & imperii* (i.e.) the proper and formal subject of power and government, or the political and ethical receptacle of it, is such and such a person, or such and such persons, as are set up according to the consent and disposition of the people and constitutions of policy, which God (who is the root of all government and order) then ratifies and confirms by his seal; and now that which, before the people's choice and God's sanction, was indifferent, becomes positive, and must be submitted to, under pain of offending God; here is man's choice and God's ratification thereof, both these seated in one subject make the supreme power and authority: this is that ordinance of man, (i.e.) of man's choice; that ought to be submitted to for the Lord's sake (i.e.) because God hath confirmed this choice of man, and tribute of due obedience is to be indispensably paid to such a power, whilst it keeps within those high conditionate ends of the people's good and welfare; and the marks and ensigns of such a supreme power (which yet in itself is nothing else but the royal standard of that virtual majesty which is in the people) is the making of peace, proclaiming of war, power of life and death, pardoning and punishing offenders, creating inferior magistrates, making and repealing laws, commanding due subjection and homage from inferiors, coinage, and the like; [7] all which are the signals of that supreme and sovereign power which is in the magistrate, and hence is the magistrate called the minister of God, and one that holds not the sword in vain; and God doth not en-

7. Bodin, *De Republica*, Lib. i, cap. 10.

trust and allow any man to have power to destroy his own image, (i.e.) to take away man's life, but him or them whom he makes gods, (i.e.) magistrates, and to whom he deputes his own place, yet this great, yea the greatest ingredient of supremacy, viz. power of life and death, that is thus affix'd to the person of a ruler, or supreme, is derived to him from that authority or government from whence he is so denominated a supreme, and it is from his authority only that his diadem is environed with such glorious rays of majesty . . .

OBJECTION 1. But admitting for argument's sake this chief ingredient of supremacy, viz. power of life and death to be so from God alone, that man should not in the least degree have any hand in it, and that the magistrate should so derive from God solely the power and prerogative of being an avenger of wrath: is the magistrate now by reason of this power from God *solutus legibus?* Is he obliged to live under the roof of no laws?

SOLUTION 1. I suppose no rational man on earth (if it should be granted he hath this power of life from God only) will deny but he is subject to the law, and to every law, penal as well as otherwise, else he crosses the end of his being elected, which was not to be above the law, and so to challenge an impunity for what offence soever he commits; but to give life to it and to execute it for the common good of his choosers, he may not, contrary to the conditionate end of his election, stride over the law, and make his own will a style to get over its hedges where he pleases. This would create and nourish a contempt of magistracy in the people from the error and wickedness of the magistrate; and instead of casting things into a mould of order and peace, deform the beauty and harmony thereof, and introduce disorder and confusion, yea this would cross and thwart those two great aims of the people's good, and God's glory, the highest ends of all governments.

OBJECTION 2. But is not the king or magistrate more worthy than the people?

It is true that Albericus Gentilis affirms that kings or magistrates are more worthy than the people, and gives this reason. *Omne id quod regitur, indignius est eo, a quo regitur,*[8] the governed is inferior in dignity to the governor; therefore saith he, *Subditi sunt principis causa,* the subject is for the prince's sake. Neither the princes of this or any former ages hath

8. *In disputatione de regia potestate.*

wanted such irrational sycophants and flattering earwigs; his inference is as absurd as his principle is untrue; is the tutor worthier than his prince? or an ordinary pedagogue than those noble plants and branches under his care and tutelage? who will affirm this? And how absurd is it to prefer any one individual man taken from amongst the people to the whole species of mankind, when the very end of magistracy (besides that supreme end of God's glory) is the people's good, let any rational man judge! He is a minister of God to thee for good; and not thou a subject to him to be a prey to his will. Aristotle tells us how a magistrate is before the people; *Magistratus hominibus proest, sed hominum causâ*, (i.e.) He hath a preference before the people, but for the people's sake, not his own. And Danæus tells us that the people are *priorius magistratu, tempore, natura et dignitate etiam, quia magistratum constituit, quia sine magistratu esse potest, sed magistratus sine populo esse non potest.* (i.e.) the people are before their magistrate in time, in nature, yea, in dignity: and his reasons are these, because the people constitute magistrates, and because they can be, and subsist without magistrates, but not the magistrates without them.

OBJECTION 3. Though the people be superior in dignity to the king or magistrate, are they proper and competent judges of his miscarriages and misgovernment, and of his degenerating into a tyrant, and may they punish him, which if they may, how far, and when?

1. We must consider the people, either as they are the universal body or community of any nation, or as they are represented by a lesser collective number chosen from among themselves, and by themselves for their own good: as now in England, Scotland, and Ireland, and in some other nations: in both and either of these capacities, it may be evinced by reason and good authorities that the people have power to depose and punish tyrants or degenerate princes, yet upon due and serious cautions and upon solemn considerations.

First it is clear in reason that those princes who are wilfully bent to destroy their people and to spill their blood like water without remorse, receding from the end for which they were chosen (viz.) the people's good, may be punished by conventions or councils of those states which they govern. For here is evident that their wills and trusts interfere, when indeed their wills should be officious handmaids to their trusts. *Voluntas imperandi & voluntas perdendi simul consistere non possunt.*[9] A

9. Grotius, *De jure belli et pacis*, lib.1, pag.91, Sect.11.

will to govern and a will to destroy the same people in the same person cannot consist together; let them that doubt of the necessity and justifiableness of even the severest temporal punishments of wicked princes and tyrants, sometimes, and in some cases, consult Barclaius, Pareus, Kekermannus, Zwinglius, Bodin, Cusmann, Althus, Danæus, Stephanus Junius, Brutus Celta, Grotius, and most learned men that write of politics, and they shall find magistrates that do grossly wander from the end of their magistracy asserted to be punishable: all of the authors before mentioned (though some of them were vehement assertors of the more than just prerogative of princes) concur to make this good. And the great judge of all the world tells us of the punishment of him or them (whosoever they be) that are murderers, that no satisfaction shall be taken for the life of a murderer, which is guilty of death, but he shall be surely put to death; and the reason is in Numbers, xxxv,33. For blood defileth the land and the land cannot be cleansed of the blood that is held therein, but by the blood of him that shed it. And how frequently and familiarly is much precious blood shed in all nations (as in this land lately) to defend the unjust greatness and prerogative of princes? (their just prerogative being nothing else but a power to do good in such cases to which the written law doth not extend). I say again, their unjust prerogative, which is nothing else but the product of a long settled tyranny, a base and sordid issue, a sperm begotten by the coition and copulation of the wills of tyrants and their flatterers in the lustiness of their usurped domination: and now God hath discovered it to all men to be a bastard and illegitimate brood that cannot derive its parentage from the consent of the people, by his stirring up of almost all men's spirits to kick it out of the world as a spurious brat. But to return again; would you have precedents to prove this? I must tell you that reason is the base of all good precedents, and all precedents in themselves, unless we put on the spectacles of reason to make an inspection into them, are but blind guides, and if the blind lead the blind, you will easily know the fate of such a manuduction; precedents are, or ought to be, for the most part but samplers or patterns for a green and childish intellect, or crutches for a lame and halting reason. But to give you some precedents: Was not Nero condemned to death by the Roman senate? Was not Tarquinius Superbus deposed by the people of Rome, with the assistance of their general? Were not some of the Lacedemonian kings even put to death, when they offended the laws of the commonwealth? as particularly, was it not the fate of one Pausanias a king of Lacedemon? . . .

2. The last thing handled was the power of councils to punish a tyrannical magistrate: now I come to the second thing: whether the people or the community have any such power of punishing their defecting princes or magistrates: and if they have such a power, when may they put it in execution, and how far may they extend the punishment? Without doubt there remains in the body of the people an unresigned sovereignty, which is their ultimate reserve against the irregularity, or overflowing tyranny of their magistrates; to which they may make retreat in clear and apparent necessities: see the place of Scripture in the margin, [1 Sam.14:43,44,45] about Jonathan's rescue from the tyranny of Saul, even by the people, and if this were not, and that the people had not such an untransferred sovereignty, and if wicked magistrates should corrupt their councils, (as oftentimes they join them with themselves in the same wicked enterprises, for the more colorable and unsuspicious actings of their wickedness,) the people would be left in a remediless condition, which God and nature never intended. And though it may be objected that this opinion may introduce anarchy and confusion, yet it cannot be denied, but the repressing of a rooted and reigning tyranny conduces to a greater good, than a momentary anarchy can do hurt: if it should prove so that anarchy should be the consequent of restraining tyranny, which yet doth not necessarily succeed it; yet anarchy cannot be of so long continuance, as the other would have been, if born withal, because (as was said before) there is inviscerated into man a prompt inclination, and a love to society and company; and this ushers in government, which necessarily follows as the thread doth the needle: and anarchy never was of any long continuance, but came as a sudden landflood or murmuring torrent, that soon reduced and confined itself again within the banks of government. It is true that there hath not been a frequent practice of this in the world of late years, yet this was a practice at Rome, as you may see in the case of Tarquinius Superbus before mentioned: and lest this instance should be thought unwarrantable which is here cited, take a Scripture pattern for it: you shall find in the first of the Kings, chap. 12., that Rehoboam king of Israel (after that the people had desired that the yoke which his father had put upon them should be made lighter, and had received counsel from the old men

to that purpose) spoke roughly to the people, and followed the counsel of the young men, and said to the people, I will add to my father's yoke, my father chastised you with whips, but I will chastise you with scorpions: but what follows: what portion (say the people) have we in David? what inheritance have we in the son of Jesse? To your tents, O Israel, &c. And so they shook off Rehoboam's tyrannical yoke, and chose to themselves Jeroboam to be king; and none of all the people of Israel lived under the government of Rehoboam, but the tribe of Judah only; and you shall find, that in the same chapter God owns this act of the people in shaking off the yoke of this tyrant: you shall find this whole story in the aforesaid 1 Kings, chap. 12. from vers. 1 to vers. 25. And the reason why the people have of late years so rarely gone the same way with the people of Israel is not because the people had no such power, or because many princes were not, or are not wicked and tyrannical enough, but because the people were so short-sighted as not to understand their own power; and because few or no tyrannical kings and magistrates have professedly and openly aimed at and driven on the destruction of the people under their government, but have subtly and cunningly ruined them under seeming and disguised pretences of good; they have made their intentions, which were first comical and baited over with pleasant and plausible shows, to appear at last openly fatal and tragical in the execution thereof. So that the issue of their designs did only discover their hearts like the heat that roasts the meat and cannot be seen but in its effects. So that tyrants had well learned the art of undoing their people before they were aware, and when undone they were become unable to help themselves by putting a check to the violent career of their tyrannical taskmasters; which makes it manifest that the people were unable to help themselves, not that it was unlawful for them to rescue themselves from tyrannical servitude, if they could.

Now if you would know when the people may repress the tyranny of their magistrates: I answer, (1) Not upon every petty error in government; for what magistrate that hath so great a burden as the care of a kingdom's weal but may sometimes slip, or start aside from the rules of strict observance of his trust. Yea, secondly, not upon some single gross acts of misgovernment, if upon seasonable admonition he see his fault, become repentant, and amend; for the end of such admonition is amendment of his government, not the punishment of his person. But thirdly, if a magistrate continue obstinate and destructive in his ways and designs after admonitions and reprehensions by words and arguments, after opposition and resistance by force of arms; then may he be proceeded against by the councils [10] and those governors of the nation or commonwealth that are under him (those *optimates regni* as Keckerman calls them) so far as the public welfare calls for it, even to death itself, if it be thought necessary: and here I shall offer this reason, why many tyrannical princes (as particularly some here in England) have not suffered death as well as deposition, because always the succeeding claiming heirs to crowns, and their potent friends have (upon politic reasons and considerations) laboured to keep themselves (in case they should offend) from being punished by precedents of their own making: in case whole councils of a kingdom will not do their duty herein, then part of them may undertake it: and if part of the councils or governors will not do it, then one of them may call the people to second him for such a work; and if none of them will do it, then another higher course may be taken as the aforesaid author urgeth, his words are these: *Si nullus plane, sit optimatum, qui patriæ salutem curet, subditi possunt vindicem aliquen & repressorem tyrannidis eligere*: (i.e.) If none of the governors of the commonwealth will need the welfare of his country, then the subjects or people may choose some one or other to be an avenger and restrainer of such a tyranny. Now if we look to the trial of the late king here, before he came to be under restraint, he was followed with inviting, advising, and reprehending declarations from the councils of two nations; he was resisted by force, he was at last imprisoned, he was again freshly importuned by the councils of England to return to his trust, to change his former mind: he amends not; he returns not: whereupon he was brought to trial, judgment, and execution, by a parliament entire in its essence, though not a full parliament. And yet in this learned man's judgment the parliament or people might have lawfully gone a great way otherwise than they did to suppress a tyrant and his tyrannies.

OBJECTION 4. But we shall meet with this objection. The house of peers are the *optimates regni*, the great men of the kingdom; they are a court of judicature: the commons never were, nor claimed any such thing, as a right, till now of late, in the trial of the king?

SOLUTION. To answer this: first, it is acknowledged that the com-

10. Keckermannus, *System Politic* lib.1,p. 434; Bodin, lib.2 cap. 5. Althusius, c.14, p.106.

mons did not exercise it of late years, though it cannot be made manifest to the contrary, but they had the power of judicature and did exercise it jointly with the lords when the peers and commons sat together in one house; and that they did sit in one house is clear by the book of *De modo tenendi Parliamenti*, and by my Lord Coke's book, called the *Jurisdiction of Courts*, in *Tit. Parliament*, and as you may see by the places in the margin cited by him. And indeed since the lords and commons were severed, and sat in distinct houses, the commons have discontinued the exercise of a judicatory power; yet it doth not appear but they had it, yea there can be no cogent and convincing reason, why they had it not *in potentia* always, though they have not put it forth till of late, *in actu*. I must confess, if mere custom were sufficient reason why the commons had no such power, something may be said; and how far mere custom ought to sway rational men is easy to judge. But secondly, whence have their lordships had this power of judicature? Was it not from the king's writ in the original of it? Yes, Master Prynne will prove it so; and now their lordships have it by a patrimonial right, a right of inheritance. I would their lordships had such a prolific virtue as to communicate their wisdoms also (I mean those lords that have any) to their posterity, as well as this pretended power of judicature. I am sure many of our peerage have entailed their vices upon their posterity and some of their successors frolic themselves with it, as no way esteeming it a *morbum hereditarium*; but what lamentable shifts have usurped powers ever had for their refuge, when reason stands aside from their cause? Doth not the election of the people (for whose good all just governments and governors are) equi-ponderat, yea over-balance the king's writ? And for hereditary succession in judicature, what reason, what honest defence hath it? Did ever any judge in Westminster hall pretend to a power or right of deriving his place of judicature to his son, or if he did or should, would it not be a senseless thing for a state to grant it him upon the sole and single consideration of being such and such a judge's son, who for many reasons may be incapable of his father's feat? This is a brat of prerogative, and though a prince's brain might be its father, I am sure it could never lay claim to reason for its mother. Thirdly, it cannot be well denied but that it was more the want of a right knowledge of their power and the extent of it, whereupon followed a disuse of its exercise, that made the commons to be believed they had no such power than any solid reason, that could or can be urged against it; and there is a far stronger reason that they should be a court of record, a judicature, than the lords, for the lords represent no shire or county, or any corporation through the kingdom, and the commons represent the whole kingdom and the lords inclusively; there is no lord that can call himself a free-holder in this kingdom but is represented in the house of commons, either by the express giving of his voice in the election of some commoner or other, or by implication, if the lord be absent at the time of election. I know that some lords the last short parliament gave their voices in election of some parliament men, and if so, we may easily know where right of supreme judicature should have been lodged, as in its proper place; and I am sure many have known to their grief where the usurpations of this right and power hath been; and it is well that our eyes are so much opened as to see our native rights, and to do the lords that courtesy, as that their two voices would no more interfere, for they have long galled one another: yea so long, that the right and genuine voice of a lord in the house of peers could at any time of the day (I mean between 11 and 12 a clock for the care of most of them for the good of the commonwealth was so great) control and give a negative to his voice by representation in the house of commons. I would not be thought to have the least evil thought of those noble lords, who have endured the heat of our late troubles, and have not fainted in work of purchasing the English freedom and taking away the badges of servitude that lay upon it. I hope they shall find their labour not to be in vain, their glory and grandeur not to be lessened, and the remembrance of their names will be as a sweet perfume to after ages.

OBJECTION 5. But may the right heirs of the crown be laid aside where the government is hereditary as it is here in England?

SOLUTION. I answer: first, the government of England by kings is not simply hereditary, the ceremony at the coronation of the English kings shows they are not so. The words that were spoken by the archbishop at the coronation (four times over) to those people that were spectators, were, viz. Will you have — to be your king, are a manifest mark of election, and therefore *non videtur desisse habere, qui nunquam habuit*. Secondly, there is no reason why an office of so great a trust as the government of a kingdom should be hereditary in respect of the miserable effects that might ensue, when all governments and governors are for the people's good; and if it should be allowed (as it hath been too long) that this title of inheritance should oversway that of election, then every fool, madman, or tyrant that draws his blood out of the prince's veins, and is next unto him, must rule before the wisest and ablest man that may be elected. It is very irrational that the people should be to no other end than to serve as a footstool for such men to ascend to their pompous majesty, though perhaps they might be esteemed justly among the refuse and offscouring of the world. Thirdly, ought not tyrants to forfeit their crowns (if it be granted they are hereditary) as well as inferior men their estates for treason? Consider that place of Cicero: there is no society or fellowship to be kept with tyrants, but the greatest distance or alienation that may be, and it is not against nature to bereave such a man of what he hath, whom it is lawful to put to death. And for the late English prince, now Charles Stuart, he hath long since, even in his father's lifetime, proved to be a pregnant scholar in his father's school, and hath learnt to write after his copy in letters of blood drawn out of the hearts of his father's then subjects, and was then confederate in iniquity with him, and now he is become the rampant heir of his father's tyranny and cruelty, and in due time (if God turn not his heart) he may inherit his father's wages and reward in suitable anathemaes.

OBJECTION 6. But whether may armies intermeddle in the change of governments and governors, or power and force be used to pull down and set up the same?

SOLUTION. Tyrannical princes (who would make their will and pleasure the people's law) do seldom or never show and unmask their hearts till they are enthroned in a popular esteem, whereby their interest may be the better settled, and they more able to stand and bear up themselves against the shocks of threatening changes. And princes of any long continuance never want numbers of people, whose ignorance and viciousness make them easy observers of their wills without ever examining the justness of their command, accounting it loyalty and religion to serve the will of princes, though they should transgress the will of God; and when kings and magistrates are thus harnessed over with popular credit, and have strongly settled and confirmed their interests, then their power shall make all their actions good, and put a stamp of lawfulness upon them; here justice must give place to powerful injustice; now I suppose none can well deny but tyrannical and destroying magistrates ought to be, upon due conviction, punished according to the nature of their offences; then if such magistrates back themselves with power to do mischief and to exempt themselves from account, may not reason and right, law and justice be seconded with might and force to overbalance tyranny if it can? Justice is never the worse for having power for its champion or second when it conflicts with armed injustice. The people of Israel in the aforesaid I King. 12. when they shook off the yoke of the tyrant Rehoboam, cried, To your tents, &c. To that refuge which God and nature allows you for your own defence, and your enemies and oppressors offence if need be; the aforesaid Tarquin was pulled down from his tyrannical throne by means of the Roman general Brutus, and you shall find that heretofore armies have not only been the means to pull down tyrants, but also have had a great hand in setting up new magistrates and governors; Grotius speaks of the choice of emperors and magistrates at Rome, who (saith he) were sometimes chosen by the people, sometimes by the senate, and sometimes by the soldiery, though the establishment and ratification of their choice was by the people; and sometimes the Roman armies chose and the senate approved of the emperors, and sometimes the senate chose and the armies approved, as you may see out of the same Grotius. So that it is no strange, though not late practice, to see armies intermeddle in the pulling down and setting up of governors and governments, the last whereof cannot be said the English army had any hand in, for ought I know or have learnt.

And now the parliament of England having chosen an aristocratical government, and made the governors thereof annual for the prevention of any settlement of tyranny, and opening a way of advancement to all ingenious and honest men to ascend by merit to the very battlements of honour and preferment, I shall give a few instances of the like government, as the present council of state is, to govern the kingdom in the interval of parliaments. In the aristocratical commonwealth of Ragousa the chief magistrates and senators were chosen and changed every year: the *Decem viri* were chosen to govern the Roman commonwealth for a year, though indeed after they found power to be so sweet, that by violence they kept it for three years, till it was wrested from them at last when they abused their power. The magistrates in Crete (saith Polybius) were annual; and certainly why magistrates have been thus chosen yearly, and the reason why they ought to be still so (if it be not thought fitter to appoint a shorter reign or continuance in power), are invincible, being for the prevention of tyranny and for encouragement to virtue.

I have at length come to a period, and make it my humble desire to the parliament of England that they will make it their business to promote righteousness throughout the land, that they will clear oppression out of the nation as well as punish oppressors, that they will take opportunities of doing good to poor Ireland by the forelock, opportunities being transient and fleeting, and must be pursued at a near distance and at view, and not by scent; opportunities are the beckonings of heaven and must not be slighted, lest God withdraw such hints of welfare from us, and we repent too late of our miscarriages and defaults therein; and how good were it that those that are in public trust should do impartial justice, which (as Aristotle saith) is *bonum alienum*, justice is a good extended to others beyond and without a man's self, a shame to those who would centre justice within themselves, and make it their work to enrich themselves and relations above an honest livelihood, when we are commanded by the great God in such time of troubles, as we are now in, not to seek great things to ourselves. If upright and public spirits would disburden themselves of the clogs of private interest, they will soon be able to master the most staring and seemingly unconquerable difficulties. God stirs up truly generous spirits to be more lively, by how much the dangers are great and more hazardous; opposition to such men do but whet and heighten endeavours and make their spirits the more masterless thereby, and what need such fear, that all the world should be against them, if the God of all the world be for them?

Finis.

A LETTER TO THE LORD FAIRFAX, AND HIS COUNCIL OF WAR

With divers questions to the lawyers, and ministers: proving it an undeniable equity that the common people ought to dig, plow, plant, and dwell upon the commons, without hiring them, or paying rent to any. Delivered to the general and the chief officers on Saturday June 9. By Gerrard Winstanley, in the behalf of those who have begun to dig upon George-Hill in Surrey. London: Printed for Giles Calvert, at the Black Spread-Eagle at the west end of Pauls. 1649.

GERRARD WINSTANLEY (b. 1609), founder of the Digger movement, was a Lancashire man who became a trader in London and lost whatever property he possessed during the civil war. Turning to speculation upon the two topics uppermost in men's minds, the nature of religion and the nature of government, he adopted in both radical ideas which were in the air, but in a fashion which stamps him as a man of original thought and of singular gentleness and sweetness of spirit. His religious faith contained the essential elements of Quakerism; Giles Calvert, his publisher, became later printer for the Friends. Winstanley shared that profound mystical conviction which Pagitt had labelled heresy, that every man has divinity in him, that God is a spirit dwelling in every individual, who will never know rest and peace until God speaks within him. In his social application of such doctrines he regarded the land as common property, and planned a communistic Utopia in which competition and poverty would cease, for society would be based on love.

In April 1649, Winstanley and some twenty followers proceeded to put such ideas into practice. They began to dig up the commons on George's Hill in Surrey, not far from Colnbrook where Winstanley had been living, and to sow corn and vegetables. When complaints were made, the Council of State instructed Lord Fairfax to break up the group. Impressed by their sincerity and soberness when he visited them in May, Fairfax determined to use no force, but to leave them ' to the gentlemen of the county and the law of the land.' In July suit was brought against them; fines of £10 apiece were eventually imposed. The local inhabitants treated harshly men who did not defend themselves. In the autumn their hovels were destroyed by a detachment of soldiers. By the end of 1650 the movement, which had spread into three other counties, was effectually stamped out. Of Winstanley's many pamphlets, the fullest is *The Law of Freedom in a Platform*, 1652, which sets forth the government and character of that commonwealth by which he vainly hoped for the realization of the ideal voiced in 1647 by Colonel Rainborow, most democratic of army leaders: ' I really think that the poorest he that is in England hath a life to live as the greatest he.'

To the Lord Fairfax, general of the English forces, and his council of war.

Sir,

OUR digging and ploughing upon George-hill in Surrey is not unknown to you, since you have seen some of our persons, and heard us speak in defence thereof: and we did receive mildness and moderation from you and your council of war both when some of us were at Whitehall before you and when you came in person to George-hill to view our works: we endeavour to lay open the bottom and intent of our business as much as can be, that none may be troubled with doubtful imaginations about us, but may be satisfied in the sincerity and universal righteousness of the work.

We understand that our digging upon that common is the talk of the whole land; some approving, some disowning, some are friends filled with love, and sees the work intends good to the nation, the peace whereof is that which we seek after; others are enemies filled with fury, and falsely report of us that we have intent to fortify ourselves, and afterwards to fight against others and take away their goods from them, which is a thing we abhor: and many other slanders we rejoice over, because we know ourselves clear, our endeavour being no otherwise but to improve the commons, and to cast off that oppression and outward bondage which the creation groans under, as much as in us lies, and to lift up and preserve the purity thereof.

And the truth is, experience shows us that in this work of community in the earth, and in the fruits of the earth, is seen plainly a pitched battle between the lamb and the dragon, between the spirit of love, humility, and righteousness, which is the lamb appearing in flesh; and the power of envy, pride, and unrighteousness, which is the dragon appearing in flesh, the latter power striving to hold the creation under slavery, and to lock and hide the glory thereof from man: the former power labouring to deliver the creation from slavery, to unfold the secrets of it to the sons of men, and so to manifest himself to be the great restorer of all things.

And these two powers strive in the heart of every single man, and make single men to strive in opposition one against the other, and these strivings will be till the dragon be cast out, and his judgment and downfall hastens apace, therefore let the righteous hearts wait with patience upon the Lord, to see what end he makes of all the confused hurleyburleys of the world.

When you were at our works upon the hill, we told you many of the country people that were offended at first begin now to be moderate, and to see righteousness in our work, and to own it, excepting one or two covetous freeholders, that would have all the commons to themselves, and that would uphold the Norman tyranny over us, which by the victory that you have got over the Norman successor is plucked up by the roots, therefore ought to be cast away. And we expect that these our angry neighbours, whom we never wronged nor will not wrong, will in time see their furious rashness to be their folly, and become moderate, to speak and carry themselves like men rationally, and leave off pushing with their horns like beasts; they shall have no cause to say we wrong them unless they count us wrongers of them for seeking a livelihood out of the common land of England by our righteous labour, which is our freedom, as we are Englishmen equal with them, and rather our freedom than theirs, because they are elder brothers and freeholders and call the enclosures their own land, and we are younger brothers and the poor oppressed, and the common lands are called ours by their own confession.

We told you (upon a question you put to us) that we were not against any that would have magistrates and laws to govern, as the nations of the world are governed, but as for our parts we shall need neither the one nor the other in that nature of government; for as our land is common, so our cattle is to be common, and our corn and fruits of the earth common, and are not to be bought and sold among us, but to remain a standing portion of livelihood to us and our children, without that cheating entanglement of buying and selling, and we shall not arrest one another.

And then, what need have we of imprisoning, whipping, or hanging laws to bring one another into bondage? and we know that none of those that are subject to this righteous law dares arrest or enslave his brother for or about the objects of the earth, because the earth is made by our creator to be a common treasury of livelihood to one equal with another, *without respect of persons.*

But now if you that are elder brothers and that call the enclosures your own land, hedging out others, if you will have magistrates and laws in this outward manner of the nations, we are not against it, but freely without disturbance shall let you alone; and if any of we commoners or younger brothers shall steal your corn or cattle or pull down your hedges, let your laws take hold upon any of us that so offends.

But while we keep within the bounds of our commons, and none of us shall be found guilty of meddling with your goods, or enclosed proprieties, unless the spirit in you freely give it up, your laws then shall not reach to us, unless you will oppress or shed the blood of the innocent: and yet our corn and cattle shall not be locked up, as though we would be proprietors in the middle of the nation: no, no, we freely declare that our corn and cattle, or what we have, shall be freely laid open for the safety and preservation of the nation, and we as younger brothers, living in love with you our elder brothers, for we shall endeavour to do as we would be done unto; that is to let every one enjoy the benefit of his creation, to have food and raiment free by the labour of his hands from the earth.

And as for spiritual teachings, we leave every man to stand and fall to his own master: if the power of covetousness be his master or king that rules in his heart, let him stand and fall to him; if the power of love and righteousness be his master or king that rules in his heart, let him stand and fall to him; let the bodies of men act love, humility, and righteousness one towards another, and let the spirit of righteousness be the teacher, ruler, and judge both in us and over us; and by thus doing we shall honour our father, the spirit that gave us our being. And we shall honour our mother the earth, by labouring her in righteousness, and leaving her free from oppression and bondage.

We shall then honour the higher powers of the left hand man, which is our hearing, seeing, tasting, smelling, feeling, and walk in the light of reason and righteousness, that is, the king and judge that sits upon this five-cornered throne, and we shall be strengthened by those five well springs of life of the right hand man, which is understanding, will, affections, joy, and peace, and so live like men in the light and power of the son of righteousness within our selves feelingly. What need then have we of any outward, selfish, confused laws made to uphold the power of covetousness, when as we have the righteous law written in our hearts, teaching us to walk purely in the creation.

Sir, the intent of our writing to you is not to request your protection, though we have received an unchristian-like abuse from some of your soldiers; for truly we dare not cast off the Lord, and make choice of a man or men to rule us. For the creation hath smarted deeply for such a thing, since Israel chose Saul to be their king; therefore we acknowledge before you in plain English that we have chosen the Lord God Almighty to be our king and protector.

Yet in regard you are our brethren (as in English tribe) and for the present are owned to be the outward governors, protectors and saviours of this land, and whose hearts we question not but that you endeavour to advance the same king of righteousness with us, therefore we are free to write to you, and to open the sincerity of our hearts freely to you and to all the world.

And if after this report of ours, either you or your forces called soldiers, or any that owns your laws of propriety, called freeholders, do abuse or kill our persons, we declare to you that we die doing our duty to our creator, by endeavouring from that power he hath put into our hearts to lift up his creation out of bondage, and you and they shall be left without excuse in the day of judgment, because you have been spoken to sufficiently.

And therefore our reason of writing to you is this, in regard some of your foot soldiers of the general's regiment, under Captain Stravie that were quartered in our town, we bearing part therein as well as our neighbours, giving them sufficient quarter, so that there was no complaining, did notwithstanding go up to George-hill, where was only one man and one boy of our company of the diggers. And at their first coming divers of your soldiers, before any word of provocation was spoken to them, fell upon those two, beating the boy, and took away his coat off his back, and some linen and victuals that they had, beating and wounding the man very dangerously, and fired our house.

Which we count a strange and heathenish practice, that the soldiery should meddle with naked men, peaceable men, countrymen, that meddled not with the soldiers' business, nor offered any wrong to them in word or deed, unless, because we improve that victory which you have gotten in the name of the commons over King Charles, do offend the soldiery. In doing whereof we rather expect protection from you than destruction. But for your own particular, we are assured of your moderation and friendship to us who have ever been your friends in times of straits; and that you would not give commission to strike us, or fire or pull down our houses, but you would prove us an enemy first.

Yet we do not write this, that you should lay any punishment upon them, for that we leave to your discretion, only we desire (in the request of brethren) that you would send forth admonition to your soldiers not to abuse us hereafter, unless they have a commission from you; and truly if our offences should prove so great, you shall not need to send soldiers for us or to beat us, for we shall freely come to you upon a bare letter.

Therefore that the ignorant, covetous freeholders, and such of your ignorant soldiers that know not what freedom is, may not abuse those that are true friends to England's freedom, and faithful servants to the creation, we desire that our business may be taken notice of by you and the highest council the parliament, and if our work appear righteous to you as it does to us, and wherein our souls have sweet peace in the midst of scandals and abuses.

Then in the request of brethren we desire we may enjoy our freedom according to the law of contract between you and us, that we that are younger brothers, may live comfortably in the land of our nativity with you the elder brothers, enjoying the benefit of our creation, which is food and raiment freely by our labours; and that we may receive love and the protection of brethren from you, seeing we have adventured estate and persons with you, to settle the land in peace, and that we may not be abused by your laws, nor by your soldiers, unless we break over into your enclosures as aforesaid, and take away your proprieties before you are willing to deliver it up. And if this you do, we shall live in quietness, and the nation will be brought into peace, while you that are the soldiers are a wall of fire round about the nation to keep out a foreign enemy, and are succourers of your brethren that live within the land, who endeavour to hold forth the sun of righteousness in their actions, to the glory of our creator.

And you and the parliament hereby will be faithful in your covenants, oaths and promises to us, as we have been faithful to you and them in paying taxes, giving free-quarter, and affording other assistance in the public work, whereby we that are the common people are brought almost to a morsel of bread; therefore we demand our bargain, which is freedom with you in this land of our nativity.

But if you do slight us and our cause, then know we shall not strive with sword and spear, but with spade and plow and such like instruments to make the barren and common lands fruitful, and we have and still shall commit ourselves and our cause unto our righteous king, whom we obey, even the prince of peace to be our protector; and unto whom you likewise profess much love by your preaching, praying, fastings, and in whose name you have made all your covenants, oaths, and promises to us: I say unto him we appeal who is and will be our righteous judge, who never yet failed those that waited upon him, but ever did judge the cause of the oppressed righteously.

We desire that your lawyers may consider these questions (which we affirm to be truths) and which gives good assurance by the law of the land, that we that are the younger brothers or common people, have a true right to dig, plow up and dwell upon the commons, as we have declared.

1. Whether William the Conqueror became not to be king of England by conquest, turned the English out of their birthrights, burned divers towns, whereof thirty towns were burned by him in Windsor Forest; by reason whereof all sorts of people suffered, and compelled the conquered English for necessity of livelihood to be servants to him and his Norman soldiers?

2. Whether King Charles was not successor to the crown of England from William the Conqueror, and whether all laws that have been made in every king's reign did not confirm and strengthen the power of the Norman conquest, and so did, and does still hold the commons of England under slavery to the kingly power, his gentry and clergy?

3. Whether lords of manors were not the successors of the colonels and chief officers of William the Conqueror, and held their royalty to the commons by lease, grant and patentee from the king, and the power of the sword was and is the seal to their title?

4. Whether lords of manors have not lost their royalty to the common land, since the common people of England, as well as some of the gentry, have conquered King Charles and recovered themselves from under the Norman conquest?

5. Whether the Norman conqueror took the land of England to himself out of the hands of a few men called a parliament, or from the whole body of the English people? Surely he took freedom from every one, and became the disposer both of enclosures and commons; therefore every one upon the recovery of the conquest, ought to return into freedom again, without respecting persons, or else what benefit shall the common people have (that have suffered most in these wars) by the victory that is got over the king? It had been better for the common people

there had been no such conquest; for they are impoverished in their estates by free-quarter and taxes, and made worse to live than they were before. But seeing they have paid taxes and given free-quarter according to their estates, as much as the gentry to theirs, it is both reason and equity that they should have the freedom of the land for their livelihood, which is the benefit of the commons, as the gentry hath the benefit of their enclosures.

6. Whether the freedom which the common people have got by casting out the kingly power lie not herein principally, to have the land of their nativity for their livelihood, freed from entanglement of lords, lords of manors, and landlords, which are our task-masters. As when the enemy conquered England he took the land for his own, and called that his freedom; even so, seeing all sorts of people have given assistance to recover England from under the Norman yoke, surely all sorts, both gentry in their enclosures, commonalty in their commons, ought to have their freedom, not compelling one to work for wages for another.

7. Whether any laws since the coming in of kings have been made in the light of the righteous law of our creation, respecting all alike, or have not been grounded upon selfish principles, in fear or flattery of their king, to uphold freedom in the gentry and clergy, and to hold the common people under bondage still, and so respecting persons?

8. Whether all laws that are not grounded upon equity and reason, not giving a universal freedom to all, but respecting persons, ought to be cut off with the king's head? We affirm they ought.

If all laws be grounded upon equity and reason, then the whole land of England is to be a common treasury to every one that is born in the land. But if they be grounded upon selfish principles, giving freedom to some, laying burdens upon others, such laws are to be cut off with the king's head; or else the neglecters are covenant, oaths and promise-breakers, and open hypocrites to the whole world.

9. Whether everyone without exception, by the law of contract, ought not to have liberty to enjoy the earth for his livelihood, and to settle his dwelling in any part of the commons of England, without buying or renting land of any; seeing everyone by agreement and covenant among themselves have paid taxes, given free-quarter, and adventured their lives to recover England out of bondage? We affirm they ought.

10. Whether the laws that were made in the days of the kings does

give freedom to any other people but to the gentry and clergy, all the rest are left servants and bondmen to those task-masters; none have freedom by the laws but those two sorts of people, all the common people have been and still are burdened under them.

And surely if the common people have no more freedom in England but only to live among their elder brothers and work for them for hire; what freedom then have they in England more than we can have in Turkey or France? For there, if any man will work for wages, he may live among them, otherwise no: therefore consider whether this be righteous and for the peace of the nation, that laws shall be made to give freedom to improprietors and freeholders, when as the poor that have no land are left still in the straights of beggary, and are shut out of all livelihood but what they shall pick out of sore bondage, by working for others, as masters over them, and if this be not the burden of the Norman yoke, let rational men judge: therefore take not away men, but take away the power of tyranny and bad government, the price is in your hand, and let no part of the nation be wronged for want of a representative.

And here now we desire your public preachers, that say they preach the righteous law, to consider these questions which confirms us in the peace of our hearts, that we that are the common people born in England ought to improve the commons, as we have declared, for a public treasury and livelihood, and that those that hinder us are rebels to their maker, and enemies to the creation.

First, we demand Aye or No, whether the earth with her fruits was made to be bought and sold from one to another? and whether one part of mankind was made a lord of the land, and another part a servant, by the law of creation before the fall?

I affirm (and I challenge you to disprove) that the earth was made to be a common treasury of livelihood for all, *without respect of persons*, and was not made to be bought and sold; and that mankind in all his branches is the lord over the beasts, birds, fishes, and the earth, and was not made to acknowledge any of his own kind to be his teacher and ruler, but the spirit of righteousness only his maker, and to walk in his light, and so to live in peace, and this being a truth, as it is, then none ought to be lords or landlords over another, but the earth is free for every son and daughter of mankind, to live free upon.

This question is not to be answered by any text of scripture or example since the fall, but the answer is to be given in the light of itself, which is the law of righteousness, or that word of God that was in the beginning, which dwells in man's heart, and by which he was made, even the pure law of creation, unto which the creation is to be restored.

Before the fall Adam or the man, did dress the garden, or the earth, in love, freedom, and righteousness, which was his rest and peace. But when covetousness began to rise up in him, to kill the power of love and freedom in him, and so made him (mankind) to set himself one man above another, as Cain lifted up himself above Abel, which was but the outward declaration of the two powers that strive in the man Adam's heart; and when he consented to that serpent covetousness, then he fell from righteousness, was cursed, and was sent into the earth to eat his bread in sorrow. And from that time began particular propriety to grow in one man over another; and the sword brought in propriety, and holds it up, which is no other but the power of angry covetousness. For Cain killed Abel because Abel's principles, or religion, was contrary to his. And the power of the sword is still Cain killing Abel, lifting up one man still above another. But Abel shall not always be slain, nor always lie under the bondage of Cain's cursed propriety, for he must rise. And that Abel of old was but a type of Christ, that is now rising up to restore all things from bondage.

2. I demand, whether all wars, blood-shed, and misery came not upon the creation when one man endeavored to be a lord over another, and to claim propriety in the earth one above another? Your scripture will prove this sufficiently to be true. And whether this misery shall not remove (and not till then) when all the branches of mankind shall look upon themselves as one man, and upon the earth as a common treasury to all, without respecting persons, every one acknowledging the law of righteousness in them and over them, and walking in his light purely? Then cast away your buying and selling the earth, with her fruits, it is unrighteousness, it lifts up one above another, it makes one man oppress another, and is the burden of the creation.

3. Whether the work of restoration lies not in removing covetousness, casting that serpent out of heaven (mankind), and making man to live in the light of righteousness, not in words only, as preachers do, but in action, whereby the creation shines in glory? I affirm it.

4. Whether is the king of righteousness a *respecter of persons* yea or no? If you say no, then who makes this difference, that the elder brother shall be lord of the land, and the younger brother a slave and beggar? I affirm, it was and is covetousness, since the fall, not the king of righteousness before the fall, that made that difference; therefore if you will be preachers, hold forth the law of righteousness purely, and not the confused law of covetousness, which is the murderer: the law of righteousness would have every one to enjoy the benefit of his creation, that is to have food and raiment by his labor freely in the land of his nativity, but covetousness will have none to live free, but he that hath the strongest arm of flesh; all others must be servants.

5. Whether a man can have true peace by walking in the law of covetousness and self, as generally all do, or by walking in the law of universal righteousness; doing as he would be done by? I affirm there is no true peace, till men talk less, and live more actually in the power of universal righteousness. Then you preachers, lay aside your multitude of words and your selfish doctrines, for you confound and delude the people.

6. Whether does the king of righteousness bid you love or hate your enemies, if you say love them, then I demand of you, why do some of you in your pulpits and elsewhere stir up the people to beat, to imprison, put to death or banish, or not to buy and sell with those that endeavour to restore the earth to a common treasury again? surely at the worst, you can make them but your enemies; therefore love them, win them by love, do not hate them, they do not hate you.

7. Whether it be not a great breach of the national covenant, to give two sorts of people their freedom, that is, gentry and clergy, and deny it to the rest? I affirm it is a high breach, for man's laws makes these two sorts of people the antichristian task-masters over the common people. The one forcing the people to give them rent for the earth, and to work for hire for them. The other which is the clergy, that force a maintenance of tithes from the people; a practice which Christ, the apostles, and prophets never walked in; therefore surely you are the false Christs, and false prophets, that are risen up in these latter days.

Thus I have declared to you and to all in the whole world, what that power of life is, that is in me. And knowing that the spirit of righteousness does appear in many in this land, I desire all of you seriously in love and humility to consider of this business of public community, which I am carried forth in the power of love, and clear light of universal righteousness, to advance as much as I can; and I can do no other, the law of love in my heart does so constrain me, by reason whereof I am called fool, mad man, and have many slanderous reports cast upon me, and meet with much fury from some covetous people, under all which my spirit is made patient, and is guarded with joy and peace. I hate none, I love all, I delight to see every one live comfortably. I would have none live in poverty, straights or sorrows; therefore if you find any selfishness in this work, or discover any thing that is destructive to the whole creation, that you would open your hearts as freely to me in declaring my weakness to me, as I have been openhearted in declaring that which I find and feel much life and strength in. But if you see righteousness in it, and that it holds forth the strength of universal love to all without respect to persons, so that our creator is honoured in the work of his hand, then own it, and justify it, and let the power of love have his freedom and glory.

Gerrard Winstanley.

The reformation that England now is to endeavour, is not to remove the Norman yoke only and to bring us back to be governed by those laws that were before William the Conqueror came in, as if that were the rule or mark we aim at: No, that is not it; but the reformation is according to the word of God, and that is the pure law of righteousness before the fall, which made all things, unto which all things are to be restored: and he that endeavours not that, is a covenant-breaker.

This letter with the questions were delivered by the author's own hand to the general and the chief officers, and they very mildly promised they would read it, and consider of it.

Finis.

THE LEVELLER

Or the principles & maxims concerning government and religion, which are asserted by those that are commonly called Levellers. London. Printed for Thomas Brewster, at the Three Bibles, at the west end of Pauls, 1659.

TOWARDS the end of January 1659, Richard Cromwell summoned a new parliament to strengthen his position as civil executive against the open conspiracy of military leaders to seize complete control of the army. It was elected according to the old system, and in it therefore appeared a powerful minority of men like Vane, Ludlow, and Cooper opposed to the Cromwellian form of government. Upon this parliament and upon England descended a rain of pamphlets and petitions from political and religious sects who, once suppressed by Oliver's firmness, now seemed to be reconstructing again the bitter scenes of a decade before. Vain and unreal their effort was; already the shadow of returning royalism was upon them.

The pamphlet printed here, which appeared early in February, presents the essentials of Leveller thought. As developed from 1645 to 1649 by John Lilburn and William Walwyn in opposition to parliamentary assumptions of sovereignty, Leveller doctrine pictured true government as a democracy responsible to the people and bound by a fundamental law from endangering personal liberty. Freedom Levellers insisted upon as an inalienable right, not only of the nation as a whole, but of every individual man, stamped as he was with God's image. Human government, they maintained, could be just only in so far as it accorded with the law of reason, and the law of reason existed because of the innate moral sense in every man. As devices to achieve such an ideal government, Levellers planned for a written constitution, to be enforced as was any other law by the courts, for biennial elections, and for a bill of rights which included religious toleration.

WHEN the sect of the Christians first arose, the tyrants wrapped them in beasts' skins to provoke the wild beasts to rend them in pieces; and when Christ their Lord descended to earth, the priests and pharisees (finding his doctrine and holiness against their interest) cast upon him all the dirt of blasphemy, drunkenness, and confederacy with the worst of sinners; and to make sure of his life they rendered him an enemy to government, and told Pilate that he was no friend to Caesar if he let him go. It hath been the common practice of all tyrants to cover the face of honesty with the mask of scandal and reproach lest the people should be enamoured with its beauty; 'tis a master-piece in their politics to persuade the people that their best friends are their worst enemies, and that whosoever asserts their rights and liberties is factious and seditious and a disturber of their peace. Did not the Gracchi in Rome by such policy perish by the people's hands, whose liberties they sought to vindicate? And do not some Englishmen now suffer deeply upon the same account, from the people's hands for whose sakes they have prodigally hazarded their estates and lives? Are not some lovers of their country defamed, and esteemed prodigious monsters, being branded with the name of Levellers, whilst those that reproach and hate them neither know their principles or opinions concerning government, nor the good they intend to their very enemies? Those that have designed to prey upon the people's estates and liberties have put the frightful vizard of Levelling upon those men's faces; and most people are aghast at them, like children at raw-head and bloody-bones, and dare not ask who they are, or peep under their vizard to see their true faces, principles, and designs. Doubtless if the people durst but look behind them upon the bugbear from which they fly, they would be ashamed of their own childish fear of the Levellers' designs to make all men's estates to be equal, and to divide the land by telling noses; they would easily discern, if they durst consider it, that no number of men out of Bedlam could resolve upon a thing so impossible that every hour would alter by the birth of some child, if it were possible once to make out equal shares; nor upon a thing so brutish and destructive to all ingenuity and industry, as to put the idle useless drone into as good condition as the laborious useful bee. Neither could the people think that any number of men fit to be feared, rather than scorned and pitied, could gain by levelling estates, for they can never have power and interest enough to disquiet the nation unless their estates be much greater than they can be possible upon an equal division; and surely it is a bugbear fit for none but children to fear any man's designs to reduce their own estates to little better than nothing; for so it would be if all the land were distributed like a three-penny dole.

But to satisfy such as desire to know what they are, who are now for destruction's sake (though formerly by their enemies scandalously) called 'levellers,' and what their designs are, I shall tell you their fundamental doctrines or maxims concerning our government; and from thence you may make a true judgment of all their plots, and either fear them or favour them accordingly.

I. First, they assert it as fundamental that the government of England ought to be by laws, and not by men; they say the laws ought to be the protectors and preservers under God of all our persons and estates, and that every man may challenge that protection as his right, without a ticket from a major general, and live under that protection and safely, without fear of a red-coat, or a pursuivant from Whitehall. They say that Englishmen ought to fear nothing but God and the breach of the laws, not to depend upon the will of a court and their council for the security of themselves and their estates. They say the laws ought to judge of all offences and offenders, and all penalties and punishments to be inflicted upon criminals, and that the pleasure of his highness, or his council, ought not to make whom they please offenders, and punish and imprison whom they please, and during their pleasure.

They say also that the laws ought to decide all controversies, and repair every man's injuries, and that the rod of the people's supreme judicature ought to be over the magistrates to prevent their corruption, or turning aside from the laws; but that the magistrates for executing the laws should not hold their offices at the pleasure of a king, or protector, lest the fear of displeasing him perverts justice. In their opinions 'tis highly criminal that a king, or protector, or court should presume to interpose by letters, threats, or promises, to obstruct the due course of the laws, or countenance and abet, or discountenance and browbeat any man's cause whatsoever. In fine, they say the laws that are incapable of partiality, interest, or passion, ought so to govern, as no man should be subject to the crooked will or corrupt affections of any man.

II. The Levellers' second maxim, or principle about government, is that all the laws, levies of monies, war and peace, ought to be made by the people's deputies in parliament, to be chosen by them successively at certain periods of time; and that no council-table, orders, or ordinances, or court proclamations [ought] to bind the peoples' persons or estates; 'tis the first principle of a people's liberty that they shall not be bound but by their own consent, and this our ancestors left to England as its undoubted right, that no laws to bind our persons or estates could be imposed upon us against our wills; and they challenged it as their native right, not to be controlled in making such laws as concerned their common right and interests, as may appear by the parliament's records in the time of Edward the second and Richard the second. The Levellers say that those whose interests are in all things one with the whole people's,

are the only proper uninterested judges of what laws are most fit to preserve and provide for that common interest: such are the people in parliament rightly constituted and methodized, and they may be depended
upon to provide remedies for the people's grievances because they themselves are sharers in every common grievance; and they will be naturally
led to study the common good, because they shall share in it. But if a
monarch's pleasure should control the people's deputies in their parliaments, the laws must be fitted for the interest of the monarch and his
family, to keep him in a condition to overtop the people, not for the
common and equal good of the whole nation: and then the monarch's
fears on the one hand, lest the people should be able to diminish his
greatness, or that he should hold his greatness at their mercy; and the
people's fears on the other hand, lest the monarch should be able to make
them slaves, and they come to hold their estates and lives at his mercy:
these I say would set two opposite interests, always at contention, in
the composing of laws; and the wisdom and industry of the people's
deputies, that should be spent in contriving the advancement of the
people's common good in the laws, would be taken up, endeavouring
to defend and preserve the people's interests against the monarch's.
Therefore, say the Levellers, 'tis equal, necessary, and of natural right,
that the people by their deputies should choose their own laws; yet they
conceive it would be of much greater good to our country if our parliaments were moulded into a better form, and some deputies were chosen
by the people, only to give their consent or dissent unto laws proposed;
and other deputies were chosen for senators, that should consult and debate of the necessity and conveniency of all laws, levies of monies, war,
and peace, and then propose all to the great assembly of the people's deputies to resolve; that so the proposing and resolving power, not being in
the same assembly, all faction and private interests may be avoided, which
may possibly arise in a single council, vested with the sole sovereign law-
making power. This second doctrine of the Levellers had been fit for
all England to have asserted some years since; and then so many father-
less and widows had not now been weeping for their lost husbands and
fathers in Jamaica and other foreign countries, nor had so many families
been ruined, nor England impoverished by the loss of trade occasioned
by the Spanish war, begun and prosecuted upon private interests or
fancies, without advice or consent of the people in parliament.

III. The Levellers assert it as another principle that every man of what quality or condition, place or office whatsoever, ought to be equally subject to the laws. Every man, say they, high and low, rich and poor, must be accountable to the laws, and either obey them or suffer the penalties ordained for the transgressors; there ought to be no more respect of persons in the execution of the laws than is with God himself if the law be transgressed; no regard should be had who is the offender, but of what kind, nature, and degree is the offence: 'tis destructive to the end of a government by law that any magistrate or other should be exempt from the obedience or justice of the laws; it dissolves the government *ipso facto* and exposeth all the people to rapine and oppression without security of their persons and estates, for which the laws are intended. Therefore, say they, great thieves and little must alike to the gallows, and the meanest man as readily and easily obtain justice and relief of any injury and oppression against the greatest as he shall do against the lowest of the people; and therefore, say they, it ought not to be in the power of any single person to defend himself from the impartial stroke of the laws, or to pervert justice by force; and that brings in their fourth principle, *viz.*

IV. That the people ought to be formed into such a constant military posture, by and under the commands of their parliament, that by their own strength they may be able to compel every man to be subject to the laws, and to defend their country from foreigners, and enforce right and justice from them upon all emergent occasions. No government can stand without force of arms, to subdue such as shall rebel against the laws and to defend their territories from the rapine and violence of strangers; and the people must either hire mercenary soldiers to be the guardians of their laws and their country, or take the care upon themselves, by disposing themselves into a posture of arms, that may make them ready and able to be their own guard. Now say the Levellers, 'tis neither prudent nor safe that the people's armies should be put into mercenary soldiers' hands. What reason can induce any people to believe that their laws, estates, liberties and lives shall be more secure in the hands of mercenaries than in their own? Who can think his estate, his liberty, or his life in safety, when he knows they are all at the mercy and will of hirelings, that are led by no other motive than that of profit or pay to serve them, and may be led by any proposal or temptation of greater profit or pay to desert them?

All ages have afforded sad experiments of trusting their strength in the hands of mercenary armies; most nations who have kept them, at least in their own bowels, having been devoured by them. Did not the Egyptian king, by trusting arms in hirelings' hands, lose both his crown and life, and brought the people to be slaves to the Mamalukes for near two hundred years? Was not the famous commonwealth of Rome ruined and enslaved by their negligent permission of Julius Caesar (upon his advantage of long continuing general) to form a mercenary army? Did not the inhabitants of Regium perish by the hands of the Roman legion left to be their mercenary defenders? And were not our neighbours of Amsterdam lately very near the loss of their estates and liberties, by their own mercenary army? And say the Levellers, the people have less reason to trust to mercenaries to defend their country from foreigners than they have to preserve their estates and liberties from domestic oppression. How can their valour or fidelity be depended upon, when a small stipend only obligeth them to either; and if they be conquered one day, they are ready to serve the conquerer next day, it being their professed principle to serve where they can have best and most certain pay. But say the Levellers, when the people which are owners of a country are disposed into a military form, they fight *pro aris et focis*; they are sensible that they have more at stake than a daily stipend, and are in no hopes to better their conditions by division amongst themselves, or by betraying their country to foreigners. Thus say they, it is prudent and safe for the people to be masters of their own arms, and to be commanded in the use of them by a part of themselves (that is their parliaments), whose interest is the same with theirs.

These four foregoing maxims contain the sum of all the Levellers' doctrine about our government in externals (whose principles without naming one of them have been rendered so prodigious and of such dangerous consequence); but let the reader judge whether the liberty, happiness, and security of every Englishman be not sought in the endeavours to establish those foundations of equal justice and safety; neither can they be charged herein with novelty or inconstancy, the same fundamentals of government having been claimed by our ancestors as their right for many hundred years.

And the late Long Parliament proposing the same to the people as the things to be defended by the late war, alleging that the king had set up courtiers to govern instead of laws, by imprisoning at pleasure, and during pleasure, and that he had attempted to make proclamations and council-table orders to be as binding as the laws that the people made by their parliaments, and that the king had exempted himself and others from subjection to the laws, and pretended a right to the militia to command the people's arms without their consent; and in confidence of the parliament's real intentions and fidelity in what they proposed, the people neither spared neither treasure nor blood to preserve themselves and their declared native rights. And therefore those called ' Levellers ' do now challenge their principles of justice and freedom as the price of their blood; and however many of the parliament's friends and adherents have since deserted their first pretences, yet the Levellers say they can give no account to the righteous God of the blood they have shed in the quarrel, nor to their own consciences of their duty to themselves, their families, and country, to preserve their laws, rights, and liberties, if they should not persist in their demands and endeavours to establish the government in what form soever, upon the foundation of the principles herein declared: and therein they would acquiesce, humbly praying the Father of all wisdom so to direct their law-makers and magistrates, that all God's people might enjoy their spiritual Christian liberties, in worshipping God according to their consciences; and they heartily wish that such a liberty may be settled, as another fundamental or corner-stone in the government.

But the designers of oppression having also thrown dirt in the faces of those whom they have named Levellers in the matters of religion, and aspersed them sometimes as Jesuits, sometimes as notorious heretics, and sometimes as licentious atheists, men of no religion, 'tis necessary that I should acquaint the reader with their principles that relate unto religion; I do not mean to give an account of their faith, for the men branded with the name of Levellers are and may be under several dispensations of light and knowledge in spiritual things, in which they do not one judge the other; yet they are all professors of the Christian reformed religion, and do all agree in these general opinions about religion and the power of men over it.

First, they say that all true religion in men is founded upon the inward consent of their understandings and hearts to the truths revealed, and that the understanding is so free that 'tis not in the power of men to compel it to or restrain it from a consent; nothing but the irresistible evidence of a truth can gain a consent; and when the evidence is clear to any man's understanding, he himself (much less another howsoever potent) cannot so much as suspend an assent. Therefore no man can compel another to be religious, or by force or terror constrain the people to be of the true religion.

Secondly, they say, that the last dictate of every man's understanding in matters of faith and God's worship, is the last voice of God to him, and obligeth him to practise accordingly. If a man be erroneously informed, yet the misconceptions he hath of truth bind him to practise erroneously; and should he resist that seeming light (though it should be in truth darkness), his sin would be much greater and of worse consequence than if he follows by his actions his erroneous conceptions. Therefore the only means to promote the true religion under any government is to endeavour rightly to inform the people's consciences, by whose dictates God commands them to be guided; and therefore Christ ordained the preaching of the Gospel as the outward means for converting souls, faith coming by hearing; and he also ordained spiritual ordinances for the conviction, instruction and punishment of erroneous and heretical persons, the scripture commanding the erroneous to be instructed with the spirit of meekness, and admonished privately, publicly, &c. And Christ never mentioned any penalties to be inflicted on the bodies or purses of unbelievers because of their unbelief.

Thirdly, Levellers say that there are two parts of true religion: the first consists in the right conceptions and receptions of God, as he is revealed by Christ, and sincere adorations of him in the heart or spirit, and the expressions or declarations of that worship outwardly, in and by the use of those ordinances that are appointed by Christ for that purpose. The second part of it consists in works of righteousness and mercy towards all men, done in obedience to the will of God and in imitation of his justice and goodness to the whole world.

The first part, being wholly built upon the foundation of revealed truths, doth in its own nature absolutely exclude all possibility of any man's being lord of his brother's faith; unless the understanding or faith of a magistrate could constrain the faith or understanding of others, to be obedient to his, or rather to be transformed into the likeness of his. And therefore therein every man must stand or fall to his own master, and having done his duty rightly to inform his neighbour, must give an account to God of himself only.

But the second part of religion falls both under the cognisance or judgment of man and the law-makers or magistrates power. Christ hath taught his followers to judge of men's religion by their works: ' By their fruits,' saith he, ' ye shall know them, for men do not gather grapes of thorns.' Whosoever (be it a court, or an army, or a single person) pretends to religion and yet remain treacherous wherein they are trusted, and continue in the breach of their promises, and are not conscientious to do to others as they would that they should do to them, but can without regard to justice seize by force of arms upon the people's rights, due to them by God's law of nature and their ancestors' agreement, and subjects their persons and estates to their wills or their ambition and covetousness, and make themselves great by oppressions out of the people's purses, those men's religion men may clearly judge, being in vain by the Scripture's judgment; yea their prayers and their preaching as abominable in God's eyes as were the fasts, new-moons, and Sabbaths of the Jews (which were then also God's ordinances), whilst their hands were defiled with blood and oppression, and the works of righteousness and mercy neglected.

It properly belongs to the governing powers to restrain men from irreligion in this second part of religion, that is, from injustice, faithbreaking, cruelty, oppression, and all other evil works, that are plainly evil, without the divine light of truths that are only revealed; and it is the duty of governing powers to compel men to this part of religion, that is, to the outward acts of justice and mercy, for the inward truth of men's religion, even in these, is beyond the magistrate's power or judgment.

Fourthly, they say that nothing is more destructive to true religion, nor of worse consequence to human society than the quarrels of nations or persons about their difference of faith and worship, and the use of force and punishments, each to compel the other to be of his belief. It cannot be denied that God, in his infinite secret wisdom, is pleased to cause his spirit to enlighten men's minds with several degrees of light, and to suffer many to remain in darkness, which be afterwards also enlightened: and therefore their faith and worship, if it be sincere, must necessarily and unavoidably differ, according to the different root of light upon which it grows. Surely babes in Christ and strong men differ much in their apprehensions and comprehensions of the objects of faith; and much more those that are not yet born in Christ, though appointed unto regeneration, and it may be instructed like Cornelius in some things.

And as to opinions about worship, the thoughts of men must naturally be different, as the mind of one exceeds another in clearness of light and capacity of judging; now when the most powerful party seeks, by force and punishments, to constrain the governed or conquered to subscribe to their faith and opinions, without regard to their own light or understandings, doth it not (as much as is in man's power) banish all dependence upon the spirit of God for light, out of men's minds, and constrain them to put out the candle of God within them, that is the light of their own understandings, and induce them for their worldly respects and safety to profess a faith and practise a worship which they neither do nor dare understand? And by continuance to contract a blindness of mind and hardness of heart; and is it possible to practise a design more opposite to true religion and the propagation of it? And it is evident that those of false religions, under a pretence of honouring God by forcing men to be religious, have blinded millions of thousands with false worships. And also, that such as have professed the true religion in substance have wickedly opposed the further enlightening work of the spirit of God, and caused thousands, for fear of punishments, to rest satisfied in the profession of a faith and worship which they understand not, and therefore can have no true religion in them. And histories will tell plentifully, how pernicious the quarrels grounded only upon difference in matters of faith have been to mankind: an honest pen would tremble to relate the murders and massacres, the dreadful wars and confusions, and the ruins and desolations of countries that have been upon this account; and the same must be to the world's end if difference in opinion about religions, worship, and matters of faith should be admitted to be a sufficient ground of quarrels. Errors and differences in men's understandings are from natural, unavoidable infirmity, which ought not to be the objects of punishments, or men's angers: it is not more likely that God should make all men's understandings equal in their capacity of judging, or give to all an equal means or measure of knowledge, than that he should make all men's faces alike. Why then (say the Levellers) should any man quarrel at another, whose opinion or faith is not like to his, more than at him whose nose is not like to his? Therefore (say they) let us be unanimous in seeking an establishment of equal freedom and security to the whole people of the best provisions for commutative and distributive justice, without partiality, and of the best means of instructing the whole people in the spirit of love and meekness: and then true religion will increase and flourish.

I have now faithfully related the sum of their principles about government and religion who have been usually called ' Levellers,' and scandalized with designs against government and religion and plots to bring the nations into anarchy and confusion. Let the reader judge what colour there is to suspect those that are thus principled, of such ill designs; or rather whether freedom, justice, peace, and happiness can be expected in our nation if these fundamentals of government be not asserted, vindicated, and practised, and made as known and familiar to the people as our ancestors intended the great charter of the liberties of England should have been, when they provided that it should be sent to every city and every cathedral church, and that it should be read and published in every county four times in the year, in full county.

I have only mentioned the fundamentals, because they claim these as their right, and humbly submit the circumstantials, as to the number whereof parliaments should consist, and the manner of their elections, and the order of their debating and resolving laws, &c. to the wisdom of the parliaments. But the reader may well enquire how those that have asserted these principles came to be called ' Levellers,' the people believing generally otherwise of them than these principles deserve? Truly the story is too tedious to relate at large, but the sum of it is, that in the year 1648 &c. the army having been in contest with some members of the Long Parliament, they constituted a general council of officers and agitators for the soldiers, and then fell into debate of proposals to be made to the Parliament for a settlement, and then some of that council asserted these principles, and the reason of them quickly gained the assent of the major part, but being contrary to the designs of some that were then grandees in the parliament and army (but most of them since dead) and had resolved of other things at that time even with the king, who was then at Hampton Court, it fell into debate in a private cabinet council how to suppress or avoid those that maintained these principles, and it was resolved that some ill name was fit to be given to the assertors of them, as persons of some dangerous design, and their reputations being blasted, they would come to nothing, especially if that general council were dissolved. Then was that council dissolved, and an occasion taken from that maxim, that every man ought to be equally subject to the laws, to invent the name of ' Levellers,' and the king, who was to be frightened into the Isle of Wight from Hampton Court with pretences that the men of these principles in the army would suddenly seize upon his person if he stayed there; he was acquainted with those men by the name of ' Levellers,' and was the first that ever so called them in print, in his declaration left on the table at Hampton Court, when he secretly (as was thought) stole away from thence; and thence it was suddenly blown abroad, with as much confidence as if they had believed it that first reported it, that a party of Levellers designed to level all men's estates; and since then the late lord protector, knowing these foundations of freedom to be inconsistent with his designs hath often mentioned the Levellers' plots with malice, scorn, and scandal; and now of late, generally, whosoever asserts the people's liberties and right of government by law and not by will, is branded as a Leveller by the flatterers.

Now I heartily wish that my countrymen may not be mistaken in my candid intentions in giving them this account. I mean not to court them, as Absalom did his father's subjects, to make them believe that those called Levellers would use them better than others, if power was trusted in their hands: for our age hath given me experience that power to enslave the people ought not to be entrusted in any man's hands, upon the fairest pretences and and most solemn oaths that that power shall be used to establish their freedom. And it is the Levellers' doctrine that the government ought to be settled upon such equal foundations of common right and freedom that no man, or number of men, in the nation, should have the power to invade or disturb the common freedom, or the common course of impartial justice, and therefore that every authority ought to be of small continuance, and the several authorities to be so balanced each by other, that without such an agreement of men, against their own interest, as human prudence cannot think possible, the people cannot suffer any common injury. But my meaning in this is only to prevent the division of my countrymen into parties, with animosities each against others, by the cozenage of names or scandals; when, it may be, they would otherwise join hands and hearts for their common rights and liberties, if they understood each others' minds, and could converse each with other, without prejudice, because of the names whereby each hath usually called the others. It is a threadbare plot of tyrants to divide the people into parties, that they may more easily master them. But I wish that my countrymen would unite in the equal principles of common right, and hearken to reason, with clearness of mind, whosoever offers it; not regarding whether he that speaks it is called a Leveller, or a Sectary, or an Anabaptist, or a Presbyter, or a Cavalier, but considering what he says; and then the number of hands to defend our liberties and properties would be so numerous that the ambition of one, or a few, could not hope for success in attempting a tyranny over us. And if this poor paper may have such an effect, that my countrymen be not deluded with the idle scandal of Levelling, cast upon honest men, into an opposition of their own welfare, I, and many that agree in the publication of this, shall have our ends.

Consider, therefore, what you here read; and the Lord make you understand the things that conduce to your peace and freedom, and the glorifying his name in righteousness in this nation.

A NEW LITANY FOR THESE TIMES

Fitted to most persons and occasions: being an essay in order to a new reformation in the three nations. *Ordered, that this* litany *be forthwith printed for public satisfaction.* London. Printed in the second year of England's redemption from the spawn of Machiavel and after the never to be lamented death of John Bradshaw.

IN this satire of unknown authorship, printed in 1660, can be seen what the average churchman and squire detested in commonwealth rule. The parody of the litany was not an uncommon device of the cavalier wit. In 1647 had appeared *The new Litanie* against the Roundheads, and *The Parliaments Letane, for the more speedy composure of Differences between them and the City, between the City and the Army, and between them all, and the King: that when they have ruined one another, the Royall Party may not by that means be Triumphant.* The temper of the latter's verse appears in these two extracts:

> From sequestring men's states unto their bare skin,
> From not caring who loses so ourselves may win,
> From a pretended holiness to cover our sin,
> > *Libera nos.*

> That it may please thee we may reign,
> And still be drivers of Charles his wain,
> And he ne'er hold the reins again,
> > *Quaesimus te.*

In 1659 there was another *New Litany,* and in the 1670's there was hawked on the streets a broadside, *The Cavalier's Litany. The Litany of John Bastwick* which caused his arrest and condemnation by the star chamber in 1637 was neither in verse nor witty, but a dull legal argument to prove that bishops were enemies of Christ's kingdom and the king's prerogative.

> From the terrible name of a Lord Protector,
> From the braves and the brags of a *Troy-novant* Hector,
> From such as drink nothing, save old Adam's nectar,
> > *Libera me,* &c.

> From putting my foot in another man's station,
> From working the ruins and plagues of a nation,
> From the terror that daily attends usurpation,
> > *Libera me,* &c.

692

From such as still aim at the publics good,
From those that have two faces under a hood,
From a reformation founded in blood,
    Libera me, &c.

From parliament men that are all for themselves,
From the equity practised by *Westminster* elves,
From splitting my bark on such dangerous shelves,
    Libera me, &c.

From a physician that kills more than he doth cure,
From a vap'ring companion that none can endure,
From the serious verily of a tradesman demure,
    Libera me, &c.

From a preacher to's humour that tortures his text,
From a Presbyterian if once he be vext,
From his brotherly love and his charity next,
    Libera me, &c.

From such as have fought for religion, and laws,
From an independent that's fierce for the cause,
From a lordly just-asse that every man awes,
    Libera me, &c.

From policy consisting in cozening, and cheating,
From a good turn not granted without much entreating,
From a senseless long prayer with a horrible bleating,
    Libera me, &c.

From inventors of plots to betray honest men,
From subject's liberty no man knows when,
From ending my days like a rogue in a den,
    Libera me, &c.

From covenants, and oaths, which no man can keep,
From the craft of a fox when he seemeth to sleep,
From a wolf that appears in the garb of a sheep,
    Libera me, &c.

From rising amornings before it be five,
From tasting the honey of another man's hive,
From a mistress whose answers are still negative,
     Libera me, &c.

From the dreadful threats of a tyrannous power,
From griping usurers that love to devour,
From marrying a wench whose beauty's her dower,
     Libera me, &c.

From a judge that a bribe did never refuse,
From a saint that did never much honesty use,
From such as are still their religion to choose,
     Libera me, &c.

From popery and its superstition so gross,
From all the grand heresies summed up by Rosse,
From a Christian that hates the sight of a cross,
     Libera me, &c.

From old John a Leyden, and all his vile crew,
From changing my name, and being christened anew,
From the news of a diurnal that seldom proves true,
     Libera me, &c.

From despising my kindred when clad poor and thin,
From a crony whose friendship is not worth a pin,
From cozening of great men that ne'er were my kin,
     Libera me, &c.

From those that live lewdly and never will marry,
From a wanton wife that's apt to miscarry,
From the pitiful fortune of Dick and Harry,
     Libera me, &c.

From meeting with rogues, and thieves in the dark,
From shooting short, over, or wide of the mark,
From Martin's devotion at Wheston's park,
     Libera me, &c.

From him that receives all and nothing disburses,
From an empty head stuffed with oaths and with curses,
From a prayer that's a prologue to picking of purses,
              Libera me, &c.

From counterfeit money which will not pass,
From an impudent quean with a face of brass,
From a city with patience rid like an ass,
              Libera me, &c.

From burying my honour and fame in the dirt,
From a bedfellow that cannot rest for the squirt,
From the gout, and the itch, and a lowzy shirt,
              Libera me, &c.

From a fiery schismatic when discontent,
From learning frugality after all's spent,
From the fag-end of the Long Parliament,
              Libera me, &c.

From falling in waters above the chin,
From a woman whose tongue is set on the pin,
From making religion a cloak to my sin,
              Libera me, &c.

From old Noll and Bradshaw now sitting in state,
From a meeting of Quakers without Alders-gate,
From acts of parliament quite out of date,
              Libera me, &c.

From the want of a cloak in a terrible shower,
From a lady that looks neither sweet nor sour,
From the Counter, Newgate, the Fleet, and the Tower,
              Libera me, &c.

From doctors and 'poth'caries when I'm in health,
From those that hate pleasure unless by stealth,
From Harrington, and his New Commonwealth,
              Libera me, &c.

From backing a mad and untoward filly,
From ignorant people and teachers as silly,
From the predictions of lying Will. Lilly,
            Libera me, &c.

From heaps of treasure as nobody prize can,
From a fool that esteems himself a wise man,
From a sequestrator and an exizeman,
            Libera me, &c.

From an evil conscience and its fierce gripes,
From whores and bawds and tobacco pipes,
From a nasty slut with her puddings, and tripes,
            Libera me, &c.

From a doctor as well read in Greek as a goose,
From a friend that playeth at fast and loose,
From leaving the world with my neck in a noose,
            Libera me, &c.

From drinking until I am fain to disgorge,
From knavish lawyers that know how to forge,
From being a soldier under Sir George—
            Libera me, &c.

From upstart nobles and new made laws,
From a pitiful preacher that looks for applause,
From red-coats, the dev'l, and the Good Old Cause,
            Libera me, &c.

From the tears of orphans, and poor widows cries,
From a parson that rails against Christmas pies,
From a sister that turns up the eggs of her eyes,
            Libera me, &c.

From a threadbare cloak and a pennyless purse,
From a knaves good esteem, and an honest mans curse,
From dying a rebel, or traitor, or worse,
            Libera me, &c.

From an impudent foolish clown given to lie,
From changing of governments, no man knows why,
From my enemies' gift and my friends' charity,
            Libera me, &c.

      Finis.

THE WAY TO BE RICH

According to the practice of the great Audley; who begun with two hundred pound in the year 1605. And died worth four hundred thousand pound this instant November, MDCLXII. *Rem, quocumque modo, Rem.* Psal.49.13. Yet their posterity approve their saying. London. Printed for E.Davis, 1662.

THE book from which the following chapter has been taken is of unknown authorship. Hugh Audley (1577–1662), its dubious hero, the ' great usurer,' was the son of a London mercer who studied in the Inner Temple and was called to the bar in 1611. His colossal fortune came from other devices than the simple one of loaning to young gallants, greeting them, as he did all his clients, with a book of devotions prominently displayed at his elbow. He held a post in the court of wards so lucrative that he was said to have lost a hundred thousand pounds by its disestablishment during the civil war. A land-speculator with sufficient acumen to see that London was expanding towards the west, he bought up a tract lying between Great Brook field and Shoulder of Mutton field. Audley street in the heart of modern Mayfair is named for him. His wealth founded several county families; the great London property of the duke of Westminster came from Audley through the marriage of a great grand-niece Mary Davies to Sir Thomas Grosvenor. Audley belongs in the category of pious moneylenders, a regular church-goer who often sighed for the simplicity of life in the days of his youth. These verses are reproduced to show how early the success formula tied itself up with religion.

. . . SECT. XI.

His discourse, and memorable sayings

I. Of men that would not thrive: 1. They would never thrive that observed not time and opportuntiy. 2. They cannot thrive that are not punctual; that by failing, looseth his friend, looseth his advantage of thriving. 3. They cannot thrive, who are of too light, voluble, and wand'ring minds. 4. They cannot thrive, who are too narrow, fixed, peremptory and resolute, and slow, and not able to meet with the great variety of occasions. 5. They cannot thrive, that are too credulous, easy, and hasty. 6. They cannot thrive, that are too anxious, diffident, and zealous. 7. They cannot thrive, that are not resolved and well-weighed. 8. They cannot thrive, who take no care of their little expenses. 9. They cannot thrive, who have not an exact account of their expenses and incomes.

698

10. They cannot thrive who meddle with more than they are well able to manage, &c.

II. His rules of thriving, which I cannot better express, than in these words:

1.

Fly idleness, which yet thou canst not fly,
By dressing, misdressing, and complement,
If those take up thy day, the sun will cry
Against these, for his light only was lent.
God gave thy soul brave wings, put not those feathers
Into a bed to sleep out all ill weathers.

2.

— — — —fool not, for all may have,
If they dare try a glorious life or grave.

3.

When thou dost purpose ought within thy power,
Be sure to do it, though it be but small,
Constancy knits the bones, and makes us stour,
When wanton pleasures beckon us to thrall:
Who breaks his own bond forfeiteth himself,
What nature made a ship, he makes a shelf.

4.

Do all things like a man, not sneakingly.
Think the king seeth thee still, for his king does:
Simpering is but a lay hypocrisy:
Give it a corner, and the chin undoes:
Who fears to do ill sets himself to task:
Who fears to do well sure should wear a mask.

5.

Slight those that say, amidst their sickly healths,
Thou livest by rule, what doth not so, but man?
Houses are built by rule, and commonwealths:

Entice the trusty sun, if that you can
From his ecliptic line: beckon the sky:
Who lives by rule, then, keeps good company.

6.

Who keeps no guard upon himself is slack,
And rots to anything at the next great thaw:
Man is shop of rules, a well trusted back:
Whose every parcel underwrites a law.
Loose not thyself, nor give thy humours way,
God gave them to thee under lock and key.

7.

Be thrifty, but not covetous, therefore give
Thy need, thine honour, and thy friend his due:
Never was scraper brave man: get to live,
Then live and use it, else it's not true
That thou hast gotten: surely use alone
Makes money not a contemptible stone.

8.

Never exceed thy income; youth may make
Even with the year: but age, if it well hit,
Shoots a bow short, and lessens still his state
As the day lessens, and his life with it,
Thy children, kindred, friends upon thee call
Before thy journey, fairly part with all.

9.

By no means run in debt, take thy own measure,
Who cannot live on twenty pound a year,
Cannot on forty; he is a man of pleasure:
A kind of thing that's for itself too dear.
The curious untwist makes his cloth too wide,
And spans himself, but would the tailor chide.

10.

Spend not on hopes, they that by pleading clothes
Do fortunes seek, when worth and service fail
Would have their tale believed for their oaths,
And are like empty vessels under sail:
Old courtiers know this: therefore set out so,
As all the day thou mayest hold out to go.

11.

In clothes, cheap handsomeness doth bear the bell,
Wisdom's a trimmer thing than shop ere gave;
Say not then, this with that lace will do well,
But this with my discretion will be brave:
Much curiousness is a perpetual wooing,
Nothing with labour: folly long a-doing.

12.

Play not for gain, but sport; who plays for more
Than he can lose with pleasure, stakes his heart,
Perhaps his wifes too, and whom she hath bore,
Servants and churches also play their part,
Only a herald who that way doth pass
Finds his cracked name at length in the church-glass.

13.

If yet thou love games at so dear a rate,
Learn this that hath old gamesters dearly cost:
Dost lose, rise up; dost win, rise in that state,
Who strive to sit out looking hands are lost:
Game is a civil gunpowder in peace,
Blowing up houses with their whole increase.

14.

Wholly abstain or wed: thy bounteous Lord
Allows thee choice of paths, take no by-ways,
But gladly welcome what he doth afford:
Not grudging that thy lust hath bounds and stays;

Continence hath its joy: weigh both, and so,
If rottenness have more, let heaven go.

15.

Drink not the third glass, which thou canst not tame
When once it is within thee, but before
Mayest rule as thou list, and pour the shame
Which it would pour on thee upon the floor.
He that is drunken may his mother kill,
Big with his sister: he hath lost the reins,
Is out-lawed by himself: all kind of ill
Doth with his liquor slide into his veins.
The drunkard forfeits men, and doth divest
All worldly right, save what he hath by the beast.
If reason move not gallantly, quit the room,
Call in a shipwreck shift there several way,
Let not a common ruin thee entomb.
Be not a beast in courtesy, but stay,
Stay at the third glass, or forego the place,
Wine above all things doth God's stamp deface.

16.

Lie not: but let thy heart be true to God,
Thy mouth to it, thy actions to them both.
Cowards tell lies, and those that fear the rod,
The stormy working soul spits lies and froth:
Dare to be true, nothing can need a lie,
A fault which needs it most, grows two thereby.

17.

Be sweet to all, is thy complexion sour,
Then keep such company, make them thy ally:
Command thyself in chief, he life's war knows
Whom all his passions follow as he goes.

18.

Think not thy fame at every twitch shall break,
By great deeds show that thou canst little do,
And do them not: that shall thy wisdom be,
And change thy temperance into bravery.

19.

Wisdom picks friends, civility plays the rest,
A toy shunned clearly passeth with the best.

20.

Towards great persons use respective boldness,
That temper gives them theirs, and yet doth take
Nothing from them, in service, care, or coldness,
Doth calculably thy fortunes mar, or make.

21.

Envy not greatness: for thou makest thereby
Thyself the worse, and so the distance greater.
Be not thine own worm: yet such jealousy
As hurts not others, but may make thee better,
Is a good spur, correct thy passions spite,
Then may the beast draw thee to happy light.

22.

Thy friend put in thy bosom, wear his eyes
Still in thy heart, that he may see what's there.

23.

Yet be not hasty if thou be a father,
Love is a personal debt I cannot give.
My children's right; nor ought he take it,
Rather both friends should die, than hinder them to live;
Fathers first enter bonds to nature's ends,
And are her sureties, ere they are friends.

24.

Calmness is great advantage; he that lets
Another chafe may warm him at his fire;
Mark all his wanderings, and enjoy his frets,
As cunning fencers suffer hence to tire.

25.

Mark what another says; for many are
Full of themselves, and answer their own notion,
Take all unto thee; then with equal care,
Balance each dram of reason like a potion.

26.

Pitch thy behaviour low, thy progress high,
So shall thou humble and magnanimous be.
Sink not in spirit; who aimeth at the sky
Shoots higher far than he that means a tree.

27.

Let thy mind still be bent, still plotting where
And when, and how the business may be done,
Slackness breeds worms; the sure traveller,
Though he alight sometimes, still goeth on.
Active and stirring spirits live alone,
Write on the others, Here lives such a one.

28.

Who say I care not, those I give for lost,
And to instruct them, 'twill not quit the cost.

29.

Scorn no man's love, though of a mean degree,
Love is a present for a mighty king.
Much less make anyone thine enemy,
As guns destroy, so may a little thing.
The cunning workman never doth refuse
The meanest tool that he may chance to use.

30.

All foreign wisdom doth account to this,
To take all that's given; whether wealth
Or love, or language, nothing comes amiss,
A good digestion turneth all to health.
And then as for our fair behaviour may
Strike off all scores none are so clear as they.

31.

Affect in things about thee cleanliness,
That all may gladly board thee as a flower;
Slovens take up their stock of noisomeness
Before-hand, and anticipate the last hour:
Let thy mind, sweetness have its operation,
Upon thy body, clothes, and habitation.

32.

In alms regard thy means, and others' merit,
Think heaven a better bargain, than to give
Only the single market-penny for it,
Join hands with God to make a man to live.

33.

Sum up at night what thou hast done by day,
And in the morning, what thou hast to do,
Dress and undress thy soul: mark the decay
And growth of it; if with thy watch that too
Be down, then wind up both; since we shall be
Most surely judged, make thy accounts agree.

34.

In brief, acquit thee bravely, play the man,
Look not on pleasures as they come, but go,
Defer not the least virtue: life's poor span
Make not an ell by trifling in thy woe:
If thou do ill, the joy fades not the pains:
If well, the pain doth fade, the joy remains.

A DISCOURSE CONCERNING SCHOOLS AND
SCHOOL-MASTERS

Offered to public consideration by M. N[edham]. London. Printed for
H.H. Anno Domini 1663.

MARCHAMONT NEDHAM (1620–1678) was the son of a gentleman of Burford, Oxfordshire, and his wife the daughter of the local innkeeper. His stepfather, the local vicar,
taught him so successfully that he became a chorister of All-Souls college at the age
of fourteen, and took his B.A. in 1637. He got an usher's place in Merchant Taylors'
school, and later became an underclerk in Gray's Inn. From 1643 to 1646 Nedham
wrote the greater part of *Mercurius Britannicus*, single-sheet weekly newspaper, violently parliamentary and satirical in tone. ' An active man in person among the rout,'
Anthony Wood describes him, ' called Captain Nedham of Gray's Inn, and what he
said or wrote looked upon as gospel.' In 1647 he left the ' blessed cause ' to kneel before
Charles I for forgiveness. An epitaph on him in that year runs:

> Here lies Britannicus, Hell's barking cur,
> That son of Belial, who kept damned stir,
> And every Monday spent his stock of spleen,
> In venomous railing on the king and queen.

He then began *Mercurius Pragmaticus* (1647–1649), ' very witty, satirical against the
presbyterians, and full of loyalty.' The Council of State found him in hiding near
Burford, committed him to Newgate, but treated him well, pardoned him, and made
him an independent again. His first pamphlet defending the new régime, *The Case of
the Commonwealth of England Stated*, appeared in 1650. From 1650 to 1660 he published
Mercurius Politicus, the official Cromwellian paper, and from 1655 to 1660 the *Public
Intelligencer*; he was ' the great Goliath of the Philistines, the great champion of the
late usurper, whose pen in comparison of others was like a weaver's beam.' At the
Restoration he fled to Holland, driven by such pamphlets as *A Rope for Politicus, or a
Hue and Cry after March. Nedham the late scurrilous newswriter* (1660). Pardoned
again, he returned to England, and took up the practice of medicine, which he had
studied in 1645. He recommended in 1675 in a preface to *A New Idea of the Practice
of Physic*, by Franc de la Boe (Sylvius) the chemical rather than the anatomical approach. During the 1670's, because of government pressure, he wrote pamphlets
attacking Shaftesbury's party.

This pamphlet represents Nedham's first public effort after his third conversion.
It shows the keenness of his sense of changing opinion, for his arguments were those
which carried weight with the cavaliers who passed the Clarendon code. But it shows
also something of the character of English education and presents that utilitarian view
of education which Locke and the eighteenth century took to heart.

THAT the education of youth is one of the greatest concernments of the
nation is a truth so obvious to every ordinary understanding that I shall

not need to insist upon the proof if it. Since 'tis plain that the scholastic state lays the groundwork and foundation of the other three states, viz. economical, ecclesiastical, and political; wherein the societies take their measures of goodness and felicity from the nature of those methods which were used and that success which hath been obtained in schools; all persons generally behaving themselves in their several stations (which providence fixes them in), according to those principles their childhood was first season'd with and that improvement of parts and manners they brought from thence. What is it that furnishes families with dutiful children, industrious servants, discreet masters? that supplies the church with able teachers, devout hearers? that keeps subjects in obedience to their prince, in a quiet and just demeanour towards one another, but the powerful impressions of an early institution, which being once well settled grow into habits and become co-natural to the temper and very constitution of the mind, not to be removed without great violence and continued efforts of ill company and constant debauches or diabolical infusions. Again, 'tis no less observable that 'tis every man's care and main design to provide well for his children after him and to transmit happiness to his posterity: and this care is visible enough in their leaving honours and estates many times purchased with their own disquiet and sin to boot. Now let me ask what those legacies of the parents' love will avail, what the laws themselves, which by bounding property are to secure those estates for them, will signify, if our children that are to succeed us are not rightly principled in piety and obedience and the rules of honesty and so prepared to a due observance of those laws, which if not kept by them as well as us, all our care and provision for them will come to nought, and the next age that treads upon our heels, if let loose to licentious or factious practices and opinions, cannot but ruin all the benefits of our peace and the interests of our religion; with this advantage, that their predecessors must bear the blame for those miscarriages which proceeded from a neglected education of their children. Nay, I shall appeal to the story of our late villainous changes, whether a few fanatic, ill-principled spirits may not get partly power to destroy partly credit to corrupt the rest of their fellow subjects from known rules of duty; as frequently those curs, which spend upon a wrong scent, are apt to mislead the whole pack.

This being, as it is among men who guide themselves by reason, agreed on, it may justly provoke the admiration of any considering person, that all sorts of people should be so remiss in this point; that amongst other provisions they seem to look upon education as the least necessary and think that charge lost which is spent in breeding their children, which their extreme lavishness on other occasions and their sordid thrift in this doth abundantly testify.

> *Res nulla minoris*
> *Constabit patri, quam filius.*
> Nothing shall stand the thrifty dad
> In less than th' breeding of his lad.

Not to mention those of quality, and take notice only of the rabble we meet with in the streets, it must needs pity any Christian heart to see the little dirty infantry which swarms up and down in alleys and lanes, with curses and ribaldry in their mouths and other ill rude behaviour, as if they were intended to put off their humanity and to degenerate into brutes. What hopes may we entertain of posterity, when the better sort are sent over to foreign schools of vice, to learn fashions, to court mistresses, dance à la mode and swear with a grace; and the worser sort are sent no whither, but learn to imitate and outdo those sorry examples they have at home.

Nor is this neglect to be charged only upon particular persons in their private sphere; but the public also may be thought to partake in the same guilt: when we consider 'tis the only way to ascertain to our posterity the fruits of our late blessed and wonderful restoration, and that so little has been done towards it, and that little too has been so little looked after and observed. Indeed it must be confessed that the public councils have in the main been very just and industrious in ordering the great concerns of our peace and in re-establishing the church in its ancient revenue and reverence. And something by the by has been touched at for the catechizing of youth, for the masters' abjuration of covenant and subscription to church orders. But that either so imperfectly worded as to afford an easy evasion, or so poorly put in execution through negligence or corruption of officers, that the law had as good never been made. I do not speak this with any imputation to the honourable assembly of parliament, but with some resentment of this inadvertency bewail the fate of the schools (which either have no patrons or their patrons no will to assist and promote their concernments), and pity the condition of posterity, which is no nearer looked to, no better provided for. It must be acknowledged, our worthy patriots have business enough before them to fill their hands and hearts, to take up their thoughts, and to employ their discourses. But when I find grievances of a meaner alloy considered and redressed, I could not but conclude that they would in their wisdom have judged (had there stood up any one to represent) school-grievances and fraud and cozenage in that mystery of as great and ill a consequence to the public and as worthy their debate and a speedy remedy as many of those which are come into acts. Whereupon, in the silence of all others, I thought my self obliged to take notice of this subject, and rather to extimulate some other, who being better acquainted with these things may make out further discoveries, than out of any confidence of an ability in myself to speak much to purpose in a thing of such moment, I have adventured to tender to public consideration my unpolished thoughts concerning the ordering of schools to the benefit and improvement of youth and the advancement of learning and religion.

And first, to speak of stipend: reward being the very life of action and the main encouragement of diligence.

> *Quis enim virtutem amplectitur ipsam, praemia si tollas?*
> For who embraces virtue's self, if you take away the pelf?

'Tis the salary which makes schools and learning flourish. *Chi ben paga, ben impara*, says the Italian. The conscience of doing public service and satisfaction of discharging one's duty is not a sufficient recompence for the toil of teaching. In courts of law and equity no under-clerk or inferior officer's place but may vie, for the profits of it, for the fairest pension of any public school. Ministers themselves, who instruct us to expect future rewards, yet without a fair present maintenance would fall into the contempt of the vulgar and their labours prove ineffectual. And this is the case of schools: no employment more publicly useful, none more toilsome and painful, yet no one more slighted even to reproach, no one less rewarded or regarded. 'Tis a great scandal to the nation, and certainly as great a grievance (if rightly considered), that no one sort of men are greater sufferers in this kind than the schoolmasters. Yet this must be said in commendation of our ancestors, that their provision was very competent and that the endowment of schools was in proportion to the estates of those times very fair and honourable. When workmen wrought for a penny a day, when that land which is now worth 40 or 50 s. an acre was then thought a dear bargain at ten groats; when everything was cheap but money, forty pound per annum was a fair livelihood and better than 200 l. now perhaps. But what do we add to our forefathers' stock? The trustees and governors in the several corporations share the improvements among themselves, take all above the salary for lawful prize, and leave the master to the bare old allowance, notwithstanding the vast increase of the old rents. So that by this means schools are become impropriations, and laymen (ignorant fellows) run away with the encouragements of learning, and receive the rewards of the masters' industry. This abuse would deserve the parliament's notice, and a severe account to be taken of the revenues of schools, which might be done by requiring all masters and governors to give in a perfect inventory of school lands, houses, etc., with their yearly value, and settling accordingly an honourable salary upon the master, with reasonable abatement for repairs and the charges of the overseers. This course would invite men of eminent parts and abilities into school-work, whereas now 'tis made the sanctuary of many idle insufficient persons, who have no hopes elsewhere; or by those, which have any merit, designed a step to some church preferment. It cannot then be expected, as things are, that the schools of this nation (excepting some few, which are illustrious and of royal foundation) should be in any tolerable condition.

Having taken notice of the mean support and slender maintenance, let us next take a view of the methods of teaching used in schools and see what disorders may be met with in them. I shall not pretend to be able to judge and give definitive sentence, what is the best method, though we ought to have that regard to antiquity and the custom of former times that we are to be very tender how we prefer our own novel conceits to their tried and approved usages; and that we do constantly adhere to that method and way which their practice, back'd with public authority, hath chalked out to us, till authority do recommend another. They do almost in all countries entertain the same grammar and go by a certain rule of teaching. Despauter obtains in France, Alvarez in Spain, and all England over heretofore Lily and Camden were in the hands of youth. And indeed, there is the same reason for uniformity in school as in church: the variety of methods (supposing they were all severally in themselves very good) doing very much mischief by not only distracting young heads, and discouraging them, and putting them back upon their removes to new masters; but also making a fundamental difference in their course as they proceed to other studies. I have heard that a bishop, at an examination in a public school, receiving an answer out of the common road from a child, which had come lately from a private school, made this reply, ' What,' says he, ' puritanism in schools too? ' And so it is with us now, since these licentious times have overthrown all order and broken us into many sects and factions; the schools have been infected with that fanatic itch, and like independent congregations have been variously administered by new lights, according to the fancy of the several teachers, that I dare say there are as many grammars taught as there are grammarians to teach, if not more. It would be well if these loose brooms were gathered again, if not into the old, yet into some one model. 'Tis likely enough the old way may have some inconvenience, many defects and redundancies; why may not the same course be taken by us as by the states of Holland, who upon such an occasion employed Vossius to revise and mend and complete the old grammars, both Greek and Latin, which are now accordingly read in the Low-Country schools; or, for better satisfaction, what if the convocation would please to order some of their number, taking to their assistance some of the most able masters, well experienced in teaching, either to correct what is amiss in the old institution, or to draw up a new body of rules and system of that art, with the advantage of later inventions. It would be a thing not unworthy the care of churchmen and that for which posterity would pay thanks to their memory. Some eminent divines in former ages have descended to that care, Dr. Colet, Dean of Paul's, Erasmus, Card. Wolsey, &c. In the mean time, I shall appeal to any man of sober judgment whether it be consistent with the nation's good to banish schism out of the church and countenance it in the schools, and whether our English youth, which is thus nursed up in faction, is like to be well taught.

When the stipends and methods are thus established, I should further propose that there should be no allowance for any one whatsoever to keep a private school upon his own account, unless it be the clerk of the parish, whose office it should be (with an allowance for it) to teach all the children of the parish at certain hours each day to write and read, and that by the direction and under the inspection of the minister; and on Saturdays to prepare them for their public answering in the church to the catechize-questions; and that when children are thus far instructed in their own parish, they should be then sent to some public school, unless the parents were of an estate to keep a tutor (to be approved by the bishop) in his house, or were of so low a fortune that he could not be at the charge of breeding his child a scholar. For without question many of those whiffling undertakers, that appear not in public stations but venture out upon their own private bottom, besides that they drain the public schools, to their great hindrance and discouragement, citizens being easily pleased with anything that is new-fangled, may very well be suspected to have no honest warrantable design if they be well inquired into. I shall readily crave pardon of any one which shall be injured in that information which I have received, but must think myself oblig'd in justice to the public to let it be understood what ill offices may be done it (as I have heard) in private. There are at this time about the city several masters of private schools which have been and are still covenanters, presbyterians, non-conformists, some of whom have been ousted out of their other mens' places for schism, who are yet encouraged by the confluence of youth from the city and by the favour of some noble families: one at Clapham, one at Totenham High-Cross, one or two at Chelsea, one or two at Newington, one at least at Hackney, &c. and so (as I am told) throughout the whole kingdom those of that party are designing the same course. Whether this be the fault of the under-officers, a sort of men that by ill execution of good laws have always brought an odium upon the episcopal authority, which employs them, and the sacred order itself, upon which they depend; or whether it be the craft and cunning of those merchants of the faction, who rather than sit out will play any game, I am not able to discern; authority may be satisfied if it may be at leisure but to make the inquiry. However, it hath a very ill face and portends unluckily enough to the peace of the nation that there are suffered such seminaries of faction, as if it were designed that posterity should retrieve the good old cause, and the children should carry on the work of the Lord in the following generation, which has proved too hot in ours (thanks be to God) for the fathers' fingers. Will not these suffering brethren have a fair opportunity of being revenged on the reverend fathers of our church for their severity in turning them out of unjust livings by training youth to a contempt of church authority and order and keeping on foot nurseries (like Barkstead's regiment) of those who may hereafter make up a schismatical army?

My lords, you had much better have continued them in the pulpit; they will do ten times more mischief now among the lambs than they could have done amongst the sheep. What they did then was like stealing of standing corn out of the field, but rubbing the ears; but what they do now is stealing the seed, the next year's crop, which the civil law hath determined to be a far greater theft. They have sufficiently spoiled the present age, must they now be turned loose to spoil the next age too? If those spirits by their religious canting could carry away men and women from their obedience to the father of their country, and from the bosom of their mother, the church, ah! my lords, are they to be trusted with the children? I am of the opinion that if the vicar-general would instead of school-licences give them licences to practise physic, he might do the whole nation a very good office; for by this means, those of their own tribe being the only persons that would probably make use of them, they might in some reasonable time give a fair account of the whole fraternity; as we used to rid our houses of rats by teaching one to eat rat's flesh and then hanging a bell around his neck he will never give over till he have ferreted all the gang away. In good earnest, it would be more prudent to advise his majesty to allow all that have suffered in that kind and are otherwise unprovided (which will not be many) a modest pension out of his exchequer, than thus to admit them to an employment which may be of so dangerous a consequence to the public peace. And whereas they pretend not to intermeddle with the institution, but to leave that to a little officer, some puny fellow they get from the university, who may subscribe according to the act, while themselves keep their own conscience free to the Godly design; besides, that it is plain enough what danger there is in their very converse and example, in their hums and haws, in their graces and family-exercises, it being so familiar with men of that principle to sow sedition in their very prayers and to make religion itself a stale to faction. I say, besides this, it will be found upon inquiry that they do too execute the teaching part, by spending considerable portions of their time in examining and taking account how their children profit; though this must be said in their behalf, that for their teaching of letters there is not that fear of a presbyterian's doing much mischief, seeing it may be supposed they cannot be very communicative of what most of them have not; but it was believed it was the intention of that act to take from them the opportunity of spreading the leaven of their factious and disloyal opinions, which they can more effectually do in the duties of a family. And it may be easily guessed by the relations on what errand those children are sent to such masters or landlord, namely, that they may learn to fear God and disobey the king and the church (as their fathers before them have done). I am somewhat the more earnest on this subject because it must be confessed that those who were censured unfit for church-work ought to be judged much less fit for the work of the school; and if the priests are denied to the fathers, much more should the children be kept from them, unless we would verify that proverb, that the fathers have eaten sour grapes, and now the children's teeth must be set on edge.

To come then to the last and chiefest consideration, how many schoolmasters themselves are to be qualified, that they may laudably perform the great trust and duty which is charged upon them. What difficulties the work has in it, to encounter all kinds of tempers and improve all sorts of wits, to be *ingeniorum & morum artifices*, to fashion minds and manners, to cultivate rude soil and dispose youth to virtuous behaviour against their natural inclinations; what care and pains, what great abilities of prudence and skill and all virtue, what a cycle of knowledge it requires to instruct others in the grounds of literature, to raise their parts, to heighten their fancy, to fix their thoughts and to crane their genius to the pitch, and so prepare them for public service, is a thing more easily discoursed than considered, more talked of than taken notice of. It is a great wonder of Providence, when we look on the present constitution of schools, how much contempt and how little encouragement is thrown to the profession, that there are any able and worthy men of that way; and sure whoever they are, it was first not the spontaneous election of their own mind, but some outward necessity of fortune, or some other fatality that condemn'd them to those galleys and tied them to that oar, seeing those that are engaged do most upon the stock of their own credit work through the flint. So true is that,

> *Quem Jupiter odit, pedagogum facit.*
>
> To whom a spite Jove takes,
> Him pedagogue he makes.

Were parents obliged but for some time to the trouble of instructing their children (they think it is trouble enough to have them in the same houses), they would quickly be convinced what respects were fit to be paid to him who undertakes such a charge, and what pardon he would deserve at their hands for small failings, when themselves cannot secure them from great ones. But were the forementioned course taken, of proportioning the salaries to the improvements of rents, there is no question to be made but schools might be well provided with gallant and able men, who might discharge that national trust with brave success, and yet with great splendour and much ease. Were that done, young scholars at the university would prepare themselves for school, as for a handsome preferment; whereas now nothing but pure necessity can put them upon that way. They would practise to talk Latin fluently, that they might readily entertain any stranger (which now many that have the reputation of good scholars are but clumsy in) and pour forth verses and declamations *ex tempore*; they would study the classical authors thoroughly and digest them, acquaint themselves with all the critical parts of philology and the elegancies of the language, and the customs of antiquity: how many Erasmuses and Melancthons and Scagligers and Puteans and Vossiusses should we have amongst us in a short time, if literature were but thus encouraged? Whereas now the pulpit is made their ultimate design; and when they set once a-preaching, they lay their studies of humanity aside.

Before I part with this, I must not forget one thing, which I take to be a main cause of the master's toil and the scholar's non-proficience: that as schools now are, the master takes too much upon him and more than he can possibly with any credit discharge; for you shall see in most schools but a master and an usher, and sometimes but one set over a company of boys whose capacities and ingenies may be sorted perhaps into seven or eight classes. It is not possible one or two men (let them work their hearts out) should suffice to this duty. Wherefore, if it were so ordered that every great school might have for each form a master, who might be as the intelligence of that sphere and wheel it about with him through the whole encyclopædia of school-learning (with a rector or president over them all), the work would go on with great facility and cheerfulness, and no less success.

This is the course which the Jesuits take and which makes them look'd on as the greatest masters of breeding up youth. And this would be very feasible, to have in every great town almost such a school, at least one or two in a county. To instance, what were it for King's College to supply Eton School, New College to supply Winchester School with half a dozen young masters, who might, as they ripened each his company, return back to his college and there, if his superiors shall judge fit, go on with those that are taken for the university through the course of philosophy. And so out of Christ Church in Oxford, and Trinity in Cambridge, seven or eight, or half a score young men should not be missed, who if they were employed at Westminster School, which furnishes both those colleges, might by dealing the work amongst so many hands make it very light and prosperous; and so of other free-schools, especially those that send scholars to certain colleges.

And this would be a pretty introduction of young masters of arts and bachelors into the world, and prepare them for a serious scene of action and keep them from growing musty in the university, where college-commons and the walks (if not good fellowship) indispose many for the duties of an active life; and to say truth, what have they those fellowships and allowances for but to serve the public, which they cannot do better at first setting out than in this way. And for places of lesser note, servitors, when they are arrived at degrees, may be sent to officiate for a time appointed and not have orders presently given them and to be put to their shifts (as heretofore) in the ministry, when their necessities recommended them to presbyterian families or poor populous corporations, where for a livelihood they studied *placentia*, preached down the church and preached up the kirk; for it has been observed that your factious little chaplains and the lecturers of your great towns proved the *boutefeus* of our late troubles. There being one or two such schools in each county, how easily will the gentry fall in, how readily the other sort of people, especially if such schools have some colleges in either university allotted for their preferment upon solemn probations, which may be easily contrived without breach of any statute. Nay, many colleges we see already so allotted, as those I mentioned before: so Saint John's for Merchant Taylors', Jesus College for the Welsh, Exeter for the Devonshire men &c., and why may not the rest be so ordered? And then for places of lesser note, as little market towns, &c. where there is a great number of children, and some that their parents would wish should do more than barely write and read, which we suppose is the clerk's work to teach them: there, as was said before, may be one or two other meaner persons with a less salary, who may be stinted too in their work, so as to teach only Latin according to grammar-rule; for those who would design further, should be obliged to attend the great schools; and no other school should have privilege to fit scholars for the university; by which means there would be a great concourse thither; and if the gentry were numerous, there might be provided masters of other faculties to take up their leisure hours and intervals of study; viz. a catechist, an arithmetician, a writing master, a master of fence, a dancing master, music masters, a rider of great horse, some old soldier to teach them their postures and to handle arms, &c. And besides this (which is the other advantage of your boarding schools) the benefits of air might be procured, in the summer quarter at least, by removing two or three miles out of the town to some convenient seat, which might with those improvements easily be purchased, as also other requisites provided for the ease and reputation of the masters and the benefit and advantage not of the scholars alone, but of those towns also where the schools are kept. Nor would this academical way tend at all to the diminution of the universities, but much advantage them in their repute by certain constant homages from all the schools in the nation, holding them *in capite*, governed by their missionaries and by their rules; and at last according to their demerit upon trial, expecting preferment from them, to which repute the mutual emulation of the masters in their several provinces being always *in fluxu* and not stationary, and the account that they must make to the college which sent them would very much conduce. Now those provinces or classes might be ordered according to the several stages scholars go in their school-learning, after some such draught as this:

The first class: grounds of grammar, declining nouns and verbs;
The second: congruity of Latin;
The third: propriety and phrase;
The fourth: oratory and rhetoric;
The fifth: poetry and verse;
The sixth: Greek grounds;
The seventh: dialect;
The eighth: antiquity and philology.

But this course may be left either to the arbitrary direction of the present master or else regulated by the head and seniors of the college to which that school shall appertain according to the occasion.

To make short, this last paragraph is offered as a scheme only upon sudden thought, on purpose to suggest to some more ingenious and better experienced head, to find out an expedient for preventing the masters' toil and yet assuring the success; nor has the whole discourse any other design than barely to represent some inconveniences in the managing of schools which are visible to any one but have not been taken public notice of by any; not that the writer of this is at all an opinionator of himself, or has the confidence of obtruding his crude and undigested sense upon the great council of the nation, or has indeed any concernment in the grievance further than his own children, whom he shall provide for, whether this have any effect or no, or can entertain any great hope to have this paper considered or looked on by any of those who may be concerned in the redress; much less was it in his aim to level satire at any one, any otherwise than honestly to discharge his own burdened thoughts, in resentment of that which his mind told him deserved to be the object of a public care, with the same freedom as he thought them. And if any one find himself aggrieved at the writer, he must not blame him for having a greater tenderness for the public good than for any private person; and withal let him take this character of him, that he is one bears that love to his country, that faith to his prince, that reverence to the church, and that honour for all true worth and desert, that he shall not be grieved himself to see his own interest, his reputation and dearest concerns lie bleeding for their sakes; and will readily allow his forgiveness for any unkindness any one shall do him on such a score.

Much more might be said concerning the exercises, especially such as are to be performed publicly, and concerning the discipline of schools by reward and punishment: wherein I should particularly advise that whipping might be, if not totally laid aside, at least very sparingly used, —and that upon moral transgressions, as swearing, thieving &c.—and then too by the hand of some servant, the beadle or lictor of the school, as an office in itself servile, not at all becoming either gentleman or divine to execute; or indeed become anything of ingenuity, either to act or suffer. Indeed the great indiscretion and intemperance of masters in that has brought a very great contempt and hatred upon the profession itself, and not to speak of the ill use some have made of it to lewdness (of which instances are not wanting, but that they are odious) it being a kind of uncovering nakedness; it does generally more hurt than good, by making those that are dull more dull, and dispiriting the ingenious; and truly, wicked boys (to whom it properly belongs) are by the frequency and commonness of it hardened; and being grown after a while shameless and senseless to the rod, having passed the last remedy (as this is accounted) do become incurable; whereas such are to be kept in a course of discipline, as not to be mended with the most severe inflictions of present smart, which is quickly worn off.

To these heads, and other expedients, I do not want store of observations taken up, both abroad from other countries and at home in our own, but think it best to reserve them till some other time, if occasion shall be offered. Again, I consider this is but a needless work peradventure; for when salaries are improved, the grounding methods settled, and masters well qualified, as to their abilities and affections, these masters will in their several companies for superstructure and discipline and other prudential ways better possibly consult for themselves than any bystander can. Let me add that in that method by me laid down, there is not any prejudice in the least intended to those masters who are at present in possession of public schools; but on the contrary great advantage of ease, of honour, and of profit. For supposing the number of schools be reduced to that paucity there mentioned, out of those masters might be chosen the *Scholarcha* or rector of each school and his colleagues too, *pro hac vice*, whose single forms would bring them in better returns than their whole huddle of scholars does now. Those of the lesser note might be planted in the lesser towns, and nothing to their loss. After these old standers were worn off the stage, then university men might take their *Qu.*

I shall conclude with an humble address to those in place and power (it being not impossible that some such may chance to let fall their eye upon this paper): that the honourable court of parliament would, as they tender the peace of three kingdoms and the preservation of their own good laws, lay to heart and take into serious consideration the necessity of wholesome institution for our children; that they would give public schools a public countenance, and remove those grievances which they labour under by settling handsome salaries and establishing some kind of uniformity; that they would not suffer those seeds to be scattered in the minds of youth which have in these late years produced such a harvest of mischiefs and confusions (upon this ground, that royal clemency is to be limited to persons, not extended to principles); that they would take up that noble design of perpetuating themselves in a well-bred posterity; and lastly, that they would not be slow in a business of so great and quick concernment, the hopes of the next age lying at stake, children growing up into men apace; and what is taken in now being hardly cured hereafter, the elder sort affording very few examples of conversion. That especially, that the right reverend and bishops would not only provide for the sheep but take care that the lambs may be fed, as the great shepherd and bishop gives them order; that they would in their dioceses visit schools as well as churches, and encourage youth in virtue; that they would please to use their power for detecting the frauds of trustees and restoring to schools their rights; and in fine, that they would enjoin their ordinaries to be very strict and careful what masters they admit, how they are qualified and affected to present government both of church and state; for he that is an enemy of one can be no friend to the other; and to call, especially all private teachers and schoolmasters (whatever their pretence may be) to a public account, it being found a task almost impossible by all methods the church of England can use to recover those persons to a sound orthodox sense whose childhood has been poisoned and prepossessed with schism.

Finis.

OMNIA COMESTA A BELO

Or an answer out of the west to a question out of the north wherein the earth is opened, and the napkin found, in which the trading talent of the nation hath been tied up, and lain hid for some years last passed; for want of which, all persons in England, from the tenant to the landlord, from the weaver to the merchant, have languished of a deep consumption.

Sir Francis Bacon, *Essay of Sedition and Troubles*, Chap.15, Pag.85. Above all things, good policy is to be used, that the treasure and monies in a state be not gathered into few hands, for otherwise a state may have a great stock and yet starve: and money is like muck, not good unless it be spread.

Idem, Pag.172. The blessings of Judah and Issachar will never meet, that the same people or nation should be both the lions whelp, and the ass between two burdens: neither will it be, that a people over-laid with taxes should ever become martial and valiant.

Hist. of Bell and the Dragon, Vers.8. So the king was wrath, and called for his priests, and said unto them, If ye tell me not who it is that hath devoured these expences, ye shall die. Vers.20,21. And the king said, I see the foot-steps of men, women and children: and the king was angry, and took the priests with their wives and children, who shewed him the privy door where they came in, and consumed such things as were upon the table.

Printed in the year, 1667.

Two editions of this anonymous pamphlet were printed in 1667. It shows one connection, at least, which the trading nonconformist drew between the enforcement of the Clarendon Code and the depression in business. England in 1667 had had three years of crisis, to which had contributed the Dutch wars, the great plague, the fire of London, the commerce-destroying Dutch fleet in the Thames, and a run on the goldsmiths.

In 1668 appeared *Et a Dracone: or, Some reflections upon a discourse called Omnia a Belo Comesta; containing some animadversions from the north, upon the letter out of the west. Correcting some mistakes, and aiming at a more full and certain discovery of the causes of the present want of money*, etc. It slyly agrees with most of the arguments in *Omnia*, but presents them in cooler fashion. It suggests that political prosperity can come only through preserving and increasing the trading stock of the nation, and that the church of England exhausts that stock by persecuting the nation's most active traders. It is a plea for tolerance from civil magistrates, and effectively argues that the enforcement of the Code is irrational and cannot prevent the spread of blasphemy or error, for they are simply opinions which change with the age.

In 1679, under the title *Omnia Comesta a Bello*, the pamphlet was twice reprinted. In that day of plots it called forth an ingenious reply, *Ananias and Saphira discovered, or, The true intent of a pamphlet called Omnia Comesta a Belo: in a letter by way of answer*. Its Tory author maintained that the original of 'this poor spiteful pamphlet' was printed at the outbreak of the rebellion to usher in the covenant, and that it is a device of the catholics to divide the church: 'the papist is the manager of all this controversy.'

SIR,

I must beg your pardon that I have so long tired your expectations, and which is worse have altogether failed them except the few scraps you find in this reply will stop the mouth of your first query; for as to the four last, I have neither time nor capacity to send you any thing that may claim the title of a resolve.

Yet that others more able may contribute towards an answer to your so seasonable and rational demands, and that you may not think I have forgot them, I shall here insert them in order as you proposed.

Query I.

Whether the great cause of impoverishing the nation, ruin of trade, and general consumption of comfort, settlement and content, which hath brought the land to a mere anatomy, is not caused by the pomp, pride, luxury, exaction and oppressions of the prelates?

Query II.

Whether, since all other reformed churches in Europe, did upon the first reformation and departure from popery, cast out all diocesan bishops, name and thing, root and branch, as an office altogether popish, together with all their hierarchical appurtenances and do to this day esteem of them no otherwise; why did not, or doth not England also do the like?

Query III.

Whether the several reformed countries beyond the seas did not take into the hands of their supreme governors all the lordly revenues of the prelates, and reserve them for public use, or dispose part of them to such persons as had well deserved of them, in the faithful service of their country; and if so, whether it might not be of good and great concern to this kingdom, for the lordships and baronies belonging to so many useless persons, to be disposed of by public authority, for public good; and more especially for the honourable maintenance of those worthy persons and their posterity, who have lost their blood and estates in the king's service, and at present lie under great discouragements, and bleeding wounds in their temporals, for want of a suitable recompense: whilst these who put them altogether never did half the service, nor if occasion should require, never can, as one of these heroic gentlemen, yet as ecclesiastics are rewarded with 2,3,4,5,6,7,8, thousand pounds *per annum,* a man?

Query IV.

Whether in those kingdoms and states where prelacy is extirpated, and a presbytery only retained, there be not as godly, able, orthodox preachers and as constant preaching as in this kingdom; and more especially, whether their subjects are not as cordially obedient, and as free from any rebellion as in these places where bishops are retained? And also whether the councils are not more free from molestations, their nobility and gentry free from affronts, and the commonalty more free from oppression where the prelates are disabled from sitting in council, from perking above the nobles, and from imposing upon the commons?

Query V.

Whether the present state of affairs in our neighbour nations, especially of France, who have a prodigious victorious army, a fleet still lying at Rochelle, a fit place from whence to invade us; and the great industry of the pope employed to divert their arms from Spain, and turning them upon some other design; whether I say it be not reasonable to consider of some way to engage all hearts and hands in this nation unanimously to oppose all invasions, rather than to multiply discouragements upon the body of the people by episcopal oppressions?

In answer to your first, I am by many reasons induced to conclude in the affirmative, That the cause of impoverishing the nation, ruin of trade, and general consumption of comfort, settlement, and content is caused by the pomp, pride, luxury, exaction, and oppression of the prelates.

It is a true maxim of the learned Verulam, ' A smaller number that spend more, and earn less, do wear out an estate sooner than a greater number that live lower and gather more: so it is with an over-grown clergy, for they bring nothing to the stock.'

That the trading stock of the nation is devoured in this prelatical gulf I shall demonstrate by laying open to view the black back-door and sink that hath drained the trading purse dry.

First, The revenues, pomp, and state of the prelates.

There are two provincial archbishops, Canterbury and York, with their princely retinue, domestic chaplains, officers for temporalities, their spiritual officers, vicar-general, guardian of the spiritualities, dean of the arches, with all their under officers and attendants.

Secondly, his courts.

> Court of faculties.
> Court of audience.
> Prerogative court.
> Delegates.

There are four and twenty bishops diocesan, with their trains, domestic servants, chaplains, officers, and courts.

To these belong,
26   chancellors and their attendants.
24   registers with their clerks.
24   gentlemen apparators.
120 inferior apparators.
48   proctors.

There are under these bishops,
60 archdeacons, and these have 60 courts, to which belong
> commissaries.
> officials.
> surrogates.
> 60 registers.
> 120 proctors.
> 200 apparators.

So that the number belonging to archbishops, bishops, archdeacons and their trade, are judged to be no less than ten thousand persons, which will require for their maintenance two hundred thousand pounds *per annum*, reckoning them at twenty pounds a man; whereas some of them have one hundred pounds, some two hundred pounds, some four hundred pounds, squeezed out of the poor people.

As for their standing rents they are well known.

Their lordly palaces, sumptuous houses, ecclesiastical dignities, baronies, &c. *vii. s. & modis*, such is their income that it amounts at least to four hundred and fifty thousand pounds a year.

They have many other ways to enrich themselves and impoverish the nation, as

First,

By ordaining deacons and ministers four times a year for money, by which they put up yearly hundreds of pounds.

Secondly,

By instituting and inducting parsons and vicars to benefices when they fall. For every such institution and induction they have three pounds at least. And in England there are 9285 parishes, so that at the rate of one in a parish, it amounts to twenty-seven thousand eight hundred fifty-five pounds.

Thirdly,

By making rural deans yearly, and for the oath taking, they pay eight shillings and six pence.

Fourthly,

By granting licences to beneficed ministers to preach in their own cures; though they be ordained before and strictly commanded to preach, yet they must not do it without a licence, and this licence costs them ten shillings, so that in 9285 parishes this comes to four thousand six hundred forty-two pounds, ten shillings.

Fifthly,

By granting, 1. Licences to curates to preach.

   2. Licences for schoolmasters to teach school.

   3. Licences for parish clerks.

   4. Licences to physicians to practise physic.

5. Licences to midwives to do their office.

6. Licences to marry, which thing of itself ariseth to a vast revenue.

For absolving excommunicated persons.

For putting men to clear themselves by oath, with their compurgators.

For commutation of penance, for so the rich come off with a round sum of money, but the poor doing their penance in kind, must stand excommunicated until they have paid their fees.

Sixthly,

By probates of wills, and granting letters of administration, which brings in constantly great sums of money.

Seventhly,

By framing new articles and forcing churchwardens to present upon oath whereby many innocent persons are brought into their courts, and squeezed both in conscience and purse; and so is the churchwarden also, if he do not take the oath prepared for him.

By their visitations for money.

First, churchwardens of every parish in England and chapel are called, who receive a book of articles to present by; if any are wanting, they are warned to appear at their courts with costs. These churchwardens pay for their book of articles every year, (though the very same) as also for writing their presentments by a clerk (which they themselves could do, but are not permitted) two shillings four pence; which in 9285 parishes cometh to one thousand fifty-eight pounds odd money, yearly.

Secondly, ministers that are licensed pay one shilling eight pence, or thereabouts, for shewing their licence to preach to the register at every bishop's visitation, though seen and allowed before; after that four shillings for procuration to the bishop; and to the gentleman apparator eight pence, though most pay twelve pence.

I shall omit the poor curates' suit and service at this court, only let you know that when any archbishop comes newly to York, all the parsons and vicars in his jurisdiction, though never so poor, and their charge never so great, give him a tenth of their livings for a benevolence, to help the poor bishop to settle himself in five or six thousand pounds a year; and if any, yea, the meanest vicar, whose poor children want bread, do through poverty omit the payment, this reverend father doth pitifully whip him to the very bones in his merciless spiritual court.

By archdeacons visitations.

These are twice a year. At Easter visitation the ministers pay their Pascal rents or synodals, which sums are not alike to all; some pay fifty-six, some less.

At Michaelmas they pay procurations, some seven shillings, some ten shillings, some less. But it is judged that ministers pay yearly at visitations five thousand pounds and upwards.

By the vast charges in collegiate churches.

There are twenty-six great deans with their attendants and servants, 544 canons, residents and prebendaries, with a numerous train of vicars, petti-canons, singing men and boys, choristers, organists, gospellers, epistlers, vergers.

Now this jovial crew have belonging to them about four hundred thousand pounds yearly in lands, rents, leases, and other revenues and profits thereunto belonging.

The excessive expenses that many thousand of the trading people of the nation are put unto, by the rigorous and tyrannical proceedings of the bishops, in excommunicating persons, for three pence, six pence, and very trivial things.

A catalogue may shortly be presented to you of the many families already undone by them; wherein it will be made manifest that more families have been ruined, more persons imprisoned, more money spent by the cruelty of the prelates' proceedings, than by all law-suits in all courts of judicature, all payments and taxes whatsoever, except upon the late extraordinary occasion.

The vast sums of money that the bishops, deans, &c. have treasured up, extorting it from the subjects for fines.

You know that for twenty years sometime by-past, their revenues were alienated and sold for great sums of money to the natives of England. Those who bought them had greatly improved them, who being some thousands of families, are undone by being turned out without any consideration. The bishops enter at a time when most of the old leases were expired, they proclaim their markets, he that gives most, friend or foe, he shall be taken tenant; they screw up the value to the height, and hereby they have drained out of the people's purses such sums of money, that amounts to so monstrous a mass that scarce any prince's treasury in Europe is able to balance it; in the mean time the money that before ran current in trading is damned up in their coffers.

Hereby the money that should carry on trade is ingrossed into the hands of a few rusty ecclesiastics, who neither serve our Lord Jesus Christ nor their country, but their own bellies, and hoard up the riches that should be as the blood in the vena ptora, to be distributed into every vein and part of the body; but by being choked up in their corban brings the whole nation into a consumption.

And it's very considerable that in all other trades men have something for their money: the farmer hath good lands for his money from the gentleman; the clothier hath good wool from the farmer for his money; the merchant hath good cloth from the clothier for his money; and thus it goes round to every one's benefit. But pray, what have we from the bishops for our money? The answer will readily be made by the major part of the land.

First,

We have all our able, godly, orthodox ministers turned out, ruined and beggared, and no manner of supply provided for the maintenance of them and their families; and in their rooms in many places a company of debauched, illiterate, superstitious, profane priests, which, blind-guides, must needs lead them that follow them to hell.

Secondly,

We have gotten most of our churchwardens perjured that do swear to present according to their visitation articles, and most of them undone that do not swear; although the imposing of such an oath is a breach of the fundamental laws of the land. Those churchwardens that are not perjured, but pursue the oath in persecuting their neighbours, are plunged into such horrid guilt, that without serious repentance, they must perish eternally, for they persecute the godly for godliness' sake, the righteous for righteousness' sake, as will appear in these following instances.

I. If a minister never so godly and able, yea, though ordained, preach without a licence from the bishop, the churchwarden is bound to present him and bring him into trouble; if he preach in a cloak and not in a garment canonical, he is bound to do the like.

II. If any person go to hear a sermon from his own parish church, though there be no preaching minister there, nor no sermon at all; and though he be bound by his vow in baptism to hear sermons, this man is to be presented.

III. If a poor man that hath not bread for his family but what he earneth by his daily labour, if he work upon a holy-day, appointed by Romish institution, he is to be presented.

IV. If any person coming to church to their service do not stand up at the creed, do not bow at the name of Jesus, do not keep off his hat all the while, he must be presented.

Now there are in all, threescore and fourteen thousand churchwardens and sides-men in England every year, and what a dreadful thing is it to have all these yearly either perjured, persecuted, or persecutors.

Thirdly,

We have gotten most of the sober trading part of the nation discouraged by citations, excommunications, writs to take them excommunicated, imprisonments upon ecclesiastical accounts; by this means thousands of families are already ruined, and many hundreds are ready to leave the land and remove into some other country, where they may have liberty of conscience and freedom from these devouring harpies.

Fourthly,

We have got instead of the gospel in the power and purity of it, a service collected out of the Romish books, the mass, breviary, &c. which service of ours King James called an ill-sung mass. We have got surplices, copes, tippets, cringings, &c. out of the Romish rituals, insomuch that the papists themselves call it an apish imitation of the mass.

Fifthly,

We have gotten a swarm of ecclesiastical officers which the Scriptures never knew, nor reformed churches ever owned.

Sixthly,

We have got a sort of proud prelates of mean extract, not of the highest rank for godliness, learning, and labour in the world, not the greatest champions for the protestant religion; witness their silence at such a time when popery hath so travailed to bring forth; so many popish books printed and published in England in affront and contempt of the reformed religion, yet not one of our bishops hath stood up in opposition to their design, nor printed any caution against popery or answer to the popish pernicious pamphlets. However very elate they are, affronting our nobility, trampling upon our gentry, grinding to powder all that put not into their mouths or offer not at their shrine; insomuch that a gentleman of quality, a person of £3000 *per annum*, speaking to one of the said prelates (lately dead) boldly, but with due respect; the prelate, in a fume, answered, ' What, Sir, do you think that it is fit for every jack-gentleman to speak thus to a bishop '; deriding the gentry of our land as not worthy to speak to a peevish prelate. Surely a gentleman of £500 *per annum* would have fallen under censure for presuming to speak to his postilion.

We have gotten all manner of misery to soul and body, plague, fire, sword, universal beggary, and without seasonable mercy, the total ruin of the whole kingdom.

But I know you will question, whether our miseries do arise from the cause assigned?

To this I answer the manifold provoking sins of the land, as adultery, blasphemy, swearing, idolatry, perjury, and contempt of God and godliness, do pull hard with heaven to bring down desolating judgments. But that the nearest cause of our impoverishments ariseth from the particular forementioned, will appear if you weigh the premises before inferred, and give them leave to speak their own conclusion: if perjury causeth a land to mourn, if oppression and rigid persecution upon the trading part of a land begets discontent and deserting of trade; if rigorous exacting and sordid hoarding up the money that should run current in trade, and that by such who contribute nothing to the public weal, be the bane of traffic, and the famishment of the poor handicrafts man, then we may lay all our calamities at the bishops' doors.

I shall call in some credible witnesses, divines, and martyrs to confirm this truth, and so leave it with you.

Bishop Jewel on Hag.I. records out of Johannes Parisiensis and others, ' That when Constantine the Great advanced bishops and endowed the church with lands and temporal possessions, there was a voice of angels heard in the air, saying, *hodie venenum infunditum in ecclesiam*, this day poison is poured into the church.'

Bernard writes, ' Since prelates increased in worldly pomp, choosing the first places in the church, they have been the chiefest in persecuting Jesus Christ; and have ever showed themselves not teachers but deceivers; not pastors but impostors; not prelates but Pilates; succeeding not Peter in teaching, but Romulus in murdering.'

Lord Cobham, that faithful martyr, saith to the bishops, ' No ground have ye in all the scriptures, so lordly to take it upon you, but in Annas and Caiaphas, who sat in judgment upon Christ and his apostles, of them only have you taken it to judge Christ's members as ye do.'

Mr. Tindal, that godly and learned martyr, writeth, ' Woe to the realm where prelates are of the council! As profitable are the prelacy to the realm with their counsel, as wolves to the sheep or foxes to the geese; for there is no mischief or disorder, whether it be in the temporal regiment or spiritual, whereof they are not the chief causes, and even the very fountain and spring; so that it is impossible to preach against any mischief, except thou begin at them; or to set up any reformation in the world, except they are first reformed: they are as indurate as Pharaoh; and therefore persecute they God's word and the preachers thereof; they stir up mischief in the world, setting princes to war; they get into the consciences of kings, and persuade them what they list, neither can any king have rest for them; they pretend they are for God and the church, but their secret intent is to bring all under their power; and when they once are set high, then are they tyrants above all tryants.'

Mr. John Frith, that worthy martyr, in his answer to Mr. More's Preface: ' Since Sylvester received such possessions hath the canker so crept into the church that it hath almost left never a sound member; then instead of God's word they preached their own commandments, and made laws to have all under them; and even as in the rooms of Moses, Aaron, Joshua, Caleb and other such faithful leaders, came Herod, Annas, Caiaphas, Pilate and Judas, which put Christ to death: so now instead of Christ, Peter, Paul, James, John, and the faithful followers of Christ, we have popes, cardinals, archbishops, and proud prelates with their proctors and malicious ministers of their master the devil, whose end shall be according to their works.'

Dr. Barnes in his supplication to Henry the eighth, ' Now it is so far come, that whosoever he be, high or low, rich or poor, wise or foolish, that speaketh against the prelates and their vicious living, he is either made a traitor to your grace, or an heretic, enemy or schismatic against holy church; as though the prelates were kings or gods: and if any man out of God's law and right conscience speak against their damnable tyranny, little will they stick to make him an heretic; and if that will not help to colour and maintain their oppression, then add they treason, sedition, rebellion, and contempt of your grace, though he be never so true a subject.'

I shall conclude with a passage of learned Mr. Tindal in his *Obedience to a Christian Magistrate*, pp.114,128,146.

' As thou canst heal no disease except thou begin at the root, even so canst thou preach against no mischief except thou begin at the bishops; whether Judas was a priest or no I care not, but of this I am sure, that he now is not only priest, but also a bishop, cardinal, and pope. Bishops that preach not, or that preach aught save God's word, are none of Christ's nor of his anointing, but servants of the beast whose mark they bear, whose word they preach, whose law they maintain, clean against God's law: bishops they are that can only minister the temporal sword, their office, the preaching of God's word laid aside; which they will neither do themselves, nor suffer any man else to do, but slay with the temporal sword (which they have gotten out of the hands of all princes) them that would. The preaching of God's word is hateful to them. Why? For it is impossible to preach Christ except thou preach against antichrist; that is to say them who with their false doctrine and violence of sword enforce to quench the true doctrine of Christ. Our prelates ought to be our servants as the apostles were, to teach us Christ's doctrine, and not Lords over us to oppress us with their own doctrines and inventions.'

Finis.

THE HISTORY OF THE ROYAL SOCIETY OF LONDON

For the improving of natural knowledge, by Tho. Sprat. London. Printed by T.R. for J.Martyn at the Bell without Temple-bar, and J.Allestry at the Rose and Crown in Duck-lane, Printers to the Royal Society. MDCLXVII.

THOMAS SPRAT (1635–1713), the son of a country parson of Beaminster, Dorset, matriculated at Wadham College, Oxford, became B.A. in 1654, and was a fellow from 1657 to 1670. There he knew the enlightened men, among them Dr. Wilkins, the warden, who promoted the Royal Society. Versatile, tactful, and facile with tongue and pen, Sprat had a knack for sensing the spirit of his environment and for attaching himself to useful friends. His laudatory poem on Cromwell was printed in 1659, with others by Dryden and Waller, and his poetic talent was nurtured by his intimacy with Crowley. His patron, the duke of Buckingham, whom he assisted in writing the *Rehearsal*, made Sprat his chaplain in 1661.

When Charles II visited Wadham in 1663, ' Sprat spoke a speech,' and the same year was proposed by Dr. Wilkins and elected to the Royal Society. Aided by John Evelyn, he patriotically refuted de Sorbières' critical observations on England, and went on, with a ' bold and liberal spirit,' to champion the new thought of the age in his *History of the Royal Society* (1667), from which the following selections are taken. Written in a style deliberately meant to be a return to ' primitive purity,' to ' a close, naked, natural way of speaking,' Sprat so exalted the pursuit of truth in this ' learned and inquisitive age ' that no book better reflects its temper.

Ecclesiastical preferment followed quickly. Sprat received from Oxford in 1669 both the B.D. and D.D. degrees, became a royal chaplain in 1676, dean of Westminster in 1683, and bishop of Rochester in 1684. For Charles II he wrote an exposé of the Rye House Plot, but he discreetly evaded James II's request that he do Monmouth's rebellion. He accepted in 1686 the hazardous appointment to the revived court of high commission, either because tempted by the vacant see of York, or as he declared two years later, in order to restrain his colleagues from violent action. He read the Declaration, he even drafted a prayer for the birth of James' son, but in 1689 he found no difficulty in taking the oaths to William and Mary and retaining his bishopric.

Sprat spent freely, rebuilding parts of Westminster Abbey and the episcopal palace at Bromley, lived handsomely himself, and died of apoplexy. His will prescribed that his body should ' be deposited in some place in Westminster Abbey . . . with as moderate expense on my funeral as is consistent with the most private decency.'

To The
KING.

SIR,

Of all the kings of Europe, your majesty was the first who confirm'd this noble design of experiments, by your own example, and by a public establishment; an enterprise equal to the most renowned actions of the best princes. For, to increase the powers of all mankind and to free them from the bondage of errors is greater glory than to enlarge empire, or to put chains on the necks of conquered nations.

What reverence all antiquity had for the authors of natural discoveries is evident by the diviner sort of honour they conferred on them. Their founders of philosophical opinions were only admired by their own sects. Their valiant men and generals did seldom rise higher than to demi-gods and heroes. But the gods they worshipped with temples and altars were those who instructed the world to plow, to sow, to plant, to spin, to build houses, and to find out new countries. This zeal, indeed, by which they expressed their gratitude to such benefactors, degenerated into superstition: yet has it taught us, that a higher degree of reputation is due to discoverers than to the teachers of speculative doctrines, nay even to conquerors themselves.

Nor has the true God himself omitted to show his value of vulgar arts. In the whole history of the first monarchs of the world, from Adam to Noah, there is no mention of their wars, or their victories: all that is recorded is this, they lived so many years and taught their posterity to keep sheep, to till the ground, to plant vineyards, to dwell in tents, to build cities, to play on the harp and organs, and to work in brass and iron. And if they deserved a sacred remembrance for one natural or me-chanical invention, your majesty will certainly obtain immortal fame for having established a perpetual succession of inventors.

I am
(May it please your majesty)
Your majesty's most humble
and most obedient
subject and servant,
THO. SPRAT.

13—The illustration opposite is the frontispiece to the first, 1667, edition of Sprat's *History of the Royal Society*. It was designed by John Evelyn, the diarist and a charter member of the society, and engraved by Wenceslaus Hollar (see illustration 5, note). Lord Brouncker, the first president of the organization, is depicted on the left; the central bust, in the new classic manner, represents the royal patron, Charles II; and Francis Bacon, whose imaginary ' Solomon's House,' an academy of wisdom, is said to have suggested the forming of the Royal Society, appears on the right. The classic architectural forms reflect the Anglo-classic style being promoted by Christopher Wren, a fellow of the Royal Society, and the many instruments of admensuration are more than mere symbols of the purpose and activities of the then recently founded scientific academy.

CAROLVS
II.
SOCIETATIS
REGALIS
AVTHOR
&
PATRONVS

SOCIETATIS PRÆSES   ARTIVM INSTAVRATOR

Evelyn inv D.D.C.   Wenceslaus Hollar f. 1667

The

HISTORY

of the

ROYAL SOCIETY.

The Second Part.

SECTION I. THE DIVISION OF THE NARRATION.

THUS I am, at length, arrived at the second part of my method, the narration itself. This I shall divide into three periods of time according to the several degrees of the preparation, growth, and complete constitution of the Royal Society.

The first shall consist of the first occasions of this model and the men who first devised to put it in execution: and shall end where they began to make it a formed and regular assembly.

The second shall trace out their first attempts, till they received the public assistance of royal authority.

The third shall deliver what they have done since they were made a royal corporation.

It may seem, perhaps, that in passing through the first of these, I go too far back and treat of things that may appear to be of too private and domestic concernment to be spoken in this public way. But if this enterprise, which is now so well established, shall be hereafter advantageous to mankind (as I make no scruple to foretell that it will), it is but just that future times should hear the names of its first promoters: that they may be able to render particular thanks to them who first conceived it in their minds and practised some little draught of it long ago. And besides, I never yet saw an historian that was clear from all affections: that, it may be, were not so much to be called integrity as a stoical insensibility: nor can I, more than others, resist my inclinations which strongly force me to mention that which will be for the honour of that place where I received a great part of my education. It was therefore some space after the end of the civil wars at Oxford, in Dr. Wilkins his lodgings in Wadham College, which was then the place of resort for virtuous and learned men, that the first meetings were made which laid the foundation of all this that followed. The university had, at that time, many members of its own who had begun a free way of reasoning; and was also frequented by some gentlemen of philosophical minds whom the misfortunes of the kingdom and the security and ease of a retirement amongst gown-men had drawn thither.

SECT.II. THE MEETINGS AT OXFORD.

Their first purpose was no more than only the satisfaction of breathing a freer air, and of conversing in quiet one with another, without being engaged in the passions and madness of that dismal age. And from the institution of that assembly, it had been enough if no other advantage had come, but this: that by this means there was a race of young men provided against the next age, whose minds, receiving from them their first impressions of sober and generous knowledge, were invincibly armed against all the enchantments of enthusiasm. But what is more, I may venture to affirm that it was in good measure by the influence which these gentlemen had over the rest, that the university itself, or at least any part of its discipline and order, was saved from ruin. And from hence we may conclude that the same men have now no intention of sweeping away all the honour of antiquity in this their new design: seeing they employed so much of their labour and prudence in preserving that most venerable seat of ancient learning, when their shrinking from its defence would have been the speediest way to have destroyed it. For the truth of this, I dare appeal to all uninterested men, who knew the temper of that place, and especially to those who were my own contemporaries there: of whom I can name very many, whom the happy restoration of the kingdom's peace found as well inclined to serve their prince and the church, as if they had been bred up in the most prosperous condition of their country. This was undoubtedly so. Nor indeed could it be otherwise: for such spiritual frenzies, which did then bear rule, can never stand long before a clear and a deep skill in nature. It is almost impossible, that they, who converse much with the subtlety of things, should be deluded by such thick deceits. There is but one better charm in the world than real philosophy to allay the impulses of the false spirit: and that is the blessed presence and assistance of the true.

Nor were the good effects of this conversation only confined to Oxford: but they have made themselves known in their printed works, both in our own and in the learned language: which have much conduced to the fame of our nation abroad, and to the spreading of profitable light at home. This I trust will be universally acknowledged, when I shall have named the men. The principal and most constant of them were Doctor Seth Ward, the present lord bishop of Exeter, Mr. Boyle, Dr. Wilkins, Sir William Petty, Mr. Matthew Wren, Dr. Wallis, Dr. Goddard, Dr. Willis, Dr. Bathurst, Dr. Christopher Wren, Mr. Rook, besides several others who joined themselves to them upon occasions. Now I have produced their names, I am a little at a stand how to deal with them. For, if I should say what they deserve, I fear it would be interpreted flattery instead of justice. And yet I have now lying in my sight the example of an elegant book which I have professed to admire: whose author sticks not to make large panegyrics on the members of that assembly, whose relation he writes. But this precedent is not to be followed by a young man, who ought to be more jealous of public censure and is not enough confirmed in the good liking of the world to think that he has such a weighty and difficult work as the making of characters committed to him. I will therefore pass by their praises in silence, though I believe that what I might say of them would be generally confessed: and that if any ingenuous man who knows them or their writings should contradict me, he would also go near to gainsay himself and to retract the applauses which he had sometime or other bestowed upon them.

For such a candid and unpassionate company as that was, and for such a gloomy season, what could have been a fitter subject to pitch upon than natural philosophy? To have been always tossing about some theological question would have been to have made that their private diversion, the excess of which they themselves disliked in the public. To have been eternally musing on civil business and the distresses of their country was too melancholy a reflection. It was nature alone which could pleasantly entertain them in that estate. The contemplation of that draws our minds off from past or present misfortunes and makes them conquerors over things in the greatest public unhappiness: while the consideration of men and humane affairs may affect us with a thousand various disquiets, that never separates us into mortal factions; that gives us room to differ, without animosity, and permits us to raise contrary imaginations upon it without any danger of a civil war.

Their meetings were as frequent as their affairs permitted: their proceedings rather by action than discourse, chiefly attending some particular trials in chemistry or mechanics: they had no rules nor method fixed: their intention was more to communicate to each other their discoveries which they could make in so narrow a compass, than an united, constant, or regular inquisition. And methinks their constitution did bear some resemblance to the academy lately begun at Paris, where they have at last turned their thoughts from words to experimental philosophy, and perhaps in imitation of the Royal Society. Their manner likewise is to assemble in a private house to reason freely upon the works of nature, to pass conjectures, and propose problems on any mathematical or philosophical matter which comes in their way. And this is an omen on which I will build some hope, that as they agree with us in what was done at Oxford, so they will go on farther, and come by the same degrees to erect another Royal Society in France. I promise for these gentlemen here (so well I know the generosity of their design) that they will be most ready to accept their assistance. To them and to all the learned world besides, they call for aid. No difference of country, interest, or profession of religion will make them backward from taking or affording help in this enterprise. And indeed all Europe at this time have two general wars which they ought in honour to make: the one a holy, the other a philosophical: the one against the common enemy of Christendom, the other also against powerful and barbarous foes that have not been fully subdued almost these six thousand years, ignorance and false opinions. Against these it becomes us to go forth in one common expedition, all civil nations joining their armies against the one, and their reason against the other without any petty contentions about privileges or precedence.

SECT. III. THEIR FIRST MEETINGS AT LONDON.

Thus they continued without any great intermissions till about the year 1658. But then being called away to several parts of the nation, and the greatest number of them coming to London, they usually met at Gresham College, at the Wednesdays' and Thursdays' lectures of Dr. Wren and Mr. Rook: where there joined with them several eminent persons of their common acquaintance: the Lord Viscount Brouncker, the now Lord Brereton, Sir Paul Neil, Mr. John Evelyn, Mr. Henshaw, Mr. Slingsby, Dr. Timothy Clark, Dr. Ent, Mr. Ball, Mr. Hill, Dr. Crone, and divers other gentlemen whose inclinations lay the same way. This custom was observed once, if not twice, a week in term time, till they were scattered by the miserable distractions of that fatal year, till the continuance of their meetings there might have made them run the hazard of the fate of Archimedes: for then the place of their meeting was made a quarter for soldiers. But (to make haste through those dreadful revolutions, which cannot be beheld upon paper without horror, unless we remember that they had this one happy effect, to open men's eyes to look out for the true remedy) upon this followed the king's return, and that wrought by such an admirable chain of events, that if we either regard the easiness, or speed, or blessed issue of the work, it seems of itself to contain variety and pleasure enough to make recompense for the whole twenty years' melancholy that had gone before. This I leave to another kind of history to be described. It shall suffice my purpose that philosophy had its share in the benefits of that glorious action: for the Royal Society had its beginning in the wonderful, pacific year, 1660. So that, if any conjectures of good fortune, from extraordinary nativities, hold true, we may presage all happiness to this undertaking. And I shall here join my solemn wishes that as it began in that time when our country was freed from confusion and slavery: so it may, in its progress, redeem the minds of men from obscurity, uncertainty, and bondage.

SECT.IV. THE BEGINNING OF THE ROYAL SOCIETY.

These gentlemen, therefore, finding the hearts of their countrymen enlarged by their joys and fitted for any noble proposition, and meeting with the concurrence of many worthy men, who, to their immortal honour, had followed the king in his banishment, Mr. Erskins, Sir Robert Moray, Sir Gilbert Talbot, etc., began now to imagine some greater thing; and to bring out experimental knowledge from the retreats, in which it had long hid itself, to take its part in the triumphs of that universal jubilee. And indeed philosophy did very well deserve that reward, having been always loyal in the worst of times: for though the king's enemies had gained all other advantages, though they had all the garrisons, and fleets, and ammunitions, and treasures, and armies on their side, yet they could never, by all their victories, bring over the reason of men to their party.

While they were thus ordering their platform, there came forth a treatise which very much hastened its contrivance: and that was a proposal by Master Cowley of erecting a philosophical college. The intent

of it was that in some place near London there should liberal salaries be
bestowed on a competent number of learned men, to whom should be
committed the operations of natural experiments. This model was every
way practicable: unless, perhaps, in two things he did more consult the
generosity of his own mind, than of other men's: the one was the largeness
of the revenue, with which he would have his college at first endowed:
the other, that he imposed on his operators a second task of great pains,
the education of youth.

The last of these is indeed a matter of great weight: the reformation
of which ought to be seriously examined by prudent men. For it is an
undeniable truth, which is commonly said, that there would be need
of fewer laws and less force to govern men, if their minds were rightly
informed and set straight while they were young and pliable. But perhaps
this labour is not so proper for experimenters to undergo: for it would
not only devour too much of their time: but it would go near to make
them a little more magisterial in philosophy than became them, by being
long accustomed to command the opinions and direct the manners of
their scholars. And as to the other particular, the large estate which he
required to the maintenance of his college: it is evident, that it is so difficult a thing to draw men in to be willing to divert an ancient revenue
which had long run in another stream, or to contribute out of their own
purses, to the supporting of any new design, while it shows nothing but
promises and hopes: that, in such cases, it were (it may be) more advisable
to begin upon a small stock, and so to rise by degrees, than to profess
great things at first, and to exact too much benevolence all in one lump
together. However, it was not the excellent author's fault that he thought
better of the age than it did deserve. His purpose in it was, like himself,
full of honour and goodness: most of the other particulars of his draft
the Royal Society is now putting in practice.

I come now to the second period of my narration, wherein I promised
to give an account of what they did till they were publicly owned, encouraged, and confirmed by royal favour. And I trust that I shall here
produce many things which will prove their attempts to be worthy of all
men's encouragement: though what was performed in this interval may
be rather styled the temporary scaffold about the building than the frame
itself. But in my entrance upon this part, being come to the top of the
hill, I begin to tremble and to apprehend the greatness of my subject.

For I perceive that I have led my readers' minds on by so long and so confident a speech to expect some wonderful model, which shall far exceed all the former, that I have acknowledged to have been imperfect. Now, though this were really so, as I believe it is, yet I question how it will look after it has been disfigured by my unskilful hands. But the danger of this ought to have deterred me in the beginning. It is now too late to look back, and I can only apply myself to that good nature which a great man has observed to be so peculiar to our nation, that there is scarce an expression to signify it in any other language. To this I must fly for succour and most affectionately entreat my countrymen that they would interpret my failings to be only errors of obedience to some whose commands or desires I could not resist: and that they would take the measure of the Royal Society, not so much from my lame description of it, as from the honour and reputation of many of those men of whom it is composed.

SECT. V. A MODEL OF THEIR WHOLE DESIGN.

I will here, in the first place, contract into few words the whole sum of their resolutions, which I shall often have occasion to touch upon in parcels. Their purpose is, in short, to make faithful records of all the works of nature, or art, which can come within their reach: that so the present age, and posterity, may be able to put a mark on the errors which have been strengthened by long prescription: to restore the truths that have lain neglected: to push on those which are already known to more various uses: and to make the way more passable to what remains un-revealed. This is the compass of their design. And to accomplish this, they have endeavoured to separate the knowledge of nature from the colours of rhetoric, the devices of fancy, or the delightful deceit of fables. They have laboured to enlarge it from being confined to the custody of a few or from servitude to private interests. They have striven to preserve it from being over-pressed by a confused heap of vain and useless particulars, or from being straightened and bounded too much up by general doctrines. They have tried to put it into a condition of perpetual increasing, by settling an inviolable correspondence between the hand and the brain. They have studied to make it, not only an enterprise of one season, or of some lucky opportunity, but a business of time, a steady, a lasting, a popular, an uninterrupted work. They have attempted to free it from the artifice and humours and passions of sects, to render it an instrument whereby mankind may obtain a dominion over things, and not only over one another's judgments. And lastly, they have begun to establish these reformations in philosophy, not so much by any solemnity of laws or ostentation of ceremonies, as by solid practice and examples: not by a glorious pomp of words, but by the silent, effectual, and unanswerable arguments of real productions.

This will more fully appear by what I am to say on these four particulars, which shall make up this part of my relation, the qualifications of their members: the manner of their inquiry: their weekly assemblies: and their way of registering.

SECT. VI. THE QUALIFICATIONS OF THE MEMBERS OF THE ROYAL SOCIETY.

As for what belongs to the members themselves that are to constitute the society: it is to be noted that they have freely admitted men of different religions, countries, and professions of life. This they were obliged to do, or else they would come far short of the largeness of their own declarations. For they openly profess not to lay the foundation of an English, Scotch, Irish, popish, or protestant philosophy, but a philosophy of mankind.

THEY ADMIT MEN OF ALL RELIGIONS.

That the church of England ought not to be apprehensive of this free converse of various judgments, I shall afterwards manifest at large. For the present, I shall frankly assert that our doctrine and discipline will be so far from receiving damage by it, that it were the best way to make them universally embraced, if they were oftener brought to be canvassed amidst all sorts of dissenters. It is dishonourable to pass a hard censure on the religions of all other countries. It concerns them to look to the reasonableness of their faith, and it is sufficient for us to be established in the truth of our own. But yet this comparison I may modestly make, that there is no one profession, amidst the several denominations of Christians, that can be exposed to the search and scrutiny of its adversaries with so much safety as ours. So equal it is above all others to the general reason of mankind: such honourable security it provides, both for the liberty of men's minds and for the peace of government: that if some men's conceptions were put in practice, that all wise men should have two religions, the one a public, for their conformity with the people, the other a private, to be kept to their own breasts, I am confident that most considering men, whatever their first were, would make ours their second, if they were well acquainted with it. Seeing, therefore, our church would be in so fair a probability of gaining very much by a frequent contention and encounter with other sects, it cannot be endangered by this assembly, which proceeds no farther than to an unprejudiced mixture with them.

OF ALL COUNTRIES.

By their naturalizing men of all countries, they have laid the beginnings of many great advantages for the future. For by this means, they will be able to settle a constant intelligence throughout all civil nations and make the Royal Society the general bank and free-port of the world: a policy which, whether it would hold good in the trade of England, I know not: but sure it will in the philosophy. We are to overcome the mysteries of all the works of nature, and not only to prosecute such as are confined to one kingdom or beat upon one shore. We should not then refuse to list all the aids that will come in, how remote soever. If I could fetch my materials whence I pleased, to fashion the idea of a perfect philosopher: he should not be all of one clime, but have the different excellencies of several countries. First, he should have the industry, activity, and inquisitive humour of the Dutch, French, Scotch, and English, in laying the ground work, the heap of experiments: and then he should have added the cold, and circumspect, and wary disposition of the Italians and Spaniards, in meditating upon them, before he fully brings them into speculation. All this is scarce ever to be found in one single man: seldom in the same countrymen. It must then be supplied, as well as it may, by a public council, wherein the various dispositions of all these nations may be blended together. To this purpose the Royal Society has made no scruple to receive all inquisitive strangers of all countries into its number. And this they have constantly done, with such peculiar respect, that they have not obliged them to the charge of contributions: they have always taken care that some of their members should assist them in interpreting all that passed in their public assemblies: and they have freely opened their registers to them, thereby inviting them to communicate foreign rarities by imparting their own discoveries. This has been often acknowledged by many learned men who have travelled hither, who have been introduced to their meetings and have admired the decency, the gravity, the plainness, and the calmness of their debates. This they have published to the world: and this has roused all our neighbours to fix their eyes upon England. From hence they expect the great improvements of knowledge will flow: and though, perhaps, they send their youth into other parts to learn fashion and breeding: yet their men come hither for nobler ends, to be instructed in the masculine and the solid arts of life: which is a matter of as much greater reputation, as it is more honourable, to teach philosophers than children.

OF ALL PROFESSIONS.

By their admission of men of all professions, these two benefits arise: the one, that every art and every way of life already established may be secure of receiving no damage by their counsels, a thing which all new inventions ought carefully to consult. It is in vain to declare against the profit of the most, in any change that we would make. We must not always deal with the violent current of popular passions, as they do with the furious eager in the Severn: where the safest way is to set the head of the boat directly against its force. But here men must follow the shore, wind about leisurably, and insinuate their useful alterations by soft and unperceivable degrees. From the neglect of this prudence we often see men of great wit to have been overborne by the multitude of their opposers and to have found all their subtle projects too weak for custom and interest: while being a little too much heated with a love of their own fancies, they have raised to themselves more enemies than they needed to have done, by defying at once too many things in use. But here this danger is very well prevented. For what suspicion can divinity, law, or physic, or any other course of life have, that they shall be impaired by these men's labours: when they themselves are as capable of sitting amongst them as any others? Have they not the same security that the whole nation has for its lives and fortunes? Of which this is esteemed the establishment, that men of all sorts and qualities give their voice in every law that is made in parliament. But the other benefit is, that by this equal balance of all professions, there will no one particular of them over-weigh the other or make the oracle only speak their private sense: which else it were impossible to avoid. It is natural to all ranks of men to have some one darling upon which their care is chiefly fixed. If mechanics alone were to make a philosophy, they would bring it all into their shops and force it wholly to consist of springs and wheels and weights: if physicians, they would not depart far from their art; scarce anything would be considered besides the body of man, the causes, signs, and cures of diseases. So much is to be found in men of all conditions of that which is called pedantry in scholars: which is nothing else but an obstinate addiction to the forms of some private life and not regarding general things enough. This freedom therefore which they use in embracing all assistance is most advantageous to them: which is the more remarkable in that they diligently search out, and join to them, all extraordinary men, though but of ordinary trades. And that they are likely to continue this comprehensive temper hereafter, I will show by one instance: and it is the recommendation which the king himself was pleased to make of the judicious author of the *Observations on the Bills of Mortality*: in whose election it was so far from being a prejudice that he was a shopkeeper of London, that his majesty gave this particular charge to his society, that if they found any more such tradesmen, they should be sure to admit them all without any more ado. From hence it may be concluded what is their inclination towards the manual arts by the careful regard which their founder and patron has engaged them to have for all sorts of mechanic artists.

SECT. VII. IT CONSISTS CHIEFLY OF GENTLEMEN.

But, though the Society entertains very many men of particular professions, yet the far greater number are gentlemen, free and unconfined. By the help of this, there was hopeful provision made against two corruptions of learning which have been long complained of but never removed: the one, that knowledge still degenerates to consult present profit too soon; the other, that philosophers have been always masters and scholars, some imposing and all the others submitting, and not as equal observers without dependence.

THE ADVANTAGES OF THIS.

The first of these may be called the marrying of arts too soon and putting them to generation before they come to be of age and has been the cause of much inconvenience. It weakens their strength; it makes an unhappy disproportion in their increase, while not the best but the most gainful of them flourish. But above all, it diminishes that very profit for which men strive. It busies them about possessing some petty prize, while nature itself, with all its mighty treasures, slips from them: and so they are served like some foolish guards, who, while they were earnest in picking up some small money that the prisoner dropped out of his pocket, let the prisoner himself escape, from whom they might have got a great ransom. This is easily declaimed against, but most difficult to be hindered. If any caution will serve, it must be this: to commit the work to the care of such men who, by the freedom of their education, the plenty of their estates, and the usual generosity of noble blood, may be well supposed to be most averse from such sordid considerations.

The second error which is hereby endeavoured to be remedied is that the seats of knowledge have been for the most part heretofore not laboratories as they ought to be, but only schools, where some have taught and all the rest subscribed. The consequences of this are very mischievous. For first, as many learners as there are, so many hands and brains may still be reckoned upon as useless. It being only the masters' part to examine and observe, and the disciples' to submit with silence to what they conclude. But besides this, the very inequality of the titles of teachers and scholars does very much suppress and tame men's spirits, which though it should be proper for discipline and education, yet is by no means consistent with a free philosophical consultation. It is undoubtedly true that scarce any man's mind is so capable of thinking strongly in the presence of one whom he fears and reverences, as he is when that restraint is taken off. And this is to be found, not only in these weightier matters, but also (to give a lighter instance) in the arts of discourse and raillery themselves. For we have often seen men of bold tempers, that have over-awed and governed the wit of most companies, to have been disturbed and dumb and bashful as children when some other man has been near who used to out-talk them. Such a kind of natural sovereignty there is in some men's minds over others, which must needs be far greater when it is advanced by long use and the venerable name of a master. I shall only mention one prejudice more, and that is this: that from this only teaching and learning there does not only follow a continuance, but an increase of the yoke upon our reasons. For those who take their opinions from others' rules are commonly stricter imposers upon their scholars than their own authors were on them, or than the first inventors of things themselves are upon others. Whatever the cause of this be, whether the first men are made meek and gentle by their long search and by better understanding all the difficulties of knowledge, while those that learn afterwards only hastily catching things in small systems are soon satisfied before they have broken their pride, and so become more imperious: or whether it arises from hence, that the same meanness of soul which made them bound their thoughts by others' precepts makes them also insolent to their inferiors, as we always find cowards the most cruel: or whatever other cause may be alleged, the observation is certain that the successors are usually more positive and tyrannical than the beginners of sects.

If, then, there can be any cure devised for this, it must be no other than to form an assembly at one time whose privileges shall be the same, whose gain shall be in common, whose members were not brought up at the feet of each other. But after all, even this cannot be free from prevarication in all future ages. So apt are some to distrust and others to confide too much in themselves: so much sweetness there is in leading parties: so much pride in following a faction: such various artifices there are to ensnare men's passions and soon after their understandings. All these hazards and many more are to be supposed, which it is impossible for mortal wit wholly to foresee, much less to avoid. But yet we have less ground of jealousy from this institution than any other, not only because they only deal in matters of fact, which are not so easily perverted, but also upon security of the inclinations of the greatest part of the members of the Society itself. This, I hope, most men will acknowledge, and I will take the permission to say in general of them that in all past and present times, I am confident, there can never be shown so great a number of contemporaries in so narrow a space of the world that loved truth so zealously, sought it so constantly, and upon whose labours mankind might so freely rely. This I speak, not out of bravery to foreigners (before whose eyes I believe this negligent discourse will never appear) but to the learned men of this nation, who are better judges of what I say. And this too, I dare affirm, in an age wherein I expect to be condemned of falsehood or partiality for this character which I have given. For so it happens that we are now arrived at that excessive censuring humour that he who takes upon him to commend anything, though never so worthy, will raise to himself far more enemies than friends. And indeed this sourness of criticism, which now bears all down before it, is very injurious to the honour of our country. For by despising men for not being absolutely excellent, we keep them from being so: while admonitions joined with praises, and reproofs with directions, would quickly bring all things to a higher perfection. But the rudeness of such critics I do not so much regard, as the objections of soberer men, who have a real good will to the promotion of this design, and yet may be a little dissatisfied in this place. For here especially they may doubt of two things. The first, whether the Royal Society, being so numerous as it is, will not in short time be diverted from its primitive purpose, seeing there will be scarce enough men of philosophical temper always found to fill it up, and then others will crowd in, who have not the same bent of mind, and so the whole business will insensibly be made rather a matter of noise and pomp than of real benefit? The second, whether their number being so large will not affright private men from imparting many profitable secrets to them, lest they should thereby become common, and so they be deprived of the gain, which else they might be sure of if they kept them to themselves.

SECT.VIII. A DEFENCE OF THE LARGENESS OF THEIR NUMBER.

To the first, I shall reply that this scruple is of no force in respect of the age wherein we live. For now the genius of experimenting is so much dispersed that even in this nation, if there were one or two more such assemblies settled, there could not be wanting able men enough to carry them on. All places and corners are now busy and warm about this work: and we find many noble rarities to be every day given in, not only by the hands of learned and professed philosophers, but from the shops of mechanics, from the voyages of merchants, from the ploughs of husbandmen, from the sports, the fishponds, the parks, the gardens of gentlemen; the doubt, therefore, will only touch future ages. And even for them too we may securely promise, that they will not, for a long time, be barren of a race of inquisitive minds, when the way is now so plainly traced out before them, when they shall have tasted of these first fruits and have been excited by this example. There was scarce ever yet any the meanest sect or the most contemptible opinion that was utterly extinguished in its cradle. Whether they deserved to live or not, they all had their course, some longer, some shorter, according as they could combine with the interests or affections of the countries where they began. What reason then have we to bode ill alone to this institution which is now so earnestly embraced and which, the older it grows, cannot but still appear more inoffensive? If we only required perfect philosophers to manage this employment, it were another case. For then I grant it were improbable that threescore, or an hundred such, should meet in one time. But here it is far otherwise. If we cannot have a sufficient choice of those that are skilled in all divine and human things (which was the ancient definition of a philosopher) it suffices if many of them be plain, diligent, and laborious observers: such who, though they bring not much knowledge, yet bring their hands and their eyes uncorrupted: such as have not their brains infected by false images and can honestly assist in the examining and registering what the others represent to their view. It seems strange to me that men should conspire to believe all things more perplexed and difficult than indeed they are. This may be shown in most other matters, but in this particular in hand, it is most evident. Men did generally think that no man was fit to meddle in matters of this consequence but he that had bred himself up in a long course of discipline for that purpose, that had the habit, the gesture, the look of a philosopher. Whereas experience on the contrary tells us that greater things are produced by the free way than the formal. This mistake may well be compared to the conceit we had of soldiers in the beginning of the civil wars. None was thought worthy of that name, but he that could show his wounds and talk aloud of his exploits in the Low Countries. Whereas the whole business of fighting was afterwards chiefly performed by untravelled gentlemen, raw citizens, and generals that had scarce ever before seen a battle. But to say no more, it is so far from being a blemish, that it is rather the excellency of this institution that men of various studies are introduced. For so there will be always many sincere witnesses standing by, whom self-love will not persuade to report falsely, nor heat of invention carry to swallow a deceit too soon, as having themselves no hand in the making of the experiment, but only in the inspection. So cautious ought men to be in pronouncing even upon matters of fact. The whole care is not to be trusted to single men: not to a company all of one mind, not to philosophers, not to devout and religious men alone. By all these we have been already deluded, even by those whom I last named, who ought most of all to abhor falsehood, of whom yet many have multiplied upon us infinite stories and false miracles without any regard to conscience or truth.

To the second objection I shall briefly answer that if all the authors, or possessors of extraordinary inventions, should conspire to conceal all that was in their power from them, yet the method which they take will quickly make abundant reparation for that defect. If they cannot come at nature in its particular streams, they will have it in the fountain. If they could be shut out from the closets of physicians or the work-houses of mechanics, yet with the same or with better sorts of instruments, on more materials, by more hands, with a more rational light, they would not only restore again the old arts, but find out, perhaps, many more of far greater importance. But I need not lay much stress upon that hope, when there is no question at all, but all or the greatest part of such domestic receipts and curiosities will soon flow into this public treasure. How few secrets have there been, though never so gainful, that have been long concealed from the whole world by their authors? Were not all the least arts of life at first private? Were not watches, or locks, or guns, or printing, or lately the bow-dye, devised by particular men but soon made common? If neither chance, nor friendship, nor treachery of servants have brought such things out, yet we see ostentation alone to be every day powerful enough to do it. This desire of glory and to be counted authors prevails on all, even on many of the dark and reserved chemists themselves, who are ever printing their greatest mysteries, though indeed they seem to do it with so much reluctancy, and with a willingness to hide still, which makes their style to resemble the smoke in which they deal. Well then, if this disposition be so universal, why should we think that the inventors will be only tender and backward to the Royal Society? From which they will not only reap the most solid honour, but will also receive the strongest assurances of still retaining the greatest part of the profit? But if all this should fail, there still remains a refuge which will put this whole matter out of dispute: and that is, that the Royal Society will be able by degrees to purchase such extraordinary inventions, which are now close locked up in cabinets, and then to bring them into one common stock which shall be upon all occasions exposed to all men's use. This is a most heroic intention: for by such concealments, there may come very much hurt to mankind. If any certain remedy should be found out against an epidemical disease, if it were suffered to be engrossed by one man, there would be great swarms swept away which otherwise might be easily saved. I shall instance in the sweating-sickness. The medicine for it was almost infallible. But, before that could be generally published, it had almost dispeopled whole towns. If the same disease should have returned, it might have been again as destructive, had not the Lord Bacon taken care to set down the particular course of physic for it in his history of Henry the seventh, and so put it beyond the possibility of any private man's invading it. This ought to be imitated in all other sovereign cures of the like nature to avoid such dreadful casualties. The artificers should reap the common crop of their arts: but the public should still have title to the miraculous productions. It should be so appointed, as it is in the profits of men's lands: where the corn, and grass, and timber, and some coarser metals belong to the owner. But the royal mines, in whose ground soever they are discovered, are no man's property but still fall to the crown.

These, therefore, are the qualities which they have principally required in those whom they admitted: still reserving to themselves a power of increasing or keeping to their number, as they saw occasion. By this means they have given assurance of an eternal quietness, and moderation, in their experimental progress, because they allow themselves to differ in the weightiest matter, even in the way of salvation itself. By this they have taken care that nothing shall be so remote as to escape their reach: because some of their members are still scattered abroad, in most of the habitable parts of the earth. By this they have provided that no profitable thing shall seem too mean for their consideration, seeing they have some amongst them whose life is employed about little things as well as great. By this they have broken down the partition wall and made a fair entrance for all conditions of men to engage in these studies, which were heretofore affrighted from them, by a groundless apprehension of their chargeableness and difficulty. Thus they have formed that Society, which intends a philosophy for the use of cities and not for the retirements of schools, to resemble the cities themselves: which are compounded of all sorts of men, of the gown, of the sword, of the shop, of the field, of the court, of the sea, all mutually assisting each other.

SECT. IX. THEIR COURSE OF INQUIRY.

Let us next consider what course of inquiry they take to make all their labours unite for the service of mankind: and here I shall insist on their expense, their instruments, their matter, and their method.

THEIR EXPENSE.

Of the stock upon which their expense has been hitherto defrayed I can say nothing that is very magnificent: seeing they have relied upon no more than some small admission-money and weekly contributions amongst themselves. Such a revenue as this can make no great sound, nor amount to any vast sum. But yet, I shall say this for it, that it was the only way which could have been begun with a security of success in that condition of things. The public faith of experimental philosophy was not then strong enough to move men and women of all conditions to bring in their bracelets and jewels towards the carrying of it on. Such affections as those may be raised by a misguided zeal, but seldom, or never, by calm and unpassionate reason. It was therefore well ordained that the first benevolence should come from the experimenters themselves. If they had speedily at first called for mighty treasures, and said aloud that their enterprise required the exchequer of a kingdom, they would only have been condemned as vain projectors. So ready is mankind to suspect all new undertakings to be cheats, and chimeras, especially when they seem chargeable: that it may be many excellent things have been lost by that jealousy. Of this we have a fatal instance amongst ourselves. For it was this fear of being circumvented that made one of our wisest kings delay Columbus too long, when he came with the promise of a new world: whereas a little more confidence in his art and a small charge in furnishing out some few ships would have yearly brought all the silver of the West Indies to London, which now arrives at Seville.

This suspicion, which is so natural to men's breasts, could not any way harm the Royal Society's establishment: seeing its first claims and pretensions were so modest. And yet I shall presume to assure the world that what they shall raise on these mean foundations will be more answerable to the largeness of their intentions than to the narrowness of their beginnings. This I speak so boldly, not only because it is almost generally found true that those things, which have been small at first, have oftener grown greater than those which have begun upon a wider bottom, which have commonly stood at a stay: but also in respect of the present prevailing genius of the English nation. It is most usually found that every people has some one study or other in their view about which their minds are most intent and their purses readier to open. This is sometimes a profusion in habit and diet, sometimes religious buildings, and sometimes the civil ornaments of their cities and country. The first of these will shortly vanish from amongst us by the irresistible correction of the king's own example: the next is of late years very sensibly abated: and it is the last of the three towards which men's desires are most propense. To evidence this, I think it may be calculated that since the king's return there have been more acts of parliament for the clearing and beautifying of streets, for the repairing of highways, for the cutting of rivers, for the increase of manufactures, for the setting on foot the trade of fishing, and many other such public works to adorn the state, than in divers ages before. This general temper being well weighed, it cannot be imagined that the nation will withdraw its assistance from the Royal Society alone, which does not intend to stop at some particular benefit, but goes to the root of all noble inventions, and proposes an infallible course to make England the glory of the western world.

This my love and my hopes prompt me to say. But besides this, there is one thing more that persuades me that the Royal Society will be immortal. And that is, that if their stock should still continue narrow, yet even upon that they will be able to free themselves from all difficulties and to make a constant increase of it by their managing. There is scarce anything has more hindered the true philosophy than a vain opinion that men have taken up that nothing could be done in it, to any purpose, but upon a vast charge and by a mighty revenue. Men commonly think that the pit in which (according to Democritus) truth lies hid is bottomless: and that it will devour whatever is thrown into it without being the fuller. This false conception had got so much ground that as soon as a man began to put his hands to experiments he was presently given over as impoverished and undone. And indeed the enemies of real knowledge had some appearance of reason to conclude this heretofore: because they had seen the great estates of some chemists melted away without any thing left behind to make recompense. But this imagination can now no longer prevail. Men now understand that philosophy needs not so great a prodigality to maintain it: that the most profitable trials are not always the most costly: that the best inventions have not been found out by the richest, but by the most prudent and industrious observers: that the right art of experimenting, when it is once set forward, will go near to sustain itself. This I speak, not to stop men's future bounty, by a philosophical boast that the Royal Society has enough already: but rather to encourage them to cast in more help by showing them what return may be made from a little by a wise administration.

SECT.X. THEIR INSTRUMENTS.

Of the variety and excellence of the instruments which it lies in their power to use, I will give no other proof than the wonderful perfection to which all manual arts have of late years arrived. Men now generally understand to employ those very tools which the ancients lent us to infinite more works than formerly: they have also of late devised a great multitude of all sorts which were before unknown: and besides, we may very well expect that time will every day bring forth more. For, according as the matter to work upon does abound, the greater plenty of instruments must by consequence follow: such a connection there is between inventions an'¹ the means of inventing that they mutually increase each other.

I might be as large as I pleased in this particular in running through some part of all the inrumerable arts of the western world, and it were not difficult to show that the ordinary shops of mechanics are now as full of rarities as the cabinets of the former noblest mathematicians. But I will leave that subject, which is so familiar to all, and choose rather to fetch a confirmation of this, even from those countries which (after the manner of the ancients) we call barbarous. And in going thither for an example, I have a farther end. In my foregoing discourse, I tried to make out the advantages of the modern times above the ancient by following the progress of learning down through their tracks, to which scholars usually confine it; I will now also strengthen that argument by briefly comparing the skill and the works of the unlearned parts of the present world with those that are past. The ancient barbarians then, those nations I mean who lay without the circle of those arts which we admire, the Gauls, the Britons, the Germans, the Scythians, have scarce left any footsteps behind them to show that they were rational men. Most of them were savage in their practices, gross in their contrivances, ignorant of all that might make life either safe or pleasant. Thus it was with them, and this all history speaks with one voice: whereas the barbarians of our times (if I may take the liberty still to use that word, which the pride of Greece first brought into fashion), the Turks, the Moors, the East Indians, and even the Americans, though they too are utterly unacquainted with all our sciences, yet by the help of an universal light, which seems to overspread this age, are in several handicrafts most ready and dextrous: insomuch that in some, they can scarce be imitated by the Europeans themselves. I shall leave it to any man to conjecture from hence, which of these two times has the prerogative, and how much better helps are probably to be found at this day in the most civil countries: when we now find so much artifice amongst those our contemporaries who only follow rude and untaught nature.

SECT.XI. THEIR MATTER.

Of the extent of the matter about which they have been already conversant and intend to be hereafter, there can be no better measure taken than by giving a general prospect of all the objects of men's thoughts: which can be nothing else but either God, or men, or nature.

As for the first, they meddle no otherwise with divine things, than only as the power and wisdom and goodness of the creator is displayed in the admirable order and workmanship of the creatures. It cannot be denied but it lies in the natural philosophers' hands best to advance that part of divinity: which, though it fills not the mind with such tender and powerful contemplations as that which shows us man's redemption by a mediator, yet it is by no means to be passed by unregarded: but is an excellent ground to establish the other. This is a religion which is confirmed by the unanimous agreement of all sorts of worships: and may serve in respect to Christianity as Solomon's porch to the temple; into the one the heathens themselves did also enter, but into the other only God's peculiar people.

In men may be considered the faculties and operations of their souls, the constitution of their bodies, and the works of their hands. Of these, the first they omit, both because the knowledge and direction of them have been before undertaken by some arts on which they have no mind to intrench, as the politics, morality, and oratory, and also because the reason, the understanding, the tempers, the will, the passions of men are so hard to be reduced to any certain observation of the senses and afford so much room to the observers to falsify or counterfeit: that if such discourses should be once entertained, they would be in danger of falling into talking, instead of working, which they carefully avoid. Such subjects therefore as these they have hitherto kept out. But yet, when they shall have made more progress in material things, they will be in a condition of pronouncing more boldly on them too. For, though man's soul and body are not only one natural engine (as some have thought) of whose motions of all sorts there may be as certain an account given as of those of a watch or clock: yet by long studying of the spirits of the blood, of the nourishment, of the parts, of the diseases, of the advantages, of the accidents which belong to human bodies (all which will come within their province) there may, without question, be very near guesses made, even at the more exalted and immediate actions of the soul, and that too without destroying its spiritual and immortal being.

These two subjects, God and the soul, being only forborne, in all the rest they wander at their pleasure: in the frame of men's bodies, the ways for strong, healthful, and long life: in the arts of men's hands, those that either necessity, convenience, or delight have produced: in the works of nature, their helps, their varieties, redundancies, and defects: and in bringing all these to the uses of human society.

SECT. XII. THEIR METHOD OF INQUIRY.

In their method of inquiring, I will observe how they have behaved themselves in things that might be brought within their own touch and sight: and how in those, which are so remote and hard to be come by, that about them they were forced to trust the reports of others.

In the first kind: I shall lay it down, as their fundamental law, that whenever they could possibly get to handle the subject the experiment was still performed by some of the members themselves. The want of this exactness has very much diminished the credit of former naturalists. It might else have seemed strange that so many men of wit setting so many hands on work, being so watchful to catch up all relations, from woods, fields, mountains, rivers, seas, and lands, and scattering their pensions so liberally, should yet be able to collect so few observations that have been judicious or useful. But the reason is plain, for while they thought it enough to be only receivers of others' intelligence, they have either employed ignorant searchers, who knew not how to digest or distinguish what they found: or frivolous, who always loved to come home laden, though it were but with trifles: or (which is worst of all) crafty, who, having perceived the humours of those that paid them so well, would always take care to bring in such collections as might seem to agree with the opinions and principles of their masters, however they did with nature itself.

This inconvenience the Royal Society has escaped by making the whole process pass under its own eyes. And the task was divided amongst them by one of these two ways. First, it was sometimes referred to some particular men to make choice of what subject they pleased, and to follow their own humour in the trial, the expense being still allowed from the general stock. By which liberty that they afforded, they had a very necessary regard to the power of particular inclinations: which in all sorts of knowledge is so strong, that there may be numberless instances given of men who in some things have been altogether useless, and yet in others have had such a vigorous and successful faculty, as if they had been born and formed for them alone.

Or else secondly, the Society itself made the distribution and deputed whom it thought fit for the prosecution of such or such experiments. And this they did, either by allotting the same work to several men, separated one from another, or else by joining them into committees (if we may use that word in a philosophical sense, and so in some measure purge it from the ill sound which it formerly had). By this union of eyes and hands, there do these advantages arise. Thereby there will be a full comprehension of the object in all its appearances, and so there will be a mutual communication of the light of one science to another: whereas single labours can be but as a prospect taken upon one side. And also by this fixing of several men's thoughts upon one thing, there will be an excellent cure for that defect which is almost unavoidable in great inventors. It is the custom of such earnest and powerful minds to do wonderful things in the beginning, but shortly after to be overborne by the multitude and weight of their own thoughts; then to yield and cool by little and little, and at last grow weary and even to loath that upon which they were at first the most eager. This is the wonted constitution of great wits: such tender things are those exalted actions of the mind, and so hard it is for those imaginations that can run swift and mighty races to be able to travel a long and a constant journey. The effects of this infirmity have been so remarkable that we have certainly lost very many inventions after they have been in part fashioned, by the mere languishing and negligence of their authors. For this, the best provision must be to join many men together, for it cannot be imagined that they should be all so violent and fiery: and so by this mingling of tempers the impetuous men, not having the whole burden on them, may have leisure for intervals to recruit their first heat, and the more judicious, who are not so soon possessed with such raptures, may carry on the others' strong conceptions, by soberer degrees, to a full accomplishment.

SECT.XIII. THEIR WAY OF INQUIRY INTO REMOTE MATTERS.

This they have practised in such things whereof the matter is common, and wherein they may repeat their labours as they please. But in foreign and remote affairs their intentions and their advantages do far exceed all others. For these, they have begun to settle a correspondence through all countries, and have taken such order, that in short time there will scarce a ship come up the Thames that does not make some return of experiments as well as of merchandise.

This their care of an universal intelligence is befriended by nature itself in the situation of England: for, lying so, as it does, in the passage between the northern parts of the world and the southern, its ports being open to all coasts, and its ships spreading their sails in all seas, it is thereby necessarily made, not only mistress of the ocean, but the most proper seat for the advancement of knowledge. From the positions of countries arise not only their several shapes, manners, customs, colours, but also their different arts and studies. The inland and continent we see do give laws to discourse, to habits, to behaviour: but those that border upon the seas are most properly seated to bring home matter for new sciences, and to make the same proportion of discoveries above others in the intellectual globe as they have done in the material.

Upon this advantage of our island there is so much stress to be laid towards the prosperity of this design, that if we should search through all the world for a perpetual habitation wherein the universal philosophy might settle itself, there can none be found which is comparable to London, of all the former present seats of empire. Babylon, that was the capital city of the first monarchy, was situated in a champion country, had a clear and uncloudy air, and was therefore fit enough to promote one part of natural knowledge, the observations of the heavens: but it was a midland town, and regarded not the traffic of foreigners, abounding with its own luxury and riches. Memphis was improper upon the same account, for Egypt was a land content with its own plenty, admitting strangers rather to instruct them than to learn anything from them. Carthage stood not so well for a resort for philosophers as for pirates, as all the African shore continues at this day. As for Rome, its fortune was read by Virgil, when he said that it only ought to excel in the arts of ruling. Constantinople, though its present masters were not barbarous, yet is too much shut up by the straits of Hellespont. Vienna is now a frontier town, and has no communication with the ocean, but by a long compass about. Amsterdam is the place of trade, without the mixture of men of freer thoughts. And, even Paris itself, though it is far to be preferred before all the others for the resort of learned and inquisitive men to it, yet is less capable, for the same reasons for which Athens was, by being the seat of gallantry, the arts of speech, and education. But it is London alone that enjoys most of the others' advantages, without their inconveniences. It is the head of a mighty empire, the greatest that ever commanded the ocean: it is composed of gentlemen as well as traders: It has a large intercourse with all the earth: it is, as the poets describe their house of fame, a city where all the noises and business in the world do meet: and therefore this honour is justly due to it to be the constant place or residence for that knowledge which is to be made up of the reports and intelligence of all countries.

To this I will add that we have another help in our hands, which almost forces this crown on the head of the English nation: and that is, the noble and inquisitive genius of our merchants. This cannot be better shown than by comparing them with those of that one country, which only stands in competition with us for trade. The merchants of England live honourably in foreign parts; those of Holland meanly, minding their gain alone: ours converse freely and learn from all, having in their behaviour very much of the gentility of the families from which so many of them are descended: the others, when they are abroad, show that they are only a race of plain citizens, keeping themselves most within their own cells and warehouses, scarce regarding the acquaintance of any but those with whom they traffic. This largeness of ours, and narrowness of their living does, no doubt, conduce very much to enrich them, and is, perhaps, one of the reasons that they can so easily undersell us: but withal, it makes ours the most capable, as theirs unfit, to promote such an enterprise as this of which I am now speaking. For, indeed, the effects of their several ways of life are as different: of the Hollanders I need say no more. But of the English merchants I will affirm that in all sorts of politeness and skill in the world, and human affairs, they do not only excel them but are equal to any other sort of men amongst us.

This I have spoken, not to lessen the reputation of that industrious people: but that I might (if it were possible) inflame their minds to an emulation of this design. They have all things imaginable to stir them up: they have the examples of the greatest wits of other countries, who have left their own homes to retire thither for the freedom of their philosophical studies: they have one place (I mean The Hague) which may be soon made the very copy of a town in the *New Atlantis*, which for its pleasantness and for the concourse of men of all conditions to it may be counted above all others (except London) the most advantageously seated for this service.

These have been the privileges and practices of the Royal Society in things foreign and native. It would now be needless to set down all the steps of their progress about them; how they observed all the varieties of generations and corruptions, natural and artificial; all the increasings and lessenings; agreements and oppositions of things; how, having found out a cause, they have applied it to many other effects: and the effects to different causes; how they are wont to change the instruments and places and quantities of matter, according to occasions: and all the other subtleties and windings of trial which are almost infinite to express. I shall only, in passing, touch on these two things, which they have most carefully consulted.

The one is, not to prescribe to themselves any certain art of experimenting within which to circumscribe their thoughts: but rather to keep themselves free and change their course according to the different circumstances that occur to them in their operations, and the several alterations of the bodies on which they work. The true experimenting has this one thing inseparable from it, never to be a fixed and settled art, and never to be limited by constant rules. This, perhaps, may be shown too in other arts, as in that of invention, of which, though in logic and rhetoric, so many bounds and helps are given: yet I believe very few have argued or discoursed by those topics. But whether that be unconfined or no, it is certain that experimenting is like that which is called decency in human life, which, though it be that by which all our actions are to be fashioned, and though many things may be plausibly said upon it, yet it is never wholly to be reduced to standing precepts, and may almost as easily be obtained as defined.

Their other care has been to regard the least and the plainest things, and those that may appear at first the most inconsiderable, as well as the greatest curiosities. This was visibly neglected by the ancients. The histories of Pliny, Aristotle, Solinus, Ælian abounding more with pretty tales and fine monstrous stories than sober and fruitful relations. If they could gather together some extraordinary qualities of stones or minerals, some rarities of the age, the food, the colour, the shapes of beasts, or some virtues of fountains or rivers, they thought they had performed the chiefest part of natural historians. But this course is subject to much corruption. It is not the true following of nature, for that still goes on in a steady road, nor is it so extravagant and so artificial in its contrivances, as our admiration, proceeding from our ignorance, makes it. It is also a way that, of all others, is most subject to be deceived: for it will make men inclinable to bend the truth much awry to raise a specious observation out of it. It stops the severe progress of inquiry: infecting the mind, and making it averse from the true natural philosophy. It is like romances, in respect of true history, which, by multiplying varieties of extraordinary events and surprising circumstances, makes that seem dull and tasteless. And, to say no more, the very delight which it raises is nothing so solid: but, as the satisfaction of fancy, it affects us a little in the beginning, but soon wearies and surfeits: whereas a just history of nature, like the pleasure of reason, would not be, perhaps, so quick and violent but of far longer continuance in its contentment.

. . . .

SECT. XXVII. THE KING'S EXAMPLE IN PROMOTING EXPERIMENTS.

When these statutes were presented to his majesty, he was pleased to superscribe himself their founder and patron, his royal highness and his highness Prince Rupert at the same time declaring themselves fellows.

Nor has the king only encouraged them by kindness of words and by acts of state, but he has also provoked them to unwearied activity in their experiments, by the most effectual means of his royal example. There is scarce any one sort of work whose advancement they regard but from his majesty's own labours they have received a pattern for their endeavours about it. They design the multiplying and beautifying of mechanic arts: and the noise of mechanic instruments is heard in Whitehall itself. They intend the perfection of engraving, statuary, limning, coining, and all the works of smiths in iron, or steel, or silver, and the most excellent artists of these kinds have provision made for their practice, even in the chambers and galleries of his court. They purpose the trial of all manner of operations by fire. And the king has under his own roof found place for chemical operators; they resolve to restore, to enlarge, to examine physic; and the king has endowed the College of London with new privileges, and has planted a physic garden under his own eye. They have bestowed much consideration on the propagating of fruits and trees, and the king has made plantations enough, even almost to repair the ruins of a civil war. They have begun an exact survey of the heavens: and Saint James's Park may witness that Ptolemy and Alphonso were not the only monarchs who observed the motions and appearances of the stars. They have studied the promoting of architecture in our island: and the beauty of our late buildings and the reformation of his own houses do sufficiently manifest his skill and inclination to that art: of which magnificence we had seen more effects ere this, if he had not been called off by this war from houses of convenience to those of strength. They have principally consulted the advancement of navigation: and the king has been most ready to reward those that shall discover the meridian. They have employed much time in examining the fabric of ships, the forms of their sails, the shapes of their keels, the sorts of timber, the planting of fir, the bettering of pitch, and tar, and tackling. And in all maritime affairs of this nature, his majesty is acknowledged to be the best judge amongst seamen and shipwrights, as well as the most powerful amongst princes.

. . . .

ANSWERS

Returned By

Sir PHILIBERTO VERNATTI

Resident in Batavia in Java Major,

To certain inquiries sent thither by order of

the Royal Society, and recommended by

Sir ROBERT MORAY

Q. 1. Whether diamonds and other precious stones grow again after three or four years in the same places where they have been dug out?
A. Never, or at least as the memory of man can attain to.

. . . .

Q. 3. Whether there be a hill in Sumatra which burneth continually, and a fountain which runneth pure balsam.
A. There is a hill that burneth in Sumatra near Endrapore; but I cannot hear of any such fountain; and I believe that the like hill is upon Java Major opposite to Batavia: for in a clear morning or evening from the road a man may perfectly perceive a continual smoke rise from the top and vanish by little and little. I have often felt earthquakes here, but they do not continue long; in the year 1656 or '57 (I do not remember well the time) Batavia was covered in one afternoon, about two of the clock, with a black dust, which being gathered together was so ponderous that it exceeded the weight in gold. I, at that time being very ill, did not take much notice of it, but some have gathered it, and if I light upon it shall send you some. It is here thought it came out of the hill: I never heard of any that had been upon this hill's top: Endrapore is counted a mighty unwholesome place, as likewise all others where pepper grows, as Jamby Banjar, Balingtone, etc. though some impute it to the hill's burning.

As for the fountain, it is unknown to us, except *oleum terrae* is meant by it, which is to be had in Sumatra, but the best comes from Pegu.

Q. 4. What river is that in Java Major that turns wood into stone?
A. There is none such to our knowledge; yet I have seen a piece of wood with a stone at the end of it, which was told me, that was turned

into stone by a river in Pegu; but I took it but for a foppery, for divers arbusta grow in rocks, which being appropriated curiously, may easily deceive a too hasty believer.

. . . .

Q. 7. Whether those creatures that are in these parts plump and in season at the full moon, are lean and out of season at the new, find the contrary at the East Indies.

A. I find it so here, by experience at Batavia, in oysters and crabs.

. . . .

Q. 24. To inquire of the divers for pearls staying long under water; whether they do it by the assistance of anything they carry with them, or by long and often use get a trick of holding their breath so long, at the Isle of Baharen near Ormus?

A. What they do at Baharen is unknown to me, but since we have had Tute Corein in Ceylon, where very good pearls grow, I hear the divers use no artifice. The manner is thus: at a set time of the year merchants come from all parts, as likewise divers with their boats; each boat hath a certain quantity of square stones, upon which stones the divers go down, and give a token to their companions when they think it time to be hauled up: each stone pays tribute to the company. The oyster or shell-fish is not immediately opened, but laid on heaps, or in holes at the seaside. When the diving time is ended, the merchants come and buy these heaps, according as they can agree, not knowing whether they shall get anything or no. So that this is a mere lottery. This pearl-fishing is dangerous, being the divers commonly make their will and take leave of their friends before they tread the stone to go down.

. . . .

Q. 27. To inquire after, and get, if possible, some of the bones of the fish called Caballa, which are so powerful in stopping blood.

A. 'Tis done, and they shall follow with the Dutch ships.

. . . .

Q. 29. Whether there be a tree in Mexico that yields water, wine, vinegar, oil, milk, honey, wax, thread and needles?

A. The Cokos trees yields all this and more; the nut, while it is green, hath very good water in it, the flower being cut, drops out great quantity of liquor, called sury, or taywack, which drunk fresh, hath the force, and almost the taste of wine; grown sour, is very good vinegar; and distilled, makes very good brandy, or areck: the nut grated and mingled with water tastes like milk: pressed, yields very good oil; bees swarm in these trees, as well as in others; thread and needles are made of the leaves and tough twigs. Nay, to add something to this description; in Amboina they make bread of the body of the tree, the leaves serve to thatch houses, and likewise sails for their boats.

. . . .

A

METHOD

For making a history of the weather

By Mr. HOOK

For the better making a history of the weather, I conceive it requisite to observe,

1. The strength and quarter of the winds, and to register the changes as often as they happen; both which may be very conveniently shown by a small addition to an ordinary weather-clock.

2. The degrees of heat and cold in the air, which will be best observed by a sealed thermometer, graduated according to the degrees of expansion, which bear a known proportion to the whole bulk of liquor, the beginning of which gradation should be that dimension which the liquor hath when encompassed with water just beginning to freeze, and the degrees of expansion, either greater or less, should be set or marked above it or below it.

3. The degrees of dryness and moisture in the air, which may be most conveniently observed by a hygroscope, made with the single beard of a wild oat perfectly ripe, set upright and headed with an index, after the way described by Emanuel Magnan; the conversions and degrees of which may be measured by divisions made on the rim of a circle, in the centre of which the index is turned round: the beginning or standard of which degree of rotation should be that to which the index points when the beard, being thoroughly wet, or covered with water, is quite unwreathed and becomes straight. But because of the smallness of this part of the oat, the cod of a wild vetch may be used instead of it, which

will be a much larger index and will be altogether as sensible of the changes of the air.

4. The degrees of pressure in the air: which may be several ways observed, but best of all with an instrument with quicksilver, contrived so as either by means of water or an index it may sensibly exhibit the minute variations of that action.

5. The constitution and face of the sky or heavens; and this is best done by the eye; here should be observed whether the sky be clear or clouded; and if clouded, after what manner; whether with high exhalations or great white clouds, or dark thick ones. Whether those clouds afford fogs or mists, or sleet, or rain, or snow, etc. Whether the under side of those clouds be flat or waved and irregular, as I have often seen before thunder. Which way they drive, whether all one way, or some one way, some another; and whether any of these be the same with the wind that blows below; the colour and face of the sky at the rising and setting of the sun and moon; what halos or rings may happen to encompass those luminaries, their bigness, form, and number.

. . . .

MEDICINAL AND ANATOMICAL.

The sixth are experiments medicinal and anatomical, as of cutting out the spleen of a dog: of the effects of vipers biting dogs: of a chameleon, and its dissection: of preserving animals in spirit of wine, oil of turpentine, and other liquors: of injecting various liquors, and other substances, into the veins of several creatures.

Experiments of destroying mites by several fumes: of the equivocal generation of insects: of feeding a carp in the air: of making insects with cheese and sack: of killing water-newts, toads, and slowworms with several salts: of killing frogs by touching their skin with vinegar, pitch, or mercury: of a spider's not being enchanted by a circle of unicorn's horn, or Irish earth, laid round about it.

Experiments with a poisoned Indian dagger on several animals: with the Maccassar poison: with Florentine poison, and several antidotes against it: of making flesh grow on after it has been once cut off: of the grafting a spur on the head of a cock and its growing: of the living of creatures by factitious air: of the reviving of animals strangled, by blowing into their lungs: of flesh not breeding worms, when secured from fly-blowings: of the suffocation of animals upon piercing the thorax: of hatching silk-worms' eggs in rarified air: of transfusing the blood of one animal into another.

. . . .

OF MOTION.

The tenth are experiments of motion: as of glass drops several ways ordered and broken: of the velocity of the descent of several bodies of divers fashions through several liquors: of determining the velocity of bodies falling through the air; tried by many ways: of the swift motion of sounds: of the irregular motion of the oil of turpentine on spirit of wine; of the strength of falling bodies according to the several heights from which they fall: of proportioning the shapes of bodies so as to make them fall together in the same time through diffusing mediums.

Experiments of the swiftness of a bullet shot with extraordinary powder: of the best figure of the weight of a pendulum for motion: of the motion of pendulous bodies of various figures: to determine the length of pendulums: to find the velocity of the vibrations of a sounding string: to find the velocity of motion propagated by a very long extended wire: for explaining the inflection of a straight motion into a circular by a supervening attractive power towards the centre in order to the explaining of the motion of the planets.

Experiments of the circular and complicated motion of pendulums, to explain the hypothesis of the moon's moving about the earth: of comparing the motions of a circular pendulum with the motion of a straight one: of the propagation of motion from one body to another: of the reflection of motion: of the vibrating motion of quicksilver in a crooked pipe: imitating the motion of a pendulum: of communicating of the strength of powder for the bending of springs; and thereby for making artificial muscles to command what strength we desire.

CHEMICAL AND MECHANICAL.

The eleventh are experiments chemical, mechanical, optical: as of reducing the flesh of animals into a liquor like blood by dissolving it in a certain menstruum: of a greater facility of raising water in pipes of a larger bore: of brewing beer with bread, barley, oats, wheat, and without malting: of precipitating tartar out of wine by several expedients: of a chemical extraction of a volatile spirit, and salt out of sponges: of examining *aurum fulminans* after explosion: of the dissolution of manna in water, and of a crystallizing it again out of it by evaporation.

Experiments of volatizing salt of tartar many ways: of examining the mucilaginous matter called star-shoot: of examining our English telescopes and microscopes and comparing them with such as have been made at Rome: of making a volatile salt with oil of turpentine and sea-salt: of the quantity of spirits in cider: of the strength of several springs: of examining a pump made with bellows: of dying silk with several Jamaica woods: of finding the strength of wood of several kinds for bearing: of finding the flexibility of various woods and determining the utmost extent of their yielding and bending.

Experiments about the gravity of bodies made on the top of Saint Paul's steeple, Westminster Abbey, and several other high places; and in a well of seventy fathoms depth: examined about the *Virgula Divina*, wherein the common assertions were found false: of the various refractions of several liquors in a new refractive engine: of common oil of tobacco made by distillation in a glass retort: of making the object-glass of a microscope to bear as large an aperture as is desired.

Of this their way of experimenting I will here produce these examples.

. . . .

SECT. XIV. EXPERIMENTS NOT DANGEROUS TO THE CHRISTIAN RELIGION.

I will now proceed to the weightiest and most solemn part of my whole undertaking, to make a defence of the Royal Society and this new experimental learning in respect of the Christian faith. I am not ignorant in what a slippery place I now stand, and what a tender matter I am entered upon. I know that it is almost impossible without offence to speak of things of this nature, in which all mankind, each country, and now almost every family do so widely disagree among themselves. I cannot expect that what I shall say will escape misinterpretation, though it be spoken with the greatest simplicity and submission, while I behold that most men do rather value themselves and others, on the little differences of religion than the main substance itself; and while the will of God is so variously distracted that what appears to be piety to some Christians is abhorred as the greatest superstition and heresy by others.

. . . .

The public declaration of the Christian religion is to propose to mankind an infallible way to salvation. Towards the performance of this happy end, besides the principles of natural religion, which consists in the acknowledgement and worship of a Deity, it has offered us the merits of a glorious Saviour: by him, and his apostles' ministry, it has given us sufficient examples and doctrines to acquaint us with divine things and carry us to heaven. In every one of these, the experiments of natural things do neither darken our eyes, nor deceive our minds, nor deprave our hearts.

SECT.XV. EXPERIMENTS WILL NOT DESTROY THE DOCTRINE OF THE GODHEAD.

First there can be no just reason assigned why an experimenter should be prone to deny the essence and properties of God, the universal sovereignty of his dominion, and his providence over the creation. He has before him the very same argument to confirm his judgment in all these, with which he himself is wont to be abundantly satisfied, when he meets with it in any of his philosophical inquiries. In every thing that he tries, he believes that this is enough for him to rest on, if he finds that not only his own, but the universal observations of men of all times and places without any mutual conspiracy have consented in the same conclusion. How can he then refrain from embracing this common truth, which is witnessed by the unanimous approbation of all countries, the agreement of nations, and the secret acknowledgement of every man's breast?

'Tis true his employment is about material things. But this is so far from drawing him to oppose invisible beings that it rather puts his thoughts into an excellent good capacity to believe them. In every work of nature that he handles, he knows that there is not only a gross substance, which presents itself to all men's eyes, but an infinite subtlety of parts, which come not into the sharpest sense. So that what the Scripture relates of the purity of God, of the spirituality of his nature, and that of angels and the souls of men cannot seem incredible to him, when he perceives the numberless particles that move in every man's blood, and the prodigious streams that continually flow unseen from every body. Having found that his own senses have been so far assisted by the instruments of art, he may sooner admit that his mind ought to be raised higher, by a heavenly light, in those things wherein his senses do fall short. If (as the apostle says) the invisible things of God are manifested by the visible, then how much stronger arguments has he for his belief in the eternal power and Godhead, from the vast number of creatures that are invisible to others, but are exposed to his view by the help of his experiments?

SECT.XVI. EXPERIMENTS NOT INJURIOUS TO THE WORSHIP OF GOD.

Thus he is prepared to admit a Deity and to embrace the consequences of that concession. He is also from his experiments as well furnished with arguments to adore it: he has always before his eyes the beauty, contrivance, and order of God's works: from hence, he will learn to serve Him with all reverence, who in all that He has made consulted ornament as well as use.

. . . .

SECT.XXIII. EXPERIMENTS NOT DANGEROUS TO THE CHURCH OF ENGLAND.

And now, having insisted so long on the parts of the Christian religion in general, it will be less needful that I should be large in vindicating this design from the imputation of being prejudicial to the church of England: for this has the same interest with that, and differs in nothing from its primitive pattern, but only in the addition of some circumstances which make it fit for this age and this place: and therefore they will both be strengthened by the same benefits and weakened by the same mischiefs.

What I have then to add concerning our church shall be comprised in these particulars: that it can never be prejudiced by the light of reason, nor by the improvements of knowledge, nor by the advancement of the works of men's hands.

For the proof of the first, it will be sufficient to consider its true design, what opinions it principally encounters, and by what arguments it ought to defend itself.

The true and certain interest of our church is to derive its doctrine from the plain and unquestioned parts of the Word of God, and to keep itself in a due submission to the civil magistrate. The extremes which it opposes are implicit faith and enthusiasm. And it is a great mistake if men think it cannot be maintained against these but by the mutual arguments of its enemies: that it cannot withstand the separatists, but by the authority of the church of Rome; nor dissent from the church of Rome, but on the tenets of the separatists. The grounds on which it proceeds are different from both: and they are no other but the rights of the civil power, the imitation of the first uncorrupt churches, and the Scripture expounded by reason: from whence may be concluded that we cannot make war against reason without undermining our own strength, seeing it is the constant weapon we ought to employ.

From this I will farther urge that the church of England will not only be safe amidst the consequences of a rational age, but amidst all the improvements of knowledge and the subversion of old opinions about nature and introduction of new ways of reasoning thereon. This will be evident when we behold the agreement that is between the present design of the Royal Society and that of our church in its beginning. They both may lay equal claim to the word reformation, the one having compassed it in religion, the other purposing it in philosophy. They both have taken a like course to bring this about, each of them passing by the corrupt copies, and referring themselves to the perfect originals for their instruction; the one to the Scripture, the other to the large volume of the creatures. They are both unjustly accused by their enemies of the same crimes, of having forsaken the ancient traditions and ventured on novelties. They both suppose alike that their ancestors might err; and yet retain a sufficient reverence for them. They both follow the great precept of the apostle, of trying all things. Such is the harmony between their interests and tempers. It cannot therefore be suspected that the church of England, that arose on the same method, though in different works; that heroically passed through the same difficulties, that relies on the same sovereign's authority, should look with jealous eyes on this attempt, which makes no change in the principles of men's consciences but chiefly aims at the increase of inventions about the works of their hands.

This was the last particular in this subject which I undertook to make good, that our church can never be impaired by the growth of the useful arts of life. But now I come nearer to it, I find that I may safely omit it: for the thing itself is so manifest that there can be no ground of raising a question about it. If our church should be an enemy to commerce, intelligence, discovery, navigation, or any sort of mechanics, how could it be fit for the present genius of this nation? What greater advantage could its adversaries have against it? How should we be able to reconcile these two titles, which so justly belong to our king, of Defender of the Faith, and Patron of Experimental Knowledge.

But in this I am not only encouraged to promise that our church will be out of all danger, but to recommend this enterprise to it as that which will become its other excellencies and is most worthy of its protection. And I shall most humbly represent to its consideration that this is not only an honourable work, but even a necessary duty, to which it is obliged by natural affection. The present inquiring temper of this age was at first produced by the liberty of judging and searching and reasoning which was used in the first Reformation. Though I cannot carry the institution of the Royal Society many years back, yet the seeds of it were sown in King Edward the sixth's and Queen Elizabeth's reign. And ever since that time experimental learning has still retained some vital heat, though it wanted the opportunities of ripening itself which now it enjoys. The church of England therefore may justly be styled the mother of this sort of knowledge; and so the care of its nourishment and prosperity peculiarly lies upon it.

VERBUM SAPIENTI

Or a short memorandum presented to the truly honourable, wise, and valiant patriots, the lords and commons in
parliament assembled.

1674

It was a grim and suspicious parliament whose members, meeting in January 1674,
received copies of this memorandum. During the preceding year their knowledge of
the facts and implications of Charles II's grand design had slowly grown. In March
the cavalier majority had forced the withdrawal of the Declaration of Indulgence,
framed to allow toleration to dissenters and catholics alike, and had clinched that
victory by a Test Act which compelled all officeholders to accept the Anglican communion. That action broke the united front of the Cabal ministry; the duke of York
and Clifford resigned, and Shaftesbury went into opposition. In June a famous pamphlet, *England's Appeal from the Private Cabal at Whitehall*, had set forth in detail
the story of the sacrifice of England to Louis XIV's ambitions and bribes. In September
had come the marriage of the duke of York to a catholic princess, Mary of Modena,
and after a bitter week behind locked doors parliament was prorogued before it could
attack the ministry. By November early peace with the Dutch seemed assured, but
whether a separate peace, or whether on stiff or easy terms, was still a question.

This memorandum, designed as lobbying propaganda, effectively marshalled the
arguments for a separate and easy peace. It repeated the disclosures of the preceding
year: the catholic complexion of the cabinet, the French dream of ' universal monarchy,' the danger to English trade, French bribing tactics, the activity of papist
agents like Father Patrick, the queen's almoner, and the disaster if a catholic heir
were born. It proposed a solution, the succession of the prince of Orange to the English
throne. It is probably to be classed among the pamphlets emanating from the prince
of Orange himself. If so, it was perhaps written by the same man who wrote *England's
Appeal*, one Pierre du Moulin, who, having been dismissed from his English employments for intriguing with Dutch agents, joined the prince and conducted a skilful
diplomatic and publicity campaign.

The text is taken from the *Calendar of State Papers, Domestic*, 1673–1675, pp.128–132.

(1674.)
(Jan.)

Verbum Sapienti, or a short memorandum presented to the truly
honourable, wise and valiant patriots, the lords and commons in parliament assembled, in these following queries:—

1. Whether the reasons of unchristian war with Holland, and im-

prudent league with France, carried on hitherto by the dark and myste-rious contrivances of a small popish cabal, are not matters fit to be taken into the serious consideration of this parliament?

2. Whether it will not be found that all the mischiefs we have felt or may hereafter fear from the Hollanders, though ten times greater than what are falsely pretended, cannot possibly be of half that dangerous consequence to us, as the advantages now given to the growth of the French power, by this pernicious league, as will plainly appear, if it be considered:— (i.) That by means hereof the French king has already made himself master of three of the seven United Provinces, and thereby so enfeebled that state (formerly the balance betwixt him and the House of Austria) that they can no longer be, as heretofore, a check to his am-bitious designs. (ii.) That he has possessed himself of all those towns on the Rhine which give him an easy passage into Germany, and also of Maestrecht and other strong towns on the Maes, opening him a wide door into that part of the Spanish Netherlands, by means whereof he has overcome the greatest difficulty in his way to that universal monarchy to which he has so long aspired. (iii.) That if to the rest of these, his new acquisitions, he should by force or agreement bring the maritime prov-inces of the Dutch Netherlands into his subjection, which not many months since he was very near effecting, he would become master of all the Dutch shipping, which must necessarily make him the unquestion-able and uncontrollable master of the sea, and by consequence master of all the trade and wealth in the world.

3. Whether, if this be true, as most undeniably it is, it be not hence demonstrable, that, if the success of this war should answer the craftily projected designs of the French councils, as certainly it had done before this if God had not miraculously prevented it, all Christendom must in-evitably be brought under the insolent and most oppressive yoke of that worse than Turkish tyranny, and England, the now foolish associate in this war, soon bear her greatest share in this common calamity?

4. Whether the states general on an impartial examination can be justly accused of the infraction of any material article of the treaty at Breda, except that only of the flag, which also was contrived on purpose to give a provocation to a war, of which 'tis manifest we were long be-fore resolved, and for which we should have wanted the least colourable pretext, if this occasion had not been given?

5. Whether, since the depression of the Lovesteyne faction, the states by their deputies, and the prince of Orange by several messages and letters, have not only offered us full satisfaction as to our right of the flag, but have also made such fair and honourable proposals as might have been a good foundation of a firm and lasting peace betwixt us and them for many generations?

6. Whether all overtures made by them have not hitherto been, and are to this day rejected, unless also full satisfaction be given to the insolent demands of the French king, according to the promissory act betwixt the two crowns, into which the king was traitorously ensnared by the pernicious practices of his plenipotentiaries, Buckingham and Arlington, in their negotiation at Utrecht?

7. Whether it be not highly scandalous to the protestant religion that the king of England, king of a protestant kingdom, should stand obliged to make war with a protestant state till they will grant a free toleration of the popish religion, restore the church lands to the popish clergy, erect public churches for popish idolatrous worship, and admit papists to an equal share in the government, which is one of the conditions insisted on by the French king?

8. Whether it be consistent with the honour of the king or the interests of the kingdom that we should stand obliged to make war with the states, till they acknowledge the French king to be their protector and restorer, and present him yearly with a medal, and pay him a tribute yearly, another insolent condition insisted on by that proud and vainglorious tyrant?

9. Whether such a league as this with France with this promissory act superinduced upon it, by which we are entangled in such an impious, dishonourable and destructive alliance, ought to be maintained with the expense of so much English blood and treasure, or rather to be voted treasonable, and burnt by the common hangman?

10. Whether the authors of this league are not guilty of the highest treason against the king and kingdom, and ought not to be proceeded against as traitors and public enemies of their country?

11. Whether the prosecution of this war, gilded at first with the specious pretences of curbing the insolency of the De Witts, and their faction, and exalting the depressed state of the House of Orange, has not in truth a manifest and direct tendency to the destruction of that

illustrious prince, whose great love to the English nation, zeal for the protestant religion, and many resplendent virtues declare him to be the most valuable pawn and most hopeful pledge of future happiness to us and our posterities, if the king should die without issue?

12. Whether a war with Spain, the necessary consequence of our adhesion to France, will not in an instant put a stop to all our manufactures at home, and to all our traffic abroad, and bring an universal poverty on all ranks amongst us?

13. Whether it will not be more prudent to accept such reasonable and honourable conditions as we may yet have from the Dutch, before they are perfectly delivered from the oppression of the French, rather than run the hazard of drawing on us the united enmity of them and all their potent allies after they have defeated the French forces, which, by the blessing of God, 'tis hoped by all good men they will do very shortly?

14. Whether, should there appear a necessity of continuing a war with Holland, we might not with more honour and greater security of our interests, and more probable hopes of success, wage war by ourselves alone than in conjunction with the French, whose friendship never yet gave anything to us, or to any that were ever in alliance with them, besides treachery and disappointment, of which we have had a sad experiment this summer in the last sea fight?

15. Whether a tax granted for carrying on this war and maintaining this league may not be more truly said to be a tax to the French king than to the king of France?

16. Whether it will not appear that the great reason of state moving to this war (next to those more religious and generous, the introducing of popery and arbitrary government) was to teach the ill-bred Dutch the proper way of addressing the great ministers of princes, viz., by large sums and yearly pensions, a finesse of policy not understood by them, as was very ingenuously confessed by a noble lord of the Cabal, who declared to one with whom the author is well acquainted that the Dutch acted more by the measures of merchants and shopkeepers than of great statesmen, and had drawn this war on themselves by the narrowness of their hearts, which could not afford to go to the price of an honourable alliance with so great a monarch as the king of England, for, to his knowledge, if they would have presented the king (I suppose, he meant himself and his brother Arlington) with £100,000, this war had never been begun?

17. Let all the world be judge whether the parliament's blindfold allowance of this war, built upon such honest, honourable and public considerations, and carried on two years without their consent or advice by two or three large-hearted gentlemen, who know how to keep up their master's reputation by setting a lusty price upon his friendship, will not be to establish corruption and bribery by a law, and to grant a monopoly of war and peace to great ministers, and give our neighbours just occasion to lay us under the dirty character with which Rome was once reproached—*Venalis Anglia, mox peritura, si emptorem invenias?*

18. Whether there be not apparent cause to suspect that those who have at present the chief direction of affairs carry on a wicked and treasonable design to subvert the fundamental laws of this kingdom by introducing popery and setting up an arbitrary government?

19. Whether the multitude of popish priests permitted to stay here in contempt of the late addresses of parliament, the continuing of many known and justly suspected papists in military and civil employments, the forming of a new standing army, the sending for one of the French king's Bassas to be their general, the imposing of soldiers upon housekeepers without paying for their quarters, the inflicting punishments on free-born Englishmen by martial law, and compelling his majesty's subjects without their consent to go into the French king's service do not afford sufficient ground for this suspicion?

20. Whether Father Patrick's bold appearing at court every day in the king's presence, his saucy and audacious confronting several members of the house of commons, his constant resort to, or rather dwelling like a domestic in Lord Arlington's house, do not justify the impudent discourses of many papists who say publicly, that the proclamation for banishing popish priests was only to humour the parliament for a while and was not intended to be executed?

21. Whether the sacred authority of parliaments and the reverence due to so great and honourable an assembly is not in danger of being quite lost if exemplary justice be not done on that foul-mouthed Scot, master of the prerogative office, the duke of Lauderdale, who, being told that the house of commons were about to draw up an impeachment against him, with an unparalleled arrogancy and rudeness answered that he had a dog in his a—— which could outbark all those curs?

22. Whether it be not absolutely necessary for the peace and safety

of these kingdoms that that great triumvirate of iniquity, Buckingham, Arlington, and Lauderdale, who have so long poisoned and perverted all councils, be forthwith removed from all public affairs and be speedily brought to condign punishment?

23. Whether the duke of York has for so long refused to receive the sacrament according to the church of England as a fanatic or as a papist?

24. Whether his compelling his last wife to apostatize from the faith she had so long professed, his choosing a second wife who is an Italian papist, descended of a father and mother who are the bastard issue of a pope and a cardinal, his open reviling the protestant religion, his bitter invectives against the protestant bishops and clergy, his intimacy with Romish priests, emissaries, and agents, his promoting bloody Irish papists to places of power and trust, his discountenancing all others, and (which is plainest of all) his denying to renounce that discriminating shibboleth of Rome, the doctrine of transubstantiation, are not warrantable grounds to conclude him to be a most confirmed papist?

25. Whether it be not much more dangerous to have the crown placed on a popish head hereafter than to have the office of admiral of England executed by a papist now?

26. Whether, therefore, it be not high time to consider of settling the succession of the crown so as may secure us and our posterities from those bloody massacres and inhuman Smithfield butcheries, the certain consequences of a popish government?

27. Whether under present circumstances a better expedient can be thought of than to give the duke's eldest daughter in marriage to the prince of Orange, his sister's son, by means whereof all future disputes about the crown will be quieted, as were those bloody controversies between York and Lancaster by the prudent marriage of Henry VII, and the administration committed to a virtuous and religious prince, who wants no accomplishments which may render him acceptable to the people, and the people happy under him, both as to their civil and religious conditions? Lastly, whether this parliament, the only hopeful remedy for this dying kingdom, can faithfully discharge their duty to God, or answer the trust reposed in them by the people, if they proceed to make any votes for a new supply till they are fully satisfied in the matters contained in these queries?

A LETTER FROM A JESUIT AT PARIS

To his correspondent in London; showing the most effective way to ruin the government and protestant religion. London. Printed, and are to be sold by Jonathan Edwin at the Three Roses in Ludgate-street. 1679.

JOHN NALSON (1638?–1686), a Cambridge man, was rector of Doddington in the Isle of Ely. He wrote a number of royalist pamphlets; his most pretentious work, which was never finished, was a collection of state papers, for the compiling of which he was given access to official files, to illustrate the period of the civil war and to serve as antidote to Rushworth's historical collections. A time-server and pusher for preferment, he got nothing for his pamphlets but a prebendal stall in Ely cathedral.

The following pamphlet, a fair sample of the fabrications of the popish plot, got Nalson into trouble with the Whig parliament of 1679. The house construed its slurs upon members of parliament who favoured the dissenters as breach of privilege; particularly did they object to the four initials which occur in the pamphlet, standing, said members, for Powle, Clarges, Titus, and Ralph Montagu. The latter was the ambassador to France who produced the letters which led to Danby's impeachment. Nalson would doubtless have fared worse than he did if Titus had not represented him as a simple clergyman meddling with affairs he didn't understand, and writing the pamphlet not, as he maintained, ' to disappoint papists, and so to serve the nation,' but to get himself a good living. He was in confinement for five weeks, and was turned out of the commission of the peace. The speaker reproved him, kneeling before the bar of the house, in these words: ' You are justly under the displeasure of the house, for meddling out of your sphere, and you are more to blame for meddling out of your calling, in personating a Jesuit in the book you have written. What you have done was beneath the gravity of your profession, and a desertion of your calling; but the house presuming that this will be a warning not to do the like offence again, and rather desiring your reformation than your ruin, they do discharge you, and you are discharged, paying your fees.'

To the reader.

Courteous reader,

THIS ensuing discourse I have perused, and find it to be an exact character of an old Jesuited Jesuit. The contents of it was their practice whilst I conversed with them, and therefore I am inclined to tell the world as much, seeing these times in which we live require that every true Englishman and protestant do understand them, to this very end, that they may detest all such practices and protest against them. And whereas they have endeavoured to deceive the simple-hearted of this nation, by fair pretences to the propagation of religion and by specious

779

shows of zeal for the salvation of souls, our countrymen may plainly see it is not us but ours they seek; if it be us, it is to destroy us, and not to save us; witness their villainous practices throughout all Christendom, and especially in this our country ever since the reformation of the church of God here with us. Reader, this is no feigned thing; the original author was an Italian, and no doubt but of the communion of that abominable whore, the mother of all harlots; and therefore we may easily be induced to believe the contents thereof; for certainly had not their practices been notoriously known, even to those of their own communion, this author could not have had the face to have published this treatise in his own country, where popish religion is generally practised and professed by every man. I tell thee, reader, when it pleaseth God to give me a little rest from this weighty affair I have now in hand, I will give the people of England such an account of the villainies of these Jesuits as will I hope make them and their votaries to be an abomination to every sober and judicious protestant, and even also to those of their own persuasion. I am confident that the eyes of the nation are open to see their base contrivances and plotting against the king, kingdom, and protestant religion; and by this little scheme we may see what would be done were they lords over us. And as I commend this treatise to thy serious consideration (dear reader) so I must also recommend to thee a piece lately set forth, entitled, *The Heart and its right Sovereign, and Rome, no Mother Church to England, in which the nullity of Rome's Church and Ordination is proved*, by that judicious and reverend divine, Thomas Jones of Oswestry in the county of Salop, and sold by Benja. Shirly under St. Dunstan's Church in Fleet Street. Both that and this I recommend to thee, to give the nation some satisfaction till God give me opportunity to do my country that service as to publish my whole narrative. I shall say no more, but beg God for a blessing on all our hearty endeavours after a more full discovery of this mystery of iniquity. And so farewell,

Thy brother in Christ,
Titus Oates

Honoured Dear Sir,

Post varios casus, post tot discrimina—After many fears and frights I thank our Blessed Lady I am safe got out of the mouth of the Lion, and have got the sea between me and danger. It would be troublesome to repeat to you the hazards I have run, how often I was upon the brink of being discovered and taken by the heretics, who have laid all the sea-ports to arrest all such as should attempt to pass over the seas; but in re-gard I have something of more moment and concern for the catholic cause to impart to you, I will not stuff out this pacquet with those re-lations, with the remembrance of which I hope hereafter to laugh away some pleasant hours with you.

I give you thanks for the account of affairs which I have now before me, and you are desired still to continue it, in regard you may do it with great security, both by reason of the way by which it comes and the character to which it is committed, which I think no person living besides yourself has a key of, and how ingenious soever some in *Haereti-copolis* may be in expounding ciphers, this will cost them some time to understand.

I understand by the enclosed proclamation, that the immortal parlia-ment, as 'twas believed, is at last dissolved, and immediately upon the receipt of yours I communicated it to their reverences, the Fathers L.C.D.F. and P. The next day they summoned together such as we put confidence in, to enter upon an immediate consult upon this traverse of our affairs. Their reverences were under as great disappointments and as many disturbances as you can well imagine, this short turn having utterly broken all the measures they had so wisely taken; and for some time they were unresolved what course to steer, being uncertain of what complexion and temper a new parliament might prove.

True it is, the late parliament were in reality, as we had reason to believe, mostly in their judgment enemies enough to catholics, but we had so well managed our affairs as to possess some of the most active and hot-spirited among them, the bellwethers of the house, who lead the whole flock. That there was an absolute necessity first to run down some great ones, who interposed, as we persuaded the world, in favour of us, and that unless they were taken out of the way, there could be nothing done to purpose, either to discover the bottom of the design, or to punish the persons principally accused of the plot, as they call it. This was a method which it was judged would take them off from the violent chase and pursuit of poor catholics, who were now upon the dreadful brink of a most terrible persecution, and to divert the storm nothing could be more conducive than to dash these black clouds one against another, and discharge their thunders mutually upon themselves: for if we could this or any other way engage the heretics deep enough in a quarrel among themselves, by the industry of our party among them, we could not tell how far these discords and oppositions might transport them, nor what would be the consequences or events of a fire-ball in the H.C. We have had no contemptible success with such engines in other occasions, and it was hoped it might at last put the nation, and especially the city, into a general mutiny upon the disappointment of their expectations, there being nothing so unanimously desired or so passionately longed for as to see all private heats laid aside, to prosecute the main business of the plot. And should it have come to a popular tumult, we should not have been wanting to have made considerable advantages of it, and under the colour of being popishly affected, and obstructing the prosecution of the plot, few of our enemies should have survived the fury of the tumult; and it may be we might have made the heretics themselves help to reduce their new Babylon to cinders a second time, and in that confusion have done some executions which I will not name. However, if that should not happen, we were hereby assured that we should for some time divert the imminent danger which threatened catholics in general, and those noble lords in particular; and no man knows what the very gaining a little time may produce in favour of us. *Multa cadunt inter poculum, supremaque labra.*

This course we knew was very pleasing to many, who, as our worthy friend, the much lamented Mr.C. had judiciously observed, to revenge their private piques had of a long time set themselves to oppose the ministers of state, and to whom such a promising opportunity was muscadine and eggs; and besides, it was infinitely taking and popular to all the discontented and factious, who, I am persuaded, would join with the catholics, the French, or the Great Turk, rather than lose the pleasure of seeing some great persons take the sommerset from the battlements of honour, especially such as they are made believe are enemies to their liberties and religion, which are but one thing with two names.

However, we were sure of this advantage, that by degrees we should persuade people that there never was any such thing as any design among the catholics against the king and government; there being no more evident demonstration that the H.C. did not believe there was any real plot than both their violent proceeding upon disbanding the army, even when 'twas said and sworn before them that there were 20,000 men in a readiness to attend the fatal blow, and that the king of France with his whole power was ready to strike in with the catholics; as also their running so furiously upon the ministers of state, instead of the catholic lords as being the more dangerous conspirators. And it may be we have lost no ground by this artifice, and thereby confirming what we did at first and have all along given out and spread abroad, that it was in reality a plot of the presbyterians against his majesty and the government, and that under the pretence of a plot of the papists, all such as were friends to the church or crown should be accused to be popishly affected; and thus by ruining the supporters, the crown must fall of course; this was the way in which they, by our assistance, so successfully proceeded in '41, and nothing could make it more plain than that the same party was playing their old lessons over again. And as we did then in a great measure happily effect our designs, and manage the heats till they burnt down all, so we were not without hopes to do the same, and like flints, by striking them one against another, to dash them in pieces, and fire the several factions; and when they were of all sides sufficiently weakened, under pretence of supporting the weaker party, to bring in the power of the most Christian king, to make them friends by subduing both, which was an advantage we might reasonably hope for now, but could not expect in the former revolutions, while his most Christian majesty was a minor, and France itself engaged in domestic troubles.

But this parliament and our hopes of it being both at an end, we are to consider how we may manage the next and succeeding parliaments so as nothing may be done to our prejudice, and by consequence that they may become advantageous to our pious design of extirpating heresy and propagating the catholic faith in England again. Upon our serious consult it has been here after mature deliberation agreed upon, to send you these following resolutions of their reverences, who have done me the honour to assign me the province of taking care to transmit their resolves to you, and receive your answers and an account of the movement of our affairs. You are therefore with all speed and secrecy to take care of the dispatch of these instructions to all such persons as we may confide in, and you shall judge qualified for an employ of so great trust and concern that I may say the whole catholic interest and hopes in England depend upon the success of this negotiation.

And first, as things previous to the elections which shall be made, let the emissaries in all counties and corporations, especially such as have burgesses, be vigilant to enquire who are to be the candidates for the succeeding elections.

Secondly, use all endeavours among the dissenters according to your interest, to get in as many of the late members as you can, especially P.C.B.M.&c. Our excellent friend M. has assured his illustriousness the N. that he will not fail to be in again, nor to do us the best service he can, now, as well as in the last.

Thirdly, if that cannot be done, but that new ones are set up, if they be persons firm in their loyalty and such as have any the remotest dependence or expectance upon the court or army, then give out among the people, though *en passant* only, as you bait at your inns, that to your certain knowledge, such gentlemen are great courtiers, and are of that party who design to reduce the nation to the model of France by the arbitrary power of a standing army, thereby to introduce and establish popery among us, which you must be sure to make most vehement and bitter declamations against. If they are persons strongly inclined to the church of England, then give out confidently that they are papists in heart and that you know where they have declared themselves such and that it is most visible by their being so much for ceremonies. This all the dissenters will not only easily credit, but will be very helpful to us in spreading and justifying the reports; these things spoken with confidence and a pretence of some intimate knowledge of them, and that you now divulge these secrets out of sincere affection to the nation, ready to be betrayed to popery and arbitrary government, will fly like wildfire among the ordinary people, who will snowball it from hand to hand and father it upon persons of repute, not knowing the original hand from whence it first came; and the repeated echo of their fears will both redouble and confirm it. By this means you shall with the assistance of the dissenters, who greedily lay hold of this occasion which they have so long wished for and expected, be sure to promote the election of such, especially burgesses, as are disaffected both to the king and church; and though possibly in many counties the loyalty and interest of the gentry will carry it against us in the knights, yet the greatest number consisting of the corporation representatives, there we shall be too hard for them. And then mark what will follow upon this: they will meet with an invincible prejudice against the king and established government, both civil and ecclesiastical; they will fall violently upon the church as well as the papists; they will be so taken up with their own affairs and embroilments our friends will engage them in, that ours will sleep; and being so hot and disorderly, they will in probability oblige the king to send them home again and seek for another.

By this means the city and country will be under the greatest disappointment and dissatisfaction imaginable, and the army which is undisbanded will be thought necessary to be kept up, but there being no money to pay them, they will be burdensome and exasperate the country and augment the jealousy of a standing army; a fleet must also be put to sea because of the alarms of the French, and when they come home the seamen must be turned adrift for their pay too; it may be a new parliament may not be called in some time, but such ways may be taken to raise money for the public necessity as may render the government odious and dispose people to a general insurrection, and then the day's our own, then my noble lords will save their heads, for they must be tried by a parliament, and if our affairs jump luckily they shall outlive Methusalem if they live to see a parliament so loyal as to give the king money or endeavour to settle the peace of the nation.

But in the second place, if the parliament shall sit and there appears any danger to us by their being unanimous and so like to continue and to bring the lords to their trial, all endeavours must be used by such as can be got to be of our party; first to run them again upon the ministers of state, as being popishly affected and designed to subvert parliaments and introduce arbitrary government. I need not speak much of this; you are sufficiently instructed how to manage it, and cannot want a cry to set it up.

Secondly, obstruct as much as possible the raising of money, and yet cry out of the imminent danger and fears of the French; it may be you will have reason and truth in that particular; however, delay the money by asking such unreasonable things in recompense of it that the money bill upon such terms may be rejected, and be sure it may not be near enough for the present necessity. Urge the misspending of the great revenue of the crown, but lay all the blame upon the ministers; you cannot miss the king if you hit the other. This will put the king out of all hopes of this parliament, and may possibly occasion either a long prorogation or a dissolution, and we shall be better provided against a new parliament than we could be now, being so much surprised in the dissolution of the last. And besides if this parliament upon which the factious have built such hopes be either prorogued or dissolved, it will still exasperate the nation, and they will be apt to receive the impressions of their own fears and jealousies as well as those we must now sow thick among the discontented; if it continues we must still play the same game, and with grievances, smart votes, and ingrateful addresses keep up and increase the misunderstandings and widen the differences between the king and the H.C.

Thirdly, asperse all that are not of our party as court-pensioners or popishly affected. This will secure ours from being discovered and will render the other odious to the people, and hinder their being elected into a future parliament, if this should happen to be hastily dissolved.

Fourthly, let our party bring in a bill for comprehension or toleration. If it does no other good, it will occasion great heats and altercations, long debates, and will be an excellent *remora* to all other affairs. It will make them highly the favourites of the separatists who will be most active against the crown and government, and if that can be passed, it is no matter how severely it excludes all catholics from the benefit of indulgence; it will certainly ruin the church, and we shall be well enough able to do our business and to prepare the people for a rebellion under the shelter of the several sects who hate both the king and church sufficiently already, and will in a little time become so numerous and confident that by their help we may be able to effect our design. This politic Janus of a toleration has also another face, for it will alienate the affections of those who are zealous for the church from the crown, when they see that give them up as a prey to their enemies; and if it does not yet, it will disable them from doing it the service they would in case of necessity; so that if it comes to a rebellion, the K. will be destitute of assistance of all sides, and must seek for aid among the catholics and from foreign power, and which way soever the game goes, we shall be sure not only to save our stakes, but to win by the hand.

Dear sir, be diligent and vigorous in the prosecution of these instructions, and be assured that nothing shall be wanting on the part of their reverences to forward the design, neither money for the present nor power for the future, if occasion offers. His most Christian majesty is now at entire liberty in case of necessity either to interpose for us or to assist us with his invincible arms, and to promote so pious and religious a cause. Doubt nothing, but be of good courage in the discharge of this high trust reposed in you, and assure yourself of success and proportionate rewards on earth, eternal fame, and eternal glory in the heavenly paradise. The fathers send you theirs and the apostolical benediction; have me recommended to all our friends. Our blessed Lady and all saints pray for you and succeed your endeavours. Fail not to advertise us how the wheel of affairs moves, that so we may be able to advise and direct accordingly, farewell.

D.P.

Paris, Feb. 12. N.St. 1678.

OF THE TRIAL OF THE SPIRITS

By John Tillotson

JOHN TILLOTSON (1630–1694), archbishop of Canterbury, was the son of a puritan clothworker of Halifax. He matriculated at Clare College, Cambridge, in 1647, became fellow in 1651, and M.A. in 1654. An eclectic in theology, he was weaned from rigid Calvinism by William Chillingworth's *Religion of Protestants* (1638), and after his ordination in 1661, he sided at the Savoy conference with the nonconforming group. Following a brief experience in country parishes he became in 1663 preacher at Lincoln's Inn, at a salary of £124 a year, a post he held till he became archbishop. He was one of few men who have preached themselves into preferment. His sermons, over which he laboured, writing and for a time memorizing every word, led to a change in the method and style of preaching; throughout the eighteenth century, when Warburton described them as 'simple, elegant, candid, clear, and rational,' they served as models both in form and content. Chaplain in 1666 to Charles II—who said of Tillotson that 'he bowed the wrong way,' leaning backwards at the name of Jesus and raising his eyes—he became prebend of Canterbury in 1670 and dean in 1672; he supported the Seven Bishops in 1688, was with Burnet an ecclesiastical adviser to William III, became dean of St. Paul's in 1689, and in 1691 replaced the nonjuror Sancroft as archbishop.

Tillotson was the most striking of the great 'latitude-men' of the late seventeenth century. To him, as to the Cambridge Platonists, truth was of two kinds, natural and revealed, and reason the faculty which apprehended and judged both. As they, he hoped to unite the church by finding a doctrinal base, limited to the essentials of natural religion, so broad that warring groups could agree on it. In 1674 and again in 1691 he tried vainly to find a formula which would open the church's doors to nonconformists. Tillotson's latitudinarianism emphasized two essentials: the fatherhood of God, and the obligation on the part of mankind to imitate the divine charity by performing good works. For him the injunction 'Depart from evil' was really 'the whole duty of man.' The laws of God were reasonable, suited to man's nature, advantageous to his interest, and not too difficult for him to obey. Thus religion became a prudential assurance of the wisdom of following in this world the paths of sobriety and piety. But Tillotson's broad and rational approach had an unexpected, if logical, result. It provided for later deists the devastating weapons by which they too could make 'trial of the spirits.'

SERMON XXI

Preached at Whitehall, 4 April 1679

I John iv, 1

Beloved, believe not every spirit, but try the spirits whether
they are of God; because many false prophets are gone
out into the world

THIS caution and counsel was given upon the occasion of the false
prophets and teachers that were risen up in the beginning of the Christian church, who endeavoured to seduce men from the true doctrine of
the Gospel delivered by the apostles of our Lord and Saviour. And
these, teaching contrary things, could not both be from God; and therefore St. John calls upon Christians to examine the doctrines and pretences
of those new teachers, whether they were from God or not. Believe not
every spirit, that is, not every one that takes upon him to be inspired
and to be a teacher come from God. But try the spirits; that is, examine
those that make this pretence, whether it be real or not, and examine
the doctrines which they bring, because there are many imposters abroad
in the world.

This is the plain sense of the words, in which there are contained
these four propositions:

First, That men may, and often do, falsely pretend to inspiration.
And this is the reason upon which the apostle grounds this exhortation:
because many false prophets are gone out into the world; therefore we
should try who are true and who are false.

Secondly, We are not to believe everyone that pretends to be inspired
and to teach a divine doctrine. This follows upon the former because
men may falsely pretend to inspiration; therefore we are not to believe
everyone that makes this pretence. For any man that has but confidence
enough and conscience little enough may pretend to come from God.
And, if we admit all pretences of this kind, we lie at the mercy of every
crafty and confident man to be led by him into what delusions he pleases.

Thirdly, Neither are we to reject all that pretend to come from God.
This is sufficiently implied in the text, for when the apostle says ' believe
not every spirit,' he supposes that we are to believe some; and when he

says ' try the spirits whether they be of God,' he supposes some to be of God, and that those which are so are to be believed. These three observations are so plain that I need only to name them to make way for the fourth.

Fourthly, Which I principally designed to insist upon these words: and that is this, that there is some way to discern mere pretenders to inspiration, from those who are truly and divinely inspired. And this is necessarily implied in the apostle's bidding us to ' try the spirits whether they are of God.' For it would be in vain to make any trial if there be no way to discern between pretended and real inspiration.

Now the handling of this will give occasion to two very material inquiries, and useful to be resolved.

I How we may discern between true and counterfeit doctrines, those which really are from God, and those which only pretend to be so?

II To whom does this judgment of discerning appertain?

I How we may discern between true and counterfeit doctrines and revelations? For the clearing of this I shall lay down these following propositions:

1. That reason is the faculty whereby revelations are to be discerned; or to use the phrase in the text, it is that whereby we are to judge what spirits ' are of God,' and what not. For all revelation from God supposes us to be men, and to be endued with reason; and therefore it does not create new faculties in us, but propounds new objects to that faculty which was in us before. Whatever doctrines God propounds to men are propounded to their understandings, and by this faculty we are to examine all doctrines which pretend to be from God, and, upon examination, to judge whether there be reason to receive them as divine, or to reject them as impostures.

2. All supernatural revelation supposes the truth of the principles of natural religion. We must first be assured that there is a God, before we can know that he has made any revelation of himself; and we must know that his words are true, otherwise there were no sufficient reason to believe the revelations which he makes to us; and we must believe his authority over us, and that he will reward our obedience to his laws and punish our breach of them; otherwise there would neither be obligation or encouragement to obedience. These and many other things

are supposed to be true, and naturally known to us, antecedently to all supernatural revelation; otherwise the revelations of God would signify nothing to us, nor be of any force with us.

3. All reasonings about divine revelations must necessarily be governed by the principles of natural religion; that is, by those apprehensions which men naturally have of the divine perfections, and by the clear notions of good and evil which are imprinted upon our natures. Because we have no other way to judge what is worthy of God and credible to be revealed by him, and what not, but by the natural notions which we have of God and of his essential perfections: which, because we know him to be immutable, we have reason to believe he will never contradict. And by these principles, likewise, we are to interpret what God has revealed; and when any doubt arises concerning the meaning of any divine revelation (as that of the Holy Scriptures) we are to govern ourselves, in the interpretation of it, by what is most agreeable to those natural notions which we have of God, and we have all the reason in the world to reject that sense which is contrary thereto. For instance, when God is represented in Scripture as having a human shape, eyes, ears, and hands, the notions which men naturally have of the divine nature and perfections do sufficiently direct us to interpret these expressions in a sense worthy of God and agreeable to his perfection. And therefore it is reasonable to understand them as rather spoken to our capacity, and in a figure, than to be literally intended. And this will proportionably hold in many other cases.

4. Nothing ought to be received as a revelation from God which plainly contradicts the principles of natural religion, or overthrows the certainty of them. For instance, it were in vain to pretend a revelation from God, ' That there is no God,' because this is a contradiction in terms.

So likewise to pretend a command from God, ' That we are to hate and despise him '; because it is not credible that God should require anything of reasonable creatures so unsuitable to their natures and to their obligations to him; besides, that such a law as this does tacitly involve a contradiction, because, upon such a supposition, to despise God would be to obey him, and yet to obey him is certainly to honour him. So that in this case to honour God and to despise him would be the same thing, and equal contempts of him. In like manner it would be vain to pretend any revelation from God, ' That there is no life after

this, nor rewards and punishments in another world,' because this is
contrary to those natural apprehensions which have generally possessed
mankind, and would take away the main force and sanction of the divine
laws. The same may be said concerning any pretended revelation from
God which evidently contradicts those natural notions which men have
of good and evil; as, that God should command or allow sedition and rebellion, perfidiousness and perjury, because the practice of these would
be apparently destructive of the peace and happiness of mankind and would
naturally bring confusion into the world. But God is not the God of
confusion, but of order, which St. Paul appeals to us as a principle naturally known. Upon the same account, nothing ought to be entertained as
a divine revelation which overthrows the certainty of the principles of
natural religion, because that would take away the certainty of divine
revelation itself, which supposes the truth of those principles. For instance,
whoever pretends any revelation that brings the providence of God into
question does by that very thing make such a revelation questionable.
For if God take no care of the world, have no concernment for human
affairs, why should we believe that he makes any revelation of his will
to men? And by this principle Moses will have false prophets to be tried:
Deut.13,1. ' If there arise among you a prophet, and giveth thee a sign
or wonder, and the sign or wonder come to pass whereof he spoke unto
thee, saying, Let us go after other gods and let us serve them; thou shalt
not harken unto the words of that prophet.' And he gives the reason of
this, ver.5. ' Because he hath spoken unto you to turn you away from the
Lord your God, which brought you out of the land of Egypt.' Here is
a case wherein a false prophet is supposed to work a true miracle to give
credit to his doctrine (which in other cases the Scripture makes the sign
of a true prophet) but yet in this case he is to be rejected as an imposter,
because the doctrine he teaches would draw men off from the worship
of the true God who is naturally known, and had manifested himself
to the people of Israel in so miraculous a manner, by bringing them out
of the land of Egypt. So that a miracle is not enough to give credit to a
prophet who teaches anything contrary to that natural notion which men
have, That there is but one God, who only ought to be worshipped.

5. Nothing ought to be received as a divine doctrine and revelation
without good evidence that it is so: that is, without some argument sufficient to satisfy a prudent and considerate man. Now (supposing there

be nothing in the matter of the revelation that is evidently contrary to the principles of natural religion, nor to any former revelation which has already received a greater and more solemn attestation from God) miracles are owned by all mankind to be a sufficient testimony to any person, or doctrine, that they are from God. This was the testimony which God gave to Moses to satisfy the people of Israel that he had sent him: Exod.4.1,2. Moses said, they will not believe me, nor harken unto my voice, for they will say, The Lord has not appeared unto thee. Upon this God endues him with a power of miracles, to be an evidence to them, that they may believe that the God of their fathers, Abraham, Isaac, and Jacob, hath appeared unto thee. And all along in the Old Testament, when God sent his prophets to make a new revelation, or upon any strange and extraordinary message, he always gave credit to them by some sign or wonder which they foretold or wrought. And when he sent his son into the world, he gave testimony to him by innumerable, great, and un-questionable miracles, more and greater than Moses and all the prophets had wrought. And there was great reason for this; because our Saviour came not only to publish a new religion to the world, but to put an end to that religion which God had instituted before. And now that the Gospel has had the confirmation of such miracles as never were wrought upon any other occasion, no evidence inferior to this can, in reason, control this revelation or give credit to anything contrary to it. And therefore, though the false prophets and antichrists, foretold by our Saviour, did really work miracles, yet they were so inconsiderable in comparison of our Saviour's, that they deserve no credit in opposition to that revelation which had so clear a testimony given to it from heaven by miracles, besides all other concurring arguments to confirm it.

6. And lastly, no argument is sufficient to prove a doctrine or revela-tion to be from God which is not clearer and stronger than the difficulties and objections against it. Because all assent is grounded upon evidence, and the strongest, clearest evidence always carries it; but where the evidence is equal on both sides, that can produce nothing but a suspense and doubt in the mind whether the thing be true or not. If Moses had not confuted Pharaoh's magicians by working miracles which they could not work, they might reasonably have disputed it with him, who had been the true prophet. But when he did works plainly above the power of their magic and the devil to do, then they submitted and ac-

knowledged that there was the finger of God. So likewise, though a person work a miracle (which ordinarily is a good evidence that he is sent by God) yet if the doctrine he brings be plainly contrary to those natural notions which we have of God, this is a better objection against the truth of this doctrine than the other is a proof of it; as is plain in the case which Moses puts, Deut. 13, which I mentioned before.

Upon the same account no man can reasonably believe the doctrine of transubstantiation to be revealed by God; because every man has as great evidence that transubstantiation is false, as any man can pretend to have that God has revealed any such thing. Suppose transubstantiation to be part of the Christian doctrine, it must have the same confirmation with the whole, and that is miracles. But of all doctrines in the world, it is peculiarly incapable of being proved by a miracle. But if a miracle were wrought for the proof of it, the very same assurance which a man has of the truth of the miracle, he has of the falsehood of the doctrine, that is, the clear evidence of his senses for both. For that there is a miracle wrought to prove that what he sees in the sacrament is not bread but the body of Christ, he has only the evidence of his senses; and he has the very same evidence to prove that what he sees in the sacrament is not the body of Christ, but bread. So that here arises a new controversy, whether a man should believe his senses giving testimony against the doctrine of transubstantiation, or bearing testimony to the miracle which is wrought to confirm that doctrine. For there is just the same evidence against the truth of the doctrine which there is for the truth of the miracle. So that the argument for transubstantiation and the objection against it do just balance one another; and where the weights in both scales are equal it is impossible that one should weigh down the other; and, consequently transubstantiation is not to be proved by a miracle; for that would be to prove to a man by something that he sees, that he does not see what he sees.

And thus I have endeavoured, as briefly and clearly as I could, to give satisfaction to the first inquiry I propounded, viz.: How we may discern between true and counterfeit revelations and doctrines. I proceed now to the

II To whom this judgment of discerning does appertain. Whether to Christians in general, or to some particular person or persons, authorized by God to judge for the rest of mankind, by whose judgment all men are concluded and bound up. And this is an inquiry of no small importance, because it is one of the most fundamental points in difference between us and the church of Rome. And however in many particular controversies, as concerning transubstantiation, the communion in one kind, the service of God in an unknown tongue, the business of indulgences, the invocation of saints, the worship of images, they are not able to offer anything that is fit to move a reasonable and considerate man; yet in this controversy, concerning the Judge of controverises, they are not destitute of some specious appearance of reason, which deserves to be weighed and considered. Therefore, that we may examine this matter to the bottom, I shall do these three things:

1. Lay down some cautions and limitations whereby we may understand how far the generality of Christians are allowed to judge in matters of religion.

2. I shall represent the grounds of this principle.

3. Endeavour to satisfy the main objections of our adversaries against it. And likewise to show, that there is no such reason and necessity for a universal infallible Judge as they pretend.

I I shall lay down some cautions and limitations by which we may understand how far the generality of Christians are allowed to judge in matters of religion.

First, Private persons are only to judge for themselves and not to impose their judgment upon others, as if they had any authority over them. And this is reasonable, because, if it were otherwise, a man would deprive others of that liberty which he assumes to himself, and which he can claim upon no other account but because it belongs to others equally with himself.

Secondly, This liberty of judging is not so to be understood as to take away the necessity and use of guides and teachers in religion, nor can this be denied to be a reasonable limitation; because the knowledge of revealed religion is not a thing born with us, nor ordinarily supernaturally infused into men; but is to be learned as other things are. And if it is to be learned, there must be some to teach and instruct others; and they that will learn must be modest and humble; and in those things, of which they are no competent judges, they must give credit to their teachers and trust their skill. For instance, every unlearned man is to take it upon the credit of those that are skilful, that the Scriptures are truly and faithfully translated; and for the understanding of obscure texts of Scripture and more difficult points in religion, he is to rely upon those whose proper business and employment it is to apply themselves to the understanding of these things. For in these cases every man is not capable of judging himself, and therefore he must necessarily trust others. And in all other things he ought to be modest, and unless it be in plain matters, which every man can judge of, he ought rather to distrust himself than his teacher.

And this respect may be given to a teacher, without either supposing him to be infallible, or making an absolute resignation of my judgment to him. A man may be a very able teacher (suppose of the mathematics) and fit to have the respect which is due to a teacher, though he be not infallible in those sciences; and because infallibility is not necessary to such a teacher, it is neither necessary nor convenient that I should absolutely resign up my judgment to him. For though I have reason to credit him, within the compass of his art, in things which I do not know, I am not therefore bound to believe him in things plainly contrary to what I and all mankind do certainly know. For example, if upon pretence of his skill in arithmetic, which I am learning of him, he should tell me that 'twice two do make not four, but five,' though I believed him to be the best mathematician in the world, yet I cannot believe him in this thing; nor is there reason I should, because I did not come to learn this of him, but knew as much of that before as he or any man else could tell me. The case is the same in matters of religion; in which there are some things so plain and lie so level to all capacities that every man is almost equally judge of them, as I shall have occasion further to show by and by.

Thirdly, Neither does this liberty of judging exempt men from a due submission and obedience to their teachers and governors. Every man is bound to obey the lawful commands of his governors; and what by public consent and authority is determined and established ought not to be gainsaid by private persons, but upon very clear evidence of the falsehood or unlawfulness of it. And this is every man's duty, for the maintaining of order, and out of regard to the peace and unity of the church, which is not to be violated upon every scruple and frivolous pretence. And when men are perverse and disobedient, authority is judge and may restrain and punish them.

Fourthly, Nor do I so far extend this liberty of judging in religion, as to think every man fit to dispute the controversies of religion. A great part of people are ignorant, and of so mean a capacity as not to be able to judge of the force of a very good argument, much less of the issue of a long dispute; and such persons ought not to engage in disputes of religion, but to beg God's direction and to rely upon their teachers, and, above all, to live up to the plain dictates of natural light and the clear commands of God's word, and this will be their best security. And if the Providence of God has placed them under such guides as do seduce them into error, their ignorance is invincible and God will not condemn them for it, so long as they sincerely endeavour to do the will of God so far as they know it. And this being the case of many, especially in the church of Rome, where ignorance is so industrially cherished, I have so much charity as to hope well concerning many of them. And seeing that church teaches and enjoins the people to worship images, it is in some sense charitably done of them, not to let them know the second commandment, that they may not be guilty of sinning against so plain a law.

Having premised these cautions, I proceed in the

II Place, To represent to you the grounds of this principle of our religion, viz. that we allow private persons to judge for themselves in matters of religion.

First, Because many things in religion, especially those which are most necessary to be believed and practised, are so plain that every man of ordinary capacity, after competent instruction in matters of religion (which is always to be supposed) can as well judge of them for himself as any man or company of men in the world can judge for him; because in these he has a plain rule to go by, natural light and clear revelation of Scripture. And this is no new principle of the protestants, but most expressly owned by the ancient fathers. Whatever things are necessary are plain, saith St. Chrysostom. All things are plainly contained in Scripture which concern faith and a good life, saith St. Austin. And nothing can be more reasonable than that those things which are plain to every man should be left to every man's judgment: for every man can judge of what is plain; of evident truth and falsehood, virtue and vice, of doctrines and laws plainly delivered in Scripture, if we believe anything to be so, which is next to madness to deny. I will refer it to no man's judgment upon earth to determine for me, Whether there be a God or not? Whether murder and perjury be sins? Whether it be not plain in Scripture that Jesus Christ is the Son of God, that he became man, and died for us, and rose again? So that there is no need of a judge in these cases. Nor can I believe any man to be so absolutely infallible as not to call his infallibility into question if he determines anything contrary to what is plain and evident to all mankind. For if he should determine that there is no God, or that he is not to be worshipped, or that he will not punish or reward men, or, which is the case that Bellarmine puts, that virtue is vice and vice virtue; he would hereby take away the very foundation of religion; and how can I look upon him any longer as a judge in matters of religion when there can be no such thing as religion if he have judged and determined right?

Secondly, The Scripture plainly allows this liberty to particular and private persons to judge for themselves. And for this I need go no farther than my text, which bids men ' try the spirits whether they be of God.' I do not think this is spoken only to the pope or to a general council, but to Christians in general; for to these the apostle writes. Now if St. John had believed that God had constituted an infallible judge in his church, to whose sentence and determination all Christians are bound to submit, he ought, in all reason, to have referred Christians to him for the trial of spirits, and not have left it to every man's private judgment to examine and determine these things. But it seems St. Paul was likewise of the same mind; and tho' he was guided by an infallible spirit, yet he did not expect that men should blindly submit to his doctrine. Nay, so far is he from that that he commends the Bereans for that very thing for which I daresay the church of Rome would have checked them most severely, namely for searching the Scriptures to see whether those things which the apostles delivered were so or not. This liberty St. Paul allowed, and though he was inspired by God, yet he treated those whom he taught like men. And indeed, it were a hard case that a necessity of believing divine revelations and rejecting impostures should be imposed upon Christians; and yet the liberty of judging, whether a doctrine be from God or not, should be taken away from them.

Thirdly, Our adversaries themselves are forced to grant that which in effect is as much as we contend for. For tho' they deny a liberty of judging in particular points of religion, yet they are forced to grant men a liberty of judging upon the whole. When they of the church of Rome would persuade a Jew or a heathen to become a Christian, or a heretic (as they are pleased to call us) to come over to the communion of their church, and offer arguments to induce them thereunto; they do by this very thing, whether they will or no, make that man judge which is the true church and the true religion; because it would be ridiculous to persuade a man to turn to their religion and to urge him with reasons to do so, and yet to deny him the use of his own judgment whether their reasons be sufficient to move them to make such a change. Now, as the apostle reasons in another case, if men be fit to judge for themselves in so great and important a matter as the choice of their religion, why should they be thought unworthy to judge in lesser matters? They tell us indeed that a man may use his judgment in the choice of his religion; but when he has once chosen, he is then for ever to resign up his judgment to their church. But what tolerable reason can any man give why a man should be fit to judge upon the whole and yet unfit to judge upon particular points? Especially if it be considered that no man can make a discreet judgment of any religion before he has examined the particular doctrines of it and made a judgment concerning them. Is it credible that God should give a man judgment in the most fundamental and important matter of all, viz. to discern the true religion and the true church from the false, for no other end but to enable him to choose once for all to whom he should resign and enslave his judgment for ever? Which is just as reasonable as if one should say that God has given a man eyes, but to look out once for all and to pitch upon a discreet person to lead him about blindfold all the days of his life. I come now to the

III Thing I propounded, which is, To answer the main objection of our adversaries against this principle; and likewise to show that there is no such reason and necessity for a universal infallible judge as they pretend. Now their great objection is this: if every man judge for himself, there will be nothing but confusion in religion, there will be no end of controversies; so that a universal, infallible judge is necessary, and without this God had not made sufficient provision for the assurance of man's faith and for the peace and unity of his church; or, as it is expressed in the canon law, *aliter Dominus non videretur fuisse discretus*: otherwise our Lord had not seemed to be discreet. How plausible soever this objection may appear, I do not despair, but if men will lay aside prejudice and impartially consider things, to make it abundantly evident that this ground is not sufficient to found an infallible judge upon. And therefore, in answer to it, I desire these following particulars may be considered.

First, That this, which they say, rather proves what God should have done, according to their fancy, than what he has really and actually done. My text expressly bids Christians to ' try the spirits,' which, to any man's sense, does imply that they may judge of these matters; but the church of Rome says they may not, because, if this liberty were permitted, God had not ordered things wisely, and for the best, for the peace and unity of his church. But, as the apostle says in another case, ' What art thou, O man, that objectest against God? '

Secondly, If this reasoning be good, we may as well conclude that there is an universal infallible judge set over the whole world in all temporal matters, to whose authority all mankind is bound to submit. Because this is as necessary to the peace of the world as the other is to the peace of the church. And men surely are every whit as apt to be obstinate and perverse about matters of temporal right as about matters of faith. But it is evident in fact and experience that there is no such universal judge, appointed by God over the whole world, to decide all cases of temporal right; and for want of him, the world is fain to shift as well as it can. But now a very acute and scholastical man, that would argue that God must needs have done whatever he fancies convenient for the world should be done, might by the very same way of reasoning conclude the necessity of an universal infallible judge in civil matters as well as in matters of religion; and their *aliter Dominus non videretur fuisse discretus*, otherwise God had not seemed to be discreet, is every whit as cogent and as civil in the one case as the other.

Thirdly, There is no need of such a judge to assure men in matters of religion, because men may be sufficiently certain without him. I hope it may be certain and clear enough that there is a God, and that his Providence governs the world, and that there is another life after this, though neither pope nor council had ever declared anything about these matters. And for revealed doctrines, we may be certain enough of all that is necessary, if it be true which the fathers tell us, that all things necessary are plainly revealed in the Holy Scriptures.

Fourthly, An infallible judge, if there were one, is no certain way to end controversies and to preserve the unity of the church, unless it were likewise infallibly certain that there is such a judge and who he is. For until men were sure of both these, there would still be a controversy whether there be an infallible judge and who he is. And if it be true which they tell us, that without an infallible judge controversies cannot be ended, then a controversy concerning an infallible judge can never be ended. And there are two controversies actually on foot about an infallible judge: One, whether there be an infallible judge or not? which is a controversy between us and the church of Rome; and the other, who this infallible judge is? which is a controversy among themselves which could never yet be decided. And yet, until it be decided, infallibility, if they had it, would be of no use to them for the ending of controversies.

Fifthly, There is no such absolute need, as is pretended, of determining all controversies in religion. If men would divest themselves of prejudice and interest, as they ought, in all matters of religion, the necessary things of religion are plain enough, and men would generally agree well enough about them. But if men will suffer themselves to be biased by these, they would not harken to an infallible judge if there were one; or they would find out some way or other to call his infallibility into question. And as for doubtful and lesser matters in religion, charity and mutual forbearance among Christians would make the church as peaceful and happy as perhaps it was ever designed to be in this world, without absolute unity in opinion.

Sixthly and lastly, Whatever may be the inconveniences of men's judging for themselves in religion, yet taking this principle with the cautions I have given, I doubt not to make it appear that the inconveniences are far the least on that side. The present condition of human nature does not admit of any constitution of things, whether in religion or civil matters which is free from all kind of exception and inconvenience. That is the best state of things which is liable to the least and fewest. If men be modest and humble and willing to learn, God has done that which is sufficient for the assurance of our faith and for the peace of his church without an infallible judge; and if men will not be so, I cannot tell what would be sufficient. I am sure there were heresies and schisms in the apostles' times, when those who governed the church were certainly guided by an infallible spirit. God has appointed guides and teachers for us in matters of religion, and if we will be contented to be instructed by them in those necessary articles and duties of religion, which are plainly contained in Scripture, and to be counselled and directed by them in things that are more doubtful and difficult, I do not see why we might not do well enough without any infallible judge or guide.

But still it will be said, Who shall judge what things are plain and what doubtful? The answer to this, in my opinion, is not difficult. For if there be anything plain in religion, every man that has been duly instructed in the principles of religion can judge of it, or else it is not plain. But there are some things in religion so very plain that no guide or judge can, in reason, claim that authority over men, as to oblige them to believe or do the contrary; no, tho' he pretend to infallibility; no, tho' he were an apostle, tho' he an angel from heaven. St. Paul puts the case so high, Gal.,1,8. 'Though we, or an angel from heaven, preach any other Gospel unto you, than what you have received, let him be accursed.' Which plainly supposes that Christians may and can judge when doctrines are contrary to the Gospel. What? Not believe an apostle, nor an angel from heaven, if he should teach anything evidently contrary to the plain doctrine of the Gospel? If he should determine virtue to be a vice and vice to be virtue? No, not an apostle, nor an angel, because such a doctrine as this would confound and overturn all things in religion. And yet Bellarmine puts this very case, and says, if the pope should so determine, we were bound to believe him, unless we would sin against conscience.

I will conclude this discourse by putting a very plain and familiar case, by which it will appear what credit and authority is fit to be given to a guide, and what not. Suppose I came a stranger into England, and landing at Dover took a guide there to conduct me in my way to York, which I knew before by the map to lie north of Dover. Having committed myself to him, if he lead me for two or three days together out of any plain road, and many times over hedge and ditch, I cannot but think it strange that, in a civil and well-inhabited country there should be no highway from one part of it to another. Yet thus far I submit to him, tho' not without some regret and impatience. But then if after this, for two or three days more, he lead me directly south, and with my face full upon the sun at noonday, and at last bring me back again to Dover pier, and still bids me follow him, then certainly no modesty does oblige a man not to dispute with his guide, and to tell him surely that can be no way, because it is sea. Now tho' he set never so bold a face upon the matter and tell me with all the gravity and authority in the world, that it is not the sea but dry land under the species and appearance of water, and that whatever my eyes tell me, having once committed myself to his guidance, I must not trust my own senses in the case, it being one of the dangerous sorts of infidelity for a man to believe his own eyes rather than his faithful and infallible guide. All this moves me not, but I begin to expostulate roundly with him and to let him understand that if I must not believe what I see, he is like to be of no further use to me, because I shall not be able, at this rate, to know whether I have a guide and whether I follow him or not. In short, I tell him plainly, that when I took him for my guide, I did not take him to tell me the difference between north and south, between a hedge and highway, between sea and dry land; all this I knew before, as well as he or any man else could tell me; but I took him to conduct and direct me the nearest way to York. And therefore after all his impertinent talk, after all his motives of credibility to persuade me to believe him, and all his confident sayings, which he gravely calls demonstrations, I stand stiffly upon the shore and leave my learned and reverend guide to take his own course, and to dispose of himself as he pleases; but firmly resolve not to follow him. And is any man to be blamed that breaks with his guide upon these terms?

And this is truly the case, when a man commits himself to the guidance of any person or church. If by virtue of this authority, they will needs persuade me out of my senses and not to believe what I see, but what they say—that virtue is vice and vice virtue, if they declare them to be so—and that, because they say they are infallible, I am to receive all their dictates for oracles, tho' never so evidently false and absurd in the judgment of all mankind; in this case there is no way to be rid of these unreasonable people, but to desire of them, since one kindness deserves another, and all contradictions are alike easy to be believed, that they would be pleased to believe that infidelity is faith, and that when I absolutely renounce their authority, I do yield a most perfect submission and obedience to it.

Upon the whole matter, all the revelations of God, as well as the laws of men, go upon the presumption that men are not stark fools, but that they will consider their interest and have some regard to the great concernment of their eternal salvation. And this is as much to secure men from mistakes in matters of belief, as God has afforded to keep men from sin in matters of practice. He has made no effectual and infallible provision that men shall not sin, and yet it would puzzle any man to give a good reason why God should take more care to secure men against errors in belief, than against sin and wickedness in their lives.

I shall now only draw three or four inferences from this discourse which I have made and so conclude.

1. That it is every man's duty, who has ability and capacity for it, to endeavour to understand the grounds of his religion. For to try doctrines is to inquire into the grounds and reasons of them; which the better any man understands, the more firmly he will be established in the truth, and be the more resolute in the day of trial, and the better able to withstand the arts and assaults of cunning adversaries, and the fierce storms of persecution. And, on the contrary, that man will soon be moved from his steadfastness, who never examined the grounds and reasons of his belief. When it comes to the trial, he that has but little to say for his religion will probably neither do nor suffer much for it.

2. That all doctrines are vehemently to be suspected which decline trial and are so loath to be brought into the light; which will not endure a fair examination, but magisterially require an implicit faith. Whereas truth is bold and full of courage and loves to appear openly, and is so secure and confident of her own strength as to offer herself to the severest trial and examination. But to deny all liberty of inquiry and judgment in matters of religion is the greatest injury and disparagement to truth that can be, and a tacit acknowledgment that she lies under some disadvantage, and that there is less to be said for her than for error.

I have often wondered why the people in the church of Rome do not suspect their teachers and guides to have some ill design upon them when they do so industriously debar them of the means of knowledge, and are so very loath to let them understand what it is that we have to say against their religion. For can anything in the world be more suspicious than to persuade men to put out their eyes, upon promise that they will help them to a much more better and faithful guide? If any church, any profession of men be unwilling their doctrines be exposed to trial, it is a certain sign they know something by them that is faulty, and which will not endure the light. This is the account which our Saviour gives us in a like case. It was because men's deeds were evil that they loved darkness rather than light. For every one that doth evil hateth the light; neither cometh he to the light, lest his deeds should be reproved. But he that doth the truth cometh to the light, that his deeds may be made manifest that they are wrought in God.

3. Since reason and Christianity allow this liberty to private persons to judge for themselves in matters of religion, we should use this privilege with much modesty and humility, with great submission and deference to our spiritual rulers and guides, whom God hath appointed in his church. And there is very great need of this caution, since by experience we find this liberty so much abused by many to the nourishing of pride and self-conceit, of division and faction; and those who are least able to judge, to be frequently the most forward and confident, the most peremptory and perverse; and instead of demeaning themselves with the submission of learners, to assume to themselves the authority of judges, even in the most doubtful and disputable matters.

The tyranny of the Roman church over the minds and consciences of men is not to be justified upon any account; but nothing puts so plausible a colour on it as the ill-use that is too frequently made of this natural privilege of men's judging for themselves in a matter of so infinite concernment, as that of their eternal happiness. But then it is to be considered that the proper remedy in this case is not to deprive men of this privilege, but to use the best means to prevent the abuse of it. For though the inconveniences arising from the ill-use of it may be very great, yet the mischief, on the other hand, is intolerable. Religion itself is liable to be abused to very bad purposes, and frequently is so; but it is not therefore best that there should be no religion. And yet this objection, if it be of any force and pursued home, is every whit as strong against religion itself, as against men's liberty of judging in matters of religion. Nay, I add farther, that no man can judiciously embrace the true religion unless he be permitted to judge whether that which he embraces be the true religion or not.

4. When, upon due trial and examination we are well settled and

established in our religion, let us hold fast the profession of our faith without wavering; and not be like children, tossed to and fro and carried about with every wind of doctrine, through the sight of men and the cunning craftiness of those who lie in wait to deceive. And, above all, let us resolve to live according to the excellent rules and precepts of our holy religion; let us heartily obey that doctrine which we profess to believe. We, who enjoy the protestant religion, have all the means and advantages of understanding the will of God, free liberty and full scope of inquiring into it and informing ourselves concerning it. We have all the opportunities we can wish of coming to the knowledge of our duty. The oracles of God lie open to us and his law is continually before our eyes; his word is nigh unto us, in our mouths and in our hearts (that is, we may read it and meditate upon it) that we may do it. The key of knowledge is put into our hands, so that if we do not enter into the kingdom of heaven, it is we ourselves that shut ourselves out. And where there is nothing to hinder us from the knowledge of our duty, there is certainly nothing can excuse us from the practice of it. For the end of all knowledge is to direct men in their duty, and effectually to engage them to the performance of it. The great business of religion is: to make men truly good, and to teach them to live well. And, if religion have not this effect, it matters not of what church any man lists and enters himself; for most certainly a bad man can be saved in none. Tho' a man know the right way to heaven never so well, and be entered into it, yet if he will not walk therein, he shall never come thither. Nay, it will be an aggravation of this man's unhappiness that he was lost in the way to heaven and perished in the very road to salvation. But if we will, in good earnest, apply ourselves to the practice of religion and the obedience of God's holy laws, his grace will never be wanting to us to so good a purpose.

I have not time to recommend religion to you at large, with all its advantages. I will comprise what I have to say in a few words and mind them at your peril: let that which is our great concernment be our great care—to know the truth and to do it, to fear God and keep his commandments. Considering the reasonableness and the reward of piety and virtue, nothing can be wiser; considering the mighty assistance of God's grace, which he is ready to afford us, and the unspeakable satisfaction and delight which is to be had in the doing of our duty, nothing can be easier. Nothing will give us that pleasure while we live; nothing can minister that true and solid comfort to us when we come to die: there is probably no such way for a man to be happy in this world; to be sure, there is no way but this to escape the intolerable and endless miseries of another world.

Now God grant that we may all know and do, in this our day, the things that belong to our peace, for his mercy's sake in Jesus Christ: To whom, with the Father and the Holy Ghost, be all honour and glory now and for ever. Amen.

THE CHARGE GIVEN BY Sʳ WILLIAM SMITH, Bʳᵗ·

At the quarter sessions of the peace held for the county of Middlesex, at Westminster, on Monday the 24ᵗʰ of April, 1682.

WILLIAM SMITH (c.1616–1696), of Redcliff, Buckinghamshire, was a son of Robert Smith, principal of New Inn, London, who fell a royalist in 1645. William matriculated at Trinity College, Oxford, in 1635, and became a barrister of the Inner Temple in 1642. In the Long Parliament, as member for Winchelsea, he delivered two speeches which were printed: one on the 'regulating of the king's majesty's prerogative, and the liberties of the subject' (1641); the other 'against the late times and prerogative.' In 1643 he left London to sit in the king's parliament at Oxford. During the war he served as governor of Chepstow Castle. At the Restoration he was created a baronet, and he sat in the cavalier parliament from 1661 to 1679.

As a justice of the peace for Middlesex, so uncompromising and hard-bitten a royalist became a special target of abuse. One Morris, for instance, was fined £3 6s.8d. and committed to New Prison till he should have paid it, for saying that Smith was a 'very pitiful fellow . . . not worth forty shillings if his debts were paid.' Noades a yeoman was fined 13s.4d. for the remark, 'I care not a turd for Sir William Smith.'

This speech is a fine example of the simple faith of a diehard Tory. Against it appeared a pamphlet called *The second part of the Ignoramus Justices; or, an Answer to the Scandalous Speech of Sir W.S. Baronet . . .*, in which Smith is accused of having been a turncoat and an unfaithful steward. Turncoat is the last term one could apply.

Gentlemen,

I HAVE had the honour to discourse to the country from this bench several times, and the advice which I gave them was to seek peace and study unity. Advice I thought very necessary, and that which would contribute most to the welfare and happiness not only of this county but of the whole kingdom. This is a trading country, and nothing can encourage and advance trade more than peace, nor can anything procure wealth sooner than trade, nor will anything secure it better than unity. The king by his wisdom and care hath hitherto preserved peace without the help of unity, for certainly no nation can be more divided than this is; it is high time for every honest man, especially magistrates and those in authority, to speak plain English: and since this honourable bench hath thought fit to command me to this service, I shall endeavour to discharge my duty and conscience in that particular. It troubles me to say it, but it is true that this is a divided nation, divided into two opposite parties, the church-party, I mean the church of England as by law established, and the anti-church, for I know not by what other name or denomination to style the dissenters (I mean dissenters of all sorts) unless I should use the scripture-word legion, for they are many; and although they are divided amongst themselves *toto cœlo*, yet they agree in this *tertio*, to torment the government. I will give you a short character of these two parties: the church-party are those who worship and serve God in the place appointed for it, the church; they honour and obey the king and submit to the laws; the dissenters do none of these, they do not approach the church, and to some of them it is an abomination; they are so far from honouring the king, that both his person and government are defamed by those pamphlets which go about the town; neither do they obey him, or submit to the laws, for very lately the king out of his great concern for the public peace thought fit by the advice of his majesty's privy council to command that conventicles should be suppressed according to law; the dissenters have been so far from obeying his majesty's command that they have contended for the conventicles as if they had been their inheritance, and have abused and reviled those officers and others who in obedience to this command have endeavoured to put the laws in execution. Now I would ask any sober-thinking person to which of these two parties his prudence would invite him to adhere, whether to that party where he may be safe under the king's protection and where his liberty and property may be well secured by the laws? Liberty and property so much talked of, and by some very unduly sought; or to that party which will lead him into a wilderness of briars and thorns where he shall never know his way, or into slippery places where he shall never be able to stand his ground, or shall, as it were, make him walk upon the edge of a knife and always be in danger. Self-preservation is natural to every creature, and methinks men who have reason should seek it much more than others.

The king and the laws have long fingers, and sometime or other they will reach the tallest malefactor. It is true the king is a gracious and merciful prince, and that perhaps may be an encouragement to some men's disobedience; but patience may be provoked too long and too far, and then *Læsa patientia fit furor*, when the lion rouseth all the beasts of the forest tremble. Notwithstanding all these provocations, the king (by the divine assistance) hath hitherto preserved peace, peace at home and peace abroad; for we have peace with all the Christian world, when at the same time most of the neighbour nations are in wars and troubles. The king hath taken care of places related to England. A terrible rebellion broke out lately in Virginia which had almost destroyed that country, the king at a great charge sent ships and soldiers thither, reduced that rebellion, and settled the country in peace. Tangier was lately attacked by a numerous and formidable enemy, and most of us here gave it for lost; some were so impudent to say it would be sold; the king sent a timely relief thither of men, money, and all other necessary provisions, and did preserve that place so that it is neither lost or sold and hath now made a lasting peace with the emperor of that country; and it is to be hoped that place will prove very advantageous for the trade of England: but this hath cost the king a great sum of money. The trade of Turkey hath been of late years very much disturbed by the pirates of Algiers and his majesty hath received notice that many of his subjects have been carried captive thither; the king to prevent those mischiefs for the future hath at a great charge for several years together maintained a considerable number of ships in the Straits, by which the Algerines have received so great losses that they are ready to beg peace. The king hath taken care of the walls and bulwarks of this kingdom, the shipping. You know the parliament appointed thirty capital ships to be built and gave six hundred thousand pound for the building of them; but when shipwrights and others came to consult about them, they found that sum of money would not do it, to make them so strong and serviceable as they ought to be; the king was forced to advance a hundred thousand pounds and more out of his own purse to perfect that work; and I have heard these several charges and disbursements do amount to near eight hundred thousand pounds. These are all accidental charges, and if the established revenue will not balance the necessary and common charge of the government (as I have heard it said in the house of commons by those who should well understand it, that it will not), where then shall these accidental charges be borne? The king cannot do it, the people then must. Why then the king hath lent this great sum of money to his subjects, and certainly it ought to be repaid with interest and with thanks, and doubtless had been long since, if the dissensions and differences which are amongst us had not prevented it. Is it not therefore high time that all possible endeavours should be used to put an end to these divisions and differences, that the kingdom may be no longer exposed to those dangers which at present it lies under? And this, very wise men are of opinion, will never be, until the conventicles (which continually blow the coals) are suppressed. The learned tell us that the plague is spread by the effluviums of the mouth, the atoms of an infected person are infected, and when they are sent out by the breath and received by those in the company of the infected, they thereby become infected; and we are told the infected person hath a strong appetite and desire to infect others. Faction is thus communicated; the venom of it by the mouths of the preachers and teachers in conventicles is transmitted into the ears of the auditors, who thereby become infected; and when they are so, they infect others. And until these effluviums, these mouths are stopped, it is not probable this plague will cease; and there is a ready way to do it, the putting the statute of 17. of the king in due execution. And do you not think this is very necessary? For if the numbers of these dissenters should be suffered to increase, in time they might be formidable to the government; for we see although they are divided in opinion, yet they agree and join together for their common interest. I have seen in a fallow field a great herd of swine, the hogs of a whole parish, the hogs of several farmers, and others, if the herdsman chastiseth any one of them for a fault, the whole herd run together in a body to condole with their companion for his misfortune, and as much as in them lies to endeavour his rescue; and these are a very untractable creature, which will neither lead or draw. Do not the dissenters do the same? If any one of them is touched by the hands of the law, they lay their heads and purses together for his relief. I would not be mistaken, I do not compare beasts to men, comparisons are odious, similes are to illustrate a proposition, not to make a parallel, *Sic parvis componere magna solebam*; but if I had done so, I have a good precedent for it. St. Paul tells us he fought with beasts at Ephesus, and those were no other but unreasonable men; and if the apostle had fought Ephesus, and all the parts about it, I am persuaded he could not have found more unreasonable men than some we have in England. I have heretofore had an indifferent good opinion of some of the dissenters, I thought they had been (as they pretended) a peaceable, quiet, and sober sort of persons, and that they had desired nothing but connivance or indulgence; they had an unruly conscience to deal with, and that they had only desired some toleration for it; but I find the crafty had a farther aim.

You know there is a lord mayor's day, and that consists of a show in the streets, and a feast at Guild-hall; the show in the streets is the pageants, they draw the vulgar, the mobile together, which gives them opportunity to make a noise, and throw about their squibs; and when they have spent some time in that and gazing upon the pageants, they go home very well satisfied; but the wiser and better sort of citizens are entertained with a feast at Guild-hall. This toleration seems to me to be a kind of pageant, held forth to entertain the vulgar and unthinking crowd with some speculations which may please them; there is something in it very taking to some people who look not far, liberty of conscience, and ease of tender consciences. But the wiser and designing sort look farther; I am afraid they aim at dominion over the lives and liberties of their fellow-subjects, and to feast themselves upon their estates: this hath been, and therefore may be. This word feast puts me in mind of a pamphlet I read the other day, where I found an invitation (by ticket) to a feast at Haberdashers' and Goldsmiths' Hall: those names made me call to remembrance the severe discipline some of the chiefest nobility and gentry heretofore had at those places; I am sure I feel the smart of those strokes to this day; I was afraid that meeting might be to view those halls, to see since they are new built, if they were fit for the old uses. This associating by tickets is an odd way, it looks like blowing the trumpet, and making proclamation, Who is on my side, who? What the law may make of it, I cannot tell, but methinks these persons adventure very far; all rebellions are not actual arms; in God's sense the rebellion of Corah and his company (which went no farther than to associate and murmur against the governors) was such a rebellion that he thought fit to punish with death. But the same pamphlet says there was a feast of the Artillery-Company (which is an anniversary feast) at which there was but 200, but at this feast there would have been 1000 of nobility, gentry, and ministers. So to me this seems to be a trial of skill; which puts me in mind of Moses and the magicians: God commanded Moses to cast down his rod, and that should become a serpent; the magicians tried their skill and threw down their rods, and they became serpents; but Moses his rod (which was but one) devoured their rods, which were many. The king he hath his rod too, which is his sceptre, which I hope will be able to break the rods of these unquiet people, that they may not again scourge and whip the nation. But what became of these magicians?

Why, when they could show no more tricks, God set a mark upon them, botches and blains; and if the law cannot reach these subtle men, divine justice may. The word magi signifies wise men, and our Saviour tells us that the children of this world are wiser in their generation than the children of light: and it appears so, for they confederate for the mutual assistance of each other upon all occasions; they will spare no pains nor cost for the advancement of each others' interest; they trade for the most part with no other but themselves; they will have no manner of commerce (if they can avoid it) with any of the church-party; so that they do not make a separation only in religion, but in all other dealings whatsoever, which is to set up a common-wealth in a kingdom, a most dangerous thing! The church-party, the children of light, they trust a good cause, put out their own eyes, and will neither see their danger or interest: most of them endeavour to build upon their own ground and raise to themselves pyramids of honour and riches, and have not much minded those of the same party who are forced to shift for themselves as well as they can; but if they should still be neglected, they must, like snails, shrink into their shells; what will be the consequence of that? The enemy when he finds his strength will quash them to pieces with his foot; what then will become of the great man's estate? It must be put into handicap with the cobbler's last, and if the cards be again shuffled, it is probable the cobbler will draw the estate, and the late rich man will have the last, and perhaps may need it to help make him a pair of shoes; what hath been, I say again may be: I have seen in the last Rebellion, noble-men and gentlemen not have a horse to ride upon or scarce a shoe to their feet. Methinks the natural body should instruct the body politic: in the natural body, if the head be assaulted, the hands are presently lifted up to defend it; if any limb be in pain, the head and heart are sensible of it; if there be but a small excrescence upon a toe, the hands are immediately at work to relieve and ease it; and thus every member gives mutual assistance to each other, by which the whole is kept in health and vigour. Should not the body politic do the like? Ought not all the members defend and support the head (where is the seat of wisdom and direction)? Ought not the head and the nobler parts of that great body encourage and succour the inferior, that so all the parts with consent and pleasure may stick close together for their common defence? Which if they did, they were invincible, *Vis unita fortior*. Rewards and punishments ever did and ever will govern the world; it is the method of heaven: 'tis true there are many generous spirits who are contented with their own virtue for their reward, but prudence should not trust to that.

> *Quis enim virtutem amplectitur ipsam*
> *Præmia si tollas?*

Virtue is like a choice plant or a tree which bears excellent fruit, but the gardener must nourish and cherish this plant and tree, or else the plant will dwindle and the tree in time bear sour fruit. I have heard it esteemed policy to make a golden bridge for an enemy to pass over, but it was that he might be gone, and trouble us no more; but I could never think it advisable to purchase enemies and put them into one's bosom, to give them places of trust and profit, this is to make them into more potent enemies than they were before. I hope for the honour of the king and safety of the government, no man for the future shall be employed until he be first sifted and winnowed, and if one grain of faction be found in him, that he shall be laid aside. This is reasonable and therefore just, and justice, gentlemen, is one of God Almighty his chiefest attributes. When there was a contention between that and his mercy, nothing but the precious blood of the Son of God could reconcile them; of that esteem is justice in heaven. This justice God hath sent into the world for the use of men, and expects it should be esteemed here; he hath not sent it by a common envoy, but by his vicegerent, not only to be distributed but to be enforced where it will not be kindly received. God tells us, By me princes decree justice; decree signifies power and authority: God hath not entrusted the prince to decree justice only, but to govern the people committed to his charge, to preserve them from themselves, and from their enemies. God says, By me kings reign, and princes decree justice, and surely he is to be believed. I wonder therefore at the strange opinion which some men have of late spread abroad, That the people make the king, and give him his authority. A strange opinion, and as presumptuous as false. Is not God the *Ens Entium?* Is not man and all other creatures emanations from that fountain? Doth he not give us our daily bread, the former and the latter rain, and all things else whatsoever? If all things are his, power and authority more; the people then cannot give it: *Nemo dat quod non habet*, and *Quicquid effecit tale est magis tale.* The king hath his authority from God, and to him alone is to be accountable;

Ipse sub nullo nisi tantum sub Deo. But I believe the mistake came from this, some men might take the law for the authority. The law it is true is the rule by which the king is to administer, but the best law and most useful that ever was made would lie still for ever if it was not acted and quickened by some authority. This authority is the king's, which he had from God, and his majesty transmits it to us and others who act by his commission to put the laws in execution. God fashioned Adam into the shape of a man, but he was a useless creature until God was pleased to give him life and motion by his breath. The laws are likewise to be quickened by that which must move and quicken them. The king, I told you, is to be accountable to God and must render an exact account of the power God hath put into his hands and how it hath been administered for the good and welfare of the people committed to his charge. The king therefore ought not to be importuned by the people to do any thing which he knows is contrary to his duty and trust, for he alone must answer for it, not they. Joshua made peace with the Gibeonites which they obtained from him by fraud, pretending they were strangers come from far and none of the Canaanites; but in two or three days the Israelites came to the knowledge that they were of the race of the Amorites (who God commanded to be destroyed), and did urge Joshua to break the peace; but he refused them and would not be unjust at their importunity and they were satisfied. Princes must be just, even against the importunities of their subjects. The king, I have heard, was pressed to exclude the duke of York, pray examine the justice of that. Can it be just to punish a man *in præsenti,* for a fault to be committed *in futuro?* If a bill had been presented to you, gentlemen of the grand jury, against any man upon presumption he would commit such or such a crime a year hence, surely you would not find that bill. This of the duke is of that nature; this could not be a fault until he was to succeed to the crown, and that is uncertain whether ever or never. It is true God hath given this crown of England to this royal family, who have enjoyed it in succession many hundreds of years, but he hath reserved to himself to determine the person of that family from time to time to the government; and when God hath made his election, is it for us to say, *Nolumus hunc regnare?* Would not this be to question the divine wisdom and to usurp upon God's prerogative, in whose hands are the issues of life and death and all other events to which all men in prudence ought to submit, because they know they must do it whether they will or no? Men ought not to pry into the arcana of heaven; God is a jealous God: the Beth-shemites were smitten for looking into the ark, and so was Uzzah for touching it, although 'twas done with a good intent. This act of wisdom and piety will make the king's name be celebrated in story; fears and jealousies ought not to transport subjects to the desire of unreasonable things of their prince, for he must answer for them, not they. I will teach you an experiment (without a crime) that you shall never fail of a good king; it is to be a good people, for God (who is infinite goodness) gives an ill king for the punishment of an ill people, and you cannot displease and provoke him more than when he hath given you a good king, if you do not treat and esteem him as you ought. The king which he hath been pleased to bless us with at this time is, I may say, with great truth, the best prince in the world (whom God long preserve) and if we honour and obey him as God expects and our duty requires, God will not fail to send a good successor. The peace of the kingdom is and ought to be the king's care, and it could not be expected that the duke should have sat still under such an indignity; and if he had, the princes of Christendom to whom he is allied (and he is allied to many, and the greatest) would have taken up the quarrel, and then our fields of peace would have been turned to fields of blood. Those who read history may find what miseries this kingdom for many years suffered when the dispute was between the two houses of York and Lancaster, how many noble families were destroyed, and many thousand of men lost their lives, and if God had not had compassion of this kingdom, and provided an expedient to unite them, the misery of war, for ought I know, might have continued to this day. Wars are not so soon or so easily ended as begun; and it is very observable that the neighbour-princes made it their business to continue that difference; some prince or other always took part with him who was conquered, and so *vicissim* with him who was down, not out of any other consideration than their own interest, that they might keep England embroiled at home, which they knew was the true way to keep wars and troubles from their own doors. I hope England for the future will never be so unwise as to give them the like advantage.

Gentlemen, the proper business of a charge is to acquaint you with the laws and statutes of this kingdom, their usefulness and penalties; that I have done heretofore to former grand juries, but it hath not had so good effect as I could have wished. Amongst others I did acquaint them with the statute of 13. of the king, which was made for the preservation of his majesty's person and government; it did provide against treason, against seditious preaching and printing, and against setting up votes of one or both houses of parliament to be effectual as laws. But notwithstanding that and other statutes, we find that persons have been lately accused for treason, and defamatory pamphlets and libels are sold about the streets as good merchantable wares, and votes of the house of commons printed to give check to laws. Men are grown to a strange boldness, and out-do Pasquil in Rome; he tells bold truths, but these here wicked and impudent lies. The sin of Ham, and that which clave to his posterity, was that he uncovered his father's nakedness; and the greatest crime of that tyrant Nero, was that he ript up the belly of his mother. Gentlemen, the king is *Pater Patriæ*, and the common-wealth is our mother, and he who rips up her bowels and shows her weakness or deformity, or abuseth his father, forfeits his very nature and is more wicked than either Cham or Nero; until men come to have a sense of religion and obey for conscience-sake, I shall be hopeless that laws will prevail; and yet I shall adventure to recommend one statute to you more, a statute not made by kings, lords, and commons, but by their king, the King of Kings, and it is this, *Statutum est omnibus semel mori*, a statute, gentlemen, which was never repealed, or ever will be; and those who shall be indicted upon this statute, no ignoramus can prevent their trial, nor shall the credit of the evidence be questioned, and the sentence will have speedy execution. Those who shall be found innocent, their sentence will be *Venite Beati*, but those who will be found guilty, *Ite Maledicti*, a dreadful sentence that, not like the sentence we have here, Go to the place from whence you came, and so to the place of execution, and there hang by the neck until you are dead: Or as we have it by tradition, to be hanged in chains alive until you are starved to death. These are easy sentences, because a little time determines the pain; but this dreadful sentence of *Ite Maledicti* sends the criminal to a place of horror and darkness, where his meat and drink will be fire and brimstone, his companions such who he durst not look upon when he was in the world, devils and furies, not to make him sport and pastime, but to torment him; and that which aggravates this punishment is that it is attended with despair, never to come out of that place of torment. If this was well considered and laid to heart, could a reasonable man be invited by any temptation whatsoever to gratify his ambition or other appetites with those things (which will be enjoyed but for a very short time), and adventure this sentence of *Ite Maledicti*? But pray let us consider what to do to avoid this fearful sentence. The psalmist instructs us he who will ascend the holy mountain must have clean hands, a pure heart, must not lift up his mind to vanity, and must not be sworn to deceive his neighbour; he must have clean hands, not subject to bribery or corruption, a pure heart, he must design nothing injurious to God, his king, or his country; he must not lift up his mind to vanity, but must lay aside all ambitious thoughts, and be contented with the station where God Almighty hath placed him; he must not be sworn to deceive his neighbour; this last is part of the law of nature and one of the precepts of the moral law, Thou shalt not bear false witness against thy neighbour. Under this head comes all perjury, subornation of perjury, lying, deceit, treachery, and falsehood; the psalmist lays before us our duty at this time, and if we perform it justly, we may avoid this sentence of *Ite Maledicti*. Gentlemen, we have all sworn you, the juries of constables, to present without favour or affection, hatred or malice, and you ought to present all those crimes which are committed within your several parishes and precincts against the laws and statutes of this kingdom; and you gentlemen of the grand jury are likewise sworn to present without favour or affection, hatred or malice, and we upon the bench are sworn to do justice according to the best of our skill and knowledge; we are not only sworn, but we have likewise made a covenant with God to be just according to our oaths; at the end of our oaths we say, So help me God, which is as much as to say we desire no help from God in our needs if we do not do that which is just according to our oaths. Now I would advise all men to consider that human nature is liable to many infirmities and accidents, to sickness, past the help of a physician, to oppression, above the help of law and lawyers; to poverty, and have no friends to afford relief. In all these cases, when human helps fail, nature points out the ways to address to God. But with that confidence can we do it when we call to mind we broke covenant with him at such and such a time? Which we cannot fail to do, for conscience is a most certain remembrancer. Is not a man a most silly creature, who shall adventure to break this covenant to gratify any appetite and please any party, and by it put himself out of God's protection and from under his care in this world, and without God's infinite mercies to come under that severe sentence of *Ite Maledicti* in the next? Gentlemen, grand juries have always been esteemed the honour of the government and the great security of the lives and liberties of the subject; they are to be *probos & legales homines*, and so is a golden chain as well for ornament as security; if they should prove otherwise, this chain of gold would be turned into gyves and fetters of iron and brass, and we should be greater slaves here in England than they are in Algiers. Our ancestors have taken great care that the grand juries should be such as they ought to be, and as you may see the statutes made in that case provide; but for all that it is happy for the people that the king hath the nomination of the sheriffs, by whom the juries are to be returned. It is a prerogative of great consequence and not to be entrusted in the hands of any subject or subjects whatsoever. The king sits aloft above all and looks down upon all his subjects, and like the sun sends forth his beams upon all alike; his spirit is as high as his place; when God intended to remove Moses and had appointed Joshua to succeed him, he commanded Moses to put some of his honour upon him, and that the text explains to be the spirit of wisdom, which is the spirit of government, and that no subject hath. He is not therefore to be equipped with too large a sail for his bottom, for fear it should overset. The king's prerogative (if it was well understood) is the subject's chiefest safety, and ought not to be in a subject's hand, for the subject's sake, and it is to be hoped no man for the future will presume to advise the king to part with any of it. Every thing is most natural when it is in its proper place; the king is to govern, the people to obey; this is harmonious, and no wise or good man will make discord; he who is for the king is for people, and he who is truly for the people is as truly for the king. They cannot be divided but they must be in danger to be destroyed; it is therefore folly as well as mutiny to say I am for the king, or I am for the country, except in conjunction; he who is not a friend to both is not a friend to either. I have ever esteemed monarchy as the best of governments (it is the government of heaven) and ours the best of monarchies, and if it be possible, I now esteem it much more than ever. I am not afraid of the king, I am sure he will do me no hurt if I keep the law, but I must confess I am afraid of some of my fellow-subjects. Story will tell you there was a great faction in Italy between the Guelfs and the Ghibellines;

the great and rich city of Florence was almost destroyed by it, sometimes one got the upper hand, sometimes the other; but God was pleased to put an end to the miseries of that city by a monarchy, under which it hath been happy ever since. Pray gentlemen, let us make it our business, as it is our interest, to preserve our monarchy from being shaken. This is to be done by universal justice, that is the chiefest pillar which supports monarchies, and if any man shall by fraud undermine that pillar or by force shake it, he will, like Sampson, pull the whole fabric upon his own head and destroy himself. But they will differ in this: Sampson had great provocation, his eyes were put out by the Philistines, and they made him their sport and pastime; but whosoever shall shake this pillar here do it from the force of a wicked inclination to destroy the government under which he may live happily and safely if he will, and so adds the sin of ingratitude to that of disobedience. Gentlemen, I have troubled you too long, but what I have said I hope will not be wholly useless. God, who is the searcher of all hearts knows I have not spoke from the spirit of bitterness, to blow the coals, or rub the old sore. I have no animosity against any man living; my design was to lay before you the danger of divisions and making parties, and so exhort you to peace and unity, and not throw away the blessings we enjoy, and make our selves ridiculous to all the world. The matter of a charge, as it respects the laws and statutes, I have caused for your ease and help to be contrived into articles which shall be read to you. Mr. clerk of the peace, pray read them.

Articles to be presented by the high and petty constables of the grand jury, and to be inquired into by the said grand jury.

1. Imprimis, You are to present all petty treason, misprisions of treasons; all priests and Jesuits and others that have received any orders from the church or see of Rome.

2. All murders, manslaughters, robberies, burglaries, breaking of houses in the day time, felonies, petty larcenies, and the accessories thereunto, committed and done within your several hundreds and precincts.

3. You are to present all popish and other recusants that do not come to their several parish churches within your divisions.

4. You are to present all unlicenced alehouse-keepers, and what disorderly alehouses you have within your divisions.

5. You are to present the neglect of hues and cries of and in whose default.

6. You are to present all highways and bridges unrepaired within your hundreds and parishes, and who are to repair them.

7. You are to present all that erect cottages or that continue cottages not having four acres of land to be occupied by the inhabitants of the said cottages within your divisions.

8. You are to present all profane swearers and cursers within your hundreds and liberties.

9. You are to present all common barrators, common disturbers, libellers, and others that break the king's peace, all outcrys and bloodsheds that happen within your liberties and precincts.

10. You are to present all forestallers, regrators, and ingrossers, all embracers of juries, that you know of within your hundreds and precincts.

Gentlemen,

It is your duty to present what shall come in proof before you upon these articles; and first you must take care of religion, to inquire after priests, Jesuits, popish recusants, and all other dissenters from the church; you must inquire after all treasons, which although they cannot be tried here by virtue of our commission, yet they ought to be presented; you are to inquire after and present all murders, burglaries, robberies, felonies, and all other crimes against the laws and statutes of this kingdom. I wind up all with this advice, that you will serve God, honour the king, love one another, and take heed to those who are given to change.

The court observing that the charge was taken in writing, commanded it should be delivered to the clerk of the peace, that it might not be published without their direction; but finding in a printed pamphlet published by R. Janeway that their chairman is very unworthily reflected upon, and some part of the charge misrepresented, they have thought fit to order it to be printed, to the intent the whole kingdom may see their opinion (which this charge unanimously is) with hopes that all his majesty's good and peaceable-minded subjects will be of the same.

Ordered by this court that the charge given in sessions by Sir William Smith be printed; and that the thanks of this bench be given to Sir William Smith for his prudent care and constant endeavour in the management of affairs for the preservation of the public peace and his majesty's government. And this court doth declare they will adhere to Sir William Smith and stand by him.

Per Cur.
Adderley.

London, Printed by Tho. Hodgkin. 1682.

AN HISTORICAL ACCOUNT OF THE RISE AND GROWTH OF THE WEST INDIA COLONIES

And of the great advantages they are to England, in respect to trade. Licenced according to order. London. Printed for Jo. Hindmarsh at the Golden Ball, over against the Royal Exchange. 1690

DALBY THOMAS (1650–c.1711) was of the parish of St. Katherine Cree, London, at the time of his marriage in 1673. In the 1680's he was a merchant trading to Virginia and the West Indies. His prosperity is attested by the clearance for Virginia in 1689 of the *Prince of Orange*, a vessel of four hundred tons, carrying twenty-six guns, owned by Thomas, John Gardner of London, and Sir Robert Davers, a member of the Barbadoes council. From his experience with Davers and the Barbadoes trade Thomas drew the materials for this account of the West Indies, one of the earliest pamphlets to argue the value of the colonies and the need for government supervision. In 1694 he appeared before the house of commons as an opponent of the Royal African Company's monopolistic privileges, and maintained the same point as in his pamphlet, that an open trade would best supply the islands with slaves. The speculative boom of the 1690's drew him from plantation interests to speedier and larger profits. He was named one of the commissioners of the Million Lottery in 1694, a surveyor of the duties on glassware and bottles in 1695, and a commissioner of the stamp duties on paper, vellum, and parchment in 1697. He was one of six promoters of the New River Company for improving London's water supply, the others being William Paterson the founder of the Bank of England, John Holland the founder of the Bank of Scotland, Francis Tyssen of the East India Company, Chief Justice Chester, and Sir John Trenchard, one of the secretaries of state. By 1699 he owned an estate in a favourite suburb of wealthy Londoners, Low Leyton, Essex, and had sufficient influence to get passed a private act of parliament altering his wife's marriage settlement. Sometime during these years he became a member of the Royal African Company, but it was not the exclusive company he had earlier criticized. By an act of 1698 independent traders were admitted to the African trade upon paying the company for the maintenance of its forts ten per cent of the value of goods shipped, exclusive of redwood, negroes, gold, and silver. In 1703, as chief director of the company, Thomas was knighted. With two frigates and two companies of soldiers, he left that same year to act as the company's governor on the Guinea coast, at a salary of £1250 a year. For the remainder of his life, at Cape Coast Castle, he fought a losing battle with the 'ten per cent men,' who by 1710 controlled twelve-thirteenths of the African trade.

To my much honoured friend

Sir ROBERT DAVERS,

Baronet, and to the rest of the gentlemen interested and concern'd in the

WEST INDIES

Gentlemen,

THE following treatise was occasioned by the great and just complaints made by you of the additional duty that was laid upon your product, and fell upon your labour and industry, though designed by the parliament to have been paid by the consumptioner; at that time the inventions of most men were at work (especially those that had any dealing with you, and a sense of your sufferings) to contrive a method whereby relief might have been given to you that are the best employed hands for the enriching and supporting this nation.

After much time had been spent in endeavouring the taking off the duty, and found that no arguments were prevalent, and almost all people despairing of relief, then Col. Waldrond, myself, and others, with no small pains nor little charge, contrived (as we thought) a method that might not only have laid the duty on the consumptioner, but also might have relieved you from the complaints of those that do charge you with being great debtors, and to have enabled every planter to make the best advantage of their plantations, by supplying them with monies, at the common interest of the colonies, by preventing numerous sellers, necessitous and ignorant sales.

And that this might run through the most strictest examination before it should have been allowed of, we proposed that his late majesty and privy council might have the first view of it, that they might be satisfied it did not lessen his majesty's revenue, and that we might have his majesty's leave to propose it to the assemblies of every individual colony, and if they did approve of it, and petitioned his majesty for the incorporating such societies, that then we and our friends might be interested in it.

But this meeting with opposition occasioned a hearing before his majesty and the lords of his privy council, and after they were satisfied it did not lessen his majesty's revenue. Our great debate with the op-

14—The illustration opposite is a map of the world which was sold about 1670 by John Seller, hydrographer to Charles II, maker of mathematical instruments, and compiler of various atlases and works on navigation. Seller had a reputation for reproducing Dutch maps, and this one is exactly the same as Johanne Blaev's *Nova et Accuratissima Totius Terrarum Orbis Tabula*. Seller simply inserted his name as draughtsman, indicated political divisions, and altered the decorations. It is the fulsomeness of the decoration, which disappeared in the following century with the advance in technical accuracy, that makes maps of the earlier periods works of art. In this one can be seen the representations of the four seasons and the four elements, the signs of the zodiac, the natural and artificial faces of the moon, the three astronomical systems, Ptolemaic, Copernican, and Brahean, and an explanation of diurnal variation.

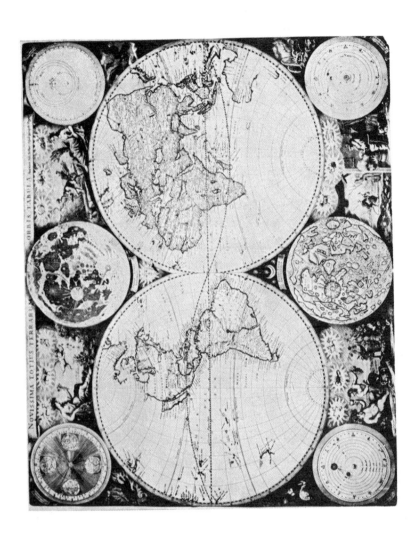

posers was about his majesty's giving leave for the sending of it to the colonies for them to try and examine it; his majesty was pleased to declare that he could not understand any reason could be given why they might not have a fight of it, for he thought Barbadoes best knew what Barbadoes wanted. I believe none will deny but that it met with a general approbation of all the lords of the council, except my lord chancellor, of whom I was informed by a friend (but at that time an opposer of this design) that he was our enemy, and accordingly we found him.

Soon after this hearing, the government began to be uneasy, and holding it not proper for a matter of this nature to be further proceeded on under an unsettled government, I rather chose to be silent, and to bear such reflections that were made by those that were totally ignorant of the method of our undertaking, though prejudicial to my particular interest, than to expose it to view, before I saw the government in a temper to consider of trade, and the great benefit you are to this nation.

Therefore I have now exposed it for your view, that you may be judges whether it might have been, or may be serviceable to you, and whether our request of sending it to you was unreasonable.

You will find by this treatise (as I humbly conceive) that our design would at least have raised the value of your goods to the price it bore before the additional duty was laid, and it was allowed at that hearing by the opposers that it would raise at least twenty per cent. Our method was to have had all your goods that came to England brought to one body of men, which we called a common factory, and they constantly to be chosen by you in your assemblies, and they to have been accountable to every consigner for the net proceeds of every parcel of goods sold, for which your charge was not to exceed what you now pay. The other part of our design was to erect a company, separate from the common factory, which should have sufficient funds in each colony, to lend what monies you had occasion of, you giving security on lands or goods, and if they did not lend it on demand, they were to forfeit to the borrower considerable for every hundred pounds demanded, the lands or goods being valued by sworn appraisers, what was lent was to be continued during your pleasure, you paying your interest when due, and you had power to pay it in when you pleased, and they obliged to lend too at least one half value of land or goods, and you not to have been confined to have borrowed it of them, but where else you pleased, so that this company might have been serviceable but could not have been hurtful, for they were bound to obey, and had no power to command.

To make it next to impossibility that the government should ever be imposed on, to permit any laws or designs of any persons whatsoever, let their pretences be ever so specious, take effect until the colonies by their assembly were consulted with: I have to the best of my knowledge given a true and just account of what import you are to this nation, by increasing of navigation, consuming the woollen manufactory, of all sorts of apparel, household-goods, &c. that are made in England, and that which was formerly foreign commodities, and cost us considerable yearly, by your industry is become native, the nation freed from that charge, and the consumptioner saves at least one half of his expense for the like quantity, besides the great advantage this nation receives by your goods exported, being over and above our consumption; and lastly, all the riches you get in the Indies by your great care, labour, and industry, is brought to England, and here it centres.

If you will be pleased to rectify my errors, that I through ignorance may have committed, that our legislators may be more fully satisfied that you are and ever must be Englishmen, and that you are much more beneficially employed there, for the benefit of this nation, than any of the like number in England, that every hardship that is put upon you, that makes your goods dearer in foreign markets, or lessens the consumption in England, is a lessening to the trade of England, and consequently prejudicial to every subject in England; and if this small treatise meets with your kind acceptance, I shall think myself very happy, and shall always be ready to demonstrate that I am your well-wisher, and

gentlemen,
your most humble and
faithful servant,
Dalby Thomas.

Chap. I

There is nothing more frequent amongst the generality of mankind than is the drawing wrong conclusions from right premises, whereby the most concise and truest maxims and sayings that wise men upon solid thinking have contrived to guide us like landmarks in the search of truth are perverted by wrong applications to drown our understandings in the gulf of error.

Thus because truth itself is not truer than that people are the wealth of a nation, those who have not time, experience, and skill to examine the fund of that undeniable verity, though in other things men of excellent understandings are apt to infer that all who set foot out of the kingdom are in some degree a diminution of its wealth; and thence take for granted that the American colonies occasion the decay both of the people and riches of the nation, when upon a thorough examination nothing can appear more erroneous, as I doubt not to make plain to every man, though my principal design is to convince the nobility and gentry of the kingdom, who, being the contrivers of our statutes and most concerned for the preservation of its grandeur, ought rightly to be informed, for fear our laws in time take a contrary bias to our trade and navigation, which are undeniably our glory and strength, as well as the only fountain of our riches.

To make this point clear it is necessary to consider and examine four things:

1. What is real wealth;
2. What is imaginary wealth;
3. How these are acquired;
4. How they may be lost.

To distinguish rightly in these points we must consider money as the least part of the wealth of any nation, and think of it only as a scale to weigh one thing against another, or as counters to reckon riches by, or as a pawn of intrinsic value to deposit in lieu of any necessary whatsoever.

True, solid, and real wealth, therefore, in respect to the nation, is the land, and what is upon or under its surface, as useful buildings, trees, quarries, mines, &c.

Thus by a good computation made by Sir William Petty, which we will take for granted till there appears a better, we may reckon the present rent of land and houses to be £10,000,000 per annum; which at twenty years' purchase amounts to £200,000,000.

The people of this nation consume annually in necessary meat, drink, and clothes, computed from their numbers, manner of living, and usual price current of things, about £50,000,000 annually, which is about £6. 10s. a head.

The imaginary wealth therefore of the nation, which consists in labour, trade, and negotiation, is four times as much as the real, and preserved in its natural channels, is to be reduced to the same value in purchase as land; whereby we may allow, that the intrinsic worth of the people and kingdom as they now stand together, is £1,000,000,000.

The money in species of the nation, though the scale by which the whole is valued and weighed, amounts not to £6,000,000.

Now such as do account the lands and buildings of the nation more valuable, because real, than the negotiation, because accidental and imaginary, will find themselves mistaken, since lands and houses without people are of no value at all, and to a naked and unindustrious nation very little more; so that labour, invention, trade, and negotiation are the only causes of as well as supports to that we call riches.

This is so self-evident that it will be superfluous to illustrate it by many examples or comparisons between civil and barbarous countries.

Therefore we must consider that when it is said, ' People are the wealth of a nation,' it is only meant laborious and industrious people, and not such as are wholly unemployed, as gentry, clergy, lawyers, servingmen, and beggars, &c. Or which is worse, employed only in disturbing the industrious and laborious, as pettifoggers, informers, catchpoles, and thieves; and, though the first sorts may be necessary, as harmless spurs to consumption, learning, or virtue, or as objects of the goodwill, mutual love, pity and compassion of human nature, as well as increasers of the numbers by children; yet the fewer such the better, whereas the last should by all imaginary ways be discouraged, tamed, or destroyed as the worst of vermin in a well-governed commonwealth.

We must likewise consider that the value of everything useful to the necessities, luxuries, or vanities of this life is measured by the industry and labour either of body or mind, which is necessary to their acquirement, whereby things of little or no price in one country, by the time spent, labour, and hazard of those which carry them to another, become dear.

From all which it is plain that only industrious and laborious people are the riches of any nation; and it will as naturally follow that these laborious or industrious which employ their talents to most advantage are of most value to such nation.

And though a man whose skill amounts to no more than to earn 3d. a day by his continual labour, can no ways add to the wealth of a kingdom like ours, because it will not supply his necessary consumption; yet such a man is a less burthen to it than one totally idle, and may increase the number by children.

So again, one that constantly by his labour can earn 6d. a day only, and consumes just so much, as he is not advantageous to the nation's wealth, so he is no burthen neither, and occasions its increase.

But that man who by industry and labour not only maintains himself and family, but makes himself rich, is to the proportion of his wealth just so much addition to the intrinsic value of the kingdom.

I have the more enlarged upon this head that I might lead the mind of the reader by a natural chain of consequences rightly to understand the true original and everlasting support of wealth, which is nothing else but labour.

As for such persons who by the faculties of the mind only acquire riches to themselves, as soldiers, lawyers, divines, bankers, retailers, victuallers, &c., they, though necessary callings, are no increasers of the nation's wealth, nor is the kingdom more rich by the fluctuating and circulation of money among such than one of them would be by putting his money out of one chest into another, or shifting it from one pocket to another.

But where soldiery becomes the trade of a people, as among the Switzers and Scots it is, who serve abroad for money, and bring it home to purchase lands there, it is of equal benefit to any other labour, by increasing the rates and value of the real wealth of those countries, which as amongst all other civil nations is land and houses.

I doubt not but the reader by this time will perceive that in what way soever a man employs his labour and industry either at home or abroad, so that at last he increases the value of the real wealth of the nation, he is in the proportion of such increase a benefit thereunto.

And on the contrary he that labours not at all, or so much as not to increase the intrinsic value of his country, is just good for nothing.

To leave this truth plain beyond dispute, I beg the doubter but to consider that if all the laborious people of the kingdom left working and were to live upon the natural produce of it, to be distributed to them in equal proportions by way of charity, as parish-poor and beggars are now supported, how long it would be before the nation became necessitous, naked, and starving, and consequently the land and houses worth nothing.

A short reflection would make him sensible that a very few years of idleness would complete the matter; whence he can no longer doubt, but that labour and industry rightly applied is the sole cause of the wealth of a nation, that money is only the scales or touchstone to weigh or value things by; and that land itself would yield no rent but as labour employed for the support of luxuries, as well as necessities, did find a due encouragement and increase.

In short, it is plain hereby,

1. That real wealth is land and houses;

2. That imaginary wealth is the laborious people.

3. That the real and imaginary wealth both increase only as industry is rightly applied by great numbers of laborious people, and not by increase of people only.

4. And the increase of people wilfully or accidentally idle is so far from being national riches that it is the surest and speediest way to inevitable poverty, famine, and nakedness, and must decay the value as well of the real as imaginary wealth of the nation, proportionably to the decay of industry.

Thus civil wars, disorders, and changes in the government of nations, by the many which become soldiers, and others that cease labouring in their trades and industry for want of security, insensibly impoverish countries much more than those slain in such changes do; by reason that those that die, as they add nothing, do consume nothing in the commonwealth; whereas the idle living add nothing and consume much to its destruction.

I shall say no more therefore on this subject, but hasten to the consideration of which hands are best employed to the advantage of the wealth of this kingdom, as our trade and negotiation now stand.

First then, the premises considered, we may lay down as an undeniable verity, that those men who add most by their labour to the increase of the intrinsic wealth of the nation, either real or imaginary, and consume least are best employed.

Again, on the contrary, those that consume most and add least are worst employed.

Now it will be impossible in the short method I design, to enumerate and clearly distinguish between every sort of employment: wherefore I shall content myself only to hint at some few ways wherein men seem to do little and yet are well employed; and others wherein they are very busy and laborious to little or no purpose.

To begin then as nature did in the cultivators of land and conductors of cattle.

The husbandman's life not only seems but is extremely careful, laborious, and painful; the grazier's and shepherd's on the contrary both seems and is a very careless, quiet, and easy way of spending time.

Yet though the first sort are usually paid most wages, and consequently can afford and do consume most upon themselves, the last notwithstanding are of much more value to the commonwealth.

For 200 sheep or 20 cows require but 40 acres of good land, and one man's easy care for a year's pasture, the profit of which by the increase of lambs, calves, wool, butter, cheese, &c., and the meliorating the wool by manufacture, is of four times at least more advantage to the commonwealth than the same number of acres employed in tillage, which requires the constant drudgery of two men and four horses at least; besides that the greatest part of what is produced by tillage is consumed in the nation; whereas manufactured wool from sheep, tallow, leather, shoes, butter, cheese, salt, beef, and many other things, arising from pasture, are staple commodities for transportation, which fetch us back silver, gold, and foreign goods, useful to the ornament and pleasure, if not necessities of life. I must affirm, the commodity which is transported is the only true increase of national strength and wealth; and that sort of reformers who would have nothing made, used, or consumed, but what nature absolutely requires, are but short-sighted and narrow thinkers as well in politics as religion: and though they may adorn their opinions and arguments with the names of Lycurgus, Cato, and other sour reasoners, yet all their discourses tend to no more but to reduce mankind back to be sheepskin-wearers, acorn-eaters, and water-drinkers; again, the bountiful God of nature supplying every country of the world with what is fully sufficient to sustain life.

Therefore to say, as many are apt to do, that England can live of itself without the assistance of any foreign nation, is to give it not the least commendation beyond any other country; but to say, and that truly, that England by the industry of its inhabitants employed in shipping, plantations, mines, manufactures, pastures, and tillage, doth not only abound in all sorts of commodities, as native meat, drink, clothes, houses, and coaches, fit for the necessities, ease, and ornaments of life, but can outvie most nations of the world for the vast plenty in varieties of wines, spices, drugs, fruits, silks, pictures, music, silver, gold, precious stones, and all other the supports of grandeur and delight, that is to speak it, a truly civilized and glorious nation indeed.

And though some men through false and envious optics look upon these things as baits to vice and occasions of effeminacy, if they would but impartially examine the truth of matters, they would discern them to be the true spurs to virtue, valour, and the elevation of the mind, as well as the just rewards of industry. For,

It is certain upon a right scrutiny, a man shall find more profaneness, dishonesty, drunkenness, and debauchery practised in nasty rags, bare walls, and alehouses than in rich habits, palaces, or taverns; and as plenty, splendour, and grandeur can have no other fountain but wisdom, industry, and good conduct; so shabbiness, indigence, and contempt rarely spring from any thing but folly, idlenesss, and vice: and where it happens otherwise by unexpected frauds, shipwrecks, fires, inundations or maims, the shame of suffering it becomes the nation's reproach, since the rarity of these accidents would make the burden which crushes a particular scarce felt when laid by a right method on the commonwealth, as I shall endeavour to make appear hereafter.

But before I return again to the consideration which part of the people are best employed for the public good, I must from what is premised, conclude, that as all who are not mischievously employed or totally idle are of some benefit to the commonwealth and should find due encouragement, so those ought to be most protected and least discouraged by the laws who are most usefully busy for the increasing the value of the real and imaginary wealth of the nation. Thus, as I said before, the shepherd and grazier is to be preferred before the ploughman and thrasher.

So the miner is to be preferred to the shepherd and grazier, because all he produces for transportaion is clear gains to the public, whereas but part of the others doth so. The mariner is to be preferred to the miner, and the like to such who contribute most to foreign trade; but in England the merchant-adventurer is to be encouraged and preferred before the mariner or any other artist, trade, or calling whatsoever. For though his labour seems a recreation rather than a toil, and consists chiefly in a regular methodizing of a punctual rotation of credit and change of commodities from one place to another, yet considering that the whole produce of nature and art would be but dead matter without a proper motion to convey it to its true end, which is consumption, all other callings receive their vigour, life, strength, and increase from the merchant, commodities rising in esteem or value as they are rightly distributed from place to place, and losing their very nature as well as worth when by overstocking the market they become contemptible, or perish for want of use or consumption. Wherefore our laws should be so contrived as never in the least to discourage or check any conception or endeavour of the venturing merchant, to whose extravagant and hazardous, as well as prudent and cautious undertaking, this nation chiefly owes all its wealth and glory. And it is a mighty pity that all laws for custom and duties, as well as for regulating navigation, erecting companies, judging maritime controversies, granting letters of marque and reprisal, and for encouraging manufactures and societies of handicrafts, should not first be debated, prepared, and begun in a great council of trade, to consist of members elected and deputed by every plantation, maritime, city, company, constitution, and trade which would desire to send members to it: from and thence after a free and full examination be represented to both houses of parliament for their approbation or dislike.

For trade is of that nature that it requires frequent pruning, lopping, and restraining, as well as cultivating and cherishing; and thrives much better under proper and rightly applied restraints, duties, taxes, and excises than in a general looseness; which being so, is it possible that a positive tonnage and poundage like ours should hit all accidents, attend the changes and mutations it receives, both at home by the plenty and scarcity of our native commodities, or abroad by the like ebbs and floods as well as the laws in foreign nations made or changed concerning it?

Or how indeed can the divines, lawyers, nobility, and great gentry of the kingdom be nice judges and right distinguishers between the clashing and tangling interests of so great a mystery as universal trade, when few or none of them have ever had the least occasion to inspect or experiment any part of it?

The defect therefore of a free and able council of trade in this nation, though it cannot destroy, yet wonderfully retards and hinders the natural and genuine increase of navigation and merchandise, and consequently of rents.

But for want of that, I will presume to go on in explaining the right and wrong application of men's industry, as they respect in general the wealth and grandeur of the nation, or in particular the interest of our American colonies, in many of which I doubt not to demonstrate one labouringman is of more advantage to England, though out of it, than any thirty the like kind can be within it.

To explain which I will take a short view of our sugar-plantations and the nature of that trade, to whose particular advantage and interest after the kingdom's I principally sacrifice my present pains.

I therefore, with all submissiveness imaginable, desire our legislators to consider:

1. That the greatest consumption of sugar is made by themselves and the rest of the rich and opulent people of the nation, though useful to all degrees of men.

2. That the quantity of it yearly produced within those sugar colonies is not less than 45,000 tons English tonnage, each comprehending £20 to the ton.

3. That about the moiety of that is consumed in England.

4. That the medium of the value of consumed sugar at the present price current is 4d. a pound.

5. That the quantity consumed in the nation at that price amounts to £800,000 sterling, and upwards.

6. That the other moiety sent to foreign markets, after it has employed seamen and earned freight, is sold for as much, and consequently brings back to the nation in money or useful goods annually £800,000, which is more than any one other commodity doth.

7. Consider too, that before sugars were produced in our own colonies, it bore three times the price it doth now, so that by the same consumption, at the same price, except we made it ourselves, we should be forced to give in money or money's worth, as native commodities and labour, £2,400,000 for the sugar we spend, or be without it to such a degree of

disadvantage of well-living, as that retrenchment would amount to. We must consider too, that the spirits arising from molasses which is sent from the sugar colonies to the other colonies and to England, which if all were sold in England and turned into spirits, it would amount annually to above £500,000, at half the price the like quantity of brandy from France would cost; and will yearly increase as brandies are discouraged, and by most are held wholesomer for the body, which is observed by the long living of those in the colonies that are great drinkers of rum, which is the spirits we make of molasses, and the short living of those that are great drinkers of brandy in those parts.

The indigo coming thence amounts to £50,000 per annum.

The logwood for which we formerly paid the Spaniards £100 per ton now comes under £15 and amounts to 1000 tons annually.

The cotton for which we paid formerly above 12d. per pound now comes at 5½d. per pound, and amounts to 1000 tons per annum, besides the hands it employs in manufacturing it.

The ginger amounts to 4000 tons per annum, and is not the sixth part in price of what the nation paid formerly for that commodity, or for pepper instead of it.

Not to speak of the many drugs, woods, cocoa, pimento, and spices, besides raw hides, &c. which come from those parts, nor of the great quantity of the gold and silver we have of the Spaniards for negroes, and the English manufactory carried by our sloops from our colonies to them.

So that it is demonstration, the nation saves and gains by the people employed in those colonies £400,000,000 sterling per annum.

Now if it be considered that in all those sugar colonies there are not 600,000 white men, women, and children, it necessarily must follow, that one with another, above what they consume, each of them earns for the public above £60 per annum.

Whereas, if the rent be £10,000,000,

And the consumption £50,000,000,

Then by reducing labour and consumption to a proper balance with the produce of rents, and supposing the imaginary wealth of the whole kingdom to increase in time of peace, the tenth part annually that will be but £4,000,000; which does not amount to 12d. a head clear increase of wealth, one with another, above necessary and constant expenses; from which it follows beyond controversy that hands employed in the sugar-plantations are one with another of one hundred and thirty times the value to the commonwealth than those which stay at home.

To this I easily foresee will be readily objected, for want of consideration, that those there consume nothing of native commodities, which if they did as those do which stay at home, their consumption would amount to £390,000 annually, at £6. 10s. per head as aforesaid, and would consequently increase the rents at least a fourth of that.

But to this I must remind the reader that I have demonstrated that whatever is consumed by idle men can never increase either the real or imaginary wealth of the nation, and that nothing but the overplus or consumption can be reckoned additional wealth; which according to our reasonable computation cannot be above 2s. a head, one with another: so that if we would grant that those in the colonies did consume nothing of our home produce, the loss by want of them here could amount only to 1,200,000s. annually, which is £60,000.

But on the contrary, this is so far from being true, that, one with another, each white man, woman, and child, residing in the sugar plantations, occasions the consumption of more of our native commodities and manufactures than ten at home do.

This cannot be doubted by those that will consider the great quantity of beef, pork, salt, fish, butter, cheese, corn, and flour, as well as beer, English mym, cider, and coals, constantly sent thither, of which commodities for the use of themselves or blacks, they have little or none of their own produce. Consider too that all their powder, cannon, swords, guns, pikes, and other weapons; their clothes, shoes, stockings, saddles, bridles, coaches, beds, chairs, stools, pictures, clocks, and watches; their pewter, brass, copper, and iron vessels and instruments; their sail-cloth and cordage, of which in their building, shipping, mills, boiling and distilling-houses, field-labour, and domestic uses, they consume infinite quantities, all which are made in and sent from England; not to speak of the great number of drudging and saddle-horses they take off, as well as of that sort of people who would in their youth be consumed in idleness, or worse at home, but there become useful to increase the nation's numbers and wealth both.

Besides, it must be remembered that there are in those colonies at least 5 blacks for one white; so that, allowing the whites to be 60,000, the blacks must be 300,000, all whose clothes and European provisions coming from England, increases the consumption of our native commodities and manufactures in a large proportion. But the axes, hoes, saws, rollers, shovels, knives, nails, and other iron instruments and tools as well as the boilers, stills, and other useful vessels of copper, lead, and pewter, which are wasted, consumed, and destroyed by the industry and profitable labour of that mighty number of slaves, are not easily to be computed, but must plainly and beyond all contradiction be of great advantage to the nation as well as to those industrious people employed at home in making them.

If these things with the vast quantity of shipping that those colonies employ be in the least reflected on, it will open the eyes of the most unexperienced person in the trade to discern the mighty advantage the nation receives from those people which go to those colonies, and the great obligation there lies upon our legislators to study their due improvement, safety, and increase.

For besides all the benefits demonstrably coming to the nation as aforesaid, they are in some kind maritime armies, ever ready not only to defend themselves but to punish the exorbitances, encroachments, piracies, and depredations of any insulting neighbouring nation; nor is it to be imagined in what awe those colonies rightly managed might keep our French, Spanish, Dutch, Danish, Brandenburg and Hamburg rivals, for wealth and maritime power, from entering into any treaties, alliances, or undertakings to our disadvantage.

What has been said shall serve for an introduction in general to the more particular parts of the nation's interest in the American trade and the due encouragement it ought to receive from the laws which may naturally make us the most rich and flourishing part, as well as the undoubted arbitrators of Europe, if not of all the maritime nations of the world. And in the next place I will show what discouragements those colonies lie under at present.

Chap. II.

The better to explain this to every capacity, it will be necessary to make a short history of sugar; that the invention, planting, and divers uses of it being known, the reader may thereby make a more perfect judgment of the national interest therein.

To which purpose it is first to be considered that the Europeans, five hundred years since, were perfect strangers to the use of it, and scarcely knew its name; but the Venetians, about that time being the great traders in East India spices, gums, and drugs, did, amongst other rarities, introduce sugar, which the physicians soon found to answer all the ends of honey, without many of its ill effects; so that it quickly became a commodity in mighty esteem, and though the price was ten times more than now, yet it prevailed so fast, and the consumption of it became so great, that an ill way of making, planting, and curing of it was, about three hundred years since, found out and practised in Greece, and some other neighbour nations, where the heat of the sun could in any degree ripen the cane.

But no nation made so considerable a progress therein as the Portuguese, who having with some success improved the art of planting it in their African colonies and islands, did at last make it their main business in Brazil, becoming thereby the only nation that set the price upon it to all the parts of the world, until the Hollanders grew their rivals for power and profit in that part of America.

But about fifty years since, during the war between those two nations in Brazil, a Hollander happened to arrive from thence upon our island of Barbadoes, where though there were good sugar-canes, the English knew no other use of them than to make refreshing drink for that hot climate, intending by planting tobacco there, to have equalled those of the Verina's, on which, ginger, cotton, and indigo they meant to rely. But this Hollander understanding sugar, was by one Mr. Drax and some other inhabitants there drawn in to make discovery of the art he had to make it; since which time by the many ingenious men the last civil war necessitated to seek their fortunes in that new world, there have been found out so many several sorts of mills, coppers, boilers, stoves, pots, and other tools and engines for planting and pressing the canes, boiling-up, separating, cleansing, and purifying the juice and sugar, as well as for drawing spirits of admirable use from the molasses, that we at present exceed all the nations in the world in the true improvement of that noble juice of the cane, which next to that of the vine, exceeds all the liquors in the world. And as our nation has been ever famous for meliorating inventions of all kinds, so in this we have gone so far, that notwithstanding the many discouragements those planters do at present and have heretofore lain under, yet they apparently set the price of it in all Europe, to the kingdom's pleasure, glory, and grandeur; which are all more advanced by that than by any other commodity we deal in or produce, wool not excepted; as I doubt not but to demonstrate beyond all dispute, before I end these papers . . .

Cotton is a commodity of great value; and the planting it of mighty advantage to the commonwealth, because we have it thereby one-third price less than formerly, when we imported it from foreign parts. Its uses are too many to be enumerated in the short method I have proposed; let it suffice therefore to say that the spinning, weaving, and working it into fustians, dimities, and many other useful stuffs, besides what is spent in candles, employs a multitude of hands, and gains the nation annually.

The manner of planting it is thus: a hundred acres of land cleared and kept for a cotton plantation requires fifty hands, whereof five must be white men-servants for the benefit of the militia, otherwise all but two might be black slaves.

It is planted in rows, as our London gardeners set their damask roses to make money of them, and rises to much about the same height in one year; and some few months time after its seeds are put into the ground, which is to be done in the wet season, when sugar-canes are planting; but sometimes it begins sooner, or later, according to the judgment of the experienced overseer. But the same hands employed in sugar can never be employed in planting and gathering the cotton, for when it is ripe, and the little bags it is contained in are opening, it is a constant labour and attendance from morning to night for the servants to go to and again in the intervals between the rows it is planted in, to take them at a critical time; otherwise it immediately damages.

There are two sorts of it called Ravell or Vine, that is yellow or white; the yellow is generally esteemed the largest staple.

An acre of ground planted therewith may produce from four hundred to two hundred pounds weight according as it hits; so that a hundred acres well looked after may produce thirty thousand pounds weight of cotton; which at 6d. a pound, as it may yield, amounts to £150.

Ginger is a useful spice for many things, and in several cases so answers the end of pepper that it is observed to rise and fall as that does.

It's planted by taking small pieces from the great races, and placing them orderly in trenches or holes, as our gardeners plant pease, and it is done in the same seasons that they plant sugar-canes.

An acre of right ground well planted will produce two thousand pounds weight of ginger; which, by its bulk in English tonnage, is accounted two tons at least.

A hundred acres require seventy-five hands, be they black or white servants, but there must by the laws always be a sufficient number of white men-servants in proportion to the black slaves, otherwise all blacks would serve, which is much cheaper than the other.

I have not set down all the casualties cotton and ginger plantations are subject to, for fear of swelling my treatise beyond its designed bulk; therefore let it suffice to say, they are subject to many, though not the same casualties, both from the alteration of seasons and other matters, as sugars are.

Indigo is more produced in Jamaica than in any other colony, by reason of the great quantity of savanna lands there, for it thrives best in light sandy ground, such as those savannas or great plains be. The seed of it from whence it is raised is yellow, and round, something less than a fitch or tare: the ground being made light by hoeing, trenches are made therein, like those our gardeners prepare for pease, in which the seed is put about March, which grows ripe in eight weeks' time, and in fresh broken ground will spire up to about three foot high, but in others not more than eighteen inches; the stalk is full of leaves of a deep green colour, and will from its first sowing yield nine crops in one year. When it is ripe they cut it and in proportionable vats steep it twenty-four hours; then they clear it from the first water, and put it into proper cisterns, where it is carefully beaten, and then is permitted to settle about eighteen hours. In these cisterns are several taps which let the clear water run out, and the thick is put into linen bags of about three foot long, and half a foot wide, made commonly of Ozenbrig cloth, which being hanged up, all the liquid part drips away. When it will drip no longer, it is put into wooden boxes about three foot long, and fourteen inches wide and an inch and a half deep. These boxes they place in the sun till it grows too hot, and then take them in till the extreme heat is over, continuing thus to do till it is sufficiently dry. In land that proves proper for indigo, the labour of one hand in a year's time may produce between eighty and an hundred pounds weight, which may amount from twelve to fifteen pounds per annum to the planter, if no accident happens: for indigo as well as all other commodities of those parts is subject to many; those most common to it are blasting and worms, to which it is very subject.

Cocoa is now no longer a commodity to be regarded in our colonies, though at first it was the principal invitation to the peopling Jamaica. For those walks the Spaniards left behind them there, when we conquered it, produced such prodigious profit with little trouble, that Sir Thomas Muddiford and several others set up their rests to grow wealthy therein, and fell to planting much of it, which the Spanish slaves who remained in the island always foretold would never thrive, and so it happened; for though it promised fair, and throve finely for five or six years, yet still at that age when so long hopes and care had been wasted about it, withered and died away, by some unaccountable cause; though they impute it to a black worm or grub which they find clinging to its root. The manner of planting it is in order like our cherry-gardens; which tree when grown up it much resembles. It delights in shade, so that by every tree they place one of plantain, which produces a fruit nourishing and wholesome for their negroes. They, by hoeing and weeding, keep their cocoa walks clear from grass continually; and it begins to bear at three, four, or five years old; and did it not almost constantly die before, would come to perfection at fifteen years' growth and last till thirty, thereby becoming the most profitable tree in the world; there having been above £200 made in one year of an acre of it. But the old trees planted by the Spaniards being gone by age, and few new thriving, as the Spanish negroes fortold, little or none now is produced worthy the care and pains in planting and expecting it. Those slaves give a superstitious reason for its not thriving, many religious rites being performed at its planting by the Spaniards, which their slaves were not permitted to see. But it is probable that wary nation, as they removed the art of making cochineal and curing vanillas into their inland provinces, which were the commodities of those islands in the Indians' time, and forbade the opening of any mines in them for fear some maritime nation might thereby be invited to the conquering them; so they might likewise in their transplanting cocoa from the Caracas and Guatemala conceal wilfully some secret in its planting from their slaves, lest it might teach them to set up for themselves, by being able to produce a commodity of such excellent use for the support of man's life; with which alone and water, some persons have been necessitated to live ten weeks together without finding the least diminution of either health or strength. But, though much more might be said, yet this shall suffice for the history of cocoa, with this addition only, that it grows on the trees in bags or cods of greenish, red, or yellow colours; every cod having in it three, four, or five kernels, about the bigness and shape of small chestnuts; which are separated from each other by a very pleasant refreshing white substance, about the consistency of the pulp of a roasted apple, moderately sharp and sweet, from which when ripe, its nuts are separated and by drying cured.

Pimento is another natural production of those islands, but principally in Jamaica, from whence many call it Jamaica pepper from the place and figure of it. The trees that bear it are generally very tall and spreading, so that the trouble of climbing them to gather it would make it incredibly dear, and those that be left, generally growing in the island, mountains, and woods, which are not taken up for planting, but remain in the king's hands. Their way is to go with their slaves into the woods, where it is plenty, and, cutting down the trees, pick it off from the branches; so that no pimento comes into Europe twice from one tree; and it happening often to miss for two or three years together, what it produces at present must be accounted an accidental benefit to the planters, rather than any thing to be relied on as a national advantage or constant encouragement.

The like may be said of lignum vitae, or Guaiacum, of red-wood, and several sorts of other trees, which come thence; for the more come the less remains, and the time required for the growing of those hard woods in the room of those cut down is in human reason so many hundreds of years, that the proposing to plant them would be rather a proof of madness than foresight; it being observable that in those spreading woods, where never axe was handled for cutting them down, nor carriage came to remove them, nor fire to burn them, there cannot be found one dotard or perishing tree of any useful kind, if of any at all.

To make and manage a Virginia or Maryland plantation for tobacco, every hand employed therein must be furnished with an axe, a saw, and other instruments for felling timber, and grubbing up its roots.

When the ground is cleared of trees and rubbish, then it is broke up with hoes, and afterwards with those and spades brought into little hillocks, like those moles turn up, into every one of which is placed one plant, so that they grow about three, four, and five foot asunder.

The tobacco plants are raised from its seed sowed in nurseries of hot-beds, skilfully prepared for that purpose in the months of January, February, March, and April, and are drawn thence and planted in the prepared little hills in the months of May and June; and will be ready for cutting in July or August following. But all the while from its planting, it is carefully to be watched, and every plant that is perceived to be dying must be taken away, and a fresh one set in the hill from whence the dead or dying plant was removed.

Tobacco plants are very subject to be undermined, eaten, and destroyed by a grub or worm that breeds about its root, which sometimes in spite of all the care and skill of the most ingenious planter will destroy his whole crop, nor do they ever escape some mischief from it; so that a tobacco plantation from January, that they sow the seed, till August, that they cut it, is a continual care and field labour in sowing, planting, hoeing, weeding, worming, succouring, and renewing: it has several accidents attend it, till it be cut and carried into the curing-house, where it is hanged plant by plant at an equal distance till it become powder-dry. At which time of the year that country is subject to great fogs and mists which makes it become waxy, and if it rises again, then it is fully cured, and becomes fit to be casked. All sweet-scented requires about three weeks' time, and Oronoco about six weeks' time; and in about three weeks more after its casking, it shows itself whether it be well cured or no. For though the experienced planter knows certainly whether his tobacco be well or ill cured, the purchaser cannot, and may be wronged if he buys it in less than three weeks' time after its casking; for if it had not been perfectly dried, it will certainly rot, perish, and become good for nothing: so that not only the prime cost but the freight home may be lost. And this the necessities of the planters sometimes only occasion, for by making too much haste not to lose his market, many times the whole year's labour and expectation is totally lost. And the care therein is very great, for there is not a leaf of tobacco put on board the ship that is well cured, but has passed at least six and thirty times through the hand of the planter or labourer. They ship it out from the month of October till April following; the annual exportation from all the tobacco colonies being an hundred and forty thousand hogsheads, at four hundred and fifty pounds weight to a hogshead.

The plantations are generally made into small parcels, not above eight or ten hands at a place, being the most beneficial and true way both for making the tobacco and raising provisions for them; and the curing-house must not be at a distance from the grounds where the tobacco grows.

The price of every pound weight of tobacco imported into the nation before we planted it was from about 4s. to 16s. a pound; and now the best Virginia is not above 7d. to the merchant, of which the king has 5d.

Two-thirds of the tobacco brought from those colonies is exported to foreign markets, which at about £3 the hogshead (which is the least the nation gets by it) amounts to above £200,000, besides the great quantity of shipping it employs.

It is not so little as a million the kingdom saves yearly by our planting tobacco; so that reckoning the white people in our tobacco colonies to be a hundred thousand men, women, and children, they one with another are each of them £12 a year profit to the nation.

There are in those colonies by a probable computation about six hundred thousand negroes and Indians, men, women, and children; and would be more, could they readily get negroes from Guinea; every one of which consumes yearly two hilling-hoes, two weeding-hoes, two grub-bing-hoes, besides axes, saws, wimbles, nails, and other iron tools and materials consumed in building and other uses, to the value of at least a £120,000 in only iron-work.

The clothes, guns, cordage, anchors, sails, and materials for shipping, besides beds and other household-goods consumed and used by them, are infinite; nor is the benefit of them to the kingdom sufficiently to be ex-plained. Therefore let it suffice in one word to say that the produce and consumption, with the shipping they give employment to, is of an infinite deal more benefit to the wealth, honour, and strength of the nation, than four times the same number of hands the best employed at home can be.

And thus much more I shall say for the colonies. As they are to the nation the most useful and profitable hands employed, and the best trade we have, both to the consuming the woollen manufactory of England and the encouraging of navigation; so those that go thither as servants, if they are industrious and just to their masters, they live much easier than in England and much more likelier to get estates, of which there are many precedents. And also they have been a great relief to many men (whose misfortunes have forced them to leave their own country) [who] by their carrying thither the remains of their shipwrecked fortunes, have recovered their lost estate, and very much conduced to that increase of wealth to this nation, as well as to the increase of shipping, which are the only true bulwarks of this nation.

That the courteous reader may readily see the benefit to England the hands employed in the colonies are, I have here made in the nature of a table, what fifty negroes with some few white hands (which are rather for security than otherwise) can make; what tonnage, what value it produces in England, what custom it pays to his majesty. It is to be understood that all they produce is clear gains to England (except some linen, wines, and brandy which is brought from foreign markets); the rest is either freight, custom, charges of merchandise, apparel, and necessaries for the plantations, or in cash, which either serves to suppport the planters when in England, or is laid out in purchasing lands; besides this, the employing of such a vast number of shipping and seamen, the benefit of which is well known to every Englishman. And since the plantations have been brought to this perfection, the consumption of England saves at least two-thirds by the abatement of the price those commodities bore before they made them; for which they never draw from England gold, or silver, but, on the contrary, by exportation of what is there made over and above our consumption does either occasion the enriching of England by monies brought from foreign parts for the sales of their product, or by bartering for other goods which must have been purchased by monies, or we must have been without them. By the hands employed in those colonies foreign commodities became native, to the great enriching of England, as aforesaid; and to the lessening the riches and strength of all other European nations that produce the like commodities.

An account of what advantage hands employed in the colonies are to this nation per annum.					
	White Men.	Blacks.	Will make.	Which is in English Tonnage.	Value in England.	Pays Custom.

	White Men.	Blacks.	Will make.	Which is in English Tonnage.	Value in England.	Pays Custom.
			C.		£	£ s. d.
Of Sugar	10	50	800	40	at 20s. per C. is 800	at 4s. 10d. per C. is 193 06 8
Of Molasses	—	—	280	14	at 8s. per C. is 112	at 9d. per C. is 10 10 0
The Excise of Molasses, when made into spirits	—	—	—			at 6d. per gall. is 56 00 0
Total	10	50	1080	54	912	259 16 8
			£			
Cotton	5	50	33000	41¼	at 6d. per lb. is 785	
Ginger	5	50	15000	7½	at 2s. per C. is 134	at 1s. per C. is 6 14 0
Indigo	5	50	5500	23	at 4s. per lb. is 1100	at 5s. per C. is 13 15 0
Total	15	150	53500	71¾	2019	20 09 0
			C.			
Tobacco Sweet-scented	21	50	1430	143	at 7d. per lb. is 4689	at 5d. per lb. is 3340 05 0
Oronoco	21	50	1712	214	at 5d. per lb. is 3954	at ½d. per lb. is 395 07 0
Total	42	100	3142	357	8643	3735 12 0

Chap. III.

From what has been said of the nature and manner of managing plantations, it is demonstrated beyond all scruple that those hands employed in our colonies are for their number the most profitable subjects of these dominions, as well to the ends of consumption and delight, as for increasing the wealth, power, and glory of the nation.

These apparent truths being once known to and generally allowed of by our nobility and gentry, it is senseless to imagine there could be one man amongst all our legislators should be so malicious to the kingdom, as to desire or endeavour the discouragement, much less ruin of such useful subjects as the planters are. But for want of experience in or intelligence of their manner of living and employing themselves in plantations, the best meaning and most upright patriots and lovers of their country, by wrong application of that right maxim, ' People are the riches of a nation,' may be most apt to study restraints, impositions, and severities on their trade and negotiation, to their present discouragement, and future ruin: which having in some degree happened already is the only cause I have used my endeavours for clearing those general mistakes, and for laying down some few useful rules for the support and encouragement of them all, but especially the sugar plantations, in whose happiness I being most at present concerned think myself most obliged to be serviceable to my power, as well as to clear my reputation; which amongst other well-meaning gentlemen is reflected on for designing a common factory for keeping up the price of their product, and a joint stock of monies to supply at common interest every industrious planter's wants till his commodity could be sold; which when rightly understood must force forgiveness, if not applause, from the most partial opposer of the design.

The better to clear which points, it is necessary to obviate that the discouragements the sugar plantations lie under have for three years last past furnished matter of complaint to all persons concerned in that commodity, as well planter as merchant; as is evident by the solemn addresses which were made to the court on that subject since the passing the act which lays an additional duty upon sugar.

The decay of those colonies being granted by all parties concerned in that advantageous negotiation, it will be necessary to be certain of the cause before proper remedies can be found out, much less applied, to that increasing distemper.

For though in gross it may be concluded that the additional duty occasioned the mischief, yet those who contrived that revenue for the crown did not intend the burden thereof should have fallen on the planter or merchant but on the consumptioner; which then had not been the least inconvenience or discouragement either to planting or trade, and consequently a more equal and less mischievous tax could not have been laid upon the nation.

But the price of sugar before the act, compared with that since, and the general fall of plantations demonstrates (beyond contradiction or dispute) that the whole burden falls on the most industrious, most useful, and best employed people for their numbers that can be found in all his majesty's dominions, which are those of the sugar colonies; besides the inequality of the thing, that sixty thousand industrious people, which the parliament intended should pay nothing, are by accident made to bear an imposition designed to be laid on the voluntary consumption of eight millions.

That the matter of fact is this, it cannot be denied by the most partial and interested against what has been proposed for the common factory, —though the natural aversion most men have to new invention, joined with the private interest of some few men who are factors at home, laziness of thought in some, and weakness of understanding in others, will, I am sensible, make it difficult, if not impossible, to establish the most compendious and proper remedy for that lingering distemper.

But this I dare boldly affirm, that what was then prescribed carried along with itself evident proofs of its innocency and well-meaning; since nothing therein could possibly take effect, until every several sugar colony in America had in their general assemblies considered and approved every part of it.

For without the sanction and laws of every several and individual colony, by their acts of assembly, the whole and every part of the proposal was utterly inconsistent and unpracticable; as those who will give themselves leave to examine it will undeniably find.

So that, if it may be supposed that the colonies themselves are proper judges of what they suffer, want, and would have, it cannot be denied but that their minds must best appear in general assemblies.

From whence it consequently follows that though the proposition might not be practicable by reason of the many different interests it was to unite, yet that the proposers were innocent, and sacrificed their labour, expenses, and time with a laudable intention.

To leave, therefore, that matter in the state it is, I will proceed to obviate the true and genuine causes of the present discouragements those colonies lie under, which may be reduced to three general heads.

1. That which is necessary to the beginning, increase, and support of a plantation comes to them much dearer than it might.

2. That what they produce by planting is forced to be sold at market

much cheaper than can be afforded, to the nation's loss as well as theirs.

3. That what they produce is carried to foreign markets at a much greater charge than they might carry it for.

To make it evident that what they want to begin, increase, and support a plantation comes to them much dearer than it might, I must desire the reader to consider (from what has been said concerning a sugar plantation) that the main support of that, as well as all other wealth, is labourers: that these labourers in plantations are either white servants or black slaves: that the white servants are either such as are hired for wages, or assigned for a term of years. Now if it appears that in the present method all these several sorts of labourers come to the planter one-third dearer than they need, then it must follow that there is a burden on that employment as heavy as if above thirty per cent were laid by way of tax upon their whole industry.

That the case of most planters is this, as well in white servants as slaves, and also in most of the tools and necessaries for managing a plantation, is too much felt to be doubted by all that are concerned in that trade or are experienced in planting. But to make it clear to others I must beg them to consider that few men leave their native country willingly who have enough conveniently to support themselves in it, except carried away by ambition or immoderate avarice, two passions little known or practised in America.

That therefore those who generally go thither comply with some urgent pressure in their fortunes or circumstances at home; so that, let them carry with them as good understandings, or strong geniuses and inclinations to planting as is possible, yet they must not hope to reap without they sow; and wheat or any other sort of grain is not a more necessary seed for its own species than wealth is seed to wealth. The Spaniards have a proverb to that purpose which says, ' He that will bring the Indies home must carry the Indies thither.' It will not be unnecessary to explain the general causes of their first thriving, that the unexperienced reader may have a just idea of the conveniences and inconveniences have attended those places by the many changes have happened in the government and laws of this kingdom since the beginning of the late civil wars.

To do which, we will make a short reflection on the unaccountable negligence, or rather stupidity, of this nation during the reigns of Henry the seventh, Henry the eighth, Edward the sixth, and Queen Mary, who could contentedly sit still and see the Spaniards rifle, plunder, and bring home undisturbed all the wealth of that golden world; and to suffer them with forts and castles to shut up the doors and entrances into all the rich provinces of America, having not the least title, or pretence of right, beyond any other nation; except that of being by accident the first discoverers of some parts of it; where the unprecedented cruelties, exorbitances, and barbarities their own histories witness, they practised on a poor, naked, and innocent people which inhabited the islands, as well as upon those truly civilized and mighty empires of Peru and Mexico, called to all mankind for succour and relief against their outrageous avarice and horrid massacres. Therefore, for a nation situated like ours for trade and navigation, being by the kingdom of Ireland the nearest eastern neighbour to that western world, to sit still and look upon all this without either envy or pity, must I say remain a lasting mark of the insensibility of those times, and the little knowledge our forefathers had of the true interest of mankind in general, or of their own country in particular.

Nor did we awake from this lethargy and wonderful dozing by any prudent foresight or formed counsel and design, but slept on until the ambitious Spaniard, by that inexhaustible spring of treasure, had corrupted most of the courts and senates of Europe, and had set on fire by civil broils and discords all our neighbour nations, or had subdued them to his yoke; contriving to make us wear his chains, and bear a share in the triumph of universal monarchy, not only projected but near accomplished when Queen Elizabeth came to the crown, as all historians of those times do plainly make appear. And to the divided interests of Philip the second and Queen Elizabeth, in personal more than national concerns, we do owe that start of hers in letting loose upon him, and encouraging those daring adventurers, Drake, Hawkins, Raleigh, the Lord Clifford, and many other braves that age produced; who by their privateering and bold undertaking, like those the buccaneers practise, now opened the way to our discoveries and succeeding settlements in America which since, as it were by chance, occasioned only by the necessities of many, wrought upon by the example, wisdom, and success of some few particulars without any formed design, help, or assistance from our state councils or legislators, in less than one century hath throve so well that they are become the example and envy, and might be the terror of all our neighbour maritime nations; and do undoubtedly maintain above half that vast quantity of shipping we employ in foreign trade: so that it can be from no other cause but want of information that many of our laws, as well as court maxims and practices, run opposite to their encouragement, protection, and increase.

The beginning of our American settlements was made in the latter end of Queen Elizabeth's reign by the encouragement of Sir Walter Raleigh, who undertook the planting of Virginia, and first brought the use of tobacco into England; but that nor any other colony of ours in the West Indies, did promise much success either to the nation or undertakers, until the reign of King James the first, whose peace with the crown of Spain restrained those bold privateers, who before, by harassing the Spanish colonies and mastering their rich ships of plate, had become very wealthy as well as numerous. But much against the will of most of them, but principally of such who had not sufficiently made their fortunes, this peace obliged them to change the prospect of their future conduct from rapine and spoil to trade and planting; so that in a very short time a considerable settlement was made in the northern parts of America, to the great increase of good shipping in the kingdom. By this means a general notion of having enough profitable lands in those parts of the world for nothing so infected the whole kingdom, that not only the necessitous and loose part of the nation flocked thither, but many nonconformists did solicit his majesty for leave to make a settlement together, under privileges and liberties, both in civil and church matters, by a constitution of their own. This combination King James prudently consented to and confirmed by his letters patent, wisely foreseeing that though a species of a commonwealth was thereby introduced into his dominions, yet the dependence thereof must be upon the crown for protection; and consequently that part of his subjects then called puritans would not be totally lost to the nation, as they must be if driven for ever to remain in foreign countries. Thus began that numerous colony of New England, where under frugal laws, customs, and constitutions, they live without applying themselves to planting any tobacco or other American commodities, except for their own private use. But by tillage, pasture, fishing, manufactures and trade, they to all intents and purposes imitate Old England, and did formerly much, and in some degree do now, supply the other colonies with provisions in exchange for their commodities, as tobacco, sugar, &c., which they carried to foreign markets, how conveniently for the nation's interest I shall not determine, being no enemy to any kind of honest industry. But this cannot choose but be allowed: that if any hands in the Indies be wrong employed for domestic interest it must be theirs and those other colonies which settle with no other prospect than the like way of living. Therefore, if any, such only should be neglected and discouraged who pursue a method [that] rivals our native kingdom, and threatens in time a total independency thereupon.

But as this cannot be said of our tobacco colonies, much less is it to be feared from our sugar plantations; except by gross mistakes at home we at last force them to part with their black slaves to the Spaniards and betake themselves to the sole planting of provisions and living upon their estates; which, should it happen, would be the greatest blow to our navigation, and consequently to the rents, that the kingdom ever received since it was a trading nation.

This digression I hope may be pardoned, since it explains a little the difference of our national interest in the several sorts of American colonies.

Nor would I be supposed to be so ignorant as to think that no kind of colonies can empty and consequently ruin the nation. No, there is a natural boundary to all worldly matters; and it becomes the wisdom of legislators truly to distinguish the depending and profitable, from the detached and undermining colonies, and rightly apply lenitives and corrosives accordingly . . .

For though to do right to the African Company, they have been wonderfully kind in the credit they have given the plantations, and that, rightly managed, a company is able to supply them with negroes cheaper than a loose trade could; yet the complaints the company continually make of the colonies' bad pay, and the complaints of the colonies for being ill supplied with negroes, allow both true, it will be necessary to inquire into the real cause of both inconveniences before proper remedies can be proposed.

To state the case truly: 'tis to be considered that when the company was first erected with exclusion to all others for trading in Guinea, the consequence thereof was never foreseen by the planters; for if it had, they could not have failed complaining against its establishment upon the foundation of such privileges they now pretend to; nor could any invention in the world have appeared a more pernicious monopoly than that would have been judged to be upon a free examination, before custom and necessity had reduced the colonies to a servile dependence thereupon.

For let [it] be granted there was a kind of a prudent necessity in the government here to unite a company for securing the gold and teeth trade in Guinea, and that it was in the power of the crown to prohibit all others, but such company to trade within the limits assigned them by their charter; yet this did not at all reach the plantations at first, nor did seem to prohibit them from buying slaves at the best market as since it has been interpreted. For, with submission to better judgments, the consequence of that interpretation seems to me to be an inlet to all manner of monopolies.

For why should not the crown by the same rule make a company who should have only power to trade thither in iron-ware, and another for wine; the like for mum, or any other commodity they want, as to prohibit bringing thither slaves but for the company's account; for the case to all intents and purposes is the same. For it is beyond all dispute known that the colonies, under a free, open, and loose trade for negroes, did flourish and increase before the company was erected.

It is certain that they could still be supplied plentifully at two-thirds the price the company makes them pay.

It is as undeniable that the company doth not supply them with the full numbers they want and could have, did not the company shut all doors to their supply.

And it cannot be denied but in these few heads are included all the several inconveniences so complained of in a monopoly.

I. For hereby a loose trade is turned into a restrained, which lessens the numbers of shipping that would trade to Guinea.

II. That comes dear to the subject that might be cheap.

III. And a useful commodity to the increase of wealth is not to be had in a sufficient quantity.

It is alleged that some part of the trade of Guinea, considering who are our rivals in it, cannot be preserved without force; and that the castle must be maintained, or that part of the trade lost; and that the castle, &c.

cannot be supported but with great cost; and that that charge falls extremely heavy upon so small a stock as that of the African Company.

The consequence of which premises is, they will always be necessitated to keep up the price of negroes one-third more than otherwise we need (though the castles are not supported or little or no ways useful to the negro trade, they keeping no forts, and seldom factors at those places where the negroes are most bought at). I confess a strong argument for the company, but a sour one for the colonies, which seem hereby deprived of their birthright, the liberty of the subject, and their possession, which consisted in a loose trade.

The premises considered, the planters may therefore justly desire that the national interest in the Guinea trade, the forts, &c., may be equally supported by all the nation as our navy's necessary forts and garrisons at home are; and not fall solely on their labour and industry. For the necessary supply of negroes to the colonies annually should not be less than £20,000.

Therefore upon a fair representation of the charge of the castle, &c., it cannot be questioned but the parliament will provide for their support, if it appear a national interest to preserve the colonies and that trade, as no doubt it is.

But as I hinted before, another cause of their selling dear is the bad pay they complain of in the colonies; and it may not be without cause that the company complains, not that the colonies give occasion for it, as matters now stand. For the country not being able to get negroes but at one-third too dear, and negroes being the main prop of a plantation, it necessarily follows, the planter must be necessitous, and thereby forced to sell his produce cheap, not being able through poverty to keep his commodity by him until it will yield a saving price.

Thus the true cause of his selling cheap is his buying dear; and both together keep the industrious planter, who is not got aforehand in his affairs, always indigent and in debt to the company. This debt being, as they allege, near £300,000, keeps the company's stock, which at first was not more than £110,000, always out of their hands; the interest of which, with the charge of the castle, falling upon so narrow a stock as £400,000. This rising at last upon the plantations makes their burden grievous at present, and must at last prove insupportable, as the debt increases; for that and their necessities will keep pace together, except some speedy remedy be found for them both.

All this taken apart and duly considered, it will appear probable to all thinking men that the plantations must speedily be ruined, and the commodities so profitable to the nation fluctuate into the hands of some neighbour colonies, who do not struggle under the like inconveniences; for which time the French, Dutch, Danes, and many other nations are at watch, and do at present increase proportionably to our discouragements. In this dismal prospect we must let them stand until we come to consider of proper remedies for these and the following inconveniences.

Another inconvenience attends them, proceeds from the wrong notion which has infected our judges, as well as the less intelligent gentry, that the people which go thither are a loss to the nation.

This, with some other more malicious but as weak suggestions, has occasioned severe and terrible sentences about exporting white servants, on pretence of spiriting; so that many have been forced to send for those who have been transported thither to produce again before the judges to acknowledge their voluntary transportation.

This occasions new offices, new fees, and new methods for sending servants thither; all which increases their price in the Indies very considerably, and falls as bad as a tax on the industry of the planter; besides makes servants so scarce that an universal languishing of such plantations as are growing happens thereby; and that want of white servants for term of years occasions the increase of wages to those they are forced to hire at great rates to supply that defect. This increase of wages is not only a new burden upon the present planters, but lessens their numbers, many choosing rather to sell their industry and labor to support themselves under others, than begin planting themselves under such visible encumbrances as daily increase upon that employment.

Thus one inconvenience begets another, to the ruin of the present and discouragement of future planting; which, before I have done, must more and more appear as national a concern as any our council can be busied about.

It is true many of the first comers, especially in Barbadoes, are got above the danger of ruin by these and other following mischiefs, that daily must, if not prevented, increase upon all who are not in the like circumstance for wealth; and peradventure to such the prospect of this general decay promises a good return and recompense for all the inconveniences they at present feel in the abatement of the value of their plantations.

Another great discouragement those colonies lie under is the arbitrary power and practices of the governors there and the court at home, which some have to their undoing felt, and all are liable to. . . .

Another inconvenience attending the colony is their being forced to bring their commodities first into England before they can carry them to any foreign market; which would appear upon a true examination not the least advantage to the nation, but a great loss. . . .

Thus in short it appears that buying the necessary matters for beginning and supporting a plantation one-third dearer than might in a right method be afforded them is one great discouraging to planting.

A second is that some of them being necessitous, they are all forced to sell their produce much cheaper than they can, under that burden, afford them.

A third, for want of a sufficient stock or credit they are not able to meliorate their sugars to a degree fit for consumption, whereby so beneficial an art is thrown away upon our Hamburg and Holland neighbours, to the mighty increase of their wealth and navigation, by our neglect as well as inconvenient customs and laws.

A fourth, by being subject to the inconvenience of complaints, suits, and removals into England, for matters sufficiently cognizable in those parts. To all which I shall only add to this section two more.

The first, a want of a true method for preserving the estates and plantations of deceased persons for the use of their relations or creditors in England.

And, lastly, by the great quantity of commodities that are sent out of the Leeward Caribbean Islands and sold to the Dutch at low prices for private lucre; for those people, saving all the duty, as well as the four and a half per cent there, as the customs in England, and having goods in barter for them directly from Holland, can afford their sugar much cheaper than their neighbours; so that there goes out of that backdoor for Holland, under the name of St. Eustace sugar, above a thousand and five hundred hogsheads of Muscovado sugar, which, refined with great advantage to that nation in Holland, keeps the markets low in all foreign parts. . . .

TO THE LORDS AND COMMONS IN PARLIAMENT ASSEMBLED.

A supplement to the proposal for a college of industry, showing a regular constant employ for the poor is the best foundation of trade and the greatest improvement to the nation and consequently support to the government, whilst the want of it tends to the poor's misery, poverty of the rich, and government's weakening. By John Bellers, 1696?.

JOHN BELLERS (1654–1725), quaker economist and poor law reformer, became by marriage joint lord of the manor of Coln St. Aldwyn's, Gloucestershire. He was a fertile projector of schemes for increasing prosperity, the general welfare, and religious knowledge. At the same time as his friend William Penn, he devised a plan for perpetual peace through a confederation of states. He advocated state-maintained hospitals and medical laboratories. He proposed that prisoners be given suitable work to avoid the evils of idleness and be instructed in the Gospel. His most important work, which influenced Robert Owen more than a century later, was entitled *Proposals for raising a College of Industry, of all useful Trades and Husbandry, with Profit for the Rich, a plentiful Living for the Poor, and a good Education for Youth* (1695). In it he suggested the capitalistic organization by private undertakers of groups of five hundred labourers each into coöperative units, which should engage in large-scale enterprise, develop production by cheapening food, eliminate waste, and so make a ten per cent or more profit to the holders of shares. It would cost £18,000 to erect such a unit, and its inmates, he figured, would make £3,000 a year over and above their keep. In these communities, communistically organized within, labour-time and not money would be the standard of value. The moral benefit to members would be incalculable.

The small pamphlet reproduced here, designed to get parliamentary sanction for the erection of such corporations, is an example of lobbying tactics used in the seventeenth century. On the Yale copy appears in longhand: ' William Brownlowe: given in the Lobby of the House of Commons: Jno. West.' Sir William Brownlowe was member for Peterborough in the 1689 and 1695 parliaments, and father of Lord Tyrconnell who pushed poor-relief projects in the 1730's. In October 1696, the house set up a committee to inspect the poor laws; the completed bill was read in March. This pamphlet was apparently struck off during those months. The act itself (8 & 9 Wm.III, c.30) shows no effect of Bellers' project. It provided that persons coming to inhabit in any parish must bring a certificate from the parish to which they belong; that persons receiving relief must wear on their right shoulder a large roman ' P,' with the initial letter of their parish, cut from red or blue cloth; that single persons hired in any parish could make no residence unless hired for a year; and that any appeal against removal of poor persons from a parish must be taken to quarter sessions.

Supposing there are seven millions of people in the nation, and that one in fourteen either will not work or want it; that is five hundred thousand men, women, and children.

And reckoning they might earn one another with sixpence a day a head, it comes to £12,500 a day, which is £75,000 a week.

That makes £3,900,000 a year the nation loseth by idleness, besides our loss in land unimproved by it, which is no small sum.

To which add but 2d. a head a day the nation is at charge in parish rates and other gifts to the poor comes to £1,300,000 a year, which account in the whole makes the loss and charge to the nation to be, £5,200,000 a year.

Though the parish rates be not much above £800,000 a year for the poor, yet the gifts otherwise given them make, I suppose, near as much more.

Now if one or two millions of this may be saved by the idle and indigent (and they better maintained and bred), what profit may be further added to the nation by the several millions of other labourers that might be employed in a better method than they are? A regular constant employment, as much excelling an irregular uncertain one for profit as a well disciplined army in order excels in strength and conduct an ignorant scattered multitude.

It's the raising more than we spend by the industry and labour of the people must strengthen the nation to support the government; all other ways and means mounting to no more than how to tax them equally, and with least sense to the people.

Some reasons for joining husbandry to manufactures for employing the poor, as proposed for a College of Industry.

1. Husbandmen are as useful and wanted as much as any mechanics, much land wanting people to manage it, and more people want bread than clothing, and as our food is double the value of our apparel and of more necessity, (the back may be promised, but the belly must be fed) if we will employ more people in manufactures or clothing than there is need for, and want them in raising food, our cloth may moth-eat for want of vent whilst the poor pine for want of bread.

2. They will less clog any market with their manufactures, some of

their hands being upon husbandry, and also the people in husbandry will take off a good part of their manufactures.

3. As they will make less to clog the market, so they will not be under a necessity of selling to buy bread (having food enough of their own) nor of selling under or before a market offers.

4. Whatever is raised or spent in the nation, the fewer hands it goes through between the raiser and user is for the advantage of the public, the raiser having the better price, or the spender buys it the cheaper, or both; and it being sent abroad to foreign markets, it may be afforded the cheaper, either to the keeping an old or gaining a new trade with strangers.

And though idle or lewd poor are (like a man's limbs out of joint) chargeable and vexatious; yet when industrious they support the rich, and the more we have of them, the stronger the nation; for if a city is of more value than a village, London than Islington, the people cannot be too numerous if every employ be but in a due proportion one to the other, husbandmen with other mechanics.

But the want of proportioning our labourers is what makes the complaint against a multitude of them, and many industrious poor groan under a dull commodity for want of vent, especially adding the increase of foreigners, who increase our manufactures (and not our husbandry) and with hard living and cheap working bring our poor mechanics to their rate of working and living (ours have not been used to) or else stand still and beg, which makes them hate the poor afflicted strangers (that fly hither from misery) as eating the bread out of our poor's mouths.

Whereas in this college method I propose consisting of temperance, industry, and a due proportioning of all trades and employments (like a due quantity of various materials in building, whilst too many of one thing, and too few of another will make the building lame, if not useless) we may employ and plentifully provide all conveniences of living for our own poor with profit, and when we have seen the experience from that copy, with the same improvement we may employ all the foreign poor that will come, who will be a treasure to the nation if well ordered (with this advantage also, that it will leave foreign princes the fewer hands to hurt us), whose children (though not their parents) will become natives of England, many of our nobility and eminent gentry and citizens (true English men) being the offspring of strangers.

And such a regular employ of our people that brings a due proportion and plenty of all things, will encourage their marriage and the coming hither of strangers (we having land enough to employ and maintain double our number, especially a well-managed fishery being added) and the increasing of our people is the best improving of our land and fishery, and increasing of our trade and seamen (transplanting as much as may be all foreign growth, to grow in our own plantations).

Therefore I pray you will permit a bill to be brought in to incorporate (with other suitable encouragements to) any persons that shall be willing to set on foot such a College of Industry.

John Bellers.

Finis.

THE DANGER OF MERCENARY PARLIAMENTS
By [John Toland?] 1698

THIS anonymous and undated pamphlet would appear to have been issued in the summer of 1698 as a piece of electioneering propaganda. The parliament of 1695–1698 had conducted an extensive investigation into bribery and corruption, and had passed a triennial act limiting the legal life of parliaments, and a place bill, vetoed by William III, designed to prevent members of the lower house from holding any government office. Admirably set forth in the pamphlet is the theory of checks and balances which lay behind such proceedings; they were both an extension of the clause in the Bill of Rights that elections should be free, and a foreshadowing of the placeman clause in the Act of Settlement. The parliament of 1695–1698, faced with a monetary crisis, issued paper money in the form of exchequer bills. They could be paid in as taxes, and when reissued and paid in a second time, returned a substantial interest rate. The Charles Duncomb mentioned in the pamphlet, a member of the house and receiver-general of the excise, falsely endorsed a number of such bills on their first issuing and pocketed the interest. The house committed him to the Tower in January 1698, and passed a bill in February to punish him; the lords rejected the bill in March and discharged him. Parliament was dissolved in July; the new parliament, of Tory complexion, met in December. This is the reference which dates the pamphlet in the summer of 1698.

It is possible that its author was the deist and political writer John Toland (1670–1722), who in 1698, after his *Christianity Not Mysterious* (1696) had lost him his Irish pulpit, was in London looking for a patron and supporting himself by odd jobs of writing and editing. That year he edited Milton's prose works, with a life of the author, in 1699 the *Memoirs of Denzil Holles*, and in 1700 Harrington's *Oceana*. His *The Art of Governing by Partys* (1701) repeats the arguments of the pamphlet and specifically cites it to support the contention that public opinion was aroused. His last work, 1722, was a reëdition of this pamphlet which, he says, was then available only in collected volumes. He added that the original was written in King William's time by the direction of Lord Shaftesbury and was printed and dispersed privately at his expense. Shaftesbury was a member of the 1695–1698 parliament. Later he partially supported Toland.

1. Several treatises have been formerly written, and more (I doubt not) will be in this juncture published, with directions and informations to the people of England for choosing fit and proper representatives for the ensuing parliament, wherein sufficient notice will be taken of the failures and defects of several who have already been entrusted in that service, and the due qualifications of such who are now to be elected. I shall therefore confine my present thoughts only to one particular

head, which yet, in my opinion, seems to involve in it the inevitable
fate of England, which wholly depends upon the choice of members
for the next session of parliament: I mean the choosing or refusing of
such persons who are now possessed of any places and preferments depending upon the gift and pleasure of the court. If herein my endeavours
prove unsuccessful I shall have nothing left but the satisfaction of my
own conscience to support me under the deplorable consequence and
effects which must necessarily attend the choice of a house of commons
filled with officers and court pensioners. This is the last struggle and
effort the people of England have left them for their properties, and
should we now miscarry in this, we may sit down and idly show our
affections for our country, and fruitlessly bewail the loss of our liberties,
but shall never meet with another opportunity of exerting ourselves in
its service. That I may therefore set the minds of people right in this
particular before it be too late, I think it will be only necessary to show
the danger of choosing members that are in places for two considerations:
first, from the nature of such a parliament, considered in itself: and
secondly, from what has already been done by parliaments so qualified.
In both which I shall be very brief, and content myself with much fewer
arguments than might be urged upon this subject. For I should almost
despair of being survived by the liberties of England, if I could imagine
there was a necessity of saying much in a case not only of such irresistible
evidence and demonstration, but also of the utmost concern and importance to us.

2. First then, we shall best be able to understand the nature of such
an ill-chosen parliament by comparing it with a true one, and with the
original design of parliaments in their institution. I hope it need not be
told that they were at first intended for a support to the king's just
prerogative, and a protection to the subjects in their as just rights and
privileges; for maintaining all due honour to the executive power, and
all suitable respect and encouragement to those who are entrusted with
the administration of the laws; for a poise and balance between the two
extreme contending powers of absolute monarchy and anarchy; for a
check and curb to insolent and licentious ministers, and a terror to ambitious and overgrown statesmen; for giving their advice to his majesty
in all matters of importance; for making necessary laws to preserve or
improve our constitution, and abrogating such as were found burdensome

and obsolete; for giving the king money for defraying the charges and expenses of the government, or maintaining a necessary war against foreign and domestic enemies, for examining and inspecting the public accounts, to know if their money be applied to its true use and purposes; in short, for the best security imaginable to his majesty's honour and royal dignities, and his subjects' liberties, estates, and lives.

3. This being the nature and true design of a parliament, let us now see whether a house of commons full of officers and court-pensioners will answer those noble and laudable ends of their constitution; and here indeed I begin already to be ashamed of my undertaking; the proof of the negative is so ridiculous that it looks too much like a jest to ask anyone in his wits whether a parliament filled with delinquents will ever call themselves to an account, or what account would be given if they should; whether an assembly of public robbers will sentence one another to be punished, or to make restitution; whether it is possible our grievances can be redressed that are committed by persons from whom there is no higher power to appeal; whether there is any hope of justice where the malefactors are the judges; whether his majesty can be rightly informed in affairs relating to himself or the public when they are represented to him only by such persons who design to abuse him; whether the public accounts will be faithfully inspected by those who embezzle our money to their own use; whether the king's prerogative can be lawfully maintained by such who only pervert it to their own sinister ends and purposes; whether a parliament can be a true balance where all the weight lies only in one scale; or lastly, whether a house of commons can vote freely who are either prepossessed with the hopes and promises of enjoying places or the slavish fears of losing them. Methinks it is offering too much violence to human nature to ask such questions as these; I shall therefore leave this invidious point.

4. Yet lest still any should remain unsatisfied or lulled into a fond opinion that these mischiefs will not ensue upon the elections they shall make, I shall further endeavour to convince those who are most moved by the force of examples by coming to my second particular, and showing how parliaments so qualified have all along behaved themselves. And here I must confess there are not many instances to be given, the project of corrupting parliaments being but of a late date, a practice first set on foot within the compass of our own memories, as the last and most

dangerous strategem that ever was invented by an encroaching tyrant to possess himself of the rights of a free-born people; I mean King Charles the second, who, well remembering with how little success both he and his father made use of open arms and downright violence to storm and batter down the bulwarks of our excellent constitution, had recourse at last to those mean arts and underhand practices of bribing and corrupting with money those who were entrusted with the conservation of our laws and the guardianship of our liberties. And herein he so well succeeded, that the mischiefs and calamities occasioned by that mercenary parliament did not terminate with his life and reign, but the effects of them are handed and continued down, and very sensibly felt by the nation to this very hour. For it is to that house of commons the formidable greatness of France was owing, and to their account, therefore, ought we to set down the prodigious expenses of the late war. It was by those infamous members that money was given to make a feigned and collusive war with France, which, at the time, was employed either in subduing the subjects at home or oppressing our protestant neighbours abroad. It was this venal parliament in effect that furnished the king of France with timber and skilful workmen for building ships, as well as expert mariners, and a prodigious quantity of brass and iron cannon, mortar-pieces and bullets from the Tower, by the help of which our own treacherous king was able to boast publicly and thank God that he had at last made his brother of France a seaman. By this means the honour of England was prostituted, and our natural and naval strength betrayed, with which, like Sampson, we should easily have broken all the cords that Europe, or the whole world, could have made to bind and enslave us, had not this parliament made a sacrifice of all to the charms of a French Delilah. To this profligate and villainous reign we are to ascribe the loss of all the considerable charters of England, the deaths of our best patriots, the encouragement and almost establishment of popery, the decay of trade, the growth of arbitrary power, the ill effects of dishonourable leagues, the shutting up of the exchequer, the progress of all sorts of debauchery, the servile compliances at court of a rampant hierarchy in the kingdom, the insolent deportment of the inferior clergy both in the universities and elsewhere, their slavish doctrine of passive obedience and nonresistance; in short, a general depravation of manners and almost utter extirpation of virtue and moral honesty. These and all the other mischiefs of that reign are justly chargeable to the account of that pensioned parliament, who either were the immediate authors or the undoubted causers of them; who, though they sat long and often and could not be ignorant of our deplorable condition, yet having their eyes blinded with the dust of gold, and their tongues locked up with silver keys, they durst not cry out for the rescue of their country, thus inhumanly ravished in their very presence. It will not consist with my designed brevity, nor is it here necessary to give the reasons that induced the court to dissolve that parliament, nor shall I take any further notice of their great and fortunate oversight in doing it, nor their unfeigned repentance afterwards for it; I shall only observe that if the nation had been so senselessly stupid to have chosen the same members a second time who were pensioners in the former parliament, we had long ago suffered the dismal consequences of our folly and madness in such a choice; nor should we now have had this liberty to warn one another against splitting upon the like rocks and falling into the same precipices. But they were wiser in those times, and the consideration of the dreadful shipwreck they had so lately escaped made them choose pilots of a quite contrary disposition, who, as far as in them lay, and as long as they were permitted to sit at the helm, repaired the shattered vessel of the commonwealth, restored its honour, revived its drooping genius, gave force to its laws, countenance to its religion, and in a great measure reduced our banished liberties and exposed the persons who sold them to the universal hatred and reproach of their fellow-subjects, a punishment indeed infinitely less than they deserved for the highest crime a member of parliament is capable of committing.

5. As for King James's reign, though it was notoriously guilty of the breach and violation of most of our fundamental laws, which sufficiently justifies our carriage towards him, yet cannot we say that his mismanagement is to be ascribed to the corruption of any parliament sitting in his time. 'Tis true indeed he reaped too much advantage from the conduct of the bribed parliament in his brother's reign, and used all possible endeavours to procure such another for himself, well knowing it to be the most effectual means for carrying on his ruinous and destructive projects; yet either from the unshaken constancy of the people, or want of dexterity in his ministers, he was altogether defeated in his expectation.

6. This miserable disappointment of King James's hopes made way for our late glorious revolution, which was brought about by the hearty endeavours, and accompanied by the most unfeigned vows and wishes of all true lovers of their country, who from hence expected a full deliverance from their present miseries and a sure remedy from their future fears: for what happiness might not the people well hope for under the government of the best of kings, supported by the best of titles, viz. the general consent and election of his people? We were filled with golden dreams not only of a bare security for our estates and lives, but an inexhausted affluence of all manner of blessings a nation is capable of enjoying. But though we have dreamt the dreams, yet have we not seen the visions. And though the nat'on is by this time sadly sensible how wretchedly they have fallen short of their former happiness, yet are they not all acquainted with the true spring and fountain from whence all their misfortunes flow, which is indeed no other than that barefaced and openly avowed corruption which, like an universal leprosy, has so notoriously infected and overspread both our court and parliament. 'Tis from hence are plainly derived all the calamities and distractions under which the whole nation at present groans; 'tis this that has changed the very natures of Englishmen, and of valiant made them cowards, of eloquent, dumb, and of honest men, villains. 'Tis this can make a whole house of commons eat their own words, and countervote what they had just before resolved on. 'Tis this could summon the mercenary members from all quarters of the town in an instant, to vote their fellow-criminals innocent; 'tis this that can make a parliament throw away the people's money with the utmost profusion, without enquiring into the management of it; 'tis this that put a stop to the examination of that scandalous escape of the Toulon fleet into Brest; 'tis this that has encouraged the mismanagements of the admiralty in relation to the loss of so vast a number of men-of-war and merchant ships, as well as other miscarriages which were by all men judged to proceed not from their want of understanding in sea affairs. 'Tis this that has hindered the passing a bill so often brought into the house for incapacitating members to bear offices: 'tis this that could not only indemnify but honour a leading member for his audacious procuring and accepting a grant of lands which by the parliament had been set apart for the public service, a vote that shall stand recorded in their own journals to the never-dying infamy of that

mercenary assembly. 'Tis this could make the same person most confidently affirm that he was sure the majority of the house would agree to what he was going to propose; 'tis this that could make men of peaceable dispositions and considerable estates vote for a standing army; 'tis this that could bring admirals to confess that our fleets under their command was no security to us. 'Tis this could make wise men act against their own apparent interest; in short, 'tis this that has infatuated our prudence, staggered our constancy, sullied our reputation, and introduced a total defection from all true English principles. Bribery is indeed so sure and unavoidable a way to destroy any nation that we may all sit down and wonder that so much as the very name of a free government is yet continued to us. And if by our wary choice of members we should happen to recover our ancient constitution, we shall with horror and amazement look back and reflect upon the dreadful precipice we so narrowly escaped.

7. Fatal experience has now more than enough convinced us that courts have been the same in all ages, and that few persons have been found of such approved constancy and resolution as to withstand the powerful allurements and temptations which from thence have been continually dispensed for the corrupting of men's minds and debauching their honest principles. Such instances of the frailty of human nature may be given within these few years past as might make a man even ashamed of his own species, and which (were they not so open and notorious) ought out of pity to mankind to be buried in perpetual silence. Who can enough lament the wretched degeneracy of the age we live in? To see persons who were formerly noted for the most vigorous assertors of their country's liberty, who from their infancy had imbibed no other notions than what conduced to the public safety, whose principles were further improved and confirmed by the advantages of a suitable conversation, and who were so far possessed with this spirit of liberty that it sometimes transported them beyond the bounds of moderation, even to unwarrantable excesses; to see these men, I say, so infamously fall in with the arbitrary measures of the court, and appear the most active instruments for enslaving their country, and that without any formal steps or degrees, but all in an instant, is so violent and surprising a transition from one extreme to another, without passing the mean, as would have confounded the imaginations of Euclid or Pyrrho. All the stated

maxims in relation to the nature of mankind, which have been long ago settled and established by philosophers and observing men, are now baffled and exploded; and we have nothing left us to contemplate but the wild extravagances of romantic fables, the sudden conveyances of nimble-fingered jugglers, the inimitable dispatches of transubstantiating priests, or the now more credible metamorphoses of men into beasts.

8. The necessity we have laid under of frequent meetings of parliament during the war has taught our managers so much dexterity and address in their applications to the members of that assembly that they are now become consummate masters in that most detestable art of corrupting our representatives by hopes and fears of attaining or losing offices and preferments. And though I here name offices, yet those offices are downright bribes and pensions, since they are held precariously from the court, and constantly taken away upon non-compliance with the court-measures; though I am not ignorant that several considerable pensions were also paid out of the exchequer to members of both houses. For places could not be had for all, though they have tried all imaginable arts for dividing among themselves the considerable posts in the kingdom; for either by splitting of offices among several persons which were formerly executed by one, or by reviving such as were sunk, or by creating others which were altogether useless and unnecessary, or by promises of preferment to those who could not presently be provided for, they had made above 200 members absolutely dependent upon them. And what points may not such a number carry in the house, who are always ready and constantly attending with more diligence to destroy our constitution than the rest were to preserve it? Who represented not their country but themselves, and always kept together in a close and undivided phalanx, impenetrable either by shame or honour, voting always the same way, and saying always the same things, as if they were no longer voluntary agents, but so many engines merely turned about by a mechanic motion, like an organ where the great humming basses as well as the little squeaking trebles are filled with but one blast of wind from the same soundboard. Yet a few of them may in some measure be distinguished from those point-blank voters, whom neither their country's safety nor their own more dear and valued interest, nor the persuasion of their once intimate friends, nor fear of reproach, nor love of reputation could ever prevail to join in an honest point, or dissent

from a question that carried in it the violation of the rights and properties of the subject. These are the men who have persuaded his majesty, or rather assumed to themselves, not to fill up any vacant offices whilst the parliament is sitting; but to keep all pretenders in a dependence till the end of the session, and bind them up to their ill behaviour, which will then be their best pretence to demand their wages of unrighteousness. Witness the commission of excise the last session, which was sued for by and promised to above thirty competitors, who all did their utmost to signalize their several merits for an office which doubtless will be at last divided amongst those who have deserved worst of their country. By these means they made their numbers and interest in the house so great that no miscarriage in the government could ever be redressed, nor the meanest tool belonging to them be punished. Some of which they did indeed take into their own hands, which raised in the people a high expectation that some extraordinary penalties would be inflicted upon them; when their design at the same time was nothing else but to protect and screen them from the ordinary course of justice. Such is now the difference in point of corruption between a common jury and the grand jury of the nation! Such a mutual assistance and support have they been to one another in the several mismanagements of their trusts; so favourable have they been to their own creatures and so implacable to those who have any way opposed their unjust proceedings, witness their scandalous partiality in the case of Duncomb, which I hope to see printed at large for the satisfaction of the public. If it were truly represented, I am sure there needs nothing more to excite in the people a universal detestation of their arrogance and injustice. And yet do these apostates pretend to value themselves upon their merit in contriving that most destructive project of exchequer bills, by which all impartial men must either think they notoriously dissemble with us, or that they have indeed lost their senses when they speak of public service; the word is so unbecoming in their mouths and so awkwardly pronounced that they seem not to breathe in their own element when they usurp the name. These are the men who have endeavoured to render our condition hopeless, even beyond the power of the king himself to relieve us. For though his majesty be deservedly loved and honoured by his people for his readiness to do them justice and ease their oppressions, yet can we not expect it from him whilst he is thus beset and surrounded, and his palaces invested by these conspirators against his own honour and the welfare of his kingdoms. The only remedy therefore that remains is to choose such a parliament who lie under no temptations, and are acted by no other motives but the real and true interest of his majesty and his dominions, a parliament that will fall unanimously upon public business and be free from those petty factions and personal piques which in the late season so shamefully obstructed and delayed the most important service of the commonwealth.

9. If it should be pretended that the nation is yet unsettled and the fear of King James has forced them upon these extraordinary methods for their own preservation, I answer that no cause whatsoever can be justly alleged in vindication of such vile arts and pernicious practices. But I would farther ask them what necessity there is upon that account for their gaining such prodigious estates to themselves in so short a time and in so merciless a way, when the nation was racked to the utmost by taxes in a long and expensive war. Is it the fear of King James that has brought such a reproach upon our revolution, as if it needed to be supported by such mean and unjustifiable practices? Is it the fear of King James that makes us content he should live so near us, or that he should be maintained at our own charge of £50,000 per annum? Or has not rather King James been made the pretence for the unwarrantable proceedings of our conspirators during the war and since the conclusion of the peace? It is very strange that King James, who is but their jest in private, should be thus made their public bugbear to frighten us out of our senses like children, so that King James must be at last our ruin abroad, who could not compass it by all his power and interest at home. And in this sense I am of their opinion, that we are not yet quite delivered from the fear of King James, who must be made the instrument of our slavery by those very persons who pretend their greatest merit to consist in delivering us from him. But what is this but making the old abdicated tyrant a footstool to ascend the throne of absolute power, and a scaffold for erecting that proud and stately edifice from whence we have so justly tumbled him down headlong. But 'tis to be hoped that the nation will be no longer imposed on by such stale pretences as these, and that a well-chosen parliament will not fail to pass their severest censures upon those who would thus jest us out of all that is dear and valuable amongst us; that they will no longer resemble a flock of sheep

(as Cato said of the Romans in his time) that follow the bell-wether and are contented when all together to be led by the noses of such whose counsels not a man of them would make use of in a private cause of his own; that they will at last vindicate the honour of England and imitate their wise ancestors in hunting down these beasts of prey, these noxious vermin to the commonwealth, rather than suffer themselves to be led in collars and couples by one mighty Nimrod, who upon the turning up his nose shall expect a full cry of sequacious animals, who must either join voices or be turned out of the pack.

10. Notwithstanding what I have said, I would not have any of them either really imagine themselves, or falsely suggest to others that I envy them their places and preferments, which I am so far from doing that I wish they rather had them for the term of their lives. I desire only that they may be subject to the laws and to some power on earth that may call them to account for their misbehaviours, that they may not be their own judges, that our sovereign remedy may not prove our chief disease, and that the kid may be seethed in something else than its mother's milk. Nor would I by any means deny them their seats in parliament, provided they are in a condition to speak and act freely, and discharged from those temptations which I find they have not constancy enough to withstand; for after all, I still believe many of them so honest that nothing but money or preferments will corrupt them. But if nothing will satisfy them but the downright subversion of our constitution, if they will be content with nothing but the utter abolishing of all laws, and the rooting up of those fences and securities provided by our ancestors for the preservation of all things that are sacred and esteemed amongst mankind, it is high time for the electors to look about them and disappoint their unreasonable and exorbitant hopes, and to spew them out as detestable members of the commonwealth, not only as unfit to be trusted with their liberties, but as unworthy to breathe in the air of a free government.

11. If any should say that the alterations in elections will stand us in no stead, since whoever are chosen will still be bought off and bribed by court-preferments, I answer, it will require a considerable time to new model and debauch a house of commons, nor can it be done but by displacing all those who are already possessed, to make way for these new-comers, which will make the trade and mystery of bribery more

plain, and consequently more abhorred. And since no parliament can now sit above three years, the court will meet with fresh difficulties to interrupt them, which may possibly at last make them weary of these practices. 'Tis true indeed, this consideration ought to make us more circumspect in our choice of members, for though we should choose but an inconsiderable number of pensioners, yet will they soon be able to work over a majority to their side; so true is the saying, ' A little leaven leavens the whole lump.' Whoever therefore out of any particular friendship or other motives of fear or private interest should vote for any one person so qualified, let him consider that as much as in him lies, he makes a complement of all the liberties of England to the unsatiable avarice and ambition of statesmen and court ministers. Since therefore we have so narrowly escaped our destruction, and one season more of the last parliament would infallibly have ruined our constitution, we cannot surely be so grossly overseen as to neglect the opportunity now put into our hands for avoiding the like hazards in time to come, which may easily be done if the freeholders and burghers in England will petition and engage their representatives to consent to a bill which shall be brought into the house, to incapacitate all members for holding offices and preferments; or if it should be thought too much to debar them altogether from the enjoyment of posts of honour and advantage, let them keep them during good behaviour and not otherwise; that such places may not be reserved in store for those who shall be from time to time elected, and thereby a continued course of corruption be carried on successively through the whole nation, who will in a few years insensibly find themselves so universally infected with this insinuating vice that we shall be thoroughly ripe for destruction, and readily expose to sale the liberties of England by auction to the fairest bidder. If it was deservedly thought one of our most dangerous grievances that the judges, who only declare the law, should hold their places *ad bene placitum*, what condition must we be in when the law-makers themselves are subjected to the same temptations? Or what advantages have we got by having our judges commissions for life, when our very legislature itself is prostituted to bribery and sordid gain? The fortune of England is now brought to the nicest point, and there are critical seasons which, if neglected, will never again be offered; and should we now fail in our duty to our country, we shall assuredly fall unpitied by the rest of the world. But if, on the other hand, we can by our foresight and diligence prevent for the future the bribing and corruption of parliaments, it is not to be imagined what security, what happiness, and what immortal reputation will be the never-ceasing concomitants of such a settlement. If the very rump of a parliament, even in the midst of domestic discontents, and beset on all sides with foreign assaults and invasions, were able by that one self-denying act to maintain the public welfare from the danger of inward convulsions at home and violent concussions from abroad; if that small and broken number, without any head and under so many disadvantages, could by this only means secure our peace and so widely extend the repute and honour of the English name, what country or what region could ever give limits to the unbounded reputation of a full and legal parliament so nobly qualified? What nation could there be so powerful as to resist our forces or so politic as to infatuate our counsels? There is nothing within the compass of human wishes that we might not assure ourselves from the wisdom and virtue of such a disinterested assembly, headed and encouraged by the most auspicious prince that ever yet swayed the English sceptre. A prince who only waits the opportunity of our own willingness to be happy, and is fired with a longing eagerness to see the nation deserve the glorious effects of his inimitable conduct and inexhausted beneficence; who only wishes a happy conjucture of a free and unbiassed parliament, that he might join with them in the rescue of himself and us from the oppression of those devouring harpies who would tear off the yet green and flourishing laurels from his majestic brows and ungratefully cast a tarnish upon the lustre of his bright and shining achievements; that he might dissipate those inauspicious vapours which have hindered him from breaking out in the height of his meridian glories and intercepted his benign and noble influence upon his inferior and dependent orbs; that he might deliver up to justice those traitorous and insinuating parasites who endeavour to inspire into his sacred breast an unworthy jealousy of his people, as if he wanted the assistance of a standing army to secure and establish to himself that throne which he has already so firmly erected in the hearts and affections of his subjects; and lastly, that he might wholly discharge himself of those wretched and perfidious statesmen who endeavour to fix the brand of their own acquired infamy upon their master, that they might make him as hateful to one party for their vices as he is already to another for his own virtues, and deprive him of the glorious title of the world's greatest benefactor, which he has so justly purchased to himself by his immortal performances.

12. I shall conclude with one word in answer to such who may possibly think I have reflected too much upon the supineness and base neglect of the people of England; as if it were possible they could be such monstrous and unnatural self-murderers as to give away with their own breath and free consent all their rights to their estates and lives. I confess I should be glad to find my labour lost on this account. But I desire such to consider that there are many honest and well-meaning Englishmen who do not distinguish between our present government and our present way of governing, whose distance from the parliament, multiplicity of business, or other circumstances in the world render them less able to penetrate the designs that are now carrying on for the total subversion of our most excellent constitution. And it is plain on the other hand that the great and unwearied diligence of the present conspirators against our government, in order to support their future elections, does infer their thoughts that the majority of the electors are capable of being imposed upon in this gross and unexampled manner. Since therefore those who are making us slaves think it no great difficulty to effect their purposes, I see no reason why I ought to be so tender as to forbear expressing my fears and apprehensions of their success.

Finis.

THE UNHAPPINESS OF ENGLAND

As to its trade by sea and land truly stated. Also, a lively representation of the miseries of the poor, the pernicious consequence of wearing swords, and the ill precedents acted at the two theatres; with effectual means to redress these growing evils; and several remarkable particulars, to which is added, an essay of the happiness of man in observing the rules of morality. By Charles Povey. London, printed for the author, living near Execution-Dock in Wapping, and to be sold by the booksellers of London and Westminster. 1701.

CHARLES POVEY (1660?–1743), who maintained that he came of an old Cheshire family, wrote an extraordinary miscellany of books and pamphlets on political, financial, religious, and moral subjects. A late eighteenth-century antiquarian described him as possessing a ' very singular cast of mind,' only a little more rational than that of one Cruden, a biblical scholar who, escaping from a madhouse, conceived himself divinely appointed to reform the nation. Politically Povey was Whig from his *A Challenge to all Jacobites* (1689) to *An Enquiry into the Miscarriages of the Four Last Years Reign* (1714). That pamphlet, which accused the late Tory ministry of plotting to support France, destroy the church, foment rebellion in Scotland, and bring in the Pretender, ran through nine editions, and was answered by Atterbury and by Swift. Later he accused the Whig ministry of stealing his schemes without reward; by 1737 he estimated that the government had made over a million pounds from the fruits of his genius. His financial pamphlets dealt with contemporary problems, a scheme in 1699 to raise funds, a plan in 1720 to replace South Sea stock with new coins. The high moral note struck in these excerpts from *The Unhappiness of England* he followed with *Meditations of a Divine Soul* (1703) and *Holy Thoughts of a God-made Man* (1704). *The Visions of Sir Hester Reily*, a penny sheet in imitation of the *Tatler*, appeared in 1710 and 1711. At the age of 80, seeing the world still unreformed in spite of his five books and more than forty shorter pieces, he was inspired by the lascivious immodesty of Richardson's *Pamela* to write a dialogue, *The Virgin in Eden, or, The State of Innocency* (1741), which he doubted not would show what holy living and dying meant.

In more practical matters Povey showed inventive fertility. He was in the coal trade in Wapping in 1700, and when hounded out by other dealers launched life and fire insurance schemes. The Sun Fire Office, which thrived for years, was begun by Povey. From 1705 to 1710 he distributed gratis *General Remarks on Trade*, which appeared thrice weekly and was supported by its advertisements. Until the postmasters general sued him for infringement of monopoly, he ran a successful penny post in London, and he broached, though never put into operation, a parcels post.

On the East India Trade

As for the East India trade, there are two companies, viz. the old and new, both confirmed by act of parliament and carried on by two select communities of men; many of these to my knowledge are persons of great parts, well skilled in the way of trade, having large estates, and are willing to increase their store. But I know not how to account for the indiscretion of both parties, who are continually striving to undermine each other by making separate interests and raising new disputes, when at the same time most of them are convinced how beneficial it would be to unite and join together in one public stock. And indeed, I dare avouch that unless such an union be effectually established by an act of parliament, the whole trade will be quite ruined within the space of a few years. Therefore it is much to be wished that they were all persuaded to agree and unanimously to reduce this noble trade to its former splendour, never suffering so honourable a society to be disgraced by stock-jobbing, a practice that enriches knaves and beggars fools. If these things were once completed, it would in some measure advance navigation abroad and promote several trades at home.

On Merchandising

There are several merchants who resort to the Royal Exchange, but few of them deal in that way for which it was designed. For I cannot but look upon it as a presage of approaching ruin, when casting my eyes on the numerous crowds I observe what an alteration there is in their demeanour and actions, and hear them talk of little else but of stocks, banks, and funds, besides a curious inquiry after state affairs both foreign and domestic; whereas about 20 years ago a man might have frequented the Exchange for several days together and not have heard a word of what was transacted in his prince's privy council; nor could he have discerned any little artifices amongst the merchants, contrived on purpose to impose on one another, which are now often practised, and may be daily discovered.

The main design of those gentlemen was to encourage trade by sea and land. Then industrious persons had an opportunity to raise themselves and families by fair dealing; but now several gain estates by the ruin of honest men, and are very far from promoting the public advantage. I could produce many instances that are not suitable to the character

15—The illustration opposite shows the fly-sheet, *The Profitable and Golden Adventure to the Fortunate*, 1695. This one, typical of hundreds which flooded the coffee-houses of the 1690's to advertise stock companies and speculative schemes, urged the public to subscribe to a government loan-lottery. Thomas Neale, who managed the lottery as master of the transfer office, was master worker of the mint under its warden, Isaac Newton. He was also groom-porter to the king with the duty of furnishing the royal lodgings with chairs, tables, cards, and dice, and of settling disputes at cards. Neale at the same time engaged in commercial, mining, and building projects of his own. He died insolvent about 1699.

The Profitable and Golden Adventure to the Fortunate.

SET out by *Thomas Neale*, Efq; Groom-Porter to his Majefty, (purfuant to his Promife late publifhed in Print) in which Fifty thoufand Tickets were to be given out at half a Guiney *per* Ticket, amounting only to Twenty five thoufand Guineas, and yet by the Method propofed, the Adventure to be drawn was to be Fifty thoufand Guineas. The Drawing, tho' Publifhed to begin on *Tuefday* the 24th of this *March*, 1695. in the Great Room at the *Swan Tavern* in *Exchange-Alley*, *London*, is put off till *Wednefday* the 25th Inftant : But the Truftees will, on *Tuefday*, meet in that Place, where any Adventurer, that pleafes, may come and fee them begin to cut off Numbers, Prizes and Blanks, and put all things in a readinefs for the Drawing, which will be certainly there the next day. And by this there will be (as is greatly defired) opportunity given of taking out Tickets, which are given out now very faft, till *Tuefday* night from any Receiver, and at the *Swan-Tavern*, where (as alfo at *Garroways* Coffe-houfe) they will be to be had ; and 'tis prefumed great Numbers will be took out that day.

The Managers to fee this exactly Performed are moft of them the fame that took care of the laft ; *viz.*

Mr. Aderman *Darwin*, Mr. *Sam.Shepheard*, Mr. *Nath*. *Herne*, Mr. *Rich. Chifwel*, Mr. *Edw. Herrys*, Mr. *Edw. Derret*, Mr. *Walter Overbury*, Mr. *Benj. Giles*, Mr. *Arthur Ingram*, Mr. *D. Foe*, and Mr. *Edw. Lawrence*.

The Receivers anfwerable for the Money by them to be received, are Mr. *John Norcot*, Weftminfter ; Mr. *Nathaniel Green*, Leicefter-fields ; Mr. *Edward Wharton* ; Mr. *John Pierfon* near Charing-crofs ; Mr. *Jo. Fells* ; Mr. *Jo. Coggs* in the Strand ; Captain *Jenkins*, Effex-ftreet ; Mr *Jo. Lund* ; Mr. *Robert Fowle*, and Mr. *Tho. Wooten* ; Mr. *James Marmian*, Fleetftreet ; Mr. *Thomas Hickin*, over againft Grays-Jnn-Gate, Holborn ; Mr. *James Hallet* ; Mr. *Edw. Harrifon*, Cheapfide ; Mr. *Edward Pinfold*, Lombard-ftreet ; Mr. *Samuel Edwards*, Cafheer to the National Land Bank, in Exchange-Alley ; Mr. *Tho. Loving* at *Grays-Inn-Gate*, next the Walks, Book-feller ; Mr. *Chaves*, at the Chocolet-Houfe , Palmal ; and Mr. *Do. Ofendo*, at the Chocolet-Houfe by St. James's-Gate. And Mr. *Richard Grabot* Bookfeller in *Briftol*. At the Receivers may be had Propofals at large.

March the 23th, 1695.   THO. NEALE.

that some bear; yet I must own that there are many others who deal considerably, but at the same time propose so low rates that men cannot subsist; nevertheless, if one refuses their offers, another is ready to accept of them.

As for the practices of merchants amongst themselves, they too often act contrary to their own interest, depriving one another of their dealers, and proffering to give a longer space for credit than such used to have, or else they sell their goods at a lower rate. Insomuch that many worthy merchants have ceased to trade, and they that are obliged to continue it for the maintenance of their families solemnly protest that their profit is very inconsiderable, which obliges them to be so hard in all their dealings, and to stoop to those mean things which a few years ago they would never have done.

It would be too tedious to rehearse how many considerable merchants that used the Exchange and were great encouragers of commerce, partly by losses, and partly by the decay of merchandising, are now reduced to the last extremity, and forced to leave their native country or suffer worse at home; although it must be granted that some are induced to take this course by an inclination to defraud rather than necessity. Now I must appeal to all that read this book, how few remain that can be reputed such traders as there used to be some years ago; indeed, it may be objected that great concerns are still transacted both on land and sea, as appears from the entries at the custom-house, which I must allow. But when the Jews and all other merchants and factors of foreign nations are excepted, the abatement will be very considerable.

However, to answer all objections that can be brought, suppose there were as great a correspondence by sea and land as there used to be, and all to be managed by our own merchants (although the contrary is evident), I am nevertheless fully satisfied that where £20 is now gained by fair dealings, not many years ago when trading was in a prosperous state, they cleared thrice as much. I never looked upon those men as rich who drove a great trade, when at the same time I knew their profit was very inconsiderable; but we live in an age where many men make a mighty reckoning of their large returns, which in a short space come to nought. Whence an estimate may be taken of the badness of the times, since merchandising is brought so very low as to occasion such disasters, especially that part of it which used to support the nation.

I heartily desire that those who are our representatives may espouse this cause, and not suffer the main pillars of this our trading city to be undermined for want of timely relief. If it were to be demanded of me by what means these grievances can be redressed, I answer, an act may be made for suppressing that pernicious trade of stock-jobbing the funds of any company whatsoever, or buying and selling any tallies, bills, or tickets, or anything else that ought to pass for specie, for more or less than designed by act of parliament, under penalty of forfeiting the whole, and to be confined in prison for the space of six months. If this were done, or something else of the like nature, I cannot persuade myself but the greatest part of that money which is now converted to so bad a use would be employed in trade, which every impartial man must allow would be a mighty advancement to it.

If it were required of me what ought further to be done, I reply, a select number of judicious men may be appointed by act of parliament to inspect into the grievances of all our merchandising, and redress them as they may think most convenient. For the support of these gentlemen, every merchant ought to allow proportionably to his dealings, so as none to exceed 3s. a quarter, nor any come under 1s., and all such persons to enter their names, with the places of their abode, at some convenient office erected for that purpose near the Royal Exchange. The same thing to be done in every port or city that is noted for trade or frequented by merchants, for I am discoursing of no other. And if any of those who are appointed for these great works should betray the trust reposed in them, that is to say, act contrary to law, in the favouring some and imposing on others, they should be fined £1000 and banished their native country, for the want of such a law is apparently prejudicial to England.

If it were further enacted that whosoever dealing in merchandises refuses to enter his name and place of abode, or delays the paying what is allotted to him into the office after 20 days, or trade contrary to the rules of the commissioners so ordained, should be deprived of the liberty of following any wholesale trade for the future; and the qualifications of wholesale dealers may be expressed in the said act.

If this or any other law of the like nature were made and put in execution, according to its true intent and meaning, I firmly believe that all our merchants would soon find the good effects of it. Then we may see our merchants' affairs flourish in their former splendour and need not doubt but our trade will be raised to the highest degree, both at home and abroad.

Some Few Remarks on our Inland Retail Trade

I am now come to a part that concerns us all, but cannot think of words to express myself. What a deluge of tears could I pour out before my mind can be refreshed and my trembling hand restored to write a perfect description of England's groans! It cannot be done by any pen that is guided by a public spirit, which is altogether incapable of reviving till it finds relief and perceives the cause removed. Therefore it may be well supposed that the misfortunes here specified are not a tenth part of those we lie under. And indeed, I can much better negatively show the advantages we are deprived of than insist too long on the misery we suffer.

First then, we want the practical part, that is to say, a full resolution to join with one consent, to make such laws and golden rules as may remove our fears and increase our hopes. Secondly, we want men of public and noble minds, to be as a vanguard in the beginning so glorious a design. For with their assistance we need not fear, but our royal army of 513 would soon engage in so fine a combat and actually relieve such as repose all their trust in their prudent conduct.

Thirdly, men of healing tempers are much wanting, who are well versed in the main points of religion and fit to make up those breaches that have happened about forms and indifferent ceremonies. Fourthly, we have great occasion for a society of men that would leave the shadows to embrace the substance and be of such a temper of mind one with another as would become all. Fifthly, there is the want of truth and faithfulness in all our dealings between man and man. Sixthly, and lastly, we want a quick trade, and many other transcendent blessings to make us completely happy.

But to return and give a faint idea of our miscarriages relating to the inland trade. Were I to go from house to house, and shop to shop, to visit every individual tradesman, and they were obliged to speak the truth as to this one single question, whether for these several years last past they have gained so much by their employment as to defray the necessary charges of life, I much fear that ten to one would answer in the negative. And if it were not for impairing their credit, I should hear many add that instead of so doing they are in a much worse condition.

To be more plain and come to particulars, I hear a general complaint in city and country amongst all sorts of dealers, as well those that drive a great trade as those that have little. As for the former, they complain that they trade chiefly upon trust, and when they receive their money, their profit is very inconsiderable. And when they meet with those that deal for ready specie, they grind them so low that a very small advance is to be made that way. And the main reason they give why they sell their goods at so low a rate is that if they refuse so to do, others are ready to accept of what is offered.

However, I am certainly assured that there is such a pernicious principle riveted in the minds of most men, that they cannot be persuaded to unite together with this one resolve, to live by what they sell, but are ready to undervalue one another's trade. Insomuch that among men who have great dealings in the world, very few get estates, but are glad to keep buckle and thong together. Nay, I am afraid that many of them, if their accounts were laid open to a public view, would be found worse than nothing; for how many instances have we had of considerable dealers who in all outward appearance were never given to any extravagancy, but to our certain knowledge have carried on a great trade for many years last past (as appears by their books) and not sustained many losses, nevertheless, at their deaths, have left their families in a mean condition? Again, others that have made large adventures in the way of trade, and whom we have had good reason to believe to be honest men, upon account of their delivering all they had into the hands of their creditors, have been forced to spend the remainder of their days in extreme penury.

Had I time, I could produce many sad examples of the like nature, besides great numbers that have failed by losses, and others by idle expenses and a design to cheat, and yet these men had all good trades. Thus we plainly see that most trades are reduced to little or no profit, and if so grievous a malady be not speedily remedied, I know not what will become of us in a short time. To conclude this article, if it be so that most men who drive a great trade can scarce maintain an even balance, what must become of those that have little or none? My heart as it were bleeds within me when I hear and see such men, especially those that strive with unwearied diligence to get an honest livelihood and are blasted by the decay of trade.

On Handicraft Trades

Many poor wanting tradesmen have laid out most of their stocks in materials to set themselves to work, and when they have gone to dispose of it in hopes of gain, to my certain knowledge they could not dispose of it for what the materials cost them before they began their work.

Men are grown so cruel one to another as to require the labour of the poor for nothing, as many handicraftsmen can testify by their own sad experience; especially weavers and shoe makers, who formerly used to gain 20 and 30s. a week by their honest day-labours. Nay, most handicraft trades are reduced to the same extremity. And as for the poor day-labouring men, their condition is much the same with the former, for many who in my remembrance were wont to maintain their families very decently can now scarce find them bread or wherewithal to cover their nakedness. I could mention many that used to get 15 or 18s. a week but are now glad of 7s. in the summer and 3 or 4s. in the winter, and too often fail at that.

. . . .

The ill consequence of wearing and using swords, and that it would be much more for the honour of our nobility and gentry, to change them for nobler tokens of honour.

I am now about to draw a scene of crimson-dye and to represent a tragedy, every act of which will usher in the streams of blood, and to open an amphitheatre not artificial but natural, wherein you may behold all ranks and degrees of men miserably massacred by sudden passion, with the instrument of pride, too keen to be trusted to the furious transports of those who stand more on the point of honour (to use the common phrase) than the life of a man, which is infinitely more precious than all the little punctilios arising from a vain-glorious conceit.

Were I to entertain you with a full view of all the duels and horrid murders that have been committed in our age, and to recount all those tragical adventures, or to inform you on what slight occasions they happened, the object would be too hideous and the theme too doleful for any mortal eye to see or ear to hear. Nay, it might cause floods of tears to flow from the eyes of those numerous widows and orphans that have been unfortunately made so by such dismal rencounters.

Therefore I shall forbear treating of any particular murders, or the circumstances of them, contenting myself only to give a short account in general of the great folly of engaging in duels, and to make some reasonable proposals by what means such rash attempts may be effectually prevented for the future, and how a much more advantageous provision may be made for the honour and distinction of our nobility and gentry.

There are very few families of any note within the kingdom of England but have had the misfortune to lose a relation or bosom-friend upon these occasions, who otherwise might have lived many years longer if the wearing of swords or other weapons of the like nature had been prohibited by act of parliament, under the severest penalty, except by such persons as are on present duty in their prince's service.

Indeed, I am seized with horror and extreme regret, whenever I consider with myself what great numbers of our nobility and gentry have lost their noble blood and suddenly expired at the point of a sword, who (if the fatal catastrophe had been timely prevented) might have performed many signal achievements for the benefit of church and state.

I can scarce persuade myself that were it possible for all that noble race who have died in the bed of honour (as some are pleased to term it) to be summoned out of their mournful tombs to be the representatives of your honourable persons in this house but their first order would be to bring in a bill against the wearing of swords, or any other instruments of sudden death. And will not you most mighty lords, nor you the most august assembly of worthy commoners espouse the cause of those your familiar friends, if not dear relations? Let their precious blood cry aloud to you to make the law, and if this will not fix your resolutions to that purpose, consider that none of you can be secured from falling as victims to a furious humour at one time or another; then surely you'll be induced to the speedy finishing so necessary an act.

But if you still continue inflexible, let those vast multitudes of the meaner sort of people that have been most cruelly and barbarously murdered prevail with you; let their sorrowful wives and innocent children, exposed to the greatest hardship and penury, raise your compassion and melt your hearts into a suitable disposition; or let the prospect of such fatal disasters that will unavoidably happen in future ages (if not timely remedied) influence your most serious and deliberate consultations.

However, if your aversion is so great that neither the number of those that have perished, nor the loss of your friends, with utter extinction of many ancient names and plentiful estates of well-descended families (of which you have so late an instance), nor the security of your own lives and fortunes, with those of your relations and friends, nor the deplorable case of many hundreds of innocent persons that have undeservedly lain weltering in their own blood, nor the mournful complaints of their poor relations that are ready to be starved for want of necessary provisions: I say, if none of these motives and affecting truths can be sufficient to gain the majority of your votes, I hope a sense of true honour and due care for the distinction of persons will at last effectually prevail.

When I consider that the people of this nation are so fortunate as to prescribe their own laws, provided they be such as do not interfere with the king's royal prerogative, and that all statutes of the realm are first proposed and agreed to by the two honourable houses of parliament; as also, that these most august assemblies are composed of persons of the highest rank and quality in the whole world, such as not only are transcendently eminent for their piety, wisdom, learning, experience, and many other excellent qualifications, but are also of noble extraction, moving in their several orbs so far above the meaner sort of people: I say, upon a due reflection on this matter, I have often admired that there is no law as yet made for the distinction of such illustrious personages from those that are inferior in station and dignity.

I can by no means be induced to believe that any sensible man will affirm that a sword makes the difference between a duke and an earl, a lord and a knight, a gentleman and a ruffian, between a person that is master of ten thousand pounds and one that is not worth so many pence, or between a real gentleman, who receives three or four hundred pounds per annum out of his own hereditary estate, a ruffling *beau* that lives by diving into every purse where he is in hopes to find a prey.

Certainly to think so would be an egregious piece of folly; for any man may much sooner distinguish a person of worth and honourable extraction by the marks of a genteel deportment and affable carriage than by the fineness of his rapier. But we live in a degenerate age, where a company of prodigal fops, that have riotously spent their substance and have scarce any thing left for their maintenance, must needs purchase a sword to credit their persons, and then are they in a fit equipage to strut it along and avouch the nobleness of their birth by an oath or direful imprecation, whereas they are well known by some to have derived their pedigree from the dregs of the people.

However, these hectoring bullies are so insolent as to affront persons of highest rank, and if the least opposition be made, they immediately require satisfaction for presuming to intrench upon their counterfeit honours. Thus many worthy persons are often set upon and barbarously assassinated by such desperate bravoes, of which numerous and fresh instances might be almost daily produced. Nay, they are of late come to that height of audaciousness that they make no scruples at all to challenge their superiors to fight duels, even those who are so far above them that the meanest of their domestic servants would scorn to undervalue themselves in contending with such sordid wretches. To conclude, these are the sparks that make us fearful to walk the streets in the evening, for the sun has no sooner withdrawn its light, but they begin to appear with their painted jilts, and breath nothing but revenge, even to the utter destruction of those that are so unfortunate as to put the least affront upon them, or so much as offer to take the wall . . .

The Regulation of Stage-Plays

This article is of great importance, and I cannot enter upon it without extreme horror and detestation, when I reflect upon the two theatres, or grand universities of all manner of vice, immorality, and profaneness, nay, blasphemy itself in the highest degree: nurseries that breed up so many children for the devil's service and their own ruin, with the utter overthrow of many families. Good God! what dreadful scenes could I present to the public view, theatres filled with tragedies, comedies, and farces acted by Satan's servants, dressed up in human shape and equipped with gaudy attire and a brazen face.

If Mr. Collier had not already treated of these abuses in an elegant style, I might have published a tract on the same subject, but in regard that my intentions are superseded, I shall desist; neither will I repeat one single line of what has been offered by that ingenious author, who cites many of their own acts and writings; but I shall only give a short character of them in general.

I must confess myself to be of that inquisitive temper as to search in the first place into the secrets of all religions, and I was ever curious to observe the different ways of worship and to hear the reasons that persons of all persuasions could give, relating to the articles of their faith.

Neither was I willing to confine my speculations within those bounds, but I was also desirous modestly to inspect public affairs, to see how the pilots steered the helm, and what latitude we were in. I had likewise a great mind to observe the clouds, whether they thickened and presaged a storm, or were ready to be dispelled in order to a favourable gale, that might waft us o'er to a safe harbour of peace and plenty, there to refresh ourselves in the pleasant streams of a silent calm.

I frequently made a diligent search into the mysteries of all merchandising, trades, arts and sciences, and was never better satisfied than to see my native country flourish in the midst of a prosperous trade.

I was also willing to gratify my curiosity in the reading and seeing several plays, that I might the better judge whether they answered the ends for which they were designed. But when I perceived how far they were degenerated, I could scarce persuade myself that I lived in a Christian nation, but rather sojourned in the lower regions, where no other plays were to be acted by the infernal fiends, but execrable blasphemies against the great God, and an absolute detestation of virtue.

For in these pompous theatres all manner of vices are strenuously maintained and set out to the best advantage. There the atheist may be confirmed in his loose principles, and the prodigal encouraged in luxury, till he consume his substance on a crowd of strumpets, and at last, perhaps miserably perishes in a duel or sudden scuffle. There you may see a buffoon dressed in the habit of a grave divine, on purpose to be made the game of the play and exposed to the public contempt. There you are told that all religion is nothing else but state policy, or a piece of vile hypocrisy. There you may hear the honourable state of matrimony derided as the meanest condition, more proper for fools than wise men, as if the marriage-bed were a far greater scandal than the lewd embraces of a harlot. There you may see a ruffian representing venerable age, and the rest of the mimics deriding him, as if the hoary head were one of the most despicable objects in the world. To conclude, you may see and hear a great deal more to the same effect, than I have declared, or am able to express.

Upon the whole, I firmly believe that were it in my power to summon all the blasphemous wretches that now live on the face of the earth, and hear them all discharging the venom of their virulent tongues, they would not utter such vile expressions as may be read and heard in many plays. Indeed, it would be too tedious to sum them up, and very improper to repeat, for fear of offending the ears of a pious auditory and corrupting the morals of unsettled persons. Moreover, were all the undiscovered atheists that lurk in the city to pull off their vizards and ascend the stage, there freely to deliver their minds, you would not hear so many pernicious notions started as are to be found in several plays.

Some time ago, I heard one of the actors speak to this effect on the public stage, ' If I knew,' said he, ' there was any wickedness that I have not done, I would go and commit it at this very instant. Don't tell me of a God and a religion, there's no such thing, it is only a state-policy, to keep fools in awe, for all things come by nature, &c.,' with many more of the like expressions.

In short, there is scarce one play that has been acted for these several years last passed but has contained some or most of the following articles, viz. 1. Blasphemous expressions, 2. Atheistical discourse, 3. Profane drollery, 4. Despising seriousness, 5. Debasing virtue, 6. Applauding vice, 7. Reflecting on the clergy, 8. Exclaiming against marriage, 9. Making a mock of infirmities, 10. Scoffing at old age, 11. Representing the pleasures of debauchery, and many other particulars that are too numerous to be recited in this little tract.

As for the intolerable mischiefs that have been occasioned by this means, it is too difficult a task for me to undertake to enumerate them; nevertheless I am very sensible that these play-houses have in a great measure corrupted this city; they have struck a damp on the minds of many which otherwise would have been better disposed; they have corrupted youth and reduced many to extreme want and penury. Lastly, they are the source of all manner of misfortunes, for there many a poor deluded wretch picks up a painted sepulchre, all over glorious without, but rotten within, more fit for an hospital than a public theatre, who soon infuses her infectious venom into the marrow of his bones; which takes up more days to cure than minutes spent in his unchaste embraces. There many gentlemen descended from noble ancestors have lost their lives in the flower of youth, and expired in a bloody scene, who otherwise might have been the ornament of their country and lived happily for many years.

To conclude, I hope none will be offended nor misconstrue what I have been treating of as to this particular. It is not the utter ruin, but a thorough reformation of the stage that I aim at, being sensible that the first institution of plays was designed for the encouragement of virtue and the discountenancing of vice. And indeed, were they made more suitable to those purposes, much greater advantage would redound to the parties concerned, for where one now frequents the houses, five would resort thither upon such a reformation.

In former times stage-plays were esteemed as an innocent diversion, and the actors gained more in six months than now in twelve; neither were they at so great an expense by one-third part as they now are. Indeed, I so far approve of such reformed play-houses as these, that I would willingly have them erected in every city. For what can be more fine than to observe the nobility, gentry, and citizens, with several others that may be worse employed, resorting in the close of the evening to see a play, where they may hear several profitable discourses concerning the wonderful works of nature, intermixed with other harmless diversions? It would be a refreshment to all sorts of men, especially such as have wearied themselves with the fatigues of the concluded day, either of body or mind. There the physician might find a description of all sorts of plants, with several curious remarks about their different nature, growth, virtues, uses, &c. The young student might be made sensible of the advantages of a liberal education and improvement in learning, by which means he may be advanced to the highest station in the church.

There the politician might receive instructions concerning the management of state affairs expressed in the most eloquent terms, with the manner of his rise from one degree of honour to another, till at last he arrives at the highest pinnacle that his prince can promote him to, that is to say, to sit on the king's right hand, to foretell an approaching storm, so that by his prudent counsel he may prevent the danger, or at least abate its fury. Otherwise, if he prove treacherous to his country, he may there behold himself portrayed in a lively scene, representing the frowns of his sovereign, the contempt offered by his equals, and the hatred of his inferiors, with an emblem of his banishment from court, imprisonment in the Tower, arraignment, trial, condemnation, and circumstances of his execution.

There the generals of numerous armies might be convinced that more advantages are often gained over a powerful enemy by well-contrived stratagems and sudden surprise than by mere force of arms. There the common soldier might be put in mind how many have raised themselves from the meanest post, by their undaunted courage, to the command of troops, regiments, and armies, and at the same time might observe the difference between flying before a cruel enemy, and the victorious pursuit of vanquished and broken forces.

There the mariner might have a view of the most useful art of navigation and maritime affairs, and be encouraged to satisfy his curiosity, in seeing most countries and learning many languages, if he were not so fortunate as to get a large share of the gold of Africa and the treasures of India. He might also be induced to steer his course to the Holy Land and view the destruction of unbelievers, with the utter overthrow of a divided people, who were furiously engaged in mutual slaughters within the city walls, whilst their enemies were contriving their ruin without, and took the advantage of their intestine broils.

In a word, the tradesman might be presented with several acts, discovering the difference between being just, upright, and fair in all manner of dealings, and the using of fraudulent, vile, and base means. He might also have a clear view of all the tricking and sinister devices that are too often used in commerce between buyer and seller. To conclude, there the artificer or handicraftsman might behold several fine scenes of arts and sciences, where ingenuity will have the general applause, whilst stupid ignorance is hissed off the stage.

Were it not for brevity's sake, I would have produced many more instances of the like nature, which are very agreeable to the sentiments of all wise men, so that most would be of my opinion, that these stage-plays, instead of corrupting the age, would serve to refine it. And indeed, I am apt to believe that the profanest atheist, the most lewd debauchee, and the vilest wretch that breathes on earth would soon get in amidst numerous crowds to see and hear such a play.

PROPOSALS FOR THE REFORMATION OF SCHOOLS AND UNIVERSITIES

In order to the better education of youth; humbly offered to the serious consideration of the high court of parliament.

[By Andrew Fletcher?]

1704

ANDREW FLETCHER (1655–1716) was the son of a country gentleman of Saltoun, East Lothian. His father was a friend of Bishop Burnet, who supervised the boy's education and turned him out not only one of the most accomplished young Scots of the age but likewise one of the most uncompromising of presbyterian radicals. In the 1670's he opposed the government's army program in Scotland; he was in the Rye House plot with Russell and Sydney; he sailed with Monmouth in 1685. During the next years this little man, pock-marked and lean of face, wandered in disguise on the continent, buying rare books in Spain, fighting the Turks in Hungary. In 1689 he joined William of Orange, but the moment he returned to Scotland he led an opposition party, almost a Scots home-rule party. As a member of the Scottish parliament in 1703 he bitterly opposed all suggestion of union with England, proposed a Scots executive to be chosen by the Scottish parliament, urged the formation of a Scots militia, and wanted to deprive the queen of the power of war and peace. It was he who struck off the well-known epigram that ' if a man were permitted to make all the ballads he need not care who should make the laws of a nation.'

This pamphlet on education has been tentatively ascribed to Fletcher. The class note which it sounded, resembling his earlier suggestion that beggars ought to be taken into the service of gentlemen on an hereditary and compulsory basis, to be bought and sold, appealed to many men south of the Tweed. Scottish education had more or less closely followed Knox's plan of 1560, which advocated a school in every parish, bursaries for poor boys of promise, the teaching of trades, competent masters. The rich were to pay for their sons' education at college, the poor were to be supported by the church, and both were to continue ' until the commonwealth have profit of them.' What wrecked Scottish education in the seventeenth century was the constant shifting of control between presbyterianism and episcopacy. Every change meant a new commission which tried to adapt the universities to its wishes. Their curricula were still medieval, and ' regents ' undertook to instruct a class in all subjects; there was no specialized professoriate. Finances were low; buildings often dilapidated. Fletcher's schemes were not original with him. From the 1690's on, new chairs were established in mathematics, law, medicine, history, oriental languages, some of them the revival of earlier discontinued chairs. Thus were laid the foundations of the eighteenth century Scottish Renaissance.

THERE has been a great decay of learning in this kingdom for many years. For instance, where we have now one who can write one single sheet, an hundred years ago we had twenty who could have written volumes in good sense and good Latin. And though the causes of the low ebb learning has sunk to among us are very obvious, yet I must confess it is no easy matter to put a stop to the growing evil. It is hard to make a scheme of education which will generally please, and harder still to put it into execution; it is difficult to alter an old constitution, though full of errors, and more difficult in our circumstances to establish a new one, though ever so just and reasonable. We have been too long pursuing the wrong road to be set easily right. We neither take just measures nor allow sufficient time for the education of our youth. However, since the encouragement and improvement of learning is certainly so much for the true interest of the nation, I shall adventure to tell my opinion frankly, and shall be heartily glad if it can be found of any use or service. At least I hope I shall excite others of greater ability to make farther inquiries into these matters, such as may convince the parliament of the necessity of reforming our schools and universities for the good and benefit of learning.

One main cause of the low estate of learning is that it is too easily and cheaply purchased; one can make his son what with us passes for a scholar at a much cheaper rate than he can breed him a shoemaker or a weaver. For a short time at the schools, and three or four years at the universities, upon little or no expense, in our way is enough to make a Master of Arts, who immediately gets into the most considerable employments which require the longest study and best qualifications, before he have years, sense, prudence, or learning. Upon which account the mechanics and poorer sort of people are encouraged to send their sons to schools and universities, finding a very little money, and as little time, sufficient to make what we call a scholar. But in my opinion were these put to the plough and other trades, it would be better for themselves (who would be kept within their proper spheres) and more for the interest of the nation, which is overstocked with scholars and in extreme want of people for mechanical employments. This is one great cause for the low condition of learning. People who are daily pinched for the back and the belly cannot bestow much time for the improvement of their minds; their spirits are depressed under their poverty; they have not money to afford them books or to bring them into the conversation of the world. And how, without these, a man can become a good scholar passes my comprehension.

But it may be said, by debarring the poorer sort from learning, some good spirits may be excluded; which as it is the only objection, so it is as easily removed.

We have as much use for good spirits to be employed in mechanical trades and merchandising as for learning, and by admitting one, upon the pretence of a good spirit, we certainly must take in an hundred of low and dull capacities. And let their genius be as good as you please, unless you give them money too they will never be able to make any tolerable advance in learning, and by the following scheme for rectifying our bursaries, a competency is provided for them, as far as the funds will go.

Another great cause of the decay of learning is the bad methods which are followed in our schools and universities, and the insufficiency of the masters, who are provided for the government of them. There are in the kingdom near one thousand parishes, and in most of them Latin is pretended to be taught, though not one of fifty of the schoolmasters is capable of teaching it; and no wonder, for not one of fifty was tolerably taught it, and not one of an hundred, however capable, has books to enable him to acquire it by his after industry. At the universities we bestow a few months upon the study of the Greek, whereas that noble language, and the learned and useful books which are written in it, may perhaps deserve our care and pains for as many years. We allow too much time upon old antiquated metaphysical jargon. And as for natural philosophy which in this and the last age has been so happily brought from an idle prattling about words of no signification to a solid science, it requires such a deep insight into the most profound parts of mathematics that I am afraid few of those who profess it are capable of teaching it. We get too hastily through our divinity. History, law, and medicine we have none.

The cheapness of our learning brings it into the hands of the poorer and meaner people. Their poverty, the wrong methods which are taken in teaching, and the insufficiency of teachers unavoidably subject them to the greatest ignorance. And both together, the ignorance and the poverty of our scholars, infallibly bring learning itself under disgrace and contempt. Poverty deprives them, as of a great many other advantages, so particularly of that due assurance, that address and that freedom of spirit, which are so natural to quality and gentry. Nay sometimes under difficult circumstances, to prevent starving, it forces them upon courses unworthy of their professions, to the no small scandal of others who should be led by their examples. And in one word, the natural tendency of our present methods is to unfit a scholar for a gentleman, and to render a gentleman ashamed of being a scholar. And, till we reconcile the gentleman with the scholar, it is impossible learning should ever flourish. But was this once done, was learning taken out of the hands of the vulgar and brought to be as honourable and fashionable among the gentry as it is now contemptible, I think it would be indeed a fair way of prospering. For were the younger sons of the nobility and gentry (who now are idle at home, or sent abroad to be knocked on the head) kept the due time at schools and universities, they being encouraged with all things proper for studying, and having their time in their own hands for reading, and not being forced out of pure necessity to enter too soon on business, would in all probability make considerable advances in learning and when possessed of employments, gentlemen would be as tender of their character as they are of their honour; besides that, being generally able to live without them, they would not lie under such temptations as poorer people do. This, as it would considerably add to the honour of learning and interest of the nation in general, so it would be no dishonourable way to dispose of the younger sons of the nobility and gentry. For besides what encouragement they might expect from the study of the laws and of medicine, there are in the kingdom at least a hundred places in the church and universities which yield two thousand marks yearly, and few of the other church benefices are under one thousand. Now in my humble opinion, the younger sons of even the best families, especially when not sufficiently provided for, might be as wisely and honourably disposed of this way as being kept idly at home or sent off to be soldiers abroad. It is plain, to dispose of them so would put them in a way of being more serviceable to God, their country, and their kindred than commonly they are. And were matters ordered after this manner, it is probable the church government would not be so ambulatory as it has hitherto been in this kingdom, since the nobility and gentry, of whom the parliaments are made up, would not readily make acts which should oblige them to take back their brothers and sons to their houses. And nothing could contribute more to the quiet and peace of the nation than that the government of the church was at last effectually secured against so frequent changes.

Now, that so good a design may take effect, it is necessary to raise the price of learning, so as to discourage the poorer sort from attempting it, that those only whose circumstances enable them to make successful advances in learning may have access to it. To make learning dearer, the number of the schools, at least, must be diminished, and the masters' salaries and fees augmented. And the time and methods of teaching in schools and universities should be regulated according to the following, or some such scheme.

I think there should be only one grammar school in a county or shire, two at most in the largest, and where two lesser lie together, one may serve for both. These schools ought to be well-endowed, and some of the best men of the nation for prudence and learning provided to be masters and ushers. A master and four doctors or ushers, at least, will be necessary for every school. And besides those public schools, at all the country churches, I would have the precentor of the parish (who needs not to be a master of arts) to teach the children to read and write English, and the common rules of arithmetic, which is all the learning that is needful or useful to the mechanics and poorer people. But it may be inquired, where shall funds be had for the maintaining of those schools? I answer, that is not my business; let the wisdom of the nation consider it. But perhaps it would be no difficult task to find our funds, if some people would apply themselves that way. There are for example in the shire of Fife about eighty parishes, and every parish has a salary, one with another, of above one hundred pounds Scots a year for a schoolmaster. Now take the one half of this salary and give to the teacher of the English language; this with the advantage of his scholars, and his emoluments as precentor and session-clerk may make him live pretty well, for he has no great character to maintain. Apply the other half to the public grammar schools; this will maintain two, being six thousand marks a year; to wit, the master of each school should have one thousand marks, and four doctors, each of them, five hundred marks a year, which, with the benefit of their scholars (for, because I would have learning dear, I would have the scholars pay much more liberally than they commonly do) would be a very comfortable and handsome provision for both masters and ushers.

My designed brevity will not allow me to be very particular in naming all the books that should be taught in schools. I shall only say in general, they ought to teach some plain and short grammar in English prose; thus they will bestow less time on grammar and have more to employ in reading authors, some of which they should read, not by shreds, as is commonly done, but from beginning to ending, such as Justin's *History*, Florus's *Epitome*, Cornelius Nepos's *Lives*, Salust, Curtius, Terence, Ovid's *Metamorphoses*, as being the completest system of the heathenish mythology, &c. Some odes, satires, and epistles of Horace may be taught, and some particular places of Virgil and other poets, at the master's discretion. And perhaps it may be very convenient, if not necessary, that boys at school be taught the rudiments of geography and chronology, so far as they are capable, that they may read their authors to the best advantage. The last year they are at school (for I would have them at least fourteen years of age before they leave it) they ought to learn the Greek grammar and some easy Greek authors, such as Æsop's fables, Lucian's select dialogues, Herodian, &c. and so we bring them to the university.

At the university, the youth must be obliged to stay six years, passing regularly through all the classes, before they can be made Masters of Arts. For examinations and trials, how rigorously soever designed, may be abused and shammed. But a long time, and due exercises performed, is the best and most profitable way to make good scholars. In Oxford and Cambridge, which are famous universities for learning all the world over, none can be made Master of Arts until he stay seven years, none Doctor of Medicine or Law till he stay fourteen; none Doctor of Divinity till he has been eighteen years about the university. Yet, after all, according to this calculation, our young men may commence Masters of Arts in the twentieth or twenty-first year of their age, which I suppose everybody will think soon enough.

In my opinion, two universities are enough for this nation, for there are no more in England. But since we are to ingraft on an old stock, we can only conveniently reform, not abolish any of our universities. As I said, the students ought to stay six years in the university, and three of these years should be employed in reading Greek and Latin jointly. Such of the Latin and Greek historians and orators as they have not read in school with the art of rhetoric will be employment enough for two years.

The poets, with the art of poetry, may furnish more than enough for the third.

Though one cannot find any great difficulty in choosing the fittest authors that are to be taught, yet for preventing all possible mistakes and preserving uniformity in all the colleges within the kingdom, it is highly convenient that some persons of good reputations for learning, and who understand the constitutions and customs of foreign universities, should be appointed to meet and particularly determine what books, and in what order they are to be read.

Perhaps it might be proper to read together Greek and Latin authors who write on the same or the like subject: for example, Dionysius Hallicarnensius and the three first books of Livy, the third book of Polybius and the twenty-first of Livy, Appianus Alexandrinus and Caesar *De Bello Civili*, the orations of Demosthenes and Cicero, the pastorals of Theocritus and Virgil, Hesiod and Virgil's *Georgics*, Homer's *Iliad* and Virgil's *Aeneas*, Pindar and Horace, &c.

A great many of the best modern books of all sorts and on all subjects being written in the style of the modern schools, it would seem necessary that short compends of logics, ethics, and metaphysics should be printed and taught in the fourth year. The professor may likewise recommend as a private task Aristotle's *Ethics* and *Politics*, some select dialogues from Plato, Xenophon's *Apoumemoneumenata*, some of Plutarch's moral treatises, Hierocles *In Aurea Carmina*, Tully's philosophic works, some books of Seneca, &c., and one day of the week may be appointed for inquiring into the diligence of students and resolving their doubts.

And seeing all the ancient orators and poets and even historians, nay, and fathers of the church too, have been addicted to the hypothesis and principles of some one or other of the philosophical sect, and often reason from their notions and use their terms and phrases, it would seem proper (besides the recommending of Diogenes Laertius, Eunapius, &c., to be diligently read and considered by the students) that some learned person or persons should compile a clear and distinct but compendious history of all the ancient philosophies, distinguishing their hypotheses judiciously, digesting their principles methodically, explaining their terms of art and phrases, and putting their notions in as clear a light as possible. This would mightily facilitate the understanding of the ancient learning.

During these four years the students should be also taught arithmetic, geography and chronology to greater perfection, the first six, with the eleventh and twelfth books of Euclid, the elements of algebra, the plane and spherical trigonometry.

The last two years are to be spent in learning mixed mathematics, or natural philosophy, viz. the laws of motion, mechanics, hydrostatics, optics, astronomy, &c. and experimental philosophy.

All along, from their first going to school till they leave the university, they ought carefully to be taught and instructed in the principles of religion, nothing being more certain that where there is not a well-directed conscience, men are rather the worse than the better for being learned in any science.

In every university there must be at least three professors of Greek and Latin, one of logic, ethics, and metaphysics, two of mathematics and natural philosophy, one of divinity, one of civil history, another of ecclesiastical, and one of Hebrew and other oriental languages. Where scholars are numerous, the number of professors ought to be augmented in proportion, for I would have many masters and few scholars. One master who pretends to teach eight or nine score of scholars (as we commonly see done) may as well undertake to teach eight or nine thousand. One master should not have above thirty scholars. And according to our scheme of making learning dear, let each of them pay 5 Lib. Sterling yearly to his master, at which rate thirty will afford 150 Lib. Sterling, which, with a small salary, may maintain the professor handsomely enough.

Besides this private teaching, I would have every professor to have once a week one public lecture in the common school, that who pleases may come and hear him. Thus we may have one or more such lectures every day, and on different subjects, according to the number and professions of the lecturers. Nothing can contribute more than this to the honour and advancement of learning.

There is nothing more deserves the consideration of parliament than that our youth are obliged to travel abroad to study physic and law, and carry so much money out of the kingdom; ten or twelve thousand pounds sterling, by modest calculation, is every year spent abroad this way. Now would the parliament but for once give two months' cess, which is but about what is spent in foreign universities in one year, the interest of it might establish professions of law and physic at home, where our youth might learn more in one year than they can do abroad in three. For they are generally sent abroad about the twentieth year of their age, which is the nicest part of it. Then their passions are strong and they have little sense to govern them, and they are just let loose from their parents and tutors, so that they acquire neither virtue nor learning, but habits of all sorts of debauchery, as we are taught by every day's experience. I would have the professions of law and physic established in the University of Edinburgh, where the students of law may have the advantage of excellent libraries for the civil law, and opportunity to hear the pleadings, and learn the form of the house, which our young men who study abroad, for all the money they have spent, are altogether ignorant of. And the physicians can have no subjects or rooms for anatomy, nor laboratories for chemistry, nor gardens for botany, but at Edinburgh.

I would have none entered into the house of advocates but such as have certificates from the professors of law that they have studied for four years with them, after they have passed the university, and none made Doctors of Medicine but such as have certificates from the professors of physic that they have studied four years with them, and none allowed to practise but such as are graduated in our own universities. And their paying liberally to their respective masters every year (and thereby saving so much from being squandered away abroad) with some salary, might prove a very good allowance to the professors. This might also hold concerning the students of divinity, that they should not be admitted into the church without testimonials from the professors of divinity that they had been a competent time (perhaps four years may be too little) at their lectures.

I do not design by this to discourage the public or private donations of charity for educating the children of honest parents, who shall be found to have good spirits. I would only have them regulated: for example, our bursaries, as we call them, are commonly but one hundred marks, or one hundred pounds which cannot maintain any person. I would therefore advise to cast four or five of them together, which, besides that it would abridge the number of pretenders to learning, might furnish sufficient funds for handsomely maintaining some few and providing them with necessaries for prosecuting their studies; neither ought this to be thought contrary to the intentions of those who made the donations since, perhaps, at the time when they were first bestowed an hundred marks might have gone farther than now four hundred do. The genuine design therefore being still pursued, it is to be presumed that it was the will of the donators that such alterations should be made when they should be found necessary.

One thing I forgot relating to the funds. Perhaps, were the funds belonging to some universities carefully and narrowly inquired into, some might be found not so usefully applied as they might be, and others yet unbestowed, which might help to erect new professions where they are wanting.

A REPRESENTATION OF THE PRESENT STATE OF RELIGION

With regard to the late excessive growth of infidelity, heresy, and profaneness: drawn up by the upper house of convocation, of the province of Canterbury, and transmitted to the lower house for their approbation.

Printed in 1711.

WHEN Francis Atterbury in 1696 tried to revive the old claim of convocation to a parity with parliament, he began a controversy that dragged on for twenty years. Atterbury represented the lower house of convocation, composed of clergymen unwaveringly high church and Tory in sympathy, while the upper house was dominated by latitudinarian and Whig bishops. In 1710–1711 the lower house had the support not only of the queen, but of a strong Tory parliament and ministry. Chosen prolocutor to preside in the lower house, Atterbury drew up a ' representation of the present state of religion,' in accord with what the queen and the Tories believed should be the chief business of the session, the devising of means to combat the ' atheism, heresy, superstition, and schism ' of the age. Violently worded, unsparing in the ' black art of spreading scandal,' it traced the ' deluge of impiety and licentiousness ' to the late monstrous rebellion, attacked such deists as Toland and Leslie and such mathematico-theologians as John Craig and William Whiston, and concluded with the recommendation that the press be again licensed and the clergy given more authority in restoring discipline. The lower house carried Atterbury's representation (printed in *The Miscellaneous Works of Bishop Atterbury*, IV,307–330); the upper house substituted the milder and shorter version printed here, which the lower would not approve. The paragraph condemning Whiston's *Primitive Christianity Revived*, which described Arianism as the true Christian creed, was the same in both representations. Other identities in wording suggest that the upper house simply edited Atterbury's copy. Both were printed, but neither by authority.

The man who undertook the defence of England against the ' black and odious ' aspersions laid upon her by her church was Matthew Tindal, who became the most significant figure of the deist movement. In *The Nation Vindicated* (printed in two parts, 1711, 1712) he concluded that England was better off than before, and because of toleration.

Atterbury was made bishop of Rochester in 1713, was banished in 1723 for complicity in a Jacobite plot, and ended his days in the service of the Old Pretender.

MAY it please your majesty;

We, the archbishop, the bishops, and the clergy of the province of Canterbury, in convocation assembled, are deeply sensible of the many blessings and advantages of your gracious and prosperous reign. Among which, there is none that more affects us than the tender care and concern shown by your majesty for the flourishing state of religion, and the godly zeal you have expressed against the wickedness of those who, by loose and profane principles and practices, have endeavoured to undermine and destroy it.

We are thankful to almighty God, who hath put it into your royal heart to repress these impious and daring attempts; and for that end, among others, to order your clergy to be called together, that they might, in synod, humbly offer their counsel and assistance.

It is, on many accounts, our duty to do the utmost that in us lies towards promoting so excellent a work. We have, therefore, applied ourselves with diligence to consider the matters to us referred; and do now, in obedience to your royal commands, humbly lay before your majesty,

A representation of the present state of religion among us, with regard to the late excessive growth of infidelity, heresy, and profaneness.

It is with the greatest affliction and concern that we enter upon a work so unpleasant in all respects, were it not for the hopes it gives us of seeing these evils in some measure removed; and, therefore, we shall not give your majesty the uneasiness of a particular relation, either of the blasphemous passages that have been published from the press, or the great impieties that have been committed. But, in discharge of the trust reposed in us by your majesty, we think ourselves obliged to lay before you such an account of the progress of infidelity, heresy, and profaneness amongst us as may let your majesty see the causes and occasions which have given the greatest rise to them, and the sad consequences with which they are attended.

It is hard to come to the beginning of these great evils, which all times have complained of; and therefore, to confine our own inquiries and lessen your majesty's trouble as much as we can, we shall look no farther back for the source of them than that long unnatural rebellion, which loosened all the bonds of discipline and order and overturned the goodly frame of our ecclesiastical and civil constitution.

The hypocrisy, enthusiasm, and variety of wild and monstrous errors which abounded during those confusions begat in the minds of many men, too easily carried into extremes, a disregard for the very forms of religion, and proved the occasion of great libertinism and profaneness, which hath ever since too much prevailed amongst us. The seeds of infidelity and heresy which were then sown did soon after appear, and the tares have sprung up in great abundance.

The authority of the present canon of Scripture hath been represented as standing upon a very precarious foundation; and the inspiration of the whole hath been called in question.

The miracles recorded in Scripture have been disputed and compared to the fabulous relations of those that occur in heathen writers.

All mysteries in religion have been exploded as absurd and useless speculations, and several fundamental articles of our most holy faith have not only been called in question, but rejected.

The Arian and Socinian heresies have been propagated with great boldness; the doctrine of a trinity of persons in the unity of the Godhead hath been denied and scoffed at; the satisfaction made for the sins of mankind by the precious blood of Christ hath been either directly renounced, or very ungratefully lessened; the established creeds of the church have been represented as unwarrantable impositions.

Even at this time when we are thus met by your majesty's writ, and exhorted by your gracious letter to consult of methods for repressing pernicious errors and impieties, a book hath been printed wherein the Arian doctrine (of which we cannot but declare our utter abhorrence) is avowed and maintained; and the truth of it is threatened to be shown by large and elaborate proofs in other treatises from the same hand, which are soon to follow. To this book, the author hath prefixed his name, and hath not been afraid to dedicate it to the archbishop, bishops, and clergy of this province in convocation assembled, with invitation to all to encourage his design by their subscriptions to it, and not without laying the imputation of antichristianism upon all those who shall not approve it.

The natural immorality of the soul hath, upon different schemes and views, been opposed as a vulgar error; and the necessity of all human thoughts and actions hath been asserted, to the overturning the foundations of all religion, whether natural or instituted, and to the rendering all notions of good and evil, of rewards and punishments, whether in this life or the next, groundless and vain.

Others have endeavoured to root out of men's minds all notions of a church, as a society instituted by Christ with peculiar powers and privileges and proper officers to administer the word and sacraments; and so to blend and confound the spiritual society with the temporal as to make everything in religion, its divine truths and most sacred ordinances, dependent on the will of the civil magistrate, as deriving solely from him their sanction and authority. Nay, these religious ordinances themselves—even the chief of them, baptism and the supper of the Lord—have been spoken of with such a degree of ungodly mockery and scorn, as to fill the hearts of good Christians with horror and astonishment.

The frauds of pagan and popish priests have been displayed in order to represent all priests as imposers upon the credulity of mankind and draw infamy upon the priesthood in general; and to render the order itself, in whatever religion it was found, equally the object of public aversion and contempt.

The books containing the errors and impieties above-mentioned have been the more easily published and dispersed, since the expiration of the act for restraining the press; and, through the greater liberty of printing which thereon ensued, have the vicious and profane had more opportunities to scatter their papers for corrupting the manners of men.

Not only several pieces formerly written on the side of infidelity, which might have been forgotten without such a revival, have been collected into volumes and published again; but mock catechisms, framed in a light manner, have been cried in the streets, to depreciate the excellent summaries of our Christian faith; and, as far as possible, to root out of men's minds the sense of those great truths that are contained in them.

This profaneness hath been much increased by the licentiousness of the stage, where the worst examples have been placed in the best lights and recommended to imitation; and the various images thus painted to the life and set out with all manner of advantage have made such impressions upon the minds of the young and unwary as are not easy to be effaced: where the bond of wedlock hath been generally treated as a ridiculous and burthensome yoke, to the great prejudice of society and virtue, and everything sacred hath been exposed: where the office of the priesthood hath been made a matter of scorn and reproach: and where, at the opening of a new theatre, the building of churches was impiously derided as a vain and useless work, the effect only of superstition and ignorance.

It is indeed for the purpose of the irreligious to discourage the building of churches where they are so much wanted and where the want of them is, in all appearance, one great occasion of the irreligion of many. For by this means vast numbers of souls have, in and about these two populous cities, been excluded from a possibility of attending the public worship of God, and from all the benefits of Christian instruction. And the natural consequence of this hath been a gradual defection from piety and virtue to irreligious ignorance, and all manner of loose and licentious living.

And as the want of churches here, so the want of competent maintenance for the service of many that are in the country, where two or three cures do not often afford enough to support a minister, is, though not a late, yet a like occasion of profaneness and ignorance there; for by this means many parishes have no minister residing among them and are several Sundays in the year without any service at all; and the ministers, by having so much duty upon them, cannot discharge it as they ought nor have time for catechising young persons, which is so necessary a part of Christian instruction.

And to the increase of this mischief both in city and country have they also contributed who have taken occasion, from the relaxation of those laws which made absence from the established church penal, to withdraw themselves entirely from all religious assemblies, although the very act of exemption, which gave liberty in one respect, equally restrained it in the other.

From these several occasions hath ensued a great neglect of the religious observance of the Lord's day, too great a part of which is spent by many in public-houses and other diversions wholly unsuitable to the time set apart for the more immediate service of God; though we have reason to think that through the care of magistrates and others some reformation hath been made of this matter.

But whatever share any of the causes and occasions above-mentioned may have had in that growth of infidelity, heresy, and profaneness amongst us, we cannot but bewail the effect, considering the dishonour it brings on our holy faith, our church, and nation; and the hurt it has done to your majesty's people, many of whom have been made worse men and worse subjects by the means of it.

It is lamentable to reflect how many souls have been lost by imbibing wicked doctrines from those books which have been scattered for several years through this kingdom; how many more are endangered by too near approaches to infidelity (though they have not as yet actually arrived to it) from a spirit of indifference and neutrality in religion which hath been infused into their minds by those means.

But what we have farther to apprehend from our impieties is that they have made us obnoxious to the displeasure of almighty God, who may justly on their account be provoked to visit us with his judgments, by stopping the continued current of success with which he has hitherto blessed our affairs, and delivering us into the hands of our enemies, by withdrawing the pure light of his Gospel from us, and letting in the abomination of popery among us.

For the emissaries from Rome have been all along very watchful to lay hold of these opportunities for the advancement of their cause, to which nothing is so serviceable as scepticism and looseness of life. These, therefore, as well as the errors and divisions amongst us, they have always encouraged to the best of their power and improved to their own advantage; representing in several books, as well as in their common conversation, the great uncertainty of the Christian religion upon protestant principles, and filling men's minds with infinite doubts, the better to make them submit to an infallible guide. They have swarmed in our streets of late years, as they do more particularly at this time, and are very busy in making converts; nor do we doubt but that divers of your majesty's subjects, either from the scandal taken at the infidelity, heresy, and profaneness they see, or from sharing the contagion of it, have by their arts been perverted.

But notwithstanding that we have these things to complain of, so much hath been done already toward taking off the causes and effects of these evils, and to prevent the further consequences of them, as to give us great hopes that through the blessing of God upon your majesty's authority and example, and the endeavours of your subjects in their several stations, we shall escape the danger we have so much reason to fear.

For as books have been published in favour of heresy and downright infidelity, so others have been written from time to time, as occasion required, in defence of the fundamental truths, whether of natural or revealed religion, with great clearness and strength of argument. The vain pleas of the several advocates for infidelity have been particularly considered and refuted, to the silencing, if not the conviction, of some of the principal of them.

A lecture was founded not many years since by Mr. Boyle, in defence of the Christian religion against all the adversaries of it, and many excellent and useful sermons have been preached and published upon that occasion.

Societies have been formed for the reformation of manners; funds of charity have been raised for the propagation of the Gospel in foreign parts, and of Christian knowledge at home, and for the pious education of poor children; great variety of plain and useful discourses have been distributed among the meaner sort for their more easy improvement; and parochial libraries have been set up for the use of ministers in the country, that they might be better provided for the instruction of those committed to their charge.

Authority hath often interposed for the countenancing these excellent designs and for withstanding the bold attempts that have been made upon our common faith; and for preventing the increase of irreligion and profaneness, royal injunctions and proclamations have issued, acts of parliament have passed, prosecutions at law have been ordered, gracious speeches from the throne have been made, and from thence such bright patterns of piety and virtue have shone forth, as have no doubt prevailed upon many, though the influence of them hath not extended so far as might have been expected.

But then the infidelity of some hath been attended with this good consequence in others, that the zeal of devout persons hath thereby been excited to do every thing that in them lay towards resisting and stemming the increase of this great evil; nor have their endeavours been altogether fruitless; our eyes daily see the happy effects of them; divine service and sacraments have of late been celebrated, and better frequented than formerly; the catechising of youth hath been more generally practised and with greater success; vast sums have been furnished by private contributions to sustain the charge of educating poor children in the pious manner above mentioned; and many other new and noble institutions of charity have been set on foot.

Many churches have been repaired and adorned at the expense of the several parishioners and other benefactors; and many chapels opened in the larger parishes, though not sufficient to answer the wants of the inhabitants. Great sums of money have been by public authority provided and applied for the building, supporting and adorning other churches; and your majesty has been graciously pleased upon our humble address to recommend to your parliament to find out means for the building of such as are still wanting; of which, from the great satisfaction with which your message was received, and the great progress made upon it, we hope to see the blessed effect; when all who are religiously disposed will have the opportunity of giving public testimony of it, and the careless be left without excuse.

In the meantime other methods of redressing these mischiefs may, we humbly conceive, be successfully tried; such as your majesty's great wisdom and piety and the foregoing observations will suggest to you.

We entertain not the least doubt of your majesty's first resolution to render the laws and proclamations set forth for the suppression of immorality and profaneness useful to that purpose, by an impartial and vigorous execution of them; and to reform the corruptions of the stage, which have been so instrumental in vitiating young and innocent minds, and have given so just offence to all serious and devout Christians.

We are entirely persuaded that your majesty will in the most effectual manner discountenance all such persons as are profligate in their lives, or the known abettors and spreaders of impious opinions; and the repeated assurances which your majesty (whom God long preserve!) hath been pleased to give your people of your care to transmit the succession of the crown in the protestant line, as established by law, give us great hopes that our enemies of the Romish communion will at last be effectually discouraged from attempting the ruin of that excellent church, of which (under Christ) your majesty is the chief governor and glorious defender.

From the application of these several means, which we do not doubt but your majesty will use, we promise ourselves very great and durable effects; but that for which we at present in most earnest and most humble manner address ourselves to your majesty is, that by your royal interposition an act may be obtained for restraining the present excessive and scandalous liberty of printing wicked books at home, and importing the

16—The illustration opposite is a *New Map of London* taken from *A New General Atlas*, London, 1721. The atlas was published by John Senex, cartographer and engraver, of Salisbury Court, Fleet Street. He was the first of the great eighteenth century map-makers and had begun his career as a bookseller. In 1708 he engraved maps of foreign countries which were collected in 1714 in *The English Atlas*. Senex's most famous work was a revision of John Ogilby's study on roads in England which appeared in 1719 as *An Actual Survey of all the Principal Roads of England and Wales*. This was frequently republished in strip-map form. For his knowledge of globular projections, Senex was elected a fellow of the Royal Society in 1728.

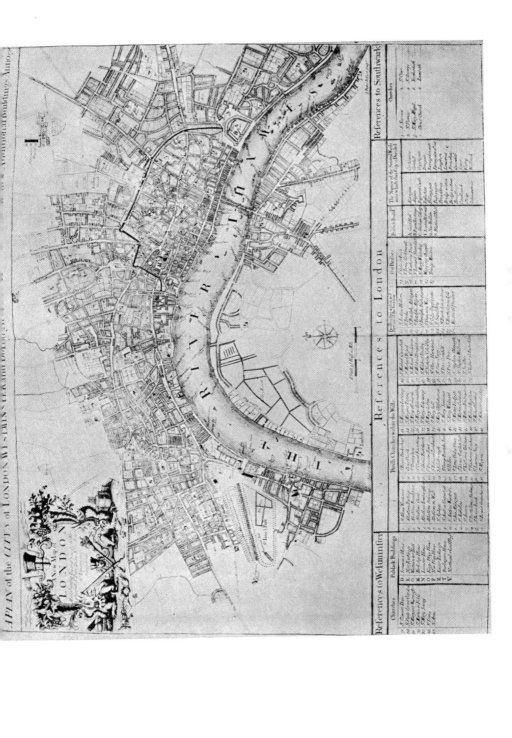

like from abroad, in such manner as to the wisdom of your majesty and your parliament shall seem most expedient. For as we take this liberty to have been one chief source and cause of those evils whereof we have spoken, so we question not but the restraint of it would go a great way in the cure of them.

There is another pernicious custom that has very much prevailed amongst us under the false notion of honour, which we beg leave to mention in this place; and that is the practice of fighting duels, which has so far obtained that your majesty hath had many occasions, and some very lately, to see the dismal effects of it.

We do therefore in all humble duty beg your majesty to take the most effectual methods to extinguish those false notions, so contrary to the laws of God and so destructive of all society, and to put a stop to this wicked and unchristian practice, by such means as your majesty in your great wisdom shall think most proper.

We have also good hope that all employed in authority under your majesty will, as we pray, ' truly and indifferently minister justice to the punishment of wickedness and vice, and to the maintenance of true religion and virtue,' and wish that some way may be found for the recovery and improvement of Christian knowledge and piety in families, which we fear is too much neglected.

We likewise hope that especial care will be taken of the education of young people at the universities, by providing that tutors make it their business to teach their pupils the principles of the Christian religion in the course of their other studies, and endeavour to make them serious in it, with a particular eye to such as are designed for holy orders.

And for ourselves who are called to this holy function, we beg leave to assure your majesty that we will take all possible care of the discharge of our own duty, and do all that in us lies, that the canons of our church may be strictly observed both by ourselves and those committed to our charge.

We have those parts of our discipline which your majesty hath in your great goodness thought fit to recommend to us for farther improvement under our most serious consideration; and hope, in some measure, to answer the wants of the church, and your majesty's expectations in referring them to us; as we shall at all times hereafter, as often as your majesty shall be pleased to require our attendance for these purposes, endeavour to make our synodical meeting subservient to the good order and establishment of this church, the interest and advantage of the Christian religion, the satisfaction of your majesty, and the honour of God.

And our daily and fervent prayer to God shall be that your majesty may be the happy instrument of these and many other blessings to this church and state, that you may be as prosperous in your designs against infidelity and vice here at home, as you have been in all your undertakings against the common enemy abroad, and may by that means add what alone is wanting to complete the glory and crown the successes of your ever memorable reign!

AN IMPARTIAL HISTORY OF PARTIES.

By William Cowper, Earl Cowper

WILLIAM COWPER, EARL COWPER (1664–1723), first lord chancellor of Great Britain, affords a rare example in English history of a man born to rank and fortune rising high in the law. He was the great-grandson of a royalist of Kent, the son of a Whig, Sir William Cowper, and his wife, the daughter of a London merchant. His only education was at a private school. An early marriage, in 1686, forced him to work at the law he had entered for its social connections; he was called to the bar in 1688, became king's counsellor in 1695 and subsequently one of the most distinguished barristers in the country. Cowper's political career, the lever by which he attained legal preferment, may be said to have begun in 1688, when he joined the prince of Orange with a handful of volunteers. As member for Hertford in 1695—his father was the other member for that county—he baited the Tories so successfully, with that charm and grace of style which led Pitt nearly a century later to regret that no copies of his speeches survived, that within a few years he led his party in the house of commons. When the Whigs came in, in 1705, he was appointed keeper of the great seal, and shortly, as he had stipulated, raised to the peerage. He was one of the commissioners for the union with Scotland. In 1710, following the Tory reaction against the Sacheverell trial at which he had presided, he resigned in spite of the queen's protests. In 1714 he was one of the lords justices who removed Bolingbroke, and was reappointed lord chancellor on 21 September, three days after George I's arrival in England.

Cowper drew up the paper printed here while one of the lords justices; it was translated into French by his wife and presented by her on 24 October, four days after the coronation, when she was appointed a lady-in-waiting. This 'impartial' survey is said to have contributed to George's decision to employ only Whigs in the principal offices of state. Flattering though Cowper had to be to George's concept of prerogative, he nevertheless deliberately pointed out the way by which crown control of parliament could be assured. Far from becoming a mere pawn in the hands of the victorious Whigs, George could and did remain the mainspring of the state.

MAY it please your Majesty,

It being probable that many of those who have had the honour of serving you as lords justices during your majesty's absence will think themselves obliged, on your majesty's arrival in your kingdom, severally to offer their thoughts concerning the first settlement of your government, as that upon which not only the security but also the tranquillity and comfort of your majesty's whole reign will entirely depend, I humbly beg leave (not being sufficiently master of the French tongue to explain myself fully, by speaking on a matter of so great consequence) to offer to your majesty's judgment, in this manner, the best information I can, together with a few thoughts on that important subject; which is done with an entire resignation to your wisdom, and a most cordial disinterested zeal for your majesty's service.

Nothing can sooner conduce to your majesty's entering on right measures at this juncture, than the giving a true idea of the parties into which, to our great misfortune, your people are divided. When that is once done, none is so well able from thence to make proper inferences and form the most useful rules of government as your majesty, whose wisdom, experience, application, and success in that particular, are known and admired by all Europe.

That part of your people which consists of papists and nonjurors, who manifest their disaffection to your majesty's government by denying to give those assurances which the laws require, are, in England, but few in proportion to the rest of your majesty's subjects; but I choose to mention these first, because all that need be suggested concerning them is in a very narrow compass. There are several penal laws in force contrived to curb and restrain them as there is occasion; and accordingly, those laws have been used to be put in execution with more or less rigour, as they who are obnoxious to them have behaved themselves with more or less duty and submission to the government, and sometimes with respect to the usage the protestants meet with in the countries of Roman catholic princes or states; and there is no question but your majesty will be advised to deal with them in the same manner.

The residue of your majesty's subjects, who take the oaths and give all the assurances the laws require, are, notwithstanding, divided into two parties with respect to the government.

These parties began to form themselves and give names to each other about the time the bill of exclusion was set on foot, in the reign of King Charles II, though some affect to carry their beginning so far back as the civil wars, which is part of the scandal one of them is pleased to fling upon the other without the least ground of truth, since, to do them right, both are sincerely for the monarchy of Great Britain and the church of England (excepting as to the church the protestant dissenters, who range themselves with those called Whigs, as the papists do with those called Tories, almost in all state controversies whatsoever).

The Tories accuse the others of being inclined to set up a commonwealth, and the Whigs them of a design to introduce popery, or at least to bring the church of England nearer to that of Rome. Whereas, on one side, there are hardly ten in the whole kingdom that may be justly suspected of being for a commonwealth; and, on the other side, whenever the danger has been near and imminent, have shown themselves firm against popery; and they among them who are projecting a union with the Gallican church are either nonjurors or as few in number and as inconsiderable as the commonwealth men have been said to be on the other side. So that, laying by the reproaches which the parties unjustly make use of, one against the other, their real differences of any consequence are but two, which began in this manner:—

King Charles II, as was believed by the influence of his brother, the duke of York, had set on foot a violent persecution against the protestant dissenters, to divide the protestant interest so that the papists might the easier take advantage of those divisions. This was mightily exclaimed against and opposed to the utmost of their power by those who were afterwards called Whigs, and was much encouraged and promoted by the other party. And hence it was that this act of toleration, or at least an exception of protestant dissenters from the penal laws, was one great point the parties at first divided upon. The other was this:—

About the year 1678, the popish plot being discovered turned the thoughts of such as were zealous for the security of the protestant religion to consider the danger it would incur if a popish successor should come to the throne; and the duke of York being known to be a Roman catholic, bills of exclusion were voted by the house of commons in three successive parliaments to set aside the duke of York, and limit the crown to the next protestant heir. One of the most forward and zealous of the members of the house of commons in this business was Sir William Cowper [father of the chancellor, and M.P. for Hertford] whose grandfather, Sir William Cowper, had been a zealous royalist.

This bill was promoted by members of the church of England (there being but two or three dissenters or thereabouts in any of those parliaments) and by such, generally speaking, who themselves or their ancestors had been royalists and taken part with King Charles I.

The court strenuously opposed it, and kept it from passing, either by getting a majority of votes against it in the house of lords, or dissolving the parliament as soon as it was seen that it would pass the house of commons.

This contest was also managed by a paper war, wherein they who were for excluding the duke of York were by their adversaries in division called Whigs; and the others, who struggled to secure the crown to him, were called Tories.

The opinions the Whigs stood upon in general were, that although the monarchy was undoubtedly hereditary and not elective, yet that for the preservation of the whole constitution and particularly to prevent a popish successor from succeeding to the crown, whom they held to be incompatible with a protestant kingdom, it was lawful for the king by act of parliament so to limit and bind the descent of the crown as to incapacitate the next popish successor or successors, and declare that it should descend and come to the next protestant heir. And this they contended very clearly would make such protestant heir, when in possession of the crown, in all respects a lawful and a rightful king.

On the other side the Tories contended that though they could not but grant that the religion of the kingdom, and consequently the constitution, would run a great hazard under a popish successor, yet that by the laws of the land and the law of God providence only was to be trusted to in such a case; and the worst that could be expected was to be borne rather than so great and national a guilt should be incurred as the setting aside, though by act of parliament, the person who was next to the crown in the course of descent according to the common law, which, in this particular, they said was unalterable; and that therefore such a statute would be void, and consequently an allegiance still due to the person so excluded.

The arguments and authorities brought to support these opinions, it would be impertinent and tedious to trouble your majesty with. It sufficeth to show what was the opinion of each of the parties at that time touching that important point, which was then agitated, and has been very lately revived on account of your majesty's succession, between the same parties in pamphlets, addresses, sermons, and laboured treatises, though not expressly in the debates or proceedings of either houses of parliament.

It is well known the Tories of that time prevailed, and the duke of York succeeded to the crown; but in less than four years' time, the foresight of the Whigs was so far justified by his government that most of the great men and leaders of the Tory party joined with them, if not led the way, to desire assistance from the then prince of Orange for the preservation of the religion, laws, and liberties of the kingdom.

The success of his glorious enterprise will ever be remembered with gratitude, and the merciful hand of God is now more visible in it than ever, when, by a plain connection of causes and effects, it has made way for your majesty's accession to the throne and the securing it to your royal family, wherein we have an unusual but most delightful prospect of safety, in so many protestant princes in being at the same time.

But the prince of Orange had no sooner overcome all difficulties, and rescued them from the danger they apprehended, than the parties began again to divide. The Tories relapsed into their former notions, and it was argued in both houses of parliament that the course of succession was not to be interrupted for any reason whatsoever; therefore, that King James and his family with him abroad were to be invited to return, that the government should be continued in his name; and because they would not trust a prince, who had in so many instances declared his design to subvert their religion and civil rights, and who had been so lately exasperated by them, they fell into an absurdity, or rather inconsistency, with their own pretences of being zealous for the prerogative, by proposing a regency over him in power though not in style, or so to restrain his authority that there should be no fear of his invading the religion and laws of the kingdom any more; choosing in that manner to alter the very nature of the monarchy and reduce it almost to a commonwealth, rather than exclude a papist from the throne and entail, after King William's decease, on the next protestant heirs.

But the majority of the convention parliament then sitting being of the Whig party, and not being willing to trust to such measures, the prince of Orange was crowned king with his queen, and the crown by an act of the 1st year of King William and Queen Mary became entailed on the heirs of the body of that queen, and after, on the Princess Ann of Denmark, and the heirs of her body; and after, on the heirs of the body of King William.

And not only so, but the other disputed point of a toleration for protestant dissenters was settled by act of parliament, as the Whigs always desired it should be; and an exemption of protestant dissenters from the penalties of all the laws which affected them was carefully and clearly enacted: the subsequent experience of which law, in bringing so much quiet and riches to the kingdom as it has done, has convinced many of the Tories of their error in that particular.

It may now reasonably be wondered at, since the two points in dispute were thus silenced by the two mentioned laws, how the parties could keep any longer divided, and what was remaining for them to continue about? This is answered by observing that the Tory party became very uneasy at seeing the opinions they had been so long contending for borne down by two acts of parliament. They could then, indeed, no longer dispute the passing those laws, but they could and did sufficiently, on all safe occasions, manifest their dislike of them and resolution to get rid of them the first fair opportunity.

So that the only change produced among the parties was this, that as the struggle before was either to procure or hinder those two important acts for the security of the protestant interest, so now it became a contest between them (covertly, at least) whether what was so obtained should be preserved and continued?

'Tis true, indeed, that by much the greater part of the Tory party, seeing a necessity either of owning the government or quitting all hopes of employments in church and state, besides being liable to double taxes (as the papists and non-jurors were), soon addressed themselves to find out such distinction as might leave them at liberty to own the then present government, and to take such preferments under it as they could get. The topic they generally went upon was, that in opposing or not helping the revolution settlement (though some of them had appeared in arms with the prince to enable him to settle things to their mind), they had acquitted themselves, in their opinions, of all guilt which they thought was contracted by those who had been busy in that work. And now that the law required them under penalties in case of disobedience to take certain oaths, they might as good christians submit to the present powers and take them accordingly, intending still to own the king only as a king *de facto*, and not *de jure*; and that they might likewise for the support of order and government, till the rightful owner should find an opportunity of being restored, conscientiously take and execute any places of profit and trust in church or state, the rather because their so doing might, in time, be a help to the setting things again, upon what they called the right foot.

Books were wrote and sermons preached, using arguments of different sorts to support, or at least colour, these and the like notions.

On these grounds, all of that party (except a very few) took the oaths of allegiance, &c., to King William and Queen Mary, and many of them were admitted into places, and some into those of the greatest dignity and trust. Several also into the church, and even of those that had made difficulties of owning the revolution settlement, and stood out till near the last minute allowed them for it, were notwithstanding countenanced and preferred.

From this false step proceeded all the difficulties and troubles which that king met with in his whole reign.

And when he found himself beset with a war against France, commotions in Scotland, and an almost total defection of Ireland, he then perceived his mistake, and that he had occasion for another kind of service than that which flowed from a principle of submission and acquiescence only to his government.

Accordingly, he made some alterations and put his principal affairs into the hands of them who had been zealous for bringing him to the throne and making a protestant settlement, so far as was then established; and these carried him through that expensive war, to the peace of Ryswick, with a zeal and application equal to their affections to his cause, at the same time effecting with success what was thought impossible though almost necessary to be done during the war, the recoinage of the whole silver species of money, without debasing the standard either in weight or fineness.

'Tis true the Tories were by the credit many of them obtained in the beginning of his reign (as before observed) so raised that though they fell very short of a majority in parliament while the court favoured the other party, yet they were able, by raising objections to and clogging the easier methods proposed for raising money, not only to make the supplies come later sometimes than was convenient, but also to necessitate raising them by way of funds, or anticipation of several excises for perpetuity or long terms of years, rightly judging that such a course would, at one time or other, load and distress the government. Whereas, if near as many duties as are now mortgaged had been given at once, those with the land tax would have maintained the current service of the war and civil government in each year by the product of the same year, and consequently the nation, not weary of the war till a good peace could be had, and out of debt, or near it, when the war was finished.

I was then in the house of commons, and one of those that proposed this method of raising the supplies within the year; but it was effectually opposed by the Tory party, they drawing into their opinion, as to that particular, several well-meaning gentlemen, by suggesting that so easy and commodious a way of raising money might prove dangerous to liberty.

'Tis true that on many occasions the party last named has had the dexterity to object this mistake of running the nation into so great a debt to their adversaries then in the ministry; but I can aver it with the greater certainty, they were far from electing that method, otherwise than that they had rather supply the king that way than not at all or unseasonably late, one of which would have fallen out, if they had endeavoured to have broke through the opposition made to the raising the money any other way.

The peace of Ryswick being made, his then majesty was prevailed on to experience once more if he could render his affairs easy, by trying to win the Tories with the principal places of trust, which they might probably execute well enough to support the government in time of peace.

The trial was made but did not answer expectation, for the king became more uneasy with them when in power than before, which together with his foreseeing the necessity of a new war made it evident that as he had begun to advise with his old servants in private, so they would quickly have been restored to their former power had his majesty lived but a little longer than he did.

It must be confessed that the act for the further limitation of the succession to the crown passed in the 12th year of this king while the Tories were in such credit and had a majority in the house of commons; it is therefore to be observed that the true reason why such a bill passed in such a parliament was that the king having, by his own inclination, and probably the advice of some of his old ministry whom he continued to hear, earnestly recommended that bill to parliament in his speech from the throne, the Tories, for fear of losing the king's favour, did not endeavour to reject it but set themselves to clog it and indeed render it absurd by some of the restrictions your majesty is undoubtedly apprised of; and to show their contempt and aversion whenever it came on, except when it was necessary to be present in order to load it, and by calling Sir J.B. to the chair of the committee for that bill, who was then thought to be distracted and was soon after confined for being so.

Thus, that bill went through the house of commons, and many there who had let it pass hoped that the house of lords, where the Whigs had yet a majority, would, by disputing at least some of those restrictions which were most absurd and impracticable, lose the bill. But the friends to your majesty's family were better advised; they took and passed the bill with all its faults and without any amendment, wisely depending that if they secured the main, the succession, whatsoever was absurdly and unreasonably annexed to it, would, at some fitting opportunity or other, be easily laid aside. Which, their opinion, has already in a great measure proved true. One of those restrictions, which enacted that all public business should be transacted only in the privy council and that every privy councillor should set his name to the resolutions drawn up in form, being repealed in the reign of the late queen; and by the same act another of those restrictions, that no officer should sit in either house of parliament after the queen's decease, was reduced so as to extend to some few officers only, and that, as well in the queen's time as after the protestant succession should take place.

King William, having passed this bill for the further limitation of the crown, soon after died, leaving that invaluable legacy to his people.

Her late majesty, upon her accession to the crown, did not only continue to employ those of the Tory party she found in power but added many others of the same, and set herself plainly and avowedly to govern by it, and as a natural consequence of so doing, was advised in her first speech from the throne to reflect on the memory of her glorious predecessor (without whose hazardous and successful expedition the sceptre had certainly been in another hand) by saying, very emphatically, that her heart was entirely English; which, however her majesty intended, they who persuaded her to use that expression, and every one who heard of it, understood to be an insinuation that King William's being born abroad had occasioned his not having the interest of this kingdom so entirely at his heart as he should have had, which was very far from having any foundation in truth, considering that he had ventured his life and fortunes more than once for our preservation, and had shown no greater favour to the states general than were necessary to cultivate a good understanding between the two nations for their common security.

Yet, notwithstanding this manifest resolution to uphold the Tory party and discountenance the other, the war had not been renewed and continued any long time before the duke of Marlborough and Lord Treasurer Godolphin, then in principal credit with the queen, discovered that they could not carry on the war with any hope of success by a set of men, who, though they were willing to profit and govern under the queen's authority, yet had not so cordial an affection to a government founded on the revolution, nor aversion to the popish line, as to induce them to bear the odium of raising the necessary supplies.

The two mentioned ministers, finding themselves under this difficulty, by the intervention of the late duke of Montague applied to some of the principal lords who had been in business under the late king and were of the Whig party, who very willingly undertook to endeavour the carrying on the queen's business in parliament on this very reasonable consideration, that some of the officers of principal trust, if not the greater part, should be in the hands of their friends, since experience had shown they had so little deserved to be run down and oppressed as they had been; that, on the contrary, they were the only persons who were willing and able to carry the queen with success through that just and necessary war; and accordingly, as an earnest of sincerity, it was insisted that the great seal should be put into the hands of Mr. Cowper, who had steadily adhered to the revolution interest in the house of commons through several successive parliaments.

This alteration was soon after made, and others following in a little time of the same nature, it was seen which way the court inclined, and thereupon in two ensuing parliaments the Whigs had a clear majority, as it will always happen whenever the court have a mind to have it so.

I need not tell your majesty how faithfully the queen was served by that ministry and those parliaments, nor with what a prodigious uninterrupted course of success, nor to what a degree the credit of the nation was raised abroad and at home—France reduced and the confederacy exalted. These things cannot but be present with your majesty, and in the clearest light.

The same ministry and parliaments showed also their affection and unwearied zeal to the interest of your majesty's house, by contriving and passing the act for the further securing the succession to the crown in the protestant line; which put it into such a method as was not to be resisted but by open force of arms and a public declaration for the Pretender, and made it high treason for any whose duty it was to be concerned in the proclamation to be so much as negligent in proclaiming the next protestant successor.

Under the same faithful and happy management passed the acts in England and Scotland for the union of the two kingdoms (the Tories vehemently opposing it) which the queen always esteemed to be the chief happiness and glory of her reign, as having been often before attempted but still in vain; and indeed, when the Tories were before commissionated to that end, they treated it as a jest or impossibility, by absenting from all meetings appointed, and so letting it drop; although nothing is more clear than that, among many other self-evident advantages, the settlement of the crown in your majesty's house had probably never been obtained in that kingdom by any other means: the evil consequences of which disunion, had it happened, are but too evident to enlarge upon.

I dare not touch upon the particular causes which drew on the disgrace and change of that ministry, nor will venture to say whether it was occasioned at first by any greater design than to change the she-favourite, which unavoidably drew on more, and those still further alterations; it being not my purpose so much to follow the springs and causes of the variations of the court measures in respect to the parties, as to show your majesty how they severally behaved themselves, when they got the ascendant in their turns, as to the protestant succession, the good of the state, and the common cause of Europe.

Your majesty was so much concerned to attend to our affairs since this last alteration, and they are so fresh in memory, that I need not be particular as to what has passed. It is enough to assert, as I think it may be done with clear truth, that immediately ensued a manifest attempt, by addresses and other occasions, encouraged by the court, to sap the very foundations or principles on which the acts for securing the protestant succession were built, by decrying all right to the crown but what was purely hereditary and in the course of descent according to the common law; that the papists and nonjurors were so far encouraged as to grow remarkable for their insolence; that a peace was in effect concluded with France in a clandestine manner, without the privity of the principal confederates, and little or no consideration had of their interests; that this neglect of them was justified by the ministry in public, by saying that the interest of Great Britain was principally aimed at in this peace (though time and experience have shown even that preference to be untrue); that our trade is almost oppressed in all its branches, and had been entirely ruined if the bill for confirming the French treaty of commerce had not been successfully opposed; that the credit of the nation at home was sunk as to the public funds, and abroad as to all our good offices or menaces, which were equally despised; that our late confederates, except the King of S——, were all more or less disgusted, and distrusted our conduct in every thing, upon the justest grounds; in short, that the power of France, which had been so happily reduced, has been restored to such a degree as to become again formidable to Europe, and consequently that the fruits of so many glorious victories as the allies had obtained were in a manner deserted and given up.

The hopes of the Pretender rose in proportion as the power of France increased; and this consequence was so natural, that one cannot avoid suspecting all this favour could not be then showed to France without a design of assisting the Pretender by that means. However it was meant, sure it is, nothing could more weaken the protestant succession than the promoting the interest of France; and yet that was done, not by any accident, inadvertence, or want of conduct, but by a continued series of contrivances, a zealous application, and an unwearied industry.

But after all this mischief the ministry had done, they still persisted to the end in declaring they had promoted and cultivated a good understanding between her late majesty and your illustrious house. The appearances of things, as far as could be discerned by those who were out of business, seemed quite otherwise. This is a subject unfit, as well as unnecessary, to be further inquired into, since your majesty must know to a certainty whether their pretences were any better founded in that particular than they were in most other things; although perhaps your majesty may receive a yet further satisfaction on this head by looking upon the instructions and letters given and sent to the earl of Clarendon.

If this short deduction or history of the two parties should give your majesty any clearer notion of them than you had before, I shall then be so fortunate as not to have trespassed on your patience in vain; since nothing can contribute more to the extinguishing them at length, and making a right use of them in the mean time, than a knowledge of their principles and practices.

Your majesty may be told, and it has been often said, that the only difference is about the places; but this is either a superficial judgment, or a desire to hinder the true causes from being discerned. For if that was true, then the struggle would only be between individuals and not between two set parties of men, which can only be kept up by some diversity of opinion, upon fundamentals, at least points of consequence; and experience shows that many who have no design on preferment, either for themselves or friends, but live retired on their estates, are yet as hot or hotter than any in these distinctions; and therefore I take those before stated to be the true causes which divide them, and which I beg leave to recapitulate in a few words—that as the Whigs always contended for the toleration of the protestant dissenters and exclusion of the popish line from the crown to be established by law, the Tories did always as earnestly and publicly oppose them till they were enacted. The former are rejoiced at their success in these great points, the latter more or less discontented to see their principles discountenanced, and those of their adversaries succeed. Both, therefore, keep and improve their strength as much as they can—the one to defend their acquisitions, the other to retake them and get rid of both the laws as soon as they safely can. Not that I would have it believed that many of the Tories are not perfectly against restoring the Pretender, by force at least, or that some few of them did not make it appear, by their actions the last year, they would not have concurred to the bringing him in even in a parliamentary way; but the true reason was, they believed their religion and liberties could not be secured if they should; and their consciences not accusing them of having done any thing towards the protestant settlement, they were well contented to enjoy the security arising from the act of others, which, though very useful, had something of unjust in it.

I have sat continually in one or other house of parliament now about twenty-four years, and observed with as much diligence and indifference as I could the inclinations and motions of both parties, and I will venture to assure your majesty as what I am very certain of, that the Whigs would venture all to support the protestant succession in your majesty's family; on the other hand, that many of the Tories would rejoice to see the Pretender restored, as they call it, even by a French power, much more if by any safer means; that the best of them would hazard nothing to keep him out, though probably do nothing hazardous to bring him in; but that if ever he should declare himself a protestant, with proper circumstances to make his conversion probable (as after the death of the French king and his mother, it is not unlikely he may do) they would greedily swallow the cheat, and endeavour by all possible means to put in practice again their old notions of divine, hereditary, and indefeasible right, by a restoration of the person in whom, by their opinion, that right is lodged.

And if any other of the popish line that are next after the Pretender should, after his decease, play the same part, your majesty will find the party last mentioned very troublesome if not dangerous; unless by prudent measures under your majesty's government, they shall be brought really and from their hearts, as well as in an outward compliance, to part with those notions which are so inconsistent with a government founded on the revolution.

I beg leave further to observe that when lately some of the heads of the Tory party made it known both by their words and actions, and I don't doubt sincerely, that they did not intend to concur in the repeal of the acts limiting the succession of the crown to your majesty's house, much less to bring in the Pretender with the assistance of France (which was a very seasonable service, and your majesty has already shown yourself sensible of it), they could bring very few of any of their party after them into the same honest measures; but on the contrary, as these leaders above mentioned appeared more zealous for your majesty's house, so in proportion they visibly lost the affections of their party, and were themselves so sensible of it that they were forced to bring in the bill against schism, only to regain the credit they had lost with their old friends.

It is an old scandal now almost worn out, thrown out by their adversaries on the Whigs, that they are against the prerogative of the crown, which I should not have thought worth mentioning but that 'tis generally believed to have made some impression on King William in the beginning of his reign to the irrecoverable detriment of his affairs; but he afterwards found that the Tories, not liking the hand which held the prerogative, were more inclined to straighten it, and the Whigs for the contrary reason to support it. And this false suggestion will certainly have the less weight with your majesty when you shall be informed, as the truth is, that the only ground for it was, the Whigs being so zealous for setting aside the popish line in favour of the protestant, which the Tories thought a high violation of the rights of monarchy and of what they erroneously called the prerogative of the crown, the descent of which they held to be unalterable by any power on earth, and thence took the liberty of branding all of a contrary opinion as anti-monarchical, or enemies to the prerogative. But in all other respects the Whigs are as zealous to support the prerogative as the Tories can be, and rather more that they are under a government founded on the revolution.

Having thus stated to your majesty the practices and dispositions of the parties, I shall only add that 'tis not to be doubted but your majesty's known goodness and experienced wisdom will necessarily incline you to such moderate counsels as will render you king of all your divided people. But I humbly conceive it not possible so to distribute your royal favours but that one or other of the parties will appear to have a superior degree of trust reposed in them: and if such a perfect equality was possible to be observed, perhaps it would follow that an equal degree of power, tending at the same time different ways, would render the operations of the government slow and heavy, if not altogether impracticable.

It remains, therefore, in my humble opinion, for your majesty to determine which of these shall have the chief share in your majesty's confidence, as most likely to support your title to the crown with the greatest zeal and most untainted affection to it. For as to their power to do it, give me leave to assure your majesty, on repeated experience, that the parties are so near an equality, and the generality of the world so much in love with the advantages a king of Great Britain has to bestow without the least exceeding the bounds of law, that 'tis wholly in your majesty's power, by showing your favour in due time (before the elections) to one or other of them, to give which of them you please a clear majority in all succeeding parliaments.

It is needless to suggest to your majesty, but for method's sake it ought just to be touched upon, that whichsoever party shall have the lower degree of your majesty's trust, it ought nevertheless to be used by those in power with very great tenderness and affection while obedient to your majesty and the laws; and as a father would a child whom he dearly loves, though he does not totally approve, and, to be more particular, should, in my humble opinion, be admitted to a fair share of such places and employments of trust, according to their several qualifications, as are during the pleasure of the crown, and not attended with the chief dependencies.

This would be very far from the usage which the last ministry of her late majesty bestowed on those who had served the queen so faithfully and successfully during the war, by turning them out of all places, even the lowest civil and military, very few excepted; by maintaining libellers, and often writing libels themselves against them; by using their power and majority in parliament to garble their predecessors' conduct, and, for want of better matter, to misrepresent and reflect on parts of it which were unblamable if not commendable; by proscribing, as far as they were able, to the contempt and hatred of the people all that did not come into their measures, and among these the majority of the house of lords (not reckoning those which that ministry plainly brought in for their own support) in calling them the faction, and even prevailing with the queen to brand them plainly enough with the same name, both in several answers to addresses and speeches from the throne, and that for no other reason but their endeavouring, in a legal parliamentary method, to oblige the ministry to make something a better peace than they were about to make, to hinder the separation of the confederate army, to rescue the trade and manufactures of Great Britain from the French treaty of commerce, and to make it evident, as they did at length, that the trade of Spain was become impracticable by the Spanish treaty of commerce.

I have but one thing more humbly to represent to your majesty, as the only and, if I mistake not, a sure means to extinguish the being and the very name of party amongst us, that your majesty would be pleased to use the utmost caution not to prefer any of those ecclesiastics whose known principles lead them to scruple the validity of a limitation of the right to the crown by act of parliament. There is a sufficient number of the clergy of the church of England, of the most learned and best livers, out of whom your majesty may choose for all preferments that shall fall vacant, who are not the least tainted with those notions which, while they continue, will ever find matter for discontents and divisions in your majesty's kingdoms. But when once it is discerned that, by a steady and uninterrupted administration, no man who is known to hold opinions inconsistent with the very foundation of your majesty's government can get into any of the crown preferments in the church, they who find themselves troubled with these inconvenient scruples will soon apply their thoughts and studies in good earnest to satisfy themselves, and then others, of the weakness of those errors, which will afterwards, in a little time, be confined to a few melancholy nonjurors, who are the less dangerous for being known; and when the clergy are brought to be of one mind as to your majesty's title, all differences in opinion among the laity on that head will soon vanish. But that part of the clergy who have always violently contended against excluding the next successor, though a papist, will never own themselves to have been in the wrong while they find they have a fair chance for the best of the church preferments without disavowing those errors, otherwise than by taking the oaths in form.

I have nothing further to importune your majesty with, nor that good providence which so visibly has placed you on the throne with any thing so earnestly as my hearty prayers that your reign may be long and glorious, and that your posterity to the end of time may rule over a happy and dutiful, and if it is not too much to ask, a unanimous people.